First Americans

First Americans provides a comprehensive history of Native Americans from their earliest appearance in North America to the present, highlighting the complexity and diversity of their cultures and their experiences. Native voices permeate the text and shape its narrative, underlining the agency and vitality of Native peoples and cultures in the context of regional, continental, and global developments. This updated edition of *First Americans* continues to trace Native experiences through the Obama administration years and up to the present day. The book includes a variety of pedagogical tools including short biographical profiles, key review questions, a rich series of maps and illustrations, chapter chronologies, and recommendations for further reading. Lucid and readable yet rigorous in its coverage, *First Americans* remains the indispensable student introduction to Native American history.

Kenneth W. Townsend earned his Ph.D. in American History from the University of North Carolina at Chapel Hill in 1991, two years after joining the faculty of the Department of History at Coastal Carolina University in Myrtle Beach, South Carolina. In addition to his teaching and university service responsibilities, Townsend served as Chair of the Department of History and established the Center for Peace and Conflict Studies at Coastal Carolina University, acting as its director for two years. He is the author of *World War II and the American Indian* (2000), *South Carolina* (2008), and varied articles.

What is this you call property? It cannot be the earth, for the land is our mother, nourishing all her children, beasts, birds, fish, and all men. The woods, the streams, everything on it belongs to everybody and is for the use of all. How can one man say it belongs only to him?

(attributed to Massasoit, Wampanoag, 1581–1661)

No tribe has the right to sell, even to each other, much less to strangers. . . . Sell a country! Why not sell the air, the great sea, as well as the earth? Did not the Great Spirit make them all for the use of his children?

(attributed to Tecumseh, Shawnee, 1768–1813)

I am a red man. If the Great Spirit had desired me to be a white man he would have made me so in the first place. He put in your heart certain wishes and plans, in my heart he put other and different desires. Each man is good in his sight. It is not necessary for eagles to be crows.

(Sitting Bull, Hunkpapa Lakota, 1831–1890)

If the white man wants to live in peace with the Indian, he can live in peace. . . . Treat all men alike. Give them all the same law. Give them all an even chance to live and grow. All men were made by the same Great Spirit Chief. They are all brothers. The Earth is the mother of all people and all people should have equal rights upon it. . . . Let me be a free man, free to travel, free to stop, free to work, free to trade . . . free to follow the religion of my fathers, free to think and talk and act for myself. . . .

(Chief Joseph, Nez Perce, 1840–1904)

The American Indian is of the soil, whether it be the region of forests, plains, pueblos, or mesas. He fits into the landscape, for the hand that fashioned the continent also fashioned the man for his surroundings. He once grew as naturally as the wild sunflowers, he belongs just as the buffalo belonged.

(Luther Standing Bear, Oglala Lakota, 1868–1939)

First Americans

A History of Native Peoples

2nd edition

Kenneth W. Townsend

Routledge
Taylor & Francis Group

NEW YORK AND LONDON

Second edition published 2019
by Routledge
711 Third Avenue, New York, NY 10017

and by Routledge
2 Park Square, Milton Park, Abingdon, Oxon, OX14 4RN

Routledge is an imprint of the Taylor & Francis Group, an informa business

First edition published by Pearson Education Ltd. 2013
Second edition published by Routledge 2019

Library of Congress Cataloging-in-Publication Data
A catalog record for this book has been requested

ISBN: 978-1-138-73588-0 (hbk)
ISBN: 978-1-138-73585-9 (pbk)
ISBN: 978-1-315-16138-9 (ebk)

Typeset in Stone Serif
by Apex CoVantage, LLC

To my wife, Diann; our children, Danielle, Brandon, and Dustin; and our grandchildren, Kaylee, Miranda, Peter, Tyler, Tristan, Alexandra, Aubree, Teagan, and Tucker

Contents

List of Figures xv
List of Maps xxi
Preface xxiii
Acknowledgments xxvii

1 **Native North America Before European Contact** 2
Stories Versus Science 3
Beginnings 5
  We Were Always Here 5
  The Scientific Evidence 6
Reading History: The Kwakiutl Story of the Deluge 7
  Clovis and Folsom Cultures 8
Changes in the West 10
  California Indians 11
  The Northwest 11
  The Great Basin and the Plains 13
Agriculture-Based Societies in the Southwest 14
  Cultural Diversity and the Arrival of Maize 14
  The "Chaco Phenomenon" 15
  Hohokam and Mesa Verde Cultures 17
Seeing History: Anasazi Sites Compared 18
Eastern Woodlands 19
  Early Eastern Woodlands Traditions 19
  Adena and Hopewell Cultures 20
  Mississippian Chiefdoms 20
  The Iroquois 22

Seeing History: Chiefdoms Maintaining Power Through Images 23
Conclusion 24
Reading History: The Iroquois Origin Story 24
Review Questions 25
Recommended Readings 25
Native American History Online 26

2 **Native Peoples and European Newcomers, 982–1590** 28
Conquests, Colonies, and Contradictions 29
An Iberian New World Order 32
  Christopher Columbus and the West Indies: The Tainos Encounter Spaniards 33
The Maya, Aztec, and Inca Worlds 35
  Maya 35
  Chichén Itzá and the Mayan City-States 36
  Maya Women and the City-States 37
  Aztecs 38
  Pre-Aztec States in Mexico 38
  Rise of the Aztec Empire 39
  Tenochtitlán 40
  Aztec Gods and Religion 40
  Aztec Women in a Warrior Culture 41
  Inca 42
  Growth of the Inca State 43
  Inca Rule 43
  The Power of Inca Women 44

Spanish Conquest, Spanish Rule   45
   Fall of Tenochtitlán   46
Profile: Malintzin, A Woman Negotiates
   With the Aztecs   46
Reading History: A Woman's Voice From
   Post-conquest Mexico: Ana Juana From
   Culhuacan   48
   Conquest of the Incas   50
Profile: Titu Cusi Yupanqui, an Inca Elite
   After Conquest   50
   Conquest of the Maya   51
Reading History: A Voice From the Maya
   New World Inquisition: Francisco Chuc
   of Sahcaba, August 11, 1562   53
French and English Newcomers   54
   Pre-Columbian Encounters in North
      America: The Norse   55
   Early Expeditions to the Northeast   55
   Native Peoples and the French Along the
      St. Lawrence River   56
   Algonquians and the English at
      Roanoke   58
Conclusion   59
Profile: Manteo, the Roanoke
   Interpreter   60
Review Questions   61
Recommended Readings   62
Native American History Online   62

3 Spanish Borderlands, 1527–1758   64
On the Fringes   65
La Florida: A Maritime Borderland   67
   The Indian Landscape of La Florida   69
   Friars and Chiefdoms   71
   Mission Life   71
   Rebellion and Decline   73
Southeast Chiefdoms and Hernando
   de Soto   75
The Southwest Borderlands   77
   Women and Caddoan Power   77
   The Texas Mission-Presidio Complex   79
The World of the Pueblos   80
   New Power in the Sword: The Spanish
      Invasion   82
   New Power in the Church: The Franciscan
      Pueblo Missions   83

New Power in Governance: Encomenderos
   and Colonial Rule   84
Rebellion: The Pueblo Revolt of 1680   85
Reading History: Declaration of the
   Indian, Juan. Place on the Río del
   Norte, December 18, 1681   86
Northern Mining Frontiers   87
   Serrano Peoples: Native Life in Sonora   87
   Miners, Ranchers, and Moving Frontiers   88
   Missionaries: Serrano Peoples and
      the Jesuits   88
   Wanderers and Communities: Native
      Resistance to Spanish Rule   89
Early Borderlands Connections in the
   Southwest   89
   Horses and Networks of Masculine Trade
      and Warfare   89
   The Rise of the Comanches   90
Conclusion   92
Review Questions   92
Recommended Readings   92
Native American History Online   93

4 Seventeenth-Century Eastern
   Woodlands, 1607–1689   94
Worlds Apart   95
Tsenacommacah   98
   The Rise of the Powhatan Confederacy   98
   Powhatan and the English: Trade and
      Conflict   100
   Indian War and the Emergence of Virginia   102
Profile: Pocahontas in the Atlantic
   World   104
Southern New England Indians
   Encounter the English   106
   Native Americans and Plymouth Bay   107
   New England Indians Face English
      Expansion   109
   Christianity and the Praying Town Model   111
Profile: Uncas, the Last Sachem of the
   Mohegans   112
Confederacies, Empires, and Villages   114
   The Huron Ascendancy   114
   War and Mourning: Five Nations' Ferocity   116
   Middle Grounding: The Pays d'en Haut   117
   Transformation of the Five Nations   118

Profile: Kateri Tekakwitha   120
Maturing Colonies Ending a Century in
   Conflict: Metacom's War and Bacon's
   Rebellion   120
   Metacom's War   121
Reading History: Mary Rowlandson's
   Captivity Narrative, 1682   123
   Bacon's Rebellion   124
Conclusion   126
Review Questions   126
Recommended Readings   126
Native American History Online   127

5 Empire, 1700–1763   128
Empires, a Chief, and a Prophet   129
Indians and Empires in the Northeast   131
   Deerfield on the Edge of Empire   132
Reading History: John Williams, *The
   Redeemed Captive Returning to Zion*,
   1774   133
   *Returning to New France and Shifting
      Strategies   134*
New England Indians "Behind the
   Frontier"   134
   Land and Indian Communities   135
   *Native Peoples and the Economics of the
      British Empire in New England   135*
   Religion, Education, and Indian Sovereignty   136
Profile: The Transient Life of Sarah
   Gardner, Indian Woman   137
Reading History: Samson Occom Tells His
   Story, 1768   139
A Mid-Atlantic Frontier   140
   Delawares and the Quest for Land   140
   The Pennsylvania Backcountry   141
   *The Indians' "Great Awakening" in
      Pennsylvania   142*
Profile: Andrew Montour: The Frontier
   Negotiator   143
Reading History: Esther: a Mahican-
   Moravian   145
Multitribal Zones and Imperial Pressure
   in the South   146
   Trading Slaves and Deerskins   147
   *Native Americans and the Costs of French
      Expansion into the Lower Mississippi Valley   148*

Tuscarora and Yamasee Wars and Breaking
      with the British   150
Profile: Mary Musgrove: A Creek Woman
   Between Worlds   152
The Seven Years' War and Indian
   Perspectives on Empire   154
   *The Redefinition of Empire and Racial
      Consciousness   156*
Seeing History: Neolin's Master of Life   157
Conclusion   160
Review Questions   160
Recommended Readings   160
Native American History Online   161

6 The Indians' Revolution, 1763–1814   162
A Disease, a Continent, and a Revolution   163
The American Revolution   166
   Questions of Iroquois Neutrality   166
   *For Liberty and Independence: New England
      Indians   169*
Profile: Molly Brant, an Iroquois Woman
   and British Loyalist   171
   Dunmore's War and the Old Northwest   172
   The South and Choosing Sides   174
Seeing History: A Draught of the
   Cherokee Country by Lieutenant Henry
   Timberlake, 1762   175
Native American Recovery, Native
   American Resistance, 1783–1814   177
   *The Revolution Continues: Treaties and
      Bloody Years   178*
   The Civilization Program   181
   Prophets and War   183
Profile: Black Hoof, Shawnee Annuity
   Chief   184
Reading History: Handsome Lake's First
   Vision, 1799   186
Profile: Hillis Hadjo, The Creek Prophet   189
Western Revolutions   190
   The Borderlands Revolution: Comanchería   191
   Comanchería: Wealth and Empire   191
   Alta California: Missionary Revolutions   192
   Mission Life   193
Profile: Indian Leaders in the Franciscan
   Missions   194
Conclusion   195

Review Questions 196
Recommended Readings 196
Native American History Online 196

7 Removal, 1801–1846 198
"Do You Want Our Country?" 199
Southern Removal 201
　Cherokee "Civilization" 202
　Cherokees Challenged 206
Reading History: The Removal
　Act of 1830 208
　Cherokee Removal 209
　The Creek Road to Oklahoma 212
　Choctaw Removal 213
Seeing History: Nanih Waiya 214
　Chickasaws Head West 216
Profile: Pushmataha, Choctaw Leader
　Caught Between Worlds 217
Resisting Removal 219
　Seminoles Fight 219
Profile: Coacoochee, the Mexican
　Seminole 223
　The Black Hawk War 223
Reading History: Black Hawk's
　Autobiography 227
Removal From the North 229
Profile: William Apess, a Pequot, Helps
　the Mashpee 231
Restoring Sovereignty in the Indian
　Territory 234
　Rebuilding the Cherokee Nation 234
　Resurgence Among Indians From the South 236
　*Indian Territory and the "Peculiar
　　Institution" of Slavery 238*
Conclusion 239
Review Questions 239
Recommended Readings 239
Native American History Online 240

**8 Western Indians and the United
States, 1800–1850 242**
Winning or Losing the West 243
Native Americans, the Corps of
　Discovery, and Constructing Empire 245
　The Plains and Missouri River Indians 246
　Pacific Northwest Indians 249

Reading History: James P. Ronda,
　The Truth About Sacagawea 250
The Pacific as the West 253
　The Russian Presence in America 254
　Tlingit Culture, Resistance, and Competition 256
　*Rocky Mountain Fur Trading and the
　　Pacific Northwest 259*
Profile: Smohalla, the Prophet 262
Winning or Losing the West? 262
　The Transformation of California 263
　*California Indians and American Manifest
　　Destiny 267*
　California's "Sexual Frontier" 269
Profile: Ishi, the Last Yahi Standing 271
　Texas Indians in Upheaval 271
Profile: Andele, the Mexican-Kiowa
　Captive 273
　The Southwest Borderlands in Transition 274
Reading History: Andele's Account 275
Conclusion 278
Review Questions 278
Recommended Readings 278
Native American History Online 279

9 The Civil War Years, 1861–1865 280
Lumbee Indians in the Civil War 281
War in Indian Territory and Minnesota 284
　Choosing Sides—The Five Civilized Nations 284
　War in Indian Territory 286
Profile: Stand Watie (Cherokee,
　1806–1871) 287
　The Upper Midwest: Sioux Resistance 290
Profile: Little Crow (Tayoyateduta or
　Thaoyate Duta, for His Red Nation),
　1810–1862 290
Seeing History: The Execution of Santee
　Sioux 293
Resistance in the Southwest and Plains 295
　Navajo Resistance 295
　Bosque Redondo 299
　War in the Colorado Territory 300
Reading History: Proclamation of
　Governor John Evans, Colorado
　Territory, June 27, 1864 303
Reading History: Letter from Black Kettle
　(Cheyenne) to Major Colley (Indian

Agent, Fort Lyon), United States Army, August 29, 1864   304
Conclusion   307
Review Questions   308
Recommended Readings   308
Native American History Online   309

10   Conflicting Postwar Directions, 1865–1877   310
Kintpuash and the Modoc War   311
Post-Civil War Directions in Indian Affairs   313
  Defining Postwar Indian Policy   314
Profile: Standing Bear (Machunazha, Ponca), 1829–1908   317
  The Powder River War   318
  Peace Overtures   320
Reading History: Report to the President by the Indian Peace Commission, January 7, 1868   321
  Renewed Resistance on the Southern Plains   325
Peace Policy, War Policy   326
  President Grant's Peace Policy   326
Seeing History: "Robinison Crusoe Making a Man of His Friday"   328
  Resistance on the Southern Plains Continues   329
Profile: Quanah Parker (Comanche)   331
  Gold in the Black Hills   332
  The Great Sioux War   333
  The Nez Perce   336
Seeing History: Custer's Last Stand   337
Conclusion   341
Review Questions   341
Recommended Readings   341
Native American History Online   342

11   The Struggle for Cultural Identity, 1877–1910   344
Wild West Shows   345
Chasing Freedom, Preserving Identity   347
  Victorio and Geronimo   348
  The Ghost Dance   351
Saving the Indian   357
  Eastern Reformers   357
  Lake Mohonk   358
Seeing History: "Give the Red Man a Chance"   359

The Attack on Indian Culture   360
  The Dawes Act   360
Reading History: General Allotment Act, or Dawes Act (1887)   361
Profile: The "Oklahoma Land Rushers, or Boomers"   365
  Christianizing the Indian   366
  Educating Native Americans   367
Seeing History: "The American Indian: Past and Present"   371
Profile: Plenty Kill, aka Luther Standing Bear (Oglala, 1868–1939)   372
Conclusion   373
Review Questions   373
Recommended Readings   373
Native American History Online   374

12   Progressivism and World War I: Charting Their Own Course in the Twentieth Century, 1900–1920   376
Simon Pokagon   377
The Progressive Spirit Among Native Americans   378
Seeing History: Dime Novels   381
  The Society of American Indians   382
Profile: Jim Thorpe   383
  Gertrude Bonnin and Laura Cornelius Kellogg   385
  Religion and the SAI   388
  Fractures Within the SAI   389
  The Peyote Issue   391
The Great War   393
  The World War I Draft   394
Reading History: Native American Citizenship and Compulsory Military Service   395
  Indians Enter Military Service   399
  Over There   400
Profile: Private Joseph Oklahombi (Choctaw)   402
  Stereotypes and Indian Military Service   403
  The Home Front   404
Conclusion   406
Review Questions   407
Recommended Readings   407
Native American History Online   408

13 Postwar Directions for Native Americans, 1918–1929   410

The "Osage Reign of Terror"   411

Coming Home   414

   Wartime Divestment of Indian Lands   415

   Wartime Resurgence of Traditional Values   418

   Citizenship for Native Americans   419

Postwar Activism   421

   The Continued Assault on Indian Lands   421

Profile: Will Rogers   422

   Pueblo Lands   423

Reading History: Letter From Commissioner of Indian Affairs Charles Burke to All Indians, February 24, 1923   426

   Fall's Removal From Office   427

Changing Directions   428

   The Emerging Path of Reform   428

Seeing History: *The Vanishing American* and Hollywood Film   429

Profile: John Collier   431

   Citizenship Revisited   434

   The Meriam Report   435

Reading History: From *The Problem of Indian Administration*, or Meriam Report, 1928   437

Conclusion   439

Review Questions   439

Recommended Readings   440

Native American History Online   440

14 The Great Depression, 1929–1940   442

The CCC Project at Bandelier National Park Near Santa Fe, New Mexico   443

Native Americans and the Early Years of the Great Depression   445

   Hard Times   446

   Reform Efforts in the Hoover Administration   448

   Health Care and Education   450

   A Brighter Prospect for Change   452

The Indian New Deal   452

   Native Americans and New Deal Reform   453

   The Public Works of Art Project   454

   The Civilian Conservation Corps—Indian Division   456

Profile: Robert Yellowtail   457

   Navajo Stock Reduction   458

   Indian Education   459

A New Direction in Federal Indian Policy   461

   The Indian Reorganization Act   461

Reading History: Excerpts from the Indian Reorganization Act (Wheeler-Howard Act), June 18, 1934   463

   Resistance to the IRA   465

Profile: Alice Lee Jemison (Seneca)   469

   An Assessment of the Indian New Deal   471

Conclusion   473

Review Questions   473

Recommended Readings   473

Native American History Online   474

15 American Indians Join the War Effort, 1940–1945   476

Lieutenant Ernest Childers Earns the Congressional Medal of Honor   477

Native Americans Enter the Armed Forces   479

   Draft Registration and Military Induction   480

   Motives for Enlistment   481

Seeing History: *Freedom's Warrior— The American Indian*   484

Defining Indian Identity   485

   Racial Identity in Virginia   485

   Tribal Sovereignty   487

Native Americans at War   488

   Indian Response to Pearl Harbor   489

   Indians at War   489

   Code Talkers   491

Profile: Postwar Ira Hayes   492

   The Popular Image of Indian Soldiers   495

Reading History: Navajo Translation of the United States Marine Corps Hymn   496

Seeing History: Military Use of Native American Imagery   497

The Home Front   498

   War Comes to the Reservations   499

   Migration to Defense Factories   501

Women and the War Effort 502
War Bond Purchases 503
Conclusion 504
Review Questions 504
Recommended Readings 505
Native American History Online 505

16 Redefining the Status of Native Americans in Post–World War II America, 1943–1962 506
John Nez (Navajo) 507
The Path to Termination 509
Senate Report 310 510
A Global Indian Reorganization Act 512
The National Congress of American Indians 513
The Immediate Postwar Direction 515
Economic Difficulties 515
Social Concerns 517
The Indian Claims Commission 518
Termination and Relocation 519
Termination Reconsidered 520
The Relocation Program 521
Seeing History: Bureau of Indian Affairs Relocation Poster "Come to Denver" 524
The Policy of Termination 525
Klamath and Menominee Termination 526
Profile: Ada Deer (Menominee) 529
Reading History: Party Platform Planks and Native Americans 532
"The More Things Change . . ." 534
The Continued Assault on Indian Lands 534
The Korean War 535
Profile: Woodrow Wilson Keeble (Sioux) 536
Hollywood Films and Television 537
Conclusion 540
Review Questions 540
Recommended Readings 541
Native American History Online 541

17 Indian Activism in the Age of Liberalism, 1961–1980 542
Bernie Whitebear and the Fort Lawton Takeover 543
A New Direction in Indian Activism 546
Fishing and Water Rights 547
Profile: Buffy Sainte-Marie, 1941– 548

Alcatraz 549
The Alcatraz Occupation 550
Profile: Vine Deloria Jr. (1933–2005) 551
Indians and the Vietnam War 553
Native Americans Enter the Armed Forces 553
Combat Service 555
Racial Consciousness 555
Red Power 556
The American Indian Movement 556
Trail of Broken Treaties 559
Wounded Knee 562
The Longest Walk 565
New Directions? 565
Seeing History: A Call for Support 566
Indian Self-Determination 567
Urbanization Patterns 568
Educational Directions 570
Reading History: Edward M. Kennedy, "Foreword" From *Indian Education: A National Tragedy—A National Challenge*, October 30, 1969 570
Mainstream Awareness 573
Conclusion 575
Review Questions 575
Recommended Readings 576
Native American History Online 576

18 Self-Determination to Decolonization: Native Americans into the Twenty-First Century 578
Ronald Reagan, Decolonization 579
Presidential Indian Policy: 1980s–1990s 582
The Reagan Years 582
Reading History: Ronald Reagan, Indian Policy Statement, January 24, 1983 583
Profile: Peter MacDonald: Navajo Leader Falls From Power in the Era of Reagan 584
George Herbert Walker Bush: Any Better? 585
Reading History: George H. W. Bush's Statement on Indian Affairs, June 14, 1991 586
Native Peoples and Activism: The 1980s and 1990s 587
Reservations and Resources 587
Casinos and Tourism 590

NAGPRA and What Is an Indian? 593
*Native American Women Take
    Charge* 596
**Reading History: James C. Chatters,
    Kennewick Man** 597
**Profile: Suzan Shown Harjo: Cheyenne-
    Creek Activist** 600
**Empowerment and Decolonization and
    Into the Twenty-First Century** 600
Literature and Art 600
Indigenous Peoples in the Academy 601
**Shifting Directions: The Obama and
    Trump Presidencies** 602
The Obama Years, 2009–2017 602
The Ascendency of Donald Trump 605

The Keystone Pipeline 606
Pocahontas 608
The Republican Agenda for Native Lands 610
*The Trump Agenda's Impact on Indian
    Country* 612
Conclusion 614
Review Questions 615
Recommended Readings 615
Native American History Online 615

*Appendix—Federally Recognized Tribes in the
    United States* 617
Glossary of Key Terms and Concepts 625
Bibliography 633
Index 643

Figures

Chapter 1 Opener—Artist's Rendition of Cahokia

1.1A 11,400 BCE Clovis point   9

1.1B 10,300 BCE Folsom point   9

1.2   Sandstone carvings at Petroglyph
      Canyon near Las Vegas, Nevada   12

1.3   Jackson stairway in Chaco Canyon,
      evidence of the engineering skills of
      the Ancestral Puebloans   16

1.4A Cave site of Mesa Verde   18

1.4B Artist's rendition of Pueblo Bonito   18

1.5   Artist's rendition of Cahokia   21

1.6   Gorget showing a falcon-man
      marine shell   23

Chapter 2 Opener—Macchu Picchu

2.1   Aztec Indians with smallpox are
      ministered to by a medicine man. As
      part of the "Columbian Exchange,"
      smallpox devastated many native
      populations even before they
      encountered the Spaniards   35

2.2   Maya glyphs carved in stone panel.
      Such glyphs show the sophistication
      of the Mayan language   36

2.3   Huitzilopochtli, the patron god of the
      city of Tenochtitlán   41

2.4   Quetzalcoatl, the feathered serpent
      god, was a deity found among pre-
      contact Mesoamerican peoples.
      Among the Aztecs, Quetzalcoatl was
      a god that moved between upper and
      under worlds and was a deity of
      creation   42

2.5   Spanish adventurers attack a native
      village on the Columbian coast of the
      Caribbean in an engraving published
      by Theodore de Bry in 1594   49

2.6   A religious dance in a drawing
      created by John White. While not
      always accurate, White's collection of
      watercolors was the first glimpse the
      English public had into the world of
      the coastal Algonquians   59

Chapter 3 Opener—Timucua Women Planting Corn or Beans

3.1   Map of the town, fort, and entrance
      to the harbor of St. Augustine and
      vicinity, Florida, 1595   68

3.2 Native men carrying The Lady of Cofitachequi of the Coosa chiefdom in Georgia on an ornamental litter; trumpeters lead the procession, which is followed by young women carrying baskets of fruit and by a contingent of bodyguards 70

3.3 A palisaded Timucuan town, with its palm-thatched houses and sentry posts at its narrow entrance 74

Chapter 4 Opener—Roger Williams Negotiating With Narragansetts

4.1 John Smith being "saved" by Pocahontas 102

4.2 Portrait of Pocahontas as Lady Rebecca Rolfe 104

4.3 Huron war chief 115

Chapter 5 Opener—Florida Indians Hunting Deer

5.1 *Samson Occom, the Reverend, sits and reads his bible* 138

5.2 Baptism of Indians in America. David Zeisberger, a Moravian missionary, preaches to the Delawares. This image, with some Delawares interested in Zeisberger and others not, demonstrates how Christianity divided some mid-Atlantic native communities 144

5.3 Delaware Prophet Neolin's chart of the paths to the Master of Life 158

5.4 There is no known image of Pontiac. John Mix Stanley, the artist of this portait, was a painter and explorer and traveler of the west, and part of a nineteenth-century movement in which artists portrayed living Native Americans in their state of existence but as a "vanishing race." In various portraits, artists like Stanley cast leaders like Pontiac as noble relics of a tragic and violent colonial past 159

Chapter 6 Opener—Payta-Kootha

6.1 Joseph Fayadaneega, called Joseph Brant, the Great Captain of the Six Nations (Thayendanegea). In this image, Brant's clothing demonstrates his pro-British position, particularly the fine clothing and gorget around his neck 168

6.2 Warrior chief Good Peter Agwelentongwas, drawn by John Trumbull 170

6.3 Map of the Draught of Cherokee Country 176

6.4 Hopothle Mico, or the Tallassee King of the Creeks 180

6.5 Black Hoof, a Shawnee leader 182

6.6 Tecumseh, sketch by Pierre Le Dru, c. 1810–1812 187

6.7 Ten-squát-a-way, The Open Door, known as The Prophet, brother of Tecumseh 188

Chapter 7 Opener—Robert Lindneux, *The Trail of Tears*

7.1 Se-Quo-Yah, a Cherokee warrior, fought in the Creek War and invented the Cherokee alphabet 205

7.2 John Ross, Cherokee Chief 207

7.3 Pushmataha 215

7.4 Osceola, leader of Seminole resistance 221

7.5 Keokuk, Sauk chief 224

7.6 Black Hawk (Makataimeshekiakiak), Sauk war chief 225

Chapter 8 Opener—Totem Pole in Saxman Native Village, Ketchikan, Alaska

8.1 One of the Jefferson Peace and Friendship medals distributed by Lewis and Clark during their expedition 246

8.2 Hidatsa village on the Knife River, a painting by George Catlin, 1832 249

8.3 This page from Lewis and Clark journals documents the

head-flattening technique used by the
Clatsop tribe   252

8.4 Fort Ross, 1840   255

8.5 *California Rancho Scene* by Alfred Sully,
c. 1849   266

8.6 Ishi, the last Yahi   272

8.7 Navajos, c. 1851   276

Chapter 9 Opener—Sioux Indians

9.1 Stand Watie   287

9.2 The Battle of Pea Ridge at Elkhorn
Tavern in March 1862, a key battle
of the Civil War, was one of the first
in which American Indian troops
engaged in combat outside Indian
territory   289

9.3 Little Crow   290

9.4 Hanging at the Santee Sioux
Reservation in Minnesota, 1862   294

9.5 Christopher Carson, known as Kit
Carson (1809–1868)   298

9.6 Navajos under guard at Bosque
Redondo, c. 1864   300

9.7 *The Battle of Sand Creek*, oil painting by
Robert Lindneux, 1936   306

**Chapter 10 Opener—Chief
Red Cloud**

10.1 William Tecumseh Sherman   316

10.2 General William Tecumseh Sherman
and the Peace Commission meet with
Cheyenne and Arapaho leaders to
draft the Fort Laramie Treaty of 1868   324

10.3 Ely S. Parker (1828–1895), Seneca chief
and Union Army officer in the
Civil War   327

10.4 Thomas Nast, "Robinson Crusoe
making a man of his Friday" (cartoon)   328

10.5 Buffalo hunters and skinners   329

10.6 Sitting Bull (c. 1831–1890) was a
Hunkpapa Lakota Sioux holy man
who led his people as a tribal chief

during years of resistance to United
States government policies   334

10.7 George Armstrong Custer   337

10.8 Chief Joseph, years after leading the
Nez Perce on their epic but failed
escape to Canada   338

**Chapter 11 Opener—Carlisle
Indian School**

11.1 Geronimo (1829–1909), leader of the
Chiricahua Apache   350

11.2 Sioux Indians performing the
Ghost Dance   353

11.3 Helen Hunt Jackson (1830–1885) was a
writer and activist on behalf of Native
Americans   358

11.4 Thomas Nast, "Give the Red Man a
Chance" (cartoon)   359

11.5 Chief American Horse (Ogala Sioux)
receiving his allotment under the Dawes
General Allotment Act   364

11.6 This 1911 advertisement from the U.S.
Department of the Interior offers former
reservation land for sale. The ad pictures
a Yankton Sioux named Not Afraid of
Pawnee   365

11.7A Chiricahua Apache children upon
arrival at Carlisle Indian School   368

11.7B Chiricahua children after four months
at Carlisle Indian School   369

11.8 *Puck Magazine* cartoon   371

11.9 Luther Standing Bear   372

Chapter 12 Opener—Princess Tsianina

12.1 Dime novels   381

12.2 Group of Siksika men and one woman
in traditional dress   382

12.3 Jim Thorpe   383

12.4 Zitkala-Sa, or Gertrude Simmons
Bonnin (1876–1938), a Yankton
Dakota Sioux writer, editor, musician,
teacher, and political activist   386

12.5   Students during mathematics class at the Carlisle Indian School   386

12.6   Dr. Charles A. Eastman (1858–1939) was a Native American physician, writer, national lecturer, and reformer. He founded 32 Native American chapters of the Young Men's Christian Association (YMCA) and helped found the Boy Scouts of America   389

12.7   Henry Roe Cloud (1884–1950) was a distinguished educator, college administrator, U.S. Federal Government official, Presbyterian minister, and reformer   391

12.8   Members of the Choctaw tribe who served as code talkers during World War I   401

12.9   Joseph Oklahombi   402

12.10   Men from Carlisle Indian School march in the Preparedness Day Parade, 1916   405

Chapter 13 Opener—Pueblo Indians at Visit to Senate Lands Committee

13.1   John Billy (Palute) farming at Duckwater Reservation   417

13.2   Pawnee dancers at the Second Annual Victory Dance to honor Pawnee veterans of World War I, August 1920   419

13.3   Will Rogers   422

13.4   Taos Pueblo, New Mexico   424

13.5   Hopi Indians performing the Antelope Dance, 1921   427

13.6   The Vanishing American poster   429

13.7   Secretary of the Interior Hubert Work and Commissioner of Indian Affairs Charles Burke meet with Osage Chiefs Red Eagle and Bacon Rind   432

13.8   Shoshone Indians perform the Sun Dance on the Fort Hall Reservation, c. 1925   433

Chapter 14 Opener—Native American Workers on the Hoover Dam

14.1   Original Gadawa family home   449

14.2   John Collier   453

14.3   This 1936 poster for the Federal Art Project exhibition of drawings from the Index of American Design shows a weather vane in the shape of a Native American   454

14.4   Civilian Conservation Corps enrollee Henry Denny, with grandchildren   456

14.5   Buying sheep from Native Americans   458

Chapter 15 Opener—Marine Corps Women Reservists

15.1   Lieutenant Ernest Childers, a Creek, being congratulated by General Jacob L. Devers after receiving the Congressional Medal of Honor in Italy for wiping out two machine gun nests, July 1944   482

15.2   Charles Banks Wilson, *Freedom's Warrior—The American Indian*   484

15.3   Raising the American flag on Iwo Jima, February 23, 1945. Ira Hayes is shown on the far left of the photo   491

15.4   Ira Hayes   492

15.5   Navajo Indian code talkers Henry Blake and George Kirk, December 1943   495

15.6A   45th U.S. Infantry Division shoulder patch, 1942–1945   497

15.6B   Shoulder sleeve insignia that was first approved for the 36th Infantry Division in November 1918   497

15.7   Apache Indians assist in the unloading of beds for evacuees of Japanese ancestry in Poston, Arizona, April 1942   500

Chapter 16 Opener—Children at Wind River

16.1   Burton K. Wheeler, Montana State Senator from 1923 to 1947   511

16.2   Representatives of various tribes attend an organizational meeting of the National Congress of American Indians, November 1944   514

16.3 Navajo hoes corn within sight of an old volcanic core in Monument Valley, Utah, 1952 516

16.4 President Harry Truman is presented with a pipe said to have once been smoked by Sitting Bull by IshTi-Opi (Choctaw), Reginald Curpy (Uncompahgre Ute), and Julius Murray (Uintah Ute) 522

16.5 Bureau of Indian Affairs relocation poster 524

16.6 Woodrow Wilson Keeble 536

Chapter 17 Opener—View of San Francisco During Occupation of Alcatraz

17.1 Buffy St. Marie 548

17.2 Sioux Indians plant an American flag on Alcatraz Island in San Francisco, California, during a demonstration in 1964 550

17.3 Vine Deloria Jr. 552

17.4 American Indian Movement leader Dennis Banks speaks before a gathering at Mount Rushmore, South Dakota 557

17.5 President Richard Nixon signs a bill giving the Taos Pueblo Indians title to Blue Lake and surrounding land in New Mexico with an interpreter and a religious leader from the tribe in attendance 560

17.6 Native American leaders refuse to obey a court order to vacate the Bureau of Indian Affairs headquarters 561

17.7 AIM member Oscar Running Bear stands with his rifle at the ready near a teepee at Wounded Knee, South Dakota on the Pine Ridge Indian Reservation, March 1973 563

17.8 American Indian Movement poster 566

Chapter 18 Opener—Protesting President Trump's Dismantling of Bear Ears Monument

18.1 LaDonna Harris (1931–) is a Comanche social activist and founder and president of Americans for Indian Opportunity 582

18.2 An early image of a Makah whaler with his own tools of the trade 595

18.3 Winona LaDuke (1959–) is a Native American activist, environmentalist, economist, and writer 596

18.4 Wilma Pearl Mankiller (1945–2010) was the first female Chief of the Cherokee Nation from 1985 to 1995 599

18.5 Foxwoods Casino 601

18.6 President Obama at the White House Tribal Nations Conferences 603

18.7 President Obama visits with Native American performers in Cannon Ball, North Dakota 604

18.8 Standing Rock protesters 608

18.9 President Trump honors Native American code talkers in which he referred to Senator Elizabeth Warren as "Pocahontas" 609

18.10 Bear Ears National Monument 611

Maps

1.1 Bering land bridge   6
2.1 Yucatan in the conquest period   37
2.2 The Valley of Mexico   39
3.1 Missions in Spanish Florida, c. 1674–1675   72
3.2 Pueblos in New Mexico, c. 1650   81
7.1 Indian removal   203
7.2 Tragic walk of the Trail of Tears   211
7.3 The Potawatomi Trail of Death   232
8.1 Tribal locations and trading establishments, Southern Plains, 1780, and Central-Northern Plains, 1785–1798   247
8.2 Major tribal groupings in California   265
9.1 Bosque Redondo, New Mexico   297
9.2 Sand Creek, Colorado   305
10.1 Powder River   319
10.2 Route of the 1877 flight of the Nez Perce from the U.S. Army   340
11.1 Western reservations   354
11.2 Federal Indian reservations nationwide, within ten years of the Massacre at Wounded Knee of 1890   356
14.1 California Census Data, 1930   447
18.1 Mineral-rich tribal lands   588
18.2 Ojibwa reservations in Wisconsin   589
18.3 New Mexican tribes   591

Preface

First Americans began as a dialogue among several historians who teach both Native American history and U.S. history. Dr. Mark Nicholas soon emerged as the principal advisor to this project, serving as co-author to the text's first edition. In my numerous conversations with him, we acknowledged the obvious—students have limited awareness of native cultures and histories, and what limited awareness they have is commonly saddled with romantic misrepresentations or traditional stereotypes. Although we agreed that several currently available Native American history textbooks effectively dispel most standard myths, they nonetheless covered inadequately many pivotal moments and issues in native histories or offered little evidence of the centrality of culture and identity in historic relations among native peoples themselves or between Native Americans and non-Indian populations.

We were troubled, too, that so many students view Native American history apart from the larger flow of human events nationally and internationally, and that U.S. history survey texts as well as Native American history texts present native studies and history as a compartmentalized subject, one seldom connected to continental or global events. It is necessary for students to be able to place Native American history into the larger context of national and international developments. Survey courses in U.S. history typically direct scant attention to native peoples in North America, the minimal space assigned to American Indians generally focused on Native Americans as momentary impediments to continental conquest or as reluctant but eventually successful adopters of mainstream American culture. Moreover, native peoples nearly vanish from sight as the twentieth century unfolds. Finally, the narrative common to existing textbooks does not include an Indian voice. This text, *First Americans: A History of Native Peoples*, provides a more complete story of American Indians and includes the native perspective.

Approach

Without the "Indian voice," the history of Native Americans is incomplete. First, providing their "voice" in their own words or in demonstrating their perspective through their actions most effectively explains native identities and behaviors over the centuries. Second, we wanted to counter directly the prevalent attitude among so many students that native peoples were consistently victims of colonial and national expansion. Corresponding to the traditionally present "victim" perspective is the argument of "inevitability." The arguments of persistent victimization and inevitability assume native peoples were unable to sway the course of history, incapable of preserving any true sense of identity, and conquered by a force vastly superior to themselves. Such a perspective holds that Indians were doomed to extinction—if not physically, then culturally—that preservation of their unique identity was beyond their ability. To the contrary, this text demonstrates routinely that American Indians were active agents in determining their own futures, evidenced in an array of resistance efforts and forms of resistance, in their effort to adapt when necessary, and ultimately in the survival of Indian identity as the United States settled into the twenty-first century.

First Americans tells the story of Native Americans and native America. The book is not just another story focused on the Cherokee and Sioux or on Native Americans as super-spiritual peoples living in some state of "communal bliss" or in perpetual harmony with nature. Students will learn about the Cherokee and Sioux peoples, to be sure, and they will read of prominent leaders including Pontiac, Tecumseh, Geronimo, and Sitting Bull, but *First Americans* balances such accounts with a detailed investigation of the lives of more obscure tribal peoples and ordinary Native Americans, moving the student among small communities, towns, villages, larger tribes and nations, and across the centuries noted for both continuity and change. *First Americans* is also about Indian homelands and histories continent-wide, stretching from Canada into northern Mexico, from the Atlantic Ocean to the Pacific Ocean. Native Americans were people adjusting, moving, and even controlling the changing circumstances within their homelands that Europeans, then white Americans, tried to wrest from them. They made hard and difficult decisions. New frameworks that historians have developed in recent years in reaction to the old story of the American frontier appear throughout the text. Geography is included as part of the larger narrative of Native American history. Native peoples have had or have maintained some control over most of North America's lands to the present, and the land itself has been, and remains, central to understanding native cultural heritage, survival, and identity. *First Americans* shows how different landscapes, as much as the peoples themselves, helped shape patterns of accommodation, adaptation, resistance, and cultural revitalization.

The narrative and chronological structure is grounded in the scholarship that has blossomed over the last 25 years. Controversial issues such as cultural authenticity, native origins, and religion are examined and contribute to a balanced perspective that shapes the fascinating and complex stories of Native American persistence, sovereignty, autonomy, and cultural change and survival, while offering students the historical context nationally and globally in which to understand more fully the native experience and perspective.

Organization

The chronological and geographic scope of *First Americans* is immense, spanning nearly 30,000 years of history and cultural change and persistence. Chapter 1 is grounded on the anthropological and archaeological record to tell the story of Native American origins and the early social and cultural patterns that created a rich history long before the arrival of Europeans. Unlike other texts, significant attention is given to Spanish colonial patterns; Chapter 2 focuses on the monumental encounters of Aztec, Mayan, and Inca peoples with the Spanish; Chapter 3 follows the creation of Spanish borderlands from a melding of cultures from present-day Florida, across North America's Deep South, and over present-day New Mexico and Southern California. Chapter 4 takes the reader into seventeenth-century territories east of the Mississippi River to explain Native Americans' first encounters with French and English colonizers and patterns of relationships that emerged. Native cultural adaptation, accommodation, and methods of resistance to English and French imperial powers to 1763 are central to Chapter 5.

Staying with a Native American-centered history, Chapter 6 treats the founding of the United States as a continental experience, one that involves and affects not only the relationship between native peoples and Euro-Americans but also the relationships among Native Americans themselves. The age of revolution is continental in scale, ranging from native roles in the American Revolution to native revolutions in the Spanish Southwest and California and a theme of continental revolution to 1814. Native American persistence and resistance throughout the United States east of the Mississippi frames Chapter 7, and Chapter 8 tracks Native Americans in the West to 1850. The narrative follows native peoples' responses to American and European economic expansion from the Missouri with Lewis and Clark through the Rocky Mountains and international fur trade into the Pacific Northwest, where Native Americans faced ocean-going competing imperial powers in Russia, the United States, and Britain, which sought the lucrative sea otter pelts. The shift from Spanish rule to American expansion and gold rush continues the story and concludes in the Southwest, where horseback native cultures clashed with an expansive United States and an ever-diminishing presence of the Mexican state.

Chapter 9 examines not only the imprint of the Civil War on Native Americans but also their inclusion in the conflict itself. Chapter 10 details federal Indian policy following the war in both its continuity with the past and in its changing direction, as well as Native Americans' determination to preserve their cultural heritage and identities. The issue of native identity remains a constant theme throughout the remainder of the text, evidenced in Chapter 11, which tracks final major efforts at armed resistance, native spiritual directions in opposition to the increasingly powerful acculturative efforts federal authorities, and privately directed reform groups. In Chapter 12, Native Americans actively define their own identity within the United States during the Progressive Era and years of the Great War and aggressively chart their own path within the system that has enveloped them, a committed direction further evidenced in Chapter 13 but one that also confronted additional challenges imposed by federal authorities and by threatening conditions on reservations. Chapter 14 details the effect of the Great Depression on native peoples nationally but also the opportunities created by the crisis for Indian economic, social, and cultural revitalization, opportunities initiated by both Native Americans and the federal government that inadvertently resulted in unparalleled inclusion in mainstream American life, as demonstrated in Chapter 15.

Chapter 16 and Chapter 17 each examine closely Washington's plan to terminate its obligations to native peoples and the rise, and ultimate power, of Native American activism that fundamentally empowered native peoples in modern America. Chapter 18 carries the story of Native Americans into the Trump presidency in the twenty-first century. Common to Chapters 9 through 18 is a focus on Indian identity and activism, a native voice, and a commitment by Native Americans to chart their own path in spite of the power brought against them by government and private reform initiatives. In contrast to other texts, *First Americans* provides a thorough treatment of Native Americans in the Progressive Era, in all major wars of the twentieth century, and post-World War II social and economic patterns. Presented throughout the text is the story of Native American activism and resistance.

This edition of *First Americans* continues the rationale for, and the objectives of, the first edition. I have restructured the narrative, provided fuller discussion of certain material, redeveloped earlier perspectives and offered new ones, and carried the subject to the present (2018) to address native affairs through the Barack Obama and Donald Trump presidencies. I want to thank Mark Nicholas for his work in drafting the text's first edition and wish him well in his current endeavors.

Features

Each chapter in *First Americans* includes many special features to enhance the narrative and the voice of native peoples throughout their history.

Opening Vignettes Each chapter begins with the story of a key person or event to set the stage for the events to come in that chapter. These stories enhance the book's focus on Native American-centered history as well as introduce students to individuals and events to help put the themes and stories in the chapter into context.

Profiles These are short biographical sketches set within the specific chronological period, personal stories to enhance the themes presented in each chapter.

Seeing History These sections offer images that speak visually about Native American history, allowing students to see and envision native peoples and their lives on native terms. These features include an introduction to put the image into historical context and critical-thinking questions to encourage critical analysis.

Reading History Each section demonstrates the printed voice of an era found in letters, diaries, publications, and government documents. These primary documents allow students to understand, in dramatic fashion, the temper of the times or discover the historical record of an era and, in so doing, gain a more complete perspective of Native Americans, the world they crafted, and the world surrounding them. Each document has an introduction and critical-thinking questions.

Chronologies At the beginning of each chapter is a chronology that is intended to give the student a broad sweep of events that will be addressed in the chapter and serve as a resource for review.

Mini-chronologies Each chapter includes mini-chronologies that allow fuller treatment of a particular issue or event.

Pedagogy We provide readers with an overview of important themes with the start of each chapter, couched in the form of broad **Key Questions** to help students organize their thinking as they read the chapter. We conclude each chapter with specific **Review Questions** that effectively compel student thought and analysis of the material presented in the narrative. The text is also rich in **charts, tables, graphs, maps, artwork,** and **photographs** that extend or supplement the narrative. At the end of each chapter is a list of **Recommended Readings** that point students to books for further study and information. At the end of the text is a **glossary** of key terms and people.

Native American History Online Students can explore the rich history of Native Americans through the links to websites that relate to the chapters' principal themes and topics. They can also visit virtually key historic places where Native American history unfolded.

Acknowledgments

I offer my appreciation and thanks to Charlyce Jones-Owen, Publisher for Arts and Sciences at Pearson, for her support, guidance, and encouragement over so many years, but especially for moving the project from its earliest stages of development to publication of the first edition. I also extend my thanks to Maureen Prado Roberts, Senior Marketing Manager; Maureen Diana, Editorial Assistant; Emsal Hasan, Associate Editor; Cheryl Keenan, Production Editor; and Kristy Zamagni of PreMediaGlobal for their work on the text's final production stages.

For this, the second edition, I want to thank Dr. Eve Mayer, Editor, *History of the Americas*, and Theodore Meyer, Editorial Assistant, *History of the Americas* at Routledge/Taylor Francis and their staff for their dedication to this project. They secured reviews and recommendations from historians in the field of native studies, offered their perspectives, provided sound guidance, and moved the second edition toward its completion. They demonstrated a level of professionalism that has been much appreciated. I also appreciate the diligent and detailed work of Kerry Boettcher in managing a final edit of the manuscript and preparing the work for the print shop. Of equal importance, if not greatest importance, Eve, Ted, and Kerry displayed remarkable patience navigating unexpected delays and a significant change of course late in the project. This book would not have been possible without their commitment and dedication.

Kenneth W. Townsend

First Americans

Native North America Before European Contact

STORIES VERSUS SCIENCE
BEGINNINGS
We Were Always Here
The Scientific Evidence
Clovis and Folsom Cultures
CHANGES IN THE WEST
California Indians
The Northwest
The Great Basin and the Plains
AGRICULTURE-BASED SOCIETIES IN THE SOUTHWEST
Cultural Diversity and the Arrival of Maize
The "Chaco Phenomenon"
Hohokam and Mesa Verde Cultures
EASTERN WOODLANDS
Early Eastern Woodlands Traditions
Adena and Hopewell Cultures
Mississippian Chiefdoms
The Iroquois

Stories Versus Science

Pawnees explain their beginnings this way: the first Pawnee man and woman received life from Tirawa, a male spirit of the upper cosmos who held the powers of thunder and lightning. The Pawnee male was represented by the Morning Star of the East, woman by the Evening Star in the West. Long ago, they and their descendants migrated from colder climates, south into the plains of North America. Pawnee origin stories vividly tell of a universe divided into male and female components. The Pawnee farmed and hunted along the Platte, Republican, and Loup rivers that interlocked parts of Nebraska, Wyoming, and Colorado, along the outer reaches of the northern plains. Their settlement patterns and gendered division of labor complemented the Pawnee bond with the stars and earth. This relationship was

Artist's rendition of Cahokia

Source: Cahokia Mounds State Historic Site/
Michael Hampshire

3

evident in a rich Pawnee ceremonial, wherein Pawnees set corn medicine bundles next to posts at the center of villages and used the stars and an understanding of four sacred cardinal directions to target fertile lands. Broken into four village divisions aligned with the four cardinal points, each village had corn and medicine bundles of different types to sustain balance between Tirawa and Mother Earth, the female cosmic being of fertility. Mother Maize was the most powerful of the corns. Pawnee gave thanks to Mother Maize through elaborate rituals that included gifts of bison meat. The cosmic balance between the Morning Star and the Evening Star—the original man and woman—was maintained in all facets of Pawnee life.

Origin stories, like the one above, explain how a people came to be. Each Native American tribal group has an origin story, which is the root of the group's cultural traditions. The numerous and diverse origin stories of Native Americans sharply counter the single origin concept posited by each of the major western religions, and, in so doing, set the stage for conflict once native peoples meet Europeans, a clash of cultures that inevitably shaped the history of the Western Hemisphere. But native origin stories also counter science, as do all religious and spiritual creation stories. The stories reference upper worlds and under worlds, concepts at odds with science. They do not follow linear time as scientists do, and they are often vague about tribal peoples' patterns of settlement and places of origin. Today, the issue is not that tribal origin stories and western religion creationism are incompatible with one another but rather that traditional native origin stories are incompatible with the archaeological record.

Scientists postulate that an ice-free corridor, the **Bering land bridge**, opened in successive periods roughly between 30,000 and 13,000 years ago, connecting Alaska and Siberia and allowing for human migration from East Asia into North America. Scientists' efforts to determine the exact timing and scale of each wave of migration are ongoing. Native Americans, however, believe the Bering land bridge argument has less to do with science and more to do with justifying native land dispossession. If native peoples did not originate in

CHRONOLOGY

30,000 BCE–13,000 BCE	Bering land bridge open
13,500 BCE–12,900 BCE	Clovis culture
11,000 BCE–6,000 BCE	Folsom culture, expansion of Paleo-Indian hunters on the Plains, and the emergence of agriculture
900 CE–1150 CE	"Chaco Phenomenon"
300 CE–1450 CE	Hohokam tradition
500 CE–1300 CE	Mesa Verde
2200 BCE–700 CE	Poverty Point mound builders
1500 BCE	Reliance on cultigens in the Eastern Woodlands
1000 BCE–200 CE	Adena complex
200 BCE–500 CE	Hopewell culture
700 CE–1200 CE	Mississippian culture and Cahokia
1200 CE–1450 CE	Expansion of Moundville and beginning of Mississippian decline
circa 700 CE–European Contact	Natchez, Coosa, and other remnant Mississippian chiefdoms in the Deep South
1000 BCE–European Contact	Growth and concentration of Iroquois cultures

North America, but only migrated there, then they were just one of many waves of colonizers of the Western Hemisphere, making their ownership of the land temporary and subject to shifting sources of power. Moreover, many Native Americans see scientific arguments as unnecessary because they believe their stories tell them everything they need to know about their own beginnings.

KEY QUESTIONS

1. How and when did people migrate to North America?
2. How did Indian life change in the West after the Clovis and Folsom cultures died out?
3. Describe and analyze the different phases of social and cultural development in the Southwest.
4. What kinds of societies and cultures developed in the Eastern Woodlands?

Beginnings

Many Native Americans insist that their people populated North America long before the dates postulated by the Bering land bridge theory. They may be right. Many Pacific coast peoples have oral traditions of great floods that carried them to the lands on which they resided. In the Bella Coola story, "When the water rose to the top of the mountain," they tied up their boats, placed their ceremonial masks on the land, and planted their villages. "The masks are still there and turned to stone," referencing the rock cliffs along the coast. The Bella Coola, like their neighbors, may have experienced flooding when the glaciers receded at the end of last Ice Age, during a period known as the Wisconsin Glaciation, when the land bridge opened between 30,000 BCE to 11,000 BCE (before the common era). If coastal peoples witnessed the rising tides of glacial warming, then they could have been in North America long before the supposed Bering corridor ever opened (see Map 1.1).

We Were Always Here

Prominent Native American scholar and activist Vine Deloria Jr. argues that native stories are "geomythology." If geologists who study the earth can use sophisticated core samples of soil to date sediment activity and the expansion of topographical features over time, such geological data should not disqualify native stories as having similar, if not more important, value as a dating technique. In fact, native stories might be as far as people need to look. There are stories that tell of receding glaciers pouring water over the landscape. Hopis and other peoples in the Southwest talk of vast fires, perhaps because of volcanic eruptions dating back hundreds of thousands of years. A few Indian stories contain precise descriptions of existing mountains and craters, possibly a topography that predates the familiar. And Pacific Northwest peoples speak of houses that were once on stilts to ward off mammoths. Students and scholars cannot dismiss all these stories as fiction. Traditionalists among Native Americans put it quite simply: "We have always been here." If Native Americans were here before the theoretical opening of the Bering land bridge, then the scientific argument that people crossed an open bridge either collapses entirely, needs much more investigation, or must include native origin stories.

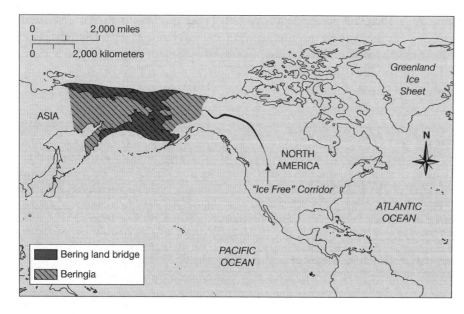

Map 1.1 Bering land bridge

The Scientific Evidence

Scientists do not know the precise details of the first population movements to the Western Hemisphere. Many paleoanthropologists (scientists who study the origins of human beings) believe that people from northeastern Asia crossed the Bering Strait using a land bridge that connected Asia to what is now Alaska. Samples of soil drilled from the seabed between Alaska and present-day Siberia confirm that the Bering land bridge once existed. There is general agreement that **hunter-gatherers** crossed the bridge by migrating through a narrow ice-free corridor. Still, questions linger. When, how, and in what numbers did these people, known as Paleo-Indians, migrate?

One recent discovery narrows the time frame. In 2013, excavations of an 11,500-year-old encampment in the Tanana River Valley of Central Alaska unearthed from a burial pit the skeletal remains of what appears to be a six-week-old girl. Named "Sunrise Girl-Child" by the team of scientists, the youngster belonged to a subgroup of migrating people who opted not to continue their journey and instead established a small community that eventually failed. A complete DNA analysis was finally completed in January 2018, and scientists at the University of Alaska and the University of Copenhagen found that about half of the child's DNA is that of Northern Eurasians, or Siberians, while the remainder is consistent with the DNA of Native Americans. This finding fits well into recent scholarship regarding the Bering Strait Theory of native origins. Most of the Canadian-Alaskan-Siberian stretch was covered completely in ice until about 12,500 years ago, note scientists at the University of Copenhagen, and therefore "incapable of sustaining human life" at any earlier time. "The land was completely naked and barren" and could not provide for migrating herds of bison for hundreds of years. The combined discoveries of ice sheets across the region and the finding of Sunrise Child-Girl certainly places humans along the path of the Bering Strait migrations and restricts their travel to an age more recent than the theory initially offered.

There are additional wrinkles to the long-accepted Bering Strait argument. What explains the presence of 12,000-year-old human remains found in an underwater Mexican cave in the early twenty-first century? The bones of a teenage girl were discovered in a 100-foot-deep water-filled pit called Hoyo Negro, or Black Hole. Her mitochondrial DNA indicated an Asian lineage, a trait exhibited by about 10 percent of the Native American population. The Bering Strait land bridge timeline now generally accepted does not mesh with the discovery of this teenage girl's bones. Meadowcroft Rockshelter, near Pittsburgh, Pennsylvania, gives archaeologists a glimpse into the lives of the earliest people of the Eastern Woodlands, a commonly used designation for the territories east of the Mississippi River, running from present-day Canada to the Gulf Coast. Skeptics have claimed that the site's **bifaces**, meaning two-sided stone tools, were not manmade artifacts. Others use radio-carbon dating (a method that tests for a steady measurable amount of carbon from archaeological site remains) to date the handmade tools to 13,000 BCE to 12,000 BCE or even as early as 30,000 BCE. If these people used the Bering land bridge, their eastward migration following big game on foot to the Eastern Woodlands would have taken just 1,000 to 2,000 years. Moreover, the stone tools at Meadowcroft were from a unique culture, unlike findings from the present-day plains and Southwest dated to the same period, and once considered the earliest tools used by people in North America.

A recent coastal find on the southern coast of Chile at Monte Verde that includes mastodon bones with human-worked stone tools raises more questions about the Bering Strait crossing. Radiocarbon dating

READING HISTORY

The Kwakiutl Story of the Deluge

Christians have the epic story of a flood in the Old Testament Book of Genesis. In that story, Noah built his Ark to save the animals and select people from certain doom. The same story appears in the Islamic Qur'an, the holy book of the Muslim world that also contains the teachings of the prophet Muhammed, the founder of Islam. The Kwakiutl of British Columbia are one of many Pacific coast peoples who have a story of a massive flood that settled over the earth. The Quatsino people that lived below the inlet knew the Flood was coming long before it happened. Some of the people hid in underground chambers safe from the waters, but most of the people built strong canoes to ride out the flood.

The largest of these canoes was made of a long cedar [for the canoe] with rope made from twisted cedar bark. Attached to this lead canoe was a large rock anchor. All the canoes were lashed together, and wooden containers of dried meat, fish, clams and berries were stored onboard.

Once the canoes were prepared, the skies darkened and torrential rains began to fall. The people noticed that the inlet's water was rising above the high tide mark. With this, some families boarded the canoes; others went underground. "I see a big wave coming," someone shouted, and they all looked and could see, in the distance, a mountain of water racing toward them. The flood hit, and the canoes rose level with the mountain tops across from their village. They avoided huge trees that were rooted up and carried by the rushing water. Pieces of their former homes dashed against the sides of their canoes. Some of the canoes broke away and were lost in the raging storm. The canoes that broke away later ended up in other places and started other tribes.

Source: James Wallas and Pamela Whitaker, *Kwakiutl Legends* (British Columbia: Hancock Publishers, 1989), pp. 37–38.

Questions

1. What might the Story of the Deluge tell us about Kwakiutl origins?
2. What are the differences between the Kwakiutl deluge account and the story of Noah and his Ark?

suggests that people may have occupied Monte Verde as early as 12,500 BCE or perhaps even much earlier. If the dating is correct, how did Paleo-Indians migrate so far south so fast? With other coastal sites in North and South America predating 20,000 BCE, some scholars have offered a new hypothesis: peopling of the Western Hemisphere might have followed water routes in addition to an ice-free corridor from Siberia. Geological evidence might support this coastal route argument. Dropping sea levels between 13,000 BCE and 14,000 BCE opened up huge ranges of ice-free land along the western continental shelf. In boats made of animal skins, people might have skirted from the Siberian region down the western coast to South America, establishing small settlements as they traveled. And in the case of the Hoyo Negro find, the *Journal of Science* has suggested that people from Southeast Asia possibly sailed or drifted eastward across the ocean, landing in Central or South America and commenced a migration from there. Indeed, the Harvard University geneticist Pontus Skoglund found DNA links between Amazon Indians and the indigenous peoples of Australia and New Guinea.

However they arrived, Paleo-Indians took full advantage of the animal and plant resources available in the Americas. Studies of contemporary hunter-gatherers, particularly in Africa, show that men hunt while women stay close to campsites, rearing children and gathering wild plants. Paleo-Indians probably lived like these present-day hunter-gatherer societies. They lived together in small bands and hunted available game such as deer and rabbits, but mostly they followed the migratory patterns of large game animals. Paleo-Indian men were skilled hunters, using a deep knowledge of the behavior and habits of their prey to bring down large animals. They developed specialized weapons to increase their chances of success and to decrease the risks the hunted animals posed to themselves. For example, Paleo-Indian men employed atlatls, hand-held tools carved out of wood, that allowed hunters to throw spears farther and with more force, thus making it possible for a hunter to make a fatal throw from a safer distance.

Clovis and Folsom Cultures

Clovis peoples flourishing from 13,500 BCE to 12,900 BCE created an important technological innovation. Clovis culture gets its name from a town in northeast New Mexico, where archaeologists first uncovered the distinctive Clovis projectile points, stone tips fixed to projectile weapons. Clovis hunters fluted their points. They flaked off the bottoms and created grooves on either side of the tip so hunters could haft the arrowheads to spears. Fluting and the distinctive chipping along the sides that made the edges of the points jagged and sharp also made tips more durable. Clovis points were quite durable, could be reused, and were sharper and harder and thus more piercing, making hunters better armed against large animals. Clovis tools also included bifaces, stone-worked tools used to cut meat and hides.

The archaeological record shows Clovis hunters particularly interested in mammoths and large bison. The remains of these animals are often found at Clovis sites, along with the distinctive fluted points and other hand-worked materials. The Lehrner site in Southeast Arizona yielded 13 mammoth remains. At Murray Springs, Arizona, archaeologists unearthed the remains of 11 bison and one mammoth, along with many hand-worked stones. Modern-day elephant movements give scientists some sense of the potential migratory patterns of bison and mammoths and thus the hunting patterns of Clovis men. Elephants travel in herds, returning generation after generation to the same places to feed and drink. Clovis people probably tracked mammoth and bison herds. Archaeologists have uncovered Clovis sites on low-lying ground, usually near rivers, ponds, or springs. Clovis hunters returned to sites like Lehrner time and time again.

Clovis people pursued large game in many parts of North America until 12,900 BCE when they begin to disappear from the archaeological record, succeeded by a host of new hunter-gatherer cultures. Paleoanthropologists offer multiple explanations for why Clovis hunters vanished. As their population grew, they may simply

1.1a 11,400 BCE Clovis point
Source: IADA/Shutterstock

1.1b 10,300 BCE Folsom point
Source: Dorling Kindersley

1.1 A Folsom point and its predecessor, the Clovis spear.

have hunted the large game animals into extinction, bringing on starvation, malnutrition, or their melding with other peoples then appearing on the scene. Another argument focuses on climate change. As the Ice Age ended, food and water sources for Clovis prey animals diminished. Without food and water, the large animals died out, leading to a tremendous decrease in the Clovis population, which was also forced to adapt to the arid landscape. In either case, native North America changed dramatically by 9,000 BCE, and new cultures replaced Clovis.

Around this time, buffalo herds became the primary target of large-game hunters. Buffalo survived the climate changes that may have doomed other large animals by adapting to low-grassland grazing. Folsom people emerged as the new buffalo-hunting culture. The Folsom cultural tradition earned its name from the town in northeast New Mexico where archaeologists first discovered the distinct Folsom fluted spear points. Folsom peoples, like Clovis bands, were excellent trackers and hunters, but Folsom peoples hunted buffalo with a more diverse set of strategies. Archaeologists have uncovered significant Folsom kill sites at Casper, Wyoming; Lindenmeier and Olson-Chubbock, in Colorado; and Cooper, Oklahoma.

All of these Great Plains sites reveal the variety and complexity of the Folsom hunting culture. At the Casper site, dated to roughly between 8,000 BCE and 7,000 BCE, Folsom hunters trapped 100 bison. Hunters often led a herd toward a cliff or steep ridge, probably dressing themselves in bison hides and making noises to scare the animals. Once the bison plummeted over the cliff, hunters butchered them and hauled their harvest back to camp. Many of these kill sites, like the one at Casper, produced more meat than one nomadic group could have consumed. Excess meat was probably traded or shared with other bands. Archaeological data also indicate that many Folsom hunters engaged in a long-distance trade in the stone materials used in tool and weapon making. Although bands were nomadic, social and economic exchanges like this were essential to settlement patterns, marriage practices, and community networks. At the Olson-Chubbock site, hunters forced 157 buffalo into a

TIMELINE 1.1 EARLY PEOPLING OF NORTH AMERICA, 30,000 BCE–8000 BCE

Date	Event
30,000 BCE–11,000 BCE	Possible window for people to cross the Bering land bridge from Siberia to Alaska
13,500 BCE–12,900 BCE	Clovis culture
9,000 BCE—8,000 BCE	Folsom culture

ravine, and the remains reveal that the hunters only killed 75 percent of the catch. The meat could have fed more than 100 people for approximately a month and was probably shared or traded through community networks of Folsom hunters. At the Cooper site, a buffalo skull was painted with a red pigment in the shape of a lightning bolt. One of the earliest examples of Great Plains art, the lightning bolt indicates both increasing cultural diversity and the emergence of a ritual and spiritual life surrounding the taking of animal life. Folsom hunters also returned to places where herds habitually grazed and drank water. At the Lindenmeier site, dated to about 8,000 BCE, archaeologists have discovered layers of encampments, suggesting that generations of hunters returned to the same spot.

Like the Folsom hunters, later generations of Great Plains hunters recognized buffalo as a source of food, pride, and spiritual power. The Assiniboine, a Siouan-speaking people once of the Northern Plains, crossing as hunters in the United States and Canada, later related their origins to the spiritual power of the buffalo. The first Assiniboine asked a spiritual guide, Inktomi, about food. Inktomi wanted the Assiniboine to avoid cannibalism, so he created buffalo. Under Inktomi's guidance, Assiniboine men learned to hunt the large beasts and make stone scrapers to remove hides. With his spiritual powers, Inktomi also taught Assiniboine women to skin a buffalo and about which sections of the animals were best to eat.

Changes in the West

The demise of the Clovis culture and the concurrent rise of the Folsom people occurred at a time when the foundations of agriculture were being laid in North America. Farming, however limited it was, depended on a climate conducive to growing crops and sufficient water to sustain their growth. Hunting continued to provide supplies of meat, and fishing still sustained those peoples residing on the coast or inland bodies of water, but, once supplemented with harvests of corn and other vegetables and fruits, the overall health of native peoples improved significantly, allowing for greater longevity and an increase in their populations. Agricultural productivity required better farm tools for cultivating croplands that expanded as populations rose. A rising reliance on agriculture carried with it the necessity of fashioning permanent communities—a sedentary existence supplanted the nomadic life of earlier cultures. Sedentary living required a more complex social order, giving rise to more formal and rigid structures of governance, interfamily relations, and property usage. In short, the rise of agriculture in North America fundamentally transformed human activity. The pace of cultural transformation depended in large measure on the land occupied by a people and the climate that governed it. There were native groups that did not develop an agrarian base for themselves but instead secured crops through trade with farming villages. Coastal natives, for example, often increased their harvest of fish, clams, and other water-based foods and actively bartered these for corn and other foodstuffs while supplementing their diet with hunted game, berries, and nuts. North America was in transition, establishing permanent and complex communities.

California Indians

Between 5000 BCE and 4000 BCE, new lifestyles and patterns of social organization emerged alongside the hunter-gatherers along the Pacific Coast. For example, between 3000 BCE and 2000 BCE, California Indians established semi-permanent villages to replace nomadic foraging communities, exploiting an array of coastal and inland resources. California Indians gathered shellfish, used the bow and arrow and harpoons to hunt large animals and seals, and caught fish. They also gathered seeds, especially those found in acorns. To facilitate the gathering and processing of acorns, villages were situated near oak forests. Women were responsible for acorn processing, grinding them with stone mortars and pestles, leeching the tannic acid out of them, and then cooking or storing them. As California villages grew in size and became more dependent on processed acorns, women developed more efficient mortars and pestles and lightweight basket designs to replace cumbersome stone or ceramic storage pots. Around 3000 BCE, climate change allowed for a dramatic increase in the population of the Pacific Coast. To meet this challenge, California Indians developed new forms of subsistence, adding small-scale agriculture to acorn gathering and hunting. The organization and planning demanded by agriculture gave rise to ranked societies led by chiefs who allocated and controlled the distribution of resources and land. Long-distance trade in goods such as shell beads suggests increased social complexity in California and the beginning of extensive tribal networks.

The Northwest

Prestigious burial goods such as fine woodcarvings and shells indicate the beginnings of hierarchical societies on the Northwest coast, present-day Alaska, British Columbia, and the coastal islands, by about 1000 BCE. The demands of ocean fishing and hunting drove Northwest peoples toward hierarchy and social specialization. Hunters needed sophisticated boats, harpoons, knives, and other blades to hunt and then remove the skins and cut the carcasses of seals and whales. Hunting such animals also required a hierarchical labor system, one in which hunters accepted the leadership roles of trackers and harpooners. Skilled wood carvers made canoes that could carry the necessary hunting implements and the weight of the crew. Craftsmen also used red and yellow cedar, fur, and spruce to build elaborate homes. The decoration of such homes marked families as members of specific **clans**, groups that associated descent within one or two specific lines and that adopted an animal as a **totem**, or spiritual symbol, to represent them. Wood carvers built gigantic totem poles decorated with depictions of their clan's mythical birds and animals, as well as mythical human spirits. An archaeological site at Ozette, Washington, that was buried by a sixteenth-century mudslide and preserved virtually intact provides a glimpse into Pacific Northwest social and cultural diversity. Archaeologists there discovered wooden boxes with artistic symbols, whale teeth, hunting tools, baskets, and carved planks and poles. Nootkan-speaking groups along Puget Sound like the Makah shared these cultural patterns with people such as the Kwakiutl of Vancouver Island and the coastal Salish peoples.

A variety of factors, including population growth, food surplus, and perhaps competition and warfare over hunting and settlement territories, contributed to the development of complex systems of social ranking among Northwest coast peoples after 1000 BCE. Such systems divided elites from non-elites and established

1.2 Sandstone carvings at Petroglyph Canyon near Las Vegas, Nevada.
Source: Wollertz/Shutterstock

each individual's social status and responsibilities. Households remained the central unit of work and consumption but were, themselves, incorporated into the ranking system. To display status and power, families with surplus food and prestige goods such as finely carved boxes, canoes, and beads and stone gathered for **potlatch ceremonies**. During these ceremonies, wealthy families recounted orally their family histories as represented in mythical accounts, and then redistributed goods to families of lesser wealth and importance to strengthen kin and community ties.

East of the coast is a vast region known as the Interior Plateau. Two main rivers bisect it: the Columbia River of the southern plateau and the Fraser River located in the more wooded north. Salish-speakers from the same linguistic stock as peoples of the coast lived along the Fraser River. Penutian-speakers who lived close to the Columbia River were famous salmon fishers. They moved their villages to follow salmon migratory patterns. After 3000 BCE, salmon fishing plateau people established long-distance trade networks with their linguistic cousins of the Northwest coast, and farther to the south into the Great Basin, a region between the Rocky Mountains and the Pacific Coastal range of the Sierra Nevada. Turquoise and shells from the South and West were exchanged for fish grease and animal hides. Wooden painted masks of mythical creatures traveled from the Northwest coast to the Interior Plateau.

The Dalles, natural rock platforms along the Columbia River, were places not only of trade but also where Indians from Plateau, Northwest coast, and Great Basin villages met to exchange prestige goods. Plateau peoples saw these meeting places as sacred and honored them with painted artwork called pictographs and carved artwork called petroglyphs that featured faces, stick people, circles of the sun, heads, eagles and other birds, sheep, deer, and images of hunters in ritual postures.

Places like The Dalles were also the site of **vision quests**, or spiritual journeys. To honor the guardian spirits who lived near sacred points of The Dalles, people made offerings, but also used different pigments of color to paint their visions as they looked for spiritual guidance in song and other rites. A present-day elder among the Flathead Lake Kutenai in Montana told one observer of how vision quests were often linked spiritually to rock formations and his peoples' long tradition of a sacred landscape. His people traveled "on top of Chief Rock, near Dayton . . . up there is a little circle of stones where we would lay. All kinds of spirits dwell up there." Among these spirits were birds and particularly the coyote, which spoke directly to people. "Coyote gave me a song," the elder recalled. "Deer gave me the power to hunt successfully." For the ancestors of people who traded at The Dalles, sacred powers to hunt, fish, trade, and maintain community balance and harmony came from visiting rock formations.

The Great Basin and the Plains

Great Basin peoples lived between the Rocky Mountains and the Pacific Coastal range. Archaeological finds, such as Lovelock Cave in Nevada, suggest that Great Basin peoples used caves as gathering places for burials and storing food. Great Basin people located their campsites near water sources where it was possible to gather piñon nuts from small pine trees and hunt small animals such as rabbits, birds, and freshwater fish. In the Western Basin region, where agricultural techniques flourished because of better rainfall, a more intensive process of planting and harvesting began around 2000 BCE. Between 400 CE and 1300 CE (the common era), cultural diversity appeared in the Great Basin archaeological record. Stone figures, ceramics, and textiles all seem to be the work of different peoples. Uto-Aztecan speakers, the ancestors of the Shoshones and Utes, had most likely moved into the Great Basin. By about 500 CE, people in Utah started planting maize near **pit houses**, building on the maize-planting traditions of the peoples of the Southwest. Pit houses were semi-subterranean dwellings, offering protection from both heat and cold as well as storage space for food and belongings. Farming in this region of pit houses was short-lived, however, as climatic change dried up arable soil.

After 3000 BCE, the Plains Indians dispersed into various bands, increasing their hunting ranges and diversifying their use of arrow and spearheads inherited from the Clovis and Folsom cultures. They used tools in mountain areas to grind nuts and developed basketwork. Around 720 CE, after a volcano eruption destroyed most of the habitable areas around the present-day Yukon Territory near Alaska, descendants of the Caddoan-speaking

TIMELINE 1.2 DIVERSITY IN THE WEST, 5000 BCE–1300 BCE

Date	Event
5000 BCE–4000 BCE	Expansion of food production and cultures in California
3000 BCE	Plains dispersal into tribal bands
1000 BCE	Cultural complexity emerges in the Northwest
400 CE–1300 CE	Cultural diversity in the Great Basin, including agricultural production

Arikaras and the Siouan-speaking Mandan and Hidatsa had already formed village settlements and farmed near rivers of the Missouri River Valley in the upper plains. Around the same time, in the northern plains, near the Black Hills of South Dakota, Athabaskan-speakers established villages and hunted bison, but they were not the mounted horseback plains people of which most people think. The plains farmers and the Northern Plains hunters engaged in far-flung networks of trade. Plains cave art from this period depicts a life of hunting small game infused with ritual. Wyoming cave rock art portrays deer and other animals with hunters and mythical figures. People in different postures, wearing masks depicting animals, indicate that the native peoples of the plains had created a rich spiritual life. Red pictographs of circles, lines, and other geometric shapes are perhaps signs that spiritual leaders used art to create a ritual and ceremonial life for Plains Indians.

Agriculture-Based Societies in the Southwest

Cultural Diversity and the Arrival of Maize

Stretching from Nevada across Arizona into New Mexico, then south into Sonora in Mexico, the Southwest had deserts and forests, mountainous territories, and regions of low to moderate rainfall. The Southwest's geographic and climatic variety in turn created diversity among the peoples who inhabited the region. Before the arrival of the nomadic Plains Indian hunters, four cultural groups, distinguished among other things by language, occupied the Southwest. Yuman-speakers dominated the Colorado River Valley and Baja California in what is today Mexico. These people were warriors and hunters, but they also relied on floodplain agriculture, growing their crops close to riverbanks to take advantage of the ready supply of water and rich riverbank soil. The O'odham and other related groups lived in southern Arizona and northern Mexico. O'odham peoples spoke a Uto-Aztecan dialect and lived in a rugged region noted for its geographical and climatic variation—remote highlands, arid deserts, and lush river valleys. Arizona and New Mexico were home to the Pueblo peoples. They spoke many different dialects but shared cultural traits. In Black Mesa, Arizona, the Hopi occupied uplands and the Zuni dwelled in six large **adobe pueblos**, which were multistory houses made of adobe (clay and straw baked into hard bricks). To the east were the Acoma, Laguna, and other Keresan- and Tanoan-speaking native peoples. All pueblos were villages made up of adobe, sometimes circular, multistoried houses connected by ladders. Some pueblos had a central plaza, and all had circular ceremonial pits known as **kivas**.

Indigenous peoples of the highlands of Mexico domesticated corn, beans, and squash approximately 9,000 years ago. Between 2500 BCE and 100 BCE, agriculture spread into the Sonoran region of northwest Mexico. The earliest variety of cultivated maize (*Zea mays*), often called Indian corn, arrived slowly in the Southwest. In time, maize cultivation and harvest came to be well-organized, labor-intensive activities. Maize would come to be grown with protein-producing crops such as beans and squash. However, the earliest variety of maize did not change life in the Southwest overnight. At first, people probably traded for maize seeds and sprinkled them on the ground, using whatever maize grew to supplement a diet of wild plants and animals that complemented their semi-sedentary ways of life.

Variations of *Zea mays* proved more adaptable to the arid climates of the Southwest. The exact timing of the arrival in the Southwest of *Chapalote*, a later variation of maize, remains in dispute. Some archaeologists contend that people of the Southwest first grew Chapalote in the second millennium BCE. Others believe that it appeared much later. *Chapalote* followed the same pattern as the earlier introduction of *Zea mays*. Native peoples scattered *Chapalote* seedlings among weeds and other plants, but they did not grow the crop intensively. People in the Southwest eventually replaced *Chapalote* maize with a more hardy and productive form, Maiz de Ocho. Requiring shorter growing seasons than *Chapalote*, easy to grind and cook, and adaptable to climatic changes and a variety of environments, *Maiz de Ocho* was the staple corn of the Southwest by the first millennium BCE, but could not support populations on its own because it lacked necessary vitamins and protein. If eaten alone, corn caused a disease known to science as pellagra. Early agriculturalists thus grew maize with beans and squash. Native peoples have referred to this combination of a nutrient- and protein-packed diet as the "three sisters." In northwest Mexico, at the Cerro Juanaqueña site, archaeologists have uncovered a 135-room pit house village along with maize cobs. Pit house villages, which replaced semi-sedentary village life, are found throughout northwest Mexico. They are the earliest examples of sedentary living based on maize production in the area.

Seasonal maize cultivation eventually changed Native American patterns of living in the Southwest. Permanent large settlements emerged there between 250 CE and 1450 CE. Known as the Mogollon cultural tradition, pit house dwellings appeared around that time throughout the Southwest. At many of these villages, certain rooms resembled storage houses. These villages were not autonomous, as luxury trade goods such as copper bells, etched shells, obsidian (volcanic glass), mica, and turquoise came from networks of long-distance trade. New ceramic styled pots and other items were used to store and cook maize, suggesting cultural variations and complexity. There are also signs of a ritual and ceremonial life surrounding crop production in the earliest kiva-like structures.

Exchange and adaptability were essential to sedentary life in the Southwest. Climatic variations and territorial diversity meant that some regions enjoyed better growing seasons than others. Facing crop failures and droughts, groups came together to exchange goods, hold rituals and ceremonies, and intermarry. Maize production and the shift to pit house villages meant that people in the Southwest became connected to each other through long-distance exchanges of people, goods, and ritual and ceremonial practices.

Until about 700 CE, pit houses were the most common social unit in the vast Southwest. From 700 CE to 1000 CE, pit house villages were replaced with adobe clay, multistoried buildings commonly known as pueblos. Agriculture contributed to a population boom, demanding more complex forms of settlement to house and feed more people. Moreover, to store maize and improve their living conditions, people had to move to larger, above-ground settlements, leaving pit houses for use as storage chambers or kivas. Change was gradual in some places, more rapid in others.

The "Chaco Phenomenon"

Chaco Canyon, New Mexico became home for a series of large adobe settlements between 900 CE and 1150 CE. Climates changed by the tenth century, with temperatures rising a few degrees in most parts of North America, and extended growing seasons during a time scientists call the Warm Period. Maize, beans, and squash dominated agricultural production during this period of warmer climates and longer growing periods and sustained the ever-increasing population. The so-called "Chaco Phenomenon" was astonishing in its size and scope. Pueblo Bonito, a large semicircular settlement of adobe apartments stacked five stories high, each apartment with its own kiva, was the centerpiece of the "Chaco Phenomenon." This settlement marked the flourishing of what archaeologists describe as Anasazi culture (a Navajo word for "ancient enemies"), ancestors to the Pueblo peoples. From Chaco Canyon, a network of similar villages spanned hundreds of square miles. Within this area, Anasazi people built at least 70 other large adobe communities known as "outliers." An intricate system of roads led back to Chaco Canyon and connected each outlier community to the others. Night-time fires from kivas ceremonially linked many Chaco Canyon outliers to Pueblo Bonito. Along with roads, Anasazi peoples carved out extensive irrigation routes in the canyon walls and on the ground. This irrigation system was crucial to successful large-scale crop cultivation in the arid climate of New Mexico. Two other "great houses," Peñasco Blanco and Una Vida, helped support the immense population of Chaco Canyon. All three great houses were

1.3 Jackson Stairway in Chaco Canyon, evidence of the engineering skills of the Ancestral Puebloans.

Source: Nagel Photography/Shutterstock

located near central drainage systems to optimize water access. The three communities shared architectural features. Each settlement consisted of rectangular rooms, built one on top of another. Large kivas stood outside the main settlement, suggesting that each great house had a community-oriented ritual and ceremonial life led by spiritual specialists and leaders. An established elite may have dominated these communities to muster laborers for construction and crop production and to control the flow of trade. Kin groups probably disputed with each other over leadership.

The discovery of bells, figurines, pottery vessels with human effigies, and macaw parrot skeletons (the colorful feathers of the birds were much prized) at Pueblo Bonito reinforces the idea that, by the tenth century, Pueblo Bonito dominated the economic, ceremonial, and ritual life of Chaco Canyon. Archaeologists believe that by about 1050 CE, a few Pueblo Bonito leaders probably controlled the roads that connected Pueblo Bonito with outlier communities. The "Great North Road," 40 miles in length, brought many people and goods to Chaco Canyon. Among Kersan-speaking Pueblos, the cardinal point of north was a symbol of their travels to their origins, where their ancestors once dwelled. Thus, in addition to its economic and other material functions, the Great North Road may have served as a cosmological guiding path toward Pueblo Bonito. Kersan-speakers, like Puebloans, also believed that four cardinal points converge at a midpoint. In a sacred-geographical layout, Pueblo Bonito appears as this mid-place, which might also help explain Pueblo Bonito's power and authority in trade relations.

Despite its grandeur and prosperity, Chaco Canyon could not withstand the dramatic climatic changes that began in 1130 CE, as the Warm Period waned. Fifty years of unrelenting drought hit the Colorado Plateau. In the face of crop failure and famine, the great houses were unable to sustain their large populations. At the same time, outliers stopped trading with Pueblo Bonito and the other great houses, preserving what they could for their own needs. Within a few generations, the great houses became ghost towns. The Chaco system collapsed, succeeded by other centralized but smaller societies in the Southwest.

Hohokam and Mesa Verde Cultures

O'odham peoples describe the Hohokam people as "those who have gone," a tribute to another grand community of pueblos in the Southwest. One of the most famous Hohokam sites is Snaketown, on the Gila River in Arizona. It earns its name from the O'odham name Skoaquick, "place of snakes." Archaeologists have excavated the 167 houses at Snaketown, along with additional dwellings at other Hohokam sites. From about 300 CE to 775 CE, most Hohokam peoples developed irrigation systems and by 1175 CE began to group houses together in a manner reminiscent of Pueblo Bonito, except Hohokam houses opened onto a grand courtyard. Archaeologists are unsure whether the Hohokam people were migrants or indigenous to Arizona. There are, however, some clues. At Snaketown there was a ball court for community rituals, a public venue found among native groups in Mexico. In addition, some of the trade goods and cultural artifacts found at Hohokam sites and dated to between 1150 CE and 1350 CE appear to have Mexican origins. Platform mounds, clay figurines, and several types of vessels are similar to Mexican forms. Nonetheless, the consensus among archaeologists now is that Hohokam was its own distinct, original culture, even if it displayed certain practices, behaviors, and some goods commonly associated with early populations of Mexico. Hohokam peoples, in fact, stood at a trading crossroads—central to California, Mexico, and other parts of the Southwest—which helps explains its rich cultural diversity.

For over 1,000 years, Hohokam settlements grew ever more sophisticated and complex. Ceremonial and ritual exchange systems centered on the ball courts and pueblo courtyards, interconnected villages, and kin and community, and gave rise to large extended clans and paramount leaders. However, between 1350 CE and 1450 CE, as archaeologists have discovered in the Salt-Gila Basin in Arizona, flooding destroyed the intricate network of Hohokam irrigation ditches. The emergence of fortified villages around the same period indicates that factionalism and warfare erupted over control of resources. By the fifteenth century, the Hohokam tradition vanished. Many scholars contend that the O'odham of the Sonora region whom the Spanish encountered in the 1500s were the descendants of the Hohokam.

The Mesa Verde cultural tradition was distinct from both the Chaco and Hohokam traditions. Mesa Verde peoples lived mostly in the San Juan Basin of Southwest Colorado. Although started by Anasazi peoples accustomed to arid regions, the Mesa Verde tradition flourished in a wetter and more fertile climate. By the twelfth century, the Mesa Verde tradition arose along the banks of rivers, particularly in cliff dwellings and deep canyons. Mesa Verde peoples abandoned their settlements in the thirteenth century as once-fertile regions turned arid under severe climatic changes. In fact, most Anasazi peoples left the "Four Corners Territory"—where Colorado, Utah, Arizona, and New Mexico meet—and migrated south and southeast to lands that became home to the Hopi, Zuni, and Rio Grande Pueblos. The adobe pueblo dwellings remained the primary social unit, and kivas were at the center of their rich spiritual life. These cultures were still in place when the Spanish arrived in the 1500s, but by this time only smaller agricultural pueblo communities remained—vestiges of a long tradition of large societies started by the arrival of agriculture thousands of years earlier.

SEEING HISTORY

Anasazi Sites Compared

The remains of archaeological structures, when linked as part of the same cultural tradition, reveal much about how Native Americans changed to meet shifting environmental circumstances. The two Anasazi cultural traditions, Pueblo Bonito and Mesa Verde, differ in architectural design and layout.

Questions

1. How did the layouts of Pueblo Bonito and Mesa Verde differ?
2. What sort of conclusions can be drawn from these differences as shown in the two images?

1.4a Cave site of Mesa Verde

Source: Nagel Photography/Shutterstock

1.4b Pueblo Bonito

Source: kojihirano/Shutterstock

TIMELINE 1.3 SOUTHWEST EXPANSION AND DIVERSITY, 2500 BCE–1450 CE

Date	Event
2500 BCE–100 BCE	Expansion of *Zea Mays* cultivation
200 BCE	Chapalote maize production
250 CE–1450 CE	Mogollon pit house cultural tradition
900 CE–1150 CE	"Chaco Phenomenon"
300 CE–1450 CE	Hohokam Culture
500 CE–1300 CE	Mesa Verde Culture

Eastern Woodlands

Early Eastern Woodlands Traditions

Far from the sacred landscapes of the Columbia Plateau and the Great Plains lived the peoples of the Eastern Woodlands, occupying the vast lands east of the Mississippi from Canada to the Gulf Coast. Exchange networks in seashells, jasper, and copper extended into the Eastern Woodlands after 3000 BCE. In time, possession of such goods came to denote rank and status. Each tribe or band lived in its own area, but they were connected to each other by trade that flowed in multiple directions. Copper came from the Great Lakes and St. Lawrence River areas. Shells from the Atlantic coast and soapstone from the Appalachians also appeared in burial sites. Shell-mound deposits also indicate a steady diet of coastal and freshwater mussels, contributing to the diversified economy and resource base necessary to support the region's increasing population. Indian Knoll, a site in Kentucky, dated to about 3000 BCE to 2000 BCE, is one of the best-preserved shell-deposit sites. Indians of the Eastern Woodlands had a spiritual life that developed from far-flung networks of esoteric knowledge and spiritually charged trade goods. Special burials based on kinship, age, and leadership indicate the presence of elite groups. Indian Knoll, for example, had more than 1,000 burials. The dead were buried in a fetal position, and some were sprinkled with ocher dust and adorned with shell ornaments such as beads.

Between 2200 BCE and 700 BCE, a unique cultural tradition emerged at a central point of the vast exchange networks among the eastern Indians. Located in the lower Mississippi Valley near the Gulf Coast, the Poverty Point culture (named after a site in Louisiana) provides evidence of dramatic cultural change among the Eastern Woodland peoples. There are more than 100 Poverty Point sites, the largest of which stands on the Macon Ridge that overlooks the Mississippi floodplain, near the confluence of the Mississippi, Arkansas, Red, Ohio, and Tennessee rivers. Strategically positioned to serve as a trade nexus, Poverty Point was comprised of large earthen mounds. The center of the Poverty Point site ranges over 490 acres, with six concentric semicircular mounds established about 130 feet from each other.

Archaeologists know next to nothing about the social organization of Poverty Point. Relying on data from later mound-building cultures, they speculate that chiefs and spiritual leaders oversaw the construction of the vast mounds that acted as centers of trade. Outlying villages produced squash and gourds, while within the mounds archaeologists have discovered immense amounts of prestige goods such as copper, galena (lead ore that often contains silver), jasper, and quartz. Scholars believe that Poverty Point developed and amassed sufficient wealth to permit social stratification and the emergence of leaders with the authority to organize and command the labor necessary to build the mounds. Poverty Point remains a puzzle, but it foreshadowed the rise of other complex societies in the Eastern Woodlands.

Adena and Hopewell Cultures

The mound-building tradition that began in the Eastern Woodlands continued in the Adena and Hopewell cultures. From about 1000 BCE to 100 BCE, the Adena complex in the central Ohio River valley was an engine for social and cultural change across the region. Adena was a vast mound-building center comprised of ceremonial burial mounds. By about 200 BCE, these mounds became more complex, becoming much larger in size and capable of accommodating more bodies, each painted with red and yellow ocher. Alongside these burial sites were circular enclosed areas where it is likely families of the deceased along with people of high status gathered to worship their ancestors. The graves included sophisticated handcrafted effigies and pipe stems in the form of both humans and animals.

A new mound-building culture emerged out of the Adena complex known as the Hopewell tradition, flourishing from 200 BCE to 500 CE. The Hopewell tradition encompassed more people and was socially and culturally more complex than the traditions that preceded it. It was a focal point of trade networks that ranged across most of North America, bringing shell, obsidian, mica, and turquoise to the craftspeople of Hopewell.

Built over centuries, Hopewell mounds were shaped like circles, octagons, and squares. The mounds had ritual and ceremonial importance, in addition to serving as burial sites. Archaeologists believe that many of these earthen mounds were aligned to reflect astronomical events, particularly sunrise and moonrise patterns. The mound building culture of Hopewell was most likely the work of **"bigmen,"** elites who gained power and authority from spiritual and mythological knowledge and the control of trade. Masks and effigies of animals and mythical spirits were used in the performance of rites that enhanced these leaders' position as directors of Hopewell spiritual life. The interment of bodies with high-prestige items suggests that "bigman" status and privilege extended into the afterlife.

Roads connected outlying villages to the center of Hopewell. These villages, which traded with Hopewell and shared its culture, might have functioned as ritual political centers with their own burial mounds, but they certainly acknowledged the larger mounds as the main centers of Hopewell life. Hopewell depended on intensive production of corn, beans, and squash for subsistence, with many villages located near floodplains to facilitate growing.

Hopewell culture went into rapid decline around 400 CE. Archaeologists believe that the introduction of maize contributed to the fall of Hopewell. With the spread of maize, clan and kinship networks became more focused on their own intensive cultivation of maize and not their connections to the larger Hopewell structure, to the detriment of the "bigmen" whose prestige and power were derived from those networks. Because the Hopewell networks facilitated cultural connections between the peoples who made up the broader cultural tradition, their decline brought with it the collapse of the tradition as a whole.

Mississippian Chiefdoms

Between 800 CE and 1200 CE, during the Warm Period, agriculture spread rapidly throughout the Eastern Woodlands, giving rise to a new age of chiefdoms in the Southeast and Midwest, known collectively as the

Mississippian tradition. The most organized chiefdoms were Cahokia, across from St. Louis, Missouri, along the Mississippi River, and Moundville in northwest Alabama. Cahokia and Moundville oversaw vast territories and featured elaborate social and political structures.

Cults played key roles in spiritual and political life at Cahokia and Moundville. A warrior cult honored elite men who had proven themselves in battle, and a fertility cult honored the harvests. The periodic rebuilding of the tops of mounds and platforms symbolized the fertility of the crops and population expansion, and created opportunities for the chiefdoms' elaborate displays of prestige.

Built along a floodplain, Cahokia served almost as a city-state, with the large mound occupied by the chiefdom at the center of a network of supporting villages. Population estimates for Cahokia itself have been placed at about 15,000 with as many as another 25,000 residing in surrounding villages. Given its service as a regional trade center, Cahokia probably drew another 50,000 guests annually. The city's base population alone in the thirteenth century equaled that of London. Among pre-Columbian Indian societies, only those in Mexico had more people. At the center of Cahokia was a magnificent mound built between the eleventh and twelfth centuries. Its size rivaled the large stone structures in Mexico and Yucatan. At Cahokia's central plaza, and atop its main mound, called Monk's Mound, priests and chiefs used myth, cosmology, and trade to cement their rule over Cahokia's population. Monk's Mound was built in four stages from the tenth to the thirteenth centuries. In a meticulously organized layout, Cahokia laborers built numerous other mounds of different sizes and shapes. Many of the mounds at Cahokia served as burial sites for the most elite of its residents. After the twelfth century, however, Cahokia began to decline as populations dispersed from the main ceremonial center, breaking up the surrounding villages that serviced the large city-state.

Lesser "Mississippian" chiefdoms existed throughout the Southeast into the sixteenth century. Like Cahokia, these chiefdoms also developed complex social, cultural, and political structures. There was a clear hierarchy of chiefs; one paramount chief oversaw chiefs of surrounding villages. The capital town was home to the paramount chief, his family, petty officials, and spiritual specialists. Subchiefs who owed loyalties to the paramount chief and managed the day-to-day agricultural production of village life lived in smaller centers. In general, chiefdoms occupied extensive lands and controlled the labor and surplus produce of villagers. The cosmology of these chiefdoms was built around dualities: an upper world versus an underworld; a fertility cult of women versus a warrior cult of men. When French and Spanish explorers came to the Southeast in the sixteenth century, they encountered the Natchez along the Mississippi and the Coosa in Georgia, the remnants of the larger remaining Mississippian chiefdoms.

1.5 Artist's rendition of Cahokia. Notice the gigantic mound behind the surrounding villagers.

Source: Cahokia Mounds State Historic Site/ Michael Hampshire

The inhabitants of these Mississippian chiefdoms led a complex spiritual life. Atop many of the numerous mounds, chiefs and priests worshipped the most important god, the sun. Craftsmen carved images of men playing a sacred bowl game known as "chunkey." The game served as a ritual, one bound by the four sacred cardinal directions that gave players the necessary sacred power for hunting and warfare. Fertility cults involving the worship of statues and figures of women tied communities to the land and the mystical potency of women. One figurine depicts a woman "cultivating" the land on the back of a serpent with the head of a panther. According to Muskogean stories, serpent-panthers from the underworld transformed themselves into food to sustain the population and only women, known for their fertility, could cultivate the back of the serpent-panther to turn the spirit into corns, beans, and squash.

Mississippian chiefs affirmed their sacred power through carvings on vessels and pendants and by controlling the production and distribution of engraved prestige goods. Geometric shapes carved on pendants, vessels, and ornaments worn around the throat all linked chiefs to the sacred powers of the sun and prized birds such as the falcon. By controlling the production and distribution of prestige goods, chiefs claimed power over the human realm. The chiefs oversaw life in surrounding villages, carried physically to those smaller communities on specially designed and adorned litters. The designs on one litter depict a chief rising from the ground to decapitate two Indians with his bare hands as he moves into the sky. The image of the decapitated heads and levitation indicates that chiefs in the Mississippian tradition also orchestrated their warriors' attacks on neighboring competitors.

The Iroquois

Iroquoian-speakers lived in the portion of the Eastern Woodlands that is now northern New York State and Southeast Canada. Iroquois people lived in rectangular longhouses made of bark and wood that could hold numerous families. The Iroquois harvested corns, beans, and squash—the "three sisters"—with women tilling the soil. The Iroquois were **matrilineal**, tracing descent through the lines of their mothers, so women had tremendous power in the appointment of clan leaders and decisions regarding warfare. At the time of European contact in the early sixteenth century and into the seventeenth century, the major Iroquoian tribes were the Huron, Erie, and Neutral in Canada, and the Five Nations Iroquois in New York State: the Seneca, Cayuga, Onondaga, Oneida, and Mohawk.

Archaeological remains of protective fences, or palisades, around villages indicate that warfare was common among the Iroquois. Sometime before 1600, several Iroquois tribes decided to resolve the factionalism, feuding, and warfare that had been so devastating for so many generations and together they formed the Iroquois League. According to Iroquois legend, a grandmother and mother recognized that a young boy, Deganawida, was a potential peacemaker. When he grew older, he traveled through Iroquoia, from west to east, carrying his message of peace to warriors and chiefs alike. One of Deganawida's converts among the Onondaga was Hiawatha. Deganawida taught Hiawatha the Condolence Ceremony, a ritual designed to facilitate the reconciliation of former enemies. Together they then carried this message of condolence to the Mohawks, who adopted the ceremony. Deganawida and Hiawatha traveled farther spreading their message of peace and encouraging intertribal unity. Soon, the Iroquois nations made peace among themselves and formed the Iroquois League. The Onondaga, Mohawk, Seneca, Cayuga, and Oneida joined symbolically into one longhouse, a sacred unity overseen by **sachems** elected from specific clans by clan mothers. The "Keepers of the Eastern Door" of the League's longhouse were the Mohawks, the most eastern tribe in New York. The "Keepers of the Western Door" were the Senecas who resided far to the west. At the center was Onondaga, in whose territory the Iroquois League would meet and light the council fires.

TIMELINE 1.4 EASTERN WOODLANDS, 3000 BCE–SIXTEENTH CENTURY

Date	Event
3000 BCE	Expansion of cultures and trade networks in the Eastern Woodlands
2200 BCE–700 BCE	Poverty Point
1000 BCE–100 CE	Adena Complex
200 BCE–500 CE	Hopewell Tradition
700 CE–1200 CE	Cahokia
1200 CE–16th century	Mississippian Tradition
Before 1600	Iroquois League founded

SEEING HISTORY

Chiefdoms Maintaining Power Through Images

Pendants, carved pottery, and other luxury items from the period of the Mississippian chiefdoms are well-preserved artifacts with images of gods and cosmic animals appearing somewhere near a carved or

1.6 Gorget showing a falcon-man marine shell, Mississippian Period, 1200–1450 CE. Excavated in 1890 at Castalian Springs Mound Group, Tennessee, by amateur archaeologist William E. Myer (1862–1923); acquired by MAI in 1926.

Source: National Museum of the American Indian Smithsonian Institution 15/853. Photo by NMAI Photo Services

etched image of a leader. Artifacts such as these are as useful as archaeological settlement sites in understanding the nature and structure of chiefdoms.

Questions

1. How do you think this artifact asserted chiefly power and authority?
2. Which image or motif is most striking?

Conclusion

The first Europeans to reach North America did not discover a "Garden of Eden" occupied by peoples who lived in a state of harmony and balance with nature. Native North America had its own rich and complex history before Europeans arrived. Scientists use archaeological dating techniques and evidence from excavated sites to investigate this history. Native peoples look to their stories to understand their past. Although seemingly incompatible, when considered together science and native traditions shed light on the beginnings of Indian life in North America. When Europeans arrived in the Americas in 1500, they encountered societies that had been changing and developing for 15,000 years. In this chapter, we focused on the societies of North America. In the next, we will turn to the societies of South America, giving particular attention to the Maya, the Aztecs, and the Inca.

READING HISTORY

The Iroquois Origin Story

Origin stories, like the one below, can tell us a lot about Native peoples. In the Iroquois origin story, their world existed on a turtle's back. In fact, Iroquoian-speakers, when first encountering Europeans, talked about living on the back of a turtle. What might sound strange or peculiar to readers had its own cultural logic.

Long before the world was created, there was an island floating in the sky, upon which the Sky People lived. They lived quietly and happily. No one ever died or was born or experienced sadness. However, one day, one of the Sky Women realized she was going to give birth to twins. She told her husband, who flew into a rage. In the center of the island there was a tree which lighted the entire island since the sun still had not been created. He tore up this tree, creating a huge hole in the middle of the island. Curiously, the woman peered into the hole. Far below she could see the waters that covered the earth. At that moment, her husband pushed her through the hole, and she tumbled towards the distant waters below.

Two birds saw Sky Woman falling, swooped down and caught her on their backs, preventing her from crashing into the water. Determined to help the woman, water creatures tried to gather mud from the sea floor with which to create new land. One after another the animals failed. Finally, Little Toad swam to the bottom of the sea, and when he reappeared his mouth was full of mud. The animals took it and spread it on the back of Big Turtle. The mud grew and grew until it became the size of North America.

Sky Woman stepped onto the land. She sprinkled dust into the air and created stars. Then she made the moon and sun. She soon gave birth to twin sons, who she named Sapling and Flint. The two boys grew into men, but they were very different from one another. Sapling was kind and gentle; Flint's heart was as cold as his name.

Sapling created what is good. He made animals that are useful to humans. He made rivers that had two opposing currents and fish without bones. He made plants that people could eat easily and nourished them. His creations eased the life of humans.

Flint destroyed much of Sapling's work and created all that is bad. He shed one current from the rivers, making them flow only in one direction. He put bones in fish and thorns on berry bushes. He tainted many plants with poison and created winter with the full bitterness of that season. His was a world of evil, danger, and difficulty.

Sapling and Flint fought for dominance, and only after a long, brutal fight was Flint finally defeated. Because he was a god Flint could not die, so he was forced to live on Big Turtle's back. Occasionally his anger is felt in the form of a volcano and other natural disasters.

Source: www.cs.williams.edu/~lindsey/myths/myths_12.html

Questions

1. What does the Iroquois Origin Story tell us about how they lived?
2. What is the cultural significance that in this story animals behaved like humans?

Review Questions

1. Why do native peoples rely on origin stories and not archaeological evidence to explain their history in North America?
2. Is the Bering land bridge a convincing scientific model for explaining the origins of human society in the Americas?
3. How did maize cultivation contribute to the rise and fall of societies in the Southwest and Mississippi Valley?

Recommended Readings

Bement, Leland C. *Bison Hunting at Cooper Site: Where Lightning Bolts Drew Thundering Herds* (Norman: University of Oklahoma Press, 1999). A great book that sheds light on bison hunting on the plains.

Blog, Stephen. *Ancient Peoples of the American Southwest* (New York: Thames & Hudson, 1997). A wonderful overview of the emergence of the various cultural traditions.

Bose, David S., James A. Brown, and David W. Penney. *Ancient Art of the American Woodland Indians* (New York: Harry N. Abrams, Inc., 1985). One of the best illustrated books of ancient art that sheds light on the complex societies that developed in the Eastern Woodlands in the Southwest.

Fagan, Brian M. *Ancient North America: The Archaeology of a Continent* (New York: Thames & Hudson, 2000). The most comprehensive study of its kind.

Keyser, James D. *Indian Rock Art of the Columbia Plateau* (Seattle: University of Washington Press, 1992). Beautifully illustrated and well organized chronologically. It also explains all the different traditions of art.

Powell, Joseph F. *The First Americans: Race, Evolution, and the Origin of Native Americans* (New York: Cambridge University Press, 2005). Powell was lead investigator for the Kennewick Man project and in this work updates evidence on native origins, with particular attention to the prevailing Bering Strait land bridge argument.

Sutton, Mark Q. *Prehistory of Native North America* (New York: Routledge, 2007). Although a university level textbook instead of a standard monograph, this book provides a thorough, balanced, and highly researched presentation of native origins and cultures from the first appearance of Native Americans in North America to their first contact with Europeans.

Wallas, James, and Pamela Whitaker. *Kwakiutl Legends* (North Vancouver, BC: Hancock House, 2002). Stories recorded over several years in the early twentieth century that shed light on Pacific coastal traditions.

Zolbrod, Paul G. *Diné bahane: The Navajo Creation Story* (Albuquerque: University of New Mexico Press, 1984). The best account of the Navajo creation story.

Native American History Online

General Sites

Rock Art Pages. www.jqjacobs.net/rock_art/ A fantastic webpage where students can explore the diversity of rock art.

Kansas City Hopewell and Plains Woodland Archeology. www.kshs.org A site dedicated to the Hopewell culture in Kansas, along with a tour of the museum collection.

Common Projectile Points of the Upper Mississippi River Valley. www.uwlax.edu/mvac/PointGuide/PointGuide.htm This site provides information about North American projectile points.

Archaeological Sites

Cahokia Mounds State Historic Site. www.cahokiamounds.org This site includes information about the historic preservation site for Cahokia.

Chaco Culture National Historical Park, Nageezi, New Mexico. www.nps.gov/chcu/ This website provides access to numerous resources for Chaco Canyon.

Indian Mounds of Mississippi. www.nps.gov/nr/travel/mounds/intro.htm A historical preservation site that offers information about the Mississippian mounds.

Macchu Picchu

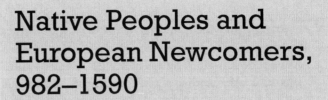
CONQUESTS, COLONIES, AND CONTRADICTIONS

AN IBERIAN NEW WORLD ORDER

Christopher Columbus and the West Indies:
    The Tainos Encounter Spaniards

THE MAYA, AZTEC, AND INCA WORLDS

Maya

Chichén Itzá and the Maya City-States

Maya Women and the City-States

Aztecs

Pre-Aztec States in Mexico

Rise of the Aztec Empire

Tenochtitlán

Aztec Gods and Religion

Aztec Women in a Warrior Culture

Inca

Growth of the Inca State

Inca Rule

The Power of Inca Women

SPANISH CONQUEST, SPANISH RULE

Fall of Tenochtitlán

Conquest of the Incas

Conquest of the Maya

FRENCH AND ENGLISH NEWCOMERS

Pre-Columbian Encounters in North America:
    The Norse

Early Expeditions to the Northeast

Native Peoples and the French Along the
    St. Lawrence River

Algonquians and the English at Roanoke

Conquests, Colonies, and Contradictions

An old African proverb posits the following perspective: "Until lions have their historians, tales of the hunt shall always glorify the hunter." To phrase it in a more commonly used form, history is written by the victors. In the early sixteenth century, Europeans entered the North and South American continents and in so doing permanently altered the course of history in the Western Hemisphere. They and those who followed well into the eighteenth century planted colonies, exploited the resources for their own gain, shattered native empires, razed cities and villages alike, corrupted cultures, spread pathogens, and reduced native populations to near extinction levels. Native Americans invariably resisted, often through warfare. At times, native peoples believed accommodation and acculturation would assure their survival, but even these efforts more often than not featured a strategy of resistance by their retention of fundamental traditional values, family structures, or spirituality in the face of forced conversion. They often resisted until treaties were accepted that allowed them to remain on traditional lands while others, at times, fled into surrounding territories to elude compulsory relocation. On occasion, they adapted themselves to the Euro-American systems that governed them and then used those same legal systems in defense of their property and cultures. Native Americans did not have written languages before the early nineteenth century, instead passing their histories through the oral tradition. Their audiences, then, were their children and their children's children. Europeans, however, penned elaborate histories and tales of their exploits in the Americas, embellishing their actions, enveloping their stories in the shrouds of courage and righteousness, and convincing readers of their own superiority over other peoples. These histories, once in print, dictated a European perspective (and later white American perspective) that later generations accepted, without question, as truth. This process commenced with the earliest of Spanish accounts in the Western Hemisphere.

Spanish accounts emphasized their superiority in firepower over Indian weaponry to make the case that the Aztec empire, the largest in the western hemisphere and numbering in the millions, fell with relative ease. Spanish chroniclers years later twisted the story to make the fall of the disease-crippled Aztec capitol of Tenochtitlán, with its numbers cut down by more than half, seem more than it was, that Hernán Cortés and his small army had accomplished the impossible against tremendous odds. Both versions promote essentially the same perspective of Spanish superiority—Spanish intelligence and creativity developed a technology capable of collapsing empires; Spanish courage and intelligence allowed their victory over a numerically superior enemy. It was essentially the same attitude all great powers have displayed throughout history toward "others."

The truth was that upon initial contact, both sides first tried to make sense of each other. Moctezuma II, the reigning lord of the main Aztec city, sent several reconnaissance missions in 1519 to the Yucatan to learn about Hernán Cortés, the leader of the Spanish party, a man who had amassed a fortune exploiting Indian labor in Cuba. To seek out and conquer the Aztecs was, in fact, not some directive from the Spanish crown, but a decision made by Cortés himself based upon his initial haphazard forays against native groups in the Yucatan. Cortés was neither a favorite within the inner circle of the Spanish crown nor liked by the imperial bureaucracy stationed in Cuba. He was a military renegade acting against the wishes of the governor of Cuba, hoping to gain fame and wealth through conquest. Moctezuma had to know about this strange man, and taking action based on revelations, he sent artists to render images of the Spanish.

One Spanish chronicler noted how the artists took interest in "the face and countenance and body and features of Cortés, and all the captains and soldiers, also the ships, sails, and horses." According to the Spanish, the Aztecs concluded that Cortés resembled one of their own lords by the name of Quintalbor, who traveled with the Aztec artists. One Aztec noticed that Spanish helmets had similarities to the headdress of their patron god of the sun, Huitzilopochtli, so they pleaded with the Spanish to gift a helmet to Moctezuma. Cortes sent a helmet to Moctezuma, who in return issued gifts to the Spanish. Aztec gifts were meant to subordinate the Spanish as tributaries, while the Spanish interpreted the gifts as Indian submission. Spaniards clad in armor and with strange animals, particularly horses, were shockingly different from the rest of the people in Mesoamerica whom the Aztecs knew and oftentimes controlled. Both sides misinterpreted the intentions and actions of the other, but it was the Spanish interpretation that prevailed in historical accounts.

Spaniards wove tales of their exploits in South America indeed to make their efforts grander than they actually were, in part because of the tremendous fame and fortune bestowed on those who conquered native populations and claimed expanses of land for the Crown and, again, because the embellished record assured Spain of its inherent superiority over other peoples. There was also a religious rationale for elaborate if not fabricated stories. Spanish Christians had engaged in a centuries-long struggle known as the **Reconquista** (718–1492) to force the Moors (Muslims with roots in North Africa) out of the Iberian Peninsula. This struggle concluded the same year Christopher Columbus launched his first voyage to the Americas. The Iberian newcomers drew comparisons between Moors and Native Americans and sometimes saw their actions in the Americas as a Catholic crusade to convert natives and to extinguish all threats to the Catholic conquest of the New World.

Spanish chroniclers certainly exaggerated their accounts of human conquest, but they also drafted heroic tales of conquistadors braving the unknown environment and mastering it. Sailing to the West Indies in 1572, nearly a century after Christopher Columbus's first landfall, the Jesuit José de Acosta observed the following: "Having read what poets and philosophers write of the Torrid Zone, I persuaded myself that when I came to the Equator, I would not be able to endure the violent heat." The writings of ancient Greek and Roman philosophers had taught him that temperatures at the equator were beyond what humans could bear, but instead of sizzling he found himself cold and confused. Acosta's experience was typical. With little or no first-hand knowledge of the Americas, Europeans turned to whatever sources were available to gather clues about what they might encounter on the other side of the Atlantic Ocean. Ancient texts, travelers' tales, and European

CHRONOLOGY

250–900 CE	Classic era of Maya civilization
900–1000 CE	Fall of Mesoamerican cities
982–14th century	Norsemen trade with Inuits and Bethouks around Canada, Greenland, Newfoundland, and Northern New England
1221	Fall of Chichén Itzá in the Yucatan
1325	Beginning of the rise of the Mexicas in Central Mexico
1426	Beginning of dynastic rule among the Aztecs
1440	Ascension of the Incas in Peru
1492	Columbus arrives
1471–1493	Efflorescence of Inca state under Tupac Yupanqui
1520s	War between Huáscar and Atahualpa weakens Inca State
1521	Conquest of Aztec Empire complete
1524	Giovanni da Verrazzano reaches present-day Rhode Island
1532	Francisco Pizarro captures Atahualpa and Spaniards takeover Inca State
1534	Jaques Cartier arrives at the St. Lawrence River
1540	Francisco de Montejo begins Mayan conquest
1544	Franciscans arrive in Yucatan
1562	Inquisition begins in the Mayan province of Mani
1585	The beginning of the English colony of Roanoake

KEY QUESTIONS

1. How did Spanish preconceptions shape their initial encounters with the peoples of the Americas?
2. What fundamental characteristics give evidence to the complexity of Aztec society and culture?
3. Describe the structure and character of the Inca State on the eve of the Spanish arrival.
4. Describe the pre-conquest Mayan world.
5. Why did the Norse sail to North America? What were the interactions between the Norse and the peoples like?
6. How did Native encounters shape French and English early attempts to settle North America?

folklore all contributed to the European vision of the previously unknown lands and the peoples who inhabited them. The absence of solid information gave them plenty of room to exercise their imaginations. White-skinned Europeans entering the "Torrid Zone," like the Jesuit Acosta, expected unbearably high temperatures, while ship captains feared deep-watered whirlpools as well as grotesque sea animals. Christian travelers also anticipated the sight of aberrations that bordered on the non-human. There were sciapodes, who had only one large leg and the cyclops with one large eye. There was a two-headed person, a dicephalus, and an acephalus, with its head in its chest. As Spanish explorers sailed for the highly prized passage to Asia, many brought with them memories of the supposed savage Moors of North Africa and such preconceptions about the strange things and experiences awaiting the few brave souls who dared to travel outside the borders of Christendom. In the Americas they encountered swamps, arid plains, mountains and cliffs, jungles, poisonous serpents, alligators, bears, a myriad of insects, unimaginably high humidity and heat, and stretches of snow and ice as far as the eye could see, and so many other obstacles of nature—all of which they overcame.

The disconnect between expectations and actual experience shaped the age of exploration and early expansion. Native and European encounters produced a mix of confusion, adjustment, hostility, violence, adaptation, and accommodation. Each encounter was different and marked the beginning of not one but many "New Worlds." For some, like the Tainos Columbus encountered on his first voyage to the Americas, the Spanish spirit of conquest nearly led to their extinction. In the Aztec and Maya of **Mesoamerica** (Central Mexico and most of Central America) and the Inca of Peru, the Spanish confronted complex and powerful civilizations. Conquest of these civilizations led to a variety of forms of Spanish rule. The history of the Spanish rule in Mesoamerica and Peru, in turn, would shape the French and English encounters with the natives of North America that would follow. The stories and accounts penned by the Spanish rested on a combination of uninformed expectations and purposeful exaltation of their own perceived heroic accomplishments.

An Iberian New World Order

Spain stood at a proverbial crossroads in the 1490s. Competing territories only recently had joined together to form the new nation under the rein of Ferdinand and Isabella, and that union was still tenuous at best. Christian forces had finally pushed the Moors from Spain bringing to an end nearly 500 years of Moorish threats and warfare. What was to be Spain's future? How would the Spanish crown provide wealth, security, and unity for its population? How would Spain fit into the broader relationship of European nations? A source of wealth was required to raise and supply a national military and naval force for national security against external threats.

Economic stability and development would have to be based on something beyond simple agriculture and fishing. The Crown gambled in 1492, providing the financing it could for Christopher Columbus' expedition to locate a western water route to the Far East and the riches it held. In October of that year, Columbus made landfall in the Americas and from that moment changed the fate of Spain, Europe, the native peoples of the Western Hemisphere, and ultimately, in time, the fate of the world.

Spanish soldiers in the Americas in the sixteenth century were known as **conquistadors**, or conquerors, and they had three basic goals: to establish Spanish rule, to extract wealth, and to convert the people they encountered to Catholicism. From their point of view, this was only right and proper. It was believed that the newly found land contained an abundance of natural resources, particularly gold, that, once extracted, would make Spain the richest nation in Europe. With wealth comes power—at home and abroad. The riches of the Americas would also be shared with those men who discovered them and then secured them for Spain—the personal motive so many conquistadors held. From the Spanish perspective, the obvious riches of the Americas had not been tapped by native peoples and, in their current state, served no one's benefit. Spain not only could put them to use but also needed to do so. And, importantly, a moral order needed to be established and maintained in a land of perceived heathenism and savagery to protect those very Spaniards who intended to exploit fully the New World. The Spanish assumed it to be their mission to bring the word of the Christian god to those who did not know Him, purging from Indians the behaviors, values, and structures that were inconsistent with biblical teaching. According to the Spanish, only good could come from the imposition of Catholicism and Spanish rule on native peoples. They reasoned that the natives' failure to fully exploit the "Garden of Eden" in which they lived justified Spanish efforts to use the natural and human resources of the Americas for their own purposes.

A set of beliefs about people, geography, and the climate were not the only things that came with Spanish exploration and expansion. Columbus's expedition began a process that historians refer to as the **Columbian Exchange**, the transfer of biological materials back and forth between Europe and the Americas. New diseases, plants, animals, and foods traveled across the Atlantic with the Spanish. In turn, potatoes, squash, corn, tomatoes, tobacco, and diseases such as syphilis were introduced into Europe. The path Spain followed from the crossroads where it found itself in the 1490s carried dire consequences for the American environment and the intensely diverse cultures that inhabited it, and the world would never again be the same.

Christopher Columbus and the West Indies: The Tainos Encounter Spaniards

Before 1492, the Tainos Indians of numerous West Indian islands—the Virgin Islands, Cuba, Jamaica, Hispaniola (present-day Haiti and the Dominican Republic), and Puerto Rico—probably numbered around six million people. The avowed purpose of Columbus's first voyage across the Atlantic was to find a passage to Asia and, with it, direct access to the riches of China and India. Thus, when he arrived at the island of Guanahaní in the Bahamas, he called the Tainos "Indians." The word would become a generic term for all of America's native populations. Columbus, and those who soon after followed, initially perceived natives of the West Indies to be living in what historian Ray Allen Billington described as "a slightly improved Garden of Eden, overflowing with Nature's bounties and peopled by a race of superior beings who lived in a perfect state of equality, without want and without masters." It was an ideal world—a pure world—apart from and superior to that of Europe, "a model that would lead decadent Europe into a better future." The humanist Pietro Martire d'Anghiera in 1550 suggested Indians lived "in that golden world of which old writers speak so much," a world free of the self-interest that plagues peoples of Europe. Amerigo Vespucci noted in his journals that native peoples lived in harmony with "neither king nor lord" governing them. Here were a people, early observers believed, that resided in a land without crime, without greed and avarice, without the shackles of rigid social and political structures, without poverty, and without disease. Indeed, in contrast to the poverty, hunger, disease, urban stench and filth, warfare, social hierarchies, political structures, and church power that shadowed all of Europe, little wonder that the initial wave of Europeans into the West Indies were in such awe. But this glowing first image changed quickly.

This purported culture of peace and purity intrigued some of Europe's most educated men, men who wanted to learn more of the Tainos and to determine if the earliest perceptions of them actually had merit. Viewing the West Indies from a sympathetic, if decidedly European point of view, Bartolomé de Las Casas traveled to Cuba at the age of 18 and found the Tainos culture to be much more complicated than earlier visitors imagined. A political and social structure governed them. Taino culture and social practices flourished under a number of chiefdoms, each composed of many villages. De Las Casas called the chiefdoms among the Tainos "kingdoms," claiming that Hispaniola had five of them. In his account, power and authority in Taino society moved downward from male and female hereditary chiefs. In one "kingdom," according to de Las Casas, a queen named Higuanama ruled. Chiefdoms oversaw districts made up of numerous villages and controlled vast social and trade networks. Local village chiefs supervised the storage of commodities for trade and redistribution among villagers, and had access to the most powerful *zemis*, the local gods they worshipped. Tainos tracked their descent through their mother's line, although all Tainos believed they originated from one cave in Hispaniola. Material wealth, prestige, status, and the right to lead were all inherited through matrilineal lines. Taino ritual and ceremonial life played out in villages, council houses, ball courts, and other public structures. *Zemis* were central to Taino ritual and social life. These West Indies natives prayed to effigies of their gods before conducting warfare against other Taino groups for control of hunting or fishing grounds, or before avenging the murder of a deceased family member. Columbus's description of the Tainos' willingness to trade "everything they had" actually was a misperception of a complicated economy of reciprocity. Reciprocal exchange created networks of obligation and kinship between Taino islanders. Tainos on the Gonáve Island, off the West Coast of Haiti, for example, made the finest wooden bowls, and Tainos from other islands traveled to trade for them. In short, De Las Casas revealed a native society far more complex than that initially imagined by Columbus and others at first encounter.

Columbus' mission was to locate an all-water route to the East and to secure for Spain the riches he found. He learned early in his second voyage to the West Indies that the wealth he desperately sought was not to be found in the West Indies. His time among the Tainos also allowed for a reconsideration of his first impression of them, and he became confident that the Tainos were, in fact, an inferior people. He still believed them to be innocent and naïve. They were willing "to trade everything they have. They all go naked as their mothers bore them." These traits alone cast the Indians into an inferior position in Columbus' eyes. That the Tainos also knew nothing of European weapons or the concept of private property further subordinated them in Columbus's mind. Their inferiority did not, however, render them useless. Columbus believed that good physical features, proportionate bodies, and an ability to repeat what was said potentially made the Tainos "good servants . . . and Christians, for they appeared to [him] to have no religion," the latter being the ultimate failing.

Because Columbus concluded that Tainos lived in a stateless society and that they were without religion, it seemed only natural to him that they should be placed under the control of the Spanish crown, whether the Tainos liked it or not. Taino defenses were no match for Spanish weapons. Even more devastating to the Tainos were European diseases, particularly smallpox. Within 30 years, war, disease, and oppression had reduced the Taino population of six million to a mere 30,000. De Las Casas saw this catastrophe through a Catholic lens, noting that "all the millions that have perished have gone to their deaths with no knowledge of God and without the benefit of the Sacraments." After witnessing firsthand the devastation of the Indians in 1515, de Las Casas became a Dominican priest and devoted the rest of his life to protecting the native peoples from Spanish oppression. For the Tainos themselves, the tragedy lay not in their failure to convert to Christianity, but in the total destruction of their way of life. The Tainos would not be the last native people to suffer under the consequences of Spanish conquest.

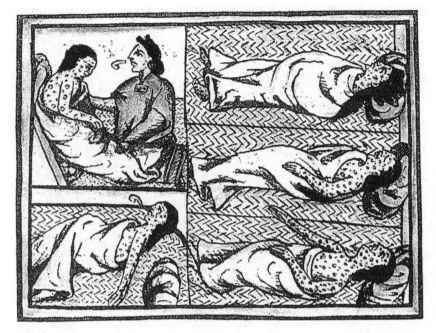

2.1 Aztec Indians with smallpox are ministered to by a medicine man. As part of the "Columbian Exchange," smallpox devastated many native populations even before they encountered the Spaniards.

Source: pnicolova/Shutterstock

The Maya, Aztec, and Inca Worlds

From Mesoamerica's eastern coastline to Peru, Spaniards encountered native peoples like none they had seen before. In the east was the Yucatan Peninsula, home of the Maya. Although geographically linked to present-day Mexico, the Maya had a distinct society, culture, and language. No central Maya capital was strong enough to establish an expansive empire, so from 250 CE to the arrival of the Spanish, rival kingdoms fought for control of the Yucatan.

Maya

A rugged landscape, fragile soil, dense tropical forests, and an unpredictable climate made the Yucatan a challenging place to live. All of this did not stop Maya from constructing massive stone pyramids and cities. In the "classic era" of Mayan civilization (250–900 CE) cities often had populations exceeding 50,000, urban centers that surpassed in both size and grandeur the cities of Europe. Local lords used the large workforces these cities could supply to drain swamps and create irrigation ditches. Mountainside terraces caught rainwater for the cultivation of maize, beans, and squash. Stone buildings from intricately carved blocks lined avenues.

Maya also made major intellectual and artistic advances. They used **glyphic writing** to communicate and trace the history of war and lordships. Paintings and glyphs contained religious motifs, as well as stories of battles and images of nobles dressed in war regalia. Masons and other stone workers constructed large structures near major centers of worship to honor gods and lords. Maya had a complex astronomical calendar that they used both for agricultural and religious purposes. Their system of mathematics included the concept of zero. Taken together, Maya writing, artwork, and intellectual advances made a major contribution to Mesoamerican culture.

2.2 Maya glyphs carved in stone panel. Such glyphs show the sophistication of the Mayan language.

Source: Granger Historical Picture Archive/Alamy Stock Photo

Chichén Itzá and the Mayan City-States

Located at the northern tip of the Yucatan Peninsula, Chichén Itzá had become the most important Mayan center of trade by the tenth century. Goods arrived at the Port of Isla Cerritos by land and sea, including prized items such as turquoise, obsidian, gold, and cacao. Pyramid-like stone structures lined its roads. Chichén Itzá's priestly lords exerted dominance through political and spiritual control. They decorated their bodies with elaborate tattoos, clothing, and jewelry to set themselves apart from lower status Maya. As divinely ordained rulers, lords spoke directly to cosmic beings. A cult of sacrifice and bloodletting connected Maya leaders to the gods and reinforced the political and social hierarchy. Maya paintings depicted many lords performing ceremonies of bloodletting from tongues, ears, and even the genitals. Bloodletting from the most elite members of the cities was the greatest gift to the Maya deities. Chichén Itzá's elites relied on a priestly class who also inherited

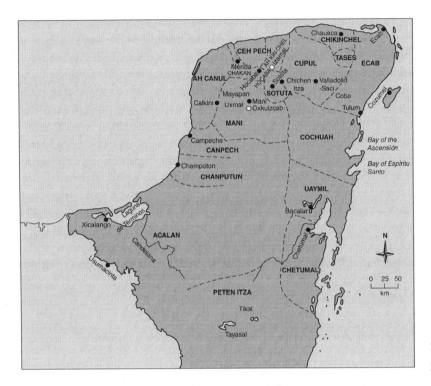

Map 2.1 Yucatan in the conquest period

their status. Through prophecies and rituals, priests determined the appropriate times for bloodletting and sacrifice. The **cenote**, a large, round, natural occurring deep well located near the city, was a ceremonial center where Maya made water sacrifices to pacify cosmic beings.

Chichén Itzá claimed political power over large portions of the Yucatan until the early thirteenth century, after which the great Maya city-states began a rapid decline from causes still unclear to scholars—the overpowering influence of, or invasions by, the Toltec empire, disease, or possibly an internal decay of its own political and social structures. After the fall of Chichén Itzá, a smaller capital arose at Mayapán. For reasons also not fully known, Mayapán's power dwindled by the mid-fifteenth century. At the time of arrival of the Spanish, Yucatan populations had dispersed into a number of lesser chiefdoms with limited political authority (see Map 2.1).

Maya Women and the City-States

Although Maya society was patrilineal, elite women played important political roles. In one famous hieroglyphic account, a famous young princess, Lady Wac-Kan-Ahaw, or "Lady Six Sky," left the powerful lineage of Dos Pilas in 682 CE to rule at the Mayan city of Naranjo. She commanded the city until her son was old enough to be crowned lord. In a tablet at Palenque from the classic period (250 CE to 900 CE), Lady Zac Kuk is depicted giving Pacal II, her son, the headdress that made him the sole ruler of Palenque. Other elite women held key positions in Maya kinship systems by linking kin groups and city-states through marriage. Women had titles within families, earned material wealth, and owned buildings and temples. They appear in glyphs next to their husbands and sons and are represented as important people.

Male Maya elites typically took the lead in public religious life, but behind the scenes women maintained household altars, produced the important calendrical ritual meals, and participated in important rituals and ceremonies. Women were sometimes represented in spiritual roles, such as the Moon Goddess. Elite women sanctioned warfare and other important actions within their lineages by contacting the spirits through their own participation in bloodletting. Many glyphs show elite women distributing weapons to the young men within their family networks. Women donned special clothing during rituals, and lords and their wives often appeared together on glyphs, participating in the public spiritual practices that gave particular dynasties the power and authority to continue their rule. Thus, elite Maya women played key roles in binding together families and sanctioning male activities important to the integrity and security of dynastic families and city-states.

Non-elite women played very different roles in Maya society. As populations increased in the Late Classic period (700 CE to 830 CE), the Maya increasingly depended on **terrace agriculture**. The building and upkeep of terrace plots required the work of women to weed, plant seeds, and cultivate gardens. Non-elite Maya women also took care of households and participated in the activities of the extended Maya kin networks called *Cah*, weaving cotton and producing ceramics. Their production of textiles and crafts helped *Cahob* (plural of *Cah*) pay tribute to the dynastic rulers of city-states and provided goods to trade with other *Cahob* for food and other staples. In short, non-elite Maya women had specific gender roles, participating in intensive and non-intensive agriculture, caring for families, and extending help to other kin within their *Cahob*.

Aztecs

Aztec origins remain somewhat cloudy, but it is generally accepted that their ancestors were hunters and gatherers who likely migrated southward into central Mexico in the twelfth century. Today, their civilization is remembered for its wealth and power, its empire that eventually spanned most of central Mexico and enveloped perhaps as many as five million people by 1500 CE, and its magnificent city Tenochtitlán with an estimated population of 150,000 residents and one that simply awed the Spanish conquistadors who arrived in the early 1500s. In some ways, Aztec society was structured similar to European societies: management of the empire rested in the hands of religious leaders and the wealthy, landed class. Slaves, servants, and free but unlanded laborers toiled in fields, constructed buildings, and performed the most basic yet essential tasks necessary to Aztec society. And, as in European nations, a military force provided domestic security and pressed the Aztec empire ever outward. Into this world ventured the Spanish only one generation after Columbus' famed voyage.

Pre-Aztec States in Mexico

Agriculture existed in Mexico centuries before the common era but exploded with massive city growth in the period of "classic era" Mesoamerican development (250 CE to 900 CE). Large-scale agricultural production at the Mesoamerican city of Palenque gave rise to a society that made advances in stone architecture, mathematics, and astronomy. In northern Mexico, the city of Teotihuacán extended its power through military aggression, economic tribute, and zealous religious worship. But for reasons still not fully understood, Teotihuacán, along with other Mesoamerican cities, fell relatively quickly to invaders from 900 CE to 1000 CE.

The Toltecs were the most powerful of the invading groups. They set up a capital at Tula and established dominance over much of Mesoamerica. But like the "classic era" city-builders, they also succumbed to invaders. However, the Toltec legacy remained important throughout Mesoamerica. The Mexica, commonly known as the Aztecs, recalled the reign of the Toltec Empire as the starting point of large-scale development in

Mesoamerica, leaving Teotihuacán's achievements mostly out of their oral tradition. Mexica lords enhanced their power, authority, and legitimacy by claiming ties to Toltec descent, and the Mexica also incorporated the Toltec pantheon of gods in their own religion.

After the fall of the Toltecs, a series of native peoples vied for dominance in the Valley of Mexico. Mayan peoples pushed in from the Yucatan, but Nahuatl-speaking peoples exerted the greatest influence. Divided into separate large territories known as *altepetls*, Nahuatl-speakers congregated in *altepetls* around Lake Tetzcoco, where they fought and struggled for control over the fertile agricultural terrain (see Map 2.2).

Rise of the Aztec Empire

In this period of confusion and war, the Mexicas migrated into the Lake Tetzcoco region of the Valley of Mexico. According to Aztec legend, approximately 10,000 Mexicas migrated to the Valley of Mexico from a northern homeland of Aztlán. Their patron god, Huitzilopochtli, known as the hummingbird of the south, or a version of the sun god, led them to the lake around 1250. In the early fourteenth century, the Mexica ascended to power following their victories in a series of wars. According to Aztec oral tradition, the Mexica saw an eagle

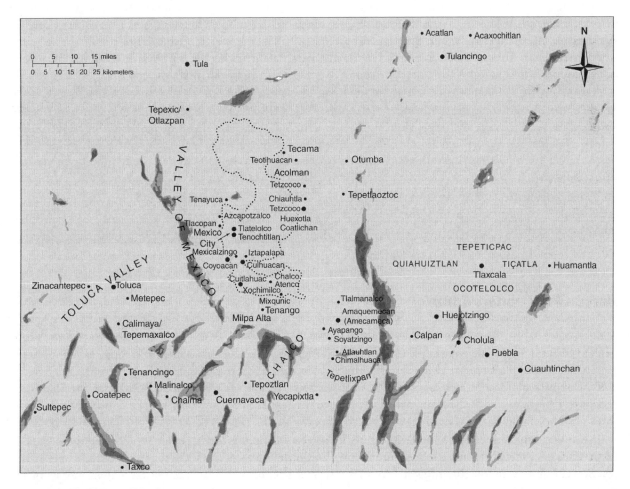

Map 2.2 The Valley of Mexico

sitting on a cactus and consuming a snake, a sure sign from the gods that the center of the lake was the best location for their capital city, Tenochtitlán. Here, Mexicas built an immense political empire under their ruler, or **tlatoani**. A succession of *tlatoanis*—including Itzcoatl (1426–1440) and Moctezuma I (1440–1468)—took control of central Mexico, exacting tribute in the form of labor, food, and fine goods from surrounding Nahua *altepetls*.

Tenochtitlán

Tenochtitlán, the city that became the center of the Aztec universe, emerged out of such conquests. On the island base in the middle of Lake Tetzcoco, Tenochtitlán formed an alliance with a "junior cousin" city, Tlateloco, which was on the island as well. Together, they dominated the Valley of Mexico, but Tenochtitlán stood as the centerpiece of Aztec power. At the time of the Spanish arrival, Tenochtitlán stretched over five square miles and was home to an estimated 150,000 people. To the Aztecs, Tenochtitlán, with its complex palaces and temples of worship, symbolized their political and spiritual dominance. In terms of architecture, stone craftsmanship, and sheer artistic beauty, Tenochtitlán rivaled many European cities. The Spanish marveled at its grandeur. One Spaniard observed, "It could not be bettered anywhere." Many compared the lake city with its intricate system of canals to Venice, Italy. Canoes and other watercraft carried food and other goods from peripheral *altepetls* to the city's center. Aqueducts supplied the city with fresh water, and many Aztecs cultivated maize, beans, and squash on floating islands. Tenochtitlán was carefully laid out to honor the sacred structure of the universe, with roads pointed in the four cardinal directions. The city was divided into districts called **calpulli**. The Aztec elite lived near the center of the city; the poor inhabited the city's periphery.

Accompanying imperial expansion and the growth of Tenochtitlán into the largest city-state in native North America was the development of distinctly Aztec social and cultural practices. Paintings and texts described lordship lineages, wars, as well as religious life in Tenochtitlán. A profound cult of war and human sacrifice helped cement Aztec power and authority over subordinate *altepetls*. There was a constant need among the Aztecs to pacify the warrior sun, Tonatiuh, and the master sun god, Huitzilopochtli. Only human sacrifices would satisfy the sun gods—the greatest gift is life. To supply the steady stream of people needed for sacrifice, the Aztecs engaged in almost constant warfare. Throughout the city, Aztecs celebrated military conquest with great displays of lordship rule and the ritual sacrifice of captives. Nahuatl pictographs dated to 1487 show 20,000 victims dying in the city's central plaza at the two main temples: one dedicated to the rain god Tlaloc and the other to Huitzilopochtli, the sun god responsible for the Aztecs' ascendancy.

Aztec Gods and Religion

A ritual calendar of the gods controlled the pulse of Aztec existence. Priestly lords turned to the gods to explain life and death, the regeneration of crops, and the movement of the planets and stars. As with other peoples, Aztecs did not recognize any separation between the sacred world and the living world. One Aztec deity, Quetzalcoatl, deserves closer examination because of its special place in the history of the Spanish conquest. Quetzalcoatl was the feathered serpent, god of the wind, of regeneration and creation, and of civilization itself. Quetzalcoatl was significant to the Aztecs because the deity linked them to the Toltecs, a people who also worshipped the serpent god. According to oral tradition, the Toltec leader Topiltzin adopted Quetzalcoatl's name, thereby giving the god human form and bringing man and spirit together. With his devoted followers, Topiltzin supposedly migrated south to the coast of Yucatan. Archaeological evidence exists of a cult of worship of Quetzalcoatl among classic era Maya. Both the Aztecs and Maya believed that Quetzalcoatl

2.3 Huitzilopochtli, the patron god of the city of Tenochtitlán.
Source: Julio Aldana/Shutterstock

would someday return to the lands of Mesoamerica. In fact, Moctezuma II, the Aztec *tlatoani* who encountered the Spanish conquistadors, had a temple honoring Quetzalcoatl.

Quetzalcoatl was supposed to return in human form, and some post-conquest Nahuatl-Spanish texts claimed Moctezuma II believed that the arrival of the Spanish conquistador Hernán Cortés fulfilled this prophecy. The Cortés-as-Quetzalcoatl story is either a monumental historical coincidence or was fabricated out of mixed accounts. The Spanish might have spread the story that Hernán Cortés arrived in Tenochtitlán on the day prophesied by the Aztec ritual calendar—the year 1 Reed—to make the conquest all the more astonishing. It is also possible that post-conquest Nahuatl writers may have used the powers associated with Quetzalcoatl to help explain Moctezuma's acquiescence in the face of Cortés. Even if the Aztecs viewed Cortés as a god, or at least the bearer of some sacred powers, they discovered their mistake very quickly.

Aztec Women in a Warrior Culture

"Thou will be in the heart of the home," observed an Aztec midwife after the conquest. At Aztec birthing ceremonies, the parents gave a boy a bow and arrow and sword, a sign of a warrior in the making. Girls received small weaving and spinning implements and a small broom, also symbols of their future life. Aztec women, both elite and non-elite, prided themselves on becoming wives to bear the next generation of Aztec warriors. At an early age, at a local House of Youth, both boys and girls learned proscribed behaviors. Except in special cases for women chosen as embroiderers in the palace, or as concubines or second wives for elite men, Aztec women sought marriage and motherhood.

Women and men in Aztec society had different spheres of influence, but these spheres were equally important and complemented each other. In line with Aztec ideas of complementary gender roles, pregnancy was the work of warrior women who went through the rigors of childbirth while men faced the rigors of fighting. The god of childbirth, Quilaztli, "She Who Makes Legumes Grow," was the centerpiece of a days-long celebration. Mexica midwives took young boys from their mothers, and the mothers recognized this as part of the warrior cult. Boys were trained to become warriors and expected to die in battle. Each time a mother placed her young son in his bed, she was to recite a passage that at once alienated her from strong maternal bonds and also reaffirmed the boy's role as an Aztec warrior. Aztec wives worked in the home and also in the markets, selling tortillas and other goods to supplement the household economy. There was no prohibition against women walking the streets of Tenochtitlán on their own. Aztec women passed down rituals, goods, and status to their daughters, and fathers passed down similar cultural and social items and practices to their sons. Goddesses and rituals dedicated to the power of women affirmed the important role of mothers and wives. The temple that housed Huitzilopochtli was called Coatepec or "Earth Mother." Becoming a wife and mother was the primary goal of all Aztec women, and rituals, cults, and goddesses reaffirmed the significance of women in a society dedicated to warfare.

Inca

The Peruvian highlands in the Andes Mountains were home to another massive empire. Like the Mexica who migrated to Mesoamerica, the Quechua-speaking Inca were migrants to the Andes. The Inca were one of

2.4 Quetzalcoatl, the feathered serpent god, was a deity found among pre-contact Meso-american peoples. Among the Aztecs, Quetzal-coatl was a god that moved between upper and under worlds and was a deity of creation.

Source: Peter Hermes Furian/Shutterstock

many small ethnic groups who looked to grow crops in the high valleys of the unique Andean environment. Quechua oral tradition has the Inca originating from Lake Titicaca; however, Inca origins still remain uncertain. The basic social units within Inca society were extended family groups called *ayllu*, and all members of a given *ayllu* claimed descent from a common ancestor. Each *ayllu* occupied and shared a large portion of land on which to grow food and graze animals such as llamas and alpacas. Among *ayllu* members was a deep sense of economic reciprocity. Clan members exchanged labor and food, cooperated in the support of the old and invalid, and assembled together for spiritual worship. With the formation of the Inca State, each *ayllu* was led by a *kuraka*, a hereditary chief.

Growth of the Inca State

The growth of the Inca State moved at a tremendous pace, beginning in 1440 in the southern Peruvian Andes only two centuries after the Incas arrived in Cuzco. Cusi Yupanqui, who changed his name to Sapa Inca ("Sole Ruler"), created the expansive Inca Empire and its dynastic rule. All subsequent leaders would also take the name of Sapa Inca, a tribute to their leader and a sign of direct descent within the Inca ruling line. Yupanqui became the absolute ruler over Cuzco by defeating a competing group known as the Chanca. From Cuzco, Yupanqui extended the Inca Empire some 600 miles in all directions. After his victory, he changed his name again, this time to Pachacutec, meaning "remaker of the world." He led the Inca Empire for 30 years, turning Cuzco from a small village into a massive imperial city. In addition, Pachacutec created the cult of worship of the sun at a new temple constructed at Cuzco. The Sapa Inca line would recognize the sun god, Inti, as the deity who founded the Inca State. Because of Pachacutec's ability to bring together political and spiritual power and authority, all subsequent Sapa Incas drew their legitimacy not only from military conquest and descent from the Sapa Inca line but also from Inti's sacred powers. At the same time, Sapa Incas allowed individual *ayllus* to remain in place, as long as they continually showed their devotion to the Sapa Inca through tribute.

Pachacutec's successor, Tupac Yupanqui, spread the reach of the Inca Empire to its fullest extent. Tupac ruled from 1471 until 1493, during which time the Incas controlled all of Peru, central Chile, and the highlands of Ecuador. There were roughly 12 million people under Inca rule. Partially accounting for the Incas' tremendous expansion was their use of an elaborate network of roads and their system of administration. Inca laborers laid an intricate road system through the rugged Andes, avenues that always remained open and accessible despite the brutal weather common to that region. Roads facilitated the flow of trade and allowed for the quick deployment of Inca military might.

Rulers also legitimated their power through a social and religious practice that was distinctly Inca. By the fifteenth century, a cult surrounding the worship of the mummified bodies of former leaders reaffirmed the dynastic line. Andean societies had always practiced ancestor worship, but the Inca took the practice to a new level. The Sapa Inca appointed men whose descent was in the Sapa Inca's line to care for the mummies. Caretakers dressed the mummies, maintained their preservation, carried them to rituals and ceremonies, and even into battles. Mummified rulers occupied their own palaces in Cuzco. This cult surrounding dead rulers ensured that any newly appointed Sapa Inca inherited wealth, the rule of the land, and divine blood within the line of descent represented in the mummies' bodies.

Inca Rule

As the Inca Empire reached its zenith in the late fifteenth century, the Sapa Inca divided the massive territory into the *Tahuantinsuyu*, or the "Four Quarters." Cities within the four quarters helped run the state.

Each quarter had a lord, or *apo*, who governed over the individual *ayllus* and *kurakas* within his quarter's borders. The *apos* were close relatives of the Sapa Inca. Underneath each *kuraka* was a series of civil servants, whose responsibilities included census taking and tribute collecting. Royal inspectors were sent to each district to ensure that civil administrators followed directions and conducted business appropriately. Communication between the empire's periphery and the center-based city relied on runners who carried messages back and forth. Incas developed the *quipu*, knotted cords used to count households and tribute. At the royal center, special men called *quipus* were responsible for recording all of the information needed to manage the state.

Mit'a tribute was an important source of income under the new regime. Tribute could come in the form of goods, but *mit'a* involved the contribution of male laborers to serve in the military, build roads and bridges, and construct temples and palaces. Other local forms of labor tribute separate from the *mit'a* system were obligations to grow crops, keep stores of food for military personnel, and offer labor support to community institutions of religious worship.

Because the Incas administered their realm much like a modern state, they faced all of the internal problems of statehood. Localities often fought one another. Ambitious men sought to overthrow local *kurakas* to increase their own land holdings and wealth. To keep the state functioning, Sapa Incas broke apart or consolidated disruptive *ayllus* under the leadership of loyal *kurakas*, or forced the migration of restive *ayllus* to more secure locations. At the higher levels of administration, infighting within the Sapa Inca line was a common occurrence, not only among *apos* but also among the Sapa Inca families. The most noted occurrence of imperial conflict was in the late 1520s between Huáscar and Atahualpa, the two sons of Huayana Capac. The struggle was long and vicious, with Atahualpa emerging victorious. Unfortunately for the Inca, the war left their state in a weakened condition at precisely the time Francisco Pizarro and a small group of conquistadors arrived in 1530.

The Power of Inca Women

The class structure of the Inca State determined the responsibilities of Inca women. They typically worked parallel and complementary roles alongside their husbands, together tending the fields of *ayllus*. However, rank within *ayllus* sanctioned different roles for elite men and women. *Kurakas* and their wives had greater claims to wealth, status, and prestige. Some women even ruled as *kurakas*. The ranking system within *ayllus* also dictated gifting between social equals and those of different status. Gifts bound men and women together, as well as particular kin groups within *ayllus*. The gifting of women to *kurakas* as second and third wives further tightened the bounds within certain *ayllus*. Overall, the labor production of men and women, and the exchange of women, organized Inca life and the communal use of resources.

The Inca State demanded the gifting of girls to the Sapa Inca line. Such girls were known as **acallas**. Civil magistrates traveled among *ayllus* and selected virgin girls to become *acallas*. For a *kuraka*, it was a tremendous honor for his daughter to become an *acalla* and move up in the Inca hierarchy. Those gifted to the Inca imperial elites played several roles. *Acallas* chosen to remain chaste were part of the divination practices of the imperial priests. Some *acallas* became concubines within an imperial harem, later to become wives of the Sapa Inca, or wives of other imperial elites.

Inca gods and goddesses also complemented each other. Women in *ayllus* worshipped Pachamama, a god of fertility that represented the reproductive forces of the earth. Pachamama complemented the male god of rain in Illapa. But the Inca elites imposed their own cosmic figures upon lower-class *ayllus* through cults of worship led by Sapa wives and husbands. To fall in favor with Inca elites, particularly elite women, lower-class *ayllu* women co-opted the image and worship of Pachamama. The Inca elite turned one of the daughters of

TIMELINE 2.1 PRE-CONQUEST MAYA, AZTEC, AND INCA WORLDS, 200 BCE—1530 CE

Date	Location	Shifting Circumstances
250 CE–900 CE	Yucatan	Rise of city-states
	Mesoamerica	Classic era of Mesoamerican civilization
900–1000	Mesoamerica	Fall of Teotihuacán, largest city-state in Mesoamerica
1220	Peru	Inca established Cuzco as the head of the Inca State
1250	Mesoamerica	Mexica (Aztecs) established center at Lake Tetzcoco that became Tenochtitlán
1325	Mesoamerica	Mexica dominated Valley of Mexico
	Mesoamerica	Succession of Aztec *tlatoani*
1422–1440		Itzcoatl
1440–1468		Moctezuma I
1440	Peru	Pachacutec established Sapa Inca line at Cuzco
1471–1493	Peru	Tupac Yupanqui extended the reach of the Inca Empire into the *Tahuantinsuyu*, or the "Four Quarters"
1520s	Peru	Civil war among the Sapa Inca line; Atahualpa became Sapa Inca

Pachamama, Saramama, the goddess of corn, into a human with divine powers. According to the Inca elite, it was Saramama as one of the first Inca queens who introduced corn to the *ayllu* women. By replacing the worship of *ayllu* goddesses with the Inca elite's divinity practices, the Inca elite solidified their position over *ayllu* women. The Inca State created a system of cosmic kinship in which *ayllu* men and women owed allegiance to a pantheon of state deities. For the Inca elite, a cosmic conquest over former local *allyus'* systems of worship meant *ayllus* would sacrifice themselves and their labor for the benefit of the state.

Spanish Conquest, Spanish Rule

Spain's quest for wealth and power, along with her crusade in the Americas to impose Christianity on native peoples, moved from the Caribbean into the lands of the Maya, Aztec and Inca early in the sixteenth century. Conquest, control, and exploitation were the goals; warfare followed by incorporation was the means to accomplish them. The seizure of vast territories and the defeat of numerous peoples with minimal forces marked the Spanish conquest. But to rule their newly acquired empire, the Spanish had to rely on indigenous households, clans, localities, politics, and economics. Thus, aspects of native society and culture survived conquest. This does not mean that Spanish rule was anything less than traumatic. Under the Spanish, the peoples of the Americas experienced brutal oppression along with wrenching social, economic, and political change.

Fall of Tenochtitlán

In 1517, an expedition led by Francisco Hernández de Córdoba set sail from the West Indies for the Yucatan. Córdoba was a landowning member of the Spanish elite in the Americas who benefited from a system of labor extraction known as the **encomienda**. The *encomienda* was a grant, under the auspices of the crown, to the labor of a certain number of Native Americans for a fixed period of time, and it usually encompassed a large area of land. In exchange for this labor, the grant holder was supposed to teach the laborers the Spanish language, train them in Catholicism, and send some of the accumulated wealth back to the crown. Córdoba's expedition was meant to bring more people and resources into this system.

Córdoba and his men encountered societies in the Yucatan that were nothing like the lesser chiefdoms of the West Indies. Maya stone masonry, a complex system of gods, and the apparent wealth of the people of the Yucatan all convinced Córdoba that he had found something special. He would not, however, live to reap the rewards of his discovery. Post-classic Mayas wearing armor made of padded cotton fought off Córdoba's force,

PROFILE

Malintzin, A Woman Negotiates With the Aztecs

Malintzin Doña Marina was born in the *atleptl* of Coatzacoalcos that stood on the outskirts of the Aztec Empire's political domination. Little is known with any certainty about her early life, but at the time Cortés arrived in the Yucatan she was a slave owned by Maya living on the shores of the Tabasco River. She spoke Chontal Mayan, Yucatec Mayan, and Nahuatl. As an enslaved woman, she probably worked in textiles, helping to produce Mayan cloth.

When Cortés arrived in the Yucatan in 1517, he battled several ethnic groups in the Tabascan region in the Putunchan and the Chontal. After their defeat, the Chontal traded 20 women to Cortés; Malintzin was part of this group. Malintzin was given a new name, Marina. Cortés's traveling party included Jerónimo Aguilar, a man who was once shipwrecked in the Yucatan and familiar with the Mayan dialect. When Aztec emissaries first arrived to talk with Cortés, he assigned Aguilar to translate, but Aguilar was unfamiliar with Nahuatl. Malintzin (now Marina) offered her services as a translator. From that point forward, Marina played an important role as the chief negotiator between Cortés and the Aztecs. She translated Nahuatl into Mayan and then conveyed the Aztec requests to Aguilar, who then told Cortés what the Aztecs wanted.

Marina became even more important once Cortés, his Spanish forces, and his Indian allies arrived in Tenochtitlán. When Cortés met Moctezuma on November 8, 1519, it was Marina who negotiated between the two leaders. Once the Aztecs were defeated, Marina continued to serve as a translator. By this time, she was already pregnant with Cortés's first child. After the conquest, Cortés resided in Coyoacan, on the outskirts of Tenochtitlán. Marina lived with Cortés, serving as a political translator so the Spanish could start to build relations with the surrounding *alteptls*. In fact, Marina was responsible for negotiating the amount of tribute each *alteptl* was to pay to the Spanish. In 1524, Doña Marina left Coyoacan for Mexico City, having married a Spaniard of high status, Juan Jaramillo. She and Jaramillo had a daughter, María, and settled on some land outside of Mexico City. In 1528, Marina's son, Martín, now six years old, left for Spain with his father Cortés. That same year, Marina died. Both her children, of mixed Spanish-Indian ancestry, moved into the ranks of Spanish nobility, her daughter becoming Doña María, and her son Don Martín.

killing Córdoba in battle. This setback did not end Spanish efforts. A second expedition to the Yucatan gathered tantalizing hints of a vast Aztec inland empire known among coastal native peoples for its immense wealth.

Hernán Cortés was selected to lead a third expedition with the expressed purpose of conquering the Aztec Empire. However, friction between Cortés and Cuba's Spanish governor, Diego Velázquez de Cuéllar, resulted in the expedition's cancellation at the last minute. Cortés ignored the order from the governor and set sail on his own initiative, leaving Cuba on February 18, 1519. Cortés commanded 11 vessels carrying 600 men, 16 horses, and 14 small cannon. He landed at Tabasco, at the base of the Yucatan, and immediately confronted fierce resistance from the local native peoples. After their defeat, Tabascan chiefdoms awarded Cortés with 20 women, one of whom was Malintzin (known among the Spanish as Doña Marina). She became Cortés's mistress and ultimately played a crucial role in the negotiations between the Aztecs and Cortés. By April 22, 1519, Cortés and his force had moved farther west along the coast of the Gulf of Mexico and established a base in a native town he captured. He named the village Veracruz and remained there over the next four months while gathering information about the Aztecs and Moctezuma II. Meanwhile, the Aztec leader sent informants to Veracruz to learn about the Spanish. Two separate forces were at work during this four-month period. First, disease inadvertently carried back to Tenochtitlán reduced Aztec numbers before the Spanish even set foot in the city. Second, Cortés learned from various sources that Aztec power was not as strong as it appeared, evidence of discord among those ruled by Moctezuma. Clearly, outlying *altepetls* in the Valley of Mexico resented Moctezuma's demands of enormous tributes, tributes that impoverished surrounding populations to maintain Tenochtitlán's grandeur and superiority.

In mid-August of 1519, Cortés moved toward the Valley of Mexico. Aztec opposition kept Cortés at bay temporarily. On several occasions, he fought off the Tlaxcalan Indians, but once defeated by advanced Spanish weaponry, the Tlaxcalans joined Cortés's forces, and he and his enlarged army arrived in Tenochtitlán on November 8, 1519. Moctezuma welcomed him into the city for reasons that remain unclear. Because the Aztecs made no distinction between the spiritual and worldly, the Spanish with their strange animals and weaponry may have appeared as foreign sacred powers, even if the Aztecs never viewed Cortés as the returning man-god Quetzalcoatl. It is also possible that Moctezuma believed he might be better able to corral Cortés's ambition by building an amicable relationship with the Spaniard or, at least, keep closer watch over his adversary. Cortés, however, took Moctezuma captive ten days later probably for the protection his captivity promised Cortes and his men. The sacred-political power of the leader was so immense that Moctezuma's seizure immobilized the upper echelons of Aztec leadership. Between the winter of 1519 and the spring of 1520, the Spanish remained in the city. After the Spanish on Cuba learned of Cortés's apparent victory in the Valley of Mexico, a seasoned explorer, Pánfilo de Narváez, set sail with 900 men as reinforcements. Cortés traveled to the Yucatan coast to greet Narváez and left Pedro de Alvarado, a senior lieutenant, in charge of Spanish operations in the Aztec city. Alvarado possessed neither Cortés's leadership nor his military skills. Recognizing the weakness of Alvarado's leadership, Aztecs plotted a counterattack. In May 1520, during a feast to honor Huitzilopochtli, the god of Aztec ascendancy, Aztecs mustered all the necessary sacred power from the deity's presence for the strike against the Spanish. They were unaware, however, that word of the Aztec plan had already reached Alvarado, who immediately launched a preemptive strike that killed a group of Aztec rulers and warriors who had gathered at a temple. Alvarado's actions prevented the planned uprising but it also ended any hope of negotiation between the Spanish and the Aztecs that Cortés believed he had fostered by holding Moctezuma. The fate of Tenochtitlán would be settled by a vicious war.

With the added power of Narváez's army, Cortés returned to Tenochtitlán and entered the city once again. The Aztecs allowed this as a means of concentrating the Spanish into one confined area and then surrounding the conquistadors with their own forces. However, after several weeks of heavy fighting, the Spanish managed to escape the city (it was at this time that Moctezuma died under mysterious circumstances). The Spanish

READING HISTORY

A Woman's Voice From Post-conquest Mexico: Ana Juana From Culhuacan

Legal documents like the one here from Ana Juana represents how Nahua peoples remained integral to the new Spanish system of governance in the Valley of Mexico. Women and men from various localities could sue in court and demand their legal rights to lands and other resources. Nahuas, of course, had to have multiple people who served as notaries to make their claims legal.

In the name of our lord Jesus Christ and of his precious mother, the heavenly lady Holy Mary, may all persons who see this document know that I, Ana Juana, whose home is here in San Juan Evangelista Culhuacan, in the *tlaxilacalli* of Santa Ana Tlacuilocan, first place my spirit and soul entirely in the hands of our lord God, because it is his creation. When I die, let him take it, and let him pardon me of all my sins. As to my earthly property that I keep for our lord God, it is my property. Let all who are my relatives know that it is my testament. Let no one invalidate my statement that I put on paper.

Thus I begin my statement: there is an enclosure of mine standing beside the road that is not yet roofed. I give it to my son named Juan Francisco. The houselot on which [the enclosure] stands is fifteen matl wide toward Xochimilco and toward Mexico City, and in length, toward the east, it is only ten matl. And I also give my son an old house that stands there facing toward Xochimilco. And there are three chinampas of mine next to the house, each one twenty [units of measure] long, next to the field of Martin Tlachochcalcatzintli. And there in the place named Quauhtenanco there are two chinampas of mine, each one twenty long, at the edge of the canal, next to the field of the late Francisco Yaoxomol. And there is one chinampa at the entrance that is ten matl, and three "Mexica lands" in the place named Ayoc. And I give all of these chinampas that are written here to my son, Juan Francisco, because he already pays tribute to them. Let no one ever take them from him.

And in Apilco there are seven chinampas of mine, each one twenty [units] long. I declare that as long as I am ill they are to be used for me, and when I die, let them be sold, and I will be buried from the money in proceeds.

And in Santiago Tetla there are sixty [units of measure] of dry land of mine; the first is in the place named Icçotitlan Ohuicanpolco, next to the field of Mateo Ilamatzin, and the second is in the place named Texallpan, next to the field of Pedro Guillermo, a poor person from Amantlan. And the third is in the placed named Temamatlac, next to the field of Pedro Itztolcatl, and here in Huixachtlan there are twenty [units of measure] of dry land of mine, next to the field of Miguel Coltzin. I give all of this dry land of mine that I record here to my son Juan Francisco. Let no one take it from him because he will pay tribute on it, he will perform community work duty on it, the hay tribute and all the various tributes.

And here is what I say concerning my husband named Gabriel Itzmalli, who is a great villain. Let him never bother my son, nor accuse him of anything. I do not know how many debts he has. He never gave me anything at all, not money nor telling me "poor you," as did the three who died, two of whom were my spouses, because we worked together to make a living. But this one, if he went to collect fruit or if he went to get maize, he would sell it himself without showing me how much he had bought. But as to the maize he just measured it out and gave it to me. Thus I say that I am afraid [of what he will do]; I declare that he should not accuse my son of anything; I beg lord don Francisco Flores, the alcalde, to speak for [my son] and to take him, because he is his godchild. Let him not abandon him.

And I said above that I gave to my son, Juan Francisco, a house that faces Xochimilco; it was the inheritance of my late sister-in-law who died. And I declare that they are not to tear it down. Let my son Juan Francisco pay something for it; he is to offer a little money to the church so that she will be helped before God our lord.

And here are the debts of my husband that I have paid, as I very well know; one peso which belongs to don Francisco Flores, alcalde, and four tomines that belong to his younger sister named Juana Xoco, and four tomines that belong to someone whose home is in San Mateo. And my husband asked me for a peso and said, "I am going to get fruit with it," and he just collected it and didn't buy the fruit. In all I paid four pesos.

This is all that I have written and put down on paper, in my testament. It was done before the *tlaxilacalli* (subunit of an *altepetl*) authorities as witnesses: Pedro Tecpanecatl; Martin Tlachochcalcatl Xochicuetzin; Diego de Tapia, church attendant; Domingo Çannen; Pedro Xochinanacaz; and before the women: Juana María, widow of Pedro Tepanecatl; Magdalena, wife of Pedro Tecpanecatl; Juana Tiacapan, wife of Diego de Tapia; Ana Tiacapan, wife of Tlacochcalcatl; Magdalenea, wife of Domingo; Ana Xoco, widow of Juan Atonemac.

Source: Matthew Restall, Lisa Sousa, and Kevin Terraciano, Eds. *Mesoamerican Voices: Native Language Writings from Colonial Mexico, Oaxaca, Yucatan, and Guatamala.* (New York: Cambridge University Press, 2005), p. 137. (Taken from The Testaments of Culhuacan, UCLA Latin American Publications Special Studies Volume 2, Nahuati Series 1.)

Question

What does the text tell us about Spanish rule in the Valley of Mexico and the role of Indian women?

retreated to Tlaxcala, where they regrouped with their allies. In a series of bloody battles, Cortés regained the initiative and fought his way back to Tenochtitlán by May 1521. Cortés benefitted from a smallpox outbreak in the city that obliterated almost the entire Aztec fighting population. Even so, the last warriors did not surrender until August 13, 1521.

The Spanish had come to establish a ruling hierarchy, extract wealth, and convert the Indian populations. But with massive Nahua populations in place, the Spanish used preexisting Nahua social organization to their advantage. To rule the Valley of Mexico, the Spanish erected the *encomienda* system regionwide and began building the institutional framework for the imposition of Catholicism. Nahua leaders remained in place, as did the local clan networks of the *calpullis*. Working

2.5 Spanish adventurers attack a native village on the Columbian coast of the Caribbean in an engraving published by Theodore de Bry in 1594.

Source: Beinecke Rare Book and Manuscript Library, Yale University

under Spanish elites, Nahuas filled all types of civic positions and created a writing system that combined Nahuatl with Spanish. An intricate system of courts was developed to litigate civil lawsuits over property and land boundaries between and among Spaniards and Nahuas. Thus, even though the Aztecs were conquered in 1521, Nahua social structures and cultural practices persisted.

Conquest of the Incas

The conquest of the Inca was even swifter than that of the Aztecs. Francisco Pizarro led the Spanish expedition into the heart of the Inca State. His goals were the same as any conquistador: to take lands and find riches for the crown to establish Spanish rule and a Spanish hierarchy and to convert the indigenous peoples. His expeditionary force consisted of 168 men, 62 of them on horseback. His party was far from a formidable opponent to the Inca. Pizarro and his men first arrived in a northern city of Cajamarca on November 15, 1532. According to one Inca account, the Spanish were referred to as *Viaracochas* (gods) because "the Indians saw them alone talking to white cloths (*paños blancos*), as a person would speak to another, which is how the Indians perceived the reading of books and letters." The next day, Pizarro and his men captured the Sapa Inca, Atahualpa, who had come to Cajamarca with a large Inca force. The Spanish offered the Sapa Inca the chance to accept Spanish rule and Catholicism, both of which Atahualpa rejected. Spaniards consequently attacked the Sapa Inca's encampment of soldiers, killing 2,000 warriors who were outmatched by Spanish military technology. Pizarro captured Atahualpa and held him in captivity until his execution in July 1533, despite the Sapa Inca offering a room filled with gold and silver as ransom. The Spanish defeat of the Inca was swift, but warfare, led by descendants of the Sapa Inca, continued sporadically well into the 1560s.

The administrative apparatus used to control the state fell into Spanish hands following the collapse of Sapa Inca power. The Spanish used the Inca social unit of the *ayllus* and the labor tribute system of *mit'a* to extract the labor necessary to operate economic enterprises such as the silver mines at Cuzco and Potosí. Quechua-speaking elites and civic officials learned Spanish, converted to Catholicism, and helped the Spanish administer the vast rural countryside of Peru. Despite the hardships of Spanish rule, the Inca ways of life did not die out entirely after Pizarro's conquest.

PROFILE

Titu Cusi Yupanqui, an Inca Elite After Conquest

Titu Cusi was probably born in 1530. He was the second to last descendant of the Inca dynasty. The rule of Huayna Capac, his grandfather, had extended from the Andes into the Amazonian lowlands, Chile, and Argentina. In 1526, Huayna and his heir, Ninan Coyoche, both died from smallpox. Titu Cusi's father, Manco Inca, received an appointment from the Spanish to help oversee the Inca State. But Manco Inca resisted the Spanish, using an army of 100,000 Inca warriors to lay siege simultaneously to Cuzco and Lima. Manco Inca successfully restored Inca rule for 30 years. As the Spanish waged their own civil war between members of two leading factions divided between the followers of Pizarro and another Spanish leader, Diego de Almagro, Manco Inca observed the events from Vilcabamba. When Manco Inca died, and his appointed successor died as well, Titu Cusi was officially made the Inca of Vilcabamba.

Titu Cusi was a smart politician. An avid supporter of an independent Inca State, Titu Cusi wore the regalia of the Inca ruler but negotiated with the Spanish to try to protect Vilcabamba. He converted to

Christianity and allowed missionaries to live at Vilcabamba. During the Inca revival known as *Taqui Onqoy*, a revitalization movement whose leaders called for outright resistance to Catholicism, literacy, and the Spanish, Titu Cusi upheld his loyalty to the Spanish. Before he died in 1571, Titu Cusi worked with an Augustinian missionary, Fray Marcos García, to have his life story written down. Titu Cusi, like many Inca rulers, recognized the importance of the written word. The text is an extraordinary and rare account of postconquest Inca society. It was also a plea to the Spanish crown to allow the Inca ruler to keep his settlement at Vilcabamba. Presented orally in Quechua, written down by García, and constructed in a linear historical fashion with Inca insights, the text, like Titu Cusi, is a representation of the hybrid Inca-Spanish culture that developed in Peru in the decades after Pizarro's invasion.

Conquest of the Maya

In 1526, Francisco de Montejo, who had served as a captain under Cortés, moved toward the Yucatan to take the region in the name of the Spanish crown. His goals were to establish Spanish rule, find a product for export to fill the coffers of the crown, and convert the local Maya population—all goals consistent with Spain's broad mission in the Americas. Within two months in the tropical climate, 50 of his men had died from disease, hunger, or exhaustion. Nine years later, in 1535, there were still few Spaniards in the Yucatan, largely because the wealth and health of the Valley of Mexico and Peru beckoned. The Yucatan became a "colonial backwater," a place in which Spaniards found no wealth but constant confrontations with Maya and overall misery. But the Maya also faced difficult times. Since the early Spanish expeditions, the Maya had endured drought and starvation. Many of the leading elite, such as the Xiu, traveled to the sacred cenote at Chichén Itzá to pray for rain, only to stumble into battle with competing *Cahob*. Such wars only compounded the Maya's problems. Montejo, in 1540, further complicated the Maya struggle by renewing relentless war against them. The Spanish easily destroyed war-torn Maya villages. Using crossbows, swords, and harquebuses, the Spaniards slaughtered thousands of Maya. Foreign pathogens also ran through Maya villages. The dual impact of disease and war reduced a native population of 850,000 to about 250,000.

The Spanish now moved to entrench colonial rule. Spanish elites allowed Maya headmen to oversee their local social units, or *Cah*, so long as *Cahob* leaders offered tributes to their Spanish masters. To position themselves within the new colonial order, Maya even went as far as to create a system of individual naming that included the name of their *Cah*. Using both Mayan and Spanish language notary records and petitions, *Cahob* leaders and family members worked within the Spanish legal system to keep a pre-conquest Maya landscape partially intact. *Cahob* members were highly litigious, suing Maya and Spaniards alike over village boundaries, property rights, and land tenure.

Intercultural relationships changed drastically once Franciscan missionaries arrived in the Yucatan. They first learned some of the native tongue in order to introduce the Maya to Catholicism and the Spanish system. Required, too, for their work to succeed was the teaching of the Spanish language to the Maya population, a process made somewhat easier for the Spanish as the Maya spoke dialects similar to the natives of Mexico, dialects learned by Franciscans.

Armed now with a developing common language, Franciscan religious zeal, under Diego de Landa's leadership, spiraled out of control. Landa arrived in the Yucatan in the late 1540s, taking control of the Franciscan order in the Yucatan, and over the following ten years pressed among the Maya the fundamentals of the Catholic faith. He preferred the willful, sincere, and heartfelt conversion of Indians to Christianity, but Landa proved more than willing to purge forcefully all traditional spiritual beliefs and practices from

TIMELINE 2.2 THE SPANISH CONQUEST, 1519–1562

Date	Location	Event(s)
November 19, 1519	Tenochtitlán	Cortés arrives and Moctezuma II welcomes the Spaniards
Winter 1519–1520	Tenochtitlán	Spanish housed in temples planning takeover because Moctezuma II captured
May 1521		Cortés moves back into Tenochtitlán
August 13, 1521	Tenochtitlán	After a long, brutal series of battles, Cortés takes Tenochtitlan
1526	Yucatan	Francisco de Montejo establishes new Spanish military presence in Yucatan
November 15, 1532	Peru	Francisco Pizarro and his 168 men capture Atahualpa and start the Spanish takeover of the Inca State
1540	Yucatan	Military conquest of Maya complete; Yucatan divided into *encomiendas*
1544	Yucatan	First eight Franciscans arrive
1562	Yucatan	Under Diego de Landa's guidance, 4,000 Maya suffer under the New World inquisition

the Maya. The Maya inquisition, as Landa's purge is now described, began in the province of Mani in 1562. Two young Maya hunters discovered stone idols in a cave. They reported their findings to Fray Pedro de Ciudad Rodrigo, who earlier that year had quelled a spiritual crisis in Mani when he pacified some newly converted Maya by assuring them that there was no stigmata (mysterious marks on the body in the places where Jesus was crucified) on a deformed baby's hands and feet. Because of his work among the recent Mani converts, Rodrigo felt betrayed learning that other Maya still worshipped their idols and practiced human sacrifice in the heartland of his Catholic evangelicalism. Rodrigo ordered the torture of hundreds of Indians by the garrucha, or the "hoist." As Franciscans pulled the Indians into the air by ropes tied to their wrists, friars attached heavy stones to their feet and flogged the accused heretics in an attempt to purge them of their sins.

Landa soon learned of the incident, but he waited a month to receive proper authority to conduct his own investigation, one that ultimately extended into eight Maya provinces. Under the terms of a Papal Bull from Rome, Landa had the power to conduct his New World inquisition in a manner similar to the inquisitions conducted during the *Reconquista* in Spain. For three months, he carried out mass arrests and brutal, selective torture of Maya suspected of non-Catholic practices or beliefs. On July 12, 1562, in the Mani province, Landa held an *auto de fe*, a ceremony involving the public display and flogging of condemned heretics just before execution. During his three-month reign of terror, Landa tortured more than 4,500 Maya. Many Maya killed themselves rather than risk interrogation and torture at the hands of Spanish inquisitors.

The year 1562, however, marked the zenith of Franciscan power and authority among the Maya. Landa's rule came to an end, and the Franciscans never again enforced Catholicism in the Yucatan with such intensity. Franciscans nonetheless continued their efforts to convert Indians by bringing them into mission compounds

READING HISTORY

A Voice From the Maya New World Inquisition: Francisco Chuc of Sahcaba, August 11, 1562

Just like the inquisition in Spain, legal documentations of confession were central to the Franciscan inquisition in the Maya provinces. Confessions gave legal credence to the friars' efforts to root out non-Christian religious practices. Francisco's account is also significant for his willingness to admit that traditional Maya religious practices, cast here as evil because of Franciscan biases, still were in practice after the Spanish had taken over the Yucatan.

Chuc's confession contains a reasonably full account of animal offerings, and the first reference to the burning of small crosses and their quenching in the blood of a sacrificed animal.

... On 11 August, Francisco Chuc, *ab-kin*, priest as they called [him] ... native of the said village of Sahcaba, ... having been [*ab-kin*] in the village [of Sahcaba] as *ab-kin* he had been present at some sacrifices made to the idols in the said village, and especially he remembered being at a sacrifice and ceremony they had made three years before through some *cuentas* [beads] one Baltasar Cocom had given to the witness so that through them they would remember to make reverence to the idols. They made a sacrifice of some birds and a pig and other animals and this witness was present at it. And perhaps three months later four idols were brought in from the forest, which they carried into the church, and they also took in wine from Castille mixed with honey and water and they offered the wine to the idols and after having offered the wine and prayed to the idols they capped the village wells in reverence and worship for the idols in the manner of fasting so that the idols should provide them with water for the *milpas*. And that then a few days after they had made that sacrifice this witness and Gaspar Zeque and Baltasar Cocom and Juan Coyi, *principals*, and Juan Yah, all natives of the village gathered together to make another sacrifice in the said church and they killed a pig ... and took a small cross that was on the altar and with six ... little sticks from which they made barbecues they burned the said sticks and the cross that was on the altar before the idols they had put in the church ... and they quenched the cross and the sticks that were burning in the belly of the pig that had been crucified there, and with the blood of the said pig they put out the said fire of the said cross and sticks. And this witness was he who put the cross and sticks in the belly of the pig to quench them with the blood, which he did twice. And later they made another sacrifice in the church in which they killed a dog and they offered the idols the heart of the dog, and those who were there roasted the said dog, and ate it. And they drank there at the sacrifice. And after these sacrifices this witness met together with the rest of the lords and the said chiefs and being together in the house of Baltasar Cocom [a chief] they discussed and agreed together to send two lords called Francisco Xeque and Andres Uc with two lengths of stick beads to purchase children for sacrifice. And so the said lords went to the villages of Quicucche and Pustunish, and in these two villages they bought two little boys who were just beginning to walk, whom they bought from Juan Puc, lord and a powerful person in the village of Pustunich, for one length of beads, and the other they bought in Quicucche from Diego Chan, a rich Indian of the said village. And the said lords brought them to the said village of Sahcaba and this witness knows from the said two lords how they had been bought from the said Juan Puc and Diego Chan and that they were children of slave women belonging to the said lords from whom they had been bought. And having brought the said children to the said village of Sahcaba about ten days after they arrived in the village this witness met with Baltasar Cocom, chief, and Diego Xibe, *principal*, now dead, and Francisco Pot, now dead, and Francisco Be, and so being together in the house of the said Baltasar Cocom, they all went from there to an ancient site a league from the village called Tabi, and they took the two boys they were holding for the said sacrifice. And when they arrived they placed the idols in a ring with the two boys in front of them and they threw them down on to the ground and as they were lying there Diego Xibbe came with a stone knife *and opened* the boys on the left side and took out their hearts and gave them to this witness and this witness received them as *ab-kin* and priest. And after he took them he raised them on high and speaking with the devil said to him, "All powerful God, this sacrifice we make to you so that you would provide us with [those things] we have need of." And then he smeared the snouts of the idols with the blood, and having finished making this sacrifice they took the blood they had from the two boys and the bodies and the heart and threw them all into a *cenote* and returned to their houses in the said village. And they left the idols there. And that when this witness was going to these sacrifices he had there four idols of his own, which he had brought out for the sacrifice of the boys. And that this sacrifice was made at the time of the hurricane a year ago because it seemed to them that their gods were angry and so they would be appeased and there would not be deaths.

He was asked if he knew if they should have made or were accustomed to make sacrifices of men or women or children or other infants in other villages or parts of these provinces and that he state in what parts and what the names were of those present at such sacrifices, he said he did not know [of] it.

Source: Inga Clendinnen, *Ambivalent Conquests: Maya and Spaniard in Yucatan, 1517–1570*. (New York: Cambridge University Press, 1987), 202–204.

Question

What does this confession tell us about the Mayan world after the conquest?

and encouraging acceptance of the faith. Brutal force to coerce conversion, they realized, only pushed Indians further away from the missionaries. The Yucatan inquisition demonstrates how far the Spanish were willing to go to impose an Iberian New World Order.

French and English Newcomers

European feet stepped on North American shores long before the travels of Columbus and those who immediately followed him. Norsemen constructed settlements and established trade with native peoples in the more frigid regions of North America in the tenth century, and European fishermen and traders conducted business across much of New England well in advance of the first encounter between Indians and the Spanish farther south. European colonization of North America, however, was neither desired at this time nor possible given the chaos of nation-building then occurring in Europe, the sweep of deadly pathogens over vast populations, the limits of technology and general knowledge, and little capability overall to plan, much less enact, a comprehensive colonial program in North America. These conditions changed by the sixteenth century. The Spanish invasion of the Americas and the wealth and power they amassed ignited a fierce determination among the French, English and Dutch for territorial claims and resources in North America. Indeed, by 1550 Spain had emerged as the principal European power, her richness and military might now determining European fortunes. "When Spain moves, the earth trembles" became an understood reality across Western and Southern

Europe. To counter Spain's burgeoning position as power-broker on the European continent, France, England, and Holland separately but deliberately committed themselves to the construction of a colonial presence in the "New World."

Pre-Columbian Encounters in North America: The Norse

The Icelandic writings, *The Saga of the Greenlanders* and *The Saga of Erik the Red*, are tales of the Norse settlement of Greenland, Labrador, and Newfoundland. In one account, Erik Thorvaldsson, known as Erik the Red, sailed west from Iceland in 982 CE and discovered a strange place he named Greenland. In 986 CE, he led 25 ships full of settlers to the new lands and established two hamlets: *Brattahlid* in the southwest portion of the island and *Godthaab*, located 400 miles north of *Brattahlid*. From these short-lived settlements, according to Icelandic tradition, Norsemen made contact with the Inuit and Bethouk peoples who hunted large sea mammals in the waters of Canada, Greenland, and Newfoundland. An informal trade relationship arose with the Norsemen swapping iron, copper, boat nails, carvings of Norsemen, and woolen cloth for ivory walrus tusks. Norsemen placed high value on walrus tusks, using them as a form of currency and shipping vast amounts of ivory back to Norway. It should not be surprising that the Norsemen saw themselves as more advanced than the Inuits and Bethouk because the Inuit and Bethouk had "no iron, but use walrus tusks for missiles (harpoons), and sharpened stones instead of knives." Ego and mere superficial glances at other cultures were traits that predated the age of European colonization.

In the 990s, Leif Eriksson, the son of Erik the Red, traveled across the North Atlantic and loaded his ship with North American timber and while there gave names to places he visited. *Helluland*, known as "Slabrock Land," probably referred to present-day Baffin Island and northern Labrador, while *Markland*, meaning "Forest Land," probably indicated central Labrador and Newfoundland. Eriksson named another place *Vinland*, probably the grapevine-filled coasts between New Brunswick and Maine.

Eriksson continued Norse trade with the Inuit and Bethouk, relations that were mostly friendly but sometimes hostile. These Europeans were not interested in colonizing the coast of North America, displacing natives, or exploiting native labor. However, there is archaeological evidence indicating the location of at least one settlement on Newfoundland, as well as trade networks Inuit and Bethouk used to spread Norse iron and other metal-worked items along the North Atlantic coast. By the late tenth century, Norsemen had settled *L'Anse aux Meadows* in northern Newfoundland. Comprised of thatch settlements, a work shed, and housing for boats, *L'Anse aux Meadows* was a prime location, with a shallow bay and fields that were good for cattle grazing. In Maine, a Norwegian penny turned up at an archaeological site dated to the fourteenth century. Iron-worked implements and raw metals continued to trickle through vast Inuit and coastal New England Algonquian trade networks long after the Norse presence ended in the fourteenth century. Their North American settlements most likely were intended as trade outposts and possibly as points of contact and supply for sea traveling Norsemen. As their long-distance travels became rarer and their trade with Inuit and Bethouk peoples assumed less importance, there was little need to maintain those far-flung settlements.

Early Expeditions to the Northeast

Long after the Norse explorers withdrew from Greenland and Newfoundland, other seafarers plied the coasts of the Northeast, particularly in the regions of Canada and New England. Encounters with native peoples were sporadic and often violent, but there were moments of cultural exchange. Indian groups had some sustained contact with Portuguese and Basque whalers, as the Europeans took their catches ashore to butcher them. Mi'kmaq around the gulf of the St. Lawrence River, Abenaki of coastal Maine, and Inuit and Bethouk traded with European fisherman and whalers for iron implements, beads, and other items. Indians did not simply replace their utilitarian items with European goods; they adapted European goods to meet their particular needs. Archaeological evidence indicates that Indians melted down Basque copper and other items to make arrowheads and scrapers, while Algonquian peoples incorporated the colorful beads into their spiritual beliefs and mortuary practices. Such European items reached inland populations through vast trade networks.

Until the late sixteenth and early seventeenth centuries, encounters between Europeans and the Indians of southern New England were also infrequent. Like the meetings farther north, they occurred mostly when Basque, Portuguese, English, and Breton fishermen explored the coastline or came ashore. Most of these sailors were in search of codfish, whales, and furs. A few were looking for new ways to reach Asia, the fabled water route of European rumor. The ships' crews typically rowed to shore to gather firewood, fill freshwater barrels, and hunt for fresh meat. Many of these explorers encountered Indians who were already seasoned traders. When Giovanni da Verrazzano, who sailed for the French, reached the Massachusetts and Rhode Island coast in 1524, he met Narragansetts and Wampanoags who had already experienced trade with Europeans. According to Verrazzano, the Indians seemed unimpressed with gold trinkets but wanted items of blue and red, particularly beads, as Algonquians saw such items as spiritually charged substances. When he showed some Algonquians his firearms, the technology did not shock them, but they did admire the weapons' craftsmanship. Algonquians of southern New England placed a high value on Verrazzano's "trinkets, baubles, and bangles" because they resembled preexisting native trade items such as **wampum** shell beads, exotic stones, and native copper. Previous interactions with Europeans had taught Algonquians not to fear Verrazzano's ship. His vessel was neither a floating island nor cannon fire thunder and lightning. Thus, when Englishmen descended on the territory in the early 1600s, Indians of southern New England saw newcomers as just another group of people to incorporate into existing trade and diplomatic networks.

Native Peoples and the French Along the St. Lawrence River

The French navigator, Jacques Cartier, sailed into the St. Lawrence River area in 1534. The St. Lawrence reached deep into the interior of North America, persuading Cartier that it might be the famed Northwest Passage to Asia. Along the St. Lawrence were the villages and cultivated fields of two primary groups of Indians: the Stadaconans and Hochelagas. Much debate surrounds the origins of these people, but most scholars agree that both the Stadaconans and Hochelagas were linguistically and culturally tied to the Huron to the north and the Iroquois to the south (see Chapter 4 for further discussion of the Huron and Iroquois). The first Indians Cartier encountered were not, however, the Stadaconans or Hochelagas. Upon entering Chaleur Bay near the entrance to the St. Lawrence River, Cartier's ship was approached by 40 or 50 canoes filled with Mi'kmaq eager to trade with the newcomers. Having gained a little knowledge of appropriate trading protocol from earlier exploratory parties, Cartier had stocked his ship with glass beads, mirrors, and other trade items to negotiate with Indians such as the Mi'kmaqs along the St. Lawrence. The French fashioned an alliance with the Mi'kmaqs after days of trading.

A young Algonquian-speaking Montagnais man near the St. Lawrence region of Canada spoke of how his grandmother marveled at the first French ship she saw, referring to it as a floating island. Unlike Atlantic-coast Algonquian speakers who had experienced waves of European traders and fishermen, the Montagnais had not encountered Europeans until the French arrived. Moreover, Algonquian oral traditions of unknown places and things had included no descriptions of European vessels. According to his grandmother's memory, the only sense she made of the bearded men on the floating island was that they must have come from strange lands with traditional spiritually charged colored gifts such as beads. Astonished, but prepared to offer the hospitality that was customary among the Montagnais, his grandmother set up wigwams for the French. In return, the Montagnais who paddled to the side of the ship in canoes received wine and a barrel of biscuits. The biscuits were dry and tasteless, and the deep red wine puzzled them. The Montagnais were appalled that the French "drank blood and ate wood" and then tossed the biscuits into the water. More impressed by the French ships than by the food and drink, the Montagnais named the French *ouemichtigouchiou* "men in a wooden canoe or boat." The coastal Mi'kmaq had an oral tradition that spoke of the French in similar ways, before the Mi'kmaq became skilled coastal traders. The biscuits were "birch tinder" from white birch trees, and the French were "cruel and inhuman" because they drank blood (the wine). The Mi'kmaq avoided the French for a period of time, wary of such a repulsive people. Indeed, just as Cartier tried to make sense of the people he encountered, the Algonquians of the northeast tried to make sense of the French.

Cartier continued up the St. Lawrence, where his dealings with the Stadaconans provoked tension, confusion, indecision, broken allegiances, and intertribal and inter-clan rivalries. On July 22, 1534, Cartier experienced his first sustained contact with the Stadaconans as traders. Unfamiliar with inland Indian trade protocol, he described the Stadaconans as the "sorriest folk there can be in the world." But the peoples he encountered were already savvy traders, securing beads, knives, and other items from previous European traders. It is most likely, too, that they had also journeyed north to the shores of Newfoundland to hunt sea mammals and there encountered other European traders and explorers. Stadaconans now received tins and glass beads during the initial exchanges with Cartier. Cartier enjoyed amicable relations with the Stadaconans until he ordered his men to erect a large cross on shore. Donnacona, a chief and leader of the Stadaconan trading party, was insulted by Cartier's actions. The French had failed to ask for permission to share the land through the proper diplomatic channels.

Cartier's relations with Donnacona improved once the explorer took two of the chief's sons, Taignoagny and Domagaya, back to France. Donnacona was at first hesitant to send his sons to France but ultimately placed his trust in the Frenchman. From a practical perspective, the long-distance travel of his sons reaffirmed his status and power as an Eastern Woodlands chief and reinforced his alliance with the French. Cartier returned with Donnacona's two sons on his second voyage in 1535. But the Frenchman soon upset Donnacona again by requesting permission to travel farther upriver to trade with a competing group, the Hochelagas. The Hochelagas received Cartier very differently than the Stadaconans. They brought out their sick hoping that Cartier could cure them, because they interpreted the metal items and glass beads as the gifts of someone with sacred powers. Seeing the Hochelagas as a fierce people but inadequate traders, Cartier left Hochelaga after only one day and returned to the Stadaconans.

Cartier soon became aware of intertribal and even inter-clan strife fomenting between Donnacona and the chief of Achelacy, a village just south of the formal settlement of Stadaconan. In a deceptive move, and perhaps at the request of their father, Taignoagny and Domagaya secretly tried to convince the Achelacy chief that the French traded worthless goods for food, essentially a plan to prevent French trade with Stadaconan competitors. Nonetheless, a variety of clan leaders, including the Achelacy chief, all courted alliances with the French. An epidemic of smallpox in Stadaconan further strained the already fragile French-Stadaconan alliance.

Cartier eventually broke relations with the Stadaconans by kidnapping Donnacona and nine villagers to help the French navigate farther inland in search of wealth, but his effort garnered little success in securing profitable trade relations. Other Frenchmen followed Cartier, but no firm trade relations and diplomatic dealings in the St. Lawrence area resulted until the late sixteenth and early seventeenth century (see Chapter 4). As smaller groups such as the Stadaconans and Hochelagas lost their importance as power brokers or were absorbed by larger tribes, the French focused on the power politics between the Huron, the Montagnais, and other Algonquian peoples who dominated the St. Lawrence territory, as well as the Iroquois to the south.

Algonquians and the English at Roanoke

Knighted in 1585 and a favorite in the court of Queen Elizabeth I, Sir Walter Raleigh was entrusted with the task of establishing the English as an imperial presence in the Americas. Both he and the Queen saw overseas expansion in economic and political terms. If England was to keep up with the major European powers, it would have to join France and Spain in the pursuit of wealth and territory in the Americas.

The competition between England and Spain took on a moral tone in the writings of Richard Hakluyt, a staunch promoter of English colonization. Drawing on Bartolomé De Las Casas's *Account of the Destruction of the West Indies*, he helped spread the "Black Legend" of Spanish atrocities in the New World. According to Hakluyt, England's colonists would never commit similar acts of brutality against the native peoples. Hakluyt's propaganda may have been useful for generating public support for colonization, but it had little bearing on Raleigh's expedition. Raleigh's goal was to establish a military outpost to fend off Spanish and French expansion along the northeastern coast of North America. Such an outpost would serve both as a base for strikes against French and Spanish vessels and a starting point for English efforts to locate the prized Northwest Passage to Asia.

In the summer of 1584, Raleigh sent two men, Philip Amadas and Arthur Barlowe, to find a site for the outpost. They discovered what they described as a "Garden of Eden" at Roanoke Island, located off the coast of present-day North Carolina. Raleigh sponsored a second expedition the following year with 108 men, including the scientist Thomas Hariot, the artist John White, and a military governor, Ralph Lane. This expedition remained on the island from August 1585 until June 1586. Hakluyt's literary campaign to gain support for English colonization cast the British as moral imperialists. In reality, however, the Roanoke colonists brutalized the Indians they encountered along the North Carolina coast much like the Spanish had done farther south.

Located near Roanoke were several prominent chiefdoms of the Sectan, Chonoac, Wepaemeoc, and Ossomoocomuck. Ossomoocomuck territory consisted of the Outer Banks of North Carolina, the thin barrier of islands that included Roanoke. Wingina was the prominent chief of the Ossomoocomuck, and he oversaw a series of well-populated villages. In describing the Indians they encountered, the English used descriptive terms with which they were familiar even though the terminology might not be accurate and was often misleading. The English commonly referred to chiefs (*weroances*) as "kings," but they did not have the extent of authority that European kings possessed; the English, then, ascribed to the *weroances* far more power than they actually enjoyed, this contributing to miscommunication between the two peoples. Before the English came, all of the Carolina coastal chiefdoms had created political, social, and cultural networks. They competed for access to inland and northern prestige goods, waged war, and cooperated with each other when it served their interests. In addition, the chiefdoms traded with shipwrecked Spaniards for metal items and other utilitarian goods. The coastal villagers turned many of these items into traditional tools, shells, and weaponry. In short, Roanoke was not a "Garden of Eden," but a world of Algonquian chiefdoms that had a long history of trading with a variety of peoples. *Weroances* such as Wingina maintained their power through persuasion and reciprocity. Such reciprocity extended outward from important villages, as Wingina and other leading men controlled trade and diplomatic networks with other chiefdoms. Thus, when the English arrived, it was the duty of Wingina and other coastal chiefdoms to negotiate reciprocal relations with the newcomers. Two Indians, Manteo and Wanchese, who had been taken back to England, learned English and became crucial cultural negotiators under Wingina's supervision. However, the English military governor, Ralph Lane, either did not understand or did not care about Algonquian protocol. Instead of offering the necessary alliances and goods to local chiefdoms in order to gain access to land and resources, he simply claimed Roanoke for the English crown.

Thomas Hariot and John White were interested in learning as much as they could about the Indians they encountered. During visits to Algonquian villages, Hariot scribbled detailed notes about native culture and customs, while White painted what would become a famous series of watercolors. Around this time, a disease that was probably some variant of influenza devastated Wingina's people as well as the interior chiefdoms. At first the strange Englishmen who roamed among villages with bibles and books, coupled with the disease's havoc, gave the English some spiritual leverage. Unfamiliar with a written language and the printed books of the English, awed by the newcomers' advanced military technology, and ravaged by foreign pathogens, coastal Algonquians proclaimed that the strange men possessed spiritual power, or *montoac*. But trouble broke when a chief refused to turn over an Indian who had stolen an English cup. Lane ordered the village burned to the ground. With English settlers plundering Roanoke villages and other coastal chiefdoms for food and supplies, any peaceful thoughts the Algonquians might have had about the English quickly vanished.

2.6 A religious dance in a drawing created by John White. While not always accurate, White's collection of watercolors was the first glimpse the English public had into the world of the coastal Algonquians.

Source: Courtesy of Library of Congress Prints and Photographs Division

In June of 1586 the English captured and beheaded Wingina. Fearing an Indian counterattack, Lane and the colonists abandoned the area and sailed home with the famous English privateer Francis Drake. John White led a second effort one year later to establish a permanent settlement on Roanoke, this time a community of families rather than soldiers. Unable to establish friendly relations with the Algonquians, White returned to England to explain conditions in the colony to his superiors. He ventured back to the colony in 1590 with supplies to find that all of the colonists had vanished. White only found the word "Croatan" carved in a wooden pole. Croatan was the name of a local group of Indians formerly allied to Wingina. The Roanoke colonists were nowhere to be found, and there were no clues suggesting what might have happened to them. The disappearance of the colonists stunned the English crown and remains an unsolved mystery.

The English experience at Roanoke foreshadowed future encounters between Indians and the English. Algonquian chiefdom leadership, land rights, reciprocity, and diplomatic protocol were of no concern to Roanoke's settlers. The sad demise of Roanoke should have prompted the English to alter their approach to the peoples of North America. Unfortunately, the English who journeyed to the Chesapeake Bay region in the seventeenth century appeared to have learned nothing from the Roanoke project. Repeating similar costly mistakes, Jamestown's settlers struggled to deal with the largest Indian confederacy in the Chesapeake under the leadership of Powhatan.

Conclusion

The arrival of Europeans in the Western Hemisphere is one of the most transformative events in world history. Europeans did not discover a new, unspoiled, pristine world but instead a world rich in complex native societies and cultures. The arrival of Columbus in the West Indies was an unadulterated catastrophe for the Tainos who lived there. Spanish weapons and pathogens destroyed complex interconnected village chiefdoms, all but

PROFILE

Manteo, the Roanoke Interpreter

In October 1584, a German traveling to London observed, "a certain Master or Captain Ral[egh] has brought two men of this country with him, and had them about his person. . . . They were in countenance and stature like white Moors." One of the two men was Manteo, a Croatan Indian. Upon his return to Roanoke, Manteo would play a critical role in sustaining relations between the local Algonquians and the English.

Arriving in England in 1584, Manteo and his compatriot Wanchese were taught English by Thomas Hariot, who had learned to speak a little Algonquian. At the same time, Manteo shared information about the customs, land, and trading practices of his people. Dressed in English garb, including leather shoes and a brimmed hat, Manteo traveled the streets of London, seeing London's sights and meeting with important sponsors of the Roanoke project.

Manteo returned to Roanoke in 1585 and immediately stepped into the role of cultural negotiator. He met with local tribesmen on the island and the coast and brokered friendships between the Algonquians and the English. Manteo served the English well, negotiating with Granganimo, the leading *weroance* on Roanoke Island, to allow the English to choose a spot on the northern tip of the island for a fort. When Ralph Lane took over operations at Roanoke, Manteo continued to serve as an intercultural broker.

Manteo even helped Lane search for gold and silver on the Carolina coast. But as the English became more brutal in their treatment of the local Indians, Manteo found it impossible to negotiate any further. In 1586, he accompanied Lane aboard the *Bark Bonner* back to England.

Still playing the role of cultural go-between, Manteo's skills with the English language helped Walter Raleigh, Thomas Hariot, and John White hatch another plan for a colony. In May of 1587, three ships with 114 colonists left Plymouth, England, for North America, this time with intentions of settling farther north near Virginia. Manteo was aboard the ship to smooth over relations with the Indians and to let the local Algonquians know of English intentions to establish a full colony with families. Stopping at Roanoke, the English encountered hostile Indians. Manteo found less hostility around Croatan Sound, but could not stop the mounting troubles between the Algonquians and the English. After a military skirmish with his own people, Manteo became the first Native American to convert to the Anglican faith on August 13, 1587. The rest of Manteo's history remains unknown.

wiping out a population that had numbered in the millions. In other areas, the impact of European arrival was more complex. In Mesoamerica, the Spanish conquistadors subdued the Aztecs, but not without the help of native allies, diseases, and the Mexica woman Malintzin who negotiated for both sides. Moreover, Nahua ways of life remained in place. In Peru, Pizarro and his band took the Inca State, but the basic native foundations of local rule and tribute continued and laid the foundation for a successful Spanish empire in the Andes. Native leaders like Titu Cusi perpetuated Inca rule in isolated Andean pockets. Some even learned how to speak and write Spanish, filling high-level civil positions in the Peruvian government. In the Yucatan, Franciscans had to learn the native tongue to convert Mayas to Catholicism, and even though the friars tried to root out Maya religious practices, Maya social structures and culture continued. When the French arrived in the St. Lawrence, the Algonquians of the northeast had already traded with Europeans for centuries and were able negotiators. The English set sail to Roanoke to establish a fort to fend off the Spanish, claiming their venture as a benevolent experiment in colonization that was in every way different from Spanish rule but actually a move to score

TIMELINE 2.3 IMPORTANT ENCOUNTERS IN NORTH AMERICA, 982–1590

Date	Location	Encounters
982	North Atlantic	Erik Thorvaldsson the Red of Iceland discovers Greenland
986	North Atlantic	Two Norse settlements establish trade relations with Inuits and Bethouks
1300s	North Atlantic	Norsemen abandon last settlement of *L'Anse aux Meadows*
1400s—1500s	North Atlantic	Lucrative coastal trade with Mi'kmaqs, Abenakis, and other northern Algonquians as Basque, Spanish, and Portuguese fisherman hunt codfish, whales, and look for furs
1517	Newfoundland	One hundred ships sail out of Newfoundland harbors for the codfishery
1524	Southern New England	Giovanni da Verrazzano sails to Cape Cod and trades with the Narragansetts of present-day Rhode Island
1534	St. Lawrence River	Jacques Cartier sails up the St. Lawrence River and trades with the St. Lawrence Iroquois in the Stadaconans and Hochelagas
1584	Carolina coast and Roanoke	Philip Armadas and Arthur Barlowe, sailing under the patronage of Walter Raleigh, establish relations with the coastal Algonquians
1585–1586	Carolina coast and Roanoke	Expedition establishing a fort at Roanoke under Ralph Lane, Thomas Hariot, and John White turns relations hostile with local Algonquian Indians
1590	Roanoke	Colony found abandoned by John White

wealth for England. Even with the benefit of the cultural negotiator Manteo, English efforts to establish a colony ended in miscommunication, violence, and a lost colony.

Spanish, French, and English explorers, as well as native peoples, all had preconceptions about the "other." However, as settlement and contact continued, as native peoples and Europeans developed better understandings of each other, new patterns of interchange developed in parts of Native North America. In the next chapter, we will examine still more patterns of cultural interaction, this time in the Spanish borderlands, the areas Spaniards attempted to control outside of Mexico and South America.

Review Questions

1. Is the concept of a "New World" useful?
2. Compare and contrast the Aztec conquest to the Inca and Maya.
3. In what ways did indigenous societies in South America remain in place after the arrival of the Spaniards?
4. Compare the encounters native peoples had with the French and the English in early stages of exploration and expansion.

Recommended Readings

Clendinnen, Inga. *Ambivalent Conquests: Maya and Spaniard in Yucatan, 1517–1570* (New York: Cambridge University Press, 1987). The best short-length study of Mayan-Spanish encounters, and the Franciscan presence in the Yucatan.

Diaz, Monica. *To Be Indio in Colonial Spanish America* (Albuquerque: University of New Mexico Press, 2017). With the focus on Central Mexico and the Andes, essayists track the multiple meanings of "Indian" identity in the early colonial era and argue that native peoples themselves shaped identity and in so doing preserved much of their original cultures.

Kupperman, Karen Ordahl. *Indians and English: Facing Off in Early America* (Ithaca, NY: Cornell University Press, 2000). Provides one of the most important interpretations of Indian-English encounters along the Atlantic seaboard.

Lockhart Nahuas, James. *The Nahuas after the Conquest: A Social and Cultural History of the Indians of Central Mexico, Sixteenth Through Eighteenth Centuries* (Stanford, CA: Stanford University Press, 1994). The best work about the Nahua people after the conquest and how their culture and society remained intact under Spanish rule.

Mumford, Jeremy Ravi. *Vertical Empire: The General Resettlement of Indians in the Colonial Andes* (Durham: Duke University Press, 2012). An intensely detailed examination of the resettlement of more than one million native people of the central Andes to Spanish colonial towns in the mid-1500s. Although an attempt to acculturate native peoples, the process, argues Mumford, strengthened Andean cultural values and character.

Schwartz, Stuart B., ed. *Victors and Vanquished: Spanish and Nahua Views of the Conquest of Mexico* (Boston: Bedford/St. Martin's, 2000). The introduction to the preconquest Aztec world is excellent, and the book comes with documents from the conquest period—a great reader for any interested student.

Trigger, Bruce G. *Natives and Newcomers: Canada's "Heroic Age" Reconsidered* (Kingston: McGill-Queen's University Press, 1986). A book that combines archaeology and history to reconstruct early French-native encounters in the Great Lakes region. A great starting point on the subject.

Native American History Online

General Sites

The Archaeology of the Inca. www.stanford.edu/~johnrick/Inca/WW/index.html An excellent site for understanding the Inca State from the archaeological perspective.

Maya-Archaeology.org. www.maya-archaeology.org Wonderful images and details regarding the preconquest Mayan civilizations.

American Journeys: Eyewitness Accounts of Early American Exploration and Settlement: A Digital Library and Learning Center. www.americanjourneys.org A great resource for primary sources from the period of early exploration.

AncientScripts.com: Aztec. www.ancientscripts.com/aztec.html This site provides views of the ancient glyphs of the Aztecs.

National Center for Public Policy Research: The Colony at Roanoke. www.nationalcenter.org/ColonyofRoanoke.html Historical documents related to the settlement of Roanoke.

Historical Sites

Machu Picchu: Ucayali Department. www.sacred-destinations.com/peru/machu-picchu Located in the Andean mountains, Machu Picchu was not discovered until 1911. Archaeologists believe it was one of the satellite cities of the Inca Empire. This website offers a stunning tour of Machu Picchu and other resources to learn more about the city.

Fort Raleigh National Historic Site, North Carolina. www.nps.gov/fora/ This site provides a collection of online resources related to the Roanoke colony.

Spanish Borderlands, 1527–1758

ON THE FRINGES

LA FLORIDA: A MARITIME BORDERLAND

The Indian Landscape of La Florida

Friars and Chiefdoms

Mission Life

Rebellion and Decline

SOUTHEAST CHIEFDOMS AND HERNANDO DE SOTO

THE SOUTHWEST BORDERLANDS

Women and Caddoan Power

The Texas Mission-Presidio Complex

THE WORLD OF THE PUEBLOS

New Power in the Sword: The Spanish Invasion

New Power in the Church: The Franciscan Pueblo Missions

New Power in Governance: *Encomenderos* and Colonial Rule

Rebellion: The Pueblo Revolt of 1680

NORTHERN MINING FRONTIERS

Serrano Peoples: Native Life in Sonora

Miners, Ranchers, and Moving Frontiers

Missionaries: Serrano Peoples and the Jesuits

Wanderers and Communities: Native Resistance to Spanish Rule

EARLY BORDERLANDS CONNECTIONS IN THE SOUTHWEST

Horses and Networks of Masculine Trade and Warfare

The Rise of the Comanches

On the Fringes

After several expeditions returned to New Spain from New Mexico with glowing reports of potential riches and Indian Catholic converts, King Philip II of Spain licensed Don Juan de Oñate to become the region's conqueror and colonizer. Oñate and a force of 129 men left Zacatecas, in present-day Mexico, in

Timucua women planting corn or beans. Drawing by Theodor de Bry.

January 1598 and reached the Rio Grande on April 20. In each Pueblo town he entered, Oñate conducted a ritual of conquest with blaring trumpets, banners, and Catholic masses. These orchestrated performances, in the minds of the Spaniards, signaled Spanish command of the community and Puebloan submission to Spanish colonial governance. The world of the Pueblo peoples, to Oñate and his fellow travelers, was now formally part of the Spanish Empire.

Pueblo Indians, however, interpreted the arrival of the Spaniards on their own terms. To many Puebloans, Spaniards were some sort of manifestation of **katsinas**, gods within the Puebloan cosmology. Many Pueblos hoped to draw on the spiritual power that *katsinas* bestowed on the conquistadores. For example, after a period of ritual fasting and worship, some Puebloans made offerings to the Spaniards as part of the gifting custom between Pueblo peoples and *katsinas*, but Spaniards made little sense of such ceremonial rites. At first, they interpreted Oñate's arrival on their own cultural terms; they considered the Spaniards as additional members of a world suffused with gods and gifts.

The Spaniards who trekked across the colonial "borderlands" of North America from Florida to California believed their various encounters with native peoples produced religious changes among the Indians and established favorable diplomatic and economic relations in spite of the armed resistance those overland expeditions often met. They assumed these alterations brought the peripheral lands far from Mexico City into the

CHRONOLOGY

1519–1621	Arrival of horses in New Spain and the Spanish Borderlands
1527–1528	Pánfilo de Narváez's failed expedition in Florida
1528–1536	Alvar Núñez Cabeza de Vaca's exploration of the South
1540	Vásquez de Coronado arrives among the Pueblos
1539–1542	Hernando de Soto's trip through the Southeast
1565	St. Augustine established in Florida
1573	Franciscans arrive in Florida
1575	Gaule Province rebellion against Franciscans in Florida
1580s–1600s	Apaches become the most devastating equestrian culture in the Southwest borderlands
1598	Don Juan de Oñate arrives in New Mexico
1608	Franciscans arrive among the Pueblos
1631	Gold discovered in Chihuahua
1650s–1670s	"Golden Age" of Franciscan work in Florida
1650s–1680s	Jesuit expansion into the mission provinces of Sonora
1656	Timucua Rebellion
1680	Pueblo Revolt
1685	La Salle contacts the Caddoans
1706	First mention of Comanches by Spaniards in New Mexico
1720s	Missionary growth in San Antonio, Texas
1758	Indian attack on San Sabá mission in Texas

KEY QUESTIONS

1. Describe the relationships among Franciscans, Indians in La Florida, and St. Augustine.
2. What were Spanish-Indian encounters and relations like in Texas?
3. Describe and analyze Puebloan relationships with the Spanish.
4. How did Indians respond to the missionaries, ranches, and mines in Sonora?
5. What kind of economy developed on the Southwest borderlands?

orbit of the Spanish Empire. But in practice, any sort of imperial control of Spain's North American outlands was more a Spanish bureaucratic vision than a reality of the day-to-day activities that shaped borderlands life. Indians were major players in the Spanish borderlands, reacting to the invaders as chance and circumstance allowed, and more often than not they continued to dominate their own homelands.

In this chapter, we will focus on a few of the zones of contact within the Spanish borderlands. In the east, the Spanish province of La Florida included present-day Florida and southern Georgia and the Indian inhabitants of those areas. In the west, the borderlands extended from Louisiana into Texas, north into New Mexico and Arizona, and west into the mining provinces of Sonora, Chihuahua, and Nueva Vizcaya in what is today Mexico. Interactions among the Spanish and native groups in these areas were so varied and complex, intense and lasting, that other Euro-American expansionists such as the British and the Americans had to deal with the Spanish legacy in their own encounters with native peoples. Indian worlds shifted along with Spanish missionaries, explorers, miners, landowners, and traders throughout these borderlands regions.

La Florida: A Maritime Borderland

Spain's venture into what is now the southeastern coastal region of the United States (Florida, northward to North Carolina), was initially spurred, in part, by France's threat to Spanish expansion in the New World. In spring 1562, a French expedition commanded by Jean Ribaut landed in northern Florida near present-day Jacksonville. Ribaut immediately laid French claim to this stretch and all lands farther north, after which his ships and 150 soldiers sailed up the coast and entered a magnificent harbor named Port Royal. He was stunned by the area's beauty and obvious bounty, noting in his journal that the harbor and the network of rivers feeding from it were filled with "so many sorts of fish that you may take them without a net or a hook, as many as you want. . . . It is one of the goodliest, best and most fruitful countries ever seen, where nothing is lacking." The French hastily constructed a small island outpost (now Parris Island, South Carolina) and dug in. It was expected that these soldiers and naval vessels could scout the region, perhaps locate sources of wealth to enrich France, and concurrently interfere with Spanish shipping along the coast. The settlement, however, fell on hard times. Food supplies dwindled rapidly. Farming the sandy island proved extremely difficult and generated few crops. Edisto Indians living on the mainland nearby offered some food, but they could not provide enough for both themselves and the newcomers. Compounding this, bickering among the settlers and a general breakdown in command erupted. The French settlers were compelled to abandon the colony. France attempted a second colony in 1564, sending 300 soldiers to Ribaut's first landing spot, and there they erected Fort Caroline on the St. John River. It seemed apparent to Spain that France intended to establish her presence in North America, particularly in the territories Spain now eyed for expansion. The clear threat to Spain's mission in America compelled a response.

3.1 Map of the town, fort, and entrance to the harbor of St. Augustine and vicinity, Florida, 1595.

Source: Courtesy of Library of Congress Prints and Photographs Division, Lowery Collection No. 76

La Florida became a Spanish province only when King Philip II of Spain responded to France's colonial efforts. On March 5, 1565, the crown contracted Pedro Menéndez de Avilés to establish a maritime outpost on the Atlantic side of the peninsula and provided him the initial funds to construct a presidio. A presidio served as a garrison to protect soldiers and civilians, and was an arm of Spanish military power and authority. In June Avilés set sail for La Florida with 1,500 soldiers, craftsmen, and colonists, but his expedition had a rocky start; only a few vessels successfully completed the perilous trek from Spain to Cuba. From there his reduced expedition finally arrived along Florida's eastern seaboard, and he did his best to avoid conflict at this time with forces based at the French outpost Fort Caroline. Avilés sought a suitable location to begin his colony, and, once finding a strategic location conducive to settlement, he claimed all of La Florida in the name of the crown and ordered the construction of the presidio of St. Augustine. Within the year, Avilés forced the French out of La Florida and attacked the French who were attempting to resettle Port Royal to the north, establishing there his own outpost, Fort San Felipe. From here, Spanish overland expeditions journeyed deep inland, reaching the Appalachian Mountains on one expedition. These missions commonly had multiple goals—locate resources that might be vital to the Spanish, determine the lay of the land, and establish amicable relations with native peoples. Hundreds of Spaniards moved into San Felipe including families, physicians, priests, and craftsmen. But the land was prone to flooding, severely limiting food production. The cattle and supply ships promised to the settlement never arrived. Hunger and malnutrition settled over the community. In desperation, settlers raided nearby Indian villages for food. The Edisto Indians retaliated, forging an alliance with other native groups and repeatedly striking at the Spanish. The outlying Spanish posts also faced a daunting Indian resistance. By 1576 the coastal Indian tribes had destroyed most Spanish settlements north of St. Augustine. Spain launched another endeavor to establish her presence in that region in 1578, but it too failed miserably as warfare erupted again, this time partly in response to Spain's effort to convert natives to Catholicism and the enslavement of Chicora Indians just north of Port Royal. In 1587 Spain discarded all plans to establish her presence and control in the regions north of La Florida. The Spanish nonetheless continued to explore Florida's inland parts, extensive waterways, and forested areas. The crown concluded that St. Augustine would become Spain's northern citadel in protecting her American empire and toward that end ultimately put all of its money for defenses in the Spanish Atlantic into the St. Augustine presidio, more than the crown gave Havana, Cuba, which was another significant maritime post.

Looking for laborers, food, and converts to Catholicism, the Spanish sought to pacify Florida's large Indian populations. Their solution, in part, was to integrate the Timucua, Guales, and Apalachees into the Spanish economic and political system. A key component of Spanish efforts in this regard was the mission system. In 1573, the crown sent 18 Franciscan friars to La Florida to serve as missionaries. They began a process that led to the creation of an interlocking chain of missions in Florida, run by friars living among the Indians. This system did not, however, evolve into absolute Spanish control over the native peoples. Negotiation and adaptation occurred on both sides of La Florida's cultural barrier.

The Indian Landscape of La Florida

Three large native groups shaped La Florida's borderlands. The Timucuan chiefdoms occupied portions of central and north Florida. Guale Indians lived along coastal Georgia. Finally, the Apalachee native peoples had villages in the northwest panhandle of Florida and portions of southwest Georgia.

Timucuan chiefdoms of the seventeenth century were composed of a number of chiefs and villages united under the leadership of one superior chief. Chiefs were known as **holatas**, but the Spanish applied the generic title of *cacique*. *Holatas* inherited their right to rule through their mothers' line and if a man was unavailable to lead, women became chiefs, or *caciques*. Villagers were sedentary agriculturalists, producing corn, beans, and squash. Archaeological evidence and early Spanish documents reveal that Timucuans lived in villages ringed with defensive stakes and containing as many as 400 residents. At the center of each village was the chiefs' council house. Villagers frequented the council house to offer gifts and perform rituals and ceremonies to show their spiritual loyalty to specific *holatas*, as well as other village elders. Outside the main village were smaller hamlets and fields of crops. Timucua chiefs organized and directed agricultural work in the fields. A head chief's authority depended on his or her ability to persuade others to follow. This was accomplished, in part, by giving gifts of food and other items to dependent villages and chiefs. Although chiefdoms tried to maintain balance and harmony in council houses, they were often at odds with each other and sometimes even at war.

3.2 Native men carrying The Lady of Cofitachequi of the Coosa chiefdom in Georgia on an ornamental litter; trumpeters lead the procession, which is followed by young women carrying baskets of fruit and by a contingent of bodyguards. Courtesy of Library of Congress Prints and Photographs Division, LC-USZ62–79801.

The arrival of the Spanish in Timucuan territory added a new and ambitious player to the already tense competition for resources and prestige.

Guale villages dotted the Georgia coastline south of the Ogeechee River when the Spanish and French first reached North America, while the Apalachee Indians lived in the westernmost portion of the Florida panhandle. Guales most likely spoke a Muskogean dialect heard among the later Creeks and, like the Timucuans, were agriculturalists, cultivating the fertile grounds. Villages were located near salt marshes that lined the coast, allowing the Guales to supplement their diet with fish and shellfish. Their chiefdoms were much like those of the Timucuans, with clusters of villages acknowledging the authority of a centrally located superior chief. Each village chief was a known as *mico*. *Micos* maintained power and authority by exercising control over the spiritual world and by participating in the continual redistribution of goods. Under the chiefs were principal men, known to the Spanish as *principales*. Individual villages had populations of 200–300 people. The establishment of the Spanish settlement of Santa Elena on Parris Island in 1567 thoroughly disrupted Guale life, as European diseases ravaged the Guales. In the face of this calamity, Guale chiefs eventually consolidated power, forming three chiefdom alliances. Far outnumbering the Guale Indians, the Apalachees were descended from the Mississippi mound-building cultures and had a more complex social, cultural, and political life (see Chapter 1).

Apalachees occupied extensive lands, with a paramount chief, subchiefs, and village chiefs controlling the labor output of village populations.

Friars and Chiefdoms

Father Diego Moreno was the leader of the first group of friars who arrived in Florida in 1573. Moreno and three others initially tried to penetrate the northern Guale province to convert the chief and his wife and ensure that local Indians posed no threat to the Spanish garrison at Santa Elena. Franciscans understood from experience that the conversion of chiefs and the giving of Christian names and gifts could play important roles in the conversion of entire native populations. In this context, the first Franciscan success story in La Florida seems to have been the baptism of the head Guale *mico* and his wife, with Spanish officials standing in as god-parents. In virtually every instance of conversion, the Guale believed the process to be nothing more than a ritual of friendship and ultimately trade.

This perceived success was not long lasting. Only two years later, in 1575, the Guales rose up against the Spanish. Three factors contributed to the rebellion. First, the Franciscans, who sometimes acted as mediators between native peoples and Spanish officials, left the province in 1574 allowing distrust and petty squabbles to surface among the Indians and sabotage their fragile unity. Second, the Spanish soldiers' demands for food from local villages undermined Indian-Spanish relations, similar to developments farther north in South Carolina. Third, the Spanish executed a rising Guale *mico* in retaliation for the killing of a Christian Guale chief. Individually, each issue carried the potential for resistance to the Spanish; collectively, the issues guaranteed armed rebellion. Indians near Santa Elena attacked in retribution, killing over 30 Spanish military men. The governor feared for the colony and worried that Indians might march south to destroy the garrison of St. Augustine. Spaniards counterattacked in 1579 by destroying the corn and other stored foods in central villages in an effort to starve the Indians, a tactic they would deploy elsewhere among La Florida chiefdoms. St. Augustine's military gleaned some valuable lessons from the uprising. They learned that they needed a permanent Franciscan presence in the Guale province. Spanish governing officials also recognized that they would have to work harder to secure and maintain the friendship of Indian leaders if they wanted to establish stability in the region.

It was in this context that a series of negotiations occurred among chiefs, friars, and the Spanish officials at St. Augustine. Chiefs traveled to St. Augustine, where friars working in the local missions on the outskirts of the maritime garrison came to baptize chiefs and give them Spanish names, again the ritual of friendship and acceptance as the Guales perceived such ceremonies. The Spanish also gave them axes and other tools in addition to European manufactured clothing. With this perception of respect, equality and cooperation, chiefs gained a heightened prestige among and authority over their own people. The Spanish viewed the results of these meetings as the Indians' acceptance of Spanish rule across the region. Once more, contrary interpretations would eventually lead to devastating results.

Mission Life

Franciscan friars continued their efforts to spread Christianity in La Florida in the 1580s and 1590s. Two types of friars journeyed into each Guale and Timucuan province, the **doctrinas** and **visitas**. *Doctrinas* were friars who established central churches at the head village of a chief. Chiefdoms had their own places of ceremony and worship such as council houses. Churches and other outlying buildings for worship either replaced the many traditional Indian structures or existed alongside them. Resident friars used Indian labor to construct churches, as well as to make some of the items necessary for Catholic religious services.

Visitas were those friars who ventured to satellite villages under the charge of the head chief. They stayed temporarily, providing prayer services and hoping to bring outlying Indian populations into the faith. One of the keys to the establishment of the mission system in La Florida was the ***camino real***. Reconstructed by archaeologists, the *camino real* was a road from east to west through the heartlands of Timucua territory on which numerous missions serviced the Timucua chiefdoms and satellite villages. The *camino real* also serviced St. Augustine with goods and laborers. This road complemented the many water-transport options available in the region.

With the chiefs' cooperation—generally the product of Spanish trade, gifting and respect—missions dramatically changed Indian life in La Florida. Around 1650, Franciscans were servicing roughly 15,000 Indians, nearly 85 percent of them in the Apalachee province. Historians call this period the "Golden Age" of La Florida's mission system (see Map 3.1).

Friars expected Indians to become good and regimented Catholics, and to participate in all of the rites of the church. Some Indians chose to live like Christians, adopting strict social and cultural patterns. Many joined Christian organizations and participated in the church hierarchy. But, as in the case of initial conversion, the Indians' acceptance of Catholicism was more often than not a shallow one—a display of cooperation with the

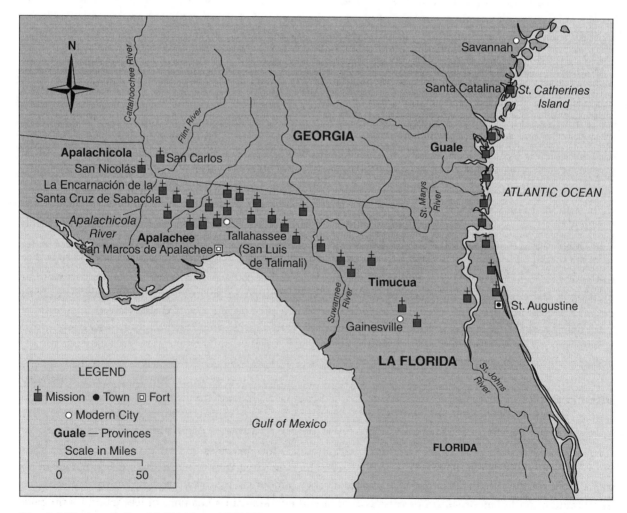

Map 3.1 Missions in Spanish Florida, c. 1674–1675

Spanish for the maintenance of peace and, perhaps, access to trade goods, as well as a means to assure some degree of cultural survival at the very moment the world they understood was experiencing drastic change. Indeed, while friars expected Indians to honor the basic Christian value of monogamous relations, many Indians continued with more traditional arrangements.

Under the orders of chiefs, Indians traveled along the *camino real* and from the Apalachee and Guale provinces to St. Augustine, and, once there, they served in labor drafts. This system was known among the Spanish as the ***repartimiento***. The *repartimiento* was really a form of tribute labor. Each mission province provided a certain number of able-bodied men to the labor draft. Chiefs never served in the labor draft; they only controlled the number of men they sent from their villages. Indian laborers performed such backbreaking tasks as carrying packs of cornmeal along the *camino real* to St. Augustine, cleaning roads, rebuilding bridges and church structures, and harvesting corn and other food. Laborers also corralled stray cattle, penned pigs, constructed chicken coops, and served in La Florida's militia. In some areas along the Panhandle, Spaniards established large ranches, known as *haciendas*, where Apalachee labor supported livestock and cattle enterprises. This labor system directly benefitted the Spanish, securing for them the resources and wealth Spain had long desired from the territory. Moreover, it pacified the native population, this allowing for regional security, stability and growth. Few Indian laborers, however, reaped tangible benefits; their service secured for the chiefs numerous goods of European origin. Tribal leaders increasingly viewed themselves as fitting into the emerging Spanish power system across La Florida and increased further their own influence, if not authority, among native peoples.

But the mission system ultimately devastated the Indian populations of Guale, Timucua, and Apalachee, forcing the restructuring of these three native societies. Harsh labor resulted in numerous deaths. Diseases such as typhoid and smallpox easily spread in a hot and damp climate and among overworked Indians, reducing native populations to less than three-quarters of pre-mission numbers. The old and the young were particularly hard hit. Native deaths left generations without elders to pass down the peoples' oral traditions, and without the young there was less hope of a future for La Florida Indians. Villages consolidated in the wake of the devastation. And, as the years passed, chiefs and the general native population recognized clearly the reality of their position in the Spanish order of La Florida—subjugation and dependency.

Rebellion and Decline

Timucua chiefdoms grew frustrated with the Spanish presence, and by the middle 1600s that frustration reached a breaking point. Rumors filtered among the Spanish and the Timucua that the English planned to attack St. Augustine. The threat of an attack came at a time when St. Augustine was already in a precarious position. Its food supplies were low, its buildings were in disrepair, and it had an insufficient number of soldiers. The governor of the province, Diego de Rebolledo, ordered his men to make repairs to those areas of St. Augustine in most need and relied on the labor draft system of *repartimiento* to provide additional workers. Rebolledo then called on the Guale, Apalachee, and Timucua chiefdoms to muster 500 men each to journey to St. Augustine to help in its security and defense. He further demanded that warriors and chiefs who made the long trek to St. Augustine bring their own supplies of corn and other foodstuffs to support them on their journey and during their stay in St. Augustine.

In making such orders, Rebolledo undermined some time-honored rules of Timucua-Spanish relations. In the past, chiefs had been exempted from the *repartimiento*. Moreover, they never carried packs of goods to St. Augustine; that was the job of laborers extracted from their villages. Having witnessed the demographic devastation brought on by intensive labor, chiefs proved unwilling to risk their positions of leadership for the sake of protecting St. Augustine.

Lúcas Menéndez, a baptized Timucua chief, came to despise Rebolledo and his policies. Menéndez, who led one of the strongest of the Timucua chiefdoms, had little trouble convincing other chiefs to take up arms against the Spanish. He ordered the killing of Spaniards within Timucua territory although he excluded Friars from the slaughter, as most Timucua chiefs were now Catholic. Violence spread from the *camino real* territory north into the large farms among the Apalachees. Trying to starve the Spaniards, Timucuans refused to participate in the spring round of crop planting. They also retreated from mission villages, and the chiefs refused to contribute further to Spanish labor drafts. The Timucuans' goal was to cut off vital food and labor supplies to the garrison in St. Augustine at the time of its greatest of need.

The Timucuans expected a Spanish response and prepared themselves by building a palisaded village to await Rebolledo's next move. In September 1656, the governor organized his counterattack. He assembled an army of 60 Spanish soldiers and 600 Apalachees and ordered them to strike deep inside Timucua territory. On their journey from St. Augustine, the joint force cleverly avoided the *camino real*, the locus of Timucua mission operations. By the end of November, the Spanish and Apalachees had entered the mission province, hanging numerous Timucua rebels as ghastly examples of what happened to rebellious Indians.

The Spanish military broke Indian resistance and restored the peace, but it could not stop the further decline of Timucua and the other mission provinces. Timucua chiefs either died or were put into prison; mission villages were burned to the ground while friars fled. Following Rebolledo's strikes, the Franciscans whose lives had

3.3 A palisaded Timucuan town, with its palm-thatched houses and sentry posts at its narrow entrance.

Source: Courtesy of Library of Congress Prints and Photographs Division, LC-USZ62-367

been spared by the Timucuans tried to rebuild Catholic life within the province. Along the *camino real*, mission villages consolidated and a few new ones were constructed, each now under a new structural arrangement governed more closely by the Spanish. The road and its missions began to resemble a chain of interlocking Catholic villages. By the late seventeenth century, depopulation and migration had pushed the mission province of Timucua to the margins of the Spanish Empire.

The Spanish at St. Augustine shifted their focus from the severely depopulated Timucua toward the Apalachee Indians who numbered anywhere from 8,000 to 10,000. Apalachees now became the main source of labor. But the distance from St. Augustine to the Apalachee villages, coupled with the influx of roaming groups of native peoples from former chiefdoms (who later became Creeks), undermined most attempts to create a successful mission system among them. At the same time, the founding of Charles Town by the British in 1670, the increase in English and French piracy, and the southward movements of the Yamasee Indians altogether collapsed the Guale coastal mission province in the late seventeenth century. Carolinians began to penetrate the southern interior, trading and allying with Westos, Yamasees, and other southeastern groups who were hostile to the Guales and Apalachees. Meanwhile, the French pushed into the Gulf region occupied by the Choctaws and Chickasaws, who were important trading partners for the Apalachees. By the end of the century, the interior mission borderlands of La Florida were slowly disintegrating. Disease, warfare, changing tribal structures, altering native alliances, human migration, and continued European expansion altogether corrupted traditional native patterns of life and now threatened a wholesale destruction of native cultures and life across La Florida.

Southeast Chiefdoms and Hernando de Soto

A little over a decade after Ponce de León's failure to take Florida, an expedition led by Hernando de Soto plundered its way across the Gulf Coast region. The Gulf Coast, contrary to what the Spaniards might have heard or believed, was not a vast, empty terrain open for the taking. De Soto was a veteran of Spanish imperial ventures in Peru. He was sure he would succeed where León had failed. De Soto secured crown approval to launch his expedition in April 1537, but he had to borrow money to help cover the many expenses involved. He set sail with nine ships, many horses, pigs, dogs, and mules, and over 600 soldiers in his party. In addition, a few women and two priests traveled with de Soto and his small army. After landing in Tampa Bay, de Soto stumbled upon Juan Ortiz, a stranded survivor of the failed Pánfilo de Narváez exploratory party that had tried to take Florida in 1527–1528. Ortiz had learned variants of the Muskogean dialects spoken by many of the Southeast's interior chiefdoms and de Soto believed his linguistic skills would help the Spanish navigate the intricate world of the Southeast Indians.

De Soto pillaged his way across several thousand miles of terrain (see Map 3.2). The chiefdoms of the Southeast were descendants of the Mississippian complex—densely settled agricultural villages with large political centers, places of worship, chiefs and priests with immense political and spiritual power and authority, and a hierarchical social structure. The largest of these chiefdoms along de Soto's route were Apalachee, Cofitachequi, Coosa, and Tascaloosa. By the mid-sixteenth century, the Mississippian complex was in sharp decline. Thus, de Soto's expedition met these large, complex societies at a moment of great vulnerability.

De Soto, with his bilingual aid, Ortiz, trekked north from Tampa. Many of the chiefdoms had earlier challenged the Narváez expedition and prepared themselves for future Spanish aggression. In the Florida panhandle, de Soto met Apalachees, Tocobagans, and various Timucuan villages. A Timucua chief named Acuera resolved not to help the Spanish at all, and the Apalachees contested de Soto's entrance into their territories. Although de Soto's aggressive assaults against the Apalachees secured for his entourage a winter stay at the main village of Anhaica, Apalachees relentlessly skirmished with the Spaniards, burning the village to the ground twice. By spring, de Soto abandoned the area and began his move farther north.

In South Carolina, de Soto's expedition encountered Cofitachequi, the largest chiefdom the Spanish had seen north of Mesoamerica. Thousands of people lived there. A large plaza and temple stood at the center of Cofitachequi, and the chiefdom extended its reach into present-day western North Carolina. In greeting de Soto's party, the Indians carried a young woman dressed in fine linen. The Spanish came to reference her as the "Lady of Cofitachequi." She was a local Cofitachequi leader, who was to govern relations with the Spanish according to Cofitachequi traditions of reciprocity, giving the Spaniards clothing and putting a string of pearls around de Soto's neck. Her gestures were meant to establish fictive kinship relations of diplomacy and trade with the Spanish, particularly important because her territory had recently been hit by a devastating epidemic, no doubt triggered by earlier Spanish forays into the Deep South. The response of de Soto's expedition was, however, anything but diplomatic. They interpreted her gestures as signs of submission and then plundered temples for riches, stole pearls, and eventually took hostage the "Lady of Cofitachequi."

Motivated to find a city of wealth like Tenochtitlán, de Soto's army moved westward into present-day Tennessee, becoming the first Europeans to traverse the Appalachian Mountains. No wealth was found, however, among the Muskogean-speaking peoples of the Tennessee territory. Frustrated, de Soto turned southward into present-day Alabama, where he entered the region of the Coosa chiefdom. Coosa had several central villages with outlying open land, probably designed for hunting and agriculture. De Soto aggressively led his men through the Indians' territory. He slaughtered or disfigured all Coosa Indians who resisted enslavement and he took hostage the paramount chief. With a train of Indian slaves and captured paramount chiefs, de Soto reached the Choctaw-speaking chiefdom of Tascaloosa, whose inhabitants had already received word of de Soto's path of destruction. By now, the pattern of Spanish behavior was clear to Indians—sweep into a region, feign friendship long enough to determine what wealth might exist nearby, take prisoners and slaves, destroy those Indians who resist, and then move onward. Under the guidance of chief Tascaloosa, the chiefdom's warriors attacked de Soto at the village of Mabila, killing many in de Soto's party and capturing horses and supplies. Armed resistance had replaced Indian friendship and accommodation.

Despite this setback, de Soto was unwavering in his quest to find wealth in the Gulf Coast region. He moved on, crossing the rugged terrain between the Alabama and Tombigee rivers. His party wintered in northeastern

TIMELINE 3.1 SPANIARDS IN LA FLORIDA AND THE SOUTHEAST, 1537–1650S

Date	Event
1537–1542	De Soto's expedition in the Southeast
1565	Pedro Menéndez de Aviles establishes St. Augustine
1567	Spanish settle Santa Elena Island among the Guale Indians
1575	Guale Rebellion
1580s–1590s	Friars create La Florida's mission provinces
1650s–1660s	"Golden Age" of mission work in La Florida
1656	Timucua Rebellion

Mississippi from late autumn 1540 to late February 1541. That spring, ancestors of the Chickasaws launched a surprise strike against de Soto's party, further weakening the expedition. A stubborn man, de Soto pushed on to become the first European to see the Mississippi River. Enticed by the sight of large villages and earthworks on the river's banks, de Soto continued his trek, motivated by the assurances of local Indians that wealth lay far beyond the Mississippi, which was probably a ruse to hurry his exit from their territory. He marched onward to present-day Arkansas, then down the Arkansas River into Caddoan territory. With men, morale, and supplies running low, de Soto put his limited understanding of the chiefdoms' cosmological beliefs to use, sending word ahead to the Natchez that he was the "son of the sun." The Natchez worshipped the sun atop great mounds. Once in Natchez territory, the untrusting Natchez leaders tested de Soto's claims, asking him to "dry up the great river." Of course, de Soto possessed no such sacred powers, and what little import the Natchez initially gave him faded abruptly. Stricken with sickness and perhaps broken in spirit, de Soto died in May 1542. The remainder of his party eventually made it back to Mexico. De Soto's failed mission in the American Southeast demonstrated the limits of Spanish control in the borderlands and the increased understanding of and resistance to the Spanish by native peoples.

The Southwest Borderlands

An expansive range of land that included stretches of the Gulf Coast, the Texas borderlands was home to both small villages and larger, more organized societies. In the 1600s, many of the people who occupied portions of central, southern, and northern Texas had already experienced massive upheaval. Once living in centralized village societies, the early excursions of the Spaniards into Nueva Vizcaya and Coahuila brought disease and a trafficking in Indian slaves to supply laborers to Spain's northern mines and ranches. The Jumanos were one large linguistic group hit hard by disease and the slave trade. Semi-sedentary groups emerged out the upheavals of the seventeenth century, relying on hunting and gathering as they searched to build new kinship and community relationships. These people, referred to as "Cohuiltecans," spoke multiple dialects. When these groups came together within missions near presidios, many indeed spoke a broken version of Cohuilteco, but this probably served to help Indians ally with each other to deal with the Spanish. Along the Gulf Coast there also existed semi-sedentary groups of which the Karankawas were the largest. They migrated with the seasons. In the spring, they moved to the upland swamps and prairies where they hunted game such as buffalo and deer and gathered fruits, nuts, and berries. In the colder months, coastal peoples gathered along the gulf, harvesting the plentiful fish and shellfish from the shores. Both inland and coastal peoples had encampments of multilingual groups, probably formed to fend off Spanish traders, raiders, military expeditions, and missionaries. Late in the seventeenth century, the Spanish pushed into Texas in search of trade partners, wealth, alliances, and potential converts. The Spanish headed in the direction of the "Land of the Tejas," where more complex and organized groups of native peoples lived.

The "Land of the Tejas," the Spanish hoped, would bring them into contact with well-organized peoples who could be converted to Catholicism and become economic allies. Instead, the Spanish encountered the Caddoan chiefdoms. The Spanish would discover that the Caddos had no wish to adapt their culture to serve the needs and desires of the newcomers.

Women and Caddoan Power

First contact between the Caddos and Europeans occurred in 1685, when the French explorer Robert de La Salle went in search of the mouth of the Mississippi River and instead ended up in Texas. He pushed inland from the Karankawas, and there he encountered an enormous group of people, the Caddos, who lived in three confederacies—Hasinai, Kadohadacho, and Natchitoches. To the Caddos, Europeans were just another people to be reckoned with. Like La Salle, Spaniards soon learned this lesson as well. The discovery of La Salle's abandoned colony clearly revealed to Spanish expeditions that the courting of Caddoan friendship might prove difficult. In the late seventeenth century, then, Spaniards began negotiations in the "Land of the Tejas." Despite La Salle's failure, French competition remained present, as the Caddos held power in the region and proved willing to negotiate with both Spanish and French traders and explorers. As the historian Juliana Barr has shown, the "Land of the Tejas" was a region where the balance of power was in Indian hands; there, in a region of large confederacies, diplomacy followed Caddoan custom.

Caddoans had a specific set of rules when it came to social conduct in diplomatic relationships. Caddos lived in scattered communities with many matrilineal agricultural settlements. Familial matrilineal households were the foundation of Caddoan society. Women who headed these families controlled the production of the harvests in mustering workers for the fields and distributing the produce. Local villages united to form the three Caddo confederacies. Among Caddoans, political and religious leaders traced their descent through their fathers' lines, but such descent functioned only as an extension of the Caddoan matrilineal framework. In other words, men would appoint nephews, uncles, or brothers of women within their matrilineal family networks, not sons, to leadership positions. The men of civic and sacred power and authority who directed each small community were known as *caddís*. The *caddís*, in turn, consulted principal men known as *canahas*. At the highest level of each confederacy was a *xinesí*, or a high priest. All of these elite men looked to the matrilineal heads of their individual households for guidance, an arrangement reflected and reinforced by Caddoan mythology (see Table 3.1).

Table 3.1 Caddoan Social Organization. This diagram shows that the male sphere of diplomacy could not function without support from matrilineal households.

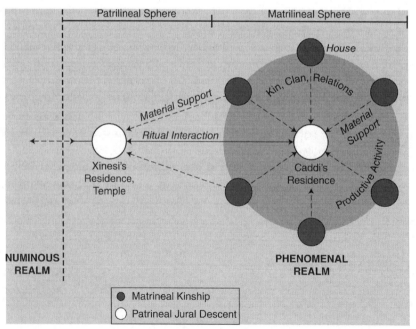

If Europeans wanted good relations with Caddoans they had no choice but to cast aside their misconceptions of Caddoan culture and society and abide by native customs. Because Caddo men took the lead in public rituals and ceremonies, Europeans assumed, at first, that men held the positions of greatest power and authority in Caddoan society. This made sense to the Europeans because it reflected the realities of their own society. When Caddoans spotted Europeans approaching a village, they would meet the strangers outside their villages, being sure to include women and children in their party as a sign of their peaceful intentions. The fact that European parties were almost exclusively male immediately aroused Caddoan suspicions because the absence of women and children, from their cultural perspective, signaled hostile intentions.

As they learned more about Caddoans, the French and Spanish did what they could to adapt to Caddoan expectations. The Spanish carried icons of the Virgin Mary and spoke of María de Jesús de Agreda, a woman of great spiritual power who according to legend had worked as a missionary in Texas nearly 100 years before the Franciscans. The presentation of female symbols and references to the "Lady in Blue," as María de Jesús de Agreda was known, had some appeal to the *Caddís*, *canahas*, and *xinesís* but the absence of Spanish women, particularly among the mendicant Franciscans who had taken vows of chastity, continued to confuse the Caddoans. Once it was obvious that the Spanish friars intended to live near or among the Caddos, the absence of women became even more disturbing. Spanish missionaries found it difficult to penetrate into village life in search of converts and receive the appropriate family titles within the Caddoan matrilineal tradition.

French traders, the earliest around Caddoan territory, probably had a little more success than Spanish missionaries. As single men, French traders could integrate themselves into Caddoan society by marrying Caddoan women. Once they were part of a Caddoan household, they were well placed to gain a deeper understanding of Caddoan social and cultural norms. Such knowledge played a crucial role in the building of fruitful diplomatic and trade relations with the Caddoans. Thus, the Spanish floundered while the French flourished.

The Texas Mission-Presidio Complex

The Spanish built missions and presidios south of the Caddoans, hoping to convert local Indians in that region and establish a firm military presence to protect their access to resources and wealth. Disease and slave raids greatly reduced the native populations, who responded by reorganizing themselves into multilingual confederacies as the Caddoans had built. These confederacies, however, were loose and less complex than the Caddoan confederacies, which made them more vulnerable to the Spanish and to other Indians in the region. Texas Indians sought diplomatic relationships with the Spanish and found the missions and the military presidios useful tools for community survival and gravitated toward those sites in the 1720s. Indians helped the Spanish erect the first missions and presidios out of wood; it was only later that the missions became formal stone structures. Indians often subsisted outside of mission compounds, only to retreat to missions and presidios in search of protection from raiding parties of Apaches. Franciscans ran the most successful missions along the San Antonio River, where missionaries and Indians constructed irrigation ditches to grow crops and raised sheep and cattle to feed local populations. Commanders at the presidios directed local affairs. Within the mission compounds, friars depended on native leaders loyal to the Catholics to secure Indian labor. Within churches, Indian-trained carpenters and artisans fused Spanish and Indian cultures. Murals reflected Christian motifs and Native American interpretations of the natural world. At the same time, Indians entered mission compounds as families and were able to hold networks of family and community together both inside and outside of the missions. Franciscans found it hard to impose Catholic ways of life on the Indians. For example, native peoples maintained traditional subsistence activities within the missions and upheld old marriage patterns. What developed was a composite Spanish-Indian society of mutual benefit.

No other areas replicated the success of the San Antonio missions. Irrigation along the lower Guadalupe, Nueces, and San Sabá rivers was less successful than along the San Antonio River, making it difficult for the Franciscans to sustain viable missions along these waterways. At the same time, the spread of disease among native populations left fewer and fewer potential Indian converts. In the 1750s, the friars constructed the San Sabá mission, along the San Sabá River, in an attempt to convert the Apache Indians, but the Apaches had established themselves as one of the fiercest horseback cultures in the Southwest. Their nomadic lifestyle was totally unsuited to sedentary mission life, and the project was an abject failure. To make matters worse, smallpox ravaged the Apache bands. War also plagued the mission effort. Apache horseback raiders had many enemies to the north who were also mounted on horses and looking for bison hunting grounds and grazing lands for their horses, as well as trade networks. The Spanish called all these enemies Norteños, although they actually included Wichitas, Tonkawas, Comanches, and smaller groups. The presidio to the north of the mission in 1758 received word that the Norteños intended to descend on the diminishing Apache population as well as the San Sabá mission. The attack on the mission could not be prevented, and it killed ten Spanish missionaries and soldiers. The San Sabá mission was not alone in its troubles. Apaches, Comanches, and other Indians raided missions for cattle, horses, and sheep. Violence stalled Spanish attempts to bring missions to the territory. By the 1760s, even the Franciscans were starting to admit that Texas was not a very fertile ground for the harvest of new Christians and that the region offered little of material worth.

The World of the Pueblos

North from Texas, in the vast lands stretching between present-day Arizona and New Mexico, lived the Puebloan peoples, adobe-dwelling descendants of the Anasazi tradition. One way to understand the Pueblo world before the arrival of the Spanish, as historian Ramón Gutiérrez has shown, is through an exploration of their oral tradition. A Pueblo origin myth that the Acoma have passed down gives us a sense Pueblo life. Before examining this story in detail, it should be noted that the Pueblo world was made up of many peoples, each with their own origin story. In addition to having different origin stories the Zuni, Hopi, Acoma, and other Pueblo dwellers spoke different languages. No centralized government oversaw the many Pueblo towns scattered across New Mexico, although Spaniards viewed all the Pueblo peoples as belonging to one society. But even with linguistic and cultural differences, Pueblo peoples shared much in common. They lived in compact settlements, some of which extended upward like apartment buildings. All Pueblos grew maize, beans, and squash. Finally, they all used stories as a part of their rich religious life. These stories conveyed both the appropriate roles and relationships between individuals within Pueblo society and the proper relationship between the natural and spiritual world.

According to the Acoma origin myth, two sisters came from the depths of the earth, arriving on a pine tree. They brought with them baskets of corn seeds. The two sisters pledged their allegiance to the sun with sacred cornmeal and pollen, begging for the earth's fertility and their security. When the sisters first touched the soil of the earth, it was not ready for planting. After praying to the sun for more guidance, Thought Woman, the sisters' original creator, appeared and gave them their names: Iatiku was Mother of the Corn clan and Nautsiti was Mother of the Sun clan. Thought Woman informed the sisters that they were to make the earth fertile and productive. Fire came the next night, and from it the sisters cooked their corn. Thought Woman taught the girls how to feed the animals with grasses and plants so the beasts could thrive and produce offspring. In one of the four sacred directions moved elks, lions, wolves, bears, and other large animals. To one of the skyworlds traveled birds including the turkey, but the turkey fell back to the human realm because of his faulty wings.

Corn Mother used her spiritual power to bring forth the seasons, represented by different spirit guides. She also made houses. Iatiku created the *katsinas*, the gods that Pueblo people would worship in their circular

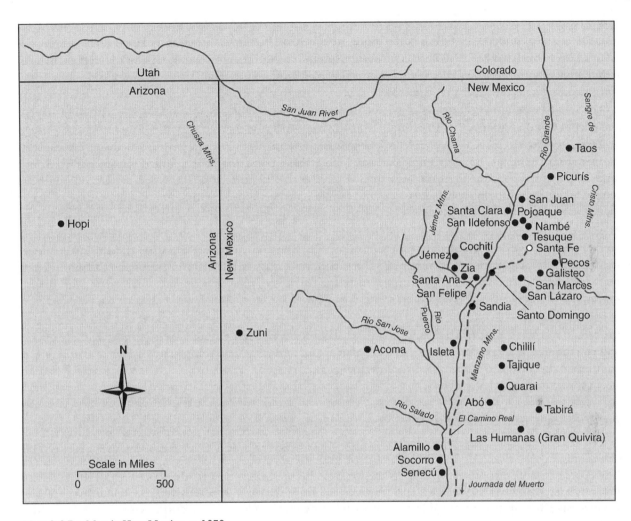

Map 3.2 Pueblos in New Mexico, c. 1650

spiritual pits known as kivas. A series of sacred rituals between Corn Mother and the *katsinas* forever bound her people to reciprocal relations with the spirit guides of the human world. She taught an old man, who became a spiritual specialist among the Pueblos, how to build kivas and maintain proper relations with the spirits through gift giving. Circular pits in the ground marking the four points of the universe, kivas also resembled the spiritual underground out of which human life and the corn and plants emerged.

Iatiku then designated a man as an outside chief of the hunters, and taught him the use of spiritually charged rocks and sticks to tame the animals. Corn Mother also created militant and civil outside chiefs. In Pueblo society, outside chiefs controlled decisions regarding warfare and diplomacy, and they worked to balance relations between young Pueblo warriors and hunters and the many human and non-human spirits outside the immediate realm of the adobe Pueblo villages. Corn Mother gave the war chief two sons, direct descendants of the utmost father, the sun. An evil snake soon returned, bringing illness to the Pueblo people, so Corn Mother created a shaman, or healer. Corn Mother taught the medicine man how to harness the sacred power of the sun to burn sticks for use only at night on a special altar. He learned how to make medicine bundles and use corn to symbolize the womb and the fertile underground world that had brought forth plants.

When there were young folk among the Pueblos who disrespected the elder Corn Mother, havoc returned again to the people as the clouds dried up along with fields. The spiritual specialists fasted and worshipped until rain returned and brought life again from the ground. So the Pueblo people would ultimately be happy, although they faced cyclical periods of hardship and crisis. Only in the circular kivas could outside and inside spiritual healers restore order to the Pueblo world.

The Acoma origin myth provides some key insights into Pueblo life. Inside and outside activities shaped the Pueblo world, routine activities within Pueblo villages versus the outside activities of hunting, diplomacy, and warfare. Women played a large role in Pueblo society. Symbolized in Corn Mother, their spiritual powers derived from giving life, building homes, cooking food, and guiding the young. Young girls moved to womanhood only by showing that spirit powers guided them as they performed such tasks and received important gifts from elders, including spiritual healers and family members. Boys, on the other hand, neither became men nor occupied the outside world of hunting and warring until they went through their own sacred rites of passage that honored the outside chiefs and the spirits of the twin gods. An outside world of taking life was the world of men, involving sacred gifting with animal spirits. The inside world of the kivas and spiritual control was also the domain of men. In kivas, inside chiefs performed rites of passage and performed the gifting that tied Puebloan peoples to the *katsinas*. With their spiritual leaders in kivas as their guides, families and the communities also found themselves connected to the four cardinal points of the sacred universe, the underworld of fertility, and the skyworld of rain and the sun. Any violations of gifting between the young and old and the inside and outside realms could result in terrible calamities, too. Only gifting to the *katsinas* and the rituals and ceremonies in kivas restored the cyclical balance and harmony. The complexity of Pueblo culture now confronted those Spaniards who ventured into the region.

New Power in the Sword: The Spanish Invasion

Spain's invasion of the Pueblo world came in several stages. Álvar Núñez Cabeza de Vaca's disastrous exploration of Florida turned into a six-year trek across the Gulf Coast and Texas. Only five survived the journey, including de Vaca's black slave Estevancio. Once back in New Spain, de Vaca's party claimed there indeed were seven cities of gold north of New Spain. The story circulated back and forth across the Atlantic. In 1536, Hernán Cortés, the conqueror of the Aztecs, sailed the California coastline searching for the cities. Hoping to find new riches, Viceroy Antonio de Mendoza sent Fray Marcos de Niza to explore New Mexico on March 7, 1539. The expedition included Estevanico. Once in New Mexico, Estevancio traveled ahead to Cíbola (the Zuni town of Hawikuh), leaving a trail of crosses behind for the others to follow. Arriving at a point one day's march from the city, Fray Marcos encountered Estevancio's men, who claimed that Estevancio had been killed at Cíbola. Marcos returned to New Spain, claiming he had personally seen Cíbola. "It is situated on a level stretch on the brow of a roundish hill," he said. He described it as a "beautiful city, the best that I have seen in these parts." Only later did Fray Marcos admit that he had not actually entered the city but instead eyed it from a distance that offered him safety from the Indian residents. Given the friar's observation, on January 6, 1540 Viceroy Antonio de Mendoza dispatched Francisco Vásquez de Coronado along with Fray Marcos to capture Cíbola. Coronado found not a city of gold but only a small village of Zuni Pueblo Indians. His expedition marked the beginning of a protracted Spanish effort to conquer the Pueblo world.

Coronado and his expedition in early summer 1540 encountered the Hawikuh Zuni. Wearing the armor of conquistadors and armed with harquebuses (Spanish firearms), the Spanish alarmed the Zuni who could make little sense of these foreign men on thundering horseback. Coronado and his entourage were just as confused by the Zuni. He had expected to find Cíbola, but discovered adobe pueblos and Indians. To the Spanish, the

Zuni and all other Indians of the Southwest, constituted a breed of savages. Conversely, Zuni viewed the Spanish as foreign and menacing *katsinas* whose entry into Hawikuh had to be prevented at all costs. Each saw the "other" as a direct threat.

The outside chiefs drew a line of cornmeal in the sand, indicating that the *katsinas* were neither to enter the town nor receive food or assistance from the Zuni. Coronado and his men claimed to be agents of God, pointing to the sun as a reference to the Creator and the power of the Catholic faith that had guided their journey. Zuni might have understood the idea of a *katsina* who claimed power from the sun, but they had no idea what the Spanish were doing when they read a document aloud in Spanish that proclaimed the subjugation of the Zuni. They responded by firing arrows across the line of cornmeal in the sand. It took no more than an hour for Coronado and his men to sweep past the cornmeal line and take the Zuni town of Hawikuh. The Zuni fled, leaving behind stores of corn, beans, turkeys, and salt. Coronado and his men occupied Hawikuh through the winter, regularly sending forays in search of riches among other Puebloan peoples, particularly the Quivira of Arizona. By April 1542, Coronado and his men abandoned the New Mexico mission and headed west to Sonora along the Pacific coast to help crush a rebellion in a mining region. Spanish invaders did, however, return to New Mexico, this time led by Don Juan de Oñate.

After several Franciscan expeditions to New Mexico in the 1580s confronted resistant Indians, Don Juan de Oñate traveled to the province to assume full control of the region and assist the friars in establishing a mission stronghold. Arriving in New Mexico in 1598, de Oñate set himself up as the *adelantado* of the New Mexican province, a Spanish word for governor of a particular province. He established his headquarters among the Tewa-speaking Puebloans, designating one of their villages as his capital and renaming it San Juan. In 1608, he moved his operations south to Santa Fe. De Oñate's success, based principally on the force of his army, emboldened Spain to claim New Mexico as a new province for the crown.

New Power in the Church: The Franciscan Pueblo Missions

The Franciscans who came to New Mexico in the wake of de Oñate confronted a complicated spiritual world, one in which a variety of spiritual powers were believed to be under the control of sacred specialists who helped guide all aspects of Pueblo life. To have any success at making converts, the friars would have to find ways to relate their beliefs and powers to the Puebloan sacred world. At first, the missionaries' approach was rather blunt. Friars claimed to control the rain, the sun, the skies, and medical marvels. At the same time, they tried to undermine the authority of native spiritual and political leaders.

The missionaries built Catholic representations of spiritual power at strategic locations that made sense within Pueblo constructions of the spiritual world. For instance, friars constructed churches at important locations, usually in the center of Pueblo towns or on top of kivas, to demonstrate how Pueblo kin and community might bind new relationships within the church body itself. They also used the spatial construction of churches to replace Pueblo interpretations of inside versus outside. They adorned the outside of churches with sacred objects like Puebloans had with their kivas and their homes, and decorated *reredos* (decorative screens that stood high above the altars) inside their churches with cardinal points of sacredness, with the holy trinity at the top. Like the *reredos*, Pueblo kivas had bearings to indicate where spirits lived, and the worship within kivas pointed to a skyworld of vast cosmic significance.

The friars also tried to subvert Pueblo ways of life to facilitate the spread of Catholicism. Friars appointed Pueblos to keep watch over Catholic worship and community affairs. Franciscans sought obedience to the Catholic ritual calendar. Celebrations and feasts commemorated important Catholic events. Puebloan women and men who converted were to assume new roles within Pueblo society. Franciscans encouraged Puebloan men to abandon hunting and become skilled at building and other labor-intensive work. Women were to remain in Pueblo homes, but friars wanted them to relinquish their normal duties of constructing Pueblo dwellings to men. Catholic Pueblo peoples were to abandon their old rules of sexuality and live in monogamous relationships. The cross with the crucified body of Christ was to supplant *katsinas* as the main symbol of spiritual power among Pueblo peoples. The Virgin Mary replaced the Pueblo Corn Mother. Committed to New World inquisitions, priests invaded homes and removed all forms of Pueblo religious practices such as kiva dolls and other idols. By introducing a mission program that tried to undermine the religious, social, and cultural ways among the Pueblos, the Franciscans sought dominance over the Pueblo peoples.

At the same time, the missionaries presented themselves as spiritual fathers to neophyte (newly converted) Pueblos. Fathers dispensed gifts to women and men to affirm their spiritual control over the world. Most important was the conversion of the young. Friars offered gifts to Pueblo children, indoctrinated them in Catholic precepts and practices, and convinced many of them that they offered a new form of spiritual paternity. In the end, however, it remains difficult to determine exactly how many Pueblo Indians were fully dedicated to the Catholic faith. Conversion was genuine in some instances, to be sure, but it is most likely that those who demonstrated publicly an acceptance of Catholicism and did not resist the Spanish move to reshape Pueblo society probably saw in this behavior a means of mitigating a much harsher and more violent action against them. The Spanish were alien to them, in possession of weapons, tools, and animals unfamiliar to them. It would take time to understand what power the Spanish actually wielded—and the limits of that power.

New Power in Governance: Encomenderos *and Colonial Rule*

Soldiers and Spanish officials remained on the outskirts of Pueblo towns. Many of the original soldiers involved in the conquest received titles as **hidalgos**, an honorary title of noble blood. Many of these men received crown grants that entitled them to extract labor from the Pueblo Indians in a form of tribute known as the *encomienda* system (see Chapter 2). These new Spanish elites fought for the most fertile lands and locations near the most populated Indian villages to increase their own wealth in colonial New Mexico. *Encomienda* tribute came from each Pueblo household. Twice every year, families provided their *encomenderos* (Spanish elites entitled to *encomienda* tribute) with bushels of maize and cloth made from cotton. From the beginning, New Mexicans also depended on Indian slaves. In 1630, for example, the population of Santa Fe included about 250 Spaniards and 700 Indian slaves.

Tensions existing between Spanish government officials and Franciscan missionaries made ruling over the realm of New Mexico difficult. Animosity between the friars and the government increased with the appointment of Bernardo López de Mendizábal as governor in 1659. The friars disliked his appointment from the start because he was not a Franciscan; he was a Jesuit, which is a different Catholic order. Tensions grew worse as Mendizábal regulated the friars' access to Indian laborers, their use of extreme punishments against wayward Indian church members, and their initiation of New World inquisitions. Mendizábal sought the loyalties of Pueblo leaders by allowing them to return to their old religious practices. The arrival of Mendizábal coincided with a famine in New Mexico, and Indians again performed the *katsina* dances as they sought food, rain, and help during this crisis. Indians had long practiced their old religion in hiding, but under Mendizábal's leadership such practices became open and public. Clearly, the conversion of Pueblos was not as extensive and thorough as earlier imagined. The friars responded to the return of the Pueblo religion with an inquisition into Mendizábal's misconduct, eventually resulting in Mendizábal's expulsion and return to Mexico City in chains as his governorship conflicted sharply with Spain's objectives. The end of Mendizábal governorship, however, did not stop the turmoil in New Mexico. With the government of the New Mexican province in disarray, the Pueblos seized upon the opportunity to rebel against the resumption of strict Spanish rule.

Rebellion: The Pueblo Revolt of 1680

A number of factors contributed to the 1680 Pueblo Revolt. The destruction of churches and killing of priests during the uprising suggest that the Pueblo Revolt was an attack against the Franciscan theocracy and a Puebloan search for a return of their old religious ways. The hardship that accompanied the famine and the abuses of the Spanish labor system also contributed to the rebellion. It has been argued, too, that cultural interaction and the rise of a class of mixed-blood **mestizos** (people of mixed European and Indian ancestry) who did not fit within the New Mexican social order helped lead the revolt. Since Spanish political authority was built on notions of racial and cultural supremacy and separation, so the mixture of cultures embodied by mestizos undermined the government and helped embolden the rebels.

The leader of the Pueblo Revolt was most likely a San Juan medicine man by the name of Popé. Displaying an immense talent for bringing together various Pueblo leaders and towns, Popé spread a message of spiritual revitalization. The answer to the Puebloans' problems could be found in unity, a return of the *katsinas*, and the overthrow of Spanish rule. With the Spanish gone, the rain would fall again, crops would regenerate, and the Pueblos could return to a life of happiness and tranquility. This message of cultural revitalization and survival would be echoed by numerous native groups over the following centuries. Popé chose the night of the new moon for the rebellion to commence, the new moon appearing August 11, 1680. Word spread from town to town of the impending revolt, but rumors of war also reached Spanish ears. Discovering the breach in secrecy, Popé initiated the rebellion one day earlier than planned, securing major roads and taking Spanish horses and mules to prevent a mounted counterattack. Then the rebels, with the help of Apache allies who hoped to gain horses by participating in the revolt, destroyed all of the Spanish towns within days except Santa Fe, which held out a little longer. On the morning of August 21, Santa Fe fell. The Spanish retreated out of New Mexico, leaving that territory once more solely in Pueblo hands. Purification began almost immediately, the Pueblos purging all Spanish traces among them both literally and through ceremonial rituals. Peace, however, never came. Drought continued to plague Pueblo

TIMELINE 3.2 TEXAS AND NEW MEXICO, 1539–1758

Date	Event
1539	Fray Marcos de Niza's expedition to New Mexico
1540	Francisco Vásquez de Coronado reaches the Zuni Pueblos in New Mexico
1598	Don Juan de Oñate arrives in New Mexico
1608	Franciscans begin their intensive mission program in New Mexico; Santa Fe becomes the capital of New Mexico
1659	Bernardo López de Mendizábal appointed governor of New Mexico
1680	Pueblo Revolt
1685	La Salle reaches the Land of the Tejas
1720s	Missionary growth in San Antonio
1758	Indian attack on San Sabá mission

farming, and hunger and malnutrition continued. Apaches and Navajos still raided Pueblo villages. For many, Popé had failed to deliver on his promised era of peace and plenty. Within one year of the rebellion, Popé was removed as the Pueblos' leader and thereafter is lost to history. It is generally speculated that the charismatic and defiant Popé died in 1688. By the end of the seventeenth century, the Spanish reconquest

READING HISTORY

Declaration of the Indian, Juan. Place on the Río del Norte, December 18, 1681

After the Pueblo Revolt, Spanish officials took confessions from some Puebloan peoples who were involved, as the Spaniards tried to make sense of how Popé, the accused ringleader of the rebellion, convinced other Indians to take up arms. In this account, an Indian named Juan described Popé's spiritual powers and abilities to persuade others into action against the Spanish.

Asked why they held the said Popé in such fear and obeyed him, and whether he was the chief man of the pueblo, or a good Christian, or a sorcerer, he said that the common report that circulated and still in current among all the natives is that the said Indian Popé talks with the devil, and for this reason all held him in terror, obeying his commands although they were contrary to the orders of the señores governors, the prelate and the religious, and the Spaniards, he giving them to understand that the word which he spoke was better than that of all the rest; and he states that it was a matter of common knowledge that the Indian Popé, talking with the devil, killed in his own house a son-in-law of his named Nicolá Bua, the governor of the pueblo of San Juan. On being asked why he killed him, he said that it was so that he might not warn the Spaniards of the rebellion, as he intended to do. And he said that after the rebellion was over, and the señor governor and captain-general had left, defeated, the said Indian Popé went in company with another native of the pueblo of Taos named Saca through all the pueblos of the kingdom, being very well pleased, saying and giving the people to understand that he had carried out the said uprising, and that because of his wish and desire the things that had happened had been done, the religious and the people who died had been killed, and those who remained alive had been driven out. He [the deponent] said that the time when he learned of the rebellion was three days before it was carried out. . . .

Asked to state and declare what things occurred after they found themselves without religious or Spaniards, he said that what he, the declarant, knows concerning this question is that following the departure of the señor governor and captain-general, the religious, and the Spaniards who were left alive, the said Indian, Popé, came down in person with all the war captains and many other Indians, proclaiming through the pueblos that the devil was very strong and much better than God, and that they should burn all the images and temples, rosaries, and crosses, and that all the people should discard the names given them in holy baptism and call themselves whatever they liked. They should leave their wives whom they had taken in holy matrimony and take any one whom they might wish, and they were not to mention in any manner the name of God, of the most holy Virgin, or of the Saints, on pain of severe punishment, particularly that of lashing, saying that the commands of the devil were better than that which they taught them of the law of God. They were ordered likewise not to teach the Castilian language in any pueblo and to burn the seeds which the Spaniards sowed and to plant only maize and beans, which were the crops of their ancestors. And he said that all the nations obeyed in everything except in the command concerning Spanish seeds, which some of them sowed because of their fondness for the Spaniards. Thus he replied.

Source: From *American Journeys Collection: Revolt of the Pueblo Indians of New Mexico and Otermín's Attempted Reconquest, 1680–1682.* © Wisconsin Historical Society 2003, pp. 232–238

Questions

1. What forces would provoke a Pueblo Indian to relate such an account?
2. Can we take his account as a useful source to understanding the revolt?

of New Mexico was all but complete. Even so, in the short run, Popé's rebellion was successful and the Pueblo sacred world had been fully restored. Under Popé's leadership, a century of Spanish rule and Catholic influences had fallen, if only temporarily.

Northern Mining Frontiers

A series of failed ocean-going expeditions from Baja California to coastal California forced the Spanish to opt for land routes in their seventeenth-century colonization of northwestern Mexico. Located just west of another mining frontier in Nueva Vizcaya was the region known as Sonora (just east of present-day Baja California and south of Arizona and New Mexico). A mix of fertile regions, deserts, and high mountains, Sonora offered both opportunities and challenges. The people of the region pursued a number of different lifestyles and spoke a variety of dialects while sharing some common cultural traits. Spanish economic, political, and religious influences upset their settlement, social, and cultural patterns. Ultimately it was the mission system in Sonora that produced the most lasting changes in tribal life ways.

Serrano Peoples: Native Life in Sonora

Sonora's rugged and complicated landscape shaped native living patterns as much as the Serrano peoples shaped the land. There were three systems of cultivation in the Sonora region. Within each region, Serrano families lived in **rancherías** as the basic units of social organization. *Rancherías*, comprised of numerous matrilineal families in village settlements, traded and warred with other native groups' *rancherías*, creating a regional network of exchange for prestige items and foodstuffs and relations of vengeance, obligation, and extended kinship. Highland and desert-dwelling Serranos utilized various skills for cultivating crops in open fields and small gardens. The Tohono O'odham of the desert plains, for example, planted short-term crops near runoff reservoirs, and developed multiple techniques to channel rainwater to their crops. Serrano peoples in less fertile areas but near rivers made use of irrigation canals. Many desert and highland dwellers, like the Hia C-e O'odham, also gathered plants to supplement their diet. For people of the desert and highlands, seasonal movements were essential. Near the foothills, in the colder months of fall and winter, they hunted and gathered wild foods with permanent sources of well water. In the summer, they organized village planting under the leadership of a head chief, who oversaw the distribution of lands, resources, and wars against invading tribes. Floodplain farmers depended on more permanent sources of water, and developed multiple ways to irrigate their fields. Flood-plain, desert dwellers, and highland Serrano peoples all supplemented their diet by hunting game. Moreover, all groups had a complex ritual and ceremonial life tied to planting and hunting.

A gendered division of labor existed within *rancherías*. Spiritual power among women came from gathering wild plants and from the fields. Rites performed for rain and fertility confirmed the deep connection between women and agriculture. Men who hunted performed a series of rituals and ceremonies to connect them with animal spirits and to gain status and honor on the hunt. Ceremonialism, labor, and exchange brought together communities, and established regional ties among Sonora's indigenous peoples. Gifting tied various native groups to the land and to each other. The Spanish arrived, and they too became part of the complex indigenous Sonoran economy of gifting and exchange.

Miners, Ranchers, and Moving Frontiers

Spaniards pushed into Sonora following the discovery of silver in Chihuahua in 1631, followed by ranchers and soldiers from Sinaloa and New Mexico. Three Spanish mines operated in Sonora by the 1640s. The Spanish population rapidly increased as livestock-raising and mining turned major profits. Roads connected Sonora to the already prosperous mining regions of Chihuahua, Nueva Vizcaya, and Nueva Galicia. Miners and ranchers relied heavily on Serrano peoples as laborers, whom Spaniards paid in heavy European cloth.

Mining, ranching, and trading frontiers shifted quickly, given that prospectors moved on as soon as a mine ceased to be productive. To support the shifting frontiers, the Spanish resorted to Indian slave labor, but they had little success in sustaining large pools of Indian slaves. The system of labor extraction in Sonora, known as the *repartimiento*, differed from that found in other Spanish settlements. The Spanish drafted native laborers but also provided some payment for their work. The drafted Indians worked as mineworkers and ranch hands, each Indian serving a set period of time determined by the needs of miners and ranchers. In the early eighteenth century, Opata and Pima Bajo pueblos were the main source of *repartimiento* labor. By the second half of the eighteenth century, the *repartimiento* had given way to another form of paid labor known as **naborías**. Under this system, the Spanish gave incentives in the form of ore and livestock to Indians who worked the mines or local ranching haciendas. The extensive trade routes, migrants, and forced labor along shifting economic frontiers brought diseases into Sonora, devastating the Sonoran Indian populations in the highlands, floodplains, and desert regions. At the same time, miners and ranchers drew from the Serrano peoples' gifting and exchange systems for supplies of food. The mission system added a new layer to the established colonial economy in Sonora that took labor, food, and other commodities from the Serrano peoples.

Missionaries: Serrano Peoples and the Jesuits

In 1591, the Jesuits began an extensive mission program of **reducciones** (also known as congregacíones), mission complexes designed to incorporate Indians into the Catholic faith and teach them about Spanish life. From the 1650s into the 1680s, the Jesuits expanded northward, bringing many Serrano *rancherías* under the control of mission operations. Sonora's many native peoples looked to the Jesuit missions as potential safe havens from the diseases and compulsory labor system that still confronted Indians in that region. But the mission system actually proved destructive to older ways of native life. Jesuits created a mission economy built around the church, supported by the Indian families they relocated from other pueblo settlements. In many cases, the Jesuits moved entire communities from their traditional homelands to new locations. Once inside the missions, native peoples inadvertently spread pathogens that had infected themselves, and they faced a direct challenge to their traditional living patterns. The Jesuits allotted new family plots of land to each household under the control of the missions and tried to impose Catholic religious practices, morality, and beliefs on Sonoran peoples. Mission chapels, replete with saint images, organs, vestments, and Catholic ritual clothing, all depended on internal production from Sonoran neophytes and laborers brought into the missions for periods of service. The Jesuits offered wages to "servants," non-mission Indians who built and repaired mission churches and houses. Wages were generally paid in foodstuffs. They also channeled food and livestock from the mission Serrano populations to herdsmen, artisans, and Indians who carried goods along the extensive networks of roads. Moreover, church leaders and institutions blended different ethnic and kin groups together, undermining traditional forms of indigenous leadership.

By the final decades of the seventeenth century, as the ranching and mining frontiers expanded outward from missions, Jesuits redirected laborers from mission pueblos to colonial enterprises. Surplus production in stores of grains and herds of livestock along with laborers no longer needed were shipped to surrounding presidios and mining camps. The mission system altered Serrano life by imposing a new mercantile system and dislocating thousands of Indians to new places of habitation. Diseases and hard labor took a tremendous toll on mission populations that had first come to the missions seeking protection from hardship.

Wanderers and Communities: Native Resistance to Spanish Rule

Many of Sonora's native peoples tried to resist this system of exploitation by staying away from missions, mines, and ranches. Some became known as ***rancherías volantes***. *Rancherías volantes* were small family groups that took flight from missions, ranches, and mines and resettled elsewhere in the Sonora region. In the seventeenth and eighteenth centuries, *rancherías volantes*, along with another group who were literally known in Spanish as *vagabundaje* (vagabonds), often allied themselves with Apache raiders who set them free from mission compounds. In the face of a growing population of indigenous wanderers who brought themselves together in new kinship and community networks, colonial policymakers created new categories to distinguish these various people. There were the **gentiles**, people who had never been part of the colonial social, religious, political, and economic order—Indians who had always wandered, in other words. Separate from the gentiles were the "new enemies," the so-called *rancherías volantes* who had once lived under colonial rule but had thrown off the yoke of Spanish imperial power. Along a northern frontier where Spanish power was weak, wandering peoples came together, remade themselves, and fought to protect the lands and resources that were now theirs.

Early Borderlands Connections in the Southwest

Horses and Networks of Masculine Trade and Warfare

Horses became extinct in North America around 13,000 years ago. The Aztec conqueror Hernán Cortés reintroduced the horse to North America in 1519. By the middle part of the sixteenth century, historians estimate that in Mexico alone there were more than 10,000 horses. Horses slowly spread north with miners, ranchers, and explorers. Spain's military also moved horses north as their expeditions stretched into distant territories, as in the case of Don Juan de Oñate who, in 1598, journeyed into New Mexico. In Chihuahua in the 1620s, Indians attacked Spanish settlements and stole horses.

Horses fundamentally altered native life as they spread into the Great Basin to the north and the trans-Missouri West. Mounted Indians at first adapted horses to existing cultural patterns of travel and subsistence, but a culture of horses in the eighteenth century soon transformed many native communities from semi-sedentary agriculturists to roaming tribal hunters. This shift resulted in new gender divisions of labor, with women taking a greater role in processing the results of buffalo hunts. Native encampments became smaller in size and changed in structure as they adapted to a nomadic lifestyle. Men extended the range of their hunting grounds, alliances, and trade networks as they encountered other horse-dependent groups. And, as Indian mobility increased, the frequency of warfare likewise increased as hunting parties competed with one another for game or ventured into enemy camps to steal their horses. Yet Indian men had not simply jumped on the backs of horses. They had to learn how to breed them, train them, care for them, and acquire the necessary items to ride them. Along the Southwest borderlands, horses became a new source of male honor, prestige, and spiritual power. Many native peoples incorporated horses into their oral traditions. The animals, in short, changed everything for Indian men.

Once mounted on horseback, Jumanos, Apaches, Comanches, Kiowas, Utes, and Wichitas, and others jockeyed for positions as they fought among themselves or against the Spanish for trade goods, horses, and captives. By the eighteenth century, a culture of horseback warfare had fully emerged, forcing the Spanish to adapt to a much different situation. Mounted Indians brought mobility to the battle—their attacks were sudden and swift, their retreats rapidly effected. Terror and uncertainty settled over the Spanish borderlands. Moreover, the developing horse culture allowed Indians to trade peacefully with peoples farther from their villages. Trading posts in New Mexico at Pecos and Taos, for example, emerged as central markets where various Indian and Spanish men came together to exchange horses, captives, guns, liquor, hides, meat, and livestock. Cultural melding became commonplace and helps explain the mutual benefits of capturing Indian women in particular. Captivity and intermarriage sometimes blurred tribal lines and brought Spaniards and Indians together in kinship and friendship, but they also perpetuated war, because war demanded more captives to replenish depleted populations. Trading and warring also resulted in community inequalities in which some men earned more honor and prestige acquiring more captives, horses, and material goods than others. As historian James F. Brooks has pointed out, Spanish and Indian male notions of honor, kinship, and exchange merged on the Southwest borderlands.

The Rise of the Comanches

The strongest of the equestrian cultures in the sixteenth and seventeenth centuries was the Apaches. By the 1580s, Apaches had developed intense networks of trade and warfare with the Pueblos. During times of peace, Apaches, who dominated the Southwest in a territorial zone known to the Spanish as *Apachería*, traded salt, buffalo hides, and the skins of smaller animals with Pueblo Indians. The arrival of the Spanish and the granting of *encomiendas* disrupted this economic system built on ties of kinship and friendship. Pueblo towns such as Pecos and Taos suffered severely when the Apache-Pueblo trade networks began to fall apart. Apaches had always participated in slave trading with other native peoples. The Spanish sought to tap this market, demanding large numbers of slaves from Apache raiders in the 1600s. Horseback Apaches now attacked the Pueblos to capture slaves for the Spanish markets in Taos and Pecos.

Apache-Spanish trade in slaves fostered an environment of raiding and trading in which other equestrian and pastoral Indian groups like the Navajos participated by the eighteenth century. A male-centered horse culture in the Southwest borderlands established new worlds of opportunity and conflict. Horses sparked the intensive movements and the displacement of Apaches, Navajos, Hopis, Jumanos, Wichitas, and Utes, in places such as the Great Basin, Northern Plains, and New Mexico.

Comanches eventually displaced the Apaches as the most dominant horseback peoples of the Southwest borderlands. They spoke a Uto-Aztecan dialect. According to oral tradition, a group of Uto-Aztecan speakers known as the Numic people advanced east and north from the Sierra Nevada territory to the south. They found new homes in the former drought-ridden but deserted territories of the southern plateau, the Great Basin, and the Rocky Mountains. There, they became Shoshones. The Shoshones' permanent home became the Northeastern Great Basin that touched the southern part of the Siouan and Athapascan territory of the Northern Great Plains. Shoshones moved with the seasons, from the Great Basin across the Rockies, chasing large game, foraging, and fishing in the Snake and Salmon rivers. By the sixteenth century, Indians moved into the bison-filled Great Plains, and a branch of the Shoshones joined this migration. These Shoshones forcibly pushed the Kiowas and other native peoples toward the Black Hills territory, taking over the northwestern plains. As was typical of Great Plains hunters, Shoshone encampments traveled with the herds, living in teepees and using dogs to drag their lightweight belongings. In the late seventeenth century, accustomed to mountain migrations, one of the splinter groups of the Great Plains Shoshones migrated into territories occupied by Blackfeet and Gross Ventres in present-day northern Montana, entering into episodic wars with the inhabitants. Pressured by other native groups who themselves sought to profit from the now lucrative fur trade coming out of French-occupied Canada, another Shoshone group moved into the Southwest borderlands, hugging the rim of New Mexico. It was this group that became the Comanches.

Through conquest, as historian Pekka Hämäläinen has persuasively argued, Comanches built an empire of their own in the early eighteenth century. Like Apaches and other Indian groups in the region, Comanches quickly learned how to play the French and the Spanish against each other. Acquiring horses, guns, and iron tools, they came to understand the dynamic power of these goods quicker than their rivals who tried to adapt the new technologies to plains ways of life. As they entered the borderlands around New Mexico, they formed a longstanding alliance with the Utes, who also made quick use of the new technology. The Utes looked to protect themselves from the more numerous Navajos who had gained strength after the Pueblo Revolt of 1680. Utes and Comanches skirted along the New Mexican borders, raiding and trading, and they became regulars at the Taos fairs where they traded robes, meat, and Navajo slaves for corn, horses, pottery, and cotton blankets.

Apaches and Jumanos, who also developed into horseback cultures, competed for dominance south of New Mexico and in west Texas. By the eighteenth century, Apaches had absorbed Jumanos. Apaches extended their range of raiding and trading across the southern plains. Within the borders of an expanse of territory known to Spaniards as *Apachería* were the northern Jicarilla Apaches and the southern Apaches with various names such as Lipans, Mescaleros, and Pelones. At the same time, the Comanche-Ute alliance dominated the northern parts of New Mexico, depleting the horse population to the point that New Mexico's northern borders were nearly defenseless.

TIMELINE 3.3 MISSIONS AND THE ECONOMY ON THE SOUTHWEST BORDERLANDS, 1519–1700

Date	Event
1519–1621	Arrival of horses in New Spain and the Spanish Borderlands
1580s	*Apachería* starts to emerge on the Southwest borderlands as a hub of economic trade
1600s	Expansion of Apache-Spanish trade in slaves along the borderlands
1621	Indians working on horseback for New Mexican *encomenderos*
1631	Gold discovered in Chihuahua
1640s	Four gold mines opened in Sonora
1650s–1680s	Jesuits incorporate Serrano *rancherías* into the Sonora mission system
1700	Jesuit missions supporting Sonora mines and ranches with Indian labor and surplus livestock and food
1706	First mention of Comanches by Spaniards in New Mexico

Comanche efforts to take over the river valleys of *Apachería* ignited war with Apaches. Apaches valued the river valleys for the water that made agriculture possible, whereas Comanches wanted the fertile freshwater grasslands primarily to feed and water their large horse populations. At first, Comanches initiated guerrilla strikes from their settlements to push Apaches into conflict with their common enemy, the Spanish. Pitting two enemies against one another reduced the fighting capabilities of each, making each more susceptible to Comanche attacks. Comanche warriors on horseback struck with such frequency and ferocity that the Spanish increasingly doubted their ability to remain in the region as their population diminished with each Indian raid and their economic ties to neighboring tribal groups and with the mining and ranching frontiers withered. With the help of the Utes, the Comanches completely severed the Apaches from commercial networks. By the eighteenth century, the unstoppable Comanches had Apaches and Spaniards—who were former enemies— allying with each other.

Conclusion

Spanish colonialism was never as successful in North America as it was in Mesoamerica and Peru. Spain's North American provinces were peripheral borderlands; territories where, in many cases, Indian social structures and cultural practices continued in spite of Spain's efforts to transform natives into their own image. As was the case elsewhere, the Spanish moved into the southern portion of North America seeking conquest, wealth, and converts. They hoped they would come to enjoy the same kind of control they had in New Spain. Yet Spanish political, economic, and religious activities remained in a state of perpetual negotiation with various Native Americans, from the chiefdoms in Florida to the Caddoans in Texas, from the Pueblo Indians, to the peoples of Sonora and the Apaches. Along the borderlands, the Spanish and Indians built mutually beneficial relationships but violence also shadowed the region. The next chapter offers a different perspective on native North America, looking at how the English and French established their earliest colonies. The native peoples of the Eastern Woodlands developed their own unique relations with the French and English.

Review Questions

1. What was the extent of the Spanish borderlands?
2. How effective were the Spanish in managing the borderlands?
3. Compare and contrast the Spanish and Indian relations in Florida to the Southwest.

Recommended Readings

Barr, Juliana. *Peace Came in the Form of a Woman: Indians and Spaniards in the Texas Borderlands* (Chapel Hill: University of North Carolina Press, 2007). This work breaks new ground in using gender to understand Spanish-Indian relations on the Southwest Borderlands.

Brooks, James F. *Captives & Cousins: Slavery, Kinship, and Community in the Southwest Borderlands* (Chapel Hill: University of North Carolina Press, 2002). A groundbreaking study of trade and slavery on the Southwest borderlands.

Gutiérrez, Ramón A. *When Jesus Came, the Corn Mothers Went Away: Marriage, Sexuality, and Power in Colonial New Mexico, 1500–1846* (Stanford, CA: Stanford University Press, 1991). Still the best study of Pueblo-Spanish relations in New Mexico.

Hämäläinen, Pekka. *The Comanche Empire* (New Haven: Yale University Press, 2008). A vastly significant study of the rise of the Comanche and the creation of their empire.

Milanich, Jerald T. *Laboring in the Fields of the Lord: Spanish Missions and Southeastern Indians* (Gainesville: University Press of Florida, 2006). A nice survey of the missionary work in Florida.

Radding, Cynthia. *Wandering Peoples: Colonialism, Ethnic Spaces, and Ecological Frontiers in Northwestern Mexico, 1700–1850* (Durham: Duke University Press, 1997). The best study of Serrano peoples, the northern mining and ranching frontiers and the Jesuit missionaries, and how Serrano peoples maintained autonomy amidst the Spanish incursions.

Weber, David J. *The Spanish Frontier in North America* (New Haven: Yale University Press, 1992). The starting point for any student interested in the Spanish borderlands.

Native American History Online

General Sites

The Journey of Alvar Núñez Cabeza de Vaca and His Companions From Florida to the Pacific 1528–1536, Together With the Report of Father Marcos Nizza and a Letter From the Viceroy Mendoza. http://books.google.com/books?id=3R0OAAAAIAAJ&printsec=frontcover&dq=cabeza+de+vaca&cd=4#v=onepage&q&f=true Cabeza de Vaca's important account of his exploration of the Gulf Coast and Texas.

The Journeys of Réné Robert Cavelier, Sieur de La Salle. http://books.google.com/books?id=l2NMAAAAIAAJ&pr intsec=-frontcover&dq=La+Salle&lr=&cd=20#v=onepage&q=&f=false This is the account of the French explorer La Salle's expedition down the Mississippi into the Gulf Coast.

American Conquest: The Oldest Written Record of Inland America. www.floridahistory.com/inset44.html Students can find an image-filled history of the de Soto expedition and other Spanish expeditions into North America.

Timucuan Ecological and Historical Preservation. https://www.nps.gov/timu/learn/historyculture/index.htm This webpage is a link to the Florida missions.

Early Texas Missions and Missionaries. www.sonofthesouth.net/texas/missions.htm This link offers a short overview of the Texas Spanish missions.

Historical Sites

St. Augustine Historical Society, St. Augustine, Florida. www.staugustinehistoricalsociety.com The site features the González-Alvarez House, which is the oldest surviving Spanish colonial dwelling in Florida.

Anasazi Heritage Center, Southwest Colorado. www.blm.gov/visit/anasazi-heritage-center and www.trailoftheancients.com/archaeology/ahc.html On these sites, students can visit many of the Pueblo communities and learn more of Pueblo history and the legacy of the Anasazi.

CHAPTER 4

King Philip (Metacomet), Sachem of the Wampanoags.

Seventeenth-Century Eastern Woodlands, 1607–1689

WORLDS APART
TSENACOMMACAH
The Rise of the Powhatan Confederacy
Powhatan and the English: Trade and Conflict
Indian War and the Emergence of Virginia
SOUTHERN NEW ENGLAND INDIANS ENCOUNTER THE ENGLISH
Native Americans and Plymouth Bay
New England Indians Face English Expansion
Christianity and the Praying Town Model
CONFEDERACIES, EMPIRES, AND VILLAGES
The Huron Ascendancy
War and Mourning: Five Nations' Ferocity
Middle Grounding: The *Pays d'en Haut*
Transformation of the Five Nations
MATURING COLONIES ENDING A CENTURY IN CONFLICT: METACOM'S WAR AND BACON'S REBELLION
Metacom's War
Bacon's Rebellion

Worlds Apart

The Wampanoag Indians of Cape Cod welcomed the Anglican Separatists, or Pilgrims, and they allowed the first Englishmen on the Cape to share their lands. But these settlers turned Wampanoag homelands into the colony of New Plymouth, and in that colony Englishmen and the Wampanoags maintained peaceful but fragile relationships. To make room for farms and houses in their new colony, the Englishmen, over the course of 40 years, stripped the Wampanoags of the most fertile soil and best harbors and beachheads. After hearing complaints, New Plymouth's leaders conceded that they would not take any more of the Indians' lands. This was nothing short of a lie. Indian-white relations in New Plymouth started to tailspin in 1663, when the colonists established the town of Swansea. Swansea's residents noticed warriors associated with the sachem, or chief, Metacom (known to the English as King Philip) around the town's borders. The settlers had taken Wampanoag hunting grounds to turn them into Swansea's farmsteads. In 1671, the colonists increased the pressure on Metacom, demanding that he cede additional Wampanoag land to Plymouth and pay tribute to the colony. Meeting these conditions would have made Plymouth sovereign over the Wampanoags. Desperate, Metacom turned to another group of English colonists for support, the residents of the Massachusetts Bay colony. Not surprisingly, the English colonists sided with each other.

In acting as they did, the English destroyed a longstanding treaty brokered in 1621 by Massasoit, Metacom's father, that allowed the English to share the Wampanoag homelands. At the time, Massasoit was on friendly terms with the colonists, but now his son Metacom faced a direct challenge to the Wampanoags' existence as an independent people. Metacom felt he had no choice but to go to war and, in 1675, King Philip's War began. The war, as it turned out, was one of the bloodiest conflicts in American history.

Around the same time, far to the west in the **pays d'en haut**, as the French called the vast territory reaching from the Great Lakes through parts of the Ohio Country into present-day Illinois, there were very different sorts of cross-cultural interactions. Horrific lighting raids out of New York by the Five Nations Iroquois Confederacy displaced many tribal peoples. Extreme violence on the part of the Iroquois turned the *pays d'en haut* into a vast multitribal zone of exiled Indians who were both physically and emotionally shattered. In this portion of the Eastern Woodlands, people desperately sought ways to keep the peace.

In the 1660s, a group of Indians welcomed the French explorer Nicholas Perrot to a village of Miami and Mascouten Indians near Green Bay. An elderly man and a woman first greeted Perrot. The Mascouten man, probably a chief, carried a pipe with a long stem, known as a calumet, a sign of his friendly intentions. The

CHRONOLOGY

1607–1608	Jamestown settlement and interaction with Powhatan Confederacy
1608	Champlain settles Quebec along the St. Lawrence River
1609–1610	Champlain and Indian alliance defeat Mohawks
1610–1614	First Anglo-Powhatan War
1621	Pilgrim treaty with Massasoit
1622–1632	Second Anglo-Powhatan War
1644	Opechancanough's last rebellion in Virginia
1640s	"Praying Town" model established in Massachusetts
1630s–1650s	Great Puritan migration to Massachusetts and development of Rhode Island and Connecticut
	First Five Nations "Beaver Wars"
1660s–1690s	Rise of the "Middle Ground" in western Great Lakes region
1675–1676	King Philip's War (Metacom's War)
1676	Bacon's Rebellion
1689	Start of King William's War in the colonies and the end of the last Iroquois "Beaver Wars"
1701	Final negotiation of grand settlement between Five Nations and New France

KEY QUESTIONS

1. How was the Powhatan Confederacy structured, and what sort of relationships did the English create with the confederacy?
2. How did intercultural encounters unfold between New England Indians and the Puritans?
3. With the creation of New France, how did the combination of trade, diplomacy, war, and Catholicism reshape Indian lives in the Northeast?
4. What made the "middle ground" different from other parts of the Eastern Woodlands?
5. What were the causes of Metacom's War?
6. What were the causes of Bacon's Rebellion?

man presented the pipe to the Frenchman for him to smoke, but first he performed a ritual, pointing the calumet in all the cardinal directions surrounding the visitors. The Indians inhaled from the calumet then blew smoke near Perrot's face as an Algonquian greeting of peace. Entering the village, Perrot witnessed the ritual practice of binding friends together. Holding their own calumets, several Miami chiefs stood at the village entrance, welcomed Perrot, and together they celebrated into the night. The following day, Perrot reciprocated the Indians' generosity. He gave the Mascoutens and Miamis a kettle and a gun. Then right before he left, Perrot proclaimed to the villagers that he was "the dawn of that light, which is beginning to appear in your lands." After years of dark times stained by bloodshed, Perrot's words in the Algonquian tongue would have brought some healing to the Indians' broken hearts. The two sides may not have fully understood each other yet, but one thing was for certain: both the French and the multitribal villagers of the *pays d'en haut* had a sincere desire to bring peace and friendship to the region.

From the moment of first encounter, Indians and those Europeans who settled in southern New England and in the western territories teetered between peace and war. Each group fashioned perspectives of the other based on their own cultural values and experiences. In so doing, neither Indians nor European fully understood the motives of one another, nor did they comprehend fully the repercussions of their own actions. European settlement of North America challenged the fundamental values and structures of Native America and compelled native peoples to seek an effective means to retain their own unique identities and properties.

As these events demonstrate, relations between Indians and Europeans in the Eastern Woodlands varied widely. Along the Atlantic seaboard, Indians and English colonists headed into war. In the *pays d'en haut*, French and Algonquian peoples worked hard to find ways to live in peace. Misunderstanding, miscommunication, and bad faith could, and did, lead to conflict, violence, and outright war. It was also true, however, that a spirit of accommodation and adaptation was sometimes enough to hold together fragile, complex relations between Indians and Europeans. And some Indian peoples took a third choice, turning inward to their communities for strength rather than relying on European goods, religions, and relationships. All of this was part of the makeup of the seventeenth-century Eastern Woodlands. This chapter begins with the Powhatan Confederacy and the English in the Algonquian homelands of *Tsenacommacah*, called Virginia by the English. It then traces Indian and English interactions in early New England. Moving into a world in the northeast near the Great Lakes region, the chapter then looks at how brewing antagonisms among the Iroquois, Huron, and surrounding Algonquian peoples became worse as the French introduced trade, disease, Catholicism, and unfamiliar diplomatic tactics. The chapter ends by looking at two major wars involving native peoples that closed out the century: King Philip's War in New England and Bacon's Rebellion in Virginia.

Tsenacommacah

Before the English arrived, Algonquian-speaking Native Americans in the region surrounding the Chesapeake Bay had already experienced significant changes to their ways of life. Historians and archaeologists remain uncertain about exactly when Chesapeake tribal groups first coalesced into larger chiefdoms, although scholars generally agree that warfare with the Iroquois to the north and the Susquehannocks to the south was the key factor in the transformation. Over time, hereditary chiefs known as *weroances* came to hold key positions in Chesapeake society. *Weroances* also mustered men for war, primarily to attack Susquehannock and Iroquois rivals. Smaller villages became tributaries to a paramount chief. The threat of raids by both northern and southern tribes compelled the chiefdoms to pursue intertribal friendships to protect settlements and trade networks. *Weroances* who traced descent through their mothers' lines entered into intertribal marriages that led to new relations of kinship. Matrilineal lines also had an important role to play in village politics. Clan mothers appointed particular village *weroances* to leadership positions, had say over the land as women tilled the soil, and often had to give their consent before men could go to war. Creating a confederacy produced frequent wars and realigned trade patterns to bring other tribes into a system of owing tribute to a leading *weroance* and his elite matrilineages.

The paramount chief in the Chesapeake was Wahunsunacock, known to the English as Powhatan. His elite village *weroances* had consolidated a massive confederacy by the time the English came to settle Jamestown in 1607. He had conquered many neighbors, created an effective system of tribute to rule over local groups, and established a shared set of beliefs. The confederacy claimed a homeland in *Tsenacommacah* ("our land") in present-day Virginia. Making comparisons with their experiences with monarchial rule, the English viewed Powhatan as a king, a man capable of ruling over lesser lords. Powhatan was no king, although in truth *Tsenacommacah* was immense. Powhatan's confederacy included close to 30 tribes in a territory extending from the southern shores of the James River up to the Potomac River. *Tsenacommacah* under Powhatan's rule generally remained unchecked by other Indians in the area.

The Rise of the Powhatan Confederacy

The Powhatan Confederacy commanded power in the Chesapeake world. In an environment of growing European trade, elite intermarriage with multiple wives, and intertribal conflict, Wahunsunacock—most likely in the 1560s or 1570s—built an Atlantic-coast Indian confederacy around *Tsenacommacah*. The size of Powhatan's confederacy was rivaled only by those of the Great Lakes Huron and New York Iroquois (see later in this chapter). Powhatan consolidated his power through war and marriage, but equally important in patterns of trade relationships he encouraged and in the actual goods exchanged. The conspicuous display of prestige items from foreign sources and the distribution of goods and food increased a *weroance's* sacred and political authority. A *weroance* of an elite lineage who accumulated more trade items and gave more to other villages could hope to rise to become a paramount chief. Thus, *weroances* were always interested in acquiring rare trade goods from distant lands, including mica, copper, shells, and various precious stones. The first European travelers to the Chesapeake coastline brought a new and exotic set of goods to this dynamic. Glass beads, mirrors, and utilitarian copper items all had their own spirit powers among coastal Algonquians like the Powhatans. Some items, such as beads and copper, had familiar colors and textures, and closely resembled traditional indigenous resources. Indians simply adapted them to existing cultural and social practices. Other items, such as mirrors which were unfamiliar in appearance and texture, brought new status and prestige to the owner. Chiefs were expected to display their wealth and to share it. In this world, decision making relied on villagers reaching a consensus. *Weroances* therefore could not coerce but only persuade. Goods secured through strong and sustained trade were crucial to the maintenance of Powhatan control over the confederacy.

The rise of the Powhatan Confederacy in the 1560s and 1570s was also linked to the incredible voyage of Paquiquineo. Paquiquineo was a young, elite Indian who traveled to Mexico City and returned to share his knowledge about the Spanish with his people. Paquiquineo most certainly traced his descent through one of Powhatan's elite matrilineal lines. In 1561, Paquiquineo boarded a Spanish vessel, the *Santa Catalina*, and headed for Spain, where he was introduced to King Philip II. It remains uncertain whether he was taken captive or sailed voluntarily. Paquiquineo was soon permitted to return home, but the expedition detoured to Mexico City. Paquiquineo became seriously ill, delaying his return to the Chesapeake for more than a year. In that time he took residence among Dominican friars, learned Spanish and converted to Catholicism. Conversion carried with it a new name; he was now Don Luís de Velasco, assuming the same name as the Viceroy of New Spain. Don Luís often spoke of his homeland, noting especially the abundance of natural resources there and the vast number of Indian souls that were ripe for Catholic conversion. He convinced the Spanish governor of La Florida, Pedro Menéndez de Avilés, a man appointed to protect Spanish provinces in North America, to send him back to the Chesapeake; on September 10, 1570, Don Luís, along with some Jesuit missionaries, landed on the shores of *Tsenacommacah*. It had been nine years since he first sailed for Spain.

Don Luís's return probably surprised the people of *Tsenacommacah*, as few natives who left aboard European ships ever made it back home. *Tsenacommacah*'s people were soon disappointed in his Jesuit companions. In their heavy black robes, the Jesuits stood out as oddities, as men who knew few survival skills, who were averse to armed conflict, and who showed little interest in learning native customs. More importantly, it was evident that the Jesuits were only interested in saving souls and had little to offer in the way of trade goods. His family hardly recognized him; he seemed more Spaniard than native. Recognizing the Jesuits as not an asset, Don Luís quickly abandoned them, jettisoned the Spanish ways he earlier adopted, and moved 40 miles upriver.

The head of the Jesuit expedition, Father Segura, blamed Don Luís for the expedition's troubles and publicly lashed out at him for his "backsliding" into Indian ways of life. Father Segura had no idea of the danger of such tirades against an Indian from an elite lineage, especially coming from someone in as weak a position as he was. Segura's slanderous tirade against Don Luís, known once more as Paquiquineo, was effectively an insult to the Indian elite class from which he came, one that merited retribution. An opportunity presented itself when Segura further insulted Don Luís by sending two Jesuits to the Indian village without proper offerings of trade. Seizing the moment, Don Luís killed the two priests. Then with a small party of warriors he went to the mission and killed Father Segura and the other Jesuits. Don Luís and his warriors made an important statement—when on *Tsenacommacah* soil, one must honor its resident population and adhere to traditional structures of trade.

The only member of the mission party to survive the attack was Alonso, a Spanish boy who had traveled with the Jesuits. Menéndez learned of Alonso's rescue and of the killings, and he organized a retaliatory expedition that he would himself lead. After a fray in which the Spanish killed 20 Indians and took 13 as captives, the Spanish entered into negotiations with the Indians. They could not find Don Luís, now using his original name Paquiquineo. The governor arranged safe passage back to his ship by freeing several of the captives. He then threatened to hang the remaining eight or nine captives if Don Luís continued to elude the Spanish. Menéndez hoped that the hangings would persuade Don Luís to surrender himself. However, in minds of the Powhatan Indians, the death of eight or nine lesser tribesmen at the hands of unwilling traders was perhaps a lesser sacrifice compared with the life of an elite chief.

Paquiquineo vanished from the historical record, but his odyssey and subsequent return had incredible consequences for Powhatan's growing confederacy. His intimate knowledge of the Spanish made Powhatan and his *weroances* more aware of European intentions and more appreciative of the power of European weapons. The Powhatan people also now realized that the European newcomers did not understand the importance of offering goods to the paramount chief and other elites. Unless Europeans learned to follow the proper rules of diplomatic and economic engagement in *Tsenacommacah*, the end result would always be violent confrontation.

Powhatan and the English: Trade and Conflict

Christopher Newport led the initial Jamestown expedition up the James River in 1607. Nearly the entire length of the James River to the falls fell within Powhatan's confederacy. The tiny settlement of Jamestown was planted 60 miles from the Chesapeake Bay. Newport and his men had selected an inappropriate place to build an outpost, particularly a settlement not of farmers but of soldiers and gentlemen. Jamestown began more as a military outpost than a self-sustaining colony. Water was brackish. Food was scarce because the soldiers and their leaders had little interest in planting and growing crops.

Some local natives were, at first, eager to trade with the English, exchanging corn for glass beads and other small items. Newport and his men, however, were not interested in establishing a minor trading post. Their goal was to bring the Indians' land under English control by any means necessary and to find profit from the lands of Virginia. To mark his intentions, Newport placed a crucifix at the head of the falls on his first expedition upriver in 1607. Because Newport had violated the rules of sharing the land only after negotiating with Powhatan, Algonquian warriors from upriver villages joined warriors from the Jamestown area in a joint attack on the English settlement. Only their guns and cannon allowed Jamestown's men to survive the offensive.

Powhatan most likely ordered the Indian strike against Jamestown as a way of gauging the colonists' intentions and their military strength. Not knowing when the next attack might come, Newport ordered the construction of fortified walls around Jamestown. This move only intensified Indian mistrust of the colonists, as it signaled English permanency on the land again without Powhatan's approval. From the beginning, Newport and the Jamestown settlers did not grasp that building a colony in *Tsenacommacah* meant getting Powhatan's approval. Newport had to first conduct business with the paramount chief. This meant trading prestige goods in an appropriate diplomatic setting and not spending time among tributary villages exchanging trinkets.

Relations with Powhatan's confederacy only deteriorated once Captain John Smith assumed command over the colony. Smith proclaimed himself Jamestown's leader in 1607–1608, right after Newport departed for England to recruit new settlers and bring back new stocks of food and goods. Jamestown faced disease and starvation in its first winter. The Indians were not interested in trading corn; their own winter stocks were low. Without Indian corn the colony could not survive. Smith was an experienced military man—aggressive and often brutal. He refused to let the colony starve. Trading where he could and using force where he could not, Smith gathered the corn required for his colony. Tributary villages traded reluctantly with what corn they could spare, but they soon grew disgruntled with Smith's aggressive tactics and lack of reciprocity.

Pamunkeys, one of the tribes within the Powhatan confederacy, captured Smith during his travels. Smith's life was spared because Powhatan's brother, Opechancanough, recognized Smith as a valuable captive, one worthy of meeting with his brother. To prevent another attack on Jamestown, Smith promised Opechancanough prestige goods from Jamestown. The captain sent a letter to his men, warning them of potential approaching Indian war parties, but also telling them to send along guns, beads, and other items.

Opechancanough took Smith to his home village where the Pamunkeys held a ceremony to prepare Smith for his introduction to Powhatan. Smith found the Pamunkey rituals strange and could make nothing of them. According to Smith, priests covered in red and white paint danced around him. Among Algonquians, rituals and ceremonies reminded villagers of the power of the spiritual world, the beginning of the human world, and what were appropriate behaviors. With offers of cornmeal as a gift, and descriptions of the earth, the Pamunkeys tried to make Smith understand that *Tsenacommacah* was a spiritual land populated by people who were hospitable in the proper settings with foreigners.

Algonquian everyday life had many ceremonies and rituals to appease spiritual beings. Virginia Indians called spirits **manitous**. *Manitous* inhabited the forests, trees, and the waters; they were among the living and the dead; they were on the earth and in the cosmos. *Manitous* were everywhere. In return for their appeasement, *manitous* provided Algonquian peoples with **manit** (power) that was essential to maintaining community balance and harmony. If Smith came to *Tsenacommacah* with good intentions, then Powhatan's confederacy and the *manitous* would offer friendship in return.

Powhatans, and probably other tribes within the confederacy, worshipped a god named Ahone as the creator of all things from the heavens and earth to the yearly bounty of corn. When it came to day-to-day activities, though, the god Okeus prevailed. With a watchful eye, Okeus made sure that men and women behaved properly and punished them when they did not. Disease, thunderstorms, and flooding were the result of Okeus punishing the Powhatans for their wrongdoings. In a stratified chiefdom like the Powhatan confederacy, having a pantheon of gods all villagers looked to for help and direction further consolidated the spiritual power and authority of both *weroances* and spiritual specialists.

After his stay with Opechancanough, Smith left for Powhatan's village of Werowocomoco, along the York River. Powhatan wanted to reinforce the bond of goodwill between Anglo-Virginians and the Powhatan people. He proposed a new relationship between the Indians and the English. To control the Jamestown settlers as a tribute village, Powhatan asked Smith to move the outpost to the York River, south of Werowocomoco. Smith also had to declare complete loyalty to Powhatan by a continuous exchange of goods. In return, Powhatan would feed the English. Smith did not agree to Powhatan's terms, and Jamestown remained as it was.

Smith remembered the event much differently. To Smith, it was another moment where he almost lost his life at the hands of Indians. During a ceremony in which Powhatan wanted to cement the new relationship, Smith believed that Powhatan's followers tried to club him to death. According to Smith, Pocahontas, the ten-year-old daughter of Powhatan, saved him from certain doom. Indeed, the story of Pocahontas saving Smith has become part of American lore. Pocahontas, who had served as a negotiator between the Powhatans and the English and would later marry the Englishman John Rolfe, had an important role as a cultural broker, which may account for why Smith gave her credit for saving his life. But most likely the ceremony was an Algonquian rite of acceptance into their culture. The clubs wielded over Smith on the altar were symbols of the captain's death as an Englishmen. Because women had their own *manit* as the givers of life, the presence of elite females such as Pocahontas brought Smith back from the dead as an adopted, elite "Anglo-Powhatan." The Powhatan Indians did not want Smith to pose a threat to the balance of relations within the confederacy, and their ritual intended to show English inclusion as equals. That Smith failed to understand its significance meant little; the English desire to control the chief and exploit the region for its resources remained unchanged.

Newport arrived in Jamestown in October of 1608. Following the London Company's orders, he staged a dramatic coronation of Powhatan in which the chief was to acknowledge his submission to the English crown. Smith returned to Werowocomoco to entice Powhatan to come to Jamestown for the coronation. Powhatan refused, insisting that the English come to him. Again, the English were in Powhatan's land, and he expected them to show the deference due him. Acquiescing to Powhatan's demand, Newport led 50 men to Werowocomoco for the coronation of Powhatan, bringing a boatload of copper, a basin, a bed, a pitcher, a bed, clothes, and a scarlet cloak and a crown. At the climax of the coronation, Powhatan was supposed to kneel, showing his submission to the English crown. Again, Powhatan refused. He did, however, take the crown and cloak as a gesture of kindness and to increase his own status and prestige among his people. The two sides saw the ceremony very differently. Newport reported to the London Company that Powhatan had submitted to the crown. To his followers, Powhatan had turned the ceremony around in his favor, demonstrating that he was a powerful man capable of bending the English to his will. Leaving the English, Powhatan—with the scarlet cloak and crown in his hands—had even more prestige items to conspicuously display.

Indian War and the Emergence of Virginia

The coronation ceremony was one of the last times Powhatan's confederacy and the Anglo-Virginians met on anything like friendly terms. Relations deteriorated quickly in the years that followed. Newport again departed for London to convince his sponsors to continue their support of the colony, leaving Smith in command at a most difficult moment. Starvation settled over Jamestown during the winter of 1608–1609, with Powhatan's people contributing to the situation by refusing to trade corn. Searching for food, and looking to reassert his authority by subduing Powhatan's people by force, Smith entered Pamunkey villages hunting for corn and other foodstuffs. In January of 1609, Smith captured Opechancanough and held him hostage, demanding corn from the *weroance*'s warriors in exchange for the safe release of their leader. That same year, Englishmen raided numerous other villages, stealing corn and killing Indians who resisted. English thievery and murder returned expected results; Pamunkeys and other Indians ambushed small English foraging parties and groups of fishermen, terrorizing the settlers into remaining inside Jamestown. Weakened by little food, increasingly malnourished, now fearful for their lives, and facing probable Indian retaliation, the settlers' only hope lay in reinforcements. In 1610,

4.1 John Smith being "saved" by Pocahontas.

solider-settlers, food, and a newly appointed governor in the person of Sir Thomas West arrived in Jamestown from London. Smith sailed for England, and West addressed the pressing issue confronting Jamestown.

Realizing that the English settlement was rescued from collapse, Powhatan's confederacy readied for war should it be necessary. It was. Jamestown's new command rebuilt the settlement, erected new defenses, deployed soldiers on foraging missions, and overtly threatened to destroy any Indian resistance that might surface. War became inevitable. The first Anglo-Powhatan war (1610–1614) raged mostly along the James River, but it did spill into the Chesapeake Bay region. The war did not go well for Powhatan and his confederated villages. Powhatan was in his sixties and physically unable to lead warriors in battle or travel among the villages to exert his influence, thus forcing Opechancanough to deal with the Anglo-Virginians. Englishmen pillaged inland villages and killed numerous Indians. They also settled on *Tsenacommacah* lands along the James River and in the interior without offering tribute to Powhatan. Opechancanough and the Pamunkeys were battered in their attempts to save their villages.

The English capture of Pocahontas in 1613 marked a turning point in the war. Pocahontas willingly abandoned her status as a Powhatan elite, converted to Anglicanism, and married an Anglo-Virginian of status, John Rolfe. With his most prized daughter and useful cultural negotiator now married to an Englishmen, and with the war shifting in favor of the English, Powhatan was a defeated man. The once mighty paramount chief of a massive confederacy agreed to English terms in the spring of 1614, receiving in return a shaving knife, combs of bone, fishhooks, and a dog and cat. By the summer of 1617, Powhatan retired to a village along the Potomac. He then officially turned his leadership duties over to Opechancanough. Grieving over his daughter's transformation, Powhatan died in 1618.

Virginia was now more secure for its English colonists, but it lacked a viable export commodity, which left the London Company without any return on its investment. In 1616, Orinoco tobacco came to Virginia from the West Indies. The tidewater soil was perfect for the crop, and early plantings and sales in London suggested a viable cash crop had been found. Indeed, demand for the tobacco soared in England and parts of Europe. Planters and indentured servants flocked to Virginia's tidewater region to strike it rich by planting as much tobacco as possible. Powhatan Indians, now in a position of subordination, supplied the colony with corn and various meats in return for continued peace and some trade items. The prospect of relatively quick wealth further complicated Indian-English relations.

After the first Anglo-Powhatan war, Opechancanough sought to preserve the Powhatan confederacy's autonomy amid the onslaught of English settlement. Tobacco profits, however, drew more and more settlers to tidewater Virginia. It became commonplace for small farmers to become rich planters from cultivating the crop—something of a "rags to riches" reality in colonial Jamestown. The English population grew rapidly, increasing the demand for lands. As families began to settle the area, the English insisted that the territory be made safe from Indians. Opechancanough tried to accommodate the new settlers, while also protecting any Native American sovereignty in *Tsenacommacah*. He allowed some Powhatans to convert to Christianity under the tutelage of the Anglican missionary George Thorpe to demonstrate that the Powhatan Indians could live side by side with the English. Opechancanough also convinced the English to allow Powhatans to train with muskets as potential allies, although the English strictly monitored the trade in guns with local Indians. And, additional lands were relinquished for Jamestown expansion.

Not all Powhatans were interested in accommodation. A medicine man named Nemattanew, called "Jack the Feathers" by the English, resented the planters and indentured servants on his people's homelands. A self-proclaimed prophet, Nemattanew preached a message of Powhatan regeneration, of a return of *Tsenacommacah* to the Indians. Nemattanew, who held immense control over sacred powers, even claimed English bullets could not kill him.

The politician and war leader Opechancanough listened to the prophet's message. When the English killed Nemattanew in 1622 for spreading his message, Opechancanough and his followers responded with raids against the English who now occupied most of *Tsenacommacah*. On March 22, 1622, Opechancanough and an alliance of the Indians once within the confederacy struck all the English settlements along the James River. Many Indians entered the lands of the English under the pretense of peace only to take English knives and axes and brutally kill the settlers. The initial rebellion resulted in the death of 347 English colonists, approximately one-quarter of the colony's total population.

PROFILE

Pocahontas in the Atlantic World

Pocahontas, the daughter of Powhatan, remains one of the most famous women in American history. As the courageous girl moving through the violent climate between her people and the settlers of Jamestown, Pocahontas became Lady Rebecca Rolfe after marrying John Rolfe in Virginia. Lady Rolfe and a few traveling friends sailed to London and were the first female migrants from the British colonies to make the trek across the Atlantic. She arrived in June of 1616 with her husband, baby boy, and ten Powhatan men. At the time of her arrival, her father's followers were waging a devastating war against the English colonists.

According to most reports, London's upper class saw Lady Rolfe as a princess, a young lady who carried herself as the daughter of a king, another English misinterpretation of leadership structures among the Virginia Indians. Lady Rolfe was also the only woman to achieve celebrity status out of numerous colonial-era voyagers to London, and the only Virginia Indian ever baptized in the Anglican Church before traveling to London. Lady Rolfe received much attention from both the crown and the church; her female friends stayed in London for five years. Pocahontas, a young girl who at one point sacrificed so much for her people, did not end her life in Virginia as the head of a Powhatan matrilineal household. As the final symbol of her transformation from Powhatan Indian to trans-Atlantic, Anglican voyager, Lady Rebecca Rolfe died in London in 1617.

4.2 Portrait of Pocahontas as Lady Rebecca Rolfe

Source: Courtesy of Library of Congress Prints and Photographs Division

Virginia's governor, Sir Francis Wyatt, mounted a counterattack. The second Anglo-Powhatan war (1622–1632) now raged across the tidewater region. Both sides hoped to exterminate the other, but by 1632 the English realized that the complete extermination of the Virginia Indians was impossible and negotiated a truce. During the long ten years of war, the united Indians showed their determination to keep some of the tidewater for themselves.

That same year, another tobacco boom had Englishmen once more demanding more land. The English population in Virginia stood at 5,200 colonists in Virginia in 1634; only six years later there were 8,100 settlers. The English pushed farther north along the York and Potomac rivers, still demanding that local Indians provide food and water. They fenced in Indian hunting grounds and allowed livestock to roam and trample Indian fields. In 1644, Opechancanough, nearly 100 years old, led the last attempt to push the English out of the tidewater. His warriors viciously struck settlements and outlying tobacco plantations killing an estimated 400–500 English colonists and taking many captives as they retreated to their interior villages. The new governor, William Berkeley, ordered his militia units to spread out over the tidewater and piedmont regions. English militia entered the remaining villages of the Powhatans, Appamattucks, Chickahomonies, Nansemonds, and Pamunkeys. Indian defenses were so weak that the English took Opechancanough hostage with little trouble and brought him to the governor at Jamestown. Opechancanough died at the old fort, shot by an insubordinate English soldier.

Indians in Virginia did not vanish after the bloody events of 1644, but the English significantly restricted native life in the region by applying the weight of English law to them. A treaty in 1646 designated a Pamunkey *weroance* named Necotawance as the sole ruler over his people. Necotawance, as a subject to the English king, enforced the colony's law that Virginia's native peoples pay an annual tribute of 20 beaver skins. Indians were not allowed to roam across colonists' lands, nor could Indians sell their land unless the governor

TIMELINE 4.1 POWHATANS AND THE ENGLISH, 1560–1644

Date	Event
1560–1570s	Consolidation of the Powhatan Confederacy
Circa 1595	Birth of Pocahontas
1561	Paquiquineo begins his trans-Atlantic voyage to New Spain
1570	Paquiquineo arrives in *Tsenacommacah* with Jesuits
1607	Establishment of the Jamestown Colony
1607–1608	Faltering relations between Powhatan Confederacy and Captain John Smith
1608	Powhatan's coronation ceremony
1609–1610	New governor Sir Thomas West arrives in Virginia
1610–1614	First Anglo-Powhatan war
1616	Pocahontas arrives in London
1616	First Tobacco boom in Virginia
1617	Powhatan turns over the leadership of the Confederacy to Opechancanough
1622–1632	Second Anglo-Powhatan war
1644	Opechancanough attacks Virginia settlements for the last time

approved the transaction. Native Americans also had to relinquish all their guns and any captives they still held. As their status changed, so too did their ability to sustain themselves. Livestock destroyed native harvests, and disputes over animal rights provoked greater tension between tidewater planters and Native Americans. The English destroyed native hunting grounds, transforming forests full of game into cleared tobacco fields and plantation homes. Virginia moved quickly to a plantation economy. To speed the growth of their new economy, Virginians relied on another group of people that they also eventually came to see as "savage"— imported African slaves.

Southern New England Indians Encounter the English

There was no massive confederacy of Indians like that of the Powhatans in New England, an area encompassing present-day Massachusetts, Connecticut, and Rhode Island. In Southern New England, particularly Massachusetts and Rhode Island, elite Indian leaders were called sachems. Sachems were not coercive leaders; they led by charisma and persuasion and inherited their positions through elite lines of descent. They were generous with the return of gifts once villagers paid tribute in meats, hides, crops, and even labor. Advised by an elite council of relations, sachems managed justice, welcomed important visitors, and upheld relations with other Indian groups. Sachem duties passed down from father to the oldest son, and, in rare moments, to the youngest son, an uncle, or even a daughter.

Before the English arrived, **sachemships**, villages linked under a sachem's control, were extended territories that also served as social units. They included numerous villages where land was held collectively, but also villages that had **usufruct property rights**. Under the latter system, sachems allowed families to grow crops on particular tracts of land, and to reap the benefits of that land for themselves. Families usually cultivated specific fields for long periods of time, and then abandoned them when the land became unfertile. This practice allowed for the sharing of resources on particular tracts, exclusive of the crops or other resources claimed by individual houses, or wigwams. Sachems also determined which families settled wigwams on unused sachemship lands and specific lands on which villagers could hunt. Because of their position, sachems claimed some power over the homeland, but they did not own the sachemship or assume absolute control over the people who used the lands. Disaffected villagers could leave at any time, for any reason, and owe tribute to another sachem. In other words, the homelands were sovereign as a sachemship, but sachems never used threats or violence to keep people bound to the land. The Indians of southern New England moved within the bounds of their homelands as the seasons and circumstances dictated. Thus, they were not wholly nomadic, but they still traveled from time to time according to the seasonal demands of fishing and hunting, to find better farming grounds, and to find new sources of a variety of other resources.

Algonquian-speaking Indians of southern New England did share cultural traits with the Virginia Indians. For example, *manitous* moved throughout all sachemships, among the villages, wigwams, hunting grounds, trails, and cultivated fields. Harvesting, fishing, hunting, warring, and trailblazing—all daily activities—occurred with rituals and ceremonies that upheld a spiritual balance between humans and the natural world. Like the Algonquian speakers of Virginia, New England Indians also believed in a universe suffused by *manit* (power). Mediating Algonquian relations between humans and spirits were medicine men—called *powwaws* in New England. New England Indians prized *powwaws* for their sacred abilities in dreaming, healing, and prophesying and these spiritual healers only maintained their respect and influence by continually demonstrating their powers.

New England's Algonquians were not wholly unfamiliar to the English before the settlement of larger colonies in New England. A stockholding firm known as the Plymouth Company established the Sagadahoc settlement in Maine in 1607 along the present-day Kennebec River where they hoped to build a productive outpost. Local Abenaki, who had some connections with the French, attacked and killed 11 of the English settlers, which led to the small outpost's demise. The Abenaki particularly hated the English seafarers for taking captives. In 1605, Captain George Weymouth captured five men and transported them to London. In 1611, Captain Edward Harlow apprehended several Algonquians from the Cape Cod region. One captive was Epenow from Martha's Vineyard. Speaking enough English to deceive his London captors into returning to the Vineyard under the pretense that the colonists would harvest gold-like corn, Epenow used the opportunity to escape and return to his people. These early contacts informed both Indian and Englishman of the "other" and exerted some influence on the future settlement of New England.

Native Americans and Plymouth Bay

Religious separatists known as Pilgrims were the first English people to build a permanent colony within the Algonquian world of sachemships and *manitous*. Dissatisfied with and harassed by England's official church, the Church of England (the Anglican Church), the Pilgrims began their emigration to the Netherlands in the late 1590s and once there settled into Dutch communities. For a myriad of reasons—economic, cultural, and the possibility of getting caught up in war between Holland and Spain—they laid plans for a large movement of Separatists to Plymouth Company lands in New England. The earliest of these families sailed on the Mayflower along with non-Separatists and arrived in the area of Cape Cod in 1620.

The non-separatists were largely soldiers led by Captain Miles Standish. Captain Standish had two missions: to secure the territory for English settlement and to establish the fish and fur trade. Standish's search for profits and the Pilgrims' search for community security free of Anglican control meant there were different English purposes for the colony and understandings of the nature of its leadership. Such confusion resulted in miscommunication and tension between the colonists and the New England Indians.

They found a most difficult land before them. While the landscape appeared empty and seemingly suited for them to plow, plant, and fence, they discovered quickly the harshness of winter and the prospect of a short growing season. They also had entered into a region populated by native peoples themselves facing an uncertain future. Diseases spread inadvertently by European fishermen and traders along the coast over the three previous years ripped through New England's Indian communities. Estimates suggest that nearly 50 percent of all Native Americans region-wide died from these pathogens, and some villages suffered a 90 percent death rate. Depopulation weakened Wampanoag leadership and many sachemships shrunk to smaller collections of villages. Long-practiced rituals and ceremonies faded, as did the power and influence of spiritual leaders who were responsible for healing the sick. These epidemics, however, proved less severe among other native groups, such as the Narragansetts of Rhode Island. Their newfound strength gave the Narragansetts profound influence over the diplomatic proceedings between the Pilgrims and the tattered remnants of both Plymouth Bay and Cape Cod sachemships. Thus, a shift in the balance of power between Wampanoags and Narragansetts had already started when the Pilgrims began their colony, and this brought greater uncertainty to the English settlers.

Struggling Pilgrims first settled at Patuxet (Plymouth). The local Patuxet Indians watched the colonists very closely. In the past, these Indians had traded with sporadic visitors, but had also witnessed captive raiders kidnapping coastal Algonquians. To compound matters, when the Mayflower originally anchored in Cape Cod Bay before reaching Patuxet, Captain Standish and his men had pilfered corn and other items from Indian stores and fields to help sustain the ship's passengers. In spite of the potential abundance of the land around Plymouth Bay, without adequate knowledge of local conditions and agricultural practices, the settlers barely lived through their first winter. Half of them died of starvation. The members of the small Plymouth Bay colony realized that without the aid of local Native Americans, their project was doomed.

After the starving time, the Wampanoags, with the aid of Samoset and Squanto (Squanto a former captive of the sea captain George Weymouth), who both spoke broken English, sought negotiations with the Plymouth Bay settlers. From the perspective of the lead Wampanoag sachem, Massasoit, an alliance with the English meant help for the diminished Wampanoags in their efforts to exert influence over nearby Indians and stymie Narraganset encroachment. In March of 1621, Squanto and Samoset arranged for a meeting between the Plymouth Bay colonists and Massasoit. Wampanoags agreed to ally with the English in times of attacks from outsiders, bear no arms during meetings, and return stolen property. Massasoit would use his authority as sachem over other local natives to exact justice against any Indians who attacked the English settlers. As in Virginia, the English granted royal powers to the leaders of southern New England tribes, referring to them as "kings," or "governors," based on familiar English structures.

But the English interpreted Massasoit's willingness to negotiate as submission to English authority and now viewed him as a subject of King James. Seeing Indians as an inferior "other," it seemed natural to cast them in a subservient position. The Wampanoags interpreted the treaty differently. Exchanges of prestige goods and assurances of peace subordinated the English to the Wampanoag sachem. Massasoit shared his lands with the newcomers and promised armed support in defense of the Separatists when needed. He allowed the settlers to farm on Wampanoag lands and hunt in their forests. He assured them the opportunity for trade, and his representatives provided the settlers with the knowledge and skills to survive in that harsh climate. In short, Massasoit saw himself as the beneficial host to whom the newcomers owed allegiance.

Competing interpretations of the treaty of 1621 strained Wampanoags' relationships with the Plymouth Bay colonists. Roaming Indians were a problem for Plymouth farmers because Wampanoag hunters jumped fences, ran across fields, and took the Pilgrims' livestock without permission. From the Indians' point of view, fences and fields changed the ecology of their hunting grounds, threatening an important source of Wampanoag men's spiritual power. Tensions rose quickly, threatening the tenuous peace. Adding to this, rumors of a Narragansett and Wampanoag alliance sifted through the countryside. The English believed that the two native powers had concluded jointly that the settlement posed dire long-term consequences for the native population and it would be best to eliminate that threat as soon as possible. Such discussions had, indeed, been held but no firm commitment to a Wampanoag-Narragansett alliance had been formally fashioned. Standish advised William Bradford, the appointed leader of New Plymouth, to fortify their tiny colony. To make matters more tense, in the winter of 1623, word spread of the Indian war in Virginia. Standish acted aggressively and moved to usurp the power of local sachems to preempt any Indian strike against the colony. He demanded sachems supply corn and furs to the colony, and he insisted they punish severely those Indians who violated English property rights or threatened violence against the community. Standish's aggressive posturing violated the 1621 treaty of friendship and hospitality, and he continued his efforts to compel the submission of natives to the north such as the Massachusetts. Standish and his men killed several Massachusetts leaders to assure Standish's standing among the Wampanoags. His actions only increased miscommunication with the Indians of southern New England, who thought they had negotiated a peace with the English.

In contrast, Edward Winslow sought peace with the Indians through the spread of Christianity. Religious conversion was his goal, and in believing conversion possible he tacitly acknowledged Indians were not primitive savages as Standish contended but instead educable and capable of adapting themselves to advanced civilization. This concept he shared with Reverend Robert Gray who, in 1609, told Virginia Company investors "It is not the nature of men but the education of men which make[s] them barbarous and uncivill." Winslow consciously rejected the claim of most Englishmen that Algonquian speakers had no religion and were beyond redemption. He offered Indians the precepts and practices of his faith by highlighting similarities between Indian and Protestant sources of sacred power. He preached that the Algonquian spirit, Kiehtan, bore a striking resemblance to the Christian God in power, purpose, and function. Winslow's favorable comparison lessened to some extent the negative image of Christianity many Indians in the region previously held and the suspicion they carried of Christian conversion efforts. Their concerns eased further as Winslow connected basic Christian human values with those of native spirituality. Yet Winslow also tried to undermine the influence of the *powwaws*, claiming that their supposed ability to cure wounds and diseases was actually the work of Satan. Asserting his own healing powers, abilities based on English medicine and Christian prayer, Winslow tended to many sick Indians, some of them recovering from their illness. Confusion settled over Indians as they contrasted the actions of Standish and the religion promoted by Winslow. Local sachems now questioned who actually led the new colony—Standish or Winslow.

New England Indians Face English Expansion

The Great Puritan Migration under the auspices of the Massachusetts Bay Company and religious leaders led by John Winthrop far surpassed the Plymouth adventure in size and scope. Between 1630 and 1633, approximately 3,000 Puritan families came to Massachusetts, and the original colony quickly expanded territorially to embrace most of New England by mid-century. They saw New England as a new "Canaan," the biblical "promised land" to which Moses led his people from bondage in Egypt. The Puritans intended to establish a new home in this distant land, one free of the constraints they confronted in England and one founded on a moral order based on biblical teachings. They believed theirs would become a "redeemer nation," a "light unto the world," a model for the nations of Europe to emulate.

These families framed their communities in what became known as the "**New England town model**," spreading out across Massachusetts and establishing small communities with fenced-in farms, fields, and common grounds. Farming and fencing quickly transformed Massachusetts's landscape, destroying the hunting grounds that were so important to the Indians' way of life. Patriarchs ruled the towns, and at the center of each town was the community church. The mass migration of Puritans to southern New England was another blow to local natives as the English immediately presumed Indians to be "savages" bound by Satan. They were to be subject to English law and brought from the world of darkness to the light of the Lord, or else.

New England's natives faced other issues as well. The Quahog clam along the Long Island shore and Rhode Island was an indispensable source of native food. Clamshells were also used to make wampum beads, sacred items painted in various colors and used among Algonquian- and Iroquoian-speaking people for rituals and ceremonies. Strung into wampum belts for circulation between villages and tribes, the beads became mnemonic devices from which Indians could translate messages. The Dutch, who had established the colony of New Netherland in advance of the Puritans in 1624 as an economic enterprise, had earlier experience with Africans who strung cowry shells to trade for slaves and goods. Building on this experience, Dutch traders provided the Narragansetts and other coastal Algonquians with metal lathes to manufacture wampum in large quantities. In a short time, once-sacred items became a form of common currency for interior Algonquian and Iroquois hunters involved in the expanding fur trade. The rising English population also placed pressure on native farming and hunting. Settlers expanded farther inland, forcing Indians to cede more land to Puritans. Increased English farming required deforestation of thousands of acres of what once was native hunting grounds. Settlers also expanded their hunting and fishing territories to sustain themselves. The search for pelts and furs to sell to the Dutch and the English put additional pressure on beavers, deer, and other animal populations closer to the Atlantic seaboard. All of these English actions reduced Indian access to crops, game, and fish and in so doing threatened the Indians' survival in their own homelands.

As their numbers increased, the Puritans moved west and south. The Puritans did not find a wilderness as they expected, but instead territories of the Narragansetts, Mohegans, Pequots, and other groups tied to the interior fur trade. One of the first Puritans to push west was not a land-hungry settler but a religious dissenter named Roger Williams. Williams had taken a public stance against theocratic rule and was banished from Massachusetts in 1636 as a result. He purchased a tract of land, the Providence Plantation, from the Narragansett Indians, and this stretch would later become Rhode Island. In 1643, Williams published his *A Key to the Language of America*, a seminal study of the Narragansett language that was designed to help English settlers deal with the Indians on a fair basis.

Unfortunately, in the 1630s and 1640s there were not many Puritans like Williams who befriended Native Americans. Seeking to increase the interior trade in wampum from which they profited, Pequots in 1633 invited the Dutch to establish a trading post in southern Connecticut. The Dutch population in North America was rather small in contrast to the English and, therefore, potentially less threatening to natives and to the environment. Moreover, Dutch traders more often than not offered Indians better returns on traded items. Puritans saw the Dutch as their enemies and as competitors for Pequot trade and property in Connecticut. For example, in 1636 William Pynchon led a party of family and friends from Roxbury to the Connecticut River, purchased lands from the local sachem, and began the community of Agawam. He profited in the beaver trade, eventually competing with the Dutch traders who had preceded him into the region. By English standards, Pynchon became an expert at dealing with native peoples. As English settlers streamed into Massachusetts as the Great Migration reached 20,000 by 1642, land-grabbing profit-minded men like Pynchon became more common and spurred English settlement into Connecticut.

Puritan New England by 1636 had expanded from its initial base to include much of Massachusetts, Rhode Island, and Connecticut. The English population was advancing rapidly, and another wave of Puritan migration to the region was anticipated, especially as Anglican and Puritan groups in England inched ever closer toward civil war. Not only was more land required for the building of a Zion in the wilderness, that new Eden envisioned by most Puritans also required control over native populations. Pequot frustrations rose. A recent epidemic had decimated their number. Moreover, the English-Dutch rivalry for trade routinely pitted the Pequot against the English. A series of skirmishes and raids between Pequot warriors and Puritans occurred in Spring 1637, including a concentrated strike against the English at Fort Saybrook. Using their Mohegan and Narragansett allies to their advantage, the Anglo-Indian alliance counter-attacked the Pequots on May 26, 1637. Uncas, the Mohegan sachem, and one of the last leaders of that group to hold power in the Connecticut region, had refused Pequot overtures to change sides, as did the Narragansetts who competed heavily with the Pequots in the trade of wampum. Surrounding the Pequot village at Mystic, the Anglo-Indian alliance completely razed the hamlet largely comprised of elders, women, and children. Fires consumed the village, and flames and billowing smoke cast an eerie scene across the horizon. English bullets ripped through homes and ceremonial structures. Outside of the fortified village, Narragansett and Mohegan warriors killed Pequots who sought to escape the carnage. Exact numbers of Indians killed in this massacre remain uncertain, but estimates place the death toll between 500 and 700 Pequots when the attack ended. Under the leadership of their sachem, Sassacus, Pequot warriors who were not in the village when it was attacked hurried west to live among the Mohawks. However, the Mohawks were allies of the Narragansetts and killed all of the Pequots who crossed their lands. Attacks on two more Pequot villages occurred by the end of July. Those Indians taken prisoner were soon afterwards sold into slavery. The 1638 Treaty of Hartford brought the brief war to an end and stated that the Pequots no longer existed as a tribe and could be sold into slavery to the West Indies.

The near obliteration of the Pequots opened a power vacuum in Connecticut. The Narragansetts and Uncas Mohegans sought to fill that vacuum and take over Pequot lands, and now waged war against one another for territorial dominance. The Mohegans signed a peace accord with the English to control the Connecticut River valley and remain allied to the English in trade and war. The Narragansett avoided such a formal arrangement. By the 1640s, an imperial rivalry for furs and wampum that extended into New York and the Great Lakes and involved Dutch, French, Algonquian, and Iroquois peoples further changed the geopolitics of Connecticut.

Christianity and the Praying Town Model

The Puritan ideal in Massachusetts was to establish a new moral order, one free of the corruption, avarice, and sinful manners common in England. It would become a glorious city of piety and purity and, hopefully, a beacon of light shining hope back on England. But having a true, godly Christian society meant Native Americans residing next to Puritans had to accept the Puritan social order or be removed from the territory. Thus, it was only a matter of time before Puritans targeted native peoples as potential converts to Christianity. Taking the lead in conversion efforts was John Eliot, a Cambridge-educated minister and head of the Roxbury Church in Massachusetts. In the early 1640s he began visiting Indian villages nearby, introducing them to the most fundamental elements of Christianity.

The seal of the Massachusetts Bay Colony demonstrated the centrality of native conversion in the Puritan world view, displaying an Indian wearing only a loincloth made of leaves, living in the original state of nature, and speaking the words "come over and help us." The image denoted native inferiority and, conversely, the Puritans' superiority. Eliot believed that successful conversion required the Indians' complete rejection of native cultures. He learned the Algonquian tongue, which allowed him greater credence among the Indians and the ability to present the word of God more quickly and efficiently from the outset. Eliot followed the strict rules of Puritan conversion among his first series of native converts. A fundamental scriptural knowledge was a requisite for full membership into any congregation, as were believable signs of a conversion experience before other "visible saints," who were people already accepted in the church. At the village of Nonatum, an aspiring spiritual leader, Waban, welcomed Eliot and encouraged him to make frequent visits. Eliot noted the fragility of mankind and praised the supremacy of God, who sent divine vengeance against sinners. He spoke of God's commandments, the benefits of life in heaven, and the fiery depths of hell. But, more important than simple oratory, Eliot recognized that he had to first link Christian tenets to native social structures to make the Indians more receptive to conversion, and converting sachems was key if he hoped to construct a tribal leadership villagers would follow. Notions of converting leaders were similar to the Spanish-Franciscan understandings of spreading mission zeal. Eliot also believed that if he could somehow display the healing power of his Christian medicine, he would undermine the work of Algonquian *powwaws*.

With some success at Nonatum and believing greater success lay ahead, Eliot in 1649 commenced his **"praying town"** model with funding from the New England Company. This would be a segregated native community adjacent to an existing Puritan town, a community structured physically the same as any Puritan village. Resident Indians would be instructed in English language, family arrangements, gender roles, attire, proper social behavior, and, of course, Puritan religion. Traditional native ceremonies, rituals, habits, and values would ultimately vanish as acculturation advanced—a process much later referred to as "killing the Indian to save the man." Natick, meaning "a place of seeking," became the first of his praying towns. Waban and his followers requested a tract of land to create their own English-styled town, and they received a grant along the Charles River. Natick was carved out of the Puritan town of Dedham, which had a population of Indians that Eliot had worked among near Roxbury. Many of the Indians who joined Natick found Algonquian cosmology inadequate in explaining the destruction English colonization wrought, and so they turned to Christianity as a new source of spiritual guidance. Other Indians found Natick a safe haven from the violence, diminishing resources, and intertribal disputes resulting from the Puritans' growing control in the region.

Natick became a model community. Indians built houses, fenced in farms, constructed a bridge, and changed traditional Algonquian gender roles. Some men no longer hunted but instead farmed, and some women imitated traditionally English women's roles. Natick laws forbade former Algonquian customs such as premarital sex and the growing of long hair. An Indian-led civil body governed the town of Natick, while Massachusetts took its own measures to guard the praying Indians by appointing Daniel Gookin in 1656 superintendent of Indian affairs. In 1660, under the watch of Gookin, Eliot, and other local church leaders, eight Indian confessors were finally brought into full communion with the church. By the close of the 1660s, Eliot and Gookin had a connected network of six additional praying towns.

In the Plymouth colony, Christianity spread among the Wampanoags from a new source along the Cape. Richard Bourne, one of the founders of the town of Sandwich, near Barnstable, began his ministry among the Wampanoags in 1660. His work soon spread to other native groups. In 1665 and 1666, a group of Christian

PROFILE

Uncas, the Last Sachem of the Mohegans

Uncas was born in 1588 near the Thames River in present-day Connecticut. He was the son of the Mohegan sachem Owaneoc. Uncas spoke broken English and Dutch. His ability to create Mohegan alliances with the English made the Mohegans a leading regional tribe of southern New England.

In 1626, Uncas married the daughter of the Pequot sachem Tatobem, a marriage designed by Owaneoc to create a Mohegan-Pequot alliance. When his father died, Uncas had to follow the guidance of Tatobem, as he had married the sachem's daughter and because of the brokered agreement of the Pequot-Mohegan alliance that put Uncas into a subordinate leadership role under the much more experienced Tatobem. When Tatobem died, Uncas began to challenge Pequot claims to dominance in an alliance where originally the Mohegans and the Pequots had a shared balance of power. In 1634, Uncas challenged Pequot power and authority to the point that the Pequots banished him to live among the Narragansett in present-day Rhode Island. Uncas went back home, only to find few Mohegans willing to follow his leadership and Mohegan lands diminished to small parcels.

Around 1635, Uncas forged alliances with leading Connecticut traders and settlers. Uncas warned the Connecticut settlers of an impending Pequot attack, as the English observed that Uncas was "faithful to the English." Uncas threw his support behind the English during the Pequot war in 1637. Uncas and his Mohegan followers led several strikes against the Pequots. Once the English-Mohegan forces defeated the Pequots, Uncas absorbed many remaining Pequots, making them Mohegans through a process of adoption. Uncas then signed the Treaty of Hartford in 1638 that made the Mohegans a "tributary" of the Connecticut colony. With the treaty, Uncas could lead the Mohegans into the former lands of the Pequots, but only under the supervision of the colony. The treaty, in short, made the Mohegans the strongest tribe in Connecticut. In 1643, Uncas lead the Mohegans into war against the Narragansetts, as both groups wanted the former Pequot lands. Uncas received help from the English. When he captured the Narragansett sachem Miantonomo, Uncas gave him to the English, and the English brought Miantonomo to court. Found guilty of war crimes, Miantonomo was sentenced to death, and the English ordered Uncas to carry out the act in Mohegan territory. Uncas's brother, Wawequa, killed Miantonomo with a blow from a tomahawk, but only after Uncas had given his approval. With their leading sachem dead, the Narragansetts had to sign a treaty of peace.

When King Philip's War broke out in 1675, Uncas again supported the English. The Mohegans assaulted both the Wampanoags and the Narragansetts. Uncas's involvement in the war was short-lived, however. By July of 1676, the Mohegans, weak in numbers, stopped any involvement in the war. Uncas, the last Mohegan sachem to play a decisive role in New England society, died in 1683 or 1684.

Indians known as the Mashpees secured a tract of land for a new praying town with Bourne's help. By the 1670s, there were both itinerant Indian and white preachers moving throughout the Cape and other parts of the New Plymouth Colony who sought to create Indian-Christian communities. Acculturation through the praying town method or through the more itinerant preachers achieved some success—at least enough success to encourage settlers in Massachusetts Bay and Plymouth. But it should be noted that native peoples in New England faced the real prospect of extermination. Disease had severely depopulated Indian villages, and warfare between the English and Pequot as well as the wars among native groups themselves had proved devastating. The territories of native control diminished as more Englishmen settled in the region and their own populations rose rapidly. Taking residency in praying towns and going through the motion of religious conversion allowed those Indians time to come to some understanding of the new reality surrounding them and to determine for themselves the best options for their own survival.

Christianity followed a different course on the island of Martha's Vineyard, where Indians were in the majority. The unique nature of Martha's Vineyard enabled Indian-Christian communities to grow and dampened any potential violence between Indians and colonists. A Wampanoag, Hiacoomes, invited Thomas Mayhew Jr. to begin Christian work among his people. Mayhew offered a brand of Puritan conversion that was not as all-encompassing and strict like the praying town model. With the help of Hiacoomes, Vineyard Indian ministers gained considerable control over religious practices and church authority on the island to tailor Christianity closely to Indian spirituality in a bid to gain more converts. Between the 1640s and 1670s, Martha's Vineyard became a stronghold of Wampanoag Christianity. John Eliot's 1663 translation of the Bible to Massachusette, a dialect closely related to Wampanoag, advanced the mission effort on the island. Puritan ministers learned the importance of "translating" Christianity into terms that made sense to the Indians such as substituting *Manitoo* for "God." Praying in church to *Manitoo* channeled the same sense of spiritual power that customarily brought community balance. On the other hand, *Cheepi* represented the god of the deceased, and in translated Puritan texts, missionaries often drew parallels between *Cheepi*, Satan, and hell. Natives who ran prayer sessions, schools, and churches cemented kinship and community networks by educating and converting family

TIMELINE 4.2 ALGONQUIANS IN AN EVER-EXPANDING NEW ENGLAND, 1606–1660S

Date	Event
1606	Establishment of the failed Sagadahoc colony among the Abenakis in Maine
1617–1619	Epidemic destroys the native populations of southern New England
1620	Pilgrims arrive and establish the colony of Plymouth Bay
1621	Wampanoag sachem Massasoit brokers peace agreement with the Pilgrims
1630–1633	Beginning of Great Puritan Migration to Massachusetts Bay Colony
1633	Pequots allow Dutch to establish a post in Connecticut to extend wampum and fur trade
1634–1638	Pequot War
1649	John Eliot establishes "praying town" model at Natick
1660s	"Praying towns" spread throughout southern New England

members and Wampanoags who resided within the boundaries of particular sachemships. At the same time, they also provided individuals and households with a source of strength to deal with emerging colonial forces on the island such as alcoholism, disease, land loss, and debt servitude. Keeping intercultural relationships on Martha's Vineyard from spiraling downward into violent conflict involved the cultivation of deeply felt religious conviction that brought together converted island Indians, their ministers, and the English missionaries.

Confederacies, Empires, and Villages

Two important institutions played key roles in Iroquois collective life: the Iroquois League and the Five Nations Confederacy. The Iroquois League represented the source of spiritual strength and political stability of the Five Nations, with a council of sachems and spiritual leaders providing a backbone of myth, tradition, peace, and unity for the Five Nations. The league was one symbolically united longhouse of the Haudenosaunee, as the New York Iroquois called themselves. The Senecas, in the setting of the longhouse, were the "Keepers of the Western Door." Moving east were the Cayugas, Onondagas, Oneidas, and the Mohawks. The Mohawks were the "Keepers of the Eastern Door" of the league's longhouse. The Five Nations Confederacy acted as the face of the league, serving in foreign diplomacy, trade, and warfare. Confederacy leaders convened at Onondaga, but league sachems did not always attend. Five Nations' chiefs and warriors from specific village clans met in council at Onondaga, the "central castle" of Iroquoia, to discuss matters concerning the overall survival of the Five Nations. If Five Nations' leaders could not reach consensus on decisions of diplomacy and war, confederacy members parted ways on good terms. Within each Iroquois nation, matrilineal longhouses grounded village life. A husband married into his wife's clan and lived in her longhouse. Iroquois women appointed clan leaders, divided between civil chiefs and war chiefs. Civil chiefs governed diplomacy, whereas war chiefs directed the activities of war. Women could remove both civil chiefs and war chiefs, and they had much power in determining the nature of diplomatic relations and whether or not specific nations went to war.

Hurons were also Iroquoian speakers. Huronia was an expansive portion of the upper Great Lakes, just northwest of Lake Ontario. Hurons shared many cultural traditions with the tribes of the Iroquois Confederacy; the Huron origin myth, for example, was much like the one of the Five Nations. They lived in extended longhouses consisting of matrilineal households, and village social structures and practices were Iroquoian in nature. Women controlled clan households and also appointed and removed leaders much like the Iroquois. The Huron differed from the Iroquois primarily in their geographical location around the Great Lakes. Such proximity to the French when they arrived gave the Huron immediate access to New France's economic lifeline and contributed to the intense warfare that eventually pitted the Huron and Iroquois against one another.

The Huron Ascendancy

Four nations were in the Huron Confederacy. Farthest to the west were the Arendarhonon, who were probably the largest of the Huron Confederacy members. To the east were the lands of the Attignawantan. Nestled in between these two groups were the Attigneenongnhac and Tahontaenrat tribes. The Ataronchronon were a fifth tribe, but other Hurons probably considered them a branch of the Attignawantan. Sparse French records indicate that only four tribes met in council as part of the Huron Confederacy.

In 1608, Samuel de Champlain established New France at Quebec. Champlain's goal was to strengthen New France's trade in furs and pelts and to fend off Dutch and English efforts to penetrate the region. Quebec's location, between the lands of the rival Iroquois and Huron confederacies, all but guaranteed that the French would be caught up in the competition between the two native groups. The situation was further complicated by the presence of a number of peoples who did not belong to either confederacy. They included the Montagnais and Algonkins, who settled along the St. Lawrence River, and the Mahicans, who lived in the Hudson River valley close to the Iroquois Mohawks.

Seeking to balance French interests with Indian ones, Champlain courted strong relations with the Indians nearest to Quebec: the Hurons, Montagnais, and Algonkins. A threat to Huron-French relations came from the Mohawks to the south, who also sought to benefit from trading with the French at Quebec at the expense of their Huron rivals. Mohawk warriors clad in their traditional wooden armor moved into French territory in 1609 and 1610. To protect his trade alliances with the Hurons and Algonquian speakers closer to Quebec, Champlain agreed to support his trading friends in two decisive blows against the Mohawks. The matchlock muskets of the French overwhelmed the Mohawks.

Trade increased the power of the Huron Confederacy at the same time as it enriched the French. From 1619 to 1629, economic interests on both sides made a trading alliance desirable. Each year, Huron traders went up the St. Lawrence to trade at Quebec, bringing with them the furs and pelts of many animals, the most important being beaver pelts. Indians seldom used beaver pelts, but Europeans found the fur to be exceptional in making men's hats and other outerwear. Demand for beaver pelts in Europe skyrocketed and pushed prices ever higher which, in turn, intensified trapping. A Montagnais hunter, tied so much to the French lifeline of goods, said, "The Beaver does everything perfectly well; it makes kettles, hatchets, swords, knives, bread—in short, it makes everything." About 6,000 pelts were taken to the Dutch posts at Fort Orange and New Amsterdam in 1626 alone by Mahican and Iroquois trappers. By the 1650s that number had increased by another 40,000. The Huron themselves traded more than 30,000 beaver pelts annually by 1640. The Huron-French trade had become an economic force to be reckoned with in the Great Lakes region. After 1630, when the trade reached its peak and

4.3 Huron war chief

Source: Dechert Collection, Kislak Center for Special Collections, Rare Books and Manuscripts, University of Pennsylvania

the beaver population appeared depleted in Huronia, Confederacy hunters used their intertribal alliances to extend Huron trade outside of their homelands. Huron traders bartered extra corn from the fields of their women for pelts from Ottawas, Algonkins, Neutrals, Eries, Petuns and other village-based Algonquians. They then traded pelts for guns, tools, and other manufactured goods. The trade in pelts increased the number of French traders and goods in the region, and with the French came European pathogens. These arrivals would soon challenge Huron culture and its population.

Beginning in 1634, Jesuits began their work among the Huron villages. Jesuits carried with them the ultimate goal of religious conversion, but their presence most immediately supported the efforts of French traders and merchants by conducting marriages that brought Frenchmen into matrilineal households. But their missionary efforts also created factionalism between Hurons who supported Catholicism and those who refused the faith. Whereas some Huron turned to Catholicism to explain their changing circumstances and to benefit from Catholic marriages for practical reasons, other Huron held the Jesuits accountable for the arrival of new diseases in their communities and turned to traditional spiritual practices to help them survive. The fracturing of Huron communities and the spread of diseases such as smallpox and typhoid combined into a spiritual and social crisis in Huronia. Many Huron turned to their spiritual leaders and their own cosmology for help against the epidemics that wiped out half of their kin and communities and some saw the Jesuits as a potential source of the evil spirits causing the unending spread of disease. Others, however, believed continued trade offered the Huron their only avenue toward survival, survival through power. By the 1640s, disease and factionalism had taken their toll and the Huron Confederacy showed signs of weakening.

Mohawks, on the other hand, grew stronger. After 1623, they turned their economic interests toward Fort Orange and the Dutch. The Dutch had established Fort Orange (present-day Albany, New York), but the Mahicans controlled Mohawk access to Dutch trade. For the Indians, the Dutch trade in furs for muskets and other metal items proved so lucrative that Mohawks called Dutch merchants *Kristoni*, meaning, "I am a metal maker." The Mahicans and their Algonquian allies had a monopoly on trade with the Dutch, a monopoly the Mohawks intended to make their own. Mohawk leaders made peace with New France and the Algonquian peoples to the north and simultaneously initiated war against the Mahicans. Four years of continuous warfare known as the Mohawk-Mahican war followed. By 1628, the Mohawks pushed the Mahicans out of important western lands and opened a trade route directly to Fort Orange, and the Mahicans settled to the north and east of the Dutch trading post. Under the terms of their pact with northern Algonquian-speakers, the Mohawks prevented Indian traders from the north from carrying furs to Fort Orange. The Mohawk conducted their battles on their own; they did not consult the other Five Nations or Iroquois League sachems. As the Mohawk-Mahican war demonstrates, the wealth that came with European trade also changed the political and military climate of Iroquoia.

War and Mourning: Five Nations' Ferocity

Iroquois warfare continued to change as epidemics hit villages and as Dutch and English traders exchanged guns with Five Nations' warriors for furs. Now armed with a new weapon, the Five Nations waged ferocious and relentless warfare from the 1640s to the 1660s to the north against New France, the Hurons, and the Algonquian speakers.

The Beaver Wars (1648–1657) were particularly intense. As the name indicates, the war centered on competition for increasingly scarce beaver pelts, a trade in which the Iroquois were equal players with the Europeans. Disease also played a role in the conflict. Daniel K. Richter has described the Iroquois' need to wage battle at this time in history as part of the Iroquois "mourning war complex." Epidemic disease took its toll on the Five Nations, who had no developed immunity to the deadly pathogens. Persistent outbreaks of disease ripped apart clans, families, and villages, killing the young and the old first, but brutalizing people of all ages. The close living conditions found in longhouses most certainly contributed to the rapid-fire spread of pathogens, as did the use of sweat lodges and other communal curing ceremonies. Seeking to replace lost kin, clan mothers grieved and commanded that young Iroquois warriors take captives from the Five Nations' enemies. Such captives could be adopted within clans after a period of indoctrination. They targeted Huron Indians.

Iroquois consistently raided Huron villages throughout the 1640s. In 1642, for instance, Senecas descended on villagers among the westernmost of the Huron, the Arendarhonon. The attack was a vicious example of the **mourning wars**. Senecas took captives, but then left the rest of the Arendarhonon for dead in the burning remnants of their village. The Senecas also took what furs were in the village along with other items. Between 1643 and 1647, the western Senecas and the Hurons continued raids against each other. To the east, Mohawks and Oneidas waged a sustained war against their northern St. Lawrence neighbors.

The Five Nations abandoned its separate western and eastern military tactics in 1648 and through coordinated operations destroyed the Huron Confederacy. The Arendarhonon fled all of their villages to live among their neighbors. In 1648, Senecas and Mohawks routed Attigneenongnahac villages. The evidence suggests that out of 400 families, 700 people either died or were taken captive. In 1649, about a thousand Iroquois conducted massive raids against the Attigneenongnahac in three major towns. Saint Ignace, a Jesuit mission town, fell to the Iroquois first, followed by the communities known as Saint-Louis and the Jesuit-run mission settlement of Sainte-Marie. Estimates suggest that the Iroquois lost one-third of their warriors, but they had spread such fear that their enemies left Huronia. After the Five Nations broke the back of the Huron Confederacy, they spent the next seven years purging other Iroquoian-speakers such as the Petuns, Eries, and Neutrals from the Great Lakes region. By the 1660s, the Five Nations had fought every tribe and village in the Great Lakes territory.

Captives that endured the brutal trek back to Iroquois villages were then put through the gauntlet, a vicious ordeal intended to exact personal vengeance against the captive. Awaiting the captives at the village gates were two lines of men, women, and children, bearing clubs and other weapons. The Iroquois pulled captives slowly through the gauntlet, as Five Nations villagers hurled insults and beat the captives with their fists and weapons. Those lucky enough to survive were enslaved among the clans. Captives were expected to acculturate themselves to Iroquois norms, behaviors, and values. Acculturation accomplished, they were assimilated fully into the Iroquois structures, receiving all of the benefits of clan membership, even to the point of adopting the name of the deceased clan member they replaced. They became Iroqouis. There are no precise numbers of how many captives were subsumed by the Five Nations, but one thing is for certain: the period of the Beaver Wars changed the entire Native American landscape of the Great Lakes region.

Middle Grounding: The Pays d'en Haut

While the Five Nations raged ferocious mourning warfare in the east, a different kind of world took shape to the west. The French called the region the *pays d'en haut* (up country). Refugee communities formed in this vast region as the Iroquois pushed thousands of Indians out of the eastern Great Lakes. Flowing west to avoid the Five Nations' wrath were Miamis, Ottawas, Kickapoos, Illinois, Foxes, Mascoutens, Ojibwas, Potawatomis, and a host of other Algonquian-speaking people—all of this a larger imprint of European colonialism in North America. They joined with the Iroquoian-speaking Huron and Siouan dialect groups such as the Winnebagos. Theirs was a multiethnic world where Indians from different groups interacted out of necessity, often living in the same village, and now sharinging cultural and social practices. A blending of cultures took place. Major *pays d'en haut* Indian settlements included Fort St. Louis and Kaskaskia, both south of Lake Michigan, and Michilimackinac, located at the northern tip of Lake Michigan. A host of other villages stood within a triangular swath of land between Lake Michigan and Lake Superior. Fertile land and easily accessible rivers, portages, and hunting grounds provided well for these people. Adding to the emerging texture of life in the *pays d'en haut* were French Jesuits, military personnel, and the **coureurs de bois**—French traders who avoided imperial restrictions on trade and lived among the Indians.

Richard White has described the *pays d'en haut* as "the middle ground," a territory in which no one power held sway. Cultural negotiation, misunderstandings, and miscommunication were all part of day-to-day life. To gain a foothold among Indian villagers, for instance, Jesuits did not present themselves as *manitous*, but only the bearers of the message of Christ. But Algonquian peoples did not understand the Christian version of Jesus, so the Jesuits adapted and referred to the "Master of Life," a native view of a Great Spirit, or being, who brought balance and harmony to their lives. Because Indians, and not the French, were in control in the *pays d'en haut*, the Jesuits did not try to dominate the Indians or attempt to eliminate the Algonquian belief system in its entirety. Instead, both the Jesuits and Indians adapted and accommodated in whatever ways were necessary to create friendly relations. Each governor of New France was known as "Onontio," which meant father. From the French perspective, this familial language implied that the Indians had subjugated themselves to the crown as its "children." From the Indians' viewpoint, the term suggested that the French were locked into a set of symbolic kinship relations that the French could not violate. Although the two sides interpreted the word differently, they both understood that they had agreed to a set of relations that carried with them specific obligations. The French offered gifts of kindness and entered villages in peace. The *coureurs de bois* were the most effective in operating in the tricky world of Indian villages. They learned the languages, often married Indian women, and formed strong friendships. Some of the French in Quebec viewed the *coureurs de bois* as white Indians, but such traders played a key role in keeping the *pays d'en haut* peaceful. In return for French gifts and friendship, the Indians remained allied to the French. If any village group broke that alliance, civil chiefs convened with the French to broker peace with the calumet ceremony. Adopted from the western Pawnees, the calumet was a long-stemmed pipe, and when smoked by all parties during rituals and ceremonies, it restored peace and order and washed away bad feelings.

At village winter posts, French traders tried to make their way into the kin networks of local Indian villages, which included the Iliniwek (Illinois), Miamis, Ojibwa, and other groups. As Susan Sleeper-Smith has noted "Marriage, either in the 'manner of the country,' or performed by missionary priests (Jesuits), assured traders inclusion as Native allies, secured personal safety, and facilitated access to furs." French traders with the good luck to marry elite women entered extensive kin networks, opening the door to greater profits from furs.

Catholicism provided another link between women and the French fur trade. An Illinois woman named Marie Rouensa used Catholic conversion to control her own personal autonomy. When her father tried to arrange a marriage between Marie and a French fur trader whose Catholic devotion was in question, Marie disobeyed her father. Marie's conversion was important in many ways. From her family's standpoint, Marie's conversion to Catholicism opened new avenues to goods from the French. Marie herself became an important promoter of the faith, eventually helping convert her entire family and village, and she received the benefits of a church-sanctioned marriage. Catholic marriages offered Indian women protection from the potential abuses of French traders. Marriage also secured the approval of the Jesuits, approval that brought important goods directly to Marie's family. French traders who married Catholic Indian women moved into their wife's household. Thus, kin, women, and Catholicism combined in a unique social system that linked Indian villagers to French traders and a frontier economy.

Transformation of the Five Nations

By the 1660s and 1670s, Five Nations villagers faced a new series of challenges. When the Dutch trader Ardent van Curler was relieved of his post, the Iroquois had to look elsewhere to trade. Treaties entered into with New France between 1665 and 1667 allowed the Five Nations to trade along the St. Lawrence at Quebec. However, one treaty provision authorized Jesuits to enter the villages of the Five Nations. They were permitted to spread Catholicism among the Iroquois and redeem captive Christian Indians. Many captives within Iroquois villages were Hurons who had converted to Catholicism before their capture, and their presence, along with the conversion of other Iroquois, factionalized village life. Catholic captives used the black-robed Jesuits and their faith as a way to stave off full integration into Iroquois society. Other Catholic Iroquois chose to leave their homes rather than face the hostility of non-Catholic villagers. Beginning in the 1660s and with a huge wave after 1673, many Catholic members of the Five Nations moved north into New France. The largest and most prominent of these migrant Catholic villages was Kahnawake (Caughnawaga). By 1679, hundreds of Catholic Iroquois had taken up residence at Kahnawake and other mission villages surrounding Quebec and along the St. Lawrence. For their home villages back in New York, the migration of Catholic members of the Five Nations only added to the ongoing demographic crisis.

A variety of issues to the east also pressured the Five Nations. In 1674, the English took New York from the Dutch. Without Dutch support, New England Indians were now in a position to target the Mohawks as enemies in reprisal for Mohawk raids a decade earlier. Southern New England Indians such as the Narragansetts and Nipmucs became permanent enemies of the Mohawks, who, like the other Five Nations, no longer so heavily depended on the wampum trade from Rhode Island and Connecticut. From New York, Governor Edmund Andros sided with a group of anti-French Iroquois in constructing the "**Covenant Chain alliance,**" an alliance between the Iroquois and the British colonies. In the 1670s, Andros intervened with the Mohawks to strike several key negotiations with New England and with the southern colonies of Virginia and Maryland (see next section). Andros and the English colonists in New York believed the Covenant Chain marked New York's ascendancy in Indian-English diplomacy. For the Five Nations, the Covenant Chain, particularly in the northeast, served as a diplomatic tool that allowed the Iroquois to assert dominance over other tribes who lacked similar powerful alliances, and this heightened the prospect of warfare in the region.

Economic insecurity worsened. Five Nations villagers, under duress, started a new series of Beaver Wars. In the early 1680s, the Iroquois found themselves in the middle of English Hudson Valley traders, the western Indian nations, and New France to the north. Warriors from the Five Nations took on the Miamis, Illinois, Ojibwas, Fox, and small settlements of Shawnees, Wyandots, and Ottawas. The Five Nations' western attacks were also part of the mourning war complex of previous years. The Iroquois brought captives home, and trade with the English prospered. With the Covenant Chain extending southward, Five Nations warriors attacked Conoys, Piscataways, and raided even as far south as among the Catawbas of South Carolina.

Under a new governor, Jacques-René de Brisay de Denonville, New France in 1687 invaded and destroyed Seneca villages that resided closest to the *pays d'en haut* where the French had worked so hard to establish valuable trading partners among the multitribal villages. Denonville commanded 2,000 soldiers, including some members of western tribes. Although only four villages were burned to the ground, and only 20 Seneca warriors died, Denonville and his party destroyed an estimated 1.2 million bushels of food. At the same time, the warriors and French unearthed the remains of Seneca ancestors, looking for buried prestige items. In short, they laid waste to the Seneca landscape and many of the sources of the lands' spiritual power. The destruction of sacred ground infuriated the Senecas and other Five Nations warriors, who mounted a counterattack against New France from multiple directions. To the north, the Iroquois raided Montreal, where the Onondagas took Fort Frontenac and captured a Jesuit priest. To the west, they attacked the numerous French-allied Algonquian speakers among the Wyandots, Miamis, and Ottawas. Along the way, the Five Nations forced the abandonment of every French fort in the western portion of the Great Lakes. Indian and European motivations to control trade and diplomacy in the *pays d'en haut* resulted in continued warfare between the French and the Five Nations.

Iroquois fortunes continued to shift dramatically. England and France waged an imperial war in Europe, known in the colonies as King William's War (1689–1697). European wars invariably spilled into North American colonies—French and English looking to extend the territory of their colonies and to expand trade among Indians. Native Americans often used colonial wars to improve their own trade relationships or use their European allies to eliminate their own enemies. Louis de Buade de Frontenac saw the opportunity and lay waste to the Iroquois to the south. New York, embroiled in an internal rebellion (Leisler's Rebellion) against a group of remaining Dutch settlers, offered little support, violating the rules of Andros's Covenant Chain. During King William's War, New France mustered support from the Ottawas and other western groups, the Abenaki

PROFILE

Kateri Tekakwitha

The most famous Catholic Iroquois was Kateri Tekakwitha, a captive whose Algonquin mother and Mohawk father both succumbed to smallpox. Their deaths left Kateri with no kinship ties in her Mohawk village. As the tension created by the Jesuits' activities among the Iroquois mounted, clan and kin pressure would sometimes pull members from the Catholic faith. In Kateri's case this was not so. She became one of the many migrants to Kahnawake. Visited daily by Father Claude Chauchetiére, Kateri was venerated throughout the Catholic community for her extreme physical and emotional devotion to the faith.

Although she lived in relative isolation, she joined a group of Catholic Five Nations women who devoted themselves to chastity, fasting, self-flagellation, and constant exposure to the pains of hot and cold. In 1680, she died at the age of 24. In death she became a powerful symbol to both Jesuits and Mohawks. She was a woman, Native American but a devout Catholic, whose devotion to the faith was as strong as any Jesuit in New France. Kateri, in life and death, blurred cultural boundaries.

bordering New England and New France, and their Catholic Iroquois friends from Kahnawake to stave off the Five Nations. Iroquois losses were enormous. The attacks left an estimated 2,000 Iroquois dead out of a total population of about 8,000. With few remaining options, the Iroquois began a peace process with New France in the late 1690s that resulted in the Grand Settlement of 1701. The Iroquois agreed to remain neutral in any conflict involving France and England and received the right to hunting grounds in the west. Yet the Iroquois still upheld the Covenant Chain with the English, allowing the Five Nations to continue to exert considerable influence over Indian affairs well into the eighteenth century.

Maturing Colonies Ending a Century in Conflict: Metacom's War and Bacon's Rebellion

Relative to population, King Philip's War was the deadliest conflict ever fought on American soil. Almost half of all towns in New England burned to the ground. In contrast, Bacon's Rebellion was not so much an Indian war as a series of raids and counter-raids between Indians and colonists that sparked a larger rebellion of small farmers against Virginia's elite planter class. In both cases, however, the fighting reflected the changing relations between and among native peoples and Anglo-Americans, as well as social and economic developments in the northern and southern colonies. Both conflicts weakened smaller Indian groups, who fell under the control of the Anglo-Iroquois Covenant Chain alliance extending into New England and as far south as Virginia. Both New England and Virginia had maturing economies and governments led by wealthy elites who asserted newer forms of racial and class authority over imported African slaves and small farmers. And although still interested in the highly lucrative trades with interior Indians for furs and pelts, after King Philip's War and Bacon's Rebellion, colonists in both regions pushed to the margins any Native Americans remaining within their borders.

Metacom's War

The rapidly growing population of Britain's North American colonies created intense pressure on native peoples, and this was a key factor in the outbreak of Metacom's War (1675–1676), also known as King Philip's War. As the British population grew naturally and from continued immigration, so did its need for more land and the construction of more towns. Settlers cut down trees, cleared forests, and dammed rivers. Following English tradition, each town had a commons area, an unfenced piece of land where all townspeople could let their pigs and cows graze. Additional grazing ranges surrounded these new towns, as did additional lands for farming by both community residents and outlying families. Forests which were once the exclusive domain of native hunters now fell under the English gun. All that Native Americans knew, all they valued, and, indeed, their very identity, was now threatened by a growing English population. For native peoples, the paradise of the colonists' new "Canaan" was an ecological disaster zone.

Not only were the 11,000 or so New England natives restricted to smaller tracts of land, their severely reduced range for hunting and farming and the near extinction of prized fur-bearing animals cut hard into the lucrative trade relations built over the previous several decades. Western tribes such as the Nipmucs had fewer beaver pelts to trade and fell into debt to trading outposts. Indebted Indians had to turn their sachem rights to lands over to merchants, who, in turn, sold these tracts to land-hungry settlers. Near the coast, in the colonies of Plymouth and Rhode Island, migration and increased birth rates also led to rising demand for Indian territories. Under the treaty of 1621, Massasoit and his Wampanoags believed they had secured some protection for their homelands. Only one generation later, his two sons, Wamsutta and Metacom, lived in an entirely new world. Christian Indians who owned their tracts sold them on the open market, undermining the power of the sachem and the social unit of the sachemship. In some areas, sachems themselves looked to profit, and they sold their homelands right out from underneath their people. Wamsutta also dabbled in the land trade. Although he had appeased the Plymouth colonists by changing his name to Alexander (Metacom changed his to Philip), he sold land to Quakers and other non-separatists from Rhode Island and elsewhere. Taken prisoner by Plymouth soldiers to curtail his land sales, Wamsutta died in custody soon thereafter. Infuriated, Metacom accused the colonists of poisoning his brother. Metacom now assumed the position of Wampanoag sachem. Bowing to pressures applied on him by colonists, Metacom reluctantly recognized the sovereignty of Plymouth in 1674 as a temporary solution to his tribe's weakened state.

Metacom recognized easily that the course of events spelled eventual doom for native peoples in the region. The English colonial population would continue to rise; additional native lands would fall into English hands, compelling families and entire communities to move farther west into territories already occupied by other Indians; the pressure to acculturate to English ways would only intensify; and, disease would further reduce the native population. He saw the destruction of native peoples—the death of Indian cultures, the corruption of native values, and Indian dependency on English colonial powers becoming absolute. Metacom, then, imagined the fate of Native Americans and called for a pan-Indian alliance to not just resist the English but rather to exterminate entirely the English presence. Warfare, if successful, would save Native Americans.

Metacom mustered his warriors for battle, while seeking to ally with the Nipmucs and the more numerous and powerful Narragansetts. One of the major problems facing a sachem on the brink of war was an inability to restrain unruly young men. Because young Wampanoag men gained sacred power, status, and prestige from going to war, Metacom's forces were more than ready to raze local villages and kill colonists. In July of 1675, a Christian Harvard-educated former counselor to Metacom, John Sassamon, was found dead in an icy pond. Apparently, Sassamon had told the English at Plymouth of Metacom's intentions to mount a pan-Indian war against the colony. Three of Metacom's enraged warriors killed Sassamon for betraying the Wampanoags. Going on little evidence other than the testimony of a Christian Indian who reported having seen the murder, two Wampanoag men were immediately apprehended, tried and convicted on the basis of circumstantial evidence, and hanged after a jury of both Englishmen and Christian Indians found them guilty. Metacom could not contain his warriors any longer.

Metacom's warriors swarmed first on Swansea, killing the settlers and torching the town. The English tried to take Metacom by surprise at his village near Mount Hope, but Metacom learned of the planned raid and he and the villagers eluded capture and death. Metacom's warriors continued their lightning raids against small hamlets throughout the Plymouth colony. In some areas, the war assumed a greater racial tone as frustrated English settlers refused to differentiate between friendly Christian Indians and their enemies, killing many praying town natives. To avoid further emotionally charged strikes on praying towns, Massachusetts's government agreed to keep Christian Indians on islands, such as Deer Island, just off of Boston's coastline. Then the English struck native villages region-wide without restraint. At Rhode Island's Great Swamp, they hit a Narragansett village with a ferocity unmatched since the Puritan strike against the Perquots 40 years earlier, killing women, children, and the elderly. Narragansetts who until now refrained from allying themselves with Metacom rose in fury, and the now-united anti-English Wampanoag, Narragansett, and Nipmuc forces moved closer and closer to Boston, burning settlements as they went. All of New England was in peril.

Mohawk intervention changed the course of the war and the state of Indian-English relations in the northeast. In January of 1676, Mohawk allies heard that Metacom was in their territory, near the Hudson River, looking for support from Mahicans and other Native Americans. Sir Edmund Andros, who received word of a planned meeting between Metacom and the Mahicans, armed the Mohawks for an attack on the would-be allies. Disease sifted among the potential allies before the meeting, taking the lives of some warriors and leaders and weakening the threat of their alliance. The Mohawks then struck hard against the Mahicans, Wampanoags, and other Algonquian speakers. To cement their position as the most important Indian group in the region, the Mohawks followed the retreating Algonquians into New England to kill them. That spring, Anglo-Indian forces faced off with Narragansetts and Wampanoags in the southwest part of New England and dealt them a devastating blow.

Tribal groups allied to the English gave colonists a numerical edge in the war. The individual colonies also struck agreements among themselves to combine their forces, evidenced when Plymouth, Connecticut, and Massachusetts Bay amassed an army of about 1,000 militia. The united militia unleashed its terror against Indian villages throughout southern New England, striking encampments and large villages alike with unrestrained ferocity. Concurrently, the fragile alliance formed by Metacom cracked, partly the result of the colonists' growing power and brutality and partly the product of weakening sympathy for Metacom's vision of purging the English from American shores. So many had benefitted from the colonial trade; some concluded that accommodation might be a better path to follow. The war turned in favor of the English, and many Indians switched sides. English raiding parties roamed the countryside. The men were promised a bounty for each Indian taken captive and the right to keep all possessions of each Indian killed or captured. Benjamin Church led one of these teams of militia and at Mount Hope in Bristol, Rhode Island on August 12, 1676 stumbled upon Metacom. A brief firefight ensued, and Metacom was killed. His corpse was beheaded and placed on public display at Plymouth.

Warfare had tremendous consequences at the local and regional level; 40 percent of the native population in southern New England were dead as a direct result of this war. According to one English account, brutality waged by "the most barbarous and cruel" enemies of the English resulted in "1,200 houses burned and 8,000 head of cattle killed," while the Indians sustained losses of upwards of 3,000 people. Englishmen sold many captured Indians into slavery, with many of the enslaved natives transported to Virginia and to the West Indies. For surviving Indians, choices were now to be made—accommodate themselves to a land governed solely by the English or relocate westward.

Both Indians and English settlers were left homeless and starving at the end of the war. For the Puritans, the devastation of such a brutal war left an indelible mark. New England lay in smoldering rubble with half its homes burned to the ground; the economy staggered, leaving many impoverished. The war also compelled many Puritans to question their faith, as the wrath of God's hand had seemingly come to New England. Why had God punished them with such ruin and death? What sins had they committed? Was the Puritan experiment in New England a failure? Such questions loomed in their minds—as did memories of the war—as they tried to rebuild their communities. The war shook the foundations of Puritan society.

Puritan memories of the war lived on in intensified animosity toward Indians. The English confined surviving New England Indians to small government-supervised tracts, the earliest forms of reservations in North America. Limited to low-paying jobs and businesses, Native Americans in New England no longer exerted an influence on the regional economy. In their place were imported slaves who now buttressed the growing urban and rural economies of New England.

Because the Mohawk joined the war on the English side, the Iroquois Confederacy extended its reach into New England in the postwar period. In April 1677, an Albany conference attended by delegates from New York, Massachusetts, Connecticut, and from the Mohawk communities set out to determine a new set of regional relationships. The Mohawks were to release any Indians who had taken refuge in Iroquoia on the condition of peaceful residency in the region. New York was to mediate between the Mohawks and New England. New York and the Mohawks, under Sir Edmund Andros's guidance, established some of the first links in the Covenant Chain alliance between English colonists and the Iroquois.

READING HISTORY

Mary Rowlandson's Captivity Narrative, 1682

Mary Rowlandson, wife to the Reverend Joseph Rowlandson, lived with her family in Lancaster, Massachusetts, on the frontier at the outbreak of King Philip's War. She and her three children, Joseph, Mary, and Sarah, all became wartime captives, enduring hardship for 11 weeks with their Native American captors. Once she returned home, Mary wrote the account of her experience, The Sovereignty and Goodness of God: Being a Narrative of the Captivity and Restoration of Mrs. Mary Rowlandson, *which is now considered a classic in the fields of early American literature and the captivity genre.*

At length they came and beset our own house, and quickly it was the dolefulest day that ever mine eyes saw. The house stood upon the edge of a hill; some of the Indians got behind the hill, others into the barn, and others behind anything that could shelter them; from all which places they shot against the house, so that the bullets seemed to fly like hail; and quickly they wounded one man among us, then another, and then a third. About two hours (according to my observation, in that amazing time) they had been about the house before they prevailed to fire it (which they did with flax and hemp, which they brought out of the barn, and there being no defense about the house, only two flankers at two opposite corners and one of them not finished); they fired it once and one ventured out and quenched it, but they quickly fired it again, and that took. Now is the dreadful hour come, that I have often heard of (in time of war, as it was the case of others), but now mine eyes see it. Some in our house were fighting for their lives, others wallowing in their blood, the house on fire over our heads, and the bloody heathen ready to knock us on the head, if we stirred out. Now might we hear mothers and children crying out for themselves, and one another, "Lord, what shall we do?" Then I took my children (and one of my sisters, hers) to go forth and leave the house: but as soon as we came to the door and appeared, the Indians shot so thick that the bullets rattled against the house, as if one had taken an handful of stones and threw them, so that we were fain to give back. We had six stout dogs belonging to our garrison, but none of them would stir, though another time, if any Indian had come to the door, they were ready to fly upon him and tear him down. The Lord hereby would make us the more acknowledge His hand, and to see that our help is always in Him. But out we must go, the fire increasing, and coming along behind us, roaring, and the Indians gaping before us with their guns, spears, and hatchets to devour us. No sooner were we out of the house, but my brother-in-law (being before wounded, in defending the house, in or near the throat) fell down dead, whereat the Indians scornfully shouted, and hallowed, and were presently upon him, stripping off his clothes, the bullets flying thick, one went through my side, and the same (as would seem) through the bowels and hand of my dear child in my arms. One of my elder sisters' children, named William, had then his leg broken, which the Indians perceiving, they knocked him on [his] head. Thus were we butchered by those merciless heathen, standing amazed, with the blood running down to our heels. My eldest sister being yet in the house, and seeing those woeful sights, the infidels hauling mothers one way, and children another, and some wallowing in their blood: and her elder son telling her that her son William was dead, and myself was wounded, she said, "And Lord, let me die with them," which was no sooner said, but she was struck with a bullet, and fell down dead over the threshold. I hope she is reaping the fruit of her good labors, being faithful to the service of God in her place. In her younger years she lay under much trouble upon spiritual accounts, till it pleased God to make that precious scripture take hold of her heart, "And he said unto me, my Grace is sufficient for thee" (2 Corinthians 12.9). More than twenty years after, I have heard her tell how sweet and comfortable that place was to her. But to return: the Indians laid hold of us, pulling me one way, and the children another, and said, "Come go along with us"; I told them they would kill me: they answered, if I were willing to go along with them, they would not hurt me.

Source: From the introduction of Mary Rowlandson, *The Sovereignty and Goodness of God: Being a Narrative of the Captivity and Restoration of Mrs. Mary Rowlandson* (1682).

Questions

1. What does Rowlandson's narrative tell us about how Indians conducted warfare in New England?
2. Did Rowlandson and her Indian captors share anything in common?

Bacon's Rebellion

In 1676, the same year Metacom's War ended in New England, Bacon's Rebellion erupted in Virginia. A rebellion that began with relatively minor skirmishes against Indians on the Virginia frontier turned into a civil war pitting small farmers against Virginia's planter aristocracy. As was the case in New England after Metacom's War, Bacon's Rebellion ended a tenuous period of peaceful coexistence in Virginia between settlers and Indians. In its wake, a new, racially defined social order emerged with sharp distinctions between the rights and opportunities of whites, blacks, and Indians. Entangled in the war from the start were Indians on the margins of the tidewater, including the Susqehannocks, Doegs, and Piscataways, as well as the tributary Indians of the tidewater, including the Pamunkeys, Occoneechee, and Mattaponi. All these Indians lived on land Virginia's small farmers believed should belong to them.

In July of 1675, a dispute between settlers and Indians over some hogs resulted in the killing of several Doegs. Seeking revenge, the Doegs murdered the servant of a local planter. It mattered little who shed first blood; Indians had killed a non-Indian and this, to Virginians, warranted a full-scale assault on the Doeg village. A Captain Brent marched with the Westmoreland County militia under the pretense of peacefully negotiating with the Doegs, but once at the village his group proceeded to kill a *weroance* and then 14 Susqehannocks nearby, assuming no difference between the two Indian groups. The Susqehannocks, pushed by the Iroquois into Maryland and living among the Piscataways, now retaliated with multiple raids in Virginia. In September of 1675 Colonel John Washington and Major Isaac Allerton, with militia units from Virginia and Maryland, descended on the Piscataways' fort. Five more *weroances* were killed, each believing Washington's party was there to negotiate a resolution to the crisis. After the attack on the fort, the Susqehannocks pushed into the forests of Virginia. Although small in number in comparison to a white male population in Virginia of 13,000, Susqehannock warriors terrorized the Virginia countryside, particularly large planters' homes. Governor Berkeley mustered men from the lower rungs of Virginia society and the tributary Indians Pamunkeys, Occoneechee, and Mattaponi.

What started as purely an armed conflict with Virginia's Indians morphed into a class struggle among the colony's white population. A measure enacted by the House of Burgesses on March 7, 1676, required the construction of defensive fortifications at the head of each river manned by 500 men drawn from the ranks of small farmers. Seeing the law as an effort to keep small farmers off of prime land and to protect the interests of elite planters, a group of men, led by Nathaniel Bacon, arose against the law and the governor's support of it. Bacon also opposed Berkeley's Indian policy in which he promised native peoples that English settlement would remain east of the Blue Ridge Mountains. As Virginia's population soared by the late 1600s, land for settlement became limited and, consequently, costlier. This, in effect, denied white men of limited means the opportunity to secure property in their own names while someone of the colony's elite might own thousands of acres and be able to purchase additional lands despite their price. It was a policy and arrangement, Bacon believed, that was purposely constructed to benefit the rich at the expense of the poor. Bacon's recommendation seemed simple: drive all Indians from Virginia, thus opening those lands to the colony's lower class. This applied even to the tributary Pamunkeys, Occonukeys, Occoneechee, and Mattaponi who had been trade partners and held the protection of Berkeley. He and those who championed his cause took Indian policy into their own hands, roaming the countryside and killing as many Indians as possible. The rebels murdered and enslaved men, women, and children and pillaged villages. The uprising against the governor and Indians became known as Bacon's Rebellion. What began as a dispute over Indians and land turned into a class war between Bacon and his militia on one side and the governor and planter elites on the other. Bacon and his men made their way to Virginia's capital, Jamestown, offering freedom to servants or slaves who joined their ranks. With them were many Indian captives, symbolic of the war's beginning. Governor Berkeley took flight from Jamestown aboard ship. On September 9, 1676, Bacon burned Jamestown to the ground. English soldiers and a militia opposed to Bacon battled the rebels, but the rebellion collapsed when its charismatic leader, Bacon, died from fever in October.

English officials forced the Virginia government to reestablish peace with the tributary Indians. The Treaty of Middle Plantation in 1677 recognized a female *weroance* as the sole leader of the Indians remaining within Virginia's borders and included provisions to control the settlement and movement of the Indians. The governor had the duty to handle any disputes or dealings between English planters and native peoples. Planters and farmers were to remain three miles from any Indian village to limit disputes over the trampling of Indian farmlands by livestock. Indians needed a local official's approval to travel, to fish, hunt, or gather berries and plants over lands not specifically allocated to them. Virginians, in short, strictly regulated the Indians on reserves.

Susqehannocks fled north. Governor Edmund Andros reached out to them, negotiating a peace that made the Susqehannocks subjects of the Iroquois Confederacy. In June 1677, Maryland and Virginia accepted Andros's terms. As a tributary group of the Iroquois, the Susqehannocks could never raid the plantation colonies again, and the Five Nations also agreed never to raid the two colonies. Now the Covenant Chain alliance had another link as it had extended its reach into the South.

Conclusion

The seventeenth century was a time of radical change and disruption for both Native Americans and Europeans in the Eastern Woodlands. French and British imperialism brought disease, war, trade, diplomacy, and new religions. Native Americans from Virginia to the Great Lakes often dictated the terms of intercultural encounters. In the *pays d'en haut*, developing peaceful relationships was a necessity for both the French and Indians who had been dispossessed by years of devastating wars with the Iroquois. At the same time, Europeans tried to impose systems of land ownership, international markets, and politics on native peoples.

As both Native Americans and Europeans competed for control of the Eastern Woodlands, efforts at coexistence were often short-lived and almost always one-sided, bent toward European designs. In Virginia and New England, the English sought to grab land as much land as possible and viewed the Indians as impediments to progress. By the 1660s and 1670s, Indians and English colonists, in both New England and Virginia, were at war. When these wars were over, it was clear that English colonists in New England and Virginia no longer saw coexistence with the Indians within their borders as a viable option. From an English viewpoint, Indians would have to submit to their authority or go. Native Americans chose their own paths, typically the polar opposite choices of accommodation or armed resistance.

Review Questions

1. Compare and contrast Native American relations in Virginia and New England.
2. How and in what ways did native peoples clash with European colonists in New France and New England?
3. Analyze the similarities and differences between King Philip's War and Bacon's Rebellion.

Recommended Readings

Brooks, Lisa. *Our Beloved Kin: A New History of King Philip's War* (New Haven: Yale University Press, 2018). A study of the complex reality of war and captivity and native resistance through the stories of two Native Americans, a Wampanoag and a Nipmuc.

Cave, Alfred. *Lethal Encounters: Englishmen and Indians in Colonial Virginia* (Lincoln, NE: University of Nebraska Press, 2013). This work argues that peaceful relations between Native Americans and English settlers in Virginia during the colony's first century of existence were impossible from the start. Conflict was inevitable given the dissimilar economic and social structures, failure of English leadership, and the strong prejudices held by Englishmen toward native peoples.

DeLucia, Christine M. *Memory Lands: King Philip's War and the Place of Violence in the Northeast* (New Haven: Yale University Press, 2018). This study looks at King Philip's War in terms of physical place—the war's direct impact on specific people and communities with attention to issues of sovereignty, resistance, culture.

Horn, James. *A Land as God Made It: Jamestown and the Birth of America* (New York: Basic Books, 2005). A new, very useful, and readable study of the Jamestown settlement and the Powhatan Indians.

Lepore, Jill. *The Name of War: King Philip's War and the Origins of American Identity* (New York: Alfred A. Knopf, 1998). A lively account of King Philip's War.

Morgan, Edmund S. *American Slavery, American Freedom: The Ordeal of Colonial Virginia* (New York: W. W. Norton, 1975). Remains a seminal study of the early settlement and development of Virginia that also focuses on English-Powhatan relations.

Richter, Daniel K. *The Ordeal of the Longhouse: The Peoples of the Iroquois League in the Era of European Colonization* (Chapel Hill: University of North Carolina Press, 1992). The best work on the Iroquois in the seventeenth century that covers their relationships with the French, Dutch, and English, and a study that offers the best analysis of the mourning wars.

Salisbury, Neil. *Manitou and Providence: Indians, Europeans, and the Making of New England, 1500–1643* (New York: Oxford University Press, 1982). The classic account of early relations between southern New England Indians and the English.

Silverman, David J. *Faith & Boundaries: Colonists, Christianity, and Community among the Wampanoag Indians of Martha's Vineyard, 1600–1871* (New York: Cambridge University Press, 2005). The most important study of Southern New England to appear in some time, and the best examination of religious change on Martha's Vineyard.

White, Richard. *The Middle Ground: Indians, Empires, and Republics in the Great Lakes Region, 1650–1815* (New York: Cambridge University Press, 1991). The most important study of the Great Lakes territory and intercultural relationships between the multitribal villages and the French.

Native American History Online

General Sites

John Eliot, *The Indian Grammar Begun: Or, an Essay to Bring the Indian Language into Rules, for the Help of Such as Desire to Learn the Same, for the Furtherance of the Gospel Among Them* (Cambridge, 1666). http://books.google .com/books?id=vz3IoF-bRi8C&printsec=frontcover&dq=John+Eliot,+Indian+Grammar+Begun:+Or,+An+Essay+ to+Bring+the+Indian+Language+into+Rules,+For+the+Help+of+Such+As+Desire+to+Learn+the+Same,+for+the+ Furtherance+of+the+Gospel+Among+Them&hl=en&ei=iq5OTpelIqL00gHDx8HkBg&sa=X&oi=book_result&ct=result& resnum=2&ved=0CC4Q6AEwAQ#v=onepage&q&f=false One of many tracts published by John Eliot, it shows how New England missionaries tried to make sense of the Algonquian tongue to spread Christianity.

Roger Williams, *A Key Into the Language of America.* http://books.google.com/books?id=wOfpAPRxlVYC&pg=PA1&dq =%22a+key+to+the+language+of+Americ%22&lr=&source=gbs_toc_r&cad=4#v=onepage&q&f=false=mgUMAAAAY AAJ&pg=PA211&dq=%22New+Netherland%22%2B%22documents%22&lr=Roger Williams's full text of the Narragansett language is an invaluable source for understanding Indian life in southern New England in the seventeenth century.

S.G. Drake, *The Old Indian Chronicle: Being a Collection of Rare Tracts, Published in the Time of King Philip's War, by People Residing in the Country* (1836). www.archive.org/details/oldindianchroni00lithgoogle A compilation of tracts published at the time of King Philip's War allows students to see how colonists viewed the war and the Indians who fought it.

Historical Sites

Mashantucket Pequot Museum and Research Center, Mashantucket, Connecticut. www.pequotmuseum.org/ The Pequot Museum provides a visual history of the Pequots and other southern New England Indians.

Jamestown Rediscovery: Historic Jamestown. historicjamestowne.org This site details the history of the colonial Jamestown settlement, with periodic updates of the on-going archaeological digs at that location, presentation of excavated artifacts, details of key native and English personalities in colonial Tidewater Virginia, the introduction of African slavery in the colony, and maps and other resources.

The New Netherland Institute and New Netherland Project, Albany, New York. www.newnetherlandinstitute.org This site provides both a virtual tour of New Netherland and access to documents and other historical resources.

CHAPTER

5

XXV.

EMPIRES, A CHIEF, AND A PROPHET

INDIANS AND EMPIRES IN THE NORTHEAST

Deerfield on the Edge of Empire

Returning to New France and Shifting Strategies

NEW ENGLAND INDIANS "BEHIND THE FRONTIER"

Land and Indian Communities

Native Peoples and the Economics of the British Empire in New England

Religion, Education, and Indian Sovereignty

A MID-ATLANTIC FRONTIER

Delawares and the Quest for Land

The Pennsylvania Backcountry

The Indians' "Great Awakening" in Pennsylvania

MULTITRIBAL ZONES AND IMPERIAL PRESSURE IN THE SOUTH

Trading Slaves and Deerskins

Native Americans and the Costs of French Expansion into the Lower Mississippi Valley

Tuscarora and Yamasee Wars and Breaking with the British

THE SEVEN YEARS' WAR AND INDIAN PERSPECTIVES ON EMPIRE

The Redefinition of Empire and Racial Consciousness

Empires, a Chief, and a Prophet

In April 1763, about ten miles from Fort Detroit, Pontiac, who at that time was an Ottawa chief, planned for an all-out war to stop the British from taking over the Ohio Valley. The French had controlled much of the territory until their recent loss in the Seven Years' War (French and Indian War), and the Indians in the region had benefitted somewhat from their presence. The British, however, now claimed the Ohio Valley, and the Indians' experiences with or understanding of the English made British authority

Florida Indians, disguised under deerskins, hunting deer.

untenable to them. Pontiac convened a council of Ottawas, Ojibwas, Potawatomis, and Hurons to win support for a strike on the newly British-occupied fort. To keep Onontio in the Ohio Valley, most warriors would not hesitate to kill the well-trained but much-despised British redcoat army who represented the new British "father." But they were drained of the necessary spiritual forces to fight because they had, for their own reasons, joined the French cause during the destructive Seven Years' War; warriors needed more than Pontiac's words to replenish their medicine bundles. Pontiac therefore not only urged Indian warriors to arm themselves but he also spread the Delaware prophet Neolin's unique prophecy of an impending sacred war and vision of a British-free existence.

Pontiac said Neolin had become "eager to make acquaintance with the Master of Life" and had "resolved to undertake the journey to paradise, where he knew he resided." Neolin traveled to the cosmic world and found three different paths, the most difficult of which led to the Master of Life. The Great Spirit told Neolin to have native peoples purify themselves spiritually and to purge themselves of the vices brought on by British trade, such as alcohol. Even more important, to accomplish this cleansing of their spirits and minds, native peoples had to abandon any prayers to *manitous*, the familiar sacred forces roaming the human realm of Algonquian peoples. Through rituals and ceremonies dedicated to the Master of Life, Indians of the trans-Appalachian west could become whole again and could carve a new path of peace and harmony across tribal lines. Only with this wholeness and harmony could they ignite a spiritual war to liberate their world from the British.

Neolin's prophecy became the catalyst for Ohio tribal unification in a war against the "whites." After receiving Neolin's message and applying it to their lives, Pontiac and about 900 Native American warriors laid siege to Fort Detroit from May through autumn. As the Master of Life had made clear to Neolin, Indians were different from whites, but to Pontiac and other British-hating native peoples, they were much different from "dogs clothed in red," a reference to British redcoats. Neolin's message had a racial component in that the British

CHRONOLOGY

1686	Reverend Williams arrived in Deerfield
1704	French and Indian raid on Deerfield
1715	Yamasee War
1721–1730	Natchez War against the French
1737	Walking Purchase in Pennsylvania
1739	Treaty of Coweta
1740s	Choctaw Civil War in Lower Mississippi Valley
1744	Lancaster Treaty
1740s–1760s	Indian Awakening among the Moravian communities in Pennsylvania
1758	Treaty of Easton
1761	Lyttelton sends 2,600 troops against Cherokee towns
1763	Treaty of Paris
	Beginning of Pontiac's War
	Beginning of the Paxton Uprising in Pennsylvania
	Proclamation of October 7, 1763

KEY QUESTIONS

1. How did events in Deerfield reflect larger trends in Indian-European relations in the Northeast?
2. How did imperial expansion in New England change the lives of Indians?
3. What shifting patterns of life in Pennsylvania prevented full-scale war into the 1750s?
4. How did patterns of imperial competition shape the Southeast?
5. What were some of the impacts of the Seven Years' War on Native Americans?

were racial "others," a perspective that increasingly resonated among western Indians. The prophet's message, one in which Indians created a world of their own, so inspired Pontiac that he united Indians across tribal lines in a massive war that resulted in the destruction of almost every British fort in the Ohio Country. The violence even spilled into the predominately Scots-Irish backcountry farms and villages of Pennsylvania and Virginia.

But how had Indian-British relations in North America deteriorated to the point where a Delaware prophet's message could inspire a militant Ottawa chief to unite diverse tribes into full-scale war against the British? How had Native Americans like Neolin and Pontiac come to make such sharp racial distinctions between Indians and Europeans? This chapter answers these questions by looking at the competition between empires in the Eastern Woodlands. It begins in the Northeast in 1700, with the British and French empires clashing on the Massachusetts frontier, which placed native peoples into difficult positions. The chapter then moves from New England into Pennsylvania and then into the South, showing how in each region native peoples dealt with the imperial ambitions of European powers. It concludes by examining the Seven Years' War, a moment of severe crisis in Native American history when the British replaced the French as the strongest imperial power in the Eastern Woodlands.

Indians and Empires in the Northeast

By the time of the raid on the small English town of Deerfield in western Massachusetts, New France had stretched its imperial holdings far from its seventeenth-century epicenter on the St. Lawrence River. The French now traded broadly with native peoples from the Great Lakes region to as far south as present-day Louisiana. New arenas for the trade of skins and furs did not diminish New France's urgency to strengthen its imperial presence on the frontiers of New England and New York. Organized by the newly appointed governor of New France, Philippe de Rigaud de Vaudreuil, raids on small English towns such as Deerfield were supposed to hold together the Indian-French relationships and thwart any hopes of further English expansion into the lucrative Western fur trade region. King Louis XIV of France was determined to protect this valuable trade by using New France as a buffer against English westward expansion. But his policy had little chance of success if New France did not strengthen its relationships with the most powerful Indian groups in the region. The 1701 peace treaty signed at Montreal ended Iroquois-French hostilities and set the course for Iroquois neutrality for the next half century, but the accord had an unintended result: The Iroquois of New York, as neutral parties between the two empires, could also turn profits by siphoning some of the fur trade to Albany, which shifted the advantage to the English. Further action was urgently needed if New France hoped to have access to furs. Raids on small towns would demonstrate that even the smallest communities could be swept up in early eighteenth-century imperial competition. Such attacks located in territories between empires in the northeast, although common, brought people of diverse backgrounds into imperial struggles that they might have otherwise avoided.

Deerfield on the Edge of Empire

The village of Deerfield sprang from Dedham, a Puritan town situated close to Boston. Its creation was not the product of a rapidly growing English population compelling territorial expansion westward but rather the imprint of colonial policy on select Puritan communities. In a bid to resolve tensions between native and English inhabitants of southern New England, the Massachusetts Bay Colony authorized the founding of Praying Towns for Indian residency—communities in which willing Native Americans were congregated for the express purposes of religious conversion and adaptation to English culture. Puritans viewed praying towns as a satisfactory and, indeed, moral solution to the vexing issue of native-white coexistence. The problem was this: establishing a praying town that abutted an existing Puritan community required acquisition of property, more often than not by relocating English families on the lands determined most suited for the praying town. This was precisely how Deerfield came into existence. English families residing on lands soon to become the Praying Town of Natick were ordered off their properties. To compensate, the Massachusetts Bay Colony government issued a grant of 8,000 acres on which those dispossessed Puritan families would build new homes and establish the town of Deerfield in 1673. Sixty-eight people received land grants and set about founding Deerfield, and within two years the new town claimed 200 villagers. As expected, Deerfield conformed to the New England town model, settling close-knit families around a commons area and placing the Congregational church and its leaders at the center of town power and authority. During King Philip's War, the residents left their farmsteads for a safer location; they did not repopulate Deerfield until 1682. In the following decades, the town found itself in the middle of an imperial conflict involving the English, the French, and numerous Indian peoples. This conflict stretched from Deerfield to New France, to scattered native villages across the Northeast, to Boston, and all the way across the Atlantic. In fact, Deerfield's position as a rather remote, frontier community made the town vulnerable to Indian raids throughout the remainder of the seventeenth century and into the early eighteenth century. It, too, was a target for the French in their incessant frontier skirmishes with English militia, especially when skirmishes were part of larger imperial wars. Such a war erupted in 1702, one commonly known as Queen Anne's War which, again, pitted Britain against France. Given Deerfield's remote location as well as the reality of a new war for empire, little wonder that French and Indians would once more strike the Puritan town.

Before sunrise on February 29, 1704, a mixed party of French and about 200 Indians (mostly Algonquian and Iroquois) descended on Deerfield from three separate directions, completely razing the town, killing Puritan residents, and taking war captives. Among those taken prisoner was the town's minister, the Reverend John Williams, and his family. A Pennacook Algonquian of some standing warned Reverend Williams's captor that he himself might kill the minister and "take off [his] scalp." Captivity carried the real possibility of death, particularly for men unless they held special value for ransom, and a minister and his family, because of their standing within the community, were prized captives. The 112 men, women, and children now under Indian control were force-marched roughly 300 miles into Canada during the height of winter. Some did not survive the trek. Forty-one residents perished in the raid, and many more were critically injured. Twenty-two French soldiers were wounded and eight Indians were killed. From the native perspective, the attack was a success.

The 200 Indians who joined the French in the raid came from five different settlements that were allied to the French. Hurons and other Algonkins came to fight from the west. Hurons who occupied a village known as Lorette also sent young men to fight. From the south came Iroquois and warriors from the Sokokis, a western Abenaki group. Some of these people became known as the Iroquois of the Mountain from the mission village of La Montagne. By far the largest contingent was the **Kahnawake Mohawks**, which was a relocated community of Catholic Mohawks who lived outside of Montreal. The Kahnawakes regularly traded with the French,

READING HISTORY

John Williams, *The Redeemed Captive Returning to Zion*, 1774

Reverend John Williams's account was one of the most popular captivity narratives of its day. It reminded English settlers of the dangers that lay lurking on the frontier, and it evoked tremendous emotions in its narrative of the hardships of captivity among feared native enemies.

On Tuesday, the 29th of February, 1703–4, not long before break of day, the enemy came in like a flood upon us; our watch being unfaithful;—an evil, the awful affects of which, in the surprisal of our fort, should bespeak all watchmen to avoid, as they would not bring the charge of blood upon themselves. They came to my house in the beginning of the onset, and by their violent endeavors to break open doors and windows, with axes and hatchets, awaked me out of sleep; on which I leaped out of bed, and, running towards the door, perceived the enemy making their entrance into the house. I called to awaken two soldiers in the chamber, and returning toward my bedside for my arms, the enemy immediately broke into the room, I judge to the number of twenty, with painted faces, and hideous acclamations. I reached up my hands to the bed-tester for my pistol, uttering a short petition to God, for everlasting mercies for me and mine, on account of the merits of our glorified Redeemer; expecting a present passage through the valley of the shadow of death; saying in myself, as Isa. xxxviii, 10, 11, "I said, in the cutting off of my days, I shall go to the gates of the grave: I am deprived of the residue of my years. I said, I shall not see the Lord, even the Lord, in the land of the living: I shall behold man no more with the inhabitants of the world." Taking down my pistol, I cocked it, and put it to the breast of the first Indian that came up; but my pistol missing fire, I was seized by three Indians, who disarmed me, and bound me naked, as I was in my shirt, and so I stood for near the space of an hour. Binding me, they told me they would carry me to Quebec. My pistol missing fire was an occasion of my life's being preserved; since which I have also found it profitable to be crossed in my own will. The judgment of God did not long slumber against one of the three which took me, who was a captain, for by sun-rising he received a mortal shot from my next neighbor's house; who opposed so great a number of French and Indians as three hundred, and yet were no more than seven men in an ungarrisoned house.

Source: Reverend John Williams, *The Redeemed Captive Returning to Zion: A Faithful History of Remarkable Occurrences in the Captivity and Deliverance of Mr. John Williams* (Boston: John Boyle, 1774).

Questions

1. What does Williams's account tell us about the captivity experience?
2. What biases might exist in the account because of his Puritan faith?

Mohawks in Iroquoia, and the Albany trading outpost. Another strong presence was the western Abenaki who occupied a village at Odanak, a settlement with close connections to New France. Eastern Abenaki known as the Pennacooks also joined. They were a group of people literally "caught between empires," living in a region they called Wôbanakik, located between New France and Massachusetts.

Returning to New France and Shifting Strategies

Eighty-nine captives survived the journey from Deerfield to Canada. Indians prized women and children as captives because many women married into Indian communities and helped replenish the population, while children did the same by assimilating into Indian culture. The number of men adopted by Indians was very small by comparison. In New France, there was conflict over what to do with the Protestant foreigners because many of them resisted adoption among the Catholic Kahnawakes. Deerfielders held on to their Protestant beliefs. French Catholics only made tensions worse. They protected many captives' lives, took many into their service as laborers, converted some widowed women to Catholicism, and used the Reverend Williams to broker a deal for French captives held by the English. In little time, the French had alienated many of the Indian warriors with whom they had gone to battle. Although Reverend John Williams, the most highly prized captive, ended up among the French, his daughter, Eunice, fully integrated into Kahnawake society. Following a series of imperial negotiations that stretched across the Atlantic, Williams eventually returned to Boston. And with the publication of his tract, *The Redeemed Captive Returning to Zion*, Williams and others made repeated attempts to redeem Eunice. But she had become a Kahnawake Mohawk, and remained so until her death.

After the Deerfield raid, Indian warriors found their movements along Massachusetts's frontier restricted. One round of warfare may have come to an end, but the Protestant-Catholic animosity that was part of French and English imperial competition continued to create division within Indian communities up through the Seven Years' War of the mid-eighteenth century.

New England Indians "Behind the Frontier"

Far from Deerfield, southern New England Indians stabilized their communities by settling on lands near English towns. The "praying town" model John Eliot established in the seventeenth century still dominated English thinking about how colonists and Indians might live together. From their perspective, the Indians had two choices: assimilation or migration. Indians themselves, however, increasingly favored a third option, adaptation. Indians in southeastern Massachusetts came to prefer living in their own communities on parcels of land connected to their homelands, even if the parcels were small, and they involved themselves in the regional and British Atlantic economy. Southern New England Indians tried to function within the New England town system and its regulations, but these efforts faced stiff resistance from English settlers who sought to exploit, marginalize, and impoverish them. Nonetheless, Indians displayed remarkable determination and resiliency. They established churches and schools on their lands, or worked closely with missionaries to become preachers and religious leaders within native communities. On the other hand, provincial leaders enacted stringent rules to regulate Indians on reserves, and by the middle of the eighteenth century, many groups fell under the protection of government-appointed guardians. Southern New England Indians tried to control their own lands and sense of community even under a system of guardianship protection. Native peoples protected common lands through community meetings, councils, their church leaders and school teachers, and the establishment of more secure legal claims to tribal acreage. Some tribes even went as far as to expel unwanted residents, particularly their sachems, who sometimes tried to sell tribal lands for personal gain. Adaptation was a conscious choice made by some Indians. Although it required them to relinquish many, if not most, of their traditional cultures, adaptation allowed for some degree of acceptance among English settlers nearby and in so doing permitted these natives to continue their residency on traditional lands—perhaps the single most important item to the majority of Native Americans.

Land and Indian Communities

In Massachusetts in the first decades of the eighteenth century, the larger reserves of Natick, Mashpee, and villages on Martha's Vineyard—all scattered remnants of former larger tribes and sachemships—experienced drastically changing relationships between land and community. Foremost among the issues they confronted was that of land ownership. Most Indian communities east of the frontier were forced to turn to English land ways, meaning a proprietorship system where land was held in common, but families had individual plots overseen by town leaders. In Natick, native peoples long valued communal ownership of property, the concept that all property was shared by all persons in the community. Opting for adaptation rather than migration, the Natick established an English system of proprietorship by 1720 in which each Indian household owned a particular tract of land. Private property ownership alienated some Indians who did not receive personal tracts and others who clung desperately to more traditional views of land ownership, but it allowed others to participate in the English land market exchange. A somewhat different proprietorship system emerged among the Mashpee Wampanoags. Mashpees governed carefully the plots assigned to individual families to prevent any sales of their traditional lands, and family tracts were not formally surveyed and regulated by law. What surfaced among the Mashpees was far less structured than the Natick system. The Mashpees guarded lands to keep for children after their parents died, and if no living heirs existed, the land was reabsorbed into the community commons to protect Mashpee sovereignty. For the Wampanoags of Martha's Vineyard, the land situation was complicated. After King Philip's War, Martha's Vineyard still retained its sachems and sachemships. There were five sachemships on the island where Indians established colonial political relationships and, in some cases, churches and schools. English colonists tried on numerous occasions to buy land fraudulently under **"sachem rights."** This was an English concept of sachem land sales where the sachem sold a particular parcel and then forced the movement of the Indians from that territory. Some Wampanoag communities reached out to government-appointed guardians and colonial lawyers to help them keep a portion of their territory, whereas other Wampanoags became landless under the "sachem rights" prerogative. By the middle part of the eighteenth century, contests over territory and power were a constant element in the Vineyard Indians' struggle to retain their lands and to sustain communities.

Native Peoples and the Economics of the British Empire in New England

With lands, trees, livestock, and other agricultural resources slowly stripped from many Indians in southern New England, Algonquian men and women ventured outside their communities for subsistence. By the eighteenth century, a system of **indentured servitude** brought many Wampanoags into the British imperial economy. Indians who entered into contracts of indenture agreed to work a set number of years in exchange for forgiveness of a debt, usually money or goods dispensed to men and women for services aboard ships, as day laborers, or in colonial homes. Some men were so heavily indebted that they indentured their children to colonial merchants and homes. Also forced to seek subsistence outside of reservation borders, Indian women indentured themselves as house servants and workers. The system of indenturing tore at the fabric of Wampanoag communities. It placed Indians into perpetual cycles of labor and debt exchange. Indenturing led to poverty, which forced many women and children to roam from one New England town to another in search of work and food.

Native men frequently signed whaling voyage agreements for expeditions sailing out of Nantucket. In return they received **lays**, which amounted to a fraction of the total catch of any particular voyage. Intense poverty, however, compelled some Indian men to barter large portions of their lays with coastal and island merchants for goods such as clothing, food, and liquor. "The case is," wrote the Congregational minister Gideon Hawley, of the Mashpees, "an Indian having gotten into debt obliges himself to a whaling till he pays." Nantucket vessels stayed at sea for years at a time. Service at sea required Indian men to leave their families and communities behind. The resulting lack of Indian men resulted in radical demographic changes in Mashpee, Natick, and Martha's Vineyard. As Hawley noted in Mashpee, the large number of widows "was the means of introducing among my people the African blood." Community men dying or deserting at sea after years of service pushed Indian women into relationships outside of reserve boundaries so women could perpetuate their communities. Although local ministers and guardians frowned on such "mixed" marriages, free African American men moved to many Indian enclaves. But Indian women served as the gatekeepers of their communities. Because of the land systems in place that protected native proprietor families, African men were excluded, in most cases, from owning Indian soil. Freed African men, however, could live with Indian women and work on the land.

In the face of a British economic system that pushed native peoples to the lower rungs of society, Southern New England Indians struggled to make a living in various sectors of colonial society. At the same time, they fought to keep family members together on what homelands they had left. Many Indians who remained on their lands turned to animal husbandry and farming. At Natick, Mashpee, and on Martha's Vineyard, Indians grew crops, raised livestock, and cut timber to trade in local markets. Land, then, remained central to community identity.

Religion, Education, and Indian Sovereignty

Missionaries, churches, and schools all served a variety of purposes among Southern New England Indians in the eighteenth century. Christian missionary efforts had long focused on Natick, Mashpee, and Martha's Vineyard, and Christianity became central to their lives. How could it have been otherwise? Religion infused every facet of New England life—government, community structures, homes, and schools. Indian ministers and school teachers labored hard within their communities. They provided a bulwark of Indian-Christian leadership, made Protestant precepts and practices and the English language palatable to Indian audiences, and used networks with Anglo-Americans and missionaries to stabilize communities on their lands. By 1757, the newly appointed Anglo-American minister Gideon Hawley and a Wampanoag preacher, Solomon Briant, together administered Mashpee's church and school. The Mashpees reached outside their community for assistance, believing Hawley might serve as a broker in legal disputes involving the government and appointed guardians—local men who seemed to care more for white interests than Mashpee sovereignty. When the Massachusetts General Court continued to ignore Mashpee legal petitions, the community went one step further. They sent a Native American school teacher, Reuben Cognehew, to England to bring the community's grievances before the King's Royal Council. By August of 1760, the Royal Council asserted its authority over Massachusetts in the case of the Mashpees and demanded that they resolve the guardianship issue. By 1763, the Mashpees managed their own acreage and resources and appointed community constables, a clerk, and five overseers, although two of the five had to be local Englishmen. The success of the Mashpees demonstrated that Christianity and education could be used to gain allies within English society, and that those allies could play useful roles in the Indians' struggle for self-preservation. It further demonstrated the extent to which those native to New England had accepted an identity separate from their ancestors.

PROFILE

The Transient Life of Sarah Gardner, Indian Woman

Sarah Gardner was born on January 16, 1730. Her father Thomas Gardner was an Indian man, perhaps a Narragansett, who lived in Warwick, Rhode Island. At an early age, Sarah was indentured to work and live in the home of David Greene, one of the more prosperous English settlers in Rhode Island.

Once she completed her indenture, Sarah Gardner began her own household in Providence, Rhode Island, and sought to establish financial independence within Providence. By the 1770s, she had 12 children. Town officials, however, saw Gardner, and all other Indian women, perhaps widowed or who had children out of wedlock, as a threat to the public good because they did not depend upon men for care. She was forced out of the town five times. Threats of whipping did not dissuade a woman desperate for local ties of friendship and employment. Town officials viewed Gardner and her family of Indian children as part of the colony's roving poor. Gardner, however, had created community networks with other women of color in Providence, and she always traveled with her children and grandchildren. Gardner's story, buried in town council records, reveals the hardships Indian women faced in a growing colonial economy in which Indian men were fewer and fewer in number, and Indian women moving from town to town struggled to find the means to feed their families.

The same religion and education that were intended to make Indians more "civilized" also united various native peoples in their efforts to resist the most pernicious effects of colonization. Samson Occom (Mohegan, 1723–1792) was perhaps the most famous Native American evangelist. His acceptance of Christianity was inspired by the teaching of radical evangelist Reverend James Davenport and by the emotional revivalism of the **Great Awakening**. From 1743 until 1747 he studied under Eleazar Wheelock at Wheelock's Moor's Indian Charity School, and in 1749 Occom became schoolmaster and minister to the Montauk tribe on Eastern Long Island with support from the London Society for the Propagation of the Gospel. This work paid little; indeed, for years he lived in poverty, but Occom's evangelizing attracted attention. The Presbytery of Long Island ordained him in 1759. Under the charge of Wheelock, in 1761 and again in 1763 Occom preached among the Oneida Iroquois in New York. At the end of 1765, he undertook a journey to England to raise funds for Wheelock's Indian school. Backed by the famous Great Awakening evangelist George Whitefield and the Second Earl of Dartmouth, Occom secured £12,000 for the new school.

Occom left Wheelock's fold and became an itinerant preacher among the various tribes of New England. By the 1760s, he hatched a plan to unite Montauks and other dispossessed Indians in a new native Christian community to be known as Brothertown in Oneida territory in New York. His own personal experience showed him that Native Americans were not, and would not be, fully accepted in the larger white society. He himself had been denied teaching or ministerial positions in mainstream, white settings although those positions had been vacant for some time. Occom understood well the difficulties faced by acculturated, or semi-acculturated Native Americans. Brothertown was intended to serve as a base of support for them. Moreover, Occom believed there was an obligation to move beyond Christian oratory and directly apply the values of Christianity to real life situations. Brothertown was Christianity in action, serving the needs of others. At the same time, a self-sustaining native community allowed for some preservation of native cultures, values, and independence. In his autobiography, *A Short Narrative of My Life*, Occom stated that his mission was to preserve native autonomy and identities. As Occom noted, "in the face of upheaval, men, women, and children from the Montaukett, Mohegan, Pequot, Narragansett, Niantic, and Farmington communities met at Mohegan . . . to envision for themselves a new future; a new pan-tribal settlement to be called 'Brotherton,' united around principles of self-determination and Christian worship."

5.1 *Samson Occom, the Reverend, sits and reads his bible.*

Source: Courtesy of Wikimedia Commons

READING HISTORY

Samson Occom Tells His Story, 1768

Samson Occom, the literate, ordained Indian minister of New England, was also a writer. In the selection here, he tells part of his life story. Historians have very few published writings by Native Americans from the eighteenth century. This adds to the significance of his writings. As they are textual productions of a literate Indian, they represent the melding of Indian and white cultures.

I was Born a Heathen and Brought up In Heathenism till I was between 16 & 17 Years of age, at a Place Calld Mohegan in New London Connecticut, in New England,—my Parents Livd a wandering life, so . . . did all the Indians at Mohegan; they Chiefly Depended upon Hunting Fishing & Fowling . . . for their Living and had no Connections with the English, excepting to [Traffic] with thim, . . . in their Small Trifles,—and they Strictly maintain'd and follow'd their Heathenish Ways, Customs & Religion—tho' there was Some Preaching among them . . . , once a Fortnight, in ye Summer Season, a Minister from N London used to Come up and the Indians . . . to attend, not that they regarded the Christian Religion. But they had Blankets given to them every Fall of the Year and for these things they would attend,—and there was a Sort of a School kept, when I was quite young, but I believe there never was one that ever Learnt to read any thing,—and when I was about 10 Years of age there was . . . a man who went . . . about among the Indian Wigwams, and where ever he Could find the Indian Child, . . . would make them read—but the . . . Children Used to take Care to Keep out of his way;—and he Used to Catch me Some times and make me Say over my Letters, and I believe I learnt Some of them. . . . But this was Soon over too—and all this Time there was not one amongst us, that made a . . . Profession of Christianity—Neither did we Cultivate our Land, nor . . . kept any Sort of Creatures except Dogs, Which We Used in Hunting; and Dwelt in Wigwams. These are a Sort of Tents, Covered with Matts, . . . made of Flags—And to this Time we were . . . unacquainted with the English Toung in general tho there were a few, who understood a little of it. . .

From the Time of our Reformation till I left Mr Wheelock—

When I was 16 years of age, we heard a Strange Rumor among the English, that there were Extraordinary Ministers Preaching from Place to Place and . . . a Strange concern among the White People—this was in the Spring of the Year. But we Saw nothing of these things, till Some Time in the Summer, when Some Ministers began to visit us and Preach . . . the Word of god; and the Common People also Came frequently . . . and exhorted us to the things of god, which it pleased the Ld, as I humbly hope, to Bless and Accompany . . . with Divine Influences, to the Conviction and Saving Conversion of a Number of us; Amongst which, I was one that was Imprest with the things, . . . we had heard. . . . These Preachers did not only Come to us, but we frequently went to their meetings and Churches. Constantly, after I . . . was convicted, I Went to all the meetings, I Could Come at; & . . . Continued under Trouble of Mind about 6 months, . . . at which time I began to Learn the English Letters; got me a Primmer and Used to go to my English Neighbours frequently for Assistance in Reading, but went to no School, . . .—And When I was 17 years of age, . . . I had as I trust, a Discovery of the way of Salvation through Jesus, and was enabl'd to put my trust in him alone for Life & Salvation.

Source: Samson Occom, "Autobiographical Narrative, Second Draft [September 17, 1768]," in Joanna Brooks, *The Collected Writings of Samson Occom, Mohegan* (New York: Oxford University Press, 2006), pp. 52–53.

Questions

1. Why does Occom describe himself as a "heathen"?
2. Describe Occom's view of the world.

A Mid-Atlantic Frontier

Unlike the colonies of New England, Pennsylvania began as a proprietor colony when the crown granted the land in 1681 to the Quaker, William Penn, to start an overseas colony. William Penn envisioned a "peaceable kingdom," one in which local Indians would live side by side with colonists. But in reality, concerns over land ownership resulted in many disputes among the proprietors (Penn's land grantees and associates), migrant settlers, and Indians. By the mid-eighteenth century, Penn's plans had floundered, and his heirs had swindled most of the land from the largest tribal group, the Delawares. The deceit of Penn's sons made the Delawares almost completely subordinate to the wishes of the colonial government and forced many of them west. Some even moved out of Pennsylvania. In the end, proprietor claims to lands and settler migration on the mid-Atlantic frontier integrated Pennsylvania into the British imperial system.

Delawares and the Quest for Land

Integration of Pennsylvania into the British imperial system of land ownership resulted from a complex set of intercultural relations. Oral tradition speaks of the Delawares as a migratory people, coming from "beyond the

TIMELINE 5.1 THE NORTHEAST IN WAR AND PEACE, 1630–1765

Date	Event
1630	Smallpox opens Deerfield land for settlement
1670	First settlement of Deerfield
1686	Reverend John Williams arrives in Deerfield with his family
1704	The French and Indian raid on Deerfield
1713	Treaty of Utrecht brings some peace to the New England frontier
1715–1763	Southern New England Indians begin to create their own proprietorships on their lands
1759	Ordination of Samson Occom
1765	Occom travels to England to raise funds for Indian education at Moor's Charity School
1700–1765	New England Indians take jobs as servants, sailors, and traders in an expanding imperial economy

Father of the Waters." When met by Penn, the Delawares were a tribal grouping that subsumed the Munsees, Unulachtigos, Unamis, and Lenni Lenapis, and they were the dominant native peoples in Pennsylvania. In the 1720s, English, German, and Scots-Irish folks migrated into Pennsylvania and jostled for land with the Delawares. Euro-Americans spread rapidly west and north from the forks of the Delaware River and demanded more land from the Indians. As they migrated, settlers pressured the Delaware for more land. Sometimes settlers purchased land rights from Indians or Pennsylvania proprietors; sometimes they made no effort to purchase land legally and simply squatted on Delaware land tracts.

After William Penn's death in 1718, his sons Richard and John fought for legal rights to their father's proprietorship. Around this time, native villages formally recognized and protected by Penn morphed into refugee communities for other Algonquian, Iroquoian, and Siouan dialect speakers displaced by English settlement across the colony and region. Indeed, Pennsylvania became home to a mixed lot. By the 1730s, the contest over land further strained intercultural relations among white settlers, proprietors, and local Indians. Penn's sons successfully secured proprietary rights to Pennsylvania and then schemed for land near the Delaware River, just north of Philadelphia. In 1734, two Delaware chiefs, Nutimus and Tishcohan, met with the Penn brothers. At the center of the discussion was a 1686 treaty, purportedly signed by Delaware leaders who had assured Penn's clear title to the desired land. An emergent Delaware leader by the name of Teedyuscung arrived at the meeting in 1735. He railed against the treaty's inclusion of Indian lands near the forks of the Delaware River as the Delawares had never received proper payment for the land supposedly conveyed in the 1686 treaty. According to Teedyuscung, the Delawares never were "paid for the Lands they agreed to sell."

Teedyuscung refuted forcefully the Penns' land claims; however, the Iroquois Covenant Chain's supposed subordination of the Delawares and threats of the cessation of trade convinced Delaware leaders to ratify the 1686 treaty. The Iroquois recognized the value of the contested land and did not want to give it up themselves. An Onondaga leader, Canassatego, argued, "We know our lands are now become more Valuable . . . but we are sensible the lands are everlasting and the few goods we receive are soon Worn out and Gone." According to proprietorship claims, the 1686 treaty had a provision that would cede land "as far as a man could walk in a day and a half." Under duress, Nutimus and Tishcohan agreed to the **Walking Purchase**, which concluded in September 1737. They ultimately relinquished 1,200 square miles as runners and surveyors, rather than walkers, measured the land in question. The sale politically subordinated the Delawares, many of whom the Iroquois forced off the acreage into western lands. Some Indians fought to stay in the Delaware Valley region, even converting to Christianity under the ministerial charge of the Presbyterian missionary, David Brainerd, who also preached among Delawares in New Jersey. Conversions might have been true or simply a practical method for remaining on the land. The status of the non-migrant Delawares among white settlers remained problematic. In the Pennsylvania backcountry, moreover, settlers and displaced Delawares and other tribes soon developed intercultural relationships that were tenuous at best.

The Pennsylvania Backcountry

In the post-Walking Purchase climate, the Delawares sought new ways to achieve community stability in a multicultural world. Western-moving Delawares formed economic, social, and cultural relations with German and Scots-Irish settlers. Confusion often resulted. Delawares negotiated fictive kinship alliances; they brought Euro-Americans into relationships through ritual and ceremony, binding traders and farmers to names of kinship such as "brother" or "cousin." Euro-Americans, however, generally misunderstood the symbolism and obligations Indians attached to such terms. Euro-American economics was not about reciprocal exchange to benefit larger communities, but about the accumulation of personal wealth to benefit immediate family members. Nonetheless, Indians and settlers negotiated trade and land agreements and tried to learn the ways of each other. Particularly important to intercultural negotiations was an emergent group of go-betweens, men like Andrew Montour, George Croghan, and Conrad Weiser. These men spoke Indian and European dialects, and at treaty tables, trading posts, and Indian villages they worked to maintain the peace in Penn's woods. Indian women were also successful at negotiating intercultural relations. A Scots-Irish man noted that he was "adopted into a great family, and now received with great seriousness and solemnity in the room and place of a great man." The Indians reminded him that "you are now one of us by an old strong law and custom." Scots-Irish fur traders were integrated into native communities through the matrilineal rules of Pennsylvania Indians, and native women extended economic and social ties to Euro-American communities through matrilineal rules of kinship networking and hospitality.

Euro-Americans, nonetheless, continued to operate within a larger economic market of empire that conflicted with the local face-to-face kinship rules guiding Indian economic behavior. Scots-Irish traders raised prices with the market and sometimes mistreated their Indian neighbors in times of exchange. But as long as disputes remained confined to local people, villages, and Euro-American towns, Indians and settlers managed to sort out their problems. Scots-Irish and German settlers even entered council ceremonies and began to make more sense of the kinship system that was so important to local native peoples. Even so, the influence of the imperial market in land and trade goods subsumed many native peoples. And by the 1740s and 1750s, Delawares understood and resented their new position in a hostile imperial world of market-oriented trade, political dominion, and land possession. With fresh memories of deceit and rightly concerned for their future, Delawares began struck back against their European neighbors, attacking homes and farms and joining with the French once the Seven Years' War erupted, believing a French victory would net Indians greater respect and a better economic deal.

The Indians' "Great Awakening" in Pennsylvania

The **Moravians** and the Great Awakening of the 1740s are not usually associated with one another; however, the German-immigrant sect established mission posts that sparked Christian revivals among Pennsylvania's Indians. In Hernhut, Saxony, a German pietist, Count Nicholas von Zinzendorf, brought the Moravians together in a more organized fashion, and in Pennsylvania he founded Bethlehem as the Moravian hub. Under the leadership of August Gottlieb Spangenberg, Moravian missionaries established a chain of mission towns along the Pennsylvania frontier. David Brainerd and other Presbyterian revivalists continued their own separate work in Pennsylvania and New Jersey, but the Moravians presented a more welcoming approach to Indian conversion and consequently had a much deeper impact on Pennsylvania's multiethnic Indian communities. From the Moravian mission perspective, conversion offered Indians the chance to enter into a peaceful and loving relationship with Christ. Baptism and devotion did not demand any knowledge of scriptures, but only a dedication from the heart to Christ's love. This stood in sharp contrast to other Christian conversion efforts in British North America. Their success spread to the Mohican community of Shekomeko, New York, but it also spilled south to the Susquehanna River Indians and farther west. Between the 1740s and 1760s, Moravians established five mission towns, with Delawares and Mahicans comprising most of the converts. With the help of baptized Mahicans, for example, Moravians built the town of Gnadenhütten, which became the cornerstone of the Moravian mission program in Pennsylvania.

PROFILE

Andrew Montour: The Frontier Negotiator

Andrew Montour was the son of Madame Montour, a prominent negotiator among Pennsylvania, New York, and the Iroquois, and Carondawana, a prominent Oneida chief. Andrew gained recognition as a negotiator between the 1740s and 1760s because of his ability to speak many Iroquois and Algonquian dialects. He first worked among the Delawares at Shamokin and traveled with Count Nicholas von Zinzendorf, the founder of the Moravian religious sect, to negotiate with the Iroquois. At the Logstown treaty conference in 1752, Montour interpreted for the Ohio Company (a group of wealthy Virginia land speculators looking to gain land in the Ohio Country), Virginia, and the Ohio Iroquois, particularly the Senecas. His tireless efforts behind the scenes convinced the Indians to give some land to the Ohio Company.

Constant work took a toll on Montour's personal life. Frequent travel, debt, and hard drinking probably ruined his first marriage to the granddaughter of a Delaware chief. By 1750, as tensions in the Ohio Country mounted between Indian villagers and the colonists, Pennsylvania employed Montour full-time to negotiate with the Shawnees, Miamis, Delawares, and the Iroquois. At the same time, he remarried, this time to an Oneida woman named Sarah Ainse. During the Seven Years' War, he served George Washington as a negotiator. His ties of friendship and kinship with the Iroquois and other groups around the Ohio River proved invaluable.

He had close relationships with the Oneida chief Scarouday, the Ohio Indians who supported the English and the Pennsylvania colonists on the frontier. Scarouday gave Montour the name *Eghisara* (no translation). Montour retired to live among the Six Nations but continued to serve as a key negotiator. Among the Six Nations, mounting debt and drinking resulted in more personal problems for Montour. Upon his death in 1772, his wife Sarah returned to live among the Oneidas. Still, Montour's ability to move among several worlds illustrated the need for such men to build relationships between native peoples and the British Empire.

Moravian mission work involved Christian proselytizing, but many Indians who remained within the Walking Purchase's boundaries used Moravian conversion to buttress political and cultural alliances. The Moravians purchased Nazareth from the Anglican evangelist, George Whitefield. Tishcohan, one of the signers of the Walking Purchase, at first distrusted the new Moravian presence and refused to leave his native lands. He argued that his conversion to Presbyterianism under David Brainerd allowed his residency among white settlers. Pennsylvania's proprietors refused to recognize his claims to autonomy as a Presbyterian Indian. Tishcohan and his followers soon found themselves trading and engaging with Moravians out of necessity. The greater contact the Indians had with the Moravians, the more they came to see this religious sect as one that sincerely valued and promoted peace and harmony. Members of Tishcohan's kin group converted under the charge of Moravians and many settled into a Christian life at Gnadenhütten. There was another reason for the move. With proprietors and settlers pushing onto Delaware lands, the Moravian mission towns provided Indians safe havens to rebuild kin and community networks. Life at Gnadenhütten allowed the Delawares to remain closely connected with their homelands—to their traditional identity—as they established peaceful cultural and social alliances with local whites. All of this is not to say that all Indian conversions were

5.2 Baptism of Indians in America. David Zeisberger, a Moravian missionary, preaches to the Delawares. This image, with some Delawares interested in Zeisberger and others not, demonstrates how Christianity divided some mid-Atlantic native communities.

Source: Library of Congress Prints and Photographs Division, LC-DIG-pga-02638

insincere. Many Indians may have truly devoted themselves to the faith as adapted from the missionaries in times of despair.

Moravian mission towns were unique places in the Pennsylvania backcountry because many Indians and Moravians established a special religious common ground. Indians shared dream experiences with Moravian brethren and sisters in an overlapping form of religious expression. Dream quests were common practice among Algonquian- and Iroquoian-speakers, but in Moravian mission towns, some Indian dreams contained Christian elements. One Mahican Indian with the Christian name Joshua remembered his dream in which "many Indians asked him to say something to them about his God." He spoke about "the Lamb who was hung on the Cross for their sins" and shared the story of Christ's blood. For Delaware and Mahican men, hunting still was a spiritual activity, but at mission towns like Meniolagomekah, missionaries taught Protestantism in Indian hunting lodges. Christianized Indians accepted the supernatural power of Christ's body and blood. Blood carried different significance among native men and women, and both discovered a new source of sacred power in images of Jesus's crucifixion and the blood that dripped from his side. To native men, blood symbolized male honor and prestige as hunters. For Delaware and Mohican women, Moravian images of Christ's blood brought them closer into the Moravian fold, as they drew corollaries between the power Indian women gained from menstrual blood and the blood of Jesus. For both, the blood of Christ

READING HISTORY

Esther: a Mahican-Moravian

A Lebenslauf, or life story, written about a new convert, was a common practice among the Moravians. An individual's Lebenslauf discussed what events precipitated a person to seek salvation. The Moravians had Indians who were working toward full conversion write down their own Lebenslaufs. They are rich sources about how Native Americans could be native and Christian at the same time.

Esther, a Mahican. The second wife of Delaware chief Memenowal/Augustus. Lived in Meniolagomekah.

March 5, 1794. "Tonight around 2 o'clock Brother and Sister Mack were called to the sick Esther. She was faint of heart, understood us all the same and was happy that we visited her. Augustus was there, as well as the Indian sisters Sarah, Bathseba, Rahel. Esther, who, for 3 nights watched and attended to her. Since Esther was in her 4th month of pregnancy, they assumed, she would deliver, which happened in a half hour after that. The child soon began to cry, the mother asked how soon it could be baptized, after all, it might not live long. Brother Josua also came to us, Augustus said: yes what my dear Esther said about the baptism of my child, that I also ask. It was small, but truly perfect and cute, looking around at all. Brother Martin baptized it 'Esther' in the death of Jesus. The sisters who were present consecrated it. Sister Sarah told Esther that now her child was baptized, she said: I thank you, dear Savior. Soon after she pulled Sarah to her and said: Soon, soon, I will die and kiss the wounds, which immediately came to pass."

March 8, 1754. "At mid-day was the burial of our Sister Esther. She appeared truly respectable. All the brothers and sisters were surprised by her kindness, as she also had her child in arm, which passed away this morning. Brother Augustus had bought her a white linen cloth, with which Anna had made a burial dress. Several of the unbaptized, whose eyes filled with tears, also paid a visit to the body."

Source: Jane T. Merritt, translator. *At the Crossroads: Indians and Empires on a Mid-Atlantic Frontier: 1700–1763* (Chapel Hill: University of North Carolina Press, 2002), p. 322.

Questions

1. What does this account say about conversion to the Moravian faith?
2. Should we view Indian conversions with an amount of skepticism?
3. Can we learn more about native life from such conversion accounts besides the religious experience?

seemed to provide true life-sustaining powers. Some Delaware and Mahican men and women gained leadership positions within the Moravian mission system. Indians adapted in many ways to life in Moravian towns, in terms of marriage, baptism, and Moravian settlement patterns. At the same time, Indians kept hold of networks of kinship and friendship that cut across the borders of Moravian mission towns and Indian villages.

And yet there were many Delawares and Mahicans who remained suspicious of the Christian missions, dividing some families into factions. One Nanticoke Indian, who believed in different worlds for Indians and whites, noted that "to the brown people he gave the sacrifice," but "to the white people he had given the Bible." Both people should never "go the same way." Traditional religious healers among Indians felt

TIMELINE 5.2 THE MID-ATLANTIC FRONTIER, 1681–1760

Date	Event
1681	Land grant to William Penn to start colony of Pennsylvania
1720s–1740s	Massive influx of Scots-Irish and German settlers to the Pennsylvania backcountry
1737	Walking Purchase concluded
1740s–1760s	Peak of Moravian mission work in Pennsylvania providing safe havens to Delawares and other Indians

particularly threatened by the spiritual powers Moravians claimed to possess and became sources of conflict as they challenged Christian teachings. Nonetheless, during the height of Moravian mission activities in the 1740s and 1750s, Pennsylvania Indians found new places of intercultural relations that kept conflict and violence in the backcountry at bay while Britain tightened its imperial hold over the region.

Multitribal Zones and Imperial Pressure in the South

By 1700, native peoples of the Southeast (including present-day South Carolina, North Carolina, Florida, Georgia, parts of northern Alabama, and Tennessee) consisted of groups who spoke Muskogee, Siouan, and Iroquoian dialects. Trade opportunities with European settlers, particularly with the English, often united Indians of small and dispersed villages into larger trade communities. By the eighteenth century, the Upper and Lower Creeks, for instance, had formed a loosely organized Creek Confederacy and established a powerful presence in the South, especially once they built strong connections to English trade. Groups of Creeks dispersed along the headwaters of the Coosa and Tallapoosa rivers in upper Alabama to form the Upper Creek towns. Principal trade towns for the Lower Creeks emerged along the Chattahoochee River in present-day Georgia. Among both Upper and Lower Creeks, the most important Muskogee towns, or *talwas*, were Coweta, Cussutia, Tuckabatchee, and Okfuskee. Cherokees in parts of present-day Georgia, North Carolina, and Tennessee also commanded power based in their four principal regional town settlements—the Overhill Towns, the Valley settlements, the Middle settlements, and the Lower Towns. "Settlement Indians," who lived closest to South Carolina's plantation system, were mostly members of the dispersed smaller tribes, but many of these groups joined the Catawba. Access to trade was the source of power, influence, and violence among Southeast Indian towns and villages, as it was for all native groups across British and French North America. Indians jockeyed to position themselves in a vast frontier network of displaced peoples and imperial trade rivalries. Competition for trade often pitted Indians against other Indians. Europe's wars of empire also ensnared Native Americans in the web of English and French alliances. Trade and war may have benefited tribes early in the century, but within one or two generations there was little left that resembled the power, the depth, and the expanse of Native America prior to European contact. The outbreak of a series of wars demonstrated the degree to which imperial commerce forced Native Americans into positions to defend local villages and towns and intertribal affairs.

Trading Slaves and Deerskins

English trade networks spanned the Southeast but centered on Charleston, South Carolina. When the English settled South Carolina in the 1670s, they entered a world already rife with imperialism and native competition. The Spanish mission system of La Florida, as discussed in Chapter 3, had extended a spiritual-military and bureaucratic system from St. Augustine on the coast, inland to the Timucua, and north into Southern Georgia. The English competed with the Spanish, brokering deals for Indian goods that undercut the Spanish.

Intense trade rivalries among diverse Indian groups surfaced soon after the founding of Charleston, rivalries often prodded by Charleston traders who saw in these contests opportunity to realize even higher returns. English-manufactured goods in demand by Southeast Indians were the same as those desired by Native Americans farther north—guns, metal tools, printed fabrics, housewares, and liquor. In exchange for these, Indians supplied the English with deerskins and slaves. Trade always returned the greatest profits to the English, but European wares invariably elevated power and influence among those natives actively engaged in trade. The Westos Indians served as key brokers between South Carolina traders and Indians of the interior and emerged as the primary suppliers of Indian slaves captured from Spanish provinces in the late seventeenth century. According to one Carolinian, the Westos and other raiding Indians sold "Indian prisoners" who were "enemies to the said Indians." But, in addition to payment for the captives, the Westos expected a steady flow of gifts to their community and to individuals. This became expensive for the English. The Kussoe Indians (Algonquian), conversely, despised the English trade, probably because they feared the effect of English competition on their long-time trade relationship with the Spanish. Carolina traders went to war with them because the Kussoes promised to side with the Spanish "to cut off the English people in this place." By the mid-1670s, the Kussoes who lived in "no certain abode" suffered defeat, allowing the English to continue their trade with "the more friendly sort of Indians." At the same time, the Guale Spanish mission province collapsed under the weight of attacks from Indians supplied with muskets from the English. Charleston leaders also firmed up trade alliances with Yamasees who devastated the mission provinces. Long tied to the Spanish mission system, native peoples in the Southeast now adjusted their settlement and trade patterns in the wake of English settlement.

The trade in deerskins was especially lucrative because of stunning investment of human energy and materials from both sides of the cultural divide. Between 1700 and 1715, for example, 54,000 deerskins went out each year from Charleston Harbor. This number increased dramatically among the Creeks, with 152,000 to 200,000 annually from 1740 to 1762. The Creeks in Alabama and Georgia alone delivered 80,000 or more to Charleston and French Mobile between 1739 and 1759. In total, the Cherokee and Creek towns supplied 1.5 million pounds of leather, with an astonishing one million deer killed.

For groups of Creek and Cherokees, the deerskin trade disrupted the pulse of daily life. The skins native women provided went into the hands of young men who then traded with Europeans for tools, cloth, and other items. White traders, who saw the benefits Creek women provided to their men in the deerskin trade and the massive influx of European trade goods, tried to marry into Creek towns. In Upper Creek country, a group of "settle idle vagrants" were telling "romancing stories to ingratiate themselves among the Indians to procure a Livelihood and get an Indian wife." Women and men both benefited from the highly rewarding deerskin trade, although prosperous young men began to assert more and more power and authority in Creek towns. As early as 1749, a British trader observed, "all Head Warriors are Men that bear great sway in their Towns even more than their beloved men." Profitability of the trade in hides for both Indians and settlers in the Carolinas was great, but the depletion of game carried profound, devastating consequences for native peoples across the region.

Native Americans and the Costs of French Expansion into the Lower Mississippi Valley

Similar transformations occurred across the Lower Mississippi Valley, although French colonists never arrived in large numbers in the Deep South. The low density of French settlers provided native peoples with tremendous leverage. Quapaws migrated to the Arkansas River valley and entered an expansive region already occupied by thousands of native peoples. By the eighteenth century, Quapaw diplomacy and trade alliances built a strong friendship that prevented the isolation and depopulation so many other Indian groups experienced. The Osages arrived at the Arkansas River valley from Ohio, and they used their numerical strength, military power, and trade to make themselves the dominant economic brokers between the French-occupied Lower Mississippi Valley and the plains and prairie regions to the north and west. For the French, diplomacy and trade occurred on multiple fronts with the newly arrived Osages and Quapaws in the Arkansas River Valley, and with the Choctaws, Natchez, Chickasaws, and Caddoan speakers who occupied portions of the Lower Mississippi Valley region. A vast regional frontier trade existed as native peoples elbowed with each other and the French for goods and positions of power.

This did not mean that the Lower Mississippi Valley was a peaceful place. Massive displacement, disease, and competition for trade took their toll on the Native American population and resulted in a series of revolts against French occupation of the Lower Mississippi Valley. The Natchez war in the 1720s and 1730s exposed weaknesses within France's multiethnic **"frontier exchange economy,"** one in which outnumbered French colonists nonetheless asserted colonial dominance. Natchez lands were located farther north from the lower Mississippi bottomlands, in a place unaffected by the Mississippi River's flood tides and offering some of the most productive soil in the Louisiana territory. In the Natchez territory, near the French Fort of Rosalie, a group of enterprising Frenchmen in 1726 established two tobacco plantations, and their laborers reflected the racial composition of the region—Indians, African slaves, and Euro-Americans. The plantations and the Natchez quickly forged strong trade relationships. Fort Rosalie's population increased, and as it grew the settlers and merchants developed a lucrative three-way trade among the fort, plantations, and Indian villages. At first, the Natchez welcomed the newcomers, but headmen came to regret the trade in guns, liquor, and cloth that disrupted their communities. More than trade, epidemics of smallpox and influenza swung the feelings of the Natchez from friendship to animosity. In 1721, the largest Natchez village located between two plantations of St. Catherine and White Earth was devastated by smallpox. Because of the triangular trade in the Natchez region, the disease spread rapidly into neighboring villages and cut in half the Natchez population. The once mighty chiefdom of sun worshippers who fended off de Soto was now reduced to a mere five villages.

The crippling imprint of disease and trade infuriated the Natchez. That the negative repercussions on Indians actually aided the French only fueled the growing rage. In 1721, French soldiers at Fort Rosalie killed several Natchez who vented verbally their frustrations and who, it is said, threatened the soldiers. Natchez warriors retaliated with a series of vengeance raids across the region, particularly against French communities and trade routes. The colonial governor assembled a party of 600 French and Indian allies that, in turn, struck Natchez towns. For the next nine years, war raged across the territory before a tenuous peace was reached.

The French found the war to be a convenient vehicle for taking additional Indian lands. Sieur De Chepart received appointment to a command post at Natchez, and from the beginning of his tenure in power he never hid his disdain for native peoples and held no regard for Natchez sovereignty. By 1725, the ongoing war along with the death of two leading Natchez Suns (chiefs), Stung Serpent and his brother, Great Sun, opened the opportunity for De Chepart to force the Natchez off prime acreage in the area. De Chepart wanted to establish his own slave-based tobacco plantation at the Natchez land known as White Earth, and Indian removal was required. Word spread quickly among Indians across the region of French actions against the Natchez homelands, and the Natchez intensified their war. The color red that represented aggressiveness appeared on poles throughout Natchez villages, and warriors painted their faces. The Indians' obvious actions understandably alarmed local settlers who had as yet not been directly threatened by the hostilities, but De Chepart, an arrogant man, ignored their concerns. Several Natchez leaders held face-to-face negotiations with De Chepart. A deal was reached; De Chepart would supply those leaders and their people with guns and ammunition for hunting in exchange for fealty and their tribute of corn and other resources. Incensed, the Natchez slaughtered more than 200 men, women, and children and took captive hundreds more. The personal arrogance and ignorance of one man, along with his greed and presumption of French superiority, fanned the flames of war and cost the lives of hundreds.

The French were determined to purge the Natchez from the Indians' traditional homeland, a move that would ultimately add to French wealth and power in North America. In December of 1729, the governor directed a force of armed slaves commanded by white officers to Chaouachas to destroy that small village of warriors. Some scholars suggest his use of African slaves rather than white Frenchmen to hit the Natchez village was an intentional act of redirecting Indian anger toward Africans, a move that might play well for white settlers. That argument is a very thin one at best. Only weeks later he joined nearby Choctaws with African slaves and 200 French soldiers for an attack on the Natchez forts. The Natchez escaped, pursued by the French across the Mississippi, while the Choctaws returned to their villages. The Choctaws had enslaved some of the Africans taken from the Natchez fort. By the summer of 1730, as the French planned to bring the Natchez war to an end, word of an African slave conspiracy spread throughout the colony. Louisiana's governor, pressed to explain to the crown exactly what had caused the troubles within the colony, lied and blamed all of the problems in French Louisiana on a united Choctaw, Natchez, African, and Chickasaw conspiracy. The fact was that the governor could not control a colony with a small French population challenged by a numerically superior and diverse collection of opponents. The Natchez war was a bloody warning to the French that in the Lower Mississippi Valley, the maintenance of peace would require much more careful management of the complicated political, social, and cultural landscape of the region.

The Choctaws earned respect from their enemies as a formidable military presence in the region and long served French interests in protecting the Lower Mississippi Valley. In the 1740s, the colony's latest governor mustered Choctaw warriors to stop Chickasaw raids and to block Chickasaw-English trade networks. For the Choctaws, the value of war was something different: to exact clan revenge and replenish their population for the lives lost in battle against the Chickasaws and English. War also protected their lucrative trade relationship. As the French applied more pressure on Choctaw warriors to fight, Choctaw society fell into disorder. They sought guns and ammunition for their persistent forays against the Chickasaws who disrupted their traditional spring and summer farming seasons. Around this time, one chief, Shulush Houma (Red Shoes), courted the British for an alliance. Making the bid more practical, the Choctaw resided in close proximity to the colony of Georgia, thus allowing easier and more regular contact between the Indians and English traders. Shulush Houma went as far as to negotiate a peace with the Chickasaws to keep a wide path of trade open with Savannah and the Carolinas. Shulush Houma's actions were inconsistent with traditional Choctaw customs of leadership which expected a leader to first consult with the civil chiefs, war chiefs, and others of the larger Choctaw nation before seeking or initiating such a significant trade arrangement or negotiating a settlement to war.

Shulush Houma's singular effort to abandon the French for the English fractured the Choctaw nation, not so much over his intent but over his breach of traditional protocol. At this time, the Choctaws numbered around 12,000 people in multiple villages within three Choctaw geopolitical units: People of the Six Towns; the Long People, located in the upper territory; and the People of the Opposite Side, living on the eastern side. Jean-Baptiste Le Moyne de Bienville, the new French governor in the 1740s, hoped to resolve the Indians' dissatisfaction with the French and arranged to meet with the multiple village chiefs. About 100 chiefs gathered for the meeting with Bienville at Mobile, a common Indian treaty ground. Bienville's meeting with Choctaw leaders resolved little, but it did temporarily patch the rift in Choctaw-French relations. Nonetheless, Shulush Houma's actions fractured Choctaw unity.

A downward spiral of events soon followed. A series of fierce battles with Chickasaws cost hundreds of Choctaw lives. An outbreak of smallpox concurrently ravaged Choctaw villages, taking the lives of hundreds more. The rising death rate among these natives was exacerbated by rising starvation and malnutrition, the product of fewer Indians available to farm, hunt, and fish for their communities. At the same time, the new governor, Pierre François de Rigaud, Marquis de Vaudreuil-Cavagnal, insisted the Choctaws wage war against the pro-British Choctaw faction led by Shulush Houma. Shulush Houma's desire for guns, cloth, and other goods from British trade now threatened civil war among the Choctaw. Choctaw villagers admonished Shulush Houma for his brazen actions of trying to negotiate with the English and rival Chickasaws, and they openly and loudly proclaimed their allegiance to the French. A young warrior took matters into his own hands, murdering Shulush Houma for the peril he brought to his people.

Civil war could not be avoided. The western district of Choctaws, pro-British and armed with British weapons, exploded in anger. They sought vengeance for the loss of Shulush Houma and war quickly engulfed Natchez, Mobile, New Orleans, and other Euro-American settlements. Slaves fled their plantations as the chaos of war spread, and the colony of Louisiana, as had been the case with the Natchez uprising, again faced the precarious situation of being outnumbered by Indians and Africans. Marooned slaves, Africans who had escaped their plantation owners and resided among Native Americans, took up arms with the Choctaws. In the winter of 1748–1749, pro-French Choctaws presented more than 100 scalps to the governor at Mobile and another 130 scalps the following year, all taken from pro-British Choctaws. The Choctaw war threatened to destroy the colony and its balance of trade. Indians did not simply fade away when the Europeans arrived; they fought back against the newcomers and against each other.

Tuscarora and Yamasee Wars and Breaking with the British

Several factors spawned war between the English and native peoples in the Southeast. Continued slave raids and disease diminished tribal numbers, traders in a competitive imperial market frustrated Indians, and intertribal alliances constrained settler land encroachments. The first major outbreak of violence occurred in North Carolina and was known as the Tuscarora War. The Tuscaroras were an Iroquoian-speaking people and, shortly before the arrival of Englishmen, one of the largest groups in the region. But disease swept through their villages, reducing their population significantly. Tuscaroras often raided nearby Indian villages for captives to sell as slaves to the English; these strikes also proved costly in Tuscarora lives. The English-Indian slave trade always tilted favorably toward the tribal group that secured the greatest number of captives and was willing to sell at lower prices. As a result, tribes that earlier had been hit by the Tuscarora now recognized the weakened status of the Tuscarora people. Power was shifting in the Carolinas. Tribal groups now attacked Tuscarora communities for supplies and captives. "Settlement Indians," such as the Catawba sponsored by the English, carried out several devastating slave raids on the Tuscaroras. Cherokees and Catawba forced the Tuscaroras closer to plantation settlements. The less-numerous Tuscaroras could no longer compete for western hunting grounds and the prized deerskins and saw in this emerging pattern their ultimate exclusion from trade and their own demise as an independent people. In retaliation, Tuscarora warriors, numbering about 500, set out on September 22, 1711, and killed about 60 Britons and 60 Swiss and Palatine migrants living within North Carolina. With little support from Virginia, North Carolina turned to Charleston to help quash the war. Backed by Yamasees, Catawba, and Apalachees, an arrogant John Barnwell accepted the task of marching into Tuscarora country and crushing the Indian uprising. Barnwell described the Yamasees as willing to "live and die with him." In a brash display of South Carolinian imperialism, Barnwell and his native allies pillaged and then torched Indian towns and took Indian captives for the slave trade. His force also nabbed Africans who had previously escaped their white owners and now resided among the Tuscarora. The punishing defeat of the Tuscaroras left them no choice but to sign a peace with North Carolina in 1715. Some Tuscarora survivors continued their residency on traditional lands but under the stern control of English overseers. A few fled into the West, avoiding Cherokee and Catawba Indians and taking root with other, more receptive native peoples. The greatest exodus of Tuscaroras traveled north, entering lands of the Iroquois Confederacy, where they were eventually embraced and included into the fold, changing the Five Nations into the Six Nations.

Little time elapsed before the Yamasee realized that alliances with the English were, at best, only temporary affairs. Trouble first surfaced in the realm of trade. English traders in the Carolinas were notoriously deceptive, increasing prices at will and routinely undervaluing the deerskins and other items Indians hauled to market. The Yamasees bore the brunt of this pattern of trade once war with the Tuscarora ended. "Did their friendship and alliance with the English mean nothing?" they wondered. Making the matter even worse, demand for deerskins skyrocketed in Europe. The exceptionally lucrative returns for deerskins drew native hunters into the Carolinas from as far away as the Iroquois Confederacy, and tribes native to the Southeast expanded their hunting range into Yamasee territory. Competition among Indians became fierce. Backcountry planters complicated these developments as they encroached into prime hunting grounds, disrupting the hunt for deer, settling on tribal properties without permission, and demonstrating clearly that the English placed no value on Indian sovereignty. These new realities certainly angered the Yamasee and elicited a call for war from many of them, but the tipping point came when English traders now targeted the Yamasee as a source of Indian slaves. War exploded in the territory in 1715. As one wealthy Virginian noted, the war erupted "in great measure owing to the Carolinians themselves, for their traders ha[d] abused and so imposed upon the Indians." The Yamasee War, as it has been termed, linked the Yamasee with new allies—Catawba, Cherokees, and some Creeks as well as members of lesser tribes from the south and east. All of them experienced the insults and intrusions presented by the English, all of them hoped to improve their positions of trade, and all of them believed that a punishing blow against the English might control British moves in the region. Altogether they attacked British traders, backcountry outposts, and plantation settlements. As late as 1720, Native Americans in South Carolina denied the English any substantial control in the colonial frontier. The alliance faded, but Yamasees and Apalachicolas continued to assault South Carolina settlements for another ten years, while Carolinians sought ways to bolster its frontier diplomacy, fortifications, and trade networks.

The 1730s and 1740s were critical years among Native Americans in the Southeast. The Cherokees on the northern frontier, the Creeks on the western frontier, and the Yamasees on the southern frontier were all internally divided into pro- and anti-British camps over questions of sustaining the deerskin trade. English efforts to spread inland threatened further Indian residency in the region as traditional lands increasingly fell to British control, over-hunting depopulated the deer and other fur-bearing animals, and trade increasingly forged dependency relationships. Natives pushed from coastal areas sought refuge in western tribes, and this often created complications for host communities. The turmoil now confronting native peoples raised the specter of armed conflict among themselves and possibly war with the British. Frontier Indians fortified their villages in preparation against English attack or raids from rival Indians; hostilities certainly erupted, often leaving tribal communities more shattered than before.

In these years the Cherokees, Creeks, and Choctaws surfaced as the most powerful Indian groups within the Deep South. Cherokees fostered kinship relationships with refugee Indians, and extended their positions from North Carolina into the land that would become Tennessee and parts of Georgia. A new generation of leaders such as Dragging Canoe learned how to fight effectively the British in the Carolina wars, and he and his followers used that knowledge successfully in subsequent battles against both English and rival Indians. The Creeks incorporated Shawnees, Yamasees, Alabamas, Natchez, and the multiethnic Florida Seminoles among which there were numerous escaped African slaves. In fact, only about half of the loosely organized

PROFILE

Mary Musgrove: A Creek Woman Between Worlds

Mary Musgrove (also known as Coosaponakeesa) was born around 1700 in the Creek town of Coweta. Her uncle was the most prominent Coweta chief, Brims, but her father was Edward Griffin, a trader out of Charles Town, and her mother a Yamacraw Creek. She moved at a young age to Pon Pon, a village along the Edisto River in South Carolina. Musgrove converted to Christianity and learned to read and write English. Of English and Creek descent, Musgrove spent her life moving between the worlds of the Creeks and the colonists of Georgia.

Musgrove had a unique position within Creek matrilineal society. She was a powerful woman, born into a powerful clan, perhaps the Wind clan, and therefore wielded authority over other Creeks. Her first marriage to John Musgrove, for example, was conducted to keep the peace between the Creeks and the Carolina Commission of Indian Trade, of which John Musgrove was a prominent member. By the 1730s, living in Pon Pon, Mary Musgrove had established herself as an important trader between the Creeks and Georgians. When John Oglethorpe established the Georgia colony on Creek lands, Musgrove negotiated talks between Oglethorpe and the Creeks. She also worked alongside Georgians to recruit Creek warriors against the Spanish, serve in diplomatic affairs, and supply Georgian settlers with beef, corn, peas, potatoes, and other crops Creek women raised in their fields.

In the late 1730s, Oglethorpe requested that Musgrove build a trading post on the Altamaha River, in Georgia. Named Mount Venture, her post soon became a meeting ground for intertribal diplomacy. Mount Venture was a place where war parties departed to fend off the Spanish and provided vital goods to sustain local colonists and Creeks. After the death of her first husband, Musgrove married a Georgian, Jacob Matthews, who once served under her as an indentured servant. Musgrove had accumulated much wealth and property in Georgia under the supervision of Oglethorpe. At her home, she welcomed the most important Creek chiefs and served as a link between Creek leadership and Georgian leadership. When the French built Fort Toulouse among the Creeks along the Alabama River, the Georgians began to fear a Creek-French alliance that would threaten the stability of their colony. Musgrove stood between the Creeks, the French, and the Georgians. When the balance of Georgian power shifted toward Savannah, she again entered into negotiations, giving presents to the Creeks to keep the peace. When a Creek warrior named Acorn Whistler killed some Cherokees outside of Charleston, Musgrove convinced the Creeks to avenge the death through the traditional channels of clan justice to uphold good relations with the English. In 1749, a Creek chief, Malatchi, arrived in Savannah, invited by her cousin Musgrove to come for gifts and to assert her right to her land grants that included St. Catherines island, off the coast of Georgia. The British ignored both Malatchi and Musgrove. This enraged her, and in her anger she proclaimed herself "queen of the Creeks." Her outburst isolated her from the British and many Creeks. Winning her own land grant on St. Catherines island, Musgrove lived out her days petitioning the Georgian government for back pay and goods for her services as an Indian agent to Oglethorpe. Mary Musgrove, or Coosaponakeesa, was a woman who easily crossed between the worlds of the Creeks and Georgians, and her life represents a microcosm of how few borders and boundaries separated Indians from colonists in the Southeast.

Creek Confederacy spoke a Muskogean dialect. Creeks pushed on three arenas, using the connections of their multiethnic newcomers. With the help of the Yamasees' Spanish supporters, Creeks brokered trade and diplomatic relations with Spanish Florida. At the same time, Upper Creek towns located along the Alabama River cultivated relations with the French, while other Creeks still tried to barter with Carolina traders. Georgia's formation as a colony in 1733 only upset a fragile balance that included Carolinian, Spanish, French, and Creek forces. In spite of James Oglethorpe's assurances that their land would be protected under the terms of the 1739 Treaty of Coweta, Creeks began to call the British in Georgia, "Ecunnaunuxulgee": "People greedily grasping at the land of the Red People." Choctaws were also diverse, but similar imperial forces worked to shift Choctaw loyalties. For a long time, Choctaws appeared loyal only to French Louisiana. But Choctaws divided into "Eastern" and "Western" villages to the north, and the "Sixtown" villages to the south.

Extending kinship, altering battle tactics, embracing native refugees and escaped African slaves, and pitting imperial powers against one another altogether aided the Cherokee, Creek, and Choctaw peoples in their pursuit of security and trade. But added to these, each nation already claimed populations far larger than other tribal groups in their respective territories, the spread of disease had proved less devastating among them because of their relative remote location from active trade centers, and trade to date had not created native dependency on the English and Spanish as it had among tribes nearer the coasts. One other benefit these interior peoples generally enjoyed was that of time—although they all encountered English, French, and Spanish explorers in the early seventeenth century, decades passed before Europeans attempted large settlement of their frontier. Time allowed the Cherokee, Creek, and Choctaw opportunity to study and assess the repercussions of European settlement and trade and to consider possible tactics of resistance.

The Southeast suffered frequent warfare through the 1760s. By the time the French and Indian War concluded, trade and warfare had reshaped the geopolitics of the interior. Creeks had pushed farther west into the French fold, many Yamasees had relocated to Florida, and Tuscarora refugees eventually migrated north to become the Sixth Nation of the Iroquois Confederacy. When the confusing state of frontier warfare subsided,

TIMELINE 5.3 MULTITRIBAL ZONES AND CONFLICT IN THE SOUTH, 1670–1740S

Date	Event
1670s	Charles Town, South Carolina, established as leading trader with Indians in the South
	Carolinians begin the Indian slave trade
1700	Multitribal zones take shape in the South
1711	Tuscarora War against Carolina Traders
1715	Yamasee War begins
1720s–1730s	Natchez Wars
1739	Treaty of Coweta; the colony of Georgia tries to establish peace with the Creeks
1730s–1740s	Continued war with the British, now involving Creeks and Cherokees
1742–1750	Choctaw civil war

large portions of the Indians' Southeast had no native peoples, and the Carolina trade economy in Indian slaves had completely collapsed.

The Seven Years' War and Indian Perspectives on Empire

The Ohio Valley was an expansive region that comprised part of New France's *pays d'en haut*. By the 1750s, Indian village life in the *pays d'en haut* had undergone a rapid and dramatic change. Ottawas and other Algonquian peoples from the Great Lakes territory had migrated south to the upper reaches of the Ohio. Into the heartland of the Ohio, Shawnees and Delawares migrated out of Pennsylvania and portions of Virginia. Added to this mix were the long-time resident Miamis and Wyandots. Intertribal associations quickly formed. Polyglot villages of Delawares and Shawnees, and disaffected Iroquois such as Mingos (a motley mobile group of Iroquoian-speakers not formally associated with the Iroquois League) and Senecas were only a few of the diverse peoples that dotted the Ohio Valley. From the perspective of the Indians who now called the region home, the Ohio River valley was attractive because the Iroquois Confederacy was less dominating and the colonial powers in New York, Pennsylvania, and Virginia held less influence there. In fact, the Iroquois Confederacy appeared more factionalized than unified, as was indeed the case. Senecas, the "Keepers of the Western Door," pushed their interests toward the French. But at Onondaga Castle where the League council fires burned in central New York, the ideal of the Covenant Chain alliance with the British still held sway among most Iroquois. The Iroquois had splintered into pro-British, pro-French, pro-Pennsylvania, and anti-Pennsylvania camps to the point that Iroquois League power in Ohio was substantially diminished.

Prompted by Pennsylvania and Virginia traders entering the Ohio Country, New France constructed a chain of outposts in the region. Led by Pierre-Joseph Céloron de Blainville, France enforced its claims to the territory and in 1754 built Fort Duquesne, near present-day Pittsburgh. A Virginia militia expedition to check French movements led by a young and brash George Washington failed miserably. Washington lost his first military engagement near the Great Meadows at Fort Necessity to a French expedition commanded by Louis Coulon de Villiers. In 1755, British redcoats under General Edward Braddock were also unsuccessful in their challenge to the French presence. These initial confrontations were the extension of a global war known as the Seven Years' War—a war known in the colonies as the French and Indian War.

Many Indians in the Ohio quickly sided with the French father, Onontio. The legacy of English actions against native peoples east of the Appalachians and new demands from English colonists for Indians to abandon lands in the Ohio underpinned their decision. Armed by the French, displaced Delawares and Shawnees raided the Virginia and Pennsylvania frontiers. Joint war parties killed settlers and burned homes. A Quaker tradition of pacifism had clearly left the province unprepared to defend its frontier borders. The Treaty of Easton in 1758 was an attempt to negotiate new political alliances and establish peace, but animosity had grown so deep that miscommunication dominated the proceedings. Teedyuscung, Delaware, pressed grievances over the Walking Purchase as he used the proper condolence ceremony to clear the throats, eyes, and ears of Quaker and Pennsylvania proprietor representatives so they might heed his words.

The English also used the language and rituals of Indian diplomacy to assert their own claims for autonomy and security. Pennsylvania turned to the Iroquois Confederacy to keep the Delawares and Shawnees in check, as the Iroquois reminded the Delawares at Easton of their role as "women." But the Six Nations could not control Delaware and Shawnee militancy. In councils, Quakers and proprietary adversaries accused each other of being responsible for the frontier bloodshed, as the language of metaphor and symbolism in Indian councils no longer kept the peace in Pennsylvania.

Frustrated by a lack of effective leadership, vigilante militias of Scots-Irish settlers took matters into their own hands, "demonizing the Delawares" and striking relentlessly at their villages. The killings along the

Pennsylvania frontier graphically displayed the intimate and personal feelings of animosity shared by both Indians and settlers, parties who used to share common space and worked to keep the peace. Militia brutality was met with equal violence from Native Americans. Indians mutilated the bodies of women, took many whites captives, and singled out farmsteads and households that had broken the fictive ties that once sustained Pennsylvania's intercultural relations.

Attempts by Carolina and Virginia traders to firm up trade alliances with both Creeks and Cherokees brought the Seven Years' War to the Southeast. Although themselves divided into pro- and anti-British factions, the Creeks collectively pursued a policy of neutrality and managed to avoid another devastating war. The Cherokees, on the other hand, could not forge a middle ground. Six hundred Cherokees from the "Overhills" towns traveled to Fort Toulouse in 1756 to court an alliance with the French. A smaller number of Cherokees fell to the pressure of the British and joined expeditionary forces against rival native peoples. More importantly, years of poor trade and land encroachment stained the relationship between the Cherokees and the British to the point of war. Stifled trade from the north provided few muskets and shot upon which Cherokee warriors had become dependent. A new governor of South Carolina, William Henry Lyttelton, sent three strikes against Cherokee towns in a preemptive move against a potential Cherokee invasion of the Carolinas. After the second attack, the Cherokees leveled major counterattacks on both the Carolina and Virginia frontiers. Cherokee warriors, in particular, laid siege to key Carolina interior forts. In 1761, Lyttelton responded, sending 2,600 British regulars and provincial soldiers into the Cherokee interior, razing approximately 15 Cherokee villages. Forced to reconcile at year's end, the Cherokee leader Little Carpenter (Attakullakulla) signed a treaty with the British that turned over a large portion of the Cherokee homelands and acknowledged the sovereignty of the British Empire. With the weakening of French ties to Indians of the Southeast and a concurrent decline in Indian power brought by internal divisions and warfare, the British became the dominant imperial presence in the Southeast.

A similar pattern emerged farther north. In 1757 William Pitt took over the British ministry and funneled additional financial and military resources into the colonies. Supplies, money, and manpower allowed the British to seize Fort Frontenac on Lake Ontario the next year, a strategic move that cut French supply lines into the Ohio Territory. Ohio Indians agreed to peace soon afterwards in the Treaty of Easton (1758), followed by the French withdrawal from Fort Duquesne, renamed Fort Pitt by the British. The war turned against the French, and by default the Indians found themselves in an increasingly precarious position. Should France lose the war, what would become of Ohio natives who had allied against Britain?

Indian alliances with the French proved fragile in this war. While native sympathies across the Ohio territory generally favored the French, longstanding tribal rivalries could not be sustained for the duration of this war. Trade, or the diminishing extent of trade, further complicated matters. The traditional dictum that successful prosecution of war requires *both* the destruction of the enemy's armies *and* his ability to wage war certainly came into play in the French and Indian War. British forces correctly struck at French lines of supply, especially those lines that provided trade goods and weapons to native allies. Without those weapons and goods, enthusiasm for their French alliance and their expectation of victory over the English waned. Moreover, the same reality that allowed the Cherokee, Creek, and Choctaw the power they wielded earlier in the century now tilted in favor of the English—numerical superiority. French and British regular armies in North America may have been at near parity, but both depended heavily on supportive forces. The English colonies during this war had a white population of over two million people, these colonists bolstered further by alliances with native groups. In short, England's manpower potential exceeded that which the French could muster in North America. Too, France placed greater import on the war in Europe itself, keeping the greater amount of supplies and money close to home. The French trans-Atlantic supply line also was targeted by the British Royal Navy, arguably the most powerful naval force on earth at that time. It seemed apparent to many interior Indian groups that the French did not display the level of determination to win as did the English. Still other Native Americans concluded that *both* the French and the English were actually their enemies; it would be self-defeating to aid either power.

The Peace of Paris (1763) shattered the many geopolitical alignments that once existed in Indian Country. Florida, New France, and parts of Louisiana were all ceded to the British Empire. The Choctaws, Chickasaws, Osages, and Quapaws now dealt exclusively with the British. Although New Orleans and trans-Mississippi Louisiana nominally remained in the hands of Spain, there was little doubt the British Empire was the dominant power in North America. It is simple to say that the balance of imperial powers in the Southeast, the Great Lakes, and the Ohio Country that Indians had used to their advantage was gone with the stroke of a pen in Europe; in reality, that ink resulted from years of brutality, terror, and uncertainty. The treaty was a punctuation mark ending one era and ushering another. No longer could Indians hope to play imperial powers and traders against one another. Postwar British Indian policy only worsened the situation. Under the leadership of Commander-in-Chief Sir Jeffery Amherst, the British established a string of outposts to control the fur trade and curtail the sale of weapons and liquor to Indians. In short, the British cut off the rituals and ceremonies of giving gifts that had secured the French presence and that had held together delicate Indian alliances. British forts constructed in the Ohio Valley during war were reinforced and signaled clearly England's permanency in the territory. The British Empire now represented the new power in Indian Country, and it displayed no interest in maintaining the proper balance between imperial motivations and Indian desires for security and autonomy.

The Redefinition of Empire and Racial Consciousness

Some Indians concluded that this new order in North America required drastic measures to secure and preserve what remained. Where Indians and British settlers may have once found some common ground, they now began to "travel two parallel campaigns of ethnic cleansing." For the Ottawa chief Pontiac, the Indian world must be purged of British intruders and British connections. Pontiac, according to historian Gregory Evans Dowd, believed in Ottawa mythology that included stories about the trickster Nanabush. **Nanabush** was a being suffused with sacred powers who brought about creative regeneration, helping replace chaos with harmony. Inspired by this image, Pontiac believed that he, too, might regenerate the Indian world.

Pontiac had another source of spiritual power to draw upon in building a **pan-Indian** union against the British. Connected by their migrant status in the Ohio Valley, Ottawas and Delawares shared rituals, ceremonies, villages, and spiritual tales. In the early 1760s, Neolin, a Delaware prophet, preached a message of Indian rebirth. His visions, in which he spoke with the "Master of Life," taught him that Indians must revive traditional rituals and ceremonies to reclaim balance between the human and sacred realm. Only through the unifying effects of sacred power could native peoples cleanse their villages of Euro-American ways of life and return the people to harmonious order. Central to Neolin's message was the idea of separate creations.

The "Master of Life" had created Indians, Africans, and whites different from one another, which is why he had originally placed them in separate parts of the world. Europeans had intruded into the Indian world. Neolin's message contained an idea of Indian racial consciousness that Pontiac now advanced. But there was another component to Neolin's prophecy. Rampant alcoholism, loss of hunting grounds, and the breakdown of community solidarity were not Euro-American problems but Indian problems. Native peoples had to follow the righteous path set by the "Master of Life," purging themselves of Euro-American trade, customs, behaviors, and religions and, through the spiritual practices of old, reunite as one people. Indians sought to recapture their cultural values and cultural identity by resisting further cultural disintegration—retrench into traditional native structures and regenerate the power and life they possessed prior to the arrival of Europeans.

By May of 1763, and with Neolin's spiritual guidance, Pontiac successfully forged a regional pan-Indian resistance movement and attacked the British-occupied Fort Detroit. Inspired by Neolin's message, Ottawas, Delawares, Shawnees, Senecas, and others swept across the Ohio region, attacking and destroying almost every single fort on the fringe of the British Empire. Within a few months, Indians scorched Britain's frontier, killing hundreds of settlers who had established themselves on the outskirts of both western Pennsylvania and Virginia. British counteroffensives forced Pontiac and his followers to retreat and regroup, but the war that would bear the Ottawa chief's name—Pontiac's War—was over by year's end. An Indian-led attempt to create a separate Indian world free of British interests had failed with the British victory, but the dream Pontiac held lived on into the nineteenth century when another Indian, Tecumseh, called for cultural and spiritual regeneration.

As Pontiac's War drew to a close, British administrators across the Atlantic fashioned a new policy—the Proclamation of 1763. The measure contained diverse objectives for equally diverse reasons, but its imprint on Native America held significant importance. The Proclamation established a line that separated Indian country from white country. This line ran the length of the Appalachian Mountains, from Quebec to west Florida. This line of demarcation established a new imperial interpretation of the Indians' status within the British empire; although residing in territories officially part of Britain, Indians would generally remain autonomous peoples. They were essentially separate peoples, living in the shadowy outskirts of the British Empire. The British were allowed to establish forts along the frontier line, and colonists were not permitted to venture into Indian country (although they did). If the Proclamation of 1763 gives any indication, Anglo-Americans had taken one step toward their own racial vision of separate worlds. One world was for whites only; the other, for Indians.

In the Pennsylvania backcountry, the idea of separate worlds also surfaced among a group of disgruntled Scots-Irish settlers. Provoked by the fear of Indian attack during Pontiac's War and the colonial assembly's inaction on their requests for soldiers and weapons, a group of settlers from the towns of Paxtang (called Paxton) just east of Harrisburg took matters into their own hands. In December 1763, armed men known as the Paxton Boys roamed the Susquehanna River valley in search of enemy Indians. They fell on a small Conestoga village with a fury. These Indians, a mixture of Senecas, Delawares and others, lived under the protection of Pennsylvania's governor, John Penn. But the Paxton Boys as they would be called either failed to realize that the Conestoga had long lived in peace in Pennsylvania and were not part of Pontiac's rebellion or they chose to ignore that reality. Most likely they viewed all Indians as enemies, just as they had "demonized Delawares" purportedly responsible for most of the attacks on backcountry hamlets in the previous years. On December 27, more than 50 Paxtonians struck the Conestogas. They killed six Indians present in the village and took captive another 14, executing all of the captives in the weeks that followed in spite of the government's order

SEEING HISTORY

Neolin's Master of Life

The only image available of Neolin's prophecy is by John McCullough. A captive during Pontiac's war, McCullough, upon his release, wrote down from memory this image of the path to the Master of Life. There are several paths in this image in light of Neolin's prophecy against Euro-American habits.

Questions

1. Which path do you think was the hardest to take and why?
2. What do you think A, B, and C represent?
3. Could the boxes represent something contained within his prophecy, and if so, what?

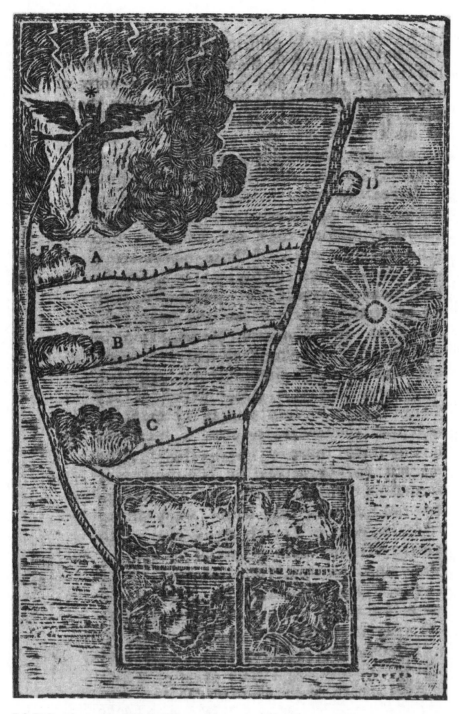

5.3 Delaware prophet Neolin's chart of the paths to the Master of Life.

Source: The Library Company of Philadelphia

TIMELINE 5.4 THE FATE OF EMPIRE, 1754–1763

Date	Event
1754	French build Fort Duquesne
1755	General Edward Braddock fails to defeat the French
1758	British successfully take Fort Frontenac; Treaty of Easton negotiated
1761	Henry Lyttelton strikes the Cherokee towns to try to quell Indian rebellion in the South
1763	Pontiac's War breaks out and the British Proclamation is issued

5.4 There is no known image of Pontiac. John Mix Stanley, the artist of this portait, was a painter and explorer and traveler of the west, and part of a nineteenth-century movement in which artists portrayed living Native Americans in their state of existence but as a "vanishing race." In various portraits, artists like Stanley cast leaders like Pontiac as noble relics of a tragic and violent colonial past.

Source: Courtesy of Library of Congress Prints and Photographs Division, LC-H27-A-4773

of protection. Early the next year the Paxton Boys targeted a village of Moravian Indians near Bethlehem, but these Indians fled their community in advance of the attack and found refuge and government protection in Philadelphia. Early in the new year, roughly 1,000 Paxton Boys marched on Philadelphia, demanding refugee Indians be surrendered. They decried the colonial government for protecting Native Americans while leaving their own hometown virtually defenseless against Indian attack. Only the intervention of reasonable men such as Benjamin Franklin prevented bloodshed. Nonetheless, a vicious pamphlet war ensued in which Paxtonians called all Indians enemies of the British Empire and argued, in vicious racial language, that their removal from the province was necessary. Paxtonians also called for greater representation in the Pennsylvania legislature. Those opposed to the Paxton position envisioned a different world, one in which Indians within the province were "fellow subjects of the king, friends, allies, or even neighbors." Paxtonians were advocates of ethnic cleansing, but, without consensus in Pennsylvania or any other colony, Indian removal on a massive scale was never realized there or anywhere else in colonial America.

Conclusion

In the eighteenth century, imperial rivalries meant shifting patterns of life in Indian Country. The English, French, and Spanish presence had many powerful implications for native peoples east of the Mississippi as traditional loyalties shaped the beliefs, values, and actions of Native Americans as much as those of the subjects of England, France, and Spain. But in the 1750s, with the outbreak of the Seven Years' War, native relations with empires began to erode. War tore across backcountry settlements. By war's end, Britain was the supreme European imperial force in North America. But in instituting relationships with Indians on the frontier that varied greatly from French patterns, British military personnel and English colonists provoked animosity. Colonists supported a strong military presence with forts on the frontier line and refused to offer the necessary gifts and follow proper diplomatic protocol, as land-hungry colonials rushed to the West.

The year 1763 marked a turning point in Native American history. After the Treaty of Paris and subsequent proclamations subordinating Indian status and sovereignty, the British presence appeared secure. The British faced a huge task in governing the trans-Appalachian west and the regions beyond. But the British made a huge mistake when they attempted to "dictate from a position of strength." British policy contributed to the emergence a racial consciousness on both sides of a new cultural divide—a deep-seated hatred imbedded in a new sense of "Indian" versus "white." Intercultural relationships were never the same after 1763.

Review Questions

1. What is "empire," and how did it change over time in different places?
2. Define racial consciousness as it was applied by Native Americans in the eighteenth century.
3. Compare and contrast how different empires were in competition with each other for good relations with various native peoples.

Recommended Readings

Dixon, David. *Never Come to Peace Again: Pontiac's Uprising and the Fate of the British Empire in North America* (Norman: University of Oklahoma Press, 2014). A richly detailed, thorough account of the causes of Pontiac's War and its consequences on both Indians and Englishmen.

Dowd, Gregory Evans. *A Spirited Resistance: The North American Indian Struggle for Unity, 1745–1815* (Baltimore: Johns Hopkins University Press, 1992). The starting point to understanding Neolin and how spiritual prophecies turned into Indian militancy.

Gallay, Alan. *Indian Slavery in Colonial America* (Lincoln, NE: University of Nebraska Press, 2015). A collection of essays that cover the breadth of Native American enslavement in British North America.

Haefeli, Evan, and Kevin Sweeney. *Captors and Captives: The French and Indian Raid on Deerfield* (Amherst: University of Massachusetts Press, 2003). The definitive study of the Deerfield Raid.

Mandell, Daniel R. *Behind the Frontier: Indians in Eighteenth-Century Eastern Massachusetts* (Lincoln, NE: University of Nebraska Press, 1996). A seminal study of New England Indians behind the frontier.

Merrell, James H. *Indians' New World: Catawbas and Their Neighbors from European Contact through the Era of Removal* (Chapel Hill: University of North Carolina Press, 1989). A groundbreaking work that discusses the intercultural relations in the Carolina region.

———. *Into the American Woods: Negotiators on the Pennsylvania Frontier* (New York: W. W. Norton, 1999). A masterful work about the Pennsylvania frontier and the role of cultural negotiators in upholding peace in a potentially violent world.

Merritt, Jane T. *At the Crossroads: Indians and Empires on a Mid-Atlantic Frontier, 1700–1763* (Chapel Hill: University of North Carolina Press, 2003). The best work on the Moravians in Pennsylvania and the collapse of intercultural peace within the colony.

Richter, Daniel K. *Facing East from Indian Country: A Native History of Early America* (Cambridge: Harvard University Press, 2001). An innovative survey of the eighteenth century.

Usner, Daniel, Jr. *Indians, Settlers, and Slaves in a Frontier Exchange Economy: The Lower Mississippi Valley before 1783* (Chapel Hill: University of North Carolina Press, 1992). The standard work on Indian-French relations in the Deep South.

Native American History Online

General Sites

Memoirs of the Reverend David Brainerd; Missionary to the Indians, On the Borders of New York, New Jersey, and Pennsylvania, Chiefly Taken From His Own Diary by Rev. Jonathan Edwards of Northampton County (reprint 1822). http://books.google.com/books?id=SS3WXnQvh1MC Presbyterian minister David Brainerd kept a very rich record of Indian daily life as he preached along the mid-Atlantic frontier.

William M. Darlinton, ed., *Christopher Gist's Journals* (1893). http://books.google.com/books?id=O3QOAAAAIAAJ Excerpts from Christopher Gist's journal at Longstown and other treaties provide a glimpse into the eighteenth-century world of a frontier negotiator and his negotiations.

Benjamin Franklin Howe, ed., *Diary of the Siege of Detroit in the War With Pontiac: Also a Narrative of the Principal Events of the Siege By Major Robert Rogers; a Plan for Conducting Indian Affairs, By Colonel Bradstreet; And Other Authentick Documents, Never Before Printed No. 4* (1860). http://books.google.com/books?id=UYUez9gwUVwC&pg=PA1&dq=pontiac In this diary, the writer talks about Pontiac's siege on Detroit. The other documents are also invaluable for understanding the British side of Pontiac's rebellion.

Historical Sites

Historic Deerfield, Deerfield, Massachusetts. www.historic-deerfield.org/ One of the best sites for students to look at early America from the perspectives of the Indians, French, and British.

Fort Ticonderoga and the King's Garden, Adirondack Park, New York. www.fort-ticonderoga.org/ A resource about the fort that also takes the native peoples' perspective into account.

Moravian Historical Society, Bethlehem, Pennsylvania. www.moravianhistoricalsociety.org The Moravian Historical Society website contains images and other resources concerning the Moravians in Pennsylvania.

Grand Village of the Natchez Indians, Natchez, Mississippi. www.mdah.ms.gov/new/visit/grand-village-of-natchez-indians Students can view a reconstructed Natchez village.

Chapter 6

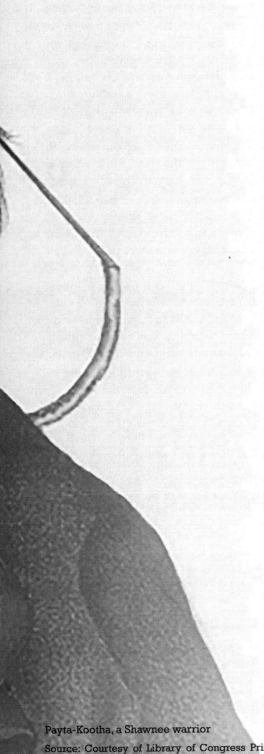

The Indians' Revolution, 1763–1814

A Disease, a Continent, and a Revolution
The American Revolution
Questions of Iroquois Neutrality
For Liberty and Independence: New England
  Indians
Dunmore's War and the Old Northwest
The South and Choosing Sides
**Native American Recovery, Native
  American Resistance, 1783–1814**
The Revolution Continues: Treaties and
  Bloody Years
The Civilization Program
Prophets and War
Western Revolutions
The Borderlands Revolution: Comanchería
Comanchería: Wealth and Empire
Alta California: Missionary Revolutions
Mission Life

A Disease, a Continent, and a Revolution

From 1775 until 1782, smallpox, or *Variola*, tore across parts of North America. A sure sign of infection was the painful, bleeding pustules that marked the body. For the people lucky to survive, the open sores healed but they left faces and bodies badly scarred. Washington scrambled for resources to combat the pestilence as it ripped through the Continental Army's ranks. *Variola* also brutalized the Oneidas and Senecas of the Iroquois Confederacy, dampening the support each Nation was able to extend to its ally during the war. This was not a disease unique to the colonial world of the Eastern Woodlands but one carried with Europeans deep into the Americas. In 1785, when a Spanish emissary traveled the Southwest territory, the Comanche refused to meet

Payta-Kootha, a Shawnee warrior
Source: Courtesy of Library of Congress Prints and
Photographs Division, LC-DIG-pga-07557

163

with him if he "brought some illness that would bring them death." *Variola* devastated Baja California's Indian communities in 1781, and then swept north and hit Alta California's Franciscan missions. The pox, without a doubt, caused a human drama of catastrophic proportions and for those tribes in the Eastern Woodlands it contributed directly to their collapse before the English.

The Indians' Revolution that began with Pontiac in 1763 (see Chapter 5) proved every bit as traumatic and as far-reaching as *Variola*. Throughout the trans-Appalachian West, bloody violence between Indians and whites made the frontier a dangerous place to live even after Pontiac's War ended. The crown, the colonies, and native peoples disputed the boundaries of the British Proclamation of 1763 and contributed to the outbreak of the American Revolutionary War in 1775, warfare that drew Native Americans east of the Mississippi into the fight.

The American Revolution concluded in 1783 with the **Treaty of Paris**, but that treaty did not in any way mark the end of the Indians' Revolution. Excluded from the proceedings of the Treaty of Paris, where a new North American order was hammered out, Indians had no voice in the geopolitical realignment of eastern North America.

Facing villages razed by war and family members killed in the conflict, a new generation of native leaders looked to repair the wreckage, fend off land-hungry Americans moving west, and sometimes to fight their own people. Chainbreaker, a Seneca warrior, recalled these troubling times in the words of his uncle, the Seneca war chief Cornplanter: "War is War, Death is Death, a fight is hard business." For Chainbreaker and other Indian leaders, the hard business of fighting did not come to a halt in 1783. The disastrous consequences of postwar Indian policy in the Old Northwest kept native peoples and whites almost in a perpetual state of war through 1815.

Just as smallpox and war changed the course of Native Americans in the East, disease ravaged Indians in Texas and New Mexico in the Southwest and farther west into California. New imperial alliances and territorial expansion in those territories also revolutionized the American West and shaped the destiny of native peoples. In the face of the Spanish, the Comanches unified the territorial boundaries of their own empire, **Comanchería**, located east of present-day New Mexico. Mounted warriors raided Spanish and Mexican settlements. Drought hit New Mexico in the 1770s, drying fields in New Mexico and leaving families to starve. Recognizing New Mexico's decline as the hub of the Spanish plains' economy, the Comanches struck New Mexico from all sides. Amid New Mexico's devastation, Comanche raiders pulled the nexus of southwest trade into Comanchería. In 1769, the Franciscans began their chain of **Alta California** missions. Franciscans revolutionized the Indian landscape of California. California Indians moved into mission compounds, where the spread of smallpox and other diseases continued. Epidemics and religious factions broke apart families. Missionaries also transformed the California ecology by introducing livestock and new plants.

KEY QUESTIONS

1. What caused the Iroquois to join the American Revolution?
2. Why did New England Indians join the patriot cause?
3. How was the Revolution fought in the Old Northwest?
4. What happened in the South during the American Revolution?
5. How were native peoples treated after the American Revolution? Think in terms of the conquest theory and the civilization program.
6. How did the Comanches build their empire?
7. What was life like for native peoples in Franciscan missions?

CHRONOLOGY

1706	Comanches begin to dominate Southwest borderlands
1757	Comanche peace with the Wichitas
1762	Treaty of Foutainbleau
1768	Treaty of Fort Stanwix
1769	Arrival of the Franciscans in Alta California
1771	Drought in New Mexico
1773–1774	Dunmore's War
1775	Sycamore Shoals Treaty
1776	Joseph Brant takes Oquaga
1777	Start of Iroquois Civil War with the Battle of Oriskany
	Dragging Canoe splits from the main Cherokee towns
1778	Battle of White Plains, New York
1779	Sullivan-Clinton Campaign through Iroquoia
1779	Battle of Vincennes
1782	Siege at Gnadenhütten
1784	Treaty of Fort Stanwix
1785	Treaty of Fort McIntosh
1785	Treaty of Dumplin Creek
	Treaty of Galphinton
1786	Treaty of Fort Finney
	Indian Confederacy Meeting at Brownstown
	Treaty between New Spain and Western Comanches
1787	Northwest Ordinance
1789	Treaty of Fort Harmar
1790	Treaty of New York
1794	Battle of Fallen Timbers
1795	Treaty of Greenville
1790–1796	Trade and Intercourse Acts and Start of the Civilization Program
1799	Handsome Lake's first vision
1805	Shawnee Prophet has first vision
1811	Tecumseh visits the Deep South
1812	Pan-Indian Unity during the War of 1812
1814	Battle of Horseshoe Bend
	Treaty of Fort Jackson

The best way to examine the Indians' Revolution is as a continent-wide event. To approach Native American history with more breadth, which means moving away from the Atlantic seaboard and Eastern Woodlands and toward the West, also involves following the United States after the American Revolution as it turned into an imperial continental force with which to be reckoned. The "Empire for Liberty," Thomas Jefferson's choice of words for American expansionism, was much like the *Variola* epidemic of 1775–1781. The "Empire for Liberty," as shown in Chapter 7 and Chapter 8, breached the Appalachian Mountains at an incredibly rapid pace. Jefferson's vision meant nothing to Native Americans; it would soon mean everything.

The American Revolution

Because of the scope of the war, and the key geographical positions of Native Americans in the Northeast, the Great Lakes and Ohio, and the South, it was inevitable Indians east of the Mississippi would find themselves joining sides during the American Revolution. The Iroquois of New York maintained their Covenant Chain of neutrality since the peace accord at Montreal in 1701. This new war, however, promised consequences far greater than any earlier conflict. Both the British and the colonists understood the critical need for a military alliance with the Iroquois once the Revolution erupted. By 1778, war between England and her enemies Spain and France raged across western Europe. Britain required a military force for both European and North American theaters. Indian alliances provided that manpower in the colonies. As for the colonists, the war garnered active support of only about one-third of the colonial British population, or roughly one million people, of whom most were children, women, and the elderly. Moreover, neither the Continental Army nor colonial militia could depend on their soldiers' unflagging participation in a war against the world's most powerful military. They, too, then, required alliances. Native Americans, approached by British and colonial representatives, confronted a dilemma—neutrality or an alliance with one of the two opposing sides. Any decision they made promised serious repercussions that depended on who ultimately won the war.

Questions of Iroquois Neutrality

A long-simmering challenge to Britain's absolute authority over her North American colonies caught fire in the 1760s and exploded in war in 1775. Inevitably, the war involved Native Americans. Unable to easily crush the colonial rebels as they initially expected, the Crown looked for allies to supplement its army in North America. King George III quickly hired about 30,000 soldiers from the German states of Hesse-Cassel and Hesse-Hanau, generally referred to as Hessians. He and his advisors also hoped to construct alliances with Native American tribal groups. Such an arrangement seemed logical. Colonists' demands for land had reduced native holdings significantly by 1775 and resulted in the expulsion of many native groups to western territories. Disease had depopulated Indian numbers and wreaked havoc on traditional tribal structures. Trade had created a dependency relationship with colonial suppliers and governments, and native cultures had become fundamentally corrupted by the colonists' insistence on acculturation. Little wonder the British readily assumed Native Americans would be willing to align themselves with English armies. Forming the alliance, however, proved more problematic than the Crown imagined, evidenced clearly in the Iroquois response to war.

British Superintendent of Indian Affairs Sir William Johnson, based in New York, championed three fundamental positions—cultivating and maintaining a positive relationship between Britain and the Iroquois; spreading the Anglican faith; and enforcing the Proclamation of 1763. The first of these three goals seemed relatively easy to accomplish. Molly Brant of the Mohawk town Canajoharie, sister to the powerful Mohawk leader Joseph Brant (Thayendanegea), was Johnson's common-law wife and mother to three of his children. He and Molly resided at his grand estate, Johnson Hall, slightly northwest of Canajoharie in New York's Hudson Valley region. The Iroquois-Johnson relationship had long been amicable, and Iroquois councils frequently convened at Johnson Hall where Johnson would dispense gifts to keep the Six Nations loyal to their British "father." Moreover, Sir William and Molly were devout Anglicans. Together, they wielded some influence over Joseph Brant, encouraging him to abandon the Presbyterian tenets he previously adopted from the New England evangelist Samuel Kirkland when both were young attendees of Eleazer Wheelock's Moor's Charity School in Connecticut. As a direct result of Molly's devotion to Anglicanism, Sir Johnson could convince Joseph Brant to convert to Anglicanism and abandon the doctrines he had learned alongside Kirkland when both were young and attended Eleazer Wheelock's Moor's Charity School in Connecticut. Johnson's ties to the Iroquois through Molly and his hospitality toward them at Johnson Hall seemed to provide an avenue toward alliance between Britain and Iroquoia when war erupted with the colonists. It was not that simple. Many Iroquois remained tied to Kirkland and his religious Presbyterian message. According to a group of Oneida warriors, they were "content with the Minister whom God hath sent to us . . . he teaches the true way of salvation." But Sir William, through his ties to the Brants, had intimate bonds of kinship within the Six Nations. Rarely did the Iroquois nations unite fully with one voice; the developing crisis between Britain and her colonies would prove no different.

Another feature of Sir William's work also encouraged him to suppose an Iroquois alliance once war came to the colonies. As Superintendent of Indian Affairs, Johnson had been the principal British negotiator with Pontiac, ending that war officially in 1766. He also had been directly involved in settling war between the Six Nations and the Cherokee in 1768. Little wonder that many Iroquois called Sir Johnson *Warraghiyagey*, which translated into "doer of great things." It was this commitment to both Native Americans and the British that garnered him the respect of both. Now he pressed the British Board of Trade to set and to formalize the boundary lines ordered in the Proclamation of 1763. Delawares, Shawnees, Mingos (an Iroquoian-speaking mixed group), and interested parties from the colonies of Pennsylvania, New York, and Virginia assembled near Rome, New York to discuss and resolve matters of territorial demarcation. The Proclamation was partly intended to establish peace along Britain's colonial frontier by denying settlers opportunity to move into Indian territory. Indeed, violence proved commonplace as colonists tried to relocate beyond the Appalachians without Indian permission to settle the lands they coveted. The resulting settlement, known as the Treaty of Fort Stanwix (1768), provided a resolution. The Iroquois agreed to surrender their claims south of the Susquehanna and Ohio rivers in return for a guarantee of their traditional homelands in New York. Johnson, representing Britain, secured Iroquois fidelity, preventing, as the treaty dictated, the expected movement of colonists onto Indian lands. The Treaty of Fort Stanwix nonetheless, opened up Kentucky, West Virginia, and non-Iroquois stretches of New York to settlement in a bid to win some favor among colonists. While this provision certainly enraged natives in those regions, particularly the Shawnee, Sir Johnson had the vested interests of those attending the negotiations. Most Iroquois did not forget this when the British solicited their help in fighting the colonists in the Revolutionary War.

Although the treaty secured the eastern lands of New York for the Iroquois, a splintering of the Six Nations nonetheless materialized by the late 1760s pitting the two easternmost Iroquois nations closest to the colonists against each other. The fracture occurred, in part, along religious lines. Anglican Iroquois, heavily Mohawk, supported William Johnson and, therefore, British interests, whereas Presbyterians were mostly Oneidas who favored Samuel Kirkland and the colonial cause. These divisions that helped push the confederacy into civil war began at villages like Oquaga, places described by contemporaries as where Indians "are disgusted with the ruling Politics of their people." At Oquaga there were Mohawks, Tuscaroras, Oneidas, and a host of other people, and to the north were the Oneida settlement of Kanowalohale and the Mohawk villages of Canajoharie and Tiononderoge. Both Oneidas and Mohawks sent chiefs to Oquaga to influence faith-based conflicts that had larger political implications. Along with the Indians were several missionaries, both Anglo-American and

6.1 Joseph Fayadaneega, called Joseph Brant, the Great Captain of the Six Nations (Thayendanegea). In this image, Brant's clothing demonstrates his pro-British position, particularly the fine clothing and gorget around his neck.
Courtesy of Library of Congress Prints and Photographs Division, LC-DIG-ppmsca-15712.

Indian. An Oneida chief "Good Peter" who first brought Presbyterianism to Oquaga in the 1740s continued to preach. Samuel Kirkland balanced his mission work between the Oneida village of Kanowalohale and Oquaga.

Such Iroquois religious-political factions on the eve of the American Revolution transformed Oquaga into a place of turmoil. After Sir William's death in 1774, his nephew Guy Johnson took the superintendent post and maintained connections with Brant and other anti-Presbyterian leaders. The British feared Kirkland's politics and anti-Anglican position as enough incentive for the Indians at Oquaga and Kanowalohale—mostly Oneidas and Tuscaroras—to claim neutrality, or worse yet, side with the colonists. Either decision would divide the Six Nations and create significant military problems. British fears proved well founded when, in June 1775, the Oneidas pledged neutrality and the more western Iroquois nations and the easternmost Mohawks declared themselves for the British. The confederacy was split. The Oneidas refused to meet at the Onondaga castle where for centuries the Confederacy held its meetings. In December 1776, Brant entered the community of Oquaga and, along with other Mohawks, took over the village. The Oneidas and other Presbyterian Indians fled to the Oneida village of Kanowalohale.

The Iroquois civil war began in earnest with the Battle of Oriskany. The battle, one of the bloodiest of the Revolution, was part of George Washington's 1777 Saratoga Campaign to try to take the Hudson River valley from the British. Loyalists from New York, the British, and Brant and his Six Nations supporters fought against colonists and patriot Oneidas and Tuscaroras. Oquaga, a Loyalist-Anglican and British stronghold, was now an open target for revolutionary colonists, and colonial forces destroyed Oquaga once they took command of the village. Even without their outpost, Brant and loyalist Iroquois continued devastating raids in the Hudson River valley and upper Susquehanna River valley of Pennsylvania. Brant's Cherry Valley campaign in eastern New York in 1778 united Senecas and British soldiers who massacred 16 officers and troops and murdered numerous settler families. Their aggression gave the **patriots** reason to harbor deep and long-lasting hostility toward the Iroquois.

By becoming patriots, the Oneidas and Tuscaroras tipped the Six Nations into civil war. To end Iroquois support of the British, George Washington ordered a scorched-earth campaign through loyalist Iroquois villages in 1779. Led by the generals John Sullivan and James Clinton, some 6,200 American troops marched into New York, laying waste to Iroquois villages and stocks of corn. Pro-British Iroquois fled to British-occupied Fort Niagara in search of food and supplies. As for the Oneidas, who had pledged neutrality in 1775, they provided warriors who served as guides and scouts for the colonists against members of the Six Nations' Confederacy. Until the end of the American Revolution, Oneidas continued to fight for the patriot cause, whereas other members of the Six Nations ferociously attacked militia units and the Continental Army in retaliation for the Sullivan-Clinton campaign. Hatred ran so deep among the Iroquois that George Washington earned the unflattering name, "Town Destroyer." By 1780, most pro-British Iroquois lived near or around Fort Niagara, and the Oneidas retained lands to the east.

For Liberty and Independence: New England Indians

Religion and tribal politics were not the only motives that brought Native Americans into the Revolutionary War. The rebels' rhetoric of "liberty and independence" resonated among many Indians in New England and inspired them to support the revolutionary cause. Trapped on small tracts of land, some New England tribal members saw the revolution as a moment of their own to seize rights to self-government and autonomy; it was an opportunity to reclaim what they had lost under the oppressive hand of English authority. They had not forgotten the colonists' central role in creating the Indians' current condition, but they did believe that without Britain's protection of the colonies, the independent states would not be in a position of strength to exert control over native peoples.

By the 1760s, there already was an Indian movement in Connecticut aimed at reclaiming liberty and independence. Samson Occom and Joseph Johnson, two itinerant Indian preachers in New England, set out to unite the Pequots, Narragansetts, Montauks, Niantics, and Mohegans and to carve out a new homeland in New York. These Indians wanted to escape the social, cultural, and economic devastation they had experienced living on ever-smaller plots of land among the colonists. Uniting in a common cause, the leaders called themselves and their followers "brethren." Occom and Johnson's efforts at tribal unification, migration, and independence became known as the **Brothertown movement**. Turmoil in Iroquoia prevented the Brothertown Indians from moving to New York immediately, but they concluded that independence for the colonies would aid their own movement and, through their ties to the Oneidas, Brothertown leaders served the patriot cause.

6.2 Warrior chief Good Peter Agwe-lentongwas, drawn by John Trumbull
Source: Yale University Art Gallery, Trumbull Collection

The Stockbridge-Housatonic Indians who lived on the fringe of Massachusetts also joined the patriot cause. A community formed in the 1730s by Mohicans, Stockbridge was a village strategically located between Massachusetts and New York. In the 1740s, missionaries encouraged the leaders of Stockbridge to become Christians and keep their traditional position as negotiators between New England Indians and the Six Nations Iroquois. During the American Revolution, Stockbridge Indians saw joining the patriot side as an opportunity to maintain a semi-independent standing but also a means to exact revenge against the Mohawks and other members of the Iroquois Confederacy. Under General Washington's guidance, the Stockbridge Indians formed their own company, trained, and became riflemen.

Other New England Indians, living closer to urban centers and towns where they were exposed to the ideas that inspired the patriot cause, fought to win the benefits of self-autonomy and preservation. Mashpee Indians apparently lost close to 80 men in the war. The Congregational minister at Mashpee, Gideon Hawley, could not

PROFILE

Molly Brant, an Iroquois Woman and British Loyalist

Molly Brant occupied a unique position during the American Revolution. Her husband, William Johnson, died before the war in 1774. However, he was a man who had earned tremendous respect among the Iroquois, particularly the Mohawks. At the same time, Molly was part of an extended matrilineal clan system. Iroquois women had a lot of power and influence in a society in which men and women traced their descent through their mothers' lines. Molly used the memory of her dead husband, as well as her position as an Iroquois woman, to exert tremendous influence among the Iroquois during the American Revolution.

After Johnson's death, Molly returned to Canajoharie with eight children. She used the money from her husband's estate to build a house out of which she redistributed goods among her family and other Mohawks. Although she was the head of her own matrilineal household, Molly used the Iroquois custom of hospitality to extend her influence among other Iroquois. Molly remained a staunch supporter of the British war effort, gathering important information about the colonists. In one instance, she warned the British that the patriots were planning an attack on Fort Stanwix. The English listened to Molly and sent a small regiment to attack the American forces in October 6, 1777 at Oriskany. Pro-British Iroquois attacked Oneida homes after their victory, and Molly earned a bad reputation among the Oneidas for her work as a British spy.

The Oneidas swept in and destroyed Molly's house, after which Molly increased her support for the British through her name as Johnson's widow. At a council meeting, she used the memory of her husband to speak about politics. In traditional Iroquois society, a husband's status did not elevate the political clout of clan mothers, but Molly's case was special. Molly moved to Fort Niagara where she continued to use her influence as a clan mother and widow to a British man to help the British cause.

At Niagara, the British lavished Molly with goods and money, as she continued to exchange information about patriot and patriot-Iroquois movements. Molly used networks of exchange and distribution to learn about Iroquois movements, dispensing money and goods out of Niagara to pro-British Iroquois. Recognizing her power among the Iroquois as a clan mother of high influence, the British continued to supply her with the necessary items to gather political information. Her influence was so strong that British General Haldimand entrusted Molly to travel from Niagara to Carleton Island to end disputes among the pro-British Iroquois living there. She continued her distribution of goods, entered into local politics, and earned the nickname among the British of "Miss Molly." After the war, Molly retired to a home in Canada and passed away in 1796. The American Revolution was a unique moment in Iroquois history, as it was in the life of Molly Brant. Using her power and authority as both clan mother and widow to a British official, Molly leveraged her position into that of a respected pro-British leader.

believe how devoted Indians were to the patriot cause. Ten days after the Declaration of Independence reached the public he exclaimed, "What can they do but enlist in the army!" The records of Colonel Nathaniel Freeman's First Barnstable Regiment listed 12 Mashpee Indians in 1775. Mohegan men served as mariners aboard patriot vessels. From Connecticut, 75 Native Americans, mostly Mohegans and Nipmucs, fought alongside Washington's forces. In Natick oral tradition, Caeser Ferrit and his son John were two of the minutemen at Concord firing at the British from the road.

Dunmore's War and the Old Northwest

Clashes between Indians and Europeans in the Old Northwest preceding the colonists' rebellion shaped the course of fighting in that region during the Revolutionary War. Although the bloody conflict between Shawnees and Virginians in 1774 known as Dunmore's War (named after the governor of Virginia) only lasted one year, its unresolved causes turned the entire Ohio territory into a powder keg waiting to be ignited. Dunmore's War began as a contest between Pennsylvania and Virginia for the lands in the Upper Ohio valley. Land speculators ventured into the territory below Fort Pitt (present-day Pittsburgh) claiming their sponsors' rights to the land. What the Indians wanted most was to hold on to the fertile lands of Kentucky, which lay west of the Kanawha River. This land was Shawnee territory, although Dunmore freely allowed Virginians to settle there.

Two attacks by Virginians in 1774, one led by Daniel Greathouse and the other by Michael Cresap, started Dunmore's War. Men like Greathouse and Cresap shared a hatred of Indians, a sentiment similar to Pennsylvania's Paxton Boys. Destruction of the Indian presence in the contested region would open that territory to settlement. Greathouse and Cresap guided their volunteers into the Ohio Valley to a tavern along Yellow Creek, just north of present-day Wheeling, West Virginia. There, Greathouse and his men stumbled upon a peaceful party of nine Mingos and promptly, without justification, killed all of them. The Mingo chief John Logan, whose brother and his entire family died in the massacre, led warriors from the clans of the killed into a mourning war against the Virginians, referred to by the Indians as "**Long Knives**" (or "Big Knives"—Indians interchanged these names to describe all Anglo-American intruders).

Shawnees joined the fray. Even their chiefs conceded that they had no control over their warriors. By July, both sides raided each other across the Ohio frontier. Northern Delawares near Moravian mission towns, among them the important civil chief White Eyes, tried in vain to stop the bloodshed. Only after Dunmore moved into the Ohio territory with a battery of Virginia militia and burned Shawnee and Iroquois settlements did both sides agree to a treaty. The Treaty of Camp Charlotte, seen as a victory for the Virginians because the Shawnees ceded their rights to lands in Kentucky, actually served as a new but porous boundary between settlers and Indians. North of the Ohio River would be Indian land; south of it, settlers were protected under the sovereignty of Virginia and the Crown. But violence and cultural mixing did not go unabated. The Bluegrass

TIMELINE 6.1 REVOLUTIONARY IROQUOIA AND NEW ENGLAND, 1763–1779

Date	Event
1763	Royal Proclamation
1774	Death of Sir William Johnson
1775	Oneidas pledge neutrality
	Mashpees enlist in Barnstable regiment
1777	Battle of Oriskany
1778	Stockbridge Indians at the Battle of White Plains
	Joseph Brant's Cherry Valley Campaign
1779	Sullivan-Clinton Campaign in Iroquoia

Region with its extensive game and fertile lands was now open to white settlers, including men such as the surveyor and famed hunter Daniel Boone. Once the American Revolution began, the Ohio territory (also known as the Old Northwest) became the scene of fierce battles between British and patriot forces. If Dunmore's War provided any indication, the Revolution in the Ohio would not be won on open battlefields with lines of riflemen; instead, multitribal villages with their own loyalties and specific agendas set the tone and pace of the fighting. Military success in the Old Northwest would depend on maneuvering through a complicated world of Native American villagers.

George Rogers Clark from Virginia and the British leader Henry Hamilton warred against each other in the Old Northwest's world of mixed villages. Hamilton seemed to have the advantage over Clark in securing Indian support. He served the Crown as Lieutenant Governor and Superintendent of Indian Affairs in the Ohio territory and was familiar with Indian rules governing diplomacy and trade, as well as the rituals and ceremonies of the warpath. In 1777, assuming commanded of British forces in the region, he ordered strikes against Kentucky and Pennsylvania backcountry settlers, abiding by Indian customs. The Algonquians called Hamilton "hair buyer" because he paid for colonists' scalps collected by warriors. Clark, on the other hand, was a Virginia "Long Knife" with a reputation for hating Indians and demonstrating no knowledge of or concern for native rituals or protocol. Clark and Hamilton's skills—and faults—collided at the battle of Vincennes in 1779 in present-day Indiana.

As they tried to court Indians and French **habitants** to join their ranks, Clark and Hamilton had to abide by the cultural norms of the *pays d'en haut*. Clark positioned his army at the French town of Kaskaskia, in present-day Illinois and, as advised by his lieutenants, reluctantly dispensed wampum belts and the appropriate diplomatic words to gain allies among Kaskaskia's Algonquians and French *habitants*. Clark knew the Indians liked the French more than the British, so he reminded them of Indian resistance to the British years earlier around the Wabash River in the Ohio territory in support of the French. Their British "father" had never treated the Indians like "Onontio." Clark also lied, telling them that the British-occupied Fort Detroit had already fallen to the Americans, implying British vulnerability. French traders moving into the Old Northwest from New Orleans also helped Clark in spreading the rumor that "Onontio" would return after the British defeat.

In the *pays d'en haut*, Hamilton did not do as well. He marched south in 1778 from Detroit as though he had a formal regiment of British soldiers. Hamilton was familiar with such rituals as gift-giving, the calumet, and ceremonies for preparation to fight including the singing of war songs, dancing, and using rum to soak a grindstone for sharpening the edges of Indian tomahawks. Algonquians performed all of these ceremonies and rituals to channel the right *manitous*, or spirits, before entering battle. While he participated in many of these rituals and ceremonies, he derided the Indians as "poor ignorant creatures," a mistimed expression of contempt not lost on the Indians.

Once the British and the Americans met at Vincennes in 1779, Clark's 200 men along with French volunteers and Algonquian warriors routed the small British garrison. Vincennes was not a typical eighteenth-century open-field battle. Clark employed guerilla tactics, similar to traditional Algonquian rules of war. In fact, the only reason Clark secured the Old Northwest for the patriot cause was that he was more successful than Hamilton in finding allies in the world of native villagers.

Securing native alliances was difficult for both the British and the Americans. Representatives of the colonists as well as experienced British diplomats were challenged by tribal protocol in conducting negotiations. Traditional rivalries among Indian groups made their alliances problematic at best, and the long, sordid relationship between Indians and Englishmen tested the limits of union for both colonists and the British military. Nowhere was this more apparent than among a group of tribally mixed communities around the village of Coshocton, located in the Upper Ohio. Situated near several Moravian towns, most of the Indians were Shawnees and Unami Delawares. The leading proponents of neutrality in the colonists' Revolutionary War came from these villages, among them Cornstalk of the Shawnees and White Eyes and Killbuck of the Delawares.

British and American representatives alike tried to convince these leaders to lead their men into war to no avail. It was not their war; neither side merited their alliance. Militant Shawnees, however, denounced neutrality, referring to the Neutrals as "cowardly." Cornstalk, White Eyes, and Killbuck were all civil chiefs, not war chiefs. As Killbuck made clear, the Delawares agreed to share information with the British *and* the colonies "in case they desire to speak as one."

War chiefs ultimately swayed the Delaware to align with the American side, but the alliance did not deter attacks by American units that refused to distinguish between friendly and unfriendly Indians. General Daniel Brodhead orchestrated an attack on Coshocton, in present-day Ohio, where many Delaware allies and their kin lived. Coshocton stood at a crossroads between Fort Pitt and Fort Detroit. The worst of these unprovoked attacks occurred in 1782 in the Moravian mission town of Gnadenhütten. Convinced the Indians of Gnadenhütten had participated in raids along the Pennsylvania frontier and at this point in time certain of the colonists' victory in the war, close to 90 "Long Knives" disobeyed orders and slaughtered 96 men, women, and children. The deaths of Cornstalk and White Eyes, and the ghastly killing of Christian Indians at Gnadenhütten, demonstrated that neutrality in the backcountry mattered little. Neutrality broke down into the chaos of frontier war.

The South and Choosing Sides

By 1775, the Cherokee population stood at about 12,000, including 3,000 warriors, down from 22,000 people at the dawn of the eighteenth century. The strategic location of Cherokee towns made them important to the Revolutionary War's Southern Campaign. The four divisions of the Cherokees—the Overhill Towns, the Valley settlements, the Middle settlements, and the Lower Towns—collectively formed a crossroad, or junction, linking colonies and major tribal groups. The Cherokees were located between the southern colonies and the Ohio Indians, between the southern colonies and the western Chickasaws and Choctaws, and between the northern colonies and the Creeks. The town was the center of Cherokee life. At one point in the eighteenth century, Great Tellico served as the seat of politics where Cherokees gathered to conduct diplomacy. By the time of the American Revolution, Chota had eclipsed the power of Great Tellico. Because of the Cherokees' geographical position, both the colonists and the British courted the leaders at Chota. They had all the more incentive to do so because Chota served as a gathering point for warring Indians from the north, like the Shawnees and Ottawas, and the powerful and aggressive native groups of the Deep South. Moreover, the town stood at an important trade location, settled on the eastern side of the Tennessee River alongside a major route to Charleston.

Chota's rise was largely due to three powerful elder chiefs: Old Hop, Attakullakulla, and Oconostota. The decision making of these three elder headmen in terms of Cherokee lands tore apart the political fabric of Chota and political life among the Cherokees. A group of North Carolina land speculators led by Richard Henderson presented the Sycamore Shoals Treaty of 1775 to the elder chiefs for their consideration in 1775. The treaty ignored the provisions housed in the Proclamation of 1763, calling on the Cherokee to cede vast acreage between the Kentucky and Tennessee rivers. In return, the Cherokee would be identified as the primary trade partners in the region. The three elder chiefs signed the treaty, but in doing so they violated the rules of Cherokee governance by consensus which, to many Indians, invalidated the treaty. Moreover, the Cherokee headmen cut off their people from prime hunting grounds in Kentucky and Tennessee and interfered with their access to trade routes along the Ohio River. River. Dragging Canoe, son of Attakullakull, demanded the Cherokee join the British to protect Cherokee country. The elders, instead, called for neutrality.

In April 1776, a combined force of Northern Shawnees, Delawares, Mohawks, and Ottawas arrived in Chota painted in black and calling for war against the colonists. Dragging Canoe and a large body of warriors from the Overhill Towns offered their support for the British and removed themselves to the Tennessee River valley in the spring of 1777. These pro-British Cherokees became known as the Chickamaugas (a name of a creek near where they lived), but they called themselves *Ani-Yunwiya*, which meant "the Real People." Chickamaugas made connections with militant Upper Creeks living to the south and established trade and communication routes with the British stationed in Alabama and the western Panhandle of Florida.

Emistisiguo, a pro-British Creek from the Creek Upper Towns, proclaimed that "if the red warriors to the northward would hold a red stick against the Virginians there, I would hold one against them here." Among the Creeks, the color red signaled hostility and war, while the color white indicated the possibility of peaceful relations. Dragging Canoe and Emistisiguo sought to unite southern pro-British Indians with their militant allies to the north. However, as with the Cherokees, Creek towns were divided over the war. Most Creeks in both the Upper and Lower Towns, for example, tried to follow a policy of neutrality.

The colonists struck major Cherokee towns in 1776, sparing only Chota. The elder headmen had no choice but to sign a truce with the Americans. By 1779, supplied with muskets from the British, the Chickamaugas and their Indian allies, which now included many Upper Creeks and an offshoot of the Creeks in the Seminoles of Florida, raged across the southern backcountry of South Carolina and Georgia. The pro-British Seminole leader Cowkeeper hoped to use the war to preserve Seminole autonomy by taking property in "slaves or cattle" from the southern colonists. By 1779, there was also a spiritual component to Indian resistance against the colonists in the South. The Cherokee Old Tassel was not among the Chickamaugas, but his spiritual message appealed to their cause. Like Neolin, Old Tassel believed that the Master of Life had created the Cherokees to be separate peoples, calling now for a final separation of Cherokees from white Americans. The anti-colonist Indians seized on this vision to sustain their war in the South and to maintain their alliances with pro-British natives farther north. However, George Rogers Clark's victory at Vincennes and the American domination of the Northwest weakened their hopes of north-south pan-Indian resistance against the colonists.

SEEING HISTORY

A Draught of the Cherokee Country by Lieutenant Henry Timberlake, 1762

Drawn by Lt. Henry Timberlake, a British writer and cartographer, the map on p. 176 appeared in his memoirs, first published in 1765. He also wrote extensively about Cherokee culture and town life, and the map is incredibly descriptive of town locations, leaders of particular towns, and the trade paths that led out of villages to important colonial trade locations such as Charleston, South Carolina. The map and his memoirs are indispensable for historians interested in eighteenth-century Cherokee life at a critical period, near the end of the Seven Years' War. In fact, his map's incredible accuracy served archaeologists working for The Great Tellico Project in the 1970s who located and excavated Cherokee Overhill towns.

Questions

1. What does the map reveal about Cherokee society?
2. What does the map tell us about Cherokee politics on the eve of the American Revolution?

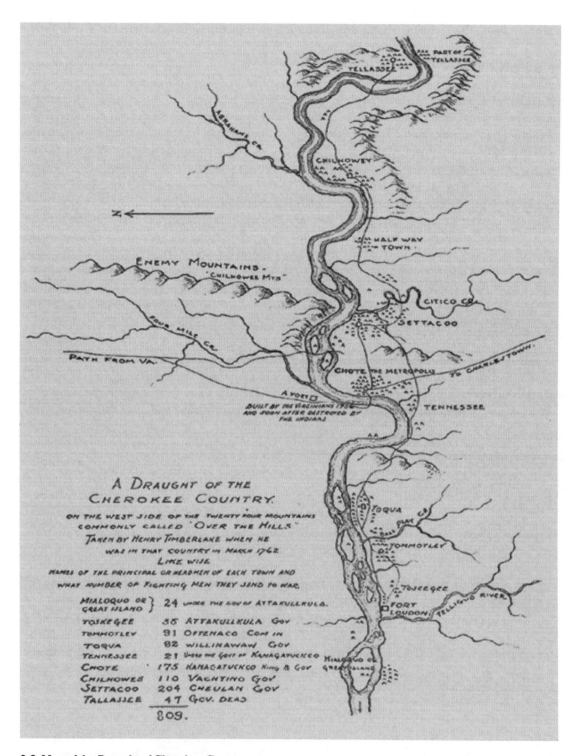

6.3 Map of the Draught of Cherokee Country

Source: Duane H. King, *The Memoirs of Lt. Henry Timberlake: The Story of a Soldier, Adventurer, and Emissary to the Cherokees, 1756–1765* (Distributed by the University of North Carolina Press for the Museum of the Cherokee Indian, 2007).

TIMELINE 6.2 THE OLD NORTHWEST AND THE SOUTH, 1774–1782

Date	Event
1774	Outbreak of Dunmore's War
	Treaty of Camp Charlotte
1775	Sycamore Shoals Treaty
1777	Henry Hamilton orders strikes against Pennsylvania and Kentucky
	Dragging Canoe breaks with Chota headmen
	Cornstalk is murdered
1778	White Eyes is killed
1779	Battle at Vincennes
	Chickamauga Cherokees attack the Carolina backcountry
1780–1781	Arthur Campbell and John Sevier attack Cherokee towns
1782	Massacre at Gnadenhütten

Between 1780 and 1781, the governor of Virginia, Thomas Jefferson, ordered Arthur Campbell and John Sevier to crush Chickamauga resistance. Campbell and Sevier massed their forces and swept through Chickamauga lands in the Overhill country, burning one village after another. Starved, emotionally traumatized, cut off from trade, isolated from supportive native tribes, and facing severe depopulation, the Chickamaugas called for peace in 1781. The Virginians presented a treaty proposal that required the complete destruction of all Chickamauga towns, the return of all captives, and their submission to American authority. The Chickamaugas, of course, refused such terms and continued to attack the southern backcountry even after the war with Britain had ended. The Cherokee nation remained divided.

Native American Recovery, Native American Resistance, 1783–1814

The 1783 Treaty of Paris ended the American Revolution but did not end the Indians' Revolution. The treaty recognized the independence of the United States and set the Mississippi River and the Great Lakes as the western and northern boundaries of the United States. However, there was no provision within the treaty for the Indians, and there was no discussion of peace made between the two powers and the tribes. The very people whose alliance was deemed critical in the war were ignored completely. With new western lands to settle, settlers pushed deep into the newly acquired territory, unencumbered by government oversight. Those Native Americans who allied themselves with the colonists, believing them incapable of threatening western tribes as an independent nation, now admitted the folly of that argument. Indians chose to resist as best they could to the wave of settlers descending into their lands. They did have, however, an unexpected resource. Under the terms of surrender, the British were to abandon all their western forts. They did not. They retained outposts around the Great Lakes territory at Michilimackinac and Detroit. British leaders in Detroit supplied Indians with guns, powder, shot, supplies, and alcohol, helping to fuel the ongoing warfare in the region. A state of perpetual war existed between the United States and Indians of the trans-Appalachian West from the Treaty of Paris of 1783 to the **Treaty of Greenville** in 1795.

The Articles of Confederation, with its governing decisions vested in the Confederate Congress, now controlled Indian policy after the American Revolution, and it did so in a reckless manner. The American Confederation saw Native Americans as subdued peoples and presented them with treaties not on a nation-to-nation basis but rather as lords dictating terms to peasants. Although some tribal leaders signed treaties to secure parcels of tribal lands, there were other Native Americans who saw things quite differently. They viewed all such treaties as fraudulent, the work of illegitimate leaders. The Miamis, Shawnees, and Wyandots of the Ohio territory in particular did not want to cede any lands at the cost of their sovereignty and autonomy. Led initially by the pro-British Mohawk Joseph Brant, a collection of tribes met at Brownstown near Detroit, forming their own union to challenge the American confederacy and protect the Ohio. War ravaged the region. In the South, Cherokees and Creeks were also willing to fight the United States in protecting their lands from white migration and securing for themselves the trans-Appalachian West.

The Revolution Continues: Treaties and Bloody Years

The United States struggled under a mountain of war debt after 1783, and the government also confronted veterans of the war who were earlier promised access to western territories once independence was gained. Many American leaders believed the sale of Indian lands once part of the British Empire might be one means for reducing the national debt and concurrently grant parcels of land in the West to former soldiers for their service. In return for the land grants, the Confederacy expected veterans to help control the actions of migrants heading west as they passed near or through Indian territories. The Confederacy's Indian policy was ill-conceived, illogical, and irresponsible.

Congress coerced Ohio Indians into signing separate treaties in 1784, 1785, and 1786. At the 1784 Treaty of Fort Stanwix, both government agents and New York policymakers insisted the Six Nations cede all claims to the Ohio territory. Commissioners then traveled south to Fort McIntosh in 1785 and met with Delawares, Wyandots, Ottawas, and Chippewas, compelling them to abandon southern and eastern Ohio. In 1786 at the Treaty of Fort Finney, commissioners again deployed the same vivid metaphor of conquest, dictating treaty provisions to the pro-British Shawnees. The Shawnees received lands west of the Ohio River. On paper only by 1786, the United States had grabbed the eastern and southern portions of the Ohio territory.

The three recent treaties enraged those native peoples who refused to acknowledge any loss of land in the Ohio Valley or tribal sovereignty as a result of the Revolutionary War or the supposed authority of the Confederation Congress. In December 1786, representatives of the Shawnee, Miami, Kickapoo, Ottawa, Potawatomi, Delaware, Iroquois, and Wyandot assembled at the Wyandot village of Brownstown, near Detroit, to set the agenda of their own confederacy. They drafted and sent a letter to Congress, disavowing the recent treaties and the theory that the Indians of the Ohio territory were conquered peoples. Knowing such a passive move would not likely accomplish anything of value, Shawnee and Miami warriors descended on farms and homes in Ohio and Kentucky. Northern Shawnee also sent emissaries, wampum belts, and war hatchets south to unite with Shawnees living among the Creeks and the Chickamauga Cherokees. Within the confederacy, warriors and military chiefs were now the decision makers, undercutting the authority of the civil chiefs, some of whom signed the treaties and sought to negotiate peace.

Indians in the South ultimately networked with the Ohio Confederacy, especially when, in 1783, North Carolina settlers pushed onto Cherokee lands, followed by speculators and agents of the government who hoped to strike an agreement with the Cherokee for lands on which a new state, Franklin, could be founded. Militant Cherokees raided the North Carolina backcountry in protest until June 1785 when the Treaty of Dumplin

Creek was signed, ceding an expanse of land to the Franklin speculators. At the Treaty of Hopewell soon afterwards, the Cherokees under the leadership of Old Tassel accepted a clear Cherokee Nation boundary on a parcel of land that spread over portions of Tennessee, North Carolina, and Kentucky. Chickamauga Cherokees, however, chose not to recognize the validity of the treaties and instead continued armed resistance to American authority in the region. The militia deployed against them took no effort to distinguish between friends and enemies, striking Cherokee villages at will and without concern. In one such strike, Old Tassel himself was killed in the town of Chilhowee by a militia unit.

Similar examples of diplomacy, miscommunication, and cross-cultural violence played out among Creek towns. Numbering around 20,000, the Creek Confederacy spread from the Upper Towns along the Coosa and Tallapoosa rivers in Alabama to the Lower Towns in Georgia. Alexander McGillivray, whose father was Scots-Irish and whose mother was Creek, claimed control of the Creek Nation in 1780 without the explicit consent of all Creek and used an inter-clan police force to secure himself in that position. Creeks opposing McGillivray and the council he manipulated turned to the famous chief Hopoithle Mico, known also as the Tallassee King. But he too conducted diplomacy without consulting Creek villagers. In 1785 at the Treaty of Galphinton, Hopoithle Mico, along with other Creek leaders, ceded to the United States a portion of Creek lands located in Georgia. Some Creeks vehemently objected to the transaction and threatened an armed response. In a series of treaties over the next year, backed by the promise of military force, the Creeks relented but steeled themselves against further actions by the United States or the state of Georgia.

Making matters worse for Native Americans was the Confederation Congress's passage of the Northwest Ordinance of 1787. The measure most immediately addressed the lingering British presence in that region, asserting America's jurisdiction and demanding British forces vacate completely the territory. It also provided guidelines for the creation of new states in the western territories, effectively announcing the government's planned distribution of tribal lands to white settlement. The United States, through the ordinance, possessed the legitimate right "to lay out the parts of the district in which the Indian titles shall have been extinguished, into counties and township." At the same time, however, the legislation stated that the "utmost good faith shall always be observed towards the Indians; their lands and property shall never be taken from them without their consent; and, in their property, rights, and liberty, they shall never be invaded or disturbed unless in just and lawful wars authorized by Congress." The Northwest Ordinance proclaimed the full weight of United States authority over all lands and people in that region and reserved the right to employ force when required to ensure compliance. These provisions, and others in the legislation, collectively established unquestioned American title to the land.

All of the treaties proposed and enforced by the United States and its agents in the 1780s along with the Northwest Ordinance diminished Native American land holding, restricted Indian movements, and supplanted their tribal autonomy and sovereignty. From its position of power and the Indians' inability to fashion and maintain a viably potent counterforce, the United States effectively exerted its will over native peoples in the recently acquired western territories.

Pockets of armed resistance, however, continued in the late 1780s and early 1790s. A loose coalition of Creeks, Shawnees, and Cherokees raged along the Tennessee and Cumberland rivers in the late 1780s. In the Northwest Territory similar unions struck newly laid farms and villages. The United States reacted as it had before, employing military force against resistant Indians followed by additional treaties that required Indians to relinquish property. The governor of the Old Northwest, Arthur St. Clair, ordered 1,133 Kentucky militiamen into northern and western Ohio to counter Shawnee and Miami raids. Josiah Harmar commanded the force in the field and marched his men toward Fort Wayne, Indiana where they were immediately challenged by the Miami war chief Little Turtle who led a collection of Ottawas, Potawotamis, Shawnees, and Miamis. The American expedition suffered significant loses and was forced to retreat to Fort Washington. Little Turtle continued his strikes against the Kentucky "Long Knives" militia.

6.4 Hopothle Mico, or the Tallassee King of the Creeks.

Source: National Anthropological Archives, Smithsonian Institution

Humiliated by Harmar's rout, President George Washington ordered St. Clair to lead an assault against the Maumee villages, now believed to be the base for native resistance in Indiana. By September 1791, St. Clair had assembled 3,200 men at Cincinnati. Rough weather and substandard equipment resulted in widespread desertions, but St. Clair marched onward toward the Maumee villages where they were confronted by Shawnees and Miamis well equipped by the British traders out of Detroit. Using guerilla tactics and led by Little Turtle and Blue Jacket (a famous Shawnee warrior), the intertribal forces descended on St. Clair's encampment. The confederacy quickly slaughtered 647 of St. Clair's regiment, forcing another American retreat to Fort Washington. As a result of these two engagements alone, nearly 800 American soldiers and militiamen lay dead. For the Indians of the Old Northwest, the governor's defeat was a glorious victory. While there appeared to be little hope for native peoples in the western lands during the 1780s, the devastation wrought by Little Turtle and Blue Jacket inspired further Indian resistance and gave hope that the Indians might check white expansion and the touted authority of the United States. Again, the confederacy sent a letter to Congress telling American policymakers the lands north or west of the Ohio were untouchable Indian territories, this time expecting a positive reply. The United States offered cash payments and trade goods in exchange for land rights. The Indians were unimpressed. Backed by the British government in Canada, particularly the governor of Upper Canada, John Graves Simcoe, the Wabash and Maumee Indians prepared for another fight with the Long Knives.

The United States appointed "Mad" Anthony Wayne to rebuild American forts on the frontier in preparation for a massive confrontation with the Indian confederacy. Fort Jefferson was garrisoned and Wayne established Fort Greenville. At the same time, Simcoe supported the Indian confederacy by building Fort Miami. Wayne's 3,500 strong well-disciplined force, which included a group of horseback Kentucky militia, left Fort Greenville on July 28, 1794. Little Turtle, meanwhile, ignored the advice of the British and with his 2,000 warriors attacked Fort Recovery where the Americans had stored munitions. The Americans staved off the attack. Little Turtle decided not to prosecute further the war, learning that the British would no longer supply the confederacy with guns, powder, and shot. With that reality, he now encouraged his fellow confederacy members to negotiate with the United States. The Ojibwas, Potawatomis, and Ottawas abandoned the fight. The remaining Indian warriors made a last stand at Fallen Timbers, located north on the Maumee River. Expecting support from the British at Fort Miami, the confederacy fought Wayne on August 20, 1794, where they incurred heavy losses. The Indians retreated to Fort Miami only to find that the British had shut the doors of the fort. Enduring irreparable losses at Fallen Timbers, the confederacy fell apart in the winter of 1794. The Indians of the

Ohio territory had faced several years of poor treaty-making and the invasion of their homelands while they attempted intertribal unity. Many Indians of the Ohio territory believed they could no longer afford to pursue a militant position against the United States.

The Civilization Program

After years of privation, the Indian confederacy, consisting mostly of Miamis, Wyandots, and some Shawnees, surrendered. The 1795 Treaty of Greenville was a grand stage upon which the United States asserted its preeminent right to a civil and ordered Old Northwest. At the treaty grounds, several key negotiations were drafted. The United States affirmed the position of George Washington as the new Indians' "father." Many of the Indian leaders accepted this position because the government agreed to dispense **annuity payments**. Annuity payments were money dispensed annually to leaders of particular tribes in compensation for the lands ceded in treaty negotiations. After 1795, annuity payments became common practice for the American government. Former confederacy militants, such as Little Turtle of the Miami and Shawnee leaders such as Black Hoof, signed the treaty and became known as annuity chiefs. Little Turtle and Black Hoof over the years turned into the most accommodating chiefs in the Old Northwest, working with William Wells at Fort Wayne, a man adopted by the Shawnees and who married to Little Turtle's daughter. The treaty marked the beginning of the American "civilization" program in the Old Northwest. With the support primarily of Black Hoof and Little Turtle, the government dispensed cattle, hogs, and farm implements in an effort to turn Ohio Indian warriors into farmers. Indian women, moreover, were expected to learn the ways of household domesticity. In short, "civilization" involved a complete transformation of the gender roles among the Ohio tribes. Along with acknowledging George Washington's place as their "father" and accepting the "civilization" program, the Treaty of Greenville secured almost the entire Ohio territory for the United States, leaving only a small parcel in the northwest corner of the Ohio for the Miamis and Shawnees. According to the treaty's terms, the United States also gained the rights to Illinois and southern Indiana territories.

Washington and Secretary of War Henry Knox had also moved to control native peoples in a series of trade and intercourse acts. Basically, these acts, on paper, blocked individual states from making treaties with Native Americans and put all such negotiations under the charge of the federal government. The first act, passed earlier on July 22, 1790 and enforced now in the Ohio Valley, gave the federal government the right to license trade. It also prohibited the sale or purchase of private Indian lands and enacted a series of laws to prevent white criminal activity in Indian territories. In 1793, the federal government gained more powers under a new series of acts. The president could mete out punishments against squatters, and he also had the authority to appoint agents in the north and south to promote the civilization program. Under the new act, the president had $20,000 per year to allot to civilizing the Indians.

In 1796, presidential authority was extended further. The new trade and intercourse acts were specifically aimed at the South, where the Cherokees and Creeks still harassed whites. The new laws established the federal factory system. Federal factories were licensed trading houses under the American government. Licensed traders operating out of federally funded and guarded trading posts were supposed to protect the Indians from the fraudulent activities of private traders, control the flow of liquor into Indian communities, and give native peoples plows, chains, hoes, axes, and other items. In essence, the trade and intercourse acts actually encouraged American expansion west by settling Indians on tracts of land that were acknowledged as the Indians' private property, at the same time as they allowed American settlers to move in and occupy surrounding territories.

Under Thomas Jefferson, elected president in 1800, the civilization program intensified. It continued to follow a racial script for Native American cultural and social change. The national government's language in negotiations with specific Indian nations possessed a racial rhetoric directed particularly at native men. Federal

6.5 Black Hoof, a Shawnee leader.

Source: Smithsonian American Art Museum

policymakers repeated time and again that an Indian man's role as a hunter had vanished with the loss of hunting grounds and game. Since Indian men would no longer be able to procure food for their communities in traditional manner, from the government's point of view, the very survival of Indian nations depended on the federal factories and farming. By trading with the federal government, Indian men who took to agriculture and animal husbandry needed less land to support families than if they remained hunters. Indian women as domestics would provide homespun cloth and take care of families. In short, Native Americans east of the Mississippi had to adopt the lifestyles of white settlers or face removal, or possibly extermination.

The civilization program had its earliest successes in three regions: New York, the Ohio territory, and in the South among the Cherokees and Creeks. Among the Senecas, who were bound to small tracts in western New York, a warrior chief named Cornplanter welcomed the civilization program to his small homelands secured from Pennsylvania along the Allegheny River. The Senecas had long-standing connections with the warring tribes of the Ohio territory; consequently, federal policymakers were particularly eager to pacify them. In New York, the federally supported Philadelphia Quakers spearheaded the civilization program, not the federal factory system. The Quakers traveled to western New York in 1796 not to preach, but only to build model farms and teach young men how to use the plow and tend livestock. By 1800, the Quakers operated a moderately successful program in western New York.

Although the federal program of civilization appeared set and Indians across the eastern United States seemed to be in compliance with that effort, there remained substantial opposition among most tribal groups to abandoning their traditional cultures. A significant number of Senecas rejected categorically the Quakers' agricultural program and instead regularly left their reserved tracts to hunt. In the Ohio territory, a small number of Miamis and Shawnees built farms, fenced fields, and raised livestock; however, many Miamis and Shawnees resented the federal factory system and the missionaries, fearing that Shawnees and Miamis on farms would eventually cede all of Shawnee and Miami lands. Resisters among them challenged the missionaries' presence on their lands and rejected the factory system completely. In the South, Alexander McGillivray and other wealthy Creeks modeled themselves on the southern planter class. They built extravagant homes on the most fertile of lands, owned African slaves, and sponsored the construction of roads for trade. In violation of Creek governance by consensus, wealthy Creeks established a council that asserted its own power and enacted laws to protect their property. Both the Creeks and Cherokees established police forces to prosecute thieves within their nations who stole slaves, horses, and other forms of property from both Indians and whites. New inheritance rights where property passed down from fathers to sons challenged Indian concepts of matrilineal descent and the importance of clan mothers. In the South especially, the civilization program gave rise to class-based societies among the Creeks and Cherokees. A few Creek and Cherokee elites held considerable property and exerted power and authority over their people, the vast majority of which did not own slaves, plantations, or large houses.

Prophets and War

The Allegany Seneca chief Cornplanter had a half-brother, also of the Wolf clan, who went by two names, Handsome Lake and Connediu. As with every Seneca man in his earlier years, Handsome Lake had earned honor and prestige as a hunter and warrior. But as a prophet, he looked beyond himself and his villages to the spiritual realm for help to sustain his friends, family, and fellow Seneca during the rough times of the 1790s. He had a series of visions between 1799 and 1800 that offered Handsome Lake a new perspective of life, one that combined elements of the civilization program and Christianity with Iroquois rituals and ceremonials. Handsome Lake's message became known as the "good word," or in Seneca, the *Gaiwi:yo:h*. His was a prophetic message of hope for Seneca sovereignty within the borders of the new American republic. *Gaiwi:yo:h* formed the bedrock of a new religion, the **Longhouse religion**, a faith that helped reestablish cultural and social balance among the Senecas.

Specifically, on June 15, 1799, Handsome Lake was in his house suffering the consequences of excessive alcohol consumption when he entered another dream state and experienced several visions that collectively spoke to Seneca men and women. In the first vision, three men approached him outside his house and offered him strawberries. A second vision carried him to the Sky World where he witnessed the crisis facing Seneca hunters. Moving deeper into the celestial realm, the prophet followed a white path; the color white, like the color red, symbolized the powers of regeneration for the Seneca. There he met a messenger who carried bows and arrows, a symbol that the end of hunting and warring was fast approaching.

With these visions and one more in 1800, Handsome Lake constructed his message. The center of the cosmic universe was the Creator. In calling on the Creator for help, Handsome Lake was much like Neolin, who called on the "Master of Life" to foster Native American unity and harmony. He singled out individual men and women as sinners who would suffer in the afterlife, clearly the imprint of Christian missionary work on Handsome Lake. He wove together multiple strands of Seneca and Eastern Woodland concepts of spiritual power and authority, and, as did other Native American prophets, borrowed the concept of a "hellish inferno" directly from Christian precepts. Angels had warned Handsome Lake in the Sky World of the celestial inferno where transgressing men and women suffered severely. If women failed to give up their sexual and mystical potency, they would be tortured at the hands of a cosmic punisher—the prophet's supernatural inversion of the benevolent Creator. The punisher also singled out men. He forced a drunkard to imbibe melted metal, representing the fired materials that an aggressive hunter needed to take life. In portions of the message, those Seneca men and women who refused to change their ways and follow the prophet's message suffered together in a cosmic doom beyond human comprehension.

Handsome Lake believed his visions had laid out a path forward for Seneca men and women. He encouraged men to become farmers and paternal males, men who cared for children and wives in individual households. For women, he encouraged acceptance of household domesticity. He warned young men to listen to their fathers, a partial move away from matrilineal rules of discipline under grandmothers and mothers. Here, the prophet combined matrilineal rules with republican ideas about virtuous fatherhood and motherhood he learned from the Quakers. Handsome Lake was the supreme Iroquois spiritual leader, giving him the power

PROFILE

Black Hoof, Shawnee Annuity Chief

Black Hoof was a member of the Maykujay branch of Shawnee Indians, a village chief born sometime after 1740. He sided with the British during the American Revolution and again during the warfare of the 1790s. After the Treaty of Greenville, Black Hoof chose a different path than other militant Shawnees did by deciding to seek assistance from the federal government. By 1800, he was the leading Shawnee chief remaining in the Ohio territory, and the federal agents stationed in Indiana and Ohio recognized him as the leader of the Shawnees. Black Hoof received annuity payments from the federal government.

Black Hoof welcomed the federal factory system at Fort Wayne, Indiana, and sought out the assistance of Quakers to help teach other Shawnees how to farm. He earned the disdain of Tecumseh and the Shawnee Prophet (see the section "Prophets and War"), becoming their bitter rival. When two of Black Hoof's followers were murdered, the chief blamed the Shawnee Prophet for their deaths, as they occurred around the same time that the prophet conducted his witch hunts. A major conference of Shawnee leaders convened, and the prophet's followers disavowed any involvement in the murders. When two white men were killed, Tecumseh and Black Hoof traveled to address the issue, and Tecumseh put his hand on Black Hoof and said, "This is the man who killed your white brother." The meeting turned violent, and the rivalry between Black Hoof and Tecumseh intensified. In 1808, when Tecumseh and the Shawnee Prophet moved their villages to the Tippecanoe and Wabash rivers in Indiana, Black Hoof confirmed his position as the leading Shawnee in the Ohio. Quaker assistance increased, and many of Black Hoof's followers abandoned the hunt for farming. When the leading Quaker, William Kirk, was dismissed under charges of misappropriating national funds, Black Hoof traveled to the capital to plead his case.

When war broke out between Tecumseh and the United States in 1812, Black Hoof offered a belt of white wampum to the federal government, an assurance that he meant to keep the peace. Black Hoof helped American troops in the Ohio territory, assisting them with knowledge about British involvement with Tecumseh's supporters. In January 1813, Black Hoof and his followers even marched to help the Americans in northern Ohio. After the war, Black Hoof still sought assistance from the federal government, but he found his people overwhelmed by white settlers who poured into the Old Northwest. Black Hoof, the annuity chief, in spite of all his efforts to change and become like white settlers, found himself pushed off his own lands. A proud Shawnee leader who believed that his people could live peaceably on their lands in Ohio, Black Hoof did not sign the treaty of 1830 that ceded all of the remaining Shawnee lands in Ohio. He never saw Kansas, to which the Shawnees were removed. He died in 1832. Black Hoof's career as a Shawnee warrior turned annuity chief illustrates that not all Indians in the Ohio saw violence against the United States as the only way to protect their autonomy and sovereignty.

to purge unwanted people from Seneca lands. In 1799, he targeted witches. In that year, one of Cornplanter's daughter's, Jiwi, had taken ill. Cornplanter asked the prophet to bring her back to proper health. According to Handsome Lake, witchcraft practiced among the scattered remnant Munsees who lived near Seneca villages had caused Jiwi's incurable state. With his indictment of the Munsees as witches, especially a chief Silverheels and some old women, the prophet demonstrated his desire to cleanse the Seneca lands of people who no longer deserved to share it.

TIMELINE 6.3 TREATIES, WAR, AND THE CIVILIZATION PROGRAM, 1783–1816

Date	Event
1783	Treaty of Paris
1784	Treaty of Fort Stanwix
1785	Treaty of Fort McIntosh
	Treaty of Dumplin Creek
	Treaty of Galphinton
1786	Treaty of Shoulderbone Creek
	Treaty of Fort Finney
	Indian Confederacy meeting at Brownstown
1790	Treaty of New York
	Josiah Harmar routed by the Indian Confederacy
1791	Arthur St. Clair defeated by Indian Confederacy
1794	"Mad" Anthony Wayne defeats the Indian Confederacy at the Battle of Fallen Timbers
1795	Treaty of Greenville
1796	Benjamin Hawkins begins civilization program among the Creeks
1800	Quakers operating farms in New York
	Moravians arrive among the Cherokees
1816	Brainerd Mission school established among the Cherokees

Handsome Lake died in obscurity in 1815. He had lived at a time of fundamental change for native peoples in the East—war, a shrunken Iroquois land base, and a depressed population forced to alter their very cultural foundations through the civilization program. He nonetheless created a spiritual message of hope and regeneration among the Seneca and created a new religion that provided his people with hope.

The civilization program also disrupted the old ways of the Shawnees. Some Shawnee adamantly rejected the transition to agriculture and animal husbandry. Black Hoof's village of Wapakoneta, by contrast, had a permanent Quaker missionary by 1807. The Quaker, William Kirk, brought hogs and cattle and helped build a blacksmith, a school, and even a sawmill. Still other Shawnees continued to hunt game that remained in the northern parts of the Ohio and still traded with British fur traders. Roaming Shawnees even traveled into Canada, where British policymakers listened to the Shawnees' angry words against the Long Knives. By 1800, the old ways of hunting and warring were nearly gone among the Shawnees, and the older generation reflected upon the days when the Master of Life had provided his men with plentiful game and wars to earn sacred power as well as honor and prestige. The old ways were dying; depression settled among many Shawnee.

Shawnees and other Ohio Indians pursued answers to the current turmoil in cultural myths and cosmological beliefs. They believed that malevolent powers in the form of serpents rose from the underworld, possessed humans, and then compelled them to wreak havoc within Indian villages. Humans who succumbed to the

READING HISTORY

Handsome Lake's First Vision, 1799

This vision was first recorded by the Quaker school teacher Henry Simmons Jr. in his journal, which still exists. Simmons was teaching on Cornplanter's grant when Handsome Lake fell into his first trance. It is an exceptional account, and it captures the power of prophetic revivalism as the Senecas faced rapid change in the early American republic.

Cornplanter was about three-fourths of a mile from his home, where he had men employed to build him a house, and where we were engaged in erecting a schoolhouse. An express came to him that his brother or step brother was dying, who had been on the decline of life for several years. Cornplanter went straightway and found a number of his people convened where his brother had been lying breathless for the space of half an hour. But about two hours later, his brother came to himself again and told Cornplanter how he was feeling and informed him of what he had seen, which was as follows. As he lay or sat in the house, he heard somebody calling. [He] arose and went out, his daughter, seeing him, asked where he was going he told her he would soon be back, and as he stood without, he saw three men by the side of the house, he then fainted and fell gently to the ground without being an Sick, the men had Bushes in their hands with berries on them, of different kinds, who invited him to take some and eat, and they would help him, and that he would Live to see such like berries ripe this Summer. He thought he took one berry off of each man's bush. They told him the great Spirit was much displeased with his people's getting drunk, and other gross Evils which they were guilty of, but as to himself they could not charge him with any thing except sometimes getting drunk, but as he had been Sick a great while, he had thought more upon the Great Spirit, and was preserved from drinking Strong drink to excess, and if he got well he must not take to it again for the great Spirit knew (not only what people were always doing) but also their very thoughts, and that there was some very bad ones among them, who would poison others, but one of them was lately killed, yet there still remained one like her who was a man. He requested his brother, to Call his people in Council, and tell them what he had said to him, and if they had any Dri'd Berries amongst them, he wished all in the Council might take it if was but one apiece.

Source: David Swatzler, *A Friend Among the Senecas: The Quaker Mission to Cornplanter's People.* (Mechanicsburg, PA: Stackpole, 2000), pp. 266–267.

Questions

1. What does this vision tell us about Seneca culture at the turn of the century?
2. What are some of the main elements in Handsome Lake's first vision?

serpent became witches. The Long Knives, according to most Shawnees, always followed the serpent's path, but now the serpent's powers had embraced their own people. By the early nineteenth century, the Shawnee communities of the Ohio territory were in disarray and grappling for answers.

As a young man, Lalawethika never won the honor and prestige as a hunter and warrior that his brother Tecumseh earned. Shamed, he turned to a life of alcoholism. One night in 1805, as he sat in his wigwam,

Lalawethika fell into a trance and experienced a vision. In this dream state he visited the top of a mountain where he could see heaven and his people who followed the path of the "Master of Life" enjoying the bounty of limitless game and fertile fields for eternity. He awoke from this vision a changed man. Where he had earlier felt despair, he now held hope for himself and for his people. The answer to the Shawnee was, in part, committing themselves to the Master's road, returning to the original Shawnee values, to traditions. He now called himself Tenskwatawa, or "Open Door." This dramatic event vaulted Tenskwatawa into the position of the Shawnee's spiritual leader. He was now the **Shawnee Prophet**. More visions followed, some reinforcing his first vision, others depicting the destruction suffered by those who did not follow the Shawnee way. Drunkards drank melted lead, and, borrowing from Christianity, the message described a hellish inferno where the bodies of evildoers were cast to burn. Like Handsome Lake, Tenskwatawa emphasized the need to revitalize rituals and ceremonies to heal the hearts and emotions of his communities. The "Master of Life" convinced Tenskwatawa that native peoples had to straighten the course of their lives that had become twisted over years of exposure to the ways of Americans. According to the prophet, "the teaching of the white people led straight to hell." Salvation for the Shawnee lay in purging white culture from Shawnee life. Only revived spiritual powers could help the Indians achieve this goal and defeat their enemies.

Tenskwatawa's movement, described by Gregory Evans Dowd as the search for "native solutions to the catastrophe of colonialism," found a permanent following. Tenskwatawa encouraged other Shawnees to abandon the ways of the Long Knives and warned the Americans that any efforts to try and put down his prophetic movement would result in the apocalyptic destruction of the universe. As Handsome Lake had done among the Senecas, the Shawnee Prophet used his spiritual powers to cleanse his world of witches. Between 1805 and 1806, he ordered the execution of several Delawares who had adopted the civilization program and demanded the killing of two of Black Hoof's followers who he claimed practiced witchcraft. In 1808, when Tenskwatawa drew near the territory of the Miamis, the annuity chief Little Turtle set out to kill the prophet. In response, Tenskwatawa called on his followers to reject annuity chiefs and cursed all annuity chiefs for taking bribes and not defending the Indian homelands. His was a movement of regeneration, of purification.

Tenskwatawa's political and spiritual message laid the foundation for a pan-Indian rebellion against the Americans. Tecumseh took his brother's message throughout the Northwest and into the South. He passed war belts among the Wyandots, Ottawas,

TECUMTHA.

6.6 Tecumseh, sketch by Pierre Le Dru, c. 1810–1812

Source: Toronto Public Library/Wikimedia Commons

TENS-KWAU-TA-WAW
THE PROPHET.

PUBLISHED BY F. W. GREENOUGH, PHILAD.ᵃ

6.7 Ten-squat-a-way, The Open Door, known as The Prophet, brother of Tecumseh

Source: Courtesy of Library of Congress Prints and Photographs Division

and Potawatomis and south to the Creeks, Choctaws, Osages, and Cherokees. By 1807, the territorial governor of Indiana, William Henry Harrison, saw increasing danger in Tenskwatawa's message of revivalism and Tecumseh's message of armed resistance to Indians across the territory. Together, they pressed for the separation of the white world from the Indian world.

Tecumseh traveled throughout the Ohio and Tennessee Valleys, arriving in the territories of the Creek and Cherokees in 1811. He could not have come to the South at a more inauspicious moment. Earthquakes shook the Creek and Cherokee towns that very year and again in 1812. Many Creek and Cherokee prophets experienced their own visions which often resembled those of Tenskwatawa and prophesied the end of their worlds unless the Creeks and Cherokees renewed the old ways of life and abandoned the civilization program. Like Tecumseh, Creeks and Cherokees also portrayed their resistance to Americans in racial terms, the work of the "red people" against the whites. Echoing the Shawnee Prophet and connecting his vision with their own visions, Cherokee seers insisted the journey to Cherokee survival lay in cultural purification, abandoning all elements of the white world. They verbally assailed those within their nation such as Major Ridge, who owned slaves, large plantations, homes, and livestock, and for selling their lands and profiting from the American government. They denounced those who signed away native lands and accepted the Christian religion. They chastised those who altered their appearances to conform to white preferences, who abandoned Cherokee rituals, and who redefined gender roles along white norms. Tecumseh's visit to the South, although less successful than he might have hoped in uniting Indians for armed rebellion, certainly ignited enthusiasm for Indian separatism among southern Indian prophets.

William Henry Harrison used Tecumseh's extended absence to strike at the mixed force of Shawnee, Winnebago, Kickapoo, Creek, and Potawatomi warriors assembled by Tenskwatawa. Harrison struck hard and razed to the ground Tecumseh's home village, but he suffered heavier losses than the Indians. Tecumseh returned from the South and immediately reached out to the British in nearby Canada for military support against the United States. Great Britain had for years supplied native warriors with weapons to harass American communities west of the Appalachians. Seeing the British as instigators of backcountry turmoil that might easily ignite another frontier war and challenging Great Britain on numerous and diverse other issues that even extended to seaborne trade, President James Madison in 1812 secured from Congress a declaration of war.

War on the frontier was rather short-lived. Tecumseh's collection of tribal warriors struck along the length of the frontier from the Great Lakes into the Tennessee Valley, but at most every battle site the American forces held their ground or routed the Indians. British supplies to the Indians also trailed off as this war with America once more drew other actors in Europe. Native Americans deserted Tecumseh's forces. Harrison tracked Tecumseh and his few British allies up the Thames River in Canada where, at the Battle of the Thames in 1813, Tecumseh was shot dead. The pan-Indian effort to retake the Old Northwest died with him, and his brother's call for revivalism collapsed. The War of 1812 was the last time the British would come to the aid of the Indians in the Old Northwest.

With the exception of a major British-American battle in New Orleans, war in the South was largely a civil war among Native Americans. Similar to the efforts of Tenskwatawa and Tecumseh, Creek prophets launched a resistance movement to regenerate native cultures. The Creek prophet Hillis Hadjo and other visionaries targeted those wealthy Creeks who, in their minds, had been corrupted by acculturation programs. The new native elite pursued personal material gain, asserted power through their wealth, and abandoned the Creeks' traditional world view by their acceptance of Christianity. Creek salvation from white America lay in resistance—resistance to so-called "civilization" programs and resistance to further land loss. Those who championed the prophets' message of regeneration assumed the name **Redsticks** because of the red battle clubs they carried. The Redstick movement fractured the Creek Nation, as Indians understood that war would most likely result from the revival initiative. They were correct, but war came not immediately from the United States government but rather from within the Creek Nation itself. By July 1813, nearly every Upper Creek town had joined the Redsticks. Gaining a few arms and supplies from the Spanish who occupied western Florida, the

PROFILE

Hillis Hadjo, the Creek Prophet

Hillis Hadjo was a Creek chief born around 1770. Also known as Joseph Francis, he was the son of David Francis, a white trader. Hillis Hadjo, or Hilis Hadsho, is a name derived from a combination of Muskogee words: "hilis," meaning medicine, and "hadsho," meaning crazy. Hillis Hadjo became a prophet around 1812. According to oral tradition, Hadjo spent ten days learning the necessary sacred powers to become a prophet. After his transformation, Hadjo earned the reputation as the leading prophet among the Creeks. He was responsible for turning other Creek resistance leaders into prophets. In June 1813, just before the outbreak of the Creek War, Hadjo encamped with a large number of followers near the Alabama River, probably making preparations for their war against the whites and wealthy Creeks in South Alabama.

Hadjo, like the Shawnee Prophet, spread a message of a return to the old ways. He emboldened the Redsticks with his message. A major battle took place at the battle of the Holy Ground or Eccanachaca. On December 23, 1813, Hadjo made a spiritual line around the Redstick encampment, claiming that the space within that circle "never would be sullied by the footsteps of the real white man." According to Hadjo's prophecy, any of General Ferdinand L. Clairborne's regiment that tried to step over the line "would fall lifeless to earth."

The Americans won the battle and under Andrew Jackson won the war, in spite of Hadjo's prophetic messages. After the battle of the Holy Ground, Hadjo fled to Florida, where he joined the rebellious Seminoles. He fought alongside the Seminoles during the First Seminole War, still carrying his prophetic message of separatism and resistance.

TIMELINE 6.4 PROPHETS AND WAR, 1799–1814

Date	Event
1799–1800	Handsome Lake has his visions
1805	Shawnee Prophet has his vision and begins the nativist movement in the Old Northwest
1811	Tecumseh travels to the Creeks and Cherokees
1811	William Henry Harrison defeats the nativists at the Battle of Tippecanoe
1813	Tecumseh defeated at the Battle of the Thames
1812–1814	Redstick Rebellion among the Creeks

Redsticks vented their anger at wealthy Creeks in the towns of Tuckabatche and Coweta. Hillis Hadjo claimed that the Master of Life spoke to him directly and selected him to guide the Redsticks in their war. Redsticks killed elite Creeks and destroyed their property—their symbols of wealth and power. One group of Redstick warriors traveled to Pensacola to get more supplies from the Spanish and there were countered by mixed-blood Creeks and white militia units from surrounding states. Redsticks withdrew but counterattacked at Fort Mims where they confronted American units gathered from Tennessee and Georgia.

Andrew Jackson led his Tennessee militia into the heart of the Creek rebellion. In March 1814, he and his men assaulted a fortified encampment of Redsticks at Horseshoe Bend. Jackson's militia, which included Cherokee, Choctaw, and Chickasaw warriors, slaughtered the Redsticks, many of whom were without guns and ammunition. Eight hundred Redstick warriors, women, and children perished in the strike. The Redstick rebellion was broken. In August 1814, Jackson arranged a truce with the Creeks, even though he had not been authorized to do so by the federal government. The treaty was between Jackson and Creek elites whose authority was no longer challenged in the Creek Nation, and it required the Indians to cede 22 million acres to Georgia, Tennessee, and Alabama.

As a final twist to a war fought between the powerful and propertied and the powerless and poor, the Creek elites who signed the treaty demanded compensation for their lost property. The U.S. government gave the Creek elites $85,000 in 1817 and an inheritance of $110,417.90 to the children of the elites who had lived during the war.

Western Revolutions

Indian rebellions had always compromised Spanish efforts in the Southwest, particularly in the area of present-day New Mexico. Beginning in the early 1760s these rebellions but an emerging revolution among Indians themselves assumed far greater importance in determining Spain's future in North America and in shaping the expansion of the United States. Indeed, Spanish control in that northern territory was diminishing at that point in time, the product of near continuous warfare with tribal groups across the region, an inability to populate sufficiently the northern stretch and develop a sustainable economy there, and a weakening of authority within Mexico itself.

In addition, the Southwest borderlands economy rested on trading, raiding, and captive exchange with principal markets at Pecos, Taos, and Santa Fe that were dominated by Comanches, Apaches, Utes, Wichitas,

Navajos, and Cheyennes. Horseback Indians traded captives for hides, buffalo meat, horses, guns, and cloth. The Spanish, in need of labor for their mines and ranches in Nueva Vizcaya and Sonora, eagerly traded with the Indians, but the sheer diversity of cultures present at the trading centers and the intensity of competition among them carried the potential for violence.

The Borderlands Revolution: Comanchería

Following prolonged and violent confrontations with Comanches in his first term as New Mexico's governor and facing continued hostilities in his second term, Tomás Vélez de Cachupín took steps to peace with the western Comanches in the early 1760s. From Spain's perspective, the treaty made the Comanches vassals of the crown of Spain and tied to trade in New Mexico; from the Comanches' perspective, the governor had acqui- esced to their authority and they were free to conduct business anywhere they chose. Given the power they commanded in the Southwest, the Comanches extended trade ties with the Kiowas, Pawnees, and Cheyennes on the western plains, with farming tribes along the Missouri River, and with a branch of the Wichitas and Taovayas. After 1763, Comanche trade increasingly included ties with the British who now commanded the Louisiana Territory recently won from France. From British forts along the Mississippi, the Taovayas acquired guns, iron hatchets, and metal utensils and, in turn, sold these goods to the Western Comanches. Comanche trade spread far and wide, ultimately controlling the horse and arms trade across the Southwest borderlands. In fact, by the 1770s, the economy of the Southwest was under Comanche control.

The Comanches divided New Mexico into distinct spheres of economic activity. In some areas, they secured captives and horses; in other areas, they purchased corn and other goods. Comanches then siphoned the cap- tives and horses to other native groups, establishing tight bonds of kinship and friendship to prevent other Native Americans from becoming potential enemies. Spain had no control over its northern provinces, as east- ern and western Comanches created domains, even moving as far south as Texas to attack the Apaches. As their empire expanded, their decentralized political system changed to meet new demands. Head chiefs emerged among both the eastern and western Comanches to control warfare, conduct diplomacy, oversee surrounding Comanche communities, and negotiate and expand economic relations.

Comanchería: Wealth and Empire

Comanchería faced significant challenges in the last decades of the eighteenth century. Even with a population of more than 40,000, the Comanches could not completely ignore actions of other native peoples. Because trade was crucial to maintaining a population of that size, a skilled enemy that succeeded in cutting off trade to Comanchería could destabilize the emerging Comanche Empire. The situation was made even trickier by the complicated, shifting diplomatic environment. Diplomatic and economic stability went hand in hand. For example, the Wichita were the Comanche Empire's economic lifeline to the Lower Mississippi Valley. Thus, when the Wichita chose to break with the Comanche and ally themselves with the Spanish, it was both a dip- lomatic and an economic blow to the Comanches.

Both the Spanish and the Comanches were under pressure in the late eighteenth century, so the time was ripe for a realignment of the relationship between the two regional powers. Negotiating with Ecueracapa, *cap- itan general* (head chief) of the western Comanches in 1786, New Spain successfully secured a peace with the western Comanches and with the eastern Comanches, ending 30 years of sporadic warfare. For the Spanish, the treaties were part of a larger effort to reform and streamline their empire. For the Comanches, peace with New Spain provided them with more secure borders at a time when they confronted both hostile neighbors and deadly disease. Comanchería faced war against former native allies who, in turn, threatened the economic networks that ran through their communities and they faced a continent-wide smallpox epidemic that took the lives of nearly two-thirds of the Comanche population in certain areas.

Into this environment the United States expanded in the early nineteenth century. Portions of the Louisiana Purchase purchased by Thomas Jefferson in 1803 were under Comanche control. As the Americans moved in, the Comanches integrated the economic opportunities associated with the American presence into the existing Comanche economy. At the same time, the American market economy began to influence Comanche life.

Some Comanches became pastoral, turning to farming and herding and connecting themselves to the American marketplace. As Americans moved into westward in the 1820s and 1830s, Comanches traded Indian slaves to slave-poor areas in Texas, Louisiana, and New Mexico. Indigenous captives among the Comanches, once part of extensive networks of kinship and community, had been transformed into market capital by the early nineteenth century. The economic changes brought about by American expansion helped create a new class order among the Comanches. Men with the most horses, slaves, and women workers were considered rich among the Comanches. Within the Comanche Empire, such wealthy men earned an elite status not for their abilities to raid, kill, and trade as in former days, but simply because they had accumulated capital. As among the Creeks and Cherokees who fell under the sway of the American civilization program, the United States' market economy created propertied and powerful Comanche men, and a poor and powerless group of younger Comanches. Young men stole the horses and wives of wealthier Comanches to compete in the open market. Changing patterns among the Comanche, predicated on American expansion, increasingly resembled those affecting tribal groups east of the Mississippi.

Alta California: Missionary Revolutions

Indians in Alta California, which encompassed most of present-day California, lived in tribal communities with social hierarchies based on village centers. Subsistence depended on the rich resources of Alta California. Moving in small encampments in seasonal patterns, tribesmen exploited coastal areas rich in sources of fish and shellfish. In the winter, groups protected stores of collected acorns and other accumulated plants, and they burned trees and grasslands to prepare for the spring harvest and to open pastoral lands to large animals. Ritual, ceremony, and goods exchange connected California peoples who protected the areas from which they gathered food.

Once the Spanish entered the region, such patterns of living changed at a rapid pace. Spanish occupation of the Monterey region came much later than the occupation of borderlands territories. After several decades of exploration along the coast and continuous conflict with coastal native peoples, Gaspar de Portolá succeeded in 1769 in taking the harbor waters. A short time after Portolá's maritime expedition, Franciscan missionaries and military and government personnel flooded Alta California, extending their reach north and south, among major groups such as the Yokuts and Chumash.

The arrival of the Spanish brought disease and environmental change that disrupted native subsistence and settlement patterns, forcing many local Indians into the mission system. Whether disease had devastated Alta California's Indians before 1769 is unclear, but once the Franciscan leader Junípero Serra began to construct a chain of missions, disease spread like wildfire (see Figure 6.3). Historian Steven Hackel's data of Indians who entered San Carlos points to the damaging effect disease had on the Indian communities of Alta California. Indians who entered the missions were largely young orphans or widows, suggesting that family structures had started to fall apart in Alta California. The arrival of animals such as horses, pigs, and cattle destroyed the delicate balance of sacredness and livelihood the California Indians had sustained with the environment of Alta California. Cattle grazed on the grasslands that Esselen and Costanoan peoples once depended on for

TIMELINE 6.5 WESTERN REVOLUTIONS, 1762–1786

Date	Event
1762	Treaty of Fontainebleau
1763	Treaty of Paris
	Rise of Comanchería as its own empire
1769	Franciscans begin chain of missions in Alta California
1771	Comanches begin sustained raids on New Mexico
1780–1781	Comanches hit by smallpox
1786	New Mexico secures peace with Western Comanches
1780s–1800s	Comanches become pastoral, increase their wealth, and encounter Americans

their crops and game. Rapidly growing livestock and cattle populations crushed Indian cornfields and entered native villages. Indians sought to check the spread of Spanish animals but were punished if they killed animals owned by missionaries or soldiers. Foreign plants invaded Alta California's ecology, completely overgrowing native territories.

Mission Life

The Franciscan missionaries who worked in the missions of Alta California were of a new generation and under new regulations. Determined to strengthen royal control over New Spain, in the eighteenth century the Spanish crown initiated a series of reforms that, among other things, curtailed the social, political, and economic power of Franciscan missionaries in the New World. In the face of these reforms, the Franciscan friars of Alta California redoubled their efforts in an attempt to prove that the Franciscan mission program still had life and was still important. At the same time, the new generation of friars came to their work with a new set of attitudes about Indians and their culture. In the seventeenth century, most friars believed that Indian spirituality was the work of the devil and the root cause of differences between Indians and Europeans. They believed that the full immersion of Indians in the Catholic faith was the key to removing the influence of indigenous religions. Accomplishing this goal required the friars to learn Indian languages and study Indian cultures. Only by communicating directly with Indians and discussing the differences between the Indians' current beliefs and practices and the "true" faith could a long-lasting transformation of Indian life ever happen.

The new generation of friars, in contrast to the earlier generation, focused on Indian "sinfulness and ignorance" and the external behaviors among native peoples that demonstrated such qualities. On the one hand, once Indians were brought within missions they were subject to strict rules designed to force mission Indians to conform to Spanish expectations of social behavior and work patterns. On the other hand, the process of baptism and conversion in Alta California became less demanding. After a century of experience in other parts of New Spain, the Franciscans had come to believe that Indians, at least at first, could only gain a child's grasp of Catholic teachings. Facing a dwindling Indian population as disease took its toll, the friars shortened the amount of time it took for an Indian to achieve baptism into the Catholic faith.

Once accepted into the faith, new converts studied and recited a version of the catechism on a daily basis, attended church services and ceremonies, and were encouraged to reflect on Catholic images in art and sculpture. Visual imagery, music, rites, confession, and celebrations within mission compounds reinforced

PROFILE

Indian Leaders in the Franciscan Missions

Franciscan missionaries became dependent on Indians to act as civil magistrates within the mission system. These California Indians, known as *alcaldes*, kept many mission records, served as godparents at baptisms, and acted as witnesses at marriages. They also served as soldiers for the missions and were rewarded with privileges such as overseeing labor and food production. Such Indian leaders, who were mostly male, were forced to straddle two worlds within the Franciscan mission system, which was often a difficult process. On the one hand, their positions as leaders depended on their service to the Franciscans. On the other hand, they were also leaders of their people and frequently rebelled to protect Indian cultural practices.

Nicolás José is a prime example of a mission Indian leader. Nicolás José was one of the first Indians to enter the San Gabriel mission, and he soon earned enough respect among the Franciscans to oversee baptisms and marriages. In 1775, Nicolás José was a witness when a nearby leader from a village sought conversion. The Franciscans made Nicolás José the first *alcalde* of San Gabriel in 1778–1779. Following a practice of redistribution common among California Indians, Nicolás José gave women to local soldiers. The Franciscans, who saw such practices as sinful, punished Nicolás José for his actions.

In October 1785, Nicolás José led a rebellion at the mission of San Gabriel. Frustrated that the soldiers and friars would not allow the California Indians to practice traditional ceremonies, Nicolás José gathered mission Indians and unconverted villagers together to revolt against the mission system. The rituals he sought to protect included the Mourning Ceremony, held in the fall "to honor the souls of those who had died in the interval" since the last Mourning Ceremony. The Mourning Ceremony was the last in a series of rites to pass the ancestor spirits from the earth to the sacred universe. Rituals such as the Mourning Ceremony bonded kin and community to the dead and were central to the California Indians' ritual calendar. The Franciscans had broken with the common practice in Alta California in which the missionaries allowed the Indians to practice such annual dances and ceremonies.

Ironically, it was Nicolás José's position as an *alcalde* that gave him the leverage to organize the rebellion. He understood the internal workings of San Gabriel, the position of the soldiers, their numbers, and the potential weaknesses that he could exploit to mount his rebellion. Prior to the rebellion, Nicolás José met with Toypurina, a 25-year-old woman living on the outskirts of the mission. She brought Nicolás José to the village leaders outside of the mission. The banning of the California Indians' religious practices was enough incentive for the Indians outside of the mission to join Nicolás José. Even unbaptized Indians faced the dual revolutions of disease and environmental change. Their lives were also in upheaval. During the attack, as a symbol of their hatred of the changes to their environment, Indians killed the Franciscans' livestock. The Franciscans punished Nicolás José for organizing the rebellion by expelling him from San Gabriel and sending him to the presidio of San Francisco where he served six years of hard labor. The rebellion of 1785, which Nicolás José led, demonstrates the precarious nature of the Alta California mission system that depended on Indians for leadership but also brought unprecedented and unwanted changes to the California Indians.

neophytes' devotion to the faith and served as social control mechanisms to prevent Indians from backsliding into native ways of life.

Mission life did not completely wipe out Native American cultural patterns. In fact, a painting by a Chumash neophyte at Mission Santa Inés of Archangel Raphael demonstrates the potential of melding Indian world views with Catholicism. Raphael appears to be a Chumash and carries a fish, representative of the Indian sacred natural world. His wings are not the soft wings of an angel, but rather they display the muscularity of an animal. One can argue that the wings might be that of the California Condor, a high-status bird within Chumash cosmology.

Over the course of the last half of the eighteenth century, the Franciscans of Alta California's missions worked hard to restructure the Indian world. Nonetheless, Native Americans did manage to maintain some degree of individual and community autonomy. Most Indians first entered missions in search of food and protection. Once inside, they discovered that mission life was not easy. As Indian families tried to rebuild themselves within missions, the close quarters, demands of labor, and food shortages all contributed to the spread of disease. Birth rates were incredibly low in the mid- to late eighteenth century, as the young and the old succumbed to a host of illnesses. Franciscans tried to enforce strict marriage and family patterns upon peoples whose adult numbers were only sustained by new arrivals to the missions. The friars put considerable effort into seeking out and punishing Indians who did not abide by Catholic rules of marriage and sexuality. Padres controlled Indian behavior with a strict regime of corporal punishment and turned Indians over to presidio soldiers to prosecute and punish them for violations of Spanish law. California native peoples faced trials for homicide and robberies, standing before military courts.

At the same time, elements of Indian leadership structures remained intact within the missions. Franciscans built on Indian systems of leadership and allowed Indians to select other Indians for certain offices. Such Indian leaders abided by Spanish rules at times and looked to subvert them at others, depending on what they saw as most important to reinforcing community security within missions. The mission Indians played an important role in the colonial economy, providing labor for mission and presidio operations. Through such work, Indians learned new artisan and craft skills that proved useful once the mission system was dismantled. However, as long as the missions dominated Alta California, Indians' talents were channeled into the colonial economic system. Indians worked as craftspeople, day laborers, herdsmen, field hands, painters, and bricklayers to advance the interests of the missions and presidios.

Keeping families intact within missions proved to be increasingly hard. Many Indians fled the missions entirely, seeking new kin and community networks outside the bounds of the colonial system. Missionaries and soldiers hunted down fugitive Indians, often inflicting brutal punishments on those they captured. After 1769, the chain of missions that stretched across Alta California became not only institutions of colonialism but also of a strict Catholic regime within which Indians struggled to hold on to old patterns of living.

The sweeping changes that affected native peoples across the Southwest in the late eighteenth and early nineteenth centuries signaled troubling years ahead for Indians, the Spanish, and the Americans. Developing economic patterns, shifting alliances and intertribal relations, and the weakening of one global power and the rise of another altogether suggested a coming struggle for survival.

Conclusion

After 1763, Native North America faced a series of revolutions sparked by both internal and external forces. Across the continent, Indians found their lives disrupted and their ways of life challenged by colonial pressure and the internal struggle within their communities to determine how best to respond to the forces that threatened them. By the early nineteenth century, the United States had emerged as the dominant force. Native peoples, however, stood in the way of the new nation's expansionist dreams. Americans quelled Indian rebellions in the trans-Appalachian West and extended the civilization program and their power into that region. As the century progressed, and after the period of Indian removal discussed in the next chapter, the struggle to maintain native sovereignty against the American new order moved west.

Review Questions

1. Explain why Indians joined the American Revolution.
2. What happened to native peoples in the trans-Appalachian west after 1783?
3. Compare and contrast the Indians' Revolution in the East versus the West.

Recommended Readings

Calloway, Colin G. *The American Revolution in Indian Country: Crisis and Diversity in Native American Communities* (New York: Cambridge University Press, 1995). Still offers the best coverage of the American Revolution among Indian communities.
———. *One Vast Winter Count: The Native American West Before Lewis and Clark* (Lincoln, NE: University of Nebraska Press, 2003). A sweeping survey of the West.
———. *The Scratch of a Pen: 1763 and the Transformation of North America* (New York: Oxford University Press, 2006). The best study of the importance of the year 1763.
Dowd, Gregory Evans. *A Spirited Resistance: The North American Indian Struggle for Unity, 1745–1815* (Baltimore: Johns Hopkins University Press, 1992). A seminal work about pan-Indian resistance, its spiritual and political components, and the factionalism that divided native peoples.
Hackel, Steven C. *Children of Coyote, Missionaries of St. Francis: Indian-Spanish Relations in Colonial California, 1769–1850* (Chapel Hill: University of North Carolina Press, 2005). The best and most balanced account of the Franciscan mission work in Alta California.
Hämäläinen, Pekka. *The Comanche Empire* (New Haven: Yale University Press, 2008). A vastly significant study of the rise of the Comanche and the creation of their empire.
Saunt, Claudio. *A New Order of Things: Property, Power, and the Transformation of the Creek Indians, 1733–1816* (New York: Cambridge University Press, 1999). One of the best studies of the Creeks and their adoption of property and how that contributed to the Redstick Rebellion.
Wallace, Anthony F. C. *The Death and Rebirth of the Seneca* (New York: Alfred A. Knopf, 1969). The classic study of the Senecas in post-Revolutionary America and the rise of Handsome Lake.
White, Richard. *The Middle Ground: Indians, Empires, and Republics in the Great Lakes Region* (New York: Cambridge University Press, 1991). An important work on the world of villages in the Old Northwest during the American Revolution.

Native American History Online

General Sites

Sullivan-Clinton Campaign: Then and Now. http://sullivanclinton.com/ This site offer a digital reproduction of the Sullivan-Clinton Campaign and demonstrates how George Washington's decision forever changed the history of Iroquoia.
R.E. Moore, *The Texas Comanches*. www.texasindians.com/comanche.htm A resource on the Comanches and their history in Texas.

Historical Sites

Johnson Hall State Historical Site, Johnstown, New York. www.parks.ny.gov/historic-sites/10/details.aspx The site provides access to Johnson Hall, the home of Sir William Johnson, where students can look at the mansion and its interior.

Old Fort Niagara, Youngstown, New York. http://oldfortniagara.org This site offers a tour of Fort Niagara, a National Historic Landmark.

Horseshoe Bend National Military Park, Daviston, Alabama. www.nps.gov/hobe/index.htm A rich resource into the history of Horseshoe Bend, a 2,040-acre park that preserves the site of the battle between General Andrew Jackson and the Upper Creek warriors.

CHAPTER 7

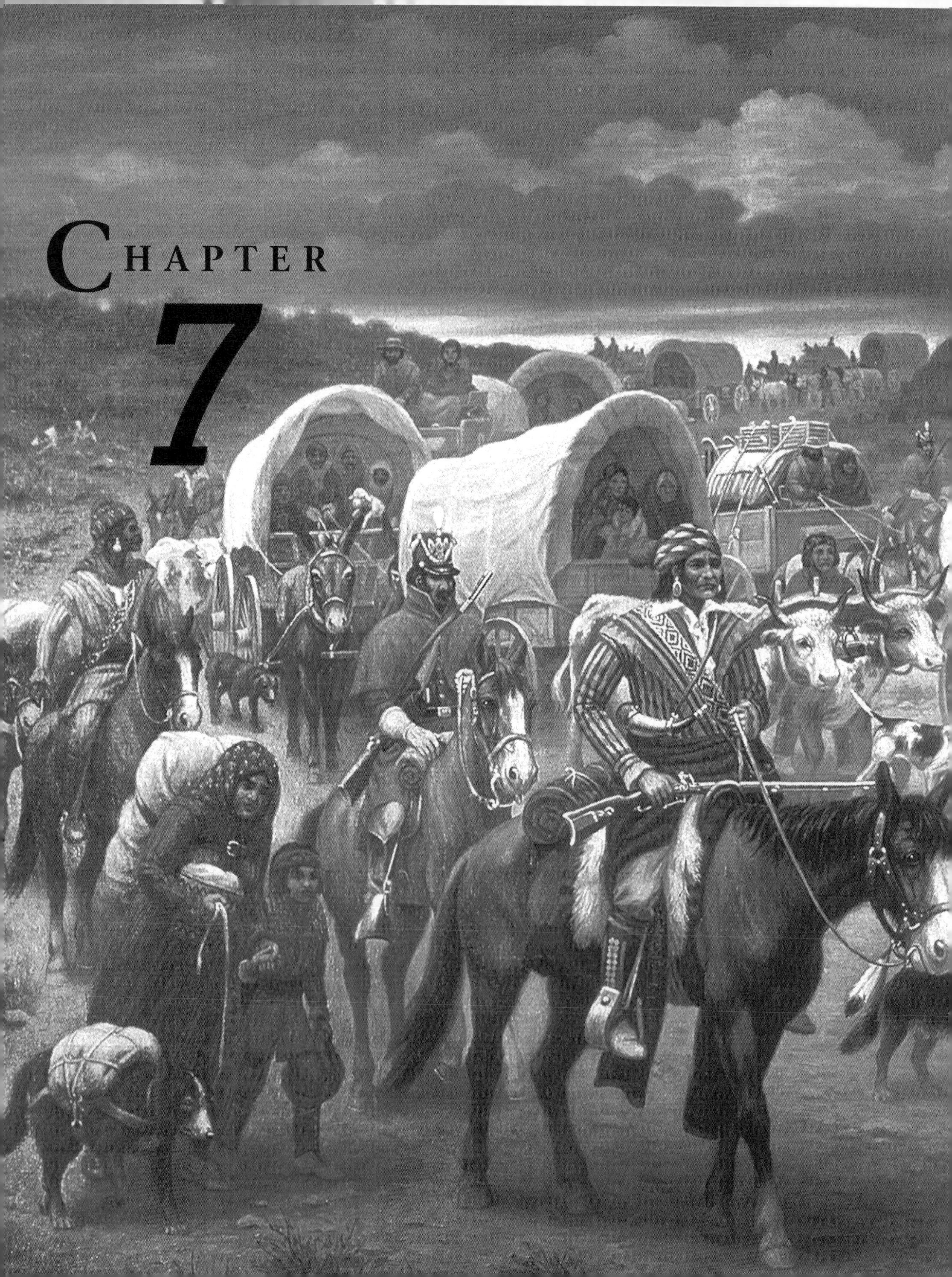

Removal, 1801–1846

"Do You Want Our Country?"
Southern Removal
Cherokee "Civilization"
Cherokees Challenged
Cherokee Removal
The Creek Road to Oklahoma
Choctaw Removal
Chickasaws Head West
Resisting Removal
Seminoles Fight
The Black Hawk War
Removal From the North
Restoring Sovereignty in the Indian Territory
Rebuilding the Cherokee Nation
Resurgence Among Indians From the South
Indian Territory and the "Peculiar Institution" of Slavery

"Do You Want Our Country?"

In the 1820s, a series of hunting-ground disputes broke out among tribes near mineral-rich lands in Minnesota and Wisconsin, lands taken over by American settlers looking to strike it rich. In the territories of the Dakota Sioux and Ojibwa, the Sauks and Mesquakies searched for game, but these lands were not their traditional hunting grounds. Soon enough, all these groups plunged into a regional war. In August 1825, the federal government entertained a council of Western Indians at Prairie du Chien, Wisconsin, along the upper Mississippi River. Federal officials expressed their concerns about the ongoing violence: "the United States of America have seen that wars have for many years been carried on between the Sioux and the Chippewas, and more recently between the confederated tribes of

The Trail of Tears is immortalized in this painting by Robert Lindneux, created in 1942 to commemorate the suffering of the Cherokee people under forced removal.

Source: *The Trail of Tears*, 1838. The removal of the Cherokee Native Americans to the West in 1838. Oil on canvas, 1942, by Robert Lindneux. Courtesy of Granger

Sacs and Foxes, and the Sioux . . . which, if not terminated, may extend to the other tribes, and involve the Indians upon the Missouri, the Mississippi, and the Lakes, in general hostilities." Judging by the turnout at

CHRONOLOGY

1801	Treaty of Chickasaw Bluffs
1804	Treaty of 1804
1805	Treaty of the Chickasaw Nation
1808	Thomas Jefferson negotiates Treaty of Removal with the Cherokees
1819	Adams-Onís Treaty
1816–1819	Cherokee Land Cessions
1821	Treaty of Chicago
1823	Treaty of Moultrie Creek
1824	First Cherokee Race Law
	Treaty of Indian Springs between Creeks and Georgia
1825	Treaty of Prairie du Chien
1826	Creation of the Choctaw Nation
1827	Removal of Creeks to Alabama
1827–1828	Full-fledged Cherokee Constitution modeled on the United States
1827–1830	Georgian Laws enacted against the Cherokees
1829	Extension of Mississippi Law over the Choctaws
1830	First Choctaws leave for the Indian Territory
1830	Andrew Jackson's Indian Removal Act
1831	Menominees give up land in Wisconsin for the Stockbridge-Brothertown and Oneidas from New York
	Cherokee Nation v. *Georgia*
1832	*Worcester* v. *Georgia*
	Treaty of 1832 between the Creeks and the federal government
	Treaty of Payne's Landing
	Black Hawk War
1835	Treaty of New Echota
	Removal of the Creeks from Alabama
1835–1842	Second Seminole War
1837–1840	Chickasaw removal
1838	Trail of Tears
1838	Treaty of Buffalo Creek
	Potawatomi "Trail of Death"
1846	Unification of the Cherokee Nation in the Indian Territory

Prairie du Chien, the region's Native Americans shared the government's concerns. Over 1,000 tribal members from the Sauk, Mesquakie, Menominee, Iowa, Dakota, Sioux, Ho-Chunk (Winnebago), and the United Band of Ottawa, Ojibwa, and Potawatomis were present. The conference resulted in a new treaty. Articles 1–12 of the treaty stipulated boundaries for the warring tribes so that there "shall be a firm and perpetual peace." It did not, however, resolve the root cause of conflict, which was the influx of white settlers into the region. In spite of the treaty, altercations over hunting grounds continued and white settlement went unabated. The Ho-Chunk speaker Little Elk in 1827, in defiance of the United States, posed a question to which most Indians and whites already knew the answer: "Do you want our Country? Yours is much larger than ours."

Indians of the Old Northwest were not alone in their anger over white encroachments. Little Elk's words would have resonated among Indians in the South who faced similar duress. Southerners wanted to push the cotton frontier into western Georgia, Alabama, Mississippi, and Florida, but their hunger for land required the removal of the so-called **"Five Civilized Tribes"**—Cherokees, Creeks, Choctaws, Chickasaws, and Seminoles. In 1808, Thomas Jefferson set a precedent when he pressured a few Cherokee chiefs to sell some lands and move to Arkansas, even though, according to Cherokee custom, a small group of chiefs had no right to cede any Cherokee soil. After 1808, the southern states took Indian removal into their own hands, beginning a decades-long struggle for white control of all southern lands.

The United States looked to establish a new order east of the Mississippi after Native American military losses in the Old Northwest and the South. This chapter examines the ways in which Indian removal intensified in the 1820s and reached its peak in the 1830s, as both Northern and Southern states, pressed by a land-hungry American citizenry, signed land cession treaties with native peoples. The chapter will also explore Native American resistance to this process. Florida Seminoles used the peninsula's difficult swampy environment to their advantage, waging the Second Seminole War for eight years and staving off large-scale removal until the 1840s. Sauks and Mesquakies in the Illinois territory under Black Hawk's leadership fought a short-lived anti-removal campaign. After tracing the unprecedented ethnic cleansing of thousands of Indians east of the Mississippi to the **Indian Territory**, or present-day Oklahoma, the chapter concludes with an examination of the efforts of removed native peoples, particularly from the South, to rebuild their sovereignty and autonomy in new lands.

Southern Removal

The removal of Native Americans from their traditional lands to properties farther west long marked the history of Indian-white relations in the eastern woods of North America. Few major concentrations of native peoples remained east of the Appalachians in the early 1800s, principally the Iroquois Confederacy, the Cherokee, and the Seminole. The Iroquois held secure title to their lands. In the Treaty of Canandaigua (1793), Congress recognized the Six Nations as an autonomous, sovereign *nation* within the borders of the United States, and that relationship between the United States and the Iroquois Nation remained protected by both parties until the early days of World War II. But the Cherokee and Seminole confronted a different reality. The Cherokee resided on lands desperately desired by southern farmers and by miners; the Seminole occupied a region somewhat conducive to agriculture but more importantly property that was strategic for securing the South's cotton economy. It became imperative in the early nineteenth century for the United States to remove those Native Americans.

George Washington and Thomas Jefferson, two of the first three presidents, and both Southerners, advanced the civilization program. Native Americans, if properly encouraged, would adapt themselves to the dominant white culture, accepting as their own the values and habits of white society and, in so doing, relinquishing all vestiges of traditional native life. They would cede their lands to the United States, except those tracts on which they would become yeoman farmers or establish businesses. Over time, they would assimilate fully with white society. Lands no longer held by tribal groups would be open for white settlement and development. Indians who refused acculturation and assimilation were to be removed to native-controlled lands west of the Mississippi River and there continue their traditional lives. From the perspective of the federal government and white citizens generally, the concept seemed logical and proper. Jefferson, however, gave even more traction to the idea of Indian removal. In 1802, he convinced Georgia to give up title to a land known as the Yazoo Strip, and promised in return that he would dispossess the Native Americans of any ownership of the land. In 1808, Jefferson convinced a group of Cherokees to cede a portion of their lands and move to Arkansas. Removal acquired priority over acculturation in the 1820s as a new group of politicians, the Jacksonian Democrats, emerged. Many Jacksonians were men born and raised on the Southern frontier or in the new western states of Kentucky and Tennessee. They believed that Indians would never fully acculturate, that assimilation was but a fanciful and misguided notion. Indians could never accommodate themselves to white society. After the admission of six new Deep South states, the Jacksonians had all they needed to focus their attention on the final removal of the Southern tribes. Under the banner of states' rights, Georgia, Alabama, Mississippi, and other Southern states called for the complete removal of the "Five Civilized Tribes." Andrew Jackson, who promoted himself as the common man's president, had the determination and popular support for the Indians' absolute removal from the South.

Although it is not well explained in most textbooks, Indian removal played out in the North as well. As a swath of migrants pushed from the Atlantic seaboard into the new northern states carved out of the Northwest Ordinance, native peoples in Ohio, Michigan, Wisconsin, and Illinois also faced removal. Combined, the removal of Native Americans in the 1820s and 1830s involved the displacement of over 100,000 Native Americans into a new Indian Territory carved out of the lands in the trans-Missouri west. From all perspectives, removal was tragic ethnic cleansing driven by greed and racism (see Map 7.1).

Cherokee "Civilization"

It had always been the goal of the colonists and now the American citizenry to eliminate the native presence either through extermination, relocation, or acculturation. "Civilizing" the Indian, as the phrase went, held the idea that there was nothing of value in native cultures and that Native Americans existed in a primitive state incompatible with advanced societies of European origin. Warfare and disease over the previous centuries certainly depopulated native populations and compelled the relocation of survivors, but concentrations of Native Americans still resided east of the Mississippi River as the eighteenth century drew to a close. The "moral high ground" among white Americans now dictated the full acculturation of those native peoples—essentially a goal that echoed the Praying Towns of colonial New England and "reform" efforts associated with

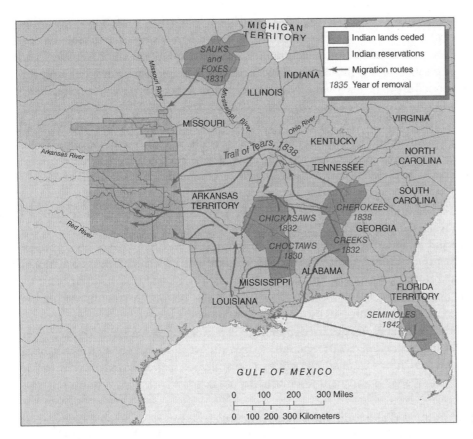

Map 7.1 Indian removal

the late nineteenth century. The Cherokee understood clearly the need to acculturate. Their earlier trade in deerskins no longer commanded market attention, and the warfare so common to the region generally and to the Cherokee particularly shrunk their territory to a fraction of what they once controlled. White settlement nearly enveloped their nation; indeed, as the white population nationally reached five million by 1800 and showed every sign of rapid growth in the coming decades, and as the South clamored for additional lands on which to cultivate the new principal cash crop of cotton, further white expansion promised to further box in the Cherokee people. Acculturation appeared the only viable course to Cherokee survival and continued residency on what remained of their traditional grounds. Toward that end, a powerful and influential leadership within the Cherokee Nation commenced a cultural redirection that promised to alter fundamentally the Indians' community structures, personal values, and world view. As the nineteenth century opened, the Cherokee framed a national governing system—a national council—and it championed full acculturation to white norms in religion, education, economics, and generally "the arts of civilized life."

Central to successful acculturation, and consequently to retaining their presence on traditional lands, was their conversion from communal property to private property concepts. The new Cherokee leadership, supported vocally by whites such as George Washington and Thomas Jefferson, encouraged Indians to take private tracts of land as their own individual farms and to cultivate marketable crops. Government agents provided plows and other farm implements, seed, and farm animals such as pigs, chickens, and cows to those willing to convert. Federal annuity payments to the Cherokee Nation added a financial base for tribal economic development. With this redirection, Cherokee farmers were expected also to alter gender roles with men performing farm labor while women directed affairs inside the home and supported their husbands outdoors as often as they could. Many male Cherokees were encouraged to establish small businesses—blacksmith work, gristmills, general stores, taverns, ferry services, and other trades supportive of an agrarian society. Remarkable change did occur. A number of Cherokees became quite wealthy enough to establish plantations, purchase slaves, and hire white field hands. Indeed, by 1809, there were 583 African slaves owned by Cherokee planters. Conforming to the expectations of "civilized" society, the wives of wealthy Cherokee men did not work in the fields; they welcomed visitors as the mistresses of fine plantation homes. Propertied Cherokees, in short, lived like their well-to-do southern white neighbors. The concepts of private property and the profit motive generated some prosperity for the Cherokee, but more importantly it signaled to white America—especially to whites living adjacent to the Cherokee—a willingness to set aside traditional patterns and embrace "the path toward civilization" as the dominant society expected. These Cherokee chose accommodation over the retention of traditional culture.

Change came to most every other facet of Cherokee life. In 1808, the Cherokee national council created a national police force (the Light Horse Guard), and this diminished the role of clan justice in Cherokee life. New laws affected property transfer and inheritance practices of matrilineal descent in Cherokee society. Between 1810 and 1824, the Cherokee National Council enacted a new series of laws and proclamations. The National Council in 1810 announced its position as supreme authority within the Cherokee Nation and asserted its right to receive and distribute all federal annuity payments. The council also denounced fraudulent treaties and land sales, and publicly declared people who sold their land and went west to be traitors to the Cherokee Nation. A last land sale in 1819 led to a series of laws strengthening the power of new Cherokee districts over the old town system. Districts had courts and marshals to handle crimes and were represented in the Cherokee national government. The Cherokee National Council by 1824 had consolidated its power, redefined the relationship between Cherokee men and women and clans, established a police force, and moved towards a new definition of Cherokee.

By 1824, the Cherokee Nation divided along the lines of geography, class, and race. Many Cherokees in the Smoky Mountain region of upper Tennessee lived according to the old ways. Such Cherokees did not own vast amounts of property or support the new laws that replaced towns with districts and courts. On the other hand, low country, wealthy Cherokees saw themselves as not only protecting their property but also building a government that could guard the rights of the Cherokees as a sovereign nation. Race officially became a component of their vision in 1824 with the passage of the first Cherokee race law. As slave owners, members of the national council had begun to view Cherokee sovereignty not only in terms of geography and the protection of individual property but also in terms of Cherokee "blood." The law tried to prevent the intermarriage of African slaves to both Cherokees and whites within the nation's borders. It also restricted the movement of free blacks into the Cherokee Nation. A petition from a well-known Cherokee warrior, Shoe Boots, reached the Cherokee council in October 1824. Shoe Boots sought admission of his children into the nation, children of his slave, Doll. The council revealed its new views of race in the Shoe Boots case. Although the council recognized his children's "inheritance to the Cherokee Country," they warned Shoe Boots to "cease begetting any more Children by the said slave woman." The Cherokee National Council, composed mostly of slave owners, began policing the sexual boundaries of other Cherokees to prevent interrelationships with blacks and the birth of children of mixed descent.

In the final step to becoming a full-fledged, sovereign republic, the National Council created the 1827 Cherokee Constitution, which was much like the Constitution of the United States. The Cherokee Constitution reaffirmed the role of district courts and marshals, created a bicameral legislature and a superior court system, and appointed a principal leader. Not all Cherokees were pleased with this development. Although the Cherokee had become the first Indian nation to have its own written constitution, the bulk of the Cherokee population resisted acculturation and clung desperately to traditional ways. Even in the face of this opposition, the national council convened, ratified the constitution in 1828, and appointed John Ross as the first principal chief. In the eyes of many white Americans, the Cherokees now had attained an acceptable level of civilization.

Sequoyah, a brilliant Cherokee man, added depth to this new standing. He created an easy way to learn and write the Cherokee language, and developing a literate population, he believed, would contribute further to the promotion of Cherokee national sovereignty and autonomy. As important as this certainly was for Indians pressing acculturation, a written Cherokee language also preserved the language itself for later generations. The use of **Sequoyah's syllabary**, which consisted of 86 syllables written in symbols, spread quickly among other Cherokees. The American Board of Commissioners for Foreign Missions (ABCFM), the most prominent Christian mission organization in Cherokee country, countered that a written form of the Cherokee language would instead prevent Cherokees from learning English. The ABCFM already faced difficult odds: only about 10 percent of the Cherokee Nation converted to Christianity in spite of effort to convert the Indians.

Christian missionaries tried a new tactic: they plucked the next generation of male Cherokee leaders from their homes and enrolled them in northern schools. Distance from their homeland and separation from anything Cherokee might hasten the acculturative process. The ABCFM sponsored two Cherokees, John Ridge and Elias Boudinot (Buck Watie), in a mission school in Cornwall, Connecticut from 1823 to 1825. While there, Ridge and Boudinot fell in love with and married white women. The town's inhabitants became outraged. Their racism fully exposed, the townspeople burned one of the couples in effigy, the newspaper published racist remarks calling the Anglo women "squaws" of "heathen barbarians," and the mission school even closed its doors. As early as 1825, Cherokees began to feel the constraints white society placed on Indians. For the Cherokees, there was a lesson in the racist backlash to the two marriages. Although a liberal spirit was beginning to sweep across much of the North at this time, one that soon gave rise to a host of reform-oriented movements, a virulent racism still commanded the hearts of most whites. No Indian, no matter how "civilized," would ever be their equal. Both Ridge and Boudinot returned to the Cherokee Nation and soon became influential leaders. Boudinot, for instance, raised enough funds to print issues of the *Cherokee Phoenix*, the first Native American newspaper and an indispensable aid to communication across the Cherokee Nation. In his early issues of the *Cherokee Phoenix*, Boudinot openly decried the volatile racial argument against native peoples that he himself had confronted with horror in Connecticut. Racism, he contended, countered the goals of acculturation and assimilation.

Virtually every feature of traditional Cherokee life had either changed or was in the process of change by the mid-1820s. Even those who resisted

7.1 Se-Quo-Yah, a Cherokee warrior, fought in the Creek War and invented the Cherokee alphabet.

Source: Courtesy of Library of Congress Prints and Photographs Division, LC-DIG-pga-07569

acculturation understood that the old ways were dying around them. Ridge and Boudinot were pleased with the apparent direction of the Cherokee Nation; becoming like their white neighbors seemed to be a practical means for securing their national sovereignty and their residency on traditional lands. Too, they believed sincerely that acculturation offered the surest means for Cherokee survival. While mainstream white society applauded the Indians' course, a darker, more sinister attitude surfaced among some whites. The talk of Indian removal again sounded in the halls of southern state legislatures and echoed across the white population by 1828. Boudinot defended Cherokee acculturation in the tone of one fully acculturated. "Sufficient and repeated evidence has been given, that Indians can be reclaimed from the savage state," wrote Boudinot in *The Cherokee Phoenix*. To remove the Cherokees to the West would only thwart their progress by taking them from "a land of civil and religious means." He accused removal advocates of racism and for promoting an impractical policy, of "building castles in the air."

Racism surely underpinned the chorus among whites for removal. Citizens of Georgia and the Carolinas believed that Indians would never become civilized enough to coexist with white people and were, therefore, better off living in the West. But another issue prompted the resurgence of aggressive racism—access to land. White Southerners frantically pursued new lands for the wealth they hoped to find in mineral extraction and agriculture. In 1799, gold was discovered on a small farm, 20 miles north of Charlotte, North Carolina. America's first gold rush resulted. Tens of thousands of people hailing from every state in the Union and from many European countries descended on the Carolina Piedmont in search of quick wealth. People panned, others placer mined, and a few with deep pockets established underground mining operations. The town of Charlotte grew in response, having a federal mint in operation by the late 1850s. Gold strikes occurred across central North Carolina and South Carolina and into northern Georgia. By the late 1820s gold hysteria dimmed as fewer strikes were made. It was thought that veins of gold probably extended into the westernmost stretches of these three southern states—into the heart of the Cherokee Nation itself—but white intrusion on Cherokee lands was not permitted by federal law. If the Indians no longer occupied that land, miners and others might gain access to the coveted properties. A second expectation of wealth for whites rested in the profitability of King Cotton. Cotton production soared following Eli Whitney's invention of the cotton gin—a crop absent from the American agrarian economy in 1790 emerged into the principal cash crop of the South by 1820. Southern planters produced 721,000 bales of cotton in 1828 alone and exported about 600,000 of those bales to European markets. Cotton sold for ten cents per pound, and each bale weighed roughly 335 pounds. Altogether, southern planters reaped $25 million that one year. They knew that demand would only increase, as it did, reaching five million bales produced in 1860. The cotton industry boosted the entire southern economy, from the expansion of port facilities, to railroad construction, new market centers, steamship production and river traffic, storage warehouses, and so many other related businesses. And, of course, cotton breathed new life into African slavery, bringing the total number of slaves in the South by 1860 to four million. Cotton growing, however, required fresh lands periodically, forcing Southern planters to expand cotton cultivation into new lands. As early as the 1820s, planters were already moving southwest into Alabama, Mississippi, and Louisiana. It should be no surprise that many contemplated the profitability of cotton on lands Cherokees currently occupied, particularly those lands in Georgia. The removal of the Cherokee from the South would give whites access to that land. The prospect of gold and the certainty of cotton, mixed with the rhetoric of racism, then, placed Georgians and Cherokees on a path toward major conflict.

Cherokees Challenged

The United States Constitution places Indian affairs under the jurisdiction of the federal government. States' rights advocates in Georgia, however, argued that, since the Cherokee resided inside the territorial boundary of Georgia, the Indians were under state authority. The "Indian problem" in Georgia was none of the federal government's business, and Cherokee removal existed as a state prerogative. John Ross, the principal Cherokee chief, countered Georgia's claims to their land, telling John C. Calhoun, the presiding Secretary of State, that Cherokees were the original owners of the land and would not leave Georgia or sell additional territory. Cherokees held a nationalist perspective, one backed by the treaty-making power of the United States. Their perspective, however, clashed with states' rights advocates in the South, as well as with the view most Americans held that the existence of a separate nation within a state was incompatible with the Constitution. Georgia approached President John Quincy Adams, insisting that he force the Cherokees to move west. When Adams refused in 1827, the state took matters into its own hands. The Georgia assembly rejected the Cherokees' sovereign nation status and asserted the right

7.2 John Ross, Cherokee Chief

Source: Courtesy of Library of Congress Prints and Photographs Division, LC-DIG-pga-07513

of Georgians to take over Cherokee lands by any means necessary. That such steps contradicted federal law and policy did not deter Georgia legislators, especially at this time when southern states routinely challenged federal authority. Although there were no tangible results from this initiative, the sentiment for absolute removal had been laid publicly.

Andrew Jackson's election as president in 1828 dealt a serious blow to Cherokees' hopes for federal protection. A Tennessee lawyer and tenacious fighter against Indians, Jackson made it clear that Indian removal would be a centerpiece of his new administration. He insisted that the existence of the Cherokee Nation within Georgia's borders violated the Constitution and, therefore, the Cherokees had no choice but to leave for the West. Jackson encouraged politicians in Washington, D.C., to determine territorial boundaries of a land west of the Mississippi on which eastern bands of Indians would be placed. Southern and Northern politicians debated Indian removal in Congress, pitting Northerners who increasingly advocated for Indian rights against Southerners who favored white expansion into Indian lands. In the end, Congress passed, and Jackson signed into law, the Indian Removal Act of 1830.

Passage of the Indian Removal Act did not stop John Ross from defending his nation, nor did it stop Georgia from taking additional steps designed to convince the Cherokees to leave the state. The state fashioned a process for seizing Cherokee property, a lottery for the redistribution of that land, and a blanket denial of the Cherokees' right to exist as a separate entity in Georgia. Furthermore, the state legislature created the Georgia Guard, a paramilitary force that monitored the borders between the Cherokees and white settlers. With the discovery of gold on Cherokee land in 1829, violence between Cherokees and Georgians erupted. Major Ridge and other Cherokees burned the homes of white squatters, and thousands of "tin pan" Georgians fought against Cherokees for the best spots to search for gold. John Ross led the more peaceful resistance, a campaign in the North to win the hearts of the ABCFM and other reformers. Encouraged by Ross, Elias Boudinot used the *Cherokee Phoenix* to tell a nationwide reading audience about the standoff between the Cherokees and Georgia. Ross traveled to Washington, D.C., and there he distributed petitions and pamphlets and gave public speeches in the hopes of swaying government officials. Ross also initiated a federal court case against Georgia's dismissal of Cherokee sovereignty. Ross and those supporting him depended on the system—the appropriate legal and moral channels—to protect the Cherokee people.

READING HISTORY

The Removal Act of 1830

On May 26, 1830, Andrew Jackson signed into law the Indian Removal Act. Georgia had already intensified pressure on Cherokees to leave the state, as had other primarily Southern states. The physical presence of the "Five Civilized Tribes" stymied the Southern states, which were determined to expand the cotton frontier westward. By passing the Removal Act through Congress in spite of opposition from benevolent reformers and congressmen, Jackson and fellow Democrats hoped to appease the Southern states, satisfy their own prejudices, and promote white economic development of the territory. Southern power advantage in Congress allowed for passage of the Indian Removal Act and actually sealed the fate of hundreds of thousands of Indians living east of the Mississippi.

CHAP. CXLVIII.—An Act to provide for an exchange of lands with the Indians residing in any of the states or territories, and for their removal west of the river Mississippi.

Be it enacted by the Senate and House of Representatives of the United States of America, in Congress assembled, That it shall and may be lawful for the President of the United States to cause so much of any territory belonging to the United States, west of the river Mississippi, not included in any state or organized territory, and to which the Indian title has been extinguished, as he may judge necessary, to be divided into a suitable number of districts, for the reception of such tribes or nations of Indians as may choose to exchange the lands where they now reside, and remove there; and to cause each of said districts to be so described by natural or artificial marks, as to be easily distinguished from every other.

SEC. 2. *And be it further enacted,* That it shall and may be lawful for the President to exchange any or all of such districts, so to be laid off and described, with any tribe or nation within the limits of any of the states or territories, and with which the United States have existing treaties, for the whole or any part or portion of the territory claimed and occupied by such tribe or nation, within the bounds of any one or more of the states or territories, where the land claimed and occupied by the Indians, is owned by the United States, or the United States are bound to the state within which it lies to extinguish the Indian claim thereto.

SEC. 3. *And be it further enacted,* That in the making of any such exchange or exchanges, it shall and may be lawful for the President solemnly to assure the tribe or nation with which the exchange is made, that the United States will forever secure and guaranty to them, and their heirs or successors, the country so exchanged with them; and if they prefer it, that the United States will cause a patent or grant to be made and executed to them for the same: Provided always, That such lands shall revert to the United States, if the Indians become extinct, or abandon the same.

SEC. 4. *And be it further enacted*, That if, upon any of the lands now occupied by the Indians, and to be exchanged for, there should be such improvements as add value to the land claimed by any individual or individuals of such tribes or nations, it shall and may be lawful for the President to cause such value to be ascertained by appraisement or otherwise, and to cause such ascertained value to be paid to the person or persons rightfully claiming such improvements. And upon the payment of such valuation, the improvements so valued and paid for, shall pass to the United States, and possession shall not afterwards be permitted to any of the same tribe.

SEC. 5. *And be it further enacted*, That upon the making of any such exchange as is contemplated by this act, it *shall and* may be lawful for the President to cause such aid and assistance to be furnished to the emigrants as may be necessary and proper to enable them to remove to, and settle in, the country for which they may have exchanged; and also, to give them such aid and assistance as may be necessary for their support and subsistence for the first year after their removal.

SEC. 6. *And be it further enacted*, That it shall and may be lawful for the President to cause such tribe or nation to be protected, at their new residence, against all interruption or disturbance from any other tribe or nation of Indians, or from any other person or persons whatever.

SEC. 7. *And be it further enacted*, That it shall and may be lawful for the President to have the same superintendence and care over any tribe or nation in the country to which they may remove, as contemplated by this act, that he is now authorized to have over them at their present places of residence: *Provided*, That nothing in this act contained shall be construed as authorizing or directing the violation of any existing treaty between the United States and any of the Indian tribes.

SEC. 8. *And be it further enacted*, That for the purpose of giving effect to the provisions of this act, the sum of five hundred thousand dollars is hereby appropriated, to be paid out of any money in the treasury, not otherwise appropriated.

Approved, May 28, 1830.

Source: Removal Act of 1830, 21st Cong. 1st sess. (1830), ch. 148

Questions

1. What does the Removal Act say about the Indians?
2. What powers were given to the federal government in the Removal Act?

Cherokee Removal

William Wirt, a Northern lawyer, presented in the U.S. Supreme Court the Cherokee argument for national sovereignty. In the fall of 1830, a Cherokee named Corn Tassel was taken to the Hall County jail for killing another Cherokee. The problem, according to the Cherokees, was that Corn Tassel had committed the crime within the Cherokee Nation's borders, and thus Georgia had no right to arrest or place Tassel on trial for murder. Tassel was nonetheless convicted and hanged in Hall County, after which Wirt brought the case *Cherokee Nation* v. *Georgia* before the Supreme Court. Wirt argued that the Cherokee Nation represented a foreign nation to which

Georgia law did not apply. Chief Justice Marshall dismissed the case in 1831, stating that the Cherokee Nation could not bring suit against Georgia because Cherokees were not a *foreign* nation. However, Marshall, in his explanation, made a powerful statement about the Cherokees' place within the American republic. The Chief Justice defined the Cherokees as a "domestic dependent nation," in that the relationship between the Cherokees and the United States "resembles that of a ward to his guardian." The concept of "domestic dependent nation" laid out by Marshall was, for John Ross and other Cherokees, confirmation of their national sovereignty, and a rejection of Georgia's right to enforce its power over them.

Georgia had expected a favorable ruling from the Court, but, even before Marshall acted on the case, the state took its next steps. The Georgia Guard officially opened Cherokee lands to settlement. State legislation put the gold rush areas of Cherokee lands under the control of the state government and directed the Georgia Guards to protect the territory using appropriate force when required. In December 1830, Georgia stipulated that no white person could reside on Cherokee lands without a state-issued license, one that required an oath of loyalty to Georgia. ABCFM missionaries, defying Georgia law and defending the Cherokees, refused to take the oath. In March 1831, the Georgia Guard took the missionaries into custody, one of whom, Samuel Worcester, was also a federal agent serving as the Postmaster General for the United States. Nine of the missionaries took the oath to avoid prison, but Worcester refused.

Worcester challenged Georgia in a case that also meandered its way to the U.S. Supreme Court. William Wirt had another chance to argue the Cherokees' case. At issue was Georgia's violation of Worcester's constitutional rights, as the state held no jurisdiction over Indian lands. In its 1832 decision in *Worcester* v. *Georgia*, the Court ruled that Worcester was arrested wrongly and was to be released. Marshall's lengthy defense of the Court's decision insisted that the federal government, and not the states, was the proper authority to deal with sovereign native tribes. In these two Supreme Court decisions, the court essentially ruled that laws affecting Native Americans could only be created and enforced by the federal government or the Indian tribes themselves. Cherokees celebrated the decision, but their joy proved premature.

A group of Cherokees—Boudinot, Major Ridge and John Ridge, Stand Watie and others—may have been generally pleased with Marshall's ruling but they believed Georgia would continue to ignore federal authority and through various means secure Cherokee lands. Indeed, President Jackson admitted in a meeting with John Ridge that he would not dispatch federal troops to coerce Georgia's obedience to federal authority. The Ridge-Boudinot faction believed the same fate awaited Cherokees in the Carolinas and Tennessee as well as other Indians across the Southeast. In short, fate would deal its hand against the Indians, with or without federal protection. Together they founded the "Treaty Party," a segment of the Cherokee Nation that operated within the realm of realpolitik to salvage what they could for the Cherokee people. In 1835, when John Ross was in Washington, D.C., to negotiate with Jackson, and with violence and factionalism erupting within the Cherokee Nation and between Cherokees and Georgians, the "treaty party" secretly signed the Treaty of New Echota. Only 20 Cherokees out of a nation numbering anywhere from 13,000 to 16,000, not all of whom were living in Georgia, signed the treaty and agreed to removal to the West under specific financial agreements. The U.S. government would pay the sum of $5 million, fund the costs of removal and the improvements on Cherokee lands, set up homes and schools and churches in the West, and accrue any legal costs. The U.S. government promised the Cherokees seven million acres of land in the West for their new homeland. The date set for Cherokee removal was May 23, 1838.

John Ross fought as hard as he could to have the treaty overturned, but it was no use. The United States Army rounded up Cherokees and put them in stockades to await removal scheduled for the summer of 1838. The Cherokees were to make the move to "Indian Territory" in separate migratory groups, scheduled at different dates, and with some of the wealthier such as Major Ridge traveling by water while the majority journeyed overland. Merchant firms that had won contracts from the government for handling the Cherokees' removal cheated the Cherokees out of food and supplies, pocketing federal dollars or selling goods intended for Indian use to whites holding cash. Hunger and disease shadowed their trek across the mountains and into the southern plains. Many were separated from family members. At a pace of about 20 to 25 miles daily at best, the 1,000 mile march carried over from late summer well into winter. Blankets were available but often thin and worn. At least 13,000 Cherokees began the trek toward an unknown land; about 4,000 perished before reaching their destination. The sad, sordid, despicable ordeal has since been termed the **"Trail of Tears"**—the horrendous loss of life, the brutal conditions endured by all, the fear and uncertainty that walked every step with them, and the absolute absence of humanity from federal authorities. The Cherokee, too, shed tears as they looked back on the mountains where they had buried their ancestors and knew they would never again see their traditional lands (see Map 7.2). About 400 Cherokee eluded the army's roundup, fleeing into the mountains and hiding there for nearly a decade before Washington granted them permission to occupy a small reservation in North Carolina, the descendants of these people forming the Eastern Band of the Cherokee Nation.

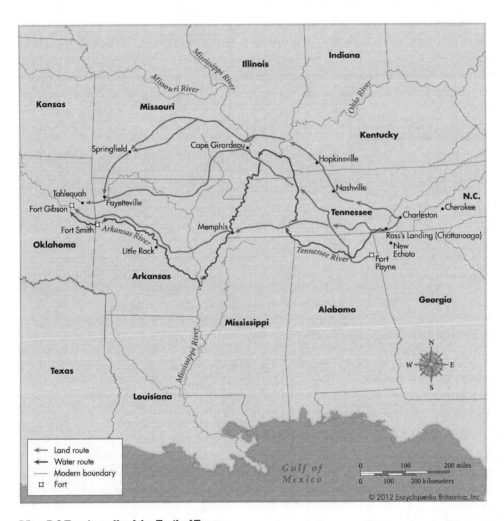

Map 7.2 Tragic walk of the Trail of Tears

The Creek Road to Oklahoma

The Creek national council in the 1820s represented towns (*talwas*) because the Lower Town Creek and Upper Town Creek divisions still were the center of Creek life. Living in portions of Georgia and Alabama, Creek town members, who numbered around 20,000, hoped that the national council represented the best interests of all Creeks. Governor Troup of Georgia began negotiations with a select group of Lower Town Creek chiefs in 1824 at a small tavern in Indian Springs owned by Chief William McIntosh, located in central Georgia. Governor Troup put forward a proposal for Creek cession of their Georgian lands. A delegation of Lower Town chiefs left the treaty table, claiming that under Creek laws of governance they had no right to sell Creek lands. But another group of leaders that included McIntosh stayed. On February 12, 1825, McIntosh, who represented the town of Coweta, claimed that his delegation represented the majority of the leading Creek chiefs and signed the Treaty of Indian Springs. According to the treaty's terms, the Creeks ceded all national lands in Georgia as well as a portion of their lands in northern Alabama. Both the Lower Creek and Upper Creek towns complained loudly that McIntosh did not have any authority over their lands. Other Creek leaders sent letters of protest to Congress, Secretary of State John C. Calhoun, and President John Q. Adams. The Senate, however, confirmed the treaty, and Governor Troup gave the Creeks until September 1, 1826, to leave Georgia.

For his violation of Creek law, the Creeks executed McIntosh and continued their challenge of the treaty. The potential for violence between white Georgians who wanted to move into the ceded territory and Creeks who refused to leave put representatives of Georgia's government in a difficult position. An emerging Upper Town Creek leader from Tuckabatchee town, Opothle Yoholo (Opothleyahola), headed opposition against Georgia's claims to Creek territory. President Adams deployed troops into Georgia to quell the potential for

TIMELINE 7.1 CHEROKEE PATH TO REMOVAL, 1808–1838

Date	Event
1805–1808	Cherokee land cessions; 1808 cession orchestrated by Thomas Jefferson
1808	First series of Cherokee laws
1810	Cherokee laws to protect property
1820–1824	Cherokees laws to strengthen national council and create district system and police force
1826	Georgia begins to challenge Cherokees
1827	Cherokee constitution
	Georgia refuses to recognize Cherokee Nation
1830	Georgia legislation in which Cherokees fell under the rule of the state
	Andrew Jackson's Indian Removal Act
	Cherokee Nation v. *Georgia*
1831	Indian Removal Act happened in 1830
1832	*Worcester* v. *Georgia*
1835	Treaty of New Echota
1838	Trail of Tears

armed conflict until there was a resolution to the Treaty of Indian Springs. In Washington in January 1826, Opothle Yoholo and other Creek leaders signed the Treaty of Washington. Replacing the Treaty of Indian Springs, the new treaty gave the Creeks more money for their lands in Georgia, but only for Creek properties situated east of the Chattahoochee River. Unsatisfied, Governor Troup put all of the Creek lands in the state into a lottery, and he mustered the Georgia militia to remove the Creeks from the state in spite of the treaty just negotiated with President Adams. Avoiding a possible violent showdown between federal and state forces, the president withdrew the federal troops; the Creeks would leave all of their lands of Georgia for a parcel of land in Alabama.

The move to Alabama was disastrous for the Creeks. In 1827, both the Upper and Lower Creek towns found themselves settled on five million acres in Alabama. It was unfamiliar and inadequate to establish large enough farms to support kin and community. As one commentator noted, the Creeks in Alabama lived "in the most miserable and wretched condition it is possible to conceive. Many of them Skeletons and their bones almost worn through their skin." Local Alabamians soon speculated in Creek lands and defrauded the Creeks in sales of food and liquor. Starvation hit many Indian homes. In response to this calamity, armed Creeks crossed back into Georgia, hoping to reach old hunting grounds along the Chattahoochee River. "A large group of Creeks, armed, are in Lee County," reported the new governor of Georgia, John Forsyth. State authorities proved incapable of preventing Creeks from moving at will across the border.

In 1832, the Alabama legislature extended its jurisdiction over the Creeks. It affirmed that Creeks did not have to pay taxes or participate in public works projects, and it assured them protection as Alabama citizens. However, Creeks could not sue whites in court; they could only sue other Creeks. More importantly, and fundamental to the state's intent, the Act of 1832 officially extinguished the power of the Creek national council, contending Creek forms of governance directly violated the power and authority of the state. In other words, Alabama assumed authority over the Creek Nation, a move that certainly challenged federal authority. Public pressure intensified to remove completely the Creeks from the state. Alabamians entered Creek lands, fraudulently speculating in the sale of tribal territory and violently forcing many Creeks from their farms and homes.

Creek negotiations in Washington resulted in another settlement, the Treaty of 1832, which signaled a watershed in Creek history. Under its terms, 90 chiefs received reserved tracts within Alabama to be divided up among heads of households. Creeks could not sell their land for a five-year period and only then with the approval of the federal government. Alabama agreed to remove all squatters and speculators from Creek lands and to treat the Creeks as citizens of the state. Despite the promises of the state of Alabama, the state never succeeded in removing white squatters from Creek lands and peace never came to the Creek reserves. One attempt to remove Alabamians involved the town of Irwington, located on Creek lands where members of former Lower Creek towns had settled. Authorities burned the town to the ground. Settlers, nonetheless, continued to move onto Creek lands, sparking violence between the Alabama National Guard and white residents. Squatters created fake deeds of sale between themselves and Creeks, stole Creek property, and violently attacked the Indians. Between 1834 and 1835, violence was rampant on the Creek reserve with settlers and Indians killing each other. Facing deprivation, harassment, and death, Opothle Yoholo and the remaining Creek leaders agreed that they had to leave Alabama if their nation was to survive. Divided into five separate groups, 14,609 Creeks left Alabama for the Western territories. As they left, looking back on the lands of Alabama and Georgia that had been home for centuries, the exiled Creeks hoped to rebuild a shattered nation.

Choctaw Removal

The Choctaws in Mississippi lived in a series of town divisions that were undergoing rapid cultural change. At the center of the Choctaw world was the earthen mound, *Nanih Waiya*, a mound that Choctaws believed was the source of their creation. In Choctaw cosmology, *Aba*, the Great Father, the sun, resided within the boundaries of a sacred circle of four cardinal points. Ancient practices that had been passed down from earlier Mississippian cultures still structured Choctaw politics and society. These included ideas about the power of *Aba* over sacred chiefs and political leaders, and chiefs as men who traded to benefit matrilineal networks.

Similar to the Cherokee and Creek, Choctaw town leaders moved toward new styles of leadership, generally combining old and new structures. In the early nineteenth century, Mushulatubbee was a leader who held firmly to traditional Choctaw forms of chiefly power and authority, with chiefs among towns distributing goods to other loyal chiefs and young men all interlocked within a specific set of matrilineal relations. Mushulatubbee, however, welcomed schools, which was a departure from the old ways. Schools became a competitive source of chiefly power and authority, just like the goods whites traded. Chiefs wanted to control the schools to influence the education of the next generation of leaders; they viewed this as a way to keep elite family status intact. The older chiefs believed that the next generation of leaders needed to learn to read and write to operate within America's market economy. David Folsom and Greenwood LeFlore led another group of chiefs. Men of both Choctaw and Euro-American descent, these new chiefs hoped to replace the township and chiefly divisions with a Choctaw national identity, one built on a constitutional government.

The rapid pace of political and social change created considerable internal tension among the Choctaw. Many chiefs had already abandoned hunting and the deerskin trade of the eighteenth-century frontier exchange economy for one of slavery, cattle ownership, and cotton farming. In fact, chiefs on both sides of the leadership debate were quite wealthy and supported schools as a new source of status and prestige. LeFlore owned more slaves than any other Choctaw. Mushulatubbee and his supporters, such as Pushmataha, dominated the three main Choctaw district divisions—Eastern, Six Town, and Western. David Folsom, in contrast,

SEEING HISTORY

Nanih Waiya

Nanih Waiya, located in present-day Philadelphia, Mississippi, is a rectangular platform mound that is roughly 25 feet high, 218 feet long, and 140 feet wide. Nanih Waiya, in the Choctaw language, means "leaning hill." Archaeologists have yet to precisely date when the ancestors of the Choctaws constructed Nanih Waiya. Pottery shards dug from the land near the mound's living area point to a possible range of 100 BCE to 400 CE. With the arrival of Europeans, and particularly by the eighteenth century, Nanih Waiya was a source of pride and strength for the Choctaw Nation. According to Choctaw oral tradition, the mound gave birth to the tribe. Choctaws came up from the underworld beneath the mound and rested on its sloping sides to dry off before settling the lands of Mississippi.

Questions

1. Why was it important for Choctaws to sustain a spiritual connection to a mound associated with ancestors who lived in the Deep South hundreds of years before the arrival of Europeans?
2. In terms of the constant pressure on the Choctaws in the 1820s and 1830s to leave Mississippi, was there something more to the mound's importance for the Choctaws than its spiritual powers?

invited the American Board of Commissioners of Foreign Missions (ABCFM) to construct the first schools among the Choctaws.

In October 1818, Mushulatubbee and his supporters signed the Treaty of Doak's Stand, an agreement ceding nearly half of the Choctaws' Mississippi territory in exchange for Arkansas lands where they planned to build new communities with their own schools and, there, live a life unmolested by whites and other Indians. His vision, however, never materialized. Instead, Washington intended to relocate the Choctaw farther west, settling them in "Indian Territory" (Oklahoma) with the Cherokee, Creek, and other tribal groups who still resided in the East. In 1826, with the prospect of compulsory removal gathering greater support in Congress, in the White House, and among whites across the South, LeFlore and his followers replaced Mushulatubbee and his town leaders, and challenged the United States' plan for Indian removal. Three district chiefs from separate town councils would govern the Choctaw Nation.

7.3 Pushmataha

Source: National Anthropological Archives, Smithsonian Institution

Folsom and LeFlore promoted a distinctly new form of Choctaw nationalism. Colonels and captains oversaw towns, while light horsemen carried the national news between towns, prevented disorder in public assemblies, organized people for gatherings, and tried to fend off the liquor trade. In August 1826, the separate councils of the Eastern and Western divisions came together and agreed that effective management of the Choctaw Nation required a constitutional government. They drafted a constitution that required the councils to meet twice annually. The new Choctaw capitol, a council house built near the federal government's outpost, was symbolic of the new direction in Choctaw politics and life in several ways. The new building, facing east, as James Taylor Carson suggests, allowed the sun god, *Aba*, to oversee all council proceedings. The new government passed a series of laws to protect property and abolish old practices such as witchcraft and pole pulling during burials—a practice that symbolized people separated into different kin groups. Legislation also established severe punishments for those involved in any form of liquor trading.

By 1828, Folsom and LeFlore turned to the missionary Cyrus Kingsbury to give the new Choctaw nationalism its own sacred power. Kingsbury offered his support to the two men and led a series of spiritual revivals among the Choctaws. The Second Great Awakening came to the Choctaw Nation, with Baptist and Methodist camp meetings exciting the converted. Protestantism and Choctaw nationalism together provided new sources of pride and strength; even still, the Choctaws combined these new patterns, continuing their belief in the importance of the guidance of the sun in *Aba*. As David Folsom observed of the new government, particularly after the deaths of Pushmataha and Mushulatubbee, "God [*Aba*] has seen fit to take those men away so that better men may be raised up in their places."

Under new leadership and with a new sense of nationhood, Choctaws confronted Mississippi and the federal government. Governor Gerard Brandon, recognizing that Andrew Jackson's election had shifted the balance of power in favor of states' rights, signed the fourth Mississippi Extension of Law Act in 1829. The law gave Mississippi jurisdiction over Choctaw lands, but not over the Indians. Andrew Jackson's Indian Removal Act of 1830 basically sealed the fate of the Choctaws in Mississippi. Cyrus Kingsbury, who had witnessed the new nationalism and spiritual revivals among the Choctaws, warned that the law was to "coerce the Indians to remove." Taking an evangelical tone, a Methodist noted that "Heaven will mark and punish the horrid crime."

With President Andrew Jackson's support, Governor Brandon moved to weaken Choctaw governance, a move that would likely collapse their nationalistic spirit. An 1830 state extension bill enabled local authorities to arrest and prosecute Choctaws for crimes on Indian lands, a measure that was intended to usurp Indian jurisdiction on tribal property. Worse yet, the bill made it unlawful for chiefs to exercise any power and authority. Any chief who tried to exert any political authority would be fined $1,000 and imprisoned for one year. At the same time, all Choctaws, as with the Cherokees, had to end all customs not in accord with the "common law" of the state. However, Mississippi extended the benefits of state citizenship to the Choctaws, including the rights to vote and to bring lawsuits to court. The exercise of these rights sounded good to Choctaws who championed acculturation and aspired to full inclusion with the general population of Mississippi. Neither Georgia nor Alabama had ever made such rights available to either the Creeks or Cherokees. But, in reality, most Indians and nearly all whites understood that the Choctaws' exercise of these rights would not likely ever be tolerated by the white population. The majority of Choctaws responded to the state law by turning inward to the civic institutions that had served as the bulwark of their new nationality, such as their churches. Churches agreed to expel members who spoke favorably of removal, and even hunt down and kill any Choctaw who went west—an interesting twist to the commandment "Thou shalt not kill." And, of course, chiefs never relinquished their power simply because a state law said they should.

In the end, the Choctaw chiefs, on both sides, came to realize that removal was the only way to save their nation. Their lands were being enveloped by white settlers, the cotton economy demanded ever more land, and the state government continually exerted its will over the Choctaw Nation and did so with the blessing of the White House. While their physical survival might not be threatened, their culture and their autonomy certainly were. Unable to challenge successfully the forces confronting them, they agreed to meet with federal agents in September 1830 and accept relocation. The result, the Treaty of Dancing Rabbit Creek, ceded the last ten million acres of Choctaw land in Mississippi. It did have a stipulation that some Choctaws could remain on specific Mississippi lands and secure legal title to those properties if they maintained their residence for ten consecutive years. This stipulation was most likely drafted to placate the outrage voiced by whites who supported the Indians' continued residency on traditional lands. Few Indians believed it possible to meet that stipulation, but there was a sizeable group who accepted that offer. Folsom, LeFlore, and others expected to make a considerable profit from the sale of their personal tracts. The first Choctaws left for Indian Territory in December 1830. Those who could afford to do so traveled aboard steamboats. Battered in many different ways, including the loss of around 2,500 Choctaws who experienced their own "Trail of Tears," the Choctaws faced an uncertain future. Around 15,000 Choctaws moved into Indian Territory, and another 5,000–6,000 stayed in Mississippi, including Greenwood LeFlore. Removal wracked and divided the Choctaw Nation.

Chickasaws Head West

North of the Choctaws were their old enemies, the Chickasaws. With only approximately 5,000 people, the Chickasaws shared cultural traits with their Mississippian neighbors. The Chickasaws had various descriptions of *Aba* (*Loak-Ishtollo-Aba*), "the great holy fire above," or the sun god. Their world, even in the nineteenth century, was one of four sacred cardinal directions, with the west also representing the place of darkness "where very bad people reside." The civilization program of the early nineteenth century had also transformed Chickasaw culture. Schools pressing general academic knowledge and the values and behaviors of white society hastened the process of acculturation. Protestant churches imposed Christianity on their communities. The cotton-based economy reshaped Chickasaw structures with the introduction of market-directed farming, the rise of plantations, African slaves, river ferries, toll roads, and cattle ranching. Certain families took advantage of the altered economic pattern and profited wildly, and, in so doing, further distanced themselves from traditional Chickasaw values. The Colbert family, particularly the brothers Levi, William, and George, became immensely wealthy. So much of the cultural redirection affecting Chickasaws looked so much like the redirection affecting the Cherokee, Choctaw, and Creek. And, like the other major native peoples in the Southeastern Woodlands, Chickasaw leaders agreed to a series of controversial treaties that ceded thousands of acres of land. The Treaty of Chickasaw Bluffs, signed in 1801, allowed the United States to refurbish "the old Chickasaw Trace," a trade route that extended from Tennessee through Mississippi. The road became a postal route, known as the Natchez Trace. Because the road cut right through northern Mississippi, the heart of Chickasaw country, prosperous Chickasaws such as George Colbert saw an opportunity to profit from increased traffic and built houses, taverns, and ferry lines along the road. However, more isolated Chickasaws did not benefit from the negotiations with the United States over such internal improvement projects. Non-elite Chickasaws had their misgivings about continued cessions of land in the corners where Mississippi met Tennessee and Alabama, as Chickasaw villages sat on the lands between the Duck and Tennessee rivers.

PROFILE

Pushmataha, Choctaw Leader Caught between Worlds

Pushmataha's career began in the 1760s and 1770s, when he earned prestige and honor as a great warrior fighting against the Creeks. Choctaw boys became men when they had proven themselves in war and gained the necessary spiritual powers from taking life. Pushmataha, also known as Apushmatahubi, translates into "messenger of death." Early in his life, Pushmataha learned as a leader how to carefully negotiate between the world of the Choctaws and that of European powers such as the French and British.

Pushmataha resided among the Six Towns Division within the Choctaw confederacy, located along the upper Leaf River in present-day Mississippi. Around 1800, Pushmataha stepped forward as a leading chief among the Six Town Division in negotiations with the United States. His wonderful speaking style won over both Choctaws and Americans. When the Creeks attacked Fort Mims, Pushmataha became a war chief and joined with Andrew Jackson against the Creeks. He was not one of the chiefs who signed the Treaty of Doak's Stand in 1820 because he understood that white settlers in Arkansas would not give up their lands to Indians. He pleaded with Jackson to give the lands to the Choctaws, but Jackson refused. Pushmataha earned his reputation through the traditional routes of chiefly power and authority, but he managed to adapt to the nineteenth century as well. He sent his children to school, recognizing that warring and spiritual powers would not enhance the status and prestige of a new generation of young men, but that education and skills in the American market economy would secure his children's elite status. Pushmataha is one of many native leaders in the South who accepted, albeit reluctantly, the necessity of adapting to the changed realities of life in the region for native peoples. He died in 1824 while attending Choctaw negotiations in Washington, D.C.

Chickasaw debts to trading houses, such as the "Chickasaw Factory," however, forced their hand. With tribesmen owing more than $50,000 dollars, Chickasaw leaders agreed to pay off the debt through a series of land cessions. The Treaty of the Chickasaw Nation of 1805 extinguished Chickasaw titles to some lands in Tennessee while it compensated some Chickasaw leaders, including the Colberts, for their cooperation. After the Redstick rebellion, the Chickasaws, under the Colberts' leadership, ceded additional lands in Tennessee, a controversial transaction given that both the Creeks and the Cherokees had claims on the land in question.

TIMELINE 7.2 CREEK, CHOCTAW, AND CHICKASAW REMOVAL, 1801–1840

Date	Creeks	Choctaws	Chickasaws
1824	Treaty of Indian Springs		
1826	Treaty of Washington		
1827	Move to Alabama		
1832	Alabama legislature passes law extending rights to Creeks		
1832	Treaty of 1832		
1834–1835	Creek removal		
1818		Leadership divisions apparent; Treaty of Doak's Stand	
1826		Revolution in Choctaw governance	
1828		Second Great Awakening	
1829		First Mississippi Extension Bill	
1830		Extension Bill outlawing Choctaw chiefs	
		Treaty of Dancing Rabbit Creek	
1801			Treaty of Chickasaw Bluffs
1805			Treaty of Chickasaw Nation
1816			Treaty of Chickasaw Council House
1820s–1830s			Chickasaw demands for land payments
1837–1840			Chickasaw removal

The Treaty of Chickasaw Council House of 1816 left the Chickasaws with little property. Of course, Charles and Levi Colbert both profited from their dealings with the United States, extending their acreage and increasing their cattle operations on the north side of the Tennessee River. After replacing his brother Charles as principal chief in 1818, Levi Colbert (Itawamba) negotiated another series of cessions and secured for himself additional tracts of land along the Tennessee River. In short, elite Chickasaw chiefs crafted a series of treaties that benefited themselves while shrinking the land base of their people.

In 1818, the federal government divided the Chickasaws into four separate districts under four separate leaders, each managing the annuity payments for their people. Resisting district divisions, the Colbert family and other large landowning elites constructed a single council house to deal with all treaty proceedings and annuity payments, a move that contradicted the Colberts' earlier tactics but now seemed practical as a means to convey the apparent wishes of all Chickasaws. In order to convene and conduct matters appropriately, political power and authority had to rest as one body on the sacred circle. Handing out decisions as a united front by the 1820s and 1830s, the leading Chickasaws, who were well aware of the Choctaw land frauds, demanded that their lands be surveyed into allotments before the removal process began. Each of these Chickasaw parcels was to be sold on an open real estate market and for good value. The council of educated, elite Chickasaws would control the proceeds from all Chickasaw land sales and distribute the annuity payments. In addition, each family was to receive an allotted parcel to live on before removal, and once that land was sold the money was to be put aside to benefit each family. When the Chickasaws left Mississippi between 1837 and 1840, the council, and individual Chickasaws who had profited from the sales of their final allotments, arrived in Indian Territory in a good financial position for resettling.

Resisting Removal

The orderly and, for some, profitable removal of the Chickasaws bore no resemblance to the violent struggle that accompanied Seminole removal in the Deep South and the removal of the Sauks and Mesquakie peoples from the mineral-rich and much-sought-after lands in Illinois. Seminoles lived principally in the Florida peninsula, an environment quite different from other lands along the cotton frontier. The peninsula, undefended and unsettled outside of the Panhandle, possessed massive stretches of swampy terrain. The Seminoles used their homelands to their advantage facing a U.S. Army that could not navigate the wetlands to round up the resistant Indians. Seminoles successfully fought off removal until 1842, and even then not all Seminoles left Florida. In the North, two different groups, the Sauks and Mesquakies, joined together under the leadership of Black Hawk to lead a small-scale conflict against the forces of removal. Resistance to removal showed just how far some native peoples were willing to go to defend their homelands.

Seminoles Fight

Seminoles were a mixed lot, most speaking variants of Muskogee languages. Many of the earliest Seminoles in Florida were eighteenth-century Creeks. A number of important Seminole resistance leaders—Cowkeeper, Payne, Bowlegs, and Micanopy—traced their descent back to Creeks. Escaped slaves who had sought refuge among the Spanish mixed with the Seminoles, and other Africans became Seminole slaves. After the Redstick rebellion of 1814, former Creek rebels also joined the Florida Seminoles. In fact, a large contingent of Upper Creeks increased the Seminole population by two-thirds. The pattern of Creek and Seminole union resembled that of tribal groups farther north that fled white expansion and brutal warfare for residency with more western native peoples who welcomed them.

The bordering cotton-producing plantation states of Georgia and Alabama understandably feared slave rebellions, but the prospect of Indians mixing with African refugees only intensified that concern—the spirit of vengeance among some former slaves now supported by a well-armed warrior population that frequently raided plantations for livestock and other goods. In March 1813, a group of 150 loyal **filibusters** (unofficial invading forces), backed financially by the United States, entered Seminole territory. For years, southern planters had coveted the upper reaches of the Florida Panhandle, looking to expand cotton growing into the peninsula. Led by Payne of the Oconees, the Seminoles successfully rebuffed the filibusters' invasion in a war that lasted two years and scarred Seminole villages.

Between 1814 and 1816, thousands of refugee Africans and Creeks built a defensive structure that Americans called the **Negro Fort**, situated in a swampy Gulf Coast stretch of land near present-day Tallahassee. Southerners' contempt for Florida as a haven for runaway slaves and rebels fed the fears of government policymakers. In an assertion of its power and authority in and around the Seminole country, the United States constructed a string of forts: Fort Jackson, Fort Gaines, Fort Mitchell, Fort Scott, and Fort Lawrence. In July 1816, two gunboats and two schooners in Apalachicola Bay laid siege to Negro Fort and destroyed it.

More whites moved south and west, hoping to spread cotton production or establish those businesses that directly supported the cotton industry. The population of southern Georgia grew quickly, as did the population of eastern Alabama. Southerners also demanded access to Spanish-held lands in Florida's panhandle. Acquisition of these properties would eliminate that stretch as a safe haven for escaped slaves and allow the federal government legal authority to employ force against Seminoles who routinely raided plantations across the Florida border. Beginning in 1817, the United States Army launched a series of strikes into the Panhandle, hitting Seminole villages and capturing runaway slaves. Although Spain objected to the American action, they commanded little power to challenge Washington's move. That inability to resist also allowed for Americans to begin settling northern Florida. What has become known as the First Seminole War ended in 1818 at the same time Spanish and American diplomats commenced negotiations for the transfer of Florida to the United States. General Andrew Jackson, however, continued military operations in the territory without explicit government authorization, razing numerous Seminole villages and capturing two Spanish forts. Despite his success, many in Washington questioned Jackson's moves, especially as President James Monroe was in negotiation with Spain. His incursions, they worried, might collapse Spain's consideration of a treaty. In spite of Jackson's rash actions, Spain and the United States signed the Adams-Onís Treaty in 1819, which ceded officially Florida to the United States. The transfer of land to the United States now brought the Seminole under American jurisdiction.

In March 1821, Jackson became territorial governor of Florida. Acting without direct approval from the federal government, Jackson tired to push all the Seminoles together into one part of the Panhandle. He showed absolute disregard for the Seminole town system and seasonal movements for food. Southern slaveholders descended into the Panhandle and reclaimed escaped Africans. At Moultrie Creek in September 1823, the Seminoles allegedly signed a treaty of removal (the Treaty of Moultrie Creek). According to the treaty, which 32 town chiefs allegedly signed, the Seminoles were to keep roughly four million acres of land in the Panhandle region and give the United States complete control over the rest of the peninsula. The Treaty of Moultrie Creek would remain a point of contention for the Seminoles, who shouted down the treaty as a fraud. Nonetheless, Washington insisted on the validity of the treaty and authorized Seminole removal. Starvation and depression prevailed among the Seminoles as they moved to their new reservation in the Panhandle.

Only a few years passed before Washington was inundated with complaints from white landowners in Florida, a population that numbered roughly 18,000 small plantation owners, farmers, merchants, and squatters. They contended that the Seminoles routinely exited the reservation and killed or stole horses, livestock, and cattle. Retaliatory skirmishes followed, raising tensions across the Panhandle. In spring 1832, in the wake of congressional passage of the Indian Removal Act, a group of Seminoles met with James Gadsden and representatives of the War Department at Payne's Landing along the Ocklawaha River. No minutes of the discussions were kept. Washington later insisted that at this meeting the Seminoles were informed of their impending relocation to Indian Territory, where they were to be melded into the Creek Nation. Neither prospect pleased them. The climate of the western land, they argued, was not suited to the Seminoles, and they demanded a separate identity apart from Creek. The Treaty of Payne's Landing was signed, the seven chiefs who affixed their names later contending they understood their signatures only to be an agreement to personally inspect the environment and climate of Indian Territory, not their acceptance of removal from Florida. The exploratory party that traveled to Indian Territory soon afterwards did note that the site proposed for Seminole residency was, indeed, acceptable and signed the Treaty of Fort Gibson acknowledging their acceptance of the lands selected by the War Department as their new home—at some undefined time in the future. Only upon arriving back home in Florida did the chiefs comprehend the treaty's full import—the Seminoles would be relocated from Florida to Indian Territory immediately. The chiefs were enraged. Several contended they had not signed the treaty, that their names had been included without their knowledge or consent. Several

7.4 Osceola, leader of Seminole resistance
Source: Library of Congress, LC-DIG-pga-00467

others maintained that they had not been fully informed of the document's provisions, being misled into signing the treaty. And a couple argued that they had been forced by the Army's representatives to put their names to the treaty, arguments corroborated by several army officers who later said the Indians were purposely misled by white negotiators while others "had been wheedled and bullied" into signing the treaty. The United States Senate approved the Treaty of Payne's Landing in April 1834. Seminole removal was sanctioned by law.

According to the treaty, the Seminoles were granted three years to prepare for relocation. For the United States, the clock had begun in 1832 with the signing of the Treaty of Payne's Landing; the Seminoles believed the time table commenced in 1834 when the Senate ratified the treaty. Washington's agent among the Seminoles was Wiley Thompson, who in October 1834 met with the chiefs to prepare them for removal only months away. The Indians initially rejected relocation, arguing that they had three more years of residency in Florida. Thompson's insistence that the three-year window would soon expire enraged the Seminole delegation, who now rebuked completely Thompson and the treaty. The Seminoles refused removal. Superintendent Thompson notified General Duncan Clinch, the U.S. Army commander for Florida, who forwarded to President Jackson the news of the Seminoles. Jackson immediately responded with a direct threat to the Indians: "Should you refuse to move," he wrote, "I have . . . directed the Commanding officer [in Florida] to remove you by force." The probability of war generated heated discussions among the Seminoles, some calling for a final armed stance against the United States and others preferring acceptance of removal to avoid bloodshed. Osceola, a young warrior at the time, vowed to fight if necessary. "I will make the white man red with blood, and then blacken him in the sun and rain . . . and the buzzard [will] live upon his flesh," Osceola purportedly responded.

Osceola and Coacoochee (Wildcat) were two of the leading resistance leaders of what soon became the Second Seminole War. Coacoochee traced his descent from two important Seminole bands, the Mikasuki and Alachuas. His mother was also the sister to Micanopy, a respected Seminole chief. Because of his elite lineage, Coacoochee became a prominent resistance leader. But it was Osceola whose name would forever be associated with war. In June 1835, Georgia militia leaders called Osceola to a meeting at Fort King to discuss the treaty, Seminole options, and the ultimate consequences of war with the United States. Enraged by the discussions at that gathering, Osceola thrust his knife into the treaty that lay on the table. The Seminole thundered that neither he nor other Seminoles would comply with removal; Florida was their home, and they intended to remain there. Words became sharp and heated among both parties. Thompson ordered Osceola's detainment, fearing the Indian's rage might sway other Seminoles to initiate war should he be allowed to return home that evening. The following morning, Osceola was released from his cell, but only if he agreed to abide by the Treaty and convince others to accept removal. He promised to do so, but he did not fulfill his pledge. In August, Army private Kinsley Dalton was transporting mail from Ft. Brooke to Ft. King. A group of Seminoles fell upon him and killed the young soldier. The army prepared for war.

The first units of Florida militia and federal troops moved into Seminole territory in mid-December 1835. Only days after their arrival, on December 28, Seminole warriors struck the soldiers near present-day Bushnell, killing all but two who fled to Ft. Brooke for safety. The Army deployed additional troops. By February 1836, Seminole warriors and runaway slaves who joined their fight struck across Florida, torching bales of cotton, raiding small towns and outposts, destroying plantations and small farms alike, and killing all who confronted them. The army and supporting militia units faced a daunting task. They floundered in the wet and swampy Florida environment, one known intimately by the Seminoles. The Americans also suffered from questionable leadership, poor equipment, and inadequate communications. On the other hand, American forces commanded a never-ending line of supplies, cannon and rifles, and a modern communications and transportation network. Perhaps of greatest importance was their numerical superiority. At the Battle of Wahoo Swamp on November 21, 1836 the Americans numbered more than 2,500 soldiers. The swamp provided Seminoles with cover and the benefit of surprise against the Americans, but the sheer number of troops routinely placed against the Indians inevitably took a serious toll on the Seminoles.

The ongoing war strained the Indians. Pockets of Seminoles had been apprehended by U.S. forces, others voluntarily surrendered. Although still fighting, Osceola, Coacoochee, and other Seminole leaders met with General Joseph Hernandez under a flag of truce to discuss some resolution to hostilities. It was a ruse. The chiefs were placed in jail under armed guard. Coacoochee and several others managed to escape, but Osceola remained incarcerated and within months died in prison, ostensibly from malaria. Their principal war chief dead, other Seminole leaders uncertain how to prosecute the war effectively, and a significant number of Indians ready to submit to federal authority, the time seemed ripe for the army to launch a major thrust across Florida that would bring the war to its conclusion. In late 1837 a multi-column push down the length of Florida began. The campaign netted some victories and met some defeats, but regardless of the battles' outcomes, the continuing war tore at the Seminoles' ability and will to resist. The Army burned homes, destroyed crops, and hounded the Indians incessantly throughout 1838 and into 1839. With each victory in battle, Seminole prisoners were shipped to Indian Territory. As the new decade opened, the war had become one of skirmishes against islands of resistance. By 1842 the war had nearly come to an end. Some Seminoles accepted removal and were quickly transported west. Others fled into swamplands and hid there; an American public that had followed the war from its beginning had developed a level of admiration for the Indians' sustained resistance and encouraged Washington to allow those in hiding to remain in Florida on a reservation.

PROFILE

Coacoochee, the Mexican Seminole

Coacoochee was a famous Seminole war leader born into an elite lineage. His father was Asin Yahola, a respected leader and warrior. During the Second Seminole War, Coacoochee gained a national reputation as one of the fiercest Seminole fighters. Once removed to Oklahoma, Coacoochee arrived with his own *italwa*, an organization of three matrilineal lineages. He assumed the Seminole position as *micco* (chief).

As a *micco* of the Seminoles living in Indian Territory during the 1850s, Coacoochee came to realize that many Seminoles were unhappy living among the Creeks. Comanches raided Seminole lands in the Indian Territory, hunting grounds were small, and the U.S. government would not allow Coacoochee to arm black slaves to help protect Seminole interests. He devised a plan to invite Seminoles who had remained in Florida to join his followers from the Indian Territory to migrate to an area along the Texas-Mexico border. There, he hoped the two groups could live together and prosper.

In 1850, Coacoochee traveled to Mexico to inspect the land where he hoped to settle his people and some escaped African slaves (maroons). He signed an agreement with the Mexican inspector and agreed to follow Mexican law. In return, Mexico would not interfere with Seminole government and customs. The land grant amounted to 70,000 acres. Coacoochee then made arrangements to return to the Indian Territory and get the rest of his people. The Mexican government reconsidered momentarily its promises but, seeing substantial advantages in Seminole settlement, reaffirmed its initial commitment to the Seminoles. The Mexican government hoped that the border would become home to good, productive citizens in the Seminoles. Moreover, the Mexican government hoped that Coacoochee and his people would help the Mexican military protect the border from Comanche raids. In 1851, Coacoochee headed to Mexico City to negotiate a new land grant so the Seminoles could settle at El Nacimiento, a town located deeper in Mexican territory and farther away from the Americans. At El Nacimiento, the Seminole migrants lived in traditional ways, following the calendar of the harvest and participating in the Green Corn Ceremony. In 1856, however, the Seminoles' fortunes took a turn for the worse. The Mexican government no longer allowed land grants to Indians, and the United States welcomed the Seminoles back to the Indian Territory, recognizing their national status. Coacoochee died in 1857, before he could witness the exodus of his people back to the Indian Territory. Coacoochee's willingness to move to Mexico to protect his people's sovereignty and autonomy enabled many Seminoles to endure removal on their terms.

The United States successfully removed approximately 4,000 Seminoles at an incredible cost of nearly $40 million. The Second Seminole War was also costly for the Indians. With towns shattered, families dispersed, chiefs captured and killed, their culture shredded, and stripped from their lands, the rebuilding of Seminole life in the Indian Territory would be a daunting task.

The Black Hawk War

Problems for the Sauks and Mesquakies began immediately after the Louisiana Purchase. The governor of the Indiana Territory, William Henry Harrison, intended to sign treaties with the Indians who lived in Indiana,

Illinois, and Wisconsin. Within these lands lived the Sauks, Mesquakies, Potawatomis, and a host of other tribes of the Northwest. The Sauks raided the Osage Indians just west of the Mississippi River, but Sauk warriors also descended on American settlements in the same area. Under the pretext of bringing the peace, Harrison negotiated the Treaty of 1804, which a group of Sauk chiefs apparently signed without understanding that the treaty required land cessions.

Facing the need to locate new lands or wage war against the United States, the Sauks and Mesquakies opted for peace. Intertribal relations were troubled, as both groups ventured west and competed for new hunting grounds on land claimed by the Dakota Sioux. The Sauks and Mesquakies also tried to assert military power over the Osages, Otoes, and Omahas along the Missouri River. Intertribal warfare erupted across the region, pulling in the Wahpeton and Sisseton bands of the Dakota Sioux, whose prime hunting territories were in present-day Iowa. The federal government intervened, sending to the territory a peace commission to Prairie du Chien in Wisconsin in August 1825. Chiefs representing the Sauk, Mesquakie, Menominee, Iowa, Dakota Sioux, Ho-Chunk, the United Band of Ottawa, Ojibwa, and Potawatomis gathered for negotiations, but the effort to settle Indian disputes over hunting territories failed miserably.

7.5 Keokuk, Sauk chief.

Source: Courtesy of Library of Congress Prints and Photographs Division, LC-DIG-pga-07519

7.6 Black Hawk (Makataimeshek-iakiak), Sauk war chief

Source: Courtesy of Library of Congress Prints and Photographs Division, LC-DIG-pga-07527

As the patterns of relocation and intertribal conflict developed, white migration into that region soared. The white population of Illinois alone more than doubled to 150,000 between 1818 and 1830. At first, settlement of Illinois was limited to the southern and central parts of the state, leaving unaffected the lands of the Sauks and Mesquakies who lived in the northwestern part of the state. The lead mines in the northwest had always turned major profits for the Sauks and Mesquakies who traded the ore with white buyers. But Illinois was now a state of the union, with specifically detailed boundaries. The Sauks and others resided within Illinois borders, and the lead mines also fell within the state's perimeter. Who owned the mines? Competing land claims over the lead region surfaced in the 1820s with the federal government ultimately deciding in its own favor. Permits to mine were soon issued to whites. Chiefs appealed to federal Indian agents to keep whites off their lands and prevent violence, but white miners continued to trespass, sometimes even sexually assaulting Indian women in the villages they entered or those they encountered near the mining district. By the late 1820s, the United

States was no longer listening to the complaints of the tribal leaders. Sauks and Mesquakies again faced some tough decisions.

Conflict rose between the Sauk leaders Keokuk and Black Hawk and fragmented the tribe as the two men battled over the appropriate response to Washington's actions. Neither man had risen to power through the traditional Sauk channels of civil chiefs and war chiefs. They instead attained influence through their wartime exploits. Keokuk was known not so much for his fighting skills as for his ability to keep the Sauks out of unnecessary conflicts. He was respected highly as a peacemaker as much as he was respected as a warrior. Black Hawk, on the other hand, had received a great medicine bundle from his father who had died when Black Hawk was in his twenties. Empowered by the medicine of war, he earned respect as a great warrior who fought and killed many enemies. Black Hawk refused to give up the traditional ways of Sauk while Keokuk pursued compromise and won the favor of the federal government for his promotion of peace. Government agents trusted him with the Sauk annuities and goods. Perhaps the most important difference between the two men was how each viewed the Treaty of 1804. Keokuk never challenged the treaty; he only sought to preserve Sauk sovereignty and autonomy on the lands they retained. Black Hawk, in contrast, vehemently opposed the treaty as a fraud and claimed that he would never cede any Sauk lands to the United States.

Differences of opinion, complicated by divergent personalities and personal histories, came to a head in 1828. In June, federal agent Thomas Forsyth tried to convince both the Sauks and Mesquakies to give up their eastern lands, lands that sat in the middle of overland trade routes between St. Louis and the lead mines and that were also hemmed in by white settlers on all sides. An important Sauk village of Saukenuk, at Rock Island, Illinois, stood at the center of the conflict. Keokuk was willing to abandon the village and move his people to the western territories, avoiding confrontation with whites and the federal government who would support its western citizens. Black Hawk, conversely, refused to relinquish the land of his ancestors. The matter was decided in the fall of 1829 when Forsyth informed the Sauks that all the land around Saukenuk had been parceled out in accord with the Treaty of 1804.

Black Hawk moved throughout the Great Lakes region in the months that followed, seeking support for his anti-removal position. He consulted a prophet of both Ho-Chunk (Winnebago) and Sauk descent, Wabokieshiek (White Cloud). White Cloud lent his support to Black Hawk, buttressing his decision in the form of prophecies and sacred power. White Cloud lived only 30 miles northeast of Saukenuk, and he did not want to see the Sauks and Mesquakies lose their prized lands. Tensions were high in the region, especially in 1830 after a group of Dakota Sioux, Ho-Chunks, and Menominees attacked a friendly party of Mesquakie chiefs traveling home from a meeting with federal officials, killing all but one. Mesquakie vengeance was certain. They, of course, damned those Indians who murdered their chiefs, but they also blamed the federal officials who had convened the council to discuss repercussions of the recently enacted Indian Removal Act. With the spiritual support of White Cloud and the attack against the Mesquakie leaders fresh in their minds, the Mesquakies threw their support behind Black Hawk. It would take only a minor incident to ignite war.

White Americans populated the town of Saukenuk in the spring of 1831. State and local officials insisted that Black Hawk and his core supporters, generally referred to as the "British Band," remain west of the Mississippi River to avoid any excuse for violence by either Indians or town residents. Keokuk echoed the state's warning. The land, however, belonged to the Sauks, countered Black Hawk. He and the British Band entered Saukenuk, forced out white squatters, and planted their own cornfields. They dared anyone to resist them. The Illinois governor hoped for peace but Black Hawk's move forced him to dispatch a state militia unit to challenge Black Hawk and his followers. On June 5, 1831, Major General Edward Gaines conferenced with leading Sauks and Mesquakies. Keokuk still argued for peace and for his people to accept removal west of the Mississippi. Black Hawk arrived in the middle of the meeting dressed in full warrior regalia and singing a war song, and he dared the state of Illinois to impede Sauk access to their lands. Tensions rose. On April 6, 1832, against the advice of Keokuk and other village leaders, Black Hawk and his Sauk and Mesquakie followers crossed the Mississippi moving toward Saukenuk for the spring planting of corn. Federal and state officials viewed Black Hawk's arrival as a sign of hostility and dispatched General Henry Atkinson's force as a countermeasure.

Atkinson camped his unit near White Cloud's village and there he waited. Located nearby, however, was a more aggressive Illinois militia unit comprised of 1,500 young men who had never before faced Indians in battle. Filled with vinegar, as the saying goes, they imagined the heroics of fighting and the ultimate destruction of a people they deemed savage. On May 14, 1832, Black Hawk sent a delegation under a white flag of peace to meet with the militia commander, Major Stillman. "Trigger happy" as the militiamen were, the troopers opened fire as the Indians approached. Black Hawk retaliated, attacking the militia, forcing their retreat, and killing 11 militiamen in the process. What started as a meeting of truce turned into the Battle of Stillman's Run.

The Black Hawk War spanned the summer of 1832. Following the Battle of Stillman's Run, Black Hawk moved into southern Wisconsin, evading as often as possible the pursuing U.S. troops. At Wisconsin Heights on July 21, Black Hawk and his British Band tangled with troops commanded by Colonel Henry Dodge. Black Hawk's band lost perhaps 60 warriors before retreating from the field. On July 26, 1832, an American force of 1,300 men again caught up with the British Band, this time south of where the Bad Axe River meets the Mississippi River. Small skirmishes marked the next several days, but on August 1, 1832, the military deployed a steamboat, the *Warrior*, whose guns fired on Indians along the river. The *Warrior* moved north to refuel, and Black Hawk took the opportunity to secure as many of his followers as he could. Black Hawk knew his force was terribly weakened. Hunger affected everyone. Most were exhausted from the repetition of fight and flight. The death toll among his warriors reduced significantly the Indians' ability to hold off many more assaults by the army that chased them. A lapse in morale compromised their will to fight. The British Band not only faced the U.S. Army but also the Dakota Sioux and their allies, a most potent force that viewed the Sauk as intruders and threats in their own territory. Black Hawk chose to lead his weakened band back across the Mississippi River. A contingent of warriors would remain in place to counter the soldiers' next strike and, in so doing, give Black Hawk time to effect escape. The Battle at Bad Axe River on August 2 broke the back of the British Band. It was a horrific fight. Ready to wage a war of extermination, the white soldiers slaughtered more than 300 warriors in addition to the Sauk and Mesquakie men, women, and children who did not move with Black Hawk. The few Indians who did cross the Mississippi died at the hands of the Dakota Sioux. Black Hawk, whom many Sauks and Mesquakies viewed as a traitor for his exit from Bad Axe, surrendered on August 27, 1832, and was sentenced to prison. The last Indian war against removal from the Old Northwest was over. The federal government successfully relocated some Sauks and Mesquakies to the Indian Territory in 1842 after buying out their western lands in Iowa.

READING HISTORY

Black Hawk's Autobiography

After the defeat of Black Hawk and the British Band, and after eight months in captivity, Black Hawk and several other leaders of the Black Hawk War commenced a trip east in April 1833. Andrew Jackson ordered them to come to Washington, D.C. These resistance Indians, by the 1830s, were a sight to behold for many Eastern Americans. After traveling by steamboat, coach, and railway, Black Hawk became somewhat of a celebrity: tourists crowded railroad stations and steamboat docks to get a look at a real Indian. After the celebrity-like tour, Black Hawk and the other prisoners continued their imprisonment in Virginia but they remained subjects of interest. Several painters had them pose for portraits. In this environment of intrigue and excitement of 1833, Black Hawk told his life story, which a newspaper reporter in Cincinnati, J.B. Patterson, finally edited and published. The following short selection is from the beginning of the book, in which Black Hawk speaks of his ancestry.

I was born at the Sac Village, on Rock River, in the year 1767, and am now in my 67th year. My great grandfather, *Na-nà-ma-kee*, or Thunder (according to the tradition given me by my father, *Py-e-sa*), was born in the vicinity of Montreal, where the Great Spirit first placed the Sac Nation, and inspired him with a belief that, at the end of four years, he should see a *white man*, who would be to him a father. Consequently he blacked his face, and ate but once a day (just as the sun was going down), for three years, and continued dreaming throughout all this time whenever he slept—when the Great Spirit again appeared to him and told him, that, at the end of one year more, he should meet his father,—and directed him to start seven days before its expiration, and take with him his two brothers *N-mah*, or Sturgeon, and *Pau-ka-hum-ma-wa* or Sun Fish, and travel in a direction to the left of sun-rising. After pursuing this course five days, he sent out his two brothers to listen if they could hear a noise, and if so, to fasten some grass to the end of a pole, erect, pointing in the direction of the sound, and then return to him.

Early next morning they returned, and reported that they had heard sounds which appeared near at hand, and that they had fulfilled his order. They all then started for the place where the pole had been erected; when, on reaching it, Na-nà-ma-kee left his party, and went alone to the place from whence the sounds proceeded, and found that the white man had arrived and pitched his tent. When he came in sight, his father came out to meet him. He took him by the hand, and welcomed him into his tent. He told him that he was the son of the King of France—that he had been dreaming for four years—that the Great Spirit had directed him to come here, where he should meet a nation of people who had never yet seen a white man—that they should be his children, and he should be their father—that he had communicated these things to the King, his father, who laughed at him, and called him a Ma-she-na—but he insisted on coming here to meet his children, where the Great Spirit had directed him. The King told him that he would neither find land nor people—that this was an uninhabited region of lakes and mountains; but, finding that he would have no peace without it, fitted out a nà-pe-quâ, manned it, and gave it to him in charge, when he immediately loaded it, set sail, and had now landed on the very day that the Great Spirit had told him, in his dreams, he should meet his children. He had now met the man who should, in future, have charge of all the nation.

Source: J.B. Patterson, ed., *Autobiography of Ma-Ka-Tai-Me-She-Kia-Kiak, or Black Hawk, Embracing the Traditions of His Nation, Various Wars in Which He Has Been Engaged, and His Account of the Cause and General History of the Black Hawk War of 1832, His Surrender, and Travels Through the United States. Also Life, Death, and Burial of the Old Chief, Together with a History of the Black Hawk War* (Rock Island, Illinois: 1833), pp. 11–12.

Questions

1. How does Black Hawk describe his great-grandfather?
2. What is the significance of Black Hawk tracing his ancestry as he does?

TIMELINE 7.3 RESISTANCE, 1804–1842

Date	Seminole Wars	Black Hawk War
1813	Payne's War	
1814–1816	Negro Fort	
1818	Andrew Jackson attacks Florida	
1821	Andrew Jackson appointed territorial governor of Florida	
1823	Treaty of Moultrie Creek	
1832	Treaty of Payne's Landing	
1835–1836	Second Seminole War combat escalates	
1837	Jesup wins at Fort Marion	
	Zachary Taylor victorious	
1842	Seminole removal begins	
1804		Treaty of 1804
1818		Illinois achieves statehood
1820		Massive migration to Illinois
1828–1829		Black Hawk and Keokuk split
1830s		Black Hawk wins supporters
1831–1832		Village of Saukenuk becomes contested ground
1832		Battle at Bad Axe River
1842		Sauks and Mesquakies removed to the Indian Territory

Removal From the North

As in the South, many Indian groups of the Old Northwest were subject to removal. A few resistance leaders such as Black Hawk challenged the order of things. Other Indians, realizing the inevitable, migrated on their own accord. A number of Indian groups in the Old Northwest had previously experienced migration when they were pushed out of the Eastern Woodlands in the eighteenth century. The Shawnees had lost their lands in Pennsylvania and Kentucky, ultimately settling in portions of the Ohio territory. Likewise, the Delawares migrated into the Ohio territory from Pennsylvania. Until 1825, most of the western Shawnees lived on a 25-mile tract of land known as Cape Girardeau, just south of St. Louis. A group of Delawares moved into the Spanish-occupied Ste. Genevieve-Cape Girardeau region, removed far from the violence of the 1780s and 1790s. These immigrant western Shawnees and Delawares used the Mississippi River as a political and economic route of communication. They took advantage of their position at a major trading crossroads, engaging with French traders operating primarily out of St. Louis. As one French merchant noted, his local storehouses "were always stocked with goods" to transport to the Ste. Genevieve-Cape Girardeau region. From the Shawnee and Delaware perspective, the Mississippi River was not as much a geographical boundary as a conduit of goods and information.

Once the United States extended its reach into the trans-Mississippi west, the western Shawnees and Delawares once again faced forced migration. After the War of 1812, American migration into the western territories accelerated. In 1820, the eastern Delawares moved into Illinois, where they reunited with many of their former kinsmen from the Spanish territories. By the 1820s, Missouri became the settling ground for western Shawnees, the Delawares, Weas, Peorias, Kickapoos, and Piankeshaws. Shawnees in Ohio under the leadership of Black Hoof and the Shawnee Prophet fought westward removal. A treaty orchestrated in 1825 resulted in the Missouri Shawnees ceding their lands and accepting a tract along the Kansas River, in present-day Johnson County, Kansas. By the 1830s, the Ohio Shawnees and some of the western Shawnees were reunited in the lands of Kansas.

The government's program of removal drove many Oneida tribesmen from New York into Green Bay, Wisconsin. An Episcopalian minister, Eleazer Williams, the great-grandson of Eunice Williams from the Deerfield Raid of 1704 and of mixed Mohawk and white ancestry, traveled with the Oneidas to Green Bay several times to look for a tract of land. In 1821, Williams joined the Oneida delegation in requesting an 18-mile-long stretch of land along the Fox River, north of Lake Winnebago. Federal policymakers negotiated with the Menominee and Ho-Chunks for the Oneida relocation, but only Menominees capitulated and even then did so reluctantly after much internal conflict and debate. In 1824, 100 Oneidas arrived at the Fox River to share the land with Menominees. By 1838, more than 650 Oneidas lived at Duck Creek, the permanent Oneida settlement in the Wisconsin territory. In the Treaty of 1838, the Oneidas got 65,400 acres carved out of the Menominee lands. On the Oneida lands of New York were also several loosely organized groups of Indians, including the Mohicans, Munsee Delaware band, Brothertown Indians, and the Stockbridge Indians formerly of western Massachusetts. Following the lead of the Oneidas to Green Bay, the Mohican, Stockbridge, Munsee, and Brothertown Indians sold their land under pressure from New York and federal officials.

The Seneca Indians living on the four reservations of Buffalo Creek, Tonawanda, Allegany, and Cattaraugus were unlike other New York tribes. Not until 1838 did government officials meet with a group of chiefs to set the terms for Seneca removal. Federal agents, working in concert with the Ogden Land Company, facilitated the Treaty of Buffalo Creek. The preemption rights to the Seneca lands were awarded to the Ogden Land Company, a group of land speculators on the Senecas' prime western New York real estate. Yet according to the preemption rules, the company could not forcibly remove the Senecas. Only through a federally approved treaty could the Senecas rightfully sell their lands. The sticking point for the Ogden Land Company and federal officials was that each reservation had chiefs representing different local interests, meaning that chiefs at one spot could never claim to speak for the interests of all of the Senecas. Preying on a select group of Buffalo Creek chiefs who sought wealth and power, government agents forced the Treaty of Buffalo Creek through Congress. The treaty required the Senecas to release the rights to all four of their reservations. With the help of the Quakers, the Seneca majority fought the treaty and finally forced the government to agree to the supplemental Treaty of 1842. In the end, the Senecas gave up the Buffalo Creek reservation, located near the growing and densely populated city of Buffalo, but kept title to their three other reservations. At no point did the Tonawanda Indians participate in the treaty process. In 1855, Allegany and Cattaraugus united as the Seneca Nation under a republican form of government, whereas the Tonawanda Senecas kept their traditional chiefs in power. Unlike the Cherokees, the Senecas successfully created and sustained an independent Indian nation within the borders of a state.

As the white American population of the Great Lakes region and the Ohio territory grew, federal policymakers placed increased pressure for removal on Menominees, Ho-Chunks, Potawatomis, and Miamis. Menominee Algonquian speakers lived in the white pine and sugar maple regions of the western Great Lakes, west

PROFILE

William Apess, a Pequot, Helps the Mashpee

Not all Indians in the North faced removal. In Massachusetts, small remnant communities remained on reserved tracts. Life in such communities, however, was not easy. In the 1820s and 1830s, the Mashpee of Cape Cod lived under the "protection" of three white overseers, men appointed by the Massachusetts state government. They were issued authority to lease Mashpee land for livestock grazing and give local white settlers rights to Mashpee woods. They also bound Mashpee Indians to indentured servitude in local white homes and whaling vessels and controlled who settled on Mashpee lands. A white minister controlled the Mashpees' church and barred the large Baptist Mashpee population from using it. Rather than protection, whites effectively restricted Mashpee life to their own advantage.

It was in this environment that the Methodist Pequot preacher William Apess lived and worked. Born in 1798 to poor Indian parents who traveled from town to town seeking employment, Apess spent his youth and young adulthood wandering throughout southern New England, taking refuge in white homes whenever he was welcomed. In New London, Connecticut, Apess converted to the Methodist faith on March 15, 1813. Formally ordained a minister sometime in the late 1820s, Apess served as an itinerant preacher. In 1829, Apess published the first autobiography ever penned by a Native American, *A Son of a Forest*. His autobiography described the hardships of living as an Indian in the Northeast; his many experiences with alcoholism, broken homes, and beatings; and his eventual conversion to Methodism.

In May 1833, Apess arrived in Mashpee, following an established circuit of Indian preaching throughout the Cape Cod area. There he became involved in the troubled politics of the region, as the Mashpees contested their overseers' authority. He helped the Mashpees draft petitions to the Massachusetts government, one of which was the first "Indian Declaration of Independence." In the document, Apess cleverly drew from American political theory: "We as a tribe, will rule ourselves, and have the right to do so: for all men are born free and equal, says the Constitution of the country." Apess's leadership in the Mashpee revolt of 1833 and 1834 gained him national fame but also prosecution and imprisonment for his political agitation. In March 1834, largely due to Apess's efforts, the Massachusetts government granted Mashpee township status. Apess died in New York in 1839. His fascinating story as a Pequot Methodist, autobiographical writer, and Native American political activist is a reminder that Indians in the Northeast used education and religion to engage in an American public arena in which they challenged the governmental powers that threatened their land. Native resistance persisted in southern New England, although their methods and tactics had changed.

of present-day Green Bay. Menominees had served the British during the War of 1812, after which Oshkosh emerged as the tribe's strongest leader. The Menominee and Ho-Chunks were part of the 1821 treaty that opened a "joint tenancy" with the New York Indians along the Fox River. They also attended the grand council at Prairie du Chien (1825), which was purportedly designed to bring peace to the region. Two years later, in the Treaty at Butte des Morts, they agreed to a new boundary with the Ojibwas but in 1831 relinquished a portion of their acreage to accommodate the New York Indians migrating into the territory. Moreover, when the United States waged a brief war against the neighboring Ho-Chunks who had long been their allies, the Menominee set aside their traditional friendship with their neighbors and gave tacit support to federal troops. During the Black Hawk War, a unit of 250 Menominee under Feather Shedder's leadership protected settlers at Green Bay who lived near a potential target of Sauk raiders. In 1831, tribal leaders agreed to cede three million acres in return for $146,500 over a 12-year period. The land ceded included the New York Indians' territory, so Congress amended the treaty to keep the lands for the transplanted New York tribes. In 1836, Menominees turned over the eastern half of their remaining land, and in 1848, they ceded the western portion. The federal government tried to push the Menominee onto a tract in Minnesota, but the continued fighting between local Ojibwas and Dakotas convinced the Menominee leader Oshkosh that it was an unsuitable place for the Menominee. A series of petitions to the federal government finally reserved a 276,000-acre tract of land for the Menominee in Wisconsin. Each of these moves demonstrated clearly the Menominee resolve for peace with Washington and further showed the Indians' willingness to adapt to ever changing circumstances. To be sure, the specter of compulsory removal lurked in the shadows, and their compliance with federal designs certainly was intended to earn them Washington's favor and hopefully avoid relocation to western territories. Still, their commitment to peace and willingness to adapt should have served as clear evidence that the Menominee posed no threat to white settlement and development of the region.

Their neighbors were Ho-Chunks (Winnebagos), who also occupied a forested landscape. They were a Siouan-speaking people, and linguistic similarities suggest that they had probably branched off at some point in their history from the Mandan, Osage, Quapaw, Omaha, or Poncas. The Ho-Chunks' hatred for the American republic's expansion made them some of the most ardent supporters of the Shawnee prophet and Tecumseh. In fact, the Ho-Chunks built their own settlement near Prophetstown (Tippecanoe) in Indiana, which was known to them as Hochungra village. They played a prominent role in the Illinois theater of the War of 1812, even helping the British hold off the American invasion of Fort Michilimackinac. By 1825, the Ho-Chunks faced American lead miners invading their rich lands. Like the Menominee, Ho-Chunks signed the treaty of peace at Prairie du Chien. In spite of the accord, Four Legs, a Ho-Chunk chief, declared that "there are a great many Americans on our land, working it without permission." Red Bird, another chief, brutally attacked squatters at La Crosse because of a rumor that the United States executed some Ho-Chunk warriors at Fort Snelling in Minnesota. Red Bird's aggression put the rest of the Ho-Chunks in an unfavorable position with the

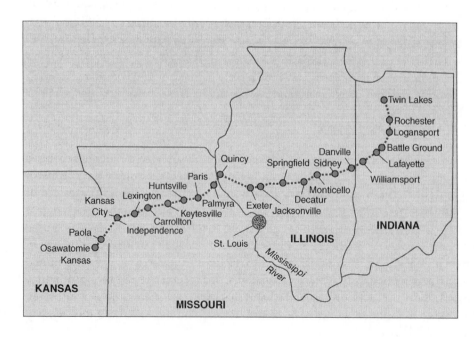

Map 7.3 The Potawatomi Trail of Death

TIMELINE 7.4 REMOVAL FROM THE NORTH, 1820S–1838

Date	Event
1820s–1830s	Shawnee removal to Kansas
1821	Oneidas travel to Wisconsin
1825	Treaty of Prairie du Chien
1831	Menominee land cession
1833	Treaty of Chicago with the Potawatomi
1837	Ho-Chunks forced into Minnesota
1838	Oneidas and other New York Indians settle on tract in Wisconsin
	Treaty of Buffalo Creek
	Potawatomi Trail of Tears

United States. Red Bird continued his assaults, striking a barge carrying lead miners and supplies near Prairie du Chien. The U.S. Army pressured the Ho-Chunks to turn over Red Bird. Once apprehended, Red Bird asked to be executed rather than shackled, stating, "I am ready . . . I do not wish to be put in irons. Let me be free. I have given away my life."

Resistance only made the Ho-Chunks more susceptible to American pressure. For Red Bird's release, the Ho-Chunks paid a heavy price: they ceded all of their lead-rich lands in Illinois. The United States also demanded all of their mineral lands south of the Wisconsin River. Internal tribal disputes resurfaced when Black Hawk's war divided the Ho-Chunks. White Cloud, the prophet, was of Ho-Chunk and Sauk descent. There were two main factions, pro-Black Hawk Ho-Chunks and those not willing to resist the United States. After the war, the Ho-Chunks' removal advanced rapidly, as the United States associated all Ho-Chunks with Black Hawk. They ceded their remaining lands around present-day Madison and Wisconsin Dells in exchange for lands in Iowa. In 1837, forced removal took them out of Iowa and into northern Minnesota. A "rebel" faction, however, never gave up, ranging between Wisconsin, Iowa, and Minnesota until Washington granted them a tract of land in south-central Minnesota.

The Potawatomis, who called themselves "Keepers of the Fire" as part of the Anishinabe, a loose confederacy that also included the Ojibwa, were one of the largest groups forced off of their Wisconsin lands and into the Indian Territory. In the eight years following the conclusion of the War of 1812, the Potawatomis were coerced into a series of treaties that successfully pushed them into Kansas. What placed the Potawatomis at the mercy of the U.S. government was a lack of centralized leadership. They were made up of loosely affiliated bands whose chiefs signed over entire tracts in the name of the entire tribe. Some of these leaders were, in fact, highly educated (known as *métis*, meaning indigenous peoples of both Indian and Euro-American heritage) and used their position as elite Potawatomis to gain the favor of the United States by selling their lands. In the fall of 1838, the United States removed 800 Potawatomis at gunpoint, transporting them over 660 miles of land from the Yellow River, located in Northern Indiana, to the Osage River, located west of the Missouri border. According to Potawatomi oral tradition, the United States cuffed and shackled the warriors and only provided rancid food. Potawatomis died each day while in transit on the "Trail of Death" (see Map 7.3). In the Treaty of

Chicago in 1833, other Potawatomis ceded their remaining territories east of the Mississippi. Anishinabes, particularly the Ojibwa, watched in fear. The Ojibwa acquiesced to major land cessions in 1837 and 1842, turning over nearly two-thirds of northern Wisconsin, large parts of central Minnesota, and most of Michigan's Upper Peninsula. By 1855, they had been settled on four reservations—Bad River, Lac Courte Oreilles, Lac du Flambeau, and Red Cliff.

The removal process showed how disconnected Potawatomi bands were. Chief Simon Pokagon, a Christian, kept his village along the St. Joseph River in Michigan; 2,000 Potawatomis from southern Wisconsin and northern Illinois fled to other parts of Wisconsin and north to Canada. Another set of bands from northeastern Wisconsin, adamantly opposed to removal, returned to their Lake Michigan villages and stayed there until 1862. The creation of Potawatomi reservations and their removal out of the state opened vast acreage in Wisconsin, Illinois, and Michigan to countless white settlers who quickly swept into the regions.

Restoring Sovereignty in the Indian Territory

Native Americans from the Deep South who arrived in Indian Territory had to rebuild their societies. The Cherokees, Creeks, Choctaws, Chickasaws, and Seminoles selected lands for their homes and farms. They established schools and government, and they sought methods to limit the violence and alcoholism borne of depression. Some Indians faced a difficult transition to life in Indian Territory, reluctantly accepting their fate and eking out a new life for themselves and their families in spite of the limited resources and opportunities. Still others prospered, especially those residing near slaveholding territories. Like their white cotton frontier planters, slave-owning Indians became very wealthy and rose to positions of power within their transplanted communities. Those who acculturated to white norms, who staked themselves into the regional or national economy, and who mirrored the values, aspirations, and behaviors of their white neighbors essentially turned away from their heritage, from tradition. It was a conscious choice they made. Living alongside them, however, were others who opted to retain as much of their traditions as they could. Indian Territory not only became a stretch of land occupied by many different tribal groups but also one that separated natives between those who remained Indian and those who emulated the very people who had dispossessed them of traditional lands and cultures. Conflict was inevitable.

Rebuilding the Cherokee Nation

Although Cherokees had a written national constitution before their removal to Indian Territory (present-day Oklahoma), they were far from a unified group at the time of their final removal from Georgia. Three distinct parties emerged among the Cherokee. The Cherokees who remained in Georgia until removal in 1838 were the largest group and called themselves the "Patriot Party." On the eve of removal, their leaders met at Aquohee Camp and vowed never to allow their nation to dissolve. A second group, the "Western Cherokees" or "Old Settlers," lived in Arkansas when the Indian Removal Act of 1830 passed Congress and by 1832 had moved into Indian Territory. They had established their own leadership and created their own laws separate from all other Cherokee groups. The final group, the "Treaty Party," included those Cherokees responsible for the Treaty of New Echota. Most relocated to Indian Territory in 1835. Thus, when John Ross stepped forward at Aquohee camp as the principal chief to unite the 14,000 Cherokees awaiting removal, there were already large numbers of Cherokees in Indian Territory who had established their own government and social structures.

The unification of the Cherokee Nation in Indian Territory became a tumultuous process. The leaders of all three parties were wealthy planters. The Old Settlers prided themselves on arriving in Oklahoma first. They insisted that the governing system and body of law they established were the true laws of the Cherokee Nation, that the constitution and set of laws carried to Indian Territory by Patriot Cherokees were not valid. The Old Settlers saw the Treaty Party, a group that included Elias Boudinot, Major Ridge, John Ridge, and Stand Watie, in the same light. To the Old Settlers, both groups were immigrants into their lands. Old Settler members, however, sought an alliance with the Treaty Party and commenced secret negotiations. Once he learned of the planned union between the Treaty Party and the Old Settlers, John Ross convened a meeting on June 19, 1839 at Takatoka where he demanded all Cherokees decide collectively who should govern. He argued that the Old Settlers' rebuff of the Patriots was an open rejection of the voice of the Cherokee people.

Ross's call for a democratically reached decision framed a sinister charade to conceal what occurred next or simply proved unpalatable to certain members of the Patriot Party. A group of approximately 100–150 Cherokees met without Ross in attendance and decided to execute the leaders of the Treaty Party. In their opinion, Major Ridge, John Ridge, Elias Boudinot, and Stand Watie were responsible for the Cherokee Nation's current predicament. They had not committed themselves to resisting removal, and their bid for power was one of self-interest that precluded unification of the Cherokee people. Honoring the traditional protocols of clan justice, the conspirators promised that clans would not exact retribution against the assassins. On June 22, 1839, 12 men carried out the murders while selected observers witnessed the executions. Major Ridge, John Ridge, and Elias Boudinot all lay dead. Stand Watie was attacked but survived his wounds. He was absolutely convinced that Ross personally ordered the murders, although he had no evidence to support his contention. Ross denied any involvement in the crime. Watie and some of his followers offered rewards for the capture of the executioners.

In July, Ross organized a meeting with some of the Old Settlers' leaders, hoping for a peaceful resolution to the factional strife. Those who killed the Treaty Party members were exonerated as proper protocol had been followed, and there was a public announcement that anyone who sought revenge for the killings would be branded an "outlaw." The assemblage formed eight police forces to protect the Cherokee people and granted amnesty to former Treaty Party members. Stand Watie interpreted Ross's police forces to be nothing more than paramilitary organizations to protect himself as he added to his own power and authority. The convention also declared the Treaty of New Echota fraudulent and adopted the Act of Union. Sequoyah and John Looney of the Old Settlers, along with John Ross, signed the act "to form ourselves into one body politic." Few Old Settler Party and Treaty Party Cherokees agreed to the Act of Union; they held their own separate conventions. Still, in September, Ross and his supporters, who now outnumbered the other two factions, enacted a new constitution that resembled the Cherokee constitution of 1827. It allowed Old Settler leaders to sit in high offices although the Ross faction held majority influence, and Ross was again chosen as the principal chief.

The new constitution accomplished little. Factional violence continued to plague the Cherokee Nation. Completely opposed to any agreements with Ross, Watie's ardent followers harassed and attacked Patriot Party supporters and murdered some in the night, riding off with the victims' horses. Ross's light horse police were instructed "to shoot first and ask questions later." For seven years the Cherokee Nation in Indian Territory endured nothing less than civil war. The violence also threatened to spill over into neighboring tribal territories. Federal negotiators journeyed to Oklahoma and in 1846 established peace, albeit a tenuous one. The light horse police were disbanded, and federally appointed sheriffs and law officers were instructed to preserve the peace.

Cherokee leaders understood that formal education was necessary for Indians in the post-removal era and, toward that end, John Ross in 1840 called for the government to provide his people with a free public education system. Legislation the following year established a school system with three districts and a superintendent to oversee related affairs. The law required each school to maintain a minimum population of 25 students to remain open. Teachers' salaries would be paid from a federal education annuity of $16,000 annually. Ross targeted the program primarily for full-blooded Cherokees who spoke no English as they required the most urgent training, but few actually attended the schools, taunted as they were by mixed-bloods who already were somewhat acculturated. Moreover, bilingual teachers were hard to find and poorer families needed their children's labor on their farms. Cherokees, however, benefited from the early education programs, as they would use the schools as models to build a stronger and more far-reaching program of internal education.

The Cherokee Nation also tackled the impact of alcohol on its communities. The Cherokee constitution made liquor illegal and instructed local district officials to arrest peddlers on the reservation. Arkansas border traffickers were especially targeted as they flooded parts of Indian Territory with alcohol. A grassroots organization also formed. The Cherokee Temperance Society (CTS) claimed 3,373 members by 1846. The CTS lobbied Cherokee leaders to promote abstinence and to lead by example, much like temperance movements across the United States were championing at the same time. Passing along the message of good citizenship and family stability were Cherokee Temperance Society branch organizations throughout the Indian nation. Local divisions recruited children, known as the Cherokee Cold Water Army, who met regularly at Tahlequah and publicly pledged devotion to temperance. The CTS even became a quasi-political body, sending petitions to the legislature of Arkansas and requesting help in patrolling the region's borders for liquor traffickers. Arkansas never responded to the petitions, but the demand for action did reach Washington and received some attention.

Resurgence Among Indians From the South

Building a new life in Indian Territory proved quite difficult for the Cherokee, and it proved just as difficult for other relocated natives as well. Drafting a constitution for the Choctaw Nation pitted the wealthy planter elite against the class of small farmers who feared the new government would ignore their concerns for those of the rich. Would sovereignty rest in the people or with an elite ruling class? Who specifically could hold positions of authority? To what extent, if any, would traditional Choctaw structures and values be maintained? And the questions continued. Under pressure from federal agents, who threatened to table the process and have Washington govern the Choctaws directly, opposing sides agreed to cooperate for the nation's welfare. The spirit of negotiation faded quickly. Once again, federal agents demanded the Choctaws resolve their political disputes or face Washington's governance. Eventually a political consensus emerged and, in June 1834, all factions accepted a new Choctaw constitution.

The constitution abandoned clan revenge, established a police force to regulate civil matters, and required each of the three districts that formed the Nation to send ten delegates to a unicameral legislature. Removal had thoroughly disrupted the system of captains and *iksas* (organized family villages), although at the local level, assemblies open to all residents would still convene to discuss local issues without interference from the new national council. The constitution also included a bill of rights, separation of powers, and trial by jury. Three district chiefs, elected to four-year terms, comprised the executive branch, and universal adult male suffrage was guaranteed.

At Doaksville in 1837, an agreement extended Choctaw Nation citizenship to Chickasaws and established for them a separate political district. The Chickasaws had to abide by all Choctaw laws, but they retained control over their own annuities and the money they might earn from any Mississippi land sales. The arrangement seemed reasonable to both parties, but in little time Chickasaws soured to the arrangement. The traditional animosity each nation had for the other still simmered in spite of the new relationship. Too, the Chickasaw district not only occupied lands extremely difficult to cultivate but also abutted the Kiowas and Comanches, who were notorious for horseback raids into Indian Territory. Poverty soon settled over many Chickasaw families, resulting in their indebtedness to local traders. Many eked out a meager living as day laborers. And in spite of the Doaksville agreement, Chickasaws refused to abandon their old ways of governance. They continued a system of an elected principal chief, and the *iksas* convened regularly. Internal squabbles also complicated matters. In 1855, Chickasaw elite planters called for separation from the Choctaw Nation and proposed features to be included in a Chickasaw constitution. The new governing structure would assume authority over annuities and land payments, replacing the earlier system in which the *iksas* regulated those items. The proposed constitution also abandoned the *iksas* structure completely. Traditional structures were directly under attack by an acculturated native upper class.

The federal government recognized the Chickasaws' right to become an independent nation in 1856. Cyrus Harris, the Nation's first governor, worked tirelessly to unify the Chickasaw, and his new government eased Choctaw discontent at losing a district by purchasing the land from the Choctaw Nation. The Chickasaws drafted and ratified their drafted constitution that provided for separation of powers, included a bill of rights, ended clan justice, established courts, controlled national funds, and divided the nation into four counties.

Turmoil and uncertainty also plagued the Creeks in Indian Territory. Longstanding tension between the Upper Towns and the Lower Towns migrated to Oklahoma with the Creek. Arriving in Indian Territory over a span of five years, from 1828 to 1833, Lower Town Creek planters settled near the Arkansas River, which became known as the Arkansas District. The chiefs chose Coweta as their main town. Removal carried the Upper Town Creek three years later to a stretch of land along the Canadian River, north of the Lower Town settlement. Conflict surfaced immediately. The federal government recognized Coweta as the capital of the new Creek Nation. Upper Creeks raged against this, demanding the capital be situated in the Upper Town Creek village of Tuckabatchee. The division of the Creeks in two separate districts led to the formation of two separate Creek chief councils, a structure that continued until 1840, when the federal government finally convinced the Creeks to create a single, unified national council. In 1844, the national council issued a written set of Creek laws. Light horse police handled local disputes, and courts in the two districts answered to a national council. The laws protected the rights of Creeks to practice traditional rituals and ceremonies and, in fact, fined individuals who did not attend. Land was jointly owned, although it was divided into a town commons and individual plots. These measures, however, did not fully unify the Creeks, and tension between the two groups continued for years.

TIMELINE 7.5 SOUTHERN INDIANS RECONSTRUCT THEIR SOVEREIGNTY

Date	Event
1832	"Old Settler" Cherokees arrive in Indian Territory
1833	Treaty of Fort Gibson signed with the Seminoles
1834	Failed attempts at Choctaw constitution
1837	Agreement at Doaksville creates fourth district for Chickasaws
1839	Cherokee convention at Takatoka
	John Ross attempts to end to hostilities
1840s	Public school system among the Cherokees starts
1842	More Seminoles living among the Cherokees than Creeks
1844	Creek laws put into place
1846	Cherokee unification
1855	Chickasaws recognized as independent nation

Federal oversight, and sometimes direct intervention, also proved necessary for the 1,069 Seminoles who were removed to Indian Territory in 1837. The Treaty of Fort Gibson, signed on March 28, 1833, required the Seminoles to settle on lands held by the Creek residing on lands just west of Ft. Gibson and there become part of the Creek Nation. It seemed a reasonable move to federal agents, believing the Seminoles would be readily absorbed into the Creek population as both nations were Muskogee speakers and, therefore, culturally compatible. The treaty was not endorsed by all Seminoles, and Chief Micanopy, who led them to Indian Territory, was one such individual.

Trouble stirred once the Seminoles arrived in Indian Territory. In a sign of defiance to the treaty, Micanopy camped the Seminoles two miles south of Fort Gibson, near the Arkansas River. The United States also underestimated the longstanding animosity between the Creeks and Seminoles, a tense relationship that made problematic the melding of these two peoples. It had been the Upper Creeks who joined with federal forces to crush Seminole resistance in Florida. Moreover, once in the West, the Seminoles found their assigned land near North Deep Fork River to be infertile. Productive lands already belonged to the Upper Creek elite. From the very moment of their arrival in Indian Territory, the Seminoles faced a series of challenges, all resulting from forced removal.

Resisting any settlement among former Creek enemies, other Seminole bands lived either near the Deep Fork River or among the Cherokees. A common argument offered by some Seminoles was that the Creeks would "look upon us as runaways, and would treat us as they would so many dogs." In 1842, 1,097 Seminoles lived in Cherokee territory along nine miles of the Grand River. In total, the number of Seminoles in Cherokee territory increased to 1,646, more than half of the total number of Seminoles in Indian Territory.

Problems continued for the Seminoles. The council was still in place, but the separation of the people in Indian Territory prevented total unity. Also, many *miccos* had died during the war or removal process, and kin and community networks had been torn apart. Living still within matrilineal clans, they continued their old spiritual ways in the Green Corn Ceremony and fended off the work of missionaries. In January 1845, a treaty was arranged among the Creeks, the Seminoles, and the United States. The treaty placed the Seminoles under direct control of the Creek national council, but it provided the Seminoles with prime lands along Little River. Known as the "Second Seminole Removal," the resettlement of 25 towns along Little River brought dispersed clans together, but town *miccos* retained their former town councils as separate entities. This effort at resolution solved little; conflict continued among the Creeks and Seminoles.

Indian Territory and the "Peculiar Institution" of Slavery

A small number of Indians from the South had owned African American slaves and plantations before removal, and they brought their slaves with them to Indian Territory, which rested below the 36°30′ parallel, the legal dividing line between slave states and free states established in the **Missouri Compromise** of 1820. Indian slaveholders were committed to the institution of slavery, in part, for the financial benefits it provided them. Many Indian slaveholders also adopted the same racial views as white Americans, an unsurprising perspective given their acculturation to white norms. But the Christian defense of slavery so thoroughly argued by white Southerners added a "supposed" moral justification to both economic and racist perspectives toward the "peculiar institution." And, from a practical position, to advocate the abolitionist cause would have emptied the seats in their schools and churches. Prior to their removal to Indian Territory, the Cherokee national council passed a series of laws concerning slave status and behavior. Slaves were forbidden from engaging in free trade without their master's consent and could not purchase or consume alcohol. The council outlawed interracial marriages between Negro slaves and Indians in 1824. The constitutions of 1827 and 1846 both denied all political rights and legal protections to African slaves within the Cherokee Nation. The "peculiar institution" followed Indians from the Deep South to Indian Territory in the 1830s, underpinning a Cherokee planter economy and class life typical of the white plantation South. Because slaves themselves were so expensive, the theft of slaves emerged as a lucrative business for some Cherokees while other Indians became wealthy as legal slave traders, traveling to places like Little Rock and New Orleans where they purchased slaves on the domestic market for sale in Indian Territory. In 1860, there were 3,500–4,000 slaves within the Cherokee Nation, owned by only 10 percent of the Cherokee families. Among the Choctaws, Creeks, and Chickasaws, the planter elite made up between 10 and 15 percent of each nation's populations. Such numbers almost exactly mirrored the proportion of slaveholders to total population in what became the Confederate States.

Conclusion

Indian removal cleared the way for a new wave of American westward migration, opening new lands in the Old Northwest and Deep South to Anglo settlers. Although Indian removal proved to be a windfall for white migration, the process shredded the unity of affected tribal groups. Those willing to relocate confronted others desperate to remain on traditional lands and willing to resist removal at all costs. It pitted relatively acculturated natives against those determined to retain traditional values and tribal structures. Those intra-tribal divisions continued in Indian Territory and, as evidenced best by the Cherokee, fueled tensions, disunity, and occasional violence over the next generation. Added to this, Indian Territory ultimately became home to the people of 25 Indian nations. Land was crowded and often contested. Native groups that historically challenged one another often found themselves sharing federally assigned tracts. Too often the land itself was not suited to agriculture and propelled Indians into poverty in an agrarian economy so unfamiliar to them. The policy of removal also raised tensions with tribal groups already in residency in the West. It was their lands on which eastern tribes were placed and their resources now being used by these strange newcomers. The Native Americans who lived in the West long before removal were terribly angered by the federal government's decision to squeeze more people into the lands that they had used for centuries. Pawnees, Comanches, Kiowas, and other groups raided Indian Territory, stealing slaves and horses from the wealthy southern tribesmen. The next chapter looks at the West more closely, and how the United States became the dominant non-native power in a chaotic world of ever-changing boundaries and peoples.

Review Questions

1. Explain why removal was such an important issue in the early American Republic.
2. How did Indian removal in the Deep South differ from removal in the Old Northwest?
3. What happened to Indians after removal?
4. Which native peoples resisted the removal process? How did they resist?

Recommended Readings

Bowes, John P. *Black Hawk and the War of 1832: Removal in the North* (New York: Chelsea House, 2007). An accessible work on the Black Hawk War.

———. *Exiles and Pioneers: Eastern Indians in the Trans-Mississippi West* (New York: Cambridge University Press, 2007). The best work yet on the removal of Indians from the Old Northwest.

Carson, James Taylor. *Searching for the Bright Path: The Mississippi Choctaws from Prehistory to Removal* (Lincoln, NE: University of Nebraska Press, 1999). This short volume provides the best ethno-historical analysis of the Choctaws and removal.

Green, Michael D. *The Politics of Indian Removal: Creek Government and Society in Crisis* (Lincoln, NE: University of Nebraska Press, 1982). Remains the standard work on Creek removal.

McLoughlin, William G. *After the Trail of Tears: The Cherokee Struggle for Sovereignty, 1839–1880* (Chapel Hill: University of North Carolina Press, 1993). An impressive work on the Cherokees' efforts to rebuild their nation in Indian Territory.

———. *Cherokee Renascence in the New Republic* (Princeton, NJ: Princeton University Press, 1986). An exhaustive study of the Cherokees in the removal era.

Miller, Susan A. *Coacoochee's Bones: A Seminole Saga* (Lawrence: University Press of Kansas, 2003). An impressive detective work that really offers the Seminole perspective.

Purdue, Theda, and Michael Green. *The Cherokee Removal: A Brief History with Documents*, 2nd ed. (Boston: Bedford/St. Martin's, 2005). A wonderful little volume that is highly accessible.

Native American History Online

General Sites

"Africans in America," Resource Bank Provided by PBS. www.pbs.org/wgbh/aia/part4/4p2959.html Offers a nice overview of the removal period. This PBS link discusses the impact of removal on the Indians, accompanied by images.

Clara Sue Kidwell, "The Effects of Removal on American Tribes." on Teacher Serve Home Page National Humanities Center. www.nationalhumanitiescenter.org/tserve/nattrans/ntecoindian/essays/indianremovalf.htm A wonderful historical overview of Indian removal that uses images and primary sources.

1827 Constitution of the Cherokee Nation. www.cornsilks.com/1827Constitution.html The site includes the constitution of the Cherokees.

"The Cherokee Phoenix From Hunter Library," Western Carolina University. www.wcu.edu/library/CherokeePhoenix/ Early issues of the *Cherokee Phoenix* reveal the changing nature of Cherokee society and culture.

Historical Sites

The Trail of Tears National Historic Trail. https://www.nps.gov/trte/index.htm This site covers the Cherokee movement from the Carolinas and Georgia into Oklahoma, providing a National Park Service support for instruction and visitation to the Cherokee route westward.

Citizen Potawatomi Nation. www.potawatomi.org Extensive resources detailing the Potawatomi removal. Among the resources are participant and observer diary entries, news reports, and government summaries documenting the removal process. This site also provides contemporary updates and news items related to the Potawatomi and to the Trail of Death.

Chapter 8

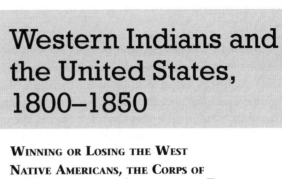

Western Indians and the United States, 1800–1850

WINNING OR LOSING THE WEST

NATIVE AMERICANS, THE CORPS OF DISCOVERY, AND CONSTRUCTING EMPIRE

The Plains and Missouri River Indians

Pacific Northwest Indians

THE PACIFIC AS THE WEST

The Russian Presence in America

Tlingit Culture, Resistance, and Competition

Rocky Mountain Fur Trading and the Pacific Northwest

WINNING OR LOSING THE WEST?

The Transformation of California

California Indians and American Manifest Destiny

California's "Sexual Frontier"

Texas Indians in Upheaval

The Southwest Borderlands in Transition

Painted wooden Alaskan totem pole in Saxman Native Village, Ketchikan, Alaska

Source: Pixachi/Shutterstock

Winning or Losing the West

Along the upper Missouri River in 1837, a smallpox (*Variola*) epidemic nearly wiped out the Mandan, Hidatsas, and Arikaras. For Mandans, as for other sedentary Indians, the traditional practices to help ailing family and friends proved more harmful than helpful. Sweat lodges, in which people huddled together for a long time, spread rather than cured people of *Variola*. Villagers without the pox and perhaps looking to escape to new lands in reality had no place to go. The equestrian Sioux, in a position of power as horseback conquerors of the upper Missouri, commanded most of the surrounding region and restricted the three sedentary groups to their traditional grounds, a frustrating strategy of territorial domination almost certainly impossible to overcome.

Consumed by horror because the pox ravaged his people, a Mandan chief of much respect, Four Bears, unleashed an inner rage. But it was not directed at the Sioux. Instead, Four Bears targeted American expansionists. As he lay dying from the disease on July 30, 1837, he condemned America's western ambitions for the outbreak of the pox. Four Bears was right to target American traders and settlers as notorious carriers of a disease that itself had no predictable pattern. The only predictability with *Variola* was that it always shook upper-Missouri societies to their very core. Four Bears shouted, "I was always ready to die for them [white people], which they cannot deny. I have done everything a red Skin could do for them, and how have they repaid it! I have Never Called a White Man a Dog, but today, I do Pronounce them to a set of Black Dogs." He

KEY QUESTIONS

1. Compare and contrast the different Indian peoples Lewis and Clark encountered during their expedition.
2. Analyze the role of Indians in the sea otter trade.
3. How did fur trading and the arrival of missionaries change life in the Pacific Northwest?
4. How did life change for California's Indians over the course of the eighteenth and early nineteenth centuries?
5. How did life change for Native Americans in Texas and the Southwest?

CHRONOLOGY

1780s–1840s	Expansion of the Pacific Coast fur trade
1803–1806	Lewis and Clark expedition
1810	Pacific Fur Company dominates the Rocky Mountain fur trade
1821	Mexico converts Alta California into a liberal state
1824	Chumash uprising
	Colonization Act
1828–1829	Estanislao rebels against Franciscan missions
1830	Mexico outlaws slavery
1834	Secularization Act in California secularizes all the Franciscan missions
1835–1836	Texas revolts against Mexico
1836	Arrival of the ABCFM on the Columbia Plateau
1837	Chimayó Rebellion against the Mexican state
1840s	Expansion westward on the Oregon Trail
1845	Texas joins the United States as a slave state
1847	Cayuses kill Marcus and Narcissa Whitman of the ABCFM
1850	Gold Rush expansion into three regions of California

had watched his own family members die before him, and now Four Bears lamented how his own pockmarked body would heighten the wolves' state of fear, as these savvy animals that ran from white people would look at his horrible disfigurement as a sign that the whites had come to stay forever.

Four Bears succumbed to the pox hours later. The native peoples of the West did, in fact, persevere. Despite their losses, the strength of the forces opposing them, and the confusion that accompanied dramatic social and cultural change, western Indians retained hope and sought ways to pull their people together. White Americans believed they had conquered the West by 1850, but in the hearts and minds of native peoples, the West was still theirs. Moreover, the United States was only one player in a larger bid to control the western half of North America. Even before the Lewis and Clark expedition laid the foundation for American expansionism, empires had reshaped the western landscape. In time, the United States would overcome its European and Euro-American competitors, claiming lands from the Pacific territories to the heart of Texas and the Southwest borderlands. American expansion in the West was indeed a long, hard-fought struggle, and native peoples were at the center of it, maintaining their own long, hard-fought struggle for survival.

Native Americans, the Corps of Discovery, and Constructing Empire

The Louisiana Purchase, which was France's 1803 sale of 800,000 square miles of land to the United States, doubled the size of the American republic for less than three cents per acre. An admitted lover of botany and geology and driven by a desire for an American westward empire, President Thomas Jefferson recruited Meriwether Lewis and William Clark to lead a Corps of Discovery to map and explore America's new territory as far as the Pacific Ocean. Lewis and Clark's expedition was not the first attempt to trace a Northwestern land route to the Pacific. Alexander Mackenzie, a Scotsman employed by the fur-trading British North West Company, in 1789 journeyed westward across Canada to initiate fur trading operations with natives and search for the fabled Northwest Passage. He, instead, reached the Arctic Ocean. Not one to dwell on failure, Mackenzie in 1793 succeeded in completing the first overland crossing of the North American continent through Canada, but, again, he discovered no direct waterway to the Pacific Ocean. Russian merchants were also active, plying the western coast for sea otters since the 1740s. Americans and Europeans alike imagined a western territory beyond the Mississippi River that promised boundless opportunities. The Lewis and Clark expedition (1804–1806) was organized and conducted with the same vision. Although the all-water route to the Pacific eluded them as it did other explorers, what the Corps of Discovery did accomplish amounted to a watershed in American history. Lewis and Clark filled their journals with maps, detailed information about the West's rich potential in resources, and indispensable ethnographic information about the Native Americans they encountered. This information would prove critical to America's effort to create a new empire in the West.

President Jefferson instructed Lewis and Clark to negotiate trade alliances with native groups they encountered. If the United States intended to take over the trans-Mississippi West, it would need well-established arteries of trade with all native peoples and a foundation of friendship with native peoples. Lewis and Clark were to gather together the chiefs at the villages they encountered, appoint one or two "head chiefs" for negotiations, enter into discussions about changing geopolitical and trade alliances, and then dispense gifts to all chiefs. They carried with them a variety of tools, adornments, and other goods for gifting along with Jefferson's "friendship medals" for the chiefs of highest standing. Alliances of trade with the western Indians, Jefferson believed, would lay the foundations for his "Empire for Liberty" in the opening of new lands to American settlers.

In the winter of 1803–1804, Lewis and Clark's team settled into St. Louis, formerly a French fur trading center and later known as America's "gateway to the West." There they gathered information and developed strategies for the Corps of Discovery's expedition. American traders who had previously ventured into the Missouri

8.1 One of the Jefferson Peace and Friendship medals distributed by Lewis and Clark during their expedition.

Source: Everett Historical/Shutterstock

River region provided ample information about tribal and village locations. The Corps of Discovery learned about the power of the Sioux, the Mandans, and the vast international trade alliances that already touched the Upper Missouri. In April 1804, their preparations complete, the expedition set out into the plains that flanked the Missouri River.

The Plains and Missouri River Indians

The territory they entered was occupied by diverse peoples, but the Sioux were recent arrivals to the region and probably wielded the greatest power in the northern plains. The Plains Sioux were divided into three groups—the Tetons, Yanktons, and Yanktonais. The Tetons (Lakota) were made up of several different bands—the Oglala, Brulé, Hunkapa, Miniconjou, and Two Kettle. By the middle of the eighteenth century, the Teton had migrated into the western plains and established a fur trade with the French at the expense of a Cree-Assiniboine trade alliance with New France. But buffalo was at the center of Sioux life and the Sioux diet. Once the Tetons overhunted a territory, they moved on, acquiring more horses and goods as they sought buffalo herds. By 1770, with an advantage in horses and guns, the Sioux commanded the lower Missouri River but had yet to conquer the large sedentary tribes of the upper Missouri—the Mandan, Arikara, and Hidatsa (see Map 8.1).

No other nomadic group by 1800 effectively challenged Teton Sioux dominance in the territory. Kiowas who earlier dictated trade in the Black Hills of South Dakota relocated to the southern plains and allied themselves with the Wichitas and Comanches. Together, they emerged as the central power in that region. The Sioux forced the Crows west into Montana. The Teton Sioux also challenged the Cheyennes and Arapahos, forcing them to either ally themselves with the Sioux or relocate to other lands. Some Cheyenne married Tetons, forming a Cheyenne-Teton alliance. Led by the Sioux, the Cheyenne and Arapahos helped displace the sedentary Pawnees, who moved permanently to the Platte River, an artery of the Missouri River. In the upper plains near the Black Hills, the Cheyennes linked up with remaining Arapahos and Kiowas and helped funnel goods to the Missouri River via the Kiowa networks with the Comanches and Wichitas. Cheyennes, who owned more horses, also turned into a fearless equestrian culture. Finally, by the early nineteenth century, a combined Cheyenne-Arapaho demand for buffalo-hunting grounds, firearms, and ammunition resulted in migration to the middle and southern plains.

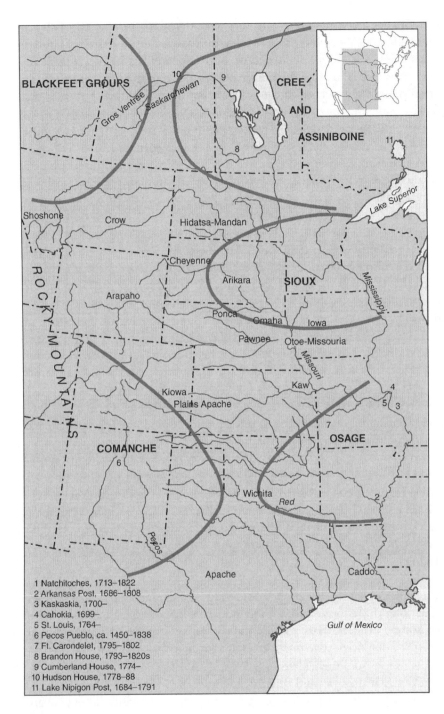

Map 8.1 Tribal locations and trading establishments, Southern Plains, 1780, and Central-Northern Plains, 1785–1798

Labels on map:

BLACKFEET GROUPS

Gros Ventree
Saskatchewan

CREE AND ASSINIBOINE

Shoshone
Crow
Hidatsa-Mandan
Cheyenne
Arikara
SIOUX
Mississippi
Lake Superior

Arapaho
Ponca
Omaha
Iowa
Pawnee
Otoe-Missouria
Missouri

R O C K Y M O U N T A I N S

Kiowa
Plains Apache
Kaw
OSAGE

COMANCHE

Wichita
Red

Pecos

Apache
Caddo

Gulf of Mexico

1 Natchitoches, 1713–1822
2 Arkansas Post, 1686–1808
3 Kaskaskia, 1700–
4 Cahokia, 1699–
5 St. Louis, 1764–
6 Pecos Pueblo, ca. 1450–1838
7 Ft. Carondelet, 1795–1802
8 Brandon House, 1793–1820s
9 Cumberland House, 1774–
10 Hudson House, 1778–88
11 Lake Nipigon Post, 1684–1791

Only approximately 3,500 strong, Cheyennes commanded the middle plains from Kansas into Colorado. The trans-Mississippi West was in transition.

Lewis and Clark realized the dramatic changes resulting from earlier European contact in the upper plains and the Sioux migrations when the Corps of Discovery reached the upper Missouri in 1804. Spanish and French traders to the south demanded buffalo hides and pemmican from the Sioux instead of furs. By pushing into new buffalo-hunting grounds around the lower and upper Missouri River, the Sioux had upset the balance of power. A massive continent-wide smallpox epidemic in 1779–1781 that hurt the sedentary Arikara, Mandan, and Hidatsa also aided Sioux expansion. Lewis and Clark, for example, noticed many abandoned Arikara villages as they traveled up the Missouri River. The Sioux took advantage of Arikara losses to force Arikaras closer to the Mandan and Hidatsa. The Sioux offered the greatest threat to American interests in the territory—they had the manpower, the necessary skills of war, and the sheer range in influence. While it was logical that Lewis and Clark initiate amicable relations with the Sioux, they believed trade might prove more beneficial with the sedentary peoples along the Missouri River as they would less able to dictate the terms of trade.

Greeting the Arikaras in 1804, the Corps of Discovery encountered a culture suffering hard times. Subsistence activities continued, but Lewis and Clark soon learned Arikara politics were in absolute disarray. Smallpox had destroyed entire villages and clans and taken the lives of many chiefs. For Lewis and Clark, whose mission depended on the chiefs, the political confusion was a logistical nightmare. They initially spent their time among the Arikara learning first how to negotiate with chiefs and then talking about shifting the Arikaras' trade alliances.

The Arapahos, Kiowas, Cheyennes, and Sioux were among some of the equestrian cultures who benefited from trading with the Arikaras for food. Although Lewis and Clark believed that the Sioux politically dominated the Arikaras, the Arikaras felt they held the advantage. They used their highly valuable corn to trade for guns and horses. The Cheyenne brought meat, fine clothing that Cheyenne women wove, and plenty of horses to trade at the Arikara market. Arikaras traded guns and shot with the Cheyenne to replenish their stock of horses for sale to the Sioux. The festival days of trading at the Arikara villages brought together many plains' people for trade. Although Lewis and Clark tried to convince the Arikara headmen to sever their trade with the Sioux, it was an impossible task. The Sioux-Arikara network was essential to the entire Midwest plains' economy.

After they left the Arikaras, the Corps of Discovery spent the winter of 1804–1805 among Mandans and Hidatsas. The center of Mandan and Hidatsa life was the village. Made up of clans and families, each village looked out for the social, economic, and political welfare of the community. Part of Mandan spiritual ceremonialism was a cedar post around which stood an open plaza. The cedar post represented the Mandans' ruling mythical hero, Lone Man. At the end of each village plaza were the *Okipa* lodges occupied during Mandan sacred *Okipa* festivals. Outside of these medicine lodges were poles with effigies dedicated to various spirits. Each household, which was an enclosed earthen lodge, had a rank among Mandans. The families of the spiritual leaders lived closest to the plaza, owning powerful medicine bundles to ward off bad spirits and protect the village. The least important families lived in the lodges most distant from the central plaza. Both Mandans and Hidatsas were horticulturists, producing large supplies of corn, beans, and squash, but they were also cultures in transition now hunting buffalo.

For the plains' equestrian cultures on the upper reaches of the Missouri River, Mandan and Hidatsa villages served as more valuable trading posts than those located southward among Arikaras. Cheyennes, Arapahos, Sioux, and Crows all traded at the Mandan-Hidatsa fairs. Horses and mules were the most tradable items brought from the West and Southwest. To obtain prestige items, the Mandans and Hidatsas bartered the animals with the nomadic cultures. To the north, from the Red River valley and southern Saskatchewan, the Cree and Assiniboine funneled British and French firearms and other goods into the Mandan-Hidatsa festivals. Lewis and Clark dispensed prestige gifts to Mandan and Hidatsa chiefs in an effort to convince them to abandon their trade with the Cree and Assiniboine. As one observer noted about the Mandan, "[they] are much more craftier than the Assiniboin in their commerce and everything." Mandans were such good traders, "they clean the Assiniboin out of everything they have." The Corps of Discovery also encouraged both groups to bring themselves into the sphere of American trade in agreeing not to negotiate with the powerful Sioux. An arrangement between the Mandans and Corps leaders allowed Lewis and Clark to erect a trading post which was appropriately named Fort Mandan. The structure was designed as a permanent political and economic

8.2 Hidatsa village on the Knife River, a painting by George Catlin, 1832.

Source: Art Resource

presence to fend off the British North West Company and French traders, as well as the Cree, the Assiniboine, and the Sioux. Moving on along the upper Missouri in 1805, Lewis and Clark had established a physical American presence in the region, but in leaving Fort Mandan unmanned and understocked Lewis and Clark could never expect to secure permanent political and trading alliances between the United States and the Mandans, Hidatsas, or Arikaras.

Pacific Northwest Indians

Before arriving at the Columbia River, the Corps encountered the Lemhi Shoshone and Nez Perce (pronounced *Nez Purse*) in the Great Basin region, particularly around Montana. Luckily for Lewis and Clark, Sacagawea and her husband now traveled with the Corps. Sacagawea was a Shoshone captive among the Hidatsa who joined with Lewis and Clark. In the Rocky Mountains and plateau region, in present-day Idaho, Sacagawea served as guide and interpreter, especially when she reunited with her brother, Cameahwait, a chief among the Lemhi Shoshone.

The northern Lemhi Shoshones had taken to horses and bison hunting. This shift in subsistence activities led to a desire for American trade items as an alternative to acquiring such goods through the difficult networks from the Spanish borderlands into the Rocky Mountains. As bison hunters, the Shoshone also wanted guns and ammunition to help stave off their enemies, primarily the Blackfeet and Sioux. The Shoshone combined a buffalo diet with more traditional salmon fishing. Lewis and Clark learned much about the Interior Plateau from the Shoshone and secured from the Indians the horses they would need to continue their travels along the Lemhi Pass through the Bitterroot Valley in southwestern Montana. Like the Shoshone, the Nez Perce they encountered also relied on horses and hunted buffalo in addition to fishing for salmon. Located close to the trade networks of the Pacific,

READING HISTORY

James P. Ronda, The Truth About Sacagawea

Sacagawea, a Shoshone woman recognized for her pivotal role in translating for the Lewis and Clark expedition, remains shrouded in mystery. Many Indian women, no matter how important they were to Indian-white relations were, like Sacagawea, receiving little attention in the written record because whites kept most written accounts, and most white men, coming from a male-dominant culture, did not elevate women into important positions. In the following excerpt, renowned historian James P. Ronda tries to make sense of Sacagawea with what accounts are available.

What is reliably known about Sacagawea makes for only a brief biographical sketch. Sometime in the fall of 1800, the young Lemhi Shoshoni girl, then perhaps 12 or 13 years old, was camped at the Three Forks of the Missouri with others from her band. As so often happened to northern Shoshonis who ventured out on the plains to hunt buffalo, the party at Three Forks was attacked by Hidatsa raiders. In the fighting that followed, several Shoshonis were killed. Among the prisoners taken were four boys and several women, including Sacagawea. Sometime between 1800 and 1804, she and one other Shoshoni captive were purchased by Toussaint Charbonneau, a trader with ties to the North West Company. When Lewis and Clark met Charbonneau at Fort Mandan on November 4, 1804, the trader and his family were living at the Awatixa Hidatsa village of Metaharta. Sacagawea was already pregnant and on February 11, 1805, she gave birth to a son named Jean Baptiste. When Toussaint Charbonneau was finally hired by Lewis and Clark as an interpreter, Sacagawea and her child became part of the Corps of Discovery.

Three questions about Sacagawea have long fascinated Lewis and Clark scholars. The name of the Indian woman—its meaning and proper spelling—continues to spark considerable debate. Sacajawea, Sacagawea, and Sakakawea have all had their partisans. The concern about spelling is not just a quibble over orthography. If the woman's name was Sacajawea, the word might be Shoshoni, meaning "boat launcher." However, if the spelling is more properly Sacagawea, the name would be Hidatsa and translate as "Bird Woman." The journal evidence from Lewis and Clark appears to support a Hidatsa derivation. On May 20, 1805, Lewis wrote: "Sah ca gah we ah or bird woman's River" to name what is now Crooked Creek in north-central Montana.

Far more important than the spelling and meaning of Sacagawea's name is the nature and scope of her contributions to the expedition. Perhaps the most persistent Lewis and Clark myth is that Sacagawea "guided" the party to the Pacific. In countless statues, poems, paintings, and books, she is depicted as a westward-pointing pathfinder providing invaluable direction for bewildered explorers. In the interest of correction, there has been a tendency to underestimate Sacagawea's genuine achievements as a member of the Corps of Discovery. Not as important as George Drouillard or John Ordway, the young woman did make significant contributions to the expedition's success.

...When the expedition left Fort Mandan in April 1805, its most immediate need was to find the Shoshoni Indians and obtain horses for what was assumed would be an easy mountain portage to Pacific waters. Lewis and Clark certainly believed that Sacagawea would be of considerable value in the Shoshoni mission. They expected that she might recognize landmarks along the route and would provide general information about the location of Shoshoni camps. When Sacagawea became ill at the Great Falls of the Missouri, Lewis admitted, "This gave me some concern as well as for the poor object herself, than with the young child in her arms, as from the consideration of her being our only dependences for friendly negotiation with the Snake Indians." But just what the captains expected from her in those talks is not plain. For reasons that are now unclear, Sacagawea was not included in Lewis's advance party that finally made contact with the Shoshonis in August 1805. Good relations between the explorers and Cameahwait depended far more on promises of guns and trade than on any intercessions made by Sacagawea.

Sacagawea was not an expedition guide in the usual sense of the word. When Lewis and Clark needed to make a critical decision in early June 1805 about the true channel of the Missouri, she took no part in the process. Much later, when the expedition needed guides, men like Old Toby, Tetoharsky, and Twisted Hair were hired for that duty. Only twice did Sacagawea provide what might be termed guide services. In late July and early August 1805, she recognized important geographical features on the way to find Shoshoni camps. On the return journey in 1806, Sacagawea accompanied Clark's party and provided the explorer with valuable information on what has since been named Bozeman Pass. For most of the transcontinental journey, Sacagawea was seeing country as new to her as it was to the captains. That she was not in the lead making trail decisions does not diminish the fact that when she did recognize a landmark, "this piece of information cheered the spirits of the party."

Success in many of the expedition's Indian missions depended on reliable communication and translation. Both diplomacy and the collection of ethnographic information demanded the sort of communication that George Drouillard's signs could not always provide. One of Sacagawea's most important roles in the expedition was that of translator, or as Clark quaintly put it, "interpretress with the Snake Indians." She often worked as part of a long and cumbersome translation chain that took each native word through many speakers before reaching the captains. Sacagawea was able to continue those duties west of the Continental Divide because of the presence of Shoshoni prisoners among groups that did not speak Shoshoni. Talks with the Flatheads at Ross's Hole were conducted through such a prisoner, as were those on the return journey with the Walulas and Nez Perces.

The expedition also benefited from the physical presence of Sacagawea and her child. Indians who might have thought the explorers part of a war party were evidently reassured when they saw a woman and an infant in the group. Clark said as much when he wrote, "The Wife of Shabono our interpreter We find reconciles all the Indians, as to our friendly intentions. A woman with a party of men is a token of peace."

Source: James P. Ronda, *Lewis and Clark among the Indians* (Lincoln, NB: University of Nebraska Press, 1984), pp. 256–258.

Questions

1. According to Ronda, who was the historical Sacagawea?
2. How does Ronda separate myth from history?
3. What was Sacagawea's influence on the Lewis and Clark expedition, according to Ronda?

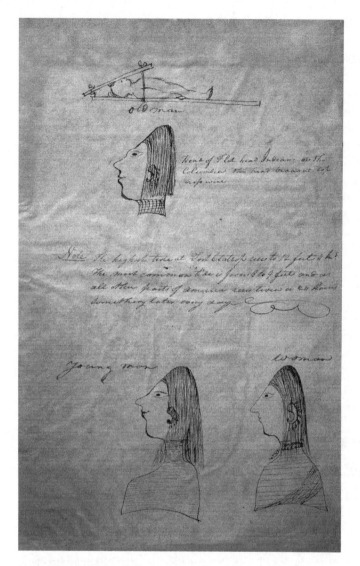

8.3 This page from Lewis and Clark's journals documents the head-flattening technique used by the Clatsop tribe.

Source: Missouri History Museum, St. Louis

the Nez Perce had goods coming in from the Columbia River. Once again, Lewis and Clark failed to make any political alliances, as the Nez Perce's primary interest was in the acquisition of guns and ammunition to fight the Blackfeet.

The Corps of Discovery in autumn 1805 made its way down the Columbia River with two Nez Perce, eventually targeting The Dalles. If there was a center of trade and a cultural crossroads that connected Pacific Northwest Indians with tribesmen of the plateau, it was The Dalles, marked by steep rocks that narrowed the water's channels. Nez Perce, Shoshone, Walulas, Umatillas, and other groups traded with river peoples to bring goods to The Dalles's cliffs, where salmon fishing was productive. From the Pacific coast, Chinook and Clatsop traders brought their own prestige items, many garnered from coastal trading with American, British, and Russian fur traders. The upper Chinooks, somewhat like the Sioux on the upper Missouri, held some power over the trade at The Dalles. Not known as aggressive peoples, Chinooks nonetheless did their best to maintain a position as the political and economic leaders of The Dalles trade networks. When at The Dalles, Chinooks looked through the bags of Lewis and Clark, examining their items very closely. The behavior was strange to the two men. To the Chinooks, this was proper protocol. Years of trading along the coast with Europeans had taught the Chinooks how to pick the best items and discard what they considered worthless.

The Corps of Discovery made it to the Pacific and there encamped for the winter of 1805–1806. A feature among the Chinooks and Clatsops Lewis and Clark noticed most was the flattening of heads among some of the tribesmen. A flat head signified elite status. Tribesmen practiced the art of head flattening, beginning in infancy. Chinook and Clatsop men, with their flattened heads, were traders more than they were aggressive warriors. Chinooks and Clatsops also followed Pacific Northwest cultural patterns of fine woodcarving and an economy based on status. Chinook peoples lived in an area along the Columbia River that extended to The Dalles. At the Columbia River drainage, Chinooks occupied the lands to the north while Clatsops occupied the lands to the south. In the summer, the two groups used highly decorated canoes to travel the Columbia to trade and visit kin and community. In the warm seasons, the sea offered plentiful food, so both Chinook and Clatsop men exploited beached whales, otters, seals, and shellfish. They were also proficient salmon and

TIMELINE 8.1 LEWIS AND CLARK'S JOURNEY

Date	Event
1803	Louisiana Purchase
1803–1804	Corps of Discovery in St. Louis
1804	Lewis and Clark travel the Upper Missouri among the Arikaras, Mandans, and Hidatsas
1804–1805	Winter at Fort Mandan
1805	Travel through the Columbia Plateau to the Columbia River
1806	Winter at Fort Clatsop on the Pacific coast

sturgeon hunters who made excellent use of the runs of these fish in the Columbia River. Both Chinook and Clatsop men also hunted interior animals such as deer and elk. Women gathered plant foods. Among both cultures, a deep respect for the environment meant that spiritual bundles and sacred practices were always involved in the procurement of food. On a big salmon catch, for example, a spiritual specialist sacrificed the first fish to honor the animals of myth that once talked and ruled the world. Both societies were hierarchical in the Pacific tradition, with clans appointing the wealthiest chiefs to lead. At the bottom of these societies were the slaves, whose status was hereditary. Chinooks and Clatsops did not carve totems, but they did specialize in carving crests that symbolized mythological creatures or clan affiliations. The arrival of trade goods from the coast made the acquisition of wealth all the more important in their society and facilitated social mobility within the ranks of Chinook and Clatsop communities.

Lewis and Clark built Fort Clatsop during that winter of 1805–1806 and looked to provision themselves for the trek home. For the Indians, the fort was a source of trade rather than a place to greet and form alliances with the Americans. The Chinooks and Clatsops viewed the Americans as petty traders carrying items of little value and consequently avoided most discussions of any long-term alliance with the United States.

Lewis and Clark journeyed home in 1806 without the trade alliances they had hoped to secure. As one historian has noted, the Corps of Discovery "failed to persuade the Indians to become children of a distant father" in Thomas Jefferson. Nonetheless, the Corps returned east with a wealth of knowledge that awed the president and stunned others. Lewis and Clark detailed in their journals the topography of the West they traveled, mapped routes through the mountains to the Pacific, noted weather patterns, determined the viability of agricultural development across the region, calculated prospects in the fur trade, and recorded tribal structures and cultural norms among the native peoples they encountered. Their failed attempt to broker trade alliances, ultimately, paled in contrast to the incentive their journals gave for further exploration and eventual settlement and exploitation of the territory. Indeed, their discoveries placed Native Americans and white America on a collision course.

The Pacific as the West

The Pacific coast was the center of a thriving trade between savvy Native American hunters and Russian merchants long before the arrival of Lewis and Clark. More often than not, Russian merchants used coercion to create a large labor force of Aleutian and other Pacific native peoples to take support trade in otter skins. The hunt for the profitable and luxurious otter skins linked the Pacific native peoples to markets as far away as China. British and American merchants sent their own ships to the Pacific coast as they too looked to make money from the labor of native otter hunters. As European and American goods flowed into Pacific Coast Indian communities, Native Americans, over time, developed more shrewd means to exact the best items to compensate for their labor and the skins they procured. Not all tribespeople welcomed the ships that plied the Pacific coast. The Tlingit, a cultural and linguistic group of discreet, stratified, and highly warlike village units, resisted the Russian presence, although they welcomed the Americans and British who looked not to establish labor regimes but to trade. In the interior, competition between American and British fur traders exploded as the Rocky Mountain fur trade yielded tremendous profits. American and British fur trappers linked Native American hunters to coastal and Canadian forts out of which tremendous numbers of furs flowed to American markets in the trans-Missouri west and the Atlantic seaboard, and to British markets overseas.

As the American presence in the Pacific eclipsed that of imperial rivals, Native Americans faced a new set of challenges as settlers in their wagons spread out across the Great Basin and Columbia Plateau, and into the new states of Oregon and Washington. American expansion came with new social and cultural values and attitudes as well as a heavy price. Zealous missionaries, disease, tribal dispossession, and intertribal warfare and coercion into the American market economy continued to reshape the Native Americans' Pacific world.

The Russian Presence in America

Trade between the Clatsop and Chinook Indians and the Russians were longstanding. In 1741, the Vitus Bering-Aleksei Chirikov outing left Russia's Kamchatka Peninsula located on the far northeastern side of Euro-Asia. Although Russians considered this a failed expedition, as the aggressive Tlingit along the Alaskan coast fended off a Russian settlement, the ships had returned home with hundreds of the highest quality sea otter skins. Russian merchants made 72 voyages to the Commander, Kurile, Aleutian, and Prilof Island chains between 1740 and 1780. By the 1790s, Russians had established outposts along the Alaskan seaboard. One company, the United American Company, which Gregory and Ivan Golikov led, made a fortune on the 100,000 sea otter furs it acquired. The company was so profitable it passed some of the wealth on to the Russian tsar, who had shares in the company. The Russian race to dominate the wealth of the otter fur trade was underway.

"The animals were the people of this country," according to a Puget Sound Indian story. A different Indian of the area remembered when otters and other animals of the earth and sea were "just the same way like man. He talk . . . fur and skin he put on and take off just like a coat." In both stories, otters spoke before the arrival of men: "this was a long time ago." Indians such as the Aleut, Nootka, Haida, Makah, Tlingit, coastal Salish, and Chinook had hunted large seals and otters, but native peoples had respected the animals that once talked, only taking furs from them to wear in cold times or for trade of immense significance with other tribesmen. Native relationships with otters changed, however, when European traders entered the Pacific seeking to acquire otter pelts, which fetched high prices in Europe, China, and the United States and returned to Indians manufactured goods that surpassed in quality and durability those made in a traditional manner.

In the vast territory stretching from the Aleutian Islands to Alaska and south to California, the Russians took the lead in developing the international market for otter pelts. If the otters in fact spoke among the Indians, they would have cast the first Russian traders, the **promyshlenniki**, in a particularly horrific light. Brutal *promyshlenniki* forced the Aleuts into their kayaks (*baidarka*) to hunt otter and frequently employed intimidation, threats, and sometimes physical violence to compel Indians to hunt longer over extended territories and to return with ever-larger hauls. *Promyshlenniki* sometimes at gunpoint forced Aleuts into their kayaks. The Aleuts were non-aggressive tribesmen, living in small, dispersed settlements along the islands. *Promyshlenniki* did not have the skills to hunt in the deep, cold, rough waters of the North Pacific in kayaks. Instead, they used their guns and iron tools to all but enslave Aleut hunters. Over the years, Aleutian men hunted the sacred animals to the point of extinction. The arrival of organized Russian companies to further exploit the area's resources only made matters worse for the Aleuts.

The United American Company organized and systematized the exploitation of Aleut hunters. Under company directions, Russian agents coerced Aleut men to hunt by holding hostage their families. As the otter population in Aleutian Island waters fell, the United American Company pressed on to the Alaskan coastline, establishing a few settlements along the way. The Russians founded St. Paul in 1792, the largest settlement and headquarters for Russian hunting operations. Alexander Baranov, the Russian colonial governor, built other forts on islands and inlets along the Alaskan coastline. The forced labor regime had a devastating impact on Aleutian society. The population of Aleut men was cut in half, and Aleutian women were targets of sexual abuse at the hands of Russians.

The low-density otter population in northern waters forced the United American Company to seek new hunting grounds. Sitka, constructed on King George Archipelago off the coast of Alaska, became the new headquarters for Russian merchants' southern operations. By the 1800s, Aleutians, *métis* (children of Russian men and Aleut women), and Russian settlers were among the hundreds of people sailing out of Sitka. Baranov in 1799 then pushed south, sending Aleutian hunters with their kayaks and harpoons into waters along northern California.

California coastal settlements proved difficult for the Russians and Aleuts to sustain. After several reconnaissance trips along the Spanish coast of Alta California, Baranov commissioned Ivan Kuskov to construct a permanent Russian settlement north of present-day San Francisco. Ninety-five Russians and 85 Aleuts, all under Kuskov's direction, built Fort Ross in 1812 on Bodega Bay. From this fort, the Russians dispatched Aleuts

8.4 Fort Ross, 1840.

Source: Courtesy of Library of Congress Prints and Photographs Division, LC-USZ62-69940

to the ocean waters to hunt, while Russian soldiers stationed at the fort protected the hunting enterprise from potential attacks by foreign competitors or interior Indians.

It was soon realized that the California otter population was not as profitable as the Alaskan population. The Russians at Fort Ross, therefore, switched their focus to agriculture, with designs to ship grain and other products as far north as the Kamchatka Peninsula. Carl Schmidt, Kuskov's successor, brought in more men and encouraged local Indians to help with farming. Aleuts received free seed to help the fort prosper. By 1823, Fort Ross had attained a level of agricultural self-sufficiency and halted food imports from Alta California.

By 1825 the Russians secured help from Pomo Indians in extending agricultural production. Pomos initially served as farmers, helping the Russians properly till the California soil with horses and oxen after the first rains in November and December, and in return Pomos received food and clothing. But like the Aleuts, the Pomos soon faced their own exploitation when the Russians tried to overcome manpower shortages. Labor incentives morphed into conscription and enslavement. The harsh labor system that developed, along with devastating diseases brought inadvertently by Russians to California, radically reduced the Pomo population. They did attempt resistance to the Russians. Organizing large-scale warfare was virtually impossible given longstanding rivalries among some clans, the impact of disease on native communities, and the distance that separated Pomo villages, which made unified armed resistance difficult at best. Nonetheless, individual clans sometimes rebelled violently, although they were quickly subdued by Russian power supported by their native allies from farther north. Less threatening to Russian operations regionally were the occasional attacks on those supervising native workers, disruptions in labor productivity, and sometimes individual and family flight toward native communities not strapped by the Russian presence. Large-scale armed resistance by the Pomos was simply not a viable option in the context of Pomo circumstances and Russian control. Their release from Russian power, however, resulted from marketplace developments. In 1840, unable to compete with cheap grain from Mexico, and without an exportable otter population, the Russians shut down Fort Ross.

Tlingit Culture, Resistance, and Competition

Densely settled Indian societies and cultures lived along the Alaskan coast. The largest of these groups was the Tlingit, who lived from Prince of Wales Island in the south to the Yakutat Bay in the north. Before the arrival of the Russians, the Tlingit dominated the Alexander Archipelago. They were divided into the Tlingit of the Gulf of Alaska, the Northern Tlingit, and the Southern Tlingit. Within each geographical grouping were numerous smaller geopolitical units known as **kwáans**. Each kwáan was a community of matrilineal clans with ties to a particular territory (see Table 8.1). Tlingit groups were not part of a single, large nation; they were Tlingit by language and social and cultural affiliation. Even so, the Tlingit clearly saw themselves as different from their neighbors, who included the Haida, Tsimshian, Eyaks, Athapaskans, Kwakiutl, and Eskimo (see Figure 8.1).

Tlingit peoples hunted and fished, constructed fine woodcarvings, and lived surrounded by totems. Salmon fishing was the chief occupation for men, but herring, cod, and candlefish also figured in the Tlingit diet. Men hunted deer and bear and used small canoes at sea to take seals, otters, and porpoises. Women gathered nuts, berries, mollusks, crabs, and seaweed. Because technical proficiency in woodcarving was needed for both fishing and seafaring, carving cedar and other woods was central to Tlingit societies. Men made small boats and weapons, including arrowheads and tipped spears. Master carvers made the totem poles. Totem poles, whether adorned with the raven, wolf, wolf-eagle, or man-raven, connected time, space, and people together in a supernatural network of relationships. Poles, home adornments, and ceremonial masks were totems that could represent past events, the environment, people, and legends. The exterior frames of homes were adorned with deer, fox, and other animals that represented Tlingit clan affiliations with specific totems. Totems acted as

Table 8.1 Social-Territorial Structure of Tlingit Society

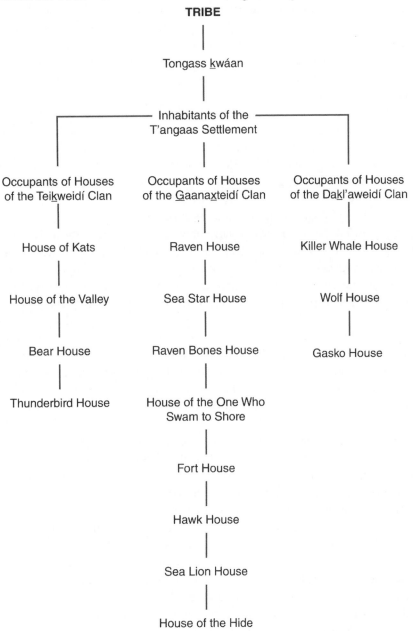

TRIBE

Tongass k̲wáan

Inhabitants of the
T'angaas Settlement

Occupants of Houses of the Teik̲weidí Clan	Occupants of Houses of the G̲aanax̲teidí Clan	Occupants of Houses of the Dak̲l'aweidí Clan
House of Kats	Raven House	Killer Whale House
House of the Valley	Sea Star House	Wolf House
Bear House	Raven Bones House	Gasko House
Thunderbird House	House of the One Who Swam to Shore	
	Fort House	
	Hawk House	
	Sea Lion House	
	House of the Hide	

social and cultural organizers. Fundamentally, totems arranged Tlingit society and politics and gave order to the cosmic relationship between Tlingits and an array of animals.

Tlingit economic and cultural diversity, an abundant resource base in stored foods, and almost constant intertribal warfare gave rise to societies based on inequality. Tlingits had what anthropologists call a "prestige economy." War was central to Tlingit society, as warriors sought to expand the territorial boundaries of particular kwáans to gain access to prime ocean grounds, wooded areas, and beachheads. Warfare was also the quickest way for a man to achieve honor and prestige. With so much emphasis on war, Tlingit parents, like the Spartans of ancient Greece, killed deformed male babies because such children would never rise within Tlingit society. The exaltation of the warrior culture entered the cosmic realm as well, where the spirit of a warrior killed in battle was considered a spirit of the highest distinction. During war, to gain more status and prestige, Tlingit groups enslaved the defeated, taking slaves home to work for their clans. Because slavery was hereditary, a substantial slave population was a constant aspect of Tlingit society. Of course, the wealthiest families with the best warriors had the most slaves.

There were other ways, besides war, that clans and families could acquire wealth. In a ranked economy, every Tlingit had tasks that when performed to their limits produced surplus goods for extended clans and for the kwáans. Hunters with excess fish stripped their catch and salted them for storage, women who gathered extra berries and shellfish stored more food for the winter months, and craftsmen who produced the finest wood totems, ships, masks, fine clothing, and copper adornments provided chiefs of kwáans with surplus prestige goods.

Accumulation of stored goods, whether for consumption or for conspicuous display, produced wealth and rank among Tlingit peoples. Kwáans used the festivals known as potlatches to show their wealth. Chiefs, who had allotted hunting grounds, taken tribute in food stores, and collected prestige items from craftsmen, used potlatches to redistribute overstocked items as a public display of their own status and prestige. Chiefs had potlatch names and ranks passed down over generations, and specific masks and clothing representative of mythic and cosmic figures. The display of totems and the distribution of prestige goods connected the chiefs to other Tlingits within a supernatural and human economy of inequality. Through the potlatch, kwáans came together, recognized the wealthy and powerful for a period of days, and then disbanded, knowing that other chiefs of wealthy kwáans would respond in kind with their own potlatches. The Tlingit, unlike the Aleut, fought to keep the Russian traders from their shores. The first significant Tlingit attack against the Russians occurred in 1793, when the Tlingits struck a Russian expedition led by Baranov. In 1799, he established the fort of Sitka on Sitka Island. It was never a secure site for the Russians, as Tlingit warriors routinely threatened the island fortification.

With a growing interest in an American trade in broadcloth, knives, and kettles, several kwáans descended on the Yakutat territory in 1801, spurred on in part when the Russians murdered a kwáan chief. I.A. Kuskov, leading the Russian defense, retreated to a small island and set up a fort with cannon. Tlingits in canoes circled the island and bombarded the Russians with arrows. Eventually, both parties agreed to a truce involving the exchange of captives. Kuskov went back to Yakutat and pressed southward toward Sitka, while the Tlingit took over a Russian defensive position, Fort Mikhailovskii. The Koloshes took Sitka in 1802. Fighting continued in the region until 1805, when Baranov and the Tlingit agreed to a treaty, but the Tlingit remained aggressive and continued to harass and threaten the Russians. Baranov relinquished his power under duress in 1818, leaving his successors to effect peace and trade with the Tlingit until 1834. Russian power in the region was in steep decline when Sitka and Fort Ozyorsk fell to the Koloshes in 1855.

The English and Americans also ventured into Tlingit territory, principally in the fur trade as pelt values soared in value. In 1834, Hudson's Bay Company traders, having withstood an outbreak of disease, established a formal trade partnership with coastal Tlingit communities. The Indians profited greatly from the British presence, as competition between American and British merchants for Tlingit furs drove up prices. Indians inspected all items, exacted high prices, and turned down flawed goods.

The shift of trade in the Tlingits' direction had a number of important consequences for Tlingit society. Kwáan accumulation of prestige items transformed potlatch festivities into more elaborate events. Competition among kwáans for access to trade, along with an influx of guns and metal weapons, led to intensified war between neighboring kwáans. Enslavement rose as well. The Hudson's Bay Company's trade through the 1840s, and the more consistent presence of American whaling ships by the 1840s and 1850s, added further to the Tlingits' prestige economy. As demands for prestige goods increased, preexisting territorial disputes grew more heated. Thus, the benefits of trade with the British and the Americans came at a considerable cost.

Rocky Mountain Fur Trading and the Pacific Northwest

The Rocky Mountain trade in beaver pelts was as competitive as the sea otter trade in the Pacific. Like sea otters, beavers were never hunted in massive numbers before the arrival of European traders. Once traders arrived in the Rocky Mountain and Plateau territories with goods desired by Indians, local tribesmen began to hunt the animals intensively, much like tribes in the American southeast did in the early 1700s, which severely depopulated the region of deer and other valued animals.

Manuel Lisa in the late eighteenth and early nineteenth centuries in part spurred the trade. Like Lewis and Clark, Lisa launched his trading expeditions from St. Louis, and, after his initial forays proved profitable, Lisa returned to St. Louis and established the Missouri Fur Company. The newly founded company erected a series of forts that extended from the Mandan country down to the Council Bluffs, in present-day Iowa. A string of trading posts exchanged goods for high-quality furs with the Omaha, Oto, Iowa, and Pawnee. Fur traders exchanged goods and furs with the Teton and Yankton Sioux at the Arikara and Hidatsa villages.

The lure of huge profits prompted American traders in the Pacific to turn their attention to the Rocky Mountains. John Jacob Astor's Pacific Fur Company successfully penetrated the Rocky Mountain region from the west in 1810, supplanting the Missouri Company, which never made any headway into the mountains. Astor was ambitious. He hoped to have a string of trading posts along the upper Missouri stretching to the mouth of the Columbia River, acquiring furs from the Rocky Mountains to the Pacific Ocean. Trade goods from the interior would follow the string of forts and reach the Rockies and the American trappers, who would then send the profitable furs by boat down the Columbia River. Astor's main trading post, and the center of the company's shipping operations, was Astoria on the coast of present-day Oregon. The Pacific Fur Company entered into direct competition with the British North West Company. With forts along the Clearwater and Willamette

TIMELINE 8.2 PACIFIC FUR TRADING AND INDIAN ENCOUNTERS, 1790S–1855

Date	Event
1790s	Russian United American Company exploits Aleut labor to expand otter trade
1799	Aleut hunters and Russian United American Company travel to California coast
1801	Tlingit attack Yakutat territory
1802	Tlingit take Fort Sitka
1805	Tlingit-Russian Treaty
1812	Russians construct Fort Ross in California and exploit local Pomo Indians
1834	Hudson's Bay Company eclipses Russian traders with local Alaskan tribes
1840	Fort Ross closes without Indian labor
1855	Sitka falls to the Koloshes

rivers, Astor's traders exchanged high-quality items for furs with the Coeur d'Alene, Pend d'Oreilles, and Flathead Indians. The Willamette Post used its access to the Nez Perce to acquire horses for the trappers. Central to Astor's operations was an overland route connecting Astoria and St. Louis. Despite his success, Astor, who feared losing it all, ended his operation and liquidated his fur trading business when conflict with the British seemed imminent just prior to the War of 1812.

Once Astor ceased operations, the Hudson's Bay Company seized control of Rocky Mountain fur trading. After the War of 1812, however, Americans entered the trade again, now with access to the Santa Fe trade, making routes to St. Louis easier and more affordable. Under the leadership of Jedediah Smith, American trappers successfully penetrated the Rocky Mountain region by 1825. Smith and others commenced lucrative operations with the Crow, Shoshone, and Salish hunters in the Great Basin. The profitable business and even intermarriage between fur traders and Indian women strengthened the American position to challenge the Hudson's Bay Company's hold on the enterprise. By the 1830s, as Smith and his partners parted ways, the Rocky Mountain Fur Company emerged as the main American trading outfit in the region, undermining British trade with the Flatheads (Salish), Bannocks, and Nez Perce. American trappers also penetrated the dangerous Crow and Blackfeet ranges along the Big Horn, Powder, and Tongue rivers. Long isolated from trappers, these rivers were a tremendous source of new beaver pelts. When John Jacob Astor reentered the trade with the American Trade Company, he once again came to monopolize fur trading in the region.

The burgeoning fur trade in and along the periphery of the Rockies brought to native groups the manufactured goods, iron products, guns and other items Indians increasingly desired—the more hides and pelts that Indians brought to the merchants, the more goods they netted for themselves and their communities. But this spawned a dark reality. The lucrative arrangement encouraged tribal groups to hunt in nearby regions controlled by traditional enemies as a means of securing more pelts and, consequently, greater returns from fur companies. As a result, intertribal warfare not only intensified but became virtually constant throughout much of the West by the 1830s. Warfare itself encouraged alliances among tribes and, in fashioning these, the existing balance of power across much of the West was altered. Increased traffic in trade also brought more Native Americans into contact with American- and English-borne diseases such as smallpox which ultimately ravaged Indian villages. Moreover, trade began to alter the nature of native identity itself. To be sure, in the early to mid-nineteenth century Native Americans in the fur-laden regions of the West retained firmly their cultural base, but the goods they secured and the relationship they cultivated with American and English traders opened the doorway to cultural change, a door that would prove nearly impossible to close. Language, spiritual beliefs, community structures, tribal leadership, healing practices and, indeed, most every element of native life would become somewhat blended with or altered by non-native cultures and values. American and English trade initiated a colonial relationship with native peoples, if not an increasing dependency relationship in some cases.

This relationship challenged the stability of Indian life in the Pacific Northwest. The challenge intensified when the gold rush hit California in 1849 and gold seekers tapped new mining regions in Washington and Oregon. The Nez Perce, Flathead, Coeur d'Alene, and other groups lived in productive valleys and near rivers that teemed with salmon and sturgeon. The people of the Pacific Northwest who had maintained their homelands to this point now faced dispossession and shrinking land bases.

To these material challenges were added changes to the religious landscape of the region. The fur traders' wealth indicated to the Indians that the traders had strong sacred power, given that among plateau peoples, such as the Nez Perce, wealth translated into a person's ability to control the spiritual world. Indians from the Columbia Plateau now sought the source of spiritual powers of the trappers. Toward that end, in the spring of 1831, seven Indians, including Nez Perce, set out for St. Louis to guide missionaries back to the plateau region.

Christians in the East viewed Indian interest in a different context, that of redemption. The Jesuit Jean de Smet spearheaded efforts in Idaho, Montana, and Washington. However, Flatheads, Nez Perce, Shoshones,

Coeur d'Alene, and Pend d'Oreille peoples were hunters who moved with the seasons, upsetting the Jesuit effort to build permanent missions of sedentary Indians. De Smet did, however, have some success as he perceived it, even if Indians converted for political and social reasons. Met by a crowd of over 1,600 Indians upon his arrival in the plateau, De Smet proceeded to baptize 600 Flatheads and Pend d'Oreilles.

The American Board of Commissioners for Foreign Missions (ABCFM) sent Protestant missionaries to the plateau region. In 1836, Marcus and Narcissa Whitman, Henry and Eliza Spalding, and William H. Gray arrived among the Nez Perce. Like de Smet, the Indians' seasonal cycles frustrated the ABCFM missionaries who hoped to shift Indians to a sedentary life where men would farm and women would work inside the home, a lifestyle common to the Christian world. Some Nez Perce and Cayuses took to agriculture, but most did not. Indian shamans warned their people to avoid missionaries who claimed to possess sacred powers. In this way, they resisted missionary efforts to convince Indians to alter their traditional lifestyle. More importantly, Christianity stood in sharp contrast to traditional native spirituality. It was, in essence, incompatible with Native American world views, and this reality, more than any argument offered by shamans, crippled the Christian missionary endeavor at this time. By the 1830s and 1840s, the missionary efforts were in steep decline among the plateau peoples.

Failed missionary work did not slow the influx of American settlers into the region. The 1840s witnessed 12,000 Americans in their "walking lodges" (wagons) arriving in the plateau territory as part of American expansionism along the Oregon Trail. The settlers brought with them disease, disruption, and a complete disregard for the interests of most Indians they encountered. Indian anger at the settlers sometimes flared into violence. The Oregon Trail cut right through the lands of the Cayuses, a people whose numbers had been radically reduced in the years since the establishment of the trail. A measles outbreak in 1847 pushed the Cayuses from anger to aggression. Finding Christianity useless in curing their ailing communities, the Cayuses killed the missionaries Marcus and Narcissa Whitman, along with a number of other people. In response, the Oregon militia retaliated. The war continued until the Cayuses who killed the missionaries turned themselves in and were hanged.

In the 1840s and 1850s, Anglo-Americans living in the Pacific Northwest began to assert control over the local tribesmen. The gold rush in California and the settlement of Oregon and Washington brought to the Pacific Northwest as many as 500,000 non-Indian residents between 1848 and 1860, and there is no realistic estimate of those individuals who ventured westward into the territory but soon thereafter returned to their eastern homes. Indeed, California statehood was granted by the United States government in 1850. The lure of quick wealth, the expectation of cheap land to farm, and opportunity to establish supporting businesses altogether drew white Americans to the West Coast. The population explosion and the concurrent economic development of the region compelled whites to remove native peoples from lands potentially rich in valuable resources. White immigrants to the fertile Willamette, Columbia, and Snake River valleys looked for ways to contain the small groups of Indians who lived alongside them. Americans looked to restrict the movements of the Cayuses, Walla Wallas, Nez Perce, and a host of smaller groups while other Americans invaded The Dalles territory, the once salmon-rich meeting place on the Columbia River, upsetting the lives of the Chinooks and Clatsops for whom The Dalles was a sacred space. In the 1850s, American territorial legislatures enacted laws to curtail the movements of local tribesmen. The Oregon Donation Law granted 320 acres of land to each adult male American settler and in so doing reduced further the land available for Indians. In the 1850s, a gold rush in Washington Territory (established in 1853) led to major outbreaks of violence between miners and warriors from area tribes. Territorial governor Isaac Stevens negotiated treaties with Rogue Valley and Puget Sound Indians, ordering the Indians to reserved tracts where they could still hunt and fish and live unmolested by whites. It was not until the end of the 1850s, however, that Congress passed into law a series of treaties that forced the Indians of Washington onto reservations. A region of numerous tribes engaged in trade networks they once dominated now faced an onslaught of Americans who intended to exploit fully native lands for their own purposes.

PROFILE

Smohalla, the Prophet

Smohalla was born into the Wanapum tribe around 1815. The Wanapum were members of the Shahaptian group, and they lived along the Columbia River, above where the Snake River begins in present-day Washington. Smohalla's name at birth was *Wak-wei* or *Kuk-kia*, which translates to "Arising from the Dust of the Earth Mother," but he was often known as Yuyunipitqana, the "Shouting Mountain," or Waipshwa, the "Rock Carrier." He earned the name "Smohalla," which means "Dreamer" in the Shahaptian tongue, when he proved his worth as a prophet.

Smohalla did not gain status and prestige through the traditional channels of Shahaptian society. Suffering from a hunched back, he was small in stature, making it impossible for him to hunt or fish. At a young age, Smohalla became unhappy with how whites, particularly traders and the Catholic missionaries, influenced his people. He traveled to La Lac, a spiritually powerful mountain, on a dream quest in search of his guardian spirit, or *wot*. He fasted and meditated for days, entering a dream state, or a state of death. The "land of the dead" sent Smohalla back to earth with a mission to save Shahaptian culture from the pressures of white society. He was instructed to resurrect the Indians' traditional religion of the *Washani*, a dream state faith that placed great emphasis on vision quests, dancing, and rituals. Christian influences had corrupted the *Washani* faith, and his task was to return it to its original form. According to Shahaptian tradition, in times of crisis a dreamer was expected to return and restore balance and harmony. Once he came back from La Lac and spread his message, Smohalla became that "dreamer."

According to Smohalla's version of the *Washani*, Shahaptians had to perform the *washat*, or dance, involving the *kookoolots*, or drums. Holding feathers of the eagle and swan, dancers looked to the sacred universe above for cultural regeneration. Following the *Washani* would return the earth to the traditional state of providing subsistence for Shahaptians and would purge their world of white ways, he told those who listened. His teachings helped spark the Yakima War of 1855–1856, fought in Oregon and Washington over white attempts to force Indians to move to reservations. Smohalla's religious teachings reached other tribes, particularly the Nez Perce. Their famous leader Chief Joseph followed the teachings of Smohalla. In the Pacific Northwest, resistance to American expansion took many forms. There was armed resistance to government policies and reservation life, and as the example of Smohalla illustrates, Indians also revitalized their traditional religions in the face of Protestant and Catholic missionaries.

Winning or Losing the West?

A familiar image presented historically in movies, Wild West shows, dime novels, and other popular forms is one in which America "won" the West by "taming" both land and native peoples. Native Americans were not set pieces in moments of encounter with American expansionists; rather, they were cultures that continued to adjust to changing circumstances as they had for hundreds of years. Moreover, America was not the only power with which tribespeople had to contend. In California, Mexico established a liberal state in 1821 to do away with Spanish rule, particularly the Franciscan missions. As Native Americans left the mission compounds, they found themselves looking to regenerate old social and cultural patterns, and with new opportunities they rebelled against the European order, especially the Franciscans. America reached the West Coast on the heels of

California's liberation from Spanish rule. American expansionists brought new ideas about the market and the state to California while adding their own layers of cultural values and beliefs to a largely native and Hispanic region. As American settlers pushed into California, they also moved into Texas, at first with the approval from Mexico. Americans brought concepts of property boundaries, slavery, and the market economy into a swirling world dominated by the unrestricted movement of equestrian Native Americans who relied on a centuries-old, local-level economy of violence and captivity exchange. Once Texans separated themselves from Mexico, statehood imposed new borders and boundaries on the equestrian cultures of Texas. Texans, driven by greed and racism, looked to exterminate the Apaches, Kiowas, Comanches, and other horseback native groups that did not share the same values of land tenure and refused to give way to American settlement. In the Southwest, particularly in New Mexico, the imposition of state power first came from Mexico. Wealthy Hispanics, people of mixed descent, and Native Americans who used the unbounded nature of the Southwest to herd sheep and trade captives and goods at local fairs all resisted the Mexican state. Local economies that fed longstanding networks of kinship and community had structured the economy of the Southwest borderlands. Mexico and then the United States desired a capitalist order in the Southwest that enhanced the power of the state and the moneyed class, not the power and authority of local communities and kin groups. The result was rebellion against the state. In terms of winning the West by 1850, the United States could not claim success, nor would Native Americans admit defeat. For native peoples who fought violently to retain their sovereignty and autonomy, the West was still their country.

The Transformation of California

The Indians of Alta California had not waited for Mexican freedom from the Spanish Empire to launch rebellions against the Franciscans. The most violent was the Chumash uprising of 1824. Conflicts between Chumash and Catholic beliefs and practices contributed to the outbreak of violence. Within the mission compounds, the Chumash, like all neophytes, had to abide by a strict Catholic regime. Among the Chumash there was a code of conduct which included siblings monitoring each other's sexual behavior. Also, Chumash chiefs had a series of priests with a cult of religious worship known as the *antap*. The Chumash worshipped an earth goddess, *Chupu*, and set up painted poles with feathers to appease the spirits. Chumash women were expected to kill their first-born child to ensure that they would have more children.

Needless to say, all of this clashed with the Catholic missions' precepts and practices. Some Chumash Indians even admitted during periods of confession to continuing dancing, constructing poles, belonging to the cult of *antap*, worshipping *Chupu*, and engaging in inappropriate sexual activity. In short, the Catholic effort among them failed miserably. Although the Catholic friars tried to impose harsh methods of social control within the confines of the missions, the Chumash clandestinely sustained many of their cultural practices. One event that contributed to the rebellion of 1824 was a Chumash woman's powerful vision years earlier, in 1801. She saw *Chupu. Chupu* told the woman that recently converted Indians, many of them recovering from epidemics, had to cleanse themselves with "tears of the sun" to avoid certain death. Many tried to follow the prophet's advice. The message of the prophet encouraged Chumash Indians, who substantially outnumbered the Franciscans; thus, the Franciscans realized they had potential Indian rebels living in the mission compounds.

Armed rebellion became more probable once the Chumash acquired weapons. Fearing pirate attacks, the missionaries armed Chumash neophytes with well-crafted bows and arrows and allowed for some military training for mission defense. One of the mission fathers at Santa Barbara even allowed the neophytes to select their own military leaders. The Franciscans overestimated the Chumash's loyalty to their cause. If provoked sufficiently, the Chumash, a people who held on to their traditional beliefs in the face of Catholic pressure and who were now well armed, would not hesitate to fight.

In 1824, the missionaries whipped a neophyte at Mission Santa Ynéz, which brought the secret worship of *Chupu* to the surface. Spiritually revitalized and armed, and angry after the whipping, mission Chumash joined Indians on the outside, assailing the mission with arrows until soldiers arrived to fight off the attack. The Chumash escaped to Mission La Purísima, where the neophytes had also risen against the Franciscans. The Indians successfully burned the mission.

The Chumash continued their rebellion against the mission system in the areas around San Buenaventura and Santa Barbara, sending messengers to tell neophytes and non-Christian Indians region-wide to take up arms. At Santa Barbara, presidio soldiers entered the mission and confronted armed Chumash who successfully held their positions. The Chumash uprising was an expression of the Indians' ability and intent to sustain their own autonomy, even in the context of mission life.

The Chumash ultimately fled, joining with local Yokut Indians in the canyons of the San Joaquin Valley. A confession from a Chumash Indian after the rebellion revealed how Chumash neophytes had concealed a revitalized culture that combined both Spanish and Chumash elements. Although they abided by Catholic marriage patterns in front of the friars, they continued traditional sibling-regulated sexual activities. A revivalism of the cult of *antap* and the worship of *Chupu* had occurred without the friars ever knowing it. After the rebellion of 1824, the neophytes who returned to the missions abandoned Chumash ways and dedicated themselves to the Catholic ritual calendar. But outside of the missions, the Indians had fused Catholic practices with Chumash ones.

Resistance from Indians outside the missions more commonly involved stealing Spanish livestock and horses. The Franciscans had hoped to build a series of missions in California's interior, but they soon discovered that groups like the Muquelemne Miwoks did not welcome the Catholic cause. Learning about horses and the equestrian culture from escaping neophytes, interior Miwoks and Yokuts used the new horseback culture to raid the missions and presidios. These interior Indians also became savvy traders, holding trading fairs to exchange stolen goods. In 1819, Spanish soldiers entered the interior, looking to capture Miwok and Yokut thieves. The expedition only found abandoned Miwok and Yokut *rancherías*. However, Spanish soldiers did eventually engage with multiple horse-thieving parties, killing numerous Miwok and Yokut Indians. Horse stealing was one way the interior Indians sought to defend themselves in a period when power was changing hands.

Winning its independence from Spain in 1821 and then slowly dismantling the chain of coastal missions, Mexican leaders severed the Franciscan missions' control over Indian labor. Mexican officials felt that Franciscans ran institutions that exploited native labor to sustain elaborate mission compounds and therefore prevented Indians from achieving self-sufficiency and making their own contributions to Alta California's economy. Some Indians who took up small plots of land and used their skills as craftsmen and blacksmiths benefited from the end of the mission system, but mission dependence on Indian labor continued, uncontrolled in some areas of Alta California (see Map 8.2).

In July 1826, the new governor of Alta California passed the Decree of Emancipation, which allowed all neophytes to leave the missions and provide their own subsistence. The decree did not end the mission system overnight. The Franciscans were not willing to let go of the neophytes—the Indians who the priests had spent years converting and controlling. In the face of Franciscan resistance, Indians who had gained some skills in reading and writing sent letters to the governor requesting his direct help in freeing themselves from the missionaries.

By 1827, Indian-Spanish relations in Alta California had deteriorated to the point where rifts even divided important interior Indians who once stood united in their hatred of the coastal missions, such as the Miwoks and Yokuts. Interior Indians, threatened on two fronts, from the Spanish along the coast and fur traders moving onto their homelands, became individual competitors rather than tribes united together. A Lakisamne Yokut neophyte named Estanislao left Mission San José to foster rebellion. From a fortified base along the Stanislaus

River, he stole Mexican livestock herds while spreading the word that other Indians should also abandon the missions. Mexican authorities were convinced that Estanislao led the horse raiders from the interior. Estanislao crushed three Mexican military parties in the interior in 1828 and 1829. A company of more than 100 Mexican soldiers, with the help of converts who hated the Lakisamne Yokuts, attacked Estanislao's fortification, eventually breaking through the walls. With few other options, Estanislao escaped, returned to Mission San José, and requested a pardon from the Franciscans. His pardon angered the Mexican troops for obvious reasons, but Estanislao and the horse-raiding rebellions from the interior speak to larger issues of change among the missions. Although there had been significant determination over time to separate themselves from the mission system and return to more traditional ways, they ultimately acted to secure their independence once it became obvious that the missions were in decline.

In the wake of these Indian rebellions, the new governor of Alta California enacted a gradual emancipation program to ease the transition from the mission compounds to freedom, but whereas Native Americans once lived with some degree of oversight and protection, they would now reside independently next to hostile indigenous neighbors from the interior. Indians with more than 12 years in the mission program and who

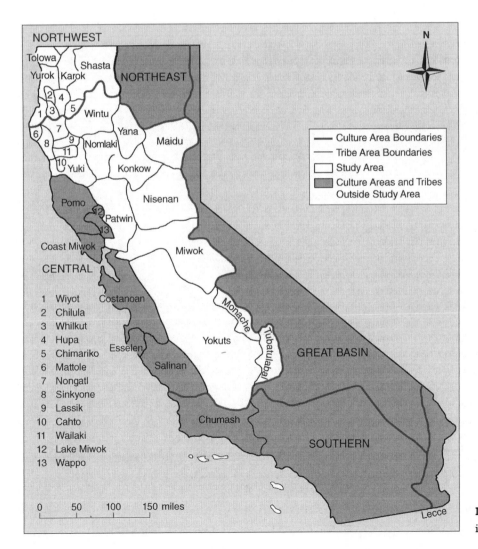

Map 8.2 Major tribal groupings in California

had children gained partial freedom. These former neophytes lived close to the parish, farming small plots of granted land, but they could be called back to serve in the missions if necessary. The gradual emancipation program only succeeded at a few missions, so Mexico ordered the secularization of all missions. By August 1834, the governor of Alta California developed a plan to distribute mission lands, implements, and livestock to create local communities of self-sufficient Indians. Each head of household received a tract of land ranging from 100 to 400 acres. To these families were parceled out mission tools, seeds, and livestock. The Mexican government denied the Indians their right to sell their land or livestock, but they could aid parish priests when necessary and serve as laborers on the large *ranchos* that emerged when land was offered to foreigners under the terms of the Colonization Act of 1824.

The Secularization Act of 1834, which officially ended Franciscan control over the missions, provided the Indians with some freedom and autonomy, but it was actually intended to dole out millions of acres to non-native Californians. Throughout Alta California between 1834 and 1840 there were small, scattered Indian settlements amid 1,000-acre *ranchos* owned by Mexican elites. Ex-neophytes, once at the disposal of the Franciscan missionaries, did achieve a level of economic independence by the 1840s, but they mostly constituted a large peasant class of small farmers, day laborers, and craft sellers. Where mission populations far exceeded the

8.5 *California Rancho Scene* by Alfred Sully, c. 1849

Source: Alfred Sully, *California Rancho Scene, Monterey*. 1849. The Oakland Museum of California Kahn Collection

available land, less fortunate Indians became part of a roving poor population, committing crimes such as stealing livestock and horses. Others moved to large *ranchos* near Los Angeles and other areas to try to work within a competitive labor market. On enormous *ranchos*, more than 100 Indians could be found laboring in the fields, tending horses and livestock, or working as blacksmiths and craftsmen. The international demand for hides and slaughtered cattle basically put the day-working Indians in the same forced labor system that had existed within the missions. Indian ranch hands received poor pay, and few Indians actually lived on the *ranchos*. Although Alta California had achieved its independence from Spain, and the Indians had their freedom from the missions, Mexican rule did little to alleviate the hardships Indians faced. By the 1850s, even under the rule of the United States, some Indians still lived in small huts near their former missions.

It is important to note two points. First, the mission system was intended to develop a solid financial return based heavily on native labor and concurrently conduct a cultural war on local native populations, a process that was consistent across North America since first encounter. In short, this was an effort to exterminate the traditional Indian and incorporate the revised model into advancing western society. Second, the Chumash and others of Alta California demonstrated clearly a determination to resist that Spanish-Mexican effort, much like native peoples across the continent had pressed since the 1490s. Resistance took the form of armed rebellion, to be sure, but also in their continuance of traditional ways and holding to traditional values in spite of public displays of acculturation.

California Indians and American Manifest Destiny

The arrival of John Sutter in the Sacramento Valley in 1838 marked a transition in California Indian relations with outsiders. Sutter established his post of New Helvetia among the Miwoks and Nisenan Indians along the American River in the Sacramento Valley and soon was a valued competitor for Indian workers. The Indians came to New Helvetia to trade with Sutter, receiving goods such as beads, sugar from Hawaii, and blankets. In return, leaders of *rancherías*, such as the Miwok chief Maximo, offered the services of village Indians. Sutter created a system of credit and debt that kept local Indians in perpetual cycles of work at New Helvetia. He introduced money and made metal necklaces into a form of currency. He also provided meager housing for his Indian workers. When wheat was harvested, Sutter employed up to 600 Indians. He also operated a distillery, a hat factory, and a tannery. Sutter had brought the American market economy into the Sacramento Valley. But in a region where disease had already ravaged the Indian population, Sutter's use of Indian workers threatened the integrity of surrounding Indian *rancherías*, who occasionally attacked New Helvetia in response.

To protect his investment in New Helvetia, in the 1840s Sutter created an Indian army of 150 foot soldiers with 50 cavalry, mostly Nisenan and Miwok Indians. He traded with the Russians at Fort Ross for army uniforms, and the Indians donned the green-and-blue uniform of the Russian army. Working with Sutter, the Native Americans used their military training to start a series of interior Indian wars against rivals and to recapture stolen horses, horses that Sutter would later sell to California *ranchos*. In 1848, as Sutter's empire continued to grow, one that depended significantly on the cooperative relationship he cultivated with local natives, a watershed moment occurred—gold was discovered on his property. Rumors spread across the continent, only to be confirmed by U.S. President James K. Polk. The rush was on. Nearly 300,000 Anglo-Americans flooded California along with another 200,000 Europeans, Mexicans, and Asians over the next few years, this beginning the transformation of an Indian-Hispanic land into a U.S. territory. Indians were largely viewed as impediments, or obstacles, to those seeking quick wealth. When expedient to do so, mining companies in gold rush California hired native laborers to supplement the non-Indian labor at hand. Indian laborers were routinely abused physically and paid far less than their actual value. The demands of their employers ripped apart Native American families, and Indian women were often raped and forced into prostitution in mining towns.

In the central mining district of California, enterprising miners brought in Pomo Indians to work alongside Nisenan and Miwoks. Not only were large mining firms digging in Indian lands, bringing native laborers in from the interior, but they were also grazing cattle for profit where Konkow Maidu once searched for food. Other Indians in the central mining district along the Feather River, such as the Konkow Maidu, fell into debt to traders who set up stores near the prime mining areas. This is not to say that Indians did not attempt to adapt and take advantage of the changed circumstances. The Indians whose economy was once based on barter now had money and quickly learned its value in a market economy. Moreover, some Indians had land and gold of their own and, with them, the ability to challenge the power and authority of leading miners and settlers who looked to abuse Indian laborers. But most California Indians witnessed not opportunity but calamity. They remained part of a mining working class, brutally mistreated by Americans who used the Indians as little more than slave labor. Oregon miners, some of whom had witnessed Indian attacks on whites, were particularly notorious for killing Indians.

The land, itself, became highly contested. American miners wanted to set up new operations wherever gold was located. Indians like the Yokut, in a rare case, actually prevented American miners from taking over their homelands along the Kings River in the southern mining district. The northwestern mining district was unique. Its rugged landscape made mining there less profitable. This reality made the region less valued to mining operations and consequently a territory over which few miners were willing to fight. Moreover, the Native American groups in the district (including the Tolowa, Hupa, Karok, and Shasta) were close to the Pacific fur trading nexus of the Hudson's Bay Company. These Indians, sharing much in common with the Pacific Northwest tribespeople, knew how to trade and were more capable of defending their lands. Nonetheless, there was still gold in those hills. Armed skirmishes did erupt on occasion, over access to land and labor.

Even though there were moments of Indian empowerment and self-preservation, long-term trends in California up to 1850 all pointed toward the Americanization of the territory. A once Hispanic-Indian region with deep roots in Spanish culture and Catholicism now had the imprint of the American market economy and the Protestant work ethic. The United States held a legal responsibility to protect Indians once it acquired California from Mexico at the conclusion of the Mexican-American War in 1848. Most Americans, however, saw Indians as racially inferior impediments to westward expansion who needed to be removed from rich lands. As mining, farming, and ranching transformed California and Indians were stripped of most rights to land tenure, California's Native Americans became a roaming, landless people.

When California achieved statehood in 1850, the federal government turned its attention to the state's "Indian problem." In a joint report, three federal Indian commissioners (Dr. Oliver M. Wozencraft, George W. Barbour, and Redick Mckee) described the issue and its potential solutions this way: "There is no further west . . . the people of California appear to have left but one alternative in relation to these remnant of once numerous and powerful tribes . . . extermination or domestication." The three commissioners negotiated 18 treaties for reservations in California, each stating that Indians would settle on lands assigned to them and be provided with livestock and other implements to support themselves. Congress, however, rejected the treaties because those arrangements left the natives as a continuing obstacle to the growing market economy of California. Many of these treaties settled California Indians on prime lands located near cattle ranches, mines, and other important resources. With Indians subsisting on fertile and mineral-rich lands next to American ranches and mines, the Indian labor pool would dry up. Too, argued many in Congress, those properties would better benefit the growing non-native population and its development of California industries. Many American leaders simply saw giving important resources to Indians as a waste of the land's potential. If the treaties were approved, "some of what are now the most populous and prosperous regions of California would be peopled by a few undeveloped natives."

Once Congress rejected the treaties, a new Indian superintendent, Edward Fitzgerald Beale, headed to California. Beale proposed a handful of reservations amounting to about 75,000 acres. Indians would not be forced onto these reservations, but invited to settle on the lands instead. Five military reservations (the Tejon, Nome

Lackee, Mendocino, Fresno, and Klamath reservations) were established in the state. Few California Indians settled on these reservations. Most of the reservations were located near or on white or Hispanic ranches, ensuring that the Indians would still serve as laborers. At the Tehama reservation, the Nomlaki people, devastated by disease, overwork, and violence, decided to work at the reserve. Some Indians, such as the Nomlaki, hoped the military reservations would guard them against white violence and a growing illicit slave trade in Indian workers. By the mid-1850s, it was clear that the reservation system, a compromise between the state and the federal government, was a failure. Indians left, removing their villages to the interior.

However, there were few options left for California's native population. Under the Act for the Government and Protection of the Indians, passed in 1850, county justices of the peace determined the fate of many California Indians. Local lands were set aside for Indian use but were quickly taken by migrant Americans. Whites could force the movement of Indian *rancherías* and there was no protection for fishing, planting, or hunting grounds, while the law allowed for Indian indentured agreements with local whites. Although local justices of the peace oversaw all labor contracts, California Indians faced a system of labor exploitation. Indians were arrested for burning and slashing acreage, a traditional practice among California Indians for the growing season. Indians who stole livestock had to pay fines, and they even faced lashings. In short, the law was not designed to protect Indians. It was designed, instead, to contain the Indian populations, protect white farms and profits, and ensure a steady supply of Indian labor.

In less than 30 years, between 1846 and 1870, California's Indian population dropped from 150,000 to 30,000. Depopulation was, in part, a result of the direct effort of some white Americans to eradicate the Indians' presence. Because California Indians were "obstacles to progress," occupying by treaty or by tradition large tracts of land needed for grazing, harvesting, and timber cutting, Americans often raided native villages in the mountains, valleys, and forests, killing Indians at will. Violence escalated as the market economy of California shifted from mines to farms, ranches, and towns. Volunteer militias took on the project of extermination. They "will succeed in totally breaking up or exterminating the skulking bands of savages," noted one newspaper reporter. One Californian, William Kibb, claimed to have murdered over 400 Indians to open new lands for cattle grazing. A newspaper reporter for the *Red Bluff Herald* wrote, "It is becoming evident that extermination of the red devils will have to be resorted to before the people . . . will be safe." Public native responses were limited. The white population had soared in the region and greatly surpassed that of Indians, making armed resistance difficult at best. They did attack remote mining camps, inadequately guarded supply lines, outlying ranches, and other targets of opportunity. They even, on occasion, took white children hostage. Each of these actions, however, resulted in vicious retaliation by state militia units or vigilantes. Moreover, each act of Indian violence further sealed their ultimate fate as the non-native population used Indian resistance to justify further the extermination of Native Americans. The California Indian Wars (1860–1865) waged in northern California against numerous native groups were devastating.

California's "Sexual Frontier"

Since the time of Spanish occupation, California had existed as what historian Albert L. Hurtado describes as a "sexual frontier," a place where sexual norms were both fluid and contested. While certainly true among settlers and in California's emerging urban centers, it definitely included direct violence against vulnerable native women. The rape of Indian women proved frequent under the Spanish, Mexicans, Russians, and now Americans. A substantially large mixed population emerged from both consensual relationships and criminal actions. In a few cases, non-native men married their Indian female partners.

After 1849, the gold rush and the American effort at Indian extermination brought Indian and Anglo men together in a violent system of labor extraction, rape, and abuse. California was a hyper-masculine environment

TIMELINE 8.3 INDIANS AND THE TRANSFORMATION OF CALIFORNIA, 1821–1865

Date	Event
1821	Mexico makes California a liberal state
1824	Chumash Rebellion
1826	Decree of Emancipation
1827	Estanislao uprising
1834	Secularization Act
1838	John Sutter arrives among the Miwok
1849	Gold is discovered
1850	California achieves statehood
	Act for Government Protection of the Indians is passed
1860–1865	California Indian Wars

with Anglo men far outnumbering Anglo women. Fur traders understood the benefits of long-term relationships with Indian women. Marriage brought them into extended Indian families, thereby opening up opportunities for reciprocal trade relations in pelts and furs. Some miners and ranchers tried to establish long-term relationships with Indian women, despite government disapproval. Government officials feared that a "mixed race" of people would come to dominate California and that Anglo-American purity would be threatened. Many whites also viewed Indian men as a danger to Anglo society. White women, if not careful, could fall prey to the "wild savage" men who would take them captive and rape them.

Poverty and the scarcity of white women in California combined to drive many Indian women into prostitution. Others served as household domestics, often becoming the mistresses of American men. Prostitution spread diseases like syphilis among both California Indian and white populations. For American men, there were plenty of opportunities to rape Indian women. With Indian men forced into labor on ranches and in mines, Indian women were left vulnerable to an American male majority. Liquor, brothels, bars, and a world filled with guns and hardworking men turned sexual violence into common practice. Rapists were never prosecuted for their violence against Indian women. Many white Californians simply considered the rape of Indian women to be a brutal but uncontrollable reality of male-dominated frontier societies. There were those who gave their tacit consent to the violent act or simply chose to ignore the barbarity of the act, in part the product of intense racism toward native peoples. In either case, the unchristian nature of those perspectives was not lost on a native population that had been subjected intensely to Christian conversion efforts over so many decades. The impact of rape and interracial sex on Indian populations was dramatic. Many Indian women died at the hands of white perpetrators. In census records from 1860, Indian men far outnumbered Indian women due to sexual assault, disease, and death. Birth rates among Indian communities dropped, and families broke apart. In some places, such as northern California, Indian women and children were left without men as a result of the pervasive wars of extermination Americans launched. Indian women struggled to find subsistence, while male Indian children became orphaned and bound out as indentured workers. Hispanicized and Anglicized populations of Indians began to replace "full-blooded" California Indian populations. Although its

PROFILE

Ishi, the Last Yahi Standing

In August 29, 1911, in a slaughterhouse near the town of Orville, California, workers stumbled on a half-naked Indian. They fetched the sheriff. Soon thereafter, two anthropologists at the University of California, Berkeley, Alfred Kroeber and T.T. Waterman, took Ishi to their museum for study.

The Yahi were a southern branch of the Yana tribe, living in the Mount Lassen Foothills of northern California. For centuries, the Yahi had subsisted in small villages in the Mount Lassen region. The United States' acquisition of California in 1848, coupled with the discovery of gold in 1849, set in motion changes that destroyed the Yahi landscape and Yahi families. American ranchers, miners, and settlers rushed in to the region, pushing the Yana people onto smaller tracts of land. The northern California wars of extermination ravaged the Yana people, as Americans sought to dispossess the Yana of their lands for grazing cattle and mining. The Yahi became wanderers, subsisting off of stolen cattle and livestock and local sources of berries and other plants. During this early period of Ishi's life, the Yahi were the fiercest of the Mount Lassen peoples, raiding ranches and homes and killing whites. Militia units responded, killing the Yahi without hesitation. When Ishi was only a child, his father was killed during one of these skirmishes with Americans. The extermination of the Yahi continued. Yahi families disintegrated until there were only 40 Yahi left hiding out in Deer Creek. By the turn of the twentieth century, local rumors swirled of a small band of "wild people" who lived in the Mount Lassen region. Ishi was part of that band. The band dwindled to four people, two men, Ishi's sister, and his mother. By the time Ishi was discovered in the slaughterhouse, he was the last of the Yahis.

impact varied by region, all in all, the sexual frontier of California thoroughly disrupted Indian life, as California became a society that targeted Indian men for death because of their alleged sexual aggressiveness and targeted Indian women for sexual abuse.

Texas Indians in Upheaval

In the early nineteenth century, Texas, unlike California, was a place where native peoples largely checked Spanish rule. The situation changed dramatically when Americans flooded the region. Two large lowland native groups, the Coahuiltecans and coastal Karankawas, fell most quickly under the weight of American expansion. Settled in the area of the Balcones Escarpment, the Guadalupe River, and the Rio Grande—collectively the lowlands of Texas—the Coahuiltecans of the 1820s were actually 55 bands that spoke a common language. Hunter-gatherers who moved through the lowlands according to the seasons, the numerous bands no longer existed as individual entities; they had been pushed by attacks into smaller areas where they were collectively known as the "Coahuiltecans." The Karankawas, living in the middle-range grounds of the Texas coast, around Matagorda Bay, San Antonio Bay, and even the northern and eastern shores of Corpus Christi, had spent centuries fending off Spanish subjugation. Like the Coahuiltecans, the Karankawas were living in bands in the 1820s. The Karankawas had stolen horses and raided Spanish missions for centuries, but the arrival of American *empresarios*—men granted large land holdings by the Mexican government—put pressure on the lands of the Karankawas. Stephen F. Austin was an example of an *empresario*. With the Mexican government's

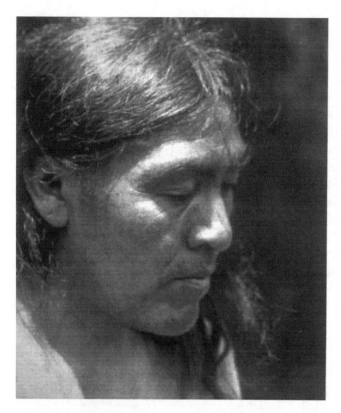

8.6 Ishi, the last Yahi
Source: The Bancroft Library, University of California

consent, Austin built a large settlement on the lower Brazos River. He was a colonizer of the territory between Galveston Bay and the Colorado River.

Continuing their longstanding defense of their homelands, Karankawas attacked Austin's settlements, prompting a series of small raids and counter-raids with the Americans. American colonists moved toward a policy of outright ethnic cleansing, shooting Karankawas without hesitation. In 1827, wealthy landholding Mexicans in the Texas territory signed a treaty with the Americans that forced large bands of Karankawas into western lands, creating unprecedented starvation because the bands could no longer follow a seasonal cycle of movement between the coast and interior in search of food. To sustain their populations, Karankawas reluctantly built trade networks with American settlers with debt and enslavement to local whites often the end result. The Texans' revolt against Mexico in 1835 and 1836 gave additional opportunity to the settlers to strike villages and further reduce the number of Karankawas. In 1845, the Texans won their desired separation from Mexico and founded their own independent republic; most Karankawas fled to the mouth of the Rio Grande River to avoid Indian policies the new nation might enact. The uncertainty and fear was justified as the Karankawas who chose to stay along the coast were devastated in a Texan attack in 1852. Those who earlier relocated to the Rio Grande, however, did not find a safe haven. Cross-border raids by native groups in Mexico took many as captives while other Karankawas were absorbed by other tribes.

At the same time as Indians in Texas were coming under pressure from early American settlement in the region, Native Americans residing in or adjacent to the Deep South fled into eastern Texas to avoid removal and disruption caused by the expansion of the cotton frontier in the South. There were approximately 200 Shawnees and Delawares to the north on Caddoan lands. The more powerful Cherokees led by Duwali (Chief Bowl or Bowles), after a series of battles with the Osages, broke from the Old Settler Cherokees in Arkansas to rebuild Cherokee town life. The Cherokees first settled on the Three Forks and Trinity rivers, but Caddos and Wichitas expelled them. By 1822, the Cherokees were living northwest of Nacogdoches. Muskogee-speaking Alabama-Coushattas lived farthest to the south in the Big Thicket region, a heavily wooded country much resembling Creek country in Georgia and Alabama. Like the Cherokees, the Alabama-Coushattas rebuilt traditional farms and became strong traders along trade routes that crossed the Big Thicket region. Texas had become an American state with a vast native population, but a population that was becoming ever more diverse and, consequently, problematic for peace.

American *empresarios*, Tejanos (Texans of Mexican or Latin-American descent), and Mexicans all feared the powerful Indian horseback cultures of Texas, which, in the decades before the Civil War, included Comanches,

Kiowas, and the Lipan Apaches. All of these cultures had deep spiritual, mythical, and ceremonial traditions surrounding their warrior-equestrian cultures. Following the herds of buffalo and establishing settlements also known as *rancherías*, the nomadic cultures of Texas frustrated American efforts to claim land, stole the property of people throughout the region, and threatened the lives of Americans, Tejanos, and Mexicans. Comanches and Kiowas also raided the western borders of the Indian Territory, stealing slaves and other property from the Choctaw and Chickasaw planters who occupied the fertile lands in the western districts.

As in other parts of the Southwest, honor and status among the horseback cultures required continual raiding for horses, goods, and particularly captives to work as slaves or replenish depleted population numbers. The result was near incessant warfare, and Kiowas, Comanches, Wichitas, and Lipan Apaches took many whites and other Indians captive. The exchange of captives became an important part of trade and diplomacy.

The American experience with slavery gave Americans some insight into the importance of captives to the economy of the powerful nomadic cultures. Most settlers who came to Texas hailed from cotton-producing southern states and brought with them the slave culture. This included an understanding of male honor sometimes associated with owning numerous African slaves and trading or selling them. And as with the domestic slave trade, in which slaves traded hands several times, captives, whether white or Indian, often moved between cultures in a continual and fluid trade. But slavery, in which bondsmen were purchased on an open

PROFILE

Andele, the Mexican-Kiowa Captive

Living on the Texas-Mexican border was risky in the 1860s. Andele, once known by his boyhood Mexican name, Jose Andrés Martínez, found himself embroiled in the intense market of captivity exchange along the Mexican-American border. Captured by Mescalero Apaches in 1866, then sold for a few buffalo robes, a red blanket, and a mule in 1867 to the Kiowa chief Heap O'Bears (Many Bears), Andele reached manhood as a Kiowa. Andele learned the ways of the Kiowa warriors. Among the Kiowa, every boy starts as a "rabbit" until he can enter one of the five orders of soldiers: the *Ti-e-pa-ko*, the *Tsai-e-ton-mo*, the *Ton-kon-ko*, the *Ah-tle-to-yo-ye*, and the *Ko-e-Tsain-ko*. The five orders made up the army of "Dog Soldiers." The Dog Soldiers were those men who had earned tremendous sacred power and prestige in battle. In time, Andele was fully assimilated into Kiowa culture and hoped to rise in rank and become a chief.

By the 1870s, Kiowa raiding for captives stopped, primarily because the U.S. government began to purchase back captives and guard the western frontier. An army general approached Andele and asked who he was. Andele, who could barely remember Spanish, recalled his former family name, and the general sent for his brother. The Kiowas turned over Andele, who became Jose Andrés Martínez again. He lived in a Methodist mission and learned Spanish and English, only to return to live among the Kiowas later. The story of Andrés's transformation into Andele illustrates the significance of captivity exchange in the Southwest. His exchange from the Mescaleros to the Kiowas upheld a delicate balance of peace and created ties of friendship. His advancement within Kiowa society was necessary to his survival as a Mexican turned Kiowa. Even though he left the Kiowas, his transformation from a Mexican into a Kiowa was complete. Andrés, or Andele, could not fit in within Mexican society and returned to his former captors. Some captives came to prefer Indian ways. Also, their lives were representative of a larger historical process, as people caught in networks of distribution and relations of kinship that sustained the local-level economies of the Southwest borderlands.

market, was also very different from the centuries-old economy of captivity. Indians adopted captives and made them part of kin and community networks; African slaves were strictly property. By the 1850s and 1860s, American officials thought they had transformed the economy and culture of the Southwest by replacing captivity exchange with the domestic slave trade. But at the local level, some Texans themselves participated in an illicit trade in captives that ranged across the Southwest into New Mexico, northern parts of Mexico that became wastelands, Arizona, and west into California. Captives were cheaper. Profiting from the use of captives on their farms and as cattle hands while connecting with local Indian communities, Texans, particularly those who could not afford African slaves, used the Indians' captive economy to their benefit.

Treaty-making with the raiding cultures was particularly difficult for the Texans, as no one chief represented the nomadic groups that moved in separate but numerous bands. Wichitas, Kiowas, and Comanches continued raids along the upper Trinity, Brazos, and Colorado rivers, ranging west to El Paso and New Mexico. On March 19, 1840, 12 Comanche chiefs, along with numerous women and children, arrived in San Antonio for a peace accord. The Texans were shocked by one of the captives who appeared half-starved and naked, a white woman by the name of Matilda Lockart. The Texas delegation demanded the immediate release of all captives, but the Comanches, whose wealth depended on captives, refused. If the Texans wanted captives, they needed to pay for the captives, just as they paid to purchase their slaves. In response, the Texas Rangers came to the council and killed all 12 of the Comanche chiefs, inadvertently killing several women and children as well. The Rangers took the remaining Comanches captive. "The Council House Fight," as it was called, angered the Comanches. They and Kiowa allies struck deep into the interior of Texas, razing towns, killing white settlers, and taking more captives. In September 1843, Houston and the Comanches negotiated a treaty to keep the peace in Texas. Tribesmen would stop stealing horses and taking captives, and in exchange, Texans would construct trading houses. The arrangement proved as minimal as it read, placing a greater burden on the Comanches than it did on the Texans. Probably for that reason in addition to the hatred each party still held for the other, sporadic skirmishes continued between the Kiowa-Comanche union and Texans.

Texas joined the Union in May 1846, and, as required by the United States Constitution, Washington assumed responsibility for negotiations with the warring tribes in Texas. The Treaty of Council Springs, negotiated with the Comanches, Lipan Apaches, Tonkawas, Caddos, and Wichitas, was intended to establish peace in Texas. Once again, the Indians agreed to turn over their captives and other stolen property to trade with licensed American traders. In exchange, the United States would respect Indian lands and trade fairly with them. The U.S. Army at that time was a numerically small force, and its units were spread thinly along the nation's coastline, across the upper plains, and into California. It maintained a minor presence in the Southwest. The upper reaches of Texas remained unprotected by federal troops, leaving that stretch largely under the watchful eyes of the Texas Rangers, whose hatred for the Indians ran deep. Rangers raided Indian villages in that territory in response to natives who swiped cattle and other farm animals from Texans or who appeared to threaten settlers in any manner. Some Comanches abandoned their traditional lives, seeking to avoid the never-ending confrontations with Texans and the white migration into the region that was then intensifying. They moved to the Indian Territory and, along with the Caddoans and Wichitas, built farms on a reserved tract of land by 1854. Most Comanches, however, remained on their lands and continued the old ways and fiercely resisted all threats to their lives.

The Southwest Borderlands in Transition

American expansion into New Mexico was slow as compared with other parts of the West. New Mexico was also not densely settled and it was far from Mexico City, so it received few funds or protection from the Mexican government. The people of New Mexico, even the Hispanic elites, provided for themselves through interlocking local-level economies.

READING HISTORY

Andele's Account

John Jasper (J.J.) Methvin was a Methodist missionary who began his work in Indian Territory in 1885. By 1887, Methvin became the official missionary to the most western tribes in Indian Territory, particularly Kiowas. His school and church, known as the Methvin Institute, tried to change the Indians in western Oklahoma, and one of his main opponents was the famous Comanche chief Quanah Parker. His publication of Andele: The Mexican-Kiowa Captive: A Story of Real Life Among the Indians *(1899), is one of three known New Mexican captivity narratives ever to be published. He met Andele, or Jose Andrés Martínez, after Andele's brother found him and took him from Fort Sill, where at some point Andele, now Jose Andrés Martínez again, became a convert to the Methodist faith under Methvin's charge.*

"Lie down, Pedro," said Andres, "keep still, they see the Mexican yonder and are started in pursuit, and when they are fully passed, if they do not discover us, we will run for yonder timber and make our escape for home. Keep still, Pedro," continued Andres, "keep still, your life depends upon it. If you make a noise, they will find us out, and we are lost. It may be they will not see up. Keep still."

As the savage band passed on, their interest fully set on the Mexican, and the boys were just in the act of slipping down through the low bushes that lined the valley to the timber beyond, they were discovered by two Apaches, who, for some reason, had wandered from the main band, and who now ran upon the boys with a wild shout of delight. Rejoicing at the prospect of becoming chiefs, each singled out his boy, ran upon him, struck him with his spear and then claimed him as a captive. This is a custom among the Indians, that whosoever first strikes a captive, or kills and scalps an enemy, becomes a hero, and great honor is done him on his return home, and he is ever after considered a great chief. His word commands attention, his wishes must be respected. It matters not whether he kills a man or captures a babe, he secures a title to chiefhood.

It may be stated here that it is not often that Indians kill little children, if they can carry them off, and it is a marvelous fact that, notwithstanding their fearful savage natures, they often show the tenderest affection for children. But it seems that the Mescaleros are among the most abandoned and cruel, and the two who had captured the boys hurried them along, calling out in mock tenderness, "Come on, come one, little boys, we will take you to see your mother, you must go to see your mother, she is crying for you now," until they reached the band who had gathered around the Mexican and his burros. They had cut the flour sacks open and scattered the flour to the prairie winds, and stripped the Mexican of every rag of clothing, till he stood there naked and trembling, his yellow skin glistening in the sunlight of the October morning, a pitiable sight.

The two boys and the naked Mexican were placed in the circle of howling Apaches and hurried along on foot, followed by a part of the band on foot, while some rode the burros and made sport as they pierced them with the points of their spears and shouted in triumph their victory over the three Mexicans.

Source: Rev. John Jasper Methvin, *Andele, or, The Mexican-Kiowa Captive. A Story of Real Life Among the Indians* (Louisville, KY: Pentecostal Herald Press, 1899), pp. 13–15.

Question

What does this account reveal about life on the borderlands?

The U.S. acquisition of New Mexico in 1848 did not disrupt these economies to any great extent as an American-directed market economy was slow to take root in the territory. Flourishing instead among some Hispanics, Indians, and Anglo-Americans was an illicit trade in captives and the bartering in buffalo hides, sheep, liquor, woven cloth, guns, and goods among Hispanics, Indians, and Anglo-Americans flourished as before, although trade goods increasingly found their way into New Mexico from the Arkansas territory by way of the Santa Fe Trail.

From afar, New Mexico looked economically bleak, a neglected colonial outpost. But wealthy Hispanics—sometimes people of both Spanish and Indian descent—Native Americans, American merchants, and even bandits thrived on a set of connected local economies. Outside of the small Pueblo settlements and main Hispanic towns of Albuquerque, Taos, Santa Fe, and Cebolleta were numerous Navajos committed to sheep pastoralism. Profiting from sheep herding in numerous ways, Navajo men were also committed to equestrian warfare and hunting. By the early nineteenth century, the Navajo had a class-based society in which chiefly power rested mostly on prosperous sheep herding, enslaving herdsmen, and an ability to link communities and kin in patronage. With so many sheep, the Navajo trading in captives and sheep with Cebolleta threatened to undermine the old routes to the western mining regions. Wealthy Navajos, whose extensive trade in sheep and captives put other Navajos in a subordinate position, mingled with local wealthy New Mexicans.

8.7 Navajos, c. 1851.

Source: Beinecke Rare Book and Manuscript Library, Yale University

Relations of trade and kinship marked relations among the Pueblo peoples, Navajos, New Mexicans, and Americans.

Leaders looked to treaties to keep the Navajos at peace. Yet violence and the constant exchange of sheep and captives fueled New Mexican demographic and economic growth. Cycles of exchange in a largely non-market-based economy among the Navajos via the burgeoning Santa Fe Trail brought in much-needed goods. Although Mexico abolished slavery in 1829, it continued in New Mexico, benefiting both the wealthy and the poor. Adopted captives added to the number of Indians and New Mexicans. Goods from the Santa Fe Trail, brought in by Americans and traded ungoverned by laws and standard rules of the market, touched all levels of New Mexican society. At trade fairs, Indians, Americans, and New Mexicans traded bison hides, captives, woolen textiles, guns, utilitarian iron goods, and agricultural produce from the Pueblos. These exchanges, according to one historian, occurred "beneath the control of [Mexican] customs officers and Indian headmen alike."

Americans, too, participated in the underground distribution of Indian captives, mostly for purposes of marriage or cheap slave labor. Some American men married Pueblo women. This made New Mexico and other parts of the Southwest borderlands more integrated into a continental market economy, extending from the eastern parts of the United States to the west. Ties to native groups in kinship allowed many American trappers and merchants to trade across the Southwest unmolested. In 1837, Apaches, Kiowas, Comanches, and Tawakoni came to a multitribal agreement allowing American traders to conduct business in the Red River region. What brought such agreements together was the market in captives. Some of the men working out of Fort Bent, in service to the American trader William Bent, were captives to the Comanches; one of those men, James Hobbs, married the chief's daughter. William Bent was married to a Cheyenne woman. Neither Mexican nor American law controlled trade in that territory, so American traders moved into the Pueblo communities, some finding wives and setting up small merchant shops. Pueblo wives linked to other pueblos through kin and community further enhanced the role of American traders in New Mexico.

Local economies of friendship and kinship benefited the people of the Southwest borderlands so much that Mexican government efforts to alter the situation led to the **Chimayó Rebellion**. In 1837, President Antonio López de Santa Anna looked to streamline his government. Included in his reform efforts was a new tax on New Mexican residents and property requirements for voting. New Mexicans and a group of Pueblo Indians retaliated in a vicious rage, decapitating and piercing the bodies of Governor Albino Pérez; his secretary of the government, Jesús María Alarid; and the previous governor, Santiago Abreú. The 1837 revolt was not an isolated Indian-led revolt, but a rebellion to protect the local economies benefiting all the people of New Mexico. Many of the rebels were textile workers from the New Mexico weaving production hub of Chimayó. These rebels took control of the capital, Santa Fe, and appointed their own governor, José Angel Gonzalez of Taos. Gonzalez embodied the cultural diversity of the revolt. He was the child of a Pueblo mother and an Indian slave (genízaro). Gonzalez sought to legitimize his power by holding a requiem for the slain governor and sending a letter of loyalty to Mexico City. The center of the rebellion became Taos, where the rebel leader Pablo Montoya had gathered his forces. The revolt was eventually crushed, but local animosities toward state power did not go away.

Brigadier General Stephen Watts Kearney arrived in New Mexico in 1846, when the United States was at war with Mexico. Seeing the Americans as just another group attempting to exert its power over New Mexicans, another intercultural rebel group rose to challenge the newcomers. Excluded from the government and fearful that the United States would clamp down on the local economy of illegal trading, 2,000 rebels, including numerous Pueblo Indians, defeated the Americans in a series of Pueblo raids. The Americans crushed this rebellion as well, but the rebellion reflected the New Mexican resistance to American occupation. It was not until after the Civil War that the Americans finally moved to contain the centuries-old intercultural, local-level trade and violence of the Southwest.

TIMELINE 8.4 TEXAS AND THE BORDERLANDS, 1820–1849

Date	Event
1820s	Coahuiltecans established as one large ethnic group in Texas
1837	Multitribal agreement to allow American traders in the Southwest borderlands Chimayó Rebellion against the Mexican state
1845	Texas becomes independent republic and begins program of ethnic cleansing of Texas Indians Texas achieves statehood Treaty of Council Springs
1849	United States takes New Mexico but cannot stop local-level economy of captivity exchange

Conclusion

Over the course of the first half of the nineteenth century, Indians in the West faced off with the United States. As they pushed westward, American migrants encountered regional and local economies that were at times difficult to understand and were nearly impossible to control. Government efforts to disrupt the political and economic relationships between the Indians of the Upper Missouri and the Sioux failed. Pacific Indians, coastal and interior, became savvy traders as Americans took over Alaska, Oregon, and Washington. American missionaries and settlers tried to change Indian lives and push native peoples onto reservations. The gold rush, American migration into the Oregon territory, and the expansion networks of trade upset the balance within California Indian communities. Forced labor, Indian rebellion, alcohol abuse, sexual violence, and a policy of extermination and interracial relationships tore at the fabric of California Indian families. In the Southwest, Americans tried to impose a market economy on a centuries-old trade in goods and captives, only to face stiff resistance. Whether the West was won or lost depends on one's perspective, but one thing is clear: a hotly contested, violent struggle for control of the West was at the center of American Indian relations by 1850.

Review Questions

1. What was the significance of the Lewis and Clark expedition for Native Americans?
2. How did the Indian landscape of California change in the first half of the nineteenth century?
3. Why did Texans, New Mexicans, and native peoples resist the imposition of state power and authority over local communities?

Recommended Readings

Brooks, James F. *Captives and Cousins: Slavery, Kinship, and Community in the Southwest Borderlands* (Chapel Hill: University of North Carolina Press, 2002). Indispensable to understanding the shifting relations on the Southwest borderlands.

Gibson, James R. *Imperial Russia in Frontier America: The Changing Geography of Supply of Russian America, 1784–1867* (New York: Oxford University Press, 1976). A short but wonderful account of Russian-American economic ventures and interactions with Indians.

Hurtado, Albert L. *Indian Survival on the California Frontier* (New Haven: Yale University Press, 1988). The best account of the California Indians and the arrival of the Americans.

La Vere, David. *The Texas Indians* (College Station: Texas A&M Press, 2004). The most accessible account of the Texas Indians.

Lightfoot, Kent G. *Indians, Missionaries, and Merchants: The Legacy of Colonial Encounters on the California Frontiers* (Oakland: University of California Press, 2006). An effective tracing of the imprint of the white American movement into California on native peoples.

Madley, Benjamin. *An American Genocide: The United States and the California Indian Catastrophe, 1846–1873* (New Haven: Yale University Press, 2017). A powerful treatment of the purposeful destruction of native California.

Ronda, James P. *Lewis and Clark among the Indians* (Lincoln, NE: University of Nebraska Press, 2002). Provides the best ethnographic reconstruction of the Lewis and Clark expedition.

Ruby, Robert H., and John A. Brown. *Indians of the Pacific Northwest* (Norman: University of Oklahoma Press, 1988). The best single survey of the Indians of the Pacific Northwest.

Native American History Online

General Sites

Lewis and Clark: The Journey of the Corps of Discovery (PBS). www.pbs.org/lewisandclark/ A link to understanding the Lewis and Clark expedition.

Welcome to Dalles Oregon. www.el.com/to/thedalles/ This site provides information about the significance of The Dalles.

PBS the American Experience: The Gold Rush. www.pbs.org/wgbh/amex/goldrush/ This webpage offers detailed information about the Gold Rush.

Indians of California–Missionization. www.cabrillo.edu/~crsmith/anth6_missions.html Traces the history of all the California missions. This provides a brief history of the mission system along with a list of California missions.

Anthony Jennings Bledsoe, *Indian Wars of the Northwest.* http://books.google.com/books?id=AfksAAAAYAAJ&printsec=frontcover&dq=california+Indian+wars&lr= A historical account of the California Indian Wars.

Rev. J.J. Methvin, *Andele, or the Mexican-Kiowa Captive.* http://books.google.com/books?id=MSATAAAAYAAJ&pg=PA3&dq=Andele's+captivity+narrative&hl=en&ei=XNSiTsTKB4O6tgeNqI2bBQ&sa=X&oi=book_result&ct=result&resnum=1&ved=0CDEQ6AEwAA#v=onepage&q&f=false The full account of Andele's captivity.

Historical Sites

Lewis and Clark State Historic Site, Hartford, Illinois. www.campdubois.com/ This site was designated as the location for one of the National Signature Events for the commemoration of the Lewis and Clark Bicentennial.

Collections and Archive Program, Smithsonian National Museum of Natural History. https://anthropology.si.edu/archives_collections.html The Collections and Archives Program includes numerous sites related to Arctic natives such as the Yupik of Alaska, sites that detail daily life, histories, languages, and cultural studies.

CHAPTER

9

The Civil War Years, 1861–1865

LUMBEE INDIANS IN THE CIVIL WAR
WAR IN INDIAN TERRITORY AND MINNESOTA
Choosing Sides—The Five Civilized Nations
War in Indian Territory
The Upper Midwest: Sioux Resistance
RESISTANCE IN THE SOUTHWEST AND PLAINS
Navajo Resistance
Bosque Redondo
War in the Colorado Territory

Lumbee Indians in the Civil War

Oppressive heat and humidity blanket coastal North Carolina in summer, and Atlantic winds drive frigid air along the shore in winter. In this climate labored African slaves constructing Fort Fisher as the Southern bulwark of a Confederate defense network around the Wilmington port. The Confederacy intended it to become the "Gibraltar of the South," and by war's end it had earned that reputation, defying Union efforts to capture it.

Construction proved slow, largely because planters in coastal Carolina required their slaves for production of cotton, the manufacture of naval stores, and the harvest of food crops. To overcome the labor shortage, the North Carolina legislature in 1863 allowed the Confederate Army to conscript all "free persons of color" to work on Fort Fisher. Emancipated slaves, free papers in hand, were gathered by the state's Home Guard units, loosely organized military units responsible for protecting the home front, and transported to the coast, as were hundreds of North Carolinians with Indian bloodlines, among them the Lumbee of Robeson County.

Conscripted labor was race based, an expected reality given the white supremacist mindset common

Sioux Indians, c. 1899

Source: Courtesy of Library of Congress Prints and Photographs Division, LC-USZ62–54813

to the region in those years. As a result, Lumbee elicited from the Home Guard units a response as vicious and as unrestrained as the one free blacks suffered. Like a few free blacks across the South, some Lumbee in Robeson County held higher economic standing than many whites. Allen Lowrie, for instance, owned a productive 200-acre farm and provided well for his wife and 12 children. But Home Guard units frequently were comprised of poorer white men who typically justified their raids against Lumbee by labeling the Indians "unpatriotic" and "traitorous." Many whites in the area and, indeed, throughout the coastal regions of the Southeast Atlantic states also regarded those claiming to be "Indian" as actually persons of African descent. Official records and white society generally considered the children of African and Indian parents to be African. With few exceptions, as early as 1773 the North Carolina colonial government listed all non-white, non-slave residents of the coastal plain as "free negroes and mullatos," a phrase reinforced as "free persons of color" in federal census reports between 1790 and 1860 and one that embraced those claiming Indian identity. Moreover, the legacy of British enslavement of Indians and the numerous wars between Native Americans and white Americans in the colonial period continued to shape white views of Indian ethnicity. For these reasons and more, Home Guard units rarely, if ever, made much distinction between former African slaves and those claiming a Native American identity.

Many Lumbee fled into the swamplands to avoid conscripted labor, slipping away from Home Guard units patrolling the countryside and the brutal punishment they inflicted on civilians evading their obligations to the South. Guardsmen frequently plundered Lumbee communities and occasionally murdered those who resisted. Lumbee men in hiding were immediately branded traitors to the Confederacy and to North Carolina, and execution awaited them upon their capture. In the swamps, too, were free blacks escaping labor conscription and poor whites evading compulsory military service. Runaway slaves and escaped Union prisoners of war from the Confederate camp in Florence, South Carolina, also hid there. They all shared a common hatred for the Confederacy, especially for the Home Guard, and a common desire to strike back at their enemies.

The Lumbee Henry Berry Lowrie (also spelled Lowry and Lowery in published works) spent most of his adult life avenging the Home Guard's treatment of his family. Guard members assaulted his mother and sisters during a raid on the Lowrie home, and his father and two brothers were arrested for possessing weapons, a violation of the state law that prohibited "free persons of color" from exercising the rights protected for white citizens. Following a sham trial, the three men were executed. The Lumbee community of Robeson County condemned openly the Home Guard's treatment of the Lowries, and many promised to aid federal forces once they arrived in the territory. In response, Home Guard units torched Indian homes, burned their crops, slaughtered Indian livestock, and confiscated property. Henry Lowrie soon assembled his own raiding party, leading Lumbee from the swamps to attack small Confederate garrisons, harassing the Rebels' lines of supply, destroying cotton still in the field, and ambushing patrols. When opportunity surfaced, they pounced on Home Guard units, more a matter of revenge than military necessity.

In early 1865, elements of the Union army, under Union General William Tecumseh Sherman's command, moved north through South Carolina. The federal plan was to lay siege to Ft. Fisher by land while the Union Navy bombarded it from the sea. Lumbee Indians welcomed Sherman's army and guided them through the swamps directly to Fort Fisher. "Their stance as guerillas in the Civil War," wrote historian Laurence Hauptman, "separates them from most other southeastern Indians." The war was "a defining experience" for the Lumbee, wrote Hauptman. It forced them to reevaluate their standing in North Carolina and take steps to protect their unique racial identity apart from white society.

The Civil War directly affected Native Americans nationally. Thousands voluntarily served the Confederacy while thousands more fought for the Union cause, differing loyalties splitting families and communities. Continued challenges to Indian residency on western lands became bloodier and more brutal, as prewar military supervision gave way to wartime militia aggression. The issue of race snared others, forcing them, as in the case of the Lumbee, to take steps to protect racial identity and place during the war and in the years that followed.

It was a pivotal moment in time for Native Americans, a war leaving its imprint on both the immediate and long-term direction in Indian affairs.

KEY QUESTIONS

1. How was the Civil War in Indian Territory also a civil war among the Cherokee?
2. In what ways were the issues leading to Santee resistance in Minnesota similar to the issues contributing to the wars that raged between Native Americans and non-Indians in the Southwest and southern plains?
3. How did America's Civil War contribute directly to the crises that emerged among the Navajo, Apache, and Cheyenne-Arapaho between 1861 and 1865?

CHRONOLOGY

1861	Congress establishes the Territory of Colorado
	Civil War begins with bombardment of Fort Sumter, Charleston, South Carolina
	Five Civilized Nations seek alliance with Confederate States of America
	Choctaw and Chickasaw Nations sign treaty of alliance with the Confederacy
	Creek Nation "neutrals" are attacked twice by the Confederate Indian Cavalry
1862	Confederate Indians fight in the Battle of Pea Ridge, Arkansas
	The Cherokee Nation capital, Tahlequah, falls to Union and pro-Union Indian forces
	Mescalero Apache surrender to federal authority in New Mexico
	Santee Sioux wage war against Minnesota settlers and the territorial militia
1863	Bosque Redondo Reservation for Apache and Navajo in New Mexico is established
	Survivors of the Santee War are relocated from Minnesota to the Dakota Territory
	In New Mexico, war erupts between the Navajo and New Mexico Volunteers
1864	War between the Territory of Colorado and bands of Cheyenne and Arapaho
	Colorado Volunteers massacre Cheyenne and Arapaho Indians at Sand Creek
1865	Congress begins its investigation of the Sand Creek Massacre
	Confederate General Robert E. Lee surrenders his army to Union General Ulysses S. Grant, effectively ending the Civil War
	Congress concludes its investigation into the massacre at Sand Creek
	The Little Arkansas Treaty provides new reservation for Cheyenne and Arapaho Indians

War in Indian Territory and Minnesota

The burst of cannon shells over Fort Sumter in Charleston Harbor on April 12, 1861 shattered President Abraham Lincoln's hopes for peace. The next day, Lincoln, with great reluctance, issued a call for 75,000 volunteers to enlist in the armed forces of the United States and in so doing committed the nation to civil war. The president did not call for the abolition of slavery in the Southern states, nor did he call for a military conquest of the recently founded Confederacy. Lincoln's goal sounded simple—preservation of the union. It seemed rational, and he expected it to be a goal that could be reached with minimal force of arms and much negotiation once both sides in the conflict realized the brutality of brother fighting brother. It proved anything but simple.

The fiery cauldron that erupted east of the Mississippi River—the deadliest war in history for Americans—pitted Northern states against Southern states, a manufacturing economy against an agrarian one, a population becoming increasingly diverse against a people becoming more homogeneous. War shredded families and alienated citizens from their hometowns and states. Two cultures sharing the same national boundaries were now at war. At stake was the identity of a nation—a people.

The regular U.S. Army fractured as Southerners abandoned their units, choosing loyalty for their home states over the United States. The War Department initially hoped it could train new recruits quickly and sufficiently to battle the Southern armies and in short order defeat the less numerous and poorly equipped Confederates. Although the War Department returned some units to the East in late spring, there seemed little need for the army to consolidate its dispersed regular units west of the Mississippi. The First Battle of Bull Run (Manassas Junction) in July 1861, however, crushed federal hopes for a short war as Southern forces routed Union armies and threatened the city of Washington, D.C. by day's end. Withdrawal of most federal forces from the West was now required, and Washington soon charged the states or territories with their own military defense.

The war quickly enveloped Native Americans. Between 20,000 and 25,000 Native Americans served in federal and Confederate armies combined. No Indian group supplied more men to the Union than did the Iroquois Confederacy, by far the largest Indian group east of the Mississippi River, but Native American groups in Indian Territory (Oklahoma) collectively contributed more manpower to the warring forces. The war in Oklahoma also exposed longstanding divisions among native peoples, divisions previously thought in Washington to be resolved. Additionally, the redeployment of federal troops from the plains and Southwest for military service in the East exposed Indians in those regions to economic, political, social, and cultural designs of territorial governments and populations. How those Native Americans responded to the challenges they faced determined their future.

The Civil War spread rapidly into Indian Territory as both the Union and the Confederacy recognized the strategic value of the area. The contest over that expanse of land threw the Indian Territory residents into the war as combatants and loyalties split between Union and Confederacy divided Indian populations as allies to either side, often pitting Indian against Indian. What developed within Indian Territory was a civil war within the Civil War. Federal and Confederate government promises, kept or broken, continually shifted Native American alliances.

Broken promises exacerbated conditions for the Santee Sioux in Minnesota. Washington's focused attention on the Civil War drew promised resources and annuity payments from the Indians. The withdrawal of federal troops exposed the Sioux to the relentless efforts of white residents in Minnesota to secure fertile Indian lands. Warfare in both Indian Territory and Minnesota between 1861 and 1865, then, was directly a product of the larger war in the East.

Choosing Sides—The Five Civilized Nations

Indian Territory (Oklahoma) was vital to the wartime interests of both Washington and Richmond. Control of the territory offered the Union a base of operations from which federal forces could move against Confederate units in neighboring Arkansas or draw forces from the South's defense of the Mississippi River, a vital supply line for the Confederacy. Oklahoma might also serve as a marshaling center from which the Union could stage military operations against Texas and Louisiana and concurrently complement federal influence in Missouri. If nothing else, the extensive Native American population potentially served as a reservoir of manpower to bolster Union ranks.

Confederates recognized their vulnerability and in early 1861 sought alliances with tribes in the region to confound Union efforts. Southerners also recognized that Indian manpower could be harnessed and placed into combat against Union armies to secure the South's western region and possibly drain federal resources needed desperately in the East. Equally important to the South was its acquisition of the Southwest, giving the Confederacy a corridor to Pacific Coast resources and ports, possible access to silver and gold deposits in the West to finance the eastern war and postwar nation-building plans, and avenues from which Confederate raiders might interdict Union transportation and communication lines between California and the East.

The Confederacy moved quickly to join those Native Americans to the Southern cause, primarily the heavily populated **Five Civilized Nations**. A shared stake in the institution of slavery meant slaveholding Indians held a vested interest in a Confederate victory. In his wide-ranging travel through the region, Confederate Indian Commissioner Albert Pike in 1861 warned tribes of the United States' challenge to their continued residency in Indian Territory. He pointed specifically to Secretary of State William Seward, who just before the war openly called for the federal government's acquisition of Five Civilized Nations' lands and their distribution to white settlers. "The Indian Territory," announced Seward, "must be vacated by the Indians." Pike's heated reference to Seward's proposal only added to the ill will for the United States that still brewed among the territory's Indians. Many personally remembered their forced removal from their eastern homes less than 30 years earlier, and the likelihood of another removal enraged them and their children. The commissioner further pointed to Washington's abandonment of federal military posts and Indian Office agents from the Indian Territory in the wake of Fort Sumter, effectively compromising the Indians' security and abandoning the government's treaty obligations to them. Pike assured Native Americans that tribal sovereignty would be preserved under the Confederate government and military protection would be provided to them. Federal authorities could offer little in response. The Five Nations understood well the truth in Pike's words. Lincoln's Indian commissioner, William P. Dole, responded weakly, promising vaguely that Washington would continue its protection of the Indians' "tribal [and] domestic institutions."

On May 25, 1861, the Chickasaw Nation sided officially with the Confederacy, and three weeks later on June 14 the Choctaw Nation allied itself with the Richmond government. Pike assured the Indians that the Confederate States of America would assume responsibility for annuity payments promised in federal treaties with the Chickasaw and Choctaw and guarantee the Indians' permanent residency on their current lands. By midsummer, each Indian nation raised its own regiment of troops, and each was baptized in combat in the Confederate victory at the Battle of Wilson's Creek near Springfield, Missouri, in late August.

In contrast to Chickasaw and Choctaw unity, the Seminole, Cherokee, and Creek nations divided internally, their people either "neutral" or openly supportive of the Confederacy. Neutrals generally agreed with the pro-Confederates' condemnation of Washington's broken treaties and their anger over the North's decision to withdraw its military protection of Indian Territory. The absence of federal troops seemed to ensure violence against Indians in the Indian Territory and possibly a civil war within Oklahoma. They also decried Seward's plan to remove land from the Five Nations. But neutrality appeared the wiser course than an alliance with the Confederacy. The war, reasoned many, would be long and bloody, and a Union victory seemed most probable given the North's manufacturing capability, its financial reserve, and its larger manpower potential. They worried, too, that the Confederacy would not necessarily reward Indian service, but that a victorious federal government would most certainly punish it. A Union victory would seal the Indians' fate in the territory. For Native Americans residing in Indian Territory, then, choosing sides was not a decision based so much on identity and prewar issues as it was a practical decision to side with the expected winners. In short, the issue for most Seminole, Cherokee, and Creek turned on a simple question: Which alliance would produce the least harm to American Indians?

War in Indian Territory

War fractured the Creek Nation. Daniel McIntosh (mixed-blood) organized and armed Creeks supportive of the Confederacy. Opothleyahola (full-blood) spoke for his settlement of 8,000 Neutrals insisting that the war in the East was only "the white man's war," not the Creeks. Blood already stained other sections of Indian Territory by summer. Fearing the Creek's internal division would lead eventually to a war among Creeks, Opothleyahola appealed to Washington for military aid to defend the tribe and to deny Confederate control of Indian Territory. The War Department, however, could not spare the materiel at that time, struggling as it was not to lose the war on Virginia's battlefields that summer and concurrently marshaling and providing for an army and navy much larger than thought necessary only a few months earlier. Washington's refusal convinced the Neutrals that once again, "Washington has turned against us." In mid-November and again two weeks later, a Confederate Indian cavalry attacked Opothleyahola's community. Although his warriors beat back their attackers, civil war soon enveloped Indian Territory and pitted Indian against Indian. On November 19, a force of Confederate Indians and Texans under Colonel Douglas Cooper's command attacked Neutrals at the Battle of Round Mountain and again in December at Chusto Talasha. The two engagements routed Opothleyahola's army and destroyed all supplies. Opothleyahola and his army escaped, moving north into Kansas on what was later termed the "Trail of Blood on the Ice" and into a period of misery, want, and death.

The debate between neutrality and alliance with the Confederacy also split the Seminoles and the Cherokee in 1861, but among the Cherokee the break fell more along old divisions dating to the Indians' removal from the East in the 1830s. John Ridge, the son of a wealthy and influential Cherokee, had reluctantly supported his peoples' relocation from Georgia, believing the move to be inevitable and hoping that Cherokee compliance would provide some positive return from Washington. Stand Watie assumed command of this group in Oklahoma following Ridge's death. Opposing the Ridge/Watie faction was John Ross and his supporters who vehemently denounced the government's acquisition of Cherokee lands in Georgia and the Indians' compulsory relocation to Indian Territory. The rift between the two groups never healed. As war washed over the nation and Washington vacated federal posts in Indian Territory, the longstanding tensions among Cherokees exploded once more into a blood feud between the Watie and Ross factions.

Stand Watie championed the Confederacy, believing Cherokee alliance with the South might yield advantages for his people in a postwar Confederate nation. He believed the Confederacy's defensive strategy for war would prove more likely of success than the Union's offensive plan. John Ross, however, feared the war's imprint on the Cherokees. At a minimum, involvement in the war guaranteed the death of many young Cherokee men. An alliance with the Confederacy also assured the wholesale destruction of tribal sovereignty and another forced removal from Indian lands should the Union win the war. Ross chose neutrality. "The Cherokees are your friends, but we do not wish to be brought into the feuds between yourselves and your Northern Brethren," he informed the Confederate Indian commissioner. "We have done nothing to bring about the conflict in which you are engaged with your own people, and I am unwilling that my people shall become its victims," he added. "Our wish is for peace. Peace at home and Peace among you," he said. Ross understood, too, that in the long run it mattered little whether the Confederacy or Union won the coming war. Indian policy under either government would not likely change fundamentally. Indeed, Ross was probably correct in his assessment. Unknown to the Cherokee, Commissioner Pike explained to President Jefferson Davis that his minimal concessions to the Indians were "really far more for our benefit than for theirs." "It is we . . . who are interested to have this country . . . opened to settlement and made into a state," he said.

In mid-July 1861, the Confederacy commissioned Stand Watie a colonel in the Southern army and approved his raising a regiment of Indian soldiers. His troops engaged Union forces in the Battle of Wilson's Creek, alongside the Choctaws and Chickasaws. That Confederate victory, coming on the heels of the Union disaster at

PROFILE

Stand Watie
(Cherokee, 1806–1871)

National Archives and Records Administration, 529026

De-ga-ta-ga (He Stands), better known in history as Stand Watie, was born near Rome, Georgia, on December 12, 1806. Little is known of his childhood, but as a young man he believed the Cherokee removal to Indian Territory best assured Cherokee cultural and physical survival, thus he signed the Treaty of Echota in 1835.

With the start of the American Civil War, Stand Watie aligned himself with the Confederacy. He was an ardent defender of slavery and blamed the federal government more than Georgia settlers for the Cherokee removal 25 years earlier. On July 12, 1861, the Confederacy commissioned him a colonel in the army, and he quickly organized a regiment of Cherokee vol-

9.1 Stand Watie

Source: National Archives and Records Administration (NARA), Washington, D.C.

unteers, the Cherokee Regiment of Mounted Rifles. During the war, Stand Watie's unit battled Union troops and Indian Neutrals in nearly 20 major engagements and numerous skirmishes throughout Indian Territory and into Arkansas. Among his most celebrated accomplishments was his remarkable defense of the Confederate retreat after the Battle of Elkhorn Tavern (March 6, 1862) and his seizure of $1,500,000 in Union supplies on September 19, 1864. The Confederacy promoted him to brigadier general on May 6, 1864, the only Native American during the war to earn that rank. Although Robert E. Lee surrendered the Army of Northern Virginia on April 9, 1865, Stand Watie continued to lead his troops in battle until June 23, the last Confederate force to lay down its arms. After the war, Stand Watie retired to his home in Honey Creek and on September 9, 1871, the General and Cherokee Principal Chief died in his sleep.

Bull Run (Manassas Junction) in Virginia, emboldened Cherokees as yet not aligned with either tribal faction or either eastern government. It also forced a change of tone from John Ross. Noted historian Phillip Weeks, "desperately hoping to block the ascendency of Watie" to greater influence among his people in the wake of victory, "Ross dramatically altered his stand" and on August 21 announced *his* intention to join with the Confederacy. Only in this manner, Ross believed, could the will of his faction receive any real consideration from the pro-Confederate Cherokees. "We are in the situation of a man standing alone upon a low naked spot of ground with the water rising all around him," said Ross. "The tide carries by him . . . a drifting log . . . [and] he is a doomed man" who refuses to latch onto it. "By seizing hold of it he has a chance for his life." Ross chose union with the Confederate States. The alliance was made official in October, and the Cherokee Nation signed a treaty with the Confederate States of America. In so doing it sealed their nation's fate with the Union. Those still desiring neutrality ventured north and joined with Opothleyahola's exiled Creeks.

In spring 1862, the war spilled furiously into Arkansas. Union strategists considered it absolutely vital to control the southern half of the Mississippi River, which the Confederates used as a highway for shipping supplies and personnel. Toward that end, forces under Union General Ulysses S. Grant struck Confederate defenses in Tennessee while one of his divisions of 10,000 soldiers moved into Arkansas and stormed Confederate defenders at Elkhorn Tavern on March 6. That battle spanned two full days, each side inflicting horrendous casualties on the other. The Battle of Pea Ridge, as it came to be known, brought 16,000 Confederates into the fight, among them 3,500 Indians. On the second day of fighting, federal troops broke the Confederate attack and forced their retreat, which Colonel Stand Watie and his Cherokee regiment protected.

The Battle of Pea Ridge at Elkhorn Tavern was a decisive victory for the Union, exposing both Arkansas and neighboring Indian Territory to possible Union control. Toward that end, federal units coordinated a military expedition deep into Indian Territory that intended to destroy the Native American alliance with the Confederacy and once more extend federal authority over the Indians there. Neutrals residing in Kansas joined with pro-Union Indians and Union armies in February.

Cherokee resistance melted across northern Indian Territory as they confronted nearly 5,000 armed Native Americans and twice that number of federal cavalry and infantry units. With the fall of the Cherokee capital Tahlequah in summer, thousands of Indians renounced their allegiance to the Confederacy and pledged their loyalty to the United States. Federal troops arrested John Ross. He, too, recanted his support for the Confederacy and assumed leadership of the pro-Union faction of the Cherokee Nation. Hearing the news of Ross's defection, Stand Watie as principal chief of the Cherokee Nation once again promised his continued support for the Confederacy. In summer 1863, another Union push across Indian Territory commenced, scattering pro-Confederate Indians.

Events elsewhere, however, overshadowed Union efforts in Indian Territory. The bloodbath at Gettysburg, Pennsylvania, in July scored a resounding victory for federal armies, driving Confederate forces under General Robert E. Lee's command southward and into a defensive struggle that continued for the next two years. It also severely drained both sides of manpower and supplies, losses the Confederacy could ill afford. It was an especially important moment in the war. Only one day after Gettysburg, Union forces under General Ulysses S. Grant compelled the surrender of Vicksburg, Mississippi, the final major Confederate defensive position on the Mississippi River. Its collapse, along with federal control of New Orleans, effectively placed the water highway in Union hands, completing one of Washington's major goals. The War Department was now in position to focus offensive operations on Richmond and split the South in half from Tennessee to the Georgia coast. Aggressive Union generals such as William Tecumseh Sherman promised to "make Georgia howl" and bring hell upon the Confederacy. In short, Washington now planned to direct every available soldier and all available supplies against the Old South. To do this, the War Department redeployed eastward most of its forces in Indian Territory.

Without a large federal presence in Oklahoma, Indian Territory became a cauldron of death for the next two years as pro-Union and pro-Confederate Indian regiments waged merciless war on one another, "turning the once bountiful Indian Territory into a no-man's-land of terror, disruption, and desolation." General Robert E. Lee surrendered his armies to General Ulysses Grant at Appomattox Courthouse on April 9, 1865, effectively ending hostilities between the North and the South, but battles continued to rage in Oklahoma until June 23 when Stand Watie, now holding the rank of general, finally conceded defeat near Doaksville, the Choctaw Nation capital.

Four years of war devastated Indian Territory. Physical wreckage littered the region, and the death rate seemed inconceivable. Equally destructive was the splintering of tribal and family lines, divisions that never healed and contributed to broader factionalizing of Indian peoples in the postwar years.

9.2 The Battle of Pea Ridge at Elkhorn Tavern in March 1862, a key battle of the Civil War, was one of the first in which American Indian troops engaged in combat outside Indian territory.

Source: Courtesy of Library of Congress Prints and Photographs Division, LC-DIG-pga-01888

After he repudiated his alliance with the Confederacy, John Ross in November 1862 had appealed to Abraham Lincoln for a presidential pardon blanketing all Cherokee who aligned themselves with the Confederate States. Lincoln promised to consider his request after the war and to give his attention to Native American issues in Indian Territory. The president did not suggest leniency, but he also did not imply punitive measures. Given Lincoln's desire for a rapid integration of Southern states back into the union and his expressed wish to heal the wounds of war quickly, it is quite possible the president would have attended to affairs in Indian Territory with the same interest and spirit of justice he intended for the South. His assassination in April 1865 took the nation down a different path.

Radical Republican rule after 1865 exposed Indians to their prewar fears. Congress imposed treaties on each of the Five Civilized Nations, each treaty requiring Indians to relinquish properties that collectively totaled the western half of Oklahoma, grant rights-of-way through Indian Territory for railroads yet to be constructed, and cede land for other tribal groups soon to be relocated to the region. Pro-Confederate Indians certainly lost much as a result of siding with the South, but Neutrals and pro-Union Indians also lost. Their cooperation or alliances with Washington mattered little. Washington began relocating more western tribes to Indian Territory, and reservation acreage decreased for those already there. There were no rewards for loyal service.

The Upper Midwest: Sioux Resistance

In the decade before war ripped apart the United States, nearly 150,000 settlers poured into Minnesota, a migration that compelled Washington to force Minnesota's Santee Sioux to accept two treaties that together stripped the Indians of nearly 30 million acres of land and confined them to a small reservation along the southern bank of the Minnesota River. By 1862, the Santee were reduced to living on a narrow strip of land one-tenth the original size of their territory. Embedded in those treaties were programs, restrictions, and expectations that collectively aimed to eradicate Native culture and to "make white men" of the Indians. The treaties and the Indians' already diminished quality of life drove a wedge among the Santee, splitting the tribe into two distinct factions. "Blanket Santee" resisted adapting to white culture, refusing to be schooled in the trades, to speak the English language, and to abandon traditional values. "Farmer Santee" feared overt resistance would encourage Minnesotans to demand Sioux removal from the territory. To remain on or reasonably close to their traditional lands, they reluctantly bent themselves toward the concept of private land ownership, Christianity, and the "white man's ways." Many, among them the venerated chief Little Crow, cut their long hair, wore settlers' clothing, moved into homes similar to those of Minnesotans, and even attempted farming. All of this was a conscious effort to attain limited accommodation to permit their continued residency on their lands, their spiritual center and source of identity.

9.3 Little Crow

Source: Library of Congress Prints and Photographs Division, LC-USZ61-83

PROFILE

Little Crow (Tayoyateduta or Thaoyate Duta, for His Red Nation), 1810–1862

Little Crow, born in 1810 in the Mdewakanton Dakota village Kaposia near present-day St. Paul, Minnesota, was by all accounts a fearless young man. He learned to read and write English so he could better defend Santee interests as white settlement expanded rapidly in Minnesota. He succeeded his father as a chief in 1846 and was one of the Sioux representatives to sign the Treaty of Traverse des Sioux with the United States that promised the Indians guaranteed and protected tribal residency along the Minnesota River. The U.S. Senate, however, retracted the assigned lands prior to ratification and compelled the Sioux to accept a revised treaty or confront forced removal from Minnesota to the Dakota Territory.

In 1858, Little Crow and other Santee representatives journeyed to Washington, D.C., and there met with President James Buchanan in a bid to secure his promise to protect Sioux land and to honor treaty provisions. Little Crow, and other like-minded Santee, adopted as his own the clothing of white Americans, the Christian religion, and farming as evidence of his willingness to accommodate himself to the society that now enveloped the Santee.

By 1862, the war between the Union and Confederacy was draining money and necessary supplies from the Santee, and Indian agents and suppliers also channeled additional funds and material earmarked for Indians into their own coffers. Moreover, white settlement in Minnesota surged, making greater demands on land. Following a series of confrontations and facing further threats to their existence, the Santee responded with a series of attacks on Minnesota farms, communities, and militia posts. Little Crow agreed with some hesitation to lead warriors into battle, knowing as he did that the Indians were at a military disadvantage. Throughout summer 1862, Little Crow and his warriors battled the Minnesota militias and citizens until the Indians were soundly defeated at the Battle of Wood Lake on September 23. He fled to Canada with many followers. In mid-June the following year, Little Crow and his son slipped back into Minnesota to gather horses and desperately needed supplies for his family and followers. On July 3, near the town of Hutchinson, a farmer named Nathan Lampson spotted Little Crow and fired on him. Little Crow fell dead. The townspeople were informed of Little Crow's death and shared in the mutilation of the Santee's body. Lampson earned not only the traditional bounty offered by Minnesota for killing an Indian but also an additional $500 for having shot Little Crow specifically. The bones of Little Crow were displayed in a local museum and later held by the Minnesota Historical Society until 1971, when his remains were sent to a surviving grandson for proper burial.

The resulting schism shattered Santee communities. The rapidly growing white population around them exacerbated Santee disunity. Hunger and malnutrition settled over the Santee as white settlement depleted hunting grounds of game and Washington failed to provide farm extension agents to aid agricultural development as promised in the treaties. Only the annual annuity payments Washington gave to the Santee averted further disaster, but these soon disappeared as they increasingly filtered into the hands of traders and reservation agents. Congress absolved itself of guilt, contending that the Santee food shortage of the 1850s was the product of the Indians' limited initiative to learn farming techniques, and annuities deferred to the war's end might compel the Santee to create the agricultural base intended by treaties.

The winter of 1861–1862 proved particularly brutal on the Santee as remaining food stores were consumed and death rates rose among the Indians. Washington's attention was focused solely on the government's withering war in the East. By summer 1862, hunger, disease, and depression shrouded every moment of Santee life. "We have no food," said Little Crow, "but there are stores, filled with food. We ask that you, the agent, make some arrangement by which we can get food . . . or else we may take our own way to keep ourselves from starving." The deep divide that had earlier corrupted Santee unity now shrank quickly, the Indians finding a common target for their anger in white settlers and Washington, especially as malnourished and dying Sioux saw all around themselves a white population fattened on former Santee lands and Indian annuities. In August, a group of Indians residing in the southern section of the reservation requested food rations from their appointed agent, Thomas Galbraith. Galbraith, backed by heavily armed local white merchants, refused the Santees' appeal. "So far as I am concerned," sneered merchant Andrew Myrick, "if they are hungry, let them eat grass or their own dung."

After a decade of land loss, cultural and personal insult, pervasive hunger, and disunion among the Santee, Minnesota's Sioux now recognized an opportunity to strike back as the few remaining federal military units in

Minnesota were redeployed to service in the East and South. Without a strong military presence in the region, many Santee determined the moment appropriate to lash out and perhaps push white settlement out of the region and reclaim much of what they had lost over the previous ten years. Tribal elders issued dire warnings should the Santee wage war on white settlers. "The white men are like the locusts when they fly so thick that the whole sky is a snowstorm. . . . You may kill one—two—ten . . . [but] white men with guns in their hands will come faster than you can count," said Little Crow.

A small party of Santee nonetheless ventured north beyond the reservation. On August 17, their path crossed a group of settlers from whom the Indians took eggs, vegetables, and some meat. A heated verbal exchange between the Indians and whites erupted into violence, and five of the settlers were killed. What actually prompted the skirmish remains unclear. White survivors insisted to authorities that they offered no physical threats against the Santee. The Indians, they claimed, approached them determined to shed white blood and wantonly murdered the five men. The Santee party returned home that evening and informed Little Crow of the firefight, insisting the incident was one of self-defense. Regardless of the cause for violence, the Santee were convinced that Minnesotans would want to visit hell upon the Indians. A fierce debate erupted among the Santee that night. Many Sioux demanded a peace overture be sent to white authorities while others called for a preemptive strike against nearby settlements. The unity that so recently emerged shattered once again, the Indians now divided between war and peace.

Several war parties formed during the night and early the next day raided nearby farms. In one of these attacks, Santee warriors killed Andrew Myrick, leaving a clump of grass in his lifeless mouth. More Santee joined the war parties that now aimed their strikes against white settlements the length of the Minnesota Valley, devastating every farm, village, and town they encountered. Settlers abandoned their homes and fled to Fort Ridgely where they reinforced the small volunteer military garrison. On August 20, the Sioux attacked the fort hoping to destroy it and continue south into the valley beyond. Defenders repelled the Santee after three

TIMELINE 9.1 THE SUMMER REBELLION, 1862

Date	Event
August 17	A small party of Santee kill five Minnesota residents near Acton
August 18	The Lower Sioux Agency explodes in open resistance
August 20–22	Various Sioux bands join together and attack Fort Ridgely
August 23	Battle at New Ulm
August 27	Colonel Henry Sibley arrives at Fort Ridgely with supplies and 250 additional troops
September 2	Colonel Sibley's troops are defeated at Birch Coulee
September 23	The Battle at Wood Lake delivers a crippling loss to the Indians
September 26	The Santee release 270 captives and surrender themselves, ending the rebellion
December 26	Thirty-eight Indians, all charged and convicted of murder and rape, are hanged
February and March	The U.S. Congress voids all treaties previously ratified with the Santee

days of bitter fighting. By August 23, the death toll for Minnesotans varied wildly depending on the source, from six hundred to "nearly a thousand, . . . and nameless outrages were committed on many." In addition to human casualties, "millions of dollars worth of property were destroyed" by the Santee, noted one observer.

General John Pope oversaw the Department of the Northwest. With no regular army forces available, Pope ordered the Third Minnesota Volunteers, under Colonel Henry Sibley's command, to "exterminate the Sioux." The Santee, he said, were uncontrollable animals fit only for destruction. Sibley was to conduct "total war" against the Sioux—kill the warriors and deny to all Santee by any means necessary both the ability to fight and the will to resist.

Sibley's army challenged a weakened Santee force at Wood Lake on September 23, 1862. Many of the warriors had abandoned the fight following their attack on Fort Ridgely. Some of them had returned home to provide for their families. Others assumed wrongly that the staggering casualty rate inflicted on settlers had effectively conveyed the message that government must attend to Indian needs. A few even believed vengeance had been accomplished. Regardless of their reason for breaking off the fight, their return home spelled doom for the Indians gathered for battle. The Battle at Wood Lake crushed Santee armed resistance. A few survivors fled into the Dakota Territory, found homes among the Teton Sioux, and contemplated their return to Minnesota.

The Third Minnesota Volunteers took 1,500 prisoners, warriors captured on the battlefield but also women, children, and men who remained neutral during the Indians' campaign. It mattered little to either Washington officials or Minnesota citizens what role, if any, individual Santee played in the recent crisis. White settlers demanded total retribution and delivered a nearly unanimous call for the systematic extermination of all Santee. General Pope shared their sentiment but tempered his emotions. He charged 390 Indian prisoners with crimes, tried them under military law, and convicted 320 of them. Of those convicted, 303 received the death sentence. Pope informed President Lincoln of the court's rulings, but the president ordered that executions be delayed until he reviewed personally the conviction of each prisoner. Based on his reading of the transcripts and advice Commissioner of Indian Affairs William Dole offered, Lincoln approved the execution of only 38 men who, he believed, had clearly murdered and raped. The evidence against these individuals was circumstantial at best and probably contrived. It has since been suggested that Lincoln could not accept the execution of more than 300 individuals, fearing a backlash among European countries then pondering an alliance with the Confederacy. At the same time, it is argued that he understood that voters in the next presidential race

SEEING HISTORY

The Execution of Santee Sioux

In 1862, Minnesota Territorial government executed 38 of 320 Santee convicted of various alleged crimes and for initiating war in the territory. President Abraham Lincoln personally sanctioned the executions. There remains significant debate regarding the president's rationale in approving the executions. Soon afterward, all Santee Indians still residing in Minnesota were relocated to the Dakota Territory.

Questions

1. What values or perspectives does the background and foreground imagery suggest?
2. How does the painting address the concept of "identity"?

9.4 Hanging at the Santee Sioux Reservation in Minnesota, 1862

Source: Courtesy of Library of Congress Prints and Photographs Division, cph 3a04167

would remember his response to the current crisis and, therefore, he felt compelled to execute a number of Santee. What is certain is that President Lincoln promised in a letter to the governor $2,000,000 to Minnesota and Washington's agreement to remove physically all Indians from Minnesota. The executions were carried out at Fort Mankato, Minnesota, on December 26.

Others continued to support the president and saw wisdom in his response. Lincoln, they contended, expected the hangings to be just and fair punishment for those who committed the most serious offenses, and his position most likely reflected his own understanding of war's brutality. His decision not to punish an entire population also revealed his developing perspective toward the Confederacy. It was Congress, they insisted, that proved less lenient. On March 3, 1863, Congress revoked its treaties with the Santee and ordered the Indians' relocation to a useless parcel of land in the Dakota Territory. Forced removal commenced in early May.

Regardless of Lincoln's motives, the fate of the Santee stood as a warning to Indians of the northern plains, especially the Teton Sioux who had opened their homes to Santee refugees. White migration into the Dakota Territory increased in 1863, and the Sioux responded with immediate, unified, and determined resistance to preserve their lands, their culture, and their identity. In spring 1863, they and the Santee refugees pledged themselves to halt all white traffic into or through the Dakota Territory and toward that end they routinely attacked wagons, stagecoaches, and anyone venturing into the region. General Pope deployed a few recently available regular army units against the combined Sioux force. The major clash Pope expected never materialized, but the presence of American troops in the Dakota Territory further enraged the Sioux, who by summer carried their raids into Nebraska and Kansas. The Sioux threat was by no means a small one. More than 14,000 Indians resided in the region, among them the 2,000 Santee removed from Minnesota.

Ineffective military operations against the Sioux continued into 1865. Pope initiated each operation, which the Sioux then effectively challenged. Indeed, by midyear Washington had spent nearly $40,000,000 on the Indian campaigns in Minnesota and the Dakota Territory, an expense that drew money from the war in the East and the South's postwar reconstruction. The cost of annuity payments and care of the Sioux that treaties required would have been but a fraction of that cost. The willingness of the federal and territorial officials to commit themselves to such an expense, not to mention the cost in lives and property, demonstrated clearly their preferred solution to the "Indian problem." The failure of the military, however, testified to the Indians' determination to resist all threats to their land, their ways of living, and their cultures. It also was evidence of the U.S. Army's weakened presence in the West as a result of the war against the Confederacy.

There were voices of peace and reason in 1865, even if many of them were based on self-interest. The governor of Dakota Territory understood the Indians preferred peace—a peace that preserved and protected their residency on the lands they cherished. He appealed to Washington and by summer a peace commission crafted treaties with one dozen bands of Sioux, each treaty pledging the right of Sioux to live on the lands over which they earlier had fought, an annuity of $15 per person per year, and supplemental food and supplies. By all accounts, the various Sioux bands remained "faithful" to the treaties they accepted as autumn faded into winter; however, government support did not materialize as promised, and many Indians endured "terrible sufferings from cold and from lack of food." Peace was tenuous at best in late 1865.

Resistance in the Southwest and Plains

The "brothers' war" that raged in the East never forced tribes of the Southwest and Great Plains to choose sides as it did those residing in Indian Territory, and the clash of blue and gray armies never threatened directly their security. Nonetheless, the war's shadow reached deep into their homeland and altered the course of their lives. The U.S. Army before 1861 maintained a presence in the territories to protect Native Americans from settlers almost as much as it was there to defend settlers from Indians. But the army's absence after 1861 gave white settlers the opportunity to attack bands of Indians and to remove them forcibly from fertile farmlands, grazing areas, and lands rich in gold and silver deposits. At its simplest level, settlers desired the elimination of all perceived threats Native Americans presented to their continued occupancy of former Indian lands. Early on, many Indian leaders pursued accommodation with white demands, not out of fear or weakness but rather as a means of preserving their people's existence, their identity. They accommodated until accommodation proved futile, after which they resorted to arms. Over the next four years, blood soaked the Southwest and Great Plains and laid the foundation for Washington's postwar redirection of Indian policy.

Navajo Resistance

Most regular U.S. Army units posted in New Mexico in spring 1861 either moved west into California to defend the state from potential Rebel activity or, as in Oklahoma and Minnesota, east to join the war against the Confederacy. New Mexico raised its own militia to provide order, enforce law, and maintain the peace with Navajos. Failure was certain. In little time after the departure of federal units, the Navajo launched a series of

Table 9.1 Navajo Removals by Month/Year and Approximate Number of Navajo

August	1863	51
October	1863	21
November	1863	455
January	1864	1,400
February	1864	2,140
March	1864	3,480
April	1864	1,650
May	1864	810
June	1864	660
August	1864	285
September	1864	275
October	1864	2,000
April	1865	920
May	1865	700

Source: Based on Neal W. Ackerly, *A Navajo Diaspora: The Long Walk to Hweeldi* (Silver City, New Mexico: Dos Rios Consultants, 1998).

raids against New Mexico settlements. Although Indian raids and counterstrikes by settlers were the norm in prewar New Mexico, settlers now viewed the routine differently. They now felt especially vulnerable to the Navajo who greatly outnumbered New Mexicans. In summer 1862, Washington repositioned federal troops from California to New Mexico to counter Confederate forces rumored to be marching into the Southwest, and their return calmed the nerves of most settlers.

General James Carleton assumed command of U.S. military forces in New Mexico and neighboring Arizona, and his friend, famed scout and trapper Colonel Kit Carson, took charge of the New Mexico Volunteers. The much-anticipated Confederate move into the Southwest failed to develop, but the War Department instructed Carleton to keep his forces in the region as a deterrent to any future consideration by the Richmond government to strike west. Without soldiers in gray to battle, the general's ears opened to the expressed fears and concerns of white settlers in the territory, and he quickly decided to end the so-called "Indian problem" in the region. He envisioned a campaign that would destroy the Indians' ability to wage war, break their will to resist, and concentrate them onto a reservation at **Bosque Redondo** on the Pecos River in southeastern New Mexico (see Map 9.1). Once there, the Navajos and their descendants would be Americanized. Noted one observer, the general's goal was for "the old Indians [to] die off and carry with them all latent longings for murdering and robbing." Indians would acculturate themselves to the behavior and values of the white world, and, in time, they would be assimilated into mainstream society. From the ashes of Navajo culture would rise Americans, contributing positively to the further development of the United States, or at the very least not impeding territorial and national development.

Carleton's view meshed well with President Lincoln's. Lincoln himself hoped to encourage development of the West during the war years, and both the president and Congress moved in that direction once it was determined that the Southern states were unable to delay Northern plans. The Lincoln administration wasted little time arranging for the financing and construction of the first transcontinental railroad. Congress and the president also granted Nevada statehood, posted federal troops and built forts in western lands rich in gold

Map 9.1 Bosque Redondo, New Mexico

and silver, and opened millions of acres for settlement under the Homestead Act. Many Americans saw the continued presence of Native Americans in the West as an impediment to Washington's plans for national expansion. The Lincoln White House agreed and proposed the removal of American Indians from lands suited to white settlement and economic return.

In New Mexico, Carleton's eyes were not fixed solely on Navajos. Mescalero Apaches also found themselves targeted by the general and the New Mexico Volunteers. Like their Navajo neighbors, the Apaches understandably resisted. The land itself defined their existence, their values, and their very understanding of life. It embodied the spirit of the Apache. They could not relinquish it without a fight. In a series of raids in August 1862, the Mescalero reportedly killed more than three dozen men and several children, taking cattle, horses, and other animals from the ranches they attacked. The Apaches viewed these strikes as acts of self-defense, essential for the protection of their own way of life and the survival of their people.

As summer 1862 waned, Carleton ordered militia units into a coordinated campaign against the Navajos and Mescalero. The militia was to exert ruthless, unrelenting brutality against all Indian warriors encountered. They were to take only women and children as prisoners, and they were to raze villages, torch crops, and feed livestock to the troops. Under Kit Carson's leadership, the volunteer army slashed across western New Mexico and eastern Arizona with unbounded ferocity. Aware of the holocaust that approached, many smaller Mescalero bands filtered word to Carleton of their willingness to halt their resistance and to relocate peaceably to a reservation. By March 1863, nearly 400 Mescalero were under federal control. Carleton established the Bosque Redondo

9.5 Christopher Carson, known as Kit Carson (1809–1868)

Source: Courtesy of Library of Congress Prints and Photographs Division, LC-DIG-cwpbh-00514

reservation and there constructed Fort Sumner to house the soldiers who would guard the Indians. For the Mescalero, resistance now turned from armed violence to more subtle tactics of cultural preservation.

In contrast, Navajos refused to surrender. Bosque Redondo lay far from their ancestral territory, their spiritual center and source of identity. In summer 1863, General Carleton sent Carson into Navajo country to utterly destroy all Indian resistance. Carson was to wage total war against the Navajo unless the Indians surrendered themselves and willingly relocated to Bosque Redondo. Carleton sent word to Navajo leaders that they had until July 20 to comply with his order of surrender or face unimaginable horrors. "After that day, every Navajo that is seen will be considered as hostile and treated accordingly," he said.

The deadline passed with very few Indians taking Carleton's offer. In midsummer 1863, only days after the battles at Gettysburg and Vicksburg back east, Carson launched his campaign against the Navajos. He led his troops from Fort Canby, ranging widely throughout Dinetah, or the land of the Dine people, in search of Navajo war parties and villages. Seldom did he engage the Indians, the Navajos generally remaining a few steps ahead of Carson's approaching soldiers. Nonetheless, his relentless search and pursuit allowed the Indians little rest and few opportunities to move their stored foods and livestock to safety. Carson confiscated Indian crops and meat and issued them to his own troops, destroying all that could not be eaten or carried away. Burned, too, were all Navajo homes, tools, blankets, baskets, pots, and other goods abandoned by fleeing Indians. In essence, Carson waged a scorched-earth strategy against his enemy, driving the Navajos into Canyon de Chelly where they awaited winter hungry and ill-clothed.

Going against common practice, Carson commenced a winter campaign that extended from mid-December 1863 through early February 1864, and he divided his army into two separate forces. His unit moved eastward through the canyon, placing into custody all who surrendered and prosecuting a war without mercy against those who resisted. He sent Captain Albert Pfeiffer north of the canyon and to the eastern rim, a move that required several days of travel. At each camp made by Pfeiffer, Navajo women and children surrendered to the soldiers, driven to submission by starvation and bitter cold. Wrote one historian, Pfeiffer "and his men did not harm these people, in spite of the fact that Apaches had killed Pfeiffer's own wife and baby." Once in position, Pfeiffer received orders from Carson instructing him to advance west through Canyon de Chelly. Carson had put into motion a classic pincer operation.

Surviving Navajos and the men under Carson's command later disagreed about the extent of actual combat during the winter campaign. The army reported few incidents of battle and very few Indian deaths. Navajos, however, insisted that attacks were frequent and often accompanied by unmatched cruelty and dismemberment of Indian bodies. Carson's campaign did not eradicate Navajo resistance. Nearly 10,000 Navajos refused surrender and straggled northwest of the canyon, deep into Hopi lands, but at least another 10,000 Indians reluctantly laid down their weapons.

Carson did not defeat the Navajo through battle. Most armed clashes between Native Americans and soldiers were brief periods of ferocity and terror followed by prolonged periods of maneuvering, retreat, and pursuit. The colonel's success was largely the product of tactics. The Indians did not anticipate Carson's winter campaign. Traditionally, Indian raids and wars occurred in warm months—the raiding months—during which the Navajo were most likely to score the foods, hides, and fabrics they wanted from more sedentary, agrarian tribes or white settlements. Winter was generally a period to settle down and endure the bitter weather. Commencing his campaign in December caught the Indians by surprise and ill-prepared for war. Retreating during winter meant there would be little food available beyond that which the Navajo could carry. As food supplies dwindled, the Navajo weakened, a situation only exacerbated by disease and extended exposure to the elements. Equally important, among the Navajo were women, children, and old folks—people who slowed the retreat and exposed warriors to more frequent battle to protect retreating Indians. Continuous retreat weakened the non-combatants and threatened the very survival of loved ones. Surrender was the Navajos' only recourse to guarantee their survival.

Bosque Redondo

Navajo relocation to Bosque Redondo began in early winter 1864, a 450-mile overland journey known since as "**the Long Walk**." To this day, the Long Walk inspires the same sense of horror as the Cherokees' Trail of Tears nearly 30 years earlier in which 4,000 Indians, or one-fifth of the Cherokee Nation, died en route to Indian Territory. Because the surrendered Navajo were temporarily held at several army posts, the Long Walk was actually multiple migrations. The first group of 1,500 Navajo left Fort Wingate heading east, followed days later by another 2,400 who exited Fort Canby. As William Young wrote in *Quest for Harmony*, "by the second day coyotes followed the contingent and hawks and crows circled overhead, waiting for Navajo to die. New Mexicans followed the convoy to pick off stragglers to sell as slaves. If a woman went into labor, she was killed. Those too weak to continue were also shot." Nine thousand Navajo found themselves at Bosque Redondo by summer's end, joining the 400 or so Mescalero Apache already there.

The living conditions at Bosque Redondo proved horrendous. The reservation was terribly overcrowded. Pneumonia, dysentery, and other diseases claimed hundreds of lives. The alkaline soil along the Pecos River produced poor-quality crops and too little food to feed such a large population. Washington earmarked $100,000 for supplies and food, but only one-third of it ever reached Bosque Redondo. The supply of housing never met demand and forced families to accommodate strangers in their already crowded homes. In November, the Mescalero fled the reservation and returned to their homeland. The army now advised Indians that all those who attempted to leave the reservation would be shot on sight. Despair settled over most Navajo.

There were, however, some positive signs for the Indians. The army never corralled the escaped Mescalero. That failure encouraged nearly 1,000 Navajo to flee the reservation in 1865 for their traditional lands. The deplorable conditions at Bosque Redondo also piqued the attention of Congress, which empaneled a joint House-Senate Committee to investigate. Their report, presented to Congress late in the year, criticized severely the state of affairs at the reservation and condemned specifically General Carleton for Bosque Redondo's pathetic condition and the army's mistreatment of Navajo during their march to the reservation the

9.6 Navajos under guard at Bosque Redondo, c. 1864

Source: National Archives and Records Administration

previous year. Such treatment of Indians, it was reasoned, would likely foster intense resistance among those still not under federal control and would probably encourage resistance among those who were already on reservations. The report reflected an emerging humanitarian spirit of reform in Indian affairs. Based on the committee's findings, Carleton was soon thereafter relieved of his command. General Ulysses Grant in November 1867 ordered Bosque Redondo removed from the War Department's jurisdiction and placed under the authority of the Indian Office. By then the reform spirit had surfaced and entrenched itself in the East, and in little time the Indian Office would initiate a fundamental change at the Navajo reservation.

War in the Colorado Territory

Gold strikes in the Pike's Peak region in 1858 and the Clear Creek area in 1859 lured to Colorado more than 100,000 prospectors, miners, businessmen, and others seeking quick wealth. As elsewhere in the mining frontier, the human tide that rushed to the territory brought with it horrific consequences to the environment and to the people native to that area. Hydraulic mining (strip mining) washed away forest-covered mountainsides. Small towns littered a landscape until recently untouched by eastern civilization, and most of which were deserted within a few months of their founding. New arrivals overhunted the forests, severely depopulated buffalo herds, deforested woodlands, and polluted water supplies. They also interfered with Indian migration patterns, carried a myriad of diseases into the region, and demanded extensive acreage for ranching and farming initiatives beyond their demanded access to gold deposits.

On February 28, 1861, Congress established the Colorado Territory, planting federal law in the region and in so doing encouraging further settlement of the area. White migration into and through the territory surged. Many easterners were escaping the carnage of the war they knew was coming, others sought business or farming opportunities in developing territories, and some simply pursued adventure. Native Americans recognized quickly the threat white settlement posed.

Colorado Indians debated their options. Many Cheyenne and Arapaho called for war to slow migration into the territory and perhaps to chase away some who had already settled there. They raided white ranchers, farmers, and mining camps hoping to drive out the unwelcome settlers. Others, however, believed a peaceful response to be more practical. The volume of white migration into Colorado was too overwhelming, and the resources available to whites in waging war against Indians seemed too abundant. Black Kettle, an older Cheyenne chief, warned that destruction of his band and others was certain should the Cheyenne and Arapaho resist with armed force. He hoped to avoid the bloodshed that elsewhere claimed so many Indian lives and collapsed Indian societies. Although he detested the loss of freedom that came with reservation life, he believed negotiation offered the only sensible solution for Cheyenne survival.

That year, Black Kettle and leaders of a few other Cheyenne bands and some Arapaho groups signed the Fort Wise Treaty, accepting a reservation south of the Arkansas River and annual payments for security against white encroachment. However, the Cheyenne Dog Soldiers, the famed warriors of the Great Plains, did not sign the treaty. Moreover, Black Kettle spoke only for those in his band willing to support his peaceful approach, and many of those who signed the treaty did so without full understanding of what they accepted.

As the white population increased, Colorado Territory Governor John Evans planned to petition Congress for Colorado statehood, but the majority of Indians still had not ceded their lands by treaty or considered seriously relocation to reservations. Maddening for the governor, too, were the Dog Soldiers' persistent raids against white intruders. Evans was an ambitious man, a man who believed his contribution to Colorado statehood would catapult him to the U.S. Senate, and possibly to higher office. By 1863, he feared his inability to corral the territory's Indians compromised his ambitions.

The governor's commander of the territory's militia was Colonel John Chivington, a Methodist minister who was roundly referred to as the "Fighting Parson." Chivington openly and unashamedly called for Indian extermination, a sentiment most white residents of Colorado shared. With the federal government and the U.S. Army understandably occupied by war east of the Mississippi River, it fell to the volunteer militia to halt Indian raids and to impose peace in the territory. Governor Evans agreed that some resolution of the "Indian problem" was required, but he initially preferred the Indians' removal rather than a protracted war against them. Removal would be cheaper for Coloradans in both money and lives, and it would satisfy the settlers' immediate demand for land. But the governor understood, too, that removal carried no guarantee of success. Little prevented Cheyenne and Arapaho from abandoning their reservations and returning to their original homes, a move certain to spark armed clashes with settlers. The potential for warfare led Evans to assume a more aggressive, hard line against Native Americans, a position consistent with Chivington's and suited to Evans's own political aspirations.

Washington in 1863 did not need another region consumed by warfare. Congressional leaders sent word that they wished to have Cheyenne-Arapaho chiefs visit Washington; meet key representatives of Lincoln's administration, Congress, and the War Department; and collectively discuss avenues toward peaceful coexistence in Colorado. They wanted Indian leaders to see for themselves the sheer enormity of power the federal government could amass against hostile Indians and to realize that white settlement of the West to date was but a trickle of what was anticipated once the Civil War concluded. In short, the trip was to demonstrate to the Cheyenne-Arapaho that their very survival hinged on their peaceful relations with settlers and most probably their voluntary relocation to reservations. In 1863, Black Kettle, Lean Bear, White Antelope, and other Cheyenne leaders along with Arapaho, Kiowa, and Comanche traveled to the nation's capital. The journey accomplished little, as the Indians who visited Washington were the very ones who consistently called for peace and accepted the Fort Wise Treaty. The trip only reaffirmed their opinions.

The government's seemingly passive approach with the Cheyenne and Arapaho enraged Colonel Chivington. The arranged treaty and reservation would permit continued Cheyenne-Arapaho residency in Colorado, a move that denied that land to prospective white settlement and economic development. Throughout the remainder of 1863 and well into the following spring, Evans and Chivington stirred the cauldron of fear among settlers, repeatedly issuing dire warnings of imminent Indian-initiated war that could be prevented only with preemptive strikes against the Cheyenne-Arapaho. To be sure, the governor's and colonel's actions were founded purely on their desire to remove Indians from the territory and not from any overtly aggressive act committed by Indians, but they carried considerable weight among settlers when placed in the context of Kit Carson's war with the Navajos to the southwest and rising tensions between whites and Lakota Indians in the Powder River region to the north. Moreover, the realization that federal troops were unavailable heightened the sense among Coloradans that their immediate action would determine their survival.

In mid-April 1864, units of the Colorado Volunteers struck several Cheyenne and Arapaho villages, killing dozens of men, women, and children. "Burn villages and kill Cheyennes whenever and wherever found," thundered one junior officer. Troopers slaughtered Indian livestock and razed encampments. Chivington justified each strike, insisting that each was in retribution for some unidentified Indian raid or was intended to stymie the Indians' grander design of total war against whites on the southern plains. On May 26, an element of the Volunteers approached a village of several hundred Cheyenne. Seeing the assembled troopers in the distance, Lean Bear, who had been among the Indian leaders to visit Washington, climbed on to his horse and rode out to assure the soldiers that he and his villagers were peaceful. The young, inexperienced Colorado lieutenant in command ordered his soldiers to fire on the lone Indian. Lean Bear died in the first volley. The soldiers retreated immediately, as they were outnumbered by warriors then gathering in the village.

Cheyenne and Arapahos decried the murder of Lean Bear and the Volunteers' recent strikes on isolated Indian villages and loudly demanded war. Throughout summer they raided wherever they could. Governor Evans's prediction of war with Native Americans came true, although it was his actions and those of the militia—not Indian aggression—that created it. In June, Evans ordered all friendly Indians to relocate to camps near military posts to ensure their safety and concurrently to expose all remaining Indians as "hostiles." Small groups of Cheyenne and Arapaho obeyed the governor's order, but anxious soldiers occasionally fired on these men and women, turning once-compliant Indians into adversaries. Little by little, event by event, and under the approving eyes of Evans and Chivington, the prospect for peace faded across Colorado, and soon hostilities spread into neighboring Kansas. It took little incentive for the Comanche and Kiowa to lend their weight to a war for Indian self-defense, warfare that with each army and Indian strike grew more brutal.

A few individuals still called for peace. George Bent, a Cheyenne chief now employed by the Colorado Territory, and Major Edward Wynkoop, the military commander at Fort Lyon, urged Black Kettle, White Antelope, and other tribal leaders to sit with Governor Evans and negotiate a truce. In September, the parties assembled with Colonel Chivington in attendance. Each Indian who attended the conference stressed his desire for peace and his willingness, although offered reluctantly, to encourage Cheyenne and Arapaho bands to settle on a reservation. Evans and Chivington also expressed their preference for peace and applauded the Indians' conciliatory position, but they assured the Indians that Colorado would most certainly use armed force to compel Indian relocation to a reservation and would not be averse to the utter extermination of the Cheyenne and

READING HISTORY

Proclamation of Governor John Evans, Colorado Territory, June 27, 1864

In summer 1864, Colorado Territory Governor John Evans was determined to reduce the Native American presence in Colorado, a move, he contended, that would allow peaceful settlement of the territory and further economic development. Placing the full burden for a peaceful resolution of the "Indian problem" on Native Americans, he issued a call for Indians in the territory to relocate immediately to reservations or face the full power of the territorial militia.

To the Friendly Indians of the Plains:

Agents, Interpreters, and Traders, will inform the friendly Indians of the Plains that some members of their tribes have gone to war with the white people. They steal stock and run it off hoping to escape detection and punishment. In some instances they have attacked and killed soldiers and murdered peaceable citizens. For this the Great Father is angry, and will certainly hunt them out and punish them. But he does not want to injure those who remain friendly to the whites. He desires to protect and take care of them. For this purpose I direct that all friendly Indians keep away from those who are at war, and go to places of safety.

Friendly Arapahoes and Cheyennes, belonging on the Arkansas River, will go to Major **Colley**, U.S. Indian Agent at Fort Lyon, who will give them provisions and show them a place of safety.

Friendly Kiowas and Camanches [*sic*] will go to Fort Larned, where they will be cared for in the same way.

Friendly Sioux will go to their Agent at Fort Laramie for directions.

Friendly Arapahoes and Cheyennes of the Upper Platte, will go to Camp Collins on the Cache-la-Poudre where they will be assigned a place of safety, and provisions will be given them.

The object of this is to prevent friendly Indians from being killed through mistake. None but those who intend to be friendly with the whites must come to these places. The families of those who have gone to war with the whites must be kept away from among the friendly Indians.

The war on hostile Indians will be continued until they are all effectually subdued.

Source: Special Collections, Tutt Library, Colorado College, Colorado Springs, Colorado

Questions

1. Why does Governor Evans create such clear imagery of unfriendly Indians and of the "Great Father," or commander in chief?
2. What is the stated directive for "friendly" Indians, and what likely is Evans's underlying motive in this decree?

Arapaho if necessary. Black Kettle and White Antelope pointedly reminded the governor that it was through their own influence that violence had remained minimal in the region. They would most certainly fight, and to the bitter end if necessary, but they wanted to make peace if possible to spare the lives of their people. Neither side could have made its position more clear. Black Kettle agreed to settle his band on a reservation near Fort Lyon in southeast Colorado. In autumn 1864, he led about 500 Indians toward the fort and in November camped on the banks of **Sand Creek** (see Map 9.2). Most of his young men rode into neighboring Kansas to hunt for food for the coming winter. Black Kettle's camp was left nearly defenseless.

Governor Evans's stated preference for peace was meaningless. He, Colonel Chivington, and the U.S. Army's regional military commander, General Curtis, agreed the time was right to launch a crippling blow against Native Americans in the territory. At daybreak on the morning of November 29, Chivington marched his 700-man force to Sand Creek. Without any provocation and without warrant, he unleashed a surprise, murderous

READING HISTORY

Letter from Black Kettle (Cheyenne) to Major Colley (Indian Agent, Fort Lyon), United States Army, August 29, 1864

Black Kettle encouraged his fellow Cheyenne to acknowledge the reality of advancing white settlement, the ultimate futility of armed resistance, and the need to relocate to reservations the government was establishing in Colorado in 1864. The Cheyenne nonetheless remained a powerful people, and, he insisted, building peace was a burden to be shared between Indians and non-Indians alike.

Cheyenne Village August 29th /64

Maj. Colley

We received a letter from Bent wishing us to make peace. We held a counsel in regard to it & all came to the conclusion to make peace with you providing you make peace with the Kiowas, Commenches [*sic*], Arrapahoes [*sic*], Apaches, and Siouxs [*sic*]. We are going to send a messenger to the Kiowas and to the other nations about our going to make [peace] with you. We heard that you [hold] some prisoners in Denver. We have seven prisoners of you which we are willing to give up providing you give up yours. There are three war parties out yet and two of Arrapahoes [*sic*]. They have been out some time and expect now soon. When we held this counsel there were few Arrapahoes [*sic*] and Siouxs [*sic*] present. We want true news from you in return, that is a letter.

Black Kittle & Other Chieves

Brought to Ft Lyon Sunday Sept 4th 1864 by One Eye

Source: Special Collections, Tutt Library, Colorado College, Colorado Springs, Colorado

Questions

1. How does Black Kettle's letter to Major Colley demonstrate that the Indians operated from a position of relative strength rather than as near helpless victims, as is popularly portrayed?

2. Based on Governor Evans's letter (see Reading History, "Proclamation of Governor John Evans, Colorado Territory, June 27, 1864," p. 303) and Black Kettle's note to Major Colley, what would be a logical perspective both Indians and Colorado settlers would hold?

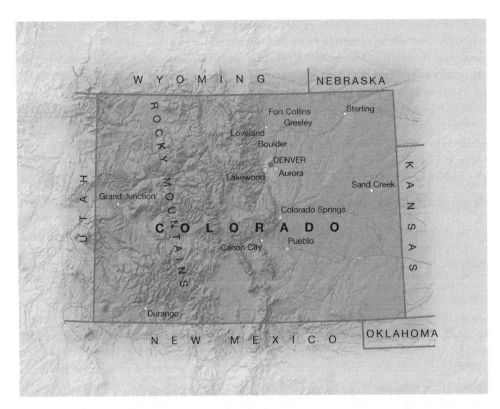

Map 9.2 Sand Creek, Colorado

assault on Black Kettle's camp. Black Kettle exited his lodge and raised an American flag given to him to demonstrate the Indians' peaceful intentions and special relationship with federal authority. The attack continued, and Black Kettle, along with his wife, fled for cover outside the camp. White Antelope was killed nearby. The Cheyenne and Arapaho fought as best they could, but their camp of mostly women, old men, and children could offer little resistance. "Indiscriminate slaughter" ensued and blood drenched the village, noted one soldier. Troopers killed every Indian they spotted—old men, warriors, women, children, and infants. Those attempting surrender met the same end. When it concluded, nearly 200 Cheyenne and Arapaho lay dead at Sand Creek, the majority being women and children.

Frenzied troopers committed the most horrific acts against the dead. Heads were removed and tossed playfully from one trooper to another. Bodies were disemboweled, scalps removed, ears taken as necklace adornments, and reproductive organs salvaged as trophies. Babies' heads were smashed on the ground or crushed by rifle butts, and the stomachs of pregnant women were sliced open. Lieutenant James Connor rode his horse slowly, tenuously, over the massacre site the next morning, carefully guiding himself around the lifeless Cheyenne and Arapaho. "I did not see a body of man, woman or child but was scalped, and in many instances their bodies were mutilated in the most horrible manner. . . . I heard one man say that he cut out a woman's private parts and had them for exhibition on a stick" and others who "stretched them over their saddle-bows and wore them over their hats." Units of the professional American army, volunteer militias, and citizen raiders had on numerous occasions over the previous 300 years waged total war on Indian peoples and massacred entire populations; however, never before had any cruel moment of war been this vicious, this barbaric. Chivington only expressed regret that more Indians were not killed. He saw himself as an agent of God.

Colorado settlers generally welcomed the news of Sand Creek. "News of their 'victory,'" wrote one scholar recently, "spread faster than rumors of gold strikes." Chivington claimed his men killed more than 500 warriors, among them Black Kettle. In his letter to Governor Evans, the colonel purposely avoided any statement of the soldiers' butchery and the wanton murder of women and children.

Rumors and unconfirmed reports of atrocities nonetheless reached Eastern newspapers. Repulsed by the stories they heard and read, Americans demanded a government investigation of the "battle" at Sand Creek. A congressional committee assembled in Denver in February 1865 to gather the testimony of Chivington and many of his soldiers. Chivington fiercely defended his attack on the camp, insisting the Cheyenne-Arapaho band was "hostile." Enlisted men and junior officers, however, countered the colonel's story, noting the passive movement of Cheyenne into southeastern Colorado and detailing the barbarity Chivington not only sanctioned but also encouraged. Although their testimony potentially placed themselves in the crosshairs of prosecution, the troopers nonetheless described what they saw and the emotions they experienced during and after the massacre. A second committee convened in March, this time in Washington, D.C., and there grilled Governor John Evans about his knowledge of and possible contribution to the Sand Creek Massacre. Evans evaded most questions posed to him, routinely stating that he was "informed" that the Cheyenne-Arapaho band had "assumed a hostile attitude before he [Chivington] attacked them." By the time the two committees concluded their work on May 30, dozens of soldiers had been questioned under oath and affidavits assembled from dozens more. General Ulysses S. Grant condemned Chivington's raid as nothing less than murder, and the army's judge advocate general denounced the strike as "cowardly and cold blooded slaughter."

Little came of the hearings. Governor Evans's vague testimony offered too little for prosecution, and witnesses could not point to anything specific that might implicate the governor of any crime. The reams of

9.7 *The Battle of Sand Creek*, oil painting by Robert Lindneux, 1936
Source: H.6130.37 (Scan #10025804), History Colorado

evidence amassed against Chivington, however, clearly proved the colonel orchestrated the massacre against a people deemed peaceful and non-threatening. He was certainly responsible for mass murder and the barbarity that followed the attack. The military uniform of the U.S. Army, concluded the Denver committee, "should be the emblem of justice and humanity," but the actions of the Colorado militia at Sand Creek stained the army's honor and that of the United States. Chivington "deliberately planned and executed a foul and dastardly massacre," it added. The Washington committee issued a similar statement. Although roundly condemned, Chivington was not prosecuted. His political aspirations, as well as Governor Evans's, evaporated as public opinion even in Colorado turned against him when the citizens learned the horrific details of Sand Creek.

Word of the massacre spread rapidly across the plains. Cheyenne and Arapaho warriors plunged headlong into full-scale war by year's end, and the nearby Kiowa and Comanche joined the rampage and raged across Texas northward into Kansas. In early 1865, nearly 1,000 warriors struck along the South Platte trail, attacking the few military posts in the territory as well as ranches, coach stations, and wagon trains. More settlers, soldiers, and travelers died in these early raids than the number of Indians killed at Sand Creek. Blood ran freely on the southern plains in early 1865 as Indian armed resistance and vengeance targeted all whites in the region. Fear swept Denver as rumors spread of an imminent Indian attack against the city. Nothing seemed safe on the southern plains, and Washington could do little. Colorado's militia units continued to chase and occasionally fight the various Indian groups, but troopers increasingly became frustrated and exhausted. Their own casualty rate soared, and by spring most viewed their job "sullenly, even mutinously," with many men simply deserting the ranks. The Civil War still commanded primary attention in the East. Even with the Confederate surrender in April, the federal government was in no position to dispatch its armies to the southern plains given the demands of postwar occupation in the South.

In October, in a feeble effort to broker a peaceful settlement, representatives of the U.S. government offered a new treaty to a gathering of Southern Cheyenne, Arapahos, Kiowa, and Comanche. The Little Arkansas Treaty, as it was termed, established a new Cheyenne-Arapaho reservation outside Colorado and one for the Comanche and Kiowa in the Texas panhandle region. A majority of chiefs rejected flatly Washington's peace overture. The reservations were not their traditional homelands, the memory of Sand Creek still burned in their hearts, and the word of Washington and its agents in previous years proved empty of honor. Many of those who refused the treaty continued their raids while others moved north to join other bands. Black Kettle, however, accepted the agents' offer, as did a small number of chiefs, and the hope of peace glimmered briefly over the southern plains. Hope proved short-lived. Not only did the reservations never materialize but also post-Civil War migrations into the West and policy redirection in Washington together ignited warfare throughout the Great Plains.

Conclusion

Much changed for Native Americans beyond the Mississippi River as a result of the Civil War. War between the blue coats and gray coats ravaged much of Oklahoma Territory, and the internal divisions among the Five Civilized Nations, especially among the Cherokee, left enduring scars. The non-Indian population of Minnesota, backed by President Lincoln, expelled the Santee Sioux to the Dakota Territory. Navajo found themselves residing on the Bosque Redondo Reservation in eastern New Mexico and hundreds of miles from their traditional home. Mescalero Apache battled militia units of the territories and some elements of the regular army, but they, too, were compelled to surrender and relocated to a reservation. The Cheyenne and Arapaho, along with the neighboring Kiowa and Comanche, were in a full-scale war with the United States in 1865. Common factors linked the experiences of these disparate Indian groups. The Civil War increasingly channeled funds previously earmarked as annuity payments for Native Americans to the war effort back east, raising the level of hardship for most Indians. The redeployment of federal troops left Native American groups in Oklahoma, Minnesota, the Southwest, and Colorado more susceptible to the policies and preferences of white settlers and their territorial governments. With reduced oversight and control from Washington, white settlers demanded greater land concessions from Indians and the tempo of white migration into these territories increased. Federal efforts to foster national economic growth further challenged continued Indian occupancy of the territories. Although the Civil War directly impacted only Indian Territory, the turmoil Indians in Minnesota, New Mexico, and Colorado faced would not likely have occurred when it did and to the extent it did without the effects of the war back East. Indians never mustered a unified response to the crises they faced. Some advocated armed resistance and others pursued conciliation and compromise.

The brutality of war in the western territories between 1861 and 1865, and particularly the arrogance and barbarity evidenced by militia units, influenced two concurrent postwar directions in Indian affairs. As you will read in the next chapter, warfare raged across the northern plains throughout the decade that followed the Civil War, in many ways an Indian resistance that mirrored wartime issues. There was also a genuine spirit for humanitarian reform and call for a redirection in federal Indian policy, a direction that surfaced first in response to the public condemnation of conditions at Bosque Redondo. Common to these twists and turns was the realization among Native Americans that the coming years would be defining ones, determining the Indians' survival and their future relationship with American society and the federal government.

Review Questions

1. What issues or concerns influenced the Cherokee in establishing alliances with Union and Confederate forces during the Civil War? How might one argue that the war in Indian Territory was largely a civil war within a civil war?
2. How were the Santee reasons for armed resistance different from those of tribes in the Indian Territory?
3. In what ways were the wartime experiences of the Santee, Navajo, Apache, and Cheyenne-Arapaho similar? How were they different?
4. What particular events in the West influenced the rise of eastern reformism? Why?
5. In what ways did the Civil War spawn the conflicts that arose in Minnesota, New Mexico, and Colorado?

Recommended Readings

Confer, Clarissa W. *The Cherokee Nation in the Civil War* (Norman: University of Oklahoma Press, 2007). An overview of the devastating loss of life, land, and sovereignty the Cherokees suffered during the Civil War.

Hatch, Thom. *The Blue, the Gray, and the Red: Indian Campaigns of the Civil War* (Mechanicsburg, PA: Stackpole, 2003). A popular history that examines warfare in the West between Native American groups and the territorial militias and federal forces during the Civil War.

Hauptman, Laurence M. *Between Two Fires: American Indians in the Civil War* (New York: Free Press, 1995). Hauptman provides a thorough, detailed study of American Indian participation in the Civil War, those who supported the Union and those who aligned themselves with the Confederacy, arguing that most Indians assumed participation would ensure tribal survival but in reality the war's results included a more rapid destruction of tribal structures.

Jackson, Helen. *A Century of Dishonor: A Sketch of the United States Government's Dealings With Some of the Indian Tribes* (New York: Indian Head Books, 1994). (Originally published in 1881). Beginning with the era of the American Revolution and continuing through the Civil War years, Jackson chronicles a long, sordid history of mistreatment and destruction of native peoples by the U.S. government.

Kelman, Ari. *A Misplaced Massacre: Struggling Over the Memory of Sand Creek* (Boston: Harvard University Press, 2015). A solid review of the famed massacre in 1864 but more importantly an examination of how that heinous event has been interpreted by each generation since 1864.

Mendoza, Patrick M. *Song of Sorrow: Massacre at Sand Creek* (Denver, CO: Willow Wind, 1993). A survey of the events leading to and contributing to the Sand Creek Massacre of 1864 and the effects of that tragic event on the Cheyenne.

Nichols, David A. *Lincoln and the Indians: Civil War Policy and Politics* (Urbana: University of Illinois Press, 2000). A thorough examination of President Lincoln's wartime Indian policy in the context of Civil War politics, with particular focus on the Oklahoma Territory, the Navajo, the Cheyenne, and the Santee Sioux.

West, Elliott. *The Contested Plains: Indians, Gold Seekers, and the Rush to Colorado* (Lawrence: University Press of Kansas, 1998). A superb study of the clash of cultures that occurred as a result of the Colorado gold rush.

Native American History Online

General Sites

Bosque Redondo. http://reta.nmsu.edu/modules/longwalk/lesson/part1/resource.htm This site provides maps tracing the Navajo Long Walk and the location of the Bosque Redondo Reservation. Included are links to photographs and documents that highlight this historical moment.

Dakota Conflict Trials. www.law.umkc.edu/faculty/projects/ftrials/dakota/dakota Housed at this website are photos of principal Santee and non-Indian players in the so-called Santee War of 1862, records of the postwar trials, accounts of the executions that followed, an extended evaluation of the notion of fair trial in this case, and letters and statements by prominent individuals at the time made public about the war and its aftermath. In addition, the site includes a brief history of the event, a chronology, and maps.

New Perspectives on the West: Documents on the Sand Creek Massacre. www.pbs.org/weta/thewest/resources/archives/four/sandcrk.htm Produced by PBS, this site includes two editorials from the *Rocky Mountain News* dated 1864, an Indian interpreter present in Black Kettle's camp at Sand Creek, and Col. John Chivington's testimony before the congressional investigation committee assembled in Denver in 1865.

"Testimony of Major Edward W. Wynkoop," Kansas Memory. www.kansasmemory.org/item/211651 The official testimony of Major Wynkoop and others associated with the Sand Creek Massacre of November 1864.

Sand Creek Papers, 1861–1864. www.libraryweb.coloradocollege.edu/library/specialcollections/Manuscript/SandCreek Digitized and available are letters Black Kettle dictated; announcements and various communiqués Governor John Evans, Commissioner of Indian Affairs William Dole, and others wrote; newspaper accounts and editorials; and various other primary source documents related to events leading to the massacre at Sand Creek and the public response to the massacre.

Historic Sites

Sand Creek Massacre National Historic Site, Eads, Colorado. www.nps.gov/sand/index.htm This historic site preserves the location of the massacre.

Bosque Redondo Memorial, Fort Sumner, New Mexico. http://www.nmhistoricsites.org/bosque-redondo The memorial preserves the history of forced march of the Navajo and Mescalero Apache Indians hundreds of miles to the Bosque Redondo Reservation.

CHAPTER

10

Red Cloud (1822–1909), war leader and head Chief of the Oglala Lakota (Sioux) from 1868 to 1909

Conflicting Postwar Directions, 1865–1877

KINTPUASH AND THE MODOC WAR

POST-CIVIL WAR DIRECTIONS IN INDIAN AFFAIRS

Defining Postwar Indian Policy

The Powder River War

Peace Overtures

Renewed Resistance on the Southern Plains

PEACE POLICY, WAR POLICY

President Grant's Peace Policy

Resistance on the Southern Plains Continues

Gold in the Black Hills

The Great Sioux War

The Nez Perce

Kintpuash and the Modoc War

The soldier bound Kintpuash's hands, fixed the noose tightly around the Indian's neck, and roughly moved him into position. With little ceremony, the officer in charge motioned for the execution to proceed, and Kintpuash fell from the platform to his death. To the U.S. Army, the hanging was an act of justice carried out against the Modoc leader charged with murder and who, for months, battled soldiers in a protracted fight in America's Northwest. Surviving Modoc, however, honored their former leader for his dogged resistance to removal from the Indians' homeland that he led over the previous many months. Their defeat and Kintpuash's execution signaled an uncertain future for the tribe. Although the Modoc War began only eight months earlier, the roots of conflict reached more than two decades into the past.

Hundreds of thousands of settlers poured into northern California and Oregon in the late 1840s, seeking wealth and land. The tide of white arrivals into the region drove Native Americans into small,

311

compact areas and occasionally forced some to abandon their ancestors' land for territories more remote and more removed from the intruders.

Kintpuash, a Modoc Indian known among whites as Captain Jack, understood well the devastating threat settlement presented and in 1864 signed a treaty relinquishing his tribe's homeland for life among the Klamath and Snake Indians. The Klamath, also pressured by migrants flowing into the region, soon found the Modoc to be a strain on their own limited resources. Kintpuash decided to return to his former homeland and took with him nearly 60 families. It was their home. The Indian Office instructed the War Department to force the Modocs' return to the Klamath and in little time troops arrived to enforce the decision.

In the early morning hours of November 29, 1872, the cavalry struck the Modoc camp, chasing the Indians across Tule Lake into a network of caverns and black lava. The army realized quickly that "Captain Jack's Stronghold" was well defended. Crossing Tule Lake exposed troopers to direct fire from the Indians, and the lava beds and caves proved adequate defense against cannon fire. Kintpuash and his warriors kept the army at bay for the next four months, and their sustained resistance garnered them news coverage across the United States and support from many white Americans.

The determined Indian resistance compelled Washington to turn to diplomatic efforts, and Kintpuash met with representatives of the federal government in spring 1873. Several Modoc leaders believed that he should have killed the peace commissioners rather than negotiate, and although this sentiment quickly gained some favor within the tribe, it remained an issue that divided the Indians. On April 11, Kintpuash and a small party

CHRONOLOGY

1865	The Five Civilized Tribes renounce treaties and alliances made with the Confederacy
1866	War erupts in the Powder River country between the Sioux and the U.S. Army
1867	The Doolittle Report is presented to Congress, the War Department, and the Department of the Interior
	The Medicine Lodge Creek Treaty is signed
1868	Fort Laramie (Wyoming) Treaty establishes the Great Sioux Reservation. A cavalry unit commanded by Col. George A. Custer attacks a Cheyenne encampment in the Washita Valley, killing Black Kettle
1869	Representatives of the Quaker religion meet with President-elect Ulysses S. Grant to promote a peace policy toward Indians
	Ely Parker (Seneca) is appointed Commissioner of Indian Affairs by President Ulysses Grant
	Sioux, Northern Cheyenne, and Arapaho settle onto the Great Sioux Reservation in the Dakota Territory
1871	Congress abandons the treaty-making process
1874	Prospectors discover gold in the Black Hills on the Great Sioux Reservation
	Modoc War rages in Oregon and Northern California
1876	Great Sioux War
	Massacre at Little Big Horn
1877	Crazy Horse surrenders and is murdered
	Chief Joseph surrenders the Nez Perce to Colonel Nelson Miles and General George Crook

KEY QUESTIONS

1. How did ideology, military circumstances, and economic progress of the United States during the period of Reconstruction contribute to federal Indian policy in the American West between 1865 and 1877?
2. Why is the Treaty of Fort Laramie considered so unique?
3. What irony is found in Grant's Peace Policy?
4. What were the principal forces that contributed directly to the military defeat of Native American resistance in the West by 1877?
5. What arguments in support of armed resistance proved common among most Indian groups in the West in the decade following the Civil War?
6. What traits and experiences did Sitting Bull, Red Cloud, Ulysses S. Grant, and George Custer have in common? How and why were the legends of these men built?

of Modoc again sat with the commissioners. As the proceedings began, he and his companions drew handguns from their coverings and opened fire, killing two representatives and seriously wounding another.

The nation's earlier sympathy now turned to rage. The U.S. Army now pursued the Modoc with revenge, not resettlement, being the motive. On June 1, Kintpuash and his closest advisors were apprehended and were hanged soon afterward. Captain Jack's head was removed and shipped to Washington's Army Medical Museum. The death of Kintpuash and the tribe's principal leaders ended Modoc resistance. In October, surviving Modoc were placed on a small reservation in Indian Territory.

The Modoc War mirrored post-Civil War patterns across the West. White migration and settlement, along with the nation's determination to exploit the continent's natural resources for national economic growth, challenged Indian residency on traditional lands and most often resulted in the Indians' forced relocation to reservations. As you will read, Native Americans resisted compulsory removal, meeting armed force with armed force as long as they believed that option remained viable. Despite some notable successes, such as the war in the Powder River country, the United States overcame armed resistance by 1877, effectively limiting Indians to defined territories that only diminished in size with each passing decade.

Post-Civil War Directions in Indian Affairs

The war was over, but death lingered long over the battlefields and the horror of war shadowed the nation. Nearly 600,000 American soldiers and an undetermined number of civilians lost their lives during the cataclysm of the Civil War, a number that dwarfed the combined deaths of all wars on the continent since the founding of Jamestown. The physical destruction the war caused also numbed Americans. Southern cities were but shells of their prewar grandeur. General Sherman's armies put Atlanta to the torch, half of Columbia lay in ash, Richmond looked more like bombed-out Berlin in 1945 than the elegant capital of the Confederacy, and the rubble of plantation homes and farmhouses lay scattered over the countryside. Union armies ripped apart railroad lines, blasted ports, and rendered useless crop land and grazing fields. Hopelessness pervaded the South. A way of life died in April 1865; one world view perished, but another world view was validated.

The United States claimed a military victory over the Confederacy, but the ideological war continued, focusing in part on the status and role of freed slaves in the postwar South. Some Northern congressmen, known as

Radical Republicans, worked to provide political and economic opportunity to former slaves, but in the South former Confederates worked just as hard to stymie black voting and to control their public movement and behavior. Former Confederate state governments enacted Jim Crow laws to segregate the races in public facilities, and Southern state legislatures passed laws that disenfranchised most black voters by 1900. Union victory reaffirmed the supremacy of the federal government over states' rights and repudiated the right of secession, but Southerners still searched for ways to protect their preference for state-based government and the racial order they saw as central to their society.

With the return of peace came a flood of European immigrants to the United States, with a growing number hailing from southern and eastern Europe—the "New Immigrants." This perceived tsunami of "others" included a large number of Catholics and Jews, persons with little education or skills, and individuals with political and social views considered "radical" by mainstream America. Most settled in the burgeoning cities of the Northeast. Many native-born Americans soon feared the immigrants would "contaminate" all that had, in their view, come to define America, a country they saw as, in its essence, white and Protestant.

Many immigrants did not stop on the East Coast but continued their trek into the Upper Midwest and western territories. They and native-born Americans alike chased dreams of quick wealth from the gold and silver strikes that dotted the West after 1865. The promise of free land contained in the Homestead Act along with supplemental congressional measures lured thousands more to open acreage beyond Missouri. The transcontinental railroad sped passengers and cargo between the Pacific coast and points east. Cattle ranching emerged as every bit the boom industry that mining was, lining the pockets of ranch owners, drawing thousands of men west as cowhands, and leading to greater demand for land. New towns multiplied west of the Mississippi River in the late 1860s and 1870s to serve mining, cattle, railroad, and farming interests across the western territories. The United States was quickly becoming a continental nation. The national economy soared to record levels of prosperity in the postwar years, and by 1900 the United States sat as the world's leading manufacturing nation, leading producer of food, and heir apparent to Great Britain as the world's principal economic force. A new national identity was emerging from the ashes of war.

The Civil War years proved catastrophic for many Native Americans. Indian resistance to white migration and settlement accomplished little for most tribes other than demonstrate to the federal government and to territorial authorities that Indians refused to be victims. Surrender to a superior military force did not necessarily mean conquest. Indeed, war continued to rage across the plains in 1865, in large measure a product of Sand Creek (see Chapter 9). It was clear to Native Americans, however, that the years directly ahead of them would determine if they were to survive as a people and, if they survived physically, the condition of their lives for generations to come. The ideas and policies that grew out of the reconstruction of the South, along with the new momentum of American expansion, had a direct impact on American Indians. Radical Republicans considered new definitions of race and ethnicity and reexamined the value of racial inclusion as they sought to remake the South. The Union victory gave rise to a stronger sense of national identity, and it contributed to the emergence of an age of economic progress and territorial expansion unparalleled in the nation's history. All of this now directly threatened Native American identities and communities.

Defining Postwar Indian Policy

On September 8, 1865, Commissioner of Indian Affairs Dennis N. Cooley informed representatives of the Five Civilized Nations at Fort Smith that their alliances with the Confederacy invalidated their earlier treaties with the United States. New treaties were to be drafted, he said. Each tribe was to pledge perpetual peace with the United States, support the government's effort "in compelling the wild tribes of the plains to keep the peace," abolish slavery in Indian Territory, acknowledge Washington's right to settle other Native American groups within the territory, and accept the union of all tribes in Oklahoma under a single territorial government. Cooley promised there would be no punitive measures against the Confederate Indians and assured tribes that Washington would not permit white citizens other than government officials to reside among them.

Cooley's remarks and the treaty stipulations provoked discussion among the Indians. Most of the Indian delegates indicated their general acceptance of the provisions, but the Confederate Cherokee hesitated. They contended that their alliance with Richmond resulted from Washington's failure to honor its treaty obligations with the Cherokee, particularly the government's assurance of military protection. Stand Watie was present at the gathering and restated his longstanding anger over the federal government's removal of the Cherokee from the Carolinas and Georgia. He condemned Washington, for it had "abolished our government, annihilated our laws, suppressed our authorities, took away our lands, turned us out of our houses, denied us the rights of men, made us outcasts and outlaws in our own land, plunging us at the same time into an abyss of moral degradation." He then demanded that the Cooley Commission create two separate Cherokee jurisdictions, one for Confederate Cherokee and one for Union Cherokee. Stand Watie's comments inflamed the Indians in attendance and resulted in a flurry of accusations against the federal government's handling of Indians prior to the war, against individual tribal leaders who aligned their people with the Confederacy without tribal consent, and between those who remained loyal to the United States and those who seceded. After three days of discussion and argument, the best that could be arranged was a statement of the Indians' allegiance to the United States, their denunciation of treaties made with the Confederacy, and Washington's willingness to ensure peace in the territory. As in the Old Confederacy, the war was over but the ideas and emotions that led to war remained alive.

A formal treaty did not emerge from the meeting, but it mattered little. Already voices in Washington called on the government to scrap the treaty system with Native Americans. Persons familiar with the recent wars in the Southwest and the plains understood, too, that many Indians would soon face relocation as postwar migration of whites and national economic development in the West intensified. Moreover, the treaty stipulations Cooley presented on September 8 indicated unequivocally that the government intended to purchase land inside Indian Territory and there place the recently defeated Plains Indians. Without a formal treaty, there existed no such financial arrangement for Washington to honor, no explicit promise to post military forces in Oklahoma to protect Native Americans, no expressed assurance of supplies or annuity payments, and no guarantee that the United States would prevent white settlement on Indian lands. The failure to secure Indian endorsement of Cooley's points turned clearly in Washington's favor and within a few years led to the transformation of Indian Territory into the Oklahoma Territory, reducing substantially the size of Indian lands to accommodate a rush of white settlement. It also encouraged eastern reformers to rethink the ultimate fate of Native Americans. Without formal treaties, Native Americans might be induced to acculturate themselves more quickly to white ways and, in so doing, purge the Indian from themselves. The precedent now existed for the government's postwar direction in Indian affairs.

Postwar interest in reforming Indian policies and treatment of Native Americans was also the product of Washington's investigations into the Sand Creek Massacre and the public's condemnation of Governor Evans, Colonel Chivington, and the Colorado Volunteers. The ferocity of warfare between Indians and settlers in recent campaigns and in the current one raging on the southern plains further encouraged politicians in the western territories to reconsider the rush to hostilities. These wars proved costly in both lives and money, and as demonstrated by the public outrage over Sand Creek and the sympathy engendered by the Long Walk, were increasingly unpopular. Dakota Territory's Governor Newton Edmunds in summer 1865 moved to bring peace between the various Sioux bands and settlers, but, as historian Robert Utley correctly notes, Governor Edmunds also acted out of self-interest. The pervasive image of the Dakota Territory ablaze in hostilities retarded migration into the region and actually caused many settlers already there to abandon their homes for a new life in more pacified areas of the West. How could Dakota develop economically and secure the population necessary for statehood if war continued to shadow the territory?

10.1 William Tecumseh Sherman

Source: Courtesy of Library of Congress Prints and Photographs Division, LC-USZ62-112190

In this climate, reformers, individuals within the Office of Indian Affairs and Congress, and military leaders all demanded the federal government fashion a final solution to the "Indian Problem," one that would bring peace to the West and open the entire region to white settlement and economic development. They agreed that the first step must be the Indians' removal from their traditional lands and their relocation to reservations. Confinement on reservations in the northern plains and southern plains would effectively open a "corridor" through the middle of the country to the West Coast for white migration and settlement. Debate surfaced among the groups over the extent of armed force to be marshaled against Indians to make this plan feasible. Interior officials, Indian Office administrators, and reformers preferred the least amount of armed force required to affect Indian removal. Better to minimize the military's role and instead lure tribes to reservations with simple promises that afforded the illusion of freedom and independence.

The army and most western settlers, however, viewed the issue differently. Native Americans typically held a spiritual connection to the land on which they lived. They would not likely vacate the land of their fathers without resistance. The army, therefore, concluded that military force would be necessary. The War Department demonstrated its commitment to that direction by appointing General William Tecumseh Sherman as commander of the Division of Missouri in September 1865, headquartered in St. Louis.

Sherman was a logical choice. "War is cruelty," he said, "and you cannot refine it"—a dictum he manifested in his Georgia campaign one year earlier. His infamous March to the Sea from Atlanta to Savannah in 1864 effectively broke the Confederacy's ability to wage war, and his relentless prosecution of "total war" through South Carolina and into North Carolina sealed the federal victory in spring 1865. "The crueler [war] is, the sooner it will be over," he said frequently. This attitude he carried into his new assignment. Sherman insisted no quarter would be given to Indians who resisted by force of arms the government's plan of removal. The general, however, was equally determined to employ only the U.S. Army should force be necessary. As Sand Creek demonstrated, the barbarity of state and territorial militias only encouraged further armed resistance by Indians.

What finally emerged by autumn 1865 was a combination of the two perspectives. All parties agreed that removal and relocation were necessary. To affect that, in the short term treaties would be offered to free-ranging tribes and force would be used against those that resisted. Once convinced that removal and relocation would occur regardless of Indian response, many tribes would willingly submit to the inevitable. Certain that

PROFILE

Standing Bear (Machunazha, Ponca), 1829–1908

By treaty in 1858, the Ponca Indians peacefully accepted a small reservation in north-central Nebraska and south-central South Dakota along the Niobrara River. There, they intended to live quietly and without external interference as promised by the U.S. government. Only a decade passed before events subverted Ponca expectations.

The Fort Laramie Treaty of 1868 ignored completely the Ponca, folding their lands into the Great Sioux Reservation, a move partly intended to placate the Lakota Sioux in the wake of recent war between the Sioux and the United States. The Ponca demanded sole occupancy of their lands, using existing legal channels and direct appeals to political figures to advance their own treaty claim to the region. Washington took no action until May 1877, when both the Interior Department and the War Department chose to relocate the Ponca to new lands in Indian Territory, away from the more contentious Lakota.

Standing Bear was one of the eight Ponca chiefs chosen to visit Indian Territory and select a reservation site. The collection of Ponca leaders found the lands unsuitable and feared relocation to the southern region would cost the tribe dearly in lives. In spite of the chiefs' objections, the U.S. Army and Interior Department ordered Ponca removal to Oklahoma.

The Ponca, indeed, found life devastating in their new home. Standing Bear's son, Bear Shield, was among those who perished that first winter. Before his death, Bear Shield asked his father to return his body to the Niobrara River region. Standing Bear and nearly three dozen others began their trek of nearly 600 miles, but General George Crook's regiment caught the Ponca, arrested Standing Bear, and held the Indians at Fort Omaha for repatriation to the Oklahoma Reservation. Using America's constitution to his advantage, Standing Bear filed suit in federal courts in Nebraska, winning the decision in *United States ex rel. Standing Bear* v. *Crook* (1879), which stated "an Indian is a person" under law. The government failed to present a valid argument for Ponca detention, and therefore the Indians were to be freed immediately. Much of the tribe returned to the Niobrara country and there resumed residency, and there Standing Bear dwelled until his death in 1908.

In October, Governor Edmunds empanelled his peace commission to meet with Sioux representatives and to secure from them an arrangement resolving the conditions that led to the current war that had spread from Minnesota. From the meeting came a peace agreement, so Governor Edmunds pronounced his mission a success. Peace advocates, reformers, and government officials who pushed minimal force and maximum acculturation efforts seemed vindicated. But, it only seemed that way. In reality, not one of the Sioux bands labeled "hostile" attended the meeting, and none of them later signed the peace agreement. The commission had met only with those bands already in peaceful residence in the territory and not likely to engage in armed confrontation with settlers or the territorial militia. "Hostiles" still ranged the Dakota Territory, sweeping into Nebraska and venturing westward, determined not to relinquish their traditional lands or abandon their cultural identity. It mattered little to Edmunds. His pronouncement of peace had been issued. He had a document proving it, and migration into the Dakota Territory now seemed assured. It would soon matter greatly to those migrating into the region and beyond.

Sherman would act aggressively on his pledge and equally certain that their survival and identity were now directly challenged, the Ponca, Bannock, Arikara, Mandan, Ute, and Gros Ventre all signed treaties presented to them between 1865 and 1877 and accepted removal to their assigned reservations with only limited resistance. Similar arrangements were made with individual bands of the Southern Cheyenne, Arapaho, Comanche, and Kiowa. Relocated Indians found their new homes intolerable. As White Eagle said about his Ponca reservation, "We found the land [there] was bad and we were dying one after another." "I thought God intended us to live, but I was mistaken," said Standing Bear (Ponca). "God intends to give our country to the White people, and we are to die." "To leave my [native] soil and go among red men who are aliens to our race," said one Quapaw, "is throwing us like outcasts upon the world." Earlier armed resistance had delayed removal, but only briefly. Relocated Indians now focused on tribal and cultural survival. For these bands, resistance against white America required a different course—passive resistance to acculturation.

The Powder River War

Gold seekers trickled into the Montana Territory in 1864, almost all of them journeying along the Missouri River. The intrusion certainly worried Native Americans, but as the migrants were largely confined to the waterway and only passing through to Montana there seemed to be little immediate danger. By summer 1865, the pace of migration increased, and the trail of miners, prospectors, and others seeking quick wealth now moved overland along the Bozeman Trail running northwest from Fort Laramie. The route crossed the buffalo-hunting range of the Teton Sioux in the Powder River country. Threats from Indians and a few scattered minor clashes resulted in the U.S. Army dispatching troops to the territory to patrol the trail and to provide a modicum of protection for both miners and Indians (see Map 10.1).

Sioux anger matched the tempo of developments. Each new miner or prospector entering the Powder River country threatened the physical well-being of Indians. Disease had devastated numerous bands across the northern plains and upper Rockies since the first intrusion of European trappers and traders a century earlier. The Sioux understood too well that rumors of new gold discoveries always led to increased white migration, in spite of Indian protests, and that wherever miners went, soldiers surely followed. The next step was always the forced relocation of Indians from their ancestral lands. The pattern of removal played out too frequently for the Sioux not to understand.

In June 1866, the United States assembled a peace commission at Fort Laramie to meet with the Teton Sioux (Sans Arc, Miniconjou, and Oglala). The principal speakers for the Sioux were Man-Afraid-of-His-Horse and Red Cloud, the latter an Oglala warrior in his early forties whom the Sioux admired for his demonstrated fighting and leadership skills. The commissioners distributed the usual gifts—food, colorful fabrics, blankets, and sundry other items—and then commenced their bid to secure the **Bozeman Trail** for the miners' use. The commissioners offered the Sioux $70,000 in annual annuity payments and recognition of the Indians' right to continued residency on their lands. They requested in return a right of passage along the Bozeman Trail into the gold fields. At best, the discussion was tense, each party expressing its desire for peace but assuring the other that they had no aversion to the use of force if that was required to protect their interests. Red Cloud informed the delegates that he wanted to consult with tribal leaders before accepting or rejecting the offer.

As the Indians discussed the proposition, a battalion of U.S. cavalry moved into Fort Laramie and with them came construction crews to build a string of military posts along the Bozeman Trail. Red Cloud erupted in anger. The Sioux, he thundered, assembled with Washington's representatives in good faith, but clearly the Americans planned "to steal the road before Indians say 'Yes' or 'No.'" He promised that the Sioux would not tolerate troops, forts, or miners in the Powder River. They would be driven out of the region, said Red Cloud as he stormed from the council. Brule Sioux representatives remained and affixed their seal to a treaty of peace.

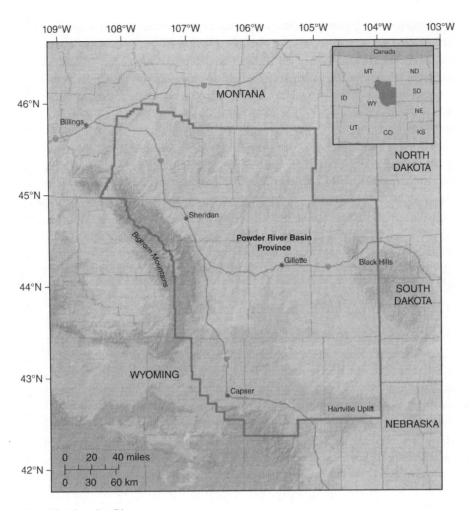

Map 10.1 Powder River

The commissioners and the Sioux genuinely desired peace, and a resolution satisfactory to both might have been possible had Washington and its agents tackled the issue differently. Miners threatened the Indians' lives. They carried diseases deadly or crippling to Indians, spoiled forests and rivers, over-hunted game, and often corrupted Indians with alcohol and eastern-made goods. Military posts, ostensibly intended to protect miners, not only increased the probability of an eventual armed confrontation but also encouraged additional white migration through the perception of stability they offered. The Sioux saw their own survival at stake. The commission stated its preference for peace and a negotiated settlement, but Washington's deployment of troops to Fort Laramie undermined the proceedings and suggested clearly to the Indians that Washington would get what it wanted, regardless of Indian preferences. Wrote one journalist at the time, "We go to them Janus-faced. One of our hands holds the rifle and the other the peace pipe, and we blaze away with both instruments at the same time. The chief consequence is a great smoke—and there it ends."

Miners plodded along the Bozeman Trail into the gold fields throughout summer 1866, and the army now manned forts along the route. Sioux fears were realized. "I remember that the white men were coming and that they were going to fight us to the finish and take away our land," said one Lakota many years later, as he recalled those pivotal days. "I thought it was not right. We are humans too and God created us all alike, and I was going to do the best I could to defend my nation. So I started out on the warpath when I was sixteen years old." Said another Sioux, "We wouldn't have fought the white men if they hadn't fought us. We would have allowed them to live among us in peace." Had white movement into the Powder River remained but a trickle, the Indians might have allowed a few settlers to reside alongside the Sioux, but the pace of white incursion understandably startled the Indians. "At the age of ten or eleven I had a six-shooter and a quiver full of arrows to defend my nation," recalled still another Indian. Resistance, most effectively armed resistance, was a natural and fully expected response.

The Sioux attacked three forts garrisoned by the army. Red Cloud and his Oglala warriors then centered attention on Fort Phil Kearny, the largest of the forts. On December 21, the Sioux set a trap to draw out troopers. One war party struck wagons hauling wood to the fort. Word of the ambush reached the garrison, and 80 soldiers led by Captain William J. Fetterman stormed through the gates to rescue those under attack. Another party of warriors, led by Crazy Horse, ambushed the reinforcements and lured the soldiers farther from the fort and away from the wagoners now fighting for their own lives. Crazy Horse artfully retreated, keeping the troopers just close enough to continue their pursuit. Fetterman led his soldiers "over the high ridge to the north and down the slope on the other side," unaware of the fury that awaited him. There the Indians sprung their trap, encircling the soldiers with nearly 1,500 warriors. In little time, the Indians killed every soldier. "The white cavalry did not know how to fight," explained Standing Bear (Lakota). "They stuck together and thus made an easy target for us."

The **Fetterman Massacre**, as the press quickly dubbed it, shocked the nation. Much of the good will and sincere calls for peace that rose among so many Americans in the wake of Sand Creek now evaporated into a general call for total war on all Indians. General William Sherman advocated the outright extermination of Native Americans, regardless of gender or age. Understandably, the U.S. Army supported Sherman's sentiment; its men were massacred and, given the sense of brotherhood that prevails across the military, it was an expected reaction to the slaughter. Rein in the Sioux by force, they agreed, "even to their extermination—men, women and children" if necessary. Similar calls echoed within Congress, with many congressmen arguing that the rifle was the most certain solution to the "Indian problem." War washed over the Powder River.

Peace Overtures

Still, some Americans defended the Sioux, particularly eastern reformers who saw duplicity in the government's behavior in sending a commission to talk peace at the same time as it sent an army to erect forts. The Indian Office specifically blamed the Fetterman Massacre on an overly aggressive U.S. Army more intent on an armed resolution than negotiated settlement.

Senator James R. Doolittle (Republican, Wisconsin) was one such advocate of peace. Doolittle had chaired Congress's Joint Committee on the Condition of the Indian Tribes and in summer 1865 led that body into the West to assess the status of Native American life and to listen to the Indian perspective regarding reservation conditions. The committee visited dozens of Indian tribes, conversed with tribal leaders, observed first-hand the impact of white westward settlement on Indian life, and listened carefully to their recommendations for peace. Visited, too, were white communities, settlers, and miners to get their suggestions for peaceful coexistence. Before an audience in Denver, Doolittle expressed his hope that a peaceful, humane policy in Indian affairs could be arranged, but the gathering instead rose to its feet and in unison shouted "Exterminate them! Exterminate them!"

Doolittle released a summary statement in January 1867. It acknowledged the obvious and significant depopulation of Indian tribes, a decline caused by starvation, malnutrition, disease, and warfare. It decried the Indians' loss of land, which contributed directly to their willingness to resist the United States with armed force. More often than not, warfare between Indians and whites was the human response to these despicable conditions and a product of the federal government's refusal to honor the treaty provisions it pressed on Native Americans. The **Doolittle Report** stated rather bluntly that the current state of affairs lent itself to the Indians' cultural disintegration and possibly to their eventual physical extinction. Doolittle and his commission insisted on a reservation system that served as a training base for Indian instruction in farming and the skills required for a productive life alongside the white world—a "civilization program" administered by the Department of the Interior—rather than a system directed by the War Department. The Doolittle Report encountered a buzz saw of opposition in the U.S. House of Representatives and from much of the general public, but the Senate received it well and pressed the War Department to temper its plans for "vigorous military retaliation." The Doolittle Report served as another step toward a revised federal Indian policy.

Red Cloud continued his war in the Powder River country. "We want these roads stopped and the soldiers kept out," said Pawnee Killer (Oglala). "War came from making the roads through the [Powder River] country. These roads scare away all the game," said another Sioux. Red Cloud echoed their sentiments, adding, "The white men have crowded the Indians back . . . until we are forced to live in a small country north of the Platte, and now our last hunting grounds . . . is to be taken from us. Our women and children will starve, but for my part I prefer to die fighting than by starvation." With Northern Cheyenne and Arapaho allies, the Indians ranged along the Upper Missouri River throughout spring and summer attacking miners, settlers, and military units in addition to their own traditional Indian enemies in the region. Their campaigns stretched the military's capabilities, spreading the greatly outnumbered troops over a vast region and in so doing exposing miners and settlers alike to frequent raids.

In September, another peace commission traveled into the plains, meeting with tribes encamped along the Missouri River. At each stop, the commission listened to Indian complaints of white aggression, but at each stop it also suggested that the Indians accept the inevitability of removal to reservations. In talks with the Sioux, commissioners recommended the Indians themselves select a territory for a reservation while they still had such an opportunity. Red Cloud, however, refused to meet with the peace commission.

READING HISTORY

Report to the President by the Indian Peace Commission, January 7, 1868

In 1867, President Andrew Johnson appointed former U.S. Congressman Nathaniel Taylor as Commissioner of the Indian Bureau. Taylor had long championed peace with Native Americans, one, he believed, best accomplished by establishing two large reservations in the plains. Later that year, Congress formed another peace commission, led by Taylor, to determine the causes of warfare on the plains and to determine avenues toward permanent peace.

To the President of the United States: . . .

When the act was passed, war was being openly waged by several hostile tribes, and great diversity of opinion existed among the officials of the government, and no less diversity among our people, as to the means best adapted to meet it. Some thought peaceful negotiation would succeed while others had no hope of peace until the Indians were thoroughly subdued by force of arms....

The first difficulty presenting itself was to secure an interview with the chiefs and leading warriors of those hostile tribes. They were roaming over an immense country thousands of miles in extent, and much of it unknown even to hunters and trappers of the white race. Small war parties ... would suddenly strike the border settlements.... Companies of workmen on the railroads ... would be attacked on the same day, perhaps in the same hour.... All safe transit across the plains had ceased. To go without soldiers was hazardous in the extreme; to go with them forbade reasonable hope of securing peaceful interviews with the enemy....

So little accustomed to kindness from others, it may not be strange that he often hesitates to confide.... Whatever our people may choose to say of the insincerity or duplicity of the Indian would fail to express the estimate entertained by many Indians of the white man's character in this respect. Promises have been so often broken by those with whom they usually come in contact, cupidity has so long plied its work deaf to cries of suffering, and heartless cruelty has so frequently sought them in the garb of charity, that to obtain their confidence our promises must be scrupulously fulfilled and our professions of friendship divested of all appearance of selfishness and duplicity.... If it should suggest to civilization that the injunction to "do good to them that hate us" is not confined to race, but broad as humanity itself, it may do some good even to ourselves....

If the lands of the white man are taken, civilization justifies him in resisting the invader. Civilization does more than this: it brands him as a coward and a slave if he submits to the wrong.... These Indians saw their former homes and hunting grounds overrun by a greedy population, thirsting for gold. They saw their game driven east to the plains, and soon found themselves the objects of jealousy and hatred.... [T]he Indians yet demand the surrender of this country to them. But they have agreed to suspend hostilities and meet commissioners next spring to treat of their alleged rights, without insisting on the previous withdrawal of the garrisons. Whether they will then insist on the abandonment of the route [Bozeman Trail] we cannot say....

If it be said that the savages are unreasonable, we answer, that if civilized they might be reasonable. At least they would not be dependent on the buffalo and the elk; they would no longer want a country exclusively for game, and the presence of the white man would become desirable. If it be said that because they are savages they should be exterminated, we answer that, aside from the humanity of the suggestion, it will prove exceedingly difficult, and if money considerations are permitted to weigh, it costs less to civilize than to kill.

In making treaties it was enjoined on us to remove, if possible, the causes of complaints on the part of the Indians. This would be no easy task. We have done the best we could under the circumstances, but it is now rather late in the day to think of obliterating from the minds of the present generation the remembrance of wrong. Among civilized men war usually springs from a sense of injustice. The best possible way then to avoid war is to do no act of injustice. When we learn that the same rule holds good with Indians, the chief difficulty is removed. But it is said our wars with them have been almost constant. Have we been uniformly unjust? We answer, unhesitatingly, yes! We are aware that the masses of our people have felt kindly toward them, and the legislation of Congress has always been conceived in the best intentions, but it has been erroneous in fact or perverted in execution. Nobody pays any attention to Indian matters. This is a deplorable fact. Members of Congress understand the Negro question, and talk learnedly of finance and other problems of political economy, but when the progress of settlement reaches the Indian's home, the only question considered is, "how best to get his lands." When they are obtained, the Indian is lost sight of. While our missionary societies and benevolent associations have annually collected thousands of dollars from the charitable, to be sent to Asia and Africa for the purposes of civilization, scarcely a dollar is expended or a thought bestowed on the civilization of Indians at our very doors. Is it because the Indians are not worth the effort at civilization? Or is it because our people, who have grown rich in the occupation of their former lands—too often taken by force or procured by fraud—will not contribute?

Indians of different tribes associate with each other on terms of equality; they have not the Bible, but their religion, which we call superstition, teaches them that the Great Spirit made us all . . . He always objected, and went with a sadder heart. His hunting grounds are as dear to him as is the home of his childhood to the civilized man. He too loves the streams and mountains of his youth; to be forced to leave them breaks those tender chords of the heart which vibrate to the softer sensibilities of human nature, and dries up the fountains of benevolence and kindly feeling, without which there is no civilization . . .

If the Indians were now in a fertile region of country, the difficulty would be less; they would not have to be removed . . . But one thing then remains to be done with honor to the nation, and that is to select a district or districts of country, as indicated by Congress, on which all the tribes east of the Rocky mountains may be gathered. For each district let a territorial government be established, with powers adapted to the ends designed. The governor should be a man of unquestioned integrity and purity of character; he should be paid such salary as to place him above temptation; . . . agriculture and manufactures should be introduced among them as rapidly as possible; schools should be established which children should be required to attend; . . . Let farmers and mechanics, millers and engineers be employed and sent among them for purposes of instruction; . . . The object of greatest solicitude should be to break down the prejudices of tribe among the Indians; to blot out the boundary lines which divide them into distinct nations, and fuse them into one homogeneous mass . . . [B]y the plan suggested we will have formed a nucleus of civilization among the young that will restrain the old and furnish them a home and subsistence when the game is gone.

Source: *The Annual Report of the Commissioner of Indian Affairs, for the Year 1868* (Washington, D.C.: Government Printing Office, 1868), pp. 26–50.

Questions

1. How does the tone and perspective of this document fit with emerging trends of the late 1860s?
2. How does the perspective of these commissioners conflict with that of existing policy and actions?
3. In this document, do Indians appear to be more the victim or the overpowered resistor?

In October, the delegation turned south and at Medicine Lodge Creek in southwestern Kansas met with war leaders and chiefs of the Kiowa, Comanche, Southern Cheyenne, Arapaho, and Apaches. More than 5,000 Indians gathered at Medicine Lodge Creek. The commission laid before the assembled Indians a plan for two separate reservations to be established in the western section of Indian Territory, Cheyenne and Arapaho on one and the other three groups sharing the other. They assured the Indians that Washington would provide all tools and seed necessary for farming, rifles and ammunition for hunting, clothing and blankets, and food. Peace would follow their signing of the treaty. The delegation offered nothing substantially different from the treaties Washington formally arranged with other tribes. The Indians accepted the treaties largely because their resistance on the southern plains over the previous year accomplished little. White migration not only continued but actually increased now that the Civil War was over. Peace, at this moment, seemed the more practical course. By month's end, with the exception of bands led by Santanta (Kiowa) and Roman Nose (Cheyenne), most Indian leaders accepted the **Medicine Lodge Creek Treaty.**

It was November when the peace commission returned north to Fort Laramie, hoping to meet with Red Cloud. He refused, and he sent word that war would continue until whites abandoned all forts on the Bozeman Trail and Washington evacuated miners and settlers from the Powder River country. Faced with the reality of an expensive and ongoing war in the region, the commission encouraged Washington to craft a treaty suited to Sioux preferences. On April 29, 1868, leaders of the Brule, Miniconjou, and Oglala Sioux gathered at Fort Laramie and signed a peace treaty with the United States that established **The Great Sioux Reservation**. It covered the western half of the Dakota Territory, and Indians were guaranteed the right to reside outside the reservation in the Powder River region above the North Platte River and east of the Big Horn Mountains. All of these lands were to be free of white settlement and intrusion. Moreover, the army would vacate its military posts throughout the Indians' newly defined territory. In what was likely a bid to win congressional and public support for the treaty, it also included a statement of the government's expectation that the Indian signatories would begin a process of acculturation. Red Cloud chose not to sign the treaty at that time, delaying acceptance until all military posts on the Bozeman Trail were abandoned. "When we see the soldiers moving away . . . then I will come down and talk," he said. In August, the U.S. Army evacuated the forts and abandoned the region, the Sioux torching each fort as the troops retreated. On November 6, Red Cloud signed the Treaty of Fort Laramie. For now, peace settled over the northern plains.

Contrary to the rhetoric of white politicians and key military officers, war in the Powder River—often called **Red Cloud's War**—ended in victory for the Sioux. The cavalry never routed Indian war parties and rarely threatened Indian villages. The Sioux commanded the countryside, moving at will and most often determining the site of combat. The various bands had a common enemy in the army and a common desire to preserve Sioux life in the Powder River as it had always been. Soldiers and miners were viewed as invaders; the Indians fought to defend their families and their land. A war of self-defense—one of survival—produced greater will to fight and to accept death in battle. Moreover, their skill in battle and even their firepower outmatched those of the soldiers and miners, and the leadership of Red Cloud and Crazy Horse proved far superior to army officers. They retreated when faced with an overwhelming force, teased the army into pursuit over great distances, which only frustrated and weakened the cavalry, and fought fiercely when the troopers did not expect to be attacked. Factored into all of this, the war proved exceedingly costly for Washington. Carl Shurz, Secretary of the Interior under President Ulysses S. Grant, estimated the government spent roughly $1 million for every Sioux, Cheyenne, and Arapaho killed in the fighting. Such a high cost of war could not be maintained indefinitely. The Sioux won the war; they compelled the United States to relinquish its hold on Sioux territory. Although a reservation ultimately was established, the treaty permitted Indians a region of "unceded" land (the Powder River) on which many chose to remain, to live as they always had lived.

10.2 General William Tecumseh Sherman and the Peace Commission meet with Cheyenne and Arapaho leaders to draft the Fort Laramie Treaty of 1868.

Source: MPI/Getty Images

The **Fort Laramie Treaty** of 1868 was a remarkable concession to Native Americans. For many Indians, it validated their commitment to resistance. The treaty effectively removed intruders from their traditional lands and in so doing acknowledged the power of the Sioux. It did not insist on Indian acculturation, only the creation of opportunities conducive to acculturation. And, from the Indians' perspective, their successful armed resistance in the Powder River emboldened them to apply force again should threats be renewed.

From another perspective, the treaty was not so remarkable. First, the United States manned and equipped only a small army in the aftermath of the Civil War. Demands on the War Department were extensive, with operations ranging from the Canadian border south through the southern plains and across the western mountains into Oregon and California. At the same time, Ku Klux Klan activities in the former Confederacy, along with efforts by state governments in the South to circumvent Washington's reconstruction agenda, compelled the government to maintain a substantial military presence in the South. The War Department did not have the manpower and materiel to wage a protracted, bloody war in the Powder River region in light of these demands. Moreover, public opinion, though leaning toward armed resolution rather than negotiated arrangement, was, nonetheless, divided. The longer the war with the Sioux persisted in the Powder River, the more divisive the war became in Congress and among the public. There simply was not enough at stake—not enough to be gained within a reasonable time frame—for the United States to continue the war.

Renewed Resistance on the Southern Plains

Tensions persisted on the southern plains. In late 1867 and early 1868, the Cheyenne, Arapaho, and other tribes waited in vain for the food supplies, clothing, and blankets promised to them in the Medicine Lodge Creek Treaty. The winter of 1868 proved especially brutal as snow and bitterly cold temperatures swept across the region. Hunger, malnutrition, and disease hit the Indian population hard, many becoming desperately ill and some dying. Not until midsummer did the long-awaited supplies finally arrive, but, by then, word of Red Cloud's apparent success had filtered across the southern plains. Angered at the government's failure to deliver on its promises and emboldened by the Sioux's successful resistance, nearly 200 young Cheyenne warriors took to raiding white farms, ranches, and settlements in Colorado and neighboring Kansas. These raids were sporadic, but General Sherman nonetheless declared the southern plains once again awash in a state of war and ordered his armies to use all necessary force to drive the Indians onto reservations in Indian Territory. He declared that all Indians not residing on their assigned reservations would be considered "hostile, and [they] will remain so till killed," regardless of their activity or purpose. Murderous skirmishes soon erupted across the territory.

Sherman commanded General Philip Sheridan to plan, organize, and implement a military campaign to destroy soundly all Indian resistance. Sheridan planned for a war of extermination. He believed a winter campaign, like that launched against the Navajo, offered the greatest chance for unequivocal success. Furthermore, winters could be quite brutal on the southern plains, but the region's topography allowed armies to maneuver against a stationary enemy, unlike in the mountainous Powder River country, where winters halted any significant movement. He informed General Sherman that he would not hesitate to strike, even if women and children inadvertently were killed. Sheridan reminded Sherman of Union campaigns against the Confederacy in which cities such as Vicksburg and Atlanta were mercilessly shelled. In battles against Indians, he said, "If a village is attacked and women and children [are] killed, the responsibility is not with the soldiers but with the people whose crimes necessitated the attack."

Black Kettle's band of Cheyenne camped on the Washita River in the westernmost strip of Indian Territory in autumn 1868. Sheridan learned that Cheyenne and Arapaho warriors known to have raided white farms and trading posts now rested in Black Kettle's camp. Indeed they did. Black Kettle spoke at length with the

Indians, and he encouraged them to avoid warfare with whites. It mattered little to Sheridan that Black Kettle had consistently promoted peace with the advancing white population, even in the wake of Sand Creek. On November 27, a regiment of the Seventh Cavalry commanded by Colonel George Armstrong Custer attacked Black Kettle's band on the Washita without advance warning. It "was all too reminiscent of Sand Creek, almost four years ago to the day," wrote one historian. More than 100 Indians died in the assault, and another 50 were taken prisoner. Black Kettle lay among the dead. Sheridan's winter campaign continued throughout December and the early months of 1869, accomplishing the general's principal goals of punishing Indian raiders, destroying the Indians' ability to fight, and forcibly moving Indians to their assigned reservations.

Peace Policy, War Policy

The plains from Canada into Texas seemed strangely quiet in early 1869. The U.S. Army's winter campaign in the southern plains muted most Indian resistance among the Cheyenne, Arapaho, Kiowa, Comanche, and Apaches. The northern region of the Great Plains was likewise quiet, Red Cloud having finally accepted the Fort Laramie Treaty and most Sioux in residence on a new reservation on a site they preferred. Peace had been attained, but at a high price. In November 1868, the nation elected a new president, placing in the White House a man commonly thought to be a "no-nonsense" individual, one who could restore order to the South while dealing effectively with white settlement and Indian resistance in the West.

President Grant's Peace Policy

As he awaited his scheduled March 1869 inauguration, the former general of the U.S. Army and now President-Elect of the United States Ulysses S. Grant believed his administration might be able to settle Indian affairs in the West. The "hero" of the Union Army in the recent Civil War was not averse to employing overwhelming military power to destroy an enemy, and Grant proved clearly his willingness to use brute force against his enemies. But the war years also left him with an intimate understanding of war's absurd brutality. Grant personally supported the preference of his long-time friends in the military to place Native Americans under the jurisdiction of the War Department rather than the Interior Department. There was, however, someone that made Grant consider seriously the Interior Department's call for humanitarian treatment of Indians and their eventual acculturation—his personal friend and advisor Ely S. Parker.

Ely S. Parker had been a chief among the Seneca Indians and Grand Sachem of the Iroquois Confederacy. Acculturated to the white world and educated in law and engineering, he served under General Grant as a Union colonel throughout the Vicksburg campaign and again in the fighting against Robert E. Lee's armies in Virginia. The two men built a close relationship with one another, and after the war Parker remained with Grant, serving as an advisor on Indian issues and from 1869 to 1871 as Commissioner of Indian Affairs—the first Native American to occupy that position. To Grant, Parker represented the promise of successful acculturation and assimilation of Native Americans, a living example of what humanitarian reform efforts could accomplish if applied to American Indians who had been removed from their traditional tribal structures.

Parker agreed with Grant's opinion, which eastern reformers shared, that Indian tribes were not equivalent to foreign powers. In 1869, he declared, "the Indian tribes of the United States are not sovereign nations, capable of making treaties." "Because treaties have been made with them, generally for the extinguishment of their supposed absolute title to land inhabited by them . . . they have become falsely impressed with the notion of national independence. It is time that this idea should be dispelled." Indians, said Parker, are "wards of the government, and the only title the law concedes them to the lands they occupy or claim is a mere possessory one."

Once inaugurated, President Grant stripped Indians of their long-time standing as independent, sovereign nations. They were now viewed as members of a "wandering tribe" living within the territorial borders of the United States and as "wards" of the federal government.

Parker's assessment conflicted sharply with the opinion and rulings of previous generations of Americans. President George Washington recognized Iroquois nationhood, affixing his signature to treaties that legitimized Indian independence from the United States despite their tribal residency within U.S. territory. Congress over the years consistently employed the treaty as a means of settling disputes between Washington, D.C., and Indian nations. Parker's view, however, carried the weight of law in 1871 as Congress now renounced Indian nationhood and halted its treaty-making with Native Americans. Washington promised to honor existing treaties, but it would no longer create new treaties with Native American tribes. Historians routinely point to this congressional move as the moment the government abruptly reversed Indian policy. It reflected a profound shift in the way the federal government perceived Native Americans. They were now viewed not as obstacles or impediments to progress but as "redeemable people" capable of accepting white American culture and genuinely, eventually, assimilating into the general population.

Parker was not the only voice seeking to influence

10.3 Ely S. Parker (1828–1895), Seneca chief and Union Army officer in the Civil War

Source: MPI/Getty Images

the president-elect's position on Indian affairs. In late January, a small group of Quakers visited Grant and presented him with a resolution adopted at their recent national convention that favored a more humane and peaceful approach to resolve the present crisis in Indian affairs. They encouraged him to appoint Quakers as reservation agents and emissaries to Indian groups not as yet relocated. Once assigned to those positions, the Quakers would spread their understanding of Christianity by word *and* by action among native peoples, manage reservations with greater humanity than that demonstrated under previous administrations, and serve as committed liaisons between Native Americans and Washington. Grant readily accepted the Quakers' recommendation, saying, "if you can make Quakers out of the Indians it will take the fight out of them. Let us have peace." Quakerism was a religion of peace, by word and by act. Equally important, and something that probably did not escape Grant, the historic failure of Christian conversion among Indians turned on the failure of the faithful to exhibit clearly and consistently the very word of God they preached. Since Quakers paid great attention to their earthy, daily deeds, perhaps they would have greater success in religious conversion.

Grant said in his inaugural address that Indian policies would be studied carefully, and he would "favor any course toward them [Indians] which tends to their civilization and ultimate citizenship," a statement that initially shocked his friends General Sherman and General Sheridan. President Grant's actual policy statement, however, proved vague. His "promise of a 'peace policy' betokened no grand design for a fresh and humane approach," but he did state his intention of placing humanity above a military solution with the caveat that "those [Indians] who do not accept this policy will find the new administration ready for a sharp and severe war policy."

SEEING HISTORY

"Robinson Crusoe Making a Man of His Friday"

This political cartoon shows President Grant "Americanizing" the Native American. The plan to Americanize Indians, or acculturate Native Americans to the traits and mores of non-Indian society, assumed national proportion under the presidency of Ulysses S. Grant in the 1870s. Replace native values and behaviors with those of the dominant race, it was believed, and Native Americans would no longer be an impediment to national progress. Moreover, reasoned reformers and political figures alike believed it was an obligation of the United States to uplift "primitives" to civilization.

Questions

1. What does the cartoon suggest about the role of Grant toward native peoples?
2. What message does the cartoonist offer regarding the Indians' receptivity of Americanization? How are these messages conveyed?

ROBINSON CRUSOE MAKING A MAN OF HIS FRIDAY.

10.4 Thomas Nast, "Robinson Crusoe making a man of his Friday" (cartoon)

Source: Courtesy of Library of Congress Prints and Photographs Division, LC-USZ61-1912

Grant gave Quakers a central role in providing humanitarian aid to reservation Indians, but under pressure from other denominations he also extended the same opportunity to all major Christian groups. He expected the transformation of Indians into hardworking, acculturated members of American society would best be accomplished under the direction of Christian missionaries. A pervasive religious presence on reservations, he hoped, might reduce the corruption and inhumanity commonly practiced on those islands of humanity. Grant's vision faded quickly as Protestants and Catholics competed fiercely to expand their roles among Native Americans, and the corruption of reservation agents increased rather than diminish.

In short order, President Grant set the tone for a policy of peace with Native Americans. From the White House, he advanced policies that made Indians the responsibility of the United States rather than persons of independent nations, emphasized the Christianization of Native Americans as a method to break their spirited resistance, pressed their acculturation of American values and their training as farmers and ranchers, and suggested their possible assimilation with mainstream society. It was, in many respects, a remarkable change of course for the United States, but it was also the antithesis of Indian desires. "If the Great Spirit had desired me to be a white man he would have made me so in the first place," said Sitting Bull. "He put in your heart certain wishes and plans; in my heart he put other and different desires. Each man is good in the sight of the Great Spirit. It is not necessary for eagles to be crows."

Resistance on the Southern Plains Continues

Two storms converged on the southern plains in the early 1870s, storms that ignited a maelstrom of violence between Indians and the United States. In 1870, hunters and skinners, those who simply stripped buffalo of their hides and left the carcass to rot, received permission from federal authorities to move their operations from the northern and central Great Plains to the southern region. There was a profitable market in the East for buffalo hides but little demand for meat. Hunters and skinners roamed the prairies slaughtering buffalo to the point of extinction. It was not uncommon for a single hunter to kill more than 100 buffalo in a single day; indeed, it was reported that William F. Cody (Buffalo Bill) alone killed at least 4,000 in an 18-month span. More than 1.25 million buffalo hides were collected and shipped east in 1873 alone. The rapid and severe depletion of buffalo crippled Indian bands that still depended on the animals for their survival. The buffalo provided almost all of the Indians' needs—food, shelter, clothing, and tools. "The buffalo were the life of the Kiowas," recalled Old Lady Horse (Kiowa) years later. "Up and down the plains those [hunters] ranged, shooting sometimes as many as a hundred buffalo a day. Behind them came the skinners with their wagons," she said. "Everything the Kiowas had came from the buffalo." Rotting carcasses offered nothing of use. Indians journeyed farther in search of herds, frequently venturing into the traditional hunting areas of other Indians

10.5 Buffalo hunters and skinners

Source: National Archives and Records Administration, 79-M-1B-3

and occasionally battling other Native Americans for access to the herds they found. Hunger soon shadowed Indians of the plains, and the freezing temperatures of winter made life almost impossible. For survival, many bands voluntarily submitted themselves to reservations where food, clothing, and shelter were promised.

There were, in fact, calls from within government, the U.S. Army, and the general civilian population to limit significantly or halt completely the destruction of the Great Plains buffalo. Stunned by the impact of over-hunting on native populations, congressmen and senators introduced bills and resolutions in Congress throughout the 1870s that called for a ban on the buffalo hunt then occurring on the prairies. One army general posted in the West described the slaughter as a "wanton waste," senseless in its magnitude. Noted one writer for *Harper's Weekly* in December 1874, "deprived of one of their chief means of subsistence . . . the [Indians] take revenge by making raids on white settlements and carrying off stocks." Ban the trade, and much of the warfare over the plains would cease, he argued. Still, General Sheridan saw certain benefit to the hunters' and skinners' work. "These men have done more . . . to settle the vexed Indian question than the entire regular army has done in the last forty years," he said. "They are destroying the Indians' commissary." "For a lasting peace," he added, "let them kill, skin, and sell until the buffalo is exterminated, as it is the only way to bring lasting peace and allow civilization to advance."

Life remained unbearable on most reservations. Government supplies and food promised under earlier agreements either failed to reach the targeted Indian groups or were damaged or spoiled beyond use before they arrived. Those few Indians who tried their hand at farming—abandoning their own cultural values to do so—seldom received the tools, seeds, and instruction promised in treaties, and much of the land on which Indians resided was absolutely unsuited to agriculture. Little wonder, then, that so many Native Americans, especially younger warriors, rose in anger at their circumstances.

On June 27, 1874, more than 300 Cheyenne and Comanche warriors struck the buffalo hunters' rendezvous site at Adobe Walls in the Texas Panhandle. Additional war parties slashed at trading posts, ranchers, farms, transportation lines, and small army outposts in Texas, New Mexico, Colorado, and Kansas. To be sure,

TIMELINE 10.1 THE DESTRUCTION OF THE BUFFALO

Date	Event
1870	The U.S. Army plans to destroy the Indians' source of life by depopulating the buffalo
1871	The House of Representatives considers a ban on the killing of buffalo in the western territories except for food
1872–1874	White hunters and skinners destroy 4,375,000 buffalo; Native Americans themselves kill 1,215,000 buffalo
1872	The U.S. Senate endorses the framing of legislation to protect buffalo and elk
1874	A bill to prohibit anyone but Indians from killing buffalo for purposes other than food is made into law
1882	Approximately 5,000 hunters and skinners are still at work depleting the buffalo population in the northern plains
1884	The buffalo of the northern plains are considered nearly extinct, with an estimated population of only 2,000 buffalo remaining

numerous military officers and politicians assigned blame correctly on the whites and on the conditions that challenged Indian survival. General Sheridan himself acknowledged that Indian resistance resulted from their continued loss of land, skyrocketing infection rates from numerous diseases whites inadvertently introduced, and Washington's conscious decision to replace native cultures with a culture alien to all they had ever known. Their lives now threatened by the rapid depopulation of buffalo, the Indians understandably rose in resistance. "Could any one expect less?" Sheridan asked rhetorically.

Regardless of the validity of their complaints, Indian resistance required a military response. Sheridan once again called for total war against all Indians not on reservations. General Sherman was of the same opinion and on July 20 authorized a full military campaign against the southern tribes, an order that received the blessing of the War Department, Interior Department, and the White House. Warfare blazed across the southern plains in what became known as the **Red River War**. Nearly 2,000 Comanche, 2,000 Southern Cheyenne, and 1,000 Kiowa fled their reservations, and most joined the fight. Sheridan's enlarged and well-equipped armies used

PROFILE

Quanah Parker (Comanche)

Born about 1850, Quanah Parker was the son of Peta Nocona, a Comanche chief, and Cynthia Ann Parker, a white captive. As a young man, he participated in raids against both Mexicans and American settlers to secure needed food and other supplies and to counter the growing presence of American settlers in the southern plains.

Parker refused to acknowledge the Medicine Lodge Creek Treaty of 1867, believing no Comanche should relinquish his land and submit to reservation life, and he continued leading raids on both sides of the border. He played a commanding role in the Comanche attack on Adobe Walls in Texas and in the Red River War of 1874–1875. In early summer 1875, Parker realized his people had reached their limit, drained by the war and the relentless pursuit of the U.S. Army. Other tribes had already surrendered. On June 2, he too resigned himself to the reservation and surrendered his band. There was no alternative, he believed; only utter destruction of his people would result if resistance continued. Parker led his band to Fort Sill in present-day Oklahoma and there began reservation life.

Despite his surrender, Quanah Parker's resistance continued, now taking on a new form. He came to see acculturation as necessary for Indian survival, but he continuously worked to preserve native cultural values, customs, and structures and in so doing retain an Indian identity. He learned English and traveled to Washington to lobby for new policies that assured the cultural survival of native peoples. He aggressively opposed government efforts to prohibit or diminish the use of peyote among southern plains Indians, arguing its use was an inherent right of native peoples and a religious right under the U.S. Constitution. Parker encouraged Comanche land allottees to lease their property to white ranchers and farmers, a move that might garner some income for landholders, and he supported the 1892 Jerome Agreement that divided the Comanche reservation. He encouraged Indians to secure a formal education and to learn "white ways," and he contributed to the development of farming and ranching enterprises among the Comanche, himself attaining some personal prosperity. Although these acts were viewed by white land speculators, government agents, and others as evidence of Parker's acceptance of non-Indian values and his evolving assimilation into white society, Parker believed them to be practical moves necessary to sustain Indian life and to preserve Comanche identity. Parker died on February 23, 1911, from an undiagnosed illness.

a series of pincer movements that masterfully enveloped the warring tribes. He targeted the Indians' food supplies and attacked villages without concern for women and children. Battles proved infrequent, but the army's pursuit was constant. With winter fast approaching and Indian groups increasingly weakened, resistance turned to desperation and bands began surrendering. The Kiowa surrendered at Fort Sill, Oklahoma, in February 1875. The Cheyenne succumbed in March, and in June the Comanche likewise turned themselves over to the U.S. Army at Fort Sill. Those who still hoped to evade the army's grasp, largely Cheyenne, moved north to join the Red Cloud Agency, a division of the Great Sioux Reservation.

President Grant, determined to coerce Indian submission, ordered the confinement of war chiefs at Fort Marion in St. Augustine, Florida, in an effort to break the warrior spirit common to the Indians' cultures, a spirit that these leaders inspired. Santanta (Comanche) was incarcerated in the Texas penitentiary and after three years of imprisonment leaped to his death from a third-floor window. The imprisonment or death of leading warriors hobbled the Indians' will to fight.

Gold in the Black Hills

By 1869, the Sioux, Northern Cheyenne, and Arapaho settled into the Great Sioux Reservation in present-day South Dakota, with a population of about 13,000 Indians. Washington added to the Indians' living space by establishing the Spotted Tail Agency in northwestern Nebraska to accommodate another 8,000 Indians. Another group opted to reside in the non-reservation territory of the Powder River area designated by the Fort Laramie Treaty. Among them lived Crazy Horse and Sitting Bull.

In 1872, trouble brewed between these Indian groups and the U.S. government. The Northern Pacific Railroad received permission to construct a rail line across the upper plains from Minnesota to the Yellowstone River Valley. The track system bypassed both the Red Cloud and Spotted Tail agencies, but its course to the Yellowstone meandered through the un-ceded lands on which Sitting Bull and Crazy Horse lived. In an effort to avoid another showdown in the Powder River country, Washington sent representatives to the Sioux asking for a route through the territory. Sioux leaders rejected flatly the request, arguing that the rail line would interfere with their hunting and encourage white settlement on Indian lands. Moreover, they added, their concession on this request would likely bring additional requests from Washington. The railway was not completed, a victim of the national financial crisis of 1873 that forced the Northern Pacific to abandon the project. Nonetheless, the Hunkpapa and Oglala Sioux of the region understood too well that this was but a brief reprieve.

In spring 1874, Colonel George Armstrong Custer with two battalions of soldiers—roughly 1,200 men—headed for the Dakota Territory with a dual assignment. First, Custer was to scout the Great Sioux Reservation for sites suitable for the construction of army posts from which troops would provide military protection to railroad companies laying track westward. The prospect of army posts within Sioux boundaries infuriated the Indians. They had not given their permission for the expedition or for the building of forts in their territory. "That is the country of the Oglala Sioux," thundered Red Cloud. Custer also escorted mineral experts and newspapermen deep into the Great Sioux Reservation. The mission was simple—confirm or refute alleged discoveries of gold in the Black Hills. They moved cautiously to the area known to the Lakota as Paha Sapa, "the heart of everything that is," the soul of the Lakota universe. There was no land considered more valuable to the Sioux—no property more central to Sioux identity—than this stretch. Custer found the precious metal he was seeking, and he wasted little time relaying word back east in September that there was "gold at the roots of the grass" on the reservation.

In response, President Grant and the War Department ordered the Black Hills off limits to white miners and prospectors and charged the U.S. Army to enforce the directive. It mattered little. Gold proved too powerful a lure. "If there is gold in the Black Hills," reported the *New York Tribune*, "no army on earth can keep the adventurous men of the west out of them." By summer 1875, the army's efforts had proved futile, and in September Washington dispatched a special commission to the Lakota, offering $6,000,000 for the Black Hills. As expected, the Sioux unequivocally rejected any bid to buy the land and promised to defend it with their lives against all intruders. By mid-October, tens of thousands of gold seekers flooded into the Black Hills.

President Grant, with the advice of the Secretary of War, Secretary of the Interior, Commissioner of Indian Affairs, and key generals of the U.S. Army, decided to suspend the government's effort at removing miners from the Black Hills. The policy had not succeeded, as miners removed from the region and released outside the reservation were found only days later panning for gold again. The administration now opted to press for the relocation of Sitting Bull's and Crazy Horse's bands onto the Great Sioux Reservation, using as justification the allegation that the Indians were raiding white settlers. Moving those bands onto the Red Cloud Agency would open the gold district to miners and allow unmolested construction of railway lines through the region.

Commissioner of Indian Affairs Edward Smith sent an order to the Sioux living in the westernmost regions that they must report to the Great Sioux Reservation by January 31, 1876, or face forced removal under the army's direction. Historians have correctly noted that Smith's order was of questionable legal validity. The Sioux and the Northern Cheyenne were permitted by the Fort Laramie Treaty to live there. They were never required to settle onto the Great Sioux Reservation nor abandon the Powder River region. Even those Indians who considered it wiser to move onto the reservation than face another war found the order's timing particularly inappropriate. The Indians could not make the journey in winter. The frigid air and abundant snowfall prevented traveling over a terrain difficult to cross even in warm months. And, the precise date, arbitrarily chosen, meant nothing to the Sioux. Their conception of time varied fundamentally from that of white civilization. January 31 meant no more to them than March 31. No Sioux arrived at the reservation by the appointed deadline.

The Interior Department wasted no time once the date passed. On February 1, it announced the Sioux, Northern Cheyenne, and Arapaho not residing on the reservation to be enemies of the United States. The War Department then instructed General Philip Sheridan to move his armies into the western Sioux country and wage relentless war against the Indians until the "hostiles" surrendered and moved to the Red Cloud Agency.

The Great Sioux War

General Sheridan directed his field commanders to implement against the Sioux the same basic plan of war used against the southern plains tribes a few years earlier—a series of pincer movements from multiple directions, pushing the Indians into a small, confined location where they could be destroyed or taken prisoner. The harsh winter of 1876, however, delayed his move against the Indians until spring. In March, General George Crook guided his force into the Powder River, unleashing cavalry units and infantry columns against the Sioux housed along the river near the Big Horn Mountains. In May, he sent his troops up the Bozeman Trail. At the same time, General Alfred Terry ordered his forces into the Dakota Territory and the Yellowstone Valley. Shoshone and Crow warriors and scouts aided the army, seeing in this campaign an opportunity to remove their traditional and common enemy from the territory. Fighting throughout the region proved as brutal as both sides initially anticipated.

On June 17, Crook's army and warriors under Sitting Bull and Crazy Horse collided in a fierce, day-long fight at Rosebud Creek that neither side could claim as a victory. Crook's troops held the field of battle, but the Sioux seriously hurt Crook's fighting capability, and their dogged resistance encouraged more Indians to join the war against the United States. The Sioux then moved to the banks of the Little Big Horn River, known to the Indians as the Greasy Grass.

Crook soon learned of Sitting Bull's general location and began repositioning his forces to converge on the Sioux. Colonel George Custer, in command of a regiment of the Seventh Cavalry, found himself a dozen miles from Sitting Bull on the evening of June 24. Certain the Indians knew of his approach, he force-marched his men that evening closer to Sitting Bull's camp for a morning strike. Custer was correct; the Sioux knew his exact location.

On Sunday morning, June 25, the plains simmered from the summer heat. Custer, eager as ever to strike the enemy and enhance his reputation, chose not to wait on the arrival of Crook's and Terry's larger forces. Little did he know that more than 1,000 Sioux, Cheyenne, and Arapaho warriors waited for him down on the Little Big Horn. The colonel planned a two-pronged attack. He would lead 225 troopers in a frontal assault against the Indian encampment, and his second-in-command, Major Marcus Reno, would guide another 115 against the Sioux flank. A third force, Captain Frederick Benteen and his 125 men, would be held in reserve to destroy those Indians fleeing the Sioux camp. All three units combined totaled no more than 465 soldiers, less than half the Sioux strength. Custer's ego crippled his chance for victory, but it was also a failure of military command. Men training to become army officers are traditionally taught several fundamental rules from which a commander does not deviate unless there is no other option—concentrate military force against the enemy and trust the intelligence scouts or agents gather. Custer did neither.

Reno struck the southern end of the three-mile-long camp, and immediately he and his soldiers realized the buzz saw they now faced. Fighting raged for nearly one hour before his troopers scattered for cover in the surrounding hills. Benteen's unit rushed to Reno's support, only to find themselves now trapped alongside Reno.

Warriors ambushed Custer as he led his force toward the Indians' camp. The Indians hit from three sides with the fury of "bees swarming out of a hive," said one Sioux chief. Rather than a fixed fight on the side of a hill as is represented in popular Hollywood films, Custer's "Last Stand," as Sitting Bull himself termed it, was a moving, fluid battle, spreading across the countryside for at least one mile before the Indians cut down Custer and his remaining soldiers. "I was not sorry . . . I was happy . . . Those Wasichus [white men] had come to kill our mothers and fathers and us, and it was our country," said Black Elk (Sioux) in an interview in the 1930s. Reno and Benteen held out until midday on June 26, when the Indians finally broke off their attack and abandoned the area in advance of General Terry's arrival. Reno lost half of his men, and Benteen's company suffered almost as many casualties.

10.6 Sitting Bull (c. 1831–1890) was a Hunkpapa Lakota Sioux holy man who led his people as a tribal chief during years of resistance to United States government policies.

Source: Courtesy of Library of Congress Prints and Photographs Division, LC-USZ62-12277

Reports flashed eastward announcing the Sioux's stunning victory at Little Big Horn. By July 5, the United States was mourning its fallen soldiers, deflating the Americans' spirited national centennial celebration the previous day. Rage quickly swept the nation. Custer's superiors, among them General Terry, were baffled by Custer's move at the Little Big Horn, their only explanation being the colonel's desire to enhance his reputation and in so doing advance his post-military political aspirations. But at what expense? General Philip Sheridan ordered reinforcements into the Dakota Territory to pursue and destroy all Sioux and Cheyenne.

Throughout the remainder of 1876, the cavalry dogged the Indians' every move, and, instead of bivouacking for winter as was the custom and as the Indians expected, Sheridan continued the campaign without rest into early spring 1877, assigning to Colonel Nelson Miles principal responsibility for crushing the Sioux and Cheyenne. Winter nearly halted the army's ability to maneuver. Bitter cold, snow, and ice whipped over the northern plains, numbing soldiers' feet and hands and making sight and breath painful. Field commanders nonetheless pressed their armies forward.

The Indians, too, suffered miserably. Hunger and disease stalked the Indians, and weather hampered their escape. Babies froze to death in the bitter winter. When Miles' units found Indian encampments, they attacked without mercy, killing as many as they could and then burning the teepees and food stores the Indians left behind in their hasty retreats. Sitting Bull, Gall, and Crazy Horse all eluded the pursuing troops when possible, but they fought fiercely when cornered. Crazy Horse frequently maneuvered his warriors into repeated battles with the cavalry to protect the Sioux as they escaped the army's clutch. The weakened and worn surrendered to the U.S. Army, but Sioux warriors, almost to a man, refused to give up their resistance.

The U.S. Army's successes against the Indians continued, but it appeared to General George Crook that Indian resistance might crumble more quickly if the Sioux and Cheyenne were offered sufficient incentive to surrender. He sent word to the Indians that a reservation could be established for Crazy Horse's people on the Tongue River. Crazy Horse trusted Crook and on May 6 brought his 800 people into Fort Robinson, Nebraska. In September, however, the War Department and Office of Indian Affairs each refused to honor Crook's promise. Angered, Crazy Horse plotted a break for the Powder River, but General Crook learned of the plan and had him arrested by the reservations' Indian police. No one is exactly sure what led to Crazy Horse being bayoneted in the back. Some argue that he struggled to free himself from the Indian police and was accidentally stabbed with an unsheathed bayonet during the scuffle. Others contend it was calculated murder, but by whom there is no firm evidence. Some witnesses and researchers point to an Indian policeman; others have suggested the killer was a soldier. On his death bed, Crazy Horse spoke his final words:

> We had buffalo for food, and their hides for clothing and our tipis. We preferred hunting to a life of idleness on the reservations . . . At times we did not get enough to eat, and we were not allowed to leave the reservation to hunt . . . We were no expense to the government then. All we wanted was peace and to be left alone. Soldiers were sent out in the winter, who destroyed our villages. Then "long Hair" [Custer] came . . . They say we massacred him, but he would have done the same to us had we not defended ourselves and fought to the last. Our first impulse was to escape with our [women and children], but we were so hemmed in that we had to fight.

Crazy Horse died late in the day on September 5.

Sitting Bull and Gall slipped across the border into Canada in February 1877, and peace settled over the northern plains. The army's relentless pursuit of the Sioux following Little Big Horn halted most Sioux and Cheyenne armed resistance. In quick succession, the federal government reduced in size the Great Sioux Reservation by 30 percent and expelled the Sioux from Nebraska. Indian lands rich in resources fell into the government's hands and from there into white ownership.

In the years that followed, Custer's reputation grew from that of an abrasive, overly ambitious, self-centered problem child of the U.S. Army who envisioned his own eventual rise to the White House to one of dutiful and obedient soldier, defender of the American Way, and victim of Indian butchery. Custer became legend—mythic. School children learned he was a patriot, a man who gave his life for his nation in a most heroic, selfless manner. The colonel was placed among America's most revered historic figures. He achieved in death the national glory he so long pursued in life, martyred in the Walt Whitman poem "A Death Sonnet for Custer." The colonel's wife, Elizabeth, added to the Custer myth, publishing three books over the next 20 years, each a glowing tribute to her fallen husband.

The Nez Perce

The Nez Perce were, like most tribes, divided in their response to relocation and their envelopment by white society. Bands that by treaty in 1855 accepted removal from ancestral lands found themselves on an Idaho reservation that shrunk in size with each subsequent gold strike in the territory. In contrast, "non-treaty Indians" lingered in their Oregon homeland and repeatedly met with peace commissions in an effort to secure an agreement with Washington that would allow them to remain there. Their determination, aided by their long history of peace, paid off. The Nez Perce were granted a small reservation in the Wallowa Valley.

Thousands of gold seekers poured into Oregon in the early 1860s to stake claims or establish businesses serving miners' needs, and many of these unwanted arrivals moved deliberately into the Wallowa Valley. Representatives from Washington again encouraged the Nez Perce to relocate and bluntly warned that the tide of white migration into the region would only rise higher. They insisted that it was in the interest of Nez Perce survival that the Indians forfeit their ancestral lands to white intruders. "We had a good country until the white people came and crowded us," said Yellow Wolf. "My people never made trouble . . . although the whites killed many of them. Only when they wanted to put us in one small place, taking from us our home country, trouble started."

Chief Joseph insisted his father (his namesake) never signed away the valley. On his death bed in 1871, the older Joseph cautioned his son, "When you go into council with the white man, always remember your country. Do not give it away." To be sure, Young Joseph (Hin-mah-too-yah-lat-kekht) honored his father's dying request, but it was not a necessary request to make of his son. He had no intention of abandoning the lands of his ancestors. "The white man has no right to come here and take our country," said Joseph. When instructed to remove his people to the Idaho reservation, Joseph responded, "Our fathers were born here. Here they lived, here they died, here are their graves. We will never leave them." Given the Nez Perce's long history of peace and their willingness to accommodate the flood of settlers into their region, Washington's delegation acquiesced and allowed the Indians to remain where they lived.

Agents, however, soon returned to the Wallowa Valley, pressured by Oregon's white population to throw open the entire region for settlement. Washington's peace commissioners were accompanied this time by representatives of the War Department. Once more the Nez Perce were asked to submit to Washington's will and remove themselves from the valley. Again, Chief Joseph refused. He recalled years later his efforts to resist removal. "I labored hard to avoid trouble and bloodshed. We gave up some of our country to the white men, thinking that then we could have peace. We were mistaken. The white man would not let us alone." In 1877, the government, without Indian permission, opened the valley to white settlement and demanded the Nez Perce move to the Idaho reservation. Proud of never having shed the blood of white settlers or having taken up arms against the United States, and certainly not wanting war given their comparative military weakness, tribal leaders reluctantly agreed to move the 800 men, women, and children of the band to Idaho.

SEEING HISTORY

Custer's Last Stand

In the quarter-century immediately following the Indians' victory over Custer's element of the Seventh Cavalry at Little Big Horn, the United States experienced the emotional rush of intense nationalism as the nation emerged as a world leader in manufacturing, in rising wealth, and in its imperial endeavors in both the Pacific and Latin America. It was widely understood that the next century, the twentieth century, would be "America's century." Artists, storytellers, and even historians increasingly enveloped the American experience and its well-known personalities in the mantle of greatness, as larger-than-life characters, and as the leader of modern civilization.

Questions

1. What perception of Custer does the artist seem to promote in this painting?
2. How does Custer represent the ideals of America in the late nineteenth century?
3. How does the image conflict with Indian perceptions of Custer and the wars against Native Americans in the 1870s?

10.7 George Armstrong Custer
Source: Everett Historical/Shutterstock

10.8 Chief Joseph years after leading the Nez Perce on their epic but failed escape to Canada.

Source: Courtesy of Library of Congress Prints and Photographs Division, LC-USZ61–2085

As the tribe moved in June, three Indian warriors strayed from the others into a small community of settlers. There they secured whiskey and, according to statements given by observers, the Indians vented their anger over their removal, became agitated, and killed four white settlers. Knowing full well that retribution was certain, the Nez Perce fled into White Bird Canyon, pursued by local militia and a small detachment of regular U.S. Army troops. The Indians turned to defend themselves. The ferocity of their fight chased away the soldiers, but now the Nez Perce were declared a hostile tribe and the weight of the U.S. Army would be directed against them.

General Oliver Howard, who participated in earlier council discussions, understood and appreciated the Nez Perce desire to remain in the valley, but he was ordered to remove the Indians by force to their new home. He sent a battalion of 400 soldiers in pursuit of the Nez Perce and at Clearwater River battled the Indians for two days. The Nez Perce fought brilliantly and escaped.

Joseph and the other chiefs gathered days later to consider their options. Of those present—Joseph, his brother Ollocot, Toohoolhoolzote, White Bird, and Looking Glass—only Looking Glass offered a viable, if extremely difficult, plan. He suggested they cross

TIMELINE 10.2 PRINCIPAL ARMED CONFLICTS BETWEEN NATIVE AMERICANS AND THE UNITED STATES, 1865–1877

Date	Event
1866–1868	War for the Bozeman Trail, or Red Cloud's War, with Sioux, Cheyenne, and Arapaho
1866–1868	Snake War in Oregon and Idaho, involving the Northern Paiute
1867	U.S. Army units engage in warfare with Southern Cheyenne and Arapaho
1868–1869	The Southern Plains War, or Sheridan's Campaign, involving bands of Cheyenne, Arapaho, Kiowa, Comanche, and Apache
1872–1873	Modoc War in California and Oregon
1874–1875	Red River War in the southern Great Plains with the Comanche, Kiowa, and Cheyenne
1876–1877	The Sioux War over the Black Hills, including the Sioux, Cheyenne, Arapaho
1877	The flight of the Nez Perce toward the Canadian border

the Bitterroot Mountains into Montana and once there either join the Crow or move north into Canada and there link with Sitting Bull. Early the next morning, the Indians commenced what historian Robert Utley described as "one of history's great—and tragic—odysseys" as troops dogged their every move.

They passed through the mountain range, exiting onto the eastern slope weary from their march, and in early August they believed the soldiers were far enough behind to rest themselves. On the morning of August 9, the soldiers surprised the Nez Perce, striking the camp and killing nearly 100 Indians. The warriors rallied and for two days held the soldiers at bay until their families could slip away.

The Nez Perce pushed onward, east into the Yellowstone, fighting when necessary and evading when possible three separate armies now converging on them. Joseph's warriors frequently humiliated, embarrassed, and outwitted the armies that gave chase by evading capture and by inflicting significant casualties on the soldiers. As summer drew to its close, Joseph's band completed its designed circular route and resumed a northward march toward Canada. Learning of Joseph's final destination, General Howard contacted Colonel Nelson Miles, posted at Fort Keogh, and instructed him to block the Nez Perce's escape into Canada (see Map 10.2).

On September 30, Miles intercepted Joseph at Bear Paw Mountain in Montana, only 35 miles from freedom. For five days battle raged, long enough for additional columns of soldiers to reinforce Miles, who by then had suffered a significant loss of men. Joseph and the other surviving chiefs considered their options and agreed on a fateful course. They chose to press the battle more fiercely during which time White Bird and a group of warriors would guide a group of about 50 women, children, old men, and wounded into Canada where Sitting Bull would care for them. On October 5, 1877, Chief Joseph implemented the plan. Once word was returned that the band had made it across the border successfully, the Nez Perce warriors ceased their fight. Joseph stepped from his defensive position and approached Colonel Miles under a white flag. He received the colonel's promise that the remaining 400 Nez Perce, once surrendered, could spend the coming winter at Fort Keogh. When spring returned, they would move to the Nez Perce reservation in Idaho. Joseph accepted Miles's offer and, with General Howard looking on, he spoke his words of surrender:

> I am tired of fighting. Our chiefs are killed. Looking Glass is dead. Toohoolhoolzote is dead. The old men are all dead. It is the young men who say yes or no. He who led the young men [Ollocot] is dead. It is cold and we have no blankets. The little children are freezing to death . . . Hear me, my chiefs! I am tired. My heart is sick and sad. From where the sun now stands I will fight no more forever.

Colonel Miles had come to respect the Nez Perce and, like General Howard, appreciate their reason for resistance. Miles's promise to Joseph was sincere, and Howard fully expected the promise to be honored in Washington. It was not. Joseph, when asked about Washington's refusal to send his people back to their homelands, said, "Miles promised that we might return to our own country. I believed General Miles, or I never would have surrendered."

Historians have long noted the respect white society extended to Joseph's committed defense of his people. He became, wrote James Wilson, "a national hero. His dignified eloquence, his chivalry and his superb generalship won him real admiration, making him—along with Crazy Horse, Sitting Bull, Geronimo and Chochise—one of the handful of genuinely famous Native Americans in history . . . His surrender speech became a widely read testament of nobility in defeat." The general public came to see Joseph as the personification of "the romantic emblem of a 'doomed race.'"

It shocked many Americans that the surrendered Nez Perce were transported not to Idaho but instead to Indian Territory, where they joined the other tribes recently removed from their lands. Influential white reformers, former adversaries, and a sympathetic public called on Washington to reconsider its placement of the Nez Perce in Oklahoma, and in 1885 Washington bowed to the pressure and permitted the Indians' relocation to Idaho. Chief Joseph, however, was not allowed to go with them. He was instead posted at the Colville Reservation in Washington. Thinking years later of his war with the United States, Joseph said, "We were like

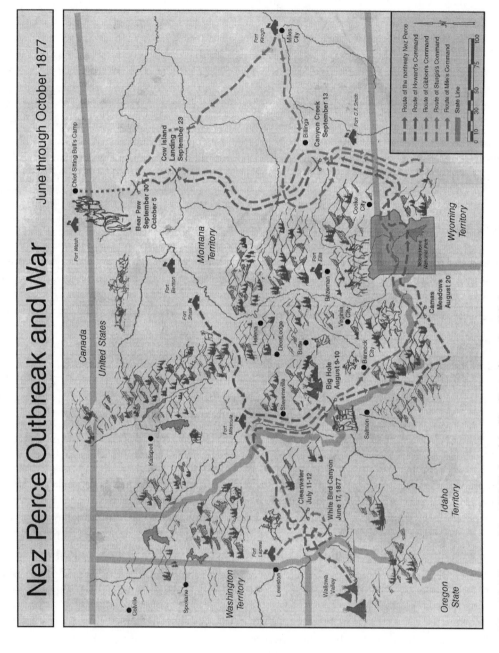

Map 10.2 Route of the 1877 flight of the Nez Perce from the U.S. Army

the deer. They were like grizzly bears. We had a small country. Their country was large. We were contented to let things remain as the Great Spirit Chief made them. They were not and would change the rivers and mountains if they did not suit them." Joseph died quietly at his Colville Reservation home in 1904.

Conclusion

President Grant's administration wielded the sword to bring "a lasting peace" to the West. Tribes that once trailed buffalo herds now found themselves boxed in on reservations. Indians who previously lived on the lands of their ancestors now dwelled hundreds or thousands of miles away on acreage alien to them in all respects. Their physical connection to the territories that rooted them to their spiritual base was now broken. The inherent right of self-determination by which they had long lived vanished. No longer were they independent nations but instead wards of the United States. In 1877, they confronted new lives, lives of confinement aimed at forcing their assimilation into a culture fundamentally different from their own.

Native Americans across the West, from the Dakotas to Oregon and throughout the Southwest, defended their lands and resisted their removal. They challenged all threats directed against their survival and did so with power and effectiveness. But the end of the Civil War unleashed a tide of white migration that washed over the West and allowed the War Department to deploy sufficient manpower to pressure Indians into submission. Washington's determination to create a unified nation from the Atlantic to the Pacific and a vibrant national economy that exploited fully available resources generally dictated the government's Indian policies. Even then, Indians were not conquered by the force of arms but instead by attrition, hunger, cold, and the weariness constant pursuit produced. For the remainder of the nineteenth century, the contest between Native Americans and the United States would turn on cultural identity and the Indians' place in the American system. Indians would now confront a policy, framed by humanitarian reformers and implemented by the federal government, that purposely and unequivocally intended to destroy all vestiges of native cultures.

Review Questions

1. What were the fundamental causes of war in the Powder River territory? What allowed the Sioux to win their war of resistance? Why is the Treaty of Fort Laramie considered so unique?
2. Why were Americans generally captivated by the flight of Chief Joseph and the Nez Perce? How did the general population view Joseph? Why? What might this suggest about American popular opinion regarding Native American resistance in the late 1860s?
3. Describe the fundamental goal of Grant's Peace Policy and identify the tactics his administration planned to employ to bring peace to the West.
4. What irony is found in Grant's Peace Policy?
5. Ulysses S. Grant, Chief Joseph, Sitting Bull, Red Cloud, and George Custer assumed near mythic proportions. What traits and experiences did they have in common? How were the legends of these men built, and why?

Recommended Readings

Cozzens, Peter. *The Earth Is Weeping: The Epic Story of the Indian Wars for the American West* (New York: Alfred A. Knopf, 2016).
Greene, Jerome. *Washita: The U.S. Army and the Southern Cheyenne, 1867–1869* (Norman: University of Oklahoma Press, 2008). A thorough study of the causes, conduct, and results of the massacre of Cheyenne at the Washita Valley. Greene argues in part that this event contributed directly to the defeat of Custer at Little Big Horn years later.

Hedren, Paul L. *Powder River: Disastrous Opening of the Great Sioux War* (Norman: University of Oklahoma Press, 2016).

Marshall, Joseph. *The Day the World Ended at Little Big Horn: A Lakota History* (New York: Viking, 2006). A thoughtful analysis of the Greasy Grass Fight (Little Big Horn) that examines combat strategy, sources of the Indians' victory, and post-battle consequences, with emphasis on the Indians' perspective.

Monnett, John H. *Where a Hundred Soldiers Were Killed: The Struggle for the Powder River County in 1866 and the Making of the Fetterman Myth* (Albuquerque: University of New Mexico Press, 2008). A study that traces the origin and course of the Powder River War, debunking long-held myths about the conflict and weaving into the analysis the war's geopolitical and environmental significance.

Neihardt, John, ed. *Black Elk Speaks: Being the Life Story of a Holy Man of the Oglala Sioux* (Lincoln, NE: University of Nebraska Press, 1979). (Originally published in 1932). The classic and powerful spiritual story of the life of Black Elk and history of the Lakota people in the late nineteenth century, following Black Elk's childhood vision through his adult life.

Utley, Robert M. *Sitting Bull: The Life and Times of an American Patriot* (New York: Henry Holt, 2008). Widely considered the most balanced scholarly treatment of Sitting Bull, accentuated by an amplified Indian perspective.

West, Elliott. *The Last Indian War: The Nez Perce Story* (New York: Oxford University Press, 2009). Considered the definitive study of Nez Perce resistance to the United States and the Indians' transition to reservation life after 1877.

Native American History Online

General Sites

The West: Fort Laramie Treaty, 1868. www.pbs.org/weta/thewest/resources/archives/four/ftlaram.htm This site contains a transcript of the Fort Laramie Treaty of 1868. The site is part of the Public Broadcasting System series "The West."

Buffalo Soldiers and Indian Wars. www.buffalosoldier.net The role of the Buffalo Soldiers, African American military units, in waging war with Native Americans in the West during the years of President Grant's Peace Policy are chronicled at this site. It includes photographs, a detailed history, and links to other Web locations.

Historic Sites

Little Bighorn Battlefield, Crow Agency, Montana. https://www.nps.gov/libi/index.htm The National Park Service manages the site of the Sioux and Cheyenne defeat of Colonel George Custer's regiment of the United States Seventh Cavalry in June 1876.

Fort Laramie National Historic Site, Fort Laramie, Wyoming. https://www.nps.gov/fola/index.htm Fort Laramie was the site of numerous meetings between representatives of the U.S. government and leaders of multiple Indian tribes and where the Sioux and United States reached a peace agreement to the Indians' favor, the Fort Laramie Treaty of 1868.

CHAPTER
11

The Struggle for Cultural Identity, 1877–1910

WILD WEST SHOWS
CHASING FREEDOM, PRESERVING IDENTITY
Victorio and Geronimo
The Ghost Dance
SAVING THE INDIAN
Eastern Reformers
Lake Mohonk
THE ATTACK ON INDIAN CULTURE
The Dawes Act
Christianizing the Indian
Educating Native Americans

Wild West Shows

Sensing the imminent passing of the frontier and the popularly termed "conquest" of the Indians, Americans in the late nineteenth century were attracted to traveling shows that brought the dying West to their own communities. None was better or more renowned than Buffalo Bill's Wild West Show, the brainchild of William "Buffalo Bill" Cody. Cody was a man of the West. He had mined for gold in California, laid railroad tracks, rode for the Pony Express, and served as an army scout. In July 1876, he helped locate Cheyenne Indians retreating from the Little Big Horn and in battle with them at Warbonnet Creek, Nebraska, is said to have personally killed Yellow Hand. He built the Wild West Show largely around his own life in the region, substantially embellishing it, and opened his first show in Omaha, Nebraska, on May 19, 1883.

Cody's two-hour show was preceded by a parade through town of his actors in full costume, along with the horses, oxen, and covered wagons featured in his show. His standard acts included sharpshooting demonstrations with both rifle and handgun, which Cody himself and his close friend Annie Oakley frequently performed. Cattle roping,

Students conduct experiments in a physics class at the Carlisle Indian School, Carlisle, Pa.

Source: Courtesy of Library of Congress Prints and Photographs Division, LC-USZ62-26787

345

feats of horsemanship, and bronco riding were routine scenes in his shows. Among Cody's special contribution to this field of entertainment were the "historical reenactments" of Indian-white battles. Indians attacked settlers' homes, stagecoaches, and wagon trains, and in each scene Buffalo Bill led soldiers to the rescue. To be sure, he presented the popular image at that time of white America's inevitable conquest over both nature and uncivilized peoples. Not until 1888 did Cody introduce his reenactment of Custer's Last Stand. According to Buffalo Bill, he delayed producing the drama out of respect for his friend Colonel Custer and in deference to Custer's wife.

Indians played a critical role in Buffalo Bill's Wild West Show. Of the 500 cast members who traveled with the show by the late 1890s, 100 were Indian men, women, and children. Uncommon for that time period, Cody paid Indian employees the same wages as white actors, allowed them to bring their families on the circuit, and encouraged them to speak their native language and practice their traditional spiritual ceremonies. Sitting Bull traveled with Buffalo Bill and performed daily with the troupe in the mid-1880s, and for a short time Chief Joseph accompanied the show. Black Elk spent several years working with Cody in the 1890s. He

CHRONOLOGY

1870	Wodziwob (Paiute) spreads his messianic message of cultural renewal among the Indians of the mountain region into Oregon
1876	San Carlos Apache Reservation is opened on the Gila River in Arizona
1879	Victorio leads a band of Apaches in a breakout from the San Carlos Reservation, leading to war on the Arizona-Mexico border
	Carlisle Indian Industrial School opens in Carlisle, Pennsylvania
	Congress appropriates $1,300,000 for Indian education
1880	Victorio is killed in battle against a Mexican army
1881	Sitting Bull crosses from Canada back into the United States and settles on the reservation
	Helen Hunt Jackson publishes *A Century of Dishonor*
1882	The Indian Rights Association is founded with the goal of aiding Native Americans and affecting reform to federal Indian policy
1883	The Indian Office issues "List of Indian Offenses," banning specific religious ceremonies
	William "Buffalo Bill" Cody opens the Buffalo Bill Wild West Show
	First annual Lake Mohonk Conference assembles to direct reform programs in Indian affairs
1887	Congress passes into law the General Allotment Act
1888	Wavoka (Paiute) has a vision that speaks of the disappearance of all whites and the return of the traditional Indian ways of life
	The Ghost Dance religion is born and starts its spread among Indians across the West
1890	Agents on the Sioux reservations ban the Ghost Dance
	Sitting Bull is arrested by reservation Indian police and in the process is shot to death
	Three hundred Sioux massacred at Wounded Knee, South Dakota
1891	Last of the Sioux bands surrender and return to their reservation
	Congress permits Indians holding individual allotments to lease their property
1893	Largest in a series of land rushes in Oklahoma

was an unknown Lakota then, but today he is a widely recognized Indian among students of Native American history for the story of his life he left to posterity in the early 1930s. Black Elk, like so many other Indians, traveled with the troupe to European capitals. In London he met Queen Victoria and purportedly called her "Grandmother England." Buffalo Bill's Wild West Show was in many respects a marvel to behold, particularly for the showmanship demonstrated in the performance ring and for the sheer logistics necessary to produce such a show. In 1899, the troupe traveled 11,000 miles within the United States over 200 days and delivered 341 performances.

Cody's show ultimately reinforced racial stereotypes and negative perspectives of Indians among white audiences. The dominant image the audience received was of Indians on horseback wearing long, flowing bonnets and Indians who whooped and screamed while attacking white settlers. They never saw the less dramatic, daily routine of Native American life. Indians in the show played the role of aggressive, bloodthirsty savages bent on killing all white intruders, and cultural variations among Indians were invisible. They were presented, too, as impediments to white progress. Equally important, Indian actors "had to re-fight a losing war nightly and their hollow victory in the Little Big Horn enactment demonstrated over and over to their audiences the justification of American conquest." The show offered audiences a skewed glimpse of the passing frontier and a distorted view of "vanishing" native peoples, but it also reinforced the popular notion that unless Indian peoples acculturated to national ways, they were destined for extinction.

KEY QUESTIONS

1. To what extent were the teachings of Wovoka and the emergence of the Ghost Dance religion reflective of a transition in the direction of Indian resistance?
2. What fundamental values and vision underpinned the direction of eastern reformers and critics of federal Indian policies by the 1880s? How did their collective vision reflect the values and aspirations of modernizing America?
3. Programs devised and implemented by eastern reformers aimed initially at the ultimate eradication of native cultures. What three principal features of Indian culture did reformers target and why? How did reformers implement their programs of "civilization"?
4. How did Native Americans resist Washington's acculturation policies in the 1880s, and to what extent were they successful in their resistance?

Chasing Freedom, Preserving Identity

Subway cars rumbled under New York City streets as horse-drawn carts and the earliest sputtering automobiles competed for space on the roads above. Electric lights lined the city's business district, and high-rise buildings with escalators elevated the skyline. Public sanitation crews removed garbage and washed the avenues, and pull-chain toilets made their entry into private homes and businesses. The middle class was expanding quickly in America, allowing for more non-essential purchasing as well as more opportunity for entertaining pastimes such as professional baseball, amusement parks, vaudeville shows, and bicycling. America's major cities were modernizing.

The nation was also assuming a new character. Immigrants continued to pour into the United States, further diversifying its racial and ethnic mix. The country's wealth increasingly came from the growth of industry, and by 1900 the United States emerged as the world's leading manufacturing nation. To further advance its wealth, America moved beyond its continental borders to secure resources and open markets, in so doing carving an empire for itself that stretched from the Caribbean across the Pacific.

The period between 1865 and 1900 was one of growing wealth and power for the United States, but it was also one of reflection and reform. Frederick Jackson Turner's article "The Significance of the Frontier in American History," Josiah Strong's short book *Our Country*, and even Brooks Adams's *The Law of Civilization and Decay* all examined America's rise to wealth and power and, most explicitly in the cases of Strong and Adams, suggested a policy of foreign imperial expansion for the United States to ensure its emerging preeminence among nations. There were also Americans who pressed for fundamental reforms in the nation's urban centers, working to match the reality of city and nation to the American rhetoric. Progressives, as they were termed, championed the extension of democracy through women's suffrage and the direct election of U.S. senators. They tackled urban political corruption, pushed for universal education and the expansion of public-funded educational opportunities, worked to reduce child labor and protect workers, addressed public health issues, and challenged unsafe factory environments and the manipulative practices of corporations.

It was an age of Americanization. Urban Progressives ventured into immigrant communities to educate and prepare new arrivals in the "American Way." They instructed immigrants in the English language and explained the nation's political structure and basic political ideology. The number of public high schools increased significantly, from 500 nationally in 1870 to nearly 10,000 by 1910, and the curriculum common to public schools stressed Civics, English, and American History. Public entertainment settings encouraged the mingling of immigrants and their inclusion with native-born Americans. The nation's expansion overseas carried with it an implied responsibility for the native persons that American business interests reached. Missionaries spread Christianity into China and Japan, educators ventured into Western Samoa, and government officials moved into all of America's overseas territories to shape values and world views. It was an age of equality and inclusion only by the narrowest of definitions, but it was expressly intended to be an era in which a common identity emerged—out of many, one people, a shared identity as Americans.

America's spirit of reform focused on urban communities and on peoples overseas, but reformers also recognized that there remained much work to be done in the western territories and states. President Ulysses S. Grant had championed a new direction in Indian affairs, calling for an active program of Americanization on Indian reservations, but little was accomplished beyond the military defeat of tribes resisting concentration on near useless lands. The reformists' agenda, however, commanded priority after 1877, now that most tribal groups resided on reservations. Americanizing the Indian proved difficult at best. Proud of their traditional values and longing to return to their earlier lives, many Indians chose to resist cultural transformation and a new identity. Government bungling and the well-intentioned but misguided tactics of reformers further complicated the effort.

Victorio and Geronimo

Said popular writer Hamlin Garland, reservation Indians are

> miserably poor, with very little to do but sit and smoke and wait for ration day. To till the ground is practically useless, and their herds are too small to furnish them support . . . Their ration . . . feeds them for a week or ten days and they go hungry till the next ration day comes round . . . Each tribe, whether Sioux, or Navajo, or Hopi, will be found to be divided . . . into two parties, the radicals and the conservatives, those who are willing to change, to walk the white man's way; those who are deeply, sullenly skeptical of all civilizing measures, are often the strongest . . . they are in the majority. Though in rags, their spirits are unbroken; from the point of view of their sympathizers, they are patriots.

Reservations across the country varied little from Hamlin's description. Reservations were places of unbridled poverty. Even in places where agriculture or ranching was practical, the tools, seeds, livestock, and especially advice necessary for success proved in short supply. Too often, the land itself was not suited to either trade. Hunting seldom offered an outlet, and few tribes enjoyed the opportunity to supplement their diet with fishing. Reservations also bred disease. Populations were large but restricted to limited acreage, facilitating the spread of communicable diseases. Homes were poorly insulated against winter's bite, food was consistently in short supply and of poor quality, and whites trading with Indian agents brought a variety of pathogens onto the reservations. Tuberculosis, smallpox, and measles routinely ravaged reservation Indians. Compounding this, there were seldom any medical services available on reservations. The few trained physicians who did treat Indians only occasionally ventured to the reservations, and once there they generally did not have access to a clinic or medicines. Tribes, through their reservation agents, sometimes requested a hospital or clinic from the Indian Office, but typically their pleas were ignored. The Yakima, for example, asked in the mid-1870s for a medical facility to be built on their reservation, but government funding was not approved until 1928. A sense of urgency arose. "Indians are destined to speedy extinction" unless the federal government provided material aid immediately and the Indians acculturated themselves to society's behaviors and labor, said President Grant shortly before leaving office. Eastern reformers believed a policy that actively worked for the Indians' physical survival was the humane, morally correct course to take, and moving Native Americans into mainstream America seemed the sensible direction to go. Now that the "Indian wars" were over, reformers believed the Americanization process could begin in earnest.

But the agony of reservation life was the result of more than material deprivation. Confinement tore at the Indians' understanding of their history and their identity. In 1878, Washakie (Shoshone) spoke of his anguish to Governor John W. Hoyt of the Territory of Wyoming:

> The white man, who possesses this whole vast country from sea to sea, who roams over it at pleasure and lives where he likes, cannot know the cramp we feel in this little spot, with the undying remembrance of the fact, which you know as well as we, that every foot of what you proudly call America, not very long ago belonged to the Red Man . . . We . . . are cornered in little spots of the earth, all ours by right—cornered like guilty prisoners, and watched by men with guns who are more than anxious to kill us off.

Washakie complained that Native Americans were now "sorry remnants" of tribes once great and powerful, their lives now dependent on government issues of seed and tools and their liberty determined by men in Washington. "Knowing all this," he concluded, "do you wonder, sir, that we have fits of desperation and think to be avenged?"

In 1876, the Indian Office opened the San Carlos Reservation on the Gila River in Arizona as a single large reservation on which all Apache Indians would reside. Reformers hoped the concentration of Apaches at San Carlos would not only allow white settlement and development of the region without fear of war but also serve as a center for Indians to master the ways of the white world. Aside from learning farming and ranching, Apaches would be schooled in English, civics, and Christianity. Eventually the Indians, especially children, would shed their Apache identity and become "true" Americans.

Bands of Apaches moved under force to San Carlos soon afterward, among them a band Victorio (Mimbres) led. By the late 1870s, Victorio had already earned a warrior reputation. As a young man in the 1850s he joined raids into northern Mexico, and in 1862 he rode with the Apache leader Mangas Coloradas in battles against the American cavalry, garnering respect as a sound tactician. But Victorio understood well that the tide of white migration threatened Indian survival. "I and my people want peace," he said in 1863. "We have little for our families to eat and wear . . . We want a lasting peace . . . We would like to live in our country, and will go onto a reservation." Throughout the decade that followed, Victorio and his people were frequently relocated

11.1 Geronimo (1829–1909), leader of the Chiricahua Apache

Source: Courtesy of Library of Congress Prints and Photographs Division, LC-USZ62-36613

from one reservation to another, each time with the promise of better circumstances and no further moves. Their forced removal to San Carlos, however, brought Victorio's patience to an end.

By all accounts, San Carlos was a miserable place. "There was nothing but cactus, rattlesnakes, heat, rocks, and insects. No game; no edible plants. Many of our people died of starvation" at San Carlos, remembered one Apache. Corrupt reservation agents were commonplace, and traditional rivalries among the various Apache groups now living together festered and frequently turned violent. Equally important, hopelessness infected the Indians. Confinement on that barren stretch of land threatened the spirit that made them Apache.

Victorio refused to remain on the reservation. In late summer 1879, he and his followers left San Carlos, determined to find a new home where they might live by the old ways or die in the process. On September 4, Victorio turned on a platoon of pursuing black cavalrymen. When word of the skirmish filtered back to San Carlos, many Apaches took heart, abandoned the reservation, and joined with Victorio's growing band. In little time, nearly 150 warriors rode with Victorio.

Throughout the following year, Victorio raided communities across western Texas and eastern New Mexico. Frequently he battled American and Mexican troops who gave chase, but by October 1880 his band was severely worn, drained of food supplies, ammunition, and physical strength. On October 15, a detachment of Mexican soldiers surprised the Apache camp and in a day-long fight Victorio and half of his warriors were killed. The remaining Apaches surrendered.

Ten months later, in August 1881, Goyathlay, better known among whites as Geronimo (Chiricahua), and 75 followers also abandoned San Carlos and took to roaming the countryside near the Mexican border. Geronimo despised both San Carlos, with its inhuman conditions, and the efforts the Indian Bureau made to transform the Apache into farmers and to replace their spirituality with Christianity. His breaking point with reservation life came in 1881 when an Apache holy man, praying, was murdered by troopers who thought wrongly that he was inciting rebellion. Geronimo and his followers lived off the land and raided outlying settlements, free of federal restraints and living as they had before.

In spring 1882, Geronimo and his warriors returned to San Carlos long enough to gather several hundred more Apaches who also wanted to escape the reservation. Troopers posted at nearby forts pursued the Indians and in so doing compelled Geronimo to change direction repeatedly in a bid to deceive the soldiers. In September, General Crook arrived and assumed regional command. The Apache termed Crook "the Gray Fox," and he carried the respect of his enemy, much as Crook respected Geronimo's honesty and fighting skill. Crook dispatched his armies to the field, roughly 5,000 soldiers and Apache scouts who began the hunt for Geronimo's band. The Apaches set up a base in Mexico's Sierra Madre and from there launched raids on both sides of the border. Gray Fox's scouts located the Indians, and Crook sent word he wished to speak with each Apache leader. Over the following weeks, individual leaders within Geronimo's band acquiesced to Crook's call for peace and his assurance that changes would be made at San Carlos. Geronimo continued his resistance until it became clear that only on the reservation would his Apaches survive. "We give ourselves up," he said to Crook. "Do with us as you please. Once I moved about like the wind. Now I surrender to you, and that is all."

Geronimo returned to the reservation, but conditions proved no better than before. In May 1885, he and 135 Apaches again abandoned San Carlos for the Sierra Madre. "We were reckless of our lives," said Geronimo, "because we felt every man's hand was against us. If we returned to the reservation we would be put in prison and killed; if we stayed in Mexico they would continue to send soldiers to fight us; so we gave no quarter to anyone and asked no favors." The same story played out. Raids to secure food and supplies attracted the army. Crook's failure to contain Geronimo on the reservation resulted in General Philip Sheridan removing him from command. Nelson Miles, recently promoted to General, replaced Crook. The army's dogged pursuit continued, wearing down the Apache warriors and reducing their number through frequent skirmishes. Finally, on September 4, 1886, Geronimo sent word to Miles of this willingness to surrender in order to preserve the lives of those who followed him. At Skeleton Canyon, Arizona, the Apaches turned themselves over to the army. Rather than return Geronimo to San Carlos, Washington ordered his removal and that of his warriors to Fort Pickens in Pensacola, Florida. Years later, still imprisoned, Geronimo said, "There is no climate or soil, to my mind, that is equal to that of Arizona. . . . It is my land, my home, my fathers' land, to which I now ask to be allowed to return. I want to spend my last days there and be buried among those mountains. . . . Could I but see this accomplished, I think I could forget all the wrongs that I have ever received." Geronimo never saw his homeland again.

The Ghost Dance

With each passing year of the 1880s, Native Americans across the West understood increasingly that their way of life—their very identity—was being destroyed. Most longed for something that would reverse the direction of events. Among the Paiute of Nevada resided a prophet, Wavoka, whose life was one steeped in cultural revivalism. His father, Tavibo (Tavio in some texts), had traveled with the holy man Wodziwob throughout the mountain country in the 1870s preaching an apocalyptic message that the Creator would soon destroy the white man's presence and return the earth in all of its original grandeur to Indians. Wodziwob encouraged his listeners to pray, sing, and dance in an effort to resurrect the natural world more quickly. The message of renewal reached tribal communities across the region, but Native Americans still believed tribal salvation might be achieved through armed resistance. It never came.

Wavoka listened to his father's stories of distant travel and to the messianic message he learned from Wodziwob. As a young man, Wavoka worked for a rancher in Nevada and in the farmlands of Oregon and California, and in these places he learned from other Indians about the diversity of Native American cultures along with the fundamental tenets of Christianity. In late 1888, probably in December, Wavoka fell sick and over the following weeks suffered fevers and lapses of consciousness. In recalling that time with anthropologist James Mooney in 1892, Wavoka said that he came face-to-face with the Creator, who shared with him a vision of a world redeemed. Lush grasslands teemed with buffalo reaching beyond the horizon, disease and sickness disappeared, and an era of peace, plenty, and contentment settled over the Indian world. Generations of Native Americans who earlier departed this world returned to their families. His was the vision of an ideal world without white men, a world purged of the horror that destroyed native cultures, a world intended by the Creator. The Creator gave Wavoka a dance to carry to the Paiute and to other Indians, a dance that was to be performed "for five consecutive days each time" and would ultimately "hasten the event."

Wrote Mooney, "God told him he must go back and tell his people they must be good and love one another." The Indians were to "have no quarrelling and live in peace with the whites; that they must work, and not lie or steal; that they must put away all the old practices that savored of war; that if they faithfully obeyed his instructions they would at last be reunited with their friends in this other world where there would be no more death or sickness or old age." Mooney's elaboration abounded in racial stereotypes, the preferences of white America, and Christianity. He missed Wovoka's most basic point that the **Ghost Dance**, as it was soon termed, was in fact the latest form of Indian resistance.

A warrior spirit still prevailed among many Indians in the late 1880s, but warfare over the previous 30 years produced little evidence to convince them that armed resistance might preserve their cultures, their lives, their identity. Wavoka's vision, therefore, found a receptive audience. Now, small groups of Indians traveled from their distant reservations to visit the Paiute and learn more of his vision. "I do not know when they will be here," said Wavoka of his ancestors, but the living were "to dance every six weeks," feast, and cleanse themselves to hasten their return and the rebirth the Creator promised.

Historians have long suggested that the Ghost Dance religion was Wavoka's melding of Indian spirituality and western Christian principles. His words referred to resurrection and rebirth, tribal and cultural salvation, the victory of goodness over evil, a life pure and simple, an era of peace and plenty. Wavoka's understanding of the basic tenets of Christianity probably framed the structure of his message, placing it into an ordered, indeed linear, context that mirrored the Christian notion of the Second Coming of Jesus, but the values embedded within his message also touched the soul of traditional Indian spirituality and identity. The core vision was uniquely Indian—a return to the methods and meaning of life that predated the arrival of white Christians, a renewal of all that forever had been Native American.

The Ghost Dance spread across the plains southward into Indian Territory and westward over the mountains into Oregon, but it received its most enthusiastic reception when it reached the Lakota in spring 1890. Said Kicking Bear, who had journeyed to Nevada to hear Wavoka's words,

> I bring to you the promise of a day in which there will be no white man to lay his hand on the bridle of the Indian's horse; when the red men of the prairie will rule the world and not be turned from the hunting grounds by any man. I bring you word from your fathers the ghosts, that they are now marching to join you, led by the Messiah who came once to live on earth with the white men, but was cast out and killed by them. I have seen the wonders of the Spirit Land, and have talked with the ghosts. I traveled far and am sent back with a message to tell you to make ready for the coming of the Messiah and return of the ghosts in spring.

Desperation had plagued the Sioux since their removal to reservations. Little wonder, then, that Wavoka's vision and the Ghost Dance seemed like "rain for thirsty souls," as Leonard Crow Dog (Sioux) observed. Said Red Cloud, "There was no hope on earth, and God seemed to have forgotten us. Someone had . . . been talking of the Son of God, and said He had come. The people did not know; they did not care. They snatched at the hope." Roughly one-third of the Lakota who were spread over five reservations embraced Wavoka's vision. The Indians' spirits rose as summer faded into autumn, but they generally believed that white America would not vanish according to Wavoka's vision without a fight. More than 3,000 Lakota assembled at the Stronghold on the Pine Ridge Reservation to dance. They passed the word that each warrior must paint symbols on his shirt representative of Wavoka's vision along with images that reflected their own spiritual values. The Creator would protect in battle those who wore the "Ghost shirt."

The sight and sound of Sioux dancing, the Indians' renewed sense of purpose, and now the addition of the Ghost shirt troubled the military. Soldiers believed they were witnessing the early signs of renewed hostilities. Newspapers, ever determined to increase their sales, hurried reporters and photographers to reservations, capturing in sensational narrative and images what they described as a rising, concerted resistance to white authority. "Indians Dancing with Guns" read a *Chicago Tribune* headline over a story that warned of imminent war on the northern plains.

Government agents among the Sioux banned the Ghost Dance in November, an order the Sioux believers openly defied. The government decided, too, that Sitting Bull should be arrested and detained until enthusiasm for the Ghost Dance waned. Although he, like Red Cloud, was not particularly supportive of the Ghost Dance, neither elder pressed the Indians to obey the ban. Agents understood Sitting Bull remained a symbol of resistance and a respected leader, and they worried that he might encourage the Indians to abandon the reservation and return to the path of war. Forty Indian police, backed by a contingent of cavalry, arrived at Sitting Bull's home early in the morning of December 15 to arrest him and in so doing break the back of the Ghost Dance movement at Standing Rock. Chaos erupted instantly. Awakened by the commotion of so many policemen and soldiers, Indians quickly gathered around the police, screaming for them not to take away Sitting Bull. Shouts turned into a scuffle, and in the excitement shots cracked the morning air, killing the venerated Sitting Bull, seven other Indians, and six policemen.

The killing of Sitting Bull enraged the Sioux, and calls for a final armed showdown echoed throughout the reservation. Their demands for war rose when they learned that thousands of additional troops were then moving into the Dakotas. A younger generation of leaders now encouraged Indians to don their Ghost shirts, take up their weapons, and once more wage war against the whites. Armed conflict countered the Creators' call for peace, but many Sioux believed violence was justified to prevent whites from snuffing out a peaceful spiritual movement. Others argued that armed resistance at this time might speed the final apocalyptic confrontation resulting in the fulfillment of Wavoka's vision.

There were groups of Native Americans who did not subscribe to either perspective, choosing instead to flee their reservations and venture north into Canada or to another reservation nearby where tensions were not quite as high. Big Foot championed this option. In mid-December, the elderly Big Foot guided approximately 300 men, women, and children toward Pine Ridge, where he expected to find a less volatile atmosphere.

The army viewed Big Foot's departure as an example to other Indians it could not tolerate. Only a few years earlier, Geronimo had led his followers from San Carlos and raided the countryside of southern Arizona. The army was determined not to allow a band of Sioux to do the same in the Dakotas. Elements of the Seventh Cavalry overtook Big Foot just north of Pine Ridge Reservation days later. The Indians were anything but an armed threat. Big Foot himself was saddled with pneumonia, his followers were short on food and blankets, and winter already swept the plains. Once surrounded, Big Foot's band surrendered without incident (see Map 11.1).

11.2 Sioux Indians performing the Ghost Dance

Source: Courtesy of Library of Congress Prints and Photographs Division, LC-USZ62-51120

On December 28, the soldiers made camp on the bank

of Wounded Knee Creek and surrounded the Indians with armed guards and Hotchkiss guns. That evening, Indians and soldiers alike settled around their fires, wrapped themselves snugly in blankets, and waited for sunrise. At dawn on December 29, the Sioux were ordered out of their teepees so that soldiers could search them and their lodges for weapons before moving the Indians onto the reservation. Nearly 100 men donned their Ghost shirts, visibly raising the tension among the already nervous troopers. One soldier discovered a rifle in Yellow Bird's possession and moved to take the weapon from the warrior. The two men wrestled and the gun discharged, killing the soldier. The cavalry opened fire on the Indians, assuming the Indians had initiated an uprising. Fighting became hand-to-hand. Troops soon broke free of the Indians and dropped back to allow the Hotchkiss guns to open fire on the Sioux. Cannon shells ripped through the air and burst among the Indians. Panic gripped the camp. Old men, women, and children tried to flee, but a flurry of shrapnel and bullets claimed many of them. In slightly more than 30 minutes, Big Foot's band suffered 150 to 200 dead and nearly half that number wounded. Big Foot lay among the dead. The Ghost shirts had not protected the Indians. Casualties among the cavalry totaled 25 killed and 40 wounded, much of this the product of friendly fire. Snow fell over Wounded Knee that afternoon, freezing bodies and preventing the burial of the dead for three days.

Reporters converged on Wounded Knee once the winter storm passed. Photographers snapped pictures of Big Foot's frozen corpse and soldiers surveying their work. Journalists recorded in words the horrid sights they found, some doing so in shame and others in joy. Dr. Charles Eastman, a Sioux educated at Carlisle Institute

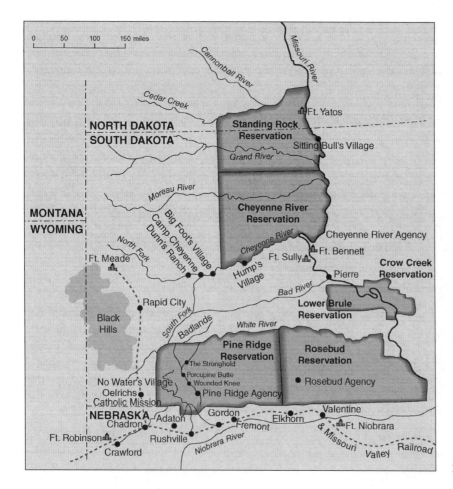

Map 11.1 Western reservations

for Indians and now a trained physician, accompanied the soldiers and newsmen to the site. "It took all my nerve to keep my composure," he said. "All of this was a severe ordeal for one who had so lately put all his faith in the Christian love and lofty ideals of the white man," he added. On January 2, the lifeless Big Foot and the others of his band killed in the skirmish were piled into a mass grave. "A people's dream, a beautiful dream, died there in the bloody snow," recalled Black Elk.

Over the next two weeks, small groups of Sioux fled their reservations and harassed troops, but General Nelson Miles deployed 5,000 fresh troops to the area. Faced with their ultimate annihilation, the Indians instead surrendered on January 15, 1891. Few people ascribed any symbolic importance to the Wounded Knee massacre at the time, but over the years that followed the massacre came to represent the closure of the "Indian frontier," and more critically the passing of the Indians' traditional identity. By the time of Wounded Knee, Native Americans had been forced onto reservations and faced the final assault on their cultural heritage and identity. In the decades to come, Indians searched for new means of preserving their cultures while concurrently adjusting themselves to the reality of America's new direction in Indian affairs (see Map 11.2).

TIMELINE 11.1 EVENTS LEADING TO THE MASSACRE AT WOUNDED KNEE, 1889–1890

Date	Event
1889	In January, Wavoka (Paiute) recounts to listeners his vision of the coming of an Indian messiah, a renewed Indian world, and the return of Indian forefathers. He calls on Native Americans to hasten the Indian resurrection through the Ghost Dance
	By summer, Wavoka's vision spreads across the western states and territories, and Indians venture to his home in Nevada to speak directly with the holy man
1890	Fear spreads among non-Indians across the territories of impending Indian-initiated war because of the Ghost Dance religion
	Sioux followers of Wovoka adopt the Ghost shirt, and hundreds of Sioux move to the "Stronghold" at the northern side of Pine Ridge
	The Indian Agent at Pine Ridge requests a battalion of soldiers to preserve order on the reservation and to provide protection should the Indians resort to warfare
	President Benjamin Harrison orders the U.S. Army to all Sioux reservations to arrest the most vocal Indian supporters of the Ghost Dance
	Governor Mellette establishes the South Dakota Home Guard, an armed citizen militia to defend citizens from Indian hostilities
	Sitting Bull is killed as Indian police and U.S. soldiers attempt to arrest him on the Standing Rock reservation
	Big Foot leads about 300 Sioux toward Pine Ridge, resulting in the Massacre at Wounded Knee
	A unit of the Seventh Cavalry apprehends the band and encamps them for the night at Wounded Knee Creek
	A struggle to disarm a Sioux warrior before the Indians are moved into Pine Ridge results in the killing of more than 200 men, women, and children and about 30 soldiers. Big Foot is among the dead

Map 11.2 Federal Indian reservations nationwide, within ten years of the Massacre at Wounded Knee of 1890

Saving the Indian

Victorio and Geronimo's raids represented the Indians' last gasp of armed resistance against life on reservations, and the Ghost Dance religion, at the time, appeared to be the Indians' final act of overt spiritual resistance. Eastern reformers, the Interior Department, and congressional leaders saw these efforts as inevitable bumps on the road toward Americanization. These bumps, however, nonetheless compelled reformers and government officials to adjust their thinking, to tweak some programs, and to emphasize more aggressively other options.

Eastern Reformers

President Rutherford B. Hayes in 1879 insisted the federal government assume a more aggressive posture and a more sincere role in the acculturation of Native Americans and their eventual movement into mainstream American life. Only through Americanization would Indians survive. The government was obligated to transform Indians into "productive and self-sufficient members of American society." Once acculturated and assimilated, the nation's historic "Indian problem" would finally be resolved. "Instead of depriving them of their opportunities, we lend them a helping hand," said Hayes. It must be the business of America, he added, "to place the Indians as rapidly as practicable on the same footing with the other permanent inhabitants of our country."

This was essentially the same message Progressive reformers delivered to immigrants in eastern cities, and it echoed white America's mantra for a single national identity. As the 1870s ended and the 1880s began, the American people and government took conscious steps to homogenize the population. In part, the effort amounted to a backlash against the rising tide of "new immigration" then entering the country—immigrants from southern and eastern Europe who were largely Catholic or Jewish, frequently illiterate and of questionable health, in possession of cultural traits and values unfamiliar to many Americans, and more inclined to support political philosophies that were different from those mainstream America accepted. The effort at Americanization was also the product of an intensifying sense of national identity among Americans and of a belief that the century to come would be an "American century." The United States' rapidly growing economy, the nation's completed territorial conquest of the continent, and the country's emerging empire in both the Pacific and Caribbean all signaled a coming age of greatness for the United States. A unified population—a common people with a common purpose—many reasoned, was fundamental to America's future success and rise in global power. Purge those groups that cannot be Americanized and absorb into the mainstream those that can acculturate fully.

Giving added weight to Washington's direction was Helen Hunt Jackson's book *A Century of Dishonor*, published in 1881. Jackson presented a most severe indictment of white aggression and federal Indian policy. "It makes little difference . . . where one opens the record of the history of the Indians," she wrote; "every page and every year has its dark stain. The story of one tribe is the story of all, varied only by differences of time and place . . . Colorado is as greedy in 1880 as was Georgia in 1830, and Ohio in 1795." Indeed, she continued, "the poorer, the more insignificant, the more helpless the band [of Indians], the more certain the cruelty and outrage to which they have been subjected." President after president, she added, formed commissions to study Indian affairs and to recommend policies. Some presidents spoke eloquently, their words reflecting Christian morality and their advisory panels offering reasonable and objective policy directions; however, speeches were typically forgotten and promises filed away in annual reports only to collect dust. Not "one American out of ten thousand ever sees them or knows that they exist," she wrote. *A Century of Dishonor* was more than a denunciation of the American treatment of Indians to 1880; Jackson called for a fundamentally new course in Indian affairs.

11.3 Helen Hunt Jackson (1830–1885) was a writer and activist on behalf of Native Americans

Courtesy of Library of Congress Prints and Photographs Division, LC-USZ62-38827

She hoped *A Century of Dishonor* would become for Indians what Harriet Beecher Stowe's *Uncle Tom's Cabin* was for American slaves. The book circulated widely, tens of thousands finding her work powerful and persuasive, supported as it was by appendices of government documents and investigations. The lingering memory of the Nez Perce's flight and Chief Joseph's brief and simple statement at Bear Paw Mountain remained an emotional base for reformers, but Jackson's history of Indian-white relations added the weight of scholarship and logic.

Spirited reformers well versed in Jackson's work and supportive of the coming age of American greatness founded organizations to promote a more humane agenda toward Indians, among them the Boston Indian Citizenship Committee and the Women's National Indian Association. Perhaps no single reform organization commanded greater influence than the **Indian Rights Association**, founded in 1882. After reading *A Century of Dishonor*, Herbert Welsh and several colleagues journeyed to the Great Sioux Reservation and surveyed the Indians' living conditions. They were dumbfounded by the near hopelessness that pervaded the Sioux, the lack of educational opportunities, the Indians' declining health, and the obvious absence of anything that would build a positive economic base for the Indians. Returning home, Welsh and his friend Henry Pancoast founded the Indian Rights Association with 30 charter members.

The Indian Rights Association used the findings of Welsh's survey of the Sioux to draft papers for public presentations and publications. Its members collected information from reservation superintendents, spoke personally with Native American leaders the IRA brought to Philadelphia and Washington, and lobbied key congressional leaders to sponsor reform projects. The organization built a strong, positive reputation for itself, partly on the strength of its membership, which included army generals such as Oliver Howard and George Crook, and partly as a result of its reliance on first-hand data collected from the reservations.

Lake Mohonk

Some of the more influential people concerned with Indian reform assembled annually at the Lake Mohonk resort, situated in the Catskill Mountains nearly 100 miles north of New York City. Lake Mohonk's elegant

SEEING HISTORY

"Give the Red Man a Chance"

The collection of eastern reformers, referred to as The Friends of the Indian, promoted a series of changes in federal Indian policy that would "Americanize" Native Americans. They called for detribalization through private property land allotment, a rigorous educational program that would strip Indians of their traditional identity, conversion to Christianity, and ultimately U.S. citizenship.

Question

What does this Thomas Nast editorial cartoon suggest about the issue of Indian citizenship and the status of Native Americans in the legal system?

GIVE THE RED MAN A CHANCE.
Make him a citizen, with all the *privileges* which that implies.

11.4 Thomas Nast, "Give the Red Man a Chance" (cartoon)

Source: Harper's Weekly

accommodations, superb service to guests, and beautiful and tranquil setting satisfied the tastes of those who attended. They first gathered in October 1883, with attendees representing the prominent Indian reform organizations based in Boston, Philadelphia, and New York; the Board of Indian Commissioners; the Indian Rights Association, respected attorneys and educators; key figures of Protestant denominations; journalists; writers; and selected politicians. Senator Henry Dawes was an annual conference guest, and Helen Hunt Jackson attended until her death in 1885. Collectively these representatives and annual guests became known as the "Friends of the Indians."

The yearly meeting allowed guests to spend one week restfully observing nature and conversing with friends and colleagues, but the primary purpose was, of course, to discuss the state of Indian affairs. Conference participants shared the belief that native cultures held no relevance to the present or future and that the Indians' only hope for survival was the shedding of all things Indian. They fully championed the Americanization of native peoples, a position they had pressed on government for years. Their professional careers had placed many of them in the very center of debate over the Indians' future since the early 1860s. They agreed that Indians must detribalize, become owners of private property, adopt Christianity, learn trades and skills to become self-reliant, assume the identity of "American," and become U.S. citizens. Their collective goal was to metaphorically "kill the Indian to save the man." "Savage and civilized cannot live on the same ground," said Commissioner of Indian Affairs Hiram Price in 1881. It was the responsibility of civilized peoples to uplift those less evolved when possible. Native Americans, reasoned attendees at the annual conference, could be acculturated and assimilated, provided the right programs were constructed. As for those who continued to resist, "the few must yield to the many." These were certainly not new ideas, but the **Lake Mohonk Conference** guests carried sufficient political clout and public influence to make each of these goals part of the framework of Indian policy.

The Attack on Indian Culture

The Indian Rights Association and the annual Lake Mohonk Conference wielded substantial influence with the public and with Congress. Their ideas grew into public statements on preferred policy directions, and their presentation of the new direction in Indian affairs was couched in moralistic rhetoric. In keeping with the larger values of western civilization at the time, it was imperative that any semblance of "primitivism" be eradicated and cultural pluralism be shunned in favor of the construction of a single, monolithic American national identity. Little time passed before their influence was felt.

The Dawes Act

Among the basic objectives of reformers was the detribalization of Indians, a goal that could be partially accomplished through the Indians' private ownership of land. From discussions among reformers at the Lake Mohonk conferences came the notion that Indians would acculturate to white ways more quickly if they had a vested interest in the American system. The foundation of Americanism, they believed, was land ownership. Toward that end, Senator Henry Dawes (Massachusetts) sponsored the General Allotment Act in Congress. President Grover Cleveland signed the act on February 8, 1887. The **Dawes General Allotment Act** allowed the federal government to divide reservation lands into individual tracts, or **allotments**, assigning each male head of household 160 acres, every single adult man 80 acres, and males under 18 years of age 40 acres each. Allotment sizes were doubled on those reservations better suited to ranching than farming. Tribal land not allotted would be sold to whites. Indian title to the allotted tracts was to be held in trust by the government for a period of 25 years, ostensibly so that allottees could not be dispossessed of their property by their own will or by deceitful tactics employed by unscrupulous white citizens. Those Indians who accepted allotment were to be offered U.S. citizenship. Congress intended the measure as an avenue by which Native Americans would become industrious individuals working their private property, develop self-reliance through their work and private property ownership, prosper, and join the larger nation as contributing American citizens. The Dawes Act was, Congress believed, the necessary first step in acculturating Native Americans.

The prospect of issuing tribal lands to individual Indian owners worried most reformers. Having had no experience in land ownership, and, indeed, given that private land ownership was an alien concept among

READING HISTORY

General Allotment Act, or Dawes Act (1887)

By the 1880s, the so-called "Indian Wars" on the plains had largely concluded. Envisioned by those calling for a new direction in federal Indian policy was a plan to acculturate Native Americans to the ways of mainstream society and, ultimately, assimilate native peoples into the fabric of America. The Dawes Act, they believed, was the critical, necessary first step toward that goal.

An Act to provide for the allotment of lands in severalty to Indians on the various reservations, and to extend the protection of the laws of the United States and the Territories over the Indians, and for other purposes.

Be it enacted by the Senate and House of Representatives of the United States of America in Congress assembled, That in all cases where any tribe or band of Indians has been, or shall hereafter be, located upon any reservation created for their use . . . the President of the United States be, and he hereby is, authorized, whenever in his opinion any reservation or any part thereof of such Indians is advantageous for agricultural and grazing purposes, to cause said reservation, or any part thereof, to be surveyed, or resurveyed if necessary, and to allot the lands in said reservation in severalty to any Indian located thereon in quantities as follows:

To each head of a family, one-quarter of a section;

To each single person over eighteen years of age, one-eighth of a section;

To each orphan child under eighteen years of age, one-eighth of a section; and

To each other single person under eighteen years now living, or who may be born prior to the date of the order of the President directing an allotment of the lands embraced in any reservation, one-sixteenth of a section:

Provided, That in case there is not sufficient land in any of said reservations to allot lands to each individual of the classes above named in quantities as above provided, the lands embraced in such reservation or reservations shall be allotted to each individual of each of said classes pro rata in accordance with the provisions of this act: . . . And provided further, That when the lands allotted are only valuable for grazing purposes, an additional allotment of such grazing lands, in quantities as above provided, shall be made to each individual.

Sec. 2. That all allotments set apart under the provisions of this act shall be selected by the Indians, heads of families selecting for their minor children, and the agents shall select for each orphan child, and in such manner as to embrace the improvements of the Indians making the selection . . .

Sec. 4. That where any Indian not residing upon a reservation, or for whose tribe no reservation has been provided by treaty, act of Congress, or executive order, shall make settlement upon any surveyed or unsurveyed lands of the United States not otherwise appropriated, he or she shall be entitled, upon application to the local land-office for the district in which the lands are located, to have the same allotted to him or her, and to his or her children, in quantities and manner as provided in this act for Indians residing upon reservations; . . .

Sec. 5. That upon the approval of the allotments provided for in this act by the Secretary of the Interior, he shall cause patents to issue therefore in the name of the allottees, which patents shall be of the legal effect, and declare that the United States does and will hold the land thus allotted, for the period of twenty-five years, in trust for the sole use and benefit of the Indian to whom such allotment shall have been made, or, in case of his decease, of his heirs according to the laws of the State or Territory where such land is located, and that at the expiration of said period the United States will convey the same by patent to said Indian, or his heirs as aforesaid, in fee, discharged of said trust and free of all charge or incumbrance whatsoever: . . . And provided further, That at any time after lands have been allotted to all the Indians of any tribe as herein provided, or sooner if in the opinion of the President it shall be for the best interests of said tribe, it shall be lawful for the Secretary of the Interior to negotiate with such Indian tribe for the purchase and release by said tribe, . . . of such portions of its reservation not allotted as such tribe shall, from time to time, consent to sell, on such terms and conditions as shall be considered just and equitable between the United States and said tribe of Indians, which purchase shall not be complete until ratified by Congress, and the form and manner of executing such release prescribed by Congress: . . .

Sec. 6. That upon the completion of said allotments and the patenting of the lands to said allottees, each and every number of the respective bands or tribes of Indians to whom allotments have been made shall have the benefit of and be subject to the laws, both civil and criminal, of the State or Territory in which they may reside; and no Territory shall pass or enforce any law denying any such Indian within its jurisdiction the equal protection of the law. And every Indian born within the territorial limits of the United States to whom allotments shall have been made under the provisions of this act, or under any law or treaty, and every Indian born within the territorial limits of the United States who has voluntarily taken up, within said limits, his residence separate and apart from any tribe of Indians therein, and has adopted the habits of civilized life, is hereby declared to be a citizen of the United States, and is entitled to all the rights, privileges, and immunities of such citizens, whether said Indian has been or not, by birth or otherwise, a member of any tribe of Indians within the territorial limits of the United States without in any manner affecting the right of any such Indian to tribal or other property . . .

Sec. 8. That the provisions of this act shall not extend to the territory occupied by the Cherokees, Creeks, Choctaws, Chickasaws, Seminoles, and Osage, Miamies and Peorias, and Sacs and Foxes, in the Indian Territory, nor to any of the reservations of the Seneca Nation of New York Indians in the State of New York, nor to that strip of territory in the State of Nebraska adjoining the Sioux Nation on the south added by executive order . . .

Sec. 10. That nothing in this act contained shall be so construed to affect the right and power of Congress to grant the right of way through any lands granted to an Indian, or a tribe of Indians, for railroads or other highways, or telegraph lines, for the public use, or condemn such lands to public uses, upon making just compensation.

Source: "An Act to Provide for the Allotment of Lands in Severalty to Indians on the Various Reservations," General Allotment Act, or Dawes Act (1887). Statutes at Large 24, 388–91, NADP, Document A 1887, at www.ourdocuments.gov

Questions

1. In what ways did the federal government ensure that allotment would be complete on all reservations?
2. How did the act intend to protect Native Americans? How did the land distribution plan potentially hold for both Indian identity and long-range policy goals?
3. What might have been a reason for excluding from the Dawes Act Native Americans living in Indian Territory?

Indian cultures, reformers feared allottees would sell or be swindled out of their property. If this occurred, it would doom the government's Americanization program. Senator Henry Teller of Colorado opposed the allotment plan and cautioned that should allotment ever become policy, the measure would inevitably lead to the Indians' extinction. The division of reservations into privately owned allotments, he warned, was "not in the interest of the Indians at all" but instead advanced the designs of men who "are clutching up this land" for their own financial windfall. Even the provision's plan for Washington to hold title to the property for a generation did not secure the Indians' property. Congress and the courts could easily negotiate new provisions to expose Indian lands to white speculators. The few critics who voiced their opinion complained that the measure would "despoil the natives of their lands and . . . make them vagabonds on the face of the earth." One congressman seethed, "If this were done in the name of greed, it would be bad enough; but to do it in the name of humanity and under the cloak of an ardent desire to promote the Indians' welfare by making him more like ourselves . . . is infinitely worse."

In the first year following passage of the Dawes Act, the Office of Indian Affairs issued 3,349 allotments and in the 1890s averaged 8,000 annually. Historian Donald Parman noted correctly that the reservations that underwent division were generally those that held lands suited to agriculture and ranching and were reasonably close to markets. Those that were "isolated and of poor quality" rarely received attention. The Navajo, groups of Utes, and others spread across the Southwest and basin regions "escaped [division], but those tribes with available agricultural or grazing lands were always allotted."

The Dawes Act was probably a genuine attempt by humanitarians of that era to create a foundation for all other Americanization efforts among Native Americans, but applying it immediately to reservations with the more valuable lands sent a signal to Indians and land speculators that could not be ignored. Developments soon after passage of the Dawes Act gave credence to the reformers' fears. Congress in 1891 attached an addendum to the Dawes Act that permitted Indians to lease their allotments without holding title to the property. Reformers initially applauded the move, believing it necessary so that Indians incapable of working their lands could nonetheless earn income through the lease. The Secretary of the Interior was to review and approve

11.5 Chief American Horse (Ogala Sioux) receiving his allotment under the Dawes General Allotment Act.

Source: Courtesy of Library of Congress Prints and Photographs Division, LC-USZ62-115669

all lease applications, and reformers believed naively that this would serve as a safety net, preventing Indians from losing their property altogether.

The Secretary of the Interior was soon inundated with lease applications. In 1893, Congress granted reservation agents the authority to determine which leases the secretary should approve, and in practice the system became one in which the secretary rubber stamped all those the agents recommended. "The rental of Indian lands after 1891 probably became the chief source of collusion between agency officials and local white interests," wrote Parman. Agents often struck deals with unscrupulous local businessmen, ranchers, and farmers determined to acquire Indian lands, and they feared no reprisal should they get caught violating the law. Indeed, a real estate firm on the Winnebago Reservation "leased 47,000 acres illegally for which it paid Indians from ten cents to 25 cents per acre but subsequently sublet to white farmers for one to two dollars per acre." The allotment plan was "poorly conceived and implemented" by eastern reformers "who had little understanding of the western geographic, economic, and social environment and no concern for Indian traditions."

The situation only got worse. In 1902, Congress passed into law the Indian Appropriation Act, which allowed the Secretary of the Interior to end its trust requirement and sell the holdings of deceased allottees on behalf of their adult heirs, while permitting the land of heirs less than 18 years of age to be sold by guardians with the secretary's approval. The purchase of heirships rose rapidly, peaking in 1904 with the sale of 122,222 acres. The **Burke Act**, which Congress approved in 1906, allowed the Secretary of the Interior the prerogative to issue an Indian title to his allotment along with U.S. citizenship, provided the allottee was determined to be "competent" by the Indian Office. The term was vaguely defined as an Indian who understood that the title allowed him full ownership of the property and that he was capable of providing a living for himself and his family on that parcel of land. In practice, there was no clear test to prove competency. As a result, Indians declared competent were soon thereafter encouraged to sell their land. The Indian Appropriations Act of 1907 contributed further to the Indians' loss of land. It allowed Indians to sell portions of their allotments as a means of raising money to purchase farm machines, livestock, and seed. This, too, took property from Native Americans and placed it into white ownership. As critics feared, Congress found ways to circumvent the intent of the Dawes Act and, in so doing, move Indian lands into white hands. It is impossible to state definitively that the sole purpose of these provisions was to divest Indians of the holdings for the benefit of white farmers, ranchers, and speculators, but the results of these measures are unambiguous. During the life of the Dawes Act, from 1887 to 1933, 60 million acres of allotted lands filtered into white ownership. If the Dawes Act was intended to facilitate the Americanization of Indians by making them landowners, it failed miserably.

PROFILE

The "Oklahoma Land Rushers, or Boomers"

Land figures prominently in the story of Indian-white relations—the settlers' determination to acquire it and the Indians' equal determination to hold on to it. Indian Territory contained more than one dozen Native American tribes living on reservations by the late 1880s. With passage of the Dawes Act in 1887, Native American reservations were to be subdivided and plots of land ranging from 160 acres to 40 acres were to be issued for private, individual ownership among tribal members. The act allowed for surplus reservation land to be purchased at minimum value from the tribes and then distributed to white settlers. The Dawes Act was touted as one of three specific requirements for Indians to become Americanized. Senator Henry Teller (Colorado), however, insisted "the real aim ... is to get at the Indians' land and open it for resettlement." The land rushes that occurred over the next decade supported Teller's claim.

On April 22, 1889, President Benjamin Harrison opened two million acres of unallotted Indian Territory for white ownership. What followed was one of the most "bizarre and chaotic episodes of town founding in world history." Nearly 50,000 settlers gathered along a designated "starting line" and at the stroke of noon and the sound of cannon they rushed into the territory to stake their claim on surveyed plots. By the end of the day, the towns of Guthrie and Oklahoma City were founded with 10,000 residents. Within the next two weeks, schools were erected and within one month Oklahoma City boasted five banks and six newspapers. On May 2, 1890, Congress established the Oklahoma Territory.

A similar rush was orchestrated on September 18, 1891, opening surplus lands of the

11.6 This 1911 advertisement from the U.S. Department of the Interior offers former reservation land for sale. The ad pictures a Yankton Sioux named Not Afraid of Pawnee.

Source: U.S. Department of the Interior

Iowa, Sac-Fox, Potawatomi, and Shawnee Indians for 20,000 settlers. Again, on April 19, 1892, some 25,000 settlers descended on lands removed from the Cheyenne and Arapaho reservations. The largest land rush occurred one year later. At noon on September 16, 1893, a cannon shot signaled the rush of 100,000 settlers to claim one of the 42,000 plots in northern Oklahoma in what was known as the Cherokee Strip. Throwing open for settlement much of the Indian Territory served the demands of land-hungry settlers from across the United States and from many European nations. In so doing, it further concentrated American Indians onto less acreage and encouraged allottees to sell or lease their lands.

Christianizing the Indian

Land ownership was one element of the Americanization effort. Central to the Americanization effort, too, was the Indians' conversion to Christianity. In 1883, the Indian Office produced a "List of Indian Offenses" intended to aid in the process of "rooting out paganism" for the advancement of civilization. Traditional feasts and dances were banned, and the various methods used among Indians for a man to secure a wife and even the "give away" ceremony were all listed as offenses. It prohibited a tribal holy man from offering spiritual understanding to his people. The bureau also banned the Sun Dance, long the soul of Plains Indian social and spiritual connection between this world and the other world. Indians, however, resisted the edict, typically performing their ceremonies in secret, out of view of reservation superintendents and other whites. "You whites assumed we were savages. You didn't understand our prayers. You didn't try to understand," complained Walking Buffalo (Assiniboine). "When we sang our praises to the sun or moon or wind, you said we were worshipping idols . . . [and] condemned us as lost souls just because our form of worship was different from yours," he added.

The Christianizing effort dated to the earliest days of the colonial period, and it had over the centuries converted many Indians, although converts typically blended Christianity with traditional Indian spirituality. Christian efforts, however, generally failed, in part because Native Americans recognized a disconnect between the words and behavior of Christians. Wrote Julius H. Seelye of Amherst College in his introduction to *A Century of Dishonor*, "it is idle to attempt to carry Christian influences to any one unless we are Christian. The first step, therefore, toward the desired transformation of the Indian is a transformed treatment of him by ourselves. In sober earnest, our Government needs, first of all, to be Christian, and to treat the Indian question as Christian principles require . . . There is no use to attempt to teach Christian duty to him in words till he has first seen it exemplified in our own deeds."

Troubling, too, for those pressing the Christianization of Indians was the obvious and sometimes heated competition among Christian denominations, all of which believed their own variation of the faith was more correct than others. Chief Joseph perhaps expressed best the Indians' dissatisfaction with missionaries: "We do not want churches because they will teach us to quarrel about God, as the Catholics and Protestants do. We do not want to learn that. We may quarrel with men sometimes about things on this earth. We never quarrel about God." Once behavior matched rhetoric and interfaith bickering ceased, reformers believed that conversion would be more easily accomplished.

There were, to be sure, some parallels between Christianity and Indian spirituality. Both believed in an afterlife, both in a supreme creator, and both in the destruction of earth on at least one occasion. They shared many of the same values—peace, charity, humility, and brotherhood. It was easy enough for Indians, especially Indian children, to meld traditional spirituality with the fundamental tenets of the Christian religion. "When

I believed the Oglala Wakan Tanka was right I served him with all my powers . . . In war with the white people I found their Wakan Tanka the superior . . . I joined the church and am a deacon in it and shall be until I die," said George Sword. But he still carried his pouch of sacred items. "I am afraid to offend it, because the spirit of an Oglala may go to the spirit land of the Lakota." Sword, like so many Native Americans, carried both in his heart. The blending of Christianity and spirituality seemed a suitable first step toward eventual full conversion. Many reformers considered it a bridge between generations. Education of youngsters would likely complete the process.

There were, however, fundamental differences between Christianity and Indian spirituality that reformers either failed to consider or wrongly believed could be altered. Certain features of Indian spiritual awareness were common to most tribal groups despite cultural variations. Vine Deloria details in his book *God Is Red* that Christianity was, and is, a linear religion. There is a beginning and end to all things. This contrasts to the continuous, circular view of life Native Americans held. Indian spirituality was spatial, tied to the land, relevant to the environment, and grounded in the interconnectedness of all things and creatures. Christianity was based on the absolute word of God, suited to all people regardless of their location, culture, or circumstance. In the Book of Genesis, God grants humans mastery over the animals and the plants. Humans are superior to all other of God's creation. Most Indians did not hold this view. As Chief Luther Standing Bear (Lakota) put it, the Creator, Wakan Tanka, was a unifying force "that flowed in and through all things—the flowers of the plains, blowing winds, rocks, trees, birds, animals—and was the same force that had been breathed into the first man. Thus all things were kindred . . . The Lakota could despise no creature, for all were of one blood, made by the same hand . . . 'Blessed are the meek, for they shall inherit the earth'—this was true for the Lakota." And, as Deloria also points out, original sin was an alien notion to Native Americans as was the concept of salvation. The reformers' focus on religious conversion, then, was a central component of the plan to detribalize Native Americans and to Americanize them. Reformers' failure to understand Indian spirituality, their refusal to see any value in native spirituality, and their belief that Christianity was the only viable religion led to their failure in this arena as much as corruption in land policy undermined that effort at Americanization.

Reformers were, however, determined to Christianize Indians. Protestant and Catholic mission schools opened on reservations, educating children in basic academics but expending greater energy on religious conversion. Christian prayers began and typically ended the school day. Regular reading of the Bible and daily instruction in the religion were routine for Indian children. Mission school teachers generally commanded positions of authority within the Indian community, their advice frequently solicited by reservation superintendents. The mission schools also erected churches on reservations, and often rations were tied to Indian attendance. Christian holidays and celebrations became centerpieces of community activity.

Educating Native Americans

Reformers hoped that an education grounded in Western academics and buttressed by vocational training and stern discipline would detribalize Native American children and, in so doing, lead to their Americanization. "We are going to conquer the Indians by a standing army of school teachers, armed with ideas, winning victories by industrial training, and by the gospel of love and the gospel of work," said one reformer. Toward that end, the Indian Office established boarding schools on the larger reservations. However, because both the children's schools and homes were on reservation land, they were able to maintain contact with their families and, through them, with their Indian identity, even if the school's curriculum muted this identity somewhat. In spite of the physical connection they were able to preserve with their youngsters, most adult Indians still disliked intensely the end result, a young adult no longer truly considered Indian among his family and friends, yet not considered white off the reservation. Native American parents often refused to part with their children and occasionally threatened agents who came for the youngsters. Agents frequently had to force parents to send their children to school, bringing with them soldiers posted at nearby forts and Indian police when they came to claim children. Although violence was generally averted, the parents' compliance was often coerced through threats of incarceration or a reduction in the families' already minimal rations. In 1907, Hopi parents were transported to and detained at Alcatraz in San Francisco Bay for hiding their youngsters.

In autumn 1879, Captain Richard Henry Pratt founded **Carlisle Indian Industrial School**, housed in out-dated and unused military barracks in Carlisle, Pennsylvania. Historian James Wilson has described Pratt as a "devoted and sincere man," but another historian, Robert M. Utley, blasted Pratt as "dogmatic, stubborn, inflex-ible, outspoken, combative, and above all determined." He "warred against the Indian bureau and its entrenched bureaucracy, which he would have abolished, along with the reservations, had he been able. He warred against ethnologists and anthropologists . . . and all others who glorified or even studied Indian culture." And, Utley adds, Pratt "warred against all critics of his ideas," especially those who criticized the Carlisle school. Both Wilson and Utley agree, however, that the captain believed Indian cultures, not the individuals, were incompatible with the modern world and were "worthless relics from an earlier stage of development which must be destroyed." "'Race' was a meaningless concept," wrote Wilson; in Pratt's mind, "all significant human differences . . . could be explained by environment alone." Remove the Indian child from his community and family, surround him with the physical trappings of contemporary American society, instruct him in Christianity and in academics, and the child would be transformed from an Indian into an American. The school's curriculum, system of discipline, and acculturation by immersion would altogether "kill the Indian and save the man." "I believe in immersing the Indians in our civilization and when we get them under, holding them there until they are thor-oughly soaked," said Pratt. The system he planned and implemented was not, at the time, considered extreme. Many schools for non-Indians nationally adhered to the same stern, rigid program Carlisle imposed on its students. Military colleges to be sure were built on the same structure, but so too were prep schools and acad-emies that served the children of America's upper crust.

11.7A Chiricahua Apache children upon arrival at Carlisle Indian School
Source: The Denver Public Library, Western History Collection, X-32903

Carlisle's curriculum centered on the basic skills common to most elementary schools—read-ing, writing, and mathematics. Classes in civics and American history shaped student percep-tions of the United States, its values, customs, and place in the world. Purposely included in all academic and religious instruc-tion was the message that native cultures possessed no value. Sci-ence courses were intended not only to advance student knowl-edge but also to demonstrate the superiority of Western civiliza-tion over Indian cultures. Stu-dents also learned manual skills such as carpentry and metal work. Pratt believed training in

11.7B Chiricahua children after four months at Carlisle Indian School
Source: The Denver Public Library, Western History Collection, X-32904

these fields would be transferable to white society or useful on the reservations once students graduated from Carlisle. The school also built a strong athletic program, fielding teams in track, baseball, and football.

Shock swept over Indian youngsters new to Carlisle as their identity was systematically stripped away. Young boys' hair was cut short, and speaking their native languages was strictly prohibited. Physical punishments were meted out for violations of school rule. Each child was issued a Christian name upon arrival. Wrote Luther Standing Bear (Lakota) in recalling his first days at Carlisle,

Instead of translating our names into English and calling Zinkcaziwin, Yellow Bird, and Wanbli K'leska, Spotted Eagle, which in itself would have been educational, we were just John, Henry or Maggie. I was told to take the pointer and select a name for myself from the list written on the blackboard. I did, and since one was just as good as another, and as I could not distinguish any difference in them, I placed the pointer on the name Luther.

Indian clothing was either discarded or burned upon arrival. Boys were issued cadet-style uniforms, typically gray and unadorned, and girls were provided very simple, matronly dresses. Students assembled in formation each morning and evening for flag-raising and lowering ceremonies and marched to meals and classes. Boys received instruction in the military's close order drill and all adhered to a stern military code of conduct. Pratt, and later the Indian Office, instructed teachers to "avoid any unnecessary reference to the fact that [the students] are Indians." The physical separation of children from their Indian heritage along with intense indoctrination of "the white way" immediately challenged the preservation of their traditional identity. "The change in clothing, housing, food, and confinement combined with lonesomeness was too much," said Standing Bear, "and in three years nearly one-half of the children from the Plains were dead . . . In the graveyard at Carlisle most of the graves are those of little ones."

In its first academic year, Carlisle served 160 students, nearly three-quarters of them young boys. The school's occasional success stories seemingly validated the rigid, rigorous curriculum and disciplinary system. Congressional appropriations for Indian education in 1877 totaled a paltry $30,000; the promise of Carlisle spurred Congress to allocate $75,000 the following year and $1,300,000 a decade later as more schools of all types were founded. Between 1877 and 1890, student enrollment nearly quadrupled at boarding schools, from 3,500 to 12,200. By 1900, more than 300 schools served Indian children, with boarding schools housing 18,000 children, roughly 75 percent of all Indian children in educational institutions (see Table 11.1).

Table 11.1 Carlisle Indian Industrial School, Enrollment by Tribes, Ten or More Students, 1879–1918

Tribe	Count	Tribe	Count	Tribe	Count
Apache	269	Iroquois	31	Potawatomi	71
Arapaho	116	Kaw	11	Pueblo	352
Arikara	26	Kickapoo	32	Puyallup	16
Assiniboine	56	Kiowa	65	Quapaw	14
Bannock	16	Klamath	69	Sac-Fox	70
Blackfoot	187	Lummi	12	Seminole	11
Caddo	41	Menominee	141	Seneca	628
Catawba	12	Miami	17	Shawnee	75
Cayuga	39	Mission	75	Shoshone	102
Cherokee	370	Modoc	17	Sioux	1126
Cheyenne	249	Mohawk	3352	Spokane	11
Chickasaw	16	Navajo	43	Stockbridge	68
Chippewa	998	Nez Perce	126	Tuscarora	103
Chitimacha	23	Omaha	124	Umatilla	10
Choctaw	82	Oneida	502	Ute	15
Clallam	15	Onondaga	136	Walla Walla	11
Colville	23	Osage	156	Wampanoag	11
Comanche	58	Ottowa	139	Washoe	15
Creek	104	Paiute	23	Wichita	35
Crow	97	Papago	16	Winnebago	164
Delaware	27	Pawnee	85	Wyandotte	42
Digger	20	Penobscot	44	Yuma	13
Flathead	19	Peoria	12		
Gros Ventre	43	Pima	71	Other	1856
Hopi	18	Pokanot	12		
Iowa	16	Ponca	46	TOTAL	13116

Boarding schools angered Indian parents, but off-reservation programs such as Carlisle made them particularly livid. Children sent to schools like Carlisle were forcibly removed from their families, from their communities, from their culture. Pratt himself traveled to Pine Ridge and Rosebud reservations in 1879 and separated 84 youngsters from their families, employing both promises and threats. As the children were carted away, their mothers' cries filled the air and their fathers' rage could barely be contained. Years passed with only the most minimal contact between parents and child. When the child returned home a nearly grown man or woman, parents and their offspring hardly recognized one another, and they most certainly did not know each other. The boarding school graduate was no longer an Indian, but instead an alien in the home of his birth.

SEEING HISTORY

"The American Indian: Past and Present"

Carlisle Indian Industrial School, along with other Indian boarding schools nationwide, built a much-respected athletic program, allowing students to participate in a variety of team and individual sports and compete with institutions similar in size to Carlisle. Best known among Carlisle's athletes is Jim Thorpe, who won gold medals in the 1912 Summer Olympics in Track and Field, and afterward became one of the most famous athletes in college and professional football.

Question

This illustration appeared in *Puck Magazine* on November 28, 1906. What message does the drawing suggest?

11.8 *Puck Magazine* cartoon

Source: Courtesy of Library of Congress Prints and Photographs Division, LC-DIG-ds-03750

PROFILE

Plenty Kill, aka Luther Standing Bear (Oglala, 1868–1939)

11.9 Luther Standing Bear

Source: Library of Congress, LC-USZ62-56421

Plenty Kill (Ota Kte) was born on the Pine Ridge reservation in Dakota Territory in 1868 and, until age 11 or 12, lived the constrained but largely traditional life of a Sioux boy. His life changed abruptly when Indian agents, reservation police, and a contingent of U.S. Army troops gathered youngsters for shipment to Carlisle Indian School in Pennsylvania. Plenty Kill was among those taken from their homes and families.

Assuming the name Luther Standing Bear at Carlisle, he resisted the compulsory haircut, school uniform, and code of behavior as best as any child could, his heart longing for the familiar and for family. Years passed, and Luther gained proficiency in English, performed well in his academic and vocational courses, and largely satisfied his teachers' expectations, but he never lost pride in his Oglala identity.

He took a variety of jobs following graduation—teacher, general store clerk, and actor in Buffalo Bill's Wild West Show, and between 1910 and 1930 he played bit parts in early Hollywood westerns. He observed a world without Indians and a nation hurrying to meld all cultures into a single people. Luther Standing Bear chose to preserve Oglala culture through literature, authoring *My People the Sioux* (1928), *Land of the Spotted Eagle* (1933), and *Stories of the Sioux* (1934). He also was active in the National League for Justice to the American Indian until his death in 1939.

Quotes from Luther Standing Bear:

"Nothing the Great Mystery placed in the land of the Indian pleased the white man, and nothing escaped his transforming hand."

"'Civilization' has been thrust upon me since the days of the reservations and it has not added one whit to my sense of justice, to my reverence for the rights of life, to my love for truth, honesty, and generosity, or to my faith in Wakan Tanka, God of the Lakotas."

"The American Indian is of the soil, whether it be the region of forests, plains, pueblos, or mesas. He fits into the landscape, for the hand that fashioned the continent also fashioned the man for his surroundings."

"The white man does not understand America. He is far removed from its formative processes. The roots of the tree have not yet grasped the rock and soil."

Conclusion

The call for reform in Indian affairs rang louder in the final quarter of the nineteenth century than at any previous moment in U.S. history. Reform was now deemed the appropriate, moral course to follow. With Native American armed resistance crushed and tribes relocated to reservations, white America took a responsibility for the people it now considered "wards" of the state. The object of the reformers was to "Americanize" the Indians through a rigid, mandatory system of education, the conversion of Indians to Christianity, the assignment of individually owned plots of land from which they were to sustain themselves and their families, and within a reasonable period of time the extension of citizenship to Native Americans. Indians, so prepared, could then free themselves of reservations and government oversight and become "real" Americans. The reformers' enthusiasm and idealism were genuine and sincere. That reformers failed to consider Indian preferences was not shocking or unusual.

Review Questions

1. What conditions existed on reservations that compelled some Indians to flee and seek an earlier form of life, even if the consequence was warfare with the U.S. Army?
2. Why did eastern reformers deem it critical to redirect federal Indian policy, and toward what goal did they guide the federal government? What was their purpose in pursuing that particular goal?
3. Which features of the reformers' goal were directly intended to eradicate Indian identity? Why were those features considered essential to completing the task?
4. What negative consequences fell on Indians as a result of the reformers' agenda?
5. In what ways did the reform efforts of eastern reformers and government officials mirror reform efforts the same groups among European immigrants to the United States initiated?

Recommended Readings

Coleman, William S. E. *Voices of Wounded Knee* (Lincoln, NE: University of Nebraska Press, 2000). A detailed study of the Ghost Dance and Wounded Knee massacre that places both in the broader context of broken treaties over decades, cultural misunderstandings, and media-driven hysteria.

Deloria, Vine, Jr. *God Is Red: A Native View of Religion* (Golden, CO: North American Press, 1992). First published in 1972, this has become the seminal work contrasting Western religions and Native American spirituality.

Fear-Segal, Jacqueline, and Susan D. Rose. *Carlisle Indian Industrial School: Indigenous Histories, Memories, and Reclamations* (Lincoln, NE: University of Nebraska Press, 2016). A collection of personal memories from Native Americans who attended and survived Carlisle Indian School.

Greene, Jerome A. *American Carnage: Wounded Knee, 1890* (Norman: University of Oklahoma Press, 2014).

Hoxie, Frederick E. *A Final Promise: The Campaign to Assimilate the Indians, 1880–1920* (Lincoln, NE: University of Nebraska Press, 1984). An intellectually stimulating and critical examination of federal Indian policy during the Progressive Era, a policy determined to crumble the structures underpinning native cultures and identity.

Standing Bear, Luther. *Land of the Spotted Eagle* (Lincoln, NE: University of Nebraska Press, 2006). First published in the 1930s, a history and explanation of traditional Lakota culture through the eyes of a traditional Lakota.

Trafzer, Clifford E. *Boarding School Blues: Revisiting American Indian Educational Experiences* (Lincoln, NE: University of Nebraska Press, 2006). A collection of essays that cover the full range of the boarding school experience for children and the origin and development of the American Indian boarding school system.

Warren, Louis S. *God's Red Son: The Ghost Dance Religion and the Making of Modern America* (New York: Basic Books, 2017). A detailed presentation of the Ghost Dance religion—its cultural origin, its role as a means for native resistance, its place in the larger context of national development and character, and its legacy in the shaping of modern America.

Native American History Online

Wounded Knee, South Dakota. www.woundedkneemuseum.org This site includes slide shows of the massacre site; a numerical count of the children, men, and women who formed Big Foot's band; and eyewitness accounts of the massacre.

"Massacre at Wounded Knee, 1890" Eyewitness to History. www.eyewitnesstohistory.com/knee This site provides a historical account of the 1890 massacre but includes the eyewitness testimony of Philip Wells, a mixed-blood Sioux and interpreter for the U.S. Army.

Archives of *The West*, Episode Eight, 1887–1914. www.pbs.org/weta/thewest/resources/archives/eight This episode of the PBS series *The West* features the Dawes Act, the Ghost Dance, and Sitting Bull's death. The site provides documents, first-person accounts, and photographs.

Carlisle Indian Industrial School/Cumberland Historical Society. www.historicalsociety.com/ciiswelcome.html This site offers a history of Carlisle Indian School.

Geronimo and His Effort to Preserve Apache Identity. Geronimo himself recounts his life in "Geronimo: His Own Story," located at http://odur.let.rug.nl/~usa/B/geronimo/geronixx.htm

Historical Sites

Wounded Knee Museum, Wall, South Dakota. www.woundedkneemuseum.org This museum chronicles the history of the Lakota Nation and devotes much of its space to the massacre at Wounded Knee in December 1890. Included are document exhibits, photographs and artwork, a scale model of the Wounded Knee Massacre site, and a Remembrance Room.

CHAPTER 12

SIMON POKAGON
**THE PROGRESSIVE SPIRIT AMONG NATIVE
AMERICANS**
The Society of American Indians
Gertrude Bonnin and Laura Cornelius Kellogg
Religion and the SAI
Fractures Within the SAI
The Peyote Issue
THE GREAT WAR
The World War I Draft
Indians Enter Military Service
Over There
Stereotypes and Indian Military Service
The Home Front

Simon Pokagon

More than 27 million people attended the World's
Columbian Exposition in Chicago between its
opening in May 1893 and its closing the following
October. The exposition, in part, commemorated
the 400th anniversary of Christopher Columbus's
first landfall in the New World, but perhaps to most
attendees its avenues and pavilions heralded a new
age for the United States and for the world—industrialization, scientific management, and the promise
of technology. The fair celebrated the advances of
civilization globally and the emerging era of progress among less-developed peoples, but it treated
Native Americans more like museum pieces of the
past than surviving cultures.

Only a few days before the expo closed, a
Potawatomi chief, Simon Pokagon, spoke before
the assembled audience. The white man, Pokagon

Princess Tsianina Redfeather Blackstone (1883–1985),
American Indian and concert performer who appeared
on stages across the country and in Europe, including
on the Metropolitan Opera stage and on the battlefields of France during World War I.

Source: Courtesy of Library of Congress Prints and Photographs Division, LC-DIG-ggbain-20485

declared, "has usurped our lands and homes." His accomplishments, "this success" that glittered so grandly at the World's Columbia Exposition and trumpeted America's greatness, "has been at the sacrifice of our homes and a once happy race . . . We have no spirit to celebrate with you." He continued his verbal assault on the national and global celebration demonstrated at this world fair now coming to its conclusion. Rather than listen carefully and critically to the Indian's words, one member of the audience was heard describing it as a "'resigned' valedictory of the 'chief of a vanishing tribe and race.'"

The choice of Pokagon as a featured speaker was a purposeful one. Born in 1830, he was the son of the Potawatomi chief credited with "selling" to the United States the land on which Chicago was constructed. He also visibly possessed the traits and skills embedded in the acculturation effort long imposed on Native Americans—a sound education, acceptance of Christianity, and accomplishments in the non-Indian world. His literary talent was already earning him the mantle "the Redskin Bard" and "the Longfellow of his Race." He certainly encouraged Indians to follow a path similar to his own, stating often that Native American survival depended on their adoption of "white ways." To fair organizers, Pokagon represented the evolution of American Indians from primitivism to civilization, and, in their minds, he was a living validation of the policies and programs of the government and reformers.

The Potawatomi's speech that October day, along with his published writings throughout the 1890s, nonetheless reflected an internal conflict so many Indians of the Progressive Era experienced. European colonization of the New World and America's expansion and development since independence irrevocably altered Indian cultures, directions, and identity. Most, like Pokagon, understood the old days—the old ways—could not continue unchanged. Acculturation to the white world, to modernizing America, was now required; however, Pokagon and many of his contemporaries were determined to preserve their Indian identity. How to protect that identity and to what extent that identity could be maintained were the essential questions with which Native Americans grappled at the turn of the twentieth century.

KEY QUESTIONS

1. In what ways were the ideals and goals of Native American Progressives similar to, and different from, those of the larger, national Progressive Movement at the turn of the century?
2. What were the principal issues that contributed to the fragmentation of the Society of American Indians?
3. How did the question of U.S. citizenship complicate the induction of American Indians into the nation's armed forces during World War I?
4. What motivated Native American men to serve in the U.S. armed forces during the war and Indian civilians to contribute their energy on the home front?
5. What changes did the Indian Office expect to see among those Indian men who served in America's military and naval forces? In what ways did Native Americans consciously preserve traditional Indian values and customs during the war?

The Progressive Spirit Among Native Americans

Opportunity and prosperity showed themselves the length of Main Street in every major American city in the early 1900s, but, just one or two streets over, a darker reality flourished, making the promise of the modern

CHRONOLOGY

1911	The Society of American Indians (SAI) is founded on Columbus Day
1912	Track and Field athlete Jim Thorpe (Sac-Fox) wins two gold medals at the Summer Olympics in Stockholm, Sweden
1917	President Woodrow Wilson issues America's declaration of war against Germany
	Native Americans are included for the first time in the nation's Selective Service System
	The first elements of the American Expeditionary Force arrive in France
	Native Americans purchase $5 million worth of Liberty Bonds
1918	The Iroquois Confederacy issues a declaration of war against Germany
	Oklahoma becomes the first state to issue a charter to incorporate the Native American Church
	The SAI denounces peyote use and calls for a federal government ban on peyote
	Commissioner of Indian Affairs Cato Sells issues a definition of U.S. "citizenship" for Native Americans
	Choctaw Indians serving at the Battle of the Argonne Forest in France become the first Indian code talkers
	By war's end, American Indians have purchased more than $25 million in Liberty Bonds

city little more than an illusion for most urban residents. Factories were notoriously hazardous for employees. In 1911, more than 140 seamstresses died in the Triangle Shirtwaist Company fire in New York City. Locked or blocked doorways and sealed windows trapped most of the women inside the burning building. Across the nation, nearly 30,000 workers annually died on the job, and hundreds of thousands more were injured. If this were not enough, wages remained absurdly low, compelling parents to send their children to the workplace to supplement their family's income. In addition, cities were becoming terribly overcrowded. America's population in 1910 stood at 92 million, nearly three times larger than it was just 50 years earlier, and almost half of these people resided in the cities. A broad spectrum of ills plagued urban America, among them prostitution, violent crime, pollution and general filth, homelessness, and the swift spread of communicable disease. City-dwelling families often suffered under the crushing impact of alcoholism, spousal and child abuse, poverty, ignorance, and poor health. The "new city," the base of "America's century," appeared wondrous and full of promise, but ever present was the "new city's" dark, seamy underbelly.

Late in the nineteenth century, a reformist spirit took root among a growing number of urban Americans awakened to the harsher reality of city life so many people endured. They were successful men and women in positions to contribute their time and money to reform work. Perhaps more importantly, they believed government held some responsibility for the individual citizen and that one person, through his own initiative, could, indeed, make a difference in the lives of others. They championed the notion that through a combination of individual initiative and collective action, aided when necessary by governmental intervention, urban society could progress, shedding itself of social problems, political corruption, and workplace dangers. It was their belief that a quality of life could be achieved in America's cities that matched the broad, grand vision of the American people.

Critical to making the urban community a glittering example of American progress was the acculturation of immigrants to the norms and values of American society. These reformers, known as **Progressives**, ventured into immigrant communities and established programs that provided job training for recent arrivals, made them politically aware and active, and prepared them to be self-reliant. Once acculturated, productive, and responsible, immigrants would be assimilated into mainstream society and there assume an American identity.

Progressives had accomplished much by 1920. They founded national voluntary associations including the YMCA and Boy Scouts, the Sierra Club, and the National Consumers League. These organizations worked to educate and empower women, children, immigrants, and the nation's dispossessed. Some Progressives spearheaded the movement to outlaw the consumption of alcoholic beverages in a bid to protect the moral fiber of Americans generally and to protect families specifically from its destructive effects. During this period, school enrollment soared, and the number of young women in post-secondary institutions rose to nearly one-third of all university students. Progressives successfully secured legislation banning child labor, criminalizing prostitution, and regulating the quality of food, drugs, and manufactured goods. Several states now provided financial aid to unemployed women with dependent children and many required regular inspection of restaurants and factories, and the federal government and most states founded public health services. In addition, Progressives expanded the nation's democratic promise, as states passed into law the referendum and initiative, the right of recall of government officials, the direct election of U.S. senators, the secret ballot, and the vote for women. The combined efforts of government, business, and individual Americans moved the nation a little closer to the ideal of American greatness so often voiced. White, middle-class Americans were not the only people involved in the Progressive Movement. A similar progressive spirit also enveloped Native Americans, one that Indians initiated and directed.

It had long been assumed among non-Indians that Native Americans were part of a vanishing race. Popular literature highlighted white America's "conquest" of native peoples through superior intellectual and physical prowess, in so doing perpetuating the idea of Indian inferiority, submission, and eventual disappearance. Wild West shows reinforced this perspective through performances in which U.S. cavalry troopers destroyed Indian attackers, opening the West to white settlement and, thus, progress. Influential, too, were the pseudoscientific racist tracts that employed a false, distorted version of Darwin's theory of evolution to "prove" the inevitability of the demise of all "primitive" cultures, including those of the Indians.

There seemed to be hard evidence to support these claims of the Indians' impending disappearance. Tribal land ownership had declined significantly since 1880, falling from 241,800,000 acres of reservation land to a mere 55,792,000 acres under tribal ownership in 1920. Moreover, the number of Indian children enrolled in public schools, boarding schools, reservation day schools, or church mission schools consistently rose, reaching 86 percent of all Indian children by 1920. In those academic settings, Indian cultural traits were to be supplanted with the norms and values of white society, and Indian children were to be trained in vocational skills for life off the reservation. By 1920, nearly 15,000 Indians were gainfully employed in towns and cities near their reservations, and more than a few Native Americans had earned college degrees and had taken professional positions in the white world. Both Catholic and Protestant officials pointed to the rising number of Indians converted to Christianity and to hundreds who had entered the priesthood or ministry. Acculturation certainly seemed to be progressing, with full assimilation of all native peoples the anticipated, and intended, outcome.

Native Americans, however, refused to disappear. Educational programs and Christianizing efforts failed to eliminate Indians' commitment to traditional familial and social relationships, tribal customs and ceremonies, and world view. In tribal communities from coast to coast, children still learned the stories of their elders and their elders before them. Urbanized Native Americans, more often than not, sent much of their earnings to family members still living on reservations, and it was common in those urban settings for a pan-Indian community to emerge as a replacement for the reservation. In a development that came as a surprise to white society, the most educated Native Americans, the ones who had secured their place in white society, were the very individuals encouraging maintenance of an Indian identity.

SEEING HISTORY

Dime Novels

In 1860, Irwin and Erastus Beadle published the first of what became known as "dime novels"—"a dollar book for a dime!" exclaimed advertisers. These mini-novels sensationalized and often romanticized America's westward expansion, making grand heroes of white hunters, cowboys, and lawmen who "civilized" the frontier, saved women from villains, and eliminated the Indian presence to settle productive or useful lands. These fictional stories routinely advanced the racist view that Native Americans were destined for extinction; only a small percentage of Indians were capable of acculturating to white norms, but their eventual assimilation would contribute to the disappearance of native peoples. By 1898, the Beadle brothers had produced more than 3,000 different titles and sold millions of copies worldwide.

Questions

1. Why would dime novels appeal to young, urban readers in the late nineteenth century?
2. How did dime novels shape the non-Indian perspective of Native Americans, and what were the consequences of this perception on Indian policy and national identity formation?

12.1 Dime novels.

Source: Courtesy of Library of Congress Prints and Photographs Division LC-USZ62-75779

12.2 Group of Siksika men and one woman in traditional dress

Source: National Archives number 517491. Department of the Interior. General Land Office. U.S. Geological and Geographic Survey of the Territories. (1874–6/30/1879)

As the national Progressive Movement worked to extend democracy to more Americans, to purge urban communities of social and corporate ills, and to move the immigrant population toward assimilation with mainstream society, a progressive spirit also embraced well-educated Native Americans. The goals of Indian Progressives bore striking similarities to those of their white counterparts. They wanted to improve the quality of reservation life for Native Americans who wished to remain there, bring the democratic promise to American Indians, and develop and extend educational programs and opportunities that would hasten Indians' acculturation and assimilation with white society.

Like the white Progressives who worked with urban immigrants and consciously promoted their maintenance of a separate cultural identity, Indian Progressives encouraged dual identity for Native Americans—full assimilation with mainstream America but also proud protection of their cultural heritage.

Indians had always resisted the destruction of their cultural identity. The work of Indian Progressives was but the most recent effort to combat the notion that pride in heritage and assimilation were mutually exclusive goals. The Progressive Movement created among Americans across the country a greater receptivity to change and reform. In this climate of reformist zeal, Native Americans found a more sympathetic audience for their concerns and preferences than had been the case in the past, and consequently they were in a better position to affect the course of Indian affairs than any time since the "Indian Wars" of the 1860s. At center stage in this moment of reform was a new pan-Indian organization, the Society of American Indians.

The Society of American Indians

A new cadre of Indian leaders emerged with the dawn of the twentieth century, a collection of individuals who agreed with the fundamental premise that assimilation was necessary. In their view, however, that goal could be achieved only with the Indians' active participation and direction. Indian Progressives who championed

PROFILE

Jim Thorpe

James Francis Thorpe (Jim) was born on May 28, 1887, in a small house near Prague, Oklahoma. His mother, Mary James Thorpe, was the wife of an Irish farmer (Hiram Thorpe) and claimed a family lineage that traced to the Sac-Fox legend Black Hawk. She insisted her son carry an Indian name, Wa-Tho-Huk, meaning "Bright Path."

In 1904, Jim Thorpe enrolled at Carlisle Industrial Indian School hoping to learn a trade more profitable than farming, and while there he involved himself in the school's athletic program. Thorpe soon starred in two sports, football and track, and he excelled in each; however, when asked years later which sport he preferred, Thorpe said "Track and Field, because it was something I could do by myself, one-on-one, me against everybody else." His talent carried him to the 1912 Summer Olympics in Stockholm, Sweden, where he won gold medals in the pentathlon and decathlon. King Gustav V presented the medals to Thorpe, congratulating him as "the greatest athlete in the world." Thorpe

12.3 Jim Thorpe

Source: Courtesy of Library of Congress Prints and Photographs Division, LC-B2-2853-15

responded in simple fashion: "Thanks, King." Only a few months later, the Olympics Committee stripped Thorpe of both gold medals and removed his name from the games' records, stating that he was not an amateur athlete at the time of the 1912 Olympics, which the committee required. It had been learned that he had been a paid member of a semiprofessional baseball team for two seasons prior to the Olympic Games. The Olympics Committee posthumously restored the gold medals to Thorpe, but not until 1982.

Sport was Thorpe's life and livelihood. In 1914, he signed with the New York Baseball Giants and played three seasons before joining the Cincinnati Reds in 1917 and the Boston Braves in 1919. But it was professional football that garnered him national attention and acclaim. The Canton Bulldogs hired the star running back in 1915 at the unparalleled sum of $250 per game, and he remained with the team for five years, leading the Bulldogs to national championships in 1916, 1917, and 1919. When the National Football League formed in 1920, Thorpe was named league president. He continued to coach and play with several teams throughout the decade and ended his football career with the Chicago Cardinals in 1929. At midcentury, Jim Thorpe was honored as "America's Greatest Football Player of the Half-Century," and the Associated Press named him "Most Outstanding Athlete of the First Half of the 20th Century." In 1951, Thorpe was inducted into the College Football Hall of Fame, and in 1963 he became a "charter enshrinee" in the Professional Football Hall of Fame at Canton, Ohio.

Thorpe's retirement from football coincided with the beginning of the Great Depression. With jobs scarce in his adopted home of Los Angeles, he traveled, occasionally found work as a paid speaker at sports events, emceed dance marathons, worked some as a day laborer, and worked as an "extra" in several minor Hollywood films. When sports enthusiasts learned that he was too poor to afford a ticket to the opening ceremony of the 1932 Summer Olympiad in Los Angeles, they raised money for him to attend the summer games and gave him a standing ovation when he arrived at the opening ceremony. Chicago employed him for a brief period as City Parks Supervisor, and he served as a consultant with the evolving NFL.

Thorpe was always proud of his Indian identity. In 1922, he founded the Oorang Indians, a professional football team comprised solely of Native Americans. He also traveled widely in the 1920s and until his death advanced his opinion publicly that the Office of Indian Affairs (OIA) needed to be abolished. Thorpe believed the OIA had bungled repeatedly programs to acculturate Native Americans and, as a result, had trapped Indians in their positions as dependent wards of the federal government. He maintained that Native Americans would never be truly free or equal citizens of the United States as long as the OIA existed. A heart attack took Jim Thorpe's life on March 28, 1953. He left behind his third wife, Patricia Askew Thorpe, and eight children. The youngest of his children, Jack, became principal chief of the Sac-Fox in the 1980s.

this perspective were themselves accomplished products of the acculturation programs imprinted on Native Americans to date—Henry Roe Cloud (Winnebago), Carlos Montezuma (Yavapai Apache), Charles Eastman (Sioux), Laura Kellogg (Oneida), Arthur Parker (Seneca), and Sherman Coolidge (Arapaho). Most had been reared in the assimilation-oriented schools the Office of Indian Affairs governed and staffed or in Christian mission schools. Many held college degrees earned in Eastern Ivy League universities and were respected members in their professions.

Henry Roe Cloud, for example, received his bachelor's degree from Yale in 1910, became an ordained Presbyterian minister following his studies at Auburn Theological Seminary, and soon afterward received a master's degree in anthropology from Yale. Arthur Parker studied anthropology and worked with leading anthropologists and ethnologists such as Franz Boas, Frank Speck, and Frederick Putnam. Dr. Charles Eastman completed his undergraduate study at Dartmouth College and earned his medical degree from Boston University. Their accomplishments in the white world proved to these men that assimilation was both possible and rewarding. They were convinced that tribal structures were incompatible with the reality of modern America. Acculturation and assimilation were essential to Indians' survival. On Columbus Day, 1911, in an elegant Columbus, Ohio, hotel they gathered with 44 others and together founded the **Society of American Indians (SAI)**, a pan-Indian association whose mission was to define the future relationship of Native Americans with mainstream society and help direct government policy and programs to advance Indians' quality of life. Said cofounder Arthur Parker, this time "Columbus was discovered . . . by the Indians."

These founders believed that assimilation should not obliterate the pride one has in his or her cultural heritage and identity. Native American children must be educated, reared in the Christian religion, and prepared for a full life in mainstream society, and they must accept the white world as their own, but Indian boys and girls must also be trained in traditional craft work, learn traditional dances, and be connected to traditional values. Each youngster, generation after generation, must be told the old stories of his or her people. Each child must not forget that he or she is Indian. SAI founders saw an analogy between the Indians' position and that of new immigrants to the United States. As the Irish immigrant pressed his child to become American, he nonetheless encouraged within his offspring a fierce pride in and deep understanding of his Irish heritage. Assimilation was the future for Native Americans; however, Indians must appreciate and honor their own unique heritage and, to the best of their ability, emulate the most "distinguishing virtues" of Indian cultures. Indians were not a vanishing race, these leaders insisted, but instead simply another race whose identity was being added to the larger American culture.

The SAI also intended to work as a lobbying organization, involving itself aggressively in congressional policymaking, seeking to "interpret correctly the Indians' heart" before Congress, state legislative assemblies, and courts of law. Toward this end, the SAI established its national headquarters in Washington, D.C., to watch closely the OIA and to interact regularly with Congress. The SAI reported on its goals and work to Indians and reform-minded groups nationally through its quarterly journal, *American Indian Magazine*. The journal routinely stressed the importance of Indian patriotism for the United States, highlighted SAI-proposed reforms in Indian affairs, championed the organization's goal of assimilation and the necessary steps to achieve it, and consistently voiced its position that Native Americans must retain cultural pride and identity.

SAI lobbyists and contributors to *American Indian Magazine* often repeated calls for government action. Of immediate concern to SAI members was the urgent need for improved health care services in tribal communities, economic development on reservations, and the settlement of Indian claims to remuneration for lost lands. Making Indians healthy and giving them the knowledge to remain healthy were prerequisites for a successful transition into the non-reservation, white world. The same rationale was offered regarding economic development on tribal lands. This included making allotted Indian farmlands productive by providing Indians with the knowledge and the tools necessary for success in agricultural labor and farm management. Advocated, too, was the teaching of job skills currently needed in urban factories so Indians could secure off-reservation employment. SAI members encouraged Native Americans to own and operate small businesses, suggesting they take out low interest rate loans, which would allow Indians to become vested members of the free enterprise system. Through these efforts, the Indians' assimilation would become more assured. Settling tribal claims, they argued, would further hasten the dissolution of the tribes themselves and leave little reason for Indians not to relocate to urban communities. As much as the association called for government remedies, it also insisted on Indian self-reliance and personal initiative. The SAI was never intended to be an organization dedicated to "antagonizing or opposing the forces of government," said one member, but rather an association in which Indians themselves could discuss issues, share opinions, and collectively shape the Indians' evolving place in American society.

The mission of the SAI, then, resembled that of urban Progressives working to improve immigrant life in America—reformers who worked within the existing political, social, and economic system to facilitate the transition of immigrants into mainstream American society. Ultimately, the immigrant would become American and possess the abilities essential for life as an independent, productive, self-reliant individual. The SAI viewed itself as that advocate for Native Americans.

Gertrude Bonnin and Laura Cornelius Kellogg

Of the 219 members of the SAI in 1912, 66 were women and most of these were educators at Indian schools. Gertrude Bonnin, also known as Zitkala-Sa (Yankton Sioux), and Laura Cornelius Kellogg (Oneida) emerged quickly as outspoken, active members of the organization. Each echoed the SAI's principal tenet of acculturation, but each also called on Indians to maintain an Indian identity greater than the one the organization suggested. One historian's suggestion that Zitkala-Sa was "always on the threshold of two worlds but never fully enter[ed] either" was probably equally true of Kellogg.

Both agreed that education was fundamental to the Indians' successful transition into white society. Not all Indian communities, however, had access to the necessary academic and vocational services or programs. Zitkala-Sa recommended the founding of "**betterment stations**," comparable to the community centers known as settlement houses Progressives established for the urban poor. Located on smaller reservations without formal schools or in loosely connected communities of allotted Indians, betterment stations would be places where Native Americans could acquire a general education and learn "social standards" common to life in non-Indian society. One such betterment station opened for Ute women at Fort Duchesne, Utah, and trained students in English, health-related matters, and general domestic skills.

12.4 Zitkala-Sa, or Gertrude Simmons Bonnin (1876–1938), a Yankton Dakota Sioux writer, editor, musician, teacher, and political activist.

Source: Courtesy of Library of Congress Prints and Photographs Division, LC-USZ62-119349

Kellogg and Zitkala-Sa hoped that betterment stations would provide sound academic and vocational training for children, but they also wanted these facilities to encourage Indian youngsters to think critically, to realize learning and ultimate wisdom derives from multiple sources, to make connections between classroom study and the surrounding world, and to appreciate one's own cultural roots. Kellogg, herself having attended Barnard College, Columbia University, Cornell, and the University of Wisconsin, criticized the quality and relevance of most existing educational programs available to Indians. She asked, What is an educated person? One who has been given a diploma following the successful completion of a prescribed course of study, or one who develops a full understanding of the natural world surrounding him or her along with an understanding of one's place in that world? "There are old Indians who have never seen the inside of a classroom whom I consider far more educated than the young Indian with his knowledge of Latin and Algebra," said Kellogg. In traditional native cultures, "there was a great regard for natural law," and this respect framed the Indians' understanding of the surrounding world. Bureau schools were purposely designed to "take away the child's set of Indian notions altogether and to supplant them with the paleface's." Why should the student not admire his or her own native heroes? "Have they not as much claim to valor as Hercules or Achilles?" Indian children should certainly learn the noble qualities and traits of white society, according to Kellogg, but they should also learn about the same things that were most admirable in their own traditional cultures.

12.5 Students during mathematics class at the Carlisle Indian School.

Source: Courtesy of Library of Congress Prints and Photographs Division, LC-DIG-ppmsca-18642

Henry Roe Cloud and Arthur Parker agreed with Kellogg's basic argument and her conclusion that the educational system itself was the problem. Typical courses of study held little relevance to Indian experiences and offered equally little benefit to unassimilated Indians. Indians should preserve the wealth of knowledge found within their cultures for its practical application in later life but also as a means of providing Indian children with a sense of their own unique heritage as they integrated with the non-Indian world. Roe Cloud and Parker felt that this would prevent Indian children from becoming poor copies of white children. "The Indian must understand the ways of the white race and follow in general the paths of enlightenment, but all civilization does not lie in the ways of the white race," Parker contended. OIA schools and Christian-directed institutions wrongly pressed the destruction of "the Indian" within Native American children. "There is something better in life for the Indian than being like a white man. An imitation is at best a cheap thing," said Parker. Let Indian children attend public high schools with white students "to accustom themselves to the ways of the country" in advance of assimilation. Then, those Indians capable and desirous of post-secondary work should enroll in an all-Indian university, the American Indian University, where the student could develop his mind "along the line for which he was best fitted by nature" and recognize "the mission of his race" to add to the common national culture.

Zitkala-Sa, Kellogg, Parker, Roe Cloud, and other Native Americans offered perspectives that mirrored much of the educational philosophy of John Dewey, the Progressive Movement's guru of modern education. Dewey encouraged schools to develop a curriculum that emphasized clear relevance to one's culture and personal experiences, a hands-on learning or interactive educational process, and a practical course of study that prepared youngsters for life as independent adults. A successful educational experience, Dewey believed, produced a graduate broadly versed in academic subjects, capable of critical analysis and rational thought, and possessed of a realistic understanding of his or her heritage and position in contemporary society and of self-reliance as an adult.

TIMELINE 12.1 COURT AND LEGISLATIVE DIRECTION IN INDIAN AFFAIRS, 1898–1908

Date	Event
1898	The Curtis Act extends allotment to the Five Civilized Tribes of Oklahoma—the Cherokee, Chickasaw, Creek, Choctaw, and Seminole—which had earlier been exempt from the Dawes Act
1899	Congress allows railroad companies blanket approval for rights-of-way through Indian lands
1902	*Cherokee Nation* v. *Hitchcock*: The Court declared that the United States can invalidate or overrule laws established by the Cherokee Nation
1903	*Lone Wolf* v. *Hitchcock*: The Supreme Court rules unanimously that Congress has the authority to abrogate treaties made with Indian tribes, as Indians are "wards" of the United States, dependent on the government for their food and protection
1906	Antiquarian Act: Congress extended to the president the right to reserve public land as federal parks and preserves, particularly to protect historic sites and sources of artifacts, initially intended to focus on Chaco Canyon and the preservation of Native American relics
	Burke Act: Congressional amendment to the Dawes Act that stated that Indians defined as "competent" to manage their own affairs could receive title to their allotted lands without completing the original 25-year probationary period, making them able to lease their holding and obligated to pay taxes on that land
1908	*Winters* v. *United States*: A ruling in favor of Indians, the Court prohibited the building of dams or reservoirs that prevent water from reaching reservations, holding that water was essential in the cultivation of agriculture and ranching enterprises among Indians still on reservations

Zitkala-Sa and Kellogg parted with many of their fellow SAI members, however, when they also insisted that Indians have the right to retain their tribal existence, rights to their lands, and sovereignty over internal community affairs, a perspective that angered many other SAI members. In her presentation at the founding of the SAI, Kellogg extolled the virtues of Indian communities and called on the SAI to support the Indians' right of self-determination, their right to join with white society or to remain apart from it. She championed the notion of **"Indian collectives,"** or "industrial villages" for Native Americans. Indians must learn "white ways," she believed, but those who preferred living more closely with traditional values and with the familiar could do so by erecting village economies based on fish, cattle, arts and crafts, or other local resources and share equally the profits from that enterprise. In so doing, argued Kellogg and Zitkala-Sa, these communities could build bridges between Indians and the national economy while retaining a clear Indian identity. As historian Tom Holm put it, Kellogg envisioned an alternative to assimilation that melded "tribalism with productivity, communalism with capitalism."

Zitkala-Sa was more directly involved with the SAI than Kellogg, hoping to work from the inside to influence the organization's direction. In 1916, she took a seat as secretary for the SAI executive council and within two years added the roles of treasurer and editor of *American Indian Magazine* to her duties. In controlling these three positions, she was able to set the organization's tone and emphasize her perspective regarding Indian education and industrial village development. She contributed articles regularly to *American Indian Magazine*, calling for the protection of Indian water and land rights and, as historian Deborah Welch noted, the maintenance of reservations as "centers of Indian cultures where all Indians, even those like herself who lived in cities, could return to reinforce their identities as Indians." Many SAI members, however, strongly opposed Zitkala-Sa's and Laura Kellogg's views and those of their supporters. In fact, splits within the SAI over positions such as those Zitkala-Sa and Kellogg maintained would ultimately lead to the collapse of the organization. Moreover, the policies these two women advocated were in direct conflict with the course being pursued by the U.S. government at the time.

Religion and the SAI

Progressives often promoted the fundamental values of Christianity in their reform work, believing as many of them did that a good Christian would work to relieve the suffering of others. Baptist minister Walter Rauschenbusch spent several years helping New York City's poor immigrants and in 1907 published his book *Christianity and the Social Crisis*. In it he demanded Christians support social programs to eradicate poverty, homelessness, hunger, and the exploitation of workers. Christians' unqualified endorsement of social reform efforts and their direct involvement in programs to aid and uplift their fellow man would give life to the word of Jesus Christ; it was, he argued, more important to demonstrate than to articulate the message of Christ.

SAI leaders were, themselves, men and women who had adopted Christianity as their religious foundation, and they were not hesitant in promoting it because they believed it was essential for successful assimilation within white society. Dr. Charles Eastman abandoned his private medical practice early in the twentieth century and spent the remainder of his life as an activist in Indian affairs and as a promoter of Christianity. Eastman traveled to Indian reservations throughout the western states promoting the formation of Young Men's Christian Associations (YMCA) in which Indian boys would learn and experience the fundamental beliefs of Christianity and Christian fellowship, which was critical, he believed, to Indians' spiritual development and their assimilation with the white world. His journey allowed him the opportunity to observe Protestant missionary work among Indians and to speak with many tribal elders who adamantly opposed religious conversion. What he witnessed and learned soon compelled him to reassess his long-held assumptions regarding the practice of Christianity in the United States. He came to wonder "how it was that our simple lives were so imbued with the spirit of worship, while much church-going among white and nominally Christian Indians led often to such very small results." Eastman concluded that modern Christianity, as practiced, was "machine-made religion . . . supported by money." Rather than concentrating on the application of Christian values in daily life, modern Christians focused on demonstrations of righteousness through public participation in ceremonies and on the superficial conversion of large numbers of non-believers to Christianity.

One Indian elder with whom Eastman spoke voiced succinctly what Eastman himself was now coming to believe: the white man "says he is a believer in God [but] he does not seem to inherit any of the traits of this Father, nor does he follow the example set by his brother Christ." "I have come to the conclusion that this Jesus was an Indian," said another elder. "He was opposed to material acquirement and to great possession. He was inclined to peace . . . and set no price upon his labor of love . . . It is strange that he [the white man] could not rise to these simple principles which were commonly observed among our people." A Sac-Fox elder offered what Eastman described as the strongest rebuke to Christianity he ever received. "The white man . . . showed neither respect for nature nor reverence toward God," the elderly man noted, but instead "tried to buy God with the by-products of nature. He tried to buy his way into heaven, but he did not even know where heaven is. As for us, we shall still follow the old trail."

In his travels, Charles Eastman, like so many other Indian Progressives, responded that Christianity is "not at fault for the white man's sins," nor was Christianity false simply because so few whites engaged in genuine Christian behavior. America, he added, is not a Christian nation, but "Christians in it are trying to make it so." Eastman, like so many other Progressives, recognized the obvious failure of Americans of all races to live truly by the words of Jesus. Intense poverty abounded in a land of immense wealth, as did hunger, homelessness, and ignorance. Racism and warfare contradicted the faith's principal tenets of brotherhood, love, compassion, peace, and the equality of man in the eyes of God. Little wonder, thought Eastman and other Indian Progressives, that assimilation of native peoples would be retarded as long as white America failed to live by the religion it purportedly valued.

12.6 Dr. Charles A. Eastman (1858–1939) was a Native American physician, writer, national lecturer, and reformer. He founded 32 Native American chapters of the Young Men's Christian Association (YMCA) and helped found the Boy Scouts of America.

Source: Courtesy of Library of Congress Prints and Photographs Division, LC-USZ62-102275

Fractures Within the SAI

The SAI accomplished little of immediate practical value in its lobbying efforts in Washington. Government appropriations remained consistent with earlier years; consequently, the deplorable state of reservation health care services and programs persisted. The OIA also believed that the traditional system of Indian education had proved sufficient and supported no change in its academic programs. The academic failure of Indians was not the result of a poor, inadequate system but rather the failure of Indians themselves to take advantage of the existing educational opportunities. The Indian Office and Interior Department also continued policies that transferred tribal and allotted lands to non-Indian ownership. The SAI had no real influence over the federal government.

The concrete accomplishments of the SAI most often came in the form of initiatives at the local level, such as the founding of betterment houses in remote Indian communities or the revamping of the curriculum at existing Indian-run schools. Money secured for these initiatives largely came from Christian missionary and relief organizations, Progressives who raised money from like-minded contributors, and from SAI collections. The SAI also had some success in publicizing Native American success stories such as those of Zitkala-Sa and Carlos Montezuma, stories that seemingly proved to native peoples and mainstream America alike the ability of Indians to acculturate and to assimilate, provided the necessary opportunities were available to them.

Some SIA members became vocal critics of the federal agencies and bureaus charged with overseeing Indian affairs. Carlos Montezuma surfaced as the OIA's most virulent antagonist, claiming consistently the Indian Office retarded rather than advanced acculturation. As long as the OIA governed Indian affairs, freedom remained an illusion for Native Americans. At the 1915 SAI annual conference in Lawrence, Kansas, Montezuma blasted delegates for not demanding the abolition of the OIA, the government office most responsible for the odious state of Indian affairs past and present. "The slimy clutches of horrid greed and selfish interests are gripping the Indian's property . . . the Indian's land and everything else is fading into a dim and unknown realm," he argued. "Being caged up" on reservations "and not permitted to develop our facilities has made us a dependent race. We are looked upon as hopeless to save and hopeless to do anything for ourselves." American Indians would remain a "dependent race" as long as there is an Office of Indian Affairs. "We must free ourselves. Our peoples' heritage is freedom." Scrap the OIA and Indians would be able to advance themselves without that agency's constraints.

Montezuma's scathing assault was understandable. As a child he was taken from his Apache family by Pima Indians and sold to a traveling photographer for $30. Immersed in the white world, he quickly learned English and the ways of white society. Later deposited in the home of an Illinois Baptist minister, he became a devout Christian, made his way through the public schools of Urbana, graduated from the University of Illinois with a degree in chemistry, and in 1889 earned his medical degree from Chicago Medical College. An admirer of Colonel Henry Pratt and the program at Carlisle Indian School, he accepted a position as medical officer at the boarding school in 1890. Over the next few years, Montezuma provided medical care to the Indian children residing at Carlisle and offered himself as an example of successful assimilation with white society. With the turn of the century, Montezuma established his private practice in Chicago. In many respects, Montezuma was the epitome of the self-made man in America—the Horatio Alger archetype. Little wonder, then, that he had nothing but scorn for the OIA, an organization that he believed retarded Indian opportunities and only gave lip service to the goal of assimilation. His accomplishments resulted from his immersion in white society and from his lack of exposure to OIA programs, programs that prevented Native Americans from escaping the shackles of poverty and ignorance and that perpetuated greedy white land speculators' victimization of native peoples.

Montezuma agreed that the betterment houses and industrial villages might provide Indian children with the practical skills necessary for assimilation, but he felt that these, too, were largely absurd projects. First, each featured the concentration of Native Americans in segregated settings, places apart from the world into which Indians would assimilate. Segregation slowed acculturation and stymied the desire for assimilation. Second, these schools, in common with the broad SAI agenda, called for the retention of cultural pride and purposely taught children Indian arts, crafts, dances, and traditions. Such classes tended to reinforce Indian identity when acceptance of white culture was more practical and relevant. Taking his own life as proof, Montezuma believed that total immersion was most conducive to assimilation. The retention of Indian culture could only hinder the progress of Indian peoples.

Like Montezuma, Henry Roe Cloud built a solid academic foundation for himself. He was a product of the bureau's educational program and graduated from Yale College with both an undergraduate degree and a master's degree in anthropology. In contrast to Montezuma, however, Roe Cloud not only insisted the OIA remain intact but also worked for the bureau as Superintendent of Haskell Institute in Lawrence, Kansas, and in various capacities with OIA agencies in Oregon. He never denied or excused corruption in the Indian Office, and he never claimed the bureau was well managed or consistent in the application of federal policy. He did, however, insist that the OIA's minimal annual appropriation from Congress compromised the bureau's success. The education, training, and basic human services Indians required in preparation for assimilation demanded a level of financial support well beyond Congress' understanding. The SAI and similar organizations could collectively pressure Congress to appropriate more funds to the Indian Office, to purge the bureau of corruption and mismanagement, to secure positions inside it for Native Americans, and to utilize the OIA more effectively as a tool for aiding Native Americans.

There were also those individuals within the association who contended the SAI failed to represent the broader Native American perspective regarding current federal policy and the path toward assimilation. The SAI viewpoint was much too narrow, said Charles Eastman. It was principally the perspective of educated, acculturated Indians themselves on the verge of assimilation. Large numbers of Indians still did not speak English. Others possessed no formal education at all.

12.7 Henry Roe Cloud (1884–1950) was a distinguished educator, college administrator, U.S. Federal Government official, Presbyterian minister, and reformer.

Source: Courtesy of Library of Congress Prints and Photographs Division, LC-USZ62-133561

Many had never visited a trained physician. Remote Indian communities had none of the services or trappings of modern society. The majority of Native Americans held none of the job skills needed in the modern economy. There still existed tribal communities along America's borders that believed they were themselves free, independent nations outside the territorial boundaries of the United States. Native peoples' attitudes toward acculturation and assimilation varied significantly and, consequently, could not be summed up by the point of view the SAI articulated. Eastman called for the founding of an "Indian Congress" to which elected representatives from each tribe would be sent. Such an organization, he reasoned, would present the full scope of Indian issues, concerns, and perspectives and, in so doing, possibly result in greater Indian influence over federal policymaking and Indian life more generally.

The Peyote Issue

Peyote use also splintered the SAI membership, as it did individual tribal communities. Found principally among the Aztecs by Spanish conquistadors of the early sixteenth century, peyote surfaced among the Apache, Comanche, and Navajo of the American Southwest by the mid-nineteenth century and among the Cheyenne, Arapaho, and Pawnee and western bands of Cherokee, Creek, and Seminole Indians by the 1880s.

Those who drank a peyote-based "tea" or chewed the peyote bean experienced effects that ranged from hallucinations to pleasant relaxation. Regardless of its physical effect, peyote offered Indians a momentary escape from the troubling world that enveloped them. The reservation system, compulsory religious conversion, tribal dissolution, allotment, and the educational process white society crafted when taken altogether promised the utter destruction of Indian cultures and identity. Resistance by any means necessary was essential for cultural preservation, and native peoples certainly resisted fiercely and continuously; nonetheless, peyote provided a brief reprieve. For others, the bean enhanced one's sense of connection to an understanding of the spiritual world—its use brought "internal peace and harmony" and inclusion with the Creator. Many Indians hoped that by using peyote they would discover the Creator's guidance or other forms of resistance to the world the United States imposed on them. In this respect, peyote usage was not fundamentally different in purpose than the Ghost Dance. The pervasive understanding that peyote linked the user to traditional Indian spirituality placed the emerging peyote cult in direct opposition to Christian missionaries.

The "peyote cult," as the growing number of users were ultimately termed, encouraged not simply escapism or union with the spirit world but also a strict code of personal conduct that encouraged the traditional Indian values of personal integrity, responsibility, honor, purity of the body and spirit, service to the community, personal accomplishment, and abstinence from alcohol and other vices the white man introduced. Although these values resembled the fundamental virtues of non-Indian Christian society, they were promoted among Native Americans as uniquely Indian values *in practice* and, as such, represented a direct challenge to the acculturative and assimilation agenda of the federal government.

Missionaries complained that peyote distracted Indians from the word of the Christian God, and they denounced what they perceived to be the uninhibited, often sinful behavior of Indians under its influence. Reservation superintendents expressed concern that Indians using peyote might become violent, and they complained that Indians under its influence often became lethargic and unresponsive to the acculturative programs of the Indian Office. In response to such negative assessment, in 1898 Oklahoma Territory became the first territory or state to outlaw peyote use. Over the next 20 years, 13 more states prohibited the practice, many of these states adding it to the ban of alcohol on reservations. Although Congress itself never criminalized peyote, the OIA used federal agents to run an interdiction campaign to halt the flow of peyote from Mexico into the United States.

Anthropologist James Mooney saw no permanent harmful effects of peyote, recognized quickly its spiritual dimension, and concluded that laws should protect peyote use as a feature of native peoples' religions. Mooney's lobbying effort, bolstered by appeals directly from Comanche war chief Quanah Parker, resulted in Oklahoma reversing its peyote ban in 1908. Ten years later, Oklahoma provided additional protection by legally incorporating the **Native American Church**, which included peyote use as a basic religious practice. With success in Oklahoma, Native Americans pressed for the church's protected legal standing in other states and eventually a national charter. By the mid-1920s, the membership of the Native American Church had grown substantially, largely the result of its appealing blend of Christian tenets with traditional native spirituality. By 1930, roughly half of all American Indians were official members of the Native American Church.

The SAI had no choice but to confront the issue. To be sure, the association wanted Native Americans to retain cultural pride and traditional skills, but peyote use seemed to pull Indians in the direction of tradition at the expense of acculturation. One should certainly recall older days, honor elders, tell the old stories, and retain pride in one's heritage; it was something entirely different to use peyote as a means of escape or resistance to the Indians' current path and to seek its legal protection.

The overwhelming majority of SAI members determined that peyote use was counterproductive and contrary to the path Indians should take, describing its usage as unchristian and an impediment to acculturation. Montezuma frequently argued that the federal government must outlaw peyote and that every effort possible must be pursued to prevent its importation from Mexico or its cultivation anywhere within the United States. A minority within the SAI, however, defended the peyote cult and the Native American Church. The cult, they argued, promoted nothing less than the identical community and personal responsibilities all Americans are taught in public schools, in their churches, and in their homes. Honesty, integrity, hard work, and individual responsibility should be allowed to flower among Indians regardless of the setting in which those values were stressed. Moreover, they continued, the Native American Church was founded as much, if not more, on Christian beliefs as it was on traditional Indian spirituality. With so many American Indians as yet unconverted, would not their membership in the Native American Church, with its admitted blend of Indian spirituality and Christianity, be more conducive to their eventual conversion than no direct exposure to the faith at all? Supporters of peyote use, however, never gained much influence within the SAI. By 1918, the association formally announced its preference for a federal law banning peyote use, and the SAI openly denounced the inclusion of peyote use in religious ceremonies of the Native American Church.

Members of the SAI, and Indian Progressives generally, frequently found themselves in conflict with one another. This should cause little surprise. The larger, national Progressive Movement directed by middle-class whites was similarly divided. Basic questions about the target, scope, and nature of reform efforts divided Progressives of all backgrounds. Little wonder, then, that Indian Progressives did not speak with a single voice. Moreover, given their minimal financial resources, their equally minimal voice in government, and the fact that the Indian population was dispersed over a large continent, it would be unreasonable to expect their reform agenda to achieve substantial success. And Native Americans themselves, nationally, did not back the SAI goals. Cultural identity remained important to American Indians, and they were determined not to vanish into the faceless, impersonal alien white world. This ongoing conflict over identity and assimilation grew even more intense in 1917 when America entered "The Great War," World War I. The government's initiation of a military draft to meet the demands of war raised crucial questions about Indian citizenship and the obligations of Indian peoples to the government of the United States.

The Great War

War ravaged Europe for more than two years before the United States committed its troops, resources, and national energy to the conflict in April 1917. In fact, Woodrow Wilson campaigned for the presidency in 1916 on the promise of keeping America out of the war. In the end, however, neutrality proved impossible to maintain, a fact driven home by Germany's sinking of three American ships bound for Britain. American diplomatic and economic interests were just too closely tied to Britain and France for the United States to stay out of the conflict, and Wilson found himself compelled to seek a declaration of war against Germany. His impassioned call for war on April 2 before a joint session of Congress brought senators and representatives to their feet. In private, Wilson said to his personal secretary, "Think what it was they were applauding. My message today was a message of death for our young men."

On April 4, the Senate voted 82 to 6 in favor of war, and the House concurred with a vote of 373 to 50 the following day. Two days later, Wilson signed the resolution that brought the United States into the European conflagration. In May, Congress enacted the **Selective Service Act of 1917** to meet the manpower needs of America's armed forces, and on June 5, nearly ten million men complied with the nation's first call for draft registration. By war's end, local draft boards held the names of 24 million men.

The initial call for war in April also sparked a level of voluntary enlistment not seen since the Confederacy's firing on Fort Sumter 56 years earlier. Hundreds of thousands of American men, eager to join the fight, rushed to army and navy recruiting offices to enlist in the armed forces. The sense of patriotic duty compelled many to leave the security of their homes, dorm rooms, and jobs to join the army. Others were swept into military ranks by the moralistic, holy crusade rhetoric embodied in Wilson's assurance that this would be a war to end all war. So many more young men were motivated by a romanticized vision of the war—it would be an adventure, a means of securing personal glory. Still others joined for practical reasons—a steady wage and specialized job training that might be useful when the fighting ended. Few, however, held a realistic view of what awaited them.

The World War I Draft

Commissioner of Indian Affairs Cato Sells realized quickly that draft registration posed certain problems peculiar to Native Americans. So many Indian men eligible for military service dwelled in extremely remote locations that lacked regular mail delivery. Even when news of the war reached remote communities, few Indians paid serious attention to Washington's call for draft registration. Only two of the 152 adult male White River Apache complied with Selective Service requirements. Among the Navajos, not more than 12 entered the armed forces. The Office of Indian Affairs informed the **Selective Service System** that time, patience, understanding, and flexibility were required in order to inform Indians of the new law and their obligation for military service. This unique circumstance compelled Commissioner Sells to assume responsibility for Indian draft registration.

Sells quickly placed draft boards on the more accessible reservations to register Indian men and to explain the concept of conscription to those who never before confronted the prospect of compulsory military service. Most difficult to clarify was the law's requirement that all men in the identified age bracket register with Selective Service, not simply those who were legal U.S. citizens. All adult males within the age spread were to register with their draft boards, but only U.S. citizens were subject to compulsory military service. Indians and draft board members alike were puzzled.

Complicating the matter was the question of citizenship. Who among the Indians were legal citizens? Given the strange and often contradictory government position on Indian citizenship over previous decades, how could an individual's legal standing be accurately determined? Rather than expend valuable time wrestling with this issue personally or committing his staff to resolve the matter, Commissioner Sells believed it simpler, quicker, and more efficient to have local draft boards make the determination.

Throughout 1917 and much of the following year, draft boards followed Sells's basic advice: "if there is any doubt whatever in your mind" regarding a registrant's citizenship status, "resolve it in favor of non-citizenship." Sells expected Native American resistance to the military draft, and he figured this directive would substantially reduce Indian opposition. In June 1918, the commissioner provided more explicit guidelines. The Indian born inside the territorial boundary of the United States but who lived "apart from his people," children of parents who were citizens, and those Indian men holding land allotments under provisions of the Dawes Act or Burke Act were all legal citizens of the United States and subject to compulsory military service. Non-citizens were to be listed "resident alien." Said one Sioux, "I am not a citizen. I am not an alien. I am an Indian. I have neither the rights of an alien nor a citizen, yet I was born in the United States. My father is a full blood Sioux Chieftain . . . I must offer myself up for service." Like so many other Native Americans, the young Sioux felt caught between two worlds.

Carlos Montezuma of the Society of American Indians contended that a nation that did not grant citizenship to Indians should not expect Indians to defend it. Through his own newsletter, *Wassaja*, Montezuma said that he was "not against the war nor against Indians going into the army if they wish . . . But is it just to force them to be soldiers?" How could the OIA specifically and the federal government in general declare Indians "competent to be soldiers but . . . not competent to be citizens," he wondered. Moreover, he argued, the United States historically took native lands, violated its own treaties with Indians, prosecuted wars against them, and treated Native Americans as inferiors. Although he respected each individual Indian's right to decide for himself to enter the military voluntarily, Montezuma insisted that Native Americans should not be forced to defend the United States. America's war was being waged to promote and defend democracy and self-determination;

Indians in the United States enjoyed neither of these. "We Indians are ready to defend the country of our forefathers as we have been doing these five hundred years," but America's "wards" should not be compelled to "protect their Protectors." Not until American Indians are granted full United States citizenship "can this country proudly draft them." The "drafting of the Indians into the army is another wrong perpetrated upon the Indian without first bestowing his just title—The First American Citizen." Montezuma was not in opposition to America's entry into the Great War or against Indian service to the United States; rather, his argument in 1917 mirrored those he posited as an SAI member against the OIA.

On the Goshute (Gosiute) reservation, eligible men adamantly refused to register with the Selective Service System. Virtually ignored by the Indian Office for decades and largely disconnected from the non-Indian world surrounding them, Goshutes were convinced they were not citizens of the United States and, consequently, were not obligated to the Selective Service System. OIA officials traveled to the Indian reservation on several occasions, each visit an effort to convince Goshutes to comply with draft registration. Unable to secure Indian compliance despite numerous meetings with tribal leaders, on February 19, 1918, the federal government dispatched a detachment of soldiers from nearby Fort Douglas to the Indian community. Once there, the soldiers arrested and charged four men presumed to be the resistance "ring leaders." Three weeks in jail convinced the Indians to comply with the Selective Service System and to instruct all eligible young men in their community to do the same.

READING HISTORY

Native American Citizenship and Compulsory Military Service

America's entry into World War I forced the federal government to address the application of the military draft on native peoples. Central to the issue was the question of U.S. citizenship for Native Americans because only U.S. citizens can be drafted into service. Were American Indians legal citizens? Although the matter initially appeared quite simple to resolve, the question of Native American citizenship ultimately proved confusing at best and spawned a series of additional concerns that continued to plague the Indian Bureau into World War II.

Letter to Jack C. Wachecha (Eastern Band of Cherokee) from Cato Sells, Commissioner of Indian Affairs, January 22, 1918

My Friends,

I have your letter of December 29 wherein you ask whether the Cherokee Indians are subject to the draft.

The law in this case subjects all Indians who are citizens of the United States to the draft, and those who are noncitizens are entitled to exemption. The question of whether you are citizens or noncitizens is one for the local boards to determine in the light of all the facts and circumstances presented by you.

If you will call upon your Superintendent he will assist you in every way possible consistent with the facts.

Your friend,

[Signed] Cato Sells

Commissioner.

Letter to the Adjutant General, United States Army from R.L. Phillips, January 30, 1918

Dear Sir:

Sometime ago I took up with you the question of sending Cherokee who cannot speak English to camps. We have registered in Graham some twenty or twenty-five Cherokee Indians who do not speak English and we would have to send an interpreter with them to get them to camps even, and I am at loss to know what to do with these people. If we could get them off our roll without being charged with them I had rather for them to be released than to have to go under the circumstances. In fact the Eastern Band of Cherokee Indians have been considered as wards of the government and not as citizens for years, as they have no right to vote, do not sit on juries, or have other privileges given to citizens.

Yours truly,

[Signed] R. L. Phillips

P.S. I am enclosing your letter from Commissioner of Indian Affairs of Washington which fails to give me much information other than if these Indians are not citizens they are not subject to draft according to his opinion.

Letter to the Provost Marshal General, War Department from E.B. Meritt, Assistant Commissioner of Indian Affairs, February 26, 1918

My dear General Crowder:

I have your letter of February 5 transmitting correspondence involving the status of the Cherokee Indians of North Carolina insofar as the draft is concerned.

The question of the status of these Indians was involved in the case of the United States vs. Boyd (83 Fed. 547–553) and passed upon by the court. For your information, I quote that portion of the decision of the Circuit Court of Appeals dealing with this matter:

"We fully agree with the statements in the complainant's bill that the Eastern Band of Cherokee Indians are wards of the nation, and that they have been treated as such since the year 1848 by the Executive and Legislative departments of the Government; and in this connection we may remark that said Indians themselves have recognized such relationship from said date down to the time during which the negotiations for the sale of the timber now in controversy were being carried on. Therefore we hold that the court below had jurisdiction of this suit and that it was not only proper but that it was the duty of the United States to take such steps and to institute such proceedings as would fully protect the interests of said band of Indians. We are unable to agree with the claim of the appellees that by virtue of the treaty of New Echota this band of Cherokees became citizens of the State of North Carolina and of the United States. By the twelfth article of that treaty it was provided in substance that those individuals and families of the Cherokee Nation that were adverse to a removal to the Cherokee country west of the Mississippi and were desirous of becoming citizens of the States where they resided and such as were qualified to take care of themselves and of their property and to become useful citizens were to be permitted to remain within said States (North Carolina, Tennessee and Alabama) and were to be entitled to receive their due portion of all the personal benefits accruing in said treaty for their claims, improvements and per capita, and to a prescriptive right to certain lands. This certainly did not confer citizenship on any portion of the Cherokee Indians, and we are unable to find any statute or any treaty that makes them citizens of the United States or that authorizes them to become citizens by naturalization. The action or assent of the United States is absolutely essential in order to enable the Indian tribes or bands or individual members of the same to renounce that dependent condition caused by the state of pupilage in which the Indians have been since the adoption of the Federal Constitution. If the treaty of New Echota can be held to authorize the members of the Eastern Band of Cherokees to apply to the courts for naturalization on showing specific proof of fitness for civilized life on their part, still it could not avail as far as this case is concerned; for there was no pretense that any of them have ever made such application or have been declared citizens of the United States by any court of the same or of the State of North Carolina. On this subject Judge Deady in the case of United States vs. Osborne (6 Sawyer, 409–3 Fed. 58–61) has well said:

> 'But an Indian cannot make himself a citizen of the United States without the consent and cooperation of the Government. The fact that he has abandoned his nomadic life or tribal relations and adopted the habits and manners of civilized people may be a good reason why he should be made a citizen of the United States, but does not itself make him one. To be a citizen of the United States is a political privilege which no one not born to can assume without its consent in some form.'"

Attention is also invited to the decision of the Supreme Court of the United States in the Cherokee Trust Fund case (117 U. S. 288–303) wherein that Court said:

> Immediately after the ratification of the treaty of 1835 measures were taken by the Government to secure its execution, and Commissioners were appointed to adjust claims for improvements and to facilitate the emigration of the Indians, but emigration proceeded slowly. Great Reluctance to go was manifested by large numbers and at last it became necessary to make a display of force to compel their removal. Major General Scott was sent to the country with troops and instructed to remove all the Indians except such as were entitled to remain and become citizens under the twelfth article of the treaty.

The number that remained was between eleven and twelve hundred. They ceased to be a part of the Cherokee Nation, and henceforth they became citizens of and were subject to the laws of the State in which they resided. The name of Eastern Cherokees accompanied those who emigrated to distinguish them from those who had preceded them and who were called "Old Settlers."

As heretofore advised, the question of citizenship is an individual one dependent upon the facts and circumstances in each case, and therefore I am unable to give you anything more definite on the subject.

The papers submitted with your inquiry are returned as requested.

Very truly yours,

[Signed] E. B. Meritt

Assistant Commissioner.

Questions

1. According to Commissioner of Indian Affairs Cato Sells, what is the legal status of Native Americans in relation to the military draft? Who determines Indian citizenship?

2. What problem did the chairman of Selective Service in Graham County, North Carolina, confront? What was his recommendation and why?

3. What ruling regarding Cherokee citizenship does Assistant Commissioner of Indian Affairs E.B. Meritt offer?

4. Given these letters, how might one accurately summarize the government and Native American understanding of U.S. citizenship in 1918 and the application of Selective Service to Native Americans?

In addition to the matter of Indian citizenship, the draft also raised the issue of treaty obligations. The Iroquois Confederacy, or Six Nations, insisted the Selective Service Act held no authority over its members. The Treaty of Canandaigua (1794), which the U.S. Senate approved and President George Washington signed, granted the confederacy "nation within a nation" status. Neither federal law nor state law applied to the Confederacy. The Six Nations comprised a separate, sovereign nation within the territorial boundaries of the United States and, consequently, compulsory military service under Congress' Selective Service Act was unenforceable among the Iroquois people. Commissioner Sells chose not to challenge the Iroquois' insistence on sovereign nationhood. The army's manpower needs were largely met nationally through voluntary enlistment and through the military draft. To challenge in court the Six Nations' legal status appeared unnecessary and potentially troublesome for the Indian Office. Moreover, many confederacy members willingly enlisted in the army and navy, and many others submitted themselves freely to draft registration and induction orders without objection. Nonetheless, the Iroquois Confederacy publicly asserted its sovereignty by issuing its own separate declaration of war against Germany in spring 1918.

Sells and federal authorities proved consistent in their response to Indian draft resistance based on treaty provisions. Pamunkey and Mattaponi Indians of tidewater Virginia argued that the Selective Service Act violated their longstanding treaty that forbade them to take up arms. Whether or not America's role in the Great War was justified, compulsory military service contradicted the Pamunkeys' and Mattaponis' special relationship with the federal government—a relationship that, to date, remained valid. Like Iroquois men, voluntary enlistment remained the prerogative of the individual, but conscription violated treaty provisions. Creek Indians presented Sells with a similar argument. Sammie Bear (Creek) of Mason, Oklahoma, insisted that earlier treaties with the federal government lawfully exempted his tribe from taking up weapons either against or in defense of the United States. Should "Higher Powers or Unseen Powers" tell him to comply with draft registration and military service, he would do so. A gathering of Creeks near Henryetta, Oklahoma, also challenged the government's authority to register and draft members of the Creek Nation. In none of these instances did federal authorities seriously consider prosecution of Indian resistors.

Commissioner Sells purposely avoided conflict. He refused to challenge treaty provisions that prevented Indian military service to the United States, ruled independently to the Indians' benefit on the question of citizenship, and placed draft boards only on reasonably accessible reservations. To be sure, Sells firmly believed military service would provide Indians with greater experience among whites and, in so doing, push them more quickly and more successfully toward assimilation with mainstream society; nonetheless, America was presently at war. Why prosecute resisting Native Americans when doing so would distract national attention from the war effort, possibly pique national interest in OIA policies, and certainly stimulate a debate with Indians that otherwise could be avoided?

Indians Enter Military Service

Government records indicate 17,303 Indians registered with Selective Service by war's end; however, the number of Indians who actually served in America's armed forces during the Great War remains uncertain. Commissioner Sells in late 1918 claimed 8,000 Indians served during the war years, but a year later he raised that figure to 10,000. More accepted among scholars today is a military service rate of 12,000 to 12,500, roughly 20 percent of the adult male Indian population at that time. The clouded picture is the product of local draft board registration documents, some of which listed Indians as "white" while others correctly identified Native American registrants as "Indian." The erroneous racial classification was largely the product of the War Department's determination, with congressional approval, to induct Native Americans into all-white military units rather than segregate them from white troops, as was the rule for African American recruits. It was a decision based on the assumption that service with whites would hurry Indian acculturation and ultimately their assimilation, a position the SAI overall favored.

Fully 50 percent of Indians who donned America's military uniform freely and voluntarily enlisted. Reasons for enlistment varied considerably. First, the Office of Indian Affairs had a vested interest in widespread Indian support for the war effort and for service in the armed forces. Years of "civilizing instruction" in boarding schools, Christian missionary work on reservations, and the government's push for private property ownership over tribal ownership of land combined to push the "Americanization" of Indians. The Indians' compliance with draft registration and especially their voluntary enlistment in the armed forces would suggest OIA success in this project. The OIA's campaign on reservations to explain the Selective Service System included a committed effort to convince Native Americans that wartime service would provide Indian veterans with easy entry into off-reservation opportunities. Native American organizations echoed the OIA's call for Indian military service. The SAI encouraged Indian participation, contending that wartime service would garner the respect of white society and hasten final assimilation, a view the Indian Rights Association and the National Indian Association shared.

Military service also provided an escape from the poverty and misery that was common on most reservations. In 1916, the annual income for Indian men nationally averaged a paltry $92, a figure roughly one-eighth that of employed white males. Disease was widespread in most tribal communities, particularly tuberculosis and trachoma. Infant mortality rates hovered near 30 percent for all children under three years of age, and the twin evils of alcoholism and suicide loomed large over Indian families. A private in the U.S. Army received $432 yearly and seamen in the U.S. Navy made even more. Clearly, a 400 percent jump in income attracted many young Indians, money that could be sent home to aid desperate families or simply be saved for postwar schooling, opening a small business, or purchasing needed farm equipment.

The armed forces also provided young men with professional medical and dental care for the first time in their lives. The military further promised to train them in skills potentially transferable to the civilian job market following military service and expose them directly to the non-Indian world within the United States and abroad. Moreover, life in the army or navy carried with it the certainty of travel to distant lands, the opportunity to interact with persons from different cultures, and most assuredly the promise of what many young men (white and Indian alike) termed "adventure."

The warrior tradition was also a powerful motive for Indian enlistment. Historically, most Indian cultures honored the warriors who defended their land, communities, and families from external threats. It was the supreme form of service a man could render to his tribe, and those who demonstrated unparalleled courage, self-sacrifice, and leadership netted glory for themselves, respect from their communities, and influence, if not power, within the tribe itself. Federal policies and treaties, however, purposely corrupted traditional Indian community structures and crippled the role of the warrior and warrior societies within tribes. Service in the

U.S. Army during the Great War, then, offered young Indian men the opportunity to follow in the footsteps of their ancestors and capture glory in battle. But the war also brought into focus for some Indian soldiers their larger connection to the United States. "I [made] up my mind . . . that I am American and I went overseas to fight for this country," said Robert Spott (Yurok, northern California).

Nearly 1,000 Indians served in the U.S. Navy, most of whom were assigned to unskilled support roles on escort ships and transport vessels. In the army, some Indian soldiers were assigned duty as truck drivers, mechanics, and clerical staff personnel, but the overwhelming majority were trained in combat arms and placed in infantry units. To be sure, the warrior tradition encouraged Native Americans to seek assignment as infantrymen. But, given their limited academic preparation, Indian servicemen found it virtually impossible to score high enough on standardized military entry examinations to qualify for skilled positions in the armed forces; consequently, they were assigned positions as riflemen rather than more specialized roles.

Entry into the army also brought forth the issue of the racial status of Indians. Were Indians to serve in white military units, be separated into all-Indian divisions, or be assigned to African American regiments? In earlier years, Canada established all-Indian battalions and companies, and it had been commonplace among the British to form military units comprised solely of the colonial subjects of a particular region or colony. Manpower demands during the Great War, however, forced both Canada and England to abandon segregation. In the United States, few officers in the armed forces and equally few political leaders saw merit in the segregation of Indians. Cato Sells, Secretary of the Interior Franklin K. Lane, and Secretary of War Newton D. Baker all refused to consider such an arrangement. First, there already existed an organizational and command structure that separated whites and African Americans; a third system, they all believed, would further complicate the armed forces' mission. Second, Native Americans had never before been separated from whites in the armed forces. Even the Indian Scout units of the mid- to late nineteenth century operated as integral parts of white combat units. Third, and more importantly, the objective of the OIA was to acculturate and then assimilate Indians into white mainstream society. Inclusion, not segregation, would move Indian servicemen toward that goal. The Society of American Indians concurred. Segregated military units would be "an affront to Indian dignity" and retard the progress of eventual assimilation. Segregation would not govern Native Americans in military uniform.

Over There

Indian servicemen arrived in France with the first contingents of the American Expeditionary Force (AEF) in late June 1917. Individual regiments, battalions, and companies of the AEF were attached to British and French armies that autumn as replacement units to bolster allied defenses in key sectors along the front. The U.S. Army did not enter the fight as a distinct, separate force until summer 1918 with campaigns at the Marne in August and at St. Mihiel in September, the latter a most vicious campaign that resulted in 7,000 American casualties, 15,000 Germans taken as prisoners, and the capture of 450 heavy guns from the enemy. From late September through October, the AEF was engaged in the bloody campaign in the Meuse-Argonne sector, northeast of Paris. In the Meuse-Argonne alone, the American death toll reached 26,277 men; tens of thousands more were wounded.

Indian servicemen distinguished themselves in battle and generally earned the respect of their white comrades. Corporal John Adams, a Siletz Indian from Oregon, served with the 42nd "Rainbow" Division and suffered multiple wounds in fighting around Chateau-Thierry in summer 1918. Proud of his Indian identity, Adams spent only a few nights in the army hospital: "I felt that no American could be or should be better than the first American," he said after the war. "I did not linger in the hospital." He quickly returned to duty although his wounds were not fully healed. Sergeant Thomas E. Rogers (Arikara) and Joe Young Hawk (Sioux) both served with the 18th Infantry Regiment. "At night, barehanded and alone," Rogers slipped along the German defensive line near Soissons and personally captured "many [German] sentinels who were taken back to the American camp for questioning," read the commendation the army awarded him. Enemy soldiers later captured Young Hawk in the same sector of operations. Determined to escape, he "turned on his captors, slew three with his hands," and captured the remaining two Germans, despite gunshot wounds to each of his own legs. Enduring excruciating pain, Young

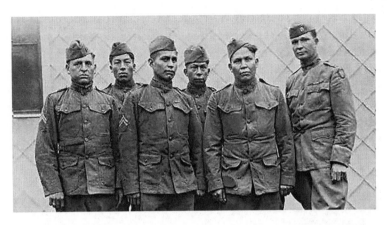

12.8 Members of the Choctaw tribe who served as code talkers during World War I.

Source: Mathers Museum of World Cultures

Hawk guided his prisoners back to the American lines. Private Arthur L. West (Winnebago) was attached to the 59th Infantry Regiment. For a week in August 1918, he scouted enemy positions along a stretch of the Vesle River, often referred to as "Death Valley," and killed German snipers lying in wait for American patrols. Private Ross, a Cherokee from Oklahoma, led a team of three men across the Vesle River, where he located a German machine gun nest and killed its two-man crew in advance of the American crossing.

Indians garnered the praise of their fellow soldiers and the men who commanded them in battle. Noted Major Tom Reilley, a battalion commander with the 165th Infantry Regiment, "when an Indian went down, another Indian stepped immediately to the front. They were always at the front [and] if a battle was on and you wanted to find the Indians, you would always find them at the front." Captain Wendell Westover, who commanded a machine gun battalion in the army's 2nd Infantry Division, recalled years after the war that the Indians in his battalion "could be counted upon to do the thing required under any circumstances, only death bringing a cessation to their performance of duty. No finer group of Americans served on the Western Front." Perhaps no single example of American Indian service captured the fortitude, the commitment, and the selflessness of Native Americans in World War I than the one Sergeant John Northrup (Chippewa) witnessed. Northrup lost a leg in the Battle of the Ourcq in summer 1918. While lying on a stretcher awaiting transport to a field hospital, he noticed another Indian soldier "crawling in on his hands and knees under heavy German machine-gun fire. On the Indian's back was a badly wounded soldier." What was beyond Northrup's comprehension was the fact that the rescuer's own two feet had been shot off.

The courage and skill of Indian soldiers during World War I caught the attention of the upper echelons of military command. Indians, said General Hugh Scott, "played a higher part in the war on the side of patriotism than the ordinary white man." They demonstrated an unparalleled "zeal for the great cause," noted General Enoch Crowder. Said France's Marshall Ferdinand Foch, "I cannot forget the brilliant services which the valorous Indian soldiers of the American armies have rendered to the common cause and the energy as well as the courage which they have shown to bring about victory—decisive victory—by attack."

On November 11, 1921, the President of the United States invited none other than Plenty Coups, the aging Crow warrior, to represent all Native Americans at a ceremony establishing the Tomb of the Unknown Soldier at Arlington National Cemetery. With 100,000 guests in attendance, Plenty Coups, dressed in full ceremonial regalia, placed his coup stick and his headdress on the coffin of the unidentified American soldier recently returned from France. In his native language, Plenty Coups expressed his gratitude to all American servicemen who fought in the recent war. He was particularly honored to represent Native Americans at "the grave of this noble warrior." "I hope the Great Spirit will grant that these noble warriors have not given up their lives in vain and that there will be peace to all men hereafter," he said. Over the next ten years, the U.S. government issued American flags and certificates of appreciation signed by the President to tribes in honor of Indian service in the Great War.

The Indians' distinguished combat record was partly the product of circumstance—finding themselves in life-or-death situations that required nothing less than a near mindless fight for the survival of themselves and their fellow soldiers. The same conditions made war heroes of whites and African Americans. Also contributing to the Indians' combat record was the warrior spirit that compelled many to perform in a manner that honored themselves, their families, and tribal traditions. To be sure, many Native American soldiers actively courted

PROFILE

Private Joseph Oklahombi (Choctaw)

No individual Native American soldier in World War I gained the fame of Private Joseph Oklahombi, a Choctaw from Wright City, Oklahoma. Oklahombi served with Company D, 141st Infantry Regiment, 36th Infantry Division, and late in the war became a "code talker." In October 1918, he and several other American soldiers found themselves separated from the rest of their company and surrounded by Germans.

Despite heavy German mortar and machine gun fire, Oklahombi "dashed to the attack of an enemy position, covering about 200 yards through barbed wire entanglements." According to the army's after-action report, he led the soldiers to a line of 50 German mortars and machine guns, captured several of the weapons, turned those against counterattacking Germans, and held the position for the next four days in spite of German artillery and poison gas fire. Over those four days, Oklahombi singly crossed "no man's land" several times to secure medical kits and additional ammunition for himself and his wounded comrades.

The American press soon learned of Oklahombi's exploits, and eager reporters were quick to write that the private's name meant "man-killer" in the Choctaw language. Unofficial records indicate Private Oklahombi killed 79 German soldiers and took another 171 as prisoners of war, a record of achievement greater than that credited to America's most remembered hero of World War I, Sergeant Alvin York. General John Pershing personally awarded Oklahombi with the Silver Star, and France's Marshall Petain bestowed the Croix de Guerre on him. Following the war, Oklahombi returned to his wife and son in Oklahoma and resumed his life as a farmer. In 1940, he was asked to give his opinion regarding America's preparation for another war with Germany. "The United States must prepare itself and really prepare immediately. Of course," he added, "I'm not in favor of war, but if the peace of the United States is molested, we must be prepared to defend ourselves." Joseph Oklahombi lost his life in an automobile accident on April 13, 1960.

12.9 Joseph Oklahombi
Source: Oklahoma Historical Society

Table 12.1 Choctaw Code Talkers of World War I 36th Infantry Division, United States Army

Billy, Albert	Edwards, James	Nelson, Jeff
Bobb, Mitchell	Frazier, Tobias	Oklahombi, Joseph
Brown, Victor	Hampton, Benjamin	Taylor, Robert
Carterby, Ben	Louis, Solomon Bond	Wilson, Calvin
Colbert, Benjamin	Maytubby, Pete	Veach, Walter

danger and voluntarily risked their own lives in battle. Ten American Indians received France's Croix de Guerre for heroism in battle, and 150 earned other medals for valor during the war. Regardless of the source of their courage under fire, Indian valor in combat proved common throughout the ranks.

One particular development late in the war did turn explicitly on the unique contributions of Indians. In October 1918, during combat operations in the Argonne Forest, officers of the 142nd Infantry Regiment realized that Germans had tapped into American battlefield telephone lines and were eavesdropping on the Allies' frontline communications. Aware that many of the Choctaw Indians in the regiment still spoke their native languages, several junior officers approached regimental commander Colonel A.W. Bloor and suggested that Native American soldiers man the telephones and transmit battlefield messages in their native tongue. Bloor agreed. The Choctaws were placed in forward observation positions along the length of enemy lines. During the first week of October, they tracked German troop movements and directed American artillery fire against enemy defenses. German losses were horrendous. Colonel Bloor recalled sometime later, "it was hardly possible that Fritz [German troops] would be able to translate these dialects." The plan worked so well that the 142nd Infantry Regiment assigned several more Indians to communications work.

Locating enough American Indians still able to speak their tribal language was not difficult; developing a standard vocabulary for Indian "**code talkers**" proved more troublesome. As there were no words in Choctaw for modern military terms and weapons, the Indians prepared a list of descriptive phrases or terms loosely corresponding to what they collectively understood. "Little gun shoot fast" referred to a machine gun, "scalps" referenced casualties, "bad air" identified poison gas, "stone" stood for hand grenade, "many scouts" represented patrol, "three grains of corn" identified Third Battalion, and "tribe" referred to regiment. Commanders of other army divisions and regiments heard of the Choctaw experiment and decided to employ their own Indian servicemen as radio operators, among them Osage, Cheyenne, Comanche, and Sioux. The war's end in mid-November, however, abruptly halted further development of the system.

Stereotypes and Indian Military Service

Thomas Rogers, Joe Young Hawk, Arthur West, and Private Ross all were "scouts" within their respective military units, a job assigned to so many American Indians in the army and one that few survived. More often than not, white officers ordered scout duty for their Indian soldiers; these officers were reared on the stereotyped images of Indian warriors and tracking abilities popularized in dime novels and Wild West shows, grossly inflated by the recollections of their grandfathers. White officers widely assumed that nature had given Indians an innate, natural ability to fight. The Indians commanded "the cunning and agility of the fox" and quickly recognized imminent danger in the bend of a branch or the turn of a leaf. They were endowed by nature with unusually keen eyesight, alertness, and sense of smell. Their patience proved remarkable, or so the stereotype went. Indian soldiers could "lie in a shell crater all day" just to take a single shot at a German. The Native American possessed the natural ability of stealth regardless of terrain and was particularly adept with the rifle and knife. The Indian soldier was instinctive and "eager to fight," his skills derived from his close personal connection with the natural world and his peoples' "ancient training" in warrior skills that continued to the present day. Noted Captain John Simpson of the 358th Infantry Regiment, Indian soldiers were "not afraid of hell itself . . . If we had had more Indians, we would have killed more Germans." It was frequently said that the Indian soldier was the Germans' "menace."

Germans were very much aware of the Indians' service in the U.S. Army and, like their white American counterparts, they held stereotyped images and grossly inaccurate ideas about Native Americans. Wild West shows had journeyed to Europe since the early 1880s, and Native Americans had performed throughout Europe for nearly 40 years before the Great War erupted. In Germany, they found their most enthusiastic audiences. Germans felt an almost kinship connection with American Indians. Germans believed they saw a reflection of their own military training and societal structures in the Indians' martial reputation and warrior societies. Moreover, the novels of German author Karl May, set in America's frontier during the late nineteenth century, highlighted the nobility of American Indians, their inherent warrior skills, and their natural ability to adopt German traits. "The Indian is closer to the German than to any other European," wrote Hans Reider, adding the Indian "is model and brother for us." During the Great War, then, numerous German soldiers, reared on the literature of Karl May and witness to Wild West shows, took special note of reports that Native Americans were in American units opposing them and often "showed considerable anxiety when learning of the high numbers and disposition of American Indians among AEF units." Wrote one historian, "Germans were so fearful over the prospect of fighting American Indians that German newspapers tried to hide the fact that Native Americans were on the Western Front." Given the Americans' own perception of Indian warrior traits and the Germans' dread in confronting Native American soldiers, it is little wonder Indians were given some of the more dangerous duties along the Western Front.

The Home Front

War requires substantial sacrifice and contribution from those who remain on the home front. Enthusiastic and sustained support from the civilian population is a critical component of modern war. From coast to coast, Americans united behind the common goal of defeating Germany regardless of cost. Liberty Bonds and Liberty Stamps, investment notes used to raise money to help finance America's war effort, were sold to people in most households nationwide. Thousands of Americans cultivated Liberty Gardens in their backyards or in vacant lots as a way of producing vegetables to supplement wartime food-rationing programs. Thousands more enrolled in the American Red Cross as nurses, fundraisers, or clerical workers. Even more volunteered their time to manufacture surgical dressings for wounded soldiers, to produce cold weather garments for servicemen, or to entertain the troops. In all of these endeavors, American Indians, like non-Indians, gave of themselves to support the war effort.

With America's entry into the European war in April 1917, Secretary of the Treasury William McAdoo commenced a program to sell savings bonds to private citizens, bonds that carried a 4 percent interest rate. Americans recognized bonds as one means for building a family nest egg, but they realized, too, that their contribution was intended immediately to finance the production of goods and weapons the nation's armed forces needed. In patriotic fashion, mingled with a twinge of self-interest, Americans invested heavily in the Liberty Bond campaigns. American Indians purchased nearly $5 million worth of bonds in the program's first sales campaign, and by war's end, Indians had bought more than $25 million in Liberty Bonds—a per capita rate of roughly $75. Impressive this figure certainly was, but perhaps even more telling of Indian support, Native Americans were, as a population, the poorest of Americans. Of the total money Native Americans spent on

Liberty Bonds, approximately $10 million came from individual and tribal purchases; purchases made before Congress in May 1918 granted the Department of the Interior the prerogative to divert a portion of tribal appropriations to Liberty Bond purchases. Commissioner Sells believed the infusion of Indian funds would certainly aid the overall war effort, and he believed bond purchases would establish among Indians the habit of saving money, a tool conducive to assimilation.

To further aid the war effort, approximately 10,000 Native American men and women volunteered their time and energy to the American Red Cross (ARC). Raising operating funds for the ARC was essential and toward that end Indians participated in auctions, performed music or dances for cash donations, or directly solicited contributions from individuals scattered across their reservations. More than $1,400 was raised in a single hour at an auction on the Pine Ridge Sioux Reservation. Even more amazing, and certainly inspiring, Pe-retta, a 75-year-old Ute woman, donated $500 to the Red Cross, leaving herself with a mere $13 in her savings account. Indians skilled in sewing and knitting manufactured scarves, mittens, sweaters, and socks for distribution to servicemen and refugees. Thousands of Indian women produced surgical dressings in Red Cross clinics, and children assembled "comfort kits" for distribution to soldiers, each kit containing razors, pencils, toothpaste, soap, paper, and other necessary items. Indian women also served as Red Cross nurses and nurse aides in hospitals located in France and England as well as in stateside facilities, some enlisting in the U.S. Army Medical Corps during the war. Still others traveled with the Young Women's Christian Association (YWCA) to France as entertainers. Tsianina Redfeather (Cherokee) was among them. Her songs, she hoped, would momentarily comfort the doughboys and "bring about a better understanding between her race and the white people." Across the United States, local tribal communities raised money to provide financial aid to returning disabled Indian veterans and their families, conserved food in concert with the nation's rationing program, educated themselves as to the causes of the war and postwar expectations domestically and globally, displayed the American flag within their communities and on their individual homes, and filled jobs in the civilian, off-reservation sector working in defense factories or as teachers, clerks, and seamstresses.

Indian farmers and ranchers likewise contributed to the war effort. Commissioner Sells aggressively encouraged Indians to increase agricultural production to meet the food needs of both civilians and the military. His patriotic call certainly inspired many Native Americans to cultivate more land, and the profit potential from increased demand for crops moved many tribal councils to place more community-owned land into farm production. Reservation farm production leaped during the war years. Shoshones at the Wind River Reservation in Wyoming cultivated 1,000 additional acres, and in Montana 12,000 more acres were put to agricultural use. Across 73 reservations, noted Cato Sells, farm production jumped 31 percent during the war, newly cultivated lands rose from 678,500 acres to 760,000 acres, and the value of Native American-produced crops nearly doubled from slightly more than $5 million in 1916 to just under $10 million in 1918.

The war effort among Indians mirrored the activities of the general white population nationally, and

12.10 Men from Carlisle Indian School march in the Preparedness Day Parade, 1916

Source: Library of Congress Prints and Photographs Division, LC-DIG-hec-06823

Native Americans and Anglo-Americans often found themselves working together, side by side. A sense of inclusion with white society surfaced among many assimilation-bound Indians. Commissioner Sells could not have been happier. According to Sells, the Indians' full participation in home front programs, their increased agricultural production for the larger American marketplace, and their growing sense of inclusion all combined to hasten assimilation. The Great War, he said, would "dissolve tribal bonds, remove interracial barriers, rescue the Indian from his retarding isolation" and ultimately "absorb him into the general population with the full rights and immunities of our American life."

Native Americans did, however, confront serious problems on the home front during the war years. Increased agricultural productivity on Indian lands fostered new demands among non-Indians for access to Native American land. In response to mounting pressure from white farmers and speculators, the OIA suggested to Indians that they lease their allotted properties and release surplus lands to more experienced white farmers and ranchers. By the end of World War I, whites farmed six times more Indian land than Native Americans worked. The leasing of allotted land rose 22 percent between 1915 and 1918, while the number of actual leases of unallotted tribal property jumped from 51 to 1,088 in those same years. In addition, Indians sold thousands of acres to whites, and Native American proceeds from these land transactions jumped significantly between 1916 and 1918, from almost $7 million to nearly $12 million. Sells hoped the leasing and purchasing of Indian lands would ultimately break the Indians' connection to the land and to tribal community life, moving them more quickly along the path to assimilation in much the same way as he envisioned military service a conduit for Indians into the general population.

The war also drained reservations of vital services. American forces in France urgently needed medical personnel and supplies. Whether lured by the clarion call of patriotism or the promise of better pay and benefits, physicians and nurses abandoned Indian communities for military service, leaving reservations with 39 percent fewer doctors and 45 percent fewer nurses in 1918 than they had in 1916. As poor as the Indian health program was before the war, the war made it much worse. Infectious disease rates soared without the minimum medical attention earlier available. Tuberculosis (TB) and trachoma (a disease that blinds its victim) ravaged Indian communities. By late 1918, one-third of all Indians suffered from TB and fully one-half were in some stage of trachoma development. Smallpox, whooping cough, and influenza also devastated Indian communities. A government investigation in 1918, however, fixed blame largely on the Indians themselves, claiming that the absence of appropriate sanitation in Native American communities and in individual homes contributed directly to the high infection rate, as did the Indians' refusal to seek medical services from white doctors.

Indian educational programs and opportunities also declined during the war. More than 30 percent of the teachers employed by Indian schools entered military service or secured more lucrative positions in white society. Wartime rationing brought additional hardships. School supplies were seldom available to the extent needed, heating fuel costs skyrocketed, and basic foodstuffs were in short supply on reservations. To compensate, Commissioner Sells suggested Indian children leave boarding schools for public schools. This, he reasoned, would ease the financial burden war placed on the Indian Bureau and would place Indian children in white social settings that would hasten assimilation. He further recommended Indian schools limit instruction in the basic academic curriculum and place greater emphasis on vocational education programs, a step that would train Indians for war-related jobs and concurrently make it easier for Indians to move into white society.

Conclusion

In 1918, the French military bestowed on Robert Spott (Yurok) medals for his heroism in battle and for his service to France. American officers approached him afterward, he recalled years later, and said, "You are all right. You fought for your country." He offered a slight smile, he said, and thought to himself, "Where is my country when I get home?"

The World War I years, and the decade that preceded it, are not typically emphasized in Indian history. Until recent years, little scholarly work centered on the Indians' participation in the Great War, and even less treated the role of the Society of American Indians and the broad themes of Indian Progressivism seriously. But the first two decades of the twentieth century were important years in the ongoing debate among Native Americans over the fundamental issue of Indian identity. Native Americans demonstrated clearly in this period that there was no consensus, no single preferred path or policy to be followed. Indeed, such disagreement only highlights the historic diversity of Native Americans, the same diversity of thought and action that precluded substantial and sustained pan-Indian efforts against European and American encroachment. The absence of a single Indian voice between 1910 and 1919 should have surprised no one, not even Native Americans.

Review Questions

1. What was the fundamental goal of the Society of American Indians? How did they expect Native Americans to attain that goal? How did they view Native American identity in the modern world?

2. In what ways were the peyote cult and the Native American Church forms of Indian resistance? Given the history of federal Indian policy, why did Washington not press the criminalization of peyote and challenge the Native American Church?

3. Why did Native Americans freely volunteer for military service in the U.S. armed forces during World War I? How were American Indian servicemen received by the nation's armed forces, and by Germans?

4. What positive benefit for Native Americans did the Indian Office believe World War I provided Indians?

5. In what ways were Indian cultures and traditions beneficial to the armed forces, and how did military service contribute to the Indians' maintenance of an identity separate from whites?

Recommended Readings

Britten, Thomas A. *American Indians in World War I: At Home and at War* (Albuquerque: University of New Mexico Press, 1997). A superb, detailed study of Native American participation in the Great War and the political, social, and economic issues surrounding their military service.

Eastman, Charles. *The Soul of the Indian: An Interpretation* (Mamaroneck, NY: Aeon, 2001). Eastman presents an overview of Lakota spiritual values along with an explanation of traditional symbols and ceremonies.

Holm, Tom. *The Great Confusion in Indian Affairs: Native Americans and Whites in the Progressive Era* (Austin: University of Texas Press, 2005). An examination of "Indian Progressives" in the late nineteenth and early twentieth centuries, particularly their commitment to the maintenance of an identity apart from mainstream, white society.

Maddox, Lucy. *Citizen Indians: Native American Intellectuals, Race, and Reform* (Ithaca, NY: Cornell University Press, 2005). A study of Native American reformers and their efforts to preserve indigenous identities in an era during which the federal government pursued actively an assimilationist agenda.

Maroukis, Thomas C. *The Peyote Road: Religious Freedom and the Native American Church* (Norman: University of Oklahoma Press, 2010). A history of the Native American Church with particular focus on the role and use of peyote and federal government challenges to its continued use.

Martinez, David. *Dakota Philosopher: Charles Eastman and American Indian Thought* (St. Paul: Minnesota Historical Society Press, 2009). A detailed examination of Charles Eastman's perspective regarding Indian assimilation and the preservation of Indian identities at the beginning of the twentieth century.

Native American History Online

General Sites

Jim Thorpe. www.profootballhof.com/players/jim-thorpe This website provides a brief biography of Thorpe with detailed attention to his professional career in sports.

Simon Pokagon. http://vos.ucsb.edu/browse.asp?id=2364 This site provides the e-text version of Simon Pokagon's (Potawatomi) writings, among them "An American Indian on the Problem of His Race" (1895) and "The Future of the Red Man" (1897). These documents present clearly the conflict that seemed inherent among Native Americans during the Progressive Era—the necessity of acculturation but the determination to retain an Indian identity.

Choctaw Indian Code Talkers of World War I. www.texasmilitaryforcesmuseum.org/choctaw/codetalkers.htm This website includes a brief history of Choctaw battlefield radio communications work late in World War I, the official report of Colonel A. W. Bloom to the Commanding General, 36th Infantry Division, and biographical sketches of most of the original Choctaw code talkers. See also "Code Talkers" at www.choctawnation.com. This site houses a brief history of Choctaw code talkers in World War I and how the use of the Indians' language confused Germans, and it provides biographical sketches of several of the code talkers.

Historic Sites

Jim Thorpe Home, Yale, Oklahoma. www.visitokc.com/listings/jim-thorpe-museum-%26-oklahoma-sports-hall-of-fame/801/ This site traces the life of Oklahoma icon Jim Thorpe.

Choctaw Nation of Oklahoma Capitol Museum, Tushka Homma, Oklahoma. www.choctawnation.com The Choctaw Nation Museum has a continuously running exhibit featuring the code talking of Choctaw Indians in World War I. Also on exhibition is the Trail of Tears and additional exhibits of Choctaw history and culture. See also www.nativetimes.com/index.php?option=com_content&view=article&id=3844

CHAPTER
13

Postwar Directions for Native Americans, 1918–1929

THE "OSAGE REIGN OF TERROR"
COMING HOME
Wartime Divestment of Indian Lands
Wartime Resurgence of Traditional Values
Citizenship for Native Americans
POSTWAR ACTIVISM
The Continued Assault on Indian Lands
Pueblo Lands
Fall's Removal From Office
CHANGING DIRECTIONS
The Emerging Path of Reform
Citizenship Revisited
The Meriam Report

The "Osage Reign of Terror"

Hunters found Anna Brown's decomposed body in a ditch near Fairfax, Oklahoma, early one morning in May 1921. It took little effort to determine the cause of Anna's death—a single bullet in the back of her head. The murder troubled local residents. Anna, an Osage Indian, was well liked and had no known enemies. A routine investigation netted no clues that pointed to the killer. Anna's death most likely would have remained unsolved, but two months later, "Old" Lizzie, Anna's mother, died suddenly. With no readily evident cause of death, the coroner cited "natural causes" in his report. More than a few local residents guessed that there might be a connection between these two tragic deaths, but suspicion ran its course and the town of Fairfax soon quieted.

Nearly two years later, on February 6, 1923, the body of Henry Roan Horse was found slumped in his car. Like his cousin Anna Brown, Roan Horse was the victim of a single gunshot to the head. And, only a few weeks later, in March, Anna's sister and brother-in-law, Rita and Bill Smith, were killed in an explosion that leveled their Fairfax home, leaving Anna's remaining sister and brother-in-law, Mollie and Ernest Burkhart, the family's sole survivors. Authorities now realized that some unidentified murderer or murderers had targeted Anna and her entire family. But why?

The Osage Tribal Council pressured local police to investigate fully the murders. Genuine, honest efforts were made to determine who was responsible for the killing of five Osage Indians. The investigation was, however, undermined by local people who appeared intimidated and frightened for their own lives and consequently worked to derail the police inquiry. The council finally requested help from the Federal Bureau of Investigation (FBI). FBI agents were soon dispatched to Fairfax and, once there, decided to focus their investigation on

CHRONOLOGY

1917	Declaration of Policy establishes a process to declare Native American allottees "competent" to manage their own property
	Senator Carl Hayden of Arizona introduces a bill to extend U.S. citizenship to all Native Americans
1918	Representative Charles Carter of Oklahoma introduces a bill to extend U.S. citizenship to American Indians
1919	Representative Homer Snyder of New York introduces a bill to grant U.S. citizenship to Native American veterans of the Great War
1920	Warren G. Harding is elected president of the United States
	Albert Fall appointed Secretary of the Interior
	Charles Burke appointed Commissioner of Indian Affairs
1921	The body of Anna Brown is discovered, starting the period known as the Osage Reign of Terror
1922	The Bursum Bill is introduced into Congress
1923	The American Indian Defense Association (AIDA) is founded
	Council of All New Mexico Pueblos denounces attacks on Indian religious ceremonies made by Secretary Fall and Commissioner Burke
	Secretary Albert Fall is forced to resign; Hubert Work is named the new Secretary of the Interior
1924	Pueblo Lands Act becomes law
	Congress passes the Indian Citizenship Act, granting U.S. citizenship to all non-citizen Indians
	The Committee of One Hundred presents investigative report on issues and concerns critical to Indian affairs at mid-decade
1926	Gertrude Bonnin founds the National Council of American Indians
	Institute of Government Research empanels a team of specialists to investigate reservation living standards and determine reforms
1928	Institute of Government Research submits its final report, *The Problem of Indian Administration*
1929	William Hale is convicted for murder and conspiracy to commit murder; the Osage Reign of Terror concludes

Roan Horse's death because his body was found on reservation lands, clearly placing that murder under federal jurisdiction. For the next three years, agents infiltrated the local community. They assumed the identities of traveling salesmen, cattle buyers, retail store employees, and oil drillers and discovered the common thread linking the deaths of Anna Brown, her cousin, her mother, her sister and her husband—oil head rights.

Unlike other Indians who received land allotments, the Osage Nation retained mineral rights on all lands allotted to individual Indians. Four times a year, the Osage received a royalty for oil and natural gas extracted from the lands and the tribal council in turn paid a percentage, or head right, to each allotted Indian. Moreover, a head right was inheritable, passed from spouse to spouse or from parent to child. FBI agents learned that with Anna's death, her head right transferred to her mother, whose death passed the head right to Henry Roan Horse; his death moved it to Rita and Bill Smith, and their deaths would send the head right to Mollie Burkhart and her husband Ernest.

As the FBI pieced together this pattern of murder and financial gain, bodies of other Fairfax residents were discovered. Among the growing list of victims were oilmen with whom agents had previously spoken, people the local police believed were about to divulge information, and individuals connected to other Indian families and their head rights. By late 1926, more than two dozen men and women had been killed in what was by then being termed the "Osage Reign of Terror."

Suspicion eventually fell on William Hale, self-proclaimed "King of the Osage Hills." Hale became wealthy as a cattleman in the 1890s and increased his net worth by securing allotted lands from Osage Indians and connecting himself to their highly prosperous oil industry. It was discovered that Hale had direct or indirect ties to each person murdered. Realizing this, agents centered their effort on Hale's nephew, Ernest Burkhart, Anna's surviving brother-in-law.

Burkhart broke under FBI pressure. It was Hale's plan to have each member of Anna's family killed, confessed Burkhart. Once Burkhart inherited a head right, he would, with substantial compensation, transfer it to Uncle William Hale. Hale made similar arrangements with other non-Indians who married into Osage families. Hale stood to gain $500,000 annually from the head rights. Burkhart said those people killed and not in the financial loop were murdered because they knew of Hale's scheme and might be a threat to the King of the Osage Hills. With Burkhart's information, the FBI charged Hale with the murder of Henry Roan Horse, and on January 26, 1929, Hale and his hired killer received life sentences in federal prison. The reign of terror ended.

KEY QUESTIONS

1. What issues challenged Native Americans on the home front during the Great War? In what ways were these issues consistent with the history of Indian-white relations? What departures were these from historic relationships?

2. In what ways were Indian Office policies and directives regarding Indians of the Southwest consistent with prewar patterns? How did the Pueblo lands issue build enthusiasm for a new direction in Native American resistance?

3. By the mid-1920s, proponents of Indian assimilation claimed their mission to be on the verge of completion. Concurrently, critics of the Indian Office and federal policy contended the government's work over the previous four decades to be an absolute failure. What points justified each side's arguments?

Coming Home

Silence—absolute and peculiar—draped the battlefields of Western Europe just before noon on November 11, 1918. The smell of death lingered in the air, fear still shrouded each soldier, and few men allowed themselves the luxury of hope that the armistice would hold. In contrast, Americans stateside rejoiced wildly upon hearing news of the armistice just before daybreak. In New York City, "the hoots of tugs in the harbor, auto horns and air-raid sirens, factory whistles and church bells" yanked residents from their sleep, bonfires blazed at street intersections, "and by noon the city was one seething celebration." New Yorkers cheered the end of war and vented their "relief, rage, triumph, hatred, [and] grief." The Great War was over.

In the weeks that followed, Americans welcomed returning troops with open arms. Communities embraced their returning soldiers as true American heroes—men who vanquished a brutal enemy and ushered in what was expected to be a prolonged era of peace. New York City's "welcome home" celebration on February 17, 1919, mirrored the nation's pride. Tens of thousands of New Yorkers jammed the sidewalks of Fifth Avenue, packed rooftops, leaned from windows, and crowded fire escape landings and ladders to hail the "defenders of democracy." A ticker tape blizzard filled the sky, martial music blared triumphantly, and troops dressed in freshly cleaned and pressed uniforms marched proudly behind waves of American flags.

The unbridled patriotic fervor temporarily masked the darker reality of the wartime home front and the early months of peace. Homeland security concerns had weakened civil liberties, as the Espionage Act and the Sedition Act together curtailed free speech and established broad definitions of treasonous behavior. The government's Committee on Public Information, which George Creel headed, had disseminated vicious anti-German propaganda and had encouraged citizens to scrutinize carefully their neighbors' actions for any semblance of disloyalty. In the private sector, manufacturers recruited millions of new workers, among them nearly one million African Americans who exited the South for employment in northern plants. Once in Chicago, Cleveland, Detroit, and other northern cities, they confronted vicious racism from white workers and residents, and racial unrest plagued the region throughout the war years and well into the next decade. In summer 1919, only months after the armistice, bloody race riots erupted in two dozen northern cities. The Ku Klux Klan resurfaced at Stone Mountain, Georgia, and quickly spread as a national menace not only to African Americans but to Catholics, Jews, and immigrants as well. Anti-Bolshevik hysteria also gripped the nation in response to the revolution that forced Russia's early departure from the Great War. Many feared that communists would attempt to undermine the United States. From 1919 to summer 1920, the Justice Department arrested, detained, and deported thousands of immigrants allegedly sympathetic to communist ideology. A variety of social and cultural issues divided the nation. Suffragettes demanded passage of a constitutional amendment to enfranchise women. Reformers pressed their call for an amendment to prohibit the manufacture, sale, and consumption of alcoholic drinks. Christian fundamentalists insisted that Charles Darwin's theory of evolution be banned from public schools and be replaced with biblical creationism in the science curriculum. Popular literary figures, later known collectively as the "lost generation," questioned the society that took America to war and condemned the seemingly dehumanizing effects of modern urban life. In spite of victory in the bloodiest war in human history to date, America appeared more confused and divided than ever, wrangling with the most fundamental of issues—its own identity.

Native American soldiers and sailors, like their non-Indian comrades, returned from the European war in early 1919 with pride in their military service and in their own individual accomplishments. From the cheering multitude that greeted them in New York Harbor to the celebrations orchestrated by their states and local communities, American Indian veterans were honored for their patriotism and the contribution to the "war to end all war."

Many American Indians sensed a new day dawning for the world, a new direction shaped by personal sacrifice and spirituality. Said Charles Eastman in 1919, the Great War exhausted the world, and it "brought home [to the United States] the realization that our boasted progress is after all mainly industrial and commercial—a powerful force, to be sure, but being so unspiritual, not likely to be lasting or stable." He believed President Wilson's noble crusade to spread the vision of self-determination globally and to eliminate ultimately the root causes of war was grounded on a spiritual base, a position in concert with American Indian values. The world now stood at an unusually opportune moment to embrace democracy and to experience fully a spiritual renewal among mankind. The nations then assembled at the Paris Peace Conference "will deliberate unselfishly in the interests of humanity" and "eliminate purely national bias and suspicion," said Eastman. The United States, he added, must assume the lead, demonstrating human compassion to its recent enemies abroad and extending full democracy to all citizens at home. "The new world order must begin at home," he continued. America was "in a position to pilot the bark of humanity into a safe harbor."

Unfortunately, Eastman's optimism was more the product of the hope and joy of victory celebrations than of careful reflection on the war's actual impact. His initial optimism mirrored popular sentiment nationally, but the darker reality that shadowed wartime America and the immediate postwar period soon settled over Native Americans. From 1917 to early 1919, western farmers continued their assault on Indian land ownership while the Department of Interior, the Office of Indian Affairs, and Christian groups attacked traditional Indian religious ceremonies and cultural values. Moreover, the notion of the "vanishing Indian" only assumed greater currency within the halls of government during the war, exaggerated by the melding of Native Americans into white military units. At stake was Indian identity.

Wartime Divestment of Indian Lands

The Great War turned Europe's once-productive croplands into battlefields, and the demands of war left too few young men on the home front to maximize production from what usable farmland was left. As a result, food shortages plagued the continent throughout the war years. Malnutrition and outright starvation ravaged populations from Russia to northern France. Europe's misery, however, resulted in sudden, albeit short-term, prosperity among American farmers who could now profit from the production of foodstuffs for both American and European markets. Crop prices jumped, and, noted one historian, "farmers bought in and out of season the way most people buy only at Christmas." Sharply increased wartime demand for food promised a stunning rise in personal prosperity, provided one was able to acquire more land and harvest more crops. The fierce competition for wartime agricultural profits meant the battle for property was fought not only in European fields but on the American home front as well.

Toward that end, western farmers intensified their pressure on the Office of Indian Affairs (OIA) to remove additional acreage from Indian control, this time cloaking their hunger for land in the flowing banner of patriotism. If Native American farmers and ranchers failed to utilize fully their land allotments for wartime food production, those properties should be withdrawn from Indian ownership and sold or leased to white farmers committed to the war food program. Secretary of the Interior Franklin Lane agreed and warned Indians to increase production or lose their lands to white farmers who would make full use of the property, a warning Commissioner of Indian Affairs Cato Sells echoed. Said Sells, "when a nation is at war, ordinary considerations do not govern." Victory and defeat stood in the balance, and, he reasoned, to secure victory government must pursue unusual policies and the general population must cooperate for the nation's welfare. The need to feed America's armed forces, the prospect of higher market prices, and Sells's warning encouraged many Indians to increase their crop output, and in 1917 they cultivated 30 percent more land than in the previous year and nearly that much more in 1918. Despite such efforts, the patriotic call to cultivation Cato Sells and others issued proved nothing more than another method by which westerners and western interests were able to secure much-coveted Indian lands (see Timeline 13.1).

Table 13.1 Changes in the Number of Indians Farming on Reservations, 1911 to 1915

Reservation	1911	1915	Percent Change	Allotted Land	Tillable Land	Percentage
Cheyenne River	500	500	0.0	920,750	5,260	0.6
Coeur d'Alene	65	93	43.1	104,077	64,640	62.1
Colville	383	570	48.8	51,653	98,480	190.7
Crow	300	379	–7.0	479,028	153,307	32.0
Fort Berthold	100	180	80.0	229,554	155,475	67.7
Kiowa	821	1,003	22.2	547,236	500,000	91.4
Klamath	75	100	33.3	207,374	10,000	4.8
Leech Lake	306	365	19.3	47,772	7,526	15.8
Lower Brule	75	90	20.0	187,356	45,696	24.4
Rosebud	900	700	–32.2	1,642,889	1,217,266	74.1
Shoshone	137	278	102.9	221,832	135,339	61.0
Spokane	75	87	16.0	64,794	35,775	55.2
Standing Rock	558	733	31.4	1,387,935	1,048,239	75.5
Uintah and Ouray	120	199	65.8	39,620	82,328	207.0
White Earth	300	300	0.0	710,466	203,000	28.6
Total	6,626	7,392	11.6	6,842,336	3,762,331	55.0

Source: United States Department of Interior, *Reports of the Department of the Interior for the Fiscal Year Ended June 30, 1915* (Washington: Government Printing Office, 1915), pp. 79–82, 115–119, 126–129.

Commissioner Sells ignored data the Interior Department collected. Since passage of the Dawes Act in 1887, the number of Indian men engaged in agriculture had risen substantially. More than 70 percent of able-bodied men residing on most reservations actively pursued farming or ranching by 1915. It was a pattern of increase noted in Interior Department documents for the five-year period before the Great War erupted, documentation that conflicted with Sells's false assertion that Indians were failing to farm their land. In spite of this apparent expansion of farming, agricultural productivity on reservations remained problematic—another point Sells failed to acknowledge. Modern farm tools and factory-manufactured fertilizers were not widely available to Native American farmers, and efficient irrigation systems rarely watered Indian lands. Access to farm loans at affordable rates proved elusive, and agricultural extension programs seldom reached the native population. Congressional acts, court rulings, and unscrupulous speculators continued to divest Indians of lands before the war, and on those reservations allotted between 1900 and 1910 only a little more than half of allotted acreage was considered "tillable land"—also a pattern consistent over the previous quarter century. Little wonder that those Indians who hoped to make a living from farming often found it difficult to sustain themselves and their families. War effort or not, many Native Americans were in no position to increase production, a reality white land speculators in the West understood well.

Regardless of the problems facing Native American farming and ranching efforts, during the war Commissioner Sells arranged the sale or lease of thousands of "surplus" (underused) acres. Thomas Campbell, head of the Montana Farming Corporation, leased 200,000 acres from the Crow, Shoshone, and Blackfeet reservations with the provision that Indians receive a mere 10 percent of the crops harvested. White ranchers, backed by the OIA, similarly called for Indians to sell their cattle, ostensibly for the war effort. Without herds, ranchers reasoned, Indians would have little need for their allotted acreage and might lease the grazing lands to white ranchers.

Wartime profits did find their way into the pockets of many Native American farmers and ranchers who retained their land. Market prices for beef and lamb jumped significantly, and the value of wool spiraled upward from 16 cents per pound in 1914 to 57 cents in 1918. Crop prices likewise climbed during the war and remained high until 1921. At the same time, however, the number of Indians who lost their land holdings climbed ever higher, plunging more Native Americans into poverty.

13.1 John Billy (Palute) farming at Duckwater Reservation
Source: Courtesy of National Archives and Records Administration

Throughout their tenure of office, Secretary Lane and Commissioner Sells sought new ways to place more acreage into non-Indian hands. In this context, America's participation in the Great War served their interest. If the U.S. armed forces considered Native Americans competent for inclusion in white military and naval forces, then it appeared reasonable to Lane and Sells that Indians on the home front might be equally ready for life without the special relationship that historically governed Indian status in America. In April 1917, as the United States entered the European war, the OIA issued its **"Declaration of Policy."** In it, Sells announced that the OIA to date had worked to improve Indian health care, educational services, and tribal economics and in so doing prepare native peoples for assimilation; now, effort would be directed toward freeing Indians from federal guardianship. The document amplified the competency clause in the 1906 Burke Act that allowed Indians the right to control their land without federal protection and oversight provided they were deemed competent to manage their own affairs. Lane appointed a "competency commission," its members charged with determining the Indians' ability to cope with and prosper in white society without federal protection. Commissioners were to make a personal visit to the home of an allotted Indian, rate his level of literacy and self-sufficiency, and based on their findings declare him competent or incompetent. In practice, interviews frequently lasted less than 15 minutes. Commissioners often found roads impassable, weather too brutal, or homes too remote to visit an allottee. In such instances, they simply pronounced the Indian competent without any visitation or interview. During the war years, the commission declared 11,000 Indians to be competent, a figure that rose to 20,000 by 1920.

Lane's competency program was clearly a sham, a program contrived to divest Indians of federal guardianship and expose allottees to property taxes they could ill afford. Unable to pay their taxes, landowners would have their property seized by local governments and auctioned to land-hungry non-Indian speculators. The absence of federal protection would open Indian landowners to tactics that encouraged or pressured their sale of the land to white speculators. Those Indians determined to be "competent" soon faced a wave of non-Indian land dealers, farmers, ranchers, bankers, and others eager to lease or purchase allotments. Many Indians succumbed to both pressure and poverty. "Reports from such reservations as the Crow, Fort Peck, and Pine Ridge indicated that some ninety percent or more sold their allotments or mortgaged them at ruinous interest rates," one scholar noted recently. The meager profits Indians gained from these land transactions vanished quickly, and poverty deepened for many Native Americans during the war years and in the immediate postwar period. Self-sufficiency and the acculturative process land ownership ostensibly promised under the allotment system were denied by policies and programs generated by the very agency calling for Indian assimilation. Of greater consequence, the land itself was the source of Indian spirituality and tribal sovereignty. As land holdings dwindled, the physical source of Indian understanding, authority, order, legitimacy, and identity diminished.

Reaction to the Declaration of Policy surprised few observers. Most Americans were oblivious to the issue. America's participation in Europe's bloody war consumed the general public's attention. Moreover, emancipation of Indians from federal guardianship and the integration of Native Americans into mainstream society had been the cornerstone of federal Indian policy for more than a quarter of a century. Congressional committees on Indian affairs, Progressive reformers, and the majority of political figures on both the federal and state levels believed that most Native Americans were now sufficiently prepared for assimilation. Even the Indian Rights Association supported, in theory, Sells's policy statement as logical, appropriate, and acceptable. The few non-Indian complaints hurled at the declaration centered on the slow process of determining competency. Native Americans who opposed Sells were most often the very ones whose voices rarely reached beyond their own homes—the least educated and acculturated Indians, Native Americans who preferred no retreat from traditional values and customs, and people already parted from their land and money.

Wartime Resurgence of Traditional Values

In 1917, Commissioner Sells acknowledged reluctantly that many Native Americans required further preparation before attaining the label "competent," and he believed that military service in white units would "hasten [their] assimilation." Much to his chagrin, the war actually stimulated in some Indians a resurgence of traditional values and behaviors and among the more disheartened rekindled overt pride in their heritage. Native American families and communities honored the new warriors with traditional going-away ceremonies that sought protection of loved ones about to enter battle. Many Indian enlistees carried with them "medicine" to ensure their safe return—pouches containing objects of spiritual importance given to them by loved ones or prepared themselves. Warrior societies, long thought by whites to be virtually extinct, resurfaced and resumed their centrality in tribal life. Their members honored the young soldiers as defenders of the tribe and often escorted the new warriors to recruitment or induction centers. Traditional war songs also reappeared, occasionally with lyrics that pronounced their loyalty to the United States but also that reminded the Indian soldier of his responsibility to his family and tribe.

At the same time that the federal government moved to limit American civil liberties in the wartime nation, Sells and the OIA leveled their sights on these traditional Native American ceremonies and customs. The Indian Office and its most ardent champions insisted that tribal dances and religious activities purportedly performed to honor Indian men entering military service revealed, in fact, a determined attachment to a primitive past and an unyielding resistance to government assimilation programs, behaviors clearly un-American and possibly treasonous. Sells's vicious condemnation mattered little to most Indians. Upon the soldiers' return home in 1918 and 1919, veterans sang victory songs of their battlefield exploits, with some alteration in lyrics making them relevant to the recent war with Germany. Entire communities participated in victory dances. Said Reverend Aaron Beede, a Christian missionary among the Sioux at Fort Yates, North Dakota, this was the "first time this [victory] dance has been held since the evening after the Little Big Horn battle of June 25, 1876."

13.2 Pawnee dancers at the Second Annual Victory Dance to honor Pawnee veterans of World War I, August 1920

Source: Courtesy of Library of Congress Prints and Photographs Division, LC-USZ62-118300

Many Indian families and communities ceremoniously cleansed the veterans' spirits of the horrors of warfare to hasten their return to the path of goodness. In these victory dances and cleansing ceremonies, veterans sometimes combined traditional garments with their military uniform, and frequently effigies of the German Kaiser were suspended from tree limbs for Indians to count coup. In all of these activities, Indians blended traditional customs and values with symbols of contemporary, non-Indian America—the melding of two worlds. And, in a manner consistent with traditional cultural norms, Indian communities frequently honored combat veterans with positions of tribal leadership. Whether the resurgence of traditional values and behaviors was a conscious rejection of the government's historic effort to eradicate all vestiges of Indian cultures under the mantle of assimilation or simply a natural expression of cultural values and behaviors that heretofore remained latent but not obliterated remains unclear; perhaps each explanation has some truth in it. In any case, it was as if Indians nationally and in unison reminded white society "We're still here."

Citizenship for Native Americans

Historian Fred Hoxie recently noted that as Native Americans turned in civilian clothing for military uniforms in 1917, the "irony of serving a nation that had dispossessed them, and of fighting to defend 'democracy' when their own communities were ruled by the Indian Office, was not lost on Indian people." To be sure, native peoples understood clearly their peculiar relationship with the United States, but for so many of the young men who joined ranks in military service and for so many of their families back home, voluntary participation in the war was seen as an opportunity to realize America's democratic promise. Exactly what framed that "democratic promise" varied from man to man.

The Society of American Indians (SAI) and the National Indian Association (NIA) each insisted that Indian loyalty to the United States during the war merited the extension of citizenship to native peoples. Responding to the mounting chorus among Indians, the thousands of letters from Native Americans and sympathetic whites that fell on the desks of congressmen, and the numerous supportive editorials that appeared in major newspapers, several prominent members of Congress introduced legislation to confer citizenship on American Indians. Senator Carl Hayden of Arizona submitted such a bill in summer 1917, and Representative Charles Carter of Oklahoma presented a similar measure to the House in early 1918; however, each also called for the immediate dissolution of the Indian Office and federal guardianship over Indians, a proposal that won few supporters in Congress and generated vocal criticism among Native Americans. "A grateful government and people will not withhold from the Native American race full rights as free men under the constitution," voiced SAI delegates at their September 1918 annual conference. In December, the NIA likewise resolved in its conference that Washington should reciprocate the Indians' voluntary service in and support for the war with full citizenship for all American Indians. Citizenship amounted to a "final solution" to the so-called "Indian problem."

Native Americans linked their own call for U.S. citizenship with President Woodrow Wilson's call at the Paris Peace Conference in 1919 for the right of self-determination to be extended to all peoples. Wrote Zitkala-Sa for the SAI's *American Indian Magazine*, "The Red man asks for a very simple thing—citizenship in the land that was once his own—America . . . The American Indian, too, made the supreme sacrifice for liberty's sake. He loves democratic ideals. What shall world democracy mean to his race?" Asked Charles Eastman, "How can our nation pose as the champion of the 'little peoples' until it has been fair to its own? . . . All we ask is full citizenship . . . We offered our services and our money in this war, and more in proportion to our number and means than any other race or class of the population." Echoing Eastman, Zitkala-Sa, and others was the American Legion, a national veterans' association that championed Indian citizenship as America's obligation for Native Americans who voluntarily served in the armed forces.

Nationally, assimilationists contended citizenship would contribute to the breaking of tribal bonds and speed movement into the general society—the Constitution serving as the Indians' protector rather than the historically inept OIA. Fiscal conservatives suggested that citizenship, elimination of the Indian Office, and the resulting inclusion of Indians in mainstream society would end an unnecessary financial burden on Washington. These disparate groups, each with its own perspective, joined with Indians to demand Congress bestow U.S. citizenship on all Native Americans.

At this time, Congressman Homer Snyder of New York chaired the House Committee on Indian Affairs. He was intimately familiar with congressional debates concerning blanket citizenship. He saw the benefits of assimilation, but he also understood, perhaps better than most in Congress, that much work remained to prepare the larger general Indian population for assimilation. On June 5, 1919, Snyder presented to the House of Representatives a bill that would grant citizenship to any Indian veteran of the Great War without loss of tribal benefits. The bill received House endorsement in September and was introduced in the Senate by Kansas Senator Charles Curtis, himself a man of Kaw-Osage heritage. Without addition or deletion, the bill sailed through the Senate in October, and President Wilson signed the measure into law on November 6.

The legislation, however, actually accomplished little. First, and not surprisingly, the OIA bungled application of the new law by making the process of securing citizenship much more complicated and frustrating than it needed to be. It required Indian veterans to complete a lengthy application form; appear before representatives of the Bureau of Naturalization, who would determine the Indian's competency; and, if approved, petition the Clerk of the Court for a certificate of citizenship. The detailed and lengthy process compelled many veterans to wonder what ultimate benefit U.S. citizenship might actually hold. State governments controlled access to the ballot box, and numerous states unapologetically still denied Indians the right to vote. It was widely assumed, too, that loss of federal protection would expose them more completely to exploitation and abuse by the government and unscrupulous non-Indians. Few veterans, therefore, saw in citizenship any fundamental improvement in their quality of life other than legal recognition. Numerous Native Americans still placed greater value on their long-standing treaty arrangements with the United States, as these earlier agreements suggested the Indians' retention of tribal sovereignty, a modicum of independence, and the preservation of their heritage. Noted one SAI member, "Our treaty rights with the government of the United States . . . are just as sacred as [a] treaty made with England or any of the foreign powers." "When our Indians become civilized and wish to quit the reservation and its mode of living," he continued, "let them receive citizenship just as the Russian or the Frenchman or the Spaniard who comes over here to make this country his home." In the end, few Indian veterans took U.S. citizenship.

Postwar Activism

The darker reality of American society, culture, and politics that lay underneath postwar victory celebrations in 1919 suggested a nation in search of itself, a nation hoping to define itself in a modernizing, socially dynamic, and clearly more threatening world. At home, the nation battled over evolution and creationism, imagined a communist wave washing upon American shores, witnessed a new direction in African American efforts to secure equal rights and recognition, and confronted a modern impulse among its youth. The image of small-town America remained firmly fixed as reality in the collective consciousness, but 51 percent of the nation's population now resided in cities. In international affairs, the United States refused to join the League of Nations in 1919 and touted isolationism as America's most reasonable policy as a means for avoiding future European wars. At the same time, however, the United States assumed a central role in fashioning multinational accords and arms reduction agreements such as the Kellogg-Briand Peace Pact and the Washington Conference. The postwar years found the United States caught between two worlds—one that looked backward and championed traits, values, and patterns believed responsible for America's exceptional development and one that pressed the nation forward as a modern, economically and politically influential player on the world stage.

Perhaps not as visible, Native Americans, too, were caught between two worlds.

Trapped by nineteenth-century policies that delivered little of what they promised, Native Americans and non-Indians increasingly sought "a final solution." In the early 1920s, lawmakers looked backward to find solutions or to fulfill those plans earlier laid. In mid-decade, new voices rose that questioned the wisdom, purpose, and goals of those pre-twentieth-century efforts and ultimately offered an assessment of the old order so profound, so shocking, that by 1929 the OIA would face fundamental change.

The Continued Assault on Indian Lands

When Warren G. Harding was elected to the presidency in 1920, he nominated Albert Fall to be the new secretary of the interior. Fall had been a practicing attorney, an elected member of the U.S. House of Representatives, and a former U.S. senator from New Mexico. He brought to the office a colorful, if checkered, past that included allegations of financial misdealing, questionable practices in his legal business, and unsavory ties with corrupt business leaders. Fall arrived at the Department of Interior filled with a determination to end, once and for all, federal guardianship of Native Americans. His choice for Commissioner of Indian Affairs was Charles H. Burke, previously South Dakota's congressional representative and author of the 1906 Burke Act. Fall and Burke carried similar opinions of Native Americans. They believed that American Indians remained a primitive, backward people virtually incapable of full assimilation. In their view, Indians were little more than impediments to progress, unworthy peoples residing on land that could be better used by non-Indian business interests. Fall and Burke moved quickly after their Senate confirmation to open Indian lands desired by white business interests.

Sometimes they supported white business interests by doing nothing, such as the case in Oklahoma after the discovery of oil on Osage land. The Osage Allotment Act (1906) purposely reduced the extent of acreage under Osage control, but it did allow for tribal ownership of all mineral rights, a provision that directly countered all previous allotment measures. To the good fortune of Oklahoma's Osage Indians, a massive deposit of oil was discovered on tribal and allotted properties, and extraction of the oil generated royalties that made the Osage people, collectively, the wealthiest of Native Americans and among the richest of all Americans nationwide.

In 1923 alone, Osage oil fields generated revenues totaling $27 million. Given the sheer abundance of "black gold" on Indian lands, it is little wonder that the Osage territory was soon inundated with land speculators, businessmen, bankers, lawyers, and others who hoped to score their own financial windfall among the Osage. Beginning in 1922 and continuing for the next four years, Osage landowners received little federal protection of their land and lives from non-Indians or from "legal Indians" who sought their wealth from oil-rich land. Fall and Burke took no steps to aid or to protect Osage property or individuals from exploitation, and federal inaction in Oklahoma garnered little attention until the FBI began its lengthy investigation into the "Osage Reign of Terror" (see chapter opening). Fall and Burke's role in New Mexico land grabs were better known to the general public before the FBI concluded its investigation.

Secretary Fall pursued development of a national park in southern New Mexico, a substantial portion of the planned reserve to be property acquired from the Mescalero Apaches. The Apaches vehemently opposed the removal of land from tribal ownership and vented their outrage in a formal, written protest sent directly to the secretary and to the Office of Indian Affairs. To no one's surprise, the letter accomplished nothing. Fall held the support of New Mexico's governor, the state's congressional delegation, and key figures in New Mexico business. A national park promised increased tourism dollars for the state and, interestingly, a financial windfall for Secretary Fall. Fall owned a ranch in the vicinity of the planned park and intended to use federal dollars to purchase a road right-of-way through that property. Without the Apaches' land, the plan for the park would likely fizzle out.

PROFILE

Will Rogers

13.3 Will Rogers

Source: Courtesy of Library of Congress Prints and Photographs Division, LC-USZ62-20553

"I never met a man I didn't like," said Will Rogers at the close of each of his radio broadcasts. The phrase became associated with him as much as the derby and mustache were associated with actor Charlie Chaplin. Rogers, whose mother and father were each part Cherokee, was born and reared near present-day Oologah, Oklahoma. He remained forever intensely proud of his Cherokee heritage and frequently quipped, "My ancestors didn't come over on the Mayflower, but they met the boat." Formal schooling appealed little to him. Capturing his heart instead was the cowboy life and the excitement of world travel. Rogers quit school after the tenth grade and devoted his energy to the family's Dog Iron Ranch until 1901, when he and a friend ventured to Argentina and there established their own cattle ranch. Despite their hard work, the enterprise failed within five months, in part because neither possessed the basic business savvy necessary to make the business succeed.

For the next two years, Rogers trained horses in South Africa and toured with a Wild West show in Australia, returning to the United States in 1904 to perform homespun comedy and lariat tricks on New York City's vaudeville stages until

1915. A brief stint with the Ziegfeld Follies led him to a movie career, first in Hal Roach's silent films and then with Twentieth Century Fox. Rogers appeared in more than 70 films, authored six books, wrote more than 4,000 articles as a syndicated columnist, and regularly hosted a radio talk show. He donated thousands of dollars to charity and to communities and families rebuilding in the wake of natural disasters.

Writing, radio broadcasts, and film altogether served as Rogers's outlets for his pointed humor and insight that typically targeted politics and social issues. Rogers believed the United States should refrain from engaging in problems not vital to the nation's security, a position that leaned increasingly toward isolationism as he aged. "No nation ever had two better friends than we have. You know who they are?" he asked. "The Atlantic and Pacific oceans." He understood that war is sometimes necessary, but, he insisted, it should be the absolute last option employed and always be soundly justified. "You can be killed just as dead in an unjustified war as you can in one protecting your own home," he said.

On August 15, 1935, Will Rogers flew as a passenger in the airplane of friend and fellow Oklahoman Wiley Post. Post refueled in Barrow, Alaska, but during takeoff the plane experienced engine failure and crashed on the runway. Both Post and Rogers died on impact. In tribute to Rogers, a statue of him stands inside the nation's capital and faces the entrance to the U.S. House of Representatives. He always said that someone should keep an eye on those politicians.

Popular Will Rogers Quotes

"We will never have true civilization until we have learned to recognize the rights of others."

"Live in such a way that you would not be ashamed to sell your parrot to the town gossip."

"It's great to be great, but it's greater to be human."

"What constitutes a life well spent? Love and admiration from your fellow men is all that anyone can ask."

"People talk peace. But men give their life's work to war. It won't stop 'til there is as much brains and scientific study put to aid peace as there is to promote war."

"I don't care how little your country is, you got a right to run it like you want to. When the big nations quit meddling then the world will have peace."

In a bid to secure Apache endorsement for the land transaction, Secretary Fall not only rigged a tribal council vote but also altered the transcript of council debate to suggest the Indians' near unanimous support for the park proposal. The national park bill passed the U.S. Senate in 1922 but was crushed in the House once Fall's unethical and possibly crooked behavior came to light.

Pueblo Lands

Fall was involved in another dubious piece of land legislation in New Mexico, this one involving nearly 12,000 non-Indians who claimed ownership of 60,000 acres of Pueblo lands under the provision of "squatters' rights." Indians asserted their legal claim to the properties, but the state government and courts refused to acknowledge Pueblo title to the land despite the U.S. Supreme Court's 1913 ruling in the Sandoval case that pronounced

Pueblos to be wards of the federal government and, as such, not permitted to sell their land. Holm Bursum, New Mexico's Republican senator and long-time colleague of Albert Fall, hoped to resolve the ongoing debate between Indians and whites by securing congressional endorsement for non-Indian ownership of the property in question. In early 1922, with the unequivocal support of Secretary Fall, he introduced the **Bursum Bill** to Congress. If enacted, the measure would legitimize the squatters' ownership. The bill required the Pueblos, not the squatters, to demonstrate rightful ownership. With little floor debate, the Bursum Bill moved easily and quietly through the Senate and was then presented to the House of Representatives for its consideration.

Indians and their allies across the Southwest rallied to challenge the bill. Antonio Luhan, a Taos Indian, traveled throughout New Mexico to raise awareness of the bill's threat to all Pueblos. Members of the Indian Rights Association and the Society of American Indians denounced the Bursum Bill as thievery and encouraged their members to actively support the Pueblos. In support, too, was the **American Indian Defense Association (AIDA)**, founded in 1923 specifically to halt passage of the proposed legislation. AIDA solicited and secured support from reformist groups across New Mexico and most visibly from the nationally recognized artist and literary communities located in Taos and Santa Fe, communities that included such prominent individuals as D.H. Lawrence, Zane Grey, Carl Sandburg, Edgar Lee Masters, and Mabel Dodge. These men and women commenced their own campaign on behalf of the Pueblos that featured personal appeals, their publication of articles in major magazines and newspapers, and the writing of letters to key political figures.

On November 3, approximately 120 Indian delegates from 19 Pueblo towns, along with a group of stalwart non-Indian allies, gathered at Santo Domingo Pueblo near Santa Fe and there, two days later, issued to Congress a statement of unanimous opposition to the Bursum Bill. Their letter pointed to the absence of Indian voices in the preparation of the legislation and the historic residency of Pueblo Indians on the land they were about to lose. They specifically insisted that the Treaty of Guadeloupe Hidalgo, which representatives of the U.S. government agreed to in 1848, required the United States to honor Mexican land grants to Native Americans. The federal government, the Indians insisted, must keep that pledge. Pueblos also appealed directly to the American people with the publication of the delegates' statement *An Appeal for Fair Play and the Preservation of Pueblo Life* in local and national newspapers. The document reminded non-Indians that the "Pueblo Indians have always been self-supporting" and "have lived in peace with our fellow Americans even while we have watched the gradual taking away of our lands and waters." Contrary to statements the OIA gave to the Senate, "we were never given the chance of having anything to say or do about this bill . . . We cannot understand why the Indian Office and the lawyers who are paid by the government to defend our interests, and the Secretary of the Interior, have deserted us and failed to protect us this time." The Bursum Bill, the statement read, "will deprive us of our happy life

13.4 Taos Pueblo, New Mexico

Source: Courtesy of Library of Congress Prints and Photographs Division, LC-USF34-002937-D

by taking away our lands and water and will destroy our Pueblo government and our customs which we have enjoyed for hundreds of years." Moreover, the bill would "take away our self-respect and make us dependent on the government." In closing, the delegates wrote, "The Pueblo, as is well-known, existed in a civilized condition before the white man came to America. We have kept our old customs and lived in harmony with each other and with our fellow Americans. This bill will destroy our common life and will rob us of everything which we hold dear—our lands, our customs, our traditions."

The *New York Times* published the Pueblo complaint in its entirety, and numerous editorials soon followed that expressly favored the Indians' argument, evidence of an emerging desire among non-Indians to protect Indian cultures and land from extinction. Non-Indian activists distributed the Pueblos' message by letter or by personal visit to civic groups across New Mexico and across the country, and they penned articles printed in popular magazines to garner broader popular attention and concern. Residents of the Taos artist colony issued their own petition in support of the Pueblos, and similar written protests quickly deluged congressmen and senators with letters in support of Indian title to their historic lands. Several Indians who had participated in the Santo Domingo meeting also traveled to Chicago and New York City where they personally presented their protest to large, enthusiastic audiences before continuing their journey to Washington, D.C., to testify before the public lands committee in the U.S. Senate. The campaign initiated by the Pueblos and supported by their non-Indian allies led to widespread popular support for their position. Faced with such a strong current of resistance from Indians and their non-Indian allies, Senator William E. Borah of Idaho recalled the Bursum Bill from the U.S. House, and in February 1923 the Senate commenced a review of the proposal and solicited alternative measures.

Commissioner Burke hoped to subvert the rising sympathy in Congress and in the general public for the Pueblo claim of legal title to the land by deflecting popular attention from the battle over property to an issue more fundamental and a value more emotionally charged—religion. In public statements, written diatribes, and personal conversations with prominent legislators, Burke openly connected Pueblo spiritual beliefs with unchristian values. Indian dances, he contended, included perverse and deviant behaviors that departed sharply from Western values. "The native dance still has enough evil tendencies to furnish a retarding influence" on Indian moral development and assimilation, he charged. Burke had his supporters. Members of the YMCA openly insisted on a ban of all "primitive dances and ceremonies," especially those which, by Christian standards, were considered "lascivious" and lewd.

Supporters of the criminalization of peyote and of Indians' access to alcohol added to the chorus. Burke recommended that government officers and well-intentioned reformers recognize the Indians' lingering reluctance to shed their immorality, and he instructed reservation superintendents to suppress their wards' "so-called religious ceremonies" and dances that contradict appropriate Christian behavior. He warned the Pueblos directly and explicitly to cease such unchristian behavior and ceremonies or face a legal order compelling them to do so.

The Council of All the New Mexico Pueblos took steps to counter Burke's charge. In May 1923, the group drafted a stinging reply to the commissioner. Titled "Declaration to the Pueblo Indians, to All Indians, and to the People of the United States," the document denounced Burke's assault on one of the most fundamental of American rights—freedom of religion. "Religious liberty," the statement read, "is threatened and is actually at this time being nullified" by the very government assigned to protect that right. "The religious beliefs and ceremonies and forms of prayer of each of our pueblos are as old as the world, and they are holy . . . Our religion is a true religion, and it is our way of life." The declaration not only defended Pueblo spirituality and practices but also condemned Burke's attack as purposely malicious and consciously misrepresentative of Pueblo ceremonies. Moreover, the Pueblo response rested on the very same issue then under debate nationally—the appropriate relationship between government and religion in civil society. Numerous state governments had already

READING HISTORY

Letter From Commissioner of Indian Affairs Charles Burke to All Indians, February 24, 1923

Commissioner of Indian Affairs Charles Burke was determined to create a climate that compelled Native Americans to acculturate with white society.

TO ALL INDIANS:

Not long ago I held a meeting of Superintendents, Missionaries and Indians, at which the feeling of those present was strong against Indian dances, as they are usually given, and against so much time as is often spent by the Indians in a display of their old customs at public gatherings held by the whites. From the views of this meeting and from other information I feel that something must be done to stop the neglect of stock, crops, gardens, and home interests caused by those dances or by celebrations, pow-wows, and gatherings of any kind that take the time of the Indians for many days.

Now, what I want you to think about very seriously is that you must first of all try to make your living, which you cannot do unless you work faithfully and take care of what comes from your labor, and go to dances or other meetings only when your homework will not suffer by it. I do not want to deprive you of decent amusements or occasional feast days, but you should not do evil or foolish things or take so much time for these occasions. No good comes from your "give-away" custom at dances and it should be stopped. It is not right to torture your bodies or to handle poisonous snakes in your ceremonies. All such extreme things are wrong and should be put aside and forgotten. You do yourselves and your families great injustice when at dances you give away money or other property, perhaps clothing, a cow, a horse or a team and wagon, and then after an absence of several days go home to find everything going to waste and yourselves with less to work with than you had before.

I could issue an order against these useless and harmful performances, but I would much rather have you give them up of your own free will and, therefore, I ask you now in this letter to do so. I urge you to come to an understanding and an agreement with your Superintendent to hold no gatherings in the months when the seed-time, cultivation of crops and the harvest need your attention and at other times to meet for only a short period and to have no drugs, intoxicants, or gambling, and no dancing that the Superintendent does not approve.

If at the end of one year the reports which I receive show that you are doing as requested, I shall be very glad for I will know that you are making progress in other and more important ways, but if the reports show that you reject this plea, then some other course will have to be taken.

With best wishes for your happiness and success, I am Sincerely yours,

Charles Burke

Commissioner

Source: National Archives, Southeast Region (Atlanta) (NRCA). ARC Identifier 279365.

Questions

1. What perspective of native cultures and of the Indian Office role does Burke's letter reveal?
2. What is Burke's tone in addressing American Indians?
3. How is it evidenced that the Indian Office will ultimately enforce its suggestion that Indians voluntarily relinquish traditional ceremonies and values?

banned teaching Darwinian evolution in public schools and added to their science curriculum compulsory instruction in biblical creationism; in so doing, government was promoting not only religion as science but also one religion over all others.

The general public gave little attention to the commissioner's strike against the Pueblos, and Burke's effort at diversion failed. Pueblos fiercely rebutted his assessment of Indian spirituality and drew the attention of politicians and others back to the original land issue. Between summer 1923 and summer 1924, several new bills were introduced into Congress that held some hope of an acceptable

13.5 Hopi Indians performing the Antelope Dance, 1921.
Source: Courtesy of Library of Congress Prints and Photographs Division, LC-USZ62-102175

resolution. Provisions found in several of these were ultimately refined and joined together to create the **Pueblo Lands Act,** passed into law on June 7, 1924. The act established a three-man board to hear all disputed land claims and it required the panel's unanimous vote in deciding all cases. Critical in determining legal title to the land was the Indian's proof of taxes paid continuously over the previous 20 years. Lands removed from Indian ownership, the act further stated, must be accompanied by financial remuneration at fair market value.

The Pueblo Lands Act ostensibly promised impartial hearings for claimants, but from its inception the new law favored non-Indian interests. The U.S. Attorney General, the Secretary of the Interior, and a third individual selected by the President of the United States comprised the three-man panel that the act required. As Indians expected, the board regularly awarded non-Indians rightful ownership of contested property, and Indian appeals in Federal District Court routinely failed.

Fall's Removal From Office

As Indians built opposition to the Bursum Bill and countered directly Commissioner Burke's irresponsible and ludicrous attacks on Indian religion, the infamous Teapot Dome Scandal ensnared Secretary Fall. The scandal centered on criminal relations between Harding administration officials and private oil companies. Fall was charged with bribery and the illegal manipulation of federal leases of two naval oil reserves. Sentenced to one year in prison, the repayment of money gained from his illegal transactions, and a $100,000 fine, Fall resigned his position in the Harding administration and spent the next year incarcerated in federal prison. Secretary Fall's disgraced exit from Washington certainly embarrassed the Republican Party, but the policies he trumpeted in matters of Indian affairs revealed a much darker, sinister intent. His harsh indictment of native cultures and his dogged effort to strip Indians of their lands was brazen, contrived, mean-spirited, narrow-minded, and increasingly at odds with America's emerging postwar values.

Fall's replacement was Secretary of the Interior Hubert Work. Work was a product of the American frontier experience, reared on the Colorado plains during and after the Civil War where the shifting winds of federal policy and Indian response often determined his life. Trained as a physician, he cared for white and Indian patients alike, founded Woodcroft Hospital in Pueblo, Colorado in 1896, and served as an army surgeon during the Great War. His medical career certainly rewarded him with the friendship and respect of many, but his demonstrated honesty and integrity won him the admiration of political figures statewide and nationally. Work accepted the position of Colorado Republican State Chair in 1912, and in 1920 he represented his state on the party's national committee. His personal friendship with the widely acclaimed humanitarian Herbert Hoover enhanced Work's standing politically and personally, and in 1922 the doctor was appointed to the position of U.S. Postmaster General. Secretary Fall's disgrace made it imperative that the Republican Party name a replacement that was beyond reproach. In 1923, Hubert Work was named Secretary of the Interior with the explicit duty of "cleaning house."

Changing Directions

When Americans thought about Indian assimilation, they imagined an inevitable process, the slow, steady working of historical forces that would bring Indians into mainstream society. The "vanishing Indian" myth was still pervasive; indeed, the notion had, perhaps, a greater hold on the American imagination in the immediate postwar era. Indian military service alongside white Americans in World War I was fresh in the minds of many Americans. Moreover, the "Indian wars" of the nineteenth century were more than a generation removed, and neither readers of dime novels nor audiences in crowded theaters watching Westerns on the silver screen recognized the stereotyped characters they saw and read about in contemporary Indians. The United States was an industrial giant, a nation whose wealth, rising standard of living, and increasingly numerous opportunities not only depended on the contribution of all Americans but also would have a transforming effect on all Americans. National progress would lead to the assimilation of native peoples, and it would do so without the harsh, coercive policies of men like Secretary Fall.

Not everyone saw things this way. There were many people, Indians and non-Indians alike, who believed that Secretary Fall's tactics were precursors of a sustained brutal war against Native Americans. Allied in this war against Indians were business interests and Christian zealots, the former motivated by greed and the latter by hostility to traditional Indian cultures. These opponents, Indians and sympathetic non-Indians, generally believed that Indians should determine their own future in America. Self-determination could only be realized if Native American voices could be heard and native peoples were empowered. Throughout the remaining years of the 1920s, a growing spirit of reform, of redress, of redirection, of humanity enveloped Indian issues.

The Emerging Path of Reform

Born during the battle that raged over the Bursum Bill, the American Indian Defense Association (AIDA) emerged quickly as a persistent critic of federal Indian policy. Founded by John Collier in May 1923, AIDA drew support from nationally acclaimed Progressives such as Harold Ickes, Hamlin Garland, and William Allen White. AIDA assigned full blame to the Office of Indian Affairs and the Department of the Interior for the failure of Indian policy. The organization accused the OIA of having only two principal goals: the utter destruction of a distinct Indian identity in America and the transfer of native lands into non-Indian hands. "The bureau leaves the family intact, or physically tears it apart," said John Collier, whichever better serves the interests of white society at a particular moment. "If Indian allotted land is coveted by white men, the bureau may, and does, lease it to them . . . Land belonging to the allotted Indian who dies is sold to white men" and his "heirs are made landless," he added. Collier and his associates condemned Commissioner Burke's attack on the Indians' "so-called religious ceremonies," insisting that it was unconstitutional for government to prohibit the acceptance or exercise of any religious belief. AIDA called for the protection of Indian cultures and tribal

SEEING HISTORY

The Vanishing American and Hollywood Film

Motion pictures of the immediate post-World War I decade continued to present farcical and stereotyped images of Native Americans, evidenced clearly in *Out West* (1918) and *Heap Big Chief* (1919). A few script-writers challenged those representations. William S. Hart required actors to learn and use the sign language of Plains Indians rather than gesture wildly on film. Others interwove authentic Indian languages into their scripts. The 1923 classic *Covered Wagon* employed 500 Plains Indians as extras, and many motion pictures of the era were filmed on location in Monument Valley or the southern plains.

An Indian perspective of postwar realities cracked slightly the wall of stereotyped presentations. *The Vanishing American* (1926) presented the theme of forced relocation and acculturation. *Redskin* (1929) highlighted the harsh conditions of boarding schools and the difficulty of "walking in two worlds."

Films of the 1920s pressed the notion that native peoples should and must acculturate to the ways and values of the dominant society. And, to be sure, stereotype, misunderstanding, and minimal concern for accuracy still clouded representations of Indian characters. Nonetheless, some films consciously attempted a slightly more developed portrayal of issues confronting Native Americans and in so doing opened the eyes of white audiences a bit wider to postwar realities.

13.6 The Vanishing American poster

Source: Archive PL/Alamy Stock Photo

Questions

1. What message does this movie poster offer?
2. How did posters such as this one suggest a new direction for native peoples?
3. Why were Hollywood films of the 1910s and 1920s pivotal in shaping popular opinion of Native Americans in the early twentieth century?

land holdings from further encroachment by the Indian Office and white interest groups, specifically demanding the termination of land allotments the Dawes Act established. AIDA further insisted on improved health and education services for Native Americans not as a prerequisite for assimilation but as something that all Indians, indeed all Americans, had a right to expect from their government. Revealing its ultimate objective, AIDA stood firm for tribal self-governance and the preservation of traditional cultural structures and values. The organization presented itself as the protector of Indians against compulsory Americanization, a position that placed it in direct opposition to the Indian Rights Association, the Office of Indian Affairs, and the course of American history.

AIDA was a national organization that focused on the rising national debate over Indian affairs. Other reform organizations, however, added regional issues and day-to-day practical matters to the agenda. One such organization was the Mission Indian Federation (MIF), founded in 1919 by Jonathan Tibbet, a non-Indian residing in Riverside, California. The MIF was a grassroots political union of southern California Indian reservations. Through collective action, its members hoped to compel basic change in federal Indian policy and to halt the abuses committed daily by Indian Affairs officers assigned to the Mission Indian Agency. Unlike AIDA, Native Americans held the MIF's leadership positions, and MIF was almost completely an Indian organization. Adam Castillo (Cahuilla) of Soboba Reservation served as MIF president for most of the organization's existence. Legal counsel, however, came from Tibbet and his colleagues. Dues paid by members financed the federation's lobbyists in Washington and Sacramento, sponsored traveling recruiters, funded legal action on behalf of the organization, and underwrote publication of the federation's magazine, *The Indian*.

Throughout the 1920s, the MIF supported the AIDA agenda and offered unwavering support to Indian initiatives and resistance efforts nationwide, such as the Pueblo land battle with Secretary Fall and Commissioner Burke. At its core, the MIF championed tribal sovereignty, or "home rule," opposed "unjust laws, rules and regulations," demanded the abolition of the Office of Indian Affairs, insisted on U.S. citizenship for all Native Americans, and called for a federal court of claims to provide compensation for tribal lands lost to the United States. On the local level, the MIF focused on water-related issues, allotment and land use, reservation boundaries, educational reform and opportunities, protection of treaty rights, and federal agents' abuse of California Indians.

The MIF's persistent criticism of the OIA and its activities on behalf of the state's Indian population garnered widespread support from Native Americans, but it also incurred the wrath of Commissioner Burke and Secretary Fall. Together they branded the MIF leaders and legal advisors, particularly Tibbet, as "Bolsheviks" and radicals, un-American, and unchristian. In the climate of the early 1920s, such charges carried potentially devastating repercussions. Indeed, in 1923 federal authorities indicted Tibbet in Los Angeles for disseminating communist ideology and promoting rebellion among Indians. He was not alone. More than 50 federation leaders and spokespeople were also arrested and accused of conspiracy against the United States.

The accusations divided Indian opinion in southern California. Most Indians recognized the charges for what they were—the OIA's purposeful effort to intimidate the MIF into a less critical posture and to silence those individuals most antagonistic to federal policies. The OIA's visible attacks on its opponents had a chilling effect among many Indians who worried that the federation's activism would lead to retaliation from Fall and Burke in the form of reductions in federal services for California Indians. The organization, however, stood firm in its defense of those who had been arrested, countered persuasively all accusations, placed correctly the accusation of bolshevism into the larger context of recent national and international hysteria, and called the OIA's effort nothing less than a tool to maintain Indian subjugation. MIF membership actually rose while Tibbet and the others awaited trial. All charges against those accused, however, were dropped before the cases reached court. Indian solidarity in California, public support for the federation from AIDA, the political

PROFILE

John Collier

Born in Atlanta, Georgia, in 1884 to a prosperous family, as a child John Collier enjoyed the luxuries afforded to the city's elite. That changed when charges of financial corruption were leveled against his father, charges that ultimately devastated the family fortune and social standing. Collier's father escaped sudden poverty and public humiliation through suicide; his mother, through a drug addiction that soon claimed her life. Orphaned as a teenager, the young Collier turned his back on high society and the pursuit of personal wealth. Instead, "he sought solace in long camping trips to the Appalachian mountains, where he found a sense of 'cosmic consciousness' in his own solitude and the beauty of the landscape."

Collier enrolled at Columbia University in 1902 and within two years moved to Paris, where he studied at the College de France. Perhaps because of the loss of his parents or his extensive study of philosophy and literature—or both—Collier came to distrust the modern industrial world. He particularly faulted America for its insistence on conformity, its acceptance of biological determinism, and its emphasis on the accumulation of wealth. He came to believe that as America industrialized, those who benefited most from industrialization sought to create a homogenous population of workers, a faceless, almost "inhuman urban America." Collier challenged this trend, arguing that the preservation of cultural traditions and identities in the United States was crucial if Americans were to retain their humanity in a modernizing world. His vision of cultural pluralism, formed early in his adult years, remained with him throughout the rest of his life.

In 1907, Collier secured employment with the People's Institute in New York City, working among immigrants to aid their transition into the social and economic fabric of America and privately encouraging their retention of cultural traditions. Over the ten years that followed, Collier spent his days in the city's immigrant communities working as an educator, a social worker, and a part-time journalist advancing the ideals of progressive reform. Collier left New York in September 1919, worn down by a decade of intense relief work. He relocated to Los Angeles and assumed a short-lived position as the city's Director of Adult Education. Collier's public support of cultural pluralism, along with his occasional positive remarks about the spirit of community that, he believed, existed in Russia, resulted in accusations that he was "un-American" and cost him his job in 1920. Unemployed, he traveled to Taos, New Mexico, to visit long-time friend Mabel Dodge who herself had earlier abandoned New York City for the artists' community in Taos.

Collier relished the natural beauty of north-central New Mexico, the spirit of the dozens of free thinkers who inhabited the colony, and conversations with his friend, but a visit to the nearby Pueblo village forever altered his life. There, Collier discovered what he had been seeking—a community, he believed, governed by peaceful cooperation, a prevalent concern for the common welfare, and a deep spiritual consciousness that made material possessions virtually insignificant. Cultural traditions and values persisted among the Pueblos despite Washington's efforts to "Americanize" the Indians. Taos Pueblo retained a fundamentally communal structure, prided itself on a rich heritage, and successfully resisted the ugly imprint of an industrializing, modernizing world. Collier described the community as a "Red Atlantis" and, to ensure its survival along with the survival of all native cultures in the United States, he committed himself to a lifelong crusade for Indian ethnic renewal in America.

turmoil that was then enveloping Secretary Fall, and the trend in American public opinion toward fair treatment of Native Americans combined to compel the OIA to abandon its attack.

It was, therefore, against a backdrop of intensified Indian activism that Secretary Work began his campaign for reform in Indian affairs. He hoped to repair the reputation of the Interior Department and the Indian Office by committing both to a program of bureau reorganization and to a sincere reform agenda. Success, he believed, was dependent on securing input from a diverse body of interested individuals and organizations. Toward that end, Secretary Work established the **Committee of One Hundred** to review federal Indian policy, survey the present quality of life for Native Americans nationally, and offer recommendations for change. Indians appointed to the committee included former SAI members Charles Eastman, Henry Roe Cloud, Sherman Coolidge, and Arthur Parker. Among the non-Indian participants were World War I icon General John J. Pershing, along with progressive reformers such as Will Carson Ryan and AIDA members William Allen White and John Collier. William Jennings Bryan was appointed to the committee for his respected standing as a legal and religious scholar, but his multiple campaigns to become president of the United States and his service as Secretary of State under Woodrow Wilson provided the committee with critical insight and important contacts in the halls of government.

The committee assembled in December and almost immediately realized that personal and philosophical divisions among them precluded any substantial alteration to federal policy. Bryan, for instance, expressed freely his opinion that Native American assimilation hinged on their Christianization. In his view, the redemption of the Indians could be attained only if he and others like him were given a free hand to "shove the Christian religion down the throat of every Indian." Parker, in contrast, restated his long-held position that "if the church and the state are sincere in their desire to bring moral and civic salvation to the American Indian, each must manfully face the conditions that has made the red man a problem." Those conditions, he continued, were the product of federal policies and the interference of hypocritical religious zealots in Indian life. Conflicting opinions also surfaced regarding congressional extension of citizenship to all American Indians, the direction of reservation educational and health care programs, and the underlying causes of failure in Indian affairs.

13.7 Secretary of the Interior Hubert Work and Commissioner of Indian Affairs Charles Burke meet with Osage Chiefs Red Eagle and Bacon Rind.

Source: Courtesy of Library of Congress Prints and Photographs Division, LC-USZ62-103938

Given the disparate perspectives among committee members, the best that could be accomplished was a statement that addressed general, common aims. The Committee of One Hundred presented its recommendations to Secretary Work in a document titled *The Indian Problem* (1924). It called for a fundamental overhaul of Indian educational programs that included the movement of more Indian children into state-funded public schools, significant alteration to boarding school curricula, access to government-funded college scholarships, and the construction of additional reservation-based schools. Committee members also chastised the OIA's failure to provide adequate health care on reservations and encouraged

Washington to commence immediately a program of health instruction among Native Americans. The committee further called for Washington's settlement of tribal claims and recommended that Pueblo title to their land be guaranteed.

The report provided little specificity regarding the implementation of committee recommendations, but as a document it signaled a new level of concern among Native Americans and non-Indians alike for the Indians' general welfare, a genuine concern that extended beyond the assimilationist goal of previous federal policy. Implied was the committees' acknowledgment of a destructive impact of federal policy over the previous two decades. More importantly, the report heightened interest in the state of Indian affairs among political leaders and encouraged reformers to continue their efforts.

The Society of American Indians held its final meeting in December 1923. The deep divisions within the SAI created by issues such as the Native American Church, peyote use, and citizenship rendered the organization ineffective as a voice for Indian policy reform. Following the SAI's collapse, Zitkala-Sa (Gertrude Bonnin) soon began traveling the lecture circuit, speaking before non-Indian reform-minded groups and tribal communities about issues she argued were critical to Native Americans. She argued that only a pan-Indian organization, created and led by Native Americans, could effectively advance the interests of native peoples. With this in mind, in 1926 Bonnin and a few close advisors founded the **National Council of American Indians** (NCAI), and she served as its president until her death in 1938.

The NCAI pressed many positions the SAI earlier trumpeted, notably pursuit of assimilation with mainstream society, but it also emphasized pride in and respect for one's Indian heritage and identity. Bonnin also encouraged Indians to accept citizenship, register to vote where permitted, and once armed with the ballot to build a powerful Indian voting bloc in state elections.

The NCAI gained a national following, but it accomplished little. Most Indians found access to the ballot elusive. NCAI lobbyists in Washington rarely carried the personal clout or financial support needed to win political influence. And, in its annual meetings the NCAI seldom issued direct challenges to federal authority, preferring instead to let well-reasoned public statements and letter-writing initiatives convince policymakers of the correctness of the organization's arguments. This approach stood in sharp contrast to the relentless public attacks AIDA launched against the OIA, attacks intended to bring the power of public opinion to bear on the struggle for Indian rights.

Native Americans working independently of the NCAI often garnered better and more practical results. Secretary Falls's rabid attack on Indian religious ceremonies piqued the attention of non-Indian society and generated among white Americans greater interest in native peoples' traditions and cultures. Traveling groups of Indian performers capitalized on this newfound curiosity. They journeyed to distant cities and there, in traditional attire, performed dances that spanned generations, played the music of their elders, exhibited tribal handicrafts, and generally demonstrated to non-Indian audiences the vitality, richness, and depth of Native American cultures. More importantly, many Native Americans openly defied

13.8 Shoshone Indians perform the Sun Dance on the Fort Hall Reservation, c. 1925.

Source: National Archives and Records Administration, 298649

federal prohibitions on certain spiritual ceremonies. The federal government banned the Plains Indians' Sun Dance in 1904, but most tribal groups resisted Washington's edict and continued their ceremonies in less traveled areas of their reservations.

Citizenship Revisited

Secretary Fall's legacy, the founding of AIDA, Secretary Work's initiative, and the tide of public opinion encouraged Congress once more to broach the issue of blanket U.S. citizenship for Native Americans. By 1920, roughly 125,000 Indians, or one-third of the total Indian population, did not hold U.S. citizenship. Some in Congress argued that citizenship would bring constitutional protections native peoples did not presently enjoy, protections that might lead to better relations between Indians and the federal government. Many Indians and non-Indians agreed but also renewed their argument that citizenship was the only moral and decent step to take on behalf of Native Americans. They saw in citizenship and assimilation not the extermination of native peoples' identity but instead the preservation of Indian rights. There were those, too, who championed citizenship as a practical method for ending federal government guardianship over Native Americans and the financial obligation it required Washington to maintain. This argument worried many passionate reformers who believed that a large number of Native Americans were still not prepared for "emancipation" and would only fall victim to further exploitation and manipulation by scandalous businessmen, land speculators, and even government officials without that guardianship. These individuals would accept blanket citizenship only if the federal government retained supervision over native peoples. Some qualified the extension of citizenship to those considered competent. Still others saw the move as a means to ultimately eliminate the OIA and, in so doing, curtail the power vested in the Department of Interior.

Indians were divided on the issue. Citizenship was the Indian Rights Association's (IRA) capstone objective, the final requirement for full integration of Native Americans into mainstream society. The IRA's position on this issue was similar to that of the Society of American Indians; to survive, the Indian "must become as other men, a contributing, self-sustaining member of society." "No nation can afford to permit any . . . body of people within it to exist in a condition at variance with the ideals of that nation," contended the SAI. The Indian must "accustom himself to the culture that engulfs him."

Numerous Indians still preferred their longstanding treaties with Washington over citizenship. Treaties stated explicitly the rights of native peoples and the limits of federal authority. Members of the Six Nations, or Iroquois Confederacy, flooded the desks of representatives and senators with letters opposing blanket citizenship. Clinton Rickard (Tuscarora) made perhaps the most convincing argument. Citizenship imposed on the Iroquois would constitute a "violation of our sovereignty," sovereignty granted by treaty with the United States in 1794 and consistently respected and honored by Congress over the previous 130 years. "We had our own citizenship . . . Our citizenship was in our own nations," said Rickard. How could the people of one sovereign nation be forced to become citizens of a "foreign nation?" he asked. Equal concern was vented among other Indian groups. "If all the Creeks and Seminoles were to become citizens [of the United States], the Creek Nation and Seminole Nation would cease to exist." At stake was tribal sovereignty and Indian identity.

On June 2, 1924, Congress passed into law the Indian Citizenship Act, granting citizenship standing to all non-citizen Indians born within the territorial boundary of the United States. Acknowledging Indian concerns such as those Rickard expressed, the new law permitted continued citizenship in tribal societies and did not negate the individual's right to tribal property. Rickard nonetheless drafted a short but terse response on behalf of the Iroquois Confederacy "respectfully declining United States citizenship" and repudiating the act as one "passed without their [the Indians'] consent."

TIMELINE 13.1 CONGRESSIONAL LEGISLATION AND AMERICAN INDIAN CITIZENSHIP

Date	Event	
1887	Dawes General Allotment Act	Native Americans who accept land allotments and who reject tribal affiliation will be citizens of the United States
1888	"Rights of Indian Women Marrying White Men" Act	Native American women who marry white men will receive U.S. citizenship, much like the process today for foreign nationals
1890	Indian Naturalization Act	Native Americans may apply for and, if approved, receive U.S. citizenship, the same process applied to immigrants seeking American citizenship
1901	Citizenship and Oklahoma Territory	Indians residing in the former Indian Territory (now Oklahoma) are U.S. citizens
1919	American Indian Citizenship Act	Native American veterans of World War I are allowed to apply for and receive citizenship
1924	Indian Citizenship Act	All Indians born within the territorial boundary of the United States are citizens of the United States

Citizenship produced little immediate or visible change. State governments determined voter qualifications, and as late as 1938 seven states still denied Native Americans access to the ballot box. But, as Clinton Rickard noted, "there was no great rush among my people to go out and vote in the white man's election."

The Meriam Report

AIDA's ongoing war with the OIA along with the Committee of One Hundred's report delivered to Secretary Work contributed to a major shift in the approach to Indian affairs the Department of Interior took, and to long-term consequences. In 1926, Secretary Work commissioned the Institute of Government Research (known today as the Brookings Institute) to empanel a team of experts to investigate reservation living conditions and the status of Native American life in the United States. The Institute's Lewis Meriam, a trained social scientist, assumed command of the team early the following year. Meriam and his collection of experts in numerous fields toured 95 reservations in 1927 and interviewed hundreds of individual Indians. Meriam's team compiled its findings and on February 21, 1928, presented Secretary Work an 847-page report titled *The Problem of Indian Administration*. More commonly referred to as the **Meriam Report**, the lengthy document was a penetrating indictment of OIA policies and governance over Indian affairs to date, policies and practices that collectively contributed to the abysmal quality of life of most American Indians.

The Meriam Report exposed not a dysfunctional health service for Native Americans but a health service that was nearly non-existent. Indians confronted a tuberculosis mortality rate of 26 percent—a rate seven times greater than that suffered by the general white population. Trachoma, a disease that causes blindness, claimed 18–21 percent of all Native Americans. Infant death added to the dismal picture; fully 26 percent of all Indian deaths occurred among children under one year of age, and 37 percent of all deaths occurred by age three, in contrast to a 16 percent rate for the general population. Venereal diseases, typhoid, pneumonia, and dysentery all occurred with greater frequency among the Indian population than among non-Indians. Team members pointed to poorly prepared or preserved foods, improper diet, inadequate personal hygiene, little community sanitation, and widespread ignorance of preventative medicine as causative agents for the outrageously high infection and mortality figures.

The report also described the Indian Health Service (IHS) as incapable of addressing effectively reservation needs. The congressional appropriation for the IHS totaled a pitifully low $756,000 from which only $200,000 was earmarked for medical field work. The IHS employed few physicians and nurses, and most of these were insufficiently trained, underpaid, and typically unconcerned. Meriam's medical experts personally witnessed reservation physicians checking only one eye for signs of trachoma rather than scanning both eyes. Complained one team member, children were "rushed through so rapidly that it is impossible to make careful diagnoses." Tuberculosis was nearly impossible to detect, noted investigators, as reservations rarely had access to chest x-ray equipment. Also contributing to the poor health of the Indian population were boarding schools that served as breeding grounds for disease and poor health—hot water was seldom available, soiled towels were routinely shared among students, and bathrooms rarely had soap. Only two toilets served 80 girls at one school. Cooks often failed to wash before preparing student meals and typically served the food on unclean plates. The $11 daily ration for food seldom included milk or fresh vegetables. "Everything in the school kitchen was covered with flies," raged one surveyor, and children were frequently given spoiled food (see Table 13.2).

Table 13.2 Findings of the Meriam Investigation: Death Rates, Native Americans and General Population From *The Problem of Indian Administration, 1928*

Deaths of Children, Age Three and Younger		
Total	**Native American**	**General Population**
	28.3%	16.2%
Highest Rates:		
Nevada	39.2	
Arizona	38.9	
Idaho	35.8	
Utah	35.8	
Colorado	32.8	
Nebraska	32.4	
Death Rate from Tuberculosis		
Total	**Native American**	**General Population**
	6.3%	0.87%
Death Rate per 1,000, All Causes and All Ages		
Total	**Native American**	**General Population**
	25.6	11.8

Source: From *The Problem of Indian Administration* (Washington: Government Printing Office, 1928).

READING HISTORY

From *The Problem of Indian Administration,* or Meriam Report, 1928

This report roundly condemned federal Indian policies over the previous 150 years that, at best, allowed for the fundamental deterioration of native peoples' communities and at worst was intended to destroy tribal communities from within. It opened with a powerful summation of general observations based on Meriam team visits to reservations spread across the North American continent.

An overwhelming majority of the Indians are poor, even extremely poor, and they are not adjusted to the economic and social system of the dominant white civilization.

The poverty of the Indians and their lack of adjustment to the dominant economic and social systems produce the vicious circle ordinarily found among any people under such circumstances. Because of interrelationships, causes cannot be differentiated from effects. The only course is to state briefly the conditions found that are part of this vicious circle of poverty and maladjustment . . .

Living Conditions. The prevailing living conditions among the majority of the Indians are conducive to the development and spread of disease. With comparatively few exceptions the diet of Indians is bad. It is generally insufficient in quantity, lacking in variety and poorly prepared. The two great preventive elements in diet, milk, and fruits and green vegetables, are notably absent. Most tribes use fruits and vegetables in season, but even then the supply is ordinarily insufficient. The use of milk is rare, and it is generally not available even for infants. Babies, when weaned, are ordinarily put on substantially the same diet as older children and adults, a diet consisting mainly of meats and starches.

The housing conditions are likewise conducive to bad health. Both in the primitive dwellings and in the majority of more or less permanent homes which in some cases have replaced them, there is great overcrowding, so that all members of the family are exposed to any disease that develops, and it is virtually impossible in any way even partially to isolate a person suffering from a communicable disease . . . Although many of them still have very primitive arrangements for cooking and heating, the use of modern cook stoves and utensils is far more general than the use of beds, and the use of beds in turn is far more common than the use of any kind of easily washable bed covering.

Sanitary facilities are generally lacking . . . Even privies are exceptional. Water is ordinarily carried considerable distances from natural springs or streams, or occasionally from wells . . .

Economic Conditions. The income of the typical Indian family is low and the earned income extremely low . . . He [the Indian] generally ekes out an existence through unearned income from leases of his land, the sale of land, per capita payments from tribal funds, or in exceptional cases through rations given him by the government . . . What little they secure from their own efforts or from other sources is rarely effectively used.

The main occupations . . . are some outdoor work, mostly of an agricultural nature, but the number of real farmers is comparatively small. A considerable proportion engage more or less casually in unskilled labor . . .

In justice to the Indians it should be said that many of them are living on lands from which a trained and experienced white man could scarcely wrest a reasonable living . . . Frequently the better sections of the land originally set apart for Indians have fallen into the hands of the whites, and the Indians retreated to the poorer lands remote from markets . . .

Suffering and Discontent. Some people assert that the Indians prefer to live as they do; that they are happier in their idleness and irresponsibility. The question may be raised whether these persons do not mistake for happiness and content an almost oriental fatalism and resignation. The survey staff found ... too much evidence of real suffering and discontent to subscribe to the belief that the Indians are reasonably satisfied with their condition.

Source: "General Summary of Findings," *The Problem of Indian Administration* (Washington: Government Printing Office, 1928), pp. 3–7.

Questions

1. How would you describe the tone of the report's introductory observations?
2. Why did the authors of the report immediately and emphatically present a negative assessment of Indian affairs?
3. How does this introductory chapter criticize not only those who created Indian policy but also the general population?
4. What do these initial points say specifically about federal policy over the previous 50 years?
5. Based on this excerpt, what would a reader expect to be the course of federal Indian policy over the decade that followed publication of *The Problem of Indian Administration?*

Investigators denounced an educational system that retarded rather than expanded Indian opportunities. Native American illiteracy averaged 36 percent nationally, with some individual reservations peaking at 67 percent. This stood in sharp contrast with the 6 percent illiteracy rate for the general population in the United States. Unqualified teachers and administrators often staffed both reservation schools and off-reservation boarding schools and openly committed themselves more to their own job security, to rigid programs that compelled the Indians' acculturation to white norms, and to a military-style disciplinary system with brutal punishment than to the true pursuit of student learning. At virtually every school surveyed, the curriculum appeared antiquated, irrelevant to student experiences and cultural background, of little use in securing gainful employment in urban settings, and utterly useless for those who remained on reservations. Moreover, students who completed their academic study at off-reservation boarding schools were generally unprepared to assimilate with mainstream society, having been trained under a classical educational curriculum.

The team understood clearly that the pathetic state of Indian health and the grossly inadequate system for Indian education exacerbated and perpetuated the miserable state of tribal economics. Eighty-four percent of all adult Indians lived on less than $200 annually. Child laborers under the age of 14 earned nine to 15 cents daily. In contrast, white Americans earned an average of $2,200 yearly for a family of four. Part of the problem lay with the Indians' lack of job skills required for off-reservation employment, an obvious failing of the current educational system and OIA programs. The team also acknowledged the Indians' hesitancy to leave reservations for work in nearby cities, a reticence spawned by the very real discrimination they confronted in the general society and by their own deep desire to retain connections with their own reservation families. Meriam's investigators further noted that nearly 50 percent of all Indians were landless and the quality of land that remained under their control was incapable of sustaining agriculture or ranching. The report blasted the policy of allotment and condemned it as central to the hideous state of Indian affairs.

The Meriam Report was "the most searching study of Indian administration ever undertaken," said Charlotte Walkup, an assistant in the Department of Interior. It "laid out, in cold blood and in a very terrifying way, what the problems were that needed to be solved." *The Problem of Indian Administration* shocked Secretary Work and Indian Office administrators, stunned those who presumed American Indians were progressing toward assimilation with white society, and shattered the complacency of many members of Congress.

The report insisted that federal appropriations be raised substantially, particularly for Indian health and education programs. It called for the abandonment of the allotment system and the protection of lands presently owned by Native Americans, a government-backed loan fund for tribal and individual business development, an education system relevant to Indian needs and circumstances, and a complete overhaul in Native American health care services. "The Meriam report," wrote one historian, "was a strange hybrid, lurching uneasily between the assimilationist views of old-style reform" and a radically new vision of cultural revitalization sounded by a rising chorus of OIA critics. The report reiterated that "the fundamental requirement of Indian policy was to enable Native Americans to be 'absorbed into the prevailing civilization.' . . . On the other [hand], it urged 'more understanding of and sympathy for the Indian point of view.'"

In November 1928, American voters sent Herbert Hoover, a Republican, to the White House. Hoover garnered widespread respect for his spirited work during World War I with the War Food Program, a program designed not only to feed American soldiers and civilians but also to provide for the large European refugee population and for the citizens of those nations devastated by war. It seemed natural to many within the United States that Hoover's humanitarianism would carry over to the White House and the administration he would soon build in Washington. Secretary Work's own service in Hoover's election hinted that the new president would address reform in Indian affairs; even vocal critics of federal Indian policy such as John Collier believed Hoover to be a suitable choice for the presidency.

Conclusion

Indian resistance to the course of federal Indian policy and to the corruption that existed throughout the Department of Interior rose substantially between the Great War and Herbert Hoover's election as president, a resistance spawned in large measure by Secretary of the Interior Albert Fall's unmasked grab for Native American lands and the scathing attack he and OIA commissioner Charles Burke together made against Indian religion and religious ceremonies. Moreover, Fall's manipulation of reports detailing tribal debate, his profiteering from the sale of tribal lands, and his willingness to twist federal and state law to suit his own desires combined generated a public outcry by native peoples and by their non-Indian supporters. True, division still remained among American Indians concerning the pace and scope of assimilation projects, the benefits of U.S. citizenship for native peoples, the relationship of tribal government to federal authority, and the ultimate disposition of tribal and personally held lands. But, in that decade, a clear desire emerged among Indians and non-Indians to achieve a fuller understanding of tribal living conditions and to plot a new course for federal Indian policy.

Review Questions

1. What tactics did non-Indians and the Office of Indian Affairs employ to remove additional property from tribal control in the decade following America's entry into World War I?
2. In what ways were the American Indian Defense Association and the Mission Indian Federation similar? How were they different?

3. What were the expected benefits of U.S. citizenship for Native Americans? Why did many Indians openly oppose blanket citizenship or, before 1924, not pursue the attainment of citizenship?

4. How might one argue that the decade following World War I marked a turning point in the relationship between Native Americans and the federal government and between Native Americans and the general American population?

Recommended Readings

Adams, David W. *Education for Extinction: American Indians and the Boarding School Experience, 1875–1928* (Lawrence: University Press of Kansas, 1997). A full account of the Indian boarding school system that was intended to supplant Native American culture with "white civilization," in so doing driving native cultures into extinction.

Britten, Thomas. *American Indians in World War I: At War and at Home* (Albuquerque: University of New Mexico Press, 1997). A thorough study of Native American participation in the Great War with special focus on their battlefield experiences, racial and cultural stereotypes, and the imprint of military service on native peoples.

Grann, David. *Killers of the Flower Moon: The Osage Murders and the Birth of the FBI* (New York: Doubleday, 2017). Superbly researched and detailed presentation of the Osage head right murders in Oklahoma.

Hertzberg, Hazel. *The Search for an American Indian Identity: Modern Pan-Indian Movements* (Syracuse, NY: Syracuse University Press, 1982). An examination of Native American understanding of self in the context of national identity during the Progressive Era.

Meriam, Lewis, et al. *The Problem of Indian Administration* (Baltimore: Johns Hopkins University Press, 1928). The seminal investigation of Native American reservation conditions in the late 1920s that ultimately gave rise to the Indian New Deal of the 1930s.

Native American History Online

General Sites

The Problem of Indian Administration. www.eric.ed.gov/?id=ED087573 and www.narf.org/nill/documents/merriam/b_meriam_letter.pdf These sites provide the full text of the government report The Problem of Indian Administration, more commonly referred to as the Meriam Report.

National Indian Law Library. www.narf.org/nill This site features the legal parameters, brief history, and Indian responses to the acquisition of U.S. citizenship by Native Americans.

Historic Sites

Taos Pueblo, Taos, New Mexico. www.taospueblo.com For more than 1,000 years, Native Americans have maintained an active, vibrant community at Taos, New Mexico. Indeed, it is the only "living Native American community" listed as a World Heritage Site by the United Nations Educational, Scientific, and Cultural Organization and identified as a National Historical Landmark. In the 1920s, Taos emerged as an artists' and writers' colony, serving as temporary home to Mabel Dodge, D.H. Lawrence, and Native American reform activist John Collier. Numerous artists continue to reside in the village and display their work for visitors, and collections of early twentieth-century artists who featured American Indian culture are on permanent exhibit.

Will Rogers Memorial Museum, Claremore, Oklahoma. www.Willrogers.com, www.quotationspage.com/quotes/Will_Rogers and https://www.imdb.com/name/nm0737259/ These sites highlight the "cowboy philosopher's" more popular quotations and his contribution to the motion pictures industry.

CHAPTER

14

Indians employed on the construction of the Hoover Dam as high-scalers, October, 1932. In this group there are six Apaches, one Yaqui, one Crow, and one Navajo.

Source: National Archives and Records Administration, 293745

The Great Depression, 1929–1940

THE CCC PROJECT AT BANDELIER NATIONAL PARK NEAR SANTA FE, NEW MEXICO

NATIVE AMERICANS AND THE EARLY YEARS OF THE GREAT DEPRESSION

Hard Times

Reform Efforts in the Hoover Administration

Health Care and Education

A Brighter Prospect for Change

THE INDIAN NEW DEAL

Native Americans and New Deal Reform

The Public Works of Art Project

The Civilian Conservation Corps—Indian Division

Navajo Stock Reduction

Indian Education

A NEW DIRECTION IN FEDERAL INDIAN POLICY

The Indian Reorganization Act

Resistance to the IRA

An Assessment of the Indian New Deal

The CCC Project at Bandelier National Park Near Santa Fe, New Mexico

The racket of sledgehammers, generators, power saws, and trucks echoed throughout the canyon and across the countryside, a wrenching sound dwarfed occasionally by dynamite explosions that ripped away rock walls. Although difficult for one to imagine, given the mounds of cliff rubble, felled trees, and scarred earth, the construction crews so feverishly at work were fashioning a visitors' park that not only put thousands of unemployed men to work but also would one day draw guests to beautiful Frijoles Canyon where visitors could catch a glimpse of the ancient culture that long ago dwelled in the area.

Pueblo ancestors migrated into and across much of New Mexico nearly 10,000 years ago, tracking animals and living off available plants. Around 1150 CE, they settled into Frijoles Canyon, living and farming there for the next 400 years. For reasons that remain unclear, they abandoned the canyon around 1550 CE and spread out along the length of the Rio Grande, establishing Pueblo communities that still exist today. President Woodrow Wilson designated the canyon and surrounding lands a national park in 1916, but the land now known as Bandelier National Park received no substantive improvements to make it accessible to the general public until 1933. That summer, as part of President Franklin Delano Roosevelt's (FDR) New Deal, a program to combat the Great Depression, Civilian Conservation Corps (CCC) workers began the arduous project of improving the park. The CCC would create the required infrastructure and facilities to attract visitors to the park and at the same time, following the lead of the reform-minded Office of Indian Affairs, preserve and display the Pueblo heritage of the region.

The CCC first laid a two-lane road through Bandelier, running from the Santa Fe highway through the park into Frijoles Canyon. Hundreds of men worked in the CCC camp over the following seven years, establishing a park that still lures tourists, artists, and scholars. The project relied heavily on local Indian enrollees, and by 1940 workers had constructed a lodge and a series of cabins to house park guests, a dining hall, craft shops, administrative offices, a guard station, and additional buildings. CCC craftsmen produced all necessary

CHRONOLOGY

1929	Herbert Hoover is inaugurated
	Charles J. Rhoads appointed the new Commissioner of Indian Affairs
	Stock market "crashes," officially beginning the Great Depression
1930	Congress allocates $1.4 million in emergency funds to the Office of Indian Affairs
1931	Indian Health Service and Indian Education Service agencies initiate emergency relief projects on reservations
1933	Franklin Delano Roosevelt is inaugurated
	John Collier confirmed as Commissioner of Indian Affairs
	Commissioner Collier crafts a redirection in federal Indian policy, presented to Congress as the Wheeler-Howard Bill
	Congress appropriates $28 million to the Office of Indian Affairs, twice the 1928 funding level
	The Civilian Conservation Corps—Indian Division is founded
	The Office of Indian Affairs begins compulsory stock reduction on the Navajo Reservation
1934	Congress passes the Indian Reorganization Act (IRA)
	The American Indian Federation (AIF) is founded to challenge the IRA
	Congress passes the Johnson-O'Malley Act
1935	The Indian Arts and Crafts Board is founded
	Roosevelt creates the Works Progress Administration, employing thousands of Native Americans in public works projects
	Henry Roe Cloud is the first Native American appointed as Superintendent of Haskell Institute
1937	The American Indian Federation challenges the Indian Reorganization Act

furniture, and artists hired by another New Deal agency, the Works Progress Administration (WPA), decorated the lodge, guest cabins, and administrative buildings with original artwork. Hiking trails and roads for touring motorists stretched through the canyon and along its rim, and CCC crews landscaped the visitors' grounds. Historical archaeologists and cultural anthropologists joined efforts to uncover, re-create, and study the canyon's early native community, a project that long outlived the CCC. Artists, likewise, continued visiting the park and with pen, watercolor, and camera captured the beauty, the serenity, and the early Native American culture tied to Bandelier.

The project at Bandelier manifested the spirit of the Indian New Deal in the 1930s, a spirit pressed by progressive reformers who understood and appreciated the value of Indian cultures and history as well as the worth of a pluralistic society. As Commissioner of Indian Affairs, John Collier hoped to reverse federal Indian policy by revitalizing traditional Native American cultures, rebuilding and protecting tribal communities, ending the allotment system, and elevating substantially the quality of reservation life. He and his progressive allies—Indian and non-Indian alike—also wanted to preserve the Indian heritage in America, a fundamental goal of the Bandelier project. The CCC's efforts at Bandelier represented that energy and that desire for renewal, and it embraced Native Americans in its labor force, as consultants on Indian history and culture, and as project supervisors and interpreters. The Indian New Deal manifested in many ways the vision and the hope of Indians and non-Indians alike that a new day in Indian affairs was dawning.

KEY QUESTIONS

1. Why was genuine reform pursued so much more aggressively during the Hoover administration years than in preceding eras?
2. To what extent was John Collier's Indian New Deal a continuation of reform work his immediate predecessor in the Indian Office initiated?
3. What arguments did Native Americans make for or against the IRA?

Native Americans and the Early Years of the Great Depression

In 1929, the American stock market collapsed. However, this catastrophic event did not cause the Great Depression that followed. The Depression was the result of numerous and significant underlying weaknesses in the American and global economies of the 1920s. The market crash did, however, mark the beginning of a decade of hard times. America slipped deeper into an economic abyss each of the three years following the stock market collapse. By 1932, the manufacturing sector produced a mere 54 percent of its 1929 output, the automobile industry operated at 20 percent capacity, and America's steel plants produced a measly 12 percent of its pre-Depression output. Private construction investments between 1929 and 1932 tumbled from $6.6 billion to a paltry $1.3 billion, and investments in business dropped 35 percent in 1931 and another 88 percent the next year. More than 9,000 banks closed their doors in the first three years of the Depression, costing depositors their life savings. Farm income continued its decade-long slide, falling to $12 billion in 1929 and crumbling to $5 billion in 1932.

The wreckage of the nation's economy produced millions of victims and seriously threatened America's capitalist system. Unemployment nationally reached 25 percent in 1932, with 12 million Americans out of work.

More than 800,000 residents of New York City were jobless, Chicago's unemployed numbered 624,000, and Detroit tallied 223,000 unable to find work. Roughly one-third of all employed persons nationally kept their jobs only by accepting part-time hours and lower wages. Banks issued foreclosure notices and evicted hundreds of thousands of families from their homes between 1929 and 1932, placing 273,000 families among the home-less ranks in 1932 alone. Bread lines and soup lines funded by some municipal governments and by charitable groups barely kept starvation at bay. Hopelessness seemed pervasive by the summer of 1932.

The Great Depression visibly and most immediately ravaged urban America, but it also tore a path through farmlands and ranchlands from coast to coast. Despite the unparalleled depth of the economic crisis, Native Americans suffered far less than non-Indians. As the Meriam Report clearly revealed, Indians were already the poorest of Americans and on the eve of the Great Depression endured the most desperate living conditions nationally. "We're all on the same level now," noted one Sioux. "The white man is in the same shape we are."

Hard Times

Joblessness, homelessness, and increasing hopelessness drove nearly half of the 33,000 urbanized Indians back to their former reservations in search of some means of support—shelter, food, family, or perhaps financial or material aid from the government. They found living conditions no better on the reservations. Migrant workers also straggled home, placing additional demands on the limited reservation resources. In 1930, as the Depression worsened, only 524 Indians resided in the major urban centers included in California's Sacramento Indian Agency jurisdiction (see Map 14.1 and Table 14.1). Opportunities for day labor diminished, the meager profits typically secured from the sale of arts and crafts nearly evaporated as tourism abruptly collapsed, and income from land leases suffered substantial decline. Compounding their deteriorating circumstances, 50 per-cent of all Native Americans remained landless in 1930. Without property, simply feeding the reservation pop-ulation became increasingly problematic. Those with land faced their own hardships. Crop prices and market values for cattle and sheep plummeted to record lows, and tribal revenue from timber harvests and oil drilling spiraled downward. Farm production was further undermined by a series of natural disasters—severe blizzards, springtime floods, oppressive summer heat, drought, and dust storms. Indian income tumbled below the abys-mally low level cited in the Meriam Report of 1928. Among the Navajos, annual per capita income stood at $135 in the early 1930s while annual per capita income for residents of the Sioux reservations collectively fell to a miserable $67. As low as that was, there were Indians who were still poorer. The annual per capita income of South Carolina's Catawba Indians plummeted to $28, and Carson Reservation Indians in Nevada actually earned half that amount.

Reservations turned desperately to state and local governments for aid, but the sad reality was that govern-ment at all levels faced a severe shortfall in revenue and channeled their modest resources to the heavily popu-lated urban centers. Clinton Rickard (Tuscarora) condemned what he believed to be New York State's disregard for relief to tribes of the Iroquois Confederacy. "After all the lobbying in Congress the New York state officials had done in the past years to obtain complete jurisdiction over the Indians, the Albany government now showed itself none too eager to provide assistance to Indians in time of crisis," he complained. The Confeder-acy had long cherished its "nation within a nation" status granted by the federal government in the Treaty of Canadaigua in 1794, and Rickard was not suggesting the dismantling of confederacy nationhood or the reduc-tion of tribal sovereignty in return for state aid. Instead, he envisioned aid in simple human, compassionate terms, much like one nation offers support to another in a period of crisis. "All we asked [for] was equality of opportunity with whites and other[s] in getting useful jobs so that we could support ourselves," he said. Native Americans historically aided and comforted white Americans in desperate times, he said. "When the white men first came to this continent, they were few, weak, and feeble. . . . We gave them land to plant corn on for

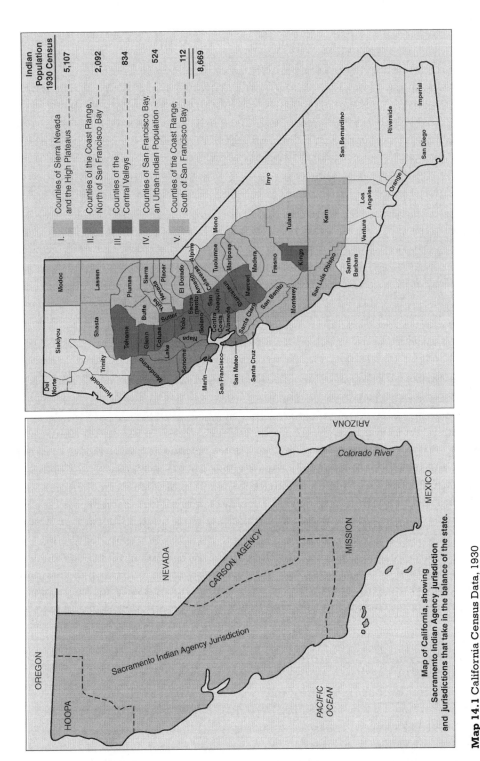

Map 14.1 California Census Data, 1930

As early as 1930, as the economic crisis deteriorated nationwide, the native population of California's Sacramento Indian Agency found urban employment almost impossible to acquire or retain, forcing most to abandon the previously lucrative San Francisco Bay region for their previous homes in more rural and less economically beneficial sections of the agency's jurisdiction, evidenced in the map. In that year, the native population in San Francisco specifically tumbled to a mere 151 residents, 37 in Berkeley, and 97 in Oakland.

Table 14.1 Indians of the Sacramento Jurisdiction in Cities of 25,000 or More, 1930 Federal Census

City	Total Population	Indian Population
Alameda	35,033	1
Bakersfield	26,015	12
Berkeley	82,109	37
Fresno	52,513	10
Oakland	284,063	97
Sacramento	93,750	85
San Francisco	634,394	151
San Jose	57,651	7
Stockton	47,963	53
	1,313,491	453

Source: Annual Report of the Superintendent, Sacramento Indian Agency, California, for the Fiscal Years 1936 and 1937, by Roy Nash, 1936–37. National Archives and Records Administration, Record Group 75: Records of the Bureau of Indian Affairs, 1793–1999. NARA ARC ID 296222.

their women and children; we gave them many plant foods unknown to them such as corn, squash, beans, and many more. When famine walked among them and their little ones cried for bread, it was the Indian who gave them meat, corn, and fish. The hand that fought for the white man in all his wars was now open to him for relief," Rickard added.

New York countered the Depression as best as it could. The state government funded public work opportunities for state residents, and some Indians secured short-term employment. State agencies also gathered food and clothing to be issued to the poorest residents, among them members of Iroquois communities. Distribution, however, was another problem. "During the winter," Rickard later recalled, "some of our men suffered frozen feet and hands while working out in the cold, but this clothing sat unused in boxes" in state-owned warehouses. In the end, direct help came not from the state government but from personal friends and from the Boy Scouts of America who, noted Rickard, "without thought of gain, collected shoes and other clothing for needy Indians" and distributed those items where they were most needed. Rickard's complaints, and those other Iroquois voiced, were not unique. Hunger, poverty, and unemployment stalked native peoples nationwide, and neither Washington nor state governments could offer as much relief as the situation required.

Reform Efforts in the Hoover Administration

Herbert Hoover's victory in the 1928 presidential election offered a glimmer of hope for Native Americans, but only a glimmer. Hoover assumed the presidency just a few months after publication of the Meriam Report and just a few months before the Wall Street collapse. But in that short time, signs of serious reform emerged. Hoover appointed Ray Lyman Wilbur as Secretary of the Interior and Charles J. Rhoads as Commissioner of Indian Affairs. Wilbur earned his medical degree from Stanford University, served as its Dean of the School of Medicine, and in 1916 became president of Stanford University, a position he maintained officially while concurrently serving as Secretary of the Interior. As a man of medicine, Wilbur reeled at the horrific findings presented in the Meriam Report and committed the Department of Interior to a program of fundamental reform of Indian reservations. Commissioner Rhoads and his assistant, Henry Scattergood, both had a more immediate connection to Indian affairs, each having recently served with the Indian Rights Association.

Wilbur, Rhoads, and Scattergood all championed Washington's longstanding plan to acculturate and then assimilate Native Americans into mainstream society. The pathetic conditions cited in the Meriam Report and the crippling effects of the Great Depression made those twin goals virtually impossible to achieve without a complete overhaul of reservation services and, ultimately, a restructuring of the Office of Indian Affairs itself. Rhoads and Scattergood insisted that the OIA tackle seriously the state of Indian health care. The Indian Office, working in tandem with the U.S. Public Health Service, was to build a more effective health care system, providing additional physicians, nurses, equipment, and clinics to treat the Indian population. It was also to establish a comprehensive disease prevention program on reservations. Rhoads promised fundamental reform in educational services, including the employment of additional teachers and a shift from boarding schools to community day schools. He also called for greater government support of tribal farming and ranching enter-prises as well as federal aid to provide job skills training that was suited to off-reservation employment opportunities. Shortly after assuming the commissionership, Rhoads laid out his vision of the steps required to move Indians toward assimilation—the creation of a special commission to adjudicate tribal claims against the United States, tribal incorporation to handle property distribution and conduct tribal business, and the elimination of the Office of Indian Affairs within 25 years. Each of these goals was specifically encouraged in the Meriam Report and applauded by the most vocal of critics of Indian affairs over the previous decade, among them John Collier. Reform, however, hinged on adequate funding.

Wilbur and Rhoads repeatedly petitioned Congress for larger appropriations to the Indian Office, frequently citing the Meriam Report in presentations before Senate and House leaders and defending higher expenditures as a cost-efficient means to ultimately free the federal government of Indian guardianship. Congressional appropriations to the Office of Indian Affairs jumped substantially, nearly doubling from $15 million in 1928 to $28 million in 1933. The growing ranks of the

Old Home of the Gadawa Family.

New Home of the Gadawa Family.

14.1 Original Gadawa family home

Source: National Archives and Record Administration

desperately poor and the emergency relief they required siphoned off much of the increased funding, ultimately reducing the funding for reform programs the commissioner envisioned. Nonetheless, Rhoads continued to pursue his restructuring of the Indian Office.

Rhoads and his advisers studied carefully the organizational framework of the OIA over the previous decades, determined its strengths and weaknesses, and devised structuring plans that they hoped would produce a more efficient, productive, and responsible office. In 1931, the commissioner implemented the broad recommendations of his advisers, creating five specialized subdivisions within the OIA: the Health Service, the Education Service, the Forestry Service, the Agricultural Extension Service, and the Irrigation Service. Each branch operated under a director, and the five directors reported to the commissioner's appointed assistants. The number of staff employees multiplied to accommodate the enlargement of services planned for each division and the need to retain records and communicate among the divisions and with Congress and non-federal support organizations. In short, restructuring consumed much of the new OIA budget and angered many Native Americans who for years demanded the dissolution of the Indian Office. The cost associated with restructuring, they now complained, deprived the hungry of food, the homeless of shelter, and the sick of medicine.

Congress itself took steps in 1930 to respond to the plight of poor Indians, earmarking $1.44 million in emergency funds for economic support projects on reservations. The Indian Agricultural Extension Service secured experts in crop production and management and sent them to Indian communities to build more profitable reservation farms and ranches. The money also helped purchase seed and feed, fertilizer, and pest control chemicals. The Irrigation Service allocated some money for the laying of lines to water crops and supplying water to cattle and sheep ranches. Money, however, consistently fell short of demand, and natural disasters exacerbated the problem. In 1931, for instance, farms and ranches across the Great Plains fell victim to locusts and prolonged drought. The economic devastation that swept over the region destroyed the will of many to recover their crops, herds, and land. Some simply abandoned their property and headed to the West Coast in search of work. The Office of Indian Affairs solicited contributions from numerous sources, finally receiving from the American Red Cross $191,000 along with carloads of flour, wheat, and other basic foods.

Wilbur, Rhoads, and Scattergood also encouraged the manufacture and sale of tribal crafts, but this effort, too, produced limited gains. They promoted and worked to implement jobs skills training programs for adult Indians, and they established a job-placement service to help Native Americans secure off-reservation employment. Construction companies increasingly hired Indians, especially on projects such as building the Hoover Dam and New York's Empire State Building in which the stereotyped Indian ability to scale cliffs and maintain balance on narrow walkways seemed to fit project needs. The Rhoads administration also recommended that each individual reservation budget a portion of its annual funding for job skills training. This proved a luxury few tribal communities could afford. The Fort Bidwell Reservation in California, however, followed Rhoads's suggestion and hired instructors to teach the basics of construction, secured materials, and with Indian labor replaced primitive shacks with simple but suitable housing for many Indian families.

Health Care and Education

Greater success during the Rhoads years resulted from the administration's initiatives to reform Indian health care and education programs. Especially appalling to readers of the Meriam Report were the horrendously high levels of infant and child mortality, tuberculosis, and trachoma infection in the Indian population. The simplest means of disease prevention proved absent among most tribal groups, and adequate community sanitation systems were equally scarce. The Rhoads Indian Office, which Interior Secretary Dr. Wilbur backed fully, aggressively pressed for heightened funding for Indian health care projects, particularly efforts centered on disease prevention. The Indian bureau also worked with the U.S. Public Health Service and state health agencies to establish workshops, classes, and mobile outreach projects to people living on larger, easily accessible reservations. By 1933, increased funding provided for 183 physicians, 13 trachoma specialists, 11 more dentists, 149 "graduate nurses," 8 more practical nurses, and 92 hospitals with a combined bed capacity of 3,000. Only 696 American Indian babies were born in OIA medical facilities in 1928, but five years later that number stood at 2,280. A government survey of 17,320 Indians residing on 24 reservations found that the trachoma infection rate had dropped to 8 percent of the total native population from the 18 percent rate cited three years earlier in the Meriam Report. The survey noted persistently high infection rates among Navajos, Flathead, Blackfeet, and San Carlos Apaches, but tribes such as the Florida Seminole, North Carolina Cherokee, and Jicarilla Apaches showed no incidence at all of the blinding disease. To be sure, some progress was being made.

Larger congressional appropriations also permitted greater attention to reforming Indian educational services. Rhoads appointed Will Carson Ryan, Jr., a professor of education at Swarthmore College, as Director of Indian Education. Ryan had directed the Meriam team's inquiry into Indian education and authored the document's stinging indictment of the Indian bureau. He endorsed unequivocally the goals of Indian acculturation, the eventual assimilation of Indians into mainstream society, and the abolition of the Office of Indian Affairs. To accomplish those goals, the Indian educational system required fundamental redirection.

Ryan argued that boarding schools should be replaced with reservation day schools, but he acknowledged readily that such a conversion required more money than was available and would take many years to complete. He also anticipated substantial resistance from non-Indian administrators and politicians. The director reluctantly accepted a slow transition period but hoped that this would be offset by a genuine overhaul in the quality of student life in boarding schools and the development of a more practical curriculum in those institutions. He ordered periodic comprehensive medical examinations for all Indian children in boarding schools, an increase in the number of physicians and nurses to conduct those examinations, sanitized kitchen facilities and meal service to students, healthful school meals, and an immediate expansion of boarding school bathroom facilities. He brought hundreds of professionally trained teachers into the service, reduced the teacher-to-student ratio in classrooms, and called for a vocational training program to replace what amounted to compulsory Indian labor in the schools. Ryan also drew up plans for the construction of more schools on reservations, a plan that would allow Indian children to be educated in their familiar, family-based environment.

Despite Ryan's hard work, only 6 of the 250 boarding schools were completely closed by the end of 1931. The failure to end the boarding school system was due, in part, to the reluctance of Congress to further increase funding for Indian affairs and the belief among some in Congress that boarding schools played an important role in the acculturation of Indian children. Boarding school administrators proved equally resistant to change. Many still had faith in the efficacy of their programs, and others' resistance stemmed from the fact that they benefited financially from the existing system. To be sure, boarding school enrollment fell from 69,000 children to 21,677 in those early years of the Great Depression. OIA construction of several dozen new reservation-based day schools contributed to the decreased enrollment, but the nation's economic calamity played a larger role. The depleted reservation economies compelled many children to abandon boarding schools and return home to help their families. Although congressional appropriations rose substantially by 1933, the concurrent rise in emergency relief needs diverted federal dollars from schools, leaving many boarding institutions without adequate funds to maintain their pre-Depression student populations.

In those boarding schools left open, Ryan instructed administrators to provide children with an academic program that included vocational training, one that offered validation of traditional Indian cultures, and one less fixed on a system of military-style order and discipline. In this, too, Ryan failed. School officers were entrenched in their positions, protected from Ryan's wrath by well-placed and powerful politicians. Seldom did administrators see any need to alter their curriculum from a classical education to a more practical one.

Moreover, most administrators believed that an instructional program that validated traditional cultural values only impeded the Americanization of Indian children. Despite his commitment to reform of Indian education, Ryan's efforts produced little in the way of tangible results.

In spite of the energy and good will of the Rhoads-Scattergood administration, Native Americans saw little fundamental redirection in Indian affairs. The Depression sharply curtailed off-reservation employment opportunities and compelled many Indian boarding school children to return to their parents' homes, further draining reservation resources. Long-embedded school administrators ignored or openly resisted reforms planned by the Rhoads administration. State governments, themselves saddled with serious revenue shortfalls, were certainly not eager to assume any responsibility for Indian education or health services, and few wanted to see any movement of Native Americans into the non-reservation job market, given the horrendous unemployment rate states already confronted. The Rhoads commissionership initially offered some hope to Native Americans. Although it failed to bring substantive change to America's native peoples, it nonetheless signaled a slight shift in Washington's willingness to repair the damage that had been done over the years.

A Brighter Prospect for Change

Native Americans watched the 1932 presidential race with little enthusiasm. Presidential candidates rarely showed any great concern for the deplorable quality of life on reservations, at best promising no more than the continued effort to assimilate American Indians into the general population. Franklin Delano Roosevelt's often-repeated reference to the "forgotten man" during the summer and autumn of 1932, along with his vague assurance of a new deal for Americans, understandably encouraged few Indians.

His inaugural address on March 4, 1933, however, inspired listeners with unparalleled hope that his campaign rhetoric was founded on conviction rather than simply a quest for votes, and faith in an FDR administration rose as the new president immediately and with genuine commitment tackled the economic crisis. Even more promising for Native Americans was Roosevelt's appointment of Harold Ickes as Secretary of the Interior. A cofounder of the American Indian Defense Association, long-time critic of the Office of Indian Affairs, and unrelenting advocate for a fundamental redirection of federal Indian policy, Ickes now occupied a seat of power within the nation's executive branch of government. Equally encouraging to Native Americans, Ickes presented the commissionership of the Office of Indian Affairs to an equally ardent champion of reform—John Collier. Only one month into the new president's term, American Indians had two outspoken proponents for fundamental change in key federal positions.

The Indian New Deal

Throughout 1933 and 1934, President Franklin Roosevelt's New Deal shook the foundations of American economic and political history. At its core, and in stark contrast with his predecessor's approach, FDR's philosophy rested on the Progressive idea that "the Federal Government has always had and still has a continuing responsibility for the broader public welfare." To lift the nation from economic depression and the American people from despair, hopelessness, and utter financial devastation, the president consciously committed his administration to a program of experimentation that fully demonstrated his belief that government held substantial responsibility for the general welfare of its citizens.

Roosevelt secured congressional passage of the National Industrial Recovery Act (NIRA) to stabilize wages and prices and, in so doing, to combat inflationary pressure in a rebounding economy. His Agricultural Adjustment Act (AAA) offered cash subsidies to farmers who agreed to limit production of particular crops, a program designed to result in higher market prices for farm products and, consequently, higher income for farmers. The Civilian Conservation Corps, the Civil Works Administration, the Works Progress Administration, and other "work relief" programs soon employed millions of Americans and helped rebuild the nation's infrastructure. The Social Security Act provided a monthly income for elderly, retired persons, an employment office to help individuals find work, unemployment compensation to those who lost their jobs through no fault of their own, and financial support to children. The Roosevelt White House further guaranteed workers the right to organize and bargain collectively, founded the Securities and Exchange Commission to oversee the stock exchange and regulate trading, and established the Federal Deposit Insurance Commission to insure bank deposits. FDR, as he had pledged in his 1932 campaign, remembered the nation's "forgotten man." The Office of Indian Affairs followed the president's lead and in spring 1933 commenced what soon became known as the "**Indian New Deal.**"

Native Americans and New Deal Reform

Commissioner John Collier launched his own New Deal for Native Americans, in tandem with Roosevelt's national campaign. In early 1933, the commissioner arranged for the Department of War to distribute surplus clothing to 30,000 poor Native Americans living on the most depressed reservations. He also secured the cancellation of $3 million in Indian debts, a step that he repeated throughout his commissionership and that resulted in the cancellation of debts totaling $12 million by 1936. At the same time, he directed the Indian Bureau to implement instructional programs in the marketing of tribally grown crops and in basic home budgeting skills. "I recall thinking at the time," said Fools Crow (Sioux), "that we had been living on less than a budget already. Poverty of the worst kind was our daily companion." Collier, with Ickes's backing, appointed an Indian to serve as Superintendent of the Klamath Reservation, began the hiring of 489 Indians to the bureau's staff, announced the cessation of Indian allotment sales, and assured Native Americans that the practice of traditional spiritual ceremonies such as the Sun Dance would be guaranteed and protected by the fed-

eral government. In short order, Collier demonstrated the sincerity of his long-held convictions and showed himself determined to affect genuine reform in Indian affairs.

President Roosevelt revealed himself to be a willing partner to Collier's reformist agenda. All New Deal emergency work relief programs embraced native peoples and placed thousands of Indians on the public payroll. The Works Progress Administration (WPA), which constructed paved roads, municipal airports, government buildings, and bridges, employed annually more than 10,000 Indians, many of whom were assigned jobs inside the OIA. The Public Works Administration hired thousands more to build new hospitals and clinics on reservations or to refurbish those in disrepair, to construct community day schools, and to lay sewage lines on reservations. The Resettlement Administration funded Indian efforts to establish and operate tribal canning and food preservations facilities, and the Civil Works Administration recruited Native Americans to construct public

14.2 John Collier

Source: Courtesy of Library of Congress Prints and Photographs Division, LC-DIG-hec-28781

schools, playgrounds, and athletic fields. The Indian Arts and Crafts Board, founded in 1935 by Collier and Ickes and funded with a separate congressional appropriation of $45,000, formed craft guilds to train Indian artists and craftsmen and to sell Indian-made goods to the general public, each item produced bearing a government stamp of authenticity. Through these programs and others, Native Americans reaped services desperately needed for their survival and found themselves now in a position to rebuild their own communities, economies, and cultures.

The public works projects drew Native Americans from reservations to nearby towns and to urban communities much farther from home. The out-migration of Indians once more fractured tribal structures and separated loved ones, but it also reduced demand on the reservations' dwindling resources. With off-reservation employment came regular pay, a portion of which was sent home to families where it stimulated, however slightly, tribal economies.

14.3 This 1936 poster for the Federal Art Project exhibition of drawings from the Index of American Design shows a weather vane in the shape of a Native American.

Source: Courtesy of Library of Congress Prints and Photographs Division, LC-USZC2-5304

The Public Works of Art Project

The Great Depression hobbled the American economy and brought the nation to an unparalleled level of poverty. Banks failed, factories collapsed, retail stores closed, personal and business investments vanished, and unemployment soared to a record 25 percent of the workforce. Plummeting tax revenues compelled federal and state governments to curtail some services and to eliminate completely non-essential programs. Public relief efforts floundered, and private initiatives often suffered from inadequate funding. In this climate of economic chaos, financial support for the arts nearly vanished.

In December 1933, President Franklin Roosevelt's Civil Works Administration (CWA) launched federal support for the arts by founding the Public Works of Art Project (PWAP). The PWAP divided the United States into 16 separate regions, each managed by a Field Coordinator responsible for selecting and hiring artists, determining which arts projects to pursue, and supervising those projects to completion. The program's mission was rather simple: "Give artists employment at craftsmen wages in the embellishment of public property with works of art." Field coordinators chose artists on the basis of personal financial need and professional ability, often drawing individuals from public relief rolls. The PWAP hired nearly 3,800 artists to paint, sculpt, and craft works of

TIMELINE 14.2 TRACKING THE PWAP AND FAP

Date	Event
November 1933	President Franklin Roosevelt establishes the Civil Works Administration
December 1933	Under direction of the CWA, the Public Works of Art Program is founded, the first federally funded program of the fine arts
April 1934	The National Exhibition of Art by the PWAP opens at the Corcoran Gallery in Washington, D.C., the project's first such exhibit; the show closes in late May
May 1934	The PWAP is terminated, but uncompleted works continue to receive funding from varied federal sources until July 1935
May 1935	By executive order, President Roosevelt establishes the Works Progress Administration
August 1935	The PWAP is reborn as the Federal Art Project, a subdivision of the WPA
June 1943	The WPA, and with it the FAP, dissolves as a federal cost-savings effort during World War II

art and placed completed pieces in tax-funded, or partially tax-funded, venues such as schools, libraries, museums, railway stations, and congressional offices.

To ensure that the program gave opportunities to Native Americans, the PWAP established a separate "Indian Division." Datus Myers was selected to be the field coordinator in New Mexico. Myers had studied art in Los Angeles and Chicago at the turn of the century and in 1923 he and his wife settled in Santa Fe. Throughout the 1920s, Myers focused his attention on the natural landscape and indigenous peoples of northern New Mexico and by the 1930s was widely recognized for his paintings of the American West and his romanticized depictions of American Indians. His deep interest in Native Americans, along with Commissioner of Indian Affairs John Collier's brief association with him in Taos, made Myers a logical choice to be field coordinator. Funding continued for the PWAP until May 1934, when President Roosevelt terminated its parent agency, the CWA, in advance of a much larger and more comprehensive relief work effort still in the design phase. For the next year, money trickled in to individual artists from a variety of federal sources.

In May 1935, Roosevelt announced the founding of the Works Progress Administration (WPA) through which millions of individual Americans and thousands of corporations would be engaged in public work. By the end of summer, the WPA had absorbed the defunct PWAP, renaming it the Federal Art Project (FAP) and expanding its mission. Central to the FAP was a program of art education and instruction. One hundred art centers opened nationwide during the last half of the 1930s. Of those, one-quarter were spread across the American West, and many of those were located on Indian reservations. Children and adults alike received training in basic art history and artistic expression. The FAP also employed professional artists using the same guidelines as the PWAP, and by 1943 FAP artists produced 240,000 prints, 108,000 paintings on canvas, 18,000 sculptures, and 2,600 wall-sized murals for public display. Among the special projects of the FAP was the Index of American Design, which generated a body of artwork that highlighted the history and daily life of the American people.

Among the hundreds of Indian artists the FAP employed, few were more productive than Tse Tsan, or Pablita Velarde (Santa Clara Pueblo). Velarde, born in 1918, attended Santa Fe Indian School and there studied art with Dorothy Dunn, a pioneer in the field of Indian art instruction. Velarde displayed a natural talent for art and in 1937 joined the ranks of WPA artists when she painted a wall mural in the entrance of the main building at the Santa Fe Indian School. She continued her work with the FAP until 1943, during which time she produced 80 paintings, most of them portraying Pueblo history and culture for the Bandelier National Park and Monument.

The Civilian Conservation Corps—Indian Division

No New Deal project reached more Native Americans or benefited more Indians directly than the Civilian Conservation Corps (CCC). Founded in March 1933, the Roosevelt administration charged the CCC with the task of reseeding barren land, planting trees, clearing forests of their underbrush, and other conservation-related jobs. The harsh and nearly unproductive condition of reservation lands had been detailed in the Meriam Report, but efforts to acquire funding for land revitalization proved futile under the Rhoads-Scattergood administration. Collier, however, believed the CCC's mission might embrace Indian reservations, and he was convinced that Indians themselves should be hired exclusively to perform reservation work. Commissioner Collier moved quickly and created the Indian Emergency Conservation Work program as a separate Native American subdivision of the CCC, a subdivision soon known as the **Civilian Conservation Corps—Indian Division (CCC—ID).**

Armed with an initial appropriation of $6 million and staffed with 14,400 Indian enrollees for the first six months, the CCC—ID in summer 1933 commenced 72 reclamation and conservation projects stretched across 56 reservations. The CCC—ID improved reservations by reseeding grasslands, planting trees, constructing dams and reservoirs, building roads and trails, removing underbrush from forests, sinking wells and laying irrigation lines, raising lookout stations for forest rangers, and clearing lands of pests and poisonous plants.

14.4 Civilian Conservation Corps enrollee Henry Denny, with grandchildren.

Source: © CORBIS/Corbis via Getty Images

Collier unsuccessfully lobbied the parent CCC to appoint Native Americans to supervisory positions in the Indian Division camps, but he was able to alter the program's operational structure to address specific Indian needs. For example, whereas the parent CCC hired only single men, the CCC—ID was allowed to accept married men. The CCC—ID allowed work camps to surpass the 225-man limit imposed on non-Indian sites, and the 18- to 25-year-old age restriction and single six-month term of employment set by Congress was waived for Native Americans. Like the national organization, the CCC—ID operated "boarding camps." Enrollees lived at the project site and had their $30 per month paychecks sent home to waiting families. The CCC—ID, however, also provided "family camps" and "commuting

PROFILE

Robert Yellowtail

Robert Yellowtail, born in 1889 in Lodge Grass, Montana, followed the same path as so many Indian children in the late nineteenth century, leaving his family at age four for full-time life at a boarding school that trained him exclusively in a non-Crow identity. He excelled in academics, continued his education at Sherman Institute in Riverside, California, and studied law at the University of Chicago. In spite of his educational training, Yellowtail remained Crow.

Throughout his adult life, Yellowtail walked two paths. On one, he followed in the footsteps of venerated, traditional tribal elders such as Chief Plenty Coups by offering a determined defense of tribal culture, structures, and land. At the same time, like many younger, acculturated Indians, he was willing to extend non-Indian interests onto the reservation and eventually meld Indians fully with the non-Indian world. Regardless of the path he traveled at any given moment, his goal remained constant—to preserve the Crow community and identity. He spoke before the U.S. Senate in 1919, calling for the Indians' right of self-determination, a position that many in his audience opposed. He also participated as a member of the Committee of One Hundred in the middle 1920s, demanding a fundamental overhaul of Indian policy and a committed effort by government to address sincerely the many pressing needs of native peoples.

Yellowtail saw in the Roosevelt administration a group of American leaders who could and would initiate a new direction in Indian affairs. Soon after Roosevelt took office in spring 1933, Commissioner John Collier removed James Hyde as Crow Reservation Superintendent and replaced him with Robert Yellowtail, the first Native American to hold such a position.

During his tenure as superintendent, Yellowtail continued the pattern of activism he demonstrated throughout his adult life. He knew too well the history of land leasing by white farmers and ranchers, a record of exploitation and financial disaster for the Crow. With federal dollars he secured high-quality horses and cattle to raise the quality of Crow herds and to stimulate tribal ranching in a concerted effort to preserve the Indians' control of their lands and to elevate tribal and individual income. He anticipated that a side benefit of this policy would be a concurrent reduction in non-Indian land leasing. Under his direction and through his political connections, he drew Works Progress Administration and Civilian Conservation Corps—Indian Division projects to Crow reservations, projects that employed Crow workers to build or repair roads, construct inexpensive houses, thin forests, lay irrigation lines, and control insects. Yellowtail also proved instrumental in securing federal dollars for the construction of day schools, the expansion of other educational programs, and the founding of the reservation's first full-service hospital. He also encouraged nullification of the government's ban on certain traditional religious ceremonies such as the Sun Dance, a ceremony that was officially resumed in 1941.

Many of Yellowtail's efforts and accomplishments mirrored those of the larger Indian New Deal, and he certainly owed his appointment as superintendent to Commissioner Collier. Nonetheless, Yellowtail never championed Collier's Indian Reorganization Act (IRA), and many Crow insist that he quietly worked against its passage. He believed the existing tribal council and governing structure of the Crow was one that had worked well over the previous 50 years. Moreover the IRA's planned reconstruction of tribal government was incompatible with Yellowtail's call for Indian self-determination.

Robert Yellowtail stepped down as superintendent in 1945, but he continued to press for the preservation of Crow tribal resources structures and identity for the rest of his life. Wrote historian Frederick Hoxie, Yellowtail "used the ways and means of whites to achieve traditional Crow goals—the preservation and perpetuation of Crow lands and ways of life."

projects," work systems that permitted the enrolled Indian the opportunity to work and learn job skills at a nearby project site while preserving his family ties, his home, and any source of income his property produced.

The success of the CCC—ID exceeded Collier's expectations. By 1941, the CCC—ID had employed more than 80,000 Indians and had completed projects on more than 150 reservations. Indian labor produced 2,500 miles of fire breaks, 9,700 miles of truck trails, 12,200 miles of fences, 91 lookout towers, 1,350 wells, 1,742 dams and large reservoirs, and 6,200 springs and small reservoirs. Enrollees cleared 263,000 acres of poisonous weeds, treated one million acres of land to eliminate pests, laid irrigation lines, planted thousands of trees, and reseeded tens of thousands of acres for both ranching operations and control of soil erosion.

Evening classes at the work site offered Indians numerous opportunities to improve their proficiency in English, math, home finance, and job skills such as small engine repair, radio communications, and drafting. Equally important, the CCC—ID eventually turned over its supervisory positions to Indians, and by late 1941 Native Americans manned more than two-thirds of these positions and administrative roles.

Navajo Stock Reduction

New Deal programs tailored to the special needs and circumstances of Native Americans netted substantial gains for reservations, but Collier's plan for ranching reform met stiff resistance among the Navajos. Navajos traditionally tied community status to the number of sheep or cattle a rancher owned. A large herd of cattle or sheep garnered much respect for the rancher regardless of its quality.

The commissioner assured Navajos that he understood fully this cultural feature, but he believed drastic changes in their ranching system were needed to reduce tribal poverty. The ranches and farms of the Great Plains and Southwest had endured hard times throughout the 1920s, and by the mid-1930s conditions had not improved. Drought covered the region, rivers and creeks for watering livestock dried up, and dust storms ravaged grasslands. Market values plummeted nationwide, forcing ranchers to sell off their herds to capture whatever financial return was possible. Navajo ranchers, however, refused to part with their cattle and sheep. Large herds, inadequate grasslands and sources of water, and the overgrazing of existing pastures combined to cripple Navajo ranching. Throughout the Rhoads administration, the Indian Affairs office recommended that Navajos reduce their herd size, arguing that underfed livestock yielded lower market prices and contributed directly to tribal economic problems. Commissioner Collier made the same argument and promoted the same solution, but the Navajo refused to change their practices.

In 1933, Collier journeyed to the reservation and appealed directly to the tribal council for stock reduction. He assured the council that stock reduction, combined with the Indian bureau's purchase of additional lands and its reseeding and irrigation projects,

14.5 Buying sheep from Native Americans

Source: National Archives and Records Administration, 295219

promised higher-quality livestock and, consequently, greater profits for ranchers. The council responded firmly that stock reduction challenged the basis of Indian status and threatened the very structure of Navajo society. It was difficult for many Navajos to grasp the logic of higher profits from fewer sheep and cattle, and from those who did understand came the charge that Collier was interfering in tribal self-determination, the much trumpeted goal of the commissioner himself.

Collier implemented the stock reduction program in spite of Indian objections. Navajos wrote angry letters to Secretary Ickes and President Roosevelt, but FDR answered them with a personal request to the tribal council that Navajos give the project a chance to work. The program was absolutely essential to raise tribal income, said the president. By March 1934, the OIA had purchased 150,000 sheep from Navajo ranchers, reducing herd size and alienating most Navajos.

Tribal council member Jacob C. Morgan blasted Collier's heavy-handed approach as evidence of the OIA's persistently overbearing posture and paternalist behavior that routinely conflicted with tribal preference. He condemned Collier's scheme as another method to impoverish native peoples and, in so doing, continue Indian dependence on and subjugation to a "beneficent" federal government. He also highlighted the inherent contradiction in Collier's actions—the commissioner's imposition of stock reduction on Navajos directly countered his public defense of Indian cultures and his advocacy for their resurgence. Finally, Morgan complained that Collier bungled the plan by employing an unfair method to reduce herd size. The Indian Office made across-the-board cuts, reducing the size of each man's herd by the same number of animals. Owners of few animals suffered what amounted to deeper cuts in their herds and consequently a greater loss of status than those who owned larger herds.

Whatever hope Navajos initially held for Collier's administration evaporated quickly, and as stock reduction unfolded they increasingly referred to him as "the devil" and, by the late 1930s, as "Hitler." A young rancher's wife named The Blind Man's Daughter recounted years later her experience with OIA agents who removed her family's sheep to a corral. "I was told to select the ones that were the best" to keep. "That hurt me and I just bowed my head. I just sent my children over and they selected some." Her husband complained: "You people are indeed heartless. You have now killed me." The Blind Man's Daughter then added, "This happened, and it wasn't long before my husband fell ill. It was no doubt the worry that sickened him. He was sick all winter, and at the beginning of spring he died."

The program did, nonetheless, result in the promised financial gain for most Navajo. A 25 percent reduction in Navajo herds produced a healthier ratio of grazing acreage to livestock. When combined with the commissioner's projects to reseed grasslands and create watering wells for animals, cattle and sheep values rose significantly. The net price per steer jumped $6.50, and wool production rose from two million pounds to three million pounds annually by 1941. Still, the Navajos remained bitter toward the commissioner.

Indian Education

John Collier attacked the problems of Indian education with a similar aggressiveness, and his dogged determination for reform, mixed with his often abrasive personality and the unqualified support of both Secretary Harold Ickes and President Roosevelt, guaranteed success. Soon after becoming commissioner, Collier appointed Willard Walcott Beatty as the new director of the Indian Education Service. Beatty's own determined character and sharp administrative skills complemented the new commissioner's, and together they presented recalcitrant boarding school administrators with an imposing force for redirection in educational services.

Collier and Beatty understood that the immediate closure of all boarding schools was impractical, but gradual elimination of boarding schools seemed feasible. They agreed to make fundamental alterations to the academic programs in those remaining open, overhaul the quality of children's living quarters and dining facilities, abandon compulsory military training for boys, and institute a less severe disciplinary code for all students. They also planned to increase the number of reservation day schools and services to embrace the entire Native community.

The commissioner and director wasted little time. By the end of 1935, the Indian Education Service transformed ten boarding schools into community day schools. Progress was readily visible in many of the boarding schools that remained open. At Haskell Institute in Lawrence, Kansas, Beatty replaced the school's superintendent with Henry Roe Cloud, the first Native American to hold the post and the first of many Indians to assume administrative duties in the Indian Education Service. Roe Cloud earlier served as a principal investigator for the Meriam Report and with his new assignment promised to bring fundamental revisions to the school. Among his earliest steps was the dismissal of Haskell's football coach, long noted for his brutal disciplinary tactics. The school's historic ties with the U.S. Army were also severed, ending Haskell's reliance on military officers as classroom instructors, military uniforms for student attire, a military code of conduct that regulated behavior and dispensed severe punishment, and compulsory military training for all male students. The academic program also shifted under Roe Cloud's direction to one more relevant to student needs and experiences, one that stressed mastery of basic subjects but also provided skills that allowed students upon graduation to sustain their lives in white society or to affect the revitalization of reservations. The example Roe Cloud set was followed in other schools. In 1936, the Santa Fe Boarding School suspended its military regimen, after which the institution became "more tolerable" according to many students. The Boys' Advisor at the Albuquerque Indian School offered a similar perspective following changes there, saying "we find a different atmosphere though the entire plant; there is more home life and more student participation."

The Community Day School program extended educational services to adult men and women. Schools provided training in the English language and courses in personal hygiene, cooking, sewing, farming, and job skills necessary for off-reservation employment. Children received instruction in a more practical, relevant curriculum within the reservation environment, allowing youngsters to remain at home with their parents and not break family bonds. Community day schools became more than just educational institutions for children; they emerged as community centers that served the larger tribal population. They also proved cost efficient. On a per-child basis, day schools cost half as much as boarding schools. By 1940, there were 226 reservation day schools in service nationwide; among the Navajo alone, the program enrolled 6,000 more children than they did ten years earlier.

Beatty also implemented a special instructor-training course to prepare college graduates for teaching positions within the Indian Education Service. Recruits pursued a two-year program that exposed prospective teachers to Indian cultures, history, and languages in addition to progressive teaching methods and field techniques. Caught in the spirit of reform, many teachers hired by the Indian Service exceeded performance expectations by working longer hours, traveling to remote areas of reservations to reach isolated families, and creating mobile libraries.

To be sure, problems persisted. Government funding remained well below actual need. Smaller and more remote reservations were sometimes purposely ignored or conspicuously bypassed to provide services to larger and more concentrated groups of Native Americans. The rebounding national economy lured many teachers and school administrators away from the Indian Education Service with the promise of higher salaries in public schools or in private industry. In spite of these difficulties, Collier's first seven years as commissioner resulted in greater progress than had been accomplished in any previous Indian bureau administration.

Congressional passage of the **Johnson-O'Malley Act** in April 1934 added to the overall plan for redirection in Indian education. Already, more Indian children attended public schools than schools managed by the Office of Indian Affairs. This legislation authorized the Secretary of Interior to arrange contracts with state governments to ease the financial burden of educating Native American youngsters in non-reservation public schools, providing federal dollars to offset newfound instructional costs. This arrangement struck down the previous, burdensome process of making deals with individual school districts. Johnson-O'Malley was intended to move more Indian children into well-funded state public schools and, as a result, expose Native Americans to educational opportunities not commonly found on reservations, even in the developing community day schools. The measure found wide approval in Congress and in the Office of Indian Affairs. Assimilationists saw this as a means by which more Indian children would be immersed in the white world and would ultimately adopt non-Indian values as their own. Although Collier feared such immersion might weaken further the Indian children's ties to native cultures, he and his supporters believed Indian children who went to public schools would then apply their advanced knowledge to their own home communities, raising the quality of life on reservations and protecting the integrity of tribal cultures.

From the moment of its implementation, the measure faced serious problems. In return for federal financial aid, Johnson-O'Malley required public schools to provide special services to Native American students, including bilingual instruction and extensive study of tribal cultures and history. Public school teachers typically knew little history of American Indians, and the image they carried of Native Americans was shaped by Hollywood films, cheap novels, and racial stereotypes. Rare was the teacher who carried any true understanding of Native cultures into the classroom. Accurate classroom materials relevant to Indian history and cultures were generally absent, and hiring qualified teachers fluent in a native language proved almost impossible. And, all too often, teachers openly displayed their own racial bias toward Native Americans. The strings Washington attached to federal dollars gave pause to most state education officials. Administrators welcomed additional money, especially at a time when economic depression drained state resources, but the apparent intrusion of federal authority into state affairs and the law's clear intention to validate native cultures at state expense angered many officials. More often than not, education officials simply placed the federal money into their schools' general operating fund accounts and made only symbolic gestures toward fulfilling the requirements of Johnson-O'Malley.

A New Direction in Federal Indian Policy

Franklin D. Roosevelt's New Deal challenged the long tradition of Washington's limited interference in the nation's economy, engaging federal authority fully in the recovery and reform of the capitalist system through a series of relief projects, oversight agencies, and managerial structures. Historians have long credited, or blamed, the Roosevelt White House with introducing to America the "welfare state" and the "imperial presidency." FDR's New Deal wrought fundamental change to the United States, setting a new path for the nation to follow. In similar fashion, the Office of Indian Affairs under John Collier hoped to reverse the direction of federal Indian policy and establish in its place a policy that acknowledged the value of Indian cultures, respected individuals and tribal groups, and permitted Native Americans a clear voice in determining their own future.

The Indian Reorganization Act

Collier's emergency relief projects addressed the immediate needs of most Native Americans and, overall, framed the Indian New Deal, but the centerpiece of Collier's work was the Indian Reorganization Act (IRA) with which he intended to reverse federal Indian policy. For more than a decade, Collier blasted the Indian bureau's determined effort to reduce tribal land holdings through an impressive array of tactics. He condemned the Indian Office for the pathetic state of reservation life detailed in the Meriam Report and for not including Native Americans directly in the government's decision-making process. He further denounced the tunnel-visioned focus of the Indian Office, Congress, and most white Americans on assimilation, arguing instead for a policy that permitted Indians the option of assimilation *or* tribal revitalization. John Collier saw in his appointment as Commissioner of Indian Affairs the clear opportunity to make his vision a reality.

Throughout spring and summer 1933, he refined his objectives, considered appropriate political strategies, and studied FDR's national program for relief, recovery, and reform. Working with Indian legal affairs expert Felix Cohen, Assistant Commissioner of the OIA William Zimmerman, and staff members of the Interior Department, Collier drafted a 48-page bill and presented it to Congress. In February 1934, Senator Burton K. Wheeler (Montana) and Congressman Edgar Howard (Nebraska), both Democrats and members of the Indian Affairs Committee in their respective houses, endorsed Collier's bill and agreed to serve as cosponsors of the measure. Wheeler and Howard were intimately aware of the 1928 Meriam Report and were initially impressed with Collier's reformist agenda.

The **Wheeler-Howard Bill**, or **Indian Reorganization Act**, departed significantly from earlier federal policies. Tribes under the IRA, said one attorney for the Department of Interior, would exist as "domestic dependent nations," each permitted to draft its own constitution, erect a system of self-government comparable to local municipalities within the states, and establish a tribal police force. Each tribe could also establish its own local courts to settle minor problems. Moreover, the IRA ended the Dawes Act of 1887, halting its system for individual land allotments, preventing further disbursement of tribal and personal lands to non-Indians, and consolidating reservation lands (allotted and otherwise) into tribal ownership with future dispersals to be made according to tribal preference. Native Americans holding allotted property were to be fairly compensated for land returned to community ownership. The act also promised substantial enlargement of community health services, educational programs suited to Indian needs and circumstances, and forest and land management initiatives. The bill further allowed the establishment of tribal business corporations that could tap into a $10 million revolving credit fund to purchase additional lands for tribal ownership, develop tribal agricultural and ranching enterprises, and issue loans to individuals who wished to pursue local business enterprises. The IRA contained a provision for a Court of Indian Affairs with jurisdiction over cases in which one or more defendants or plaintiffs were Native American. As remarkable a redirection in Indian policy the IRA signaled in content, Collier's stated willingness to allow each individual tribe the right to accept or reject the IRA as policy proved startling. At no time in the federal government's history did Native Americans have the opportunity to opt out of any Washington plan. As Collier envisioned it, the Wheeler-Howard Bill would reverse the course of federal Indian policy by preserving native cultural traditions and making assimilation with white society optional rather than compulsory.

The IRA received careful scrutiny in each house of Congress and generated some heated debate, particularly among members of the House of Representatives who took exception to the consolidation of Indian lands into tribal ownership. Common ownership of land directly countered traditional American values, they argued, and denied access to private property ownership for the more acculturated, assimilation-bound Indians. Members of Congress also expressed doubt in the Indians' ability, or competency, to manage their own political and financial affairs.

Collier and several close assistants traveled across the United States to gauge the Indians' initial response and concurrently encourage Native American support of the IRA. The commissioner held ten separate meetings with tribal representatives between early March and late April 1934, and in each Indians presented Collier with a myriad of opinions. He was stunned to find substantial resistance to the Wheeler-Howard Act among Native Americans themselves, many of them concerned about land consolidation and the loss of individual allotments. More than a few Indians objected to what they viewed as a compulsory retrenchment into traditional community values and structures, a policy that would slow acculturation and ultimately threaten Indian assimilation with mainstream society. To Jacob C. Morgan, the proposed legislation would push native peoples "a step backwards." Morgan pointed out that the Navajo population had grown fivefold over the previous 60 years, and poverty gripped the reservation as the man-to-arable-soil ratio declined. Housing remained

READING HISTORY

Excerpts from the Indian Reorganization Act (Wheeler-Howard Act), June 18, 1934

The Indian Reorganization Act, enacted in 1934, was an effort championed by Commissioner of Indian Affairs John Collier to restructure fundamentally the relationship of Native Americans to the federal government, improve substantially living conditions on Indian reservations, and revitalize many traditional features of native cultures.

An Act to conserve and develop Indian lands and resources; to extend to Indians the right to form business and other organizations; to establish a credit system for Indians; to grant certain rights of home rule to Indians; to provide for vocational education for Indians; and for other purposes.

BE IT ENACTED by the Senate and House of Representatives of the United States of America in Congress assembled, that hereafter no land of any Indian reservation, created or set apart by treaty or agreement with the Indians, Act of Congress, Executive order, purchase, or otherwise, shall be allotted in severalty to any Indian.

Section 2. The existing periods of trust placed upon any Indian lands and any restriction on alienation thereof are hereby extended and continued until otherwise directed by Congress.

Section 3. The Secretary of the Interior, if he shall find it to be in the public interest, is hereby authorized to restore to tribal ownership the remaining surplus lands of any Indian reservation heretofore opened, or authorized to be opened, to sale, or any other form of disposal by Presidential proclamation, or by any of the public land laws of the United States....

Section 4. Except as herein provided, no sale, devise, gift, exchange or other transfer of restricted Indian lands or of shares in the assets of any Indian tribe or corporation organized hereunder, shall be made or approved: Provided, however, That such lands or interests may, with the approval of the Secretary of the Interior, be sold, devised, or otherwise transferred to the Indian tribe in which the lands or shares are located or from which the shares were derived or to a successor corporation....

Section 5. The Secretary of the Interior is hereby authorized, in his discretion, to acquire through purchase, relinquishment, gift, exchange, or assignment, any interest in lands, water rights or surface rights to lands, within or without existing reservations, including trust or otherwise restricted allotments whether the allottee be living or deceased, for the purpose of providing lands for Indians. For the acquisition of such lands, ... there is hereby authorized to be appropriated ... a sum not to exceed $2,000,000 in any one fiscal year....

Section 7. The Secretary of the Interior is hereby authorized to proclaim new Indian reservations on lands acquired pursuant to any authority conferred by this Act, or to add such lands to existing reservations ... for the exclusive use of Indians entitled by enrollment or by tribal membership to residence at such reservations....

Section 10. There is hereby authorized to be appropriated ... the sum of $10,000,000 to be established as a revolving fund from which the Secretary of the Interior ... may make loans to Indian chartered corporations for the purpose of promoting the economic development of such tribes and of their members....

Section 16. Any Indian tribe, or tribes, residing on the same reservation, shall have the right to organize for its common welfare, and may adopt an appropriate constitution and bylaws, which shall become effective when ratified by a majority vote of the adult members of the tribe . . . Such constitution and bylaws when ratified as aforesaid and approved by the Secretary of the Interior shall be revocable by an election open to the same voters and conducted in the same manner as hereinabove provided. . . .

Section 18. This Act shall not: apply to any reservation wherein a majority of the adult Indians, voting at a special election duly called by the Secretary of the Interior, shall vote against its application. . . .

Questions

1. As stated in the act's introduction, what was the purpose of the Indian Reorganization Act and to what extent did the act's introduction suggest a reversal in the direction of federal Indian policy?
2. What were the principal provisions of the act that signaled clearly a fundamental shift in policy?
3. In what ways did this act actually reinforce federal policy over the previous 50 years?

grossly inadequate, educational opportunities were limited, and health services proved incapable of serving the peoples' basic needs. Revitalization of traditional tribal structures and cultural values, he argued, would only perpetuate poverty and prevent assimilation, which he considered the Indians' only avenue toward survival. Many white Americans who opposed the Wheeler-Howard Bill echoed Morgan's assessment, saying that the legislation "does not give Indians much leeway not to be Indian, and to walk Main Street like the rest of us." The commissioner returned to Washington and drafted more than two dozen amendments to the Wheeler-Howard bill that addressed Indian concerns.

Congressional discussions and the Indians' comments netted some alterations to the Wheeler-Howard Bill. The legislation ultimately did not include the provision for special Courts for Indian Affairs. Slight changes were made to education services and land policies, and native peoples in both Alaska and Oklahoma were exempted from the IRA. The bill then passed through both houses of Congress and received President Roosevelt's signature on June 18, 1934. Collier expected the IRA to signal a "new day dawning" for American Indians.

The Indian Reorganization Act now went to each reservation for approval or rejection. Collier traveled personally to those communities where passage of the IRA appeared doubtful and answered questions, clarified IRA provisions, and assured Indians that the new law would permit both the revitalization of traditional culture and a path toward assimilation depending on the tribe's or individual's preference. His presence at council meetings often tilted the vote in favor of the IRA.

Collier expected Native Americans to offer a ringing endorsement of the IRA. Some Arapahos saw in the IRA a "better governmental break than ever" as it allowed the Indian, said one, "to participate actively in his own problems and in the common good." Said another tribal council member, the new policy provided for "the first intelligent system of Indian education . . . ever offered" and a "practical method of guaranteeing to all tribes the ability to learn to run their own affairs." Antonio Luhan (Taos Pueblo) journeyed to Hopi villages encouraging support for the IRA. "I told them that in past times, the Government tried to make white people out of us . . . but it looks now they have turned around and are giving us back to our own Indian ways and this bill helps us do that. . . . I have property myself in my Pueblo and why should I come here and advise you to take this bill if it wasn't any good? I am in the same place as you are. . . . We have got a real friend in John

Collier." But Luhan's promotion of the IRA also addressed the consequences of not supporting the measure. He reminded his listeners of their "white neighbors" who will certainly continue efforts to take tribal land, and he routinely highlighted his own experience in the Pueblo land crisis in the 1920s. "Maybe they see gold. They might see coal." Under the current system, he reminded his listeners, the sale of land allotments would continue and only ensure Native Americans a lifetime of poverty. "That is enough to finish the Indians. You have no place to hang your hat or shawl. No house, no home."

Resistance to the IRA

Tribes voted individually on the IRA over the following months and years. Of the 263 that ultimately voted, 192 accepted the Indian Reorganization Act. This was certainly not an overwhelming victory for Collier; indeed, tribal debates and votes on the IRA revealed a degree of division among Native Americans that Collier and most non-Indians had not expected. The slimmest of vote margins often gave tribal passage of the IRA. A mere two votes decided the contest in favor of the act among the Capitan Grande people of California's Mission Indian Federation, and a single vote determined acceptance among the Alturas of the Sacramento Agency. The margin of victory for the IRA certainly was large on many reservations, but that in itself did not necessarily imply wide-spread support for the new policy. Many Indians simply chose not to vote. Non-participation demonstrated Indian defiance of the IRA, a form of protest that many Indians viewed as a logical tactic in resisting a measure they had little direct voice in creating and an election process many considered alien to traditional cultures. Only one-third of the Arapahos cast ballots against the IRA, but observers contended that the act would have been defeated easily if all eligible voters had participated. A one-vote margin gave Shoshones the IRA until absentee ballots were counted (see Table 14.2).

Reasons for resisting the IRA varied widely among Indians. Navajos defeated the IRA partly because they were still angry at Collier's stock reduction program. Some tribes that had little direct contact with Washington specifically or with the outside world generally feared the IRA might compromise their historic independence and fracture their traditional structure and values. Cynicism and suspicion understandably pervaded many Indian communities. Policies over the previous century were uniformly bent toward the removal of Indians from their land and their eventual makeover as whites. In contrast, the IRA promised to return property to tribal ownership and halt the longstanding allotment system. In place of compulsory acculturation, Native American cultures and values would be renewed, revitalized, and protected by law. Collier himself noted in a message to OIA field workers that the "cultural history of Indians in all respects is to be considered equal to that of any non-Indian group." Instead of imposing a policy on Native Americans, the IRA allowed for Indian self-determination. Such a dramatic and abrupt reversal in the course of history understandably created suspicion. "There is some big wolf circling around to see its way to take what we have got," said one Arapaho. Indians from coast to coast sounded a preferred desire "to be left alone just where we are."

Resistance also centered on the IRA's requirement for a governmental system not of Indian origin. The Iroquois Confederacy noted, as did many other tribal groups, that a formal, written constitution actually countered traditional tribal systems of self-government. "It's not self-government," said Ramon Roubideau (Sioux), "because self-government by permission is no self-government at all. Everything that the Indian Reorganization Act brought in under the guise of self-government was subject to the approval or the concurrence of the Secretary of the Interior or his authorized representative—the superintendent. . . . It's just like the rich kid with the rich father. Everything is planned for him. He never develops this mind of his." "The IRA did not allow the Indians their independence. . . . It did not protect their sovereignty," said Rupert Costo, a Cahuilla from California and later president of the American Indian Historical Society.

Table 14.2 Indian Tribes, Bands, and/or Communities that Voted on the Indian Reorganization Act

Tribe	Reservation Population	Eligible Voters	Affirmative	Negative
ARIZONA				
Colorado River Agency	1,169	648	225	16
Fort Apache Agency	2,718	1,340	726	21
Hopi Agency	2,538		519	299
Navajo Agency (AZ, NM)	43,135	15,900	7,608	7,992
Papago Agency	5,899	3,431	1,443	188
Pima Agency	6,092	3,098	1,500	204
San Carlos Agency	2,843	1,473	504	22
Truxton Agency	1,103	621	221	45
CALIFORNIA				
Fort Yuma	819	402	192	32
Hoopa Valley Agency	3,500 (est.)	1,105	250	508
Mission Agency	2,794	1,725	229	855
Sacramento Agency		1,396	745	435
COLORADO				
Consolidated Ute Agency	834	354	94	13
FLORIDA				
Seminole Agency	580	295	21	0
IDAHO				
Northern Idaho Agency	2,121	849	319	332
Fort Hall Agency	1,839	971	375	31
IOWA				
Tomah Agency	419	198	63	13
KANSAS				
Potawatomi Agency	1,860	914	419	144
LOUISIANA				
Choctaw Agency	128	35	25	3
MINNESOTA				
Consolidated Chippewa Agency	14,405	7,179	1,316	368
MICHIGAN				
Great Lakes Agency	. . . .	653	512	36
Tomah Agency	. . . .	424	237	112

Tribe	Reservation Population	Eligible Voters	Affirmative	Negative
MISSISSIPPI				
Choctaw Agency	1,792	736	218	21
MONTANA				
Blackfeet Agency	3,962	1,785	823	171
Flathead Agency	2,964	1,218	494	166
Fort Belknap Agency	676	344	179	7
Tongue River Agency	1,541	757	418	96
Crow Agency	2,082	982	112	689
Fort Peck Agency	2,663	1,027	276	578
NEBRASKA				
Winnebago Agency	4,498	2,209	669	102
NEVADA				
Carson River Agency	6,250	1,611	616	334
Western Shoshone Agency	718	489	225	17
NEW MEXICO				
Mescalero Agency	722	367	273	11
United Pueblos Agency	11,667	6,333	1,959	327
Navajo Agency (AZ, NM)	43,135	15,900	7,608	7,992
NEW YORK				
New York Agency	. . . .	3,125	272	1,540
NORTH CAROLINA				
Cherokee Agency	3,254	1,114	700	101
NORTH DAKOTA				
Ft. Berthold Agency	1,569	61	477	139
Standing Rock Agency	3,775	1,559	668	508
Turtle Mountain Agency	6,034	1,181	257	550
OREGON				
Klamath Agency	1,364	666	56	408
Umatilla Agency	1,140	681	155	299
Grand Ronde-Siletz Agency	821	446	156	191
Warm Springs Agency	992	461	308	75
SOUTH DAKOTA				
Cheyenne River Agency	3,288	1,420	653	459

(*Continued*)

Table 14.2 *Continued*

Tribe	Reservation Population	Eligible Voters	Affirmative	Negative
Crow Creek Agency	1,556	548	158	285
Flandreau School	345	193	79	5
Pine Ridge Agency	8,370	4,075	1,169	1,095
Rosebud Agency	8,380	4,117	1,091	595
Sisseton Agency	2,658	1,170	266	335
UTAH				
Uintah and Ouray Agency	1,524	780	424	28
Fort Hall Agency	137	109	37	26
WASHINGTON				
Colville Agency	3,925	2,035	513	725
Taholah Agency	2,156	1,345	390	288
Tulalip Agency	3,480	1,280	587	238
Yakima Agency	2,942	1,392	361	773
WISCONSIN				
Great Lakes Agency	4,517	2,471	816	289
Menominee Agency	2,077	1,020	596	15
Tomah Agency	3,728	2,070	854	127
WYOMING				
Wind River Agency	2,196	1,032	339	469

IRA opponents often demanded instead the maintenance of existing treaties. The Quapaw of Oklahoma vented their rebuttal to Collier's plan, saying, "We [already] have a treaty with the United States, describing by metes and bounds the size and shape of our allotments, and it states that its purpose is to provide a permanent home for the nation." The Yakima tribal council extended the perspective: "We feel that the best interests of the Indians can be preserved by the continuance of treaty laws" entered into with the United States in 1855. New York's Oneida insisted Washington honor "the terms of the Treaty of Canandaigua between our nation, our confederacy, and the United States government of November 11, 1794."

Hotly contested, too, was the apparent redirection of Native Americans from the course toward assimilation to what many referred to as a "return to the blanket." The IRA only perpetuated the segregation of Indians from mainstream society and, in so doing, retarded their prospects for assimilation, the Indian Rights Association complained. Jacob Morgan led Navajo opposition. Morgan, himself a product of the boarding school system and founder of the Navajo Progressive League in 1918, argued that the Indians' only salvation from intense poverty, the horrific state of Indian health, and overall stagnation on the reservation was assimilation with the white world. "Our future under this plan," said Morgan, "is a sunset" for the Navajo people. The Indian Rights Association denounced the IRA for its plan to reinvigorate tribal societies, thereby continuing the Indians' segregation from mainstream America. Segregation meant death to Native Americans; it would eventually make real the notion of the vanishing Indian.

Collier's forceful and often arrogant personality alienated many Indians who otherwise might have been supportive of the IRA. The commissioner was determined the IRA be accepted by tribal councils and was often livid when Native Americans challenged his vision. Said Rupert Costo (Cahuilla), "his autocratic administration and repressive administration damned him before the Indians."

The sharpest and most coordinated attack on the IRA came from the American Indian Federation. Founded in Washington, D.C., on June 8, 1934, only ten days prior to congressional passage of the IRA, the American Indian Federation (AIF) at year's end boasted a membership of 3,500 Indians, most from tribal groups spread across the Southwest. The AIF advanced the assimilationist arguments trumpeted by Carlos Montezuma during the Progressive Era—U.S. citizenship, a sound education received in public schools, and Indian adoption of Main Street values. The organization's most extreme tenet called for the complete abolition of the Office of Indian Affairs "with its un-American principles of slavery, greed, and oppression." The AIF challenged any policy that might "return Indians to the blanket" and argued that Collier's reformist zeal promised to contribute to "the strengthening, not the diminishing, of bureaucratic control in the lives of American Indians." American Indians must "take their place beside all other people in this land of opportunity," said AIF president Joseph Brunner (Oklahoma Creek).

Brunner and a small group of allies pressed the federation's argument in a harsher tone. They alleged that "vicious Communist features" were included in the IRA and that it was Collier's intention to instill "communal bliss" rather than true American values among Native Americans. They claimed, furthermore, that Collier and the new federal Indian policy he promoted intended to subvert the Christianization of Native Americans. Said Elwood Towner (Hoopa), "Indians and gentile Christians" must battle "the forces of evil" found in the Roosevelt administration. The IRA "is communism working in the Indian Service." Native Americans

PROFILE

Alice Lee Jemison (Seneca)

No member of the American Indian Federation delivered a more vicious, protracted, and scathing assault on federal Indian policy under John Collier than Alice Lee Jemison. Jemison's close friend described the Seneca as a "cultured woman . . . and skillful speaker and writer," but a woman people often misunderstood. Historian Laurence Hauptman agreed, and he noted that her personal accomplishments and rise to influence within the American Indian Federation proved all the more remarkable given the trials she faced in her younger years. Hers was a life "of hardships, against almost insurmountable difficulties," he wrote. Poverty shadowed her childhood, slowed her education, and forced her into a series of poor-paying jobs beginning at age 12. Throughout the 1920s, she worked as a nursemaid, housekeeper, store clerk, peddler, theater usher, door-to-door salesperson, and factory worker before securing a minor position with a Buffalo law firm. For reasons that remain unclear, her marriage failed after only two years, and she was left with two small children to rear. Her Christian faith gave her solace, and her law office job taught her skills desired by the Seneca Tribal Council whose president, Ray Jimerson, hired her to conduct legal research for the tribe. In many ways her life modeled the American Dream, and her success—indeed, her survival—contributed to her favorable view of the Office of Indian Affairs' Americanization policy.

She saw in John Collier a direct threat to Native Americans. The Indian Reorganization Act he drafted in 1933 intended the revitalization of traditional Indian cultures and tribal communities. His program, she believed, contradicted policies that encouraged Indian assimilation with mainstream society and consequently ensured continued segregation, poverty, and the eventual disappearance of Indians as a people.

In 1934, Alice Jemison joined with others to found the American Indian Federation and became the AIF's executive secretary. She quickly moved beyond her official role and emerged as the AIF's most unrelenting, bitter crusader against the IRA, Collier, and the Office of Indian Affairs. Jemison raged that the IRA was nothing less than a concerted effort by Collier and the Roosevelt White House to impose Communism on the United States. The IRA ended private property and replaced it with a system of common land ownership. It resurrected traditional tribal cultures, including the promotion of traditional Indian spiritual ceremonies and beliefs. The policy, she insisted, was unchristian. "The fundamental ideas of the commissioner's plan or program are Communistic," she thundered, and they compelled "Indians [to] live in a state of communal bliss." She blasted the IRA's education program, denouncing it as one based on ideas trumpeted by John Dewey to homogenize a population and one that recommended textbooks that shed favorable light on communist ideals. The agricultural reform agenda pushed by Collier, she added, resembled the system of Soviet collectives. Jemison further railed against the Indians' loss of independence to "Washington directed policies" that only produced a "dominant, omnipotent government"—again, a system comparable to the Soviet Union. "The Office of Indian Affairs," she claimed, "is . . . the most dangerous, Christ-mocking, Communist-aiding, subversive, and seditious organization in the nation." Her fundamental argument was that of the federation, but Jemison's tirades proved exceptionally vicious, scathing, and incendiary.

Jemison's seething attack captured the attention of pro-Nazi organizations throughout the United States, particularly the German-American Bund, the Silver Shirt Legion, and the James True Associates. Encouraged by Jemison's bitter rhetoric, these groups hoped to use her as a conduit through which their fascist message could be spread among Native Americans. Each of these organizations published articles that blended Nazi propaganda with Jemison's anti-Communist assault against Washington, twisted her critique of what she saw as America's unchristian direction into an anti-Semitic argument, and boldly called on Indians and fascists to work together against the Roosevelt government. But Jemison also used the fascist organizations to advance her attacks on Collier, the OIA, and the IRA. She accepted monetary donations to finance her speaking tour in 1936 and 1937, and she appeared on speakers' platforms alongside swastika-wearing American fascists to denounce the communist direction she and the other speakers saw the White House and OIA taking the nation, believing any help she could get in the fight against the government's new Indian policy was worth having.

Her activities and associations quickly earned the watchful eye of the Federal Bureau of Investigation, which tracked her movements and detailed her activities. In 1937, she was called to testify before the Senate Committee on Indian Affairs, and two years later she was called before the House Committee on Un-American Activities. In each setting, Jemison fired a hail of accusations against Collier and the Indian Office, reiterating her belief that the commissioner was taking the agency in a Communist and unchristian direction.

Was Alice Lee Jemison a supporter of Nazism? No, she was not. Nazi racial ideology disgusted her. She repeated in each public presentation her uncompromising devotion to personal freedom and her opposition to overpowering governments that ignored the will of the people. She did, however, choose to "dance with the Devil" in an effort to reverse the new federal Indian policy. Regardless of her intent, the AIF eventually decided it had to split with Jemison. In 1939, the FBI broadened its focus from Jemison to the federation, and public sentiment toward perceived Nazi sympathizers became increasingly hostile as Germany took Europe into the cauldron of war. Unable to quiet Jemison, the AIF asked for and received her resignation.

listened to Brunner's and Towner's arguments against the IRA, but they generally considered their accusations of an alleged communist conspiracy in the OIA ludicrous. Towner garnered less respect than Brunner. His rant seemed out of touch with reality, especially when he accused President Roosevelt and John Collier of being partners in a global Jewish conspiracy against democracy and capitalism. Said one observer, Indians showed Towner "little regard" because of the "sentiments he expressed." The close ties he built with pro-Nazi groups inside the United States also alienated the Native American population. There remained, however, substantial support for the AIF. Despite Brunner's extremist words, the federation nonetheless expressed the views of many Native Americans and, through the AIF's central tenets, maintained a certain continuity with previous Indian progressive groups.

An Assessment of the Indian New Deal

Collier's Indian New Deal accomplished much. Most Native Americans welcomed the increased federal funding, the reclamation of tribal lands, and the acquisition of additional acreage. The effort to close boarding schools and to end the dehumanizing disciplinary system and compulsory military program in those boarding schools that remained open also found favor among Native Americans. The construction of reservation day schools, the fundamental alteration in school curriculum, and the expansion of adult education programs further signaled a positive direction to Indians. Expansion of health services on tribal lands, including the construction of hospitals and clinics and the employment of additional physicians and nurses, gave hope where previously there was little. The commissioner's validation of traditional values and cultures, his rhetoric of tribal self-determination, and the truly unique opportunity to reject or accept by tribal vote the IRA as policy all signaled a profound change in federal Indian policy.

Between 1933 and 1940, most reservations experienced a facelift, and the expectation of continued progress seemed genuine. "Despite much backfiring and waste motion," said Oliver La Farge on the eve of World War II, "the program does move forward." Between 1934 and 1940, more than 200 full-time physicians resided on reservations, 175 other doctors provided their services on a part-time basis, 800 nurses were employed full-time by the Indian Office, and 1,300 health specialists worked directly with native peoples maintaining medical facilities and providing health-related instruction. Ninety-seven full-service reservation hospitals with a bed capacity of 5,000 patients treated 64,000 Indians as in-patients and another one million as outpatients annually. The tuberculosis infection rate dropped from 21 percent of the Indian population in 1928 to 15 percent by 1938, and the level of infection continued downward over the three years that followed. Infant mortality rates also declined, as did the incidence of trachoma and most other infectious diseases the Meriam Report cited ten years earlier.

Through the IRA and Collier's broader Indian New Deal, the OIA purchased land adjacent to reservations and ceded those properties to tribal councils. The Shoshones and Arapahos together netted 1.25 million acres in April 1940, and, by tapping into the New Deal's Resettlement Administration, John Collier was able to secure another 1.2 million acres that same month for other tribes. The Collier administration returned four million acres of land to Indian control.

The IRA's provision for a revolving credit fund of $10 million also contributed to the renewal of reservations. Tribal councils secured loans from which individual Indians borrowed money for farm equipment, seed, and other necessities to make farming productive. Agricultural extension field agents worked directly with Native American farmers and provided practical instruction in community day schools. Collier secured money, material, and manpower through various New Deal agencies for irrigation projects on reservations and land reclamation, and the OIA employed nutritionists and other experts to instruct Indians in meal preparation and food preservation. With Collier's Navajo stock reduction program and the aid provided by the Indian Office to Native American ranchers nationally, Indians owned 100,000 more steer in 1940 than they did ten years earlier. In 1928, Indian ranchers grossed $263,000. In 1940, they grossed $3,125,000. The Indians' total agricultural income jumped from almost $2 million to $49 million while Collier was commissioner. The IRA's emphasis on building profitable tribal economies resulted in an annual per capita income of $600 for Indians nationwide, an amazing achievement given that annual per capita incomes on some reservations were as low as $14 in 1928. Native Americans nationally experienced remarkable improvements in their tribal economies, health care, and educational services at the very time when most Americans suffered the weight of economic depression. And, government promotion of self-government and traditional cultural values, and its effort to preserve the Indian heritage altogether signaled a new spirit in Washington and generally garnered Indian approval.

To be sure, Collier and the IRA failed to solve many problems, and it often had the unintended consequence of raising tension between Indians and the federal government and fracturing tribal communities between those who supported and those who opposed the IRA. Collier's program gave the illusion of tribal self-government, of self-determination. Boilerplate constitutions regulated tribal affairs under the IRA as governing structures were to be approved by the Commissioner of Indian Affairs and the Secretary of the Interior or not be implemented. Majority rule now replaced the more traditional method of community consensus. Moreover, the commissioner frequently threatened and intimidated hesitant Indian communities and largely bulldozed passage of the IRA where he could. Collier generally ignored the diversity of Indian cultures and was rightly criticized for having a more romantic than realistic perception of native peoples.

Nonetheless, in 1941 Native Americans could scan the preceding 100 years and find no better example of a genuine reformist spirit that valued Indian cultures than that which existed under Collier's administration. Said Reverend C. Aaron (Mahican) in 1934, "My common sense tells me that John Collier is a member of the White Race, but my heart tells me John Collier is an Indian. . . . John Collier is an Indian with a heart as big and broad as the day is long . . . [and] through the provisions of [the IRA] we see a new day dawning." Less effusive but certainly approving of the IRA and Collier, one San Carlos Apache noted, "I think the IRA was the best thing that ever happened to Indian tribes. . . . For many years, the San Carlos Apaches held a celebration on June 18 to commemorate the birth of this legislation." Said Benjamin Reifel (Sioux), "we had the most sickening poverty that one could imagine" in 1930. Many Indians survived by eating their horses. An observer on the Qualla Reservation (Cherokee) in North Carolina complained that before Collier's New Deal Cherokee homes were "worse than filthy. . . . I don't see how they live and they are not living, but just existing." Philleo Nash, an anthropologist who worked among Indians in the 1930s and was appointed Commissioner of Indian Affairs in 1961, credited Collier and the IRA with reversing the abysmal conditions faced by most Native Americans. "The tribes were dying in 1932," he said. The reformist agenda of Collier, embodied in the IRA and in numerous supplemental programs he fashioned, provided Native Americans the necessary tools for survival.

Nash was only partly correct. He failed to credit Indians themselves. Were it not for the Indians' own initial complaints against the IRA, the number of tribal communities that rejected the IRA, the narrow vote that occurred in so many other tribal elections, the Indians' persistent willingness to challenge Collier, and even the reactionary positions advocated by some Indians, the IRA would have never evolved in form and substance as it did. Moreover, Native Americans participated extensively in Indian New Deal projects, made use of new or improved services, and took advantage of newfound opportunities. The IRA and related programs framed only the outline in which individuals and tribal communities themselves detailed the course of renewal and growth.

Conclusion

Throughout the 1930s, John Collier's administration of the Office of Indian Affairs sought to overturn the previous 100 years of federal Indian policy. Rather than compel Indians to the path of assimilation, Collier and the programs he constructed allowed Native Americans, for the first time under federal government supervision, to choose for themselves assimilation or renewal of traditional tribal cultures and structures. The Indian Reorganization Act he crafted along with the New Deal programs he extended to reservations were largely responsible for the revitalization of reservations, the return of lands long lost to the government or to white speculators, the development of generally prosperous tribal economies, improvements in the state of Indian health care and education, and the creation of opportunities for Indian self-determination. Native Americans used the new federal Indian policy and its subsidiary programs to move into administrative positions, gain a stronger educational foundation, advance themselves financially, secure their families, and place themselves in positions where they could ultimately choose and direct their own course in life. Although much of Collier's IRA reflected his own personal agenda for the revitalization of tribal communities, often ignored Indian voices, and frequently turned on his romanticized vision of Native Americans, it was heavily influenced by decades of reformist activity and rhetoric led by or championed by Indians themselves.

Review Questions

1. How did the 1928 Meriam Report shape the reform programs of the 1930s under the Hoover and Roosevelt White Houses?
2. Of what significance was the Rhoads commissionership of the Office of Indian Affairs to the work John Collier pursued?
3. In what ways was the Indian Reorganization Act a fundamental redirection of federal Indian policy? How might one argue that the IRA inadvertently accelerated Native American opportunities for assimilation with white society?
4. What reasons did Indians give for resisting the Indian Reorganization Act? How did they demonstrate their opposition?
5. How effective and of what consequence to Native Americans was Collier's Indian New Deal?

Recommended Readings

Cohen, Felix S. *On the Drafting of Tribal Constitutions* (Norman: University of Oklahoma Press, 2007). Cohen, who helped draft the Indian Reorganization Act, offered in this document guidelines for tribes then writing constitutions under the IRA.

Deloria, Vine. *The Indian Reorganization Act: Congresses and Bills* (Norman: University of Oklahoma Press, 2002). A collection of the historical documents from the earliest years of John Collier's efforts to alter the course of federal Indian policy.

Hosmer, Brian, and Colleen O'Neill, eds. *Native Pathways: American Indian Culture and Economic Development in the Twentieth Century* (Boulder: University of Colorado Press, 2004). Essays that examine Native American adaptation to and participation in twentieth-century economic directions and the imprint of their participation on cultural identities.

Kelly, Lawrence C. *The Assault on Assimilation: John Collier and the Origins of Indian Policy Reform* (Albuquerque: University of New Mexico Press, 1983). A significant treatment of the Indian Reorganization Act and the effort to preserve traditional native cultures before World War II.

Philp, Kenneth R. *John Collier's Crusade for Indian Reform, 1920–1954* (Tucson: University of Arizona Press, 1977). The classic study of John Collier and the transformation of federal Indian policy in the years he served as Commissioner of the Bureau of Indian Affairs.

Native American History Online

General Sites

Felix Cohen, *Handbook of Federal Indian Law* (1941). http://thorpe.ou.edu/cohen.html This site includes the nearly 700 pages of legal history, documents, constitutions, and other material compiled by Felix Cohen during the 1930s and published by the Government Printing Office in 1941. Cohen's work details the field of Indian Law, treaties, the scope of federal power over Indian affairs, tribal and individual rights, tribal self-government, tribal property, taxation, and federal services to Native Americans. It is the definitive legal statement regarding Native Americans on the eve of World War II. It also contains an annotated table of federal statutes and treaties, federal court cases and Department of Interior rulings, and Attorney General opinions.

University of Oklahoma and the National Indian Law Library, *Native American Constitution and Law Digitization Project*. http://thorpe.ou.edu/ This is the broader website in which Felix Cohen's *Handbook of Federal Indian Law* is located. Of particular interest are recent revisions to tribal constitutions, post-1941 court rulings and federal statutes, research guides, and information and links specifically tied to Indian affairs in Oklahoma and Alaska.

Adobe Gallery: Art of the Southwest Indians. www.adobegallery.com Adobe Gallery specializes in Pueblo pottery and fine art in a variety of presentation forms including baskets, paintings, sculptured works, furniture, and jewelry. Presented in the gallery's collection is the artwork of Pablita Velarde.

The Avery Collection of Native American Art, Tucson, Arizona. www.statemuseum.arizona.edu Located in the Arizona State Museum, the museum encourages awareness of, understanding of, and respect for Arizona's cultural heritage. Central to this mission is the Avery Collection of American Indian Art, which includes more than 300 paintings produced by Native American artists since the mid-1930s.

Museum of Indian Arts and Culture. www.indianartsandculture.org In 1909, Edgar Lee Hewett founded the Museum of New Mexico to gather and preserve artifacts, artwork, and crafts of Native American cultures. Nearly 20 years later, John D. Rockefeller established the Laboratory of Anthropology to study Southwest Indian culture. The museum and laboratory merged in 1947, creating the Museum of Indian Arts and Culture (MIAC).

Historic Sites

Bandelier National Park, New Mexico. www.nps.gov/band/index.htm Located between Santa Fe and Taos, the park includes Frijoles Canyon, the ancestral home of the Pueblo peoples. The park's website includes a brief history of the Pueblo peoples in the region, timelines, an online collection of Pueblo artwork, and multimedia presentations.

Navajo Nation Council Chamber, Window Rock, Arizona. www.nps.gov/history/nr/feature/indian/2005/navajo.htm The Navajo Nation Council Chamber was a project of the New Deal agency Public Works Administration (PWA) completed in 1935. Admirers of the facility described it as "the single-most significant building . . . symbolizing the New Deal revolution in federal Indian policy." Its octagonal shape, east-facing doorway, and red sandstone exterior were all intended to honor Navajo cultural traditions as was Gerald Nailor's mural "The History and Progress of the Navajo Nation," which adorns an interior wall. On June 16, 2004, the Council Chamber was first listed as a National Historical Landmark.

CHAPTER 15

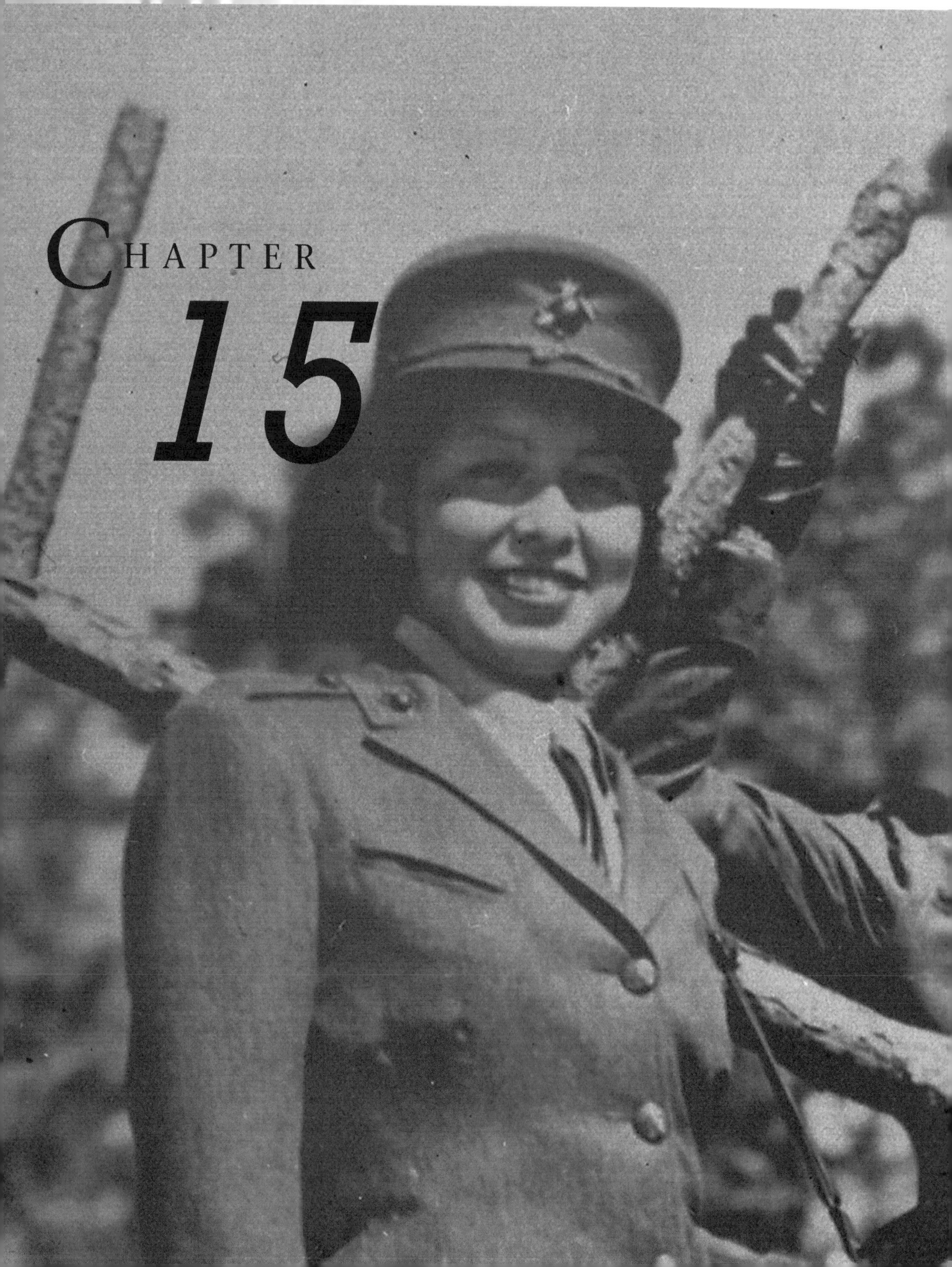

Marine Corps women reservists at Camp Lejeune, North Carolina, October, 1943

Source: National Archives and Records Administration, 535876

American Indians Join the War Effort, 1940–1945

LIEUTENANT ERNEST CHILDERS EARNS THE CONGRESSIONAL MEDAL OF HONOR
NATIVE AMERICANS ENTER THE ARMED FORCES
Draft Registration and Military Induction
Motives for Enlistment
DEFINING INDIAN IDENTITY
Racial Identity in Virginia
Tribal Sovereignty
NATIVE AMERICANS AT WAR
Indian Response to Pearl Harbor
Indians at War
Code Talkers
The Popular Image of Indian Soldiers
THE HOME FRONT
War Comes to the Reservations
Migration to Defense Factories
Women and the War Effort
War Bond Purchases

Lieutenant Ernest Childers Earns the Congressional Medal of Honor

Among the 25,000 Native Americans who served in the U.S. Army during World War II was Ernest Childers (Creek). Born in Broken Arrow, Oklahoma, in 1918 and educated at Chilocco Indian Agriculture School, Childers entered the Army National Guard in 1937. Military service provided supplemental income, specialized training, and leadership skills transferable to civilian employment. As important, Childers viewed military service as a patriotic duty to the United States and a way of making a personal connection to his Indian heritage. Commissioned a Second Lieutenant, the army sent Childers to present-day Fort Drum, New York, where he became platoon leader for C Company, 180th Infantry Regiment, 45th Infantry Division.

On September 8, 1943, Lieutenant Childers landed with American and British forces on a beach near Salerno, Italy, some 150 miles south of Rome. The next day, he led his platoon inland in search of enemy gun positions and soon came under direct fire from a German observation post protected by snipers and machine guns. Stumbling for cover, Childers fractured his foot. He nonetheless assessed the situation quickly. His men were pinned down under intense enemy fire, and already there were casualties. With more thought for the safety of his men than concern for himself, Childers moved forward from one minimally concealed position to another, from each position firing his carbine and killing a sniper. He then slipped undetected to a spot nearly behind the machine gun crew, and from there he fired his rifle until all of the Germans lay dead.

The lieutenant's fractured foot forced him to remain in camp as his battalion moved against another German strongpoint near the town of Oliveto on September 22. Radio reports soon confirmed the battalion had encountered strong enemy resistance. Lieutenant Childers gathered eight men and, despite his own injury, guided them to the site of the firefight. He and his soldiers flanked the Germans without being noticed and grouped themselves behind a rock wall that overlooked a cornfield with enemy machine gun and mortar

CHRONOLOGY

1939	Germany invades Poland, officially igniting World War II in Europe
	The American Indian Federation denounces Nazi ideology
1940	The Navajo Tribal Council states its unanimous support for the United States, should America decide to enter the European war
	California's Mission Indian Federation announces its full support for national military preparedness efforts
	The U.S. Congress passes the Selective Training and Service Act
	U.S. Army forms Indian code-talking teams for each army division
	Draft registration begins
	St. Regis Mohawk Nation announces its intention to resist compulsory military service
1941	Federal District Court in Washington State rules against Indian exclusion from the Selective Service Act
	The U.S. Circuit Court of Appeals rules against Iroquois exemption from the Selective Service Act
	Japanese naval air forces strike Pearl Harbor, forcing the United States into World War II
1942	War Department issues Memo 336 to resolve American Indian racial classification in the nation's armed forces
	U.S. Marine Corps forms the Navajo Code Talker unit
	War Relocation Authority establishes an internment camp on tribal lands for Japanese American relocatees
1943	Lieutenant Ernest Childers earns Congressional Medal of Honor
1944	Wartime farming and ranching operations on Indian lands generate record productivity and profits
1945	Marine Corps Corporal Ira Hayes participates in raising the American flag on top of Mount Suribachi, Iwo Jima
	World War II in Europe ends
	Japan surrenders, ending the war in the Pacific

emplacements. While his men laid covering fire, Childers crossed the field alone, running toward a small house held by German soldiers. Years later, Childers recalled that he "felt the heat from the bullets" as they zipped past him, but he killed two snipers housed there and darted for cover closer to the enemy machine guns. After destroying the German guns, Lieutenant Childers inched forward to capture the German mortar position. With the enemy snipers, machine guns, and mortar silenced, German resistance crumbled. When asked afterward how many Germans he probably killed, Childers calmly responded, "I wouldn't want to make a statement about that." Another officer, however, credited him with 17 "kills" in that one engagement.

For "conspicuous gallantry and intrepidity at the risk of life above and beyond the call of duty in action on September 22, 1943," the United States awarded Lieutenant Ernest Childers the Congressional Medal of Honor on April 8, 1944. His "exceptional leadership, initiative, calmness under fire, and conspicuous gallantry" proved an inspiration to his men and was directly responsible for the elimination of enemy resistance in the area. Childers was the first American Indian in U.S. military history to receive the honor.

Recalling his wartime exploits during a commemorative ceremony at the annual Chilocco Indian School reunion in summer 2001, Ernest Childers expressed both the pride he carried for his Indian heritage and his deep affection for the United States. "Being an American means that you are of many diverse heritages. We are a nation of ethnicities: Anglo-American, Native American, Afro-American, Hispanic, [and] Asian-American," he said. "We Americans have had our differences, and we probably will continue to have our differences, just like any family, but . . . we are all Americans." "The American Indian," he added, "has only one country to defend and . . . the American Indian never turns his back." He was Creek, but he was also American.

KEY QUESTIONS

1. What reasons did Native Americans offer for their compliance with draft registration and their willingness to volunteer for military service?
2. To what extent and in what ways did Native Americans resist wartime challenges to their Indian identity?
3. How did the Indians' cultural characteristics and the stereotyped images of Indians many whites held combine to shape the role of Native Americans in the armed forces?
4. How did the war effort alter Native American life on the home front?

Native Americans Enter the Armed Forces

In late summer 1939, the Great Depression seemed to be coming to an end; however, any relief Americans might have felt as their financial future brightened was tempered by new threats looming on the horizon. War erupted in Europe when Adolf Hitler unleashed his German armies against Poland on September 1; two days later, England and France rose to Poland's defense. In the Far East, Japan's continued grip on Manchuria and coastal China severely strained American-Japanese relations, and rumors of eventual war between the United States and Japan were heard in the corridors of the war and navy departments.

Congress, backed by popular opinion, sought to keep the United States neutral, although American sympathies clearly rested with Great Britain, France, and China. Nonetheless, President Franklin Delano Roosevelt intended America to be prepared should war descend on the United States. In the closing months of 1939 and throughout the following year, FDR ordered factories to commence the production of war materiel—airplanes, tanks, ships, firearms, ammunition, and other equipment required of modern military forces. He intensified intelligence-gathering efforts, strengthened naval power in the western Atlantic, and directed the army and navy to fortify defenses in the Philippines. Congress in September 1940 authorized the nation's first peacetime military draft, calling into the U.S. Army nearly one million men. All male citizens aged 21 through 35 were to file their names with the Selective Service System on October 16 and await selection for military duty.

Native Americans largely supported the nation's preparations. Within weeks of Hitler's invasion of Poland, the American Indian Federation (AIF) publicly denounced Nazi ideology and all organizations in Europe and the United States connected in any way to the current German regime. By year's end, the AIF further pledged its full loyalty to the United States and its total cooperation with defense preparedness efforts. The Navajo Tribal Council at Window Rock, Arizona, unanimously passed a resolution on June 3, 1940, that assured its complete allegiance to the federal government should war come to America. The Navajo people, the resolution read, "stand ready to aid and defend our Government and institutions against all subversives and armed conflict," and the council further promised that un-American activities on the reservation would be "dealt with severely." In southern California, the Mission Indian Federation sent President Roosevelt "a message of loyalty and readiness to serve our great nation" and deferred until the crisis passed all attempts to secure financial remuneration for lands lost to whites over the previous 90 years. Passage of the Selective Service Act transformed rhetoric into action.

Draft Registration and Military Induction

Despite bitterly cold temperatures and mounding snow, hundreds of Navajo men on October 16, 1940, trekked to the draft registration center at Fort Defiance, Arizona, and filed their names with the Selective Service System. Many carried their own personal firearms, assuming registration meant immediate induction into the army. Draft registration continued over the following months, and by year's end 5,000 Navajos had complied with Selective Service requirements. The Navajos were not alone; from reservations scattered coast to coast, 42,000 Indian men representing nearly all tribal communities in the United States registered their names for military service by early autumn 1941. Commissioner of Indian Affairs John Collier boasted almost 100 percent cooperation among Native Americans.

Although registration rates certainly impressed officials in the Office of Indian Affairs and the War Department, the actual number of Native Americans who voluntarily enlisted in the armed forces proved even more surprising. Of the 4,500 Indians in uniform by November 1941, fully 60 percent had enlisted rather than waiting to be drafted. Commissioner Collier told the press that the rate of Indian volunteerism proportionately surpassed that of any other race in America, including whites. "If the entire population enlisted in the same proportion as Indians," voiced another observer, "there would be no need for selective service."

Indian enlistment would likely have been much greater were it not for an unexpectedly high rejection rate; fully one-third of all Native Americans were classed "unfit" for military service. To be sure, Indian New Deal programs had substantially improved the health of American Indians and reservation medical services. Nonetheless, much more improvement was needed. Military examiners in 1940 found disease and malnutrition still prevalent among Indian draft registrants. Trachoma remained pervasive, as did pulmonary and cardiovascular problems. Excessive weight caused by improper diet also prevented entry into the armed forces. Newspapers nationwide ran the response of one overweight Indian rejected by the army. "Don't want to run," said the man, who belonged to different tribes depending on which paper ran the story. "Want to fight!" In Arizona alone, 45 percent of American Indians fell below the military's acceptable level of personal health, in contrast to 27 percent of white registrants.

Failure to meet the army's minimum educational and psychological standards further complicated Indian induction. Although the number of reservation-based day schools skyrocketed during the Depression years and boarding school curricula underwent fundamental changes, the educational reforms of the Indian New Deal came too late to help Indian men at the upper age limit of draft eligibility. Most of those who failed entrance exams resided in the Southwest and Great Plains, living in areas far removed from educational services offered by the OIA. One problem that perplexed officials in both the OIA and War Department was the preponderance of Indians who still spoke only their native language, making their induction into the armed forces virtually impossible. Also, common to standardized testing even today, the army's exams favored more acculturated Indians and, as a result, suggested many Indians were not "socially prepared" for military service. Nearly half of Arizona's native population scored below the minimal passing mark for this area of measurement. In contrast, only 12 percent of the state's white registrants fell below the passing mark.

Motives for Enlistment

Why were Indians overwhelmingly in compliance with the Selective Service Act and so willing to enlist in the nation's armed forces? After all, only 50 years earlier war with the United States still raged on the Great Plains, and nationwide Indian living standards still remained poor in 1940. Commissioner Collier's answer startled few listeners. "Indians," he said, "have identified the struggle of democracies the world over with their own struggle of the last century." Native Americans historically fought "to retain their cultural independence" and battled against a "super-race dominating, absorbing, and reducing to serfdom the small minority group of a different culture." Congressman John Coffee of Washington agreed: "After the injustices the Indian has suffered, he is still ready for an all-out defense of democracy." Individual Indians and entire tribal communities support the United States, he continued, "because America has made a conscientious effort to right old wrongs and improve the life of Indians," as evidenced by the leadership of John Collier over the previous decade. "Democracy gradually corrects those injustices," he concluded.

Many Native Americans concurred. The Navajo Tribal Council resolution of June 1940 confirmed Collier's and Coffee's assessments. The council pledged loyalty "to the system which recognizes minority rights," and

TIMELINE 15.1 NATIVE AMERICANS IN MILITARY SERVICE

Date	Event
September 1940	U.S. Congress enacts the Selective Training and Service Act, establishing the nation's first peacetime military conscription law
October 1940	The first national day of compulsory registration for service is on the 16th; most eligible Native American men comply with the law and register with the draft
November 1941	By November, 42,000 American Indian men have registered their names with the Selective Service office, and 4,500 have entered military service
December 1941	On December 7, Japanese naval forces attack American naval and military installations on the island of Oahu, Hawaii, forcing the United States into World War II
January 1942	Approximately 10,000 Native Americans are in military service
January 1945	Federal government records indicate a total of 25,000 American Indians in the nation's armed forces

15.1 Lieutenant Ernest Childers, a Creek, being congratulated by General Jacob L. Devers after receiving the Congressional Medal of Honor in Italy for wiping out two machine gun nests, July 1944.

Source: National Archives and Records Administration, 191, American Indian select list

encouraged opposition to the "threat of foreign invasion and the destruction of the great liberties and benefits which we enjoy on our Reservation." Said Cozy Stanley Brown: "My main reason for going to war was to protect my land and my people. . . . There are Anglos and different Indian tribes living on the earth who have pride in it. . . . I wanted to live on the earth in the future. . . . The Anglos say 'Democracy,' which means they have pride in the American flag. We Navajos respect things the same way they do." Ernest Childers (Creek), like so many young men in the late 1930s and early 1940s, viewed military service in part as a citizen's responsibility to serve and defend his nation, as we saw at the beginning of the chapter.

Indeed, a clearer sense of identity with the United States induced thousands of Indians to comply with draft registration and spurred many to military service. Collier's Indian New Deal countered the long-standing policy of compulsory assimilation, revived traditional Indian ceremonies and community structures, and trumpeted self-determination for Native Americans. Indian Office programs elevated the quality of reservation life for most Indians and widened opportunities for those who sought inclusion within the general population. For the first time in their relationship with the U.S. government specifically and American society generally, many Indians perceived a nation ready to embrace them fully as citizens, with all of the rights, privileges, and responsibilities citizenship carried.

An emerging sense of national identity was only one of many reasons for Indian compliance with Selective Service and enlistment. Fear also compelled their movement into the armed forces. Stories of German and Japanese atrocities were commonplace in newspapers in 1940 and 1941, particularly stories of the brutality inflicted on Polish Jews by Hitler's occupation forces and the earlier, infamous "rape of Nanking" conducted by the Japanese army. Understood, too, was the racist foundation of both Nazism and Japanese imperialism. "Germany is right now deliberately exterminating the Poles, who are about as numerous as the Indians," said Collier in early December 1941. "The same thing is happening to the Greeks right now. That is what we face if we lose the war." News reports and Collier's words struck a sensitive nerve among Indians. Over the course of four centuries, Indians themselves had lost their lands and suffered near extermination at the hands of an invading race-conscious power. The massacre of Big Foot's band at Wounded Knee still shadowed the memory of older Sioux, and the images of the Long Walk, Sand Creek, the flight of the Nez Perce, Geronimo's resistance, and dozens of other bitter days remained scorched in their minds. The horror of genocide once experienced would not be repeated. Said one Indian enlistee, "I'm doing this for my people" and for "the many American people, also [for] the unborn children which would be the generation to come."

Protection of the land itself prompted still other young men to enlist. Albert Smith (Navajo) said, "this conflict involved Mother Earth being dominated by foreign countries. It was our responsibility to defend her."

Cozy Stanley Brown shared Smith's perspective. He joined the Marine Corps "to protect my land and my people because the elderly people said that the earth was our mother. . . . The Navajo people get their blessings from the four sacred mountains, our mother the earth, father the sun, and the air we breathe." The land was more than property, more than territory arbitrarily divided by imaginary lines, and more than regions governed by certain political ideologies. The earth itself was the source of life, identity, and spirituality in Native American cultures. It was to be defended against destructive peoples and forces.

The opportunity to recapture a traditional "warrior spirit" attracted some Indians into the nation's armed forces. Treaties entered into with the United States decades earlier forbade Native Americans from taking up arms, and warrior values that historically framed tribal structures slowly disintegrated with each passing year since the conclusion of Indian-white hostilities. Rank, status, and influence within tribal communities were no longer predicated on a warrior's reputation and skill as in earlier days. Participation in this war, then, offered many young men the opportunity and the means to renew their tribal warrior tradition, gain personal honor and respect, and assume responsibilities within the tribe in the manner of their ancestors. "Go and fight as your forefathers did . . . our Great White Father is calling us to help. We must go," said Three Calves to the younger Blackfoot men on his reservation.

There were still other significant motivators. Having been reared on stories of their fathers' "adventures" in the last European war, many imagined their own journey to London or Paris, or to strange and exotic Pacific islands, returning home with their own stories of war and travel to pass onto their children and grandchildren years later. The promise of an adequate, regular income enticed others, while the lure of specialized job training transferable to a postwar civilian economy attracted other men. And, like so many Americans coast to coast, Japan's aerial assault on Pearl Harbor unleashed a profound determination to exact revenge. Joe Big Son (Blackfoot) enlisted just days after Pearl Harbor was attacked. "I'll scalp the Japs if I get near one" and use the trophies to "decorate the town of Arlee after the war is over," he promised family and friends.

For all of these reasons and many more, Native Americans complied with draft registration and accepted military service. Between December 7 and December 31, 1941, all but three single men from the Grand Portage Ojibwa Reservation in Minnesota joined the armed forces. Of the 500 residents on the Mesquakie Sac-Fox Reservation, 19 donned uniforms within days of Pearl Harbor. Ten thousand Indians were in military service by the end of January 1942, more than twice the total number in service one week before Japan's strike on the United States. In a short letter to John Collier in early spring 1942, Mae Williamson (Blackfoot) informed the commissioner that 100 young men from her community were already in the armed forces, among them her husband's five brothers. "Thus it is throughout the tribe," she wrote. Less than one year later, six Indian families in Montana each contributed five sons to the war effort. By spring 1943, 40 percent of all able-bodied Crows were soldiers or sailors, and 100 Ojibwa from the Lac Court Oreilles Reservation in Wisconsin, with a total population of only 1,700, were in service by that same time. Two thousand Sioux enlisted in the various military branches; 22 of these came from the Little Eagle community that had only 300 permanent residents, and only two of these men were drafted. Clearly, Native Americans viewed World War II as their war. By 1945, Washington's records identified 25,000 Indians in the nation's armed forces, representing most tribal groups and every cultural region (see Table 15.1).

Table 15.1 Native American Servicemen, Spring 1945

Army	Navy	Marine Corps	Coast Guard
21,767*	1,910*	723*	121*

* Figure does not include Commissioned Officers.
Source: Department of the Interior, *Indians at War*. Washington, D.C.: Government Printing Office, 1945.

SEEING HISTORY

Freedom's Warrior—The American Indian

Charles Banks Wilson, born in 1918, devoted much of his career as a professional artist to capturing on canvas the history of Oklahoma and its prominent citizens. He also published books about the American West, the Texas Rangers, and Native Americans, among them *Indians of Eastern Oklahoma* (1956). His masterful portraits of Will Rogers and Jim Thorpe along with his paintings of the people and landscape of the state hang in the Oklahoma State Capitol building. In 1995, at the age of 77, Wilson painted *Freedom's Warrior— the American Indian* to honor the service of Native Americans to the United States in times of both war and peace.

Questions

1. What perspective or theme does Wilson portray in this piece representing Native American service during World War II?
2. In what ways does the artwork mirror the wartime rhetoric of American policymakers, military personnel, and press concerning Native American participation in World War II?

15.2 Charles Banks Wilson, *Freedom's Warrior—The American Indian*

Source: Courtesy of Library of Congress Prints and Photographs Division, LC-USZ62-87996

Defining Indian Identity

The United States portrayed the war as the ultimate conflict between good and evil, between the forces of God and Satan. Although Americans of every faith answered the call to war, Protestant governing bodies hesitated to offer official sanction for military action until summer 1942 when each, reluctantly and with very liberal interpretations of biblical teachings, validated armed force as the nation's only recourse. Even then, not all devout Christians relinquished their fundamental doctrine of peace and brotherhood. Thousands of American citizens placed their religious identity above their national identity and refused induction into the armed forces. The Selective Service System exempted from conscription anyone "who, by reason of religious training and belief, is conscientiously opposed to participation in war in any form." More than 70,000 individuals filed applications for **conscientious objector** (CO) status; approximately 40,000 received the classification and were instead assigned non-military work in hospitals and public service projects.

Resistance to compulsory military service also surfaced among Native Americans. Commissioner Collier suggested the occasional dissent emanating from some reservations was not necessarily opposition to military service on religious grounds but instead simple misunderstanding of the law. "Indians on these reservations are not slackers," he noted in a letter to Selective Service chief General Lewis B. Hershey. "They are not radicals or agitators. It is a case of merely making them understand" the law and its purpose. "There are many patriotic Indians who find the Selective Service Act distasteful not because they object to military service, but because they consider it a reflection on their loyalty to the country." Collier's explanation seemed plausible. Indian condemnation of compulsory service partly turned on the idea that everyone should fight, not simply those randomly selected by the draft. "Since when has it been necessary to conscript the Sioux as fighters?" asked one Indian on the Rosebud Reservation. Collier's interpretation of Indian resistance, however, proved quite limited. Resistance to the draft rested on much more serious issues—racial identity and tribal sovereignty.

Racial Identity in Virginia

Walter Ashby Plecker directed Virginia's State Office of Vital Statistics throughout the 1930s and the war years that followed. He insisted that all individuals in Virginia who claimed Indian identity were actually African Americans hoping to escape Jim Crow race segregation. Plecker justified his sweeping assessment with an 1894 Bureau of American Ethnology report that determined that Virginia natives and African Americans had intermarried in the nineteenth century and formed a single race. He cited scholarly works that claimed Indian "blood has so largely mingled with that of the Negro race as to have obliterated all striking features of Indian extraction." Plecker demanded Virginia strip Pamunkey Indians of their Native American identity and relegate the Gingaskins, Nottoways, Chickahomineys, and all other Tidewater natives to the African American listing. The Selective Service Act required Indians to be registered as "white" and inducted into white military units. Determined to protect white society from "racial amalgamation," Plecker ordered Virginia's draft boards to list all individuals claiming Indian identity as "colored" and to assign them to African American military training centers.

J. L. Adams (Chickahominey) wrote a letter of protest to the Selective Service System, the Department of Interior, and the OIA. Adams reminded federal officials that "the other time our boys registered [for World War I], they registered as Indians and went with the whites. Now, it seems as if they want to send us with the colored. . . . We don't mind our boys going [into service] if they can be sent right and not with the colored," he complained. The War Department in March 1941 responded, ordering draft boards to investigate the "ethnic origin" of all Indian registrants before attaching them to any training unit, but Virginia's State Director for Selective Service instructed boards to list Native Americans as "Indian mix" and to induct them as "white recruits." Confusion reigned until January 1942, when the War Department issued **Memo 336**. It reaffirmed the earlier order for boards to investigate the racial heritage of draft registrants and to class as "Negro" those Indians with any "ascertainable Negro blood." The memo also directed draft boards to consider "whether their [Indian] associates are Negro and whether they are treated as Whites in the social patterns of their community and State," a much simpler and quicker method for determining racial identity.

Virginia's Indians resisted the ruling from Washington. In the February draft call, one dozen Chickahominey inductees were shipped to an all-black training camp. Once there, each man refused to leave the barracks until reclassified as "White" or "Indian." They assured the military that only armed force would dislodge them until their racial identity was changed. "Indians are not trying to avoid the draft or serving in the United States Army," wrote tribal chief O. Oliver Adkins in a stinging note to the War Department. Racial classification was the sole issue. Adkins reached to the heart of the Indians' argument: "What have we to fight for? For the individuals who deny us our Birth Rights . . . and classify us to a creed that we do not belong, to which we may be mistreated as Negroes? My people are American Indians of the State of Virginia. They will not go as Colored or as Negroes." The Indians' resistance, along with the lack of a record of Chickahominey association with African Americans, ultimately won them reclassification.

Oliver Fortune (Pamunkey) did not fare as well. He registered with the Selective Service in February 1942 and enlisted in the army days later, but he was assigned to the Negro Training Facility at Fort Meade, Maryland. Fortune refused induction and was immediately slapped with the federal charge of "refusal to serve." As he awaited his October 30 trial, Commissioner John Collier admitted that "something should be done" to support Fortune's claim of Indian identity, but the Selective Service System, not the Indian Office, had jurisdiction in the matter. Tribal leaders sought the intervention of Governor Colgate Darden and in their letter voiced "distress and alarm" that Fortune and other Pamunkeys were listed as black recruits. "This action simply blots out our Tribe, our race, our descent, and places us as negroes [*sic*]." Identification as African Americans, the letter continued, "would be an act of death to us—death to what we value in life, our Indian heritage." Not wanting to make an enemy of Plecker, Governor Darden did nothing to help Fortune.

Prosecutors during the trial produced evidence that one of Fortune's grandparents and his mother were each listed in state records as "colored," a term that generally referred to African Americans. Moreover, Fortune had attended an all-black school. The defense argued that state documents only presented two racial categories—white and colored. That his grandparent and mother were listed as "colored" did not mean they were African American, only that they were not considered "white." The "colored" identifier for his mother precluded Oliver Fortune's admission to white schools as a child; consequently his association with African Americans was one the state imposed on him. Nonetheless, Fortune was convicted and sentenced to two years in the federal prison at Petersburg.

University of Pennsylvania anthropologist Frank Speck continued Fortune's battle and aided the resistance effort among all Virginia Indians. In public speeches, interviews with the news media, and letters to government officials, Speck attacked Memo 336 and Walter Plecker's efforts to classify Virginia Indians as people of African descent. Speck pointed out that Plecker's oft-quoted scholarly passages were taken out of context. Specifically, he noted, the phrase "not a little" Negro blood in fact read, "There has been considerable intermixture of white blood in the tribe, and not a little of that of the Negro." Speck argued that if Pamunkeys were to be listed in a racial category other than Indian, the "white" designation applied as much as "colored." Equally important, he produced the Laws of the Pumunkey Indian Town, written in 1896, that clearly prohibited Indian marriage with African Americans: "No member of the Pamunkey Tribe shall intermarry with anyy [*sic*] Nation except the white under penalty of forfeiting their rights in town." Speck further pointed to the Bureau of American Ethnology bulletin Plecker was so keen to reference, providing the author's own assessment that the Pamunkeys appeared more Indian than black and would ultimately assimilate fully with Virginia's white population. The evidence Speck amassed and the increasing number of angry letters, petitions, and public demonstrations by both Indians and whites across Virginia compelled draft boards to set aside Memo 336 and induct into white military units all men who claimed Indian identity. Fortune won reclassification as a conscientious objector and was released from prison.

Virginia's native population initiated and continued a defense of their Indian identity and with Speck's supportive work gained state recognition as Indian. The issue, nevertheless, persisted throughout the remaining war years. Eighteen Pamunkeys and dozens of other Indians from Virginia tribes served in white military units, but the state's *Gold Star Honor Roll* in 1946 listed only one Indian among Virginia's servicemen killed in action. Tribes found the names of lost sons listed instead as African American. The setback embittered tidewater Indians, and in the postwar years they moved to define themselves as a separate race in Virginia, apart from both African Americans and whites. Because of their own lobbying efforts and legal battles, by 1950 state records showed 1,056 Indians in the state, a marked increase over the 1940 listing of 198. The battle over state records reflected the new spirit among the state's native population to assert its unique identity.

Tribal Sovereignty

Indian resistance in Washington State to draft registration and compulsory military service turned on a different issue. The Yakima Nation enjoyed tribal sovereignty protected by treaty with the U.S. government since the 1850s, but in 1941 Washington, D.C., insisted the Selective Service Act negated all treaties with Indians and now required Native Americans to submit themselves to conscription. Watson Totus was of military age. Totus did not object to military service, but he believed the Selective Service Act threatened Yakima tribal sovereignty and identity. Specifically, the 1855 treaty forbade Yakimas from taking up weapons against or on behalf of the United States. Enforcement of the Selective Service Act would invalidate that longstanding treaty and, in so doing, eliminate tribal sovereignty. Second, the treaty had not extended American citizenship to the Yakima people. They remained non-citizens residing inside the territorial boundaries of the United States. Totus and many others within the tribal community reasoned that the Selective Service Act applied only to U.S. citizens and therefore held no authority over the Yakima Nation. In May 1941, Totus and 70 supporters filed suit in Federal District Court to prevent enforcement of draft registration and compulsory military service on their separate nation.

On May 28, Judge Lewis B. Schwellenbach ruled against the Yakimas in *Totus et al. v. The United States.* The Citizenship Act of 1924, he determined, proclaimed all Native Americans within the United States as natural citizens, regardless of existing treaties. The **Nationality Act of 1940** only reaffirmed the 1924 legislation. In a final, compelling statement, the judge pointed to the Selective Service Act itself, which "superseded" all treaties with Indian nations and permitted Congress to suspend "all laws or parts of laws in conflict" with Selective Service "for the period in which the act is in force." Yakima claims for exemption from compulsory military service were, therefore, denied. Totus and his codefendants reluctantly accepted the court's decision and submitted themselves for draft registration.

A more protracted battle over tribal sovereignty was already in progress in upstate New York. The Treaty of Canandaigua (1794) legally recognized the Iroquois Confederacy, or Six Nations, as an independent, sovereign nation within the United States. That special relationship with Washington was one of mutual agreement that Congress sustained throughout the nineteenth and early twentieth centuries. The Six Nations demonstrated its national sovereignty when, in 1917, the Confederacy issued its own declaration of war against Germany, separate from that of Congress, and in November 1924 when the Confederacy sought admission to the League of Nations. Passage of the Selective Service Act in 1940 and Washington's insistence that it applied fully to the 4,200 Indians of the Six Nations carried a direct challenge to the Confederacy's continued national independence.

On October 8, 1940, the St. Regis Mohawk Council resolved that draft registration was not applicable to the Confederacy as member tribes were "foreign nations, not United States citizens." "Under our treaty with the United States of America, we are a distinct race, nation, and people owning, occupying, and governing the lands of our ancestors," a Seneca declaration read. Clinton Rickard (Tuscarora) put it more succinctly: "How can a citizen have a treaty with his own government?" Those young men who wished to enlist in America's armed forces were certainly free to do so; however, the Selective Service Act commanded no authority over the independent, sovereign Six Nations.

Leaders within each Confederacy tribe told their young men to register with the draft but immediately file petitions for exemption from military service; America's legal authority over the Six Nations would be tested. Seventy-three Tuscaroras and dozens from each of the other five tribes registered in February 1941, and many of these soon thereafter submitted their appeals for exemption. In the meantime, attorneys for the Six Nations searched for someone to volunteer himself as a "test case" in federal court. Warren Eldreth Green (Onondaga) offered himself to tribal lawyers that spring. He had not only registered with the draft but, on April 26, had been inducted into the army as well. Wilfred Hoffman, a Syracuse attorney hired to represent Green, immediately filed a writ of habeas corpus to secure the Onondaga's release from service despite Green's personal desire to remain in the army. The issue at stake, however, was much more important than Green's wish to serve.

Federal District Court judge Frederick H. Bryant on May 14 recognized the seriousness of the fundamental issue and its broader implications for Indians nationwide and quickly rejected Green's petition, permitting Hoffman to appeal the matter to a higher court. The United States Court of Appeals, Second Circuit, heard the Indians' argument in *Ex Parte Green* in October and rendered its unanimous decision against Green and the Confederacy on November 24. Each of the three appellate judges—Thomas W. Swan, Harrie Brigham Chase, and Jerome Frank—admitted his sympathies rested with Green, but, said Frank, "We have taxed our ingenuity in vain to find any interpretation which would result in a decision in his [Green's] favor." "We find ourselves compelled to decide against Green, although . . . we reach that conclusion most reluctantly." As in *Totus et al.* v. *the United States*, Frank, Chase, and Swan determined the Citizenship Act and Nationality Act constitutional and applicable to all Native Americans. With or without their consent, American Indians were legal citizens of the United States. Domestic law commanded priority over treaties. Moreover, noted Frank, the Selective Service Act negated all treaties for the duration of the conflict.

Court rulings in *Ex Parte Green* and *Totus et al.* v. *the United States* favored the federal government and, in those decisions, probably contributed more immediately and concretely in placing Native Americans clearly on an assimilationist path than did any other government act or court interpretation since the Dawes Act of 1887. Treaties were declared null and void, and there was no longer any confusion over Indian citizenship as far as Washington was concerned. The Confederacy nonetheless persisted in presenting itself as an independent, sovereign nation. The Iroquois formally declared war on Germany and Japan in June 1942, a symbolic gesture indicating the Confederacy's intention to continue the fight for recognition as a separate, sovereign nation within a nation.

Native Americans at War

The earliest radio reports of Japan's strike on Pearl Harbor, Hawaii, shocked most stateside listeners. Although casualty figures were not yet available, Americans fully understood death and destruction cloaked the island of Oahu that Sunday morning, December 7, 1941. Personnel at American naval and military installations in Hawaii struggled to extinguish raging oil-fed fires, and rescuers feverishly retrieved the wounded and dead from the harbor while hundreds more frantically struggled to save sailors still trapped on the battleships *Arizona* and *Oklahoma*. Teams of nurses treated the rising number of wounded as best as they could, frequently making the wrenching decision of who should receive medical attention and who among the injured were beyond hope. Soldiers and Marines hurried to erect a defensive ring around the island against an expected Japanese troop landing that never came. Under the veil of smoke that towered over Oahu at midday, the U.S. Navy lay crippled and military aircraft smoldered in piles of twisted wreckage on the island's air bases. Throughout the nation, Americans that day realized Japan had brought the United States into war. They realized, too, that Japanese sights now focused on American forces in the Philippines.

There was much concern among Indians at Santa Clara Pueblo. Young men from the village were posted on Oahu and many more were attached to a New Mexico National Army National Guard regiment stationed in the Philippines, islands the Japanese forces would certainly soon attack. "There was a general acceptance of the war as their own," noted Oliver La Farge during his visit to Santa Clara that Sunday morning. "There were expressions of regret for the many boys, not just of their own people, but American boys in general, who were going to be killed" in the war than now washed American shores.

Indian Response to Pearl Harbor

Anxiety was plainly evident at Santa Clara Pueblo. "There was an unexpectedly keen sense of Hawaii and the Philippines" in which many of their own sons served, said Oliver La Farge. But Santa Clara was not exceptional. Families of Indian men already in service knew their loved ones were now fighting for their lives or would soon go to war. Thousands more would watch their fathers, brothers, and sons rush to recruiting offices in the days that followed.

Native American response to Japan's attack and Hitler's declaration of war on the United States three days later manifested itself in tribal action. Cheyenne Indians denounced the Axis powers as an "unholy triangle whose purpose is to conquer and enslave the bodies, minds, and souls of all free people." Tribal communities in Arizona discontinued their use of the swastika, a longstanding symbol of friendship, on clothing, blankets, and pottery. In an indisputable show of tribal sovereignty, the Jemez Pueblo Indians and the Ponca Indians each issued their own, separate declarations of war on Japan and Germany, and the Chippewa of Michigan promised to "stand by Uncle Sam to the end" in their pronouncement of war with all Axis powers. The following June, representatives of the Iroquois Confederacy assembled on the steps of the U.S. Capitol with Vice President Henry Wallace to call for the Indians' full participation in the war. "It is the unanimous sentiment among Indian people that the atrocities of the Axis nations are violently repulsive to all sense of righteousness of our people, and that this merciless slaughter of mankind can no longer be tolerated. . . . Now," the declaration continued, "we do resolve that it is the sentiment of the council that the Six Nations of Indians declare that a state of war exists between our Confederacy of Six Nations on the one part and Germany, Italy, and Japan and their allies against whom the United States has declared war, on the other part." American Indians immediately joined the nation's war effort. Individuals and entire tribal communities set aside past differences with the United States and committed themselves to winning the war against the Axis nations; it was, they all agreed, a war of national survival and a war against evil.

Indians at War

Approximately 25,000 Indians served in America's armed forces during World War II, nearly one-third of all eligible young Indian men. It is suspected that even more actually served. The Selective Service System registered Indians as "whites" on official documents; the 25,000 known to have served also identified themselves as Native Americans, but, for whatever reason, many others never listed their Indian identity.

Throughout World War II, the Office of Indian Affairs' monthly publication, ***Indians at Work***, kept Native American readers abreast of individual and tribal contributions to the war effort. It highlighted home front conservation programs, scrap material collection drives, war bond sales, agricultural production, off-reservation employment, job-training courses, and emerging directions in federal Indian policy. To connect readers on the home front to Indians in the armed forces, the magazine tracked Indian enlistment rates, published letters Indian servicemen sent to the OIA, described specialized training recruits received and the possible application of those skills to postwar reservations, and detailed, when possible, the combat performance of individual Indian soldiers, Marines, and sailors. National news organizations occasionally pulled stories from *Indians at Work* for publication in national and regional newspapers.

Indians at Work and major newspapers reported the service and sacrifice of General Clarence L. Tinker (Osage). Tinker assumed command of the Army Air Corps in Hawaii just days after Pearl Harbor and throughout spring 1942 substantially increased its operational capacity and readiness for war in the Pacific. During the Battle of Midway on June 3 and 4, Tinker's B-17 and B-24 bombers flew 55 sorties against the Japanese fleet, directly contributing to America's pivotal victory over Japanese naval forces. Three days later, Tinker personally led a bomber force against the Japanese garrison on Wake Island, 1,000 miles west of Midway. He refused "to assign anyone else the task." For reasons still unknown, Tinker's plane crashed into the Pacific only 40 minutes into the flight. No trace of the general or his crew was ever discovered. In *Indians at Work*, Commissioner Collier revealed Tinker's Osage heritage (an identity he seldom shared with others) and linked the general to the larger participation of Indians in the war, writing that Tinker "exemplified the modern Indian soldier"—courageous and selfless.

Reports filtered stateside over the next three years from both the European and Pacific Theaters of Operation of Native American combat duty. From the Philippines came the story of Lieutenant Colonel Edward McClish (Choctaw). A graduate of Haskell Institute in Lawrence, Kansas, and Bacone College in Muskogee, Oklahoma, McClish in December 1941 commanded a Filipino force resisting the Japanese invasion of Mindanao. With the collapse of allied resistance in April 1942, McClish led his men into the mountainous countryside. From there he directed a persistent and successful guerilla campaign that included more than 350 engagements against Japanese occupiers until the island was liberated in spring 1945. His protracted action resulted in approximately 3,000 Japanese killed and another 600 wounded.

While battling Japanese troops in 1943, Army Private Ben Quintana (Keres) grabbed the machine gun from the lifeless hands of his comrade and "delivered a withering fire into the enemy, inflicting heavy casualties." His effort halted the Japanese attempt to envelop the American position, but in so doing Quintana lost his own life. For his courage, Private Quintana received posthumously the Silver Star. Marine private Leonard Webber (Shoshone) saw action in November 1943 on the Pacific island Tarawa. He frequently exposed himself to enemy guns while running messages from battalion headquarters to frontline tank units. The following summer, Webber landed on Saipan and later on Tinian Island, and in each battle, under heavy mortar and small arms fire, he individually scouted routes ahead of advancing American tanks. Sergeant Nathaniel Quinton found himself locked in battle with Germans in the Hurtgen Forest in November 1944, a campaign in which the United States suffered 20,000 casualties. The army credited him with killing or wounding 55 enemy soldiers before being captured himself. Quinton, however, soon overpowered one guard, killed another, secured maps that detailed German defensive positions, and successfully made his way back to American lines. Army private Houston Stevens (Kickapoo) faced a German warplane, the dreaded Me-109, as his landing craft approached the beaches of southern France in August 1944. Although machine gun rounds from the plane tore through his side, hip, and legs and he found himself surrounded by flames that threatened to detonate crates of ammunition, Stevens fired his .50 caliber machine gun at the German plane and forced its retreat. Also commended in *Indians at Work* was Private First Class Albert Wahweotten (Potawatomi), who charged 200 yards ahead of his platoon to clear a German-occupied house. Armed with an M-1 rifle and a rocket-firing bazooka, Wahweotten destroyed the enemy's machine guns, rushed the house, and captured 12 prisoners.

Native Americans served in every branch of America's armed forces, held every rank from private and seaman to general and admiral, and performed most every military task in military service. Ira Hamilton Hayes (Pima) captured the imagination of the American public and ultimately came to represent Indian contribution to the war effort. He was later memorialized in one Hollywood film, praised in one published biography, honored most recently in James Bradley's popular book *Flags of Our Fathers*, and enshrined forever in the Iwo Jima Memorial at Arlington National Cemetery just outside Washington, D.C. Hayes enlisted in the Marine Corps in 1942 and served with distinction in combat across the South Pacific. More than once he was offered promotion to

15.3 Raising the American flag on Iwo Jima, February 23, 1945. Ira Hayes is shown on the far left of the photo.

Source: National Archives and Records Administration, 80-G-413988

a higher rank for his courage and leadership skills, but each time Hayes refused the responsibility. Instead of ordering other Marines into life-threatening assignments, he would say "I'd rather do it myself."

In February 1945, the Fifth Marines landed on Iwo Jima, a volcanic island laced with a network of tunnels and defended by 25,000 Japanese soldiers. Three days into the month-long battle, Hayes's platoon moved up Mount Suribachi, the highest point on the island from which enemy cannon fire pinned down Marine movements below. Slowly, methodically, and with heavy casualties, Hayes's platoon reached the peak, and there he and five others raised the American flag in front of the watchful camera of combat photographer Joe Rosenthal. The photo captured the essential spirit of the Marine Corps and America's inevitable victory in the Pacific, and it soon graced the cover of magazines across the United States. To the Indian Office and news media, the image of Hayes highlighted a "warrior spirit" among American Indians in the war against Axis nations. Hayes (now a corporal) and two other survivors of the flag-raising were returned stateside to help sell war bonds. Hayes never reveled in the honor and accolades given him, preferring instead to return to his combat unit still fighting the Japanese. Until his death he insisted he was only doing his duty.

Code Talkers

Modern technology permitted armies in both World War I and the early years of World War II to intercept battlefield radio and telephone transmissions and, in so doing, gain information that might determine the course of combat. The existing methods of encryption and decoding transmissions were notoriously time consuming and not suited to the hectic pace of the battlefield. Shortly before America entered World War II, the U.S. Army Signal Corps considered a variety of solutions to the problem of protecting battlefield communications from enemy listeners. Signal Corps officers recalled the army's impromptu use of Choctaw Indians to send telephone messages during the closing days of war in 1918.

PROFILE

Postwar Ira Hayes

15.4 Ira Hayes

Source: National Archives and Records Administration, 519164

James Bradley's popular book *Flags of Our Fathers* captured superbly the stories behind the six men who together raised the American flag on top Mount Suribachi, Iwo Jima, in February 1945 and explained with compassion and understanding the postwar lives of those men immortalized in Joe Rosenthal's photograph.

Ira Hamilton Hayes (Pima) was discovered lifeless on the bitterly cold morning of January 24, 1955, lying face down in his own blood and vomit outside a small hut on the Gila River Reservation, where he had spent the previous night playing cards and drinking. Hayes was only 32 years old. A local coroner listed his death accidental, the product of alcohol and exposure. Regarded widely as a hero of Iwo Jima—indeed, an American military icon—Arizona's governor ordered his body to be laid in state under the capitol rotunda where thousands of men, women, and children passed by his casket, honoring his wartime service and the inspiration he ignited among many Americans in the waning months of war. Former governor Rose Mofford recalled 40 years later that Hayes's funeral on January 26 was "the biggest funeral I've ever seen in Arizona." His body was then transported to Arlington National Cemetery for burial. After his death, Hollywood "honored and memorialized" the Pima Indian in two films, country and western singer Johnny Cash paid tribute to Hayes in song, and one writer penned a book of the Indian's life and death. Hayes in death moved from hero to legend.

Bradley's *Flags of Our Fathers*, however, presented a more complex story of each flag raiser and revealed in Hayes the turbulence of his postwar life. Reporters, tourists, neighbors, and coworkers all made his life intolerable, pestering him for his photograph, an autograph, or a piece of his clothing. They begged him for interviews and for the gory details of war and his own description of that brief moment immortalized in a photograph. Hayes hated the attention. "He'd never talk about the event. Or the war," said Urban Giff, a fellow Marine and Pima. Hayes grew increasingly "distant." He despised the label "hero" and felt tortured by the word. Said Giff, "It wasn't just that Ira had seen others do much more than he, and pay for it with their lives. His problems were made worse by the fact that in our culture, it's not proper for a person to seek recognition." Although Hayes did not seek attention, it found him. "I think he always struggled" with his notoriety, said Giff.

Hayes rarely held any job for more than a few months and generally kept himself physically close to few friends. He occasionally developed genuine emotional relationships with other combat veterans. He was particularly distressed that his friend Harlon Block was not identified as one of the six flag raisers, and the Marine Corps insisted that Hayes not reveal the mistake. In May 1946, Hayes simply walked off the Gila

River Reservation and hitchhiked to southern Texas, covering 1,300 miles in three days to visit the Block family and confess that Harlon was, indeed, among the men in Rosenthal's photograph. Hayes spoke only a few minutes with Harlon's father, Ed, the two men standing uncomfortably in the Blocks' cotton field. Once he set the record straight for the family, Hayes abruptly said, "Okay, well, I guess I'll be off." The two men shook hands, and Ira walked away.

The mental and emotional chaos that plagued Hayes never diminished, even with the Corps' eventual admission that Block was among the flag raisers. Memories of war consumed Ira. Between summer 1942 and Japan's surrender, he had witnessed unimaginable horror. Hayes experienced nothing more personal, nothing more intimate, nothing more hellish in his life than war. The Pima suffered extreme "combat fatigue," or post-traumatic stress disorder, as American society today terms the condition. Like many veterans, he sought momentary relief "in the bottle." His police records in Phoenix and Chicago list more than 50 arrests for public drunkenness and disorderly conduct, but the label "alcoholic" misrepresents Hayes. Those closest to Hayes knew him to have a low tolerance for alcohol and maintained that days often passed between binges. His drinking, they contend, was for Hayes simply a tactic for escaping the demons of war that haunted him. Wrote Bradley, "Ira's war would never end" until his life came to an end. In death, Ira Hayes found peace.

In autumn 1940, the 32nd Infantry Division enlisted a small group of Chippewa and Oneida Indians expressly for communications service. An Iowa National Guard unit, the 19th Infantry Division, enrolled members of the Sac-Fox tribe for similar training, and 17 Comanche were inducted into the 4th Infantry Division. During army maneuvers in Louisiana in August 1941, all of these Indians used their native languages to relay battlefield directives, and commanders noted some success. The Comanche seemed particularly proficient and in October relocated to Ft. Benning, Georgia, for additional training.

In his book *The Comanche Code Talkers of World War II*, historian William C. Meadows notes that the Comanche fashioned a simple code within their language. "Well, we kind of sat around in groups . . . and we kicked it around and we all agreed on something and we'd go with it," said Roderick Red Elk. A bomber aircraft, for example, was termed "pregnant bird" and its bombs "baby birds." A "turtle" represented a tank, and a bayonet was "gun knife"—each term spoken in Comanche. "We almost went crazy ourselves figuring out the original code," remembered Haddon Codynah years later. Certain words, they realized, could not be tied easily to animals, geographic features, or tools, so the Indians crafted a system in which one Comanche word matched each letter of the English alphabet. "Saddi" (dog) stood for the letter D, "tuhka" (eat) for E, and so forth. "I often wondered what those Krauts thought when they heard it. They probably said, 'What the heck is going on there anyway?'" mused Forrest Kassanavoid. The army used the code in November 1941 during mock battles at Fort Jackson, South Carolina, and again in the larger Carolina Maneuvers in summer 1942. In each, the Signal Corps seemed satisfied with Comanche radio work and recommended the Indians' deployment to the European Theater of Operations.

The army, however, bungled the effort. Division commanders and many staff officers in the War Department failed to recognize the full potential of these Indian specialists. Standard radio communications systems, they contended, sufficed in the heat of frontline battle. Second, the army selected no single group of Indians exclusively for code talking (see Table 15.2). Although special attention was given to the Comanche code-talking project, each infantry division was allowed to recruit Indians from areas closest to its stateside base. Recruits hailed from at least four different broad language groups, spoke at least two dozen dialectical variations, and represented more than one dozen tribes. With a collection of Comanche, Sac-Fox, Choctaw, Chippewa, Oneida, Hopi, Pawnee, Sioux, Kiowa, and others, interdivision communication proved virtually impossible. Moreover, only a few code talkers served in each division; without a large complement of code

Table 15.2 Known Native American Code Talkers in the United States Army, World War II

Assiniboine	Co. B., 163 Inf. Div. (ID)
Chippewa/Oneida (17)	32nd ID
Choctaw	K Co., 180th Inf. Reg. 45th ID
Comanche (17)	4th Signal Co., 4th ID
Hopi (11)	223rd Battalion
Kiowa	689th Fld. Art. Batt., XX Corps.
Muscogee/Creek and Seminole	195th Fld. Art. Batt.
Sac and Fox (19)	18th Iowa Inf.
Sioux (Lakota and Dakota)	302nd Rec. Team, 1st Cav. Div. and 32nd Fld. Art. Batt./19th RCT.

Notes:
Numbers in parentheses indicate the number of Native Americans known to serve as code talkers in that particular military unit.
The Cherokee and Pawnee served as code talkers, although no specific military unit has been identified in military records.
Source: William C. Meadows, *The Comanche Code Talkers of World War II* (Austin: University of Texas Press, 2002), Appendix H, pp. 241–242.

talkers and an established, uniform training program in the United States to prepare more Indians for this service, code capabilities would likely disappear as casualty rates rose. Finally, rather than use the trained Indians solely for sending and receiving messages, the army employed code talkers in the laying and repairing of telephone lines, one of the most hazardous duties given to any soldier in combat.

The Marine Corps approached the program in a more systematic and organized manner. It selected only Navajos as code talkers. Few German academics and no Japanese scholars in the interwar period studied the language. Additionally, Navajo was understood to be a very difficult language to master, certainly much too difficult for enemy combat radiomen to learn in addition to English. There were also thousands of Navajos who still spoke their native language, allowing the Marine Corps to have a steady supply of code talkers.

The first 29 Navajos were recruited as code talkers in 1942 from boarding schools at Fort Defiance, Shiprock, and Fort Wingate and sent to San Diego for boot camp, advanced infantry training, and communications school. After mastering basic radio operations, the Navajos created a code in their own language for combat use. Two methods were devised. The simpler system assigned specific words to specific weapons, tactics, military units, geographic formations, and directives. "Tsidid" (bird) represented airplane; "tsisi-bewol-doni" (bird shooter) stood for anti-aircraft gun; "annasozi" (cliff dweller) was fortification; "chal" (frog) represented amphibious. A "words for alphabet" system was also created. Unlike the Comanches, the Navajos assigned multiple words to each letter to eliminate repetition and in so doing prevent the Japanese from breaking that code.

In autumn 1942, the first contingent of Navajo code talkers arrived on Guadalcanal with the Second Marine Division to support the American offensive that began there on August 7. Commanders immediately put the Navajos to work. They sent messages among platoon, company, battalion, and division commanders, and they directed shore bombardment from naval ships. Until the end of World War II, code talkers participated in every major Marine campaign in the Pacific Theater, including battles on Saipan, Iwo Jima, and Okinawa. Within the first two days of the Iwo Jima campaign alone, the Navajos radioed more than 800 messages without error. "Were it not for the Navajos," said Major Howard Conner, "the Marines would never have taken" the island.

The same level of respect and admiration surfaced from officers and enlisted men in each battle from Guadalcanal to the doorstep of Japan itself.

Eight hundred Navajos served in the Marines during World War II, but only 450 were code talkers. All but 30 saw action against the Japanese, and, of these, eight were killed performing their duty. The service of the Navajo code talkers remained officially a military secret during the war and for years afterward. The Pentagon in the 1950s believed there might be an occasion one day to resurrect Indian code talking, but technology evolved so rapidly that in 1969 the Nixon White House no longer deemed Indian code work vital to modern military service and declassified the Navajos' contribution to World War II. In 1981, President Ronald Reagan issued certificates of appreciation to surviving code talkers, and in September 1992 the Pentagon opened a permanent exhibit commemorating the Navajos' special service.

15.5 Navajo Indian code talkers Henry Blake and George Kirk, December 1943

Source: National Archives and Records Administration, 532395

The Popular Image of Indian Soldiers

The older, harsher image of Native Americans had softened in the minds of most non-Indians by World War II, although Hollywood films continued to portray Native Americans as vicious, throat-cutting savages. As noted earlier, many white Americans believed Indians to be a vanishing race.

It is easy to be understanding of and compassionate toward one's historic enemy when that enemy is nearing extinction. Moreover, white Americans now viewed the historic confrontation between American Indians and whites as a matter relegated to the distant past, and Indian armed resistance to white expansion the previous century now seemed understandable, if not justified. Indians had fought to defend their lands and families against conquest and destruction by a vicious, aggressive enemy, hardly an ignoble motive for warfare and certainly a motive that paralleled the Allies' current struggle against the Axis.

There also existed a pervasive curiosity about Indians among white troops, largely the product of prewar segregation and Hollywood-based stereotypes. Of particular interest was the Indians' spirituality. Although it was (and is) common for soldiers to carry good luck charms into battle, white soldiers were particularly interested in "Indian medicine"—the small pouches of personal items over which prayers for protection had been offered by one's family or tribal community. Some Indians recounted special religious ceremonies given them by their communities and families prior to deployment, ceremonies that sought the Indian's safe return home. Still others collected small items from dead enemy soldiers for use in purification rituals upon their return home. And Indians, either individually or in small groups, often conducted ceremonies that sought their Creator's protection before a coming battle. Popular war correspondent Ernie Pyle scribbled one story about Indians who danced and sang, seeking protection just before they landed on Okinawa, and Richard Tregaskis described in

READING HISTORY

Navajo Translation of the United States Marine Corps Hymn

We have conquered our enemies
All over the world,
On land and on sea,
Everywhere we fight.
True and loyal to our duty,
We are known by that,
United States Marines,
To be one is a great thing.
Our flag waves
From dawn to setting sun.
We have fought every place
Where we could take a gun;
From northern lands
To southern tropic scenes,
We are known to be tireless,
The United States Marines.
May we Live in peace hereafter,
We have conquered all our foes,
No force in the world we cannot conquer
We know of no fear.
If the Army and the Navy
Ever look on Heaven's scenes,
United States marines will be
There living in peace.

Nin hokeh bi-cheh a-na-ih-la
Ta-al-tso-go na-he-seel-kai
Nih-bi-kah-gidotahkah-gi
Ta-al-tso-go en-da-de-pah
Ay be nihehozeen
Washindon beAkalh Bi-kosi-la
Ji-lengoba-hozhon
Ni-he ha-na-ah-tajihla
Yelkhol-go e-e-ah
Day-ne tal-al-tsogoenta-she-jah
Tal-tso-go entas-se-pah
Ha-kazdineh-ih be-hay-jah
Ado taaokhek-ash-shen
Do ni-din-da-hi ol-yeh
Hozo-go nay-yeltay to
A-na-oh bi-keh de-dlihn
Ni-hi-keh di-dlini ta-etin
Yeh-wol-ye hi-he a-din
Sila-go-tsoidochah-lakai
Ya-ansh-go das dez e e
Washindon be Akalh-bi Kosi la
hozo-g-kay-ha-tehn

Source: www.oldcorps.org

Question

Why was the conversion of the Marine Corps Hymn into the Navajo language important or significant for Navajo Marines?

SEEING HISTORY

Military Use of Native American Imagery

Throughout modern American military history, images of Native Americans and those popularly associated with American Indian cultures have been used as military emblems. The 45th Infantry Division's use of the Thunderbird emerged as the most widely recognized Indian symbol in the European Theater of Operation during World War II. Each point of the red square field represents a state from which the division drew its soldiers—Colorado, Oklahoma, Arizona, and New Mexico. The Thunderbird was intended to represent respectfully the cultural heritage of Native Americans in those states, a life-giving force, hope, power, and strength. Although the Thunderbird was not a tribal symbol for most Indians who served in the 45th Infantry Division, it nonetheless held a broad cultural meaning for them. Indians comprised about 25 percent of the division's manpower strength.

Another emblem with Native American roots was the one the 36th Infantry Division adopted. The 36th Infantry Division was based in Texas and Oklahoma. The established symbol of Oklahoma was the arrowhead, which symbolized the state's heritage and the heritage of Native Americans who long resided there. The "T" represented Texas, the division's headquarters. Indians made up about 20 percent of the 36th Infantry Division.

Questions

1. What messages did the U.S. Army hope to convey in using these images?
2. What might the symbols suggest to Native American soldiers who served in those divisions?
3. Although smaller, specialized units used more stereotypical Indian imagery, how do these divisional patches relate to the broader national perception of Native Americans at this time in history?

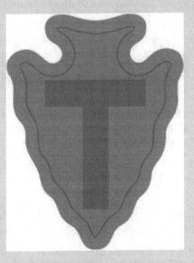

15.6a 45th U.S. Infantry Division shoulder patch, 1942–1945.

Source: U.S. Army

15.6b Shoulder sleeve insignia that was first approved for the 36th Infantry Division in November 1918.

Source: U.S. Army

his book *Guadalcanal Diary* a similar scene he witnessed among Indian Marines before their baptism by fire. On Leyte Island in the Philippines, one Indian who earlier spoke of the protection ceremony his family gave him dashed for cover underneath several wood planks with a white Marine hard on his heels. When the gunfire ceased and they both uncovered themselves, they found the boards chewed by enemy fire, but neither man suffered a scratch. "In fact," said the Indian, "I came out of the war without being touched by the enemy." His white comrade attributed his own safety to his closeness with his newfound Indian friend.

On the national level, however, the image of the Indian warrior assumed almost mythic proportions. Born in the embellished stories fathers told their sons, dime novels, and Hollywood films, Indian warriors were presented as possessing near superhuman combat skills—persistent, committed to victory, willing to die for their cause if necessary, able to track an enemy through any terrain and in any weather, stealthy in their movement, and masters of the ambush. The general population viewed them as "natural" fighters.

Both scholars and government officials took the "natural fighter" image as reality in the 1940s. Said the prominent academic Stanley Vestal, the Indian "was a realistic soldier; he knew that war meant killing, and he never gave quarter or expected it." Indians, he added, pursue an "offensive approach to life," especially in battle. Government officials touted the Indians' "inherited talents . . . uniquely valuable" to the current war. Of particular importance was the Indians' "endurance" and "rhythm" for combat, their "feeling and timing, [and] co-ordination" in battle and the Indian soldiers' "uncanny ability to get over any sort of terrain at night." The Indian, said one White House insider, "takes a rough job and makes a game of it. Rigors of combat hold no terrors for him." "American Indians are crack marksmen," noted one congressman. "They excel as scouts and trailsmen and lookouts." Said one army commander, "The sense of perception of many Indians is so acute that they can spot a snake by sound or smell before they can see it. They have an uncanny faculty at weaseling over any kind of terrain." The Indian "takes to commando fighting with gusto. Why not? His ancestors invented it," one army officer insisted.

As a result of these exaggerated descriptions and stereotyped images, Native American frontline soldiers often found themselves assigned the more hazardous duties. Platoon leaders, aware of Native Americans in their units, frequently placed an Indian as point man on patrol inside enemy territory, believing he would be able to "smell" or sense the enemy's presence or effectively track the enemy's retreat. Officers frequently assigned Native Americans to nighttime commando raids against enemy positions, scaling cliffs or serving as snipers—tasks thought to be suited to natural Indian skills, according to their white commanders.

Indian soldiers and Marines generally understood the rationale that placed them in the most dangerous assignments. They appreciated the respect implied by their white officers, but they knew too well that such duty made them easier targets for enemy guns. Nonetheless, they obeyed their orders with few objections. Said one Native American soldier, "we figured we were dead men any way you look at it. At some point, on some battlefield, the enemy would eventually get us."

The Home Front

The war embraced all Americans on the home front. Sixteen million men donned military uniforms between 1940 and 1945, leaving behind worried parents, wives, and children. Service Star flags hung in living room windows, each blue star representing one family member in the armed forces. As the war progressed, gold stars replaced blue, indicating a loved one who paid the ultimate price in battle. Another 15 million Americans migrated from farm to town, from city to city, and from state to state to secure lucrative jobs in defense factories. The pattern of daily life altered as Washington rationed civilian access to gasoline, home heating fuel, tires, meat, coffee, sugar, cigarettes, and dozens of other items desperately needed by the military. Communities gathered scrap metals, worn-out rubber goods, animal fat and meat drippings, and old newspapers for recycling into war-related materiel. Unnecessary travel was discouraged, air raid drills became routine, war bond sales were frequent, patriotic parades were regularly held in small towns and cities alike, and newspapers daily followed allied action overseas along with the training and deployment of local servicemen. No American escaped these daily reminders that the United States was at war.

War Comes to the Reservations

"Now and then as we went about our tasks in the evening, the crisp air would carry to us the voices of elderly people singing plaintive war songs about young people who would not return home alive," remembered one elderly Sioux of the war years. Among Native Americans on reservations and among those working in urban-based defense plants nationwide, the reality of war seldom strayed far from their minds. So many young men had left for war, many others soon would, and many would never come home.

Native communities faced World War II much like all other American towns and cities. Reservations organized local civil defense organizations to prepare themselves against possible enemy attack against the United States and to lend direct support to the army and navy should their help be required. Indians within a few hundred miles of the coast and along the more remote stretches of the U.S. borders with Mexico and Canada erected observation posts that volunteers manned on rotating shifts, 24 hours daily, scanning the skies for enemy aircraft while others patrolled on foot areas most suited to saboteur movement. Many tribal communities formed Home Guard paramilitary units to provide defense of local bridges, dams, and power plants. On the Kaschia Reservation near Stewart's Point, California, 17 tribal members, each toting his own shotgun, rifle, or handgun, routinely patrolled the countryside looking for saboteurs and commandos who may have slipped ashore from enemy submarines. With so many men absent from home, one group of Chippewa women formed their own home guard. "We have rifles, we have some ammunition, and we know how to shoot," one woman said. On most reservations, community day schools operated longer hours to provide courses in auto mechanics, welding, and electronics—skills desperately the armed forces desperately needed. Patriotic posters written in English with native-language captions covered storefront windows or were tacked onto telephone poles and fences.

American Red Cross (ARC) offices opened on many reservations. They initially opened to support reservation hospitals that lost medical personnel to military service, but as the war progressed they treated wounded servicemen. ARC nurses also offered residents courses in first aid, and Red Cross programs included instruction in food preservation, personal hygiene, and community sanitation. Indian women volunteered their time with the ARC to manufacture surgical dressings for overseas field hospitals and to knit scarves and mittens for distribution to soldiers and sailors stationed in cold climate areas. The Red Cross also conducted national fund-raising drives to help support the organization's national and global reach. The 1942 ARC fundraiser kicked off at Zuni Pueblo during a blinding snowstorm, but each household contributed money or stored crops "and in each case the wheat, corn, or hay was ready when someone called." In one home, the family donated all it could—six dollars and two gold rings. In another, a little girl gave her only nickel to the Red Cross drive.

Reservations, like all other communities in America, looked to redirect local resources to the war effort. The Blackfoot Agency in Browning, Montana, offered the War Department its entire manufacturing center for national defense, a center that specialized in filing and polishing castings and assembling mechanical parts. The 2,500 residents of the Crow Indian Agency in southern Montana not only placed "their entire tribal resources . . . in the hands of President Roosevelt" but also further contributed $10,000 of tribal funds for the government's purchase of "bombs and guns." Klamath Indians of Oregon donated $150,000 for the construction of a national defense training center on their land, and the Cheyenne dropped all outstanding financial claims against the U.S. government.

15.7 Apache Indians assist in the unloading of beds for evacuees of Japanese ancestry in Poston, Arizona, April 1942.

Source: National Archives and Records Administration, 536128

The land itself proved a valuable resource for America's armed forces. Reservation farming and ranching operations witnessed substantial growth and profitability during the war, largely generated by the military's demand for food. Between 1939 and 1941, reservations, such as the Rosebud Agency in South Dakota, organized National Defense committees to determine and categorize tribal resources and to lay production plans in the event of war. The committees served as advisory boards, encouraging Indian farmers to produce particular crops that would not only contribute to armed forces demand but also generate a lucrative income. The Hoopa Valley Indian Agency in California founded a Young Farmers' Club, which applied for and received $1,300 from the Indian Education Service to purchase a tractor, plow, disc harrow, and a mowing machine. The club rented the equipment to members for a mere $2 per cultivated acre and used the fee to cover the cost of fuel.

More than 100 Eastern Cherokees entered military service by summer 1942, and dozens more migrated to defense jobs in urban centers. The labor shortage forced the Cherokees to solicit agricultural support from the U.S. Army. The War Department studied the Indians' problem and crafted a solution. The army had recently transformed its traditional cavalry divisions into "mechanized divisions." The horse was now obsolete in the armed forces. Rather than destroy the horses, as the War Department previously ordered, Washington called on one cavalry division to transfer its horses to the Cherokees for plowing fields. The War Department also assigned one platoon of soldiers to temporary duty at the Cherokee reservation to help cultivate farmlands.

Nationwide, Indians cultivated 35 percent more acreage in December 1942 than they did just before Japan's attack on Pearl Harbor one year earlier. Commissioner John Collier noted that Indian farm production in 1942 provided cereal goods to 367,000 soldiers, vegetables to 52,000 men, and fruit to 38,000. Similar productivity continued throughout the war years. In 1944 alone, Indians produced 4.8 million bushels of cereal valued at $5,000,000, vegetables netted $3,700,000, and fruits earned $775,000. By mid-1945, the value of all Indian-produced farm goods stood at nearly $23,000,000.

Ranching performed even better. Reservations increased cattle holdings 35 percent and sheep nearly 15 percent just before Pearl Harbor, anticipating America's entry into war and the nation's sudden need for meat. By the end of 1942, Indian ranchers earned $13,000,000 supplying meat and dairy goods to the armed forces, more than $14,000,000 one year later, and $16,000,000 by the end of 1944.

Both the army and navy required isolated acreage for pilot training facilities and military airfields. They also needed unoccupied property for gunnery and bombing ranges. Across the United States, particularly in the South, federal courts condemned tens of thousands of acres, forced property owners to relocate, and authorized use of the newly acquired land for target practice. Most lands that the federal government secured from Indians came from reservations in the Great Plains and Southwest. The Pine Ridge Sioux alone lost 300,000 acres to the War Department, which converted much of the land into an artillery practice range. Nationwide, Washington took control of more than 840,000 acres of Indian lands for military purposes. Although that acreage was returned to Indian control following the war, the short-term loss nonetheless impeded full wartime development of Indian agriculture and ranching operations and renewed some distrust of Washington among older Indians who retained vivid memories of land loss decades earlier. The federal government also needed land for the housing of 120,000 Japanese Americans taken into custody and forcibly removed from the West Coast by a Presidential Executive Order shortly after Pearl Harbor. The **War Relocation Authority (WRA)** established a 90,000-acre camp with 7,500 Japanese Americans on Indian lands at Poston, Arizona, in 1942, and another facility to accommodate 5,000 detainees was planned for the Gila Reservation in southern Arizona.

Migration to Defense Factories

Forty thousand Indians moved from reservations to urban communities during the war years, most of them securing employment in the nation's defense industry. Wives and children often followed the married men who migrated. As evidence of impending change within American Indian societies, a sizeable portion of the migrants were single women. The Indian Office estimated that another 14,000 Indians might have gained off-reservation employment had placement and transportation services been available for the more remote or isolated native communities. In 1942, aircraft manufacturers in southern California hired 200 Indians, representing at least one dozen different tribes, and more than 700 gained work at airplane plants in Wichita and Tulsa. Shipyards in Seattle and San Francisco employed 75 Native Americans in early 1942, a number that leaped over the next three years. The army ordnance depot at Fort Wingate, New Mexico, hired 1,500 Navajos, fully one-third of the total workforce there. Thousands more gained jobs with construction companies and railroads, and still others took work in factories producing military vehicles and chemicals, in government offices, and in hospitals. Noted one reservation superintendent in a telegram to Commissioner Collier, there were "workmen leaving in every direction in search of work." The wartime migration of Indians constituted the largest single movement of Indians from their reservations in American history.

Indian migration, as one would suspect, was initially regional and largely followed defense work. Lumbee Indians of North Carolina first spread across the Tarheel State, but as war production increased and more jobs opened, many Lumbee moved north to Baltimore and Philadelphia, many eventually settling in Detroit. New York's Iroquois initially took jobs in Buffalo, Rochester, Syracuse, and New York City, gaining positions with Bausch and Lomb, General Motors, Kodak, Alcoa, National Gypsum, and Curtis-Wright. By late 1942, the expanding defense industry lured Iroquois men and women to Chicago, Detroit, Akron, and cities as far away as Tulsa. Off-reservation employment generated an income level most Native Americans never previously enjoyed. Salaries typically averaged $2,000 to $2,500 annually, which was roughly four times the national average for Indians in the late 1930s.

Alaskan natives found prosperity much closer to home. In 1940, the War Department commenced the construction of airfields, army posts, and highways into Alaska as part of a coastal defense ring around the United States that stretched through the Aleutian Islands. To combat the bitterly cold Alaskan winter, army officials in February 1942 contracted the Nome Skin and Sewers Cooperative, formed earlier under the New Deal, to manufacture 10,000 reindeer parkas, seal skin trousers, mittens, snowshoes, caps, and fur socks. Alaska's two salmon canneries supplied military personnel and civilian construction crews with food and earmarked their entire 1942 production for America's armed forces.

The native population in the Aleutians, however, confronted a much different wartime reality. In summer 1942 Japanese forces landed on the islands of Attu and Kiska and remained there for the next year. Rather than realize newfound business opportunities and higher paying jobs, native families faced occupation by an enemy force and deportation to Japan as prisoners and laborers. About 25 percent of the nearly 200 Aleuts held in Japanese POW camps did not survive. Those not swept under the Japanese boot confronted removal from their homes and loss of their property to American military demands. United States forces torched their homes and other community buildings to prevent their use by the Japanese. The relocated families were transported to southeastern Alaska where the military had hastily constructed relocation camps in which native families could reside safely for the war's duration, but these facilities failed to provide the most basic services. There had not been sufficient time for adequate planning, Army officials contended. However, since 1940 the War Department had considered a Japanese invasion of the Aleutians and Alaska to be a possible move should war erupt between the two nations and had commenced the enlargement of defense capabilities across those regions. Relocation camps were grossly overcrowded. Electricity and running water reached few people, essential survival supplies such as cold weather clothing were not provided, food was generally inadequate to feed the population and frequently poor in quality, and medical services were nearly non-existent. Indeed, tuberculosis and pneumonia sifted widely through relocation centers. "The overcrowded [living] conditions were an abomination," recalled Philemon Tutiakoff. Sickness struck almost every relocated family, and death was not an uncommon visitor. Not until late 1945 were Aleuts permitted to return to their home communities where they struggled to rebuild their prewar lives. In 1987 the United States Congress finally granted each surviving relocatee a sum of $12,000 for their wartime losses.

Women and the War Effort

With so many men in the armed forces or relocated to urban defense work, women increasingly found greater job opportunities and assumed increased tribal responsibilities within their communities. Local construction and maintenance work crews hired female labor, and women became truck drivers, heavy equipment operators, and engine mechanics. They poured concrete roads, built small bridges, manned firefighting teams, and erected housing for Japanese American detainees. Among Zuni and Navajos, the number of female silversmiths increased significantly, working now in a trade traditionally reserved for men. Washington contracted many of these women to produce military rank insignia worn by army and naval officers.

Like their male counterparts, unmarried Indian women also left home for jobs in defense factories. Of the 40,000 Indians who secured employment in urban areas, fully 12,000 were women. Douglas Aircraft Corporation and Martin Aircraft hired hundreds of Indian women as riveters, sheet-metal cutters, and electronics specialists. They worked in shipyards, produced tanks and jeeps, manufactured ammunition, test-fired weapons, and assembled radios. Thousands more gained positions in the nursing field, took jobs as secretaries, and became teachers in overcrowded school districts. Women who worked in technical fields generally received their training on the job, but many Indian boarding schools also offered courses that provided these women their skills. Chilocco Indian School in Oklahoma actively encouraged young women to enroll in its sheet-metal cutting classes; one such class in 1942 included 24 students, only three of whom were men. Sherman Institute in California offered women seats in arc welding classes and machine courses. Female graduates typically earned $40 to $50 weekly, an income level far greater than available to them before the war and a salary commensurate with white employees who performed the same jobs. Certainly the desire to aid the war effort led many women to seek jobs in defense factories, but the promise of good pay and personal independence lured many others from home.

Lydia Westlund (Ojibwa) was employed in a non-medical position in a Minnesota hospital in 1941 but soon realized the opportunity to secure a substantially higher income by taking a job in defense work. "It was easy getting a job," said Westlund. "I went to work at Wood Conversion for the money. . . . I was only making thirty dollars a month at the Indian hospital. My wage . . . tripled at the mill." She left the company to give birth to her child, but months later she reentered the workplace, securing an even better-paying job at a nearby paper mill. Lily Laveau (Ojibwa) worked alongside Westlund at Wood Conversion but was soon lured by higher wages and training opportunities at a Boeing Aircraft plant in Seattle, Washington. Laveau received two weeks of instruction and was then assigned a place on the assembly line. "All we did," said Laveau, "was sleep and work." Her journey to Seattle, however, resulted in more than good pay. Laveau was unsure just what to expect from the non-Indian Seattle population, a population so recently diversified by the explosive job market there. Much to her surprise, "no one at Boeing" appeared concerned about her Indian heritage. "No one asked what nationality anybody was," said Laveau, and "bigotry posed no problem." Maria Carpenter also left her Minnesota home soon after the war began for work at a plutonium plant in Hanford, Washington. Wages were very good, but defense work in distant states had other results. Said Carpenter, she had not expected to be so homesick in Washington. She returned to Minnesota only to realize that her short stay in Hanford had changed her. She learned that she "no longer tolerated her father's strict household rules" and soon afterward left home once more, this time for work in Illinois.

Eight hundred Indian women exchanged their civilian clothes for military uniforms in the army's Women's Auxiliary Corps (WACs) and the navy's WAVES (Women Accepted for Voluntary Emergency Service). A few joined the Marines' women support service. "I went into the WAVES," recalled Hilda Rogers (Ojibwa) "because my older brother was in the service." Rogers trained as a medical corpsman and in 1943 was assigned to a military hospital in Norman, Oklahoma, to care for wounded sailors and soldiers returned stateside from the South Pacific. Women in the auxiliary services were also trained for a wide range of other duties; some were typists, others drove trucks or worked on small engines, and still others staffed supply depots and communications centers.

Whether in auxiliary military branches or in off-reservation civilian employment, Indian women received far more than exceptional pay; they gained "financial independence and participation in everyday American affairs" apart from their families. "I learned how to do things for myself . . . how to get along with other people and be out in the public. . . . I have a lot more confidence," said Lily Laveau (Ojibwa).

War Bond Purchases

The U.S. government increased taxation to help cover the costs of war, but Washington also raised money through the sale of war bonds. These federal notes were sold for $18.25 and upon their maturity netted the buyer $25, providing Washington with funds to help finance the war and purchasers a positive return for their investment.

Most Native Americans bought war bonds as individual investors, as did most Americans in the general population. It was common to set aside personal or family funds for the purchase of one bond monthly. The largest transactions, however, were made by tribes that used portions of their annual congressional appropriations to buy bonds. The Shoshones authorized Washington to redirect $500,000 of tribal funds for bond purchases, and Creek Indians in Oklahoma invested $400,000 in war bonds by the end of World War II. Tribal purchases in 1942 stunned BIA officials and clearly indicated the depth of Indian support for the war effort: the Klamaths invested $228,000; the Cheyenne River Sioux spent $15,000; Pine Ridge Sioux purchased $106,000; and Kiowas invested $93,000. The Quapaw, however, far surpassed all other tribal investments, purchasing $1,018,000 in war bonds by year's end. Whether individual or tribal purchases, total Indian bond sales totaled $50,000,000 by spring 1945.

Conclusion

By war's end, Native American servicemen had created a remarkable record of military service. At least 25,000 Indians wore America's military uniforms during the war, the majority of whom entered service as volunteers. That number would have been much greater were it not for health and educational deficiencies that prevented many would-be Indian recruits from meeting the armed forces' minimal entry standards. Indian servicemen were fully integrated into the military, where they were recognized and treated as full and equal citizens. They served in both theaters of war, performed every military occupation, and served at every rank in both the army and navy. Their combat record netted Indians 71 Air Medals, 34 Distinguished Flying Crosses, 51 Silver Stars, 47 Bronze Stars, and nearly 700 Purple Hearts. The United States bestowed on Lieutenant Ernest Childers (Creek) and Lieutenant Jack Montgomery (Cherokee) the nation's highest recognition for valor, the Congressional Medal of Honor. Five hundred fifty Indians paid the supreme price, giving their lives in service to the United States.

The war also brought significant change to Native Americans on the home front. At least 40,000 Indians left their reservations and secured training and employment in defense factories situated in urban communities. They learned new skills and trades that promised postwar employment in cities and towns, earned record high wages during the war, and generally found full inclusion in the larger dominant society. Reservations marshaled their resources for military use, and tribal communities contributed directly in all national security efforts and programs. But the war also instilled a new identity among many Indians. Racial prejudice, evidenced in Virginia and elsewhere, along with the federal government's negation of historic treaties that derailed tribal sovereignty combined to forge among many Indians a determination to carve their own place in society, a place separate from both whites and African Americans. This new determination was in direct conflict with the emerging consensus in the federal government that it was time to move toward final termination of all services to Native Americans and full assimilation of Indians with white society, a consensus that was the direct consequence of the successful wartime inclusion of Indians in the military and civilian sectors.

Review Questions

1. In what ways did Native Americans assert their separate identity as Indians during World War II? How did the federal government and non-Indians generally demonstrate the full and equal inclusion of Native Americans in the war effort?

2. How did the Selective Service Act and Nationality Act of 1940 affect tribal sovereignty and the Indians' heretofore special relationship with the U.S. government?

3. Why was the Native American response to the military draft and Indian enlistment into the armed forces so overwhelmingly positive? What was the basis for some Indians' resistance to compulsory military service?

4. In what ways did American Indians on the home front demonstrate their support for the nation's war effort? How did these activities also aid Indians themselves?

5. "Native American participation in the armed forces, in domestic wartime programs, and in debates concerning their identity and status within the United States together suggested an emerging spirit of activism by Indians, for Indians." Explain.

Recommended Readings

Golodoff, Nick. *Attu Boy: A Young Alaskan's World War II Memoir* (Anchorage: University of Alaska Press, 2015). The author's personal recollection of the Japanese invasion of Attu, his imprisonment in Hokkaido for the war's duration, and his fight for survival. This work includes the voices of other Attu natives as well.

Hemingway, Albert. *Ira Hayes: Pima Marine* (Lanham, MD: University Press of America, 1988). A biographical portrait of the famed Marine Corporal Ira Hayes who helped raise the American flag on top of Mount Suribachi, Iwo Jima, during World War II.

Kohlhoff, Dean. *When the Wind Was a River: Aleut Evacuation in World War II* (Seattle: University of Alaska Press, 1995).

Meadows, William. *Comanche Code Talkers of World War II* (Austin: University of Texas Press, 2002). An examination of the U.S. Army's effort to use Native Americans in frontline radio communication prior to and during World War II with particular attention to Comanche recruits.

Paul, Doris. *The Navajo Code Talkers* (Philadelphia: Dorrance, 1973). The first comprehensive study of the Marine Corps' use of Navajo for battlefield communications during World War II.

Townsend, Kenneth William. *World War II and the American Indian* (Albuquerque: University of New Mexico Press, 2000). A thorough, critical examination of Native American participation in World War II and interpretation of the war's imprint on native peoples.

Native American History Online

General Sites

The Navajo Code Talkers' Dictionary, Naval History and Heritage Command. www.history.navy.mil This sites provide the actual code used by Navajo talkers during World War II and video recollections of surviving code talkers.

Alamo Scouts: The U.S. Sixth Army Special Reconnaissance Unit of World War II. www.alamoscouts.org Lieutenant General Walter Krueger founded the Alamo Scouts in November 1943. For the remainder of the war, the 250 scouts, of whom 14 were American Indians, operated behind Japanese lines in support of the Sixth Army Ranger Battalion, freeing 198 American prisoners of war on New Guinea and providing intelligence service in the liberation of 500 POWs at the Cabanatuan POW Camp at Luzon, Philippines, in February 1945. The website includes the story of the unit, the Indians' service as Alamo Scouts, and photographs of Native American members.

"Indians in the War." www.archive.org/details/IndiansInTheWar_997 This document, printed and released by the Office of Indian Affairs in November 1945, includes the personal stories of several Native American combat soldiers, the work of American Indians on the home front, a list of the men who earned military service medals, and those killed or wounded in combat.

Historic Sites

The United States Marine Corps Memorial, Washington, D.C. www.nps.gov The memorial commemorates the flag raising on Mount Suribachi, Iwo Jima. The site provides a brief history of the memorial, suggests "things to do" while visiting the memorial, and gives basic information for visitors.

The 45th Infantry Division Museum, Oklahoma City, Oklahoma. www.45thdivisionmuseum.com The museum is dedicated to the army's historic 45th Infantry Division (the Thunderbird Division). Among the galleries honoring the division's military contributions to America is one that highlights the role of Native Americans in that unit during World War II.

The Pentagon, Washington, D.C. www.defense.gov Built in 1942, the Pentagon displays exhibits highlighting the nation's military history. "Native Americans in Defense" and "Navajo Code Talkers" are among the rotating exhibits.

CHAPTER

16

Redefining the Status of Native Americans in Post–World War II America, 1943–1962

JOHN NEZ (NAVAJO)
THE PATH TO TERMINATION
Senate Report 310
A Global Indian Reorganization Act
The National Congress of American Indians

[handwritten note: NSA Accounts 225-8516]

Children at the Wind River Agency, c. 1948.

John Nez (Navajo)

The war was over for John Nez. He had survived. Like 15 million other American veterans of World War II, Nez hoped to place the war behind him and pursue what he expected to be a peaceful, prosperous, and rewarding life. He returned home in 1945 to find instead a reservation in disrepair, job opportunities limited, and a life far from satisfying.

Nez's journey to war was not much different from the 25,000 other American Indian men who wore their nation's military uniforms in World War II. Born in 1917, he received his education near his home on the Navajo Reservation and excelled academically, graduating with honors and earning an all-expense-paid graduation trip to Los Angeles. The summer vacation proved a watershed event for Nez.

His brief visit to Los Angeles, he said later, "opened new vistas of the white world," and for the first time he seriously considered the possibility of a life among non-Indians. The Great Depression, however, limited Nez's job opportunities, and throughout the 1930s he took whatever jobs were available near home.

Nez was drafted in January 1941. Over the course of the war, he endured the horror of combat in North Africa, Italy, France, and Germany. His experience in World War II convinced him that he was "a respected equal in the white world," and he embraced fully the acculturative experience of military service. Indeed, said one anthropologist who spoke with Nez following the war, for the young Navajo "white ways were more than a veneer." They were, he added, "integral parts of his motivational system." That observation was, perhaps, exaggerated.

Nez planned to open a trading post on the Navajo Reservation following the war. He applied for a GI small business loan under provisions of the Servicemen's Readjustment Act Congress passed into law only one year earlier, but without prior store management experience or formal training in business, his application was rejected. Nez, then, turned to farming, but without collateral he could not secure funds to purchase a tractor and other necessary tools. His bid to enroll in business school also failed when he found it impossible to get financial aid. Dejected, he turned to alcohol and was repeatedly jailed for public drunkenness and disorderly

CHRONOLOGY

1937	Senator Burton K. Wheeler calls for congressional repeal of the IRA
1942	Congress cuts federal appropriations to the Office of Indian Affairs
1943	Senator Burton K. Wheeler introduces Senate SR 310 to cut OIA funding and activities
	The Association of American Indian Affairs publishes the first edition of *The American Indian*
1944	The National Congress of American Indians is founded in Denver, Colorado
1945	In January, John Colliers resigns as Commissioner of Indian Affairs
	William Brophy is appointed Commissioner of Indian Affairs
1946	Congress establishes the Indian Claims Commission
	Acting Commissioner of Indian Affairs William Zimmerman indicates tribes ready for termination of federal services
1947	Drought ravages farming and ranching on Indian reservations across the Southwest
1948	New Mexico and Arizona extend the right to vote to Native Americans
1950	Dillon Myer is appointed Commissioner of Indian Affairs
1951	The Indian Relocation Program is established
1953	Glenn Emmons is appointed Commissioner of Indian Affairs
	House Concurrent Resolution 108 states congressional intent to terminate the federal government's special services to Native Americans
1958	Nearly 100,000 Native Americans have migrated to urban centers since 1950
1960	The Democratic Party pledges protection of programs to preserve Indians' cultural heritage
1961	The National Indian Youth Council is founded

conduct. By 1949, poverty and hopelessness had enveloped the 32-year-old World War II combat veteran and prewar academic achiever.

Nez's story was not an exceptional one. To be sure, the war stimulated Indian acculturation with the white world, and a substantial portion of the Native American population certainly viewed the war as an avenue into mainstream society. But for so many others like John Nez, the immediate postwar era brought hardship and uncertainty. Prewar programs that aimed at strengthening tribal economies and community services disintegrated under the war's financial demands, leaving many reservations in conditions close to those condemned in the 1928 Meriam Report. Compounding the problem, many in Congress, and many in the public at large, felt the time had come for the termination of federal guardianship over Native Americans. This posed a potential threat to the continued existence of tribal communities and Indian identity itself. The immediate postwar era, then, were years in which native peoples found themselves at another crossroad.

KEY QUESTIONS

1. Why did Congress during the World War II years consider the elimination of the Indian New Deal and renewal of compulsory assimilation as federal Indian policy?
2. How was the policy of termination in part a product of the Cold War?
3. What was the purpose of the bureau's Indian relocation program? By the late 1950s these programs were considered failures. Why?
4. What responses or patterns of behavior among Indians in the postwar years remained consistent with prewar norms? What responses or patterns of behavior were in contrast to prewar patterns?

The Path to Termination

The course of war in early 1942 offered Americans little comfort. Adolf Hitler's armies and air force dominated central and western Europe, pushed deeper into Russia, continued their aerial campaign against England, and swept across North Africa. German U-boats prowled the waters of America's Atlantic and Gulf coasts and sent to the ocean floor nearly five million tons of supplies the Allies desperately needed. Air raid drills regularly reminded civilians as far inland as Atlanta, Georgia, that they, too, were vulnerable to enemy attack. In the Pacific, Japanese forces conquered the Philippines and in so doing captured 70,000 defenders of whom 10,000 were Americans. The Bataan Death March that followed took the lives of 1,500 prisoners. By summer 1942, Japan held most of Asia in its grip, stretched its control to the central Pacific, had commenced operations against New Guinea, and was planning the invasion of Australia.

In the face of numerous setbacks, America steeled itself for a long war. The United States mobilized its manpower and resources, factories accelerated their conversion to defense production, and civilians committed themselves to a total war effort. Said one judge in Greenville, South Carolina, "Let us make Japan as free of Japanese as the Sahara is free of oases." The nation's commitment to victory carried with it three obvious conclusions: national unity was essential; achieving victory would be an expensive endeavor; and the United States must be prepared to accept a central role in postwar international affairs.

By 1943, the Roosevelt administration had sharply curtailed funding for programs that were not essential to the war effort and was searching aggressively for additional budget items to cut. The administration was also anticipating the postwar era, looking beyond eventual victory over the Axis powers to consider America's place in the world once the war was over. Central to such considerations were concerns about the postwar relationship between the United States and the Soviet Union.

The Tehran Conference in November 1943 and the Yalta Conference in February 1945 exposed serious rifts within the Grand Alliance of Great Britain, the United States, and the Soviet Union. Soviet Premier Josef Stalin publicly acknowledged his appreciation for American aid at Tehran, but at each conference he insisted that the Western nations concede Eastern Europe to Soviet control, accept the permanent dismemberment of Germany, and not impede Soviet access to the Kurile Islands and influence in East Asia. Many in the White House and Congress came to believe that Germany would be replaced by an expansion-minded Soviet Union, determined to impose its will and root Communism across Europe and the Far East. By war's end, the United States saw the Soviets as a very real threat to global peace. A hot war was now being replaced with a "cold war," two opposing powers determined to exert their influence globally, tempered only by the prospect of mutual nuclear annihilation. This emerging postwar confrontation required America's commitment to a central role in international affairs, a willingness to focus the economy and national budget on Soviet containment, and national unity of purpose.

By early 1943, reservations nationwide were feeling the sting of reduced tribal appropriations and the government's elimination of job-training programs, road-building and school construction projects, and irrigation initiatives. Money previously spent on educational and health services now went into the defense budget. Given the demands war imposed, Congress wasted little time scouring the national budget for any and all programs that might be suspended. Among those considered was the Indian Reorganization Act (IRA).

Senate Report 310

Significant opposition to the IRA surfaced long before the attack on Pearl Harbor. Senator Burton K. Wheeler, himself the original co-sponsor of the bill, claimed in 1937 that both the Office of Indian Affairs and Congress misunderstood the legislation he championed only a few years earlier. The IRA, he argued, was never intended to promote tribal revitalization; it was intended to cultivate educational programs, medical services, and economic opportunities that collectively prepared Indians for assimilation. Wheeler believed the IRA significantly addressed many of the problems condemned in the 1928 Meriam Report, but the next sensible step was the melding of Indians into mainstream society. The senator now called for the IRA's repeal and the clear promotion of assimilation as federal Indian policy.

Wheeler's recommendations fell on deaf ears until the United States entered World War II. The heavy financial burden of war compelled a reassessment of all domestic programs then receiving federal funds. Congress had no choice but to curtail or to end completely all programs not considered indispensable to the war effort. Programs central to the New Deal such as the Works Progress Administration and Civilian Conservation Corps were discontinued as cost-savings measures. The Indian Office would not be spared. OIA appropriations plummeted 15 percent, from $33 million in 1941 to $28 million in 1942, with additional reductions scheduled for each year of war that followed. The expanding departments of War and Navy also desperately needed office space in Washington, D.C. In 1942, Congress informed Commissioner of Indian Affairs John Collier of the OIA's compulsory relocation to Chicago to accommodate military and naval space requirements in the nation's capital.

In this environment, Senator Wheeler's prewar critique of the IRA gained newfound appreciation. By 1943, the House and the Senate considered scrapping the IRA as another method to cut non-defense spending. In June, Senator Wheeler introduced **Senate Report 310 (SR 310)**. The measure recommended the immediate cessation of research and surveys commissioned by the OIA, and it called for the complete elimination of all tribal rehabilitation programs. SR 310 further demanded all money allocated for tribal land purchases be withdrawn; federal government control over forests, irrigation, hospitals, and schools on Indian reservations would be transferred to the jurisdiction of state governments; and tribal trust funds were to be divided into equal individual shares. Finally, SR 310 insisted on immediate staff reductions within the Indian Office leading ultimately to the closure of the bureau itself. Wheeler's plan simply was to remove Indians from federal supervision and protection, dismantle reservations, and move individual Indians into mainstream life. He couched SR 310 in the rhetoric of wartime cost saving; if enacted into law, federal appropriations to the OIA would drop to a mere $5 million by 1945, with the savings channeled into military defense.

The widespread inclusion of Native Americans in the war effort added weight to Wheeler's measure. The exodus of 65,000 Native Americans from reservations to military service and defense employment in urban centers suggested to congressmen the Indians' successful acculturation to date and their overt desire to assimilate with white society. Wheeler and many others in Congress reasoned that the Indians' acceptance by whites, the wartime training Indians received, their exposure to the larger non-Indian world, and the further accultura-

16.1 Burton K. Wheeler, Montana State Senator from 1923 to 1947.

Courtesy of Library of Congress Prints and Photographs Division, LC-USZ62-77522

tive imprint on Indians caused by military service would combine to encourage Native Americans to abandon reservations for life in the general population following the war. Moreover, the collapsing reservation safety net resulting from reduced federal appropriations would compel the more recalcitrant to move into mainstream American society. In short, congressional sentiment had cycled back to assimilation as federal policy. Assimilation was justified as a necessary redirection to help finance the current war, as reasonable given the Indians' present level of acculturation, and as required in the larger context of the government's preparation for the postwar world. The time had come finally to terminate the federal government's guardianship over Native Americans.

The new mood in Congress caught the attention of Indians nationwide and generated considerable concern. Said Hazel Lohah Harper (Osage), here was "the word 'terminate' again—terminate the Indians. I don't know what is going to happen to the Indians [over] the next fifty years." The **Association on American Indian Affairs** (AAIA) rallied and lobbied aggressively against passage of SR 310. In its first edition of *The American Indian*, released in late 1943, the editors openly condemned the emerging sentiment in Congress, and Oliver La Farge's article "The Brothers Big Elk" personalized the Indians' perspective.

The Big Elk brothers, wrote La Farge, were two combat-experienced airmen in Europe who personally valued assimilation but did not believe Washington should force it on all native peoples. Forced assimilation contradicted the right of self-determination long cherished among Americans and guaranteed expressly to Indians under the IRA. The Indians' special relationship with the federal government certainly encouraged acculturation and assimilation, but assimilation had historically been based on the individual Indian's personal choice and level of preparation rather than on some arbitrary, fixed time table. Tribal sovereignty, long a centerpiece of Native American cultures and affirmed once more by the IRA in recent years, would be cast aside by the federal government should Washington adopt a policy of termination. Especially galling to the brothers was that Congress now spoke of termination at a time when so many Native Americans were away from home working in the nation's defense industries or serving in America's armed forces. The Big Elk brothers "hope the American people will repay loyalty with loyalty, but experience keeps them from being quite sure," wrote La Farge.

The AAIA proposed an alternative to SR 310. Rather than enact the measure immediately, termination of Indian Office supervision and support programs among Native Americans should be a gradual process, implemented only according to each tribe's readiness for termination and with the explicit consent of tribal members. Continued federal aid and protection remained essential for less acculturated Indians, the AAIA insisted. Concurrently, state governments should construct and fund their own programs to replace federal support for and oversight of education, health, and legal services for Indians. Particularly critical, noted the AAIA, was the enfranchisement of Indians in all states of the union.

Commissioner Collier echoed the AAIA's sentiment. Neither Arizona nor New Mexico in 1944 allowed Native Americans the right to vote. "These states should do the American thing and grant Indians the franchise," Collier insisted, especially when "we are preaching democracy" worldwide. What new injustice awaited Native Americans without the protection of the federal government? he wondered. "Right now, when the Indians are fighting and dying in far places all around the globe for the freedom of us all—right now, serious attempts are publicly being made to destroy all the protections and all the rights they have so recently won," said Collier. Senate Report 310 was nothing less than a surreptitious scheme "to betray and wreck their lives while they are at war and unable to raise their voices in defense," he thundered.

Counterarguments offered by the AAIA, the Big Elk brothers, and Commissioner Collier weakened support for SR 310's passage. Perhaps more important in 1943, however, was the urgency of war as it moved into Sicily and across the Solomon Islands in the Pacific. Termination could wait until the war ended. SR 310 failed to gain passage into law; nonetheless, its initial support in the Senate signaled a changed mood within the federal government.

A Global Indian Reorganization Act

In 1943, Commissioner of Indian Affairs John Collier faced a U.S. Congress and an American population increasingly inclined to scrap the Indian Reorganization Act and cut federal services to Native Americans, making more real the notion "out of many, one." He understood correctly the ultimate fate of the IRA, but he believed its principal features still held merit and could benefit underdeveloped Pacific Islanders in the postwar period.

The commissioner presented his idea to both President Franklin Roosevelt and Secretary of the Interior Harold Ickes, emphasizing the IRA's fundamental support of cultural diversity. The diversity among Pacific peoples could not be more extensive than that found among American Indians, he reasoned. "What the Indians have shown, the peoples of China, India, and Indonesia . . . just as certainly will show if granted liberty, responsibility, and intellectual nurture," said Collier. Ickes agreed and advised Roosevelt that "because of the Department's unique experience with primitive people," the Indian Office "should participate actively in the administration of . . . islands in the Pacific which may be occupied and governed by the United States" following the war.

The plan first aimed at supplying food, shelter, and medicine to islanders. The Indian Office would then develop island agriculture, build modern health facilities, create educational services, and establish democratic governments. Roosevelt concurred and in January 1943 directed the departments of State, Interior, War, and Navy to establish a committee to oversee "recruitment and training of civilian personnel for work in occupied areas," setting up a program comparable to the Indian New Deal. FDR insisted "we have no imperialistic intention" in the Pacific, but he added that "the interests of this country will dictate either the permanent acquisition of some of these territories in defense of our western coast or some continuing friendly relationship." A policy similar to the IRA would protect the "inherent rights of these native peoples" and concurrently support American interests, he said.

The plan for globalizing the IRA, however, sputtered and soon stalled. The immediate demands of war made planning for postwar redevelopment of Pacific Island peoples much less important. Moreover, the president and key members of the various departments recognized the substantial financial burden the plan would impose on the United States, money the nation could ill afford given postwar domestic and global responsibilities. And, already heard throughout Congress was the determined call for reduced government and the elimination of unnecessary spending, evidenced clearly by congressional discussion of Senate Resolution 310. Roosevelt abandoned Collier's plan, expanding his own vision of a postwar United Nations. By autumn 1944, the commissioner found no support in Washington for the globalization of the IRA.

The National Congress of American Indians

A new definition of the Indians' status in America was clearly to be a product of the nation's experience in war, and Native Americans increasingly moved to shape and influence the eventual outcome. With that purpose in mind, 80 Indians representing 50 tribes from 27 states assembled in Denver, Colorado, in November 1944 and founded the **National Congress of American Indians** (NCAI). A pan-Indian organization comprised of both assimilationists and traditionalists, founding members agreed that it was imperative that Indian rights, both individually and tribally, be protected and that the NCAI should serve as a "national instrument to make [Indian] voices heard in legislation and implementation of federal Indian policy."

The NCAI saw itself as a national mouthpiece for Native Americans, articulating the Indians' collective argument for equality and freedom of choice. "Indians as a distinct cultural group cannot survive . . . unless they speak as one people with a common voice," the Denver gathering announced. The delegates agreed on a number of points. Individual Indians and tribal communities alike should "control their own destinies"—by their own choice, pursuing either assimilation or the retention of tribal life. Federal services remained essential to prepare Native Americans for assimilation and to protect tribal communities from the usurping authority of state governments. Should termination become federal policy, then certain prerequisites were to be completed. Specifically, NCAI founders insisted on the establishment of an Indian Claims Commission to make financial settlements with tribal communities. It also demanded Indian suffrage in Arizona and New Mexico. Commissioner Collier echoed the NCAI's position, saying those two states "should do the American thing and grant the Indians the franchise, for all over the world we are preaching democracy and should grant a little more of it at home."

In some respects, NCAI founders comprised a new generation of Indian leaders. They were born in the era of land allotments, tempered by two global wars and a worldwide economic crisis, and molded by the reformist agenda of the 1920s and 1930s. Many of them were politically experienced, having held positions in the Indian Office since 1934. They understood, too, that World War II would be a watershed event in determining the future of both the United States and Native Americans. But NCAI founders also promoted continuity with the past. Like the earlier Society of American Indians, they called for the maintenance of their Indian identity and respect for their traditional cultures regardless of the path Native Americans might pursue after the war.

John Collier's resignation as Commissioner of Indian Affairs was among the earliest major issues the NCAI addressed. Twelve years at the OIA helm exhausted Collier. Most wearing on him were the war years, which carried crumbling appropriations, a general deterioration of reservation services, relocation of the OIA to Chicago, and a growing sentiment in Congress for scrapping Washington's historic special relationship with native

16.2 Representatives of various tribes attend an organizational meeting of the National Congress of American Indians, November 1944.

Source: National Archives and Records Administration, 298658

peoples. Convinced he was no longer effective, Collier tendered his resignation on January 19, 1945; President Roosevelt accepted it reluctantly.

The NCAI hoped Collier's replacement would be a Native American. The postwar Congress would decide questions critical to Indian identity. Did tribes exist as domestic dependent nations, or were tribal communities to be dissolved as political units and their members placed under the jurisdiction of state governments? If the latter, to what extent would the federal government provide material aid during the period of transition, and what pressure would Washington bring against state governments to ensure the equal treatment of Native Americans no longer under federal guardianship? A Native American commissioner of the Indian Office would reasonably be in a position to present forcefully the Indians' points of view and perhaps influence decision making in Washington.

NCAI secretary Dan Madrano and Robert Yellowtail, who served as superintendent of the Crow Reservation, approached Secretary of the Interior Ickes. The secretary listened to their argument but selected instead

William Brophy as commissioner. Brophy previously worked as the principal attorney for the Pueblo Indians and was well known as an Indian New Deal supporter and "friend" of Indians. His nomination nonetheless angered the NCAI because it blatantly ignored Indian preferences. The Senate Committee on Indian Affairs endorsed Brophy's nomination, and on March 6, 1945, the Senate unanimously confirmed him as Commissioner of Indian Affairs.

As World War II drew to its close, the stage was set for a postwar debate over the Indians' special relationship with the government and people of the United States. The impending confrontation would determine Indian identity in America. As he left office, John Collier reflected on the distinguished service Native Americans made in the war effort but noted that "the final battleground is at home."

The Immediate Postwar Direction

The war took 60 million lives globally, left homeless nearly 30 million people, and leveled the structures of modern civilization. The extent of its carnage confounded the comprehension of most survivors and left both hope and fear as its dual legacy. Many hoped the war's sheer brutality and the development of weapons of mass destruction made warfare such an abhorrent prospect that civilization would seek alternate means for settling disputes. The newly established United Nations seemed to promise an age of negotiation and a path to remove the principal causes of war. For Americans, the $142 billion amassed in wartime personal savings offered unparalleled opportunity for elevating standards of living and greasing national economic growth. Concurrently, however, the world now watched as global power shifted from the prewar imperial giants to two new players with fundamentally different political ideologies and economic agendas, the United States and the Soviet Union. A "cold war" now simmered as the new power brokers challenged one another over the division and occupation of Germany, Polish elections, influence on the Korean peninsula, and postwar security needs. In addition, fear of economic recession and rising unemployment pervaded much of America, and many worried about the impact of returning combat veterans on civilian life. It was an age of hope; it was an age of fear.

Economic Difficulties

Peace silenced defense factories. Munitions plants, shipyards, aircraft manufacturers, and producers of all other war-related materiel laid off two million employees in 1945. Many Native Americans who had relocated to urban centers for wartime employment now found themselves unemployed or facing severely reduced wages, and all were hit by a rising inflation rate and confronted with stiff competition for jobs with veterans who received preferential treatment from employers. The odious specter of racism surfaced once more as Native Americans and African Americans lost jobs to returning white veterans. Indians had few opportunities open to them in urban America in late 1945. Urban Indian income fell from $3,600 in 1944 to $1,200 annually five years later. Nearly 75 percent of those Native Americans who had ventured from their homes to urban centers during the war had trekked reluctantly homeward by 1949.

Reservations fared no better. Washington's suspension of New Deal programs and funds halted economic development projects, closed day schools, and curtailed reservation health care services. Wartime military wages and dependency allotments disappeared with the end of war, as did government contracts for reservation-produced vegetables, meat, timber, and other items earmarked for the armed forces. The average income for Native Americans living on reservations slid closer to prewar levels. Navajos averaged $471 annually in the immediate postwar years, the Sioux just under $600, Arizona's Indians at $525, and Oklahoma's Native

Americans near $625. The median income for Indians nationally in 1949 stood at $950, a figure better than the prewar median but 50 percent below the 1944 level.

Conditions on the Navajo Reservation proved similar to those elsewhere. In summer 1947, drought settled over the reservation, devastating the Indians' livestock and agricultural base. Irrigation projects planned before the war had vanished with the New Deal. The reservation in the immediate postwar period held more cattle and sheep than it could sell in a peacetime market. Without an adequate supply of water, crops withered and livestock weakened or died from thirst. Market values plummeted for what little the Navajos actually produced. Reduced income denied seed and tools to many farmers, and postwar inflation placed new equipment completely out of financial reach. Hunger soon shadowed much of the Navajo population. Said one Navajo, "Well, you see, sometimes I don't eat for two or three days." Especially despicable, these Americans who supported the war effort at home and through military service now received less attention and care than the enemy America had recently defeated. "The [food] intake . . . is several hundred calories below that which we [the United States] provide the Germans in the territory we occupy," complained Oliver La Farge. Finally, in December, President Harry Truman approved the allocation of $2 million in emergency aid to the Navajos. The funds helped, but the reservation's economic woes remained serious. Blizzards hit the reservation in the winter of 1948–1949. The hard-frozen ground prevented the planting of winter crops. Cattle now froze in the fields. Federal relief came more quickly than before as National Guard units and the Civilian Air Patrol delivered food, fuel, animal feed, and clothing by air drops, but fully 10 percent of all livestock still perished.

Most Indian veterans hoped the United States would guarantee economic opportunities on their reservations or in urban settings in return for their military service. "I'm a mechanic," said a Winnebago soldier. "I want a real job. They're not going to send me back to live in a shack and loaf around in a blanket." Acceptance among white soldiers convinced one Sioux veteran that the postwar era would be a positive period for him and others like him. Being Indian, he said, "is no bar . . . to securing jobs in a great many fields of commerce and industry . . . [or] to succeed in a great many professions." "When we Indian servicemen get back [from war] we're going to see that our people are set free to live and act like American citizens," said another Winnebago. Thousands of Indian veterans and Native Americans previously employed in defense industries did secure postwar employment and took residency in Los Angeles, San Francisco, Detroit, Chicago, New York, and other major urban centers nationwide. They earned respectable wages and continued their education. Success, however, depended heavily on the Indian's level of prewar acculturation and military training in non-combat skills.

16.3 Navajo hoes corn within sight of an old volcanic core in Monument Valley, Utah, 1952.

Source: Courtesy of Library of Congress Prints and Photographs Division, LC-USZ62-133885

Social Concerns

The returning veterans themselves also caused concern. Many came home with wounds that left them unable to contribute to the work of their families and communities. Memories of the sheer horror of war shadowed others. Fatigued by the horrors of battle, numbed by man's capacity to destroy, and conflicted about their own wartime actions, many found momentary solace in alcohol. Others found adjustment simply impossible. This pattern was ultimately the cause of Pima Indian and World War II icon Ira Hayes's untimely death. And many Indian servicemen did not return home, leaving behind orphaned children and grieving parents. "The wounds of war were too deep," said one Sioux elder. Indian servicemen had also witnessed and experienced a life alien to the reservations. Veterans were, said one Sioux, a "younger generation with a taste for new and non-Indian things and ways." Added another, "the exposure of the young people to city life was too disturbing" for their return to reservation life.

In 1946, renowned anthropologist John Adair journeyed to Window Rock, Arizona, to survey reservation conditions and to talk with war veterans. He found 2,000 Indian veterans in residence at Window Rock, but the Veterans Administration (VA) provided only two representatives to handle loan applications, educational benefits, and readjustment issues. Moreover, the VA and local banks refused to make loans against Indian lands, the property generally being considered insufficient collateral. Without loans, few Indian veterans could open small businesses or purchase equipment required for their postwar careers. The 100 veterans Adair interviewed acknowledged their acceptance by and full inclusion among white soldiers during the war, but most felt they had been "dumped" back into civilian life and that racial discrimination now colored the VA office.

Adair and other specialists who examined the Navajo Reservation found living conditions even more disturbing. The absence of teachers and the meager facilities available permitted only 6,000 of the eligible 25,000 Navajo children to attend school in 1947. The Indian Office, now known as the Bureau of Indian Affairs (BIA), funded a medical staff and services that would have been hard-pressed to handle a population half the size of the Navajos. Scarlet fever, typhoid fever, measles, and smallpox spread through the Navajo Reservation.

The postwar conditions that faced reservation and urban Indians spawned much resentment. "We went to Hell and back for what?" asked one veteran. "For the people back here in America to tell us we can't vote? Can't do this! Can't do that! Because you don't pay taxes and are not citizens! We did not say we were not citizens when we volunteered for service against the ruthless and treacherous enemies, the Japs and the Germans!" And, added to this, Arizona and New Mexico still denied the right to vote to Native Americans, and alcohol consumption was prohibited by law. "I have a false eye, cheekbone, [and] a silver plate in my head," complained another Indian veteran, "but I can't buy liquor in a bar like any [other] American."

Oliver La Farge spoke at the annual meeting of the AAIA in November 1947 and echoed Adair's findings and the comments of so many veterans. "Indians cherished the *delusion* that in return [for military service] their country would pay attention to the Indians' needs . . . and give them a full opportunity to share in the good things of our way of life," said La Farge. The cessation of government work programs, the end of New Deal services to individuals and to reservations, rising unemployment, reduced personal income, and the failure of the Veterans' Office to provide basic services to Indians subverted the Indians' hope for a better life for himself and his people. "When [the Indian] came back, he had great hopes. He spoke better English. He had his mustering-out pay, he had the GI Bill of Rights, he had seen the world, he had lived and fought and played as an equal among white men," said La Farge. Indians now felt "boxed in," their expectations dashed by "hopelessness and destitution."

The Indian Claims Commission

Native Americans had long pursued government restitution for lost lands, and some tribal groups received minimal compensation in the two decades before World War II. The Yankton Sioux, for example, netted more than $300,000 in 1928, and ten years later Congress awarded the Shoshones $4,000,000 and the Klamath $5,000,000. By the end of World War II, settlements through the existing Court of Claims reached $47,000,000. Given the recent history of cash settlements made to tribal communities and the expressed will of Congress to end its responsibility for Native Americans, the call for a final resolution of all Indian claims surprised few people.

House Resolution 4497, a bill proposing the creation of the **Indian Claims Commission (ICC)**, arrived on the floor of the House of Representatives in early 1945 and immediately became the subject of intense debate. The bill coincided with Ickes's resignation as Secretary of the Interior and President Truman's selection of Julius A. Krug as his replacement. Thousands of letters supportive of the ICC bill swamped Krug's desk, and NCAI lobbying efforts intensified. The Indians' aggressive lobbying of the new secretary proved unnecessary. Krug personally desired the immediate emancipation of Indians from federal guardianship, a move he believed would free Washington from an unnecessary financial burden. Believing the settlement of claims to be the first step toward emancipation, Secretary Krug fully endorsed the ICC bill.

In 1946, Congress established the Indian Claims Commission to settle outstanding tribal financial claims against the United States, a plan explicitly demanded by the NCAI at its founding two years earlier. Said NCAI president Napoleon Bonaparte Johnson, Native Americans would not break their tribal bonds or take residency in urban centers until a permanent and fair resolution of their claims was complete. Many Indian proponents of the ICC and most all non-Indian advocates championed the commission as the final step to end Indian dependency on the federal government and, in so doing, eliminate the historic special relationship between Washington and native peoples. It was intended to produce an economic "leveling" of Native Americans with the white population. President Truman approved the bill, saying, "I am glad to sign my name to a measure that removes a lingering discrimination against our First Americans and gives them the same opportunities that our laws extend to all other American citizens."

The process seemed simple enough. The ICC gave Native American tribal communities a five-year window in which to file their monetary claims for tribal lands lost to the federal government. After August 13, 1951, the commission would receive no more claims. Once filed, the commission would review the claims, determine the legality of the Indians' title to the land, and reach a financial settlement, a period of review itself not to exceed a five-year limit.

Napoleon Johnson and the NCAI called on President Truman to appoint to the commission individuals intimately familiar with Native American history, cultures, and law, and one of the commissioners, he contended, should be Native American. Johnson contacted tribal leaders nationwide, asking them to appeal personally to Truman. Again, letters and telegrams from tribal leaders and individual Indians poured into Washington, most recommending the appointment of noted Indian legal expert Felix Cohen. Truman instead opted for the political appointment of three men with virtually no experience in or knowledge of Indian affairs. The goodwill initially given the ICC by Indians dissipated quickly.

Once empanelled, the commission learned that the filing of claims and the settlement of cases would be more complicated than expected. Disputes swirled around conflicting tribal claims to a given parcel of land. To which tribal community would the land be restored? In 1951, the Colville Confederated Tribes of Washington, for example, filed a claim for the same lands claimed by the Nez Perce of Idaho. The method of payment also spawned debate within tribes, some members calling for a per capita payment and others demanding awards be invested fully in the tribal economy. The Crow Tribal Council opted to assign half of its award as per capita payments of $3,000 with the stipulation that the windfall payment be spent solely on housing, health, education, or farm development. The remainder of the settlement was to be invested in tribal land purchases, community economic development, and local social services. Angering many Native Americans was the assertion of Indian identity by people who suddenly "discovered" their Indian bloodline, individuals who had not previously resided on the reservation and had never before taken an interest in Indian affairs. Just before the Miami received their settlement of $8 million the tribal roster held 317 names; within two years, more than 3,000 people claimed Miami identity. Many tribal groups initially refused a monetary settlement, instead insisting on the return of the actual lands taken from them. It was the land itself they wanted, not the cash. Land was the source of tribal spirituality and culture; it was the core of tribal identity. The Taos Pueblo insisted on title to Blue Lake rather than accept a cash award of $10 million. "My people will not sell our Blue Lake. That is our church. . . . We cannot sell what is sacred. It is not ours to sell," complained Taos tribal leader Paul Bernal. Pit River Indians of California filed their claim in 1951 for the return of 3.3 million acres lost since the early 1850s. The ICC conceded in 1956 that the land was illegally taken from the Indians but offered only monetary compensation for the loss. Not until 1963 did the commission arrive at an appropriate sum for restitution, an amount that totaled 47 cents per acre. The Pit River Indians, like the Taos, rejected the settlement. The ICC decided early in the process not to grant lands to tribes, believing that divesting current owners of the land would only create another class of claims.

The ICC found it virtually impossible to assign an accurate value to lands taken from Native Americans a century or more earlier. In some cases, commissioners erred on the side of higher land values for compensation and frequently accepted without discussion the legitimacy of the amount of land claimed by Indian attorneys. On occasion, the commission credited more acreage to a tribe than the tribe itself claimed. In 1957, the commission issued an award to the Pawnees for 23 million acres of land taken from them in Kansas and Nebraska, although Indian attorneys claimed a much smaller figure.

The ICC awarded extremely large settlements to numerous tribal groups. Utes netted $32 million; the Chiricahua Apaches, $16 million; Oklahoma Cherokees, $14 million; the Cheyenne-Arapaho, $15 million; and the Crows, $10 million. On a per capita basis, however, the settlements often proved insignificant. Prairie Potawatomi, for example, received an award of $1 million, but that translated to a mere $490 per person.

The ICC found it impossible to resolve Indian claims within the ten-year period as planned and ultimately continued the process beyond 1956 to 1978. In that span of time, the commission decided 341 claims, or 62 percent of all claims made, and awarded more than $1.3 billion, or an average of $2.5 million per case. What the ICC and the entire claims process accomplished unintentionally was the creation of political and legal networks to represent Indian perspectives, a growing knowledge among Native Americans about how to use the existing government systems to the Indians' advantage, a younger generation of Indians who now pursued legal training and careers in law, and a new determination among Indians to preserve a tribal anthropological and archaeological record for tribal identity and for use in future battles with government agencies.

Termination and Relocation

In 1946, the Eightieth Congress came into session determined to combat what it perceived as a growing global Soviet menace. Many members of Congress openly talked of an inevitable armed confrontation with the Soviet Union. They believed a resolute, united American people bound by a common world view, determined not to appease Soviet demands, and committed to the use of force in defense of the Western world would stymie the Soviets' global master plan. The defense of the American way of life would require the development of a vibrant and prosperous postwar economy, the maintenance of a common national identity, and the immediate reconstruction of Europe and Japan. Agencies and bureaus not deemed essential to this effort were to be dissolved and their appropriations reallocated appropriately. In this emotionally charged climate, the issue of terminating federal services to Native Americans surfaced once more as a potential cost-saving step for the federal government.

Termination Reconsidered

In 1946, the U.S. Senate instructed Acting Commissioner of Indian Affairs William Zimmerman to prepare a list of cost-saving initiatives that Congress could act on immediately. Zimmerman purposely stalled. He was a staunch supporter of John Collier's Indian Reorganization Act and feared the Senate's directive would lead directly to the dismantling of the IRA and to the termination of federal services to Native Americans. He was right. Congress finally ordered his cooperation and insisted he decide immediately which tribes could be "removed at once from government supervision." Zimmerman considered levels of acculturation, tribal economic development to date, state government ability and willingness to assume a financial and moral responsibility for Native Americans, and probable non-Indian support structures within the states. Critical to his assessment was the Indians' likely acceptance of, or consent for, termination. The Acting Commissioner proceeded slowly, again hoping congressional enthusiasm might wane, but under pressure he eventually submitted his list of those tribes he believed might survive without federal aid (see Table 16.1).

Soon afterward, William Brophy received confirmation of his appointment to be Commissioner of Indian Affairs. Like Zimmerman, Brophy opposed immediate termination of federal services to Native Americans, but he, too, was in no position to stop the inevitable. He did, however, pressure Washington to secure Arizona and New Mexico's guarantee of voting rights for Native Americans before implementing termination as federal policy. Two years passed before voting rights were granted in those two states, an issue resolved in the Arizona Supreme Court case *Harrison* v. *Laveen* (1948).

Table 16.1 Acting Commissioner of Indian Affairs William Zimmerman's Ranking of Indian Tribes Ready for Termination of Federal Services and Supervision

Group 1: Predominantly Acculturated and Ready for Termination, by Indian Agency

Flathead	New York
Hoopa	Osage
Klamath	Potawatomi
Menominee	Sacramento
Mission Indian Turtle Mountain	

(Combined population of about 53,000)

Group 2: Semi-Acculturated but Short-Term Service Continuation Required, by Indian Agency

Blackfeet	Cherokee	Cheyenne River	Colville
Crow	Fort Belknap	Fort Peck	Fort Totten
Grande Ronde	Great Lakes	Northern Idaho	Quapaw
Taholah, Tulalip	Tomah	Umatilla	Warm Springs
Wind River	Winnebago	Consolidated Chippewa	

(Combined population of about 75,000)

Before the 1948 presidential election, Congress empaneled the **Commission on the Organization of the Executive Branch** to recommend ways the executive branch could be reorganized to save money. Former Republican president Herbert Hoover chaired the commission and planned to dismantle Franklin Roosevelt's New Deal. He saw a federal government suffering from overlapping services and weighed down by a budget grossly inflated by both the New Deal and World War II. Hoover planned for the commission to reduce big government, eliminate what he and his fellow Republicans considered to be wasteful and unnecessary programs, and limit federal expenditures wherever possible. Republicans expected Hoover's goals to be realized through the commission, believing Harry Truman's tenure in the White House would end with the November election. Truman's surprise reelection, however, stunned Hoover and his Republican colleagues, and the commission found itself forced to make concessions to the Democratic administration. Indeed, the final report of Hoover's commission, delivered to President Truman and to Congress in 1949, actually institutionalized much of Roosevelt's New Deal. At the same time, the Hoover Commission surveyed carefully the recent history of Indian affairs and carefully scrutinized John Collier's Indian Reorganization Act. The IRA had proved very expensive, and the commission concluded quickly that a cheaper, more cost-efficient Indian policy was readily available. It recommended Indian affairs become the responsibility of the individual states and not the obligation of the federal government.

The committee's report stated, without evidence, that Indians nationally desired assimilation and preferred it to the tribal revitalization programs of Collier's IRA. Tribal self-government was but a "stage in the transition from federal tutelage to full Indian participation in state and local government." Lands should no longer be tax exempt, and tribal lands should be transferred to Indian-owned corporations to avoid controlling efforts by tribal councils. Tribes would reorganize as county political units rather than retain tribal government. The commission claimed its recommendations reflected Indian preferences, but it never solicited Native American input.

The NCAI had acknowledged at its founding that assimilation was a reasonable goal for many Native Americans. It added, however, that most Indians were still not acculturated sufficiently to consider seriously the termination of federal services and that explicit Indian consent must precede the removal of government supports. The NCAI challenged the Hoover Commission report, hinting that the rushed pace toward emancipation was nothing more than another tactic by which white speculators could secure tribal lands and gain controlling financial interests in Indian-owned business freed from government supervision. Said Ruth Muskrat Bronson (Cherokee), executive secretary of the NCAI, immediate termination carried with it the "cessation of education, health, and welfare services now supplied by the Federal Government . . . without assurance that these would be provided by the States or local communities." Moreover, the rapid movement toward termination "is being decided upon without, nay, over the protests, of the Indians concerned." If termination must be the new federal policy, then it should proceed gradually, allowing Native Americans the opportunity to prepare themselves for their own successful transition into mainstream society.

Congress and Secretary Krug assured tribes of continued financial assistance for Indians to develop jobs skills suited to urban economies. Both houses passed the **Indian Loan Act**, which gave Native Americans access to low-interest federal loans to supplement their voluntary relocation from reservations to urban centers. In addition, funds would be available for reservations to combat tribal poverty, illiteracy, and inadequate health care until they were better able to provide for themselves. Termination, however, remained the federal government's goal.

The Relocation Program

In May 1950, President Truman appointed Dillon Myer as the new Commissioner of Indian Affairs. It seemed to be a logical choice. The new commissioner was widely regarded as a highly efficient bureaucrat and servant of the public. His work as director of the War Relocation Authority that removed 120,000 Japanese Americans from the West Coast and held them at inland detention centers earned the respect of most Americans. His views of Native Americans and termination were also in concert with a termination-minded Congress. Indians, he said, possessed no "legitimate culture" of their own. Acculturative policies of the past had moved Indians ever closer to the values and characteristics of the dominant white society; all that was now required was the withdrawal of federal services to and federal responsibility for Native Americans. Under his tenure as commissioner, he planned to direct Indians "into the sunlight of full independence," to "free the Indian from government control" and to "free the government from undue expenditures." More succinctly, Myer wanted Washington "out of the Indian business."

Little by little, Myer's administration withdrew federal services from Native Americans. He began the transfer of BIA hospitals and medical clinics to state or local government control. He commenced the closing of reservation day schools and reenergized off-reservation boarding schools. The bureau poured more than $2 million into local public school districts under the Johnson-O'Malley Act to merge Indian youngsters into local, predominantly white public schools. Within the BIA, he ended the employment of personnel sympathetic to John Collier's vision of cultural pluralism, and in autumn 1950 he publicly called for the Indians' inherent right of self-determination, which he defined as the Indian's right to free himself from federal support and from a Native American identity. Once this freedom had been claimed, Indians would simply become "Americans" and take their place in mainstream society as equal, contributing members.

16.4 President Harry Truman is presented with a pipe said to have once been smoked by Sitting Bull by IshTi-Opi (Choctaw), Reginald Curpy (Uncompahgre Ute), and Julius Murray (Uintah Ute).

Source: Courtesy of Library of Congress Prints and Photographs Division, LC-DIG-ds-00308

Most Native Americans held a very different view of self-determination. They believed self-determination was an inherent right of the individual or the tribe to determine if, and when, the time was right for termination and assimilation. The NCAI added that Washington retained responsibility for tribal economic development and for providing the services necessary to place Indians in a position where they could decide for themselves which path to follow—assimilation with white society or continued tribal residency and identity as Indian. Commissioner Myer, however, gave scant attention to the NCAI.

In 1951, Myer inaugurated his **Indian Relocation Program** as a method to hasten Native American movement from federal aid and supervision. The program encouraged Indians to relocate to Cleveland, Tulsa, Dallas, Los Angeles, San Francisco, Seattle, St. Louis, or Chicago—the "cement prairies" as one Indian relocatee described them. Urban communities offered greater likelihood of steady employment, a better income, a higher standard of living for Indian relocatees, and a sense of personal investment in the existing system. Moreover, cities provided easier access to modern health care services, public schools, and vocational programs. The Indians' immersion in predominantly white urban communities would speed their overall acculturation and assimilation. Christianity, the English language, and mainstream values and behavior would quickly supplant Indian spirituality, native languages, and tribal values. "The old people can die on the reservation, but they want the young ones to move to the city, intermarry, forget their traditions, and disappear," complained one Pine Ridge Sioux who relocated to Cleveland. Added Blackfeet Tribal Council chairman Earl Old Person, "Why is it so important that Indians be brought into the mainstream of American life?"

Relocation was voluntary in that one could choose to move from the reservation now with some financial support or wait until termination became legal federal policy and be set adrift without any kind of federal safety net. Advertising touting only the positive features of relocation littered reservations. The program promised that in cities Indians would find nice homes, abundant food, access to good health care, and a golden future for their children.

Myer promised adequate financial aid for those who volunteered for relocation, but in practice the BIA issued only enough money to cover an Indian's transportation to the closest major city and subsistence until the relocatee received his or her first paycheck. The bureau spent a mere $300,000 in the first year of the program. In 1952, the bureau raised its offer to Indians. The BIA would now pay for transportation costs for the Indian seeking urban employment *and* for his immediate family. Second, the BIA would provide $50 for the shipment of household items, another $50 for the purchase of work tools required at the new job, and family subsistence for four weeks—longer if the Indian relocatee lost his job through no fault of his own. The bureau also urged commercial loan offices to consider Indian loan applications favorably and established Indian Relocation Centers in the cities to provide support in locating housing and jobs, directing Indians to inexpensive medical services, placing children in schools, and serving as advocate and legal advisor when needed. The centers assumed a role comparable to inner-city offices the National Urban League established for African Americans. The minimal aid offered by the BIA was grossly insufficient, but it was much more than Myer had originally planned.

Myer worried particularly over the prospect of segregated Indian neighborhoods forming within the cities. The emergence of "little reservations" would undermine his plan to immerse Native Americans in white society. To prevent this, the Relocation Program refused to allow more than two Indian families to take residence in the same city block. The ban mattered little. Relocated families often welcomed relatives and friends who independently migrated to the city. Homes quickly became crowded, with relocatees and their extended families pooling income for common benefit. A survey of urban Indian residency in Detroit found 16 Indians of all ages living in one stuffy attic without furnishings. Children were discovered sleeping in hallways and in shared bathrooms in another apartment building. Two years into the Relocation Program, the Welfare Council of Minneapolis noted that "one Indian family of five or six, living in two rooms, will take in relatives and friends who come from the reservations seeking jobs until perhaps fifteen people will be crowded into the space."

SEEING HISTORY

Bureau of Indian Affairs Relocation Poster "Come to Denver"

The relocation program Commissioner of Indian Affairs Dillon Myer established relied on Indians' voluntary participation. More than 30,000 Native Americans chose to accept the limited BIA financial support and take residency in one of the major cities nationally supported by the BIA program. "Come to Denver" is one of the promotional posters the BIA prepared to encourage Indian involvement with the relocation program.

COME TO DENVER

THE CHANCE OF YOUR LIFETIME !

Good Jobs

Retail Trade
Manufacturing
Government-Federal, State, Local
Wholesale Trade
Construction of Buildings, Etc.

Happy Homes

Beautiful Houses
Many Churches
Exciting Community Life
Over Half of Homes Owned by Residents
Convenient Stores—Shopping Centers

Training

Vocational Training
Auto Mech., Beauty Shop, Drafting,
Nursing, Office Work, Watchmaking
Adult Education
Evening High School, Arts and Crafts
Job Improvement, Home-making

Beautiful Colorado

"Tallest" State, 48 Mt. Peaks Over 14,000 Ft.
350 Days Sunshine, Mild Winters
Zoos, Museums, Mountain Parks, Drives
Picnic Areas, Lakes, Amusement Parks
Big Game Hunting, Trout Fishing, Camping

16.5 Bureau of Indian Affairs relocation poster.

Source: National Archives and Records Administration, 75-N-REL-G (box 32, folder 1)

Questions

1. What features of the poster would likely entice Indians to volunteer for relocation to Denver?
2. What goal does the poster suggest awaits participating Native Americans? What is absent from the poster?

Native Americans frequently found it difficult to adapt themselves to the strange communities in which they now lived. The incessant traffic, the constant presence of police, a much faster pace of life, and a general absence of open space bothered many. As one scholar described it, "the entire culture of middle-class European Americans . . . was alien to many Native Americans. Raised in non-competitive, non-capitalistic cultures, they often had little concept of budgeting or saving, preferring to share their money or material goods with others as a way of surviving." Said Richard McKenzie (Sioux), who served as director for the Indian Relocation Center in San Francisco, "The simplest facts of life in the city were new to them: gearing your entire day by a clock, when to go to work, when to eat lunch." They, too, were unsure how to obtain necessary services. "On the reservations, their health care had been free, rents and other costs low. Overwhelmed by unforeseen expenses, thousands drifted into city boweries. For them, the white man's road led straight from homeland to ghetto," noted one scholar. In a span of only 13 days, the Minneapolis Welfare Council found 450 cases of Indians appearing before local courts of law, roughly 20 percent of these individuals charged with public drunkenness. The council further discovered that among urbanized Indians in Minneapolis in 1955, the "average age of death" was 37 years, which contrasted starkly with 46 years for all Minnesota Indians and 68 years for all state residents. In cities such as Baltimore, Maryland, entire city blocks became Indian. As more Indians moved into the area, they gravitated toward one another, finding security among other Native Americans and comfort among the familiar. Historian Don Fixico noted that government officials "failed to comprehend the existing strength of Native American cultures and the tenacity with which Indians would try to preserve their heritage."

Relocation was a disaster. The bureau's financial aid fell far short of need, and Myer failed to comprehend the Indians' determination to maintain family ties. He and his successors wrongly assumed, like so many others in Washington, that decades of acculturative programs and experiences had prepared all Indians for their transition into the non-Indian world. Most Native Americans were not fully ready for assimilation, but more importantly most did not want to relinquish their Indian identity. The BIA encouraged Indians to relocate without consideration for their marketable job skills, their ability to be self-reliant in an urban location, and the quality of their interpersonal skills with strangers. Moreover, Myer evaluated reservation superintendents in part on the number of Indians they enrolled in the Relocation Program; consequently, superintendents frequently pressed Native Americans to volunteer for relocation. Complained one Pine Ridge Sioux, "a lot of the people were pushed into this program" without concern for their likely success or survival in the city. Indeed, more than 50 percent of the Pine Ridge Sioux who relocated to urban centers returned to Pine Ridge before the decade ended. Leonard Bear (Creek) enlisted in the relocation program and moved his family of seven to Los Angeles in 1956. The limited funds and support provided him through the Indian Relocation Office proved grossly inadequate for a family that included five children. They found a tiny house in desperate need of repair on the city's outskirts, and his minimal job skills allowed him the most menial income. "They did not tell us it would be like this," said his wife.

Approximately 100,000 Native Americans had relocated to urban communities by 1958, but only one-third did so with federal aid under the Relocation Program. Nearly 75 percent of all Indians returned to their reservations by decade's end. Relocation was a dismal failure. The program did not even save money for the federal government. Relocation costs rose from $575,000 in 1952 to a staggering $3,000,000 in 1957.

The Policy of Termination

President Dwight D. Eisenhower was inaugurated as president in January 1953. Two months later, he replaced Commissioner Myer with New Mexico banker Glenn Emmons, a man who also championed termination as federal Indian policy and enthusiastically embraced House Concurrent Resolution 108 (HCR 108), which

Congress passed unanimously in August. HCR 108 was not law, but it sanctioned unequivocally the placement of American Indians under the "same laws . . . as are applicable to other citizens of the United States" and the extension to them of the same benefits and responsibilities of all citizens. It encouraged the government to conclude its special relationship with native peoples "at the earliest time possible." Recommended for immediate termination were Indians in California, Florida, New York, and Texas along with the Klamath, Menominee, Flathead, Potawatomi, and Turtle Mountain Chippewa. Said Senator Arthur Watkins (Utah), "they [Native Americans] want all the benefits of the things we have . . . but they don't want to help pay their share of it." Termination, he added, would bring Indians into the larger family of Americans.

Within a few weeks, Congress passed **Public Law 280**, which gave California, Minnesota, Nebraska, Oregon, and Wisconsin jurisdiction over criminal and civil law for tribes in those states. It further stated that all other states could assume similar jurisdiction provided state legislation were to be crafted authorizing that responsibility. Congress neither required nor expected Native American consent for the process to commence. D'Arcy McNickle (Flathead), an associate of John Collier and supporter of the IRA, contended that Indians "saw the action as a threat to one of the remaining areas in which they exercised local autonomy; and beyond that lay the possibility that the states would want to tax Indians lands." Earl Old Person (Blackfeet) expressed a darker and widely shared fear. "In our language," he said, "the only translation for termination is to 'wipe out' or 'kill off.'" It would be impossible, he added, for the Blackfeet to build programs necessary for tribal economic, education, and health care development when, at the same time, the federal government moved to end its services and to remove its safety net. "It is like trying to cook a meal in your teepee when someone is standing outside trying to burn the teepee down," he said. The NCAI hurriedly assembled an emergency meeting to prepare a unified response. Members agreed to lobby Congress to sway sentiment toward a reevaluation of termination, if not the complete abandonment of the plan. NCAI lobbyists argued forcefully that measures making their way through Congress violated treaties between the tribes and the federal government and that Native American consent to the new policy direction had never been given. According to McNickle, "the treaties made them a distinctive people, the abrogation of which would cut them off from their own past." Indian opposition mattered little. A string of termination bills became law over the next few years, measures that dissolved tribal constitutions and eliminated tribal governments.

Klamath and Menominee Termination

The Indian Bureau and Congress believed the Klamath of Oregon were prepared for termination, and their successful "emancipation" was certain. Members of the bureau and Congress widely assumed the notion that the Klamath were among the most acculturated Indian groups nationwide—they were well educated and skilled and their acceptance as state citizens would be universal in Oregon. They, too, owned and managed a thriving timber business that returned to employees an annual income of $4,000, a figure consistent with the national average. Surely emancipation would be a simple process, many reasoned.

A survey of the Stanford Research Associates countered that assessment. Thirty-nine percent of the Klamath had no more than a grammar school education. Slightly less than half of Indians 18 years of age or older had any steady employment record. The survey team also learned that Oregonians openly feared the Indians would become a serious public financial burden, especially once their ICC cash settlement was spent. In fact, the Stanford team "flatly warned" Congress that the Klamath were not ready for termination and that the move would be disastrous if imposed on the Klamath within the decade.

Underneath the conflicting perspectives lay another reality. Nearly 15 million Americans changed their permanent residency during the war years. Seeking employment and training in the financially lucrative defense industries, they relocated from rural farm belts to cities or migrated from one region of the country to another.

Half a million Southerners abandoned the Old Confederacy for jobs in the Midwest, replaced by one million Northerners who moved into the South to construct military and naval bases or work in shipyards in Virginia, South Carolina, Florida, Alabama, and Louisiana. At the same time, the population of the West Coast grew at a phenomenal pace. Wrote historian David Kennedy, "as if the entire continent had been tilted westward, people spilled out of the South and Great Plains into the Pacific coastal states." The population of California, Oregon, and Washington collectively jumped one-third between 1940 and 1945, the largest number of migrants settling in San Diego, Los Angeles, San Francisco, Portland, and the Tacoma-Seattle area. Wartime airplane manufacturers and shipbuilders resumed commercial production after the war, and new technologies developed for wartime purposes became peacetime industries. Migration to the West continued after 1945. California had a 72 percent higher population in 1950 than it did just one decade earlier. "Some eight million Americans had lifted their heels for the Pacific Coast" by 1950, wrote Kennedy.

The western population surge threatened tribal communities such as the Klamath. The migrants' demand for property rose in proportion to the population, and a natural increase in population—the baby boom—was already a visible byproduct of the war. Industries multiplied in those coastal states and with them came greater demand for land and resources. Arguments Congress issued for Klamath termination turned fundamentally on the long-held goal of assimilating Native Americans, and they were consistent with earlier Indian Office efforts and the current Relocation Program as well. Postwar demand for property along the West Coast, however, made termination an immediate, practical policy to pursue. The same duality of purpose contributed to Menominee termination.

Most Klamath initially opposed termination, seeing in it another means for "the white man to get our land," but the clear determination of Congress to press the policy convinced Indians that termination was a fait accompli. Given that resistance was not a viable option, they reasoned that reluctant cooperation might better suit the moment. In 1958, the Klamath voted in favor of termination by a vote of 1,659 to 474. The Klamath would become another political unit within the state and be expected to manage their own lumber industry and assume financial responsibility for health care, education, and community welfare. Tribal assets

TIMELINE 16.1 TERMINATION ACTS, 1950S

1953	House Concurrent Resolution 108 calls for the immediate suspension of federal supervision of and services to Native Americans, removing from Indians the status of federal "ward" and extending to native peoples all the privileges and responsibilities as U.S. citizens
	Public Law 280 authorized the states of California, Nebraska, Minnesota, Wisconsin, and Oregon to assume responsibility for and jurisdiction over Indian affairs
	The Klamath Termination Act ended federal government services to and responsibility for the Klamath Indians of Oregon
1954	The Menominee Termination Act removed the Menominee Indians from federal guardianship status
	The Western Oregon Indian Termination Act brought to an end federal services to and supervision of all 61 Indian tribes in Oregon residing west of the Cascade Mountains
1958	The California Rancheria Termination Act terminated federal responsibility for all California Indians and provided for the distribution of Indian tribal properties and assets to individual tribal members

were valued at $100,000,000. The Indians opted to sell their holdings and distribute the earnings on a per capita basis, a distribution of about $50,000 per person. Tribal lands totaling one million acres were to be sold at auction, but few speculators offered bids and the property was ultimately purchased by the United States Forest Service. The Indians were now required to purchase the property on which they lived, draining money from their settlement. Medical costs, taxes, and school-related expenses consumed even more. With termination, the tribe lost protected fishing and hunting rights, which resulted in steep fines for fishing or hunting out of season or for catching or killing beyond a state-imposed legal limit. They were on their own, without federal support or safety net. The lumber mill lost government contracts to more efficient and less costly companies, and Indian unemployment soared. The per capita distribution slipped quickly through Klamath hands. As the money vanished, families tapped into the trust accounts of their minor children. Said one Klamath, "It was like throwing steak to the dogs."

Klamath termination ultimately cost the federal government much more than it expected. Administrative costs reached $3.5 million and the Forest Service's timber purchase totaled $70 million. The Forest Service certainly sold tracts of land and averaged $1.6 million yearly from those transactions, but the investment return proved inconsequential. Ironically, before termination Klamath timber sales covered fully the BIA's administrative expenses, and the bureau could have netted a much greater investment profit through other opportunities.

In 1951, the Court of Claims awarded an $8.5 million settlement to the Menominee of Wisconsin, but Senator Arthur Watkins who chaired the Senate Subcommittee on Indian Affairs halted its issue on the condition of tribal acceptance of termination. In 1953, the Menominee voted 169 to 5 in favor of termination. Senator Watkins hailed the vote as the Indians' acceptance of progress, but neither he nor Congress acknowledged that only 5 percent of eligible Indian voters cast a ballot. Their refusal to participate in the voting process was the Indians' method of demonstrating their resistance to termination. "Most of our people chose to be absent from the meeting in order to express their negative reaction to termination," wrote the editor of DRUMS, a Menominee anti-termination newsletter. Indeed, continued the editorial, a second balloting a few weeks later resulted in a 197 to 0 tally. "Our feelings did not matter," and termination was implemented on June 17, 1954. Congress then issued a per capita distribution of funds.

Tribal property was valued at $35 million, owned collectively by 3,270 tribal members. Income from wildlife, tribal businesses, agriculture, timber sales, and other sources in 1953 reached more than $3 million. Faced with termination, the Menominee opted to create their own county and assume responsibility for their own community services rather than be absorbed by a neighboring county. The tribe founded Menominee Enterprises, Incorporated (MEI) as legal owner of tribal lands and the Indians' lumber mill, and each tribal member was made a shareholder in MEI. In this manner, the Menominee believed they could retain profits from the sale of tribal lands and continue to reap benefits from the timber industry following termination.

In the transitional period that continued to 1961, disaster struck the Indians. Once incorporated, Menominee County had the lowest population among the state's 72 counties, and it ranked last in income, employment, housing, farmland, and high school graduates. The community hospital closed without the safety net of federal appropriations. Diseases such as tuberculosis, long controlled by the Indian Health Service, now resurfaced and ultimately spread across 30 percent of the tribe, and infant mortality soared well above the national average. The lumber mill, now a private business, lost its guaranteed timber contracts with the federal government. Profits plummeted, and MEI was forced to scale down production and lay off workers. In a bid to raise funds to cover its newfound tax liability, MEI forced Indians to purchase from the corporation the land on which they lived. Property not sold to Indians was offered to white buyers. "Because our land is now being sold to non-Menominee, termination is doing to us what allotment has done to other Indian tribes," read a DRUMS editorial. The cost of the property, along with the new burden of paying for medical services, taxes, and numerous other new expenses, cut deeply into the Indians' ICC award. Poverty gripped the Menominee.

PROFILE

Ada Deer (Menominee)

Born in August 1935 on the Menominee Reservation in Wisconsin, Ada Deer was the daughter of Joseph Deer, a Menominee with little formal education who was determined to instill in his child an understanding of and respect for her cultural heritage. Ada's mother, Constance Stockton Wood Deer, came from an upper-class white family on the East Coast and became a registered nurse. She secured employment with the Office of Indian Affairs, holding a position at the Rosebud Sioux Reservation before relocating to the Menominee Reservation, where she met and married Joseph. Together, Joseph, and Constance Deer proved influential in shaping the life of their daughter.

With the exception of a period of residence in Milwaukee just before and during World War II Ada spent most of her childhood on the reservation. She excelled in school and while in high school was appointed to the Youth Advisory Board of Wisconsin's Human Rights Commission, a position she retained after entering the University of Wisconsin in 1953. At the same time, the drive to terminate federal government responsibility for Native Americans took sharp focus on the Menominee. Her work with the Youth Advisory Board had exposed her to social issues that confronted residents statewide, and the reality of termination facing the Menominee compelled her to involve herself more directly in issues directly affecting Native Americans. Deer changed her major from pre-med and in 1957 graduated with a bachelor's degree in social work. From Wisconsin, she enrolled in graduate studies at Columbia University and, in 1961, earned a Master of Science degree in social work. She had been shaped by her Menominee roots, influenced directly by her mother's life that was spent working for the welfare of others, matured by her involvement in human rights work and the challenges imposed by tribal termination. The direction for her adult life was now set.

By 1970, Ada Deer had become an outspoken advocate for reform in Indian affairs, and she had dedicated herself to improving the quality of life for Native Americans nationwide. She served the urban Indian community in Minneapolis; was employed by the Bureau of Indian Affairs and traveled across the United States surveying the social and economic conditions of Indian communities; worked with the Urban Indian Task Force, a division of the U.S. Department of Health, Education, and Welfare; was on the board of directors of the Americans for Indian Opportunity; and helped organize the Menominee in their fight against Menominee Enterprises, Incorporated efforts to sell tribal property to non-Indians. And, in 1971, she testified in Congress for the repeal of the termination policy and the restoration of the Menominee tribe.

Deer continued her work over the decades that followed. She served as a senior lecturer in the School of Social Work and Native American Studies at the University of Wisconsin, assumed a position with the Native American Rights Fund (NARF), and was the NARF board chair throughout the late 1980s. She involved herself with the Democratic Party and proved instrumental in shaping the party's plank on Indian affairs for both the 1978 and 1982 presidential elections, and she was central in securing Walter Mondale's nomination at the 1984 Democratic Convention. She ran unsuccessfully for public office on several occasions, but in 1993 she was nominated by President Bill Clinton and confirmed by the Senate to be Assistant Secretary for Indian Affairs, the first woman to hold the office. During her four years in the position, she continued the work of restoring federal recognition to Native American tribal groups, 12 tribes being successful in their bid. She regularly advised Congress on Indian issues, efforts that helped produce necessary changes for the benefit of Indians to the American Indian Religious Freedom Act and the Indian Self-Determination

Act. Challenging the administration's position on tribal sovereignty and taxation, she left her White House position.

Ada Deer was one of the new breed of Indian leaders who emerged in the wake of World War II. She was well educated, personally influenced by depression and war, and directly challenged by the policies of termination and relocation. Like her colleagues of the 1950s and 1960s, she refused to accept the Indians' disappearance through assimilation and instead channeled her energy into preserving both Indian identity and tribal integrity.

Unemployment rose to 25 percent, and county aid to those in desperate need more than doubled. The Indians' access to fishing and hunting now fell under state regulation, and many Indians spent time in jail for fishing and hunting out of season, while others could not afford to pay the required licensing fees. Tribal members turned to selling what land they owned individually to cover personal expenses, and many reluctantly abandoned their community for homes and jobs elsewhere.

The cases of the Klamath and the Menominee highlighted the crushing impact of termination on Native Americans, and it showed that the policy carried with it unplanned and excessive financial obligations for the federal government. Their cases reveal, too, that Congress and the BIA were determined to press ahead with emancipation despite warnings of imminent failure. The perceived financial benefits of emancipation colored congressional attitudes. Common to the cases of both Klamath and Menominee, Congress and the BIA did not solicit Indian consent or consider seriously Indian dissent.

Some tribes successfully prevented termination. The Osage Indians, for example, held oil leases worth $131 million in 1953. Wealth allowed the Osage Nation to retain superb attorneys, to wield influence with state congressmen and senators, to lobby effectively in Washington and, as a result, to avoid termination completely. Other tribes were not so fortunate. The Catawba Indian Nation, located near Rock Hill, South Carolina, was not wealthy and its population also was tiny, numbering less than 700. In 1959, Congress presented termination to the Catawba Indian Nation. Neither the tribal council nor individual tribal members could afford the legal fees necessary to challenge successfully the preservation of their federally recognized tribal status. They also feared recrimination from area whites should they not consent to tribal dissolution. The Tribal Council voted 40 to 17 in favor of "emancipation." There seemed to be no viable alternative. Tribal property was appraised, and the Indians were offered the option of land or cash payment. Three hundred and forty-five took title to five acres each and the remaining 286 each received a settlement of $296.

Termination crippled tribes. "To us," said John Wooden Legs (Cheyenne), "to be Cheyenne means being one tribe—living in our own land—in America, where we are citizens. Our land is everything to us. . . . It is the only place where Cheyenne remember [the] same things together. I will tell you one of the things we remember on our land. We remember that our grandfathers paid for it—with their lives."

Termination failed to deliver on its promise of freedom; indeed, the government's view of freedom stood in sharp contrast with that of reservation Indians. Following the advance of white society, freedom lay on the reservation, protected by treaties with the federal government. There, and only there, could Indians live as Indians, clinging to a social structure of their choice, holding to a spiritual awareness they preferred, and preserving an identity they cherished despite the acculturation programs of the Indian Office. Termination in both intent and practice imposed on Native Americans a direction contrary to Indian preferences. "Choice" under termination was non-existent—self-determination was an illusion. Said Felix Cohen, "If a government repudiates its obligations to a white man we speak of 'governmental bankruptcy.' . . . If a government repudiates its obligations to an Indian, this is commonly referred to as 'emancipating the Indian.'"

Termination fever waned by the late 1950s. The program actually increased BIA expenses, and bureau employment rose 20 percent. Indian complaints, failed cases such as the Menominee, and the persistent lobbying activities of the NCAI combined led Secretary of the Interior Fred Seaton to announce that termination would no longer proceed without explicit Indian consent, a position President Eisenhower eventually encouraged. The Republican Party Platform for the 1960 presidential race called the "precipitous termination" of federal Indian trusteeship unacceptable and maintained that the party would not terminate "any tribe which has not approved such action."

Like the Republicans, Democrats distanced themselves from the Indian policies of the 1950s. Democratic presidential candidate John Kennedy in 1960 promised "no change in treaty or contractual relationships without the consent of the tribes concerned," and in a Kennedy administration there would be no effort by the federal government "to impair the cultural heritage of any group" of Native Americans. The party platform echoed Kennedy's pledge. The federal government held a "unique legal and moral responsibility" for Native Americans given "the injustice that has sometimes been done to them" by Washington and by white society. Instead of compulsory termination, the party called for "full development of [the Indians'] human and natural resources . . . while preserving their cultural heritage." Indian claims were to be settled promptly and err to the Indians' benefit, and the historic patterns of land removal would be halted. Once elected in November, Kennedy tapped Stewart Udall of Arizona as Secretary of the Interior. Udall not only followed the president's lead but also preferred that federal Indian policy pursue "maximum development" of tribal communities rather than their termination. Kennedy's promise and Udall's work lifted Indian expectations.

In June 1961, the NCAI sponsored a pan-Indian conference at the University of Chicago that attracted more than 400 Native American leaders from both reservations and urban communities. The assembly produced very little of consequence—it largely restated the broad transgressions of the United States against Native Americans, denounced the intent and the implementation of termination and relocation policies since World War II, emphasized the Indians' continued survival in America, and restated their determination to retain what they still had.

Less noticed was another Indian conference, comprised of young, college-educated Indians. Echoing the rhetoric of the rising national youth revolt that ultimately captured global attention in the 1960s, these Indians turned against the NCAI leadership, denouncing them as a collection of "Uncle Tom-a-hawks" who cooperated with the federal government and who had collectively allowed tribal power, traditional values, and a genuine Indian identity to disappear under their leadership. Although angry at Indian elders within the NCAI, the conference reserved its most damning words for the federal government and white society. The conference founded its own organization—the **National Indian Youth Council (NIYC)**. "The Indian problem *is* the white man," read the NIYC founding statement. In the view of the NIYC, white America was determined to accomplish "unilateral cultural extinction" of Native Americans.

The NIYC condemned the dark reality of Indian life. Disease, malnutrition, little access to quality medical care, inadequate home and community sanitation, and alcoholism contributed to an average life expectancy of 40 years for American Indians by the early 1960s. Infant mortality among Indians was twice that of the general population, illiteracy far surpassed any other ethnic group in the nation, and unemployment stood ten times higher than the national average. More than 50,000 Indians lived in substandard housing, often in shacks and occasionally in abandoned cars. Racism pervaded much of America, and opportunities for education and employment seldom reached Native Americans. NIYC founders agreed that government promises held little credibility—even those made by the Kennedy administration. Said NIYC member Robert Thomas (Cherokee), "As I look around at the Indian situation, it looks like one big seething cauldron about ready to explode." Indeed, it was. The founding of the NIYC signaled a significant departure from the cooperative relationship earlier native organizations promoted with white, mainstream America and federal policies. Whereas the Society for American Indians (SAI) had encouraged the maintenance of an Indian identity, it pressed

READING HISTORY

Party Platform Planks and Native Americans

The policy of termination, Dillon Myer's urban relocation program, and the resistance to and increased activism of the National Congress of American Indians in response to postwar federal initiatives drew national and international attention throughout the 1950s. By 1956, Republicans and Democrats alike recognized the need to address native issues and offered in the presidential campaigns of 1956 and 1960 what each believed to be adequate and equitable solutions.

Republican Party Platforms

"Indian Affairs," 1956

We shall continue to pursue our enlightened policies which are now producing exceptional advances in the long struggle to help the American Indian gain the material and social advantages of his birthright and citizenship, while maintaining to the fullest extent the cultural integrity of the various tribal groups.

We commend the present administration for its progressive programs which have achieved such striking progress in preparing our Indian citizens for participation in normal community life. Health, education, and employment opportunities for Indians have been greatly expanded beyond any previous level, and we favor still further extensions of these programs.

We favor most sympathetic and constructive execution of the Federal trusteeship over Indian affairs, always in full consultation with Indians in the management of their interests and the expansion of their rights of self-government in local and tribal affairs.

We urge the prompt adjudication or settlement of pending Indian claims.

"Indian Affairs," 1960

As recently as 1953, 30 percent of Indian school-age children were unable to obtain an education. Through Republican efforts, this fall, for the first time in history, every eligible Indian child will be able to attend an elementary school. Having accomplished this, we will now accelerate our efforts to open up both secondary and higher education opportunities for every qualified Indian youth.

As a result of a stepped-up health program there has been a marked decrease in death rates from tuberculosis and in the infant mortality rate. Also substantial progress has been made in the modernization of health facilities. We pledge continued progress in this area.

We are opposed to precipitous termination of the federal Indian trusteeship responsibility, and pledge not to support any termination plan for any tribe which has not approved such action.

Democratic Party Platforms

"American Indians," 1956

Recognizing that all American Indians are citizens of the United States and of the States in which they reside, and acknowledging that the Federal Government has a unique legal and moral responsibility for

Indians which is imposed by the Constitution and spelled out in treaties, statutes, and court decisions, we pledge:

- Prompt adoption of a Federal program to assist Indian tribes in the full development of their human and natural resources, and to advance the health, education and economic well-being of Indian citizens, preserving their traditions without impairing their cultural heritage;
- No alteration of any treaty or other Federal-Indian contractual relationships without the free consent of the Indian tribes concerned; reversal of the present policies which are tending toward erosion of Indian rights, reduction of their economic base through alienation of the lands, and repudiation of Federal responsibility;
- Prompt and expeditious settlement of Indian claims against the United States, with full recognition of the rights of both parties; and
- Elimination of all impediments to full citizenship for American Indians.

"American Indians," 1960

We recognize the unique legal and moral responsibility of the Federal Government for Indians in restitution for the injustice that has sometimes been done them. We therefore pledge prompt adoption of a program to assist Indian tribes in the full development of their human and natural resources and to advance the health, education, and economic well-being of Indian citizens while preserving their cultural heritage.

Free consent of the Indian tribes concerned shall be required before the Federal Government makes any change in any Federal-Indian treaty or other contractual relationship.

The new Democratic Administration will bring competent, sympathetic, and dedicated leadership to the administration of Indian affairs which will end practices that have eroded Indian rights and resources, reduced the Indians' land base and repudiated Federal responsibility. Indian claims against the United States can and will be settled promptly, whether by negotiation or other means, in the best interests of both parties.

Source: Ralph Roberts, Platforms of the Democratic Party and the Republican Party, 1960. Washington, D.C.: United States House of Representatives, 1960. See www.babel.hathitrust.org

Questions

1. To what extent, if any, did Republicans and Democrats each alter their party platforms between 1956 and 1960? What might have accounted for those changes?
2. In what ways, if any, were the two parties similar in their party platforms?
3. How was each party's position in both 1956 and 1960 consistent with, or different from, its own actions in the first half of the twentieth century?
4. In 1960, which party seemed closer to the demands of Native American activists, and in what way(s)?

acculturation and assimilation as the ultimate goal for Native Americans. The NIYC in contrast acknowledged the need to adapt to the realities of modern American life but insisted on the fundamental rights of tribal self-determination, tribal sovereignty, and cultural preservation and the supremacy of existing treaties. In short, the NIYC reversed the SAI position and in so doing placed native traditionalism above the long-held objectives of federal Indian policies. It was this new organization, writes Bradley Shreve in his recently published *Red Power Rising* (2014), that rewove the fabric of native activism and ultimately gave rise to the Red Power Movement later in the decade.

"The More Things Change . . ."

Between 1945 and 1961, the average American gave little attention to Indian affairs. After two decades marked by economic depression and global war, the general population embraced the apparent promise of a new era, an age of affluence and consumerism, technological innovation, the "new American home," personal advancement and national progress, and domestic tranquility. At the same time, Americans understood there were serious challenges confronting the nation—the cold war that threatened humankind's very survival and the civil rights movement domestically that promised a redefinition of American society. Confronted with such hopes and fears, government and mainstream society alike consciously pursued the two goals of progress and security, viewing anything and anyone not directly associated with either goal as unimportant and inconsequential. As a result, the general population ignored Indian issues, and prewar and wartime policies and popular attitudes toward American Indians continued into the postwar era.

The Continued Assault on Indian Lands

During World War II, in the face of new demands created by war industries and population migration, America faced a sudden need to increase its electrical power supply, and the government responded to the problem with the construction of new hydroelectric power plants. The postwar economic boom and population explosion only increased the demand for power and, once again, dams were a central part of the government's response. In 1943, the Army Corps of Engineers commenced an extensive project in North Dakota that included the building of six dams. Garrison Dam was one of the six, located on the Missouri River where it ran through the Fort Berthold Reservation, home to Arikara, Hidatsa, and Mandan Indians. Completed in 1953, the project required the flooding of one-quarter of all reservation land, a section that accounted for most of the Indians' agricultural and ranching base.

In 1943, Colonel Lewis Pick, U.S. Army Corps of Engineers, and William Sloan of the Bureau of Reclamation planned for the construction of five major dams north of Sioux City, Iowa, 18 tributary dams, and a string of levees running 1,500 miles south of Sioux City. They believed the network, once completed, would effectively control flooding along the Missouri River, provide irrigation for agricultural development, and generate electricity for commercial and private use. Congress approved the next year what quickly became termed the Pick-Sloan Plan.

Congress viewed the project as a means of building a solid economic base in the region, but the power generated by the hydroelectric power plants served defense needs as well. The War Department had expanded significantly the military's presence in the upper plains by 1944, and soon after the war many in Congress anticipated the maintenance of a large postwar military presence in the region as America's relationship with the Soviet Union became more confrontational. Some members of the House and Senate cautioned that the plan could be disastrous for Native American reservations located along the length of the project, but sentiment in

Washington already leaned toward the termination of federal services to Indians and their postwar integration with mainstream, non-Indian society.

The Pick-Sloan Plan affected 23 reservations. The five large dams included Garrison Dam in North Dakota and Gavins Point, Fort Randall, Oahe, and Big Bend in South Dakota. The project immediately withdrew land from the Standing Rock Reservation and Cheyenne River Sioux Reservation, as well as the Yankton, Crow Creek, and Lower Brule Sioux. It flooded nearly 600 square miles of reservation lands that had been fertile for the Indians. Those driven from the flooded areas were compelled to seek new acreage or find day labor work. The project also displaced 1,000 families and fractured community structures.

Congress assured Native Americans that it would provide displaced Indians with property comparable in size and quality to the lands lost to the dam project. Garrison Dam flooded a portion of the Fort Berthold Reservation. The tribal council twice rejected compensatory lands offered them by Congress and ultimately, with great reluctance, accepted a $7.5 million cash settlement. The other reservations also opted for a financial settlement. This further split tribal communities, now between those who favored a per capita distribution of the settlement and those who preferred the money be used for reservation economic and social project development.

The joint efforts of government and private business replicated the Pick-Sloan project on many other Indian lands in the late 1940s and throughout the 1950s. Among the Iroquois Indians, two Mohawk communities in upstate New York lost sizeable land holdings to the St. Lawrence Seaway Project, and the Seneca along the New York-Pennsylvania border lost 10,000 acres to the Kinzua Dam. The same story played out nationwide, affecting dozens of reservations and tens of thousands of Native Americans. At each site, in the wake of dam construction, Native Americans found themselves landless and forced to accept property of poor quality, take residency with extended family, or relocate to nearby towns and cities.

The Korean War

As Indians confronted postwar dam construction projects, Dillon Myer's Relocation Program, and termination as federal Indian policy, attention both nationally and globally settled on a distant peninsula in East Asia. In June 1950, North Korean military units armed with Soviet weapons stormed across the 38th parallel into South Korea, opening a hot front in the cold war. North Korean forces quickly brushed aside defenders and streamed south, trapping the South Korean armies at Pusan on the southeastern tip of the peninsula. President Harry Truman insisted the United Nations marshal armies to drive back the invaders. He was certain this invasion was constructed by the Soviet Union, determined to breach containment. "The relationship between the Soviet Union and North Korea," he said, "is the same as Walt Disney to Donald Duck." The United Nations hesitated, and Truman unilaterally committed American troops to another ground war in Asia.

Native Americans once again answered their nation's call to arms, as they had in all of America's previous wars. Indeed, approximately 30,400 served in the armed forces during the war years. Many were men who had extended their World War II military service into the postwar era as members of their state National Guard units. Many others had entered the armed forces prior to this war as a means of securing decent pay, education, and job skills suited to off-reservation employment. Still others followed family tradition.

As in previous wars, Indian soldiers typically found themselves in the infantry and deployed for combat. Furthermore, the stereotyping common to Indians in the two world wars continued into the Korean War. "My platoon leader always sent me out with our patrols. He called me 'Chief' like every other Indian. . . . Maybe he thought I could track down the enemy. I don't know for sure, but I guess he figured that Indians were warriors and hunters by nature," said Jack Miles (Sac-Fox-Creek).

PROFILE

Woodrow Wilson Keeble (Sioux)

16.6 Woodrow Wilson Keeble

Source: 615 collection/Alamy Stock Photo

On March 3, 2008, President George W. Bush stepped onto a small stage and bestowed posthumously the Congressional Medal of Honor (CMH) on U.S. Army Master Sergeant Woodrow Wilson Keeble (Sioux) for his battlefield valor 57 years earlier in the Korean War. On two separate occasions, Master Sergeant Keeble was recommended unanimously for the award by the men of G Company, 164th Infantry Regiment, North Dakota Army National Guard—the men with whom he fought in Korea. Twice the required paperwork was purportedly lost. His family, friends, army comrades, and state officials all tried numerous times over the following years to move the Department of Defense into changing Keeble's Distinguished Service Award into the CMH, but no action was ever taken in Washington. In 1982, Woodrow Keeble suffered a massive stroke and died. Not until December 2007 did the Department of Defense respond to initiatives by senators from North Dakota and South Dakota and authorize President Bush to grant Keeble the Medal of Honor.

In the public ceremony, President Bush stood in front of two empty chairs, one representing "Woody" Keeble and the other his deceased wife Blossom. The president acknowledged the previous attempts to secure authorization for the medal: "Some blamed the bureaucracy for a shameful blunder. Others suspected racism. . . . Whatever the reason," continued Bush, "the first Sioux to ever receive the Medal of Honor died without knowing it was his. A terrible injustice was done to a good man, to his family, and to history. . . . I deeply regret this tribute comes decades too late."

Keeble was born on the Sisseton-Wahpeton Reservation in 1917. In 1942, the Dakota Indian opted for military service with the 164th Infantry Regiment, North Dakota National Guard rather than accept a lucrative offer to play professional baseball with the Chicago White Sox. By year's end, Keeble found himself fighting Japanese forces on Guadalcanal. He remained with the National Guard following the war, and the regiment was deployed to Korea in early 1951.

The 164th endured bitter fighting with North Korean and Chinese forces, and in October he assumed temporary command of G Company's three platoons after all commissioned officers had been killed or severely wounded. Keeble personally led three assaults against a fortified Chinese position, each time his company being repulsed. Keeble then moved against the enemy by himself. With a bag of hand grenades and a Browning Automatic Rifle (BAR) he slipped into a protected position and destroyed one pillbox. He weaved his way to the second pillbox, eliminated it, and then took out the third. One eyewitness recalled that Keeble was under constant enemy fire. "There were so many grenades coming down on Woody that it looked like a flock of blackbirds," he added. Said Keeble sometime after the war, "There were terrible moments that encompassed a lifetime, an endlessness when terror was so strong in me that I could feel idiocy replace reason."

Russell Hawkins accepted the Medal of Honor for his stepfather. "Woody epitomized our cultural values of humility, compassion, bravery, [and] strength," said Hawkins. He was "the embodiment of the Sioux word 'woyonihan,' or honor." In a separate tribute given by the National Congress of American Indians the next day, First Vice President Jefferson Keel said, "He served this country with dignity and honor and it was only fitting that his heroism was honored by the President of the United States in such a respectful and meaningful way."

During or shortly after the war, three American Indians were awarded the Congressional Medal of Honor for their actions in Korea. On November 5, 1950, Corporal Mitchell Red Cloud Jr. (Winnebago) was attached to the 19th Infantry Regiment, 24th Infantry Division, near Chonghyon, South Korea. Standing night watch on a ridge facing elements of the Chinese Army, Corporal Red Cloud spotted enemy forces moving toward his encamped company and sounded a warning. He immediately opened fire on the advancing troops. Multiple bullets tore into Red Cloud, but he refused to retreat and propped himself against a tree for support. He continued to fire on the enemy until he was mortally wounded. His valor slowed the Chinese advance, allowing his company time to gather its wounded and retreat. Captain Raymond Harvey (Chickasaw) commanded a company of soldiers near Taerni-dong. In March 1951, his company was ordered to take a North Korean-held hill, where his men encountered three reinforced enemy pillboxes. Acting alone, Captain Harvey moved against the enemy and destroyed each pillbox, killing all defenders with hand grenades and carbine fire despite suffering multiple wounds himself. He refused evacuation until his company completed its mission. Private First Class Charles George (Cherokee, Eastern Band) earned his Medal of Honor near Songnae-dong on November 30, 1952, while serving with the famed 45th Infantry Division. Private First Class George's raiding party attacked an entrenched enemy position situated along a ridgeline to secure prisoners for interrogation. Heavy mortar and machine gun fire nearly repelled the Americans. George reached the crest of the ridge, leaped into the trench, and fought and killed several enemy soldiers in hand-to-hand combat. With a prisoner in tow, George and his unit began their retreat to American lines. An enemy soldier hurled a hand grenade at the fleeing Americans. George purposely fell on the grenade, absorbing its full blast and, in so doing, saved the lives of his fellow soldiers.

Americans on the home front gave scant attention to Native American military service during the Korean War. Individual tribes, however, praised the service of their young men and, as in past wars, sent them to combat with "medicine pouches" and received them home with honor ceremonies and, for some, spiritual cleansing rituals. Their service in war also catapulted many veterans into positions of tribal leadership, as was the custom historically among many Indian cultures, and in time some of these men assumed prominent roles in the National Congress of American Indians and were elected to public office off the reservation. Ben Nighthorse Campbell (Cheyenne), for example, served in the United States Air Force during the Korean War and in the mid-1980s was elected to the U.S. House of Representatives from Colorado.

Hollywood Films and Television

Major Hollywood films often reflect the social and political issues of the years in which a movie is produced, and films of the postwar era were no different. The "Western" remained a popular film genre in the 1950s, and, using the setting of the "Wild West" of the previous century, scriptwriters and producers occasionally commented on America's postwar role in international affairs, threats to the United States both foreign and domestic, individualism in a corporate society, corruption in government, human failings, and the hope for personal redemption. Hollywood also drew attention to race relations and the current struggle for racial equality in America, offering perspectives seldom presented in prewar films.

It is little wonder that Hollywood Westerns in the 1950s focused audience attention on Native American assimilation with white society, given the policy of termination and the government's relocation program. *Broken Arrow* (1950), for instance, featured James Stewart playing the lead role of Tom Jeffords, a "friend" to the Apaches who came to understand that Indians, like white settlers, value honesty and courage, love their families, and have hopes and fears common to all peoples regardless of race. Jeffords appreciated the Apaches' unique cultural traits and concluded that Indians "are valuable in their own right." This understanding and acceptance of the Apache pitted him against the local white community, especially when Jeffords married an Apache woman. *Broken Arrow* certainly exposed and condemned the racism historically directed at Native Americans. Jeffords's evident respect for Apache culture and his marriage to an Apache woman suggested his acceptance of Indian assimilation with white society, given that he finds Indian values compatible with those of his own culture and his new bride follows him, not the other way around.

The Great Sioux Uprising (1953) featured a white doctor among the Sioux who insisted that he never looked at "the color of a man's skin." Wars with plains tribes, such as the Sioux, were more often the product of unscrupulous Indian agents and government officials or greedy miners than the fault of Indians. *Drum Beat* (1954) presented the story of a white man who risked his own life to save a young Indian warrior from vengeful white settlers, and, by doing so, jeopardized his own position within white society. *Walk the Proud Land* (1956) also attacked racism and segregation, with Indian agent John Clum (Audie Murphy) helping San Carlos Apaches acculturate themselves to the white world in advance of their eventual assimilation. Each of these films emphasized the commonality of man, regardless of race or ethnicity, and through their principal characters encouraged mutual understanding, respect, and the idea that Indians and non-Indians could live together as one people. These films were notable for their messages of inclusion, and the perspective of these films reflected the federal government's policy of termination and assimilation, not necessarily the will of American Indians.

Few Westerns, however, focused as much emotion on Indian-white racism as did producer John Ford in his film *The Searchers* (1956). Ford cast John Wayne in the lead role of Ethan Edwards. Little is revealed of Ethan's life, other than that he is a veteran of the Civil War and that Comanche Indians killed his family. He appears unexpectedly at the door of his sister's family and offers no explanation for the years that he has been out of touch with them. Evident, however, is his intense hatred for Native Americans, a trait first introduced in his reunion with Martin Pawley, the part-Cherokee adopted son of Ethan's brother, Aaron. Early in the film, a Comanche raiding party led by Chief Scar attacks Aaron's home while Ethan is away, killing Aaron and his wife and taking Aaron's two daughters, Lucy and Debbie. The remainder of the film features Ethan's vengeance-filled search for the girls, one that spanned several years. He and Martin learn that Lucy was killed, and Ethan remarks that she was better off dead than forced to live like a Comanche. The search continues for Debbie. Ethan and Martin eventually locate Chief Scar's camp and find Debbie still alive; however, they discover that she has forgotten much of her white culture and has for all purposes become Comanche. As a result, Ethan is determined to kill her along with Chief Scar, and in the final scenes of fighting with the Indians Ethan is stopped from killing Debbie by Martin, but also by his own sudden awareness that Debbie is still white and a blood relation. Debbie can be "redeemed."

The Searchers clearly exposed the rabid hatred Ethan carried for Native Americans, a product of personal family tragedy. Ford also shows that Chief Scar had suffered the loss of family and friends, and Scar clearly understood that Comanche culture would not likely survive continued white expansion. There is, then, little difference between Ethan Edwards and Chief Scar, and this is one theme of the film—that the brutality both Indians and whites exhibited in the previous century was often the product of man's most basic motivations, vengeance and survival. Debbie's anticipated "redemption" suggested that continued efforts at Indian acculturation will result positively with the blending of native peoples and mainstream society.

These messages increasingly filtered into the new medium of the era—television. *Cheyenne* was a weekly drama that stood slightly apart from the standard formula Westerns. Actor Clint Walker played Cheyenne Brodie, a white man reared by the Cheyenne and skilled in both Indian and non-Indian ways. He was a drifter who moved from one job to the next—an army scout one week, a rancher the next, a lawman later. In each episode he confounded black-hat villains and invariably "saved the day." Brodie was proud of his Cheyenne ties and slipped easily between the Indian and non-Indian worlds, suggesting to audiences the commonality of core values between whites and Indians. In most episodes he expressed the Indians' collective fears, expectations, and determination to survive but concurrently acknowledged that Native American survival hinged on the Indians' merging with the white world. Brodie served as the "enlightened" promoter of Indian acculturation and assimilation during the era of termination and relocation.

The Lone Ranger first aired as a radio program in the 1930s but made a successful transition to television in the 1950s. The Lone Ranger, or "masked man," was the quintessential American hero, apprehending thieves and cattle rustlers, protecting women and children in distress, always representing the law and goodness over evil. His sidekick was Tonto, an Indian every bit the hero of the Lone Ranger but relegated to the role of

TIMELINE 16.2 MAJOR HOLLYWOOD FILMS IN THE 1950S WITH ANTI-RACISM MESSAGES REGARDING INDIANS

1950	*Broken Arrow* criticizes white settlers for their racism toward Native Americans and promotes Indian inclusion with white society
1952	*The Savage,* the story of a white child who comes to reject white society, calls on Indian resistance to white encroachment
1953	In *The Great Sioux Uprising,* a white physician serving the Sioux challenges the racism of his white community toward native peoples
1955	*White Feather* presents the marriage of an Indian woman to a white man and the bigotry and prejudice exhibited by white settlers
1956	*Walk the Proud Land* features an Indian agent on the San Carlos Apache reservation who teaches Apache men the skills and knowledge necessary for inclusion with white society
	The Last Hunt condemns the heartless behavior of white settlers toward native peoples and the slaughter of buffalo with its life-threatening repercussions on Indians
	John Ford's *The Searchers* examines the bitter racism whites historically felt for Native Americans
1957	In *Run of the Arrow,* a defeated Confederate war veteran finds a home among the Sioux
1959	In *The Unforgiven,* a child of Kiowa parents, reared as a white child by settlers who kept her Indian heritage secret until her biological brother demands her return, confronts her heritage and white bigotry

"faithful companion." Tonto, played by Jay Silverheels, was the acculturated Native American, respected by the Lone Ranger and, in many episodes, superior intellectually and in refinement than whites. The television series today is often remembered for certain stereotypical traits that Tonto could not shed and the Lone Ranger's occasional condescending comments to Tonto, his subordinate, but child audiences in the 1950s found in the pair of heroes a level of equality, mutual respect, and trust not common to earlier representations; moreover, that perspective reached a larger audience than Hollywood films as television became the primary source of filmed entertainment in the 1950s.

To be sure, many films and television programs still presented the worn stereotype of American Indians. Youngsters who played "Cowboys and Indians" continued to assign negative traits to those identified as "Indian." Even in those films that attempted to convey a more respectful and inclusive image of native peoples, little effort was taken to present accurately Native American cultures and even less attention was directed toward current realities. Nonetheless, films and television shows of the 1950s offered a slightly modified view of American Indians and, in so doing, encouraged audiences to question their long-held views on Indian cultures and Indian-white relations.

Conclusion

The unparalleled cost of waging war compelled the United States to slash the budgets of most programs deemed non-essential to the war effort, a cost-saving strategy that resulted in a substantial reduction in appropriations to the Indian Office. In many instances, budget cuts significantly curtailed or ended completely programs that had proved immensely beneficial to Native Americans only a few years earlier. This, along with what many Americans considered to be the Indians' successful and near seamless transition into military service or defense work, suggested to Congress that it was time to press once again for Native American assimilation with mainstream society. Sentiment in favor of ending the Indians' special relationship with the United States only intensified following World War II, as America confronted a new challenge—the excessive costs of the cold war and, once more, the perceived need for a single American identity. Federal Indian policy in the 1950s, then, became one of terminating federal responsibility for and services to Native Americans. In response, the National Congress of American Indians, founded in 1944, lobbied Congress to slow the pace of termination and to continue basic government services necessary for the Indians' successful movement into the general population, but NCAI efforts were only minimally effective. Termination, and the Bureau of Indian Affairs' concurrent program of relocating Indians to urban communities, failed because they, ironically, proved too costly and ineffective. In 1961, the founding of the National Indian Youth Council signaled the emergence of a new Indian leadership and a new direction in Native American activism. The NIYC would soon employ the tactic of direct public confrontation to challenge federal and state laws and to press for the Indians' right of self-determination, a tactic and goal that realized success in the 1970s.

Review Questions

1. How did global events and issues contribute directly to the redirection of federal Indian policy between 1943 and 1960?

2. The government expected the policy of termination to be the final step in assimilating Native Americans into mainstream society. Why were political leaders and bureau officials so confident of the success of this policy at this time, given the limited assimilation of Indians to date?

3.   Termination and relocation proved to be failures for the federal government. What issues or developments contributed to the failure of these policies? How did these policies affect native communities the federal government targeted for termination?

4.   How did the National Congress of American Indians respond to federal policy directions in the postwar years? To what extent did the NCAI prove itself to be successful in defending Indian interests? Why did many younger Indian leaders deem the NCAI a failure in its defense of native peoples in the 1950s?

Recommended Readings

Cowger, Thomas W. *The National Congress of American Indians: The Founding Years* (Lincoln, NE: University of Nebraska Press, 1999). Cowger presents the history of the founding of the NCAI and tracks its role in the postwar age of native activism.

Fixico, Donald L. *Termination and Relocation: Federal Indian Policy, 1945–1960* (Albuquerque: University of New Mexico Press, 1986). A critical examination of the imprint of federal policies on native peoples in the Truman and Eisenhower administrations.

Fixico, Donald L. *The Urban Indian Experience in America* (Albuquerque: University of New Mexico Press, 2000). A thorough study of the effects of urban migration and residency on contemporary Native American identity.

Philp, Kenneth R. *Termination Revisited: American Indians on the Trail to Self-Determination, 1933–1953* (Lincoln, NE: University of Nebraska Press, 1999). A penetrating examination of shifting ideologies in federal Indian policy from 1933 to 1953.

Shreve, Bradley G. *Red Power Rising: The National Indian Youth Council and the Origins of Native Activism* (Norman: University of Oklahoma Press, 2014). A groundbreaking study of the NIYC and its influence on the rise of 1960s Indian activism.

Native American History Online

General Sites

Indian Claims Commission Decisions. http://digital.library.okstate.edu This website provides ICC decisions on claims Indians tribes filed between 1946 and 1978, including the rationale for supporting or rejecting tribal claims and the amount of payment awarded to those approved by the commission.

The Korean War Veterans Memorial. www.abmc.gov/about-us/history/korean-war-memorial Presented on this site is a detailed history and description of the Korean War Veterans' Memorial, including the position of the statue representing American Indian servicemen.

National Native American Veterans Memorial. www.nmai.si.edu/nnavm/memorial This sites detail the Smithsonian's planned addition, one that will trace the history of Native American military service to the United States and honor those who served both abroad and at home.

The National Congress of American Indians. www.ncai.org The homepage for the National Congress of American Indians, this website provides news regarding current policy issues and policy research, NCAI-sponsored initiatives, and a calendar of events.

National American Indian Veterans. www.navavets.com This site provides online access to the organization's newsletter, *The Warrior*, and to information regarding veterans' benefits, news, and events of interest to American Indians. Through this site, native veterans have an outlet through which they can voice their personal stories and their personal opinions on military-related issues.

Historic Sites

The Korean War Veterans Memorial, Washington, D.C. www.nps.gov/kowa/index.htm The memorial honors those Americans who served during the "forgotten war" from 1950 to 1953. Specifically identified among the statues of soldiers is an American Indian, symbolically representing the 30,000 Native Americans who served in uniform during that war.

The National Museum of the American Indian, Washington, D.C. www.nmai.si.edu/ The museum presents varied exhibits in Washington, DC and New York City as well as traveling exhibits nationwide. These exhibits often feature Native American military service and contemporary society and culture.

CHAPTER

17

A canvas teepee on a summit overlooking the Golden Gate Bridge during the takeover of Alcatraz by Native Americans.
Source: Bettmann/Getty Images

Indian Activism in the Age of Liberalism, 1961–1980

BERNIE WHITEBEAR AND THE FORT LAWTON TAKEOVER
A New Direction in Indian Activism
Fishing and Water Rights
Alcatraz
The Alcatraz Occupation
INDIANS AND THE VIETNAM WAR
Native Americans Enter the Armed Forces
Combat Service
Racial Consciousness
RED POWER
The American Indian Movement
Trail of Broken Treaties
Wounded Knee
The Longest Walk
NEW DIRECTIONS?
Indian Self-Determination
Urbanization Patterns
Educational Directions
Mainstream Awareness

Bernie Whitebear and the Fort Lawton Takeover

"People were injured . . . equipment was destroyed . . . [and] barracks were torched," recalled Randy Lewis of the Indians' March 8, 1970, attempted occupation of Fort Lawton, a decommissioned military installation just north of Seattle, Washington. Although the *Seattle Times* reported a much less violent confrontation between Native Americans and military police, the persistence of the protesters' efforts spoke to their determination. Over the four weeks that followed, Indians attempted to breach the fort's perimeter three more times, but Military Police (MPs) and a contingent of soldiers from nearby Fort Lewis forcibly removed them. The Fort

Lawton effort attracted a national audience, garnered substantial support from non-Indians in the Seattle area and across Washington, and engaged prominent politicians.

Bernie Whitebear led the effort. His call for local Native Americans to take over Fort Lawton grew from his desire to use a portion of abandoned military property as a site for a larger, more effective Indian center for Seattle's Indian population. The city's Indian population had more than quadrupled between 1950 and 1970, from less than 1,000 to about 4,000, and Seattle claimed the largest urban Indian population on the West Coast. Federal policies of termination and relocation accounted for part of this demographic change, but the "Third World poverty" commonplace on Indian reservations forced many others to abandon their homes and move to cities in the hope of employment.

Whitebear was born in 1937 on the Colville Federated Reservation in Washington. "I don't think there was anyone poorer than us," said Whitebear. He did well in school and was able to take advantage of federal assistance to attend the University of Washington, majoring in engineering. After serving in the U.S. Army, he found work at Boeing Aircraft. His accomplishments matched the goals of federal Indian policies in the post-World War II years—relocation and assimilation. But Whitebear remained proud of his Indian heritage, and he committed himself to improving living conditions among Seattle's urbanized Indians. He immersed himself in national Indian affairs and, like many young Americans in the 1960s, came to see direct action as the best way to achieve social and economic change.

In 1969, the federal government announced plans to decommission Fort Lawton and sell the property to private developers and local government. Whitebear and others hoped to secure some of the land to accommodate a new Indian Center, but city officials intended to convert Fort Lawton into a public park. Whitebear believed it imperative for Indians to press their demand aggressively. In February 1970, he assembled those of similar opinion and called for Indians to move onto the fort's grounds, occupy it, and from that position negotiate a settlement with the city.

On March 8, Whitebear led more than 100 protesters to Fort Lawton and breached the south perimeter. With the media present, Whitebear announced, "We, the Native Americans, reclaim the land known as Fort Lawton in the name of all American Indians by right of discovery." He based the Indians' claim to Fort Lawton on 1865 treaty provisions that promised the return of "surplus military lands to their original owners." His long-time friend, Bob Satiacum (Puyallup), restated Whitebear's proclamation and then read a formal statement drafted by the United Indian People's Council that claimed "this place [Fort Lawton] does not resemble most Indian reservations. It has potential for modern facilities, adequate sanitation facilities, heath care facilities, fresh running water, educational facilities, and transportation facilities." An estimated crowd of 500 Indians and non-Indians gathered outside the front gate in support of Whitebear's initiative. Soldiers stationed at nearby Fort Lewis quickly reinforced the Fort Lawton MPs and broke up the small encampments already raised inside the army post. Protesters were arrested, loaded into trucks, and hauled away to the post jail where they were soon issued letters of expulsion and escorted to the front gate. For weeks, the pattern of "invasion, arrests, jailings, letters of expulsion from military property, physical escort off the fort, [and] re-invasion" continued.

The American Indian Fort Lawton Occupation Force soon became the United Indians of All Tribes Foundation (UIATF); Whitebear served as its director to initiate and develop the tactics required to secure the federal property. Whitebear presented the Indians' arguments before a congressional investigation committee chaired by Senator Morris Udall, won public support from Washington State's congressional delegation, secured backing from the National Congress of American Indians, and received the endorsement of presidential candidate Senator Henry Jackson. He also filed the necessary forms with the federal government to purchase the decommissioned military grounds before the City of Seattle was able to do so. The General Service Administration ultimately demanded Seattle and the UIATF reach a settlement. Talks began in

June 1971 and concluded in November with an agreement that allowed for the establishment of Seattle's Discovery Park and the assignment of a 20-acre tract to accommodate Daybreak Star Indian Cultural Center. Said Whitebear of the settlement, "It's not a treaty. The white man doesn't keep treaties. It's a legal, binding, agreement."

The $1.2 million construction cost for Daybreak Star Indian Cultural Center came from grants, Seattle city funds, and private contributions. In May 1977, the facility opened and commenced serving the needs of Seattle's urban Indian population. Today, the center has a staff of more than 100, manages a $5 million budget, and directs a variety of federal programs and community initiatives.

Whitebear displayed the traits common to Indian activists of the 1960s and 1970s. These activists generally found established Indian reform or advocacy organizations too modest in their vision and too compliant with federal and state government. Whitebear's UIATF championed direct action—aggressive action—to press Indian issues locally and nationally through news agencies; to inform and gain support of a broad, diverse audience; and to compel government response. These tactics became increasingly common among America's youth in the 1960s and early 1970s, evidenced most visibly in the civil rights movement and anti-war movement. This chapter highlights the spirit of rebellion among Native Americans in those two decades and the radicalization of Indian protest.

CHRONOLOGY

1963	The National Indian Youth Council initiates "fish-ins" across the Pacific Northwest to protest state game laws
1964	Native Americans take brief occupation of Alcatraz Island in San Francisco Bay
1966	Department of Justice enforces fishing rights as provided in existing treaties with Native Americans
1968	The American Indian Movement (AIM) is founded in July in Minneapolis
	President Lyndon Johnson issues his statement "The Forgotten American," officially ending the Policy of Termination
1969	Nearly 80 Indians begin an 18-month occupation of Alcatraz Island
1970	More than 100 American Indians attempt the takeover of Fort Lawton, a decommissioned U.S. Army post near Seattle
1971	The occupation of Alcatraz concludes in summer
1972	Nearly 1,000 Native Americans occupy the Bureau of Indian Affairs
	Congress passes the Indian Education Act
1973	AIM takes over the South Dakota town of Wounded Knee and begins a three-month occupation
1974	The "Boldt Decision" upholds Indian treaty fishing rights
1975	Congress enacts the Indian Self-Determination and Education Assistance Act
1978	The Longest Walk, an AIM-sponsored demonstration in Washington, D.C., is held in summer
	Congress passes into law the American Indian Religious Freedom Act

KEY QUESTIONS

1. What new tactics did Indian leaders of the early 1960s initiate to protect and defend treaty provisions and native interests, and why did they deem those tactics appropriate? How did Native American dissent reflect the current of dissent nationwide?

2. In what ways was Native American military service during the Vietnam War consistent with Indian participation in America's previous wars of the twentieth century? How was Indian military service in the 1960s different from that of World War I and World War II?

3. What explains the radicalization of Native American dissent in the late 1960s and early 1970s? To what extent did radicalization affect favorably and negatively the national response to native issues?

4. How did the state of Indian affairs at the end of the 1970s reveal both consistency and contrast with previous decades in the twentieth century?

A New Direction in Indian Activism

It was early autumn, 1964. The nation was almost one year removed from the tragedy of President John F. Kennedy's assassination in Dallas, Texas. His successor, Lyndon Baines Johnson, had taken advantage of the growing myth of Kennedy liberal reform to press passage of a civil rights bill and to commence his own vision of a Great Society. A spirit of reform, of redirection, settled over much of America, a spirit that particularly influenced university and college students.

But the winds of dissent blowing in the mid-1960s predated Kennedy's assassination. In 1960, two graduate students at the University of Michigan, Tom Hayden and Alan Haber, established Students for a Democratic Society (SDS). In the 1962 Port Huron Statement, SDS decried persistent racism, denounced the nuclear arms buildup and Cold War, condemned the continuance of poverty in a land of such abundance, insisted on the equality of all humans, and called for the realization of participatory democracy. The Free Speech Movement (FSM), founded in 1964 and led by Mario Savio, born in part out of the civil rights struggle, echoed the values of SDS and specifically targeted America's escalating involvement in Vietnam. What President Johnson touted in 1964 as the "Kennedy Spirit"—human equality and equal opportunity for all Americans—drew more young people into the rising movement for reform in the United States.

As the 1960s progressed, peaceful protest turned violent. The predominantly African American Watts Community in Los Angeles exploded in bloody rioting in summer 1965 and set the pattern for urban racial unrest for the remainder of the decade. The civil rights movement championed by Martin Luther King Jr. splintered into increasingly radical divisions, among them the Student Non-violent Coordinating Committee and the Black Panthers. At the same time, the United States became mired in war. By summer 1967 there were more than 500,000 American troops deployed in Vietnam, and despite President Johnson's contention that he could see the "light at the end of the tunnel," victory seemed increasingly elusive. This perspective appeared accurate in early 1968 when North Vietnam unleashed its Tet Offensive. The anti-war movement, like the civil rights movement, radicalized and was marked with campus rebellions and building takeovers, mass demonstrations exceeding 100,000 protesters, and draft evasion and draft card burning. In May 1970, four students at an anti-war demonstration at Kent State University in Ohio were shot to death by National Guard soldiers, an incident that drew a sharper line between mainstream America and dissenting America. And, as the 1960s came to a close, the Weather Underground was founded and advocated full-scale revolution in the United States—violent revolution if required.

It seemed to be a watershed moment in American history. The intellectual discourse of dissent heard in cafés and art galleries late in the 1950s evolved into peaceful confrontation by the mid-1960s and into radical, often violent, confrontation by decade's end. This pattern was evident, too, among Native American activists.

The National Congress of American Indians had emerged as the principal advocate for Native American issues following World War II (see Chapter 16). It was largely comprised of young, college-educated individuals tempered by the Great Depression and war who, like members of previous pan-Indian organizations, still believed that working within the existing political, social, and economic institutions could lead to positive change. The founding of the National Indian Youth Council (NIYC) in the early 1960s, however, signaled a shift toward a more activist approach to Indian issues. Soon after its establishment, the NIYC demonstrated its separation from the NCAI and other Indian organizations that predated it by employing direct, but peaceful, confrontation to bring Indian issues to a national audience and to compel government to address those concerns.

Fishing and Water Rights

The leadership of the National Indian Youth Council found existing pan-Indian advocacy groups ineffective and called for a more aggressive approach in advancing Indian issues. Rather than continue holding conferences and meetings and periodically issuing NIYC statements of purpose or support, leaders like Clyde Warrior (Ponca) believed direct action—public protest akin to that demonstrated during the civil rights movement—would garner greater attention and produce more immediate and more positive results. At the NIYC meeting in December 1963, Warrior received the enthusiastic support of Hank Adams (Sioux/Assiniboine) and together they targeted government restrictions on Indian fishing rights in the Pacific Northwest for direct action.

Native American fishermen relied on the region's rivers and streams as a source of food, and the United States had consistently guaranteed the Indians' unabated use of those waterways in treaties made with Indians of Oregon and Washington. State governments, however, routinely ignored treaty rights and by the early 1960s required all fishermen, including Indians, to purchase fishing licenses and to submit to other fishing restrictions that generally favored commercial interests. Much of this was made possible under Public Law 280, which authorized tribal termination and the extension of state jurisdiction over Native Americans and Indian lands, in many instances without Indian approval. Native Americans who ignored state game laws found themselves criminally convicted, fined, and occasionally jailed. At the same time, commercial fishing rivals often destroyed Indian fishing nets, denied them fuel for their boats, and maliciously damaged boat motors. Fights frequently erupted at boat landings and docks, and in most cases local authorities blamed the Indians and not white fishermen.

In March 1964, the NIYC called for a series of "fish-ins" across the Pacific Northwest to bring to national attention the Indians' lost free use of the region's rivers and streams previously protected by treaties. Hundreds of Indians gathered at Puget Sound to protest state game laws, and the NIYC orchestrated a demonstration at the state capital in Washington. Adams, Warrior, and others also secured the participation of popular Hollywood actor Marlon Brando to ensure full media coverage. Brando, long sympathetic to Native American issues, joined the Indians' protest and was taken into custody by the local game wardens, although authorities soon released him in an effort to avoid additional national exposure for the demonstration.

NYIC-sponsored fish-ins continued for the next two years. With each staged fish-in, dozens of Indians were beaten and arrested, many of them serving months in local jails. Media coverage of the demonstrations, particularly scenes of physical abuse against Indians, drew the attention of an increasingly interested American public. As with African Americans' struggle for civil rights, violent efforts to suppress Indian protests shifted public opinion in the protesters' favor. Clyde Warrior and other leaders of the NIYC genuinely wished for peaceful

PROFILE

Buffy Sainte-Marie, 1941–

Buffy Sainte-Marie was born on the Piapot Cree Indian Reservation in Saskatchewan, Canada, in 1941 or 1942. Orphaned at an early age, a family in Maine adopted and reared her. As a child Buffy knew little of her Cree heritage, but her family did make her somewhat aware of the family's Indian traditions and values and more generally of the history of Indian-white relations in the United States. She earned a bachelor's degree in Eastern Philosophy in 1962 from the University of Massachusetts and later a Ph.D. in Fine Arts from the same university.

Sainte-Marie began playing the guitar at age 16 and by the early 1960s was part of the café scene in Greenwich Village, New York, playing and singing both popular and her own original songs. Her music demonstrated a power, a feeling, and a perspective common to the early '60s folk music genre that was just starting to gain the attention of middle America's youth. Sainte-Marie's songs were sharply critical of racism, incest, drug abuse, and war, and she quickly earned a reputation as a singer/songwriter of protest music. Her song "The Universal Soldier," performed by pop singer Donovan, condemned the foolishness of war and contended that soldiers are as much responsible for war as the leaders who initiate war. Young men have a choice—to serve, or not to serve. Without soldiers, there would be no war.

Sainte-Marie is especially proud of her Indian identity. She has published articles in which she discusses current Indian issues, and worked with Dennis Banks and Russell Means in the early days of the American Indian Movement. "Now That the Buffalo's Gone" became one of her most respected songs. It not only criticized the government's historic treatment of native peoples but also challenged listeners to think critically about their own views of native peoples and Native American issues. Her music extended the reach of activist Indians into the culture of mainstream young America, cultivating awareness of and garnering support for native issues among non-Indians. Her reputation as a protest singer was rewarded with a place on President Lyndon Johnson's "performers to suppress" list and President Richard Nixon's famed "enemies list."

Her music and her Indian activism has carried her to appearances on *The Tonight Show* in the 1960s and a regular role on the children's program *Sesame Street* from 1976 to 1981 in which she educated youngsters about American Indian cultures. Sainte-Marie's popularity rose even more when her song "Up Where We Belong" became the theme song for the feature film *An Officer and a Gentleman* in the mid-1980s.

Sainte-Marie put musical performances on hold to rear her son. During those years she trained herself in digital arts and has since produced highly respected works featuring Native American cultural heritage. Her work is displayed in museums across the United States.

17.1 Buffy St. Marie
Source: Pictorial Press Ltd/Alamy Stock Photo

confrontation with state authorities, but they understood the gain that widespread reports of violence against peaceful demonstrators would bring to the fish-ins. And, to assure continued news coverage and to suggest cross-racial support for Indian fishermen, fish-in organizers routinely encouraged celebrities such as activists Jane Fonda and Dick Gregory to participate.

In 1966, the United States Department of Justice officially reasserted Indian fishing rights under the 1850s treaties, a measure sustained in 1974 by U.S. District Court Judge George Boldt in *United States* v. *Washington*. Generally referred to as the "**Boldt Decision**," the court ruled that "non-treaty fishermen shall have the opportunity to take up to fifty percent of the harvestable number of fish . . . and treaty right fishermen shall have the opportunity to take up to the same percentage." Similar disputes arose between Native Americans and non-treaty fishermen in states from coast to coast, and throughout the 1970s federal courts repeatedly upheld treaty provisions in place of state laws, highlighted in the decision in the case of *United States* v. *Michigan* (1979) that assured Ottawa and Anisnhinaabe Indians continued fishing rights in the Great Lakes.

Victories in the fight against state fish and game laws encouraged Indian activists to use direct action to recover reservation lands lost to state governments over the previous century. In the 1970s, a range of Indian tribes filed suits for the return of traditional tribal lands. The Penobscot and Passamaquoddy asserted claim to more than half of Maine; South Carolina's Catawba Indians pressed for the return of a much smaller tract, but one on which sat the highly profitable Carowinds Theme Park that straddled the South Carolina-North Carolina state line between Rock Hill and Charlotte. These efforts had little success. Although the American public was generally sympathetic to calls to restore fishing rights, Indian claims on land—land that was often in the hands of powerful non-Indian individuals and organizations—were another matter.

Nonetheless, the shift to direct action in full view of a national audience generally proved successful. Fish-ins drew much-needed attention to a pressing issue among Pacific Northwest Indians and in so doing ignited interest in Indian affairs more broadly among non-Indians. Moreover, the NIYC's activism was initiated and led by a group of younger Native Americans. These new leaders were born during the years of the Indian Reorganization Act, challenged by the policies of termination and relocation, and better educated than their parents. They were a generation of emerging activists reared in an age of new national communications systems in which "real-time" news coverage was increasingly common, and in a period of increased Indian transience and urbanization that only furthered a pan-Indian consciousness.

Alcatraz

In 1963, the federal government closed its penitentiary on Alcatraz Island in San Francisco Bay. The next year, on March 8, about 40 Indian activists, among them Russell Means, Richard McKenzie, and Belva Cottier, boated to the abandoned island and attempted to reclaim the property for Native Americans. Within 24 hours, U.S. marshals removed them. The Indians soon filed suit in federal court, insisting they were entitled to the island under Article 6 of the Fort Laramie Treaty of 1868. The treaty had promised the Sioux surplus federal land "which is not mineral land, nor reserved by the United States for special purposes other than Indian occupation."

According to the Indians' interpretation of the treaty, now that the United States no longer required the property to accommodate a federal prison, the island was to be returned to Indian ownership. In short order the court dropped what it considered to be a bizarre if not absurd suit.

In their book *Like a Hurricane: The Indian Movement from Alcatraz to Wounded Knee*, Paul Chaat Smith and Robert Allen Warrior concede that those who ventured onto Alcatraz that day most likely "saw the action as a publicity stunt"; they knew their claim to the 1868 treaty was terribly weak. Nonetheless, "they were quite serious about the central point: treaties were not irrelevant and Indians had not forgotten them." The media

17.2 Sioux Indians plant an American flag on Alcatraz Island in San Francisco, California, during a demonstration in 1964.

Source: Bettmann/Getty Images

treated seriously the fish-ins farther north partly because of the support given to them by high-profile celebrities and partly because the NIYC protests were grounded on issues and arguments understood generally by most non-Indian observers. On the other hand, the contention that Alcatraz should be returned to Indian control on the basis of a century-old treaty appeared foolish at best and ludicrous at worst to television audiences and newspaper subscribers nationally.

The situation changed markedly over the next five years. Indian enrollment in colleges and universities increased as a result of slightly improved family income and Great Society programs that channeled tuition assistance to racial minorities. At many institutions of higher education, Indian students representing a wide range of tribal affiliations joined together to form Native American student unions. Universities increasingly established academic programs of study in Native American cultures and history, patterns of growth similar to the founding of the Black Student Union and African American culture and history academic programs that occurred during the same period. At the same time, urban Indian Centers not only grew in number but also expanded significantly the services they provided, including community fairs, exhibits, and programs that educated non-Indians about Native American cultures and history and celebrated Indian identity. The Fort Lawton takeover and fish-ins in the Pacific Northwest grabbed national attention and succeeded in securing some opportunities and policy reversals for Native Americans. Alcatraz in 1964 garnered no positive return for Indians, but five years later activists concluded that the island's takeover should be revisited.

The Alcatraz Occupation

On November 9, 1969, Alcatraz once again captured national attention. A collection of Indians, mostly college students and those directly involved in urban-based Indian programs, packed a few boats and motored to the island in an effort to occupy "the Rock," but federal authorities arrested and removed them the following day. Another, larger effort was made on November 20. Almost 80 Indians, again largely of local residency, boated to Alcatraz Island and announced their occupation "in the name of all American Indians." Explaining their actions to the attending newsmen, they detailed Alcatraz's suitability to serve as an Indian reservation. "Alcatraz Island is more than suitable for an Indian Reservation" as "this place resembles most Indian reservations." The island "is isolated from modern facilities . . . has no fresh running water . . . has inadequate sanitation facilities . . . no oil or mineral rights . . . no health care facilities . . . [and] no educational facilities." Moreover, "there is no industry, and so unemployment [will be] very great; . . . the soil is rocky and unproductive, and the land does not support game." And, they pointed to the recent use of the island as a federal penitentiary, saying that "the [Indian] population has always been held as prisoners and kept dependent on others"; in this, living on Alcatraz proved no different than residing on a typical reservation. Seventy more Indians joined them over the next few days.

The Indians' aims were simple. First, the **Alcatraz Takeover** would serve as a means by which public attention would be dramatically drawn to native issues and concerns. Chief among these issues was the desperate need of urbanized Native Americans for Indian community centers that could provide basic support services. Second, they hoped the takeover would help create a unified Indian movement working toward the common goal of self-determination. As a symbol of Indian conditions and Indian protest, Alcatraz might spark the founding of a truly pan-Indian movement. "We want all Indian people to join with us," said occupation leader Richard Oaks. He called for the unity of "all our Indian Brothers behind a common cause" rather than accomplishing nothing "by working alone as individual tribes."

Television news teams gave the occupation wide coverage over the next few weeks, as did the print media. Reporters routinely conducted street-level interviews to sample popular opinion of the Indians' actions, and most residents of the San Francisco-Oakland area voiced support for the occupiers. "A former prison became the symbol of a renewed Indian quest for freedom, a declaration of independence from the strangling embrace of white society and compliant Indian leaders," wrote Edward Lazarus, whose father was a highly respected attorney representing Indian causes in the 1960s. The Federal Bureau of Investigation (FBI) created plans to forcibly remove what it politely termed "trespassers," but the FBI never received authority from the White House to implement its operation. Instead, President Richard Nixon chose to let the takeover run its own course, trusting that internal tensions among the Indians would lead to the occupation's collapse.

Nixon's patience was rewarded. Disagreements among the leaders surfaced soon after the occupation began. Most of the original occupiers left the island and were replaced by people new to the cause and by those pressing their own, separate agenda. Factions quickly emerged. There seemed to be no single voice, no firm set of expectations or goals, no idea of what constituted "victory." The occupation ended on June 10, 1971. "The Alcatraz occupation could have gone much more smoothly," said Lanada Boyer (Shoshone), reflecting on the takeover 25 years later. "We made many mistakes," she added, "but this is how we learn and grow."

PROFILE

Vine Deloria Jr. (1933–2005)

Born in Martin, South Dakota, in 1933, Vine Deloria Jr. (Lakota) emerged as the "most significant voice" for his generation of Native Americans. His family history mirrored the principal directions in Indian affairs and federal Indian policy over the previous century. His great-grandfather was a Yankton Sioux holy man, his grandfather a Yankton chief who converted to Christianity in the 1860s, and his father a Progressive Indian who held a prominent national post in the Episcopal Church and who called for assimilation while retaining pride in the family's Indian heritage.

Deloria served with the United States Marine Corps in the mid-1950s before earning a bachelor's degree in 1958 from Iowa State University and a master's degree in theology from Lutheran School of Theology at Rock Island, Illinois, in 1963. In 1964, he accepted the appointment of Executive Director of the National Congress of American Indians (NCAI) and held that position for the next three years. From this position, he witnessed first-hand the government's manipulation of tribal communities and saw just how limited the Indians' options were within the existing political structure of the United States. He also learned quickly how internal arguments over issues, strategy, and tactics undermined the NCAI, prompting many Indians to abandon the organization and later join the more radical American Indian Movement. Deloria left the NCAI in 1967, returned to school, and earned his law degree in 1970 from the University of Colorado. He then began a teaching career that spanned the next three decades, teaching Indian and Ethnic Studies at Western Washington State College, University of California at Los Angeles, University of Arizona, and University of Colorado. At the same time, Deloria worked to educate Native Americans about Indian law, particularly tribal and individual rights, and he worked to help Indians gain access to legal aid services.

Deloria is best known for his highly respected books published between 1969 and his death in 2005, of which there are more than 20. His first, *Custer Died for Your Sins: An Indian Manifesto* (1969), became an immediate bestseller. He damned the general history of Indian-Euro-American relations over the previous 500 years, blasted the federal government's failure to honor its treaties with native peoples, condemned non-Indian determination to strip Native Americans of their own rich culture and heritage, and insisted that the United States recognize tribal self-determination as new federal Indian policy. The book's publication could not have been better timed, coinciding as it did with the Alcatraz takeover and the growing youth militancy of the era. He published *We Talk: You Listen* the following year, describing America's current crises in environment, race, political power, and economics as symptoms of a corrupted nation's sickness, and he encouraged a rebirth of traditional tribal governing and social structures as a logical alternative. *Behind the Trail of Broken Treaties* (1974) explained the Indians' perspective on the issues that gave rise to the American Indian Movement, its 1972 occupation of the BIA building in Washington, D.C., and the takeover of Wounded Knee, South Dakota. He consistently criticized non-Indians for providing only intellectual or verbal support for Native American rights and identity rather than joining in direct action with Indians to advance the movement. His 1972 book *God Is Red: A Native View of Religion* compared and contrasted Indian spirituality with Christianity and the Judeo-Christian world, stressing his belief in the superiority of the Native American understanding of life, values, and relationship of man to nature.

17.3 Vine Deloria Jr.

Source: Cyrus McCrimmon/The Denver Post via Getty Images

Vine Deloria Jr. provided a necessary voice to the Indian activism of the 1960s and 1970s. Although he was far less known nationally than those activists who aggressively and publicly challenged government through fish-ins, occupations, and marches, Deloria produced a much-needed, coherent, intellectual, ideological perspective that explained Native American resistance to a non-Indian audience, a perspective that grew quickly within mainstream society and, as a result, contributed directly to creating a climate conducive to a fundamental redirection in Indian policies and popular sentiment. Vine Deloria Jr. was not a warrior in the traditional sense, but his work for Native Americans was every bit as vital.

Despite its collapse, the takeover succeeded in placing before the American population a better awareness and understanding of Native American issues in the late 1960s. Moreover, it demonstrated to Native Americans that direct action might not accomplish all Indian goals, but it certainly served as a useful and emotionally rewarding tool. "We took the island because we wanted the federal government to honor our treaties and its own laws . . . and to focus attention on Indian reservations and communities throughout the nation where our people were living in poverty and suffering great injustice," said Lanada Boyer. Boyer was cofounder of and executive secretary for the Bay Area Native American Council (BANAC), a union of all Bay Area Indian organizations in support of those on Alcatraz Island. "The United States is always the first [nation] to point out human rights violations in other countries, without regard to its own treatment of Native Americans, Blacks, Chicano, Asians, and poor people," she added. The occupation, said John Mohawk (Seneca), demonstrated the Indians' "general discontent" and signaled "their intent to survive as a people." "Alcatraz was the birth of a new movement in the sense that it served as a touch post for Native people who were seeking change, and it demonstrated to them that concerted action could have some results, however faltering those efforts may seem to us now," said John Mohawk. "We have a long way to go before we can live in a balanced world and be the best people that we can be. . . . Our hardships have made our spirits grow strong. We give thanks for our many blessings and pray that the sacred circle of life continues forever," said Boyer.

Indians and the Vietnam War

The American military presence in Southeast Asia rose each year after the Gulf of Tonkin Incident in 1964, reaching 500,000 American troops deployed inside Vietnam by 1967. Conversely, popular support for the war among Americans declined with each passing year, dropping from 80 percent immediately following the Gulf of Tonkin Resolution to 40 percent in spring 1968. This drop in support was due in large measure to the growing casualty rate, which topped 57,000 American deaths by war's end. It was a war with limited objectives, one that propped up a corrupt South Vietnamese government, and one that created a disillusioned generation of younger Americans. Native Americans participated in the war as their fathers and grandfathers had in earlier conflicts, but Vietnam forced many to reconsider their racial identity in mid-twentieth-century America.

Native Americans Enter the Armed Forces

Federal records do not give an accurate number of American Indians who served in the armed forces during the Vietnam War era. As was the case in World War II and World War I, Selective Service registration papers during the Vietnam War years did not offer an "American Indian" racial category. Registrants and inductees were expected to identify themselves as "white," "negro," or the catch-all category "other." Many Native American men did, in fact, list themselves in the third category, identifying themselves as American Indian or more specifically as members of a particular tribe. In his book *Strong Hearts, Wounded Souls*, historian Tom Holm noted that only 40 percent of the Indians presented themselves as American Indian on registration and induction papers. Among those interviewed by Holm, 20 percent admitted they had "no idea what racial category" was ultimately assigned to them, and 48 percent knew they were inducted as "Caucasian"; generally, recruiters, gave a racial identity to Indian recruits and draftees based on physical appearances, surnames, or racial bias.

Approximately 62,000 American Indians served in the U.S. armed forces during the Vietnam War era, and of those about 42,000 were deployed to Vietnam for at least one tour of duty. In Vietnam, 226 lost their lives. As in the two world wars, the number of American Indians in military service was greater in proportion to their representation in the United States as a whole. Nearly one of every four eligible Indian men served in contrast to one of every 12 men in the general population. As in previous wars, American Indians once more served principally in combat roles, largely joining infantry and specialized infantry units such as the Marines' Force Recon and the army's Special Forces, Airborne, and Ranger units.

Holm focused on the Readjustment Counseling Survey (RCS) conducted by the Veterans Administration that questioned 170 Indian veterans of the Vietnam War, representing 77 tribal groups (see Table 17.1). These were politically active men, energized and politicized by the tempo of 1960s resistance nationally and by their military service. One-third worked with the American Indian Movement, the National Indian Youth Council, or the National Congress of American Indians before or soon after their military service.

Seventy-five percent of the RCS respondents cited their sense of family and tribal obligation and heritage as a reason for entering military service during the Vietnam era; 75 percent also listed "duty, country," or "patriotism" as a very important motive for serving in the armed forces. Holm added that the Indian respondents also "were patriots in the tribal sense of the word." He noted that many of the interviewed Indians felt "honor-bound and obligated legally to defend the country not because they were citizens of the United States but because their individual nations had signed treaties with the whites." He pointed to one respondent who said, "My people have always honored our treaties, even when the whites haven't. I went in [to service] because our treaties say that we're allied to the U.S." "I went to Vietnam," remarked another Indian veteran, "not because I have any particular loyalty to the United States but because I have loyalty to my own people, my own tradition."

To be sure, financial gain was also an important motivation for enlistment. The acquisition of technical skills that might be transferrable to civilian jobs lured many into the armed forces. High rates of unemployment on reservations and the limited opportunities for urban jobs because of insufficient education or racial bias compelled many others to enlist.

The warrior spirit that encouraged so many young men to serve in earlier wars also drove many Indians to serve in Vietnam. Wrote Holm, "Many truly wanted to be warriors in the older tradition . . . they could form a link to their warrior ancestors." He referenced a Cherokee whose family members fought against white America and those who fought alongside white soldiers in World War I and World War II. "I tried to live up to the ways of my ancestors and be a warrior," he said. They generally saw "military service as an honorable method of gaining respect within their home communities." Following the "path of the old-time warriors" led many inductees into the combat arms units of the ground forces. "I went eleven-bravo (Army infantry) so I could get into the war. I wanted to be a warrior," said one RCS interviewee.

Table 17.1 Native Americans' Reasons for Entering Military Service, Based on the RCS Survey, Reported as Percentage of those Interviewed

	Very Important	Somewhat Important	Not Very Important	Not Important
Sense of Duty	44	31	14	11
Family Tradition	51	24	12	13
Tribal Tradition	44	32	13	11
Respect from Indians	35	27	18	20
Financial Gain	21	29	28	22
Respect from Non-Indians	15	24	25	36

Source: "Native Americans' Reasons for Entering Service, Percentages" based on RCS Survey in Tom Holm, *Strong Hearts, Wounded Souls: Native American Veterans of the Vietnam War* (Austin: University of Texas Press, 1996), p. 119.

Combat Service

As in America's earlier wars, Native American soldiers were "often singled out for some perilous jobs simply because they were Indians." The pervasive popularity of Hollywood Westerns following World War II and television's Western-themed weekly programs exaggerated longstanding stereotypes about Indian fighting skills. Platoon leaders frequently assigned Indians the more dangerous duties because they believed Indians still possessed natural talent as hunters, trackers, and fighters having "[grown] up in the woods," recalled one Menominee veteran. A Cherokee veteran said he volunteered to work with Long Range Reconnaissance Patrols (LRRPs) because his platoon commander "kept running me on point . . . and putting me out on listening posts at night" because of his perceived natural ability to locate the enemy. He soon chose to work with LRRPs because he "knew the people around me knew what they were doing. . . . I figured my best shot at living through Vietnam was to be a LRRP. Crazy, ain't it?"

Consistent with earlier wars, too, many Native American soldiers carried medicine bundles into battle. Some carried sacred tobacco, small arrowheads, carvings given by family and friends, pebbles, a small pouch of earth, or sacred corn pollen, the latter, said a Navajo veteran, "to keep me safe and to give me strength and courage." They relied on vision and prayer to get them through their tour of duty in Vietnam.

Racial Consciousness

The Vietnam War experience for American troops was unlike any previous war in certain respects. In this war of attrition, success turned on the "body count," tallying the actual number of enemy killed and elevating that number with "presumed killed" rather than on territories gained and placed under American control. It was also a war experience that prompted many participants to make connections between racial consciousness and larger political and social issues. For Native Americans, the racial consciousness, although always present, assumed new dimensions as Indians occupied Alcatraz, attempted the takeover of Fort Lawton, pressed the sanctity of earlier treaties, promoted cultural awareness programs, established the American Indian Movement, and pressed an array of native issues. Little wonder that Native American soldiers drew comparisons between what they witnessed in Vietnam and the history of Indian-white relations in the United States. "We went into their country and killed them and took land that wasn't ours. Just like the whites did to us," said one veteran. Often they noted that "instead of fighting for the government in a far-off country, they should have taken up arms against it in this land," wrote Holm. Said a Creek-Cherokee, "my job was to run missions into what everybody called 'Indian country.' That's what they called enemy territory. . . . I woke up one morning fairly early in my tour and realized that instead of being a warrior like Crazy Horse, I was a scout used by the army to track him down. . . . I was fighting the wrong people, pure and simple, and I've never gotten over it."

Enemy territory across Vietnam was commonly termed "Indian Country." General Maxwell Taylor testified before the Senate Foreign Relations Committee soon after the Gulf of Tonkin Resolution swept through Congress that the U.S. Army would employ a "pacification" program in Vietnam. Elaborating on the policy, he said, "it is very hard to plant the corn outside the stockade when the Indians are still around. We have to get the Indians farther away in many provinces to make good progress." In his article "America and Vietnam: The Indian Subtext," David Espey referenced a veteran of the infamous My Lai massacre who "equated 'wiping the whole place out' with what he called 'the Indian idea . . . the only good gook is a dead gook.' The Indian idea was in the air of Vietnam." Vine Deloria noted in his famed book *Custer Died for Your Sins* that 15 percent of Indians surveyed insisted the United States should get out of Vietnam, and 85 percent believed they should get out of America." Said Ben Chitty, "War taught us some things . . . politicians tell lies and call themselves 'patriots,' . . . We knew that the honesty and loyalty and sacrifice required of us in war were worth a lot more than the dishonest, manipulative, greedy politics which sent us into combat. . . . We saw," he added, "the 'American way of life' from a different angle, at the edge of the empire. We enforced it. Made it work. Nations occupied. Populations terrorized and decimated. Countrysides laid waste. Societies and cultures destroyed. For what?" Service in Vietnam revealed itself as a "bitter irony" to many Indian veterans. Native Americans who over the centuries battled against the United States for the preservation of their own independence and right of self-determination now fought to extend America's imperial power over a people that preferred national independence and self-determination. Chitty drew a comparison between the "Indian wars" of the nineteenth century and the war in Vietnam—"the 'Wild West' was a free-fire zone. General Custer was on a search-and-destroy mission at Little Big Horn. Not much to choose between Wounded Knee and My Lai, or between forced relocation to new reservations and the resettlement camps we built in Vietnam." "The real war," he and other Indian veterans concluded, "was here at home."

The war left deep scars on so many combat veterans. Said one Indian veteran, "I was a happy, healthy boy, and I felt in harmony with my family, my people, and the earth because of the teachings my grandfather shared." His service in the Marine Corps and combat in Vietnam changed that. "I had to swallow the anger and shame when [fellow Marines] jokingly called me 'chief,'" and "I stayed [in Vietnam] for three tours because I lived so much with death that I couldn't come home." The war "hardened me to the point where I didn't believe in a lot of things I had been taught to believe in," said Jerald Lytle. "The goodness of man and God, and trust, things like that. . . . [Vietnam] destroyed a lot of things in me."

Most Indian veterans of Vietnam returned home to resume their earlier lives, securing jobs on or near reservations. Others took advantage of the GI Bill of Rights to enroll in colleges and universities, establish their own businesses, gain job skills, or purchase a house. Many chose to become politically active, working within the political system rather than opposing it from outside. They gained seats on tribal councils, became lawyers specializing in Indian issues, and served as teachers, tribal law enforcement officers, and Indian Center staffers. As much as anything else, wartime experiences compelled many returning veterans to become active in Indian affairs, work on behalf of native peoples, and counter the historic and prevailing image of American Indians.

Red Power

By the late 1960s and early 1970s, many Native Americans had come to believe that even more aggressive action was necessary to compel federal and state authorities to address fully Indian concerns and produce more tangible results than those gained by fish-ins and the Alcatraz occupation. Many emerging Indian leaders now concluded that the gains achieved by Native Americans in the early to mid-1960s were but minor concessions government made, minimal changes intended only to resolve local Indian problems the media turned into national issues. Beginning in 1968, Native American activism splintered with those calling for greater aggressiveness taking a more radical and often violent direction. They increasingly used the term **Red Power,** a term that was intended to convey the idea that Native Americans would themselves determine their own course in America as free peoples.

The American Indian Movement

In 1968, the greater Minneapolis area was home to about 10,000 American Indians, mostly Sioux and Anishinaabe. On almost any given day, nearly 70 percent of all individuals held in the city jail were Native American.

17.4 American Indian Movement leader Dennis Banks speaks before a gathering at Mount Rushmore, South Dakota.

Source: Everett Collection Historical/Alamy Stock Photo

Emerging leaders in the local Indian community argued that white authorities purposely singled out Native Americans in Minneapolis much like blacks were singled out in Oakland or Los Angeles. This, they insisted, was the product of racism, ignorance of Indian cultural traits and living conditions, and general indifference to justice. Indian activists in the city formed "Indian patrols" to monitor police radios and provide a Native American presence in Indian communities long targeted by law enforcement. Over the 12 months that followed, the number of Indians jailed dropped 60 percent. On the heels of this successful initiative, a small group of Native Americans, among them Dennis Banks and Clyde Bellecourt, organized a new activist group on July 28, the **American Indian Movement (AIM)**.

In late 1967, Dennis Banks was serving a six-month prison term for forgery. Smith and Warrior note in *Like a Hurricane* that Banks "read obsessively," educating himself about the ongoing civil rights movement and anti-war effort and studying Native American histories and treaties. "I began to see that the greatest war was going to go on right here in the United States, and I began to realize that there was a hell of a situation in this country," said Banks. He committed himself to fighting in defense of Indian rights. Clyde Bellecourt, also doing time in the same prison, read material on Ojibwa religion and culture and in so doing found both his spirit and mission. Banks and Bellecourt left prison in 1968 determined to defend American Indian interests and advance a rebirth and broader awareness of native cultures. In founding AIM, they initially intended to unite the 20 or so independent Indian organizations in the greater Minneapolis metropolitan area and concentrate Indian influence on local politics. AIM also involved itself in the local Indian Center, encouraged and directed cultural awareness programs, and promised to defend urban Indian residents by force if necessary. In this, AIM mirrored the community focus of the Black Panthers as well as the willingness of most radical groups at the time to accept violence as a proper response to government and society's oppressive policies and structures.

AIM founders saw three forces as most responsible for the undermining of Indians: "Christianity, white-oriented education, and the federal government." Few could argue with AIM's assessment given the dark history of Indian-white relations over the previous five centuries, but organization leaders intended their message for Indians as much as they did for non-Indians. Banks, George Mitchell, Bellecourt, and others in AIM faulted the NYIC for not being more aggressive in pressing Indian issues, the NCAI for being too conciliatory to Washington, Indian New Deal tribal governments and leaders for being so easily duped by the BIA and Indian Commissioner John Collier, and earlier pan-Indian groups and leaders for encouraging Native Americans to acculturate and assimilate with mainstream society. According to AIM, the policies and positions of these organizations would ultimately make the older "vanishing Indian" myth a reality. AIM's message was resistance and rebirth. It called on Indians to defy the forces that guaranteed the Indians' final destruction and to join in the process of producing a rebirth of traditional Native values. AIM members "returned to the old religions of their tribes." Theirs was a "spiritual movement, a religious rebirth, and . . . a rebirth of Indian dignity." "The American Indian Movement sees itself as a new warrior society for Indian people," not one that is rooted on

TIMELINE 17.1 EXAMPLES OF AMERICAN INDIAN PROTEST ACTIVITIES

1964	Survival of American Indians (SAI) is founded and initiates "fish-ins" across Washington State
1968	Mohawk Indians stop traffic on Cornwall International Bridge between the United States and Canada to protest U.S. restriction of Indian free movement across the border
1970	On Thanksgiving Day, members of AIM occupy *Mayflower II*, a replica of the original *Mayflower*, and paint Plymouth Rock red
1971	AIM occupies Mount Rushmore on July 4 to highlight the irony of a nation celebrating its independence when that same nation stripped another people of their independence
1976	Un-Thanksgiving Day is established to honor those Indians who occupied Alcatraz Island and to commemorate native resistance historically

military power as perceived by "white persons" but rather a warrior society in the traditional sense of Indian understanding—"The men and women of the nation who have dedicated themselves to give everything that they have to the people," said one early member of AIM. And, in concert with traditional Native American values, "Its role [is] a peaceful one, to work within the system toward its goals, *unless* pushed by counter forces into a military stand."

Trail of Broken Treaties

By early 1972, AIM had already demonstrated its capacity for aggressive action in defense of Native Americans, but in the aftermath of the killing of a Native American that year the organization's notoriety rose significantly. The murder of 51-year-old ranch hand Raymond Yellow Thunder (Oglala Sioux) in February by several "white racists" and the general failure (or refusal) of local authorities and the BIA to investigate fully brought AIM and 1,400 supporters to the small town of Gordon, Nebraska. Days of Indian rage and demonstration, often violent, followed until Gordon officials and the state legislature agreed to create a human rights commission, investigate thoroughly the murder, and convict those responsible for the crime. Said one Indian man of AIM's response to the Yellow Thunder murder, "I think people around here know that we're not just a bunch of little Indians" anymore. "Yellow Thunder wasn't the first of us to be mistreated," said one Lakota woman, "but he'd better be the last." Soon after AIM departed Gordon, a small group of activists "visited" a trading post near Wounded Knee, South Dakota, operated by James Czwczynski. Czwczynski had allegedly "choked" an Indian boy in his store days earlier. These members of AIM destroyed some store goods and property (although far less than the $50,000 worth of damage later claimed by Czwczynski) and threatened his life should he ever lay hands on another Indian. In spring, AIM denounced tribal councils generally for their refusal to take up arms to counter non-Indian exploitation of tribal resources, and members brandished their own weapons at an Indian convention in Minnesota demanding the Chippewa Tribal Council protect its fishing rights by force if necessary. AIM's willingness to present itself as an armed activist organization and to employ force when needed drew a growing national audience and the attention of government at all levels.

In summer 1972, AIM leaders decided the time was right for a national demonstration. Robert Burnette suggested all Indian organizations unite "under the banner of the **Trail of Broken Treaties** and proceed to Washington where we will show the world what Indians truly stand for." Vern Bellecourt, AIM national coordinator, echoed Burnette's call and announced that AIM would arrange for a meeting of Indian groups to be held in Denver.

Bellecourt recalled in *The Road to Wounded Knee* that on September 30, 50 representatives of several Indian groups, among them AIM, the NIYC, and the Native American Rights Fund, assembled as planned at the New Albany Hotel in Denver and crafted plans for the national demonstration. It would be a peaceful demonstration in Washington, D.C., intended to "educate the general public, the president, and Congress" on issues affecting Native Americans. AIM leaders Dennis Banks and Russell Means were to arrange caravans in Los Angeles, San Francisco, and Seattle; guide them eastward gathering supporters along the route; and converge on Minneapolis-St. Paul on October 23. From there, the Indians would proceed en masse to Washington, D.C., at the end of October and officially present a statement of Indian demands and expectations. At the same time, Bellecourt and others were to make arrangements in the nation's capital for accommodations, demonstration permits, conference facilities, publicity, and administration contacts.

The caravans with 600 travelers reached Minneapolis on October 23. Once there, members of AIM briefly occupied the BIA building. At the same time, caravan leaders and demonstration organizers met and drafted a document that came to be known as the Twenty Points, a list of AIM demands that they intended to present in Washington. As Paul Smith and Robert Warrior noted, "people joined the caravan[s] because their communities were in pain, and nothing of real substance was being done" to resolve their problems.

The media grossly exaggerated the number of Indians heading to the nation's capital, often citing a figure of 30,000–40,000. Russell Means, remembered Robert Burnette, laughed and said, "I don't know where the hell they're all coming from. All I've got here is eight hundred." The inflated figures reflected real fears among the general population. Violent demonstrations and riots had been common across the United States since 1964. The frustration and anger of African Americans in South Central Los Angeles erupted in urban warfare in summer 1965, with riots occurring in other metropolitan centers over the following years. The Black Panthers' determination to defend African American inner-city communities led to gun battles in Oakland and other major cities in the late 1960s, and the melee at the 1968 Democratic National Convention in Chicago was burned into the collective consciousness of Americans. Little wonder that the prospect of an Indian demonstration in Washington only days before the 1972 presidential election concerned so many people.

Internal dissention, however, weakened the Indians' effort. Most participants were determined to make this a peaceful demonstration. Their goal was to educate both politicians and the general public about the harsh realities facing Native Americans. More than a few considered it "terribly unfair" to criticize the Nixon administration. The president, they insisted, had personally called for the right of self-determination for Native American communities and denounced the policies of termination and relocation. Nixon had also returned Blue Lake to the Taos Pueblos in New Mexico, added nearly $1 million to the federal college scholarship fund for Indians, doubled appropriations to the Indian Health Service, established the Office of Indian Water Rights, and supported new programs that addressed Native American alcoholism and drug abuse. Indeed, many American Indians credited the Nixon White House with addressing native issues more seriously than any president since Franklin Delano Roosevelt.

Others, however, expected a violent response from federal authorities. It was Nixon, they reminded administration supporters, who had routinely unleashed brute force against peaceful demonstrations since his election in 1968. It was Nixon, they said, who issued no note of condemnation for the shooting death of four university students at Kent State in May 1970. And it was Nixon, they added, who turned loose the FBI and administration-created "special investigation" units to infiltrate and destroy from within groups and organizations that exercised their First Amendment right to public dissent. How could those involved with the Trail of Broken Treaties expect anything less from an administration that has so clearly demonstrated its willingness to suppress dissent? These Native Americans were determined to meet force with force.

17.5 President Richard Nixon signs a bill giving the Taos Pueblo Indians title to Blue Lake and surrounding land in New Mexico with an interpreter and a religious leader from the tribe in attendance.

Source: Courtesy of The Richard Nixon Presidential Library and Museum (National Archives and Records Administration)

The caravan from Minneapolis pulled into Washington on Wednesday, November 1. Participants were unsure what to expect upon their arrival in Washington, but they soon confronted an unanticipated problem. Rather than finding a support network ready to provide food and shelter, the arrivals found instead no housing for demonstrators, no provisions for food service, and no established communication with government officials. Churches that had earlier promised aid now reversed their decision to help, fearful of being perceived as supporters of a demonstration that quite likely would turn violent. The advance team, which Robert Burnette led, had failed in its sole duty, complained many demonstrators. Given the need to shelter nearly 1,000 people from the cold and rain, caravan leaders directed the Indians to the Bureau of Indian Affairs office, "a place they never even intended to visit," wrote Smith and Warrior, and there found sleeping space in the auditorium and access to the cafeteria. The matter might have been settled with this, but police gathered and at dusk rushed into the building, ordering the Indians to evacuate. The confrontation quickly devolved into a furious fight that chased the police back to the streets. The Indian occupants were now determined not to leave the BIA building.

In the days that followed, White House officials and Trail of Broken Treaties leaders sought ways to avoid further violence and secure a peaceful evacuation of the BIA, but police, armed with court orders, continued to test Indian defenses that only became tighter daily and assumed more ominous signs. Doorways were barricaded, "war paint appeared on the faces of Indian men. Occupiers prepared Molotov cocktails by the dozens; by the hundreds." Increased national attention focused on the standoff in Washington and, predictably, opposing sides only hardened their respective positions. Still, there remained hope for a negotiated settlement.

By Monday afternoon, November 6, federal courts sanctioned police removal of the BIA occupants, but in a bid to avoid further conflict, the White House invited a small group of Indian leaders to the Executive Office Building to negotiate a settlement. Frank Carlucci, representing the Nixon administration, assured Indians that a special committee would be empanelled to review the Twenty Points. He added that there would be no prosecution of demonstrators for the BIA takeover, and a small amount of money, generally less than $100 per person, would be given to those requesting it for their journey home. On Thursday morning, November 9, the Indians vacated the BIA building and began their homeward trek.

Participants interpreted the Trail of Broken Treaties in varied ways. Some saw the occupation as a strike against the great oppressor, the United States. They had

17.6 Native American leaders refuse to obey a court order to vacate the Bureau of Indian Affairs headquarters.

Source: Bettmann/Getty Images

traveled across the continent to present the Indians' perspective, and in Washington the government and the national population heard them. Others felt defeated. They had journeyed to Washington in peaceful protest, seeking to garner understanding from the general population and genuine promises of aid from political figures only to be overshadowed by the presidential election and manipulated by the Nixon White House.

AIM's move on Washington and the $2 million damage to the BIA building, however, garnered little sympathy from non-Indians. Mainstream America in 1972 was exhausted by nearly a decade of demonstrations and riots. Many Americans had grown tired of relentless criticism of the government and the American way of life. The war in Vietnam continued, but public opinion polls routinely showed Americans generally had faith in Nixon's handling of the war. The civil rights movement continued, but the Black Panthers, SNCC, and other radicalized groups had become or were becoming marginalized and less threatening as African Americans were now moving into elected office and the majority of Americans publically supported equal rights. The resurgent conservative political ideology that arrived in Washington in 1968 received an unparalleled mandate in 1972 when Nixon won reelection in a landslide vote.

Wounded Knee

Since its founding, AIM condemned New Deal-era tribal governments for "selling out" to Washington, of being Washington's puppet, and of not representing sincerely Indian preferences and genuinely defending Indian interests. Tribal councils often responded angrily to AIM's attacks, arguing that they—the more moderate Indians—used the existing governing structures to secure the funds and services necessary to raise the overall quality of reservation life. The confrontation was split along generational lines as much as it was an obvious clash between moderates and traditionalists.

AIM also contended that tribal governments were rife with corruption and sometimes employed intimidation to retain power. Such was the case on the Pine Ridge Sioux Reservation where Dick Wilson served as tribal chair, said AIM leaders. The Pine Ridge Reservation in 1973 was one of the poorest Indian communities in the United States. Poverty and unemployment exceeded rates found on most reservations of similar size, ranging from 50 percent to 70 percent. Compounding that, Wilson routinely awarded the few available reservation jobs to family, friends, and associates who gave him their unyielding support as tribal chairman in return. Health and education systems on the reservation had deteriorated since the Indian New Deal to a level reminiscent of conditions described in the 1928 Meriam Report. AIM also secured some evidence that Wilson had arranged the sale of reservation lands to area non-Indians and to commercial enterprises, sales that rewarded him with questionable income and further reduced the ability of individual Indians to provide adequately for themselves and their families. AIM also accused Wilson of misusing tribal funds and permitting strip-mining operations on the reservation, a process responsible for the contamination of reservation water supplies that resulted in unusually high rates of sickness, birth defects, and death. AIM members also contended that Wilson, a "mixed blood," held no personal attachment to and saw no value in the 1868 Fort Laramie Treaty that protected the Black Hills from the federal government and white land speculators, and that the chairman placed no spiritual significance on the territory as was common among the Oglala people. Moreover, those who challenged Wilson incurred his wrath. He had built around him an armed force, what Wilson termed an auxiliary police force, to intimidate opponents. The group was known as Guardians of Our Oglala Nation, or **GOONs**. In 1972, while AIM leaders occupied the Bureau of Indian Affairs building in Washington, Wilson coerced the tribal council to ban AIM from Pine Ridge.

Throughout January and February 1973, Russell Means, Dennis Banks, and other AIM leaders planned and initiated a series of protest rallies and demonstrations in towns surrounding Pine Ridge and sponsored a move by tribal traditionalists to impeach Wilson. The impeachment effort collapsed on February 22. With Wilson's firm grip on the reservation and the BIA's refusal to investigate the tribal council and its chairman, AIM concluded that it had no alternative but to resort to force. On February 27, about 200 Indians, mostly AIM members, armed themselves with rifles, shotguns, and handguns; marched into the town of Wounded Knee; and commenced an occupation that lasted 71 days. AIM leadership publicly condemned the failure of the BIA to defend Native American interests nationally as the bureau was charged to do, blasted the federal government's persistent failure to honor its historic treaties with Native Americans, and demanded the immediate removal of Dick Wilson from office. In a more dramatic and symbolic effort, AIM announced the resurrection of the Oglala Sioux Nation, proclaimed its independence from the United States, and asserted Sioux rights under the 1868 Fort Laramie Treaty.

Within hours of AIM's move, scores of heavily armed federal agents descended on the town, supported by National Guard soldiers. Indians and soldiers alike erected roadblocks, sealing off entry to or escape from Wounded Knee. The media quickly followed federal agents to the town and by the next day provided film footage of armored personnel carriers, attack helicopters, a variety of field guns, and well-equipped troops ready to contest the Indian occupation. The national television audience saw a scene strangely similar to what Indian-white military confrontations a century earlier would have looked like. Spokespeople from both sides stated that they did not desire or anticipate an armed showdown, but few people present in and around Wounded Knee expected anything less than violence. Robert Burnette believed that Russell Means did not expect to survive the occupation. "I hope by my death and the deaths of all these Indian men and women," said Means, "there will be an investigation into corruption on the reservations and there's no better place to start than Pine Ridge." The Wounded Knee Takeover, or **Wounded Knee II** as it is often termed, captured national and international attention and in so doing accomplished one of AIM's fundamental goals.

Wounded Knee II occasionally appeared to be a circus event. News reporters and cameramen jockeyed for interviews and routinely put onto film the most sweeping and dramatic imagery to hook viewers. Hollywood celebrities sometimes called news conferences to state publicly their emotional and intellectual attachment to the Indians' cause or offered a supportive sound bite as they signed autographs. Actor Marlon Brando, although genuinely supportive of Indian action, added to the circus atmosphere when he refused to accept the Academy Award for his role in *The Godfather* as a protest statement on behalf of Native Americans. Speaking for him at the Academy Award Presentation on March 27, Sasheen Littlefeather said, "Marlon Brando has asked me to tell you . . . that he cannot accept this very generous award" because of "the treatment of American Indians today by the film industry." Brando received widespread criticism for not appearing himself and rejecting the honor.

The takeover also served as a publicity event for many politicians. Senator George McGovern, South Dakota Democrat and recently defeated presidential contender, flew in by helicopter and was present among the

17.7 AIM member Oscar Running Bear stands with his rifle at the ready near a teepee at Wounded Knee, South Dakota on the Pine Ridge Indian Reservation, March 1973.

Source: Bettmann/Getty Images

National Guard troops for much of the occupation, purportedly to serve as a mediator if needed. President Nixon called for a negotiated settlement to the standoff, but he assured his law-and-order constituency that federal authorities would treat AIM properly.

There was, however, the darker and more serious side to the confrontation. Gun battles erupted frequently between the Indian occupiers and surrounding soldiers, occasionally ending with casualties—primarily Indians. On March 7, the federal government ordered occupiers to surrender or face a full military assault. The National Guard backed up the threat, moving up six armored personnel carriers, each with a mounted .50 caliber gun. Responded Means, "We came here and bet our lives that there would be historic change for our nation," and said that either death or a meeting of Indian demands would create that new direction. Washington's treatment of American Indians "has not changed from Wounded Knee to My Lai and back to Wounded Knee," he added. Means was convinced that this moment would define the path of Indian-federal government relations. There was, indeed, a genuine spirit supportive of fighting to the last man among the occupiers. "If I die here at Wounded Knee," said Leonard Crow Dog, "I will go where Crazy Horse and Sitting Bull and our grandfathers are." Recalled Robert Burnette, "some sang war songs. Others walked around with prayers on their lips. . . . Some of the men were Vietnam veterans, and they must have felt a curious bitterness about digging in to face the fire of the same country they had risked death for in Asia." It would be a defining moment, as Indian activists across the United States promised armed retaliation against federal government military decision at Wounded Knee. Federal authorities called off its move against the town and ordered a withdrawal of the National Guard's advanced unit, but confusion of the moment and a breakdown in communications sparked a furious gun battle that left thousands of rounds spent and multiple casualties.

The standoff continued, each side blaming the other for starting that firefight and those that followed over the course of the next month. Representatives of AIM and the federal government issued public statements and occasionally met with one another in an effort to resolve the occupation. On April 6, federal authorities proposed a settlement. It called for Means's arrest, high-level discussion with White House representatives in Washington, a federal inquiry into Pine Ridge issues that led to the Wounded Knee takeover, a Justice Department investigation into Pine Ridge tribal council and Chairman Dick Wilson's violation of civil rights, and a review of the 1868 Fort Laramie Treaty. Means and most others within the AIM leadership accepted the proposal; Dennis Banks rejected it. The deal collapsed, however, over the issue of disarming the Indians. Means understood the proposal to say that Indians would disarm and relinquish their occupation of Wounded Knee only when discussions in Washington were well underway and appeared promising. Federal officials insisted that disarmament precede the talks. Said Means, "the government broke it [the arrangement] before the ink was dry."

With negotiations broken, sporadic fighting resumed until Buddy LaMonte was cut down by machine gun fire on April 27. His mother begged AIM and its supporters in the town to cease the standoff before others were killed, especially the many women and children who had moved into Wounded Knee with husbands, fathers, and brothers. Her request perhaps tipped the balance of opinion among the occupiers, but AIM leaders were already looking for a favorable way to end the occupation. They concluded that they had already accomplished much. The earlier peace proposal certainly addressed most of AIM's immediate concerns, and they believed federal officials would be eager to implement it rather than continue a siege that cost the government popular support each day. By late April, public opinion polls showed nearly 80 percent of college-educated Americans were sympathetic to Indian activism, and most expressed understanding if not support for the occupation of Wounded Knee. On May 7, the Indians began disarming themselves and preparing for the court hearings, trials, and government investigations that would continue for the remainder of the decade.

Ending the takeover did not end the violence at Pine Ridge Reservation. Over the next three years, there were at least two murders of Indians at Pine Ridge, and another two dozen Indians who opposed Dick Wilson and the moderates were listed as missing. Moreover, agents of the FBI were dispatched to the vicinity purportedly to investigate the murders, arrest suspects, and ensure the preservation of law on the reservation, but it was widely assumed among Indians and generally acknowledged among agents that the FBI directed its activities solely against AIM's presence in and near Pine Ridge.

The Longest Walk

In March 1978, AIM organized another major public demonstration in Washington, D.C. Eleven bills had been introduced in Congress over the previous few months. Most of these bills, which the Washington State congressional delegation initiated, collectively intended to restrict Native American fishing and hunting rights, close many Indian schools and hospitals, and limit significantly tribal sovereignty. It was widely believed among Indian and non-Indian political watchdogs that the bills stood little chance of passage, but AIM leaders perceived the bills' introduction as a possible harbinger of future trends in Congress. They agreed that the current Congress and Jimmy Carter White House should be reminded forcefully that Native American resistance remained alive and well and that American Indians would challenge any government effort to diminish Indian rights or reverse recent gains. Leaders concluded that another march on Washington would best serve their purpose.

Dubbed **The Longest Walk**, AIM began the march in San Francisco within clear view of Alcatraz Island, still a symbol of Native American resistance. For nearly five months, a core group of Indians moved on foot across the country, joined by Indian and non-Indian supporters who accompanied them for part of the trek. On July 15, a little more than 2,000 demonstrators arrived in the nation's capital.

Unlike the Trail of Broken Treaties six years earlier, the media gave scant attention to The Longest Walk. Most journalists considered it to be a "non-event"—no violent confrontation, no destruction of public property, no screams for revolution, and no backlash from the White House. AIM's advance team, Washington-area churches, and White House officials worked together to avoid a repeat of the disaster of November 1972. Churches volunteered to provide demonstrators with food and some lodging. The federal government supplied military kitchens, tents, water tanks, and bus transportation from a federal park across the river in Maryland. Taxpayers picked up the $250,000 cost. President Carter, a genuine and sincere advocate for human rights, was determined that Native Americans would have the opportunity to express their dissent and to do so peacefully. Twelve days later, on July 27, Indian demonstrators left the city.

The bills that drew Indian protest failed in Congress, as expected, but there were other important results of the Longest Walk. First, AIM's march and peaceful demonstration and the cooperation given by the White House helped improve the organization's image in the public mind. In this sense, the Longest Walk was a public relations victory. It also signaled to policymakers, the general public, and native peoples alike that AIM remained committed to the defense of Indian rights and that Native Americans would continue to press for change. Finally, on August 11, just two weeks after the Indians' departure from Washington, Congress passed into law the American Indian Religious Freedom Act (AIRFA), which President Carter promptly signed. The measure asserted the federal government would "protect and preserve for American Indians their inherent right to believe, express, and exercise [their] traditional religions." President Carter acknowledged that the United States historically "denied Native American access to particular sites and interfered with religious practices and customs." The AIRFA would ensure that Indian sacred sites would be secured to them and that government would not violate traditional ceremonies.

New Directions?

Indian activism drew popular attention to the dark history of Indian-white relations in the United States and the horrific conditions under which many Native Americans continued to live. Alcatraz, fish-ins, demonstrations,

SEEING HISTORY

A Call for Support

AIM created and widely distributed the poster "Prevent a 2nd Massacre at Wounded Knee" in early 1973, during its occupation of Wounded Knee, South Dakota. By associating the current standoff in Wounded Knee with the cavalry's destruction of Big Foot's band nearby in December 1890, AIM suggested the latter confrontation to have equally pivotal results for native peoples unless significant support surfaced quickly among Native Americans and those understanding the current crisis in Indian affairs.

17.8 American Indian Movement poster

Source: Courtesy of Library of Congress Prints and Photographs Division, LC-DIG-ppmsca-08113.

Questions

1. How does the poster bridge past and present?
2. What broad messages are conveyed through the poster's banner and artwork?
3. To what extent is the narrative necessary in soliciting solidarity?
4. To whom is the poster directed?

and Wounded Knee II collectively convinced many that a new direction in Indian policy was long overdue. In the late 1960s and throughout the 1970s government leaders responded to Indian protests and popular opinion and in so doing began the long process of redefining the status of Indians in the United States.

Indian Self-Determination

In 1968, President Lyndon Johnson issued a White House statement titled "The Forgotten American." The brief announcement acknowledged the long history of paternalistic management of native peoples by the federal government, denounced the recent policy of termination as destructive of native peoples, and promised a new direction in government's relationship with Indians. Said Johnson, Washington must ensure Indians' "freedom of choice"—the individual right to remain on tribal lands or meld with mainstream society. Indians, he added, must be permitted "full participation in American life"—particularly the right to secure employment and education. Above all, Native Americans must be allowed "self help, self development, and self determination." The White House admitted the president's statement was in part a response to recent Indian activism, but it added that the basic ideals embedded within the statement were an extension of the president's Great Society program. It was an important announcement, but virtually nothing of substance materialized during the waning Johnson administration.

Richard M. Nixon, however, took a more aggressive posture. In July 1970, a little more than one year into his first presidential term, Nixon issued his statement on Indian affairs. Nixon said that historically Indians were "oppressed and brutalized, deprived of their ancestral lands, and denied the opportunity to control their own destiny." Termination as federal policy was now officially ended, with tribal communities now considered permanent "sovereign institutions" responsible for managing their own affairs. As was the case with Lyndon Johnson, Nixon felt compelled to make this broad statement of self-determination. Protests over fishing rights and treaty provisions continued into his administration, new court cases were fought over the rightful ownership of lands removed from Indian control, individual tribal groups pressed the Nixon White House on local service issues such as inadequate education and health care, the Alcatraz Occupation was well underway, and public opinion was already becoming fixed in favor of Native Americans. As Nixon faced the ongoing challenges of the civil rights movement and the war in Vietnam, he looked for opportunities both foreign and domestic to improve his public image with relatively little effort. Indian self-determination was one of those opportunities. Shortly after Nixon issued his statement, the White House drafted legislation to make good on his promises. What emerged from Congress was the Indian Self-Determination and Education Assistance Act.

On January 4, 1975, Congress passed into law the Indian Self-Determination and Education Assistance Act, formally halting the termination policy and inaugurating tribal self-determination as new federal Indian policy. According to the law, Congress acknowledged the "obligation of the United States to respond to the strong expression of the Indian people for self determination." Congress intended to continue the "federal government's unique and continuing relationship with and responsibility to the Indian people." Under the Indian Self-Determination and Education Assistance Act, individual tribes were empowered to determine their own needs and affect plans by which those tribal needs would be met without the interference of the federal government. Tribes could enter into federal grant-funded contracts with agencies to provide for or to expand their community human services such as health care and day centers, strengthen and improve their tribal government, and acquire additional land.

As many expected, the new law generated few positive gains. Federal agencies complicated the process of issuing federal grants and found it difficult to relinquish their supervision of tribal affairs. Amendments were attached to the act in the late 1980s and again in the mid-1990s that ultimately gave some teeth to the act.

TIMELINE 17.2 MAJOR LEGISLATION, COURT DECISIONS, AND EXECUTIVE DECISIONS IN THE 1970S

1970	The U.S. Senate votes to return 48,000 acres of land to Taos Pueblo Indians in New Mexico
1971	Alaska Native Claims Settlement Act provides a $962 million settlement to Alaskan native peoples for lands lost to the federal government in addition to title to 40 million acres of land
1972	Indian Education Act passes, allowing for the federal funding of bilingual and bicultural programs in public schools and the founding of the Office of Indian Education in the U.S. Department of Education
	President Richard Nixon returns ownership of Mount Adams in Washington State to the Yakima people
1975	Indian Self-Determination and Education Assistance Act provides community social and educational opportunities and recognizes the tribal right of self-governance
1978	Indian Child Welfare Act, passed into law by President Jimmy Carter, recognizes the legal rights of Indian extended families and the authority of tribal courts to determine guardianship issues
	American Indian Religious Freedom Act protects traditional Indian religious ceremonies, sites, rituals, and sacred objects
	Tribally Controlled Community College Assistance Act allows federal grants to establish tribally governed colleges, with curricula relevant to tribal preferences
	The U.S. Supreme Court rules that decisions regarding tribal enrollment are matters solely decided by the individual tribe
1980	The U.S. Supreme Court rules that the United States pay the Sioux Indians $105 million for lands lost to the federal government in 1877, but the Lakota reject the monetary settlement and continue demanding the return of the land itself

Nonetheless, the measure officially redirected federal Indian policy once again, this time in a direction that native peoples overwhelmingly preferred.

Urbanization Patterns

Between 1960 and 1980, the American Indian population jumped by 818,000, reaching an approximate total of 1,500,000. Three-quarters of that increase, roughly 603,000, occurred in the 1970s. Natural increase certainly accounted for the greatest growth in the population, with approximately 477,000 children surviving to age three over those two decades. This growth reflected improved prenatal care for Indian women, both in urban communities and on reservations. The remainder of the growth came from individuals who, for the first time, officially identified themselves as Native American. The 1960s and 1970s saw heightened pride in American Indian identity and, as a result, many individuals who had earlier sought closer affiliation with mainstream society now asserted their native ancestry. Moreover, federal services to Native Americans increased appreciably in those two decades. Unfortunately, sudden access to government services and money proved attractive to people of minimal or dubious Indian descent, prompting them to make their legal claims to Indian identity solely for material gain.

As the Indian population rose, the number of urban Indians likewise increased. Historians James Olson and Raymond Wilson noted in their book *Native Americans in the Twentieth Century* that "the single greatest change in the structure of the Native American community in the 1960s and 1970s was the mass migration of young people to major urban centers." In 1940, only 13 percent of Native Americans lived in urban areas, but that figure skyrocketed to more than 50 percent 40 years later, by which time roughly 827,000 resided in towns and cities and 707,000 lived in rural areas or on reservations.

Urban Indian centers were first established in the 1950s in those cities that were part of Dillon Myer's relocation program, and by 1970 an Indian Center was present in most major cities nationwide. Centers offered Native Americans a variety of services including legal aid, employment assistance, avenues to secure reasonably priced health care, job skills training programs, and liaisons to federal programs. By the mid-1970s, the federal government annually appropriated funds to Indian Centers under the Native American Program Act.

Native American income averages rose throughout the 1960s and 1970s, especially for urbanized Indians. Indian income, however, still trailed that of any other race in the United States. In 1980, the median Indian household income stood at $12,227 in contrast to $17,710 (or $37,600 and $54,225 respectively in 2018 US dollar value) for the general population. Income levels for Indians employed during their prime employment years, ages 25–54, averaged only $15,905 annually (see Table 17.2). This income level, however, was significantly higher than that of 1970. In 1970, the median for urban males was $4,700 in contrast to $2,800 for reservation males, or $1,000 annually on a per capita basis for all workers on reservations. At the same time, white American men had a median income of $9,000, and African American men had a median income of $5,500.

The median income for urban Indians in both 1970 and 1980 was higher than that of reservation or rural Indians because those who migrated to or were reared in cities were generally better educated. On average, urban Indian men completed 11.2 years of school, whereas rural Indian men only completed 8.7 years. Education opened doors to better-paying employment; in 1980, 48 percent of urban Indian males held jobs as professionals, craftsmen, and managers. Unemployment rates also were significantly different for urban and rural Indians, averaging 11 percent for urbanized Indians in 1975 in contrast to 40 percent for rural residents. Again, Native American unemployment remained much higher than unemployment in the white population. In spite of these gains, fully 23 percent of all Native Americans in 1980 lived in poverty.

Table 17.2 Native American Income, 1980, by Number of Households

Income Range	Number of Households	Percent
Less than $5,000 annually	88,977	21
$5,000–15,000	162,812	38
$15,000–25,000	102,138	24
$25,000–50,000	67,508	16
$50,000 or more	8,125	1

Source: United States Bureau of the Census, 1980.

Educational Directions

In spite of noteworthy gains Indian activists made, American Indians still faced numerous serious problems—high rates of alcoholism, inadequate health care that allowed for the nation's highest rates of infectious disease, and unemployment rates that still exceeded those of other minority groups in America. Still a serious matter, too, was the fact that Indians remained the least educated citizens in America.

In 1967, the U.S. Senate empaneled a committee to investigate the current status of Native Americans, with Senator Edward (Ted) Kennedy serving as committee chair. The committee issued its findings in a 1969 report titled *Indian Education: A National Tragedy, A National Challenge*, better known as **The Kennedy Report**. The document effectively summarized the history of Indian-white relations. America's long policy of "assimilation by education" was fundamentally an "Indian land policy," a conscious plan to secure Indian land for white profit while training Indians to assume minor roles in the national economy. Noted the committee, "the 'Indian problem' raises serious questions about this Nation's most basic concepts of political democracy . . . the most precious assumptions about what this country stands for—cultural pluralism, equity and justice, the integrity of the individual, freedom of conscience and action, and the pursuit of happiness." The document then highlighted the history of Indian relations with the United States and its people, consistently demonstrating America's "failure" of justice.

The Kennedy Report revealed the consequences of America's failed policies. In South Dakota, juvenile delinquency rates were nine times the national average, 20 percent of Indian homes had no adult male present, the

READING HISTORY

Edward M. Kennedy, "Foreword" From *Indian Education: A National Tragedy—A National Challenge*, October 30, 1969

The following document and the larger text from which it is excerpted drew national attention to an array of problems in Indian education, problems, according to the report, that had remained constant despite a myriad of programs over decades that intended to reform Indian education. Senator Edward Kennedy and the committee he chaired drew a direct line from the failed programs of Indian education to the deplorable living conditions and opportunities native peoples faced in the United States. The report resulted in a reformist impulse equal to that which emerged in the wake of the Meriam Report 40 years earlier.

The American vision of itself is of a nation of citizens determining their own destiny; of cultural difference flourishing in an atmosphere of mutual respect, of diverse people shaping their lives and the lives of their children. This subcommittee has undertaken an examination of a major failure in this policy: the education of Indian children. . . .

The responsibility for the education of Indian children is primarily in the hands of the Federal Government. Of the 160,000 Indian children in schools—public, private, mission, and Federal—one-third are in federally operated institutions. In addition, the Federal Government has a substantial responsibility for Indian children enrolled in public schools. Under the Johnson-O'Malley Act of 1934, the Secretary of the Interior was authorized to contract with States and other agencies to provide an effective education for Indian children. Last year, more than 68,000 Indian children were covered by this act. . . . To a substantial extent, then, the quality and effectiveness of Indian education is a test of this Government's understanding and commitment.

Has the Federal Government lived up to its responsibility? The extensive record of this subcommittee, seven volumes of hearings, five committee prints, and this report, constitute a major indictment of our failure.

Drop-out rates are twice the national average in both public and Federal schools.

Some school districts have dropout rates approaching 100 percent;

Achievement levels of Indian children are 2 to 3 years below those of white students; and

the Indian child falls progressively further behind the longer he stays in school;

Only 1 percent of Indian children in elementary school have Indian teachers or principals;

One-fourth of elementary and secondary school teachers—*by their own admission*—would prefer not to teach Indian children; and

Indian children, more than any other minority group, believe themselves to be "below average" in intelligence.

What are the consequences of our educational failure? What happens to an Indian child who is forced to abandon his own pride and future and confront a society in which he has been offered neither a place nor a hope? Our failure to provide an effective education for the American Indian has condemned him to a life of poverty and despair.

Fifty thousand Indian families live in unsanitary, dilapidated dwellings, many in huts, shanties, even abandoned automobiles;

The average Indian income is $1,500, 75 percent below the national average;

The unemployment rate among Indians is nearly 40 percent—more than 10 times the national average;

The average age of death of the American Indian is 44 years;

for all other Americans it is 65;

The infant mortality rate *is twice* the national average; and

thousands of Indians have migrated into cities only to find themselves untrained for jobs and unprepared for urban life. . . .

These cold statistics illuminate a national tragedy and a national disgrace. They demonstrate that the "first American" has become the "last American" in terms of an opportunity for employment, education, a decent income, and the change for a full and rewarding life . . . clearly, effective education lies at the heart of any lasting solution. . . . The findings and recommendations contained in this report are a call for excellence, a reversal of past failures, and a commitment to a national program and priority for the American Indian equal in importance to the Marshall plan following World War II. . . .

U.S. Senate Committee on Labor and Public Welfare, *Indian Education: A National Tragedy—A National Challenge* (Washington, D.C.: Government Printing Office, 1969), pp. ix–x.

Questions

1. The committee report cites the federal government as the responsible agent for the failures associated with Indian education. Why?
2. What would be probable reasons for the committee not assigning blame to the states and to individual school districts?
3. In what ways does this foreword suggest that the failures in Indian education are a national tragedy?
4. From your reading of earlier chapters, how does this description of Indian education compare or contrast with previous government reports and private assessments?
5. What might account for the continuity with or divergence from previous evaluations?

number of Indian children placed into foster homes was five times greater than for the general population, and there was "extreme and severe alcoholism" across the Indian population. Among Indians of the Pacific Northwest, adolescent suicide was "epidemic." In Oklahoma, 34 percent of prison inmates were Native American although Indians only comprised 5 percent of the total state population. Fully 90 percent of Oklahoma Cherokees in Adair County lived on welfare, and 40 percent were functionally illiterate. In McCurtain County, 99 percent of Choctaws lived below the poverty line. Schools, read the report, "blame their own failures on the Indian student."

According to the report, to turn the current state of Indian affairs around, the federal government had to develop a sound educational program for Native Americans; education "must become a high priority objective," and full use of national resources must be employed. The report further called for government to directly involve Indians in building a strong educational system, including Indian parents directly in the educational development of their children. The government should also develop effective vocational and technical training programs; provide greater access to college work-study; provide bilingual instruction; create and implement special educational programs to prevent alcoholism; investigate and, where necessary, prosecute discrimination against Indians in schools receiving federal funds; create and implement adult education programs in native communities; train and recruit Native American teachers; establish a network of Indian-based community colleges; and develop curriculum that includes the study of native cultures, history, and contemporary life at all levels of instruction. The committee noted that implementation of its recommendations would prove costly, but it insisted the federal government must and could cover the expense.

The Kennedy Report mirrored the 1928 Meriam Report, condemning the historic failures of federal government and calling for a fundamental redirection in government responsibility. It also called for programs and plans first initiated under the leadership of Commissioner of Indian Affairs John Collier in the 1930s. The Kennedy Report's near duplication of Meriam and Collier's recommendations was evidence by itself that the government had failed miserably in its fundamental responsibility to Native Americans—again.

The report set in motion the passage of the **Indian Education Act** in 1972, legislation that channeled federal dollars into colleges and universities to train Indian students as teachers and social workers, provided for the creation of adult education programs in Indian communities, and led to the founding of the National Board of Indian Education. Although a few Indian community colleges existed before the Kennedy Report, many more were founded after the report was issued (see Table 17.3).

Table 17.3 Tribal Colleges, Founded 1968–1979

Dine College	Arizona	1968
United Tribes Technical College	North Dakota	1969
Oglala Lakota College	South Dakota	1971
Turtle Mountain Community College	North Dakota	1972
Fort Berthold Community College	North Dakota	1973
Sitting Bull College	North Dakota	1973
Nebraska Indian Community College	Nebraska	1973
Blackfeet Community College	Montana	1974
Cankdeska Cikama Community College	North Dakota	1974
Keweenaw Bay Ojibwa Community College	Michigan	1975
Fort Peck Community College	Montana	1978
Sisseton Wahpetan College	South Dakota	1979
Northwest Indian College	Washington	1979

Mainstream Awareness

The activities of NCAI, NYIC, and AIM along with the news coverage given to Indian activism collectively raised the consciousness of non-Indians for native history, cultures, anthropology, and contemporary issues. As a result, colleges and universities increasingly offered courses dealing with Native American issues. Scholarly publications rose in number and quality to meet the interest of students and academics alike, including works that are still widely read today. William T. Hagan's *American Indians* (1961); Stan Steiner's *The New Indians* (1967); Hazel Herzbert's *The Search for an American Indian Identity: Modern Pan-Indian Movements* (1971); Francis Jennings's *The Invasion of America: Indians, Colonialism, and the Cant of Conquest* (1975); Margaret Szasz's *Education and the American Indian* (1974); and Robert Berkhofer Jr.'s *The White Man's Indian: Images of the Indian from Columbus to the Present* (1978): each transformed the scholarly literature of the 1960s and 1970s and contributed directly to serious, detailed, and critical study of Indian history and cultures.

Two books were perhaps most responsible for elevating the intensity of interest in and sympathy for Native Americans among non-Indians. Vine Deloria Jr.'s *Custer Died for Your Sins: An Indian Manifesto* (1970) sharply condemned the long history of abuse native peoples suffered under America's political, religious, and economic systems, tracing the Indians' historic response to white territorial and cultural expansion. It also offered suggestions for the direction of Indian response in the decade to come. Deloria called on non-Indians to look past their long-held stereotyped view of American Indians, but in so doing he encouraged Native Americans to reevaluate themselves and recapture traditional values lost through the acculturative process of previous decades.

The second book, Dee Brown's *Bury My Heart at Wounded Knee: An Indian History of the American West* (1970), focused principally on the period just before the American Civil War to the immediate aftermath of the Wounded Knee Massacre in 1890. Brown presented a scathing, bitter indictment of politicians, the military, and members of the public who worked for the destruction of vibrant, culturally rich peoples and left Indians as subjects of the United States. Its tone and message to the non-Indian world and its sympathy for Native Americans appealed immediately to the younger generation of Americans in 1970. Although Brown occasionally, and perhaps inadvertently, cast Indians as victims, he successfully melded into his narrative a clear Indian voice and, in so doing, gave readers greater insight into the historical record and native perspectives. *Bury My Heart* became an instant bestseller in 1970, and it remains an important work having sold more than five million copies.

As important as these books were, Hollywood films reached a much larger audience. Three films released in 1970 set the studios' tone for the decade in representing Native Americans. *Soldier Blue* commanded short-term popularity in the theaters and renewed interest three years later during the media frenzy that followed AIM's occupation of Wounded Knee. In the film, Candice Bergen plays Cresta Lee, the young, beautiful fiancée of an army officer. Cresta had been taken captive by a Cheyenne warrior two years earlier but was recently "liberated" from the Indians during a military raid. As the film opens, she was being returned to her fiancé. A Cheyenne war party attacks the soldiers, killing all but one, who escaped. Cresta eludes the Indians. The film shows the smirks of soldiers who contemplated Cresta's "virtue" as a result of her captivity, contrasting their vile expressions with Cresta's admission of love for her Indian husband and the Cheyennes. Determined to exact vengeance on the Cheyenne for killing a platoon of his soldiers, Colonel Iverson orders his troops to "raze the village! Burn this pestilence!" The resulting slaughter is a gory representation of the Sand Creek Massacre of 1864, highlighting the barbarity and savagery of white soldiers against Indian men, women, and children. *Soldier Blue* exposes the virulent violence, racism, and cultural arrogance white America directed against Native Americans and conversely the Cheyenne's humanity. In 1970, the film marked a clear departure from earlier films in the genre. Although some movies of the 1950s and 1960s presented Indians in a relatively respectable manner, the intensity of violence and white racism directed toward them was significantly understated. *Soldier Blue* broke that trend.

That same year, Richard Harris starred in the movie *A Man Called Horse*, which was based on Dorothy Johnson's 1940 short story of the same title about an English aristocrat captured by Sioux while hunting. Abused and treated as a horse by his captives, the captive, who assumed the name "Horse," ultimately gains the Indians' respect after killing several Shoshone warriors scouting the Sioux encampment. Native Americans justifiably criticized the film at the time of its release, largely in response to Horse taking command of Sioux warriors, instructing them in European tactics of warfare, and leading them to victory in battle against the attacking Shoshone in the climatic scenes. Once more, Indians were shown as dependent on the skills of whites, which devalued the warrior ability of the Sioux and in so doing detracted from the somewhat favorable treatment given the Indians earlier in the story. But, for its time, *A Man Called Horse* made a genuine, albeit misguided at times, effort to present an accurate and detailed representation of Sioux culture. Horse witnesses Sioux mourning rites, initially finding them primitive and repulsive, but he comes to understand them and ultimately adopts them as his own. He learns the intimate details of male-female relationships, community structures and cooperative work, spiritual values, and tribal governance. Horse studies and learns the Indians' sense of duty, responsibility, courage, and sacrifice. Sioux culture becomes his own, to the point that Horse submits himself to the Sun Dance. Horse's evolution is a reversal of the government's program of acculturation and assimilation, a rejection of Euro-American values and structures for what he deems not only a simpler but also a more human and more rewarding life.

Contrasting native and non-Indian cultures, too, was *Little Big Man*, starring Dustin Hoffman in the title role. Jack Crab (Hoffman) moves between the white world of the post-Civil War years and the Cheyenne world; in so doing, the film contrasts the two cultures, finding white society and its religious, political, and military leaders significantly inferior to the Cheyenne. Crab, who is given the name Little Big Man by his adopted Indian family, nonetheless finds it difficult to abandon completely his birth identity. He witnesses Custer's attack on the Cheyenne camp at the Washita Valley and is present with Custer at Little Big Horn, in each case finding Custer and his troops thoroughly reprehensible. Like *A Man Called Horse*, *Little Big Man* at times oversimplified issues and cultural variations while at other times greatly exaggerated them, and showed little objectivity in representing Indian and non-Indian cultures. Nonetheless, these three films collectively captured the imagination of a viewing public generally unfamiliar with native cultures and history beyond the misrepresentations of earlier Hollywood films and public school textbooks. In capturing mainstream America's attention, they increased popular interest in and concern for current Indian affairs.

Hollywood films, popular literature and academic publications, the Kennedy Report, and news media coverage of Indian activism in the 1960s and 1970s collectively shaped a rising perspective among non-Indians of nothing less than a program of American genocide against Native Americans, a program long understood by native peoples themselves. Treaties, removal, the reservation system, Americanization programs, and incessant warfare were all aimed at the utter destruction of Indian lives, community structures and values, native cultures, and identity—the Euro-American colonization of a continent and eradication of peoples and cultures who resisted. By the early 1990s, the argument of genocide had gained widespread support in academia, but it also generated substantial controversy. David Stannard's *American Holocaust: The Conquest of the New World* (1993) emerged as the principal narrative on the subject as it tracked 400 years of violence against native people in the Americas, violence resulting in a 95 percent depopulation of Native Americans over that time frame. At the core of Stannard's argument was his conviction that American genocide rested fundamentally on values rooted in the Christian religion itself. Indian activism in the 1960s and 1970s that generated popular interest in Indian affairs, history, and cultures created a receptive audience for *American Holocaust* but they also set into motion a determination among native peoples to assert themselves politically, to secure themselves, and to shape their identity in contemporary America.

Conclusion

The 1960s and 1970s witnessed a rapid evolution in American Indian activism. The era opened with the National Congress of American Indians (NCAI) as the principal pan-Indian agency through which native peoples pressed their issues nationally. In the early 1960s, the National Indian Youth Council (NIYC) formed and championed direct action in place of written treaties and political lobbying in Washington, D.C. Among its earliest efforts were the fish-ins held in the Pacific Northwest. Such localized demonstrations resulted in some positive gains; however, what became known as the "Indian Movement" assumed a more radical dimension with the founding of the American Indian Movement (AIM) in 1968, an organization that took Indian protest to a national level and proved willing to exert armed force against armed force directed against Indians. The pattern of evolution resembled that of the civil rights movement by African Americans and the anti-war movement aimed at the Vietnam War, but Indian radicalization centered on Indian issues rather than the broader rights of American citizens. The Indian Movement focused its energy on the reaffirmation and maintenance of earlier treaties made with the federal government, the reclamation of tribal lands, and the commitment among Indians to revitalize their own traditional tribal structures and cultural values. The Indian Movement promoted individual and tribal self-determination—the right of Indians to chart their own directions and the determination to have government protect that most basic right. To be sure, Indian activism in the 1960s and 1970s alienated some Native Americans who either retained preference for strictly local resolutions or continued to believe working within the existing national political system would garner greater results. Nonetheless, a greater level of pan-Indian activism was evident in those two decades than was evident at any time in the past.

Much was accomplished. Indian enrollment at colleges and university rose significantly, many institutions of higher learning began offering programs of study in Indian history and anthropology, and more Indian children moved into school settings. In addition to educational advances, Indian centers were founded in most major urban communities to support and aid the needs of Native American residents, self-determination became federal Indian policy, and income levels rose. At the same time, the general American population grew much more aware of native issues and history, offering their voices in support of Indian activism and government redress. Although much changed for Indians during the 1960s and 1970s, much work remained. Poverty continued to shadow native communities, as did low literacy rates and poor health. Further complicating matters, Ronald Reagan's election to the presidency in 1980 caused much concern among Native Americans, who feared the conservative president would attempt to reverse the gains of the previous decades.

Review Questions

1. In what ways did the Indian issues of the 1960s and 1970s reflect continuity with native issues of the past?
2. What evidence is there that the 1960s and 1970s might be considered a watershed era in Native American history?
3. How was Indian activism of the 1960s and 1970s similar to the civil rights and anti-war movements? How was Indian activism different from those movements?
4. Why did general, mainstream American society confront Native American issues? How was this helpful or harmful to the Indian Movement?
5. How was the primary goal of Indian self-determination evident in the efforts and arguments of Indian activists during the 1960s and 1970s?

Recommended Readings

Banks, Dennis, and Richard Erdoes. *Ojibwa Warrior: Dennis Banks and the Rise of the American Indian Movement* (Norman: University of Oklahoma Press, 2005). The autobiography of Dennis Banks, cofounder of the American Indian Movement and icon of post-World War II native activism.

Bellecourt, Clyde, and Jon Lurie. *The Thunder Before the Storm: The Autobiography of Clyde Bellecourt* (St. Paul, Minnesota: Minnesota Historical Society, 2016). Bellecourt's own story of his childhood on the White Earth Reservation, his turbulent life as a young adult, his centrality in the founding of the American Indian Movement and its internal battles and its confrontation with the American system, and his continued fight for justice.

Brown, Dee. *Bury My Heart at Wounded Knee: An Indian History of the American West* (New York: H. Holt, 2007; first published in 1970). This work, often considered controversial, counters the traditional representation of Native Americans and national expansion by challenging long-held assumptions and popular myth and by detailing the Indian perspective.

Cobb, Daniel, and Loretta Fowler, eds. *Beyond Red Power: American Indian Politics and Activism Since 1900* (Santa Fe: School for Advanced Research, 2007). A collection of essays that offer insight into how Native Americans have employed political and non-political tactics other than AIM-style militancy to influence policymaking, tribal sovereignty, and the preservation of Indian identity.

Deloria, Vine, Jr. *Custer Died for Your Sins: An Indian Manifesto* (New York: Macmillan, 1969). A critical examination of American race relations, religion, social norms and behaviors, and the role of government as they relate to native issues.

Krause, Susan Applegate, and Heather A. Howard, eds. *Keeping the Campfires Going: Native Women's Activism in Urban Communities* (Lincoln, NE: University of Nebraska Press, 2009). A collection of essays that trace and evaluate the work of urbanized indigenous women in the United States and Canada since World War II.

Matthiessen, Peter. *In the Spirit of Crazy Horse: The Story of Leonard Peltier and the FBI's War on the American Indian Movement* (New York: Penguin Books, 1992). A superb survey of living conditions and political activism on the Pine Ridge Reservation in the 1970s and the effort of federal offices to crush native dissent.

Smith, Paul Chaat, and Robert Allen Warrior. *Like a Hurricane: The Indian Movement From Alcatraz to Wounded Knee* (New York: New Press, 1996). A thorough, detailed treatment of the founding of the American Indian Movement and its work to advance justice for native peoples.

Stannard, David E. *American Holocaust: The Conquest of the New World* (New York: Oxford University Press, 1993).

Native American History Online

General Sites

Wounded Knee. youtube.com/watch?v=Opbxnuw0Dw0 This website features an online broadcast titled "Wounded Knee," which is a PBS documentary of the Indian occupation of Wounded Knee, South Dakota, in 1973. Tabs are included that take the viewer to additional episodes in the PBS series.

Federal Bureau of Investigation. http://foia.fbi.gov/room.htm In the search bar, type "Wounded Knee" to view and read the texts of FBI investigations and reports related to the Indian occupation of Wounded Knee, South Dakota, in 1973, violence on the Pine Ridge Reservation throughout the 1970s, and government documents related to the American Indian Movement nationwide.

Kennedy Report. www.eric.edu.gov/?id=ED034625 At this website, the viewer will find the full online text of the 1969 report *Indian Education: A National Tragedy—A National Challenge*, commonly referred to as the Kennedy Report.

National Indian Youth Council. www.niyc-alb.com Links provide viewers with a history of the NIYC as well as current activities.

Historic Sites

Alcatraz Island, San Francisco, California. https://www.nps.gov/alca/index.htm This National Park Service website provides viewers with an overview of the Indians' use of and protest occupancy of the island.

National Native American Vietnam Veterans Memorial. https://www.thehighground.us Dedicated in 1995, the National Native American Vietnam Veterans Memorial is the first national memorial to honor the participation of American Indians in the war in Vietnam. The monument lists the names of all Native American servicemen who died in Southeast Asia.

CHAPTER
18

UTAH
STANDS WITH
BEARS EARS

PROTECT
BEARS EARS

WWW.STANDWITHBEARSEARS.ORG

YOUR
ANDS

Self-Determination to Decolonization: Native Americans into the Twenty-First Century

RONALD REAGAN, DECOLONIZATION
PRESIDENTIAL INDIAN POLICY: 1980s–1990s
The Reagan Years
George Herbert Walker Bush: Any Better?
NATIVE PEOPLES AND ACTIVISM: THE 1980s AND 1990s
Reservations and Resources
Casinos and Tourism
NAGPRA and What Is an Indian?
Native American Women Take Charge
EMPOWERMENT AND DECOLONIZATION AND INTO THE TWENTY-FIRST CENTURY
Literature and Art
Indigenous Peoples in the Academy
SHIFTING DIRECTIONS: THE OBAMA AND TRUMP PRESIDENCIES
The Obama Years, 2009–2017
The Ascendency of Donald Trump
The Keystone Pipeline
Pocahontas
The Republican Agenda for Native Lands
The Trump Agenda's Impact on Indian Country

Protesters against President Trump's speech to dismantle Utah's Bears Ears National Monument, at the state capitol in Salt Lake City, Utah.
Source: Johnny Adolphson/Shutterstock

Ronald Reagan, Decolonization

A participant in the 1988 summit meeting in Moscow asked Republican President Ronald Reagan about the U.S. government's relationship with Native Americans. The president's unfamiliarity with the present state of native peoples at that time was painfully obvious. His response to the question sent shock waves throughout Indian country:

Let me tell you just a little something about the American Indian in our land. We have millions of acres of land for what are called preservations—or reservations, I should say. And they're free to leave the reservations and be American citizens among the rest of us, and many do. Some still prefer, however, that way—that early way of life. And we've done everything we can to meet their demands as to how they wanted to live. Maybe we made a mistake. Maybe we should not have humored them in that wanting to stay in that kind of primitive state. Maybe we should have said no, come join us.

Elected to the White House for two terms after serving as California's governor, Reagan never established a consistent and practical Indian policy. A former Hollywood actor, Reagan's "Indians" seemed like characters he plucked from 1950s or 1960s Western films or cowboy dime novels. In the 1988 Moscow summit, Reagan failed to mention the many educated Native American community leaders still pressing the political fight for self-preservation and self-determination. He and his cabinet members made little effort to understand or help Native Americans on their terms. During Reagan's two terms, native leaders felt betrayed by the federal government.

Nearly two decades later, a group of indigenous educators and activists published *For Indigenous Eyes Only: A Decolonization Handbook* in 2005. The end product of a conference organized by leading indigenous studies scholars Waziyatawin Angela Cavendar Wilson (Wahpetunwan Dakota) and Devon Mihesuah (Choctaw), *For Indigenous Eyes Only* is a seminal text in the field of American Indian Studies. Although each made individual contributions to the book collections, the authors collectively argued that colonization acted like a disease, robbing native peoples of their lands, cultures, and identities. If colonization was the disease, the authors further argued that decolonization was the antidote. **Decolonization** involved individuals and native communities making a conscious effort to move toward self-empowerment, a position actively pursued since the founding of the NIYC. By 2005, indigenous studies programs had blossomed throughout academia. Guided by their own people within the academy, Native Americans who followed the path of decolonization no longer needed the federal government to facilitate change. Instead they could rely on themselves to disarm the remaining forces of colonization. According to *For Indigenous Eyes Only*, "Decolonization is the intelligent, calculated, and active resistance to the forces of colonialism that perpetuate the subjugation and/or exploitation of our minds, bodies, and lands, and it is engaged for the ultimate purpose of overturning the colonial structure and realizing Indigenous liberation."

KEY QUESTIONS

1. What were the differences between Ronald Reagan's policies and those of George W. Bush?
2. How have the so-called "energy tribes" tried to take greater control over natural resources?
3. What have casinos and tourism done for Native Americans?
4. In what ways have Native American women become politically active?
5. Describe and analyze the "Native American literary tradition" and the "Indian aesthetic."
6. Why is decolonization an important shift in Native American activism?

Between the era of Ronald Reagan and the emergence of decolonization, Native Americans faced many of the same challenges of previous decades. Federally appointed officials tried to control Native American self-determination and sovereignty, while native peoples fought through the avenues of activism and litigation to empower themselves. But in a number of areas in the 1980s and 1990s, native peoples gained some control over their own destinies, from the rise of Indian gaming to the fight for the repatriation of sacred objects and

CHRONOLOGY

1982	Massive increase in Native American unemployment due to Ronald Reagan's economic programs
1983	Federal recognition of the Pequots
	Ronald Reagan's first presidential statement on Indian policy
	Wilma Mankiller chosen to run as deputy chief of the Cherokee Nation
	Ojibwa spearfishing rights recognized
1986	Star Lake Incident with Ojibwa spearfishers
	Pequots start high-stakes bingo
1987	Landmark decision in *California* v. *Cabazon Band of Mission Indians*
1987– 1995	Wilma Mankiller serves as first female president of an Indian tribe in the Cherokee Nation
1988	IGRA (Indian Gaming Regulatory Act) put into federal law
	Revised version of Alaska Native Claims Commission Act passes Congress
	Tribal Controlled School Act passes Congress
1989	Winona LaDuke wins Reebok Human Rights Award
1990	NAGPRA passes during George W. Bush's administration
1992	Columbus Quincentenary
	Pequots open Foxwoods Casino
1993	Ten of New Mexico's tribes have gaming
1996	Winona LaDuke's first run as vice-presidential candidate on the Green Party ticket with Ralph Nader
	Kennewick Man discovered
1997	Tribal revenues grow 30-fold because of tribal gaming
1999	Landmark launch of Makah whaling voyage
2000	Winona LaDuke makes second bid as vice-presidential candidate on Green Party ticket with Ralph Nader
2002	Forty-five California Indian groups have gaming
2003	Harrah's Casino opens among the eastern band of the Cherokee Nation
2004	Ninth District Court of Appeals rules that Kennewick Man has no cultural affiliation to any tribes in the state of Washington
2005	Seminal publication of *For Indigenous Eyes Only: A Decolonization Handbook*

their ancestors' remains. As American Indians entered the twenty-first century, they turned more inward, looking to reinvigorate their communities with tailored programs of decolonization. The future for native North America, although uncertain, in many respects is not entirely bleak. Greater numbers of native peoples are in higher education, reservations have established better schools and medical programs, leaders have striven for native-centered definitions of self-determination, and there exists the potential that Native American leaders will rise to prominence at both the state and national levels.

Presidential Indian Policy: 1980s–1990s

The Reagan Years

"Less is more" was the motto for Reagan's two terms in office; that motto also determined the White House's treatment of Native Americans. Reagan's desire to "cut the growth of government spending," for example, meant cutting social programs that had benefited the lives of native peoples. Staff members, appointed by the president to oversee Indian affairs, assured native leaders that reducing the role of government in Indians' lives was in line with the federal policy of self-determination. After all, self-determination "was about getting government out of the way." James G. Watt, appointed secretary of the interior, and Kenneth L. Smith (Warm Spring Wasco) were the first staff members who shaped Indian policy during the Reagan years. Both Watt and Smith were dedicated to the core Reagan ideology of reining in government spending and the expansion of the economy in the private sector.

They fell out of favor with many Native Americans. As Smith explained to the National Tribal Chairman's Association (NTCA), "all of us here would like these budget cuts to come in other programs other than Indian programs—but if we are realistic and reasonable we have to expect to share in some of the cuts." Cuts to programs impacting Native Americans hit them as an ethnic minority greater than any other group of Americans. In 1982, for instance, the Kickapoo tribe's federal funds were cut by two-thirds. Navajo unemployment rates skyrocketed from 38 percent to 72 percent because many Native American jobs came from federal programs. The NTCA reacted by arguing that self-determination required federal funding, not cuts. "In order to be economically self-sufficient," argued Wendell Chino, chair of the NTCA, "we must continue to receive aid to educate and train our people, to plan and implement economic programs, and to help support our governments and provide basic services to our people." In short, the Reagan administration, as one historian has argued, "treated Indian programs as line items in a Federal budget." So much of the Republican rhetoric echoed that of Washington's call for termination in the 1950s.

Secretary of the Interior Watt only made matters worse on January 19, 1983. He compared the Indian situation to socialism. As Watt said, "I tell people if you want an example of the failures of socialism don't go to Russia—come to America and go to the Indian reservations." LaDonna Harris (Comanche), who spearheaded activism for the Pueblo peoples and the Menominee of Wisconsin against termination and relocation, reacted immediately in a letter to the president. "He has undoubtedly undermined the spirit and intent of your policy, but even more damaging than that is the perpetuation of racist, stereotypical attitudes from one man in the Federal government most intimately involved with American Indian people." Soon after Watt's scathing words and unexpected resignation, Reagan finally released his presidential statement on Indian affairs, reaffirming the government's commitment to less federal government and more Indian self-determination. To help forward this goal, Reagan's staff decided to create the

18.1 LaDonna Harris (1931–) is a Comanche social activist and founder and president of Americans for Indian Opportunity.

Source: MPI/Getty Images

Presidential Advisory Commission on Indian Reservation Economies. The commission consisted of six native leaders and three members appointed by the president. The most recognizable Indian name on the commission was Ross O. Swimmer, then presiding chief of the Cherokee Nation. The commission found many problems standing in the way of Native American economic development, everything from weak tribal management of economic resources to an "unfavorable business climate." The commission recommended that tribal governments "make private ownership or private management of tribal enterprises an objective of their involvement in business activity." In line with "Reaganomics," outside groups encouraged Indians to privatize land and then transfer unused lands to the private sector. Again, the position taken by this White House sounded all too familiar with those championed by earlier administrations. Reagan, however, vetoed several key bills Congress passed that would have actually given tribal governments more control over their resources. For example, he vetoed HR 5118, the Southern Arizona Water Rights Settlement Act. The bill established a way for Arizona tribal peoples to negotiate with other tribes, the state, and the federal government to create equitable sharing of water. Reagan vetoed the bill because he did not want federal monies involved in the settlement of water rights.

When it came to the federal acknowledgment of tribes during the Reagan era, Native Americans also faced obstacles. Reagan vetoed a bill that would have recognized the Mashantucket Pequot, arguing that the bill of tribal recognition was too costly. The bill was amended, putting more financial onus on the state of Connecticut. Reagan signed the revised bill, the Connecticut Indian Land Claims Settlement Act, on October 18, 1983.

READING HISTORY

Ronald Reagan, Indian Policy Statement, January 24, 1983

President Reagan's views of Native Americans.

Throughout our history, despite periods of conflict and shifting national policies in Indian affairs, the government-to-government relationship between the United States and Indian tribes has endured. . . .

Our policy is to reaffirm dealing with Indian tribes on a government-to-government basis and to pursue the policy of self-government for Indian tribes without threatening termination. . . .

This administration pledges to assist tribes in strengthening their governments by removing Federal impediments to tribal self-government and tribal resource development. This administration affirms the right of tribes to determine the best way to meet the needs of their members and to establish and run programs which best meet those needs. . . .

A lingering threat of termination has no place in this administration's policy of self-government for Indian tribes, and I ask Congress to again express its support of self-government.

Source: For Reagan's full policy statement, see "American Indian Policy, January 24, 1983" at www.cms.gov

Questions

1. What does Reagan's statement have to say about Indian-federal relations overall?
2. How did the policy reflect Reagan's "less is more" philosophy?
3. Why was Reagan focused on termination?

The Gay Head Wampanoags also had to revise their federal recognition bill to shift costs away from the federal government, and Reagan signed it on August 21, 1987.

Budget cutting marked the first term of Reagan's presidency and the vetoing of important bills, both of which signaled that Reagan wanted a less involved federal government in Indian affairs. Native peoples felt the impact of Reagan's approach to economics. As another example of "Reaganomics" at work in Indian country, the federal government transferred the control and costs of day schools to state governments.

Two major developments marked the second term of Reagan's presidency: the establishment of a federal law for Indian casinos and the revival of some congressional activity for Native American interest groups. The 1988 **Indian Gaming Regulatory Act** (IGRA) tried to balance control of Indian gaming between the tribes and states. The law established three classes of gaming, as well as a National Indian Gaming Commission. Class I gaming included traditional Indian gaming activities, overseen by the tribes directly. Class II gaming included games such as bingo that would fall under the regulation of the tribes and Gaming Commission. The third

PROFILE

Peter MacDonald: Navajo Leader Falls from Power in the Era of Reagan

Peter MacDonald was a Navajo engineer who had worked for years in urban California. He returned to the Navajo reservation and took a leadership position in the Navajo Office of Economic Opportunity. From that position, he swiftly rose to head of the Navajo tribe. "He served three four-year terms until 1983, throughout the era when tribal governments were transformed into modern full-fledged governments supported by extensive federal funds." MacDonald is cited for beginning the new era of tribal government for the Navajo people.

At the same time, however, MacDonald became an example of how too much tribal power in the hands of one leader in the Reagan era led to graft and corruption. He was in favor with the Reagan administration and was at one point considered for commissioner of Indian affairs. As one Reagan aide reported, "Peter MacDonald has been most cooperative and helpful. He supported Reagan in 1980 and organized support for the Watt nomination."

MacDonald's rise to power was rapid, and he increased the power of the office of tribal chair. MacDonald himself reflected on his own power: "As chairman of the Navajo Nation I had all the power that accompanies the ruler of a country. People sought political favors from me. People were anxious to do my bidding." When a Senate Special Committee on Investigations looked into MacDonald's dealings with other Navajos, they discovered that he had accepted bribes. MacDonald justified his acceptance of bribes as part of Navajo custom. As MacDonald said, "The Navajo consider gifts as expressions of love and respect." The Navajo purchase of Big Boquillas Ranch, 491,000 acres west of Flagstaff, Arizona, resulted in his eventual demise. Third-party investors made over $8 million as a result of MacDonald's political actions and connections, and the Navajo Nation acquired land "that would otherwise have been impossible to get." MacDonald was brought up on federal charges of racketeering, bribery, and political abuse. He was found guilty. MacDonald's fall exemplifies how Reagan-era investigative committees tried to make Indian self-determination and self-government a reality, but after MacDonald's fall the committee abandoned any efforts to reform other tribal governments. This reflected the Reagan presidency's overall ineffectiveness in Indian policy.

type, Las Vegas-style gaming, involved compact agreements between particular tribes and the states. And, with the revision of the Alaska Native Claims Settlement Act in 1988, Congress gave power directly to the tribes to control lands and resources. The Tribally Controlled School Act of 1988 gave more power to tribes to control their own schools.

George Herbert Walker Bush: Any Better?

When Reagan's vice president George H. W. Bush ran for president in 1988, he departed from Reagan's Indian policies. Bush promised better education and economic development for Native Americans and a continued push toward self-government and self-determination. He compared himself to Abraham Lincoln, "who fully recognized the importance of Indian sovereignty in a nation of sovereign states." However, Bush, too, was detached from the reality of Indian-federal relationships that seemed part of 1980s Republican politics. Lincoln advocated "civilizing" native peoples, not tribal sovereignty. In fact, during his one term as president, Bush's overseas diplomacy became the core of his presidency, particularly in Kuwait and Iraq. In light of this, Bush showed very little concern for domestic affairs. The president relegated most domestic affairs issues to cabinet members, such as his secretary of the interior, Manuel Lujan. At first, the Bush presidency seemed like the Reagan presidency all over again.

Manual Lujan selected Eddie F. Brown (Pascua Yaqui) as assistant secretary of Indian affairs, however Cliff Alderman and Mary McClure, both White House staff members, ultimately managed most Indian affairs issues with the help of an interagency task force. When prodded to submit a presidential statement on Indian affairs, Bush, under the advisement of his staff members, finally gave a statement on June 14, 1991 (see Reading History).

Although the statement and the president's way of handling Indian affairs did not mark a clear departure from the Reagan years, there were some significant advances in Indian public programs and education during Bush's presidency. Lauro F. Cavasos, Secretary of Education, created the Indian Nations at Risk Task Force to evaluate problems within the Indian education system. The result was that the Bush Administration sanctioned the Tribally Controlled Community College Assistance Act of 1978. Sections 1102–1105 of the bill were a step closer to Indian sovereignty in that the legislation publicly endorsed the use of native languages in the classroom. Concurrently, the BIA went through a process of reorganization to streamline the office, work with tribal leaders, and create better programs in Indian education. The greatest achievements during the Bush years, however, came instead from the Democrat-dominated Congress. With the support of Senator John McCain (R-Arizona), Senator Daniel Inouye (D-Hawaii) argued for the construction of an Indian museum to house the collections of George G. Heye. Bill S1722, issued in 1987, called for the construction of a new National Museum of the American Indian on the Mall with the Smithsonian museums. Inouye was proud that, as a result of the law, "there will be a great museum established on the National mall that will be home to the priceless artifacts of Indian culture, history, and art." Bush signed the bill into law, and construction of the museum began. Tribal peoples were consulted on every phase of the design of the museum. In 1990, Congress passed the Native American Graves Protection and Repatriation Act (NAGPRA) (discussed later). To help native peoples control tribal membership and protect their sovereignty, Congress also authorized the Indian Arts and Crafts Act (IACA). The bill established criminal penalties for non-Indian artists who claimed to make Indian art, which gave more power to the Indian Arts and Crafts Board to regulate the flourishing art trade among tribal communities. Indian artists, as one historian has argued, "became the only card-carrying ethnic group of the United States, forced to present their 'papers' to display their art publicly." Not all tribal groups agreed with IACA, but with an expanding tourist economy (discussed later) in various parts of Indian country, the act did protect the authenticity of tribal art production to prevent non-Indians from profiting on fakes.

READING HISTORY

George H. W. Bush's Statement on Indian Affairs, June 14, 1991

George Bush reaffirms the government-to-government relationship.

This government-to-government relationship is the result of sovereign and independent tribal governments being incorporated into the fabric of our nation, of Indian tribes becoming what our courts have come to refer to as quasi-sovereign domestic dependent nations. Over the years the relationship has flourished, grown, and evolved into a vibrant partnership in which over 500 tribal governments stand shoulder to shoulder with the other governmental units that form our Republic.

This is now a relationship in which tribal governments may choose to assume the administration of numerous Federal programs pursuant to the 1975 Indian Self-Determination and Education Assistance Act.

This is a partnership in which an Office of Self-Governance has been established in the Department of the Interior and given the responsibility of working with tribes to craft creative ways of transferring decision-making powers over tribal government functions from the Department to tribal governments.

An Office of American Indian Trust will be established in the Department of the Interior and given the responsibility of overseeing the trust responsibility of the Department and of insuring that no Departmental action will be taken that will adversely affect or destroy those physical assets that the Federal Government holds in trust for the tribes.

I take pride in acknowledging and reaffirming the existence and durability of our unique government-to-government relationship.

Within the White House I have designated a senior staff member, my Director of Intergovernmental Affairs, as my personal liaison with all Indian tribes. While it is not possible for a President or his small staff to deal directly with the multiplicity of issues and problems presented by each of the 510 tribal entities in the Nation now recognized by and dealing with the Department of the Interior, the White House will continue to interact with Indian tribes on an intergovernmental basis.

The concepts of forced termination and excessive dependency on the Federal Government must now be relegated, once and for all, to the history books. Today we move forward toward a permanent relationship of understanding and trust.

Source: "Statement Reaffirming the Government-to-Government Relationship Between the Federal Government and Indian Tribal Governments" at www.presidency.ucsb.edu

Questions

1. Does Bush's statement mark a clear departure from the Reagan administration's position?
2. What is the government-to-government relationship?
3. How does Bush view Native American self-determination?

Overall, presidential support for Native Americans as sovereign people with unique identities was greater during the Bush administration than during Reagan's two terms. For example, in 1991, President Bush declared a national Indian heritage month. However, in 1992, the celebration of Columbus's quincentenary enraged native peoples who thought the federal government was finally making significant advancements in favor of native identity. As Suzan Harjo (Cheyenne and Hodulgee Muscogee) said: "For Native people, this half-millennium of land grabs and one-cent treaty sales has been no bargain." Some Native Americans led demonstrations against the quincentenary festivities, which they felt made them relive the genocide and subsequent centuries of abuse they endured after Columbus's arrival in North America. Thus, although there were some advances during the Bush years, his term ended on a sour note.

Native Peoples and Activism: The 1980s and 1990s

Reservations and Resources

Some reservations sat on land rich in oil, gas, coal, or uranium. Tribes that lived on these lands were dubbed "energy tribes." Despite the presence of these resources, in the 1980s many of these tribes still lived in poverty. For energy tribes, tribal governments working with and against outside pressure groups have defined their sovereignty, but not always to the benefit of all group members. They have certainly worked to protect the profits from their resources from the state and private sector interests, but internal tribal divisions have led to on-reservation fights over who should have access to the money. For example, among the Sioux in South Dakota, concerns surrounding land and resources have led to a multitude of political problems. By the mid-1990s, to contain the reservation infighting that prevented the Sioux from full self-determination and reservation sovereignty, tribal councils started to work closely with grassroots movements.

Earl Bordeaux, a council member of the Rosebud Sioux reservation, commented on the state of affairs of the Sioux in South Dakota: "Look what the state of South Dakota is doing to her Indians. . . . They won't recognize our Treaty Rights. They won't recognize our jurisdiction." Located in western South Dakota, the tracts of Sioux land are enormous. Pine Ridge has 3.1 million acres; Rosebud, 3.2 million acres; Cheyenne River, 2.8 million acres; and Standing Rock, 2.7 million acres. Despite the large size of these tracts of land, their populations remain low, which encourages both local whites and the state to try to take unscrupulous advantage of the Sioux and benefit from their natural resources. It was in this context that Sioux on a number of reservations developed a new form of grassroots-based political mobilization to protect their own interests.

This was a major change for the Sioux, particularly those at Pine Ridge (Oglala Sioux) and Rosebud (Sicangu Oyate or Brulé). The Sioux were earlier known for tribal political divisions that separated most people into two camps, the "hostiles" and "friendlies," and whose inability to get along provoked violence on the reservations and contributed to the corruption of tribal politics. A shift toward grassroots politics did not mean all Sioux got along, but many Sioux in the 1990s now recognized the benefit of united grassroots efforts to address the abuses perpetuated by local whites and the state. This resulted in much less tribal fragmentation. The Oglala at Pine Ridge created a more responsive system of tribal government with local districts and with leaders who petitioned against decisions of the tribal council and effectively managed the decision making of the council. In fact, tribal councils had to respond to the voice of the people, as the representatives themselves were elected from the districts.

For many Sioux, sovereignty remained the most important issue—how to attain it and how to protect it. Insisting that the "Black Hills are not for sale," Sioux leaders resisted efforts to establish dumps and oil pipelines on their land. For the Sioux, the Black Hills territory has always been sacred ground, land that could never be sold or leased. Local whites and the state repeatedly challenged the Sioux rights to their lands as the century closed. Many outsiders pushed onto Sioux lands without permission, while the state, in violation of treaty rights, snatched up large tracts of Rosebud, Cheyenne River, and Standing Rock land for the construction of dams, roads, and other projects under the right of "eminent domain" (the right of the state to use up acreage for public works) and all but destroyed the reservation economies. The Sioux, through grassroots petitions and gatherings, have pressured the state to compensate them for their lost land.

Local grassroots organizations also challenged the state on issues of criminal justice, education, and health care reform. South Dakota's penal system seemed to purposefully target the Sioux. In the 1980s, roughly 60 percent of young men in the prisons of South Dakota were of Sioux descent. Alcohol distribution is another issue tribal councils and grassroots leaders addressed. Tribal leaders tried to ban the off-reservation sale of alcohol to protect reservation sovereignty. Councils and local leaders encouraged the construction of schools and the establishment of tribal-run colleges, and they established their own game and departments of fishing and housing. These organizations manage relations with the state and Bureau of Indian Affairs on issues of health care, resource rights, and poverty. The determination of Sioux grassroots activists was reflected in the fact that local petitions for change often develop into lawsuits filed in federal courts.

Western energy tribes such as the Apache, Hopi, Navajo, Pueblo, and Arapahoe, as well as native peoples in California and Washington, worked to secure their mineral-rich lands as sources of economic revitalization and as a way to loosen their bonds of dependence on the federal government. Prior to the mid-1970s, the government or private sectors carried out most of the mineral extraction on native lands; they produced little in return for native peoples. Indian leaders, however, began to force a shift in this dynamic, pressuring the Department of the Interior to better regulate private sector efforts to benefit from mineral resources on Indian lands. Tribal leaders also gained substantial ground in the U.S. Supreme Court, where it was decided that native peoples could tax various energy producers; by the 1980s, native peoples actually negotiated contracts that gave work to reservation populations and generated revenue for entire tribes. Energy-generated income has helped the Apache, Hopi, and Pueblo grow and develop their local economies (see Map 18.1).

By the late 1970s and early 1980s, a pan-tribal organization of energy tribes began to assume an active role in Washington D.C. LaDonna Harris (Comanche), wife to Congressman Fred R. Harris, took an active role in leading the **Council of Energy Resource Tribes (CERT)**. The CERT put together accurate statistics about acres of mineral lands per reservation and developed leasing programs that would fall under the control of tribes

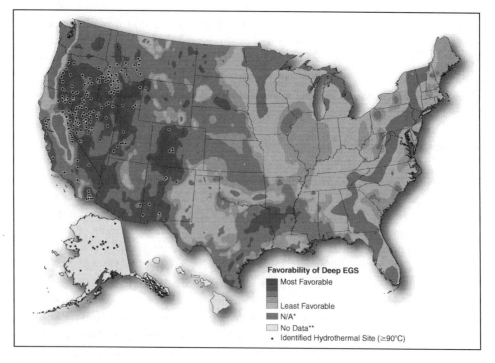

Map 18.1 Mineral-rich tribal lands

rather than private companies. CERT forced the federal government to allow reservation Indians in the West to create more profitable contracts with private sector energy companies. By the mid-1980s, CERT tribes earned a total of $400 million from energy-related contracts. Individual owners of allotted acreage among the western energy tribes also profited. In the 1980s, families and clans with individual allotments joined with tribal governments, lawyers, geologists, and other scientists to profit from their own private parcels of energy-rich land.

The cultivation of energy resources created problems such as controlling pollution and managing water. Several landmark cases enabled native peoples to take a more active role in stopping the dumping of waste on reservation lands. In 1984, both the Jicarilla Apache tribe and Navajo tribe threatened lawsuits against the San Juan Basin coal lease. Such coal excavations polluted reservation water sources, and the federal government had no body to regulate the pollution of reservation waters. Eventually, the state of New Mexico put a stop to the San Juan Basin coal lease. The Northern Cheyenne tribe, in an important case, used the Clean Air Act to prevent pollutants from entering the environment surrounding the Cheyenne reservation. The Yakima Nation set a precedent in using CERT to establish a viable database to demonstrate how destructive nuclear waste dumps were to reservation lands. Under the Nuclear Waste Policy Act of 1982, tribes extended their control over nuclear dumping. By the 1990s, native peoples had taken a substantial role in energy control and development.

Energy tribes were not the only native peoples fighting to control local environmental resources. In Wisconsin, a conflict over walleye fish and the lakes from which fishermen caught them broke out into a regional battle between natives and non-natives. The key players were the Lac du Flambeau band of Lake Superior Chippewa (Ojibwa) Indians, other Chippewa communities, proprietors of a local vibrant tourist economy that attracted seasonal fishers, and state- and federal-run organizations (see Map 18.2). In 1983, after nine years

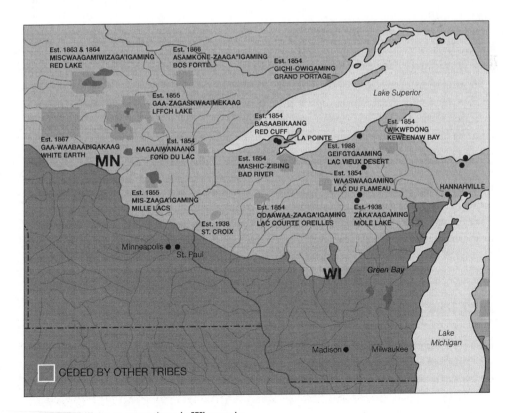

Map 18.2 Ojibwa reservations in Wisconsin

of court battles, the U.S. Court of Appeals validated the Chippewa bands' rights to fish and hunt off of their reservations in surrounding lakes and woodlands. The court decision upheld the right of the Ojibwa hunters to catch the walleye fish using traditional methods of spearing. Before the decision, Ojibwa had not spearfished for over a century. The owners of local resorts objected, arguing the Ojibwa spearfishing would deplete the stocks of fish in the surrounding lakes. Local whites published newspaper complaints once the spearfishers began their activities in the winter of 1983. Spearfishing resulted in a cultural and spiritual revitalization among the Ojibwa, particularly at Lac du Flambeau, but it provoked racial animosity among local whites and attracted the attention of state and federal officials.

Eventually, the Great Lakes Indian Fish & Wildlife Commission formed as a federally funded agency that offered assistance to the 13 Ojibwa bands in Wisconsin. Mike Chosa and Gilbert Chapman, both men with experience off the reservation in urban politics, used the Lac de Flambeau tribal council as a powerful force to negotiate with the state for fishing rights. They also helped form the Wa-Swa-Gon Treaty Association (WTA) that stood in direct opposition to any tribal negotiations from tribal councils for state monies in exchange for renouncing Ojibwa treaty rights.

In 1986, a nine-day fishing season began at Star Lake. It faced outside opposition from the Protect Americans' Rights and Resources, a group that opposed what it saw as "special rights" for Indians. In response, Ojibwas ignited a spiritual revitalization at Star Lake, celebrating the image of the eagle, singing songs, and playing drums on shore before fishing. When Wayne Valliere started his first song, non-Indian protesters tried to intimidate him as they surrounded him in their orange hunting garb. But the spiritual powers of the event were confirmed when an eagle flew overhead. In Ojibwa tradition, an eagle was the most powerful spiritual animal, so the presence of the eagle shocked even the angry protesters. Said Valliere, "I saw them look up and I looked up and I saw an eagle make twenty-foot circles over the drum. Then we walked through the whole town, carrying that drum."

After the Star Lake episode, the controversy became more than local, as regional and state papers published stories about the controversy between the Ojibwa and local whites. Racial remarks against the Ojibwa reached the newspapers, while the Ojibwa cast the first spearfishers as "Walleye Warriors." A radical organization, Stop Treaty Abuse/Wisconsin worked to defeat the Ojibwa. To fund anti-fishing ads on television and in newspapers, they produced "Treaty Beer." The racist images on the beer cans were meant to incite support for a rejection of Ojibwa treaty rights. In the late 1980s, violent threats against the Ojibwa continued to mount because they had secured the right to hunt each spawning season; the National Guard was dispatched to protect the Indians. The Ojibwa, themselves, were divided. Among the Lac de Flambeau, for example, Ojibwa WTA members accused the tribal council of negotiating for money to abandon fishing treaty rights. The Walleye War was a fight over natural resources in which the Ojibwa became politically active and used a local movement of spiritual and cultural revitalization to support their rights to fish from surrounding lakes, even as whites verbally and violently opposed Ojibwa fishing. The centerpiece for change that filtered across the landscape of Indian affairs in the 1980s and 1990s was native activism, the spirit of determining for themselves what was in the best interest of Native Americans nationally and locally and taking action when necessary to resist federal and state directions.

Casinos and Tourism

In 1987, a landmark Supreme Court case, *California v. the Cabazon Band of Mission Indians*, opened the floodgate to tribal casino operations throughout the United States. The Supreme Court ruled that Indians could operate gaming enterprises without state regulation. The result was a boom in Indian gaming operations in the late 1980s and 1990s.

"From 1988 when the IGRA (Indian Gaming Regulatory Act) was passed, to 1997, tribal gambling revenues grew more than 30-fold, from $212 million to $6.7 billion." However, not all tribes experienced the windfall of tribal gaming, as only certain states negotiated with tribes to permit different levels of gaming. Two states, New Mexico and Connecticut, emerged first as the most profitable tribal gaming areas in the United States. In both states, tribal peoples used the profits of gaming to establish health care and education programs, and diverted gaming revenue to other tribal members so all could benefit. Gaming, in short, became a form of tribal empowerment.

New Mexico's tribes, including 27 groups of Navajo, Apache, and Pueblo peoples, filed lawsuits in the 1980s to establish gaming on their reserved tracts. High-stakes bingo had predated IGRA, established among several Pueblo groups in 1983. Bingo reduced unemployment among many Pueblo peoples to about 4 percent by 1985. By 1993, ten New Mexico tribes had gaming on their reserved tracts, the Jicarilla Apache and Mescalero Apache tribes and the Pueblos of Acoma, Sandia, Pojoaque, San Juan, Taos, Isleta, Santa Ana, and Tesuque (see Map 18.3). In all, gaming operations employed 597 people and paid out more than $4.8 million in salaries and

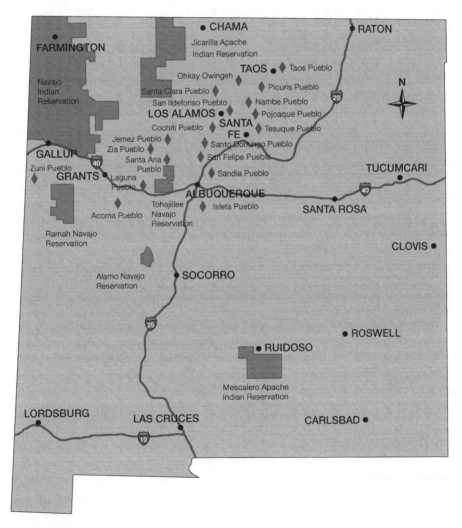

Map 18.3 New Mexican tribes

daily wages. Pueblo peoples used some of their profits to bolster political campaigns in support of tribal gaming, using litigation, lobbying, and electoral pressure, to secure more rights to gaming. By 1995, New Mexico's population spent $172 million on gaming, casinos took in $231 million, and tribes distributed $184 million in wages and salaries. In facing off any political opposition to tribal gaming, the New Mexican groups joined together to form a pan-Indian gaming alliance. For New Mexico's native peoples, gaming was more than just money to help their communities; it was a war for tribal sovereignty and empowerment.

Richard (Skip) Hayward became nationally recognized as one of the most active supporters of tribal gaming. Hayward started his career by encouraging people who claimed Pequot descent to settle on and protect their 200-acre reservation in an isolated part of Connecticut. In 1983, federal recognition of the Pequot, and the allocation of $900,000 of federal money, opened the door for Pequot gaming operations. In 1986, Hayward and the Pequot started high-stakes bingo with the help of the Penobscot, who had been denied the right to run bingo operations in Maine. Although the road to the Pequot bingo parlor was hard to find, eventually the Pequot had over 1,000 tourists coming to play bingo each day.

In 1991, Hayward made the move to open slot-machine gaming, and he negotiated an agreement with Connecticut that would allot 25 percent of all Pequot royalties to the state. With a $60 million investment from Malaysian investor Lim Goh Tong, the Pequot opened the Foxwoods Casino on February 1, 1992.

The Mashantucket Pequot set an example that other tribes and states tried to imitate. New York Oneidas and Senecas opened large-scale casino operations with the help of foreign investments. Sun International, a South African investment company, helped the Mohegans open the Mohegan Sun casino, near the Mashantucket Foxwoods casino. The profits and generation of jobs were tremendous. By 1998, Foxwoods employed 41,000 people and pumped $1 billion into the state economy. In an area suffering for years from economic depression, the Foxwoods casino became a major tourist attraction that revived the local economy. The Pequot also used their money to build up tribal infrastructure. The Pequot built better schools, established better health care programs, and established a $180 million tribal museum and research center. Foxwoods has become the most profitable casino in the United States. Following the Connecticut model, California also began to allow tribal gaming. By 2002, there were 45 Indian groups running gaming operations. Gaming, although criticized as an abuse of federal tribal recognition, has received support from state governments that have come to view tribal gaming as one path to tribal economic development and empowerment. In many cases, however, as has happened among the Seneca, tribal gaming monies have fallen into the hands of a few tribal leaders. And among smaller tribes, large profits have not necessarily resulted in improvement for all members of the tribe. Indians without casinos still suffer under the weight of economic depression. Thus, casinos have benefited some—but not all—native peoples.

Casinos are almost certainly tied to a rise of tourism among native tribes, but gaming is not the only way tribes have sought to bring tourists to reservation lands. The Eastern Band of Cherokee have created a very prosperous tourist industry, one that combines traditional Cherokee culture with other Native American customs that white tourists find attractive. They have used tourism as a way to reinforce Cherokee sovereignty and autonomy along the borders of North Carolina and Tennessee.

The Eastern Band of Cherokees or Eastern Band of the Cherokee Nation (EBCN) live in an area known as the "boundary." Located on the border of North Carolina and Tennessee's Great Smoky Mountains National Park, the EBCN has taken advantage of their location to promote a distinct brand of tourism. Cherokees have mixed perceptions about the tourist industry. As one woman said, "I didn't like foolin' with the tourists. They ask dumb questions. . . . when the tourists came, they wanted to see an Indian. They all wanted to take my picture too. I guess I look like an Indian." To create an "authentic Cherokee" environment to appeal to tourists, the EBCN has established "**The Trail of Tourism**." Small groups, under the guidance of a member of the EBCN, move through different stations. The first station has women creating beadwork. The Cherokees call the beadwork *wampum*, although the word *wampum* is not a traditional Cherokee word for beads. At the next station, white tourists can view Cherokee women at work making pottery, and the next station has women making baskets. There is a station that is a reconstructed log cabin from 1750, a sweathouse, although not constructed in traditional Cherokee fashion. After that is a station dedicated to pre-contact society: a Cherokee house from 1540. Led by their guides, the tourists then visit a station where men knap flint arrowheads and make traps. Next is a canoe-making station, where men carve out canoes from yellow poplar trees, followed by another station where Cherokee men make woodcarvings. After passing through all the artists' stations, the tourists enter the Cherokee council house. Here, the tourists sit and listen to the guide talk about ancient Cherokee customs and culture. Tourists also can watch members of the EBCN perform the play *Unto These Hills*. The plot centers on the story of Tsali and is a mythical account of Cherokee survival against white invasion in the Smoky Mountain region.

Millions of tourists visit the EBCN each year. For non-natives, it offers the opportunity to "play Indian," to imagine themselves as Cherokees existing on the frontier of America. They can take pictures of Cherokee chiefs wearing headdresses, Indians living in tepees, carving elaborate totem poles, or hunting buffalo although these are not part of the Eastern Cultural region and specifically alien to the Cherokees. But these are the types of Indians white tourists expect to see. Tourists can shop for Cherokee artists' wares, many authenticated by signatures and strict rules. The EBCN's fair and the building the of Harrah's Cherokee Casino have only increased the number of tourists along the boundary. By 2003, the Harrah's Cherokee Casino was so profitable that the Cherokees funneled money back into their community, with each Cherokee receiving a check. Tourism has served as a path to tribal and personal independence, and it has given the Cherokees the economic resources to assert their sovereignty along the boundary.

NAGPRA and What Is an Indian?

Under the presidency of George H. W. Bush, Congress passed the **Native American Graves Protection and Repatriation Act (NAGPRA)**. The act established a set of criteria for the repatriation of tribal ancestors and other items deemed sacred. Under NAGPRA, tribes had to "consent" to the removal of remains from any archaeological sites, and archaeologists had to consult tribes if they discovered any excavated remains. By November 16, 1993, because of NAGPRA, all museums and universities funded by the federal government had to take inventory of Indian remains and objects contained within their collections. They then had to establish the nature of each item and the way it came into the institution's collection. Collection curators had to consult with tribal members, and then repatriate any bodies or sacred items directly tied to a tribe by heritage or cultural identity.

NAGPRA resulted in the immediate repatriation of the remains of many tribes' ancestors. Some Indians, who might have viewed anthropologists and museums with a degree of skepticism if not outright anger, now could consider themselves on an equal playing field with the scientific community. Suzan Shown Harjo (Cheyenne), head of the National Congress of American Indians (NCAI), for years had demanded the return of her ancestors killed at the Sand Creek Massacre in Colorado in 1864. As Harjo put it, "It wasn't enough that these unarmed Cheyenne were mowed down by the Cavalry . . . many were decapitated and their heads shipped back to Washington as freight." Because of NAGPRA, the Cheyenne remains went home under the supervision of a Cheyenne delegation. Smithsonian curators and a group of Blackfeet worked together to return 15 Blackfeet skulls sent in 1892 to the Army Medical School. To ensure that the Blackfeet received the correct skulls, the Smithsonian put together a team of bioarchaeologists that determined which skulls were of Blackfeet ancestry. The skulls, returned to Montana, now have their own monument. In another case, the Jemez Pueblo received word from the Robert S. Peabody Museum that "we have a lot of your stuff." The Pueblo carried the bodies in ceremonial fashion back to Pecos Pueblo for proper interment. Another case involved the remains of the last Yahi Indian, Ishi. In May 1997, Arthur Angle of the Butte County Native American Cultural Committee made public that Mt. Lassen would be Ishi's grave. There was one problem: California scientists had removed Ishi's brain upon his death, and, to many of the local native peoples, interring Ishi's body without his brain violated the rules of ceremonial burials. The search for Ishi's brain began. It turned up, hidden in a jar since 1917 on a shelf in the Smithsonian's facility in Silver Springs, Maryland. The brain of the last Yahi went to the Redding Rancheria and Pitts River tribes of Northern California. Ishi's cremated remains were buried with his brain, thanks to NAGPRA.

The NAGPRA legislation had some ambiguous and controversial language. Many groups like the Pequot, Makah, Zuni, and Navajo had their own cultural resource centers and, in the case of the Pequot, a state-of-the-art series of museum displays. Even for communities with their own teams of archaeologists and anthropologists, the thorny language of NAGPRA had made the repatriation of sacred items more difficult than expected. Particularly troublesome are the following phrases: "culturally affiliated," or "culturally unidentified"; "cultural patrimony" versus private ownership; and the definition of "tribe." There is no one legally recognized definition of "tribe," and, in any case, native peoples identify themselves with their groups not in the legal jargon of court cases but by cultural and social patterns specific to their communities. NAGPRA uses the word "tribe" and more open-ended phrases such as "culturally affiliated" or "culturally unidentified." Under NAGPRA, sacred objects must have a cultural affiliation to a specific native tribe to be worthy of repatriation. If objects remain "culturally unidentified," then the items do not need to return to any one particular group.

The word *patrimony* has also posed its own set of problems. Patrimony assumes that items were owned communally by a tribe "rather than property owned by an individual tribal member." However, some native communities, particularly in the Pacific Northwest, were stratified where private property trumped communal ownership. All of this linguistic confusion has clogged the legal channels, even with groups with community-based cultural resource outreach programs. As they attempt to use NAGPRA to regain sacred objects, native peoples are consistently confronted with the problem of defining what it means to be Indian.

For the Makah of the Pacific Northwest, the lack of clarity in NAGPRA has made repatriation a politically divisive issue. In the 1970s and 1980s, extensive excavations began at the **Ozette site**, a centuries-old Makah village. The Makah tribal council sought to control the objects found at the site, forming the Makah Cultural Resource Center (MCRC) to help in this effort. All of the materials excavated from Ozette now reside at the MCRC. NAGPRA, as it applied to artifacts found at the Ozette site and in other museums, however, has caused political discord among the Makah. Because the Makah traditionally believed in a form of private property ownership among whalers rather than tribal ownership, community members have fought over important sacred objects related to the Makah tradition of whaling. "Whale is the sacrament in our communion with the sea," observed one Makah community member in 1997. Whaling, at one point, was everything to the Makah. Individual Makah owned objects associated with Makah whaling, including sacred masks, harpoons, and woodcarvings. But NAGPRA's definition of ownership meant that only tribal claims, not individual claims, were recognized. What it meant to be Native American, or in this case Makah, was therefore thrown into question, particularly when the Makah earned the right to start whaling again in the 1990s.

The Makah had not whaled for centuries. However, under a 1998 ruling of the International Whaling Commission (IWC), the Makah were allowed to start whaling hunts in traditional style from their traditional beachheads along Neah Bay. In a watershed moment in twentieth-century Native American history, the Makah launched their first hunt on May 17, 1999. Once whaling reentered the Makah community as a cultural practice, oral stories about Makah whaling and the sacred objects tied to the practice began to emerge. The MCRC started to record these stories from elders, and they learned from such stories that whaling relied on the individual property of Makah clan and family members. Therefore, the idea of a Makah "tribe" was a recent creation, as families, clans, and village affiliations defined Makah identity in the past. Therefore, any sacred objects associated with whaling in museums belonged to the descendents of Makah whalers. Families began to claim certain items, either from the Ozette site or museums, as belonging to their clans. Others made similar claims. The NAGPRA wording of "patrimony" and "tribe" left the Makah locked in a struggle to make individual property claims rather than communal or "tribal" claims to repatriation. The MCRC has tried to mediate the process, but the result is that the MCRC has become a politicized body, supported by some community members and resented by others.

Another instance where native identity and NAGPRA has created discord among Native Americans was in the repatriation of Kennewick Man, an Indian whose skeletal remains were discovered July 28, 1996, by chance along the banks of the Columbia River in Kennewick, Washington. Radiocarbon dating and scientific testing determined that Kennewick Man was between the ages of 45 and 50 when he died sometime between 8400 and 9000 BCE. Because of NAGPRA, the remains were at the center of a debate involving science, native peoples, and legal definitions of Indian cultural identity. Five Native American groups—the Nez Perce, Umatilla, Yakama, Wanapum, and Colville—made claims to Kennewick Man, wishing to bury his remains according to tribal custom. Because Kennewick Man's remains were discovered on lands formerly occupied by the Umatilla tribe, that group took their case to the United States Court of Appeals for the Ninth Circuit. In 2004, the ruling was handed down that anthropologists or historians could not directly link Kennewick Man to the Umatilla. Because Kennewick Man was discovered on land overseen by the Army Corps of Engineers, his remains are at the Burke Museum, at the University of Washington, as the legal property of the Army Corps of Engineers. Scientists have sent countless teams to study the remains.

The case, however, had greater implications. Questions surfaced about the "500-year-old rule" passed down by the Department of the Interior that any human remains older than 500 years were automatically "Native American." Kennewick Man, when analyzed by scientists, did not fit the typical physiology of native peoples. Was Kennewick Man really a Native American? The language of NAGPRA and the Kennewick remains converged in the case to raise important questions about Native American identity. What is still at stake with NAGPRA are the legal meanings of "Native American" and "indigenous." As in tribal recognition cases, the law still wields power into the twenty-first century in defining who native people are in legal terms, although Native Americans do not view themselves as belonging to the categories handed down by the courts.

18.2 An early image of a Makah whaler with his own tools of the trade.

Source: Library of Congress, LC-USZ62-73626

Native American Women Take Charge

American society has eroded many of the matrilineal traditions of tribal peoples. In matrilineal societies, those in which ancestry is traced through the female line, women hold tremendous political power. In the twentieth century, Native American men, even the men in the American Indian Movement (AIM), began to push women to the margins of reservation political life. Much of the transition from female- to male-dominated native societies stemmed from the American political system itself, which has always seen Native American males as the only legitimate Indian political leaders. Sarah Winnemucca (Paiute) remembered having to dress like an "Indian princess" and being "well versed" in the ways of white society before she could lecture about the abuses against native peoples. In the 1980s and 1990s, following the example of indigenous political women from the 1970s such as LaDonna Harris, many native women became more assertive as political figures. Winona LaDuke (Ojibwa) and Wilma Mankiller (Cherokee), for example, maneuvered through the complicated world of male politics to claim their own important positions.

"When I was little, I used to be made fun of," remarked Winona LaDuke about her early childhood in Ashland, Oregon. It was an environment of harsh racism, but it paved the way for LaDuke's decision to become a Native American activist. Her parents, Betty and Vincent, were both activists in the 1960s. Growing up, LaDuke always heard the words "Go out and do the right thing." By the 1970s, LaDuke was at Harvard, helping form an on-campus organization for ethnically diverse people. With other like-minded people, LaDuke staked out strong political positions concerning native peoples and the outside world. While conducting research in Harvard Library, she stumbled on an article that noted most uranium mines were on Indian reservations. "It means probably they should not be living there," said LaDuke. To make such documents accessible to Indian communities, LaDuke put her sharp intelligence to work, translating legal documents into simple English for reservation-based political organizers. After graduation in 1982, LaDuke had no doubts that she wanted to return to the White Earth Reservation in Minnesota, her ancestral homeland, and work at the grassroots level.

"This is the land I feel most comfortable in the world," observed LaDuke about the White Earth Reservation. Whereas most of her fellow Harvard graduates went on to lucrative jobs, LaDuke lived in a trailer on the White Earth Reservation in Minnesota. The White Earth Reservation faced many problems that demanded immediate attention. White Earth had one of the lowest levels of household income in the United States, with 85 percent of the reservation population unemployed. Schooling was also a problem, as nearly half of all White Earth teens dropped out of school. High levels of alcohol abuse, untreated mental illness, and family and community-level violence also marred life in White Earth. For LaDuke, the cure to many of the ills facing the Ojibwa was the return of sacred tribal lands. While working as principal

18.3 Winona LaDuke (1959–) is a Native American activist, environmentalist, economist, and writer.

Source: Scott J. Ferrell/Congressional Quarterly/Alamy Stock Photo

READING HISTORY

James C. Chatters, Kennewick Man

The Gerasimov method aims to produce a very specific image, one as close to that of the deceased as possible. Practitioners of this school, who tend to have an extensive background in osteology and anatomy, begin by closely studying the bones of the face, and observing asymmetries in bone structure and variations in the development of muscle markings. These are clues to the personal characteristics of the dead. Heavily used muscles, for example, leave prominent spurs or ridges in facial bone and show what expressions the person most often held.

Next, after placing the tissue thickness markers, the Gerasimov-style artist fashions 18 major muscles from clay and places them on the face according to their standard thickness in human beings. These include the oval sphincters that surround the mouth and eyes, the massive muscles that close the jaws, and the delicate muscles that manipulate the corners of the mouth and wrinkle the brows and nose. Once these are in place, the face begins to take on a human look, albeit a macabre one. Using the muscles now as a secondary superstructure, the artist lays a thin clay "skin" over the face to the height of the tissue markers, taking into account the topography created by the musculature. The resultant face is immediately quite life-like and gives the artist less latitude in crafting the finished face. As with the American school, the sculptor ages and lines the face following advice from the team's scientific members, taking cues from the asymmetries and markings noted in the initial inspection of the skull. In the case of Kennewick Man, evidence for severe injuries suggested that the man lived many of his 40-plus years in frequent if not chronic pain. Prominent muscle markings above the chin and beneath the eye sockets confirmed this, revealing a face held in an expression of determined endurance. For this reason, our approximation of Kennewick Man, which we created in about three days using the Gerasimov method, shows the weariness of a middle-aged man in perpetual discomfort. Like the American method, the Gerasimov approach has proved useful for forensic identification, but its best application is for approximating the appearance of the long dead. Forensic anthropologists ordinarily rely on this method for recreations of our earlier hominid ancestors. Well-known examples include the *Homo erectus* created by museum artist John Gurche of the Denver Museum of Natural History and the Neanderthal approximation crafted by Gary Sawyer, a preparator at the American Museum of Natural History. Because we have no artistic standards for how these hominids looked, approximators must produce them with as much scientific rigor as possible. As well founded in science as they may be, facial approximations, as their name suggests, are not literal portraits of the dead. No means yet exist for doing that. Nevertheless approximations constitute the only way we have of gazing at our early ancestors and thereby seeing them as vital beings like ourselves.

Source: James Chatters, *Meet Kennewick Man*, Central Washington University NOVA. Full text at www.pbs.org/wgbh/nova/tech/meet-kennewick-man.html

Questions

1. What sorts of problems does the discovery of Kennewick Man create for the scientific community?
2. Explain how there could be a resolution to the question of to whom Kennewick Man's remains belong.

of White Earth's high school in the 1980s, LaDuke lobbied the federal government for the return of Ojibwa lands. During her campaign, she joined and visited other activists on other reservations.

LaDuke discovered that at the local level, beneath the face of tribal councils, women were most active in health care and education reform. With the help of women from other reservations, LaDuke began a strong environmental campaign against nuclear waste and pollution of reservation lands with other poisons. In her mind, there was a direct connection from the depressed state of women to the rampant sexual violence perpetrated against them to the degradation of reservation lands. American colonialism, in conquering the soil and upending matrilineal clan structures, also "raped the soil" by making land the domain of men and not of women. In traditional matrilineal societies, the conquest of soil meant the disempowerment of native women. For LaDuke, an environmentalist campaign on a national scale would not only result in the protection or even the return of Native American soil but also the protection of Native American women's rights.

In 1985, LaDuke and eight other activists formed the Indigenous Women's Network (IWN). The organization grew, meeting each year to address problems common to many Native American women. IWN sponsored community-based women's activism, usually projects starting small, such as the diaper service on the Cree Reservation. However, as women asserted more and more power within their communities, according to LaDuke, such small movements would grow much bigger and wield more influence. In 1989, because of her tireless work with IWN, LaDuke received the 1989 Reebok Human Rights Award of $20,000.

LaDuke used the money to form the **White Earth Land Recovery Project (WELRP)**, and from there she soon emerged as a nationally recognized Native American environmental activist. By 2000, WELRP had reclaimed 1,200 acres of Ojibwa land for the White Earth people. Through WELRP, LaDuke has argued that Ojibwa people must reconnect with the soil in traditional ways if they were to solve such problems as suicide, alcoholism, crime, and high drop-out rates. In 1991, LaDuke's efforts were further recognized when she became a board member of Greenpeace. She joined the relentless attack against the James Bay Project (second phase) that would have polluted reservation lands the size of Maine, Vermont, and New York combined. The first phase had poisoned large Cree fisheries by allowing mercury to seep into the rivers and streams. Bringing together students, Greenpeace, IWN, and other activists, LaDuke successfully convinced the Canadian power company to abandon the $60 million James Bay II Project. In 1997, she published her first book, *Last Standing Woman*, which interwove White Earth oral traditions and the fictional story of a woman, Alanis Nordstrom. In 1996, Winona was selected as the vice-presidential candidate on the Green Party ticket. She became an even more recognizable face on the national scene as "No Nukes LaDuke," running alongside presidential candidate Ralph Nader. Her vice-presidential nomination was confirmation on a national stage of LaDuke's abilities to move through the world of male politics while fighting for a clean environment and Native American rights.

Like LaDuke, Wilma Mankiller's (Cherokee) childhood experiences instilled in her the drive to become active in Native American politics. Her family moved from Oklahoma to San Francisco as part of a massive urban relocation movement in the 1960s. It was at San Francisco's Intertribal Friendship House that Mankiller learned at an early age about Native American solidarity and activism. She was part of the 1969 occupation of Alcatraz and worked among the Pit River Indians who sought to reclaim land from the Pacific Gas and Electric Company. Mankiller married at age 17 and had two children. The marriage, however, ended in divorce and in 1976 Mankiller decided to move back to Oklahoma. When Mankiller relocated to Cherokee country at Talequah, her children faced the same problems that many urbanized children confronted once they returned to reservation life. Whereas Mankiller had confronted racism at an early age in urban America, her children talked and dressed differently than other Cherokees and were considered outcasts.

Mankiller quickly entered community-based politics among the Cherokees. Working with Chief Ross Swimmer, she helped the Bell Community Revitalization Project. Her tireless efforts to help poor Cherokee families get jobs had achieved much success by the early 1980s. Her work with the Bell Community convinced Mankiller that poverty, education, and health care reform at the local level were the keys to Cherokee sovereignty. Bell was considered a ghetto of eastern Oklahoma, and Mankiller's work to stabilize the community's economy brought attention to her within the larger Cherokee Nation. When Chief Swimmer ran for reelection in 1983, he chose Mankiller as his deputy chief. Mankiller was unprepared for high-level national politics, particularly the male-oriented nature of Cherokee politics that was critical of women playing an active role on the national scene.

In her successful efforts to become deputy chief and then the first female principal chief of the second largest Indian nation, Mankiller had to confront sexism inherent in male-oriented Cherokee politics. Her run for deputy chief in 1983, then chief in 1987, provides ample evidence of the sexism that pervaded Cherokee politics. "The big issue seemed to be my being a woman," observed Mankiller. The matrilineal structure of Cherokee society, "of balance between men and women seemed to be long forgotten," Mankiller remembered. Her election as deputy chief, however, revealed that many Cherokees saw Mankiller as more than just a woman: they saw her as someone who was willing to take on some of the toughest issues that faced their communities. Her plans for grassroots economic and cultural renewal appealed to many Cherokees in the poorest of districts. Her bid for chief in 1987 also reflected the sexist nature of Cherokee politics. Her opponent criticized her for not taking her husband's last name. She also had to contend with the feeling among some Cherokee that "women should [not] be in leadership positions." In both elections, Mankiller, an ardent feminist, challenged the issue of gender head on.

18.4 Wilma Pearl Mankiller (1945–2010) was the first female Chief of the Cherokee Nation from 1985 to 1995.

Source: Buddy Mays/Alamy Stock Photo

Once elected chief of the Cherokee Nation in 1987, Mankiller began to attack the most important issues that threatened Cherokee sovereignty by working on community development. She was able to acquire federal funds to finance local hospitals and other health care facilities, as well as to improve Cherokee district schools to lower the drop-out rate among Cherokee children and teenagers.

One of the most important achievements of Mankiller's political career as chief was the signing of the security of a self-governance pact with the federal government. According to the terms of the agreement, the United States would "conduct relations on a government to government basis." In other words, the United States agreed to officially acknowledge Cherokee sovereignty. For Mankiller, the pact meant that the Cherokee tribal government would be able to use "its authority to buy back some of our land base, to build and operate our own health care system, or sign a government-to-government agreement." Mankiller, in the face of tremendous opposition from within the Cherokee Nation and from other tribes, looked to shore up Cherokee identity by more effectively policing the admittance of new members into the Cherokee Nation. People had to secure their heritage through clear documentation on the census rolls; they could not simply claim Cherokee descent. For Mankiller, a nation could not be sovereign unless its Indian identity was guarded and protected.

As a result of Mankiller's grassroots movements to better the health and welfare of the Cherokee Nation, there was a population boom among the Cherokees. Between 1987 and 1991, the Cherokee population increased from 77,043 to 116,053. Many Cherokees drew inspiration from Mankiller's leadership. Many of these were Cherokee women who had faced powerlessness, degradation, and rape as the Cherokee Nation shifted toward a more male-centered society. Mankiller's tireless attacks against gender stereotypes and her immense success as a leader of the second largest Indian nation in the United States shows how much progress native women had made since the male-dominated Indian activism of the 1960s and 1970s.

PROFILE

Suzan Shown Harjo: Cheyenne-Creek Activist

Suzan Shown Harjo is a nationally recognized Native American activist. Her activism began in the 1960s when she began her own radio show, and it continued into the 1970s. Jimmy Carter appointed Harjo to serve as a liaison between the government and Native American communities. It was during this period that Harjo became deeply concerned with Indian health care and education.

Harjo's efforts resulted in several landmark pieces of legislation. Harjo had a hand in the passage of the 1978 American Indian Religious Freedom Act, the creation of the National Museum of the American Indian in 1989, and the passage of NAGPRA in 1990. She became president of the Morning Star Institute and dedicated herself to protecting Native American sovereignty, arts, and indigenous-focused academic research. An extension of Morning Star was *Just Good Sports*. Spearheading attacks against Indian mascots in sports, Harjo tried several times to have images of stereotypical Indians removed as sports mascots in intercollegiate and professional sports. Like LaDuke and Mankiller, Harjo serves as an example of how Native American women have broken into a male-dominated world of politics to defend the rights of native peoples.

Empowerment and Decolonization and Into the Twenty-First Century

Literature and Art

A recent explosion in Native American literature has become an outlet for indigenous expression of sovereignty and self-determination. Native writers draw on many literary genres to give Indian peoples voices and to create authentic tribal and pan-Indian identities. At the same time, they challenge Western assumptions about literature in the creation of a literary style that is distinctly Native American.

Native women writers have been particularly successful at rescuing Indian women's voices that were marginalized by colonialism and undermined by the new male-centered world of many native communities. Many of these new female writers of the late twentieth and early twenty-first centuries have staked out strong feminist positions in their work. Louise Erdrich (Turtle Mountain Chippewa) began her career with three books of poetry. Many of her early poems drew from Ojibwa oral tradition while reflecting on the tragic history between native peoples and the federal government. Her first book, *Love Medicine* (1984), interwove the story of four Ojibwa families. In the book, Erdrich draws on the voices of many of the family members but focuses particularly on how Catholicism has eroded Ojibwa spirituality and the role of native women in Ojibwa life. This book was the first in a series of three that traced these families as they confronted the pressure to assimilate. Her later works delved deeper into the complex gender relations among present-day Ojibwa. *Tales of Burning Love* (1996) focused on a husband and wife, the difficulties of the urban experience, and how urban life shaped particular ideas about Ojibwa relationships between men and women. Anne Lee Walters's (Pawnee) autobiography *Talking Indian* (1992) is a deep reflection on the boarding school experience from a woman's perspective. Walter experienced an identity crisis when the schools told her to not look for answers in the "tribal voice." Another writer, Luci Tapahonso (Navajo), has emerged as one of the most fearless of Navajo authors. Her two collections of poems, *Shiprock Night* and *Seasonal Woman*, both appeared in 1981, and both reflected on Navajo womanhood, Navajo families, and the Navajo cultural heritage. Her acclaimed collection of stories and poems, *Blue Horses Rush In* (1997), also emphasized Navajo female roles (illustration). These native writers have not only suffused their poems, stories, novels, and autobiographies with the female voice but also have sought to recover cultural traditions and heritages in which womanhood had a large role to play. In bringing the female voice to the center, they have helped forge a distinct Native American feminist literary tradition. Such works are empowering for the authors and native women who read them.

There has never been a Native American men's movement, yet male writers have used a variety of literary traditions to reclaim masculine roles within Native American societies. In recent years, three authors in particular, Simon Ortiz (Acoma Pueblo), Louis Owens (Choctaw-Cherokee), and Gerald Vizenor (Chippewa), used "humor as a powerful point of cultural criticism." All three authors draw on the native tradition of the trickster "as a means by which humor and the surreal can be used to challenge and subvert cultural stereotypes and preconceptions." Through their trickster stories, Ortiz, Owens, and Vizenor discovered a deeply expressive literary method to voice the anger of Native American men and empower twenty-first-century Indian men.

Indigenous Peoples in the Academy

Indigenous scholars approach life in academia sometimes with more conflicting interests than mainstream academics. For years, Native Americans were marginalized by Euro-American colleagues and peers who wrote about Indians and set the terms of Native American scholarship. Devon Mihesuah (Choctaw) describes such academics as "gatekeepers." According to Mihesuah, "by purposely ignoring Indigenous voices, publishing repetitive monographs that offer little to tribes, hiring unqualified faculty, graduating unprepared students, and devaluing Indigenous programs and concerns on campus, many scholars and universities are still supporting, promoting, and acting upon many of the same colonial ideologies." There has been a tremendous growth in Indigenous studies programs throughout American colleges and universities. Some Indian scholars are, however, critical of such programs. The academy, Mihesuah suggests, is too restrained by Western thinking and theories. In her opinion, academia itself needs to be decolonized. By decolonizing the academic realm and by teaching indigenous studies from an indigenous perspective, academics like Mihesuah intend to take their decolonization program outside of the academic arena to empower their communities. In short, Mihesuah and her supporters believe that the scholarly study of Indians should be focused on helping present-day native peoples who live under the weight of serious problems such as language loss, sexual violence, health problems, and poor education.

18.5 Foxwoods Casino

Source: Andre Jenny/Alamy Stock Photo

Angela Cavender Wilson (Wahpetunwan Dakota) agrees with Mihesuah that academia is trapped in a box of "intellectual imperialism." Indigenous scholars must break out of that box. As part of this effort, indigenous-centered research should help present-day native communities, not pander to a small circle of white scholars who claim to write "Indian history" but have no interest in the people they study. Wilson would argue that if native intellectuals engage in the process of decolonization and empowerment within the academy, they have to extend that program to tribal communities. Recovering indigenous knowledge is at the center of this project. With so many more Native Americans entering universities and colleges, the opportunity exists. Indigenous scholars like Wilson must carefully lay out the program of decolonization and empowerment so that it is unthreatening to tribal communities, far-reaching in its impact, and interested in "worldview, oral tradition, ceremonial life, language, values, and relationship with the land."

Shifting Directions: The Obama and Trump Presidencies

The ten years between 2008 and 2018 were peculiar and often discomforting ones, to say the least. War in Afghanistan continued with no visible path toward settlement; in the minds of so many Americans it had become "perpetual war." By 2018, the nation's armed forces were recruiting young men and women whose fathers had been among the first to fight in Kandahar, Bagram, and Kabul some 17 years earlier. America's war in Iraq settled to an official closure by 2011, but troops remained in-country as trainers and advisors. A new war surfaced, featuring the Islamic State in Iraq and Syria (ISIS), and this drew U.S. funds to resistance forces and, again, American special forces units as "advisors." The nation's economy suffered its greatest threat in 2008 since the years of the Great Depression. Home foreclosures skyrocketed as unemployment soared, business profits plummeted and thousands of small firms closed, some large corporations which had become fixtures in the American business sector downsized significantly or sought financial bailout from Washington, and most academic institutions curtailed services while some shut their doors. It seemed to be the worst of times. In that stretch of ten years, the very character of America seemed to change. The sentiment of retrenchment emerged among a large segment of the general population—withdraw from the depth and complexity of the global stage and focus solely on American domestic security, focus on American economic strength by restructuring trade agreements and reducing America's relationship to the global economy, develop the nation's energy independence from foreign sources and supplies, reduce the country's financial obligations even to its own people by making individuals more personally responsible for their own lives, and recapture what many termed "traditional American values." In contrast, a large segment of the population promoted America's continued leadership in the world in security matters, economic development, and human rights and called for an expansion of federal protection of and opportunities for American citizens. The opposing perspectives settled along established political party lines, Republican and Democrat. Polarization ensued. So many of these issues, if not all, fell, too, upon Native Americans.

The Obama Years, 2009–2017

The presidential campaign of Barack Obama in 2008 was one that promised "hope" for America—for the nation and for individuals. Obama, the Democratic contender for the White House in 2008, touted the need for America to maintain its global responsibilities, for the federal government to steer the economy to recovery, and to move all Americans toward an age of greater opportunity and equality. He stood in direct contrast to the actions of his predecessor, George W. Bush. For Native Americans particularly he promised to give special attention to Indian complaints about federal mismanagement of services and Washington's continuous neglect of treaty obligations. "Few have been ignored by Washington for as long as Native Americans," he said in a speech to the Crow Nation in Montana.

Early in his presidency Obama signed into law the American Recovery and Reinvestment Act of 2009. This extensive measure was principally directed at recovering the nation's economy in the wake of collapsing real estate and financial sectors that began in the final years of George W. Bush's administration. This legislation included specific measures beneficial to Native Americans, including the allocation of $510 million for

18.6 President Obama at the White House Tribal Nations Conference

Source: USDA Photo/Alamy Stock Photo

salvaging native community housing projects and settling an existing suit against the U.S. Department of Agriculture that alleged discrimination against Indians in the Farm Loan program. He reconstituted the White House Tribal Nations Conference, an annual summit including the president, his advisors, and Indian leaders initiated by President Bill Clinton in November 1990. The summit during his two terms in office assembled each December for eight consecutive years, and from this gathering the president listened to the concerns and hopes offered by tribal leaders and engaged with them on a government-to-government basis and on a person-to-person level.

In 2010 President Obama signed into law the Tribal Law and Order Act which allowed tribal courts to extend and expand sentences for those convicted in criminal cases. This gave tribal courts greater authority within native communities, removing state justice departments from interference in reservation-based crimes and essentially extending the jurisdiction of tribal courts. Obama's Executive Order 13175 required the federal government to consult directly with tribal governments on policy directions and on programs affecting tribal communities. That same year, the Department of Education concluded a survey of Indian Education and released its report "Tribal Leaders Speak: The State of Education." The document called for better and more frequent communication between tribes and the federal government in determining funding for Indian schools, services, and educational opportunities. In 2012 his administration crafted the State-Tribal Education Partnership (STEP) which authorized $42 million in grants to tribal education agencies and programs.

Lawsuits brought by 17 tribes against the federal government over the previous decade were settled during the Obama years. These suits alleged poor federal management of funds, lands, and resources, and the plaintiffs were collectively awarded $492 million. In fact, throughout his eight years in the White House more than 100 claims made by Native Americans and tribal groups were resolved at a cost to Washington of $3.3 billion. "Settling these long-standing disputes reflects the Obama Administration's continued commitment to reconciliation and empowerment for Indian Country," said Secretary of the Interior Sally Jewel. The administration also increased land holdings to some tribes through direct reassignment of federal properties and through a government program to purchase lands for assignment to tribal governments. President Obama made numerous personal visits to reservations to meet with tribal leaders, many of which were focused on energy projects and federal investment in reservation-based businesses.

18.7 President Obama visits with Native American performers in Cannon Ball, North Dakota.

Source: JIM WATSON/AFP/Getty Images

In 2010 he also accepted the United Nations Declaration on the Rights of Indigenous Peoples, adopted by the UN in September 2007 but not approved by the United States and three other countries at that time. The declaration asserted the right of all indigenous people globally to protect their cultures; to receive government-funded health care and education; to secure the basic rights of life, liberty, and property; and to create and manage their own governments and economies. The United States initially objected to the UN declaration, arguing that the measure provided no clear definition of what constitutes an indigenous person, community, or culture. Washington had earlier balked at the measure, too, because its wording provided little clarity regarding the right of self-determination for native peoples—to what extent is an indigenous population able to pursue its own ends? President Obama held meetings with Native American leaders on multiple occasions to discuss the UN policy and received more than 3,000 comments from individual Indians before making his decision.

Perhaps the hallmark piece of legislation enacted during the Obama presidency was his Affordable Care Act (ACA), initially termed "Obamacare" by his detractors but eventually adopted universally as the identifying label. Although not aimed solely at native peoples, the ACA was a plan to bring more Americans under the services of health insurance plans as a means to counter the grotesquely high cost of medical care in the United States. Native Americans residing on reservations already had access to medical care through the Indian Health Service, but nearly 60 percent of American Indians were urban residents and many of them could not afford the high cost of health insurance. On the surface, the ACA held the promise of affordability and access, but compromise measures placed into the act to secure its passage into law in fact limited competition among insurance companies in states and this drove up individual costs. Numerous states also opted out of the program's offer of federal supplemental financing of insurance costs. The ACA also included a "mandate," a measure that required individuals to purchase health insurance or pay an annual fine. All told, the ACA generated confusion among Native Americans. Who has access to reservation medical services? In the non-reservation population, can an individual Native American rely on the Indian Health Service for medical attention or must he purchase his own insurance? If the former, who is Indian when so many with native lineage also have non-Indian branches in the family tree? The ACA stated that one must have documentation of his or her tribal membership to receive IHS care. "I'm no less Indian than I was yesterday," said Liz DeRouen of North Carolina. "Just because the definition of who is Indian got changed in the law doesn't mean that it's fair for people to be penalized. . . . If I suddenly have to pay for my own health insurance to avoid the fine, I won't be able to afford it." The mandate certainly hurt many Native Americans, as did the steep cost of insurance coverage for individual subscribers, especially when one recognizes that fully 25 percent of native people in the United States live below the current poverty line.

Roughly 70 percent of registered Native American voters identify themselves as Democrat. Obama was their president certainly by party affiliation, but the attention given by his administration to Indian affairs surpassed that of his predecessors over the previous four decades. This does not mean to imply that there was no opposition to his administration. Complaints were lodged with the BIA, landed on the desks of U.S. representatives and senators, found coverage in the news media, and echoed across Indian Country regardless of one's party affiliation. Dam construction projects sometimes resulted in the flooding of individual homes and in several instances removed significant acreage from tribal and personal use. Federal projects on or near Indian lands sometimes interfered with hunting and fishing enterprises. The mining of precious metals and the extraction of oil was reduced by the Obama White House as more land fell under federal protection. In spite of Obama's numerous visits with tribal leaders and his annual conference each December, many Native Americans felt their voices went unheard, and tribal governments felt less like governing bodies when meeting with the president and more like simple shareholders. And, obviously, the ACA proved more a financial liability than a health benefit.

The Ascendency of Donald Trump

President Obama's successor brought to office the polar opposite approach to America's global responsibility, economic development, and human rights. On November 8, 2016, the Republican candidate Donald Trump won the United States presidency, defeating Democrat challenger Hillary Rodham Clinton in a battle widely deemed vicious and often absurd. Trump promised throughout the campaign to "Make America Great Again" although he never truly identified what previous period in the nation's history was "great," nor did he ever define his vision of national greatness or how such a platitude applied to the people themselves. His speeches fomented an exaggerated fear of Muslim terrorism inside the United Sates and a fear of Muslim refugees flooding America's shores. He promised to ban all Muslims from entering the United States "until we can figure out what the hell is going on." He damned Mexicans illegally crossing the porous southern border of the United States, labeling them "rapists" and "murderers" of Americans. While it was true that millions of men, women, and children were entering the country illegally, the rate of entry had actually diminished over the previous years and there was in fact a significant population abandoning their residency in the United States for the homes they earlier left behind. Nonetheless, Trump insisted he would construct a border wall to make America safe and force Mexico to pay for its construction. Trump also harped incessantly on Clinton's alleged responsibility for the death of four Americans at the U.S. embassy in Benghazi, Libya, among them the American ambassador to that country, and he constructed the narrative that her failure with Benghazi was tantamount to treason. He further decried her use of email, suggesting criminal intent with the chant "lock her up" echoing at his campaign events and soliciting the help of Russia to uncover her 30,000 emails.

But Trump was probably more obsessed with his predecessor in the White House, President Barack Obama. Trump's agenda once in office appeared to be intensely focused on reversing each and every specific measure Obama achieved in the course of eight years through congressional legislation or executive order. He aimed squarely at killing the Affordable Care Act ("Obamacare"). He also promised a major redirection in the tax code—one that would reward middle-class Americans with the greatest tax break in history. The bill his Republican-controlled Congress pieced together, as revealed by most economists and even by federal bureaus and agencies, was in fact one that would raise the national debt by at least one trillion dollars over ten years and place a greater tax burden on those people earning less than $75,000 annually while benefiting the richest 1 percent of Americans. Trump had little to offer Native Americans, but Indian affairs snagged him in his first year as president.

The Keystone Pipeline

The Keystone Pipeline System was commissioned in 2010 as an oil delivery system to move crude oil from extraction facilities in Canada to production facilities in Illinois and also to reception depots in Texas. Three construction stages were initially planned and constructed, but eventually a fourth, referred to as Keystone XL (KXL), was deemed necessary by TransCanada Corporation. KXL was to originate at Hardisty, in Alberta, Canada, and run to Baker, Montana, then angle southeast through a portion of North Dakota, stretch through South Dakota to Steele City, Nebraska, and turn eastward toward Illinois. The entire system, once completed, had the intended goal of securing oil for America's use at a cost cheaper than that being purchased from members of the Organization of Petroleum Exporting Countries (OPEC). Moreover, the purchase of Canadian oil would ostensibly liberate the United States from the web of political intrigue and the messy entanglement of American foreign policy in the Middle East and North Africa. The proposed pipeline, however, faced a series of hurdles, largely environmental protection regulations imposed by the Environmental Protection Agency (EPA). It also confronted an American public increasingly worried about the destructive effects of carbon emissions on the environment and on human life itself. This had been a growing concern since passage of the Air Pollution Control Act in 1955, the first legislative act to address air quality in the United States. In the 55 years following its enactment, the federal government implemented the Clean Air Act (1963), established the Environmental Protection Agency (1970), and set pollution control standards on aviation, automobiles, and factories. Private enterprise and government investments increasingly focused on clean energy initiatives and sustainable energy systems. The general public followed the direction, influenced heavily by popular films such as *The Day After Tomorrow* and former U.S. Vice President Al Gore's documentary *An Inconvenient Truth*. The Obama administration had joined the United States to an international recognition of global climate change secured in conference at Paris, an agreement that held the potential of limiting harmful carbon emissions that affect climate change and promoting sustainable, clean energy. Largely because of this dire threat to human life on earth and in the context of a half-century of trying to mitigate the effects of fossil fuel usage, the White House under President Barack Obama sounded opposition to the KXL project. So, too, did the EPA and the National Resources Defense Council. From a more narrow perspective, the extracted oil came from "tar sands"—"one of the dirtiest, most carbon-intensive fuels on the planet." It was estimated that its extraction and refinement process would generate 17 percent more greenhouse gases than standard oil production.

Native Americans added another argument against the KXL pipeline. The Indigenous Environmental Network warned that KXL would inevitably suffer oil leakage, damaging the land and drinking water supplies available to people along the line's route generally and to Native American reservations more specifically. Contaminated water would also affect negatively the agricultural industry of the entire region, contributing to poorer quality fish and crops harvested and an agricultural production harmful to humans more broadly. Numerous tribal governments voiced the same concern, and thousands of individuals—native and non-native alike—joined the chorus of opposition. As doubt rose that Keystone XL would be approved, TransCanada in June 2014 proposed an additional line known as the Dakota Access Pipeline (DAP). TransCanada routed the DAP through northwestern North Dakota, across South Dakota and Iowa to Illinois, a $4 billion project. The same environmental issues were raised to counter DAP construction, but added to those arguments was another one largely unique to Native Americans. TransCanada's application for a permit to the South Dakota Public Utilities Commission for construction approval noted clearly that the project would probably disturb or destroy "prehistoric or historic archaeological sites . . . buildings, structures, objects and locations with traditional value to Native Americans and other groups." "We would never put a native pipeline underneath Arlington Cemetery," said Faith Spotted Eagle (Yankton Sioux). Again, Native Americans complained that the pipeline would leak and contaminate water supplies relied on by tribal communities and despoil the land, plants, and animal life along the route. Moreover, there had been very little interest in securing native input during the planning stages of the project; moving the line over tribal lands was a violation of tribal sovereignty, many Native Americans insisted.

Native people did not speak with a single, common, united voice; they never have. There were those along the pipeline routes who supported the projects. Construction jobs might possibly be acquired, and financial gain in the nation's economy might trickle down to tribal communities and to individuals. Others claimed the potential damage to land, water, and cultural heritage would be tolerable and certainly not as extensive or dangerous as project opponents claimed, putting significant trust in corporate assurances. There were those such as Robert Fool Bear Sr. (Standing Rock Sioux) who contended that there were, indeed, numerous public hearings on the pipeline project for nearly two years prior to the start of construction, but very few Sioux attended them. He added that the protests that soon emerged were in fact not initiated by or dominated by Sioux but rather by outsiders from across the country who promoted their own personal agendas. President Obama rejected Keystone XL on November 6, 2015.

Although KXL had been stymied for now, construction on the DAP project commenced in June 2016. An executive order halted construction but not until the pipeline had neared the Standing Rock Sioux Reservation in southern North Dakota. Another reprieve. A grassroots protest surfaced that summer to draw national attention to the issues confronting native peoples as well as the impact continued fossil based fuel usage would have on the environment. Centered at Cannonball, North Dakota near the Standing Rock Reservation, the number of protesters who made their way to the developing encampment ranged initially in the hundreds but by autumn surpassed 3,000. The Rosebud Sioux contended that the pipeline, if continued, constituted an "act of war" against Native Americans. North Dakota governor Jack Dalrymple ordered the camp abandoned and the protesters dispersed, but his promise of state action only solidified opposition and drew even more opponents to the Standing Rock camp. State and local authorities essentially surrounded the camp ostensibly to control the growing population and to prevent violence that they claimed was being initiated by protesters.

Winter was fast approaching. November faded into December. Warnings were issued by the governor and by law enforcement to suspend protests and dissolve the encampment. Others cautioned encamped protesters to vacate the area in advance of the stinging and bitter cold weather common to the northern plains. Instead, more protesters arrived at the camp, not only more Native Americans but nearly 2,000 veterans of America's armed forces who supported the Standing Rock protest. Again, Governor Dalrymple ordered a mandatory evacuation of the camp by December 5, again to break the resistance movement but under the allegation that demonstrators had become violent, igniting fires and throwing rocks at police and guardsmen surrounding the camp. The protesters countered by arguing that the fires were lit by police to chase them from the camp. News reports airing on nationwide television and social media did reveal violence. Law enforcement was seen employing pepper spray and tear gas against groups of protesters that often included babies, children, and the elderly. Rubber bullets targeted demonstrators, and water cannons were directed at large groups as well as housing structures despite the frigid weather. Protesters "were attacked with water cannons. It is 23 degrees out there," said LaDonna Brave Bull Allard (Standing Rock Sioux). The reservation Medical and Healer Council issued a statement that read, "As medical professionals, we are concerned for the real risk of loss of life due to severe hypothermia under these conditions." One of the leaders of the Standing Rock protest, Dave Archambault II, called on the United Nations and President Obama to "take immediate action to prohibit North Dakota from engaging in its retaliatory actions and practices." "We call on the president," he said, "to take all the appropriate steps to ensure 'water protectors' (the name many attributed to protesters) are safe and that their rights to free speech and peaceful assembly are protected." Given the deteriorating conditions at and surrounding the camp, the U.S. Commission on Civil Rights sent representatives to monitor the affair for civil rights violations.

18.8 Standing Rock protestors

Source: ROBYN BECK/AFP/Getty Images

But Standing Rock protesters, Native Americans more generally, and all those who nationally who supported their struggle confronted a stark reality: the president-elect, Donald Trump, was a friend of big business and not inclined to support any delay in the Dakota Access Pipeline project. Moreover, he denied the science behind climate change, called on greater exploitation of America's natural resources, championed the growth of fossil fuel industries such as oil and coal, and repeatedly announced his intent to reduce government regulations and oversight in all matters. On January 24, 2017, just four days into his presidency, Trump announced his wish to revive the KXL and DAP projects. Toward that end, he ordered the expediting of federal environmental reviews that he described as an "incredibly cumbersome, long, horrible permitting process." Construction began immediately although the president did not sign TransCanada's permit until March 24. Trump's move allowed Governor Dalrymple to order once more the evacuation of the Standing Rock Camp, and by February 21 most protesters had dispersed. Oil began rushing through the pipeline in late April 2017. The matter was closed, or was it? Just as taps were opened in April, thousands of gallons of oil spilled from the Dakota Access line in two locations near Menno, South Dakota. Another sprung open in November 2017 from the KXL line near Lake Traverse Reservation, also in South Dakota near Amherst. Native protesters continued their resistance, this time in court. They secured representation of Earthjustice, a non-profit environmental law firm, which filed suit against the U.S. Army Corps of Engineers for letting a permit that allowed construction to violate existing environmental regulations. After hearing arguments, federal judge James Boasberg on June 14 ruled that permits allowing DAP construction near Standing Rock and approved by the president actually violated federal law. Judge Boasberg decided that the potentially destructive effects of oil spills "on fishing rights, hunting rights, or environmental justice" were inadequately considered and addressed. He added that the Corps was "silent, for instance, on the distinct cultural practices of the Tribe and the social and economic factors" that might be affected. "This is a major victory for the Tribe and we commend the courts for upholding the law and doing the right thing," responded Dave Archambault II. The Obama White House, he continued, studied seriously the potential damage but "President Trump hastily dismissed these careful environmental considerations in favor of political and personal interests." The court ruling, however, was not the "major victory" Archambault claimed it was. The judge did not ban further construction or use of the pipeline. Further investigation by the Corps of Engineers was required before any stoppage would occur. Since summer 2017, the Dakota Access Pipeline has continued to move oil through the system. At this point in time—mid-2018—Native American resistance to the pipeline continues in court while oil is pumped through DAP and KXL.

Pocahontas

Throughout the 2016 presidential campaign, Republican candidate Donald Trump—in both primary and general election races—debased contenders in the simplest manner possible. Routinely he assigned disparaging adjectives to his opponents' names—"Little" Marco Rubio, "Weak" Jeb Bush, and "Crooked" Hillary Clinton, for example. And, Trump was not averse to referring to individuals by race and ancestry. At one campaign stop he pointed to one of the few African Americans in the crowd and shouted, "There's my African American!" Indeed, on June 16, 2015 as he announced his intent to seek the presidency, he denounced Mexicans who illegally entered the United States saying, "They're bringing drugs. They're bringing crime. They're rapists. And some, I assume, are good people." One moniker he repeatedly used was the name he assigned to U.S. Senator Elizabeth Warren (D-Mass.) who routinely, forcefully, and publicly countered most of Trump's remarks. Trump called her Pocahontas, using the name derisively and accusing her of falsely claiming a Native American ancestry. He continued using this name for the senator throughout his campaign and, indeed, throughout his first year in the presidency. On November 27, 2017, he used the term at a most unlikely event.

That day, the president was scheduled to speak at a ceremony that honored Navajo code talkers from World War II. He approached the speaker's platform which interestingly was positioned in front of a large portrait of President Andrew Jackson, who Trump admires. Jackson was responsible for the Indian Removal Act and the relocation of Cherokee and other native groups from the Southeast to Oklahoma in the late 1830s, a move that caused the death of thousands of Indians. Beside the president were three surviving code talkers. Breaking from his planned remarks, Trump said, "You're very, very special people. You were here long before any of us were here. Although we have a representative in Congress who they say was here a long time ago. They call her Pocahontas. But you know what? I like you. Because you are special." The National Congress of American Indians (NCAI) immediately denounced the president's comment as a racial slur against both Senator Warren and Native Americans. "We regret that the President's use of the name Pocahontas as a slur to insult a political adversary is overshadowing the true purpose of today's White House ceremony," stated NCAI President Jefferson Keel. "Today was about recognizing the remarkable courage and invaluable contributions of our Native code talkers. That's what we honor today and everyday—the three code talkers present at the White House representing the ten other elderly living code talkers who were unable to join them, and the hundreds of other code talkers from the Cherokee, Choctaw, Comanche, Lakota, Meskwaki, Mohawk, Navajo, Tlingit, and other tribes who served during World Wars I and II." With pointed reference to the historical figure Pocahontas, the NCAI noted that she, her family, and the Pamunkey people held a valued role in American history; using her name as a disparaging term, said John Norwood of the Alliance of Colonial-Era Tribes, "smacks of racism. . . . The reference is using a historic American Indian figure as a derogatory insult and that's insulting to all American Indians." Navajo Nation President Russell Begaye offered a more measured response: "First and foremost, we appreciate the honor and recognition that has been bestowed upon the Navajo Code Talkers, who truly are National Treasures and protectors of freedom." In an oblique reference to the president's aside, Begaye added that "In this day and age, all tribal nations still battle insensitive references to our people. The prejudice that Native American people face is an unfortunate historical legacy." Others were not so diplomatic.

18.9 President Trump honors Native American code talkers in which he referred to Senator Elizabeth Warren as "Pocahontas."

Source: Oliver Contreras-Pool/Getty Images

"The reckless appropriation of this term [Pocahontas] is deeply offensive," said Amber Kanazbah Crotty (Navajo). The president's words were but the "latest example of systemic, deep-seated ignorance of Native Americans." She chastised Trump, adding that the code talkers are not "pawns to advance a personal grudge, or promote false narratives." Senator Warren responded, saying, "It was deeply unfortunate that the President of the United States cannot even make it through a ceremony honoring these heroes without throwing out a racial slur."

Trump's slur, intended or not, is more than a simple example of racism or ignorance; it is, argue many scholars, a clear example of the historic myth regarding native peoples pressed upon generations of non-Indians and exemplifies the "colonial tool of domination." Schoolchildren across the United States are given an ahistorical perspective of the Pamunkey child who, the myth goes, welcomed the English at Jamestown Colony in the early 1600s, saved Captain John Smith from execution by her people, linked the colonists to the growing and curing of tobacco which ultimately saved the failing settlement, and willingly abandoned her people by marrying John Rolfe and accepting Christianity. The grossly skewed story is premised on the notion that Indian people were "redeemable" if they cast off their own cultures and accept that of Europeans. They existed in a primitive state prior to contact with an allegedly more advanced people, one relegated to extinction as it possessed little, if any, value in contrast to the European civilization. Their survival, the concept holds, turned not on resistance to European values, ideals, systems, and structures but rather their embracing of the superior. The Indians' demise was inevitable, as one culture or civilization was inherently supreme. And, as spirituality was, and remains, the centerpiece of cultural definition, the colonial tool concept further "insinuates that Christianity is better than traditional indigenous religion," contends Roxanne Dunbar-Ortiz, professor emeritus at California State University. It is, then, at its core, a simple argument waged relentlessly since first contact between native peoples and Europeans: the concept of "otherness" as historian James Axtell once defined it. The slur offered by Trump while purportedly honoring Navajo code talkers slammed not only the real Pocahontas and detracted from the very purpose of that Oval Office ceremony to honor men of courage and contribution but reinforced the centuries-old perspective of the racial superiority of Europeans and Euro-Americans—all of this in one brief, thoughtless quip.

The Republican Agenda for Native Lands

For the entire year in which he vied for his party's presidential nomination and throughout the following four months of his campaign against Democratic challenger Hillary Rodham Clinton, Donald Trump insisted that one of his first acts as president would be to erect an actual wall across America's southern border that abuts Mexico. This, he contended, would halt the illegal flow of Mexicans and others into the United States. The wall would be funded not by Americans but rather by the Mexican government, he thundered. Moreover, he promised to remove those Mexicans already illegally inside the United States, even if he had to create special paramilitary units to round up those people, detain them, and then deport them. At his campaign rallies, he verbally countered those who denounced his plan, saying "the wall just got taller!" Trump never addressed any of the obvious problems associated with his ranted promises. How could he possibly compel Mexico to pay for the wall? Would the paramilitary units and their actions be constitutional? How would the United States secure the property on which to construct such a wall—payment to private citizens and corporations owning the land or the exercise of the government's right of eminent domain? The Tohono O'odham Nation, which is about the size of Connecticut, straddles 62 miles of the U.S.-Mexico border in Arizona. Trump's wall would cut right through the reservation, in places separating burial lands from the remaining reservation, breaking the physical ties of some families, and disrupting basic human and community services. As of mid-2018, the wall remains but an idea and a promise; funding has not been approved by Congress as the Mexican government vehemently and understandably refuses to finance the project, no prototype has been chosen, and no lands have been acquired as yet on which the wall would be erected. Although the wall has not materialized, and it may never materialize, the idea of it clearly shows the president's perspective regarding the sanctity of private property and tribal lands, and this remains a certain threat to reservations.

The Republican Party Platform of 2016 posed a direct threat to lands owned by or protected for native peoples in the United States. Trump and his closest advisors have called on the privatization of Indian lands by ending tribal land holding, reclaiming lands not actively used by native groups or individuals, and selling those properties to individual Indians or non-Indians who would develop the lands for economic returns or allow government and corporate access to the resources found on those lands. This would counter nearly one century of federal Indian policy. Privatization has been the goal since colonization—"to strip Native Nations of their sovereignty," their property, and their culture, contended Tome Goldtoth (Navajo, Indigenous Environmental Network). Trump surrounds himself with advisors who echo loudly his own thoughts. Markwayne Mullin, a Cherokee from Oklahoma, co-chairs the president's Native American Affairs Coalition (NAAC). Mullin, purportedly speaking for Native Americans nationally, assured Trump that "we will have broad support [for this] around Indian country." His colleague on the NAAC, Ross Swimmer (Cherokee), concurred and suggested that tribal land sales be aimed more toward non-Indians than to native peoples. The planned move to divest lands from Indian ownership is based largely on securing the abundant natural resources found on native lands. Trump and the party were—and remain—acutely conscious of the seemingly inexhaustible reservoir of natural resources on Native American lands. Although existing reservations cover only 2 percent of the territorial United States, they hold an estimated 20 percent of the oil, natural gas, and coal in America according to testimony given to Congress by the Bureau of Indian Affairs in 2008. In 2009, the Council of Energy Resource Tribes, a tribal energy consortium, estimated tribal energy resources to be valued at $1.5 trillion. Tribal leasing of energy-rich lands has garnered substantial profits. The Crow of Montana and Southern Ute in Colorado have engaged in mining and drilling that reap significant revenue for tribal members and support health services, educational programs, and infrastructure development on their reservations. Removing tribal ownership and control of those lands could open an avenue for wealthy non-Indians and corporations to secure those resources, divert income to themselves and their own interests, and allow for the overall collapse of human services on those reservations. Trump's NAAC is comprised of 27 members. Three of the four co-chairs have direct ties to the oil industry. Investigations have revealed that several have received substantial campaign donations from energy companies and in response have touted the concept of privatization. Publicly, Mullin and Swimmer both have noted they want to preserve tribal control of reservations and continue federal appropriations to them at their current level, but continued federal funding for reservations is not identical to opening lands for mineral speculation by outsiders. Mark Fox, chairman of the Three Affiliated Tribes in Fort

18.10 Bear Ears National Monument
Source: THoffman/Shutterstock

Berthold, North Dakota which is an energy tribe says, "if privatization has some kind of meaning that rights are given to private entities over tribal land, then that is worrying. But if it has to do with undoing federal burdens . . . there might be some justification." Worrying?

Privatization of native lands has commenced. One of Barack Obama's final acts as president was to pronounce the 135 million acres of Bears Ears National Monument in southern Utah and the 300,000 acres of Gold Butte National Monument in Nevada as federally protected lands. "These places—the rocks, the wind, the land—they are living, breathing things that deserve timely, lasting protection," said Russell Begaye (President, Navajo Nation). "The place of my ancestors will now be preserved for all future generations." "Our connection with this land," said Alf Lomahquahu of the Bears Ears Coalition, "is deeply tied to our identities, traditional knowledge, histories, and cultures." President Obama, noted Native Americans, issued federal protection for more land and water than any previous president; his designation of Bears Ears and Gold Butte was the twenty-ninth time he took such action. But in his first year in office, Trump rescinded Obama's declaration, removing the federal protection standing for both Gold Butte and Bears Ears. Trump's plan was principally to open those lands to energy companies for the extraction of precious resources. Senator Orrin Hatch (R-Utah) contended that Obama's decree was nothing less than "an attack on an entire way of life"—corporate and individual access to natural resources that feed the American economy. "They declared war on us today," said Shaun Chapoose (Ute). Five tribal groups—the Hopi, Navajo, Ute Mountain Ute, Ute, and Pueblo Zuni—immediately filed suit in federal court to halt the White House's move against Bears Ears. In similar fashion, Secretary of the Interior Zinke called on the president to open the Cascade-Siskiyou National Monument in Northern California to let "traditional" activities like mining, logging, and drilling resume in those protected areas. Again, the power present in Washington reflects a slant toward native peoples, cultures, and lands consistent with policies and preferences of the late nineteenth century.

The Trump Agenda's Impact on Indian Country

The Trump Administration has pursued a very simple agenda—reverse each accomplishment of the Obama presidency, stimulate the national economy by providing a significantly expanded freedom to corporate interests, and craft both foreign and domestic policies in terms of their explicit and immediate benefit to the United States' financial and power interests. There are, indeed, numerous problems confronting Americans, problems that have existed for decades and problems that have constrained American growth, security, and welfare. Native Americans specifically face continued difficulties. The Native American population of Alaska is about three million in number (five million when those with minimal ties to a native ancestry are included, or 2 percent of the total U.S. population). The poverty rate among them stands at about 25 percent, the highest rate for any race in the United States. The infant mortality rate for Indians stands at nine per 1,000 births while it sits at seven per 1,000 for the general population. Male life expectancy for American Indian and Alaskan Native (AIAN) men is currently 71 years, compared to 78 years for white men. The AIAN population has, on average, lower birth weights than that found in the general population and a higher rate of diabetes, heart disease, and cancer. Native peoples continue to lag behind non-natives in other important categories. While 92 percent of all non-natives over the age of 25 have earned high school diplomas, only 82 percent of the AIAN population has met that standard. Seventeen percent of AIAN men and women hold a bachelor's degree whereas 33 percent of non-natives have reached that level of education. Twelve percent of non-natives have attained graduate degrees whereas only 6 percent of the AIAN population hold a master's or doctoral degree. As of 2012, the median household income for AIAN families stood at $37,300, but the median level for white families was $56,500. The disparity between Native Americans and the non-Indian population in each of these categories has been consistent throughout American history, especially noticed since the government's first landmark study in 1928, known as the Meriam Report. Much more needs to be accomplished. The one positive statement that can be offered regarding current figures is that the gaps between Native Americans and the general population have narrowed slightly. Having noted that, it is imperative to recognize that the pattern of slow improvement will likely be reversed directly or indirectly if the current administration effects the policy changes it desires.

The Republican/Trump agenda has a direct impact on native peoples. The ill-defined, brief, bullet-point budget proposal made public in March 2017 called on the reduction of Indian housing block grants by 25 percent from $650 million to $500 million, and it planned for the complete elimination of Community Development Block Grants. The realization of both efforts is expected to affect negatively individual and tribal community programs aimed at securing opportunity, livability, and security on reservations. The recommended budget also called for the end of 241 positions in the Bureau of Indian Affairs, a reduction of $21 million in tribal legal and justice programs, a drop of $50 million in direct federal financial support in reservation non-housing construction projects, and a $27 million reduction in government management of tribal resources. Moreover, Indian education will realize a $64 million cut and another $23 million in curtailments to human services on reservations nationwide. "Tribal programs are rooted in the United States' trust responsibilities and treaty obligations towards Indian Tribes and Native Americans," responded the National American Indian Housing Council. The Trump White House contends funding cuts are necessary across the board in a bid to reduce the federal debt; however, the Administration's tax reform legislation that passed Congress in December 2017 is certain to raise the national debt by at least one trillion dollars according to every respected economic analyst and financial institution. Human and community services have been, and remain, fundamental provisions in the government's treaty obligations to native peoples. More importantly, funding reductions proposed by the Trump administration compromise basic human services and needs, particularly on reservations. How does the median family income of Native Americans rise if government cuts money for school construction, the hiring of trained teachers, providing adequate school materials and programs, and financially aiding post-secondary education opportunities? How does the health of AIAN improve if government reduces appropriations for medical facilities, curtails access to health care by reducing supplemental funds for medical insurance and services, eliminates health education programs and opportunities, halts certain preventative care programs, and refuses to halt expansion or operation of pipeline services that leak oil onto land and into water reservoirs? Evidence of this surfaced in the president's tax reform legislation in December 2017. The measure, effective January 1, 2018, halted the government "mandate" that each American have medical insurance, a key provision in President Obama's Affordable Care Act, popularly referred to as Obamacare. Said Tom Perez, Chair of the Democratic National Committee, "The United States has long guaranteed Native Americans access to healthcare" largely through treaty provisions and long-established federal Indian policies. "Repeal of Obamacare would put much of this tribal health care at risk, including the care received by more than 290,000 American Indians and Alaska Natives through the Medicaid expansion," he added. Moreover, what does it mean for a people who have their legal relationship with government altered fundamentally as tribal sovereignty is challenged? Implicit in the constriction of funds is a return to the 1950s goal of termination as the president and his advisors have openly questioned the relationship of the federal government to Native Americans and started to move toward termination of support services.

It must be noted that there exists a body of support for Trump and his agenda among some Native Americans. In autumn 2016, shortly before the presidential general election, the Native American Coalition (NAC) formed specifically in support of Trump's candidacy and to advance an Indian perspective rarely highlighted. The NAC, representing tribal groups across 15 states, has contended that federal governance of Indian affairs in fact restricts development of tribal communities. The litany of regulations, argues the NAC, "keep Indian Country from becoming self-sufficient." "Indian Country is prevented from harnessing our own energy resources by ever-increasing regulations. . . . The Trump administration will ease restrictions on American energy reserves."

That Trump previously challenged tribal development of gaming on reservations, claiming without evidence that Indian casinos were run by organized crime and staffed by "fake Indians," resumed pipeline construction across or near native lands without listening to native concerns, routinely refers to Senator Elizabeth Warren as Pocahontas, and proposed a budget that would reduce federal services to native peoples is all secondary to the prospect of windfall profits some Native Americans expect from exploitation of the land and its resources. Others argue that the Obama administration and those that preceded it maintained policies and added new ones that prevented native peoples from securing independence from federal subjugation, an argument that was also offered during the New Deal years. Still others who have become part of mainstream society see in Trump a president who will direct the United States into an age of greatness, into a nation fixed on the prosperity and security of its own people rather than a nation obligated to global demands.

As noted previously, there is no single Native American voice; there never has been. There is, nonetheless, a resistance among native peoples in the United States that remains stronger and louder than the work of some who champion a desire to link arms fully with mainstream America. This has been the history of Native America, and it is the present as well—a cultural and spiritual connection to the land still not comprehended by most non-natives, the maintenance of a unique and special identity, a determined spirit of independence and worth, and a world view that is inclusive rather than exclusive. Change comes to all life forms. This has certainly been true for Native Americans. Over the course of their history they have not succumbed to an ever-growing dominant people but instead determined the method and scope of their response and acted on those choices. Their resistance, their activism, their voice, and their decisions have allowed for the refrain "We are still here."

Conclusion

Scholars involved in the decolonizing agenda have to center all of their research and writing on rescuing indigenous knowledge. As Angela Cavender Wilson has argued, "Reclamation of Indigenous Knowledge is more than resistance to colonial domination; it is also a signifier of cultural revitalization and mounting Native nationalism." If there has been a major shift from the era of Ronald Reagan to the twenty-first century, it is in how Native Americans approach the obstacles they have faced for decades. Since the 1960s, the federal government has tried to control definitions of self-determination and sovereignty and even what it meant to be a tribe. For native peoples of the twenty-first century, legal definitions do matter in terms of defining legal citizenship. They also matter in the government-to-government relationship that helps tribes build casinos and control their own resources and try to ensure that money flows back into their communities and not into state or federal agencies. At the same time, however, Native Americans look less to the law to define how they see themselves as culturally distinct peoples. Whether at the grassroots level or in unions between tribes, native peoples have taken a variety of activist positions to claim what is theirs. Energy tribes, working with the private sector, state governments, and federal authorities, have asserted a stronger role in controlling the resources on their lands to make money and better their communities. Casinos and tourism have opened Native American tribes to the outside world, but they have also helped native groups funnel monies back into tribal infrastructures to provide better medical care and create jobs and native-run schools and universities. Using NAGPRA as the starting point, indigenous groups have reclaimed ancestral remains and sacred objects from universities and museums. And in taking charge of cultural preservation projects, many tribes use archaeological evidence and reclaimed items to reconstruct tribal histories. Artists and writers have used painting and literature to create a Native American artistic tradition that continues to grow. With growing numbers of Native Americans in higher education, indigenous scholars have used their positions as faculty members to set a powerful agenda for the twenty-first century. Whether at Native American-run universities or larger, public and private institutions of higher education, native peoples have started programs of language and cultural retention. With so many educated Native American leaders and community members, American Indians no longer need to rely solely on the federal government to provide definitions of "self-determination" and "self-government." Through education, tribal communities can wrest themselves from Western imperialistic knowledge and colonizing bureaucracies to turn inward toward their people and empower themselves. The twenty-first-century movement toward decolonization has gained considerable speed. Decolonization is one way native groups have set a new course to tackle many of the problems that have beset their peoples for centuries, and therefore it holds the promise of a better future.

Review Questions

1. What is the decolonization movement?
2. Compare the roles of Native American leaders in the 1980s and 1990s.
3. How do Native American men and women approach literature?
4. What is NAGPRA? How has this measure benefited native peoples and what problems has it created?
5. How have Native Americans pursued claims to resources on and off reservations?
6. In what direction are Native Americans headed in the twenty-first century?

Recommended Readings

Ambler, Marjane. *Breaking the Iron Bonds: Indian Control of Energy Development* (Lawrence: University Press of Kansas, 1990). An exceptional study of energy rights and Native Americans' fight to control their mineral-rich lands.

Beard-Moose, Christina Taylor. *Public Indians, Private Cherokees: Tourism and Tradition on Tribal Ground* (Tuscaloosa: University of Alabama Press, 2009). Probably the best local-level anthropological study of Native American tourism.

Bordewich, Fergus M. *Killing the White Man's Indian: Reinventing Native Americans at the End of the Twentieth Century* (New York: Doubleday, 1996). A reflection on issues of Indian sovereignty.

Castile, George Pierre. *Taking Charge: Native American Self-Determination and Federal Indian Policy, 1975–1993* (Tucson: University of Arizona Press, 2006). A survey of the years of Ronald Reagan and George H. W. Bush.

Eisler, Kim Isaac. *Revenge of the Pequots: How a Small Native American Tribe Created the World's Most Profitable Casino* (New York: Simon & Schuster, 2001). A study of the Pequots' fight to build their casino.

Janda, Sarah Eppler. *Beloved Women: The Political Lives of LaDonna Harris and Wilma Mankiller* (DeKalb: Northern Illinois University Press, 2007). A comparative study of two important Native American women activists.

Nesper, Larry. *The Walleye War: The Struggle for Ojibwe Spearfishing and Treaty Rights* (Lincoln, NE: University of Nebraska Press, 2002). The best work on this little-known struggle.

Tillett, Rebecca. *Contemporary Native American Literature* (Edinburgh: Edinburgh University Press, 2007). A scholarly analysis of Native American literary traditions.

Tweedie, Ann M. *Drawing Back Culture: The Makah Struggle for Repatriation* (Seattle: University of Washington Press, 2002). This anthropological work makes the important linkage between Makah concepts of property, the activity of whaling, and NAGPRA.

Native American History Online

General Sites

Writings of Luci Tapahonso. www.hanksville.org/storytellers/luci/ This site offers a brief biography of Tapahonso and has access to many of her writings.

Artwork of Edgar Heap of Birds. http://heapofbirds.ou.edu Students can view more of the startling art of Heap of Birds, as well as learn about him as a teacher and activist.

NAGPRA. www.nps.gov/nagpra The full text of the NAGPRA legislation is provided here.

Artwork of Colleen Cutschall. www.rpearce4.wixsite.com Another site of an important Native American artist with a biography and pictures of her stunning work.

Historical Sites

National Congress of American Indians. www.ncai.org/ The National Congress of American Indians has been operational since its founding in 1944. This site, its Internet home, provides visitors with the NCAI history, its position on numerous current government policy issues, and its own initiatives to advance native concerns.

Eastern Band of Cherokees, Cherokee, North Carolina. www.visitcherokeenc.com The site talks about the history of the Eastern Band of Cherokees and about their growth and development over time.

The Makah Indians, Olympic Peninsula, Washington. The Makah Indians www.makah.com This website provides an overview of Makah history and culture, along with numerous images of their homeland and people. The webpage for the museum offers a wonderful history of the Makah, as well as some images of artifacts and access to important contact information if students are interested in archival work about the history of the Makah.

Mashantucket Pequot Museum and Research Center, Mashantucket, Connecticut. www.pequotmuseum.org/ There is a link provided to interactive online exhibits that tell a visual history of the Pequot, and there is a list of archival materials under the link to the library and archive for students interested in pursuing any research into the Pequot.

Appendix

Federally Recognized Tribes in the United States

Indian tribal entities within the contiguous 48 states recognized and eligible to receive services from the United States Bureau of Indian Affairs.

Absentee-Shawnee Tribe, *Oklahoma*

Agua Caliente Band of Cahuilla, *California*

Ak Chin, *Arizona*

Alabama-Coushatta Tribes, *Texas*

Alabama-Quassarte Tribal Town, *Oklahoma*

Alturas Indian Rancheria, *California*

Apache Tribe, *Oklahoma*

Arapahoe Tribe, *Wind River Reservation, Wyoming*

Aroostook Band, *Micmac, Maine*

Assiniboine and Sioux Tribes, *Fort Peck Reservation, Montana*

Augustine Band, *Cahuilla Mission, California*

Bad River Band, *Lake Superior Chippewa, Bad River Reservation, Wisconsin*

Bay Mills Indian Community, *Sault Ste. Marie Band of Chippewa, Bay Mills Reservation, Michigan*

Bear River Band, *Rohnerville Rancheria, California*

Berry Creek Rancheria, *Maidu, California*

Big Lagoon Rancheria, *California*

Big Pine Band, *Owens Valley Paiute-Shoshone, Big Pine Reservation, California*

Big Sandy Rancheria, *Mono, California*

Big Valley Band, *Pomo Indians, Big Valley Rancheria, California*

Blackfeet Tribe, *Blackfeet Reservation, Montana*

Blue Lake Rancheria, *California*

Bridgeport Paiute Indian Colony, *California*

Buena Vista Rancheria, *Me-Wuk Indians, California*

Burns Paiute Tribe, *Burns Paiute Indian Colony, Oregon*

Cabazon Band, *Cahuilla Mission Indians, Cabazon Reservation, California*

Cachil DeHe Band, *Wintun Indians, Colusa Rancheria, California*

Caddo Indian Tribe, *Oklahoma*

Cahuilla Band of Mission Indians, *Cahuilla Reservation, California*

Cahto Indian Tribe, *Laytonville Rancheria, California*

Campo Band of Diegueno Mission Indians, *Campo Indian Reservation, California*

Capitan Grande Band, *Diegueno Mission Indians, California:*

    Barona Group, *Capitan Grande Band, Mission Indians, Barona Reservation, California*

    Viejas (Baron Long) Group, *Capitan Grande Band, Mission Indians of Viejas Reservation, California*

Catawba Indian Nation (aka Catawba Tribe of South Carolina)

Cayuga Nation, *New York*

Cedarville Rancheria, *California*

Chemehuevi Indian Tribe, *Chemehuevi Reservation, California*

Cher-Ae Heights Indian Community, *Trinidad Rancheria, California*

Cherokee Nation, *Oklahoma*

Cheyenne-Arapaho Tribes, *Oklahoma*

Cheyenne River Sioux Tribe, *Cheyenne River Reservation, South Dakota*

Chickasaw Nation, *Oklahoma*

Chicken Ranch Rancheria, *Me-Wuk Indians, California*

Chippewa-Cree Indians, *Rocky Boy's Reservation, Montana*

Chitimacha Tribe, *Louisiana*

Choctaw Nation, *Oklahoma*

Citizen Potawatomi Nation, *Oklahoma*

Cloverdale Rancheria, *Pomo Indians, California*

Cocopah Tribe, *Arizona*

Coeur D'Alene Tribe, *Idaho*

Cold Springs Rancheria, *Mono Indians, California*

Colorado River Indian Tribes, *Arizona and California*

Comanche Indian Tribe, *Oklahoma*

Confederated Salish & Kootenai Tribes, *Flathead Reservation, Montana*

Confederated Tribes, *Chehalis Reservation, Washington*

Confederated Tribes, *Colville Reservation, Washington*

Confederated Tribes, *Coos, Lower Umpqua and Siuslaw Indians, Oregon*

Confederated Tribes, *Goshute Reservation, Nevada and Utah*

Confederated Tribes, *Grand Ronde Community of Oregon*

Confederated Tribes, *Siletz Reservation, Oregon*

Confederated Tribes, *Umatilla Reservation, Oregon*

Confederated Tribes, *Warm Springs Reservation, Oregon*

Confederated Tribes and Bands, *Yakama Indian Nation, Washington*

Coquille Tribe, *Oregon*

Cortina Indian Rancheria, *Wintun Indians, California*

Coushatta Tribe, *Louisiana*

Cow Creek Band, *Umpqua Indians, Oregon*

Coyote Valley Band, *Pomo Indians, California*

Crow Tribe, *Montana*

Crow Creek Sioux Tribe, *South Dakota*

Cuyapaipe Community, *Diegueno Mission Indians, Cuyapaipe Reservation, California*

Death Valley Timbi-Sha Shoshone Band, *California*

Delaware Nation, *Oklahoma* (formerly Delaware Tribe, *Western Oklahoma*)

Delaware Tribe of Indians, *Oklahoma*

Dry Creek Rancheria, *Pomo Indians, California*

Duckwater Shoshone Tribe, *Duckwater Reservation, Nevada*

Eastern Band of Cherokee Indians, *North Carolina*

Eastern Shawnee Tribe, *Oklahoma*

Elem Indian Colony, *Pomo Indians, Sulphur Bank Rancheria, California*

Elk Valley Rancheria, *California*

Ely Shoshone Tribe, *Nevada*

Enterprise Rancheria of Maidu Indians, *California*

Flandreau Santee Sioux Tribe, *South Dakota*

Forest County Potawatomi Community, *Wisconsin*

Fort Belknap Indian Community, *Fort Belknap Reservation, Montana*

Fort Bidwell Indian Community, *Fort Bidwell Reservation, California*

Fort Independence Indian Community, *Paiute Indians of the Fort Independence Reservation, California*

Fort McDermitt Paiute and Shoshone Tribes, *Fort McDermitt Indian Reservation, Nevada and Oregon*

Fort McDowell Mohave-Apache Community, *Fort McDowell Indian Reservation, Arizona*

Fort Mojave Indian Tribe, *Arizona, California & Nevada*

Fort Sill Apache Tribe, *Oklahoma*

Gila River Indian Community, *Gila River Indian Reservation, Arizona*

Grand Traverse Band of Ottawa & Chippewa Indians, *Michigan*

Greenville Rancheria of Maidu Indians, *California*

Grindstone Indian Rancheria of Wintun-Wailaki Indians, *California*

Guidiville Rancheria, *California*

Hannahville Indian Community of Wisconsin Potawatomie Indians, *Michigan*

Havasupai Tribe, *Arizona*

Ho-Chunk Nation, *Wisconsin* (formerly known as the Wisconsin Winnebago Tribe)

Hoh Indian Tribe, *Washington*

Hoopa Valley Tribe, *California*

Hopi Tribe, *Arizona*

Hopland Band of Pomo Indians, *Hopland Rancheria, California*

Houlton Band of Maliseet Indians, *Maine*

Huron Potawatomi, Inc., *Michigan*

Inaja Band of Diegueno Mission Indians, *Inaja and Cosmit Reservation, California*

Ione Band of Miwok Indians, *California*

Iowa Tribe, *Kansas and Nebraska*

Iowa Tribe, *Oklahoma*

Jackson Rancheria of Me-Wuk Indians, *California*

Jamestown S'Klallam Tribe, *Washington*

Jamul Indian Village, *California*

Jena Band of Choctaw Indians, *Louisiana*

Jicarilla Apache Tribe, *New Mexico*

Kaibab Band of Paiute Indians, *Kaibab Indian Reservation, Arizona*

Kalispel Indian Community, *Kalispel Reservation, Washington*

Karuk Tribe, *California*

Kashia Band of Pomo Indians, *Stewarts Point Rancheria, California*

Kaw Nation, *Oklahoma*

Keweenaw Bay Indian Community, *L'Anse and Ontonagon Bands of Chippewa Indians, L'Anse Reservation, Michigan*

Kialegee Tribal Town, *Oklahoma*

Kickapoo Tribe of Indians, *Kansas*

Kickapoo Tribe, *Oklahoma*

Kickapoo Traditional Tribe, *Texas*

Kiowa Indian Tribe, *Oklahoma*

Klamath Indian Tribe, *Oregon*

Kootenai Tribe, *Idaho*

La Jolla Band of Luiseno Mission Indians, *La Jolla Reservation, California*

La Posta Band of Diegueno Mission Indians, *La Posta Indian Reservation, California*

Lac Courte Oreilles Band of Lake Superior Chippewa Indians, *Lac Courte Oreilles Reservation, Wisconsin*

Lac du Flambeau Band of Lake Superior Chippewa Indians, *Lac du Flambeau Reservation, Wisconsin*

Lac Vieux Desert Band of Lake Superior Chippewa Indians, *Michigan*

Las Vegas Tribe of Paiute Indians, *Las Vegas Indian Colony, Nevada*

Little River Band of Ottawa Indians, *Michigan*

Little Traverse Bay Bands of Odawa Indians, *Michigan*

Los Coyotes Band of Cahuilla Mission Indians, *Los Coyotes Reservation, California*

Lovelock Paiute Tribe, *Lovelock Indian Colony, Nevada*

Lower Brule Sioux Tribe, *South Dakota*

Lower Elwha Tribal Community, *Lower Elwha Reservation, Washington*

Lower Sioux Indian Community, *Minnesota Mdewakanton Sioux Indians, Lower Sioux Reservation, Minnesota*

Lummi Tribe, *Washington Lytton Rancheria, California*

Manchester Band of Pomo Indians, *Manchester-Point Arena Rancheria, California*

Manzanita Band of Diegueno Mission Indians, *Manzanita Reservation, California*

Mashantucket Pequot Tribe, *Connecticut*

Match-e-be-nash-she-wish Band of Pottawatomi Indians, *Michigan*

Mechoopda Indian Tribe, *Chico Rancheria, California*

Menominee Indian Tribe, *Wisconsin*

Mesa Grande Band of Diegueno Mission Indians, *Mesa Grande Reservation, California*

Mescalero Apache Tribe, *New Mexico*

Miami Tribe, *Oklahoma*

Miccosukee Tribe, *Florida*

Middletown Rancheria of Pomo Indians, *California*

Minnesota Chippewa Tribe, *Minnesota (Six component reservations: Bois Forte Band (Nett Lake); Fond du Lac Band; Grand Portage Band; Leech Lake Band; Mille Lacs Band; White Earth Band)*

Mississippi Band of Choctaw, *Mississippi*

Moapa Band of Paiute Indians, *Moapa River Indian Reservation, Nevada*

Modoc Tribe, *Oklahoma*

Mohegan Indian Tribe, *Connecticut*

Mooretown Rancheria of Maidu Indians, *California*

Morongo Band of Cahuilla Mission Indians, *Morongo Reservation, California*

Mualapai Indian Tribe, *Arizona*

Muckleshoot Indian Tribe, *Washington*

Muscogee (Creek) Nation, *Oklahoma*

Narragansett Indian Tribe, *Rhode Island*

Navajo Nation, *Arizona, New Mexico, & Utah*

Nez Perce Tribe, *Idaho*

Nisqually Indian Tribe, *Washington*

Nooksack Indian Tribe, *Washington*

Northern Cheyenne Tribe, *Montana*

Northfork Rancheria of Mono Indians, *California*

Northwestern Band of Shoshoni Nation, *Utah (Washakie)*

Oglala Sioux Tribe, *Pine Ridge Reservation, South Dakota*

Omaha Tribe, *Nebraska*

Oneida Nation, *New York*

Oncida Tribe, *Wisconsin Onondaga Nation, New York*

Osage Tribe, *Oklahoma*

Ottawa Tribe, *Oklahoma*

Otoe-Missouria Tribe of Indians, *Oklahoma*

Paiute Indian Tribe, *Utah*

Paiute-Shoshone Indians, *Bishop Colony, California*

Paiute-Shoshone Tribe, *Fallon Reservation and Colony, Nevada*

Paiute-Shoshone Indians, *Lone Pine Reservation, California*

Pala Band of Luiseno Mission Indians, *Pala Reservation, California*

Pascua Yaqui Tribe, *Arizona*

Paskenta Band of Nomlaki Indians, *California*

Passamaquoddy Tribe, *Maine*

Pauma Band of Luiseno Mission Indians, *Pauma & Yuima Reservation, California*

Pawnee Nation, *Oklahoma*

Pechanga Band of Luiseno Mission Indians, *Pechanga Reservation, California*

Penobscot Tribe, *Maine*

Poria Tribe of Indians, *Oklahoma*

Paiute-Shoshone Chukchansi Indians of *California*

Pinoleville Rancheria of Pomo Indians, *California*

Pit River Tribe, *California (includes Big Bend, Lookout, Montgomery Creek & Roaring Creek Rancherías & XL Ranch)*

Poarch Band of Creek Indians, *Alabama*

Pokagon Band of Potawatomi Indians, *Michigan*

Ponca Tribe, *Oklahoma*

Ponca Tribe, *Nebraska*

Port Gamble Indian Community, *Port Gamble Reservation, Washington*

Potter Valley Rancheria of Pomo Indians, *California*

Prairie Band of Potawatomi Indians, *Kansas*

Prairie Island Indian Community of Minnesota Mdewakanton Sioux Indians, *Prairie Island Reservation, Minnesota*

Pueblo of Acoma, *New Mexico*

Pueblo of Cochiti, *New Mexico*

Pueblo of Jemez, *New.Mexico*

Pueblo of Isleta, *New Mexico*

Pueblo of Laguna, *New Mexico*

Pueblo of Nambe, *New Mexico*

Pueblo of Picuris, *New Mexico*

Pueblo of Pojoaque, *New Mexico*

Pueblo of San Felipe, *New Mexico*

Pueblo of San Juan, *New Mexico*

Pueblo of San Ildefonso, *New Mexico*

Pueblo of Sandia, *New Mexico*

Pueblo of Santa Ana, *New Mexico*

Pueblo of Santa Clara, *New Mexico*

Pueblo of Santo Domingo, *New Mexico*

Pueblo of Taos, *New Mexico*

Pueblo of Tesuque, *New Mexico*

Pueblo of Zia, *New Mexico*

Puyallup Tribe, *Washington*

Pyramid Lake Paiute Tribe, *Nevada*

Quapaw Tribe, *Oklahoma*

Quartz Valley Indian Community, *California*

Quechan Tribe of the Fort Yuma Indian Reservation, *California & Arizona*

Quileute Tribe, *Washington*

Quinault Tribe, *Washington*

Ramona Band of Village of Cahuilla Mission Indians, *California*

Red Cliff Band of Lake Superior Chippewa Indians, *Wisconsin*

Red Lake Band of Chippewa Indians, *Minnesota*

Redding Rancheria, *California*

Redwood Valley Rancheria of Pomo Indians, *California*

Reno-Sparks Indian Colony, *Nevada*

Resighini Rancheria, *California* (formerly known as the Coast Indian Community of Yurok Indians of the Resighini Rancheria)

Rincon Band of Luiseno Mission Indians, *Rincon Reservation, California*

Robinson Rancheria of Pomo Indians, *California*

Rosebud Sioux Tribe, *South Dakota*

Round Valley Indian Tribes, *California* (formerly known as the Covelo Indian Community)

Rumsey Indian Rancheria of Wintun Indians, *California*

Sac & Fox Tribe of the Mississippi, *Iowa*

Sac & Fox Nation of Missouri, *Kansas and Nebraska*

Sac & Fox Nation, *Oklahoma*

Saginaw Chippewa Indian Tribe, *Isabella Reservation, Michigan*

Salt River Pima-Maricopa Indian Community, *Arizona*

Samish Indian Tribe, *Washington*

San Carlos Apache Tribe, *Arizona*

San Juan Southern Paiute Tribe, *Arizona*

San Manual Band of Serrano Mission Indians, *California*

San Pasqual Band of Diegueno Mission Indians, *California*

Santa Rosa Indian Community, *Santa Rosa Rancheria, California*

Santa Rosa Band of Cahuilla Mission Indians, *Santa Rosa Reservation, California*

Santa Ynez Band of Chumash Mission Indians, *Santa Ynez Reservation, California*

Santa Ysabel Band of Diegueno Mission Indians of the Santa Ysabel Reservation, *California*

Santee Sioux Tribe of the Santee Reservation, *Nebraska*

Sauk-Suiattle Indian Tribe, *Washington*

Sault Ste. Marie Tribe of Chippewa Indians, *Michigan*

Scotts Valley Band of Pomo Indians, *California*

Seminole Nation, *Oklahoma*

Seminole Tribe, *Florida, Dania, Big Cypress, Brighton, Hollywood & Tampa Reservations*

Seneca Nation, *New York*

Seneca-Cayuga Tribe, *Oklahoma*

Shakopee Mdewakanton Sioux Community, *Minnesota (Prior Lake)*

Sheep Ranch Rancheria of Me-Wuk Indians, *California*

Sherwood Valley Rancheria of Pomo Indians, *California*

Shingle Springs Band of Miwok Indians, *California*

Shoalwater Bay Tribe, *Washington*

Shoshone Tribe, *Wind River Reservation, Wyoming*

Shoshone-Bannock Tribes, *Fort Hall Reservation, Idaho*

Shoshone-Paiute Tribes, *Duck Valley Reservation, Nevada*

Sisseton-Wahpeton Sioux Tribe, *Lake Traverse Reservation, South Dakota*

Skokomish Indian Tribe, *Washington*

Skull Valley Band of Goshute Indians, *Utah*

Smith River Rancheria, *California*

Snoqualmie Tribe, *Washington*

Soboba Band of Louiseno Mission Indians, *Soboba Reservation, California*

Sokaogon Chippewa Community of the Mole Lake Band of Chippewa Indians, *Wisconsin*

Southern Ute Indian Tribe, *Colorado*

Spirit Lake Tribe, *North Dakota* (formerly known as the Devils Lake Sioux Tribe)

Spokane Tribe, *Washington*

Squaxin Island Tribe, *Washington*

St. Croix Chippewa Indians, *Wisconsin*

St. Regis Band of Mohawk Indians, *New York*

Standing Rock Sioux Tribe, *North & South Dakota*

Stockbridge-Munsee Community of Mohican Indians, *Wisconsin*

Stillaguamish Tribe, *Washington*

Summit Lake Paiute Tribe, *Nevada*

Suquamish Indian Tribe, *Port Madison Reservation, Washington*

Susanville Indian Rancheria, *California*

Swinomish Indians, *Washington*

Sycuan Band of Diegueno Mission Indians, *California*

Table Bluff Reservation—Wiyot Tribe, *California*

Table Mountain Rancheria, *California*

Te-Moak Tribes of Western Shoshone Indians, *Nevada (Four constituent bands: Battle Mountain Band; Elko Band; South Fork Band and Wells Band)*

Thlopthlocco Tribal Town, *Oklahoma*

Three Affiliated Tribes of the Fort Berthold Reservation, *North Dakota*

Tohono O'odham Nation, *Arizona*

Tonawanda Band of Seneca Indians, *New York*

A: Tonkawa Tribe, *Oklahoma*

Tonto Apache Tribe, *Arizona*

Torres-Martinez Band of Cahuilla Mission Indians, *California*

Tule River Indian Tribe, *California*

Tulalip Tribes, *Washington*

Tunica-Biloxi Indian Tribe, *Louisiana*

Tuolumne Band of Me-Wuk Indians, *California*

Turtle Mountain Band of Chippewa Indians, *North Dakota*

Tuscarora Nation, *New York*

Twenty-Nine Palms Band of Luiseno Mission Indians, *California*

United Auburn Indian Community, *California*

United Keetoowah Band of Cherokee Indians, *Oklahoma*

Upper Lake Band of Pomo Indians, *California*

Upper Sioux Indian Community, *Minnesota*

Upper Skagit Indian Tribe, *Washington*

Ute Indian Tribe of the Uintah & Ouray Reservation, *Utah*

Ute Mountain Tribe, *Colorado, New Mexico, & Utah*

Utu Utu Gwaitu Paiute Tribe of the Benton Paiute Reservation, *California*

Walker River Paiute Tribe, *Walker River Reservation, Nevada*

Wampanoag Tribe of Gay Head (Aquinnah), *Massachusetts*

Washoe Tribe, *Nevada & California (Carson Colony, Dresslerville Colony, Woodfords Community, Stewart Community, & Washoe Ranches)*

White Mountain Apache Tribe, *Fort Apache Reservation, Arizona*

Wichita and Affiliated Tribes (Wichita, Keechi, Waco, & Tawakonie), *Oklahoma*

Winnebago Tribe, *Nebraska*

Winnemucca Indian Colony, *Nevada*

Wyandotte Tribe, *Oklahoma*

Yankton Sioux Tribe, *South Dakota*

Yavapai-Apache Nation of the Camp Verde Indian Reservation, *Arizona*

Yavapai-Prescott Tribe, *Arizona*

Yerington Paiute Tribe of the Yerington Colony & Campbell Ranch, *Nevada*

Yomba Shoshone Tribe, *Nevada*

Ysleta Del Sur Pueblo, *Texas*

Yurok Tribe, *California*

Zuni Tribe, *New Mexico*

Native entities within the state of Alaska recognized and eligible to receive services from the United States Bureau of Indian Affairs.

Village of Afognak

Native Village of Akhiok

Akiachak Native Community

Akiak Native Community

Native Village of Akutan

Village of Alakanuk

Alatna Village

Native Village of Aleknagik

Algaaciq Native Village (St. Mary's)

Allakaket Village

Native Village of Ambler

Village of Anaktuvuk Pass

Yupiit of Andreafski

Angoon Community Association

Village of Aniak

Anvik Village

Arctic Village (see Native Village of Venetie Tribal Government)

Native Village of Atka

Asa'carsarmiut Tribe (formerly Native Village of Mountain Village)

Atqasuk Village (Atkasook)

Village of Atmautluak

Native Village of Barrow Inupiat Traditional Government (formerly Native Village of Barrow)

Beaver Village

Native Village of Belkofski

Village of Bill Moore's Slough

Birch Creek Tribe (formerly listed as Birch Creek Village)

Native Village of Brevig Mission

Native Village of Buckland

Native Village of Cantwell

Native Village of Chanega (aka Chenega)

Chalkyitsik Village

Village of Chefornak

Chevak Native Village

Chickaloon Native Village

Native Village of Chignik

Native Village of Chignik Lagoon

Chignik Lake Village

Chilkat Indian Village (Klukwan)

Chilkoot Indian Association (Haines)

Chinik Eskimo Community (Golovin)

Native Village of Chistochina

Native Village of Chitina

Native Village of Chuathbaluk (Russian Mission, *Kuskokwim*)

Chuloonawick Native Village

Circle Native Community

Village of Clark's Point

Native Village of Council

Craig Community Association

Village of Crooked Creek

Curyung Tribal Council (formerly Native Village of Dillingham)

Native Village of Deering

Native Village of Diomede (aka Inalik)

Village of Dot Lake

Douglas Indian Association
Native Village of Eagle
Native Village of Eek
Egegik Village
Eklutna Native Village
Native Village of Ekuk
Ekwok Village
Native Village of Elim
Emmonak Village
Evansville Village (aka Bettles Field)
Native Village of Eyak (Cordova)
Native Village of False Pass
Native Village of Fort Yukon
Native Village of Gakona
Galena Village (aka Louden Village)
Native Village of Gambell
Native Village of Georgetown
Native Village of Goodnews Bay
Organized Village of Grayling (aka Holikachuk)
Gulkana Village
Native Village of Hamilton
Healy Lake Village
Holy Cross Village
Hoonah Indian Association
Native Village of Hooper Bay
Hughes Village
Huslia Village
Hydaburg Cooperative Association
Igiugig Village
Village of Iliamna
Inupiat Community of the Arctic Slope
Iqurmuit Traditional Council (formerly Native Village of Russian Mission)
Ivanoff Bay Village
Kaguyak Village
Organized Village of Kake
Kaktovik Village (aka Barter Island)
Village of Kalskag
Village of Kaltag
Native Village of Kanatak
Native Village of Karluk
Organized Village of Kasaan
Native Village of Kasigluk
Kenaitze Indian Tribe
Ketchikan Indian Corporation
Native Village of Kiana

Agdaagux Tribe of Kind Cove
King Island Native Community
Native Village of Kipnuk
Native Village of Kivalina
Klawock Cooperative Association
Native Village of Kluti Kaah (aka Copper Center)
Knik Tribe
Native Village of Kobuk
Kokhanok Village
New Koliganek Village Council (formerly Koliganek Village)
Native Village of Kongiganak
Village of Kotlik
Native Village of Kotzebue
Native Village of Koyuk
Koyukuk Native Village
Organized Village of Kwethluk
Native Village of Kwigillingok
Native Village of Kwinhagak (aka Quinhagak)
Native Village of Larsen Bay
Levelock Village
Lesnoi Village (aka Woody Island)
Lime Village
Village of Lower Kalskag
Manley Hot Springs Village
Manokotak Village
Native Village of Marshall (aka Fortuna Ledge)
Native Village of Mary's Igloo
McGrath Native Village
Native Village of Mekoryuk
Mentasta Traditional Council (formerly Mentasta Lake Village)
Metlakatla Indian Community, *Annette Island Reserve*
Native Village of Minto
Naknek Native Village
Native Village of Nanwalek (aka English Bay)
Native Village of Napaimute
Native Village of Napakiak
Native Village of Napaskiak
Native Village of Nelson Lagoon
Nenana Native Association
New Stuyahok Village
Newhalen Village
Newtok Village
Native Village of Nightmute
Nikolai Village

Native Village of Nikolski
Ninilchik Village
Native Village of Noatak
Nome Eskimo Community
Nondalton Village
Noorvik Native Community
Northway Village
Native Village of Nuiqsut (aka Nooiksut)
Nulato Village
Nunakauyarmiut Tribe (formerly Native Village of
    Toksook Bay)
Native Village of Nunapitchuk
Village of Ohogamiut
Village of Old Harbor
Orutsararmuit Native Village (aka Bethel)
Oscarville Traditional Village
Native Village of Ouzinkie
Native Village of Paimiut
Pauloff Harbor Village
Pedro Bay Village
Native Village of Perryville
Petersburg Indian Association
Native Village of Pilot Point
Pilot Station Traditional Village
Native Village of Pitkis Point
Platinum Traditional Village
Native Village of Point Hope
Native Village of Point Lay
Native Village of Port Graham
Native Village of Port Heiden
Native Village of Port Lions
Portage Creek Village (aka Ohgsenakale)
Pribilof Islands Aleut Communities of St. Paul &
    St. George Islands
Qagan Tayagungin Tribe of Sand Point Village
Rampart Village
Village of Red Devil
Native Village of Ruby
Village of Salamatoff
Organized Village of Saxman
Native Village of Savoonga
Saint George Island (see Pribilof Islands Aleut Com-
    munities of St. Paul & St. George Islands)
Native Village of Saint Michael
Saint Paul Island (see Pribilof Islands Aleut Commu-
    nities of St. Paul & St. George Islands)

Native Village of Scammon Bay
Native Village of Selawik
Seldovia Village Tribe
Shageluk Native Village
Native Village of Shaktoolik
Native Village of Sheldon's Point
Native Village of Shishmaref
Native Village of Shungnak
Sitka Tribe of Alaska
Skagway Village
Village of Sleetmute
Village of Solomon
South Naknek Village
Stebbins Community Association
Native Village of Stevens
Village of Stony River
Takotna Village
Native Village of Tanacross
Native Village of Tanana
Native Village of Tatitlek
Native Village of Tazlina
Telida Village
Native Village of Teller
Native Village of Tetlin
Central Council of the Tlingit & Haida Indian
    Tribes
Traditional Village of Togiak
Tuluksak Native Community
Native Village of Tuntutuliak
Native Village of Tununak
Twin Hills Village
Native Village of Tyonek
Ugashik Village
Umkumiute Native Village
Native Village of Unalakleet
Qawalangin Tribe of Unalaska
Native Village of Unga
Village of Venetie (see Native Village of Venetie
    Tribal Government)
Native Village of Venetie Tribal Government
    (Arctic Village and Village of Venetie)
Village of Wainwright
Native Village of Wales
Native Village of White Mountain
Wrangell Cooperative Association
Yakutat Tlingit Tribe

Glossary of Key Terms and Concepts

acallas   Girls gifted by *ayllus* to the Sapa Inca line.

adobe pueblos   Multistory houses made of adobe clay (clay and straw baked into hard bricks).

Alcatraz Takeover   The occupation of Alcatraz Island that began in November 1969 and continued for 18 months.

allotment   A piece of land ranging in size from 40 to 160 acres issued to an individual Indian man from territory previously determined tribal property.

Alta California   "Upper California," name for the northern portion of New Spain after the Viceroyalty of New Spain was divided into two provinces.

altepetls   City-states founded by Nahuatl-speakers in the Yucatan.

American Indian Defense Association (AIDA)   Indian advocacy group founded in 1923 by John Collier to fight passage of the Bursum Bill.

American Indian Movement (AIM)   Indian activist organization founded in 1968 in Minnesota that employed confrontational and occasionally violent tactics to challenge government and tribal council policies and to promote the preservation of traditional Indian cultures.

annuity payments   Payments made to chiefs in exchange for their cooperation with the American government.

Apachería   A territory in New Mexico out of which Apaches conducted their trade, diplomacy, and warfare.

Association on American Indian Affairs   A pan-Indian organization that assembled periodically to discuss the direction of federal policies and programs and to advocate Native American perspectives and preferences to political and non-government offices.

ayllu   Inca extended family group in which each member claimed descent from a common ancestor.

Bering land bridge   An ice-free land bridge connecting Siberia and Alaska. According to most scientists, the Americas were first populated by migrants from Asia who used this bridge.

betterment stations   Indian community-based and Indian-directed educational centers designed to provide general education, job skills training, and social skills necessary for transition into mainstream society.

bifaces   Two-sided stone tools.

bigmen   Hopewell elites whose power was based on their control of trade and spiritual life.

Boldt Decision   Court ruling in *United States* v. *Washington* (1974) that upheld Native American fishing rights as provided by treaties.

Bosque Redondo   A reservation in eastern New Mexico to house Navajo and Mescalero Apache in the 1860s.

Bozeman Trail   Overland route running northwest from Fort Laramie into the Powder River country of the Montana Territory.

Brothertown movement   Movement led by Samson Occom and John Johnson with the goal of uniting the Pequots, Narragansetts, Montauks, Niantics, and Mohegans of Connecticut and creating a new homeland in New York.

Burke Act   Congressional legislation passed in 1906 that allowed the Secretary of Indian Affairs to issue an Indian man legal title to his allotment if the Indian were deemed "competent" to handle his own public affairs.

Bursum Bill   A bill presented to Congress in 1923 that intended to legitimize white squatters' rights on Pueblo Indian lands.

cacique   The generic title given by the Spanish to all chiefs in the Southeast.

Caddís   Selected leaders who oversaw villages within the Caddoan confederacy.

Cahob   Mayan kin networks.

calpulli   A district within Tenochtitlán.

camino real   The road and chain of missions that crossed through Florida in the seventeenth century.

Carlisle Indian Industrial School   An off-reservation boarding school founded in 1879 whose program for acculturating Native American children became the model for most Indian boarding schools.

Civilian Conservation Corps—Indian Division (CCC–ID)   A subdivision of the Civilian Conservation Corps, a New Deal agency, that was manned solely by Native Americans for conservation work on Indian reservations.

Century of Dishonor   A book authored by Helen Hunt Jackson and published in 1881 that detailed and condemned the destruction of Native American nations and cultures in North America since the earliest establishment of European settlements.

cenote   A large, round well located near the center of Mayan cities and used for religious ceremonies.

Chimayó Rebellion   1837 uprising against the imposition by the government of Mexico of new taxes on the people of New Mexico.

clans   Groups of families or household who claim descent from a common ancestor.

code talkers   Indians who used their native language to transmit battlefield messages during World War I and World War II.

Columbian Exchange   The exchange of biological material between the Americas and Europe.

Comanchería   The empire of the Comanches located near present-day New Mexico.

Commission on the Organization of the Executive Branch   Also known as the Hoover Commission, the panel was established to consider and recommend tactics to implement a reorganization of the federal branch and reduce federal expenses, in so doing cutting substantially federal appropriations and programs to Native Americans.

Committee of One Hundred   Committee empanelled by Secretary of the Interior Hubert Work to review federal Indian policy, to survey the quality of reservation life nationally, and to offer suggestions for changes in programs for Native Americans.

conquistadors   Spanish professional soldiers who carried out the Spanish conquest of portions of the Americas.

conscientious objector   An individual deferred legally from compulsory military service for his moral or religious opposition to war.

Council of Energy Resource Tribes (CERT)   An organization put together in the 1980s to help energy-rich tribes protect and control their resources.

coureurs de bois   French traders who avoided imperial restrictions on trade and lived among the Indians.

Covenant Chain alliance   An alliance between the Iroquois and the British colonies brokered in the 1670s.

Dawes General Allotment Act   Passed into law in early 1887, the Dawes Act intended to detribalize Native Americans by dividing reservations into individual land allotments and encouraging economic self-sufficiency among Native Americans.

Declaration of Policy   An Indian Office statement that established a commission to determine if an Indian was competent to manage his own public and business affairs and therefore ready to live in white society as a self-sufficient individual.

decolonization Native Peoples' deliberate attempt to create self-sufficient methods to protect themselves and their communities without outside interference.

doctrinas Franciscan friars who established central churches and were responsible for church administration and policy.

Doolittle Report Issued by Senator James Doolittle in 1867, based on travels his commission made across the West, that called for a "civilization program" for Native Americans based on reservations and the transfer of authority for Indian Affairs from the War Department to the Interior Department.

empresarios Americans invited to settle in Texas by the Mexican government.

encomienda Spanish system of labor extraction in which Spanish elites were granted the right to the labor of a certain number of Indians for a certain period of time.

Ex Parte Green A decision rendered in federal district court in 1941 that treaties with Native Americans existed solely at the will of Congress and that the Selective Service Act negated all treaties for the duration of the war.

Fetterman Massacre The annihilation of 80–100 U.S. cavalry soldiers under Captain William Fetterman's command on the Bozeman Trail at the hands of Sioux Indians in December 1866.

filibusters Unofficial invading forces with financial backing from the United States sent to provoke the Seminoles into rebellion.

Five Civilized Nations A term that identified collectively those Native Americans removed to Indian Territory in the 1830s under the federal government's removal policy. The tribes included the Cherokee, Seminole, Chickasaw, Choctaw, and Creek.

"Five Civilized Tribes" The five southern nations seen by white Americans as having acquired the most attributes of civilization. They included the Cherokees, Creeks, Choctaws, Chickasaws, and the Seminoles.

Fort Laramie Treaty Established the Great Sioux Reservation in the western half of the Dakota Territory and guaranteed protected Indian occupancy of the Powder River country.

"frontier exchange economy" The colonial economy of French-occupied colonial Louisiana and surrounding territories that interlocked Native Peoples, a small number of French colonists, and African slaves in face-to-face trade to help sustain individual interests and the interests of the colony and the French overseas empire.

gentiles Serranos who had never been part of the Spanish colonial order.

Ghost Dance A spiritual movement of cultural preservation and rebirth among Native Americans that commenced in 1889, based on a vision of a messianic salvation promoted by the Paiute holy man Wovoka.

glyphic writing Carved or inscribed symbols, in the case of the Maya made up of pictograms.

GOONs Anagram for Guardians of Our Oglala Nation, an auxiliary "police force" founded by Pine Ridge tribal chairman Dick Wilson.

Great Awakening Evangelical Christian movement that swept British North America beginning in the 1730s.

Great Sioux Reservation Established by the Fort Laramie Treaty, the reservation covered the western half of the Dakota Territory—the Black Hills region.

habitants French settlers who farmed in what is present-day Quebec, and also a generic name for the French who settled in Indian country.

hidalgos Spaniards who had received honorary titles of nobility for their service in the Americas.

holatas Timucuan chiefs.

hunter-gatherers Participants in a nomadic lifestyle centered on hunting and the gathering of wild edible plants.

iksas Organized family villages of the Choctaw.

indentured servitude Contractual servitude for a set period time, usually to satisfy a specified debt, used in New England to keep Indian men and women bound to work.

Indian Claims Commission Created by the United States to resolve the financial claims Indian tribes made against the United States.

Indian collectives   A plan by which Indian communities would pool their labor, share costs of production, and divide equally the profits of production.

Indian Education Act   Passed into law in 1972, the act channeled federal dollars into programs to improve the quality of Indian education, training Indians to become classroom teachers and social workers, and developing two-year institutions of higher learning for Native American students.

Indian Loan Act   Congressional legislation that provided Indian access to low interest rate federal loans to supplement the relocation of individuals from reservations to urban communities.

Indian New Deal   The generic term to denote the Roosevelt administration's extension of New Deal services and programs to native peoples.

The Indian Problem   The report of the Committee of One Hundred, delivered to Secretary Work, which recommended a complete overhaul in educational and health care programs provided to Indians by the federal government.

Indian Gaming Regulatory Act   Passed in 1988, IGRA established various layers of rights for native peoples to build casinos on reservation lands.

Indian Relocation Program   A plan pressed by the Bureau of Indian Affairs by which individual Native Americans would leave their reservations for residency in urban communities.

Indian Reorganization Act   The official title given to the Wheeler-Howard bill once passed into law by Congress in June 1934.

Indian Rights Association   Founded in the early 1880s, the association advocated fair treatment of Native Americans, federal protection of Indian rights, and the Indians' full access to the tools suited for acculturation.

Indian Territory   The name given to the expanse of land, essentially present-day Oklahoma, designated by the federal government as a general reservation beyond the range of white settlement for Indian peoples removed from eastern states. Ultimately, more than 25 Indian nations or parts of Indian nations were relocated to Indian Territory.

Indians at Work   A monthly publication issued by the Office of Indian Affairs that informed readers of developments on reservations and Indian wartime activities.

Johnson-O'Malley Act   Congressional legislation that authorized the Secretary of the Interior to provide federal money to state governments to supplement the financial cost of educating Indian children in public schools.

Kahnawake Mohawks   A group of Catholic Mohawks who moved from New York to New France to avoid persecution by fellow Iroquois for their religious beliefs. They played a prominent role in the raid on the town of Deerfield.

katsinas   The gods that Pueblo spiritual specialists called on to return balance and harmony to Pueblo life. Katsinas could also appear in evil forms.

The Kennedy Report   The name given to a report titled Indian Education: A National Tragedy— A National Challenge, which was produced by a congressional investigation committee chaired by Senator Edward Kennedy in 1969.

kivas   Large chambers, usually subterranean, used for religious ceremonies.

kwáans   Subdivisions of the main geographical divisions of the Tlingit. Each kwáan was a community of matrilineal clans with ties to a particular territory.

Lake Mohonk Conference   A series of meetings held each summer throughout the 1880s and attended by educators, policymakers, and social reformers in the Catskill Mountains who ultimately formulated the ideology and political tract for the Americanization of Indians in the United States, resulting in the Dawes General Allotment Act of 1887.

lays   Compensation for participation in a whaling voyage amounting to a set fraction of the total catch.

"Long Knives"   Indian term for colonists and then Americans who were hostile to Indians.

The Long Walk   The movement of thousands of Navajo and Apache from the "four corners" area over hundreds of miles to Bosque Redondo in the mid-1860s. It has been compared to the Cherokee Trail of Tears 30 years earlier.

The Longest Walk   AIM's peaceful demonstration in Washington, D.C., in 1978.

Longhouse religion   Seneca religion based on Handsome Lake's prophetic message.

kuraka   An Inca hereditary chief.

manit   Power provided to Algonquian peoples by manitous. This power was essential to the maintenance of community balance and harmony.

manitous   The spirits that occupied the worlds of the Algonquian-speaking peoples in Virginia and New England.

Medicine Lodge Creek Treaty   Accepted by bands of the Kiowa, Comanche, Southern Cheyenne, Arapaho, and Apache in October 1867, the treaty provided two reservations in western Indian Territory.

Memo 336   A directive from the Selective Service System in 1942 for local draft boards to investigate the racial heritage of registrants to determine the assignment of recruits in racially segregated military units.

métis   Indigenous peoples of both Indian and Euro-American heritage.

matrilineal   Inheritance or determination of ancestry through the female line.

Meriam Report   Formally known as The Problem of Indian Administration, the Meriam Report was an 800-page assessment of the state of Native American life, communities, resources, and policies as they existed in the late 1920s.

Mesoamerica   The region of the Americas that includes central Mexico and most of Central America.

mestizos   Persons of mixed European and Indian ancestry.

micco   The Creek term for chief.

micos   Guale chiefs.

Missouri Compromise of 1820   Act of Congress that established a dividing line between slave and free states.

mit'a   Inca system of labor obligation in which male subjects contributed military service and participation in the construction and maintenance of public buildings and infrastructure.

Moravians   Members of a German Christian sect that was particularly successful in religious outreach to Indians.

mourning wars   The cycle of warfare carried on by the Iroquois sparked by disease, the trade in furs and muskets, and the death of family members.

naborías   A system of labor recruitment in which the Spanish gave the Indians incentives to work in mines or on ranches.

Nanabush   The cosmic trickster in Ottawa oral tradition who could remake the world for the better.

National Council of American Indians (NCAI)   A pan-Indian advocacy organization that surfaced in 1926 following the collapse of the Society of American Indians.

National Congress of American Indians   A pan-Indian organization founded in 1944 to advance and protect Indian rights individually and tribally and to lobby government at all levels on behalf of Native Americans.

National Indian Youth Council   A pan-Indian organization comprised of young college-educated Indians who challenged the National Congress of American Indians for influence in government and in shaping the direction and attitudes in Indian affairs.

Nationality Act   A congressional act in 1940 that clarified the 1924 Citizenship Act and affirmed the citizenship of all Native Americans born within the territorial boundaries of the United States.

Native American Church   Religious organization founded in the early twentieth century that combined Christian and traditional Indian religious beliefs and practices.

Native American Graves Protection and Repatriation Act (NAGPRA)   A bill passed during the administration of George H.W. Bush requiring the immediate return of Indian remains and sacred objects to native communities.

Negro Fort   Defensive structure built between 1814 and 1816 by Africans and Creeks on the Gulf Coast of Florida.

New England town model   Small farming communities with fenced farms and fields and common grounds, led by town patriarchs and centered on the community church.

origin stories   Stories that describe and explain the beginnings of a society or people.

Ozette site   A Makah archaeological site that has provoked controversy among the Makahs about private versus "tribal" property under the rules of NAGPRA.

pan-Indian Movement emphasizing common characteristics, conditions, and goals of all Indian groups.

patriots Colonists in British North America who favored independence during the Revolutionary War.

pays d'en haut The name the French gave to the vast territory stretching around the Great Lakes that was home to Indians forced out of the Northeast by the Iroquois.

peyote Hallucinogen derived from the agave cactus.

pit houses Semi-subterranean dwellings that offered protection from both heat and cold, as well as storage space for food and belongings.

potlatch Festival in which chiefs demonstrated their power and wealth by distributing goods to their followers and allies.

powwas Medicine men who mediated relations between spirits and the Algonquian speakers.

praying town Town established for New England Indians who had converted to Christianity.

Progressives Reformers dedicated to combating the ills of late nineteenth and early twentieth century urban America by working for social and political progress.

promyshlenniki Independent Russian traders who forced the Aleuts to work and hunt for them.

Public Law 280 A congressional act that gave five states full jurisdiction over civil and criminal law for Native Americans in those states.

Pueblo Lands Act, 1924 Established a three-man board to hear and resolve land claims cases between Pueblo Indians and non-Indians.

rancherías The basic social unit among the Indians of the Sonora territory and other mining regions in the Southwest and southern California.

rancherías volantes Small family groups that took flight from missions, ranches, and mines and resettled elsewhere in the Sonora region.

Reconquista The centuries-long struggle by Christians to force the Muslim Moors out of the Iberian Peninsula.

Red Cloud's War Warfare between the U.S. Army and bands of Sioux and Northern Cheyenne in the Powder River country, 1866–1868, considered the only war Native Americans won against the United States.

Red River War U.S. cavalry operations against the Kiowa, Cheyenne, and Comanche in the Texas panhandle and in parts of New Mexico, Colorado, and Kansas in summer 1875 through spring 1875.

Redsticks Term for Creeks who resisted the civilization program of the United States. The term derives from the red clubs such Creeks carried into battle.

reducciones Mission complexes designed to incorporate Indians into the Catholic faith and teach them about Spanish life.

repartimiento A Spanish form of labor tribute in which each mission district was responsible for contributing a certain number of men for a defined amount of time.

reredos Decorated screens placed above churches in Spanish New Mexico.

sachems Elite leaders of the League of the Iroquois, elected to their positions by clan mothers; also the leaders among New England Indians who oversaw sachemships and ruled by persuasion.

sachemships The vast territories in New England overseen, but not owned, by sachems.

"sachem rights" A fraudulent system of land exchange established by English colonists whereby a sachem could sell the lands supposedly under his or her control.

Selective Service Act (1917) Congressional act that established the military draft, or compulsory military service, in the United States.

Sand Creek The site of a Cheyenne-Arapaho encampment in Colorado in 1864 at which the Colorado Militia attacked and killed more than 200 Indians, an event that sparked warfare across the plains.

Selective Service System The agency of the U.S. government charged with the responsibility of raising manpower for the nation's armed forces.

Senate Report 310 (SR 310) A statement introduced into the U.S. Senate in 1943 that called for the end of federal tribal rehabilitation programs and the Indian Reorganization Act, advocating, too, the closure of the Office of Indian Affairs.

Sequoyah's syllabary Sequoyah's set of 86 syllables written in symbols that comprised his written form of Cherokee.

Shawnee Prophet Name for Tenskwatawa, the brother of Tecumseh, after he had a series of prophetic visions.

Society of American Indians (SAI) Progressive pan-Indian association intended to define the future relationship of Native Americans with mainstream society and help direct government policy and programs to advance the Indians' quality of life.

terrace agriculture A form of agriculture in which terraces are cut into hillsides to help capture water runoff and limit soil erosion.

tlatoani Term for a Mexica leader.

totem An object or animal imbued with sacred powers and associated with a particular family, clan, or people.

Totus et al. v. the United States A ruling issued by federal district court in 1941 that held Yakima Indians were obligated to comply with draft registration and compulsory military service, regardless of the Indians' earlier treaty provisions.

Trail of Broken Treaties AIM's cross-country demonstration that concluded in Washington, D.C., with the Indians' occupation of the Bureau of Indian Affairs building in 1972.

"The Trail of Tears" The forced march of 13,000 Cherokees made over 1,000 miles to Oklahoma.

"The Trail of Tourism" The Eastern Band of Cherokee Indians has given this name to one of their main tourist attractions, a series of booths and displays, to attract the attention of white visitors.

Treaty of Greenville (1795) Treaty that was signed following the Battle of Fallen Timbers in which large portions of Ohio were ceded to the United States.

Treaty of Paris 1763 peace agreement that brought the Seven Years' War to a close and left Native Americans along the frontier to deal with the British as the dominant imperial force in North America.

Tsenacommacah The vast territory in Virginia claimed by the Powhatan Confederacy.

usufruct property rights System in which sachems allowed families to grow crops on particular tracts of land and reap the benefits of that land for themselves.

vision quests The ritual seeking of personal connection with the spirit world.

visitas Franciscan friars who traveled from village to village spreading the Catholic message.

Walking Purchase Agreement between the Delawares and the heirs of William Penn that the Delawares would cede as much land as could be "traversed in a day's walk."

wampum Highly prized sacred beads made from quahog clamshells.

War Relocation Authority (WRA) A federal agency created during World War II responsible for the relocation and detention of Japanese Americans for the war's duration.

weroances Village leaders among the Indians of Virginia selected to lead through elite matrilineal lines.

Wheeler-Howard Bill A legislative bill introduced into Congress in 1933 to reorganize the political relationship between Native Americans and the federal government and to revitalize tribal communities and cultures.

White Earth Land Recovery Project (WELRP) Founded by Winona LaDuke, WELRP worked to protect the resources of the White Earth reservation in Wisconsin.

Wounded Knee II The 1973 Indian takeover and occupation of Wounded Knee, South Dakota.

Xinesís High priests among the Caddoans.

zemis Local gods worshipped by the Tainos.

Bibliography

Chapter 1

Bement, Leland C. *Bison Hunting at the Cooper Site: Where Lightning Bolts Drew Thundering Herds*. Norman: University of Oklahoma Press, 1999.

Blog, Stephen. *Ancient Peoples of the American Southwest*. London: Thames & Hudson, 1997.

Bose, David S., James A. Brown, and David W. Penney. *Ancient Art of the American Woodland Indians*. New York: Harry N. Abrams, Inc., 1985.

Fagan, Brian M. *Ancient North America: The Archaeology of a Continent*. London: Thames & Hudson, 2000.

Keyes, James D., and Michael A. Klassen. *Plains Indian Rock Art*. Seattle: University of Washington Press, 2001.

Keyser, James D. *Indian Rock Art of the Columbia Plateau*. Seattle: University of Washington Press, 1992.

Powell, Joseph F. *The First Americans: Race, Evolution, and the Origin of Native Americans*. New York: Cambridge University Press, 2005.

Wallas, James, and Pamela Whitaker. *Kwakiutl Legends*. North Vancouver, BC: Hancock House, 2002.

Whitaker, Pamela. *Kwakiutl Legends*. British Columbia: Hancock Publishers, 1982.

Zolbrod, Paul G. *Diné bahane: The Navajo Creation Story*. Albuquerque: University of New Mexico Press, 1984.

Chapter 2

Axtell, James. *Natives and Newcomers: The Cultural Origins of North America*. New York: Oxford University Press, 2000.

Bauer, Ralph. *An Inca Account of the Conquest of Peru*. Boulder: University of Colorado Press, 2005.

Clendinnen, Inga. *Aztecs: An Interpretation*. New York: Cambridge University Press, 1991.

Diaz, Monica. *To Be Indio in Colonial Spanish America*. Albuquerque: University of New Mexico Press, 2017.

Greenblatt, Stephen. *Marvelous Possessions: The Wonder of the New World*. Chicago: University of Chicago Press, 1991.

Kupperman, Karen Ordahl. *Roanoke: The Abandoned Colony*. New York: Rowan & Littlefield Publishers, 1984.

Lockhard Nahuas, James. *The Nahuas After the Conquest: A Social and Cultural History of the Indians of Central Mexico, Sixteenth Through Eighteenth Centuries*. Stanford, CA: Stanford University Press, 1994.

Miller, Mary, and Karl Taube. *An Illustrated Dictionary of the Gods and Symbols of Ancient Mexico and the Maya*. London: Thames & Hudson, 1993.

Mumford, Jeremy Ravi. *Vertical Empire: The General Resettlement of Indians in the Colonial Andes*. Durham: Duke University Press, 2012.

Powers, Karen Vieira. *Women in the Crucible of Conquest: The Gendered Genesis of Spanish American Society, 1500–1600*. Albuquerque: University of New Mexico Press, 2005.

Quinn, David Beers. *Set Fair for Roanoke: Voyages and Colonies, 1584–1606*. Chapel Hill: University of North Carolina Press, 1985.

Restall, Matthew. *The Maya World: Yucatec Culture and Society, 1550–1850*. Stanford, CA: Stanford University Press, 1994.

———. *Seven Myths of the Spanish Conquest*. New York: Oxford University Press, 2004.

Restall, Matthew, Lisa Sousa, and Kevin Terraciano, eds. *Mesoamerican Voices: Native-Language Writings from Colonial Mexico, Oaxaca, Yucatan, and Guatemala*. New York: Cambridge University Press, 2005.

Rouse, Irving. *The Tainos: Rise and Decline of the People Who Greeted Columbus*. New Haven: Yale University Press, 1992.

Schwartz, Stuart B., ed. *Victors and Vanquished: Spanish and Hahua Views of the Conquest of Mexico*. Boston: Bedford/St. Martin's, 2000.

Silverblatt, Irene. *Moon, Sun, and Witches: Gender and Class in Inca and Colonial Peru.* Princeton, NJ: Princeton University Press, 1987.

Townsend, Camilla. *Malintzin's Choices: An Indian Woman in the Conquest of Mexico.* Albuquerque: University of New Mexico Press, 2006.

Vaughn, Alden. *Transatlantic Encounters: American Indians in Britain, 1500–1776.* New York: Cambridge University Press, 2006.

Chapter 3

Barr, Juliana. *Peace Came in the Form of a Woman: Indians and Spaniards in the Texas Borderlands.* Chapel Hill: University of North Carolina Press, 2007.

Brooks, James F. *Captives and Cousins: Slavery, Kinship, and Community in the Southwest Borderlands.* Chapel Hill: University of North Carolina Press, 2007.

Bushnell, Amy Turner. *Situado and Sabana: Spain's Support System for the Presidio and Mission Provinces of Florida.* Athens: University of Georgia Press, 1995.

Calloway, Colin G. *One Vast Winter Count: The Native American West Before Lewis & Clark.* Lincoln, NE: University of Nebraska Press, 2003.

Galloway, Patricia K., ed. *The Hernando de Soto Expedition: History, Historiography, and Discovery in the Southeast.* Lincoln, NE: University of Nebraska Press, 2006.

Gutierrez, Ramon A. *When Jesus Came, the Corn Mothers Went Away: Marriage, Sexuality, and Power in Colonial New Mexico, 1500–1846.* Stanford, CA: Stanford University Press, 1991.

Hämäläinen, Pekka. *The Comanche Empire.* New Haven: Yale University Press, 2008.

Milanich, Jerald T. *Laboring in the Fields of the Lord: Spanish Missions and Southeastern Indians.* Gainesville: University Press of Florida, 2006.

Radding, Cynthia. *Wandering Peoples: Colonialism, Ethnic Spaces, and Ecological Frontiers in Northwestern Mexico, 1700–1850.* Durham: Duke University Press, 1997.

Chapter 4

Axtell, James. *Beyond 1492: Encounters in Colonial North America.* New York: Oxford University Press, 1992.

Brooks, Lisa. *Our Beloved Kin: A New History of King Philip's War.* New Haven: Yale University Press, 2018.

Cave, Alfred. *Lethal Encounters: Englishmen and Indians in Colonial Virginia.* Lincoln, NE: University of Nebraska Press, 2013.

Cronon, William. *Changes in the Land: Indians, Colonists, and the Ecology of New England.* New York: Hill & Wang, 1983.

DeLucia, Christine M. *Memory Lands: King Philip's War and the Place of Violence in the Northeast.* New Haven: Yale University Press, 2018.

Horn, James. *A Land as God Made It: Jamestown and the Birth of America.* New York: Basic Books, 2005.

Lepore, Jill. *The Name of War: King Philip's War and the Origins of American Identity.* New York: Alfred A. Knopf, 1998.

Mandell, Daniel. *Behind the Frontier: Indians in Eighteenth-Century Eastern Massachusetts.* Lincoln, NE: University of Nebraska Press, 1996.

Pulsipher, Jenny Hale. *Subjects unto the Same King: Indians, English, and the Contest for Authority in Colonial New England.* Philadelphia: University of Pennsylvania Press, 2005.

Silverman, David J. *Faith & Boundaries: Colonists, Christianity, and Community Among the Wampanoag Indians of Marth's Vineyard, 1600–1871.* New York: Cambridge University Press, 2005.

Sleeper-Smith, Susan. *Indian Women and French Men: Rethinking Cultural Encounter in the Western Great Lakes.* Amherst: University of Massachusetts Press, 2001.

Trigger, Bruce G. *The Children of Aataentsic: A History of the Huron People to 1660.* Montreal: McGill-Queen's University Press, 1976.

———. *Natives and Newcomers: Canada's "Heroic Age" Reconsidered.* Montreal: McGill-Queen's University Press, 1985.

Chapter 5

Calloway, Colin G. *The Scratch of a Pen: 1763 and the Transformation of North America.* New York: Oxford University Press, 2006.

Dixon, David. *Never Come to Peace Again: Pontiac's Uprising and the Fate of the British Empire in North America.* Norman: University of Oklahoma Press, 2014.

Dowd, Gregory Evans. *War Under Heaven: Pontiac, the Indian Nations, and the British Empire.* Baltimore: Johns Hopkins University Press, 2004.

DuVal, Kathleen. *The Native Ground: Indians and Colonists in the Heart of the Continent.* Philadelphia: University of Pennsylvania Press, 2006.

Gallay, Alan. *The Indian Slave Trade: The Rise of the English Empire in the American South, 1670–1717.* New Haven: Yale University Press, 2002.

Haefeli, Evan, and Kevin Sweeney. *Captors and Captives: The French and Indian Raid on Deerfield.* Amherst: University of Massachusetts Press, 2003.

Hahn, Steven C. *Invention of the Creek Nation, 1670–1763.* Lincoln, NE: University of Nebraska Press, 2004.

Mandell, Daniel R. *Behind the Frontier: Indians in Eighteenth-Century Eastern Massachusetts.* Lincoln, NE: University of Nebraska Press, 1996.

Merrell, James H. *Into the American Woods: Negotiators on the Pennsylvania Frontier.* New York: W. W. Norton, 1999.

Merritt, Jane T. *At the Crossroads: Indians and Empires on a Mid-Atlantic Frontier, 1700–1763.* Chapel Hill: University of North Carolina Press, 2003.

Oatis, Steven J. *Colonial Complex: South Carolina's Frontiers in the Era of the Yamasee War, 1680–1730.* Lincoln, NE: University of Nebraska Press, 2005.

O'Brien, Jean. *Dispossession by Degrees: Indian Land and Identity in Natick, 1650–1790.* New York: Cambridge University Press, 1997.

Pencack, William, and Daniel K. Richter, eds. *Friends and Enemies in Penn's Woods: Colonists, Indians, and the Racial Construction of Pennsylvania.* Harrisburg: Pennsylvania State University Press, 2004.

Piker, Joshua. *Okfuskee: A Creek Indian Town in Colonial America.* New York: Harvard University Press, 2004.

Silverman, David J. *Faith and Boundaries: Colonists, Christianity, and Community Among the Indians of Martha's Vineyard, 1600–1871.* New York: Cambridge University Press, 2005.

White, Richard. *The Middle Ground: Indians, Empires, and Republics in the Great Lakes Region.* New York: Cambridge University Press, 1991.

Chapter 6

Brooks, James F. *Captives and Cousins: Slavery, Kinship, and Community in the Southwest Borderlands.* Chapel Hill: University of North Carolina Press, 2002.

Dowd, Gregory Evans. *A Spirited Resistance: The North American Indian Struggle for Unity, 1745–1815.* Baltimore: Johns Hopkins University Press, 1992.

Edmunds, R. David. *Tecumseh and the Quest for Indian Leadership.* New York: HarperCollins Publishers, 1984.

Fenn, Elizabeth A. *Pox Americana: The Great Small Pox Epidemic of 1775–1782.* New York: Farrar, Straus, & Giroux, 2002.

Glatthaar, Joseph T., and James Kirby Martin. *Forgotten Allies: The Oneida Indians in the American Revolution.* New York: Hill & Wang, 2006.

Hackel, Steven C. *Children of Coyote, Missionaries of St. Francis: Indian-Spanish Relations in Colonial California, 1769–1850.* Chapel Hill: University of North Carolina Press, 2005.

Horsman, Reginald. *Expansion and American Indian Policy, 1783–1812.* Norman: University of Oklahoma Press, 1992.

Martin, Joel W. Martin. *Sacred Revolt: The Muskogees' Struggle for a New World.* Boston: Beacon Press, 1991.

McConnell, Michael N. *A Country Between: The Upper Ohio Valley and Its Peoples, 1724–1774.* Lincoln, NE: University of Nebraska Press, 1997.

Taylor, Alan. *The Divided Ground: Indians, Settlers, and the Northern Borderlands of the American Revolution.* New York: Alfred A. Knopf, 2006.

Chapter 7

Atkinson, James A. *Splendid Land, Splendid People: The Chickasaw Indians to Removal.* Tuscaloosa: The University of Alabama Press, 2004.

Beck, David R. M. *Siege and Survival: History of the Menominee Indians.* Lincoln, NE: University of Nebraska Press, 2002.

Bowes, John P. *Black Hawk and the War of 1832: Removal in the North.* New York: Chelsea House, 2007.

Champagne, Duane. *Social Order and Political Change: Constitutional Governments Among the Cherokee, the Choctaw, the Chickasaw, and the Creek.* Stanford, CA: Stanford University Press, 1992.

Jackson, Donald P., ed. *Black Hawk: An Autobiography.* Urbana: University of Illinois Press, 1964.

Lancaster, Jane E. *The Seminoles' Struggles to Survive in the West, 1836–1866.* Knoxville: The University of Tennessee Press, 1994.

Loew, Patty. *Indian Nations of Wisconsin: Histories of Endurance and Renewal.* Madison: Wisconsin Historical Society Press, 2001.

Mahon, John K. *History of the Second Seminole War, 1835–1842.* Gainesville: University Press of Florida, 1967.

O'Brien, Greg. *Choctaws in a Revolutionary Age, 1750–1830.* Lincoln, NE: University of Nebraska Press, 2005.

Young, Mary Elizabeth. *Redskins, Ruffleshirts, and Rednecks: Indian Allotments in Alabama and Mississippi.* Norman: University of Oklahoma Press, 1961.

Chapter 8

Brooks, James F. *Captives and Cousins: Slavery, Kinship, and Community in the Southwest Borderlands.* Chapel Hill: University of North Carolina Press, 2002.

Calloway, Colin G. *One Vast Winter Count: The Native American West Before Lewis & Clark.* Lincoln, NE: University of Nebraska Press, 2003.

Cebula, Larry. *Plateau Indians and the Quest for Spiritual Power, 1700–1850.* Lincoln, NE: University of Nebraska Press, 2007.

Gibson, James R. *Otters, Skins, and Boston Ships: The Maritime Fur Trade of the Northwest Coast.* Seattle: Washington University Press, 1999.

Grinev, Andrei Val'terovich. *The Tlingit Indians in Russian America, 1741–1867.* Lincoln, NE: University of Nebraska Press, 2008.

Hackel, Steven C. *Children of Coyote, Missionaries of St. Francis: Indian-Spanish Relations in Colonial California, 1769–1850.* Chapel Hill: University of North Carolina Press, 2005.

Hämäläinen, Pekka. *The Comanche Empire.* New Haven: Yale University Press, 2008.

Judson, Katherine Berry. *Myths and Legends of the Pacific Northwest.* Lincoln, NE: University of Nebraska Press, 1999.

La Vere, David. *The Texas Indians.* College Station: Texas A&M Press, 2004.

Lightfoot, Kent G. *Indians, Missionaries, and Merchants: The Legacy of Colonial Encounters on the California Frontiers.* Oakland: University of California Press, 2006.

Madley, Benjamin. *An American Genocide: The United States and the California Indian Catastrophe, 1846–1873.* New Haven: Yale University Press, 2017.

Rawls, James J. *Indians of California: The Changing Image.* Norman: University of Oklahoma Press, 1986.

Ronda, James P. *Lewis and Clark Among the Indians.* Lincoln, NE: University of Nebraska Press, 2002.

Ruby, Robert H., and John A. Brown. *Chinook Indians.* Norman: University of Oklahoma Press, 1976.

Sandos, James. *Converting California: Indians and Franciscans in the Missions.* New Haven: Yale University Press, 2004.

Smith, F. Todd. *From Dominance to Disappearance: The Indians of Texas and the Near Southwest, 1786–1859.* Lincoln, NE: University of Nebraska Press, 2008.

Wallas, James, and Pamela Whitaker. *Kwakiutl Legends.* New York: Hancock House, 1989.

Wishart, David J. *The Fur Trade of the American West: A Geographical Synthesis.* Lincoln, NE: University of Nebraska Press, 1999.

Chapter 9

Armstrong, William H. *Warrior in Two Camps: Ely S. Parker, Union General and Seneca Chief.* Syracuse, NY: Syracuse University Press, 1990.

Colton, Ray Charles. *The Civil War in the Western Territories: Arizona, Colorado, New Mexico and Utah.* Norman: University of Oklahoma Press, 1984.

Confer, Clarissa W. *The Cherokee Nation in the Civil War.* Norman: University of Oklahoma Press, 2007.

Cox, Hank. *Lincoln and the Sioux Uprising of 1862.* Nashville: Cumberland House Publishing, 2005.

Cunningham, Frank. *General Stand Watie's Confederate Indians.* Norman: University of Oklahoma Press, 1998.

Dunlay, Thomas W. *Kit Carson and the Indians.* Lincoln, NE: Bison Books, 2005.

Gordon-McCutchan, R. C., ed. *Kit Carson: Indian Fighter or Indian Killer?* Niwot: University Press of Colorado, 1996.

Hämäläinen, Pekka. *The Comanche Empire.* New Haven: Yale University Press, 2009.

Hatch, Thom. *The Blue, the Gray, and the Red: Indian Campaigns of the Civil War.* Mechanicsburg, PA: Stackpole, 2003.

Hauptman, Laurence M. *Between Two Fires; American Indians in the Civil War.* New York: Free Press, 1995.

Hoig, Stan. *Sand Creek Massacre.* Norman: University of Oklahoma Press, 1974.

Jackson, Helen Hunt. *A Century of Dishonor: A Sketch of the United States Government's Dealings with Some of the Indian Tribes.* New York: Indian Head Books, 1994.

Kelman, Ari. *A Misplaced Massacre: Struggling Over the Memory of Sand Creek.* Boston: Harvard University Press, 2015.

Nichols, David A. *Lincoln and the Indians: Civil War Policy and Politics.* Urbana: University of Illinois Press, 2000.

Ostler, Jeffrey. *The Plains Sioux and U.S. Colonialism from Lewis and Clark to Wounded Knee.* New York: Cambridge University Press, 2004.

Roessel, Ruth. ed. *Navajo Stories of the Long Walk Period.* Tsaile, AZ: Navajo Community College Press, 1973.

Schultz, Duane. *Over the Earth I Come: The Great Sioux Uprising of 1862.* New York: St. Martins, 1993.

Sides, Hampton. *Blood and Thunder: The Epic Story of Kit Carson and the Conquest of the American West.* New York: Random House, 2007.

Thompson, Gerald. *The Army and the Navajo: The Bosque Redondo Reservation Experiment, 1864–1868.* Tucson: University of Arizona Press, 1976.

Utley, Robert M. *The Indian Frontier of the American West, 1846–1890.* Albuquerque: University of New Mexico Press, 1984.

Weeks, Philip. *Farewell, My Nation: The American Indian and the United States, 1820–1890.* Arlington Heights, IL: Harlan Davidson, Inc., 1990.

West, Elliott. *The Contested Plains: Indians, Gold Seekers, and the Rush to Colorado.* Lawrence: University Press of Kansas, 1998.

Wilson, James. *The Earth Shall Weep: A History of Native America.* New York: Grove Press, 1998.

Chapter 10

Ambrose, Stephan. *Crazy Horse and Custer: The Parallel Lives of Two American Warriors.* New York: Anchor Books, 1996.

Armstrong, William. *Warrior in Two Camps: Ely S. Parker, Union General and Seneca Chief.* Syracuse, NY: University of Syracuse Press, 1990.

Blaine, Martha Royce. *Pawnee Passage: 1870–1875.* Norman: University of Oklahoma Press, 1990.

Bray, Kingsley M. *Crazy Horse: A Lakota Life.* Norman: University of Oklahoma Press, 2008.

Connell, Evan S. *Son of the Morning Star: Custer and the Little Big Horn.* New York: North Point Press, 1997.

Cozzens, Peter. *The Earth Is Weeping: The Epic Story of the Indian Wars for the American West.* New York: Alfred A. Knopf, 2016.

Dippie, Brian W. *The Vanishing American: White Attitudes and United States Indian Policy.* Lawrence: University of Kansas Press, 1991.

Greene, Jerome. *Stricken Field: The Little Big Horn Since 1876.* Norman: University of Oklahoma Press, 2008.

Gwynne, S. C. *Empire of the Summer Moon: Quanah Parker and the Rise and Fall of the Comanches.* New York: Scribner, 2011.

Hardorff, Richard. *The Death of Crazy Horse: A Tragic Episode in Lakota History.* Lincoln, NE: Bison Books, 2001.

Hedren, Paul L. *Powder River: Disastrous Opening of the Great Sioux War.* Norman: University of Oklahoma Press, 2016.

Howard, Oliver, and Duncan McDonald, Chief Joseph. *The Pursuit of the Nez Perce: The Nez Perce War of 1877.* Kooskia, ID: Mountain Meadows Press, 1993.

Larson, Robert. *Gall: Lakota War Chief.* Norman: University of Oklahoma Press, 2009.

Lazarus, Edward. *Black Hills, White Justice: The Sioux Nation Versus the United States, 1775 to the Present.* New York: HarperCollins Publishers, 1991.

Marshall, Joseph. *The Journey of Crazy Horse: A Lakota History.* New York: Penguin Books, 2005.

Murray, Keith. *The Modocs and Their War.* Norman: University of Oklahoma Press, 1984.

Ostler, Jeffrey. *The Plains Sioux and U.S. Colonialism from Lewis and Clark to Wounded Knee.* New York: Cambridge University Press, 2004.

Pennington, Jack. *Battle of Little Big Horn: A Comprehensive Study.* El Segundo, CA: Upton & Sons, 2001.

Sharfstein, Daniel J. *Thunder in the Mountains: Chief Joseph, Oliver Otis Howard, and the Nez Perce War.* New York: W. W. Norton, 2017.

Utley, Robert. *Frontiersmen in Blue: The United States Army and the Indian, 1848–1865.* Lincoln, NE: University of Nebraska Press, 1991.

———. *The Indian Frontier of the American West, 1848–1890.* Albuquerque: University of New Mexico Press, 1984.

West, Elliott. *The Contested Plains: Indians, Gold Seekers, and the Rush to Colorado.* Lawrence: University of Kansas Press, 2000.

Reclamations. Lincoln, NE: University of Nebraska Press, 2016.

Fritz, Henry E. *The Movement for Indian Assimilation, 1860–1890.* Philadelphia: University of Pennsylvania Press, 1965.

Greene, Jerome A. *American Carnage: Wounded Knee, 1890.* Norman: University of Oklahoma Press, 2016.

Hittman, Michael. *Wavoka and the Ghost Dance.* Lincoln, NE: University of Nebraska Press, 1997.

Kasson, Joy S. *Buffalo Bill's Wild West: Celebrity, Memory, and Popular History.* New York: Hill & Wang, 2000.

Kraft, Loius. *Gatewood and Geronimo.* Albuquerque: University of New Mexico Press, 2000.

Prucha, Francis Paul. *Americanizing the American Indian: Writings by the "Friends of the Indians," 1880–1900.* Boston: Harvard University Press, 1973.

———. *The Churches and the Indian School, 1888–1912.* Lincoln, NE: University of Nebraska Press, 1979.

Smoak, Gregory E. *Ghost Dance and Identity: Prophetic Religion and American Indian Ethnogenesis in the Nineteenth Century.* Berkeley: University of California Press, 2006.

Trafzer, Clifford E. *Boarding School Blues: Revisiting American Indian Educational Experiences.* Lincoln, NE: University of Nebraska Press, 2006.

Utley, Robert M. *The Lance and the Shield: The Life and Times of Sitting Bull.* New York: Henry Holt, 1993.

Vuckovic, Myriam. *Voices from Haskell: Indian Students Between Two Worlds, 1884–1928.* Lawrence: University Press of Kansas, 2008.

Warren, Louis S. *God's Red Son: The Ghost Dance Religion and the Making of Modern America.* New York: Basic Books, 2017.

Young, William A. *Quest for Harmony: Native American Spiritual Traditions.* New York: Seven Bridges Press, 2002.

Chapter 11

Adams, David Wallace. *Education for Extinction.* Lawrence: University of Kansas Press, 1995.

Carlson, Leonard. *Indians, Bureaucrats and Land: The Dawes Act and the Decline of Indian Farming.* Westport, CT: Greenwood Press, 1981.

Chamberlain, Kathleen. *Victorio: Apache Warrior and Chief.* Norman: University of Oklahoma Press, 2007.

Child, Brenda. *Boarding School Seasons.* Lincoln, NE: University of Nebraska Press, 1998.

Coleman, William S. E. *Voices of Wounded Knee.* Lincoln, NE: University of Nebraska Press, 2000.

Faulk, Odie. *The Geronimo Campaign.* New York: Oxford University Press, 1993.

Fear-Segal, Jacqueline, and Susan D. Rose. *Carlisle Indian Industrial School: Indigenous Histories, Memories, and*

Chapter 12

Adams, David Wallace. *Education for Extinction: American Indians and the Boarding School Experiment, 1875–1928.* Lawrence: University of Kansas Press, 1997.

Britten, Thomas A. *American Indians in World War I: At Home and at War.* Albuquerque: University of New Mexico Press, 1997.

Crawford, Bill. *All American: The Rise and Fall of Jim Thorpe.* New York: John Wiley & Sons, 2004.

Fixico, Donald. *Daily Life of Native Americans in the Twentieth Century.* Westport, CT: Greenwood Press, 2006.

Hauptman, Laurence. *The Oneida Indians in the Age of Allotment, 1860–1920.* Norman: University of Oklahoma Press, 2006.

Hertzberg, Hazel W. *The Search for an American Indian Identity: Modern Pan-Indian Movements.* Syracuse, NY: Syracuse University Press, 1971.

Holm, Tom. *The Great Confusion in Indian Affairs: Native Americans and Whites in the Progressive Era*. Austin: University of Texas Press, 2005.

Hoxie, Frederick, ed. *Talking Back to Civilization: Indian Voices from the Progressive Era*. New York: Bedford-St. Martin, 2001.

Maddox, Lucy. *Citizen Indians: Native American Intellectuals, Race, and Reform*. Ithaca, NY: Cornell University Press, 2005.

Maroukis, Thomas C. *The Peyote Road: Religious Freedom and the Native American Church*. Norman: University of Oklahoma Press, 2010.

Meadows, William. "The Origins of Native American Code Talking." In *Comanche Code Talkers of World War II*. Austin: University of Texas Press, 2002.

Nabokov, Peter. "A Twentieth Century Indian Voice." In *Native American Testimony: A Chronicle of Indian-White Relations from Prophecy to the Present, 1492–2000*, edited by Peter Nabokov. New York: Penguin Books, 1999.

Stewart, Omer C. *Peyote Religion: A History*. Norman: University of Oklahoma Press, 1993.

Welch, Deborah. "Gertrude Simmons Bonnin (Zitkala-Sa)." In *The New Warriors: Native American Leaders Since 1900*, edited by R. David Edmunds. Lincoln, NE: University of Nebraska Press, 2001.

Zitkala-Sa. *American Indian Stories, Legends, and Other Writings*. New York: Penguin Books, 2003.

Chapter 13

Adams, David W. *Education for Extinction: American Indians and the Boarding School Experience, 1875–1928*. Lawrence: University of Kansas Press, 1997.

Aleiss, Angela. *Making the White Man's Indian: Native Americans and Hollywood Movies*. Westport, CT: Praeger, 2005.

Burke, Flannery. *From Greenwich Village to Taos: Primitivism and Place at Mabel Dodge Luhan's*. Lawrence: University Press of Kansas, 2008.

Child, Brenda. *Boarding School Seasons: American Indian Families, 1900–1940*. Lincoln, NE: University of Nebraska Press, 2000.

Cobb-Greetham, Amanda. *Listening to Our Grandmothers' Stories: The Bloomfield Academy for Chickasaw Females, 1952–1949*. Lincoln, NE: Bison Books, 2005.

Debo, Angie. *And Still the Waters Run: The Betrayal of the Five Civilized Tribes*. Princeton, NJ: Princeton University Press, 1973. (Originally published in 1940).

Fey, Harold E., and D'Arcy McNickle. *Indians and Other Americans: Two Ways of Life Meet*. New York: Harper & Row, 1970.

Grann, David. *Killers of the Flower Moon: The Osage Murders and the Birth of the FBI*. New York: Doubleday, 2017.

Hoxie, Frederick. *A Final Promise: The Campaign to Assimilate the Indians, 1880–1920*. Lincoln, NE: University of Nebraska Press, 2001.

Krouse, Susan Applegate. *North American Indians in the Great War*. Lincoln, NE: University of Nebraska Press, 2007.

Lewis, David Rich. *Neither Wolf Nor Dog: American Indians, Environment, and Agrarian Change*. New York: Oxford University Press, 1994.

Lomawaima, K. Tsianina. *They Called It Prairie Light: The Story of Chilocco Indian School*. Norman: University of Nebraska Press, 1995.

Matthews, John Joseph. *Sundown*. Norman: University of Oklahoma Press, 1988.

McAulife, Dennis. *Bloodland: A Family Story of Oil, Greed, and Murder on the Osage Reservation*. Tulsa, OK: Council Oak Books, 1999.

Oakley, Christopher A. *Keeping the Circle: American Indian Identity in Eastern North Carolina, 1885–2004*. Lincoln, NE: University of Nebraska Press, 2005.

Olson, James, and Raymond Wilson. "Native American Reaction and the Seeds of Reform." In *Native Americans in the Twentieth Century*. Urbana: University of Illinois Press, 1986.

Parman, Donald. "From War to Depression." In *Indians and the American West in the Twentieth Century*. Bloomington: Indiana University Press, 1994.

Riney, Scott. *The Rapid City Indian School, 1898–1933*. Norman: University of Oklahoma Press, 1999.

Vuckovic, Myriam. *Voices from Haskell: Indian Students Between Two World Wars, 1884–1928*. Lawrence: University Press of Kansas, 2008.

Wenger, Tisa. *We Have a Religion: The 1920s Pueblo Indian Dance Controversy and American Religious Freedom*. Chapel Hill: University of North Carolina Press, 2009.

White, Richard D., Jr. *Will Rogers: A Political Life*. Lubbock, TX: Texas Tech University Press, 2011.

Yagoda, Ben. *Will Rogers: A Biography*. Norman: University of Oklahoma Press, 2000.

Chapter 14

Bilosi, Thomas. *Organizing the Lakota: The Political Economy of the New Deal on the Pine Ridge and Rosebud Reservations*. Tucson: University of Arizona Press, 1992.

Collier, John. *From Every Zenith: A Memoir and Some Essays on Life and Thought*. Denver, CO: Sage Books, 1963.

———. *The Indians of the Americas*. New York: W. W. Norton, 1947.

Cowger, Thomas. *The National Congress of American Indians: The Founding Years*. Lincoln, NE: University of Nebraska Press, 1999.

Daily, David W. *Battle for the BIA: G. E. E. Lindquist and the Missionary Crusade Against John Collier*. Tucson: University of Arizona Press, 2004.

Deloria, Vine. *The Indian Reorganization Act: Congresses and Bills*. Norman: University of Oklahoma Press, 2002.

Fey, Harold E., and D'Arcy McNickle. *Indians and Other Americans: Two Ways of Life Meet*. New York: Harper & Row, 1970.

Fowler, Loretta. *Arapahoe Politics: 1851–1978*. Lincoln, NE: University of Nebraska Press, 1982.

Graymont, Barbara, ed. *Fighting Tuscarora: The Autobiography of Chief Clinton Rickard*. Syracuse, NY: Syracuse University Press, 1973.

Hauptman, Laurence M. "The American Indian Federation and the Indian New Deal: A Reinterpretation." *Pacific Historical Review* 52 (November 1983).

———. *The Iroquois and the New Deal*. Syracuse, NY: Syracuse University Press, 1999.

Hoefer, Jacqueline. *A More Abundant Life: New Deal Artists and Public Art in New Mexico*. Santa Fe: Sunstone Press, 2003.

Hoxie, Frederick. *Parading Through History: The Making of the Crow Nation in America, 1802–1935*. New York: Cambridge University Press, 2008.

Iverson, Peter. *Dine: A History of the Navajos*. Albuquerque: University of New Mexico Press, 2002.

Littlefield, Alice, and Martha C. Knack, eds. *Native Americans and Wage Labor: Ethnohistorical Perspectives*. Norman: University of Oklahoma Press, 1996.

Lomowaima, K. Tsianina. *They Called It Prairie Light: The Story of Chilocco Indian School*. Lincoln, NE: University of Nebraska Press, 1995.

McNickle, D'Arcy. *Native American Tribalism: Indian Survivals and Renewals*. New York: Oxford University Press, 1973.

O'Neill, Colleen. *Working the Navajo Way: Labor and Cure in the Twentieth Century*. Lawrence: University Press of Kansas, 2005.

Oakley, Christopher. *Keeping the Circle: American Indian Identity in Eastern North Carolina, 1885–2004*. Lincoln, NE: University of Nebraska Press, 2005.

Reyhner, Jon, and Jeanne Eder. *American Indian Education*. Norman: University of Oklahoma Press, 2006.

Schrader, Robert. *The Indian Arts and Crafts Board: An Aspect of New Deal Indian Policy*. Albuquerque: University of New Mexico Press, 1983.

Szasz, Margaret Connell. *Education and the American Indian: The Road to Self-Determination, 1928–1998*. Albuquerque: University of New Mexico Press, 1999.

———. *Between Indian and White Worlds: The Cultural Broker*. Norman: University of Oklahoma Press, 2001.

Taylor, Graham D. *The New Deal and American Indian Tribalism: The Administration of the Indian Reorganization Act, 1934–1945*. Lincoln, NE: University of Nebraska Press, 1973.

Weeks, Charles. "The Eastern Cherokee and the New Deal." *North Carolina Historical Review* 53 (July 1976).

Wunder, John R. "Native Americans and Constitutionalism." In *Retained by the People: A History of American Indians and the Bill of Rights*. New York: Oxford University Press, 1994.

Chapter 15

Akweks, Aren. *Six Nations Iroquois Confederacy Record (World War II)*. Hogansburg, NY: Akwesasne Mohawk Counselor Organization, 1946.

Bixler, Margaret. *Winds of Freedom: The Story of the Navajo Code Talkers of World War II*. Darien, CT: Two Bytes Press, 1992.

Bradley, James, and Ron Powers. *Flags of Our Fathers*. New York: Bantam Press, 2006.

Collier, John. "The Indian in a Wartime Nation." *The Annals of the American Academy* 223 (1942): 310–34.

Cowger, Thomas W. *The National Congress of American Indians: The Founding Years*. Lincoln, NE: University of Nebraska Press, 2001.

Franco, Jere. *Crossing the Pond: The Native American Effort in World War II*. Austin: University of Texas Press, 1999.

Golodoff, Nick. *Attu Boy: A Young Alaskan's World War II Memoir*. Anchorage: University of Alaska Press, 2015.

Gouveia, Mary. " 'We Also Serve': American Indian Women's Role in World War II." *Michigan Historical Review* 20 (Fall 1944): 153082.

Graymont, Barbara, ed. *Fighting Tuscarora: The Autobiography of Chief Clinton Rickard*. Syracuse, NY: Syracuse University Press, 1973.

Greenberg, Henry, and Georgia Greenberg, eds. *Carl Gorman's World*. Albuquerque: University of New Mexico Press, 1984.

Hauptman, Laurence M. *The Iroquois Struggle for Survival: World War II to Red Power*. Syracuse, NY: University of Syracuse Press, 1986.

Johnson, Broderick, ed. *Navajos and World War II*. Tsaile, AZ: Navajo Community College Press, 1978.

Kirtland, John C. *The Relocation and Internment of the Aleut People During World War II: A Case in Law and Equity for Compensation*. Anchorage: Aleut-Pribilof Islands Association, 1981.

Kohlhoff, Dean. *When the Wind Was a River: Aleut Evacuation in World War II*. Seattle: University of Washington Press, 1995.

Meadows, William. *Comanche Code Talkers of World War II*. Austin: University of Texas Press, 2002.

Nez, Chester, and Judith Schiess Avila. *Code Talker: Memoir of WWII Navajo Marine Chester Nez*. New York: Berkley, 2011.

Takaki, Ronald. *Double Victory: A Multicultural History of America in World War II*. New York: Back Bay Books, 2001.

Townsend, Kenneth. *World War II and the American Indian*. Albuquerque: University of New Mexico Press, 2000.

Westerlund, John S. *Arizona's War Town: Flagstaff, Navajo Ordnance Depot, and World War II*. Tucson: University of Arizona Press, 2003.

1934–1945. Lincoln, NE: University of Nebraska Press, 1980.

Valandra, Edward Charles. *Not Without Our Consent: Lakota Resistance to Termination, 1950–1959*. Urbana: University of Illinois Press, 2006.

Chapter 16

Aquila, Richard, ed. *Wanted Dead or Alive: The American West in Popular Culture*. Urbana: University of Illinois Press, 1996.

Biskind, Peter. "Cochise, Si! Geronimo, No!" In *Seeing Is Believing: How Hollywood Taught Us to Stop Worrying and Love the Fifties*. New York: Henry Holt & Co., 2000.

Cobb, Daniel. *Native Activism in Cold War America: The Struggle for Sovereignty*. Lawrence: University of Kansas Press, 2008.

Cowger, Thomas W. *The National Congress of American Indians: The Founding Years*. Lincoln, NE: University of Nebraska Press, 1999.

Fixico, Donald. *The Urban Indian Experience in America*. Albuquerque: University of New Mexico Press, 2000.

Grounds, Richard, George Tinker, and David Wilkins, eds. *Native Voices: American Indian Identity and Resistance*. Lawrence: University of Kansas Press, 2003.

Hauptman, Laurence. *The Iroquois Struggle for Survival: From World War II to Red Power*. Syracuse, NY: Syracuse University Press, 1986.

LaGrand, James B. *Indian Metropolis: Native Americans in Chicago, 1945–1975*. Urbana: University of Illinois Press, 2002.

Lawson, Michael. *Dammed Indians: The Pick-Sloan Plan and the Missouri River Sioux*. Norman: University of Oklahoma Press, 1982.

Lenihan, John H. *Showdown: Confronting Modern America in the Western Film*. Urbana: University of Illinois Press, 1985.

Lobo, Susan. *American Indians and the Urban Experience*. Lanham, MD: AltaMira Press, 2001.

Metcalf, R. Warren. *Termination's Legacy: The Discarded Indians of Utah*. Lincoln, NE: University of Nebraska Press, 2007.

Parman, Donald. *Indians and the American West in the Twentieth Century*. Bloomington: Indiana University Press, 1994.

Peroff, Nicholas. *Menominee Drums: Tribal Termination and Restoration, 1954–1974*. Norman: University of Oklahoma Press, 1982.

Philp, Kenneth R. *Termination Revisited: American Indians on the Trail to Self-Determination, 1933–1953*. Lincoln, NE: University of Nebraska Press, 1999.

Shreve, Bradley G. *Red Power Rising: The National Indian Youth Council and the Origins of Native Activism*. Norman: University of Oklahoma Press, 2014.

Szasz, Margaret Connell. *Education and the American Indian: The Road to Self-Determination, 1928–1973*. Albuquerque: University of New Mexico Press, 1974.

Taylor, Graham D. *The New Deal and American Indian Tribalism: The Administration of the Indian Reorganization Act,*

Chapter 17

Banks, Dennis, and Richard Erdoes. *Ojibwa Warrior: Dennis Banks and the Rise of the American Indian Movement*. Norman: University of Oklahoma Press, 2005.

Bordewich, Fergus M. *Killing the White Man's Indian: Reinventing Native Americans at the End of the Twentieth Century*. New York: Anchor Books, 1996.

Cobb, Daniel, and Loretta Fowler, eds. *Beyond Red Power: American Indian Politics and Activism Since 1900*. Santa Fe: School for Advanced Research, 2007.

Crow Dog, Mary. *Lakota Woman*. New York: Harper Perennial, 1991.

Deloria, Vine, Jr. *Behind the Trail of Broken Treaties: An Indian Declaration of Independence*. New York: Dell Publishing, 1974.

———. *God Is Red: A Native View of Religion*. Golden, CO: North American Press, 1994. (Originally published in 1972).

———. *We Talk, You Listen: New Tribes, New Turf*. Lincoln, NE: University of Nebraska Press, 2007. (Originally published in 1970).

Edmunds, David, ed. *The New Warriors: Native American Leaders Since 1900*. Lincoln, NE: University of Nebraska Press, 2001.

Fixico, Donald L. *The American Indian Mind in a Linear World: American Indian Studies and Traditional Knowledge*. New York: Routledge, 2003.

Fortunate Eagle, Adam, and Tim Findley. *Heart of the Rock: The Indian Invasion of Alcatraz*. Norman: University of Oklahoma Press, 2002.

Holm, Tom. *Strong Hearts, Wounded Souls: Native American Veterans of the Vietnam War*. Austin: University of Texas Press, 1996.

Jenkins, Philip. *Dream Catchers: How Mainstream America Discovered Native Spirituality*. New York: Oxford University Press, 2004.

Johnson, Troy, and Donald Fixico. *The American Indian Occupation of Alcatraz Island: Red Power and Self-Determination*. Lincoln, NE: University of Nebraska Press, 2008.

Josephy, Alvin. *Now That the Buffalo's Gone: A Study of Today's American Indians*. Norman: University of Oklahoma Press, 1984.

Kipp, Woody. *Viet Cong at Wounded Knee: The Trail of a Blackfeet Activist*. Lincoln, NE: University of Nebraska Press, 2008.

Krause, Susan Applegate, and Heather A. Howard, eds. *Keeping the Campfires Going: Native Women's Activism in Urban Communities*. Lincoln, NE: University of Nebraska Press, 2009.

LaGrand, James B. *Indian Metropolis: Native Americans in Chicago, 1945–1975*. Urbana: University of Illinois Press, 2002.

Lobo, Susan, and Kurt Peters, eds. *American Indians and the Urban Experience*. New York: Rowman & Littlefield, 2001.

Lobo, Susan, Steve Talbot, and Traci Morris. *Native American Voices: A Reader*. New York: Prentice Hall, 2010.

Mihesuah, Devon A. *American Indians: Stereotypes and Realities*. Atlanta, GA: Clarity Press, 2009.

Nagel, Joane. *American Indian Ethnic Renewal: Red Power and the Resurgence of Identity and Culture*. New York: Oxford University Press, 1997.

Owings, Alison. *Indian Voices: Listening to Native Americans*. New Brunswick, NJ: Rutgers University Press, 2011.

Reyes, Lawney L. *Bernie Whitebear: An Urban Indian's Quest for Justice*. Tempe: University of Arizona Press, 2006.

Reyhner, Jon A. *American Indian Education: A History*. Norman: University of Oklahoma Press, 2006.

Sayer, John William. *Ghost Dancing the Law: The Wounded Knee Trials*. Boston: Harvard University Press, 2000.

Szasz, Margaret Connell. *Education and the American Indian: The Road to Self-Determination, 1928–1998*. Albuquerque: University of New Mexico Press, 1999.

Chapter 18

Bordewich, Fergus M. *Killing the White Man's Indian: Reinventing of Native Americans at the End of the Twentieth Century*. New York: Doubleday, 1996.

Castile, George Pierre. *Taking Charge: Native American Self-Determination and Federal Indian Policy, 1975–1993*. Tucson: University of Arizona Press, 2006.

Cobb, Daniel M., and Loretta Fowler, eds. *Beyond Red Power: American Indian Politics and Activism Since 1900*. Santa Fe: School for Advanced Research, 2007.

Darian-Smith, Eve. *New Capitalists: Law, Politics, and Identity Surrounding Casino Gaming on Native American Land*. Belmont, CA: Wadsworth/Thomson Learning, 2004.

Frantz, Klaus. *Indian Reservations in the United States: Territory, Sovereignty, and Socioeconomic Change*. Chicago: The University of Chicago Press, 1999.

Lobo, Susan, and Kurt Peters, eds. *American Indians and the Urban Experience*. Lanham, MD: AltaMira Press, 2001.

Mason, W. Dale. *Gaming: Indian Tribal Sovereignty and American Politics*. Norman: University of Oklahoma Press, 2000.

Mihesuah, Devon Abbott. *Indigenous American Women: Decolonization, Empowerment, and Activism*. Lincoln, NE: University of Nebraska Press, 2003.

Mihesuah, Devon Abbott, and Angela Cavender Wilson, eds. *Indigenizing the Academy: Transforming Scholarship and Empowering Communities*. Lincoln, NE: University of Nebraska Press, 2004.

Rushing, W. Jackson, III, ed. *Native American Art in the Twentieth Century*. New York: Routledge, 1999.

Wilson, Waziyatawin Angela, and Michael Yellow Bird, eds. *For Indigenous Eyes Only: A Decolonization Handbook*. Santa Fe: School of American Research, 2005.

Index

1912 Summer Olympics, Stockholm, Sweden **379**, 383
1968 Democratic National Convention protests 560

Abenakis 56, **61**, 107, **113**, 119, 132–3
accommodation 30, 32, 76, 97, 103, 122, 126, 204, 290, 295
acculturation 111, 113, 117, 121, 137, 166, 189, 202–6, 216–17, 234, 237–9, 267, 296, 315, 324–9, 331, 347, 349, 357, 360–1, 378, 380–2, 384–5, 390–2, 399–400, 418, 429, 438, 449, 451–2, 457, 462, 465, 481, 509, 511–12, 516, 520–5, 531, 534, 538–40, 558, 573–4; by immersion 368; of immigrants 379–80; passive resistance to 318; vs. segregation 390
Achelacy 57
Acoma Indians 14, 80–2; origin story of 80–2
Acoma Pueblo 601
Act for Government Protection of the Indians **270**
Act for the Government and Protection of the Indians (1850) 269
Adair, John 517
Adams, Brooks 348
Adams, Hank (Sioux/Assiniboine) 547
Adams, John Quincy 207, 212–13
Adams-Onís Treaty (1819) **200**, 220

adaptation 134
Adena culture **4**, 20, **23**
Adobe Walls attack 330–1
Affordable Care Act (ACA) ("Obamacare") 604–5, 613
Afghanistan: war in 602
African slaves 106, 120, 148–9, 151, 153, 182, 204, 206, 217, 222, 238, 273–4, 281–2
Agreda, María de Jesús de ("Lady in Blue") 79
Agricultural Adjustment Act (AAA) 452
agriculture in North America **4**, 10–11, 13, **13**, 14–15, 17, 20, 33, 38, 76, 88, 92, 182, 185, 202, 206, 239, 256, 261, 323, 330, 349, 363, **387**, 416, 439, 501, 512, 528; floodplain 14; in Mesoamerica 38; terrace 38
Air Pollution Control Act (1955) 606
Alabama 21, 76, 146–7, 151–3, 175, 179, 189–90, **200**, 201–2, 206, 212–13, 216–17, **218**, 220, 272, 396, 527
Alabama River 152–3, 189
Alabama-Coushattas 272
Alabamas 151
Alaska 4, 6, **10**, 254–5, 464, 501–2, **568**, **581**, 585, 612–13; Sitka 255, 258; Ketchikan *242–3*
Alaska Native Claims Commission Act (1988) **581**
Alaska Native Claims Settlement Act (1971) **568**

Alaska Native Claims Settlement Act (1988) 585
Alaskan natives 501
Albuquerque Indian School 460
alcaldes 194
Alcatraz Island: occupation by Native Americans *542–3*, **545**, 549–53, *550*, 555–6, **558**, 565, 567, 598
alcoholism 114, 156, 186, 231, 234, 379, 399, 531, 560, 570, 572, 598
Aleutian Islands 254–5, 501
Aleuts 254–6, 258, **259**; held as POWs by Japan 502; moved to relocation centers 502
Alger, Horatio 390
Algonkins 115, 132
Algonquian language 56, 91, 106, 109, 111, 115–17, 119, 122, 144, 230; dialects 141, 143
Algonquians 56–7, 59–60, *59*, **61**, 97–8, 100–1, 107, 110, 130, 132, 154, 173; coastal 109; trade networks 55
Allegany Senecas 183–4
Allegheny River 182
Alliance of Colonial-Era Tribes 609
Allies, the 495, 509
allotment policy/system 385, **387**, 392, 406, *416*, 417–18, 439, 445, 465, 589
allotment sales 453

Alta California 164, **165**, 192–5, **193**, **244**, 255–6, 263–7; Colonization Act (1824) 266; Decree of Emancipation 264–5; Franciscan mission system in 164, 192–5, **193**; *rancherías* 267; *ranchos* 266–7, *266*; Secularization Act (1834) 266; tribal groupings in 265

Alturas 465

Alvarado, Pedro de 47

Amazon Indians 8

American Board of Commissioners for Foreign Missions (ABCFM) 205, 208, 215, **244**, 261; on Columbia Plateau **244**; missionaries of 210

American century 357, 379

American citizenship 487; *see also* U.S. citizenship

American colonialism 598

American Confederation 178

American Dream 469

American empire 348

American expansionism/expansionists 67, 166, 244–5, 261–3, 271

American Expeditionary Force (AEF) **379**, 400, 404; arrival in France **379**

American identity 414

American Indian and Alaskan Native (AIAN) 612–13

American Indian Citizenship Act (1919) **435**

American Indian Defense Association (AIDA) **412**, 424, 428, 430, 432–5, 452

American Indian Federation (AIF) **444**, 469–71, **478**, 480

American Indian Fort Lawton Occupation Force 544

American Indian Historical Society 465

American Indian Movement (AIM) **545**, 548, 552, 554–5, *557*, 557–65, **558**, *563*, **566**, 573, 575, 596; Twenty Points 560, 562

American Indian racial classification in armed forces **478**

American Indian Religious Freedom Act (AIRFA) (1978) 529, **545**, 565, **568**, 600

American Legion 420

American market economy 268

American national identity 360

American Recovery and Reinvestment Act (2009) 603

American Red Cross (ARC) 404–5, 450, 499

American Revolution *see* American Revolutionary War

American Revolutionary War 164, 166–71, 173–4, 177–8, 184

American River 267

American Trade Company 260

Americanization of Indians 399, 431

Americanization program 348–9, 357, 359–60, 363–4, 366–7, 373, 430, 452, 469, 574; and allotment program 360–5, 373; citizenship as part of 373; conversion to Christianity as part of 366–7, 373; education as part of 367–8, 373; Indian boarding schools 368–70, 370; detribalization as part of 367

Americans for Indian Opportunity 529, *582*

Amherst, Sir Jeffery 156

Anasazi peoples 15, 17; tradition 80

ancestors' remains, repatriation of 581, 593–5, 614; "500-year-old rule" 595

Andele (Jose Andrés Martínez) 273, 275

Andes Mountains 42–3, 60

Andros, Edmund 119, 122–3, 125

Anglican Church 104

Anglicanism 60, 103, 167

Anglo-Virginians 101–3

Anishinaabe 556

Anishinaable Indians 549

Anishinabes 234

annuity chiefs 181, 187

annuity payments 203–4, 219, 226, 236–7, 284–5, 291, 295, 307, 315, 318

anti-Bolshevik hysteria 414

Antiquarian Act (1906) **387**

anti-war movement 545–6, 575

Apaches **66**, 79–80, 85, 89–92, **91**, 190–1, 247, 263, 275, 277, 298, 304, 323, 326, **338**, **346**, 349–51, *442–3*, 390–1, *500*, 538, **539**, 588, 591; as horseback culture 80; Jicarilla 91; Lipans 91; Mescaleros 91; Pelones 91

Apalachees 69, 70–5, 72, 150

Apalachicola Bay 220

Apalachicolas 151

Apess, William 231

Appalachian Mountains 69, 76, 157, 166, 431

Appamattucks 105

Appomattox Courthouse 288

Arapaho reservation 366

Arapahos 246, 247, 248, **283**, 301–7, **312**, 318, 321, 323–6, *324*, 332–4, **338**, 384, 391, 464–5, 465, 471, 588

Archambault, Dave, II 607–8

Arctic Ocean 245

Arendarhonon 114, 116–17

Arikaras 14, 243, 246, 247, 248–9, **253**, 259, 318, 400, 534

Arizona 8, 14, 17, 67, 80, 83, 87, 274, 296–7, **346**, 349, 351, 353, **412**, 419, **436**, **466**, 480–1, 488–9, 492, 497, 501, *500*, **508**, 512–13, 515, 517, 521, 531, 552, **572**, 583–5, 610; Flagstaff 584; Phoenix 493

Arkansas 19, 77, 201–2, 215, 217, 234, 236–7, 272, 276, **283**, 285, 287–8, 301, 236

Arkansas River 77, 148, 237–8, 301, 303

Arlington National Cemetery 491–2, 606

Army Corps of Engineers 534, 595, 608

Army National Guard 477

arrowhead symbol 497

Articles of Confederation 178

Asia 6, 32–3, 56, 58, 322, 509, 535, 564

assimilation 202, 205, 296, 326, 329, 331, 341, 357, 360, 380–2, 384–6, 388, 390–3, 398–400, 405–6, 417–19, 428, 430, 432–4, 438–9, 449, 451–2, 461–2, 464–5, 469–71, 473, 482, 488, 504, 510–11, 521, 523, 525, 530, 534, 538, 540, 544, 551, 558, 574, 600; alternative to 388; and immersion 390; of immigrants 380, 382, 385; vs. segregation 390

Assiniboines 10, 246, 247, 248–9, 547

Assistant Secretary for Indian Affairs 529

Associated Press 383

Association of American Indian Affairs (AAIA) **508**, 511–12, 517; *The American Indian* **508**, 511

Astor, John Jacob 259–60

Ataronchronon 114

Athabaskan language 14

Athapascan territory 90
Athapaskans 256
Atkinson, Henry 227
Atlantic Coast 509
Atlantic Ocean 19, 31, 33, 55–6, **61**, 68–9, 82, 97–8, 103, **105**, 109, 132, 134, 140, *144*, **146**, 155, 157, 166, 202, 254, 281–2, 341, 423, 480, 509
Attakullakulla (Cherokee) 174
Attignawantans 114
Attigneenongnahacs 114, 117
Attu: Japanese occupation of 502
Austin, Stephen F. 271–2
Australia 422, 509; indigenous peoples of 8
Avilés, Pedro Menéndez de 68–9
Axis powers 489, 491, 495, 510
Aztecs 22, **31**, **35**, 38–42, *42*, 45–7, **45**, **52**, 60, 391; cult of war and human sacrifice 40; empire 30, 32, 38; Huitzilopochtli (master sun god) 40, *41*, 42, 47; Itzcoatl 40; Moctezuma I 40; Spanish conquest of 40, 47–50, 60, 82, 89; Tenochtitlán 30, 38, 40–2, *41*, 46–7, 49, 76; Tlateloco 40; warrior cult of 41–2; women in 41–2; *see also* Cortés, Hernán; Malintzin; Mexica; Moctezuma II; Quetzalcoatl

baby boom 527
Bacon Rind (Osage) *432*
Bacon, Nathaniel 125
Bacon's Rebellion **96**, 97, 124–6
Baja California 87, 164
Baker, Newton D. 400
Baltimore 501, 525
Bandelier National Park and Monument 444–5, 456
Banks, Dennis 548, *557*, 557–9, 563–4
Bannocks 260, 318
Baranov, Alexander 255, 258
Barnwell, John 150–1
Bataan Death March 509
Battle at Bad Axe River 227, **229**
Battle at Birch Coulee 292
Battle at New Ulm 292
Battle at the Thames 190
Battle at Vincennes **177**
Battle at Wood Lake 292, 293
Battle of Chusto Talasha 286
Battle of Fallen Timbers **165**, **185**
Battle of Gettysburg 288, 298

Battle of Guadalcanal 494–5, 536
Battle of Horseshoe Bend **165**
Battle of Iwo Jima 494
Battle of Midway 490
Battle of New Orleans 189
Battle of Okinawa 494
Battle of Oriskany **165**, 169
Battle of Pea Ridge at Elkhorn Tavern, Arkansas **283**, 288, *289*
Battle of Round Mountain 286
Battle of Saipan 494
Battle of Sand Creek *see* Sand Creek Massacre
Battle of Stillman's Run 227
Battle of the Argonne Forest **379**
Battle of the Holy Ground (Eccanachaca) 189
Battle of the Thames 189
Battle of Tippecanoe **190**
Battle of Vicksburg 288, 298, 325
Battle of Vincennes **165**, 173, 175
Battle of White Plains, New York **165**
Battle of Wilson's Creek 285–6
Battle of Wood Lake 291
Bay Area Native American Council (BANAC) 553
Beadle, Irwin and Erastus 381
Beale, Edward Fitzgerald 268
beans 14–15, 20, 22, 35, 40, *65*, 69, 80, 83, 86, 248, 448
Bear Ears National Monument *578–9*, *611*, 612; Bears Ear Coalition 612
Bear Paw Mountain 339
Beatty, Willard Walcott 459–60
beaver fur/pelts 105, 109–10, 115–17, 121, 259–60
Begaye, Russell 609, 612
Bella Coola: origin story 5
Bellecourt, Clyde 557
Bellecourt, Vern 559
Benghazi, Libya: U.S. embassy attack 605
Bent, George 302, 304
Benteen, Frederick 334
Bergen, Candice 574
Bering land bridge theory 4–8, **4**, <u>6</u>, **10**
Berkeley, William 105, 125
Bethouk **31**, 55, 56, **61**
Bible 367
Bienville, Jean-Baptiste Le Moyne de 149–50
Big Foot 353–5, **355**, 482, 566
Big Horn Mountains 324, Mountains 333

bison *see* buffalos
Bitterroot Mountains 339
Black Elk (Sioux) 334, 346–7, 355; in Buffalo Bill's Wild West Show 346–7
Black Hawk (Makataimeshekiakiak) 201, 219, *225*, 226–9, **229**; "British Band" of 226–7
Black Hawk (Sac-Fox) 383
Black Hawk War **200**, 227, 231, 233
Black Hills 90, 246, 332–3, 562; sacred to Sioux 587
Black Hoof (Shawnee) 181, *182*, 184–5, 187, 230; acceptance of annuity payments 184
Black Kettle (Cheyenne) 301–2, 304–7, **312**, 325–6
Black Panthers 546, 558, 560, 562
Blackfeet 91, <u>247</u>, 250, 252, 260, 451, 526, 593
Blackfeet Reservation 416
Blackfeet Tribal Council 523
Blackfoot 483
Blackfoot Agency 499
Blackstone, Princess Tsianina Redfeather *376–7*
Blainville, Pierre-Joseph Céloron de 154
Blue Jacket 180
Blue Ridge Mountains 125
Bluegrass Region 172–3
Board of Indian Commissioners 360
boarding schools 367, 369, 371, 370, 380, 390, 399, 406, 429, 432, 436, 438, 449, 451–2, 457, 459–60, 468, 471, 480, 494, 502, 523, 600; system 468
Boas, Franz 384
Boasberg, James 608
Boldt Decision **545**, 549
Bonnin, Gertrude Simmons *see* Zitkala-Sa
Boone, Daniel 173
Borah, William E. 425
Bordeaux, Earl (Sioux) 587
Bosque Redondo Reservation **283**, 296–300, <u>297</u>, *300*, 307–8
Boston 122, 132, 134, 360
Boston Indian Citizenship Committee 358
Boudinot, Elias (Buck Watie) 205–6, 208, 210, 235
Bourne, Richard 112
Bowlegs (Seminole) 219

Boy Scouts of America 380, *389*, 448
Bozeman Trail 318, 322, 324, 333
Braddock, Edward 155, **159**
Bradford, William 108
Bradley, James 492–3; *Flags of Our Fathers* 491–2
Brainerd Mission school **185**
Brainerd, David 142–3
Brando, Marlon 547, 563–4; Academy Award refusal 563–4; Sasheen Littlefeather as spokesperson 564
Brandon, Gerard 216
Brant, Joseph (*Thayendanegea*) **165**, 166–9, *168*, 178
Brant, Molly 166–7, 171; as clan mother 171
Briant, Solomon 136
British Board of Trade 167
British Empire 143, 154–7, 160, 178
British imperial economy/system 126, 135, 140
British North West Company 245, 249, 259
British Proclamation **159**
British Royal Navy 155
British, the 58, 67, 75, 104, 119–20, 129–31, 149, 151–7, **153**, 160, 166–9, 171, 173–5, 177–78, 180, 184, 188–9, 191, 231–2, 249, 258–60, 400
Brodhead, General Daniel 174
Bronson, Ruth Muskrat (Cherokee) 521
Brophy, William **508**, 515, 521
Brothertown Indians 230
Brothertown movement 169
Brown, Dee 573; *Bury My Heart at Wounded Knee: An Indian History of the American West* 573
Brown, Eddie F. (Pascua Yaqui) 585
Brownstown 178
Brulé Sioux 318, 324, 587
Brunner, Joseph (Oklahoma Creek) 469, 471
Bryan, William Jennings 432
Buchanan, James 290
Buffalo (city) 230, 501
Buffalo Bill's Wild West Show 345–7, **346**, 372; Indians in 346–7; reenactment of Little Big Horn battle 346–7
buffalo hunters and skinners 329–30, *329*, **330**, 539

buffalos 246–8, 250, **330**, 335, 341
Bureau of American Ethnology: report on Virginia natives 485, 487
Bureau of Indian Affairs (BIA) 503, 517, 523–5, *524*, 528, 528–31, 540, 558–9, 563, 585, 588, 605, 611, 613; AIM occupation of Minneapolis office 560; AIM occupation of Washington, D.C. office **545**, 552, 561–3, *561*
Bureau of Naturalization 420
bureau schools 386
Burke Act (1906) 364, **387**, 394, 417, 421; competency clause 417
Burke, Charles H. **412**, 421–2, 425–6, 430, *432*, 439
Burnette, Robert 559–61, 563–4
Bursum Bill **412**, 424–5, 427–8
Bursum, Holm 424
Bush, George H. W. **581**, 585–6, 593; administration 585–6
Bush, George W. 536, 602
Butte County Native American Cultural Committee 594

Cachupín, Tomás Vélez de 191
Caddoan speakers 13–14, 148
Caddoans **66**, 77, 92, 272
Caddos 77–9, <u>247</u>, 272, 274; confederacies of 78, 79; matrilineal households of 78–9, *78*; social organization *78*; women of 77–9; *see also* Hasinai; Kadohadacho; Natchitoches
Cahokia chiefdom **4**, 21, *21*, *23*
Cahokia Mounds *2–3*, 21, *21*; Monk's Mound 21
Cahuilla Indians 430, 469
Calhoun, John C. 207, 212
California 11, **13**, 17, 66, 82, 87, 164, 192–6, **244**, 254–6, *259*, 262–71, *266*, **270**, 274, 278, 285, 295–6, 311, **312**, 325, **338**, 351, 400, 430, 432, 446, <u>447</u>, 450, 457, **466**, **478**, 480, 499–501, 502, 519, 526–7, **527**, *550*, 552, 580, **581**, 584, 588, 590, 592, 594, 610, 612; gold rush 260–1, 345; *rancherías* 269; Sacramento 267, 430; as "sexual frontier" 269–71; statehood 261, 268, **270**, 271; *see also* Alta California; California reservations; gold rush
California Indian Wars 269, **270**

California Indians 11, 164, 192, 194, 268–9, 430
California reservations 268–9; Fresno 269; Klamath 269; Mendocino 269; Nome Lackee 268–9; Tehama 269; Tejon 268–9
California Secularization Act (1834) **244**
California v. Cabazon Band of Mission Indians **581**, 590
California's Mission Indian Federation 465
calumet (pipe) 96–7, 118, 173
Cameahwait (Shoshone) 249, 251
Camp Lejeune, North Carolina *476–7*
camp meetings 215
Campbell, Arthur 177, **177**
Campbell, Ben Nighthorse (Cheyenne) 537
Canada 7, 10, 19, 22, **31**, 55–6, 91, 132, 134, 171, 180, 185, 188, 234, 245, 291, 326, 335, **338**, 339, **346**, 353, 400, 446, 499, 548, **558**, 606
Canyon de Chelly 298
Cape Cod **61**, 95, 112–13, 107, 231; Bay 107
capitalism 388, 471
Capitan Grande people 465
captivity exchange **278**
captivity narratives 123, 133, 275; of Andele 275
Carleton, James 296–300
Carlisle Indian Industrial School *344–5*, **346**, 355, 368–72, *368*, *369*, *370*, 383, *386*, 390, *405*,
Carlucci, Frank 561
Carolina Commission of Indian Trade 152
Carolinas 147, 149–51, 155, 206, 210, 315
Carolinians 75, 151, **153**, 281
Carson Reservation Indians 446
Carson, Kit (Christopher) 296–9, *298*, 302
Carter, Charles **412**, 419
Carter, Jimmy 565, **568**, 600
Cartier, Jaques **31**, 56–7, **61**
Cascade-Siskiyou National Monument 612
Cash, Johnny 492
Castilian language 86
Castillo, Adam (Cahuilla) 430
Catawba Indian Nation 530
Catawbas 119, 146, 150–1, 549

Catholicism 33, 46, 49–52, 60, 69, 72, 77, 83–4, 97, 99, 116, 118, 134, 195, 268, 600

Catholics 72, 134, 314, 329, 366, 414

Catlin, George *249*

Catskill Mountains 358

cattle ranching 217, 314

Cavasos, Lauro F. 585

cave rock art 14

Cavendar Wilson, Waziyatawin Angela (Wahpetunwan Dakota) 580

Cayugas 22, 114

Cayuses **244**, 261

Central-Northern Plains 247

Cerro Juanaqueña site 15

Chaco Canyon 15–17, *16*, **387**

Chaco Phenomenon **4**, 15. **19**; Peñasco Blanco 15; Una Vida 15; *see also* Anasazi peoples; Pueblo Bonito

Chainbreaker 164

Champlain, Samuel de **96**, 114–15

Charbonneau, Toussaint 250

Chattahoochee River 213

Cherokee Cold Water Army 236

Cherokee Country 176

Cherokee language 205, *205*

Cherokee Nation 179, 203–7, 209–10, **212**, 234–6, 238–9, 285–6, 288, 299, **387**, 396–7, **581**, 583, 599, *599*; Act of Union 235; and African slaves 238–9; annuity payments to 203–4; capital Tahlequah 283, 288; civil war of, in Indian Territory 235; constitution of 1827 235, 238; constitution of 1839 235; constitution of 1846 238; Eastern band **581**; schools 235–6; treaty with Confederacy 288; unification in Indian Territory 200, 234, **237**

Cherokee Nation v. Georgia **200**, 209–10, **212**

Cherokee Nation v. Hitchcock **387**

Cherokee National Council 204, 238

Cherokee Phoenix newspaper 205–6, 208

Cherokee Strip 366

Cherokee Temperance Society (CTS) 236

Cherokee Trust Fund case 397

Cherokees **130**, 146–7, 150–3, **153**, 155, **159**, 165, 167, 174–5, 177, **177**, 178–9, 181–2, 184, **185**, 188, 190, **190**, 192, *198–9*, 201–11,

214–18, 230, 234–6, 238–9, 272, 287, 289, 307, 315, 362, **387**, 391, 395–7, 401, 405, 422, 504, 534, 555, 572, 592–3, 596, 598, 601, 609, 611; Chota 174–5; Confederate 315; Constitution **200**, 204, **212**; convention at Takatoka 237; Georgian laws against **200**; Great Tellico 174; Land Cessions **200**, **212**; Light Horse Guard 204; light horse police 235; matrilineal structure of 599; national council laws **212**; Old Settlers 272, 397; Overhill towns 174–5, 177; "Patriot Party" 234–5; property laws **212**; public school system 237; relocation of 609; removal of 203, 210–11, 234; self-governance pact 599; "Treaty Party" 234–5; Treaty of Removal (1808) **200**; Union 315; "Western Cherokees" ("Old Settlers") 234–5, **237**; *see also* Cherokee Nation; Treaty of New Echota; Trail of Tears

Cherry Valley campaign 169

Chesapeake Bay 59, 98–100, 103

Cheyenne reservation 366, 589

Cheyenne River Sioux Reservation 354, 535, 587

Cheyenne River Sioux: war bond purchases 503

Cheyenne-Arapaho: compensation for lost lands 519

Cheyennes 191, 246–8, 247, 277, **283**, 301–7, **312**, 324–6, *324*, 330, 334–5, **338**, 345, 391, 403, 489, 499, 530, 539–40, 574, 587, 593, 600; Dog Soldiers 301

Chicago 384, 414, 425, 446, 455, 493, 501, 510, 513, 516, 523, 560

Chicago Tribune 353

Chichén Itzá **31**, 36–7, *37*; cenote 37, 51

Chickahomineys 485–6

Chickahomonies 105

Chickamaugas (*Ani-Yunwiya*/"the Real People") 175, 177–9, **177**

Chickasaw Factory 218

Chickasaw Nation **200**, 237, **237**; treaty of alliance with Confederacy **283**, 285

Chickasaws 75, 77, 148–50, 156, 174, 190, 201, 216–19, 234, 273, 286, 362, **387**; *Aba (Loak-Ishtollo-Aba)*

216; acceptance into Choctaw Nation 236; annuity payments to 219; break from Choctaw Nation 237; Doaksville agreement 236, **237**; *iksas* 236–7; planter elite of 239; recognized as independent nation 237; removal of **200**, 203, 218; *see also* Chickasaw Nation; Treaty of 1804; Treaty of Chickasaw Bluffs; Treaty of Chickasaw Council House; Treaty of the Chickasaw Nation

Chicoras 69

Chief American Horse (Ogala Sioux) *364*

Chief Joseph ((Hin-mah-too-yah-lat-kekht; Nez Perce) 262, **312**, 336, 338–9, *338*, 341, 358, 366; in Buffalo Bill's Wild West Show 346; removal to Colville Reservation 339, 341; statement at Bear Paw Mountain 358

Chief Plenty Coups 457

Chihuahua 66, 67, 88–9, **91**

Childers, Ernest (Creek) 477–9, **478**, 482, *482*; Congressional Medal of Honor awarded **478**, 479, *482*, 504

Chilocco Indian Agriculture School 477, 479

Chilocco Indian School 502

Chimayó 277

Chimayó Rebellion **244**, 277, **278**

China 33, 254, 348, 479, 512

Chino, Wendell 582

Chinooks 252–4, 261; head flattening 252

Chippewa Tribal Council 559

Chippewas 178, 199, 401, 489, 493–4, 499, 601

Chiricahua Apaches *368*, *369*; compensation for lost lands 519

Chivington, John (the "Fighting Parson") 301–2, 304–7, 315

Chochise 339

Choctaw "Trail of Tears" 216

Choctaw Civil War **130**, **153**

Choctaw confederacy 217

Choctaw language 76, 214

Choctaw Nation 214–16, 236; acceptance of Chickasaws 236; constitution for 236; creation of **200**; Doaksville 288; treaty of alliance with Confederacy **283**, 285

Choctaws 75, 148–50, 153, 155, 156, 174, 188, 190, 201, 213–17, 219, 234, **237**, 273, 286, 362, **379**, **387**, *401*, 490, *522*, 572, 601, 609; *Aba* (Great Father) 214–15; as code talkers **379**, *401*, 402–3, 491–5; Eastern 214–15; Long People 149; matrilineal networks 214; Mississippi Law imposed on **200**; *Nanih Waiya* 213–14; nationalism 215; People of the Opposite Side 149; People of the Six Towns 149, 214, 217; planter elite of 239; removal of <u>203</u>; removal to Indian Territory **200**, 215–16, 219; Western 214–15; *see also* Choctaw Civil War; Choctaw confederacy; Choctaw Nation; Choctaw "Trail of Tears"; Treaty of Dancing Rabbit Creek; Treaty of Doak's Stand
Chonoac 58
Chota **177** nationalism 215
Christendom 32
Christianity 34, 45, 51, 71, 103, 108–9, 113, 136–7, 139, 141, *144*, 152, 183, 187, 189, 205, 217, 261, 290, 327, 348–52, 359–60, 366–8, 373, 378, 380, 388–9, 393, 523, 551–2, 558, 610; blending with Indian spirituality 367; linearity of 367
Chumash 192, 195, 263–4, <u>265</u>, 267; *antap* 263–4; *Chupu* 263–4
Chumash Rebellion **244**, 263–4, **270**
church mission schools 380, 384
Church of England 107 *see also* Anglican Church
Church, Benjamin 122
Citizenship Act (1924) 487–8
citizenship qualifications: denial of tribal affiliation **435**; land allotments **435**; naturalization process **435**; residence in Indian Territory **435**; women marrying white men **435**; World War I veterans **435**; *see also* U.S. citizenship
civil rights movement 534, 545–6, 547, 558, 562, 567, 575
Civil War 272, 277, **283**, 284–5, *289*, 307–8, 313–14, 323, 325–6, *327*, 341, 427, 538, 573–4; in Colorado Territory 300–7; in Indian Territory 286–9; Lumbee Indians in 281–3;

and Navajo 295–300; and Sioux 290–5
Civil Works Administration (CWA) 453–5, **455**
Civilian Conservation Corps (CCC) 444–5, 453, 456, *456*, 510
Civilian Conservation Corps—Indian Division (CCC—ID) **444**, 456–8
Civilization Program **165**, 182–3, 185, **185**, 187, 189, 192, 196, 217, 321
Clairborne, General Ferdinand L. 189
clan mothers 183
Clark, George Rogers 173, 175
Clark, William 245, 247–53, **253**, 259
Clatsops 252–4, *252*, 261; head flattening 252, *252*
Clean Air Act (1963) 589, 606
Clearwater River 338
Cleveland, Grover 360
Clinch, Duncan 221
Clinton, Bill 529, 603
Clinton, Hillary Rodham 605, 609–10
Clinton, James 169
cloth trade 148
Cloud, Henry Roe (Winnebago) **444**
Clovis culture **4**, 8–9, 10, **10**, 13; Lehrner site 8
Clovis point 8, *9*
Coacoochee (Wildcat) 222–3
Coahuila 77
Coahuiltecans 271, **278**
coal deposits 587
code talkers **379**, *401*, 402–3, 491–5, *494*, 609, *609*, 610
Cody, William "Buffalo Bill" Cody 329, 345–6, **346**
Coeur d'Alenes 260–1
Coffee, John 481–2
Cofitachequi 75–6; "Lady of Cofitachequi" 76
Cohuiltecans 77
Cohuilteco (language) 77
Colbert family 217–19
cold war 510, 515, 534–5, 540, 546
College Football Hall of Fame 383
Collier, John 428, 428–2, 439, **444**, 449, 445, 452–65, *453*, 468–73, 480–3, 485–6, 490, 500–1, **508**, 510, 512–13, 515, 520–1, 523, 526, 558, 572; resignation of 513–14
colonial militia 166
colonialism 187, 580, 600
colonization 580
Colonization Act (1824) **244**

Coloradas, Mangas (Apache) 349
Colorado 3, 9, 17, 100, 247, 357, 363, 365, 427, **436**, **466**, 497, 537, 552, 593, 611; Denver 304, 306–7, 320, **508**, 513, 524, 559, 597; Plateau 17
Colorado River 14, 272, 274
Colorado Territory 301–8, 325, 330
Colorado Volunteers **283**, 302, 307, 315
Columbia Plateau 19, **244**, **253**, 254, 260
Columbia River 249, 252–3, **253**, 262, 595; Valley 261
Columbian Exchange 33, *35*
Columbus Day **379**, 384
Columbus Quincentenary **581**, 586–7
Columbus, Christopher 31–4, **31**, 38, 54, 377, 384, 587
Colville 595
Colville Confederated Tribes 518
Colville Federated Reservation 544
Comanche Empire 191–2
Comanchería 164, 191–2, **193**
Comanches **66**, 80, 90–2, **91**, 163–4, **165**, 190–2, **193**, 223, 236, 239, 246, <u>247</u>, 263, 272–5, 277, 302–4, 307, 318, 323, 326, 330–2, **338**, 391–2, 403, 538–9, 582, *582*, 596, 609; as code talkers 493, 494; "The Council House Fight" 274; -Ute alliance 91; Uto-Aztecan dialect of 90
combat fatigue 493
Commission on the Organization of the Executive Branch (Hoover Commission) 521
Commissioner of Indian Affairs 293, **312**, 314, 326, 333, 360, **379**, 394, 396, **412**, 415, 421, 426, **444**, 445, 448, 455, 462–3, 472–3, 480, 510, 512, 584
Commissioner of Indian Affairs **508**, 515, 520–2, 524, 572
Committee of One Hundred **412**, 432–3, 435, 457; *The Indian Problem* 432
Committee on Public Information 414
communalism 388
Communism 470–1, 510
communists 414
community day schools *see* day schools
compulsory military service **478**
Conestogas 157

Confederacy (Confederate States of America) 281–2, **283**, 284–9, 293–5, **312**, 313–16, 325, 393
Confederacy Congress 178–9
Confederate Army 281
Confederate Indian Cavalry **283**, 286
Confederate Indians **283**
Confederate States 239
Congress's Joint Committee on the Condition of the Indian Tribes 320
Congressional Medal of Honor **478**, 479, **482**, 504, 536–7
Connecticut **96**, 106, 110, 112, **113**, 119, 122–3, 139, 167, 169, 171, 205, 231, 579, 583, 591–2, 610; New London 139, 231
Connecticut Indian Land Claims Settlement Act (1983) 583
Conoys 119
conquistadors 31, 33, 38, 41, 44, 47, 60, 82, 391; as *katsinas* 66
Conscientious Objector (CO) status 485, 487
containment policy 535
Continental Army 163, 166, 169
Continental Divide 251
Cooley Commission 315
Cooley, Dennis N. 314–15
Coolidge, Sherman (Arapaho) 384, 432
Coosa **4**, 21, *70*, 75, 76
Córdoba, Francisco Hernández de 46–7
corn 14–15, 17, 20, 22, 33, 45, *65*, 69, 71, 73, 80–1, 91, 100–3, 107–8, 115, 149, 152, 169, 191, 193, 226–7, 248, 403, 446, 448, 499, *516*, 555; *see also* maize
Corn Mother 80–2
Corn Tassel 209
Cornplanter 164, 182, 183–4, 186
Cornstalk 173–4, **177**
Cornwall International Bridge traffic stop **558**
Coronado, Francisco Vásquez de **66**, 82, **85**
Cortés, Hernán 30, 41, 46–7, 49, 51, **52**, 82; and horses 89
Coshoctons 173–4
Costanoans 192
Costo, Rupert (Cahuilla) 469
cotton 38, 46, 84, 91, 201–3, 206, 208, 214, 216–17, 219–20, 222, 234, 272–3, 281–2, 493
cotton gin 206

Council of All New Mexico Pueblos **412**, 425; "Declaration to the Pueblo Indians, to all Indians, and to the People of the United States" 425, 427
Council of Energy Resource Tribes (CERT) 588–9, 611
count coup 419
coureurs de bois 117–18
Court of Claims 518, 528
Covenant Chain alliance 119–20, 123, 126, 141, 154, 166
Cowkeeper (Seminole) 175, 219
Crazy Horse **312**, 320, 324, 332–3, 335, 339, 555, 564
creationism 414, 421, 427
Creator (Wakan Tanka) 351–2, 367, 372, 392
Cree Indians 246, <u>247</u>, 248–9
Cree Reservation 598
Creek Confederacy 146, 153, 179
Creek Nation 189–90, 213, 221, 237–8, 285–6, 398, 434; Coweta as capital 237; national council 212–13, 237; Neutrals **283**, 286; "Trail of Blood on the Ice" 286
Creek War 189, *205*
Creeks 70, 75, 147, 151–3, **153**, 155, 174–5, 178–9, 181–4, **185**, 188–90, **190**, 192, 201, 213–14, 215–18, 223, 234, **237**, 272, 288, 362, **387**, 391, 398, 434, 479, 482, *482*, 504, 525, 555, 600; in Florida 219; Lower 146, 175, 212–13, 237; matrilineal society of 153; as Muskogee speakers 238; planter elite of 239; removal from Alabama **200**, <u>203</u>, 213, **218**; removal to Alabama **200**, <u>203</u>, 213, **218**; Upper 146–7, 175, 212–13, 219, 237–8; war bond purchases 503; *see also* Creek Confederacy; Creek Nation; Creek War; Treaty of 1832; Treaty of Indian Springs; Treaty of Washington
Creel, George 414
Cresap, Michael 172
Croatan 59, 60
Croghan, George 142
Croix de Guerre: awarded to American Indians 402–3
Crook, General George **312**, 333–5, 350–1, 358; as "the Gray Fox" 350
Crow Creek 535

Crow Creek Reservation <u>354</u>
Crow Indian Agency 499
Crow Nation 603; Tribal Council 518–19
Crow Reservation 417–18, 457, 514
Crows 246, <u>247</u>, 248, 260, 333, 339, 483, 402, *442–3*, 457, 611; compensation for lost lands 519; *see also* Crow Indian Agency; Crow Nation
Cuba 30, 33–4, 47, 68; Havana 69
cultural diversity 512
cultural pluralism 360, 431, 523, 570
Cumberland River 179
Curtis Act (1898) **387**
Curtis, Charles 420
Custer, Col. George Armstrong **312**, 326, 332–7, *337*, 556, 574; "Last Stand" 334, *337*, 346

Dakota Access Pipeline (DAP) 606–8; leaks from 608
Dakota Indians 201, 232, 580
Dakota Sioux 199, 224, 226–7; Sisseton band 224; Wahpeton band 224
Dakota Territory **283**, 290, 293–5, 307, **312**, 315, 317, 324, 332–3, 335, 372
Dalles, The 12–13, 252, 261; trade at 252
Dalrymple, Jack 607–8
Darwin, Charles 414; theory of evolution 380
Davenport, Reverend James 137
Davis, Jefferson 286
Dawes General Allotment Act **346**, 360–5, *364*, **387**, 394, 416, 430, **435**, 488; termination of 462
Dawes, Henry 360
day schools 380, 449, 451–2, 453, 457, 460–1, 471–2, 480, 499, 515, 523; funding of 584
Daybreak Star Indian Cultural Center 545
De Chepart, Sieur 148–9
De Las Casas, Bartolomé 34, 58
De Mendoza, Antonio 82
De Niza, Fray Marcos 82, **85**
De Oñate, Don Juan 65–6, **66**, 83, **85**, 89
De Smet, Jean 260–1
De Soto, Hernando **66**, 75–7, 148
De Vaca, Alvar Núñez Cabeza **66**, 82

Declaration of Independence 171
decolonization 580–1, 601–2, 615; of academia 601–2
Decree of Emancipation **270**
Deep South **4**, 148, **165**, 202, 219, 234, 239, 272
Deer, Ada (Menominee) 529–30
Deerfield **130**, 131–2, 134, **140**
Deerfield Raid 230
deerskin trade 214
Deganawida 22
Delaware River 141
Delawares 140–5, *144*, **146**, 154, 156–7, 167, 172, 174, 178, 187, 229–30, 272
Deloria, Vine, Jr. (Lakota) 551–2, *552*, 555, 573; *Custer Died for Your Sins: An Indian Manifesto* 573
democracy 348, 382, 394, 415, 419–20, 471, 481–2, 512–13, 546, 570
Democratic Party **508**, 529, 532; National Committee 613
Denonville, Jacques-René de Brisay de 119
Department of Defense 536
Department of Education 603; "Tribal Leaders Speak: The State of Education" 603
Department of Justice **545**, 549
Department of State 512
Department of the Interior **312**, 321, 326, 331, 333, 357, *365*, 389, 405, 415–16, 421, 428, 432, 434–5, 439, 449, 462, 485, 512, 586, 588, 595; Office of American Indian Trust 586; Office of Self-Governance 586
Department of the Navy 510, 512
Department of the Northwest 293
Department of War see War Department
detribalization 359–60, 367
Detroit 180, 414, 446, 501, 516, 523
Detroit British outpost 177
Dewey, John 387, 470
dime novels 381, *381*, 403, 428, 498, 580
Dinetah 298
Division of Missouri 316
DNA analysis 6, 8
Doaksville agreement 236, **237**
Dodge, Henry 227
Dodge, Mabel 424, 431
Doegs 124–5

Dole, William P. 285, 293
domestic dependent nation, concept of 210, 462, 514
domestic slave trade 273–4
Donnacona 57
Doolittle Report **312**, 321
Doolittle, James R. 320
draft registration 393–5, 398–9, **478**, 480, 482–3, 487–8
Dragging Canoe (Cherokee) 151, **165**, 174–5, **177**
Drake, Francis 59
dream quests 144, 262
drop-out rate 598–9
Drouillard, George 251
Duck Creek 230
Duck River 217
Duckwater Reservation *417*
Dunmore's War **165**, 172–3, **177**
Dunn, Dorothy 455
Dutch, the 109–10, **113**, 115–16, 118–19
Dutch language 112
Dutch traders 109
Duwali (Chief Bowl/Bowles) 272
dysentery 299, 436

Earthjustice 608
East Asia 510
East Coast 314, 529
Eastern Band of the Cherokee Nation (EBCN) 211, 592–3; "boundary" 592–3; tourism 592; "The Trail of Tourism" 592–3; *Unto These Hills* 593
Eastern Cherokees 395–7, 500
Eastern Europe 314, 357, 510
Eastern reformers 315, 320, 326, 349, 357, 359, 364
Eastern Woodlands **4**, 7, 19–20, 22, **23**, 57, 92, 96–7, 126, 131, 163, 166, 217, 229
Eastman, Charles (Sioux) 355, 384, 388–9, *389*, 391, 414–15, 420, 432; "Indian Congress" 391
economy of captivity 274
economy of violence and captivity exchange 263
Ecueracapa 191
Edisto Indians 69
Edmunds, Governor Newton 315
Eisenhower, Dwight D. 525, 531
Eliot, John 111–13, **113**, 134
Elizabeth I (England) 58

eminent domain, right of 587, 610
Emistisiguo 175
Emmons, Glenn **508**, 525
Empire for Liberty 166, 245
Empire State Building 450
encomienda 46, 49, *52*, 84, 90
energy tribes 587–9, 612, 614
energy-generated income 588–9
England 55, 58–61, 100, 103, 109–11, 136–7, **140**, 160; London 104
English language 108, 111–12, 139, 152, 205, 235, 273, 290, 331, 348–9, 372, 385, 390–1, 396, 458, 460, 494, 499, 517, 523, 596
English law 105
Environmental Protection Agency (EPA) 606
Epenow 107
epidemics 57, 76, 107, 110, **113**, 116, 148, 164, 166, 192, 243, 248, 263, 572; *see also* influenza; smallpox
Episcopal Church 551
equestrian culture **66**, 90, 246, 248, 263–4, 273
Erdrich Louise (Turtle Mountain Chippewa) 600
Eries 22, 115, 117
Erik the Red (Erik Thorvaldsson) 55, **61**
Eriksson, Leif 55
Eskimos 256
Espionage Act 414
Esselens 192
Estanislao **244**, 264–5; uprising **270**
ethnic cleansing 160, 201–2, 272, **278**
Europe 33–4, 109, *376–7*, **478**; reconstruction of 520
European Theater of Operation 490, 493, 497
Europeans 4, 22–4, 30–2, 34, 55–6, 59–61, 76, 77–9, 97, 99, 115–16, 126, 131, 147, 150, 153, 156, 163, 172, 193, 214, 245, 252, 267, 610
Evans, John 301–4, 306–7, 315
evolution, theory of 380, 414, 421; banning of teaching of 427
Ex Parte Green 488
Executive Order 13175 603
Eyaks 256

Fall, Albert **412**, 421–4, 427–8, 430, 432–4, 439; and Teapot Dome Scandal 427
Fallen Timbers, battle at 180

Far East 510

Farm Loan program: discrimination against Indians 603

Farmington 138

Fayadaneega, Joseph (Six Nations) *168*

Feather Shedder (Menominee) 231

Federal Art Project (FAP) 455–6, *454*, **455**; Index of American Design 455, *454*

Federal Bureau of Investigation (FBI) 412–13, 422, 470, 551, 560, 564

Federal Deposit Insurance Commission 453

federal factory system 181–2, 184

federal guardianship 417–18, 420–1, 434, 509, 511, 514, 518

federal Indian policy 308, 321, **346**, 357, 359, 361, 418, 428, 430, 432, 439, **444**, 445, 452, 461–2, 469–71, 473, 490, 510, 513, 525, 531, 535, 540, 551–2, 567–8, 575, 611

Ferdinand and Isabella (Spain) 32

Fetterman Massacre 320

films: *Broken Arrow* (1950) 538, **539**; *Covered Wagon* 429; *Drum Beat* (1954) 538; *The Great Sioux Uprising* (1953) 538, **539**; *Heap Big Chief* 429; *The Last Hunt* (1956) **539**; *Little Big Man* 574; *A Man Called Horse* 574; *Out West* 429; *Redskin* 429; *Run of the Arrow* (1957) **539**; *The Savage* (1952) **539**; *The Searchers* (1956) 538–9, **539**; *Soldier Blue* 573–4; *The Unforgiven* (1959) **539**; *The Vanishing American* 429, *429*; *Walk the Proud Land* (1956) 538, **539**; westerns 580; *White Feather* (1955) **539**

First Amendment right to public dissent 560

First Anglo-Powhatan War **96**, 103, **105**

First Barnstable Regiment 171

First Battle of Bull Run (Manassas Junction) 284, 286–7

First Cherokee Race Law **200**, 204

First Mississippi Extension Bill **218**

First Seminole War 189, 220

First series of Cherokee laws **212**

fishing and hunting rights 565

fishing rights 549

fish-ins **545**, 547, 549–50, 552, 556, **558**, 565, 575

Five Civilized Nations (Tribes) 201–2, 208, 285, 289, 307, **312**, 314; alliance with Confederacy **283**, 285; of Oklahoma 387; *see also* Cherokees; Chickasaws; Choctaws; Creeks; Seminoles

Five Nations "Beaver Wars" **96**, 116–17, 119

Five Nations Iroquois Confederacy 22, 96, **96**, 114, 116–20, 123, 125–6; acceptance of Tuscaroras into 151; *see also* Six Nations

Flatheads 251, 260–1, 451, 526

Florida 66–7, **66**, 146, 156–7, 201, 526–7; Panhandle 69–70, 73, 75, 175, 219–20; Pensacola 190, 351; St. Augustine 66, <u>68</u>, 69, 71–5, **76**, 147, 332

Florida Indians 73, *128–9*

Foch, Ferdinand 401

Folsom culture **4**, 9–10, **10**, 13; Casper site 9; Cooper site 10; Lindenmeier site 10; Olson-Chubbock site 9–10

Folsom point *9*

Folsom, David 214–16

Fonda, Jane 549

For Indigenous Eyes Only: A Decolonization Handbook 580, **581**

Ford, John 538, **539**

Forsyth, John 213

Forsyth, Thomas 226

Fort Bent 277

Fort Berthold 611–12

Fort Berthold Reservation 534–5

Fort Bidwell Reservation 450

Fort Brooke 222

Fort Canby 298–9

Fort Clatsop 253, **253**

Fort Defiance 480, 494

Fort Detroit 129–30, 156, 173–4

Fort Douglas 395

Fort Drum 477

Fort Duchesne 385

Fort Duquesne **159**

Fort Fisher 281–2

Fort Frontenac 119, **159**

Fort Gaines 220

Fort Greenville 180

Fort Hall Reservation *433*

Fort Jackson 220

Fort Jackson, South Carolina 493

Fort Jefferson 180

Fort Keogh 339

Fort King 222

Fort Laramie (Wyoming) Treaty (1868) **312**, 303, 318–19, 324, *324*, 325–6, 332–3, 549, 562–4

Fort Larned 303

Fort Lawrence 220

Fort Lawton: Indians' attempted occupation of 543–4, **545**, 550, 555

Fort Lewis 543–4

Fort Lyon 302–4

Fort Mandan 248–51

Fort Mankato 294

Fort Marion **229**, 332

Fort Miami 180

Fort Michilimackinac 232

Fort Mikhailovskii 258

Fort Mims 190, 217

Fort Mitchell 220

Fort Niagara 169, 171

Fort Orange (Albany) 115–16

Fort Ozyorsk 258

Fort Peck Reservation 418

Fort Phil Kearny 320

Fort Pitt (Pittsburgh) 172, 174

Fort Recovery 180

Fort Ridgely 292–3, **292**; attack **292**

Fort Robinson 335

Fort Ross 255–6, *255*, **259**, 267

Fort Scott 220

Fort Sill 275, 331–2

Fort Smith 314

Fort Snelling 232

Fort Stanwix 171

Fort Sumner 298

Fort Sumter **283**, 284–5, 393

Fort Washington 179–80

Fort Wayne 181, 184

Fort Wayne, Indiana 179

Fort Wingate 299, 494, 501

Fort Wise Treaty 301–2

Fort Yates 418

Fortune, Oliver (Pamunkey) 486–7

Four Bears (Mandan) 244–5

Four Legs (Ho-Chunk) 232

fourth Mississippi Extension of Law Act (1829) 216

Fox Indians 117, 119, 200, 362; removal of <u>203</u>

Fox River 230–1

Fox, Mark 611–12

France 55, 57–8, 67–8, **96**, 119–20, 131–2, 148, 154–5, 160, 166, 191, 228, 245, *376–7*, **379**, 393, 400–3, 405–7, 415, 479, 491, 508; Paris 400, 431, 483, 606

France's "frontier exchange economy" 148

Franciscans 31, 52, 66, 85, 164, 165, 193, 262–6; in Alta California 193–5; *doctrinas* 71; missionaries 51–4, 60, 69, 71–2, 74–5, 79–80, 83–4, 193–5; missions 72, 85, 193, 244, 262–7; mission secularization 266; *visitas* 71–2

Franklin, Benjamin 160

Free Speech Movement (FSM) 546

free speech, right to 607

freed African men 136

freed slaves 313

Freeman, Colonel Nathaniel 171

French and Indian War 153–5

French explorers 21

French, the 32, 54, 56–7, 67–9, 75, 79, 91–2, 96–7, 107, 110, 114–15, 117–19, 126, 129–32, 130, 134, 140, 142, 148–50, 152–6, 159, 173, 217, 246, 406, 421

Friends of the Indian, The 359–60

Frijoles Canyon 443–4

Frontenac, Louis de Buade de 119

Ft. Benning, Georgia 493

fur trade/trading 91, 107, 109, 113, 116, 118, 131, 142, 156, 185, 245–6, 252–4, 258–9, 264, 268, 270; Pacific Coast 244, 259–60, 259; Rocky Mountain 244

Gadsden, James 220

Gaines, Edward 226

Galbraith, Thomas 291

Gall 335

Galveston Bay 272

Garden of Eden 23, 33, 58

Garland, Hamlin 428

Garrison Dam 534–5

gas deposits 587

Gaule Province rebellion 66

Gay Head Wampanoags 584

gender roles 188

Genesis, Book of 367

genocide 482, 574, 587

George III (England) 166

George, Charles (Cherokee, Eastern Band) 537; Congressional Medal of Honor 537

Georgia 21, 67, 69, 70, 146–7, 149, 151–3, 153, 175, 179, 190, 200, 201–2, 206–10, 212–13, 212, 216, 220, 222, 234, 272, 286–8, 315–16,

357, 414, 431, 493, 509; Atlanta 313, 316, 325, 431, 509; Savannah 149, 152, 316; Stone Mountain 414

Georgia Guard 207, 210

Germany 379, 393, 398, 402, 404, 418, 470, 478, 482, 487–9, 508, 510, 515; America's declaration of war against 379

Geronimo (Chiricahua Apache) 339, 350–1, 350, 353, 357, 482; imprisonment at Fort Pickens, Pensacola 351; surrender at Skeleton Canyon 351

Ghost Dance 346, 352, 353, 355, 357, 392; banned 346, 353; "Ghost shirt" 325–4, 355; as Indian resistance 352

GI Bill of Rights 517, 556

Gila Reservation 501

Gila River 346, 349

Gila River Reservation 492–3

Gingaskins 485

global climate change 606, 608

Gnadenhutten massacre 177

God 34, 48–9, 54–5, 82, 86, 108, 111, 113, 123–4, 133, 144, 167, 215, 305, 318, 320, 327, 352, 366–7, 372, 389, 392, 485, 556

gold 33, 36, 50, 56, 60, 66, 82, 91, 107, 206–8, 210, 244, 260–1, 267–9, 270, 271, 278, 285, 296–6, 301, 305, 312, 314, 318–19, 322, 332–3, 336, 345, 371, 465

Gold Butte National Monument 612

gold rush: Black Hills 312; California 244, 260–1, 267–9, 270, 271, 278; Charlotte, North Carolina 206, 210; Colorado 300–1; Oregon 336; Washington Territory 261

Golikov, Gregory and Ivan 254

Gonzalez, José Angel 277

Good Peter Agwelentongwas 170

Gookin, Daniel 112

Gore, Al 606; *An Inconvenient Truth* 606

Goshute (Gosiute) reservation 395

Goshutes 395

Governor Mellette 355

Goyathlay *see* Geronimo

Grand Alliance 510

Grand Portage Ojibwa Reservation 483

Grand Settlement of 1701 120

Grant, Ulysses S. 283, 288, 300, 306, 312, 324, 326–9, 332, 341, 348–9

Gray, Robert 108

Gray, William H. 261

Great Awakening 137, 142

Great Basin 12–13, 13, 89–90, 249, 254, 260; Lovelock Cave site 13

Great Britain 132, 188, 314, 479, 510

Great Depression 383, 444, 444, 445–6, 448–9, 451, 454, 479–80, 508, 547, 602

Great Lakes 19, 96–8, 110, 114–15, 117, 119, 126, 131, 154, 156, 166, 177, 189, 200, 226, 230, 549, 590

Great Lakes Indian Fish & Wildlife Commission 590

Great Plains 9–10, 19, 90–1, 295, 301, 307, 326, 329–30, 338, 450, 458, 481, 501, 527; art 10; hunters 10

Great Puritan migration 96, 109–10, 113

Great Sioux Reservation, The 312, 324, 332–3, 335, 358

Great Sioux War 312

Great Smoky Mountains National Park 592

Great Society 546, 550, 567

Great Spirit 130, 186, 228, 323, 329

Great War *see* World War I

Great White Father 483

Greathouse, Daniel 172

Green Corn Ceremony 223, 238

Green Party 581, 598

Green, Warren Eldreth (Onondaga) 488

Greenland 55, 61

Greenpeace 598

Gregory, Dick 549

Grey, Zane 424

Gros Ventres 91, 318

Guale Spanish mission province 147

Guales 69, 70–1, 72, 73, 75; *micos* (chiefs) 70–1

guerilla tactics 173

Gulf Coast 7, 19, 75, 76–7, 82, 220, 509

Gulf of Tonkin Incident 553

Gulf of Tonkin Resolution 553, 555

guns trade 148

Gustav V (Sweden) 383

Haber, Alan 546

Haidas 254, 256

Hakluyt, Richard 58

Hale, William 412, 413

Hamilton, Henry 173, 177

Handsome Lake/Connediu **165**, 183, **190**, 185–7; and Creator 183; "good word" (*Gaiwi:yo:h*) 183; as prophet 183

Harding, Warren G. **412**, 421; administration 427

Hariot, Thomas 58, 60, **61**

Harjo, Suzan Shown (Cheyenne) 593, 600; *Just Good Sports* 600

Harlow, Captain Edward 107

Harmar, Josiah 179–80, **185**

Harper's Weekly 330

Harrah's Cherokee Casino **581**, 593

Harris, Cyrus 237

Harris, LaDonna (Comanche) 582, *582*, 588, 596

Harris, Richard 574

Harrison, Benjamin **355**, 365

Harrison, William Henry 188–9, **190**, 223–4

Harvey, Raymond (Chickasaw) 537; Congressional Medal of Honor 537

Hasinai 78

Haskell Institute 391, **444**, 460, 490

Hatch, Orin 612

Haudenosaunee 114

Hawaii: Oahu **481**, 488–9

Hawkins, Benjamin **185**

Hawley, Gideon 136, 170

Hayden, Carl **412**, 419

Hayden, Tom 546

Hayes, Ira Hamilton (Pima) **478**, 491–3, *491*, *492*, 517

Hayes, Rutherford B. 357

Hayward, Richard (Skip) 592

Hernandez, Joseph 222

Hessians 166

Heye, George G. 585

Hiawatha 22

hidalgos 84

Hidatsas 14, 243, 246, <u>247</u>, 248–50, *249*, **253**, 259, 534

high-stakes bingo 591–2

Hillis Hadjo (Hilis Hadsho) 189–90

Hispaniola 34

Hitler, Adolf 479–80, 482, 489, 509

Hoboithle Mico (the Tallassee King) 179, *180*

Hochelagas 56–7, **61**

Ho-Chunks (Winnebagos) 201, 224, 226, 230–3, 233; removal to Iowa 233; removal to Minnesota 233, **233**

Hodulgee Muscogee 587

Hoffman, Dustin 574

Hoffman, Wilfred 488

Hohokams **4**, 17, **19**; Snaketown site 17

Holland 55, 107

Hollywood 334, 372, 383, 461, 491–2, 495, *495*, 498, 537–40, **539**, 547, 555, 563, 573–4, 580

home rule 430, 463; *see also* tribal sovereignty

Homestead Act 297, 314

Hoopa Valley Indian Agency 500

Hoover Commission *see* Commission on the Organization of the Executive Branch

Hoover Dam *442–3*, 450

Hoover, Herbert 428, 439, **444**, 448, 521

Hopewell culture **4**, 20, **23**; "bigmen" 20

Hopis 14, 17, 80, 90, 299, 348, 368, *427*, 464, 493, 588, 612; Antelope Dance *427*; origin story 5

horseback Indians 191

horses 30, 47, **66**, 75, 76, 80, 85, 89–91, **91**, 183, 191–2, 220, 235, 239, 246, 248, 250–1, 256, 260, 264, 267, 271, 273–4, 291, 297, 345, 422, 457, 472, 500; horseback warfare 90; and Indian men 89–90

Horseshoe Bend 190

House Committee on Indian Affairs 420

House Committee on un-American Activities 470

House Concurrent Resolution 108**508**, 527

House Indian Affairs Committee 462

House Resolution 4497 518

Howard, Edgar 462

Howard, Oliver 338–9, 358

Hoyo Negro (Black Hole), Mexico 6, 8

Hoyt, John W. 349

Hudson River 115, 119, 122, 166, 169

Hudson's Bay Company 258, **259**, 260, 268

Hunkpapa Lakota Sioux *334*

Hunkpapas 332

hunter-gatherers 6, 8, 11, 271

Hupas 268

Huron Confederacy 114–17; *see also* Arendarhonon; Ataronchronon; Attignawantan; Attigneenongnahac; Tahontaenrat

Huronia 114–17

Hurons 57, 97–8, 114–18, *115*, 130, 132; origin myth of 114; *see also* Huron Confederacy

hydraulic mining (strip mining) 301

hydroelectric power 534–5

Iberian Peninsula 31

Ice Age 5, 9

Iceland 55, **61**

Ickes, Harold 428, 452–4, 459–60, 512, 514, 518

Idaho 249, 260, 336, **338**, 339, 425, **436**, **466**, 518

Iliniwek (Illinois) 117–18

illegal Mexicans 610

Illinois (state) 96, 173, 225–7, **229**, 230, 232–4, 390, 503, 551, 606

Illinois Indians 117–19, 225

Illinois territory 181, 201–2, 219, 224

illiteracy: Native American 438

immigrants 235, 261, 314, 347–8, 357, 379–80, 382, 384–5, 388, 414, 431, **435**; Catholic 314, 357; Jewish 314, 357

imperial presidency 461

imperialism 147; British 126; South Carolinian 150; French 126; intellectual 602; Japanese 482

Inca 22, **31**, 32, 42–5, **45**, **52**; *ayllus* 43–5, 50; cult of ancestor worship 43; Cuzco 43; Inti (sun god) 43; Lake Titicaca 43; *mit'a* system 44, 50; mummification of leaders 43; revival (*Taqui Onqoy*) 51; Sapa Inca ("Sole Ruler") 43–4, 50; Spanish conquest of 50–1; State (Empire) 43–5, 50, 60; *Tahuantinsuyu* 43–4; Tupac Yupanqui 43; women in 44–5; Yupanqui (Pachacutec) 43; *see also* Manco Inca; Pachamama; Pizarro, Francisco; Titu Cusi

indentured servitude 135, 231

India 33, 512

Indian activism 545, 552, 564, 567, 573, 574–5; male domination of 598–9

Indian Affairs office 333, 458

Indian Affairs officers 430

Indian Appropriation Act (1902) 364

Indian Appropriations Act (1907) 364

Indian Arts and Crafts Act (IACA) 585

Indian Arts and Crafts Board **444**, 454, 585

Indian Awakening **130**
Indian Bureau 321, 350, 368, 395, 406, 451, 453, 458, 461–2, 526
Indian Centers 550, 569, 575
Indian Child Welfare Act (1978) **568**
Indian citizenship 393–4, 398, 420, **435**, 488
Indian Citizenship Act (1924) **412**, 434, **435**
Indian claims 532–3
Indian Claims Commission (ICC) 518–19, 526, **508**; monetary awards instead of land 519
Indian Confederacy **185**; meeting at Brownstown **185**
Indian Country 156–7, 160, 555, 579, 584–5, 603, 605, 611, 613
Indian cultural identity 382, 384–5, 388, 390, 392–3, 595
Indian dances 425–6
Indian debts, cancellation of 453
Indian Education Act (1972) **545**, **568**, 572
Indian education appropriation **346**
Indian Education Service **444**, 459–61, 500
Indian education system 585
Indian fishing rights 547
Indian free-movement across border, restriction of **558**
Indian frontier, closure of 355, 357
Indian gaming 580, 590–2
Indian Gaming Regulation Act (IGRA) (1988) **581**, 584, 591
Indian guardianship 449
Indian health care 449
Indian Health Service (IHS) 436, **444**, 528, 560, 604
Indian heritage 369, 433, 445, 472, 477, 479, 486, 503, **539**, 544, 551, 586
Indian identity 282, 331, 367, 378, 380, 384–5, 388, 390, 400, 407, 415, 428, 434, 485–7, 489, 509, 513–15, 519, 525, 530–1, 534, 548, 550, 569, 573, 599
Indian Knoll site 19
Indian land claims 518–19
Indian land ownership 415
Indian Loan Act 521
Indian messiah 352, **355**
Indian Movement 575
Indian nationhood, concept of 327
Indian Nations at Risk Task Force 585

Indian Naturalization Act (1890) **435**
Indian New Deal 452–3, 457, 461, 471–3, 480–2, 512, 515, 558, 562
Indian Office 300, 312, 316, 320, **346**, 349, 364, 366–7, 369, 419–20, 425, 449–51, 459, 461, 471–2, 482, 511–14, 517, 527, 531, 540; "List of Indian Offenses" **346**, 366, 389–92, 395, 398, 430, 432, 439, 486, 491, 501
Indian Problem 156, 207, 268, 295–6, 301, 303, 316, 320, 357, 420, 531, 556, 570
Indian Progressives 382, 389, 393, 407
Indian prophets 188
Indian religious ceremonies and cultural values 415
Indian Relocation Program **508**, 523–5, 526, 528, 532, 535; Indian Relocation Centers 523–5
Indian removal 148–9, 160, 184, 196, *198–9*, **200**, 201–2, 203, 206–7, 210–11, 215, 239, 316; *see also* Indian Removal Act
Indian Removal Act (1830) **200**, 207–9, 216, 220, 226, 234, 609
Indian Reorganization Act (IRA) (1934) **444**, 457, 461, 464–5, 465–73, **508**, 510–13, 520–1, 526, 549; excerpt 463–4; termination of 526–32, 535; votes by tribe/band/community **466–8**
Indian reservations 348, 354, 356, **387**, 388, 395, 430, 449, 455–6, 463, **508**, 511, 544, 550, 553, 582, 596; poverty on 348–9; *see also names of individual reservations*
Indian rights 207, 433–4, 513, 533, 558, 565
Indian Rights Association (IRA) **346**, 358, 360, 399, 418, 424, 430, 434, 449, 468–9
Indian Scout units 400
Indian self-determination 457, 465, 473, 567, 582, 584; *see also* self-determination
Indian Self-Determination Act 529–30
Indian Self-Determination and Education Assistance Act (1975) **545**, 567–8, **568**, 586
Indian separatism 188
Indian slave trade **153**
Indian slaves 76–7, 84, 88, 147, 150–1, 154, 192, 238, 277

Indian sovereignty 151, 585; *see also* sovereignty
Indian spirituality 113, 193, 352, 366–7, 392–3, 418, 427, 523, 552; differences from Christianity 367, 552; parallels with Christianity 366–7; as spatial view 367
Indian suffrage **508**, 512–13, 517, 521; *Harrison v. Laveen* 521
Indian Territory (Oklahoma) **200**, 201–2, 210, 215–16, 219, 221–3, 227, **229**, 233–9, **237**, 273–5, 284–9, 295, 299, 308, 313–15, 317, 323, 325, 339, 352, 362, 365–6, **435**; slavery allowed in 238
Indian veterans 517
Indian Wars 267, 269, **270**, 349, 361, 382, 428, 556
Indiana 173, 179–81, 184, 188, 223, 231, 233
Indiana Territory 223
Indians: as wards of U.S. federal government 341, **387**, 395–6
Indians' cultural heritage **508**
Indians' Revolution 164, 166, 177
Indigenous Environmental Network 606, 611
indigenous knowledge 614
indigenous religions 193
Indigenous Women's Network (IWN) 598
Indonesia 512
infant and child mortality 399, 436, 450, 471, 528, 531–2, 571, 612
influenza 59, 406
Inouye, Daniel 585
Institute of Government Research (Brookings Institute) **412**, 435; *The Problem of Indian Administration* (Meriam Report) **412**, 435–9, 436
intellectual imperialism 602
Interior Department *see* Department of the Interior
Interior Plateau 12
International Whaling Commission (IWC) 594
internment camp **478**
Inuit **31**, 55, 56, **61**
Iowa (state) 224, 227, 233, 259, 493, 534, 551, 606
Iowas 201, 224, 247, 259, 366
Iraq 585; war in 602
Iroquoia 22, 114, 116, 123, 133, **165**, 167, 169, **172**

Iroquoian language 22, 24, 109, 114, 117, 144, 150, 154; dialects 141, 143, 146
Iroquois Civil War **165**, 169
Iroquois communities 448
Iroquois Confederacy (Six Nations) 151, 153–4, 163, 169–70, 201, 284, 326, **379**, 398, 434–5, 446, 465, 487–9; 1917 declaration of war against Germany **379**, 398, 487; 1942 declaration of war against Germany, Italy, and Japan 487–9; as independent, sovereign nation within United States 487
Iroquois League 22, **23**, 114, 116, 154; Condolence Ceremony 22; *see also* Deganawida; Hiawatha
Iroquois Nation 202
Iroquois nationhood 327
Iroquois of the Mountain 132
Iroquois peoples **4**, 22, 57, **61**, 97–8, 110, 114–15, 118–120, 125–6, 131–2, 137, 141, 143, 154, 166–7, 171–2, 178, 183, 185, 201, 398, 501, 535; the gauntlet 117; matrilineal culture of 114, 171; "mourning war complex" 116–17, 119; origin story 24–5; religious conflicts 167–8; rituals 183; sachems 22, 116; *see also* Cayugas; Five Nations Iroquois Confederacy; Haudenosaunee; Hurons; Mohawks, Oneidas; Onondagas; Senecas
Ishi, last of the Yahis 271, *272*, 594
Islam 7
Islamic State in Iraq and Syria (ISIS) 602
isolationism 421, 423
Italy 478, *482*, 508
Iwo Jima Memorial 491
Iwo Jima, battle for 491–2, *491*

Jackson, Andrew 189–90, **200**, 202, 207–8, 210, 216–17, 220–1, 227, **229**, 609
Jackson, Helen Hunt **346**, 357–8, *358*, 360; *A Century of Dishonor* **346**, 357–8, 366
Jackson's Indian Removal Act **212**
Jacksonian Democrats 202
James Bay II Project 598
James I (England) 108
James River 98, 100, 103–4

Jamestown 59, 98, 100, 102–5, 125, 313
Jamestown Colony **96**, **105**, 610
Japan 348, **478**, 479, 483, 489, 493, 495, 500, 509; reconstruction of 520
Japanese Americans, wartime relocation of 501, *500*, 501, 522, **478**
Japanese army 482
Japanese imperialism 482
Japanese naval air forces **478**
Japanese naval forces **481**
Jaramillo, Juan 46
Jefferson, Thomas 166, 177, 181, 192, **200**, 201–3, **212**, 245, 253; Peace and Friendship medals 245, *246*
Jemez Pueblo Indians 593–4; declaration of war against Germany and Japan 489
Jemison, Alice Lee (Seneca) 469–70
Jerome Agreement (1892) 331
Jesuits **66**, 88–9, **91**, 99, **105**, 116–20, 260–1; among Hurons 115–17; missionaries 99
Jesup **229**
Jesus Christ 117–18, 139, 144, 388–9; Second Coming of 352
Jewel, Sally 603
Jews 414
Jicarilla Apaches 451, 589, 591
Jim Crow laws 314
Jim Crow race segregation 485
Johnson, Andrew 321
Johnson, Joseph 169
Johnson, Lyndon **545**, 546, 548, 567; "The Forgotten American" **545**, 567
Johnson, Napoleon Bonaparte 518
Johnson, Sir William (*Warraghiyagey*) 166–8, 171
Johnson-O'Malley Act (1934) **444**, 460, 522, 570
José, Nicolás 194
Jumanos 77, 90–1
Justice Department 414, 564

Kadohadachos 78
Kahnawakes (Caughnawaga) 119–20, 132, 134
Kamchatka Peninsula 254, 256
Kansas 184, 230, 233, **233**, 247, 286, 288, 295, 302, 304, 307, 323, 325, 330, 390–1, 420, 519; Lawrence 390–1, 460, 490

Kansas River 230
Karankawas 78, 271–2
Karoks 268
Kaschia Reservation 499
Kaw-Osages 420
Kaws <u>247</u>
Keeble, Woodrow Wilson (Sioux) 536–7; Congressional Medal of Honor 536
Keel, Jefferson 609
Kellogg, Laura Cornelius (Oneida) 384–8; "Indian collectives" 388
Kellogg-Briand Peace Pact 421
Kennebec River 106
Kennedy Report, The (*Indian Education: A National Tragedy, A National Challenge*) 570–2, 574
Kennedy, Edward (Ted) 570
Kennedy, John F. 531, 546; administration 534; assassination of 546
Kennewick Man **581**, 595, 597; Gerasimov method 597
Kent State University shooting 546, 559
Kentucky "Long Knives" militia 179–80
Kentucky 19, 167, 172–4, **177**, 178–80, 202, 229
Kentucky River 174
Keokuks *224*, 226–7, **229**
Keres Indians 490
Kersan language 14, 16
Keystone Pipeline System 606; Keystone XL (KXL) 606–8; leaks from 608
Kickapoos 117, 178, 188, 230, 490, 582
Kicking Bear 352
Killbuck 173–4
King Philip (Metacom) *94–5*, 96
King Philip's War (Metacom's War) 96–7, **96**, 112, 120–24, 132, 135
King William's War **96**, 119
King, Martin Luther, Jr. 546
King's Royal Council 136
Kingsbury, Cyrus 215–16
Kintpuash (Captain Jack) 311–13
Kinzua Dam 535
Kiowas 90, 191, 236, 239, 246, <u>247</u>, 248, 263, 273–5, 277, 302–4, 307, 318, 323, 326, 329, 331–2, **338**, 493, **539**; Dog Soldiers of 273; war bond purchases 503

Kirk, William 184–5
Kirkland, Samuel 167–8
Kiska: Japanese occupation of 502
kivas 14–17
Klamath Indians 312, 499, 526–8, 530;
    compensation for lost lands 518;
    war bond purchases 503
Klamath Reservation 453
Knox, Henry 181
Koloshes 258, **259**; capture Sitka **259**
Konkow Maidus 268
Korean peninsula 515
Korean War 535–7
Krug, Julius A.518, 521
Ku Klux Klan 325, 414
Kurile Islands 510
Kuskov, Ivan 255–6, 258
Kussoe Indians (Algonquian) 147
Kuwait 585
Kwakiutls 11, 256; flood story 7

La Farge, Oliver 489, 511–12, 516–17
La Florida **66**, 67–75, <u>72</u>, 92,
    99; *camino real* 72–5; French
    settlements in 67; *repartimiento* 73;
    Santa Elena 70–1; Spanish mission
    system 147; St. Augustine *66, 68,*
    69, 71–3, 75
La Lac 262
La Montagne 132
La Salle, Robert de **66**, 78, **85**
Labrador 55
Lac Court Oreilles Reservation 483
LaDuke, Winona (Ojibwa) **581**, 596,
    596, 598, 600; "No Nukes LaDuke"
    598; Reebok Human Rights Award
    581, 598
Laguna 14
Lake Michigan 117, 234
Lake Mohonk Conference **346**, 360
Lake Ontario 155
Lake Superior 117
Lake Superior Chippewa (Ojibwa)
    Indians 589; Lac du Flambeau band
    of 589–90
Lake Traverse Reservation 608
Lake Winnebago 230
Lakotas 302, 319, 332–3, 352, 367,
    367, 372, 559, **568**, 609
Lalawethika 186–7; as Shawnee
    Prophet 187; as Tenskwatawa
    ("Open Door") 187, *188,* 189; *see
    also* Shawnee Prophet
Lancaster Treaty (1744) **130**

land allotments 359, 394, 413, 415,
    430, **435**, 462, 513; sale of 465
Land of the Tejas 78, **85**
land rushes 346, 365–6; Oklahoma
    346, 365–6
land: common ownership 470; as core
    of tribal identity 519; leases 446;
    tribal ownership of 462, 464–5
Landa, Diego de 51–2; *auto de fe* of
    Mayans 52
Lane, Franklin K. 400, 415, 417–18;
    competency program 417–18
Lane, Ralph 58, 60, **61**
Latin America 337
Lawrence, D. H. 424
Le Dru, Pierre *187*
League of Nations 421, 487
Lean Bear 302
Lee, Robert E. **283**, 288, 326
LeFlore, Greenwood (Choctaw)
    214–16
Leisler's Rebellion 119
Lemhi Shoshone 249–50
Lenni Lenapis 141
Leonard Crow Dog (Sioux) 352
Lewis and Clark expedition **244**,
    245, 250, **253**; Corps of Discovery
    245–53, **253**; journals *252*
Lewis, Meriwether 245, 247–53, **253**,
    259
Leyte Island 498
Liberty Bonds **379**, 404–5
Liberty Gardens 404
Liberty Stamps 404
Lincoln, Abraham 284–5, 289, 293–4,
    296–7, 301, 307, 585
Lindneux, Robert *198–9, 306*
Lipan Apaches 273–4
liquor trade 148, 215
Lisa, Manuel 259
Little Arkansas Treaty (1865) **283**, 307
Little Big Horn River (Greasy Grass)
    333–5, 337, 345; battle **312**, 347,
    418, 556, 574
Little Carpenter (Attakullakulla) 155
Little Crow (Tayoyateduta or Thaoyate
    Duta) 290–2, *290*
Little Eagle community 483
Little Elk (Ho-Chunk) 201
Little Turtle (Miami) 179–81, 187
London **105**, 483
London Company 101, 103
London Society for the Propagation of
    the Gospel 137

Lone Wolf v. Hitchcock **387**
Long Island 137; shore 109
Long Knives ("Big Knives") 172–4,
    185–7
Long Walk 315, 482
Longest Walk, The **545**, 565
Longhouse religion 183
Looking Glass 338–9
Looney, John 235
Los Angeles 267, 383, 430–1, 455,
    507–8, 516, 523, 525, 527, 546,
    557, 559–60
lost generation 414
Louis XIV (France) 131
Louisiana Purchase 192, 223, 245, **253**
Louisiana territory 67, 131, 148–50,
    153, 156, 191; Fort Frontenac
    155; Fort Rosalie 148; Mobile 147,
    149–50
Lower Brule Reservation <u>354</u>
Lower Brule Sioux 535
Lower Mississippi Valley 19, **130**,
    148–9, 191
Lower Sioux Agency **292**
Lujan, Manuel 585
Lumbee Indians 281–2, 501
Luther Standing Bear (Lakota) 367
Luther Standing Bear (Plenty Kill;
    Oglala/Lakota) 369, 372, *372*
Lyttelton, William Henry **130**, 155,
    159

Macchu Picchu *28–9*
MacDonald, Peter (Navajo) 584
Mackenzie, Alexander 245
Madison, James 188
Madrano, Dan 514
Mahicans 115–16, 122, 142, 144–5,
    472
Maine 55–6, 106, **113**, 548–9, 592,
    598
maize (*Zea mays*) 4, 13–15, **19**, 20,
    35, 40, 48, 80, 84, 86; *Chapalote*
    variety 14; *Maiz de Ocho* 14–15;
    and pellagra 15
Makahs 11, 254, 594–5, *595*; Makah
    Cultural Resource Center (MCRC)
    594–5; Ozette site 594–5; and
    whaling **581**, 594–5, *595*
Malintzin (Doña Marina) 46, 47, 60
Man-Afraid-of-His-Horse (Sioux) 318
Manchuria 479
Manco Incas 50
Mandan-Hidatsa trade festivals 248

Mandans 14, 232, 243–4, 246, _247_, 248–9, **253**, 259, 318, 534; _Okipa_ festivals 248

Manitoo 113

manitous 101, 106–7, 130, 173

Mankiller, Wilma (Cherokee) **581**, 596, 598–600, _599_; Bell Community Revitalization Project 598

Manteo (Croatan) 60–1

Marine Corps _see_ U.S. Marine Corps

market economy 192, 214, 217, 254, 263, 267–9, 276–8

Marshall, Chief Justice 210

Martha's Vineyard 107, 113–14, 135–6

Maryland 119, 125, 486, 525, 565, 594

Mascoutens 96–7, 117

Mashantucket Pequot 583, 592

Mashpees 113, 135–6, 170–1, 231; "Indian Declaration of Independence" 231

Massachusette (language) 113

Massachusetts (state) 56, 230–1, 360, 548

Massachusetts Bay colony 96, **96**, 106, 109–13, **113**, 122–3, 131–6, 170

Massachusetts Bay Company 109

Massachusetts Indians 108

Massasoit 96, **96**, 108, **113**, 121

Master of Life 130, 156–7, _158_, 175, 183, 185, 187, 190

Masters, Edgar Lee 424

matrilineage 98

matrilineal descent 22, 183, 204; lineages 34, 98–9, 223

matrilineal social structure 78–9, _78_, 87, 114, 116, 142, 183, 214, 238, 256, 596, 598–9

matrilineal societies/traditions 596, 598–9

Mattaponi Indians 124–5, 398

Maumee Indians 180

Maumee River 180

May, Karl 404

Maya 22, **31**, 32, 35–8, 39, 40–1, 45–6, **45**, **52**, 60; astronomical calendar of 35; _Cah_ (kin network) 38, 51; cult of sacrifice and bloodletting 36, 38, 52–3, 60; glyphic writing of 35, _36_, 37–8; Inquisition imposed on 51–2; Lady Wac-Kan-Ahaw ("Lady Six Sky") 37; mathematics of 35; Mayapán 37; Naranjo 37; Pacal II 37; pyramids of 35; Spanish conquest of 51–4; women in

37–8; _see also_ Chichén Itzá; Landa, Diego de; Montejo, Francisco de; Palenque; Quetzalcoatl; Rodrigo, Pedro de Ciudad; terrace agriculture; Yucatan

Mayan language 51

Mayflower 107, 422, **558**

Mayflower II occupation **558**

Mayhew, Thomas, Jr 113

McAdoo, William 404

McCain, John 585

McClish, Edward (Choctaw) 490

McCullough, John 157

McGillivray, Alexander 179, 182

McGovern, George 563

McIntosh, Daniel 286

McIntosh, William 212

Meadowcroft Rockshelter 7

Means, Russell 548–9, 559–60, 563–4

measles 261, 349, 517

Medicaid 613

medicine bundles 4, 81, 130, 226, 248, 555

Medicine Lodge Creek Treaty (1867) **312**, 323, 325, 331

medicine pouches 367, 537, 555

Mendizábal, Bernardo López de 84, **85**; inquisition of 84

Menéndez, Lúcas 74

Menominee Reservation 529

Menominees **200**, **201**, 224, 226, 230–2, 526, 528–31, 555, 582; ICC award 528; land cession **233**; Menominee Enterprises, Incorporated (MEI) 528–30

Meriam Report 435–9, _436_, 446, 448–9, 450–1, 456, 460, 461–2, 471, 509–10, 562, 570, 572, 613

Meriam, Lewis 435

Mesa Verde peoples **4**, 17, **19**; site _18_

Mescalero Apaches 273, 275, **283**, 297–9, 307, 423, 591

Meskwaki 609

Mesoamerica 30, **31**, 32, 35, 38–9, 41–2, _42_, **45**, 60, 76, 92

Mesquakie Sac-Fox Reservation 483

Mesquakies 199, 201, 223–7; removal of 219, 227, **229**

mestizos 85

Metacom (Philip) 121–2

Metacom's War _see_ King Philip's War

Methodism 231

Methvin, John Jasper (J.J.) 275; Methvin Institute 275

metis 233, 255

Metropolitan Opera _376–7_

Mexica **31**, 38–40, 42, **45**, 60; midwives 41

Mexican border wall 605, 610

Mexican-American War 268

Mexico 14–15, 17, 21, **31**, 32, 35, 38, 40, 46–7, 51, 61, 65, 67, 77, 87, 89, 190, 223, **244**, 256, 262–3, 266, 268, **270**, 272, 274, 277, **346**, 349, 351, 392, 499, 610; independence from Spain 264, 267; slavery abolished **244**, 277; _see also_ Valley of Mexico

Mexico City 46, 48, 66, 84, 99, 223

Mi'kmaq 56–7, **61**

Miamis 43, 96–7, 117–19, 154, 178–82, 187, 230, 362, 519

Micanopy (Seminole) 219, 222, 238

Michigan 202, 234, **467**, 489, **572**

Michilmackinac British outpost 177

Middle East 606

Middle Ground, western Great Lakes region **96**

Mihesuah, Devon (Choctaw) 580, 601–2

Miles, Colonel Nelson **312**, 335, 339, 351, 355

military draft 393–5, 398, 480, **481**

Mindanao, Japanese invasion of 490

mineral resources on tribal lands 588, 588

Mingos 154, 167, 172

Miniconjou Sioux 324

mining 67, 83, 87–9, 92, 206, 225, 260, 267–9, 276, 300–1, 314, 605, 611–12

Minneapolis 525, 529, **545**, 556–60

Minnesota 199, 232–4, **233**, **283**, 284, 290–5, **292**, _294_, 307–8, 317, 332, 483, 503, 525, 526, **527**, 559, 596

minutemen 171; Concord 171

Mission Indian Agency 430

Mission Indian Federation (MIF) 430, 432, **478**, 480; _The Indian_ 430

mission Indians 193–5

Mission La Purísima 264

Mission San José 264–5

Mission Santa Barbara 263

Mission Santa Ynéz 264

Mississippi (state) 77, 200, 213, 215–17, **218**, 219, 236

Mississippi River 7, 19, 21, 77–8, 148, 160, 164, 166, 177, 182, 192,

199–202, 207, 224, 226–7, 229–30, 245, <u>247</u>, 284–5, 288, 301, 307, 314, 396

Mississippian tradition **4**, 20–2, **23**, *24*, 70, 75

Missouri (state) 21, 230, 233, 285, 314, 316; Cape Girardeau 229

Missouri Compromise 238

Missouri Fur Company 259

Missouri River 14, 191, 200, 224, 243, 245–6, <u>247</u>, 248, 318, 321, 534–5

Mitchell, George 558

Miwoks **270**

Moctezuma II 30, 41, 46–7, **52**

Modoc War 311, **312**, 313, **338**

Modocs 311–13

Mogollon cultural tradition 15, **19**

Mohawk-Mahican war 116

Mohawks 22, **96**, 110, 114–17, 119, 122–3, 132–3, 166–71, 174, 178, 230, 535, **558**, 609; Canajoharie 166–7, 171; "Keepers of the Eastern Door" 114; Tiononderoge 167

Mohegans 109–10, 112, 137, 138–9, 169, 171, 592; Mohegan Sun casino 592

Mohicans 142, 144, 170, 230; Shekomeko, New York 142

Monroe, James 220

Montagnais 56–7, 115

Montana 13, 91, 246, 249–50, 260, 318, 339, 406, 457, 462, **467**, 499, *511*, **572**, 593, 603, 606, 611

Montana Farming Corporation 416

Montana Territory 318

Montauks 137, 169

Monte Verde, Chile 7–8

Montejo, Francisco de **31**, 51, **52**

Montezuma, Carlos (Yavapai Apache) 384, 390–2, 394–5, 469

Montgomery, Jack (Cherokee): Congressional Medal of Honor 504

Montour, Andrew 142–3

Montoya, Pablo 277

Montreal 119, 131–2, 166, 228

Mooney, James 351–2, 392

Moor's Indian Charity School 137, **140**, 167

Moors 31–2

Moravian Indians 160

Moravians 142–6, *144*, **146**, **185**; Gnadenhütten 142–3, 174; Nazareth 143; towns **130**, 172–3

Morgan, Jacob (Navajo) 468

Morning Star Institute 600

Moscow summit 579–80

Mother Earth 482

mound building cultures 19–20, 70

Moundville chiefdom **4**, 21

Mount Adams: returned to Yakima people **568**

Mount Rushmore *557*; occupation **558**

Mount Suribachi, Iwo Jima **478**, 491–2

Mourning Ceremony 194

Muhammed, prophet 7

Mullin, Markwayne (Cherokee) 611

Munsee Delaware band 230

Munsees 141, 184

Muqlemne Miwoks 264, *265*, 267–8

Murphy, Audie 538

Musgrove, John 152

Musgrove, Mary (Coosaponakeesa) 152

Mushulatubbees 214–15

Muskogean stories 22

Muskogee language 70, 75, 76, 189, 219, 272; dialects 146, 153

Muskogees 146

My Lai massacre 555, 564

Myer, Dillon **508**, 522–6, 532, 535, 569

Myers, Datus 455

Mystic massacre 110

Nader, Ralph **581**, 598

Nahuas 48–50, 60

Nahuatl language 39, 46, 50

Nansemonds 105

Nanticokes 145

Nantucket 135–6

Narragansett language 110

Narragansetts 56, **61**, 107–10, 112, 119, 121–2, 137–8, 169

Narváez, Pánfilo de 47, **66**, 75

Nash, Philleo 472

Nast, Thomas *328*, *359*

Natchez **4**, 21, 77, 148, 150–1

Natchez trace 217

Natchez Wars **130**, 148–50, **153**

Natchitoches 78

Naticks 135–6, 171

nation within a nation status 446

National American Indian Housing Council 613

National Board of Indian Education 572

National Congress of American Indians (NCAI) **508**, 513–15, *514*,

518, 521, 523, 526, 531–2, 537–8, 540, 544, 547, 551–2, 554, 558, 573, 575, 593, 609

National Consumers League 380

National Council of American Indians (NCAI) 433, **412**

National Exhibition of Art by the PWAP **455**; Corcoran Gallery, Washington, D.C. **455**

National Football League 383–4

National Guard 477, 516, 537, 563–4, 590; Alabama 213; Iowa 493; and Kent State shooting 546; New Mexico 489; North Dakota 536

national identity 214, 314, 357, 360, 482, 485, 519

National Indian Association (NIA) 399, 419

National Indian Gaming Commission 584

National Indian Youth Council (NIYC) **508**, 531, 534, 540, **545**, 547, 549–50, 554, 558–9, 575, 580

National Industrial Recovery Act (NIRA) 452

National League for Justice to the American Indian 372

National Museum of the American Indian 585, 600

National Tribal Chairman's Association (NTCA) 582

National Urban League 523

Nationality Act (1940) 487–8

native activism 534, 590

Native American activism 540, 556

Native American Affairs Coalition 611

Native American Church **379**, 392–3, 433

Native American Coalition (NAC) 613

Native American cultures 351, 434, 445, 465, 483, 511, 525, 540, 550

Native American feminist literary tradition 600–1

Native American Graves Protection and Repatriation Act (NAGPRA) (1990) **581**, 585, 593–5, 600

Native American Program Act 569

Native American Rights Fund (NARF) 529, 559

Native American self-determination 580; *see also* self-determination, right of

Native American sovereignty 103, 580, 600; *see also* sovereignty

Native Americans: below poverty line 604; education 570–2; health issues 575; income levels 569–72, *569*, 575; literacy 572, 575; servicemen 483; unemployment 570–1, **581**, 582

native spirituality *see* Indian spirituality

nativist movement **190**

Natural Resources Defense Council 606

naturalization 397

Navajo language 15, 494–5, *496*

Navajo Nation 609, 612; purchase of Big Boquillas Ranch 584; Tribal Council **478**, 480, 482

Navajo Office of Economic Opportunity 584

Navajo Progressive League 468

Navajo Reservation **444**, 507–8, 516–17, 584

Navajos 85, 90–1, 191, 276–7, *276*, **283**, 295–9, *300*, 302, 307, 325, 348, 363, 391, 394, *442–3*, 446, 451, 458–60, 464–5, 468, 480, 482, 501–2, 508, 515–16, *516*, 555, 582, 584, 588–9, 591, 594, 600–1, 609–16; as code talkers 494–5, *495*, 609–10; "the Long Walk" 299; ranching practices 458–60; stock reduction program 472; *see also* Navajo Nation

Navy Department 479

Nazism 470–1, **478**, 480, 482

Nebraska 3, 295, 317, 332, 335, 345, 362, **436**, 462, 519, 526, **527**, 559, **572**, 606; Omaha 345

Necotawance 105

Negro Fort 220, **229**

Negroes 282, 286, 486

Neolin (Delaware prophet) 130–1, 156–7, *158*, 175, 183 and "Master of Life" 183

Netherlands, the *see* Holland

Neutrals 22, 115, 117, 174

Nevada 12–14, *12*, 90, 296, 351–2, **355**, **436**, 446, **467**, 612; statehood 296

New Amsterdam 115

New Brunswick 55

New Deal 444–5, 452–4, 458, 461–2, 471–3, 501, 510, 515–17, 521, 562, 614

New England **31**, 54–6, **61**, 97, 106–10, 112–13, **113**, 119–24, 126, 13–2, 134–7, 139, **140**, 167, 169–70, **172**, 202, 231; as new "Canaan" 109, 121; town model 132

New England Company 111

New France **96**, 114, 116, 118–20, 131–4, 154, 156, 246

New Guinea 509; indigenous peoples of 8

New Helvetia 267

New Immigrants 314

New Jersey 141–2

New Mexico 8–9, 14–15, 17, 65, **66**, 67, 81, 81*-91, **85**, **91**, 164, **165**, 190*-2, **193**, 263, 274, 276*-7, **278**, **283**, 295*-7, 297, 307*-8, 330, 350, **412**, 421*-5, *424*, 431, 444, 455, **467**, 489, 497, 501, **508**, 512*-13, 517, 521, 526, 560, *560*, **568**, **581**, 589, 591*-2, 591; pueb los 81; tribes of 591; U.S. acquisition of 276; Volunteers **283**, 296–7

New Netherland 109

New Orleans 150, 156, 173, 239, 288

New Plymouth colony 95–6, 108, 112–13; Swansea 95–6

New Spain 65, **66**, 82, **91**, 92, 99, **105**, **165**, 191, 193

New World 31–3, 52, **52**, 54–5, 58, 67, 84, 90, 121, 193, 377–8, 415; European colonization of 378

New York (state) 22, 96, 98, 110, 114, 119, 123, 131, 137, 142, 154, **165**, 166–7, 169–70, 178, 182, **185**, **200**, 230–2, **233**, 362, **412**, 420, 446, 448, **467**, 468, 477, 487, 501, 526, 535, 592, 598; Albany 116, 123, 131, 133, 446

New York City 347, 360, 379, 388, 414, 422, 425, 431, 446, 450, 501, 516, 548

New York Times 425

New York Tribune 332

Newfoundland 55, 57, **61**; *L'Anse aux Meadows* 55

Newport, Christopher 100–2

Nez Perce 249–52, 260–2, **312**, 336, 338–9, *338*, 340, 518, 595; flight to Canadian border **338**, 358, 482; removal to Idaho reservation 336, 339; removal to Indian Territory 339; reservation in Wallowa Valley 336

Niantics 138, 169

Nipmucs 119, 121–2, 171

Nisenans 267–8

Nixon, Richard 548, 551, *560*, 562, 564, 567, **568**; administration/ White House 495, 560–2

Nomlakis 269

Nootkan language 11

Nootkas 254

Norsemen **31**, 54, **61**

Norteños 80

North Africa 508–9, 606

North America 4–5, 7–11, 15, 20, 23–4, 30, 32, 40, 54–6, 58–61, 66–7, 70, 89, 92, 97, 99, 110, 117, 119, 121, 123, 131, 142, 146, 149, 155–6, 160, 163–4, 166, 190, 195, 201, 245, 267, 437, 581, 587; European trade with 54

North Atlantic 55, **61**

North Carolina 58, 67, 76, 146, 150–1, 174, 178–9, 206, 211, 281–2, 316, 396–7, 451, 472, *476–7*, 501, 549, 592, 604; Home Guard 281–2

North Carolina Cherokee 451

North Dakota 418, 534–6, **572**, *604*, 606–7, 612

North Korea 535

North Platte River 324

North Vietnam 546; Tet Offensive 546

Northern Cheyenne **312**, 321, 332–3, 589

Northern Great Plains 90

Northern Pacific Railroad 332

Northern Paiutes **338**

Northern Plains 3, 10, 14, 90, 246, 294, 308, 316, 318, 324, **330**, 335, 353, 607

Northwest coast 11–12

Northwest Ordinance **165**, 179, 202

Northwest Passage 56, 58, 245

Northwest, the **13**, 175, 187, 224

Norway 55

Norwood, John 609

Nottoways 485

nuclear dumping: on reservation lands 589

Nuclear Waste Policy Act (1982) 589

Nueva Galicia 88

Nueva Vizcaya 67, 77, 87–8, 191

Numic people 90

O'odham peoples 14, 17

Oakland riots 560

Oakley, Annie 345

Obama, Barack 602–5, *603, 604,* 607–8, 612–13; administration 603, 606, 614

Obamacare *see* Affordable Care Act (ACA)

Occom, Samson 137–9, *138,* **140,** 169; Brothertown idea 137–8

Occoneechees 124–5

Occonukeys 125

Ocklawaha River 220

Oconostota (Cherokee) 174

Office of Indian Affairs (OIA) 316, 335, 363, 384–6, 389–92, 394–5, 398–400, 406, 415, 417, 418, 420–1, 423, 425, 428, 430, 432–5, 439, 444, **444,** 449–54, 459, 462, 465, 470–73, 480–1, 485, 490, **508,** 510–11, 513, 529; Agricultural Extension Service 450; Americanization policy 469; "Declaration of Policy" 417; Education Service 450; Forestry Service 450; Health Service 450; *Indians at Work* 490–1; Irrigation Service 450; schools 386

Office of Indian Education **568**

Office of Indian Water Rights 560

off-reservation employment 385, 438, 449, 450, 452, 454, 460, 490, 501–3, 537

Ogden Land Company 230

Oglala Sioux 324, 332, 559, 587

Oglala Sioux Nation 563

Oglalas 320, 367, 562

Oglethorpe, James 152–3

Ohio 148, 154, 166, 174, 179, 184, 202, 357, 383–4, 546; Cleveland 360, 414, 523

Ohio Company 143

Ohio Country 96, 131, 143, 154, 156

Ohio Indian Confederacy **165,** 178–81; meeting at Brownstown 178

Ohio Iroquois 143

Ohio River 20, 143, 154, 167, 172, 174, 178

Ohio Territory 155, 172–3, 178, 181, 186, 229–30

Ohio Valley 129–30, 154, 156, 172, 178, 181

oil deposits 587

Ojibwa reservations <u>589</u>; Bad River 234; Lac Courte Oreilles 234; Lac du Flambeau 234; Red Cliff 234

Ojibwas 117–19, 130, 180, 199, 201, 231–4, 483, 503, 558, **581,** 589–90, 596, 598, 600; recognition of spearfishing rights **581,** 589–90; spirituality 600; treaty rights 590

Okinawa, battle for 495

Oklahoma 9, 201, 215, 223, 234–5, 237, 275, 284–6, 288–9, 295, 308, 315, 317, 331–2, 339, 365–6, **379,** 383, **387,** 392, 398, 401–2, 411, **412,** 419, 421, 422–3, **435,** 464, 469, 477, 484, 490, 497, 502–4, 515, 519, 572, 598–9, 609, 611; land rush **346**

Oklahoma Cherokees: compensation for lost lands 519

Oklahoma Territory 307, 315, 365, 392, **435;** criminalization of peyote use 392; incorporation of Native American Church 392

Oklahombi, Joseph (Choctaw) 402

Old Hop (Cherokee) 174

Old Lady Horse (Kiowa) 329

Old Northwest 164, 172–3, **177,** 179–81, 184, 189, **190,** 201, 227, 229, 239; *see also* Ohio territory

Old Tassel (Cherokee) 175, 179

Old Testament *Book of Genesis* 7; flood story 7

Omahas 224, 232, <u>247</u>, 259

Oneidas 22, 114, 117, 137, 143, 163, 167–9, 171, **200,** 230, **233,** 384, 468, 493–4, 592; Kanowalohale 167–9; Oquaga 167–9; travel to Wisconsin **233;** Treaty of 1838 230

Onondaga Castle 154, 169

Onondagas 22, 114, 119, 141, 488

Onontio 118, 130, 154, 173

Oorang Indians professional football team 384

Opata pueblo 88

Opechancanough **96,** 100–5, **105**

Opothle Yoholo/Opothleyahola (Creek) 212–13, 286, 288

Oquaga **165**

oral tradition 30

Ordway, John 251

Oregon 254, 259–62, 268, 278, 311, **312,** 325, 336, **338,** 341, **346,** 351–2, 391, 400, **467,** 499, 526–7, **527,** 547, 596

Oregon Donation Law 261

Oregon territory 278

Oregon Trail **244,** 261

Organization of Petroleum Exporting Countries (OPEC) 606

origin stories 4–5; Acoma 80, 82; Bella Coola 5; Hopi 5; Iroquois 24–5; Pawnee 3–4

Orinoco tobacco 103

Ortiz, Simon (Acoma Pueblo) 601

Osage Allotment Act (1906) 421

Osage Nation 413, 530; oil head rights 413; oil leases of 530; retention of mineral rights on land allotments 413, 422; Tribal Council 412

Osage Reign of Terror **412,** 413, 422

Osage River 233

Osages Indians 148, 156, 188, 224, 232, <u>247</u>, 272, 362, 403, 411–13, 421, 490, 511, 530; *see also* Osage Nation

Osceolas *221,* 222

Oshkosh Indians 231–2

Ossomoocomuck 58; weroance (chief) Wingina 58–9

Otoe-Missourias <u>247</u>

Otoes 224, 259

Ottawas 115, 117, 119, 129–31, 154, 156–7, 174, 178–80, 187, 201, 549; Nanabush 156

otter trade **259**

Owens, Louis (Choctaw-Cherokee) 601

Pachamama 44–5

Pacific Coast 314, 527

Pacific Fur Company **244,** 259–60

Pacific islanders 512–13

Pacific Northwest 260, **545,** 547, 575

Pacific Northwest Indians 11–12, **13,** 252, 268, 549

Pacific Ocean 245, **253,** 509, 512

Pacific Theater of Operation 490, 494

Paha Sapa 332

Paiute Indians 351–2, 596

Palenque 37–8

Paleo-Indians 6, 8

Palute *417*

Pamunkeys 100, 102–3, **105,** 124–5, 398, 485–7, *486,* 609–10

Pancoast, Henry 358

Pan-Indian Unity **165**

Paquiquineo (Don Luís de Velasco) 99, **105**

Paris Peace Conference 414, 420

Parker, Arthur (Seneca) 384, 386–7, 432

Parker, Ely S. (Seneca) 326–7, *327;* appointed Commissioner of Indian

Affairs **312**, 326; as Seneca chief and Grand Sachem of Iroquois Confederacy 326, *327*

Parker, Quannah (Comanche) 275, 331, 392

Pascua Yaqui 585

Passamaquoddy 549

patriot cause 169–71, 173

patriots 171

Patuxet 107; *see also* Plymouth

Patuxet Indians 107

Pawnee Killer (Oglala) 321

Pawnees 118, 191, 239, 246, <u>247</u>, 259, 391, *419*, 493, 519, 600; origin story 3–4

Paxton Boys (Paxtonians) 157, 160, 172

Paxton Uprising, Pennsylvania **130**

Payne (Seminole) 219

Payne of the Oconees 220

Payne's Landing 220

Payne's War **229**

pays d'en haut 96–7, 117–19, 126, 154, 173; Ft. St. Louis 117; Kaskaskia 117, 173; Michilmackinac 117

Payta-Kootha *162–3*

peace commissions 224, 295, 312, 317, 318, 321, 324, *324*, 336

Peace of Paris (1763) 156

peaceful assembly, right to 607

Pearl Harbor attack **478**, **481**, 483, 489–90, 500, 510

Pecos 90, 190

Pecos Pueblo 594

Pecos River 299

Pedro Menéndez de Avilés 99

Pend d'Oreilles 260–1

Penn, John 157

Penn, William 140–1, **146**

Pennacook Algonquian 132

Pennacooks 133

Pennsylvania 7, **130**, 131, 140–4, 146, **146**, 154, 157, 160, 167, 169, 172–4, **177**, 182, 229, 288, 372, 486, 535; Bethlehem 142, 160; Carlisle **346**, 368; Fort Duquesne (Fort Pitt) 154–5; Pittsburgh 154; as proprietor colony 140

Penobscots 549, 592

Pentagon 495

Penutian-speakers 12

People's Institute 431

Peorias 230, 362

Pequot war (1637) 112, **113**

Pequots 109–10, 112–13, **113**, 122, 138, 169, 231, **581**, 592, 594; federal recognition of **581**, 592; Foxwoods Casino **581**, 592, *601*; high-stakes bingo **581**, 592

Perez, Tom 613

Perrot, Nicholas 96–7

Pershing, John 402, 432

Peru **31**, 32, 35, 42–3, **45**, 50–1, **52**, 60, 75, 92

Petain, Marshall 402

Petroglyph Canyon *12*

petroglyphs *12*, 13

Petuns 115, 117

peyote 331, **379**, 391–3, 433; criminalization of 425; cult 392

Pfeiffer, Albert 298

Philadelphia 141, 160, 182, 214, 358, 360, 501

Philip II (Spain) 65, 68, 99

Philippines 480, 489, 490, 498, 509

Piankeshaws 230

Piapot Cree Indian Reservation 548

Pick-Sloan Plan 534–5

pictographs 14

Pike, Albert 285–6

Pilgrims (Anglican Separatists) 95, **96**, **113**, 107; treaty with Massasoit 96

Pima Bajo pueblo 88

Pima Indians 390, 491–3, 517

Pine Ridge Sioux 501, 523, 525: war bond purchases 503

Pine Ridge Sioux Reservation 3, 52–4, <u>354</u>, **355**, 370, 405, 418, 562–5, *563*, 587

Piscataways 119, 124–5

pit house villages 15

pit houses 13, **19**

Pit River Indians 519, 598

Pitt, William 155

Pitts River tribe 594

Pizarro, Francisco **31**, 44, 50–1, **52**, 60

Plains Indians 13–14, 315, 331, 429, 434

Plains Indians' Sun Dance: banning of 434

Plains Sioux 246; Tetons (Lakota) 246, 259; Yanktons 246, 259; Yanktonais 246; *see also* Tetons (Lakota)

Platte River 246, 321

Plecker, Walter Ashby 485–7

Plenty Coups (Crow) 401–2

Plymouth 107

Plymouth Bay colony 107–8, **113**, 121–2

Plymouth Company 106–7

Plymouth Rock **558**

pneumonia 299, 436, 502

Pocahontas (Lady Rebecca Rolfe) 101, *102*, 103–4, *104*, **105**, 609–10, 614

Pokagon, Simon (Potawatomi) 234, 377–8

Poland **478**, 479–80; Jews in 482

Polk, James K. 267

Pomos 256, **259**, 268

Ponca Indians 232, <u>247</u>, 318, 547; declaration of war against Germany and Japan 489

Ponce de León, Juan 75

Pontiac 129–31, 156–7, *159*, 164, 167

Pontiac's War **130**, 157, **159**, 164, 167

Pony Express 345

Pope, John 293, 295

Portland 527

Portolá, Gaspar de 192

Post Traumatic Stress Disorder 493

Potawatomi "Trail of Death" **200**, <u>232</u>, 233, **233**

Potawatomis 117, 130, 178–80, 188, 201, 224, 230, 233–4, **233**, 366, 377–8, 519, 526; as "Keepers of the Fire" 233; as part of Anishinabe 233; removal to Indian Territory 233; *see also* Potawatomi "Trail of Death"; Treaty of Chicago

potlatch ceremonies 12

Potomac River 98, 103, 105

Poverty Point culture **4**, 19–20, **23**

poverty rate 612

Powder River country **312**, 313, 318, <u>319</u>, 320–1, 324–5, 332–5

Powhatan 59, 98–100, 103–4, **105**

Powhatan Confederacy **96**, 98–104, **105**

Powhatan Indians 104–6

powwaws (medicine men) 106, 109, 111

Prairie du Chien 232–3; council of Western Indians at 199, 201, 231

Prairie Potawatomi: compensation for lost lands 519

Pratt, Richard Henry 368–9, 370, 390

praying town model **96**, 111–13, **113**, 121; Natick 111–12

Praying Towns 132, 134, 202; Natick 132

Preparedness Day Parade *405*

Presbyterianism 167–8

Presidential Advisory Commission on Indian Reservation Economies 583
Price, Hiram 360
primitivism 360
private property 135, 181, 359–61, 399, 462, 470, 594, 611; concept of 34, 203–4, 363; vs. tribal ownership 399
Proclamation of 1763 **130**, 157, 164, 166–7, 174
Professional Football Hall of Fame 383
Progressive Era 378, 469
Progressive Movement 380, 382, 387, 393
Progressives 348, 357, 379–80, 382, 385, 388–90, 393, 418, 428
Progressivism 452
Protect Americans' Rights and Resources 590
protection ceremony 498
Protestant work ethic 268
Protestantism 215
Public Law 280 526–7, 547
Public Works Administration 453
Public Works of Art Project (PWAP) 454–5, **455**; "Indian Division" 455
Puck Magazine 371
Pueblo Bonito 15–17, *18*
Pueblo Indians 277, *410–11*, 423–6, 431, 433, 444, 456, 515, 582, 588, 591; Acoma 591–2; Isleta 591–2; lands 423; Pojoaque 591–2; religion 425, 427; San Juan 591–2; Sandia 591–2; Santa Ana 591–2; Taos 591–2; Tesuque 591–2; as wards of federal government 424
Pueblo Lands Act (1924) **412**, 427
Pueblo Revolt **66**, 85–6, **85**, 91; leader Popé 85–6
Pueblo Zuni 612
Puebloan peoples 14–15, 66, **66**, 80, 82; *katsinas* 80–5; *kivas* 81–3; Spanish invasion of 82–3; Tewa-speaking 83; women of 82; *see also* Acoma; Corn Mother; Hopi; Quivira; Zuni
pueblos 14, 15, 90
purification rituals 495
Puritans 109–11, 113, 122–3, 132; and "New England town model" 109
Pushmataha (Apushmatahubi) (Choctaw) 214–15, *215*, 217
Puyallup Indians 544
Pyle, Ernie 495

Quahog clam 109
Quakerism 327
Quakers 121, 140, 155, 182–6, **185**, 230, **312**, 327, 329; tradition of pacifism 154
Qualla Reservation (Cherokee) 472–3
Quapaws 148, 156, 232, 318, 468; war bond purchases 503
quasi-sovereign domestic dependent nations 586
Quatsino people: flood story 7
Quebec **96**, 114–14, 118–19, 133, 157
Quechua (language) 42–3, 50–1
Queen Anne's War 132
Quetzalcoatl 40–1, *42*, 47
Quintana, Ben (Keres) 490; posthumous Silver Star 490
Quinton, Nathaniel 490–1
Quivira 83
Qur'an 7

race riots 414
racial classification 486
racial consciousness 160, 555
racial discrimination 517
racial identity 485
racial rhetoric 181–2
racism 202, 205–6, 263, 270, 389, 414, 515, 534, 536, 538, **539**, 546, 548, 557, 574, 590, 596, 598, 609–10
Radical Republicans 314
radiocarbon dating 7–8
Raleigh, Sir Walter 58, 60, **61**
rape of Nanking 482
Rauschenbusch, Walter 388
Reagan, Ronald 495, 575, 579–80, **581**, 582–6, 614; administration 582, 584
Reaganomics 583–4
Rebolledo, Diego de 73–4
Reconquista 31, 52
Red Bird 232–3
Red Cloud 318, 320–1, 324–6, 332, 352–3
Red Cloud Agency 332–3
Red Cloud, Mitchell, Jr. (Winnebago) 537; Congressional Medal of Honor 537
Red Cloud's War 324, **338**
Red Eagle (Osage) *432*
Red Power Movement 534, 556
Red River War 331, **338**
Redding Rancheria tribe 594
Redstick movement 189

Redstick rebellion **190**, 218–19
Redsticks 189–90
religion, freedom of 425
religious ceremonies: banned **346**
religious right 331
relocation policy/program **508**, 523–6, 528, 532, 535, 538, 540, 544, 549, 560, 569, 582
Reno, Marcus 334
Republican Party 427–8, 531; Platform of 2016 611
reservation day schools *see* day schools
reservation farming and ranching 500–1
reservation lands 598; tribal ownership of 380
reservation life 262, 301, 331, 349–50, 382, 445, 461, 482, 517, 562, 598
reservation schools 438
reservation sovereignty 587–8
reservation superintendents 358, 366–7, 392, 425, 457, 501, 525
reservation system 391, 574
reservation-based schools 432
Resettlement Administration 453, 471
Rhoads, Charles J. **444**, 448–52, 456, 458
Rhode Island **31**, 56, **61**, **96**, 106–7, 109–10, 112, 119, 121–2, 137; Providence 137
Ribaut, Jean 67
Rickard, Clinton (Tuscarora) 434–5, 446, 448, 488
Ridge, John 205–6, 210, 235, 286
Ridge, Major 207, 210, 235
Rigaud, Pierre François de 150
Rights of Indian Women Marrying White Men Act (1888) **435**
Rio Grande 66, 271–2, 444
Rio Grande Pueblos 17
Roanoke colony **31**, 58–60, **61**; *see also* Manteo
Robert S. Peabody Museum 594
Rocky Mountain Fur Company 260
Rocky Mountains 12–13, 90, <u>247</u>, 249–50, 259, 323
Rodrigo, Pedro de Ciudad 52
Roe Cloud, Henry (Winnebago) 384, 386–7, 390–1, *391*, 432, 460
Rogers, Will 422–3, *422*, 484
Rolfe, John 101, 103–4, 610
Roman Nose (Cheyenne) 323
Roosevelt, Franklin Delano 444, **444**, 452–4, **455**, 459–62, 464, 470–1,

479–80, 499, 512–14, 521, 560; administration 456–7, 469, 509
Rosebud Agency 500
Rosebud Creek 333
Rosebud Sioux 607
Rosebud Sioux Reservation 354, 370, 485, 529, 587
Rosenthal, Joe 491–3
Ross, John 204–5, 207–8, *207*, 210, 234–5, **237**, 286–9
Rouensa, Marie 118
Rowlandson, Mary 123–4
Rowlandson, Reverend Joseph 123
Russia 254, 414–15, 509, 605
Russian merchants/traders 245, 253–6, 258, *259*, 267, 269
Ryan, Will Carson 432, 451–2

Sac Nation 228
Sacagawea 249–51
Sac-Fox Indians 366, 383–4, 389, 493–4
Sac-Fox-Creek 537
sachems 22, 106–9, 110–11, **113**, 114, 116, 121, 134–5; rights 135; sachemships 106–7, 114, 121, 135
Sacramento Agency 465
Sacramento Indian Agency jurisdiction 446, *447*, *448*,
Sacramento Valley 267
sacred objects, repatriation of 580, 593–5, 614
Sacs 200, 362
Sagadahoc colony 106, **113**
Sainte-Marie, Buffy (Cree) 548
Salish Indians 11; coastal 254, 260
Salish language 12
Sammie Bear (Creek) 398
Samoset 108
San Antonio River 80
San Carlos Apache Reservation **346**, 349–51, 353
San Carlos Apaches 451, 472, 538, **539**
San Diego 494, 527
San Francisco 194, 255, 368, 447, 501, 516, 523, 527, 551, 559, 565, 598; Intertribal Friendship House 598
San Francisco Bay **545**, 549
San Gabriel mission rebellion 194
San Juan 83, 86
San Juan Basin coal lease 589
San Sabá mission attack **66**
Sand Creek Massacre **283**, 304–7, 305, *306*, 314–15, 320, 326, 482, 574, 593

Sandburg, Carl 424
Sandoval Case 424
Santa Anna, Antonio López de 277
Santa Clara Pueblo 489
Santa Fe 83–5, **85**, 190, 276–7, 424, 455
Santa Fe Boarding School 460
Santa Fe highway 444
Santa Fe Indian School 455–6
Santa Fe trade 260
Santa Fe Trail 276–7
Santa Inés mission 195
Santanta (Comanche) 332
Santanta (Kiowa) 323
Santee Sioux **283**, 284, 290–3, **292**; annuity payments to 291; "Blanket Santee" 290; "Farmer Santee" 290; Minnesota River reservation 290, *294*; removal to Dakota Territory 293–4, 307
Santee War **283**
Santo Domingo Pueblo 424–5
Saratoga Campaign 169
Sassacus (Pequot sachem) 110
Sassamon, John 121
Satan 109, 113, 485
Satiacum, Bob (Puyallup) 544
Saukenuk **229**
Sauks 199, 201, 223–7, 232–3; annuity 226; removal of 203, 219, 227, **229**; Saukenuk 226&-7; *see also* Treaty of 1804
Savio, Mario 546
Saxmans *242–3*
scarlet fever 517
Scattergood, Henry 449, 450, 452, 456
Schmidt. Carl 256
scorched-earth strategy 298
sea otters 245, 253–4, 259
Seaton, Fred 531
Seattle 501, 503, 523, 543–5, **545**, 559; Discovery Park 545
secession, right of: repudiation of 314
Second Anglo-Powhatan War **96**, 105, **105**
Second Great Awakening 215, **218**
Second Seminole War **200**, 201, 222–3, **229**; Battle of Wahoo Swamp 222
Secretary of Education 585
Secretary of State 432
Secretary of the Interior 324, 333, 362, 364, 400, **412**, 415, 421, 425, 427–8, *432*, 439, 448–9, 452, 460, 463–4, 465, 472, 512, 514, 518, 531, 570, 582, 585, 603, 612

Sectan 58
Secularization Act **270**
Securities and Exchange Commission 453
Sedition Act 414
segregation 468–9, 470, 538; in armed forces 400
Selective Service Act (1917) 393, 398
Selective Service registration 553
Selective Service System **379**, 394–5, 399; inclusion of Native Americans **379**, 394
Selective Training and Service Act (1940) **478**, 480–1, **481**, 485–8; Indian exclusion from **478**; Iroquois exemption from **478**; as negation of treaties 487–8; registration of Indians as "whites" 485, 490
self-determination 482, 551, 556, 567, 575, 580–2, 585, 587, 600; definition 614–15; federal policy of 582
self-determination, right of 341, 388, 394, 415, 420, 428, 457, 465, 472, 511, 523, 540, 560, 604
self-government 585; definition 615; right of 532
Sells, Cato **379**, 394–5, 398–400, 405–6, 415–19
Seminole Nation 285–6, 434
Seminoles 151, 175, 189, 201–2, 219–23, *221*, 234, **237**, 238, 362, **387**, 391, 434, 451; Alachuas 222; filibusters' invasion of 220; matrilineal clans of 238; *miccos* 238; Mikasuki 222; move to El Nacimiento 223; move to Panhandle reservation 220; as Muskogee speakers 238; removal of 203, 219–20, 222–3, **229**, 238; "Second Seminole Removal" 238; *see also* Seminole Nation; Treaty of Fort Gibson; Treaty of Moultrie Creek; Treaty of Payne's Landing
Senate Committee on Indian Affairs 470, 515
Senate Foreign Relations Committee 555
Senate Indian Affairs Committee 462
Senate Lands Committee *410–11*
Senate SR 310 **508**, 510–13
Senate Subcommittee on Indian Affairs 528

Seneca language 183
Seneca Nation 230, 362; Tribal Council 469
Seneca reservations: Allegany 230; Buffalo Creek 230; Cattaraugus 230; Tonawanda 230
Senecas 22, 114, 116–17, 119, 143, 154, 156–7, 163–4, 169, 182, 185–7, 230, 326, 384, 488, 535, 553, 592; "Keepers of the Western Door" 114; *see also* Seneca Nation; Treaty of 1842; Treaty of Buffalo Creek
Sequoyah 205, *205*, 235
Serra, Junípero 192
Serrano peoples 87–8, **91**; Hia C-e O'odham 87; Jesuit mission system among 88–9, *91*; *rancherías* 87, *91*; Tohono O'odham 87
Service Star flags 498
Servicemen's Readjustment Act 508
Settlement Indians 146, 150
Seven Years' War (French and Indian War) 129–31, 134, 142–3, 154–5, 160, 175
Sevier, John 177, **177**
Seward, William 285
sexism 599
sexual violence 598, 601
Shahaptian group 262; *Washani* faith 262
Shahaptian language 262
shamans 261
Shastas 268
Shawnee Prophet **165**, 184, 187–9, *188*, *190*, 230, 232
Shawnees 118, 143, 151, 154, 156, *162–3*, 167, 172–4, 178–81, 182, *182*, 185–8, 229–30, 272, 366; Maykujay branch 184; removal to Kansas **233**
Sheridan, Philip 325–7, 330–1, 333, 335, 351
Sheridan's Campaign **338**
Sherman Institute 502
Sherman, William Tecumseh 282, 288, 313, 316, *316*, 318, 320, *324*, 325, 327, 331; Georgia campaign 316; March to the Sea 316; "total war" 316
Shiprock 494
Shoe Boots case 204
Shoshone Reservation 416

Shoshones 13, 90–1, <u>247</u>, 249–52, 260, 333, 406, *433*, 465, 471, 490, 551, 574; compensation for lost lands 518; war bond purchases 503
Shoshonis *see* Shoshones
Shulush Houma (Red Shoes) 149–50
Shurz, Carl 324
Sibley, Colonel Henry **292**, 293
Sicangu Oyate Sioux 587
Siege at Gnadenhutten **165**
Sierra Club 380
Sierra Madre 351
Sierra Nevada 90
Siksika Indians *382*
Siletz Indian 400
silver 295, 297, 314
Simcoe, John Graves 180
Simmons, Henry Jr. 186
Siouan dialects 117, 141, 146
Siouan territory 90
Siouan-speakers 14, 232
Sioux 199–201, 243, 246–50, <u>247</u>, 278, *280–1*, 303–4, **312**, 315, 318–21, 324–6, 332–5, **338**, **346**, 348, 352–5, *353*, **355**, 358, 384, 394, 400, 403, 418, 446, 465, 472, 482, 483, 485, 493, 499, 515–17, 525, 536–7, 538, **539**, 547, 549, 556, **568**, 574, 587–8; migrations 247; reservations **346**, 446; Sun Dance 574; *see also* Plains Sioux
Sioux War over the Black Hills **338**
Sisseton-Wahpeton Reservation 536
Sitting Bull (Hunkpapa Lakota Sioux) 329, 332–5, *334*, 339, **346**, 353, *522*, 564; in Buffalo Bill's Wild West Show 346; killing of 353, **355**
Six Nations 143, 151, 153–4, 167–9, *168*, 170, 178, 398, 434, 488–9; as autonomous, sovereign nation 202
Sky World 183
slave rebellions 220
slave trade 77, 150–1, **153**, 239, 269, 273–4
slavery 110, 122, 206, 214, 238, **244**, 258, 263, 273, 277, 284–5, 287, 314, 469
smallpox (*Variola*) 34, *35*, 49–50, 57, 73, 80, 116, 120, **140**, 148, 150, 163–4, 166, 192, **193**, 243–4, 248, 260, 349, 406, 517
Smith, Captain John 100, 102–3, *102*, **105**, 610
Smith, Edward 333

Smith, Jedediah 260
Smith, Kenneth L. (Warm Spring Wasco) 582
Smithsonian Museum 585, 593–4
Smohalla (Wak-wei/Kuk-kia/Yuyunipitqana/Waipshwa) 262
Smoky Mountain region 204, 593
Snake Indians 251, 312
Snake River 262; Valley 261
Snake War **338**
Snyder, Homer **412**, 420
Soboba Reservation 430
social organization: development of 11–12
Social Security Act 453
socialism 582
Society of American Indians (SAI) **379**, 382, 384–5, 388–95, 399–400, 407, 419–20, 424, 432–4, 513, 534; *American Indian Magazine* 385, 388, 420
Sokokis 132
Sonora 14, 17, **66**, 67, 83, 87–9, **91**, 92, 191; gentiles 89; *naborías* labor 88; *rancherías volantes* 89; *repartimiento* labor 88; silver mines in 88; *vagabundaje* 89
South America 8, 23, 30–1, 61
South Carolina 67, 71, 76, 119, 146–7, 151–2, 155, 175, 206, 282, 316, 446, 493, 509, 527, 530, 549; Charleston 147, 152, 174–5, **283**, 284; Charles Town **153**
South Carolina's Catawba Indians 446
South Dakota 14, 246, 317, 332, **346**, **355**, 421, **468**, 500, 535–6, **545**, 551–2, *557*, 559, *563*, 564, 566, 572, **572**, 587–8, 606, 608
South Dakota Home Guard **355**
South Korea 535, 537
South Pacific 503
South, the 182–3, 188–9, 201, 203, 206, 217, 238, 285–6, 288, 307, 314, 325–6, 414, 527; reconstruction of 314, 325
Southeast Asia 553
Southern Cheyennes 318, 323, 331–2, **338**
Southern Plains 91, 211, 246, <u>247</u>, 302, 307, 315–16, 323, 325–6, 329, 331, 333, **338**, 429
Southern Plains War **338**
southern planter class 182
Southern Ute 611

Southwest borderlands 66, 90–1, **91**, **165**, 190–1, 245, 263, 273, 277, **278**

Southwest, the 5, 14–15, 17, **66**, 80, 83, 90, 163–4, 190–1, 195, 263, 273–4, 277–8, 285, 295–6, 308, 315, 341, 363, 391, 424, 469, 481, **508**

sovereignty 598, 600; definition 614

Soviet Union 470, 510, 515, 519, 535

Spain 31–4, 45–6, 51–5, 58, 65, 67–9, 73, 77, 82–4, 89, 92, 99, 107, 156, 160, 166, 190–1, 220, 264, 267

Spalding, Henry and Eliza 261

Spangenberg, August Gottlieb 142

Spanish borderlands 66–7, **66**, **91**

Spanish Empire 66–7, 75

Spanish explorers 21

Spanish language 46, 50–1, 60, 273

Spanish law 195

Spanish, the: arrival of 17; "Black Legend" of atrocities 58; conquest 45–7

Speck, Frank 486–7

spiritual cleansing rituals 537

Spotted Tail Agency 332

Squanto 108

squash 14–15, 19–20, 22, 33, 35, 40, 69, 80, 248, 448

St. Clair, Arthur 179–80, **185**

St. Joseph's River 234

St. Lawrence River 19, **31**, 56–7, 60, **61**, **96**, 115, 118–19, 131

St. Lawrence Seaway Project 535

St. Louis 21, 117, 226, 229, 245, **253**, 259, 260, 316, 523

St. Regis Mohawk Council 488

St. Regis Mohawk Nation **478**

Stadaconans 56–7, **61**; *see also* Cartier, Jaques; Donnacona

Stalin, Josef 510

Standing Bear (Lakota) 320

Standing Rock protesters 607–8, *608*; Standing Rock Camp 608

Standing Rock Sioux 607

Standing Rock Sioux Reservation 353, 354, **355**, 535, 587, 607

Standish, Captain Miles 107–8

Stanley, John Mix 159

Star Lake Incident **581**, 590

states' rights 206–7, 216, 314

State-Tribal Education Partnership (STEP) 603

Ste. Genevieve-Cape Girardeau region 229–30

Stevens, Houston (Kickapoo) 490

stock exchange 453

stock market "crash" (1929) **444**, 445, 448

Stockbridge Indians 230

Stockbridge-Brothertown **200**

Stockbridge-Housatonic Indians 170

Stowe, Harriet Beecher 358; *Uncle Tom's Cabin* 358

Strong, Josiah 348

Student Non-violent Coordinating Committee (SNCC) 546, 562

Students for a Democratic Society (SDS) 546; Port Huron Statement 546

suffragettes 414

suicide 399, 598

Sullivan, John 169

Sullivan-Clinton campaign **165**, 169

Sully, Alfred *266*

Sun Dance 366, *433*, 453, 457

Sunrise Child-Girl 6

Survival of American Indians (SAI) **558**

Susqehannocks 98, 124–5

Susquehanna River 167; valley 157

Susquehanna River Indians 142

Sutter, John 267, **270**

swastika: as symbol of friendship 489; use discontinued by tribal communities 489

sweat lodges 116, 243

Swimmer, Ross O. (Cherokee) 583, 598–9, 611

Sycamore Schoals Treaty (1775) **165**, 174, **177**

syphilis 270

Tacoma-Seattle 527

Tahontaenrat 114

Tainos Indians 32–4, 59; *Zemis* 34

Tallahassee 220

Tanoan-speakers 14

Taos 86, 90–1, 190, 276–7, 424, 431, 455

Taos artist colony 424–5, 431

Taos Pueblo 424, *424*, 431, 464, 519, 560, *560*, **568**; Blue Lake 519, 560, *560*

Taovayas 191

Tapahonso, Luci (Navajo) 600–1

Tascaloosa 75, 76

Tatobem (Pequot sachem) 112

Tawakonis 277

Taylor, Nathaniel 321

Taylor, Zachary **229**

Teapot Dome Scandal 427

Tecumseh 157, **165**, 184, 186–9, *187*, **190**, 232

Teedyuscung (Delaware) 141, 155

Tehran Conference 510

Tejanos 272–3

television shows: *Cheyenne* 539–40; *The Lone Ranger* 540; *Sesame Street* 548

Teller, Henry 363, 365

temperance movements 236

Tennessee 19, *24*, 76–7, 146, 151, 174–5, 179, 188, 190, 202, 204, 207, 210, 217–18, 288, 396, 592

Tennessee militia 190

Tennessee River 174–5, 179, 217, 219

Tennessee Valley 189

Teotihuacán 38–9

termination policy 430, **508**, 509, 511–13, 520–3, 526–32, 535, 538, 540, 544, 547, 549, 560, 567, 582–3, 586, 613; ended **545**

Territory of Colorado **283**

Territory of Wyoming 349

Terry, Alfred 333–5

Teton Sioux 293–4, 318; Miniconjou 318; Oglala 318; Sans Arc 318

Tetons (Lakota) 246, 259; Brulé band 246; Hunkapa band 246; Miniconjou band 246; Oglala band 246; Two Kettle band 246

Texas 66, 67, 77, 79–82, 91–2, 164, 191–2, 223, **244**, 245, 263, 271–4, **278**, 285, 307, 326, 330–2, 350, 493, 497, 526, 546, 606; admission to United States **244**, 272, 274, **278**; *empresarios* 271–2; independence 272, **278**; missions in 79–80; presidios in 79–80; revolt against Mexico **244**, 272; San Antonio 66, 85; San Sabá mission 80, *85*

Texas Rangers 274, 484

Third Minnesota Volunteers 293

Thompson, Wiley 221–2

Thorpe, George 103

Thorpe, Jim (Sac-Fox) 371, **379**, 383–4, *383*, 484

Three Affiliated Tribes 611

three sisters 15, 22

Thunderbird symbol 497

Tibbet, Jonathan 430, 432

Timberlake, Lt. Henry 175, <u>176</u>
Timucua *64–5*, 69–75, <u>*72*</u>, *74*; *holatas* (*caciques*) 69
Timucua Rebellion **66**
Tinker, Clarence L. (Osage) 490
Tippecanoe River 184
Tishcohan 141, 143
Titu Cusi 50–1, 60
Tlaxcala 49
Tlaxcalan Indians 47
Tlingit-Russian Treaty (1805) **259**
Tlingits 254, 256–9, **259**, 609; attack Yakutat territory **259**; capture Fort Sitka **259**; kwáans 256–8; matrilineal clans 256; Northern Tlingit 256; potlatches 258; "prestige economy" of 257–9; social structure *257*; Southern Tlingit 256; Tlingit of the Gulf of Alaska 256; warrior culture of 257–8; woodcarving 256
tobacco 33, 103, 105–6, **105**, 148, 555, 610
Tocobagans 75
Tohono O'odham Nation 610
Tolowas 268
Toltecs 38–9, 40; empire 37, 38; Topiltzin 40; Tula 38; *see also* Quetzalcoatl
Tomb of the Unknown Soldier, Arlington National Cemetery 401
Tongue River 335
Tonkawas 80, 274
totems/totem poles 11, *242–3*, 253, 256–7
Totus et al. v. The United States 487–8
tourism 423, 446, 592–3, 614
Towner, Elwood (Hoopa) 469
trachoma 399, 406, 436, 451, 471, 480
Trade and Intercourse Acts **165**, 181
trade: deerskin 147; slaves 147
traditional Indian cultures 451
Trail of Broken Treaties 559–2, 565
Trail of Tears *198–9*, **200**, <u>203</u>, 210–11, <u>211</u>, **212**, 299
trans-Appalachian West 177–8
TransCanada Corporation 606, 608
transcontinental railroad 296, 314
trans-Mississippi west 230, 245, 247
trans-Missouri west 89, 202, 254
Treaty at Butte des Morts 231
Treaty between New Spain and Western Comanches (1786) **165**
Treaty of 1804 **200**, 224, 226, **229**

Treaty of 1832 **200**, 213, **218**
Treaty of 1838 230
Treaty of 1842 230
Treaty of Buffalo Creek (1838) **200**, 230, **233**
Treaty of Camp Charlotte (1774) 172, **177**
Treaty of Canandaigua (1794) 201, 398, 468, 446, 487
Treaty of Chicago (1821) **200**
Treaty of Chicago (1833) 233–4, **233**
Treaty of Chickasaw Bluffs (1801) **200**, 217, **218**
Treaty of Chickasaw Council House **218**, 219
Treaty of Council Springs 274, **278**
Treaty of Coweta (1739) 153; 130, 153
Treaty of Dancing Rabbit Creek 216, **218**
Treaty of Doak's Stand (1818) 215, 217, **218**
Treaty of Dumplin Creek (1785) **165**, 178–9, **185**
Treaty of Easton (1758) **130**, 154–5, **159**
Treaty of Fort Finney (1786) **165**, 178, **185**
Treaty of Fort Gibson (1833) 221, **237**, 238
Treaty of Fort Harmar (1789) **165**
Treaty of Fort Jackson (1814) **165**
Treaty of Fort McIntosh (1785) **165**, 178, **185**
Treaty of Fort Stanwix (1768) **165**, 178
Treaty of Fort Stanwix (1784) **165**, 167, **185**
Treaty of Fountainbleau (1762) **165**, **193**
Treaty of Galphinton (1785) **165**, 179, **185**
Treaty of Greenville (1795) **165**, 178, 181, 184, **185**; annuity payments 181; "civilization" program 181
Treaty of Guadeloupe Hidalgo 424
Treaty of Hartford (1638) 110, 112
Treaty of Hopewell 179
Treaty of Indian Springs (1824) **200**, 212–13, **218**
Treaty of Middle Plantation (1677) 125
Treaty of Moultrie Creek (1823) **200**, 220, **229**
Treaty of New Echota (1835) **200**, 210, **212**, 234–5, 396–7
Treaty of New York (1790) **165**, **185**

Treaty of Paris (1763) **130**, 160, **193**
Treaty of Paris (1783) 164, 177–8, **185**
Treaty of Payne's Landing (1832) **200**, 221, **229**
Treaty of Prairie du Chein (1825) **233**, **200**
Treaty of Removal (1808) **200**
Treaty of Shoulderbone Creek (1786) **185**
Treaty of the Chickasaw Nation (1805) **200**, 218, **218**
Treaty of Traverse des Sioux 290
Treaty of Utrecht (1713) **140**
Treaty of Washington 213, **218**
Treaty Party 210
treaty rights 421, 430, 434, 547, 587, 590
Triangle Shirtwaist Company fire 379
tribal casinos 590, 614
tribal colleges *572*
Tribal Controlled School Act (1988) **581**, 585
tribal gaming **581**; classifications 584–5
tribal identity 519
tribal incorporation 449
tribal lands 134, 179, 363, 430, 462, **478**, 518, 521, 528, 567, <u>588</u>, 607, 611; leasing of 611; privatization of 611–12; sale of 611
Tribal Law and Order Act (2010) 603
tribal revitalization 462, 510, 521
tribal self-determination 459, 471, 534, 552, 567, 575; *see also* self-determination
tribal self-governance 430; right of **568**
tribal self-government 472, 583
tribal sovereignty 178, 285–6, 418, 421, 430, 434, 446, 485, 487–9, 504, 511, 530, 534, 565, 585, 592, 607, 613; *see also* sovereignty
tribal spirituality and culture 519
tribal trust funds 511
tribalism 388
Tribally Controlled Community College Assistance Act (1978) **568**, 585
tribe: definition 594, 614
trickster 601
Troup, Governor 212
Truman, Harry 516, 518, 521–2, *522*, 535
Trumbull, John *170*

Trump, Donald *578–9*, 605, 608–14, *609*; administration 612–13

Tsenacommacah 97–101, 103–4, **105**; *see also* Virginia

Tsianina Redfeather (Cherokee) 405

Tsimshians 256

tuberculosis 349, 399, 406, 450, 471, 502, 528, 532; Indian mortality rate 435, *436*

Turner, Frederick Jackson 348

Turtle Mountain Chippewa 526, 600

Tuscarora War 150, **153**

Tuscaroras 150–1, 153, 167–9

typhoid 73, 116, 436, 517

U.S. Air Force 537

U.S. Army 210, 219–21, 227, 233, 274, 284, 295, 301, 304, 307, 311–13, **312**, 316, 318, 320, 324, 330–3, 326, **330**, 335–6, 338, 340, **338**, **355**, 372, 399–400, 404, 460, 477, **478**, 480, 486, 493–4, 499–500, 501–4, 544, **545**, 555; Indian code-talking teams **478**

U.S. Army Medical Corps 405

U.S. Army Signal Corps 491

U.S. Attorney General 427

U.S. Capitol *410–11*

U.S. citizenship 359, 361, 364, **379**, 395, **412**, 420–1, 430, 433–4, **435**, 439, 469

U.S. Commission on Civil Rights 607

U.S. Congress 188, 201, 207–8, 212, 215, 230, 232, 234, 261, 268, **283**, **292**, **312**, 316, **346**, 361, **478**, **481**, 512

U.S. Constitution 206–7, 231, 274, 331, 420, 533; Indian affairs within 206

U.S. Department of Agriculture 603

U.S. Department of Education **568**

U.S. Department of Health, Education, and Welfare 529; Urban Indian Task Force 529

U.S. Forest Service 528

U.S. government 190, 210, 223, 233, 273, 307, 317, 332, 388, 402, 424, 482, 487, 499, 503, 579

U.S. House of Representatives 208, 299, 301, 321, **330**, 361, 420–1, 423–4, 449, 462–3, 518, 537

U.S. Marine Corps *476–7*, **478**, 483, 491, 492, 494–5, 498, 503, 551, 556; Hymn in Navajo *496*; Navajo Code Talker unit **478**

U.S. Navy 399–400, 489, 499–500, 503–4

U.S. Postmaster General 428

U.S. Public Health Service 449, 451

U.S. Senate 208, 212, 221, 290, 299, 321, **330**, 361, 393, 398, 420–1, 423–5, 449, 457, 463, 470, **508**, 510, 512, 515, 520, 529, 535, **568**, 570

U.S. Supreme Court 209–10, **387**, 397, 423, 521, **568**, 588, 590

Udall, Morris 544

Udall, Stewart 531

Uintah Ute *522*

Umatillas 252, 595

Unami Delawares 173–4

Unami Indians 141

Uncas (Mohegan sachem) 110, 112

Uncle Sam 489

Uncompahgre Ute *522*

Union Army 313, 326, *327*

Union Navy 282

Union, the 281, 284, 289

United American Company 254–5, **259**

United Band of Ottawa, Ojibwa, and Potawatomis 201, 224

United Indian People's Council 544

United Indians of All Tribes Foundation (UIATF) 544–5

United Nations 513, 515, 535, 607

United Nations Declaration on the Rights of Indigenous Peoples 604

United States v. Michigan 549

United States v. Washington ("Boldt Decision") 549

United States vs. Boyd 396–7

United States vs. Osborne 397

United States: independence of 177; treaty-making power of 207, **312**, 327

Un-Thanksgiving Day **558**

Unulachtigos 141

Upper Midwest 314

Upper Missouri River 243, 246–9, 252, **253**, 259, 278, 321

Upper Ohio valley 172

Upper Platte 303

uranium deposits 587, 596

urban vs. rural Indians 569–71

usufruct property rights 106

Utah 13, 17, 385, **436**, **468**, *516*, 526, 612; Monument Valley *516*; Salt Lake City *578–9*

Ute Mountain Utes 612

Utes 13, 90–2, 190, 318, 363, 385, 405, 612; -Comanche alliance 91; compensation for lost lands 519

Uto-Aztecan speakers 13–14

Valley of Mexico 39–40, 39, **45**, 47–9, 51; Lake Tetzcoco region of 39–40

Valliere, Wayne (Ojibwa) 590

van Curler, Ardent 118

vanishing Indian myth 415, 428, 469, 558

vaudeville 422

Vaudreuil, Philippe de Rigaud de 131

Velarde, Pablita (Tse Tsan; Santa Clara Pueblo) 455–6

venereal diseases 436

Veracruz 47

Verrazzano, Giovanni da **31**, 56, **61**

Vespucci, Amerigo 33

Veterans Administration (VA) 517, 554

Vicksburg Campaign 326

Victoria, Queen (England) 347

Victorio (Mimbres) **346**, 349–50, 357

Vietnam War 553–6, 562, 567, 575; American involvement in 546; Indian service in 553–6, *554*; pacification program 555; veterans 564

Villiers, Louis Coulon de 154

Virgin Mary 79, 84, 86

Virginia 60, **96**, 97–8, 100–6, **105**, 108, 119–20, 122, 124–6, 131, 143, 150–1, 154–5, 157, 167, 172–3, 175, 177, 228, 286–7, 326, 398, 485–7, 504, 527; House of Burgesses 125; plantation economy 106; Richmond 284–5, 288, 296, 313, 315

Virginia Company 108

Virginians 106, 125, 172, 175, 177

vision quests 13, 262

Vitus Bering—Aleksei Chirikov 254

Vizenor, Gerald (Chippewa) 601

vocational training 367, 386, 451–2

vote, right to 396, 420, 435, **508**, 512, 517, 521

Wabash River 184

Wabashes 180

Wabokieshiek (White Cloud) 226–7

Wahpetunwan Dakota 580, 602

Wahunsunacock 98; *see also* Powhatan

Wahweotten, Albert (Pottawatomi)
490
Wake Island, battle for 490
Walking Buffalo (Assiniboine) 366
Walking Purchase **130**, 141, 143, **146**,
154
Walla Wallas 261
Wallace, Henry 489
Walleye War 589–90
Walters, Anne Lee (Pawnee) 600
Walulas 251–2
Wampanoag language 113
Wampanoags 56, 95–6, 107–8,
112–14, **113**, 121–2, 135–6
wampum beads 109–10, **113**, 119,
593; belts 178
Wamsutta (Alexander) 121
Wanapums 262, 595
war belts 187
war bonds 491, 503
War Department 220–1, 284, 286,
288, 296, 300–1, 312, **312**, 316–17,
321, 325–6, 331–3, 335–6, 341,
399, 453, **478**, 479–81, 485–6, 493,
500–2, 512, 535; Memo 336, **478**,
486–7, 510, 535
War for the Bozeman Trail **338**
War of 1812 **165**, 189, 230–3, 260
War Relocation Authority (WRA) **478**,
501, 522
Warbonnet Creek 345
wards, Indians as 341, 373, 384, 396,
424–5
Warm Period 15, 17, 20
Warm Spring Wasco 582
Warren, Elizabeth 609–10, *609*; called
Pocahontas by Trump 609, *609*,
614
warrior societies 418
warrior spirit 483, 491, 554
Warrior, Clyde (Ponca) 547
Washakie (Shoshone) 349
Washington (state) **478**, 487, 544, 552,
558, 565, **568**
Washington Conference 421
Washington Territory 261
Washington, D.C. 171, 207–8, 210,
213, 215, 217, 220–2, 226–7, 232,
236, 254, 260–1, 262, 274, 284,
290, 306, 327, 385, *410–11*, 425,
455, 469, **483**, 487, 491, 510, **545**,
552, 559, 565, 575
Washington, George 143, 154, 163,
169–70, 180, 202–3, 327, 398;

as Indian father 181; as "Town
Destroyer" 169
Washita River 325–6
Washita Valley **312**, 574
Wa-Swa-Gon Treaty Association (WTA)
590
water rights 583
Watie, Stand 210, 235, 286–8, 315
Watt, James G. 582, 584
Watts riot 546
WAVES (Women Accepted for
Voluntary Emergency Service) 503
Wavoka (Paiute) **346**, 351–3, **355**
Wayne, "Mad" Anthony 180, **185**
Wayne, John 538
Weas 230
Weather Underground 546
Webber, Leonard (Shoshone) 490
Weiser, Conrad 142
welfare state 461
Wells, William 181
Welsh, Herbert 358
Wepaemeoc 58
weroances 98–9, 101–2, 105, 125
Werowocomoco 101
West Coast 34, 261–2, 316, 450, 501,
522, 527–8, 544
West Indies 31, 33–4, 46, 59, 103, 110,
122
West Virginia 167, 172
West, the 151, 160, 166, 178, 206–7,
210, 238–9, 245, 248, 253, 260,
262–3, 274, 278, 284–5, 295–7,
302, 307, 313–16, 320, 326, 330,
341, 345, **346**, 351, 380, 416, 527,
589; winning 263
West, Thomas 103, **105**
Western Hemisphere 4–6, 8, 30, 33, 59
Westos 75, 147
Weymouth, Captain George 107–8
whaling voyage agreements 135
Wheeler, Burton K. **508**, 510–11, 462,
511
Wheeler-Howard Bill **444**; *see* also
Indian Reorganization Act (IRA)
Wheelock, Eleazar 137, 139, 167
White Antelope 302, 304–5
White Bird (Nez Perce) 339
White Bird Canyon 338
White Cloud 233
White Eagle (Ponca) 318
White Earth Land Recovery Project
(WELRP) 598
White Earth Reservation 596, 598

White Eyes 173–4, **177**
White House Tribal Nations
Conference 603
White River Apaches 394
White, John 58, *59*, 60, **61**
White, William Allen 428, 432
Whitebear, Bernie 544
Whitefield, George 137, 143
Whitman, Marcus and Narcissa **244**,
261
Whitman, Walt 336
Whitney, Eli 206
whooping cough 406
Wichitas 80, 90, **165**, 190–1, 246, <u>247</u>,
272–4
Wilbur, Ray Lyman 448, 450
Wild West shows 262, 345, 380,
403–4, 422
Willamette River Valley 261
Williams, Eleazer 230
Williams, Eunice 230
Williams, Reverend John **130**, 132–4,
140
Williams, Roger 110
Wilson, Angela Cavender
(Wahpetunwan Dakota) 602, 614
Wilson, Charles Banks 484, *484*
Wilson, Dick 562–5; Guardians of Our
Oglala Nation (GOONs) 563
Wilson, Woodrow **379**, 393, 415, 420,
432, 444
Wind River Agency *506–7*
Wind River Reservation 406
Window Rock 517
Winnebago Reservation 364
Winnebagos 117, 188, 226, 384, 401,
516
Winnemucca, Sarah (Paiute) 596
Winslow, Edward 108–9
Winters v. United States 387
Winthrop, John 109
Wirt, William 209–10
Wisconsin 199, **200**, 202, 224, 227,
230, 232–4, **233**, 320, 386, 483,
526, **527**, 528–9, 582, <u>589</u>, 590;
Green Bay 96, 230–1; Prairie du
Chien 199, **200**, 201, 224, 232–3
Wisconsin Dells 233
Wisconsin Glaciation 5
Wisconsin River 233
Wisconsin territory 230
Wôbanakik 133
Wodziwob (Paiute) **346**, 351
Women's Auxiliary Corps (WACs) 503

Women's National Indian Association 358

women's suffrage 348, 380

Worcester v. Georgia **200**, 210, **212**

Worcester, Samuel 210

Work, Hubert **412**, 427, 432–5, *432*, 439

Works Progress Administration (WPA) 443–5, **444**, 455, **455**, 457, 510

World War I *376–7*, 393, 395, 398–402, *401*, 404, 406–7, **412**, 415–17, 420, 428–9, 432, **435**, 439, 485, 491, 553, 554; American Indian veterans of **412**, 420–1; armistice 414; Indian service in 399–403; Pawnee veterans of *419*; Western Front 401, 404

World War II 202, 395, **455**, 471, 477, **478**, **481**, 483, 489, 491, 494–5, 497–8, 503, 507–10, 513, 515, 517–18, 521, 529–31, 534, 537, 540, 544, 547, 553, 554, 571, 609

World's Columbian Exposition, Chicago 377–8

Wounded Knee Creek massacre **346**, 354–5, **354**, **355**, 356, 357, 482, 556, 559, 564, 566, 573

Wounded Knee Takeover (Wounded Knee II) **545**, 552, 563–7, *567*, 574

Wyandots 119, 154, 178, 181, 187

Wyatt, Francis 105

Wynkoop, Edward 302

Yahi Indian 594

Yakama Indians 595

Yakima Indians 349, 487

Yakima Nation 487, 589; tribal council 468

Yakima War 262

Yakutat territory 258

Yalta Conference 510

Yamasee War **130**, 151, **153**

Yamasees 75, 147, 150–1, 153

Yana tribe 271; Yahis 271

Yankton 535

Yankton Sioux *365*, 385, *386*, 551, 606; compensation for lost lands 518

Yaqui *442–3*

Yavapai Apaches 384

Yazoo Strip 202

Yellow Bird (Sioux) 354

Yellow Hand 345

Yellow River 233

Yellow Thunder, Raymond (Oglala Sioux), murder of 559; Gordon, Nebraska 559

Yellow Wolf (Nez Perce) 336

Yellowstone River Valley 332–3, 339

Yellowtail, Robert (Crow) 457, 514

Yokuts 192, 264, 265, 268; Lakisamne 264–5

York River 101, 105

York, Alvin 402

Young Men's Christian Association (YMCA) 380, 388, *389*, 425

Young Women's Christian Association (YWCA) 405

Yucatan 21, 30, **31**, 35–7, *37*, 39–40, **45**, 46–7, 51–2, **52**, 60; Inquisition 52–4

Yuman (language) 14

Yurok 406

Zacatecas 65

Zeisberger, David *144*

Ziegfeld Follies 423

Zimmerman, William **508**, 520–1, *520*

Zinke 612

Zinzendorf, Count Nicholas von 142–3

Zitkala-Sa (Yankton Sioux) 385–8, *386*, 390, **412**, 420, 433; betterment stations/houses 385–6, 390

Zuni Pueblo 499

Zunis 14, 17, 80, 82–3, **85**, 502, 594; Hawikuh (Cíbola) 82–3

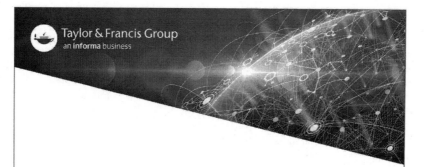